D0088666

CAROLINAS & GEORGIA

JIM MOREKIS

© AVALON TRAVEL

Contents

DISCOVER

the Carolinas & Georgia

When people around the world think of the American South, it's some archetypal image from the Carolinas and Georgia that comes to mind, whether they know it or not. Spanish moss hanging from a live oak, a tangy pulled-pork barbecue sandwich, hiking the Appalachian Trail, classic lines from *Gone with the Wind,* the robust smell of a tobacco field, enjoying a cold Coca-Cola while listening to bluegrass music... This is the vivid, iconic backdrop of a real or imagined experience of the South, both for the people who've always yearned to visit as well as for those who call it home.

This is a huge area with a huge history to match. The three states covered in this guide encompass about 150,000 square miles and contain nearly 10 percent of the American population, living in enormous metropolitan areas, tiny crossroads hamlets, and everything in between. Among them, the Carolinas and Georgia have been the birthplace of four U.S. presidents and seminal American figures like Martin Luther King Jr.

In the enormous swath of America between the Blue Ridge and the Atlantic Ocean you'll find a marvelously diverse geography, with peat-filled swamps and Appalachian balds, salty ocean waves and bass-rich lakes, sandhills and deep forest, slow-moving blackwater rivers and rushing mountain streams.

Quite simply, there's a lot to see and do here, whether your taste runs to rock climbing, fishing, beachcombing, kayaking, or following Southern Gothic literature. Or even just enjoying good food and drink—many of the nation's best chefs practice their trade in restaurants in Atlanta and Charleston. You could make an entire vacation exploring down-home barbecue joints and comparing the various regional sauces that even today inspire impassioned good-natured debate.

It may seem folly to attempt to try and tie it all together, but one common thread does run through the Carolinas and Georgia: that fabled Southern hospitality and the easy, welcoming laughter that comes with it.

END OF 1ST FLIGHT
TIME: 12 SECONDS
DISTANCE: 120 FT.
DEC. 17, 1903
PILOT: ORVILLE

Planning Your Trip

Where to Go

The Outer Banks and the Coastal Sounds

Probably the most culturally unique area in this guide, the Outer Banks of North Carolina still harbor charming pockets of a centuries-old seafaring tradition all along its wave- and wind-battered beach strands. The nearby Coastal Sounds provide a relaxing, sheltered counterpart to the Outer Banks' heavy traffic during the high season.

Wilmington and the Cape Fear Region

The northernmost outpost of the antebellum rice plantation culture, classy little Wilmington has transformed itself into one of the most active film production centers outside California. The surrounding Cape Fear region features several beautiful, accessible beaches for family enjoyment.

Central North Carolina

This culturally and politically diverse area isn't only a big golf getaway and center of the stock-car racing universe; it features the region's second-largest city, the financial powerhouse and ethnic melting pot of Charlotte, as well as the highly progressive, university-dominated "Triangle" of Chapel Hill, Durham, and Raleigh.

Asheville and the Blue Ridge Parkway

A left-of-center oasis in conservative Appalachia, Asheville nestles a surprisingly large amount of progressive culture, great food, and live music into the foothills. The Blue Ridge Parkway is a pleasant, peaceful meander amid the mountains, wildflowers, and various state parks and campgrounds along its 250-mile length in North Carolina

The live oak is an iconic image of the South.

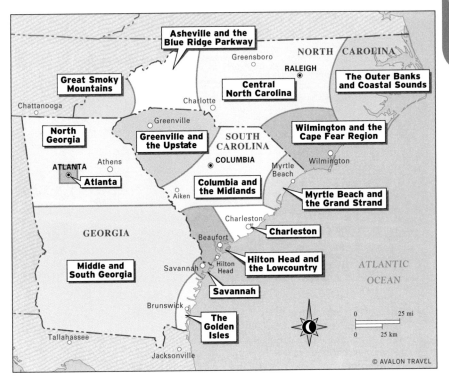

bordering thousands of acres of national forest.

Great Smoky Mountains

America's most traveled National Park, these deep mountains along the Tennessee border combine the culture of old Appalachia with friendly, kitschy tourist attractions. Skiers will enjoy the many slopes available in winter, and the warmer months offer plenty of camping, hiking, and nature-loving activities.

Myrtle Beach and the Grand Strand

The 60-mile Grand Strand focuses on the resort activity of Myrtle Beach and its adjacent, faster-growing sister North Myrtle Beach. Down the strand are the more peaceful areas of Pawleys Island and Murrells Inlet, with historic Georgetown anchoring the bottom portion of the long, skinny peninsula.

Charleston

One of America's oldest cities and an early national center of arts and culture, Charleston's legendary taste for the high life is matched by its forward-thinking outlook. The birthplace of the Civil War is not just a city of museums resting on its historic laurels; the "Holy City" is now a vibrant, creative hub of the New South.

Hilton Head and the Lowcountry

The Lowcountry's mossy, laid-back pace belies its former status as the heart of American plantation culture and the original cradle of secession. Today it is a mix of history (Beaufort and Bluffton), natural beauty (the ACE Basin), resort development (Hilton Head), military bases (Parris Island), and relaxed beaches (Edisto and Hunting Islands).

Rainbow Row, Charleston

Columbia and the Midlands
The state capital and home of South Carolina's largest university, Columbia is still a very manageable, fun place. The surrounding area, the "real" South Carolina, offers a look at a small-town way of life usually seen in Norman Rockwell paintings. A resurgent polo scene is bringing affluent but accessible Aiken back to its full equestrian glory.

Greenville and the Upstate
Fast-growing Greenville could teach many other cities a lesson in tasteful, efficient renovation. A short drive away are the treats and treasures of South Carolina's Blue Ridge region—a more user-friendly, less expensive version of the trendy mountain towns over the border in North Carolina.

Atlanta
There's always something to do in one of America's most dynamic cities, a burgeoning multiethnic melting pot that also has a friendly flavor of the old South beneath the surface. For every snarled intersection, a delightfully bucolic neighborhood tantalizes with cafés, shops, and green space. Adventurous restaurants and quirky nightlife venues are particular specialties.

North Georgia
The Blue Ridge Mountains are the backdrop for this inspiring, scenic area full of waterfalls, state parks, and outdoor adventures for the whole family. The influence of the enormous University of Georgia in Athens reigns supreme in the rolling green Piedmont region.

Middle and South Georgia
From Macon to Columbus, the rhythmic heart of Georgia is the soulful cradle of the state's rich musical tradition—and where its best barbecue is located. Its therapeutic value isn't only found in the legendary Warm Springs that gave solace to FDR. Farther south is the state's agricultural cornucopia and home of former president Jimmy Carter, along with the mighty and mysterious Okefenokee Swamp.

Savannah
Georgia's grand old city isn't just full of

history, though that's very much worth exploring. It has found new life as an arts and culture mecca, with as many or more things to do on any given day than cities two or three times its size. Come prepared for high tea or a rowdy party; either way, Savannah's got you covered.

The Golden Isles

History and salt-kissed air meet in the marshes of Georgia's chains of relatively undeveloped barrier islands. The feeling is timeless and tranquil. The Golden Isles are one of the country's hidden vacation gems and one of the most unique ecosystems in North America.

When to Go

First things first: Most portions of the Carolinas and Georgia can get scorching hot in the summer. For heat-prone areas, August is the month you probably don't want to be here. Obvious exceptions are the mountainous areas along and in the Blue Ridge, and beach and resort areas such as the Outer Banks, the Cape Fear region, Myrtle Beach, and Hilton Head, all of which see their highest visitor traffic during late summer.

Winter tends to be quite mild in South Carolina and Georgia. However, in the deep Blue Ridge and much of the interior portion of North Carolina, winters can be cold, and in the upper mountainous regions, snowy. If you do venture into the mountains in the colder months, keep in mind that many businesses there are seasonal and might be closed during your visit.

Autumn leaf-watching season throughout the Blue Ridge Mountain area, from North Georgia all the way up to the Virginia border, is extremely popular. While there are plenty of picturesque and practical state parks in the Carolinas and Georgia, they fill up very quickly during the colorful leaf-turning season. Book well in advance.

Savannah's beautiful Forsyth Park

summer on Myrtle Beach

The hurricane threat along the mid-Atlantic and Southeast coast is highest in August and September. Obviously there's no way to plan in advance to avoid a hurricane, but that is when trips, especially by plane, are most likely to be disrupted.

In Savannah hotel rooms are difficult to get around St. Patrick's Day in the middle of March. Same goes for Charleston during Spoleto in late May-early June. The Masters golf tournament in Augusta in April fills lodging for many miles around, spilling into South Carolina. In metropolitan areas like Atlanta and Charlotte, you'll have no problem finding the lodging you need.

In the many college towns throughout the Carolinas and Georgia—such as Chapel Hill and Durham in North Carolina, Columbia and Clemson in South Carolina, and Athens in Georgia—lodging is at a premium during home football weekends (basketball in North Carolina). Expect a dearth of available lodging and high prices for the lodging that is available.

Before You Go

Because of the expansive size of the region covered in this guide, and its generally blasé attitude toward public transportation, a car is a must for travel throughout the Carolinas and Georgia. Atlanta is an exception; its public transit system, MARTA, is extensive and reasonably priced.

While the weather tends to be on the hot-to-mild side, anywhere near the mountainous regions, the weather can change on a minute-to-minute basis, from uncomfortably warm to bitingly cold and wet in a flash. If you're camping anywhere in the mountains, keep in mind that the Blue Ridge region has some of the highest rainfall totals in the country. Plan and pack your gear accordingly.

Many people flying into the region do so through Hartsfield-Jackson International Airport in Atlanta, Delta Airlines' headquarters and the busiest airport in the world. When there is a delay there, there's a delay pretty much everywhere. Other key airports are in Charlotte, Columbia, Savannah/Hilton Head, Charleston, and Raleigh/Durham.

The Best of the Carolinas & Georgia

This three-week circle route begins and ends in the centrally-located airport hub of Charlotte. Explore the scenic Blue Ridge and Smoky Mountains, see the highlights of Georgia, soak up the history and beaches of the Atlantic coast, and experience the Outer Banks.

Charlotte
DAY 1

Start in Charlotte with a day of exploring museums. Visit the Levine Museum of the New South for an engaging introduction to North Carolina and Southern history, and then stop in at the Mint Museums to see their stellar collections of art and modern craft. Dine at any of Charlotte's hundreds of delicious international restaurants, and spend a night of Old South luxury at the Duke Mansion or the VanLandingham Estate.

Blue Ridge Parkway
DAY 2

Begin your two-day trek down the Blue Ridge Parkway with a visit to fun little Boone. Head down to Blowing Rock, then visit the Linville Caverns, and spend the night at Eseeola Lodge.

Asheville
DAY 3

Continue south on the Blue Ridge Parkway, with stops at the Folk Art Center, the Museum of North Carolina Minerals, and Mount Mitchell. This afternoon, take a walk around downtown Asheville, before dining at Salsa's and settling in for the night at one of the city's bed-and-breakfasts.

Charlotte, North Carolina

Great Smoky Mountains National Park

Great Smoky Mountains National Park
DAY 4
Get an early start and hit Highway 28, winding along Fontana Lake (don't miss the dam!) into Tennessee. Spend the day touring Great Smoky Mountains National Park, making sure to see Cades Cove, Clingmans Dome, and the elk at Cataloochee. Spend the night in Bryson City (at the edge of the park), or at the Pisgah Inn near Waynesville (about an hour away).

Greenville and Athens
DAY 5
Drive down to Greenville and have lunch in the progressively restored downtown area. Head west to Athens, Georgia, taking a stroll on the scenic north campus of the University of Georgia. After dinner at The National, take in a rock 'n' roll show tonight at the 40 Watt Club. Stay the evening at Hotel Indigo.

Atlanta
DAY 6
Head west into Atlanta and go to Centennial Olympic Park to visit the Georgia Aquarium and World of Coca-Cola. Tonight, take in a Braves game, if they're in town, or maybe a show at the Fox Theatre. Settle into a night in your room across Peachtree Street from the Fox in the Georgian Terrace Hotel.

FDR Country
DAY 7
Head southwest to the Warm Spring-Pine Mountain area to FDR's Little White House and explore the lasting legacy of the president's time in Georgia. Stay in a historic lodge tonight at nearby Franklin D. Roosevelt State Park.

Plains
DAY 8
Today, head southeast into little Plains and visit the several sites dedicated to native son Jimmy Carter. Make the short drive to the site of the notorious Civil War POW camp at Andersonville and tour the adjacent National Prisoner of War Museum. Spend the night in the ornate Victorian Windsor Hotel in nearby Americus.

Okefenokee and Jekyll Island

DAY 9

Get up early and make the three-hour drive to the Okefenokee Swamp to spend the day padding, hiking, and bird- and alligator-watching. This evening, head up to Jekyll Island and your stay at the legendary Jekyll Island Club.

Savannah

DAY 10

After a walk on the beach, head north to Savannah and stroll the downtown squares, with maybe a tour of the historic Owens-Thomas House. Enjoy your night's stay at a B&B like the Green Palm Inn or a boutique room at the Bohemian Hotel.

DAY 11

Ride out to Bonaventure Cemetery to enjoy its calming beauty and then on to Fort Pulaski to take in all the history there and the scenic grounds. Tonight splurge on a meal at Elizabeth on 37th.

Charleston

DAY 12

Before leaving Savannah, do some shopping on Broughton Street. Head an hour north to Beaufort, South Carolina, to walk around their charming waterfront for a while. This evening, head into Charleston and a night at a historic B&B like the John Rutledge House or an evocative hotel like The Vendue.

DAY 13

Stroll the streets of Charleston's French Quarter, Rainbow Row, and The Battery. Do some shopping on King Street. This afternoon, head across the Ashley River to historic Drayton Hall.

Myrtle Beach

DAY 14

Head north to the surf-and-sun playground of Myrtle Beach for a day on the sand and kitschy, family-friendly activities like Ripley's Believe It or Not! Enjoy the view from your balcony at the Tilghman Beach and Golf Resort.

Ripley's Believe it or Not! in Myrtle Beach

Grandfather Mountain State Park, North Carolina

The 250-mile length of the Blue Ridge Parkway in North Carolina is one of the most scenic and enjoyable drives in the country. Here are some highlights and suggested detours, north to south:

- **Milepost 238 to 244: Doughton Park** has hiking trails, a lodge, a restaurant, a picnic area, and a campground.
- **Milepost 272: E.B. Jeffress State Park** features a trail to a waterfall simply called the Cascades.
- **Milepost 292 to 295: Moses H. Cone Memorial Park** offers hiking, fishing, and equestrian trails and features the Parkway Craft Center.
- **Milepost 295 to 298: Julian Price Memorial Park** has trails, a campground, and a large lake, the only lake on the parkway where you can do some paddling.
- **Milepost 304:** The **Linn Cove Viaduct** runs alongside Grandfather Mountain. A visitors center leads to a trail under the viaduct.
- **Milepost 316: Linville Falls Recreation Area** has trails with overlooks of the namesake falls, along with a nice campground.
- **Milepost 331:** The little **Museum of North Carolina Minerals** explores the state's mining background.
- **Milepost 363 to 369: Craggy Gardens** is a great place to see blooming purple rhododendron in June.
- **Milepost 382:** The **Folk Art Center** sells and exhibits traditional Appalachian crafts.
- **Milepost 384:** The brand-new, LEED-certified **Blue Ridge Parkway Visitors Center** includes a large theater showing a very good film about the region's history and culture.
- **Milepost 431: Richland Balsam** is the highest point on the parkway at 6,053 feet. A trail takes you through a small old-growth forest.
- **Detours: Mount Mitchell State Park** (via Hwy. 128); **Grandfather Mountain State Park** (via Blowing Rock Hwy./U.S. 221); **Linville Caverns** (via U.S. 221).

Wilmington
DAY 15

After a morning swim, make the short trip into North Carolina to visit historic Wilmington. Take a walking tour of the gorgeous historic district. At night, attend a concert at Thalian Hall, and take your pick of beautiful bed-and-breakfasts for your night's lodging.

The Outer Banks
DAY 16

Head up to New Bern for lunch, allowing at least a couple of hours for travel time. Spend the afternoon touring historic Beaufort, making sure to leave time for a visit to the Maritime Museum and the Old Burying Ground. For supper, visit a legend, Morehead City's Sanitary Fish Market.

DAY 17
Explore Down East in the morning, visiting Harkers Island's Core Sound Waterfowl Museum. Wend your way up to Cedar Island, and catch the ferry to Ocracoke, a 2.5-hour voyage. Stay the night at the Captain's Landing in Ocracoke.

DAY 18
Explore Ocracoke in the morning, and then, early in the day, catch the ferry to Hatteras (40 minutes on the water). From there, head up Highway 12, tracing the Outer Banks northward. Cross onto Roanoke Island, visiting the Aquarium or Fort Raleigh National Historic Site, and staying at the White Doe Inn; or keep driving north to Nags Head, and spend the night at the First Colony Inn.

The Triangle
DAY 19
Take U.S. 64 west to visit the state museums of Raleigh: the North Carolina Museums of History, Natural Sciences, and Art. Pick up a hot dog for lunch at the Roast Grill—don't ask for condiments!—or have a more elegant lunch inside the Museum of Art. This evening, make the jaunt over to Chapel Hill spending a luxurious night at the Carolina Inn.

DAY 20
This morning tour the campus of the University of North Carolina, and if you're a sports fan, visit the Carolina Basketball Museum. Mosey the nine miles over to Durham for lunch at the Thai Café or one of the city's great taco stands. Check out campuses at North Carolina Central University and Duke University. In the evening, catch a Durham Bulls game, or head back to Chapel Hill for some live music at Cat's Cradle or Local 506.

Lexington and Back to Charlotte
DAY 21
Get on I-85 for the drive back down to Charlotte—but budget time to stop for some of Lexington's amazing barbecue along the way!

The Paths of the Civil War

This itinerary for Civil War buffs, customized for those flying into and leaving from Atlanta, hits the conflict's historical highlights in Georgia and South Carolina. Because the CSS *Hunley* exhibit in Charleston toward the end of the trip is only open on weekends, ideally you should begin this trip on a Sunday or Monday.

Day 1
Head to Atlanta's Grant Park neighborhood to visit the Cyclorama, a unique Victorian-era portrayal of the Battle of Atlanta (Zoo Atlanta is right next door). This afternoon drive a bit east to Stone Mountain Park to see the huge relief sculpture of Robert E. Lee, Stonewall Jackson, and Jefferson Davis

on the granite outcropping that gives the park its name.

Day 2
Take a road trip in your rental car to North Georgia. See the burgeoning Kennesaw Mountain National Battlefield. Spend the rest of the day touring the expansive Chickamauga battlefield near the Tennessee border.

Day 3
Drive down I-85 to I-185 and head into Columbus for a visit to the National Civil War Naval Museum, chronicling the lesser-known maritime aspect of the conflict. After lunch drive southeast on Highway 26

Chickamauga battlefield

and spend the afternoon at the site of the notorious Andersonville POW camp and adjacent National Prisoner of War Museum. Spend the night in nearby Americus at the Windsor Hotel.

Day 4

Head down I-75 and a bit east to little Irwinville and the site of the arrest of Confederate President Jefferson Davis. After lunch head on into Savannah for a stay at an antebellum B&B like the Foley House.

Day 5

Tour Savannah's downtown squares, including a stop at the Green-Meldrim House, General Sherman's headquarters while he was in town. Stroll along River Street, focal point of Savannah's huge antebellum cotton shipping industry.

Day 6

Head east along the road to Tybee Island for a long visit to the scenic grounds at Fort Pulaski, which Robert E. Lee helped construct before the war. Once considered the most impregnable fortress in the world, Fort Pulaski's Confederate garrison was forced to surrender by the first use of rifled cannons in warfare. Close the day with the two-hour drive to Charleston and a night at the Mills House Hotel, which once hosted Lee himself.

Day 7

Take the ferry and spend the morning at Fort Sumter in Charleston Harbor, where the Civil War began in April 1861. This afternoon visit the CSS Hunley facility in North Charleston, where the first submarine ever to attack an enemy vessel is being painstakingly restored (book tickets well in advance). Tomorrow you drive back in time to catch your flight out of Atlanta.

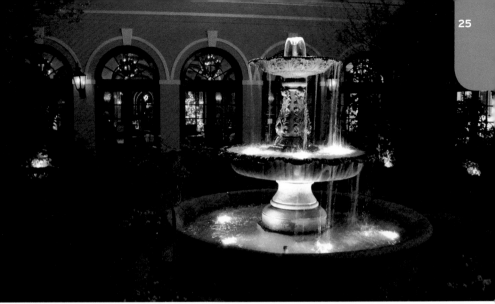
historic Mills House Hotel, Charleston

Literary Lights

This week-plus driving tour takes you from the Appalachians to the ocean in the footsteps of the region's most legendary authors.

Day 1
Your first stop is in Asheville, North Carolina. Enjoy a relaxing walk through the vibrant downtown, capped by a visit at the centrally located Thomas Wolfe home. A short drive away in Flat Rock is the home of poet Carl Sandburg. Retire to your swank room at the Grove Park Inn.

Day 2
Get up bright and early for a drive down to Nantahala Outdoor Center on the Georgia-South Carolina border for some white-water rafting on the scenic Chattooga River, setting of the 1972 film adapted from James Dickey's novel *Deliverance*. Tonight, enjoy a hearty dinner at the nearby Dillard House in Dillard, Georgia, also a B&B where you'll stay the night.

Day 3
Make the short drive to Atlanta and a visit to the Margaret Mitchell House, a.k.a. "The Dump," where the former newspaper reporter wrote the novel *Gone with the Wind* over a 10-year period. After a Southern comfort food lunch at nearby Mary Mac's Tea Room, venture into west Atlanta for a visit at the Wren's Nest, home of Joel Chandler Harris, author of the tales of Uncle Remus. Enjoy your night's stay at the Georgian Terrace hotel, where Clark Gable and Vivien Leigh stayed while in town for the *Gone with the Wind* premiere.

Day 4
Visit Milledgeville, former state capital and stately town where Flannery O'Connor wrote all her most important works. Visit her family farm at Andalusia and see the room where she worked, then head downtown to see the O'Connor collection of memorabilia at her alma mater, Georgia College & State University.

Day 5

On the way out of town head to nearby Eatonton and visit the recreated boyhood home of Joel Chandler Harris, author of the Uncle Remus stories. Take the Alice Walker Driving Trail, highlighting important local sites in the life of the great African American author who also called Eatonton home. Tonight, you spend the night in Savannah, at the Hamilton-Turner Inn, once owned by "Mandy," a character in John Berendt's *Midnight in the Garden of Good and Evil.*

Day 6

Tour the squares of downtown Savannah, including a stop at the Flannery O'Connor Childhood Home and the nearby, ornate Cathedral of St. John the Baptist, where she and her family attended mass. Enjoy lunch at Mrs. Wilkes' Dining Room, mentioned prominently in *Midnight in the Garden of Good and Evil.*

Day 7

An hour away, walk around charming little Beaufort, South Carolina, which inspired so much of the work of novelist Pat Conroy. The grave of his father, James, a.k.a. "The Great Santini," is in the National Cemetery near downtown. Stay the night in the historic Cuthbert House Inn, which hosted cast members such as Barbra Streisand during the filming of *Prince of Tides.*

Day 8

For an optional additional day, head to the "Holy City" of Charleston for a visit to Fort Moultrie on Sullivan's Island, where a young Edgar Allan Poe was stationed as a U.S. Army officer and inspired to write *The Gold Bug.* Eat a pub lunch at nearby Poe's Tavern. Spend the rest of the day and evening in downtown Charleston, soaking up the atmosphere that inspired the tale *Porgy and Bess,* first novelized by native son DuBose Heyward and then popularized by George Gershwin's opera.

The African American Experience

The Carolinas and Georgia were critical not only in the U.S. civil rights movement but also in the history of African Americans since before the nation's inception. Here are some black history highlights:

North Carolina

- Greensboro: Visit the International Civil Rights Center and Museum in the former F. W. Woolworth retail store, site of a 1960 sit-in to protest segregation.

- Wilmington: This coastal city was the site of notorious race riots in 1898.

- Rodanthe: At the Chicamacomico Life-Saving Station, learn about the exploits of the African American crew at the Pea Island Life-Saving Station.

South Carolina

- St. Helena Island: This Gullah community features the Penn Center, where Martin Luther King Jr. once organized civil rights activists.

- Beaufort: African American Civil War hero Robert Smalls has a memorial at the Tabernacle Baptist Church. See his former home on Prince Street. View the Berners Barnwell Sams House, where Harriet Tubman once worked as a nurse.

- Daufuskie Island: The Mary Field School is where author Pat Conroy once taught a group of African American schoolchildren. The experience gave him new insight into African American culture.

WHITE WATER, BLACK WATER, BLUE WATER

The Carolinas and Georgia provide a wealth of water-based enjoyment, whether by kayak, canoe, fishing boat, or just plain enjoying the beach.

WHITE-WATER RAFTING

- The **U.S. National Whitewater Center** in Charlotte offers a variety of well-supervised activities, including rafting, paddling, and kayaking, as well as dry-land activities like zip-lining.
- **Nantahala Outdoor Center** offers rafting and tubing opportunities on the scenic Nantahala River in North Carolina.
- The **Chattooga River** at the border of the Carolinas and Georgia was the setting of the movie *Deliverance* and provides a range of rafting opportunities along Sections III and IV, designated Wild and Scenic.
- Columbus, Georgia, is tearing down obsolete earthen dams on the **Chattahoochee River** to make white-water rafting an eco-tourism attraction.

BLACKWATER KAYAKING

- The Cape Fear River of North Carolina is rife with kayaking and canoeing possibilities. The 147-mile **Cape Fear River Trail** starts in J. Bayard Clark Park in Fayetteville and takes you all the way to the mouth of the river in Southport.
- **Cape Romain National Wildlife Refuge** north of Charleston, has hundreds of square miles of sheltered and ecologically significant wetland within its borders for your paddling enjoyment.
- The **Edisto River** in coastal South Carolina is the world's longest blackwater river. Kayaking and canoeing opportunities abound, whether on your own or through numerous chartered trips.

- The **Congaree River** running through Columbia, South Carolina, is a friendly and fun place to kayak. Nearby you can paddle through the ancient wetland of **Congaree National Park,** one of the last old-growth forests left in the United States.
- The **Altamaha River Canoe Trail** in southeast Georgia takes you down one of the East Coast's largest and most protected rivers.

BLUE-WATER ADVENTURE

- In addition to its miles of windswept beaches, the Outer Banks offer an amazing look at an old maritime heritage. Farther down the coast is the **North Carolina Maritime Museum** in Beaufort.
- The beaches on the North Carolina coast near Wilmington—**Wrightsville Beach** and **Kure Beach**—are a perfect blend of beauty and family-friendliness.
- **Little River,** North Carolina, seemingly offers as many fishing charters as there are people in this little town.
- At **Myrtle Beach,** South Carolina, you can enjoy a water park or a banana ride or a Jet Ski—all in one afternoon.
- Take a 90-minute boat ride around **Charleston Harbor** on **SpiritLine Cruises.**
- There may not be a better beach to ride your bike on than **Hilton Head,** South Carolina.
- Hop a ferry to one of Georgia's Golden Isles, such as **Cumberland Island** or **Sapelo Island,** and enjoy peace and quiet along with a bit of history.

REV. MARTIN LUTHER KING, JR.
1929 ~ 1968
"Free at last, Free at last,
Thank God Almighty
I'm Free at last."

CORETTA SCOTT KING
1927 ~ 2006
"And now abide Faith, Hope,
Love, These Three; but the
greatest of these is Love."
1 Cor. 13:13

Martin Luther King Jr. National Historic Site

- Walterboro: The Tuskegee Airmen Memorial pays tribute to the World War II heroes.

- Charleston: Explore history at the Old Slave Mart museum. The Avery Research Center for African American History and Culture is at the College of Charleston. Boone Hall Plantation has 10 of the best-restored antebellum slave quarters in the country. The Bench by the Road is a monument to the million or so enslaved people who first arrived in the New World at Sullivan's Island.

Georgia

- Albany: The Albany Civil Rights Institute explores the Albany Movement of the early 1960s, a critical early phase of civil rights and of Martin Luther King Jr.'s legacy.

- Atlanta: An influential collection of historically black colleges and universities (Spelman College, Morehouse College, and Clark Atlanta University), the Atlanta University Center occupies a contiguous space near Downtown. The centerpiece of

study of the civil rights movement's greatest hero, the Martin Luther King Jr. National Historic Site comprises his birth home, the King Center for Nonviolent Social Change, the tomb of King and his wife, Coretta Scott King, the central Visitors Center, and Historic Ebenezer Baptist Church. The site is within Sweet Auburn, the most influential traditionally black neighborhood in Atlanta.

- Sapelo Island: This Sea Island retains ancestral African American communities with direct links to General Sherman's "40 Acres and a Mule" order.

- Savannah: The oldest black congregation in the United States worships at First African Baptist Church, in a historic downtown building built by enslaved people. Formerly a black-owned bank, the Ralph Mark Gilbert Civil Rights Museum interprets Savannah's key role in civil rights in Georgia. The Pin Point Heritage Museum outside Savannah chronicles the oystering community where Supreme Court justice Clarence Thomas grew up.

THE OUTER BANKS AND COASTAL SOUNDS

The Outer Banks are like a great seine net set along the northeastern corner of North Carolina, holding the Sounds and inner coast apart from the open ocean, yet shimmying obligingly with the forces of water and wind. The Outer Banks can be—and on many occasions have been—profoundly transformed by a single storm. A powerful hurricane can fill in a centuries-old inlet in one night, and open a new channel wherever it pleases. As recently as 2003, Hatteras Island was cut in half—by Hurricane Isabel—though the channel has since been artificially filled. This evanescent landscape poses challenges to the life that it supports, and creates adaptable and hardy plants, animals, and people.

The Sounds are often overlooked by travelers, but they are an enormously important part of the state and the region. Collectively known as the Albemarle-Pamlico Estuary, North Carolina's Sounds—Albemarle, Pamlico, Core, Croatan, Roanoke, and Currituck—form the second-largest estuarine system in the country after Chesapeake Bay. They cover nearly 3,000 square miles and drain more than 30,000. The diverse marine and terrestrial environments shelter crucial plant and animal communities as well as estuarine systems that are essential to the environmental health of the whole region and to the Atlantic Ocean.

Sheltered from the Atlantic, the Inner Banks are much more accommodating, ecologically speaking, than the Outer Banks. Wetlands along the Sounds invite migratory

© DREAMSTIME.COM

THE OUTER BANKS

HIGHLIGHTS

◖ **Fort Raleigh National Historic Site:** Here at the site of the Lost Colony, the mysterious first chapter of English settlement in the New World unfolded in the 1580s (page 40).

◖ **Ocracoke Island:** On this remote island, you'll find a historic village that is the home of one of America's most unique local communities, as well as some serious water sports and walking opportunities (page 48).

◖ **Cape Lookout National Seashore:** The more than 50 miles of coastline along Core and Shackleford Banks, now home only to wild horses and turtle nests, were once also the home of Bankers, who made their livings in the fishing, whaling, and shipping trades (page 51).

◖ **Beaufort's Old Burying Ground:** Even if it weren't the final resting place of the "Little Girl Buried in a Barrel of Rum," this little churchyard would still be one of the prettiest and most interesting cemeteries in the South (page 56).

◖ **Core Sound Waterfowl Museum:** Actually a museum about people rather than ducks, the Waterfowl Museum eloquently tells of the everyday lives of past generations of Down Easterners, while bringing their descendants together to reforge community bonds (page 59).

◖ **North Carolina Aquarium:** Sharks and jellyfish and their aquatic kin show their true beauty in underwater habitats at the aquarium, while trails and boat tours lead to the watery world outdoors (page 62).

◖ **The Great Dismal Swamp:** This natural wonder straddling the Virginia-Carolina line is an amazing place for canoeing or kayaking, bird-watching, or sightseeing (page 64).

◖ **Somerset Place Historic Site:** The graceful architecture and exotic setting of this early plantation contrast with the tragic history of its slavery days (page 69).

◖ **Mattamuskeet National Wildlife Refuge:** The landmark lodge on Lake Mattamuskeet towers over a dramatic waterscape that attracts migratory birds by the tens of thousands (page 72).

◖ **Tryon Palace:** The splendid and, in its day, controversial seat of colonial government in North Carolina is reconstructed in New Bern's historic district, a significant destination worthy of a whole day's leisurely exploration (page 73).

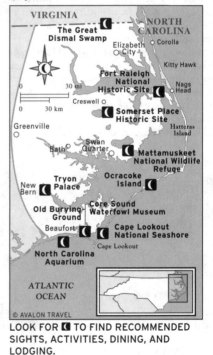

LOOK FOR ◖ TO FIND RECOMMENDED SIGHTS, ACTIVITIES, DINING, AND LODGING.

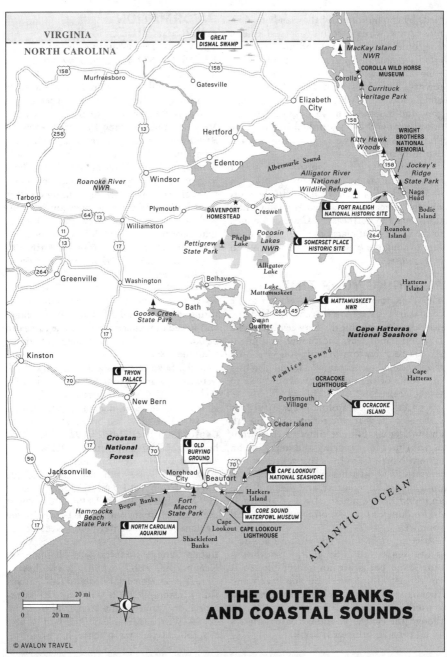

VIRGINIA
NORTH CAROLINA

GREAT DISMAL SWAMP

MacKay Island NWR

COROLLA WILD HORSE MUSEUM

Corolla

Currituck Heritage Park

158   Murfreesboro

Gatesville

158   Elizabeth City

258   13

Hertford

Kitty Hawk Woods

WRIGHT BROTHERS NATIONAL MEMORIAL

Edenton

158   Jockey's Ridge State Park

Roanoke River NWR

Windsor

Albermarle Sound

Alligator River National Wildlife Refuge

Nags Head

Bodie Island

11   13

Tarboro

64   13   Plymouth

DAVENPORT HOMESTEAD

64   Creswell

FORT RALEIGH NATIONAL HISTORIC SITE

Roanoke Island

Williamston

17

Pettigrew State Park

Phelps Lake

Pocosin Lakes NWR

SOMERSET PLACE HISTORIC SITE

264

264   Greenville

Washington

Belhaven

Alligator Lake

Hatteras Island

Goose Creek State Park

Bath

Lake Mattamuskeet

264   45   MATTAMUSKEET NWR

17

Swan Quarter

Cape Hatteras National Seashore

Kinston

70

Pamlico Sound

Cape Hatteras

TRYON PALACE

OCRACOKE LIGHTHOUSE

New Bern

Portsmouth Village

OCRACOKE ISLAND

Croatan National Forest

70

Cedar Island

50

Jacksonville

17

OLD BURYING GROUND

Morehead City   Beaufort

70   CAPE LOOKOUT NATIONAL SEASHORE

Harkers Island

17

Hammocks Beach State Park

Bogue Banks

Fort Macon State Park

CORE SOUND WATERFOWL MUSEUM

ATLANTIC OCEAN

NORTH CAROLINA AQUARIUM

Cape Lookout

CAPE LOOKOUT LIGHTHOUSE

Shackleford Banks

0   20 mi
0   20 km

THE OUTER BANKS AND COASTAL SOUNDS

© AVALON TRAVEL

birds by the hundreds of thousands to shelter and rest, while pocosins (a special kind of bog found in the region) and maritime forests have nurtured a great variety of life for eons. Here is where North Carolina's oldest towns—Bath, New Bern, and Edenton—set down roots, from which the rest of the state grew and bloomed. In Washington County, 4,000-year-old canoes pulled out of Lake Phelps testify to the region's unplumbed depths of history.

You may hear folks in North Carolina refer to any point on the coast, be it Wilmington or Nags Head, as "Down East." In the most authentic, local usage of the term, Down East really refers to northeastern Carteret County, to the islands and marsh towns in a confined region along the banks of Core Sound, north of Beaufort.

PLANNING YOUR TIME

The standard beach-season rules apply to the coastal areas covered in this chapter. Lodging prices go up dramatically between Memorial Day and Labor Day, and though you might score a rock-bottom price if you visit on a mild weekend off-season, you might also find that some of the destinations you'd like to visit are closed.

Coastal North Carolina is beautiful four seasons of the year, and for many people fall and winter are favorite times to visit, wonderful times for canoeing and kayaking on eastern North Carolina's rivers, creeks, and swamps. The weather is often more than mild enough for comfort, and the landscape and wildlife are not so obscured by tropical verdancy as they are in the spring and summer.

Late summer and early autumn are hurricane season all through the Southeast. Hurricane paths are unpredictable, so if you're planning a week on the beach and know that a hurricane is hovering over Cuba, it won't necessarily hit North Carolina, although the central Carolina coast is always an odds-on favorite for landfall.

INFORMATION AND SERVICES

The **Aycock Brown Welcome Center** (milepost 1.5, U.S. 158, 877/629-4386, www.outerbanks. org, Dec.-Feb. daily 9am-5pm, Mar.-May and Sept.-Nov. daily 9am-5:30pm, June-Aug. daily 9am-6pm) at Kitty Hawk, the **Outer Banks Welcome Center** (1 Visitors Center Circle, Manteo), and the **Cape Hatteras National Seashore Visitors Center** (Cape Hatteras Lighthouse, Memorial Day-Labor Day daily 9am-6pm, Labor Day-Memorial Day daily 9am-5pm) on Ocracoke are all clearinghouses for regional travel information. The **Outer Banks Visitors Bureau** (www.outerbanks. org) can be reached directly at 877/629-4386. Extensive travel information is also available from the **Crystal Coast Tourism Authority** (3409 Arendell St., 877/206-0929, www.crystalcoastnc.org).

North Carolina Sea Grant (919/515-2454, www.ncseagrant.org) provides wallet cards listing the seasons for different seafood caught and served in Carteret County. The cards can be ordered by mail or downloaded and printed from the website.

Major **hospitals** are located in Nags Head, Windsor, Washington, Edenton, Ahoskie, and Elizabeth City. On Ocracoke, only accessible by air or water, nonemergency medical needs can be addressed by **Ocracoke Health Center** (305 Back Rd., 252/928-1511, afterhours 252/928-7425). Note that 911 works on Ocracoke, like everywhere else.

Other hospitals in the area include **Carteret General Hospital** (3500 Arendell St., Morehead City, 252/808-6000, www. ccgh.org, where the author was born), **Craven Regional Medical Center** (2000 Neuse Blvd., New Bern, 252/633-8111, www.uhseast.com), **Duplin General Hospital** (401 N. Main St., Kenansville, 910/296-0941, www.uhseast. com), **Lenoir Memorial Hospital** (100 Airport Rd., Kinston, 252/522-7000, www.lenoirmemorial.org), and **Wayne Memorial Hospital** (2700 Wayne Memorial Dr., Goldsboro, 919/736-1110, www.waynehealth.org).

Nags Head and Vicinity

The Outer Banks are a long sandbar, constantly eroding and amassing, slip-sliding into new configurations with every storm. The wind is the invisible player in this process, the man behind the curtain giving orders to the water and the sand. The enormous dune known as Jockey's Ridge was a landmark to early mariners, visible from miles out to sea.

According to legend, Nags Head was a place of sinister peril to those seafarers. Islanders, it's said, would walk a nag or mule, carrying a lantern around its neck, slowly back and forth along the beach, trying to lure ships into the shallows where they might founder or wreck, making their cargo easy pickings for the land pirates.

It was the relentless wind at Kill Devil Hill that attracted the Wright brothers to North Carolina. Today, it brings thousands of enthusiasts every year, hang gliders and parasailers, kite-boarders and kite flyers. Add to these pursuits sailing, surfing, kayaking, hiking, birding, and, of course, beach-going, and the northern Outer Banks are perhaps North Carolina's most promising region for outdoor adventurers. Several nature reserves encompass large swaths of the unique ecological environments of the Banks, though increasingly the shifting sands are given over to human development.

SIGHTS
Wright Brothers National Memorial
Although they are remembered for a 12-second flight on a December morning in 1903, Wilbur and Orville Wright actually spent more than three years coming and going between their home in Dayton, Ohio, and Kitty Hawk, North Carolina. As they tested their gliders on Kill Devil Hill, the tallest sand dune on the Outer Banks, the Wright brothers were assisted by many Bankers. The locals fed and housed them, built hangars, and assisted with countless practicalities that helped make the brothers' experiment a success. On the morning of December 17, 1903, several local people were present to help that famous first powered flight get off the ground. John Daniels, a lifesaver from a nearby station, took the iconic photograph of the airplane lifting off. It was the first

THE OUTER BANKS

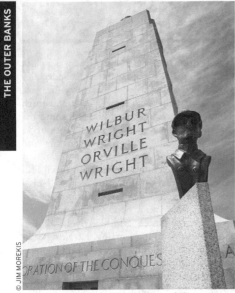

© JIM MOREKIS

Wright Brothers National Memorial

acres of a strange and amazing environment, the largest active sand dune system in the eastern United States. Ever-changing, this oceanside desert is maintained by the constant action of the northeast and southwest winds. Visitors can walk on and among the dunes. It's a famously great place to fly kites, go sand-boarding, and hang glide (hang gliding requires a valid USHGA rating and a permit supplied by the park office).

Nags Head Woods Ecological Preserve

Bordering Jockey's Ridge is another unique natural area, the Nature Conservancy's **Nags Head Woods Ecological Preserve** (701 W. Ocean Acres Dr., about 1 mile from milepost 9.5, U.S. 158, 252/441-2525, www.nature. org, daily dawn-dusk). Nags Head Woods is over 1,000 acres of deciduous maritime forest, dunes, wetlands, and interdune ponds. More than 50 species of birds nest here in season, including ruby-throated hummingbirds, green herons, and red-shouldered hawks, and it is also home to a host of other animals and unusual plants. Maps to the public trails are available at the visitors center.

Kitty Hawk Woods

Slightly smaller but no less important is the Nature Conservancy's **Kitty Hawk Woods** (south of U.S. 158 at Kitty Hawk, trail access from Woods Rd. and Birch Lane, off Treasure St., 252/261-8891, www.nature.org, daily dawn-dusk). These maritime forests harbor the unusual species of flora and fauna of the maritime swale ecosystem, a swampy forest sheltered between coastal ridges. Kitty Hawk Woods is open to the public for hiking and birding, and can be explored from the water as well. A canoe and kayak put-in is next to the parking lot of **Kitty Hawk Kayaks** (6150 N. Croatan Rd./U.S. 158, 252/261-0145, www. khkss.com).

Currituck Heritage Park

The shore of Currituck Sound is an unexpected place to find the art deco home of a

and only photograph he ever made. He was later quoted in a newspaper as saying of the flight, "I didn't think it amounted to much." But it did, and that flight is honored at the **Wright Brothers National Memorial** (milepost 7.5, U.S. 158, Kill Devil Hills, 252/441-7430, www.nps.gov/wrbr, park year-round daily, visitors center June-Aug. daily 9am-6pm, Sept.-May daily 9am-5pm, free). At the visitors center, replica gliders are on display, along with artifacts from the original gliders and changing displays sponsored by NASA. You can also tour the reconstructed living quarters and flight hangar, and, of course, climb Kill Devil Hill to get a glimpse of what that first aviator saw.

Jockey's Ridge State Park

Jockey's Ridge State Park (Carolista Dr., off milepost 12, U.S. 158, Nags Head, 252/441-7132, www.jockeysridgestatepark.com, Nov.-Feb. daily 8am-6pm, Mar. and Oct. daily 8am-7pm, Apr.-May and Sept. daily 8am-8pm, June-Aug. daily 8am-9pm) contains 420

© JIM MOREKIS

Jockey's Ridge State Park

1920s industrial magnate. The **Whalehead Club** (1100 Club Rd., off milepost 11, Hwy. 12, 252/453-9040, www.whaleheadclub.com, visitors center 11am-5pm daily, standard tours 9am-4pm daily, specialty tours require 24 hours advance notice, $5-15) was built as a summer cottage by Edward Collings Knight Jr., an industrialist whose fortune was in railroads and sugar. This beautifully simple yellow house—only a "cottage" by the standards of someone like Knight—sits on a peaceful spit of land that catches the breeze off the sound. It's the centerpiece of Currituck Heritage Park, where visitors can picnic, wade, or launch from the boat ramp, in addition to touring the house.

Next to the Whalehead Club is the **Outer Banks Center for Wildlife Education** (Currituck Heritage Park, Corolla, 252/453-0221, www.ncwildlife.org, daily 9am-5pm, free). With exhibits focusing on the native birds, fish, and other creatures of Currituck Sound, the center also has a huge collection of antique decoys—an important folk tradition of the Carolina coast—and offers many special nature and art programs throughout the year; check the website for a program calendar.

The 1875 **Currituck Beach Lighthouse** (Currituck Heritage Park, 252/453-4939, Apr.-Nov. daily 9am-5pm, closed in rough weather, $8, free under age 7) stands on the other side of the Center for Wildlife Education. It is one of the few historic lighthouses that visitors can climb. The 214-step spiral staircase leads to the huge Fresnel lens and a panoramic view of Currituck Sound.

Corolla Wild Horse Museum

In the town of Corolla, the circa-1900 Corolla Schoolhouse has been transformed into a museum honoring the wild horses of the Outer Banks. The **Corolla Wild Horse Museum** (1126 Old Schoolhouse Lane, Corolla, 252/453-8002, summer Mon.-Sat. 10am-4pm, off-season hours vary, free) tells of the history of the herd, which once roamed all over Corolla but now live in a preserve north of the town.

PRONUNCIATION PRIMER

The Outer Banks are a garland of peculiar names, as well as names that look straightforward but are in fact pronounced in unexpectedly quirky ways. If you make reference publicly to the town of Corolla, and pronounce it like the Toyota model, you'll be recognized right away as someone "from off." It's pronounced "ker-AH-luh." Similarly, Bodie Island, site of the stripy lighthouse, is pronounced "body," as in one's earthly shell. That same pattern of pronouncing o as "ah," as in "stick out your tongue and say 'ah,'" is repeated farther down the coast at Chicamacomico, which comes out "chick-uh-muh-CAH-muh-co." But just to keep you on your toes, the rule doesn't apply to Ocracoke, which is pronounced like the Southern vegetable and Southern drink: "OH-kruh-coke."

Farther south along the banks is the town of Rodanthe, which has an elongated last syllable, "ro-DANTH-ee." On Roanoke Island, Manteo calls out for a Spanish emphasis, but is in fact front-loaded, like so many Carolina words and names. It's pronounced "MAN-tee-oh" or "MANNY-oh." Next door is the town of Wanchese. This sounds like a pallid dairy product, "WAN-cheese." Inland, the Cashie River is pronounced "cuh-SHY," Bertie County is "ber-TEE," and Chowan County is "chuh-WON."

ENTERTAINMENT AND EVENTS

Chip's Wine and Beer Market (milepost 6, Croatan Hwy./U.S. 158, Kill Devil Hills, 252/449-8229, www.chipswinemarket.com) is, in addition to what the name suggests, the home of **Outer Banks Wine University.** In at least two classes a week, Chip himself and other instructors host wine and beer tastings with an educational as well as gustatory bent.

Nightlife

The **Outer Banks Brewing Station** (milepost 8.5, Croatan Hwy./U.S. 158, Kill Devil Hills, 252/449-2739, www.obbrewing.com) was founded in the early 1990s by a group of friends who met in the Peace Corps. The brewery-restaurant they built here was designed and constructed by Outer Bankers, modeled on the design of the old lifesaving stations so important in the region's history. The pub serves several very gourmet homebrews at $4.50 for a pint, $6 for four five-ounce samplers. They've also got a nice lunch and supper menu, with elaborate entrées as well as the requisite pub fare.

   Bacu Grill (Outer Banks Mall, milepost 14, U.S. 158, Nags Head, 252/480-1892), a Cuban-fusion restaurant, features live jazz and blues music, and serves good beer, wine, and snacks into the wee hours of the morning. **Kelly's Outer Banks Restaurant and Tavern** (milepost 10.5. U.S. 158, Nags Head, 252/441-4116, www.kellysrestaurant.com, Sun.-Thurs. 4:30pm-midnight, Fri.-Sat. 4:30pm-2am) is also a good bet for live music and has a long wine list with some lovely vintages. **Lucky 12 Tavern** (3308 S. Virginia Dare Tr., Nags Head, 252/255-5825, www.lucky12tavern.com, daily 11:30am-2am) is a traditional sports bar with TVs, foosball, and New York-style pizza.

SPORTS AND RECREATION
Kayaking

Coastal Kayak (make reservations at North Beach Outfitters, 1240 Duck Rd., Duck, 252/261-6262, www.coastalkayak.org) offers tours throughout the northern Outer Banks, including guided trips through the Alligator River National Wildlife Refuge and the Pea Island National Wildlife Refuge, as well as the Pine Island Audubon Sanctuary and Kitty Hawk Woods. Tours last 2 to 3.5 hours and cost $35-50.

Diving

The **Outer Banks Dive Center** (3917 S. Croatan Hwy., 252/449-8349, www.obxdive.

com) offers instruction and guided tours of wrecks off the coast of the Outer Banks. Guided wreck dives are only available April-November. All levels of divers are welcome.

Hiking and Touring
The **Currituck Banks National Estuarine Preserve** (Hwy. 12, 252/261-8891, www.nc-coastalreserve.net) protects nearly 1,000 acres of woods and water extending into Currituck Sound. A 0.3-mile boardwalk runs from the parking lot to the Sound, and a primitive trail runs from the parking lot 1.5 miles through the maritime forest.

Back Country Outfitters and Guides (107-C Corolla Light Town Center, Corolla, 252/453-0877, http://outerbankstours.com) leads a variety of tours in the Corolla region, including Segway beach tours, wild horse-watching trips, kayaking, and other off-road tours.

Surfing
The North Carolina coast has a strong surfing culture, not to mention strong waves, making this a top destination for experienced surfers and those who would like to learn. **Island Revolution Surf Co. and Skate** (252/453-9484, www.islandrevolution.com, must be over age 8 and a good swimmer, group lessons $60 pp, private lessons $75) offers private and one-on-one surfing lessons as well as board rentals. So does **Ocean Atlantic Rentals** (Corolla Light Town Center, 252/453-2440, www.oar-nc.com, group lessons $50 pp, private lessons $75, couples $120, must know how to swim), which also has locations in Duck, Nags Head, and Avon, and **Corolla Surf Shop** (several locations, 252/453-9283, www.corollasurfshop.com, age 9 and up).

Online resources for Outer Banks surfing include the website of the Outer Banks District of the Eastern Surfing Association (http://outerbanks.surfesa.org), www.wrightcoastsurf.com, www.obxsurfinfo.com, and www.surfkdh.com.

Kayaking
The Outer Banks combines two very different possible kayaking experiences—the challenge of ocean kayaking and the leisurely drifting zones of the salt marshes and back creeks. **Kitty Hawk Sports** (798 Sunset Blvd., 252/453-6900, www.kittyhawksports.com) is an old and established outdoors outfitter that leads kayaking and other expeditions. Another good bet is **Kitty Hawk Kayaks** (6150 N. Croatan Hwy., Kitty Hawk, 866/702-5061, www.khkss.com), which teaches kayaking and canoeing, rents equipment for paddling and surfing, and, in cooperation with the Nature Conservancy, leads tours, including overnight expeditions, through gorgeous waterways in pristine habitats.

Kitty Hawk Kites (877/359-8447, www.kittyhawk.com), which *National Geographic Adventure* magazine calls one of the "Best Adventure Travel Companies on Earth," has locations throughout the Outer Banks, including at Corolla. They too teach and lead hang gliding, parasailing, Jet Skiing, kite-boarding, kayaking, and lots more ways to ride the wind and water.

ACCOMMODATIONS
Under $150
The **₵ First Colony Inn** (6720 Virginia Dare Tr., Nags Head, 800/368-9390, www.firstcolonyinn.com, $69-299, depending on season) is a wonderful 1932 beachfront hotel. This regional landmark has won historic preservation and landscaping awards for its 1988 renovation, which involved moving the entire building, in three pieces, three miles south of its original location. The pretty and luxurious guest rooms are surprisingly affordable.

Bed-and-breakfasts include the sound-front **Cypress Moon Inn** (1206 Harbor Court, Kitty Hawk, 877/905-5060, www.cypressmooninn.com, age 18 and over, $200 summer, $175 spring and fall, $135 winter), with three pretty guest rooms. The **Baldview B&B** (3805 Elijah Baum Rd., Kitty Hawk, 252/255-2829, www.baldview.com, no children or pets, $125-200) is a modern residence located on a beautiful property along the sound, with four nicely appointed guest rooms and a carriage house.

The **Cypress House Inn** (milepost 8, Beach

Rd., Kill Devil Hills, 800/554-2764, www.
cypresshouseinn.com, $99-199, depending on
season) is a very traditional coastal Carolina-
style house, built in the 1940s and an easy walk
to the beach. Its hurricane shutters and cypress-
paneled guest rooms will give you a taste of
Outer Banks life in the days before the motels
and resorts.

In Kitty Hawk and Nags Head, you'll
find an abundance of motels, from chains to
classic 1950s mom-and-pops. The **Surf Side
Hotel** (6701 Virginia Dare Tr., Nags Head,
www.surfsideobx.com, 800/552-7873, from
$55 off-season, from $165 high season) is a
favorite for simple and comfortable accommodations, with standard rooms and efficiencies in a location right on the dunes. All guest
rooms at the **Blue Heron** (6811 Virginia Dare
Tr., Nags Head, 252/441-7447, www.blue-
heronnc.com, from $50 off-season, from $130
high season) face the ocean. The Blue Heron
has a heated indoor pool as a consolation
on rainy days. Super-affordable is the **Sea
Foam Motel** (7111 Virginia Dare Tr., Nags
Head, 252/441-7320, www.outer-banks.
nc.us, from $62 off-season, from $110 high
season), an old-timer with a lot of retro appeal. Other good choices in the area include
the **Colony IV by the Sea** (405 S. Virginia
Tr., Kill Devil Hills, 252/441-5581, www.
motelbythesea.com, $68-163, depending on
season) and **Beach Haven Motel** (milepost
4, Ocean Rd., Kitty Hawk, 888/559-0506,
www.beachhavenmotel.com, from $65 off-
season, from $105 high season).

$150-300

The **Colington Creek Inn** (1293 Colington
Rd., Kill Devil Hills, 252/449-4124, www.
colingtoncreekinn.com, no children or pets,
$168-198, depending on season) is a large out-
fit with a great view of the sound and the creek
it's named for.

The **Sanderling Resort and Spa** (1461
Duck Rd., near Duck, 877/650-4812, www.
thesanderling.com, $130-450) is a conventional
full-size resort, with three lodges, a spa, three
restaurants that include the Lifesaving Station,

housed in an 1899 maritime rescue station, and
various sports and recreational rental options.

FOOD

Sam & Omie's (7728 S. Virginia Dare Tr.,
Nags Head, 252/441-7366, www.samandom-
ies.net, Mar.-mid-Dec. daily 7am-10pm, $10-
25) was opened during the summer of 1937, a
place for charter fishing customers and guides
to catch a spot of breakfast before setting sail.
It still serves breakfast, with lots of options in

the eggs and hotcakes department, including a few specialties like crab and eggs benedict. It also has a dinner menu starring seasonal steamed and fried oyster, Delmonico steaks, and barbecue.

Tale of the Whale (7575 S. Virginia Dare Tr., Nags Head, 252/441-7332, www.taleofthewhalenagshead.com, spring-fall daily 4pm-9pm, closed winter, dinner entrées $15-50) sits at a beautiful location, at the very edge of the water with a pier jutting into Roanoke Sound. There's outdoor music from a pier-side gazebo and a dining room with such a great view of the water that it feels like the inside of a ship—but the real draw is the incredibly extensive menu of seafood, steak, and pasta specials. They also have an imaginative cocktail menu.

Grits Grill and Bakery (5000 S. Croatan Hwy., Nags Head, 252/449-2888, daily 6am-3pm, $7-12) is a favorite for breakfast, famous for its biscuits, Krispy Kreme donuts, eggs, and, of course, grits.

The **(** **Blue Point** (1240 Duck Rd., Duck, 252/261-8090, www.goodfoodgoodwine.com, lunch Tues.-Sun.11:30am-2:30pm, dinner daily 5pm-9:30pm, closed Mon. in winter, $20-35) has a nouveau Southern menu, with staples like catfish and trout done up in the most creative ways. Among the specialties, fresh Carolina shrimp is presented on "barley risotto," with broccolini, wine-soaked raisins, and lemon arugula pesto. Try the key lime pie with raspberry sauce, Kentucky bourbon pecan pie, or seasonal fruit cobblers. After-dinner drinks (among them espresso martinis and special dessert wines) complement an amazing wine list that is, if anything, even more impressive than the menu. There are at least a dozen vintages in almost every category, with prices ranging from $7 per glass to $250 per bottle, and several top-notch single-malts and small-batch bourbons. The Blue Point also occupies an amazing building, a custom-built waterside home with diner-style seating, an open kitchen with a counter and bar stools running its length, checkered floors, and a big screen porch. Reservations can be made online as well as by phone up to a month in advance, and are very necessary:

Peak hours in season are booked two to three weeks in advance, while even winter weekends are usually booked solid several days ahead.

Owens' Restaurant (milepost 16.5, Beach Rd., Nags Head, 252/441-7309, www.owensrestaurant.com, daily 5pm-9pm, $12-25) has been in operation at Nags Head for more than 60 years, and in addition to their good seafood menu, visitors enjoy looking over the owners' collection of historical artifacts from Outer Banks maritime life. New in 2009, **Blue Moon Beach Grill** (4104 S. Virginia Dare Tr., Nags Head, 252/261-2583, www.bluemoonbeachgrill.com, daily 11:30am-9pm, $12-25) is rapidly becoming a local favorite. Known for its seafood dishes, Blue Moon is also a popular place to grab a draft beer after work. **Tortuga's Lie** (milepost 11.5, U.S. 158/Beach Rd., 252/441-7299, www.tortugaslie.com, Sun.-Thurs. 11:30am-9:30pm, Fri.-Sat. 11:30am-10pm, $10-20) has a good and varied menu specializing in seafood (some of it local) cooked in Caribbean-inspired dishes, with some good vegetarian options.

For casual and on-the-go chow options at Nags Head, try **Maxximuss Pizza** (5205 S. Croatan Hwy., Nags Head, 252/441-2377, Sun.-Thurs. noon-9pm, Fri.-Sat. noon-11pm, $12-20), which specializes in calzones, subs, and panini, in addition to pizza; **Yellow Submarine** (milepost 14, U.S. 158 Bypass, Nags Head, 252/441-3511, Mon.-Sat. 11 am-9 pm, Sun. noon-9pm May-Sept., Tues.-Sat. 11:30am-8pm, Sun. 1pm-8pm Mar.-Apr., Oct.-Nov., $7-16), a super-casual subs and pizza shop; or **Majik Beanz** (4104 S. Virginia Dare Tr., Nags Head, 252/255-2700, Sun.-Wed. 7am-3pm, Thurs.-Sat. 7am-10pm) for coffee and shakes.

The **Kill Devil Grill** (2008 S. Virginia Dare Tr., 252/449-8181, $13-20) serves hearty meals for brunch, lunch, and dinner. Entrées include excellent seafood and steaks. Vegetarians will find limited options, but meat eaters will be well satisfied. **Food Dudes Kitchen** (1216 S. Virginia Dare Tr., Kill Devil Hills, 252/441-7994, daily 11:30am-9pm, $10-17) has great seafood, wraps, and sandwiches. **Rundown**

Café (5218 N. Virginia Dare Tr., Kitty Hawk, 252/255-0026, daily 11:30am-9pm, $10-15) is a popular local eatery with affordable Caribbean-influenced fare.

GETTING THERE AND AROUND

The closest major airport to this region is the **Norfolk International Airport** (ORF, 2200 Norview Ave., Norfolk, VA, 757/857-3351, www.norfolkairport.com), approximately one hour's drive from the northern Outer Banks.

Raleigh-Durham International Airport (RDU, 2600 W. Terminal Blvd., Morrisville, NC, 919/840-2123, www.rdu.com) is 3 to 5 hours' drive from most Outer Banks destinations.

Only two bridges exist between the mainland and the northern Outer Banks. U.S. 64/264 crosses over Roanoke Island to Whalebone, just south of Nags Head. Not too far north of there, U.S. 158 crosses from Point Harbor to Southern Shores. Highway 12 is the main road all along the northern Outer Banks.

Roanoke Island

Roanoke Island was the site of the Lost Colony, one of the strangest mysteries in all of American history. Its sheltered location—nestled between the Albemarle, Roanoke, and Croatan Sounds, and protected from the ocean by Bodie Island—made Roanoke Island a welcoming spot for that party of ocean-weary English people in the 1580s. Unhappily, they lacked the ability to make one of the bed-and-breakfast inns in Manteo or Wanchese their home base, so that after a hard day of fort-building they could relax with a hot bath and free wireless Internet. Instead they cast their lots in the wilderness, and what befell them may never be known.

At the northern end of Roanoke Island is the town of Manteo and the Fort Raleigh National Historic Site. This is where most of the attractions and visitor services are concentrated. At the southern end is Wanchese, where some of Dare County's oldest families carry on their ancestral trades of fishing and boatbuilding.

◖ FORT RALEIGH NATIONAL HISTORIC SITE

Fort Raleigh National Historic Site (1401 National Park Dr., Manteo, 252/473-5772, www.nps.gov/fora, park daily dawn-dusk except Christmas Day, visitors center Sept.-May daily 9am-5pm, June-Aug. daily 9am-6pm, park admission free, admission charged for Elizabethan Gardens and *The Lost Colony*) covers much of the original site of the first English settlement in the New World. Some of the earthworks associated with the original 1580s fort remain and have been preserved. The visitors center displays some of the artifacts discovered during this restoration effort. Two nature trails in the park explore the island's natural landscape and the location of a Civil War battle.

Within the National Historic Site, two of Manteo's most famous attractions operate autonomously. About 60 years ago, Manteo's **Elizabethan Gardens** (252/473-3234, www.elizabethangardens.org, hours vary, $9 adults, $6 children) was conceived by the Garden Club of North Carolina as a memorial to the settlers of Roanoke Island. Much of the beautifully landscaped park recreates the horticulture of the colonists' native England in the 16th century.

Also within the park boundaries is the Waterside Theater. North Carolina has a long history of outdoor drama celebrating regional heritage, and the best known of the many productions across the state is Roanoke Island's ***The Lost Colony*** (Fort Raleigh National Historic Site, Roanoke, 252/473-3414, www.thelostcolony.org, $30 adults, $28 seniors, $10 children). Chapel Hill playwright Paul Green was commissioned to write the drama in 1937 to celebrate the 350th anniversary of Virginia Dare's birth. What was expected to be a single-season production has returned almost every year for over 75 years, interrupted only occasionally for emergencies such as prowling German U-boats.

OTHER SIGHTS

The **North Carolina Maritime Museum** (104 Fernando St., Manteo, 252/475-1750, www.obxmaritime.org, hours vary, free), whose mother venue is located in Beaufort, operates a branch here on Roanoke Island. In addition to the many traditional Outer Banks working watercraft on display, the museum holds boat building and handling courses at its George Washington Creef Boathouse. Visitors not enrolled in classes can still come in and watch traditional boat builders at work in the shop.

The **North Carolina Aquarium on Roanoke Island** (374 Airport Rd., 3 miles north of Manteo, 866/332-3475, www.ncaquariums.com, daily 9am-5pm, $10.95 adults, $8.95 children) is one of three state aquariums on the North Carolina coast. It's a great place to visit and see all sorts of marine fauna: sharks and other less ferocious fish, crustaceans, octopuses, turtles, and more. Like its sister aquariums, it's also a research station where marine biologists track and work to conserve the native creatures of the coast.

Roanoke Island Festival Park (1 Festival Park, Manteo, 252/475-1500, www.roanokeisland.com, Feb. 19-Mar. and Nov.-Dec. daily 9am-5pm, Apr.-Oct. daily 9am-6pm, $8 adults, $5 ages 6-17, free under age 6) is a state-operated living history site. The highlight is the *Elizabeth II,* a reconstruction of a 16th-century ship like the ones that brought Walter Raleigh's colonists to the New World. There are also a museum, a reconstructed settlement site, and several other places where costumed interpreters will tell you about daily life in the Roanoke colony.

THE OUTER BANKS

THE LOST COLONY

On July 4, 1584, an expedition of English men commissioned by Walter Raleigh dropped anchor near Hatteras Island. Within a couple of days, local Native Americans were coming and going from the English ships, scoping out trade goods and offering hospitality. They got on famously, and when the English sailed back to Europe to tell Raleigh and the queen of the land they had found, two Indian men, Manteo and Wanchese, came along as guests. It seems that Wanchese was somewhat taciturn and found London to be no great shakes, but Manteo got a kick out of everything he saw and took to the English.

In 1585 a new expedition set out for Roanoke, this time intending to settle in earnest. When they reached the Pamlico Sound, their bad luck began. Most of their store of food was soaked and ruined when seawater breached the ship, so from the moment they arrived on shore they were dependent on the goodwill of the indigenous people. Manteo and Wanchese went to Roanoke chief Wingina to discuss the plight of the English. Wanchese, a man of superior insight, tried to convince Wingina to withhold help, but Manteo pled the colonists' case convincingly, and the English were made welcome. Winter came, and the colonists, having grown fat and happy on the local people's food, were doing precious little to attain self-sufficiency. Then a silver cup disappeared from the English compound. It was posited that the thief came from a nearby village, which was promptly burned to the ground. Worried about his own people, Wingina cut off food aid, hoping the English would either starve or go away. Instead, they killed him. Three weeks later, an English supply ship arrived with reinforcements of men and material, but they found the colony deserted.

Yet another attempt was made, this time with whole families rather than gangs of rowdy single men. A young couple named Eleanor and Ananais Dare was expecting a child when they landed at Roanoke, and soon Virginia Dare was born, the first English child born in the New World. Relations with the Native Americans grew worse, though, when the Roanoke people, now under the leadership of Wanchese, were unwilling to aid a new wave of colonists. Manteo, still a friend, tried to enlist the help of his kinfolk, but they were facing lean times as well. John White, leader of the expedition and grandfather of Virginia Dare, lit out on what he planned would be a fast voyage back to England for supplies and food. Through no fault of his own, it was three years before he was able to return. When he did, he found no sign of the settlers, except "CRO" carved on a tree, and "CROATOAN" on a rail.

Thus began 400 years of unanswered questions and speculation that will probably never be resolved. Some believe that the English colonists were killed by the local people, some that they were captured and sold into slavery among Native Americans farther inland. Several communities in the South of uncertain or mixed racial heritage believe themselves to be descendants of the lost colonists, and some evidence suggests that this might in fact be possible. The answers may never be found, and for the foreseeable future, the mystery will still hang heavily over Roanoke Island and its two towns: Manteo and Wanchese.

SPORTS AND RECREATION

The **Outdoors Inn and Outfitters** (406 Uppowoc Ave., Manteo, 252/473-1356, www.theoutdoorsinn.com) offers scuba instruction, beach dives, dive boat charters, and swimming lessons. Kayak tours include wildlife and dolphin watching, birding, salt marsh, and photography tours.

TOURS

The **Downeast Rover** (sails from Manteo waterfront, 252/473-4866, www.downeastrover. com, daytime cruises $30 adults, $15 ages 2-12, sunset cruises $40) is a reproduction 19th-century 55-foot schooner that sails from Manteo on daytime and sunset cruises. Cruises last two hours and depart three times daily at 11am,

Waterside Theater, where *The Lost Colony* is performed

2pm, and sunset. To see the Outer Banks from the air, your options include a World War II biplane or a closed-cockpit Cessna through **Fly the Outer Banks** (410 Airport Rd., Manteo, 252/202-7433, $38-98), or a biplane through **Barrier Island Aviation** (407 Airport Rd., 252/473-4247, www.barrierislandaviation. com, $40-150).

ENTERTAINMENT AND EVENTS

Outer Banks Epicurean Tours (252/305-0952, www.outerbanksepicurean.com) are a wonderful way to dine royally while learning about the rich culinary traditions of this region and how the Banks' natural history creates this unique cuisine. The four-hour tours, which start at $95 pp (not including alcohol), give a good introduction to the native fish and shellfish of the area and the heritage of the people who harvest them, as well as bees and beekeeping, local wineries and microbreweries, coastal barbecue, indigenous and colonial cuisines, and many other topics.

SHOPPING

Manteo Booksellers (105 Sir Walter Raleigh St., 252/473-1221 or 866/473-1222, www. manteobooksellers.com, daily 10am-6pm) is a great independent bookstore, specializing in Outer Banks history and nature, but with a wide selection for all tastes.

Endless Possibilities (105 Budleigh St., 252/475-1575, www.ragweavers.com, Mon.-Sat. 10am-5pm) is an unusual sort of a shop where you can buy purses, boas, rugs, and other adornments of home and body made from recycled secondhand clothes. All the profits go to support the Outer Banks Hotline Crisis Intervention and Prevention Center, a regional help line for victims of rape and domestic violence, as well as an HIV/AIDS information center. And if you happen to be in Manteo long enough, you can even take lessons here to learn how to weave.

ACCOMMODATIONS
Under $150

The **Island Guesthouse** (706 U.S. 64,

252/473-2434, www.theislandmotel.com, rooms from $60 off-season, from $85 high season, cottages from $125 off-season, from $200 high season, pets welcome for a fee) offers simple and comfortable accommodations in its guest house, with two double beds, air-conditioning, and cable TV in each room. They also rent out three tiny, cute cottages. Another affordable option is the **Duke of Dare Motor Lodge** (100 S. U.S. 64, 252/473-2175, from $42 high season). It's a 1960s motel, not at all fancy, but a fine choice when you need an inexpensive place to lay your head.

A top hotel in Manteo is the **Tranquil House Inn** (405 Queen Elizabeth Ave., 800/458-7069, www.1587.com, $109-239). It's in a beautiful location (though it's hard not to be on this island), and downstairs is one of the best restaurants in town, 1587. The **Scarborough Inn** (524 U.S. 64, 252/473-3979, www.scarborough-inn.com, $75-125, depending on season) is a small hotel with 12 guest rooms and great rates, the sort of old-time hotel that's hard to find these days.

Over in Wanchese, the **Wanchese Inn** (85 Jovers Lane, Wanchese, 252/475-1166, www.wancheseinn.com, from $69 off-season, from $129 high season) is a simple and inexpensive bed-and-breakfast. It's a nice Victorian house with modern guest rooms, and there is a boat slip and available on-site parking for a boat and trailer. The **Island House** (104 Old Wharf Rd., 866/473-5619, www.islandhouse-bb.com, $85-175) was built in the early 1900s for a local Coast Guardsman, with wood cut from the property and nails forged on-site. It's very comfortable and quiet, and a big country breakfast is served every day.

$150-300

The **❰ White Doe Inn** (319 Sir Walter Raleigh St., 800/473-6091, www.whitedoeinn.com, from $175 off-season, from $350 high season) is one of North Carolina's premier inns. The 1910 Queen Anne is the largest house on the island and is on the National Register of Historic Places. Guest rooms are exquisitely furnished in turn-of-the-century finery. Guests enjoy a four-course breakfast, evening sherry, espresso and cappuccino any time, and a 24-hour wine cellar. Spa services are available on-site, and you need only step out to the lawn to play croquet or boccie.

The **Cameron House Inn** (300 Budleigh St., Manteo, 800/279-8178, http://cameronhouseinn.com, $130-210) is a cozy 1919 arts and crafts-style bungalow. All of the guest rooms are furnished in a lovely and understated craftsman style, but the nicest room in the house is the porch, which has an outdoor fireplace, fans, and flowery trellises.

The **Roanoke Island Inn** (305 Fernando St., 877/473-5511, www.roanokeislandinn.com, $150-200) has been in the present owner's family since the 1860s. It's a beautiful old place with a big porch that overlooks the marsh. They also rent a single cottage on a private island, five minutes away by boat, and a nice cypress-shingled bungalow in town.

FOOD

Located in the Tranquil House Inn, with a great view of Shallowbag Bay, **❰1587** (405 Queen Elizabeth Ave., 252/473-1587, www.1587.com, June-Aug. daily 5pm-9pm, Sept.-Oct. Wed.-Sun. 5pm-9pm, Jan.-Feb. Fri.-Sat. 5pm-9pm, closed Nov.-Dec. dinner entrées $18-29) is widely regarded as one of the best restaurants in this part of the state. The menu is of hearty chops and seafood, with local ingredients in season, and a full vegetarian menu is also available on request. The wine list is a mile long.

Basnight's Lone Cedar Café (Nags Head-Manteo Causeway, 252/441-5405, www.lonecedarcafe.com, spring-fall Mon.-Wed. 5pm-close, Thurs.-Sat. 11:30am-3pm and 5pm-close, Sun. 11am-close, lunch entrées $6-18, dinner entrées $18-31) is a water-view bistro that specializes in local food—oysters from Hyde and Dare Counties, fresh-caught local fish, and North Carolina chicken, pork, and vegetables. It's one of the most popular restaurants on the Outer Banks, and they don't take reservations, so be sure to arrive early. The full bar is open until midnight.

The **Full Moon Café** (208 Queen Elizabeth

St., 252/473-6666, www.thefullmooncafe.com, high season daily 11:30am-9pm, call for off-season hours, $10-30) is simple and affordable, specializing in quesadillas and enchiladas, wraps, sandwiches, a variety of seafood and chicken bakes, and quiches. Despite the seemingly conventional selection, the food here is so good that the Full Moon has received glowing reviews from the *Washington Post* and the *New York Post*—quite a feat for a little café in Manteo.

The **Magnolia Grille** (408 Queen Elizabeth St., 252/475-9787, www.roanokeisland.net, Sun.-Mon. 7am-4pm, Tues.-Sat. 7am-8pm) is a super-inexpensive place for all three meals and snacks in between. They've got a great selection of breakfast omelets, burgers, salads, soups, and deli sandwiches, with nothing more than $7.

GETTING THERE AND AROUND

Coming from the mainland, you'll reach the town of Mann's Harbor on the inland side of Croatan Sound, and there you have two choices for crossing to Roanoke Island. If you take U.S. 64/264, to the left, you'll cross the sound to the north, arriving in Manteo. If you stay straight at Mann's Harbor you'll be on the U.S. 64/264 Bypass, which crosses to the middle of the island, south of Manteo. Proceed until you get to the main intersection, where you can turn left onto U.S. 64/264 to go to Manteo, or right onto Highway 345 toward Wanchese.

To reach Roanoke Island from the Outer Banks, take U.S. 158 or Highway 12 to Whalebone Junction, south of Nags Head, and cross Roanoke Sound on the U.S. 64/264 bridge.

Cape Hatteras National Seashore

To many Americans, Cape Hatteras is probably familiar as a name often repeated during hurricane season. Hatteras protrudes farther to the southeast than any part of North America, a landmark for centuries of mariners and a prime target for storms. Cape Hatteras, the "Graveyard of the Atlantic," lies near Diamond Shoals, a treacherous zone of shifting sandbars between the beach and the Gulf Stream. Two channels, Diamond Slough and Hatteras Slough, cross the shoals in deep enough water for a ship to navigate safely, but countless ships have missed their mark and gone down off Cape Hatteras. The 1837 wreck of the steamboat *Home* on the Shoals, which killed 90 passengers, led Congress to pass the Steamboat Act, which established the requirement of one life vest per passenger in all vessels.

In 2003 Hurricane Isabel inflicted tremendous damage and even opened a new channel right across Hatteras Island, a 2,000-foot-wide swash that was called Isabel Inlet. It separated the towns of Hatteras and Frisco, washing out a large portion of the highway that links the Outer Banks. For some weeks afterward, Hatteras residents had to live as their forebears had, riding ferries to school and to the mainland. The inlet has since been filled in and Highway 12 reconnected, but Isabel Inlet's brief reign of inconvenience highlighted the vulnerability of life on the Outer Banks.

BODIE ISLAND

The 156-foot **Bodie Island Lighthouse** (6 miles south of Whalebone Junction), whose huge Fresnel lens first beamed in 1872, was the third to guard this stretch of coast. The first light was built in the 1830s, but it leaned like the Tower of Pisa. The next stood straight but promised to be such a tempting target for the Union Navy during the Civil War that the Confederates blew it up themselves. An unfortunate flock of geese nearly put the third lighthouse out of commission soon after its first lighting, when they collided with and damaged the lens. The lighthouse is not open to the public, but the keeper's house has been converted into a **visitors center** (252/441-5711, call for hours). This is also the starting point for self-guided nature trails to Roanoke Sound through the beautiful marshy landscape of Bodie Island.

The **Oregon Inlet Campground** (Hwy. 12, 877/444-6777, $20), operated by the National Park Service, offers camping behind the sand dunes, with cold showers, potable water, and restrooms.

HATTERAS ISLAND

Cape Hatteras makes a dramatic arch along the North Carolina coast, sheltering the Pamlico Sound from the ocean as if in a giant cradling arm. The cape itself is the point of the elbow, a totally exposed and vulnerable spit of land that's irresistible to hurricanes because it juts so far to the southeast. Along the Cape Hatteras National Seashore, Hatteras Island is just barely wide enough to support a series of small towns—Rodanthe, Waves, Salvo, Avon, Buxton, Frisco, and the village of Hatteras—and a great deal of dramatic scenery on all sides.

Sights

Lifesaving operations are an important part of North Carolina's maritime heritage. Corps of brave men once occupied remote stations along the coast, ready at a moment's notice to risk— and sometimes to give—their lives to save foundering sailors in the relentlessly dangerous waters off the Outer Banks. In Rodanthe, the **Chicamacomico Life Saving Station** (milepost 39.5, Hwy. 12, Rodanthe, 252/987-1552, www.chicamacomico.net, mid-Apr.-Nov. Mon.-Fri. noon-5pm, $6, $5 over age 62 and under age 17) preserves the original station building, a handsome gray-shingled 1874 structure, as well as the 1911 building that replaced it—and which now houses a museum of fascinating artifacts from maritime rescue operations—along with a complex of other buildings and exhibits depicting the lives of lifesavers and their families.

Cape Hatteras Lighthouse (near Buxton, 252/473-2111, www.nps.gov/caha, mid-Apr.-May and Labor Day-mid-Oct. daily 9am-4:30pm, June-Labor Day daily 9am-5:30pm,

$8 adults, $4 children, children smaller than 3 foot 5 not permitted), at 208 feet tall, is the tallest brick lighthouse in the United States. It was built in 1870 to protect ships at sea from coming onto the shoals unaware. It still stands on the cape and is open for climbing during the warm months. If you have a healthy heart, lungs, and knees and are not claustrophobic, get your ticket and start climbing. Tickets are sold on the premises beginning at 8:15am; climbing tours run every ten minutes starting at 9am.

Sports and Recreation

Pea Island National Wildlife Refuge (Hwy. 12, 10 miles south of Nags Head, 252/987-2394, www.fws.gov/peaisland) occupies the northern reach of Hatteras Island. Much of the island is covered by ponds, making this an exceptional place to see migratory waterfowl. Two nature trails link some of the best bird-watching spots, and one, the 0.5-mile North Pond Wildlife Trail, is fully wheelchair-accessible. Viewing and photography blinds are scattered along the trails for extended observation.

The Outer Banks owe their existence to the volatile action of the tides. The same forces that created this habitable sandbar also make this an incredible place for water sports. **Canadian Hole,** a spot in the sound between Avon and Buxton, is one of the most famous windsurfing and sailboarding places in the world, and it goes without saying that it's also perfect for kite flying. The island is extraordinarily narrow here, so it's easy to tote your board from the sound side over to the ocean for a change of scene.

As with any sport, it's important to know your own skill level and choose activities accordingly. Beginners and experts alike, though, can benefit from the guidance of serious water sports instructors. **Real Kiteboarding** (Cape Hatteras, 866/732-5548, www.realkiteboarding.com) is the largest kiteboarding school in the world. They offer kiteboarding camps and classes in many aspects of the sport for all skill levels. **Outer Banks Kiting** (Avon, 252/305-6838, www.outerbankskiting.com)

© JIM MOREKIS

Pea Island National Wildlife Refuge

also teaches lessons and two-day camps, and carries boarders out on charter excursions to find the best spots.

There are all manner of exotic ways to tour Hatteras. **Equine Adventures** (252/995-4897, www.equineadventures.com) leads two-hour horseback tours through the maritime forests and along the beaches of Cape Hatteras. With **Hatteras Parasail** (Hatteras, 252/986-2627, www.hatterasparasail.com, parasail ride $60, kayak tour $35), you can ride 400 feet in the air over the coast, or even higher with **Burrus Flightseeing Tours** (Frisco, 252/986-2679, www.hatterasisland-flightseeing.com, $35-63 pp).

Accommodations
UNDER $150
Among the lodging choices on Hatteras Island is the **Cape Hatteras Bed and Breakfast** (46223 Old Lighthouse Rd./Cape Point Way, Buxton, 800/252-3316, $119-159), which is only a few hundred feet from the ocean. Guests rave about the breakfasts.

Simpler motel accommodations include the clean, comfortable, and pet-friendly **Cape Pines Motel** (47497 Hwy. 12, Buxton, 866/456-9983, www.capepinesmotel.com, $49-159, depending on season, $20 pets); the **Outer Banks Motel** (47000 Hwy. 12, Buxton, 252/995-5601 or 800/995-1233, www.outerbanksmotel.com, $49-120), with both motel rooms and cottages; and the **Avon Motel** (Avon, 252/995-5774, www.avonmotel.com, $43-131, $10 pets), a pet-friendly motel that has been in business for more than 50 years.

$150-300
Another good choice on Hatteras Island is the very fine **Inn on Pamlico Sound** (49684 Hwy. 12, Buxton, 252/995-7030 or 866/995-7030, www.innonpamlicosound.com, $120-320, depending on season). The inn is right on the sound, with a private dock and easy waterfront access. The dozen suites are sumptuous and relaxing, many with their own decks or private porches.

CAMPING

Rodanthe Watersports and Campground

(24170 Hwy. 12, 252/987-1431, www.watersportsandcampground.com) has a Sound-front campground for tents and RVs under 25 feet, with water and electrical hookups and hot-water showers. Rates are $19.25 per night for two people, $4.75 for each additional adult, $3 for children and dogs, and an extra $4.75 per night for electrical hookups.

The National Park Service operates two campgrounds ($20) in this stretch of the National Seashore: The **Frisco Campground** (53415 Billy Mitchell Rd., Frisco, 877/444-6777) opens in early April, and **Cape Point Campground** (46700 Lighthouse Rd., Buxton, 877/444-6777) opens in late May. At Frisco, you actually camp in the dunes, while at Cape Point, like the other National Park Service campgrounds in the area, the campsites are level and located behind the dunes. Both have cold showers, restrooms, and potable water.

Frisco Woods Campground (Hwy. 12, Frisco, 800/948-3942, www.outer-banks.com/friscowoods, $30-90) has a full spectrum of camping options, from no-utilities tent sites and RV sites with partial or full hookups to one- and two-bedroom cabins. The campground has wireless Internet access, hot showers, and a coin laundry.

Food

Though the **Restaurant at the Inn on Pamlico Sound** (Hwy. 12, Buxton, 252/995-7030, www.innonpamlicosound.com, $15) is primarily for guests of the inn, if you call in advance you might be able to get a reservation for dinner even if you're staying elsewhere. The chef likes to use fresh-caught seafood, sometimes caught by the guests themselves earlier in the day. Vegetarian dishes and other special requests are served.

For breakfast, try the **Gingerbread House** (52715 Hwy. 12, Frisco, 252/995-5204), which serves great baked goods made on the premises.

◖ OCRACOKE ISLAND

Sixteen miles long, Ocracoke Island is the southernmost reach of the Cape Hatteras National Seashore. The history of Ocracoke Island is, frankly, a little creepy. First of all, there's the remoteness; one of the most geographically isolated places in North Carolina, it's only accessible today by water and air. Regular ferry service didn't start until 1960, and it was only three years before that that Ocracokers had their first paved highway. In 1585, it was one of the first places in North America seen by Europeans, when the future Lost Colonists ran aground here. It may have been during the time they were waylaid at Ocracoke ("Wococon," they called it) that the ancestors of today's wild ponies first set hoof on the Outer Banks. Theirs was not the last shipwreck at Ocracoke, and in fact, flotsam and goods that would wash up from offshore wrecks were among the sources of sustenance for generations of Ocracokers.

In the early 18th century, Ocracoke was a favorite haunt of Edward Teach, better known as the pirate Blackbeard. He lived here at times, married his 14th wife here, and died here. Teach's Hole, a spot just off the island, is where a force hired by Virginia lieutenant governor Alexander Spotswood finally cornered and killed him, dumping his decapitated body overboard (it's said to have swum around the ship seven times before going under), and sailing away with the trophy of his head on the bowsprit.

All of **Ocracoke Village,** near the southern end of the island, is on the National Register of Historic Places. While the historical sites of the island are highly distinctive, the most unique thing about the island and its people is the culture that has developed here over the centuries. Ocracokers have a "brogue" all their own, similar to those of other Outer Banks communities, but so distinctive that, in the unlikely event that there were two native Ocracokers who didn't know each other already, and they happened to cross paths somewhere out in the world, they would recognize each other right away as neighbors (and probably cousins) by the cadences of their speech.

Ocracoke Lighthouse

A lighthouse has stood on Ocracoke since at least 1798, but due to constantly shifting sands, the inlet that it protected kept sneaking away. Barely 20 years after that first tower was built, almost a mile stretched between it and the water. The current **Ocracoke Lighthouse** (village of Ocracoke, 888/493-3826) was built in 1823, originally burning whale oil to power the beam. It is still in operation—the oldest operating light in North Carolina and the second oldest in the nation. Because it's on active duty, the public is not able to tour the inside, but a boardwalk nearby gives nice views.

British Cemetery

The **British Cemetery** (British Cemetery Rd.) is not, as one might suppose, a colonial burial ground but rather a vestige of World War II.

During the war, the Carolina coast was lousy with German U-boats. Many old-timers today remember catching a glimpse of a furtive German sub casing the beach. Defending the Outer Banks became a pressing concern, and on May 11, 1942, the HMS *Bedfordshire*, a British trawler sent to aid the U.S. Navy, was torpedoed by the German *U-558*. The *Bedfordshire* sank, and all 37 men aboard died. Over the course of the next week, four bodies washed up on Ocracoke—those of Lieutenant Thomas Cunningham, Ordinary Telegraphist Stanley Craig, and two unidentified men. An island family donated a burial plot, and there the four men lie today, memorialized with a plaque that bears a lovely verse by Rupert Brooke, the young poet of World War I and member of the British Navy, who died of disease on his way to the battle of Gallipoli.

Sports and Recreation
Ride the Wind Surf Shop (486 Irvin Garrish

Hwy., 252/928-6311) gives individual and group surfing lessons, for adults and children, covering ocean safety and surfing etiquette in addition to board handling. A three-day surf camp ($200, or $75 per day) for kids ages 9 to 17 gives an even more in-depth tutorial. Ride the Wind also leads sunrise, sunset, and full-moon kayak tours around the marshes of Ocracoke ($35).

The **Schooner Windfall** (departs from Community Store Dock, Ocracoke, 252/928-7245, www.schoonerwindfall.com, tours $40), a beautiful 57-foot old-fashioned-looking schooner, sails on three one-hour tours a day around Pamlico Sound. Passengers are allowed, and even encouraged, to try their hand at the wheel or trimming the sails.

Accommodations

The **Captain's Landing** (324 Hwy. 12, 252/928-1999, www.thecaptainslanding.com, from $200 high season, from $100 off-season), with a perch right on Silver Lake (the harbor) looking toward the lighthouse, is a modern hotel owned by a descendant of Ocracoke's oldest families. Suites have 1½ baths, full kitchens, comfortable sleeper sofas for extra guests, and decks with beautiful views. They also have a bright, airy penthouse with two bedrooms, an office, a gourmet kitchen, and even a laundry room. The Captain's Cottage is a private two-bedroom house, also smack on the water, with great decks and its own courtyard.

The **Pony Island Motel and Cottages** (785 Irvin Garrish Hwy., 866/928-4411, www.ponyislandmotel.com, from $108 high season, from $60 off-season) has been in operation since the late 1950s and run by the same family for more than 40 years. It has regular and efficiency motel rooms as well as four cottages on the grounds. Clean guest rooms, a good location, and year-round good prices make this a top choice on the island.

Edwards of Ocracoke (226 Old Beach Rd., 800/254-1359, www.edwardsofocracoke.com, from $53 spring and fall, from $90 summer) has several cozy bungalows typical of coastal Carolina, referred to here as "vintage

accommodations." The mid-20th-century vacation ambiance is very pleasant, the cabins are clean and well kept, and the prices are great.

The **Island Inn** (25 Lighthouse Rd., 252/928-4351, www.ocracokeislandinn.com, from $60 off-season, from $100 high season, no children) is on the National Register of Historic Places and bills itself as the oldest operating business on the Outer Banks. It was built in 1901 and first used as an Odd Fellows Hall; during World War II it was used as a barracks. The building is made of salvaged shipwreck wood. The resident ghost is believed to be a woman, because she seems to enjoy checking out female guests' cosmetics and clothes, which will sometimes turn up in the morning in places other than where they were left the night before.

CAMPING

At **Ocracoke Campground** (4352 Irvin Garrish Hwy., Ocracoke, 877/444-6777, $23), campsites are right by the beach, behind the dunes. Remember to bring extra-long stakes to anchor your tent in the sand.

GETTING THERE AND AROUND

The northern part of Cape Hatteras National Seashore can be reached by car via Highway 12 south from Nags Head. Following Highway 12, you'll go through the towns of Rodanthe, Waves, Salvo, and Avon, then around the tip of the cape to Buxton, Frisco, and Hatteras, where the highway ends. From there, you have two choices: backtrack or hop a ferry.

Ocracoke can only be reached by ferry. The **Hatteras-Ocracoke Ferry** (800/368-8949, May 13-Oct. 5 5am-midnight on the half-hour, Apr. 1-May 12 and Oct. 7-Dec. 31 5am-midnight on the hour, Jan. 1-Mar. 31 4:30am-12:30am alternating half hours, 40 minutes, free) is the shortest route to Ocracoke. If you look at a map, Highway 12 is shown crossing from Ocracoke to Cedar Island, as if there's an impossibly long bridge over Pamlico Sound. In fact, that stretch of Highway 12 is a ferry route too. The **Cedar Island-Ocracoke Ferry**

(800/856-0343, www.ncdot.org/transit/ferry, May 20-Sept. 29 7am-8pm every 90 minutes, Mar.18-May 19 and Sept. 30-Oct. 27 7am-4:30pm every 3.5 hours, Jan. 1-Mar. 17 and Oct. 28-Dec. 31 7am-4:30pm every 3.5 hours), which is a 2.25-hour ride, costs $15 per regular-size vehicle one-way. There's also a ferry between **Ocracoke and Swan Quarter** (800/345-1665, May 20-Sept. 29 6:30am-4:30pm every 3 hours, Jan. 1-May 19 and Sept. 30-Dec. 31 7am-4:30pm every 6.5 hours, 2.5 hours, regular-size vehicle $15 one-way).

Lower Outer Banks

The southern reaches of the Outer Banks of North Carolina have some of the region's most diverse destinations. Core and Shackleford Banks lie within the Cape Lookout National Seashore, a wild maritime environment populated by plenty of wild ponies but not a single human. On the other hand, the towns of Bogue Banks—Atlantic Beach, Salter Path, Pine Knoll Shores, Indian Beach, and Emerald Isle—are classic beach towns, with clusters of motels and restaurants, and even a few towel shops and miniature golf courses. Both areas are great fun, Cape Lookout especially so for ecotourists and history buffs, and Bogue Banks for those looking for a day on the beach followed by an evening chowing down on good fried seafood.

◖ CAPE LOOKOUT NATIONAL SEASHORE

Cape Lookout National Seashore (office 131 Charles St., Harkers Island, 252/728-2250, www.nps.gov/calo) is an otherworldly place, with 56 miles of beach on four barrier islands, a long tape of sand so seemingly vulnerable to nature that it's hard to believe there were once several busy towns on its banks. Settled in the early 1700s, the towns of the south Core Banks made their living in fisheries that might seem brutal to today's seafood eaters—whaling and catching dolphins and sea turtles, among the more mundane species. Portsmouth, at the north end of the park across the water from Ocracoke, was a busy port of great importance to the early economy of North Carolina. Portsmouth declined slowly, but catastrophe rained down all at once on the people of the southerly Shackleford Banks, who were driven out of their own long-established communities to start new lives on the mainland when a series of terrible hurricanes hit in the 1890s.

Islands often support unique ecosystems. Among the dunes, small patches of maritime forest fight for each drop of fresh water, while ghost forests of trees that were defeated by advancing saltwater look on resignedly. Along the endless beach, loggerhead turtles come ashore to lay their eggs, and in the waters just off the strand, three other species of sea turtles are sometimes seen. Wild horses roam the beaches and dunes, and dolphins frequent both the ocean and sound sides of the islands.

Pets are allowed on a leash. The wild ponies on Shackleford Banks can pose a threat to dogs that get among them, and the dogs, of course, can frighten the horses, so be careful not to let them mingle.

Portsmouth Village

Portsmouth Village, at the northern tip of the Cape Lookout National Seashore, is a peaceful but eerie place. The village looks much as it did 100 years ago, the handsome houses and churches all tidy and in good repair, but with the exception of caretakers and summer volunteers, no one has lived here in nearly 40 years. In 1970 the last two residents moved away from what had once been a town of 700 people and one of the most important shipping ports in North Carolina. Founded before the Revolutionary War, Portsmouth was a lightering station, a port where huge seagoing ships that had traveled across the ocean would stop and have their cargo removed for transport

© AVALON TRAVEL

LOWER OUTER BANKS

Pamlico Sound

Swan Quarter

Swan Quarter Ocracoke Ferry

Ocracoke

Portsmouth

Cedar Island Ocracoke Ferry

CAPE LOOKOUT NATIONAL SEASHORE

Cedar Island Bay

Cedar Island

West Bay

Rose Bay

Pungo River

Raccoon Bay

DOWN EAST

Core Banks

Core Sound

CAPE LOOKOUT LIGHTHOUSE

ATLANTIC OCEAN

92

Bath

Pamlico River

306

33

33

306

55

Neuse River

Oriental

101

306

70

OLD BURYING GROUND

Morehead City

Beaufort

Harkers Island

CORE SOUND WATERFOWL MUSEUM

Shackleford Banks

Fort Macon State Park

Atlantic Beach

Pine Knoll Shores

Theodore Roosevelt Natural Area State Park

New Bern

TRYON PALACE

Croatan

National

Forest

Havelock

58

Peletier

Swansboro

Bogue Sound

Bogue Banks

NORTH CAROLINA AQUARIUM

0   10 mi

0   10 km

43

Pollocksville

Trenton

41

Hofmann

Forest

70

Hubert

24

Camp Lejeune

New River

172

Hammocks Beach State Park

Topsail Island

11

Kinston

258

Jacksonville

Topsail Beach

Surf City

17

210

50

To Wilmington

70

Goldsboro

Cliffs of the Neuse State Park

Seven Springs

Neuse River

55

258

50

40

Wallace

421

across the shallow sounds in smaller boats. There is a visitors center located at Portsmouth, open April-October with varying hours, where you can learn about the village before embarking on a stroll to explore the quiet streets.

Once every other year in the spring, an amazing thing happens. Boatloads of people arrive on shore, and the church bell rings, and the sound of hymn singing comes through the open church doors. At the Portsmouth Homecoming, descendants of the people who lived here come from all over the state and country to pay tribute to their ancestral home. They have an old-time dinner on the grounds with much socializing and catching up, and then tour the little village together. It's like a family reunion, with the town itself the family's matriarch.

Shackleford Banks

The once-busy villages of Diamond City and Shackleford Banks are like Portsmouth in that, though they have not been occupied for many years, the descendants of the people who lived here retain a profound attachment to their ancestors' homes. Diamond City and nearby communities met a spectacular end. The hurricane season of 1899 culminated in the San Ciriaco Hurricane, a disastrous storm that destroyed homes and forests, killed livestock, flooded gardens with saltwater, and washed the Shackleford dead out of their graves. Harkers Island absorbed most of the refugee population (many also went to Morehead City), and their traditions are still an important part of Down East culture. Daily and weekly programs held at the Light Station Pavilion and the porch of the Keepers' Quarters during the summer months teach visitors about the natural and human history of Cape Lookout, including what day-to-day life was like for the keeper of the lighthouse and his family.

Cape Lookout Lighthouse

By the time you arrive at the 1859 **Cape Lookout Lighthouse** (visitors center, 252/728-2250), you'll probably already have seen it portrayed on dozens of brochures, menus, business

signs, and souvenirs. With its striking diamond pattern, it looks like a rattlesnake standing at attention. Because it is still a working lighthouse, visitors are allowed in on only four days each year. Visit Cape Lookout National Seashore's website (www.nps.gov/calo) for open house dates and reservation information. The allotted times fill up almost immediately.

Accommodations

Morris Marina (877/956-5688, www.cape-lookoutconcessions, $65-100) rents cabins at Great Island and Long Point. Cabins have hot and cold water, gas stoves, and furniture, but in some cases visitors must bring their own generators for lights as well as linens and utensils. Rentals are available only April-November. Book well in advance.

CAMPING

Camping is permitted within Cape Lookout National Seashore, though there are no designated campsites or services. Everything you bring must be carried back out when you leave. Campers can stay for up to 14 days.

Getting There

Except for the visitors center at Harkers Island, Cape Lookout National Seashore can only be reached by ferry. Portsmouth, at the northern end of the park, is a short ferry ride from Ocracoke, but Ocracoke is a very long ferry ride from Cedar Island. The **Cedar Island-Ocracoke Ferry** (800/856-0343, regular-size vehicles $15 one-way) is part of the state ferry system, and pets are allowed. It takes 2.25 hours to cross Pamlico Sound, but the ride is fun, and embarking from Cedar Island feels like sailing off the edge of the earth. The **Ocracoke-Portsmouth Ferry** (252/928-4361) is a passenger-only commercial route, licensed to Captain Rudy Austin. Phone to ensure a seat. There's also a vehicle and passenger ferry **from Atlantic to Long Point,** Morris Marina Kabin Kamps and Ferry Service (877/956-6568), on the North Core Banks; leashed or in-vehicle pets are allowed. Most ferries operate between April and November.

Commercial ferries cross every day **from mainland Carteret County** to the southern parts of the national seashore. There is generally a ferry route between Davis and Great Island, but service can be variable; check the Cape Lookout National Seashore website (www.nps.gov/calo) for updates.

From Harkers Island, passenger ferries to Cape Lookout Lighthouse and Shackleford Banks include Calico Jacks (252/728-3575), Harkers Island Fishing Center (252/728-3907), Local Yokel (252/728-2759), and Island Ferry Adventures (252/728-6181) at Barbour's Marina.

From Beaufort, passenger ferries include Outer Banks Ferry Service (252/728-4129), which goes to both Shackleford Banks and to Cape Lookout Lighthouse; Island Ferry Adventures (252/728-7555) and Mystery Tours (252/728-7827) run to Shackleford Banks. Morehead City's passenger-only Waterfront Ferry Service (252/726-7678) goes to Shackleford Banks as well. On-leash pets are generally allowed, but call ahead to confirm for Local Yokel, Island Ferry Adventures, and Waterfront Ferry Service.

VILLAGE OF CEDAR ISLAND

For a beautiful afternoon's drive, head back to the mainland and follow U.S. 70 north. You'll go through some tiny communities—Williston, Davis, Stacy—and, if you keep bearing north on Highway 12 when U.S. 70 heads south to the town of Atlantic, you'll eventually reach the tip of the peninsula, and the fishing village of Cedar Island. This little fishing town has the amazing ambience of being at the end of the earth. From the peninsula's shore you can barely see land across the sounds. The ferry to Ocracoke departs from Cedar Island, and it's an unbelievable two-hour-plus ride across the Pamlico Sound. The beach here is absolutely gorgeous, and horses roam freely. They're not the famous wild horses of the Outer Banks, but they move around as if they were.

A spectacular location for bird-watching is the **Cedar Island National Wildlife Refuge**

(U.S. 70, east of the town Atlantic, 252/926-4021, www.fws.gov/cedarisland). Nearly all of its 14,500 acres are brackish marshland, and it's often visited in season by redhead ducks, buffleheads, surf scoters, and many other species. While there are trails for hiking and biking, this refuge is primarily intended as a safe haven for the birds.

Accommodations and Food

The Driftwood Motel (3575 Cedar Island Rd., 252/225-4861, www.clis.com, $70-80) is a simple motel in an incredible location, and since the ferry leaves from its parking lot, it's the place to stay if you're coming from or going to Ocracoke. There's also camping ($16 tents, $18-20 RVs) here, with electricity, water, and sewer.

The Driftwood's **Pirate's Chest Restaurant** (3575 Cedar Island Rd., 252/225-4861, Apr.-Oct., call for hours, $10-20) is the only restaurant on Cedar Island, so it's a good thing that it's a good one. Local seafood is the specialty, and dishes can be adapted for vegetarians.

BEAUFORT AND VICINITY

It's an oft-cited case of the perversity of Southern speech that Beaufort, North Carolina, receives the French treatment of "eau"—so it's pronounced "BO-furt"—whereas Beaufort, South Carolina, a rather similar Lowcountry port town south of Charleston, is pronounced "BYEW-furt."

The third-oldest town in North Carolina, Beaufort holds its own with its elders, Bath and New Bern, in the prettiness department. The little port was once North Carolina's window on the world, a rather cosmopolitan place that sometimes received news from London or Barbados sooner than from Raleigh. The streets are crowded with extremely beautiful old houses, many built in a double-porch, steep-roofed style that shows off the early citizenry's cultural ties to the wider Caribbean and Atlantic world.

In the late 1990s a shipwreck was found in Beaufort Inlet that is believed to be that of the *Queen Anne's Revenge,* a French slaver

© JIM MOREKIS

the town of Beaufort

captured by the pirate Blackbeard in 1717 to be the flagship of his unsavory fleet. He increased its arsenal to 40 cannons, but it was nevertheless sunk in the summer of 1718. Blackbeard was killed at Ocracoke Inlet a few months later, and it took five musket balls and 40 sword wounds to finish him off. Incredibly cool artifacts from the *QAR* keep emerging from the waters of the inlet. Beaufort had been a favorite haunt of Blackbeard's, and you can find out all about him at the North Carolina Maritime Museum.

Sights
NORTH CAROLINA MARITIME MUSEUM

The **North Carolina Maritime Museum** (315 Front St., 252/728-7317, www.ah.dcr.state. nc.us/sections/maritime, Mon.-Fri. 9am-5pm, Sat. 10am-5pm, Sun. 1pm-5pm, free) is among the best museums in the state. Even if you don't think you're interested in boatbuilding or maritime history, you'll get caught up in the exhibits. Historic watercraft, reconstructions, and models of boats are on display, well presented in rich historical and cultural context. There's also a lot to learn about the state's fishing history—not only pertaining to the fisheries themselves but also to related occupations, such as the highly complex skill of net-hanging. Far from being limited to the few species caught by today's fisheries, early North Carolina seafarers also carried on a big business hunting sea turtles, porpoises, and whales.

Across the street from the museum's main building, perched on the dock, is the **Harvey W. Smith Watercraft Center.** For many generations, North Carolina mariners had an international reputation as expert shipbuilders, and even today, some builders continue to construct large seaworthy vessels in their own backyards. This has always been done "by the rack of the eye," as they say here, which means that the builders use traditional knowledge handed down over the generations rather than modern industrial methods. Their exceptional expertise is beautifully demonstrated by the craft in the museum and by boats still working the waters today.

BLACKBEARD AND BONNET: THE BOYS OF 1718

In the 18th century the Carolina coast was positively verminous with pirates. For the most part they hung out around Charleston Harbor, like a bunch of rowdies on a frat house balcony, causing headaches for passersby. Some liked to venture up the coast, however, into the inlets and sounds of North Carolina. The most famous local pirates were Blackbeard and Stede Bonnet. They did most of their misbehaving in our waters during 1718.

Blackbeard is said never to have killed a man except in self-defense, but clearly he was so bad he didn't need to kill to make his badness known. He was a huge man with a beard that covered most of his face, and his hair is usually depicted twisted up into ferocious dreadlocks. He wore a bright red coat and festooned himself with every weapon small enough to carry; as if all that didn't make him scary enough, he liked to wear burning cannon fuses tucked under the brim of his hat. He caused trouble from the Bahamas to Virginia, taking ships, treasure, and child brides as fancy led him.

Poor Stede Bonnet. With a name like that, he should have known better than to try to make a living intimidating people. He is said to have been something of a fancy-pants, a man with wealth, education, and a nagging wife. To get away from his better half, he bought a ship, hired a crew, and set sail for a life of crime. Though never quite as tough as Blackbeard,

with whom he was briefly partners, Bonnet caused enough trouble along the Southern coast that the gentry of Charleston saw to it that he was captured and hanged. Meanwhile, the Virginia nabobs had also had it with Blackbeard's interference in coastal commerce, and Lieutenant Governor Alexander Spotswood dispatched his men to kill him. This they did at Ocracoke, but it wasn't easy; even after they shot, stabbed, and beheaded Blackbeard, his body taunted them by swimming laps around the ship before finally giving up the ghost.

Blackbeard has in effect surfaced again. In 1996 a ship was found off the North Carolina coast that was identified as Blackbeard's flagship, the *Queen Anne's Revenge*. All manner of intriguing artifacts have been brought up from the ocean floor: cannons and blunderbuss parts, early hand grenades, even a penis syringe supposed to have been used by the syphilitic pirates to inject themselves with mercury. (During one standoff in Charleston Harbor, Blackbeard and his men took hostages to ransom for medical supplies. Perhaps this explains why they were so desperate.) To view artifacts and learn more about Blackbeard, Stede Bonnet, and their lowdown ways, visit the North Carolina Maritime Museum in Beaufort and in Southport, as well as the websites of the *Queen Anne's Revenge* (www.qaronline.com) and the Office of State Archaeology (www.arch. dcr.state.nc.us).

◖ OLD BURYING GROUND

One of the most beautiful places in all of North Carolina, Beaufort's **Old Burying Ground** (Anne St., daily dawn-dusk) is as picturesque a cemetery as you'd ever want to be buried in. It's quite small by the standards of some old Carolina towns and crowded with 18th- and 19th-century stones. Huge old live oaks, Spanish moss, wisteria, and resurrection ferns, which unfurl and turn green after a rainstorm, give the Burying Ground an irresistibly Gothic feel. Many of the headstones reflect the maritime heritage of this town, such as that of a sea

captain whose epitaph reads, "The form that fills this silent grave / Once tossed on ocean's rolling wave / But in a port securely fast / He's dropped his anchor here at last."

Captain Otway Burns, an early privateer who spent much time in Beaufort, is buried here; his grave is easy to spot, as it is topped by a canon from his ship, the *Snap Dragon*. Nearby is another of the graveyard's famous burials, that of the "Little Girl Buried in a Barrel of Rum." This unfortunate waif is said to have died at sea and been placed in a cask of rum to preserve her body for burial on land. Visitors

THE OUTER BANKS

© JIM MOREKIS

Old Burying Ground

often bring toys and trinkets to leave on her grave, which is marked by a simple wooden plank. Feel free to add to her haul of goodies, but it's not karmically advisable to tamper with those already here.

BEAUFORT HISTORIC SITE

The **Beaufort Historic Site** (130 Turner St., 252/728-5225, www.beauforthistoricsite.org, Dec.-Feb. Mon.-Sat. 10am-4pm, Mar.-Nov. Mon.-Sat. 9:30am-5pm, $8 adults, $4 children) recreates life in late 18th- and early 19th-century Beaufort in several restored historic buildings. The 1770s "jump-and-a-half" (1½-story) Leffers Cottage reflects middle-class life in its day, as a merchant, a whaler, or, in this case, a school-master would have lived in it. The Josiah Bell and John Manson Houses, both from the 1820s, reflect the graceful Caribbean-influenced architecture so prevalent in the early days of the coastal South. A restored apothecary shop, a 1790s wooden courthouse, and a haunted 1820s jail that was used into the 1950s are among the other important structures. There are tours led by costumed interpreters as well as driving tours of the old town in double-decker buses.

Sports and Recreation
DIVING

North Carolina's coast is a surprisingly good place for diving. The **Discovery Diving Company** (414 Orange St., 252/728-2265, www.discoverydiving.com, $65-110 per excursion) leads half- and full-day diving trips to explore the reefs and dozens of fascinating shipwrecks that lie at the bottom of the Sounds and ocean near Beaufort.

CRUISES AND WILDLIFE TOURS

Coastal Ecology Tours (252/247-3860, www.goodfortunesails.com, prices vary) runs very special tours on the *Good Fortune* of the Cape Lookout National Seashore and other island locations in the area, as well as a variety of half-day, day-long, overnight, and short trips to snorkel, shell, kayak, and watch birds, as well as cruises to Morehead City restaurants and other educational and fun trips. Prices range from

$40 pp for a 2.5-hour dolphin-watching tour to $600 per night plus meals for an off-season overnight boat rental. **Lookout Cruises** (600 Front St., 252/504-7245, www.lookoutcruises.com) carries sightseers on lovely catamaran rides in the Beaufort and Core Sound region, out to Cape Lookout, and on morning dolphin-watching trips. **Island Ferry Adventures** (610 Front St., 252/728-7555, www.islandferryadventures.com, $10-15 adults, $5-8 children) runs dolphin-watching tours, trips to collect shells at Cape Lookout, and trips to see the wild ponies of Shackleford Banks. **Mystery Tours** (600 Front St., 252/728-7827 or 866/230-2628, www.mysteryboattours.com, $15-50 adults, free-$25 children, some cruises adults only) offers harbor tours and dolphin-watching trips as well as a variety of brunch, lunch, and dinner cruises and trips to wild islands where children can hunt for treasure.

Accommodations

◖ Outer Banks Houseboats (324 Front St., 252/728-4129, www.outerbankshouseboats.com) will rent you your own floating vacation home, sail it for you to a scenic spot, anchor it, and then come and check in on you every day during your stay. You'll have a skiff for your own use, but you may just want to lie on the deck all day and soak up the peacefulness. Rates run from $1,200 per weekend for the smaller houseboat to $3,000 per week for the luxury boat, with plenty of rental options in between.

The **Inlet Inn** (601 Front St., 800/554-5466, www.inlet-inn.com, $110-170) has one of the best locations in town, right on the water, near the docks where many of the ferry and tour boats land. If planning to go dolphin-watching or hop the ferry to Cape Lookout, you can get ready at a leisurely pace, and just step outside to the docks. Even in high season, rates are quite reasonable.

The **Beaufort Inn** (101 Ann St., 252/728-2600, www.beaufort-inn.com, $200-250) is a large hotel on Gallants Channel, along one side of the colonial district. It's an easy walk to

the main downtown attractions, and the hotel's outdoor hot tub and balconies with great views make it tempting to stay in as well. The **Pecan Tree Inn** (116 Queen St., 800/728-7871, www.pecantree.com, $135-175) is such a grand establishment that the town threw a parade in honor of the laying of its cornerstone in 1866. The house is still splendid, as are the 5,000-square-foot gardens. Catty-corner to the Old Burying Grounds is the **Langdon House Bed and Breakfast** (135 Craven St., 252/728-5499, www.langdonhouse.com, $120-185). One of the oldest buildings in town, this gorgeous house was built in the 1730s on a foundation of English ballast stones.

Food

Among the Beaufort eateries certified by Carteret Catch as serving local seafood are the **Blue Moon Bistro** (119 Queen St., 252/728-5800, www.bluemoonbistro.biz, Tues.-Sat. 5:30pm-10pm, $17-35) and **Aqua Restaurant** (114 Middle Lane, "behind Clawsons," 252/728-7777, www.aquaexperience.com, Tues.-Sat. 5:30pm-9:30pm, $15-25).

If you're traveling with a cooler and want to buy some local seafood to take home, try the **Fishtowne Seafood Center** (100 Wellons Dr., 252/728-6644) or **Tripps Seafood** (1224 Harkers Island Rd., 252/447-7700).

◖ Beaufort Grocery (117 Queen St., 252/728-3899, www.beaufortgrocery.com, lunch and dinner Wed.-Mon., brunch Sun., $20-36), despite its humble name, is a sophisticated little eatery. At lunch it serves salads and crusty sandwiches along with "Damn Good Gumbo" and specialty soups. In the evening the café atmosphere gives way to that of a more formal gourmet dining room. Some of the best entrées include boneless chicken breast sautéed with pecans in a hazelnut cream sauce; Thai-rubbed roast half duckling; and whole baby rack of lamb, served with garlic mashed potatoes, tortillas, and a margarita-chipotle sauce. Try the cheesecake for dessert.

The waterfront **Front Street Grill** (300 Front St., 252/728-4956, www.

frontstreetgrillatstillwater.com, Tues.-Sat. lunch 11:30 am-2:30pm, dinner 5:30pm-9:30pm, Sunday brunch 11:30am-2:30pm, $15-22) is popular with boaters drifting through the area, as well as diners who arrive by land. The emphasis is on seafood and fresh regional ingredients. Front Street Grill's wine list is extensive, and they have repeatedly won *Wine Spectator* magazine's Award of Excellence.

Aqua (114 Middle Lane, 252/728-7777, www.aquaexperience.com, dinner Tues.-Thurs. 6pm, Fri.-Sat. 5:30pm, small plates $8-14, big plates $23-28) divides its menu into "small plates" and "big plates," so you can make up a dinner tapas-style and sample more of the menu. The fare ranges from Southern classics like shrimp and grits to more exotic fare like a Japanese bento box with yellow fin tuna, calamari, and shrimp spring rolls. Vegetarians will find limited options, but if you're looking for local seafood, you're in luck.

HARKERS ISLAND

The Core Sound region, which stretches to the east-northeast of Beaufort many miles up to the Pamlico Sound, is a region of birds and boats. Consequently, hunting has always been a way of life here, almost as much as fishing. In earlier generations (and to a much lesser extent today), people who fished most of the year did a sideline business in bird hunting; not only would they eat the birds they shot, but they made money selling feathers for women's hats, trained bird dogs for their own and other hunters' use, and served as guides to visiting hunters. Many Down Easterners also became expert decoy carvers. This art survives today, partly as art for art's sake, and also for its original purpose.

To get to Harkers Island, follow U.S. 70 east from Beaufort, around the dogleg that skirts the North River. A little east of the town of Otway you'll see Harkers Island Road. Take a right on Harkers Island Road and head south toward Straits. Straits Road will take you through the town of Straits, and then across a bridge over the straits themselves, finally ending up on Harkers Island.

◖ Core Sound Waterfowl Museum

The **Core Sound Waterfowl Museum** (1785 Island Rd., Harkers Island, 252/728-1500, www.coresound.com, Mon.-Sat. 10am-5pm, Sun. 2pm-5pm, free), which occupies a beautiful modern building on Shell Point, next to the Cape Lookout National Seashore headquarters, is a community labor of love. The museum is home to exhibits crafted by members of the communities represented, depicting Down East maritime life through decoys, nets, and other tools of the trades, everyday household objects, beautiful quilts and other utilitarian folk arts, and lots of other things held dear by local people. This is a sophisticated, modern institution, but its community roots are evident in touching details like the index-card labels, written in the careful script of elderly women, explaining what certain objects are, what they were used for, and who made them. The museum hosts monthly get-togethers for members of Down East communities, a different town every month, which are like old home days.

Core Sound Decoy Carvers Guild

Twenty years ago, some decoy-carving friends Down East decided over a pot of stewed clams to found the **Core Sound Decoy Carvers Guild** (1575 Harkers Island Rd., 252/838-8818, www. decoyguild.com, call for hours). The Guild, which is open to the public, gives demonstrations, hosts competitions, and holds classes for adults and children, and it has a museum shop that's a nice place to browse.

Events

The Core Sound Decoy Carvers Guild also hosts the **Core Sound Decoy Festival,** usually held in the early winter. Several thousand people come to this annual event—more than the number of permanent residents on Harkers Island—to buy, swap, and teach the art of making decoys.

Food

Captain's Choice Restaurant (977 Island Rd., 252/728-7122, Fri.-Sun. 7am-9pm, Tues.-Thurs. 10am-9pm) is a great place to

THE OUTER BANKS

try traditional Down East chowder. Usually made of clams, but sometimes with other shellfish or fish, chowder in Carteret County is a point of pride. The point is the flavor of the seafood itself, which must be extremely fresh, and not hidden behind lots of milk and spices. Captain's Choice serves chowder in the old-time way—with dumplings.

MOREHEAD CITY

Giovanni da Verrazzano may have been the first European to set foot in present-day Morehead City when he sailed into Bogue Inlet. It wasn't until the mid-19th century that the town actually came into being, built as the terminus of the North Carolina Railroad to connect the state's overland commerce to the sea. Despite its late start, Morehead City has been a busy place. During the Civil War it was the site of major encampments by both armies. A series of horrible hurricanes in the 1890s, culminating in 1899's San Ciriaco Hurricane, brought hundreds of refugees from the towns along what is now the Cape Lookout National Seashore.

They settled in a neighborhood that they called Promise Land, and many of their descendants are still here.

The Atlantic and North Carolina Railroad operated a large hotel here in the 1880s, ushering in Morehead's role as a tourist spot, and the bridge to the Bogue Banks a few decades later increased holiday traffic considerably.

Morehead is also an official state port, one of the best deepwater harbors on the Atlantic Coast. This admixture of tourism and gritty commerce gives Morehead City a likeable, real-life feel missing in many coastal towns today.

Sights

Morehead City's history is on display at **The History Place** (1008 Arendell St., 252/247-7533, www.thehistoryplace.org, Tues.-Sat. 10am-4pm, free). There are many interesting and eye-catching historical artifacts on display, but the most striking exhibit is that of a carriage, clothes, and other items pertaining to Emeline Pigott, Morehead City's Confederate heroine. She was a busy girl all through the

THE CAROLINA SOUNDER

© JIM MOREKIS

Morehead City is a longtime maritime center.

Civil War, working as a nurse, a spy, and a smuggler. The day she was captured, she was carrying 30 pounds of contraband hidden in her skirts, including Union troop movement plans, a collection of gloves, several dozen skeins of silk, needles, toothbrushes, a pair of boots, and five pounds of candy.

Entertainment and Events

Seafood is a serious art in Morehead City. North Carolina's second-largest festival takes place in town every October—the enormous **North Carolina Seafood Festival** (252/726-6273, www.ncseafoodfestival.org). The city's streets shut down and over 150,000 visitors descend on the waterfront. Festivities kick off with a blessing of the fleet, followed with music, fireworks, competitions (including the flounder toss), and, of course, lots and lots of food.

If you're in the area on the right weekend in November, you'll not want to deprive yourself of the gluttonous splendor of the **Mill Creek Oyster Festival** (Mill Creek Volunteer Fire Department, 2370 Mill Creek Rd., Mill Creek, 252/247-4777). Food, and lots of it, is the focus of this event. It's a small-town fete, a benefit for the local volunteer fire department, and the meals are cooked by local experts. You'll be able to choose from all-you-can-eat roasted oysters, fried shrimp, fried spot (a local fish), and more, all in mass quantities. The oysters may not be local these days (and few served on this coast are), but the cooking is very local—an authentic taste of one of North Carolina's best culinary traditions. Mill Creek is northwest of Morehead City on the Newport River.

Sports and Recreation

Many of this region's most important historic and natural sites are underwater. From Morehead City's **Olympus Dive Center** (713 Shepard St., 252/726-9432, www.olympusdiving.com), divers of all levels of experience can take charter trips to dozens of natural and artificial reefs that teem with fish, including the ferocious-looking but not terribly dangerous eight-foot-long sand tiger shark. There are at least as many amazing shipwrecks to choose from, including an 18th-century schooner, a luxury liner, a German U-boat, and many Allied commercial and military ships that fell victim to the U-boats that infested this coast during World War II.

Food

The **Sanitary Fish Market** (501 Evans St., 252/247-3111, www.sanitaryfishmarket.com, daily 11:30am-9:30pm, $15-20) is probably Morehead City's best-known institution. The rather odd name reflects its 1930s origins as a seafood market that was bound by its lease and its fastidious landlord to be kept as clean as possible. Today it's a huge family seafood restaurant. Long lines in season and on weekends demonstrate its popularity. Of particular note are its famous hush puppies, which have a well-deserved reputation as some of the best in the state. Be sure to buy a Sanitary T-shirt on the way out; it'll help you blend in everywhere else in the state.

The **Bistro-by-the-Sea** (4031 Arendell St., 252/247-2777, www.bistro-by-the-sea.com, Tues.-Thurs. 5pm-9:30pm, Fri.-Sat. 5pm-10pm, entrées $10-25) participates in Carteret Catch, a program that brings together local fisherfolk with restaurants, fish markets, and wholesalers to ensure that fresh locally caught seafood graces the tables of Carteret County. In addition to seafood, specialties here are steak, tenderloin, and prime rib.

Café Zito (105 S. 11th St., 252/726-6676, www.cafezito.com, dinner Fri.-Mon. from 5:30pm, entrées $17-27), located in a pretty 1898 house, serves elegant Mediterranean fare and also participates in Carteret Catch.

Captain Bill's (701 Evans St., 252/726-2166, www.captbills.com, daily 11:30am-9:30pm, $12-20) is Morehead City's oldest restaurant, founded in 1938. Try the conch stew, and be sure to visit the otters that live at the dock outside. Another famous eating joint in Morehead City is **El's Drive-In** (3706 Arendell St., 252/726-3002, daily 10:30am-10pm, $10), a tiny place across from Carteret Community

College. El's is most famous for its shrimp burgers but serves all sorts of fried delights.

BOGUE BANKS

The beaches of Bogue Banks are popular with visitors, but they have a typically North Carolinian, laid-back feel, a quieter atmosphere than the fun-fun-fun neon jungles of beaches in other states. The major attractions, Fort Macon State Park and the North Carolina Aquarium at Pine Knoll Shores, are a bit more cerebral than, say, amusement parks and bikini contests. In the surfing and boating, bars and restaurants, and the beach itself, there's also a bustle of activity to keep things hopping. Bogue, by the way, rhymes with "rogue."

◖ North Carolina Aquarium

The **North Carolina Aquarium at Pine Knoll Shores** (1 Roosevelt Blvd., Pine Knoll Shores, 866/294-3477, www.ncaquariums. com, Aug.-June daily 9am-5pm, July Fri.-Wed. 9am-5pm, Thurs. 9am-9pm, $10.95 adults, $8.95 children) is one of the state's three great coastal aquariums. Here at Pine Knoll Shores, exhibit highlights include a 300,000-gallon aquarium in which sharks and other aquatic beasts go about their business in and around a replica German U-Boat (plenty of originals lie right off the coast and form homes for reef creatures); a "jellyfish gallery" (they really can be beautiful); a pair of river otters; and many other wonderful animals and habitats.

Trails from the parking lot lead into the maritime forests of the 568-acre **Theodore Roosevelt Natural Area** (1 Roosevelt Dr., Atlantic Beach, 252/726-3775).

Fort Macon State Park

At the eastern tip of Atlantic Beach is **Fort Macon State Park** (2300 E. Fort Macon Rd., 252/726-3775, www.ncsparks.net/foma.html, park daily 9am-5:30pm, fort Oct.-Mar. daily 8am-6pm, Apr.-May and Sept. daily 8am-7pm, June-Aug. daily 8am-8pm, bathhouse area Nov.-Feb. daily 8am-5:30pm, Mar.-Oct. daily 8am-7pm, Apr.-May and Sept. daily 8am-8pm, June-Aug. daily 8am-9pm, bathhouse $4 adults, $3 children). The central feature of the park is Fort Macon itself, an 1820s Federal fort that was a Confederate garrison for one year during the Civil War. Guided tours are offered, and there are exhibits inside the casemates. For such a stern, martial building, some of the interior spaces are surprisingly pretty.

Sports and Recreation

The ocean side of Bogue Banks offers plenty of public beach access. In each of the towns, from the northeast end of the island to the southwest end—Atlantic Beach, Pine Knoll Shores, Salter Path, Indian Beach, and Emerald Isle—there are parking lots, both municipal and private, free and paid.

Aside from the fort itself, the other big attraction at **Fort Macon** is the beach, which is bounded by the ocean, Bogue Sound, and Beaufort Inlet. Because there's a Coast Guard station on the Sound side, and a jetty along the Inlet, swimming is permitted only along one stretch of the ocean beach. A concession stand and bathhouse are located at the swimming beach.

Atlantic Beach Surf Shop (515 W. Fort Macon Rd., Atlantic Beach, 252/646-4944, www.absurfshop.com) gives individual ($50 per hour) and group ($40 per hour) surfing lessons on the beach at Pine Knoll Shores. Lessons are in the morning and early afternoon. Call for reservations.

Accommodations

The **Atlantis Lodge** (123 Salter Path Rd., Atlantic Beach, 800/682-7057, www.atlantislodge.com, $70-220) is an old established family-run motel. It has simple and reasonably priced efficiencies in a great beachfront location. Well-behaved pets are welcome for a per-pet, per-night fee. The **Clamdigger** (511 Salter Path Rd., Atlantic Beach, 800/338-1533, www.clamdiggerramadainn.com, $40-260) is another reliable choice, with all oceanfront guest rooms. Pets are not allowed. The **Windjammer** (103 Salter Path Rd., Atlantic Beach, 800/233-6466, www.windjammerinn.com, $50-200) is another simple, comfortable motel, with decent rates through the high season.

Food

The **Channel Marker** (718 Atlantic Beach Causeway, Atlantic Beach, 252/247-2344, daily 11am-9:30pm, $15-25) is a more upscale alternative to some of the old-timey fried seafood joints on Bogue Banks (which are also great—read on). Try the crab cakes with mango chutney, or the Greek shrimp salad. The extensive wine list stars wines from the opposite side of North Carolina, from the Biltmore Estate in Asheville.

White Swan Bar-B-Q and Chicken (2500-A W. Fort Macon Rd., Atlantic Beach, 252/726-9607, Mon.-Sat. 7am-2pm, $8) has been serving the Carolina trinity of barbecue, coleslaw, and hush puppies since 1960. They also flip a mean egg for breakfast.

The ◀ **Big Oak Drive-In and Bar-B-Q** (1167 Salter Path Rd., 252/247-2588, www. bigoakdrivein.com, Fri.-Sun. 11am-3pm) is a classic beach drive-in, a little red-white-and-blue-striped building with a walk-up counter and drive-up spaces. They're best known for their shrimp burgers (large $5), a fried affair slathered with Big Oak's signature red sauce, coleslaw, and tartar sauce. Then there are the scallop burgers, oyster burgers, clam burgers, hamburgers, and barbecue, all cheap, and made for snacking on the beach.

Frost Seafood House (1300 Salter Path Rd., Salter Path, 252/247-3202, Fri.-Sun. 7am-9pm, Mon.-Thurs. 4:30pm-9:30pm, $10) began in 1954 as a gas station and quickly became the restaurant that it is today. The Frost family catches its own shrimp and buys much of its other seafood locally. Be sure to request a taste of the "ching-a-ling sauce." Yet another community institution is the **Crab Shack** (140 Shore Dr., Salter Path, 252/247-3444, daily 11am-9pm, $9-25). You'll find it behind the Methodist church in Salter Path. Operated by the Guthries (a family name that dates back to the dawn of time in this area, long before anyone thought of calling their home the "Crystal Coast"), the restaurant was wiped out in 2005 by Hurricane Ophelia, but they have since rebuilt, rolled up their sleeves, and plunged their hands back into the cornmeal.

GETTING THERE AND AROUND
By Car
One of the state's main east-west routes, U.S. 70, gives easy access to almost all of the destinations in this chapter. From Raleigh to Beaufort is a little over 150 miles, but keep in mind that large stretches of the highway are in commercial areas with plenty of traffic and red lights. U.S. 70 continues past Beaufort, snaking up along Core Sound through little Down East towns like Otway and Davis, finally ending in the town of Atlantic. At Sea Level, Highway 12 branches to the north, across the Cedar Island Wildlife Refuge and ending at the Cedar Island-Ocracoke Ferry.

Down south, to reach the Bogue Banks (Atlantic Beach, Emerald Isle, and neighboring beaches) by road, bridges cross Bogue Sound on Highway 58 at both Morehead City and Cedar Point (not to be confused with Cedar Island).

By Ferry
A 20-minute free **passenger ferry crosses the Neuse River** between Cherry Branch (near Cherry Point) and Minesott Beach in Pamlico County every half-hour (800/339-9156, vehicles and passengers, pets allowed).

Albemarle Sound

Referred to historically as the Albemarle, and sometimes today as the Inner Banks, the mainland portion of northeastern North Carolina is the hearth of the state's colonial history, the site of its first European towns and the earliest plantation and maritime economies.

The Great Dismal Swamp is here, a region thought of by early Carolinians and Virginians as a diseased and haunted wasteland, the sooner drained the better. They succeeded to some extent in beating back the swamp waters and vapors, but left enough for modern generations to recognize as one of the state's crown jewels.

Early cities like Edenton and Bath were influential centers of government and commerce, and today preserve some of the best colonial and early federal architecture in the Southeast. The vast network of rivers and creeks include some of the state's best canoeing and kayaking waters, and along the Albemarle Regional Canoe-Kayak Trail, there are a growing number of camping platforms on which to spend an unforgettable night listening to owls hoot and otters splash.

◖ THE GREAT DISMAL SWAMP

Viewed for centuries as an impediment to progress, the Great Dismal Swamp is now recognized for the national treasure that it is, and tens of thousands of acres are protected. There are several points from which to gain access to the interior of the Dismal Swamp. A few miles south of the North Carolina-Virginia line, on U.S. 17, is the **Dismal Swamp Welcome Center** (2294 U.S. 17 N., visitors center 2356 U.S. 17 N., South Mills, 877/771-8333, www.dismalswamp.com, late May-Oct. daily 9am-5pm, Nov.-late May Tues.-Sat. 9am-5pm). Should you be arriving by water, you'll find the Welcome Center at mile 28 on the Intracoastal Waterway. You can tie up to the dock here and spend the night, if you wish, or wait for one of the four daily lock openings (8:30am, 11am,

1:30pm, and 3:30pm) to proceed. There are also picnic tables and grills here, and restrooms open day and night.

Another area of the swamp to explore is the **Great Dismal Swamp National Wildlife Refuge** (Suffolk, VA, 757/986-3705, www.albemarle-nc.com/gates/gdsnwr, daily dawn-dusk), which straddles the state line. Two main entrances are outside Suffolk, Virginia, off the White Marsh Road (Hwy. 642). These entrances, Washington Ditch and Jericho Lane, are open April-September daily 6:30am-8pm, October-March daily 6:30am-5pm. In the middle of the refuge is Lake Drummond, an eerie 3,100-acre natural lake that's a wonderful place for canoeing. (Contact refuge headquarters for directions on navigating the feeder ditch that lets out into Lake Drummond.) You may see all sorts of wildlife in the swamp—including poisonous cottonmouths, canebrake rattlers, copperheads, and possibly even black bears. One more word of caution: Controlled hunting is permitted on certain days in October through December, so if you're visiting in the fall, wear brightly colored clothing, and contact refuge staff in advance of your visit to find out about closures.

GATESVILLE

Near the town of Gatesville, a little way west of South Mills on U.S. 158, is another gorgeous swampy natural area, **Merchant's Millpond State Park** (176 Millpond Rd., Gatesville, 252/357-1191, http://ncparks.gov, office daily 8am-4:30pm except holidays, park Nov.-Feb. daily 8am-6pm, Mar.-May and Sept.-Oct. daily 8am-8pm, June-Aug. daily 8am-9pm). This is a great spot for canoeing or kayaking, with miles of beautiful blackwater backwaters. The park has a canoe rental facility, charging $5 per hour for the first hour and $3 per hour for each additional hour; or, for those camping, $20 for 24 hours. There are several hiking trails through the park, totaling about nine miles.

Merchant's Millpond has several campsites for three kinds of campers. The family campground, near the park office, is easily accessible, accommodates trailers as well as tents, and had a washhouse with restrooms, showers, and drinking water. Off the park's Lassiter trail are five backpack campsites. All supplies, including water, must be packed in, and there is a pit toilet nearby. There are also two canoe camping areas reached by canoe trails. These sites also have pit toilets, and campers must bring water and other supplies.

ELIZABETH CITY

The **Museum of the Albemarle** (501 S. Water St., 252/335-1453, www.museumofthealbemarle.com, Tues.-Sat. 9am-5pm, Sun. 2pm-5pm) is a relatively new and growing museum. It explores the four centuries of history in northeastern North Carolina since the first English settlers arrived at Roanoke. Come here to learn about the Lost Colonists, the pirates who swarmed this region, the folkways of the Sound country, and more.

To stay in Elizabeth City, you have several options. The **Pond House Inn** (915 Rivershore Rd., 252/335-9834, www.thepondhouseinn.com, $99-165) sits on the banks of the Pasquotank River. Each of the large guest rooms has its own fireplace in this pleasant 1940s house. The **Culpepper Inn** (609 W. Main St., 252/335-9235, www.culpepperinn.com, $90-145), just a few blocks from the Albemarle Sound, has several comfortable guest rooms in the main house, and cozy accommodations in a carriage house and cottage.

There are also chain motels in the area, including the **Travelers Inn** (1211 N. Road St., 252/338-5451, www.travelersinn.webs.com, around $70, small pets allowed), **Econo Lodge** (522 S. Hughes Blvd. B, 252/338-4124, www.econolodge.com, around $70, pets allowed), **Holiday Inn Express** (306 S. Hughes Blvd., 252/338-8900, www.hiexpress.com, $75-125), and **Hampton Inn** (402 Halstead Blvd., 252/333-1800, www.hamptoninn.com, around $100).

HERTFORD

If you're traveling between Edenton and Elizabeth City, don't miss Hertford, a pretty little Spanish moss-draped town on the Perquimans (per-KWIH-muns) River. The historic **Newbold White House** (151 Newbold White Rd., 252/426-7567, www.newboldwhitehouse.org, guided tours Mar.-late Nov. Tues.-Sat. 10am-4pm, $5 adults, $3 students) is the oldest brick house in North Carolina, built in 1730 by one of the region's early Quakers. The grounds include a seasonal herb garden and a 17th-century Quaker graveyard. While you're in Hertford, stop in at **Woodard's Pharmacy** (101 N. Church St., 252/426-5527), an old-fashioned lunch counter and soda fountain in the heart of downtown, where you can grab a pimiento cheese sandwich and an ice cream cone. If you're making it an overnight, stay at **1812 on the Perquimans** (385 Old Neck Rd., 252/426-1812, $80-85) or at the **Beechtree Inn** (948 Pender Rd., 252/426-1593, $90). At the Beechtree, guests stay in restored pre-Civil War cottages. Children and pets are welcome.

EDENTON

Incorporated in 1722 but inhabited long before that, Edenton was one of North Carolina's most important colonial towns, and it remains one of its most beautiful.

Historic District

The whole town is lined with historic buildings, and several especially important sites are clustered within a few blocks of each other near the waterfront. The easiest starting point for a walking tour (guided or on your own) is the headquarters of the **Edenton State Historic Site** (108 N. Broad St., 252/482-2637, www.edenton.nchistoricsites.org, Apr.-Oct. Mon.-Sat. 9am-5pm, Sun. 1pm-5pm, Nov.-Mar. Mon.-Sat. 10am-4pm, Sun. 1pm-4pm), also referred to as the Edenton Visitors Center. The 1782 **Barker House** (505 S. Broad St., 252/482-7800, www.edentonhistoricalcommission.org, Mon.-Sat. 10am-4pm, Sun. 1pm-4pm), a stunning Lowcountry palazzo, was the home of Penelope Barker, an early revolutionary and organizer of the Edenton Tea Party. It's now the headquarters of the Edenton Historical Commission, and the location of their bookstore. The 1758 **Cupola House** (108 Broad St., 252/482-2637, www. cupolahouse.org, daily 9am-4:30pm, tickets available at Edenton Visitors Center, $10) is a National Historical Landmark and a home of great architectural significance. Although much of the original interior woodwork was removed in 1918 and sold to New York's Brooklyn Museum, where it remains, the Cupola House has been restored meticulously inside and out and its colonial gardens recreated. Also a designated National Historical Landmark is the **Chowan County Courthouse** (111 E. King St., 252/482-2637, www.edenton.nchistoricsites.org, hours vary, $1), a superb 1767 brick building in the Georgian style. It is the best-preserved colonial courthouse in the United States.

Accommodations and Food

The 🌙 **Broad Street Inn** (300 N. Broad St., 888/394-6622, www.edentoninn.com, from $170) occupies not one but four exceptional historic buildings: the 1901 main White-Bond House, the 1801 Satterfield House, a 1915 tobacco storage barn remodeled with beautiful guest rooms, and the 1870 Tillie Bond House cottage. Each one of these is artfully restored, with soft and restful furnishings. Breakfast cook Janie Granby prepares specialties like lemon soufflé pancakes, and North Carolina native and star chef Kevin Yokley prepares four-course dinners that are dazzling. Entrées include grilled swordfish with artichoke vinaigrette, lamb porterhouse chops with dried cherry sauce, and breast of Muscovy duck with red currant sauce.

The **Granville Queen Inn** (108 S. Granville St., 866/482-8534, www.granvillequeen. com, $95-140) is a rather splendid early-1900s mansion decorated in a variety of early 20th-century styles. Breakfasts are as ornate and elegant as the house itself, featuring poached pears, potato tortillas, crepes, and much more.

WINDSOR

A small historic town on the Cashie River, Windsor is the seat of Bertie County. Historic architecture, good food, and wetlands exploration are equally compelling reasons to visit this lesser-known treasure of the Albemarle region. Pronunciation is a little perverse here: The county name is pronounced "ber-TEE," and the river is the "cuh-SHY."

Sights

Hope Plantation (132 Hope House Rd., 252/794-3140, www.hopeplantation.org, Apr.-Dec. Mon.-Sat. 10am-4pm, Sun. 2pm-4pm, $11 adults, $6 children) was built in 1803 for the former governor David Stone. Stone did not live to see his 50th birthday, but by the time of his death he had been the governor of North Carolina, a U.S. senator and congressman, a state senator, a Superior Court judge, and a seven-times-elected member of the State House. He graduated from Princeton University and passed the bar when he was 20; he was the father of 11 children and one of the founders of the University of North Carolina. High among his most impressive accomplishments was the construction of this wonderful house. Characterized by a mixture of Georgian and federal styles with significant twists of regional and individual aesthetics, Hope House is on the National Register of Historic Places.

The **Roanoke-Cashie River Center** (112 W. Water St., Windsor, 252/794-2001, www. partnershipforthesounds.org, Tues.-Sat. 10am-4pm, $2 adults, $1 children) has interpretive exhibits about this region's history and ecology. There is a canoe ramp outside where you can get out into the Cashie River, and canoe rentals are available ($10 per hour, half-day $25, full day $35).

Southeast of Windsor on the Cashie River, the **Sans Souci Ferry** (Woodard Rd. and Sans Souci Rd., 252/794-4277, Mar. 16-Sept. 16 daily 6:30am-6pm, Sept. 17-Mar. 15 daily 6:45am-5pm) operates, as it has for generations, by a cable and a honk of the horn. To cross the river, pull up to the bank, honk your horn, and wait. The operator will emerge directly and pull you across.

Recreation

The headquarters of the **Roanoke River National Wildlife Refuge** (114 W. Water St., 252/794-3808, www.fws.gov/roanokeriver) are located here in Windsor. The Refuge, however, stretches over nearly 21,000 acres in Bertie County, through the hardwood bottomlands and cypress-tupelo wetlands of the Roanoke River Valleys, an environment that the Nature Conservancy calls "one of the last great places." The Refuge is an exceptional place for birdwatching, with the largest inland heron rookery in North Carolina, a large population of bald eagles, and many wintering waterfowl and neotropical migrant species.

Food

Bunn's Bar-B-Q (127 N. King St., 252/794-2274, Mon.-Tues., Thurs.-Fri. 9am-5pm, Wed. and Sat. 9am-2pm, from $5) is a barbecue and Brunswick stew joint of renown, an early gas station converted in 1938 to its present state. Super-finely chopped barbecue is the specialty, with coleslaw, cornbread, and plenty of sauce from those little red bottles you see on every surface.

WILLIAMSTON AND VICINITY

Williamston is at the junction of U.S. 17 and U.S. 64. If you're passing through town, Williamston is a great place to stop for barbecue or a fresh seafood meal.

Sights

A little west of Williamston on U.S. 13/64 Alternate, you'll find the town of Robersonville and the **St. James Place Museum** (U.S. 64 Alt. and Outerbridge Rd., call Robersonville Public Library at 252/795-3591, by appointment, free). A Primitive Baptist church built in 1910 and restored by a local preservationist and folk art enthusiast, St. James Place is an unusual little museum that fans of Southern craft will not want to miss. A serious collection of traditional quilts is the main feature of the museum. Of the 100 on display, nearly half are African American quilts—examples of which are much less likely to have survived and find their way into museum collections than their counterpane counterparts made by white quilters. Getting a glimpse of the two traditions side by side is an education in these parallel Southern aesthetics.

On the same highway is **East Carolina Motor Speedway** (4918 U.S. 64 Alt., 252/795-3968, www.ecmsracing.com, usually Apr.-Oct., pits open at 3pm, grandstands from 5pm), a 0.4-mile hard-surface track featuring several divisions, including late-model street stock, modified street stock, super-stock four-cylinder, and four-cylinder kids class.

Food

Come to Williamston on an empty stomach. It has an assortment of old and very traditional eateries. The ◖ **Sunny Side Oyster Bar** (1102 Washington St., 252/792-3416, www.sunnysideoysterbarnc.com, Sept.-Apr. Mon.-Thurs. 5:30pm-9pm, Fri.-Sat. from 5:30pm, Sun. 5pm-8pm, $12-20) is the best known, a seasonal oyster joint open in the months with the letter *r*—that is, oyster season. It's been in business since 1935, and is a historic as well as gastronomic landmark. Oysters are steamed behind the restaurant, and then hauled inside and shucked at the bar. Visit the restaurant's website to get acquainted with the shuckers. In eastern North Carolina, a good oyster shucker is regarded as highly as a good artist or athlete, and rightly so. The Sunny Side doesn't take reservations, and it fills to capacity in no time flat, so come early.

Down the road a piece, **Martin Supply** (118 Washington St., 252/792-2123), an old general store, is a good place to buy local produce and preserves, honey, molasses, and hoop cheese. **Griffin's Quick Lunch** (204 Washington St., 252/792-0002, Mon.-Fri. 6am-8:30pm, Sat. 6am-2pm, $8) is a popular old diner with good barbecue. Back on U.S. 64, **Shaw's Barbecue** (U.S. 64 Alt., 252/792-5339, Mon.-Sat. 6am-7pm, $7-10) serves eastern Carolina-style barbecue, as well as good greasy breakfasts.

© JIM MOREKIS

Cypress Grill in Jamesville

East of Williamston at the intersection of U.S. 64 and Highway 171, the small Roanoke River town of Jamesville is home to a most unusual restaurant that draws attention from all over the country (it's even been featured in the *New York Times*). The **❰ Cypress Grill** (1520 Stewart St., off U.S. 64, 252/792-4175, mid-Jan.-Apr. Mon.-Sat. 11am-8pm, $7-10) is an unprepossessing wooden shack right-smack on the river, a survivor of the days when Jamesville made its living in the herring industry, dragging the fish out of the water with horse-drawn seine nets. Herring— breaded and seriously deep-fried, not pickled or sweet—is the main dish here, though they also dress the herring up in other outfits, and serve bass, flounder, perch, oyster, catfish, and other fish too. The Cypress Grill is open for the three and a half months of the year, from the second Thursday in January through the end of April, and you could hardly have a more intensely authentic, small-town dining experience anywhere else.

EAST ON U.S. 64

The eastern stretch of U.S. 64 runs along the Albemarle Sound between Williamston and the Outer Banks, passing through the towns of Plymouth, Creswell, and Columbia before it crosses over to Roanoke Island. Here you'll encounter evidence of North Carolina's ancient past in the form of old-growth forests; of the recent past in a plantation with a long and complex history of slavery; and the present, in art galleries and abundant wildlife-watching and recreational opportunities.

Plymouth

Plymouth is an attractive little town on the Roanoke River with a rich maritime and military history. Most notably, it was the site of the 1864 Battle of Plymouth, the second-largest Civil War battle in North Carolina, fought by more than 20,000 combatants. At the **Roanoke River Lighthouse and Maritime Museum** (W. Water St., 252/217-2204, www.roanokeriver-lighthouse.org, Tues.-Sat. 11am-3pm and by appointment, $3.50), visitors can explore a pretty replica of Plymouth's 1866 screw-pile lighthouse and, across the street in an old car dealership, the maritime museum itself, featuring artifacts and photographs from the region's water-faring heritage. On East Water Street is the **Port O'Plymouth Museum** (302 E. Water St., 252/793-1377, www.livinghistoryweekend. com, Tues.-Sat. 9am-4pm, $3.50 adults, $2.50 ages 12-17, $1.50 ages 8-11). This tiny museum is packed with Civil War artifacts, including a collection of beautiful pistols, telling the story of the Battle of Plymouth.

Davenport Homestead

West of Creswell is the **Davenport Homestead** (3 miles from U.S. 64 exit 554, 252/793-1377, by appointment only, free), a small 18th-century cabin built by Daniel Davenport, the first state senator from Washington County. In 1800 this diminutive homestead was home to 14 people—six members of the Davenport family, and eight slaves. Visitors can take a self-guided tour of the Davenport Homestead, but for a closer look, ask Loretta Phelps, who lives across the road and is a Davenport descendant, to unlock the buildings and show you around.

◖ Somerset Place Historic Site

Somerset Place Historic Site (2572 Lake Shore Rd., Creswell, 252/797-4560, www. ah.dcr.state.nc.us, Apr.-Oct. Mon.-Sat. 9am-5pm, Sun. 1pm-5pm, Nov.-Mar. Tues.-Sat. 10am-4pm, Sun. 1pm-4pm, free) was one of North Carolina's largest and most profitable plantations for the 80 years leading up to the Civil War. In the late 18th and early 19th centuries, 80 enslaved Africa-born men, women, and children were brought to Somerset to labor in the fields. The grief and spiritual disorientation they experienced, and the subsequent trials of the enslaved community that grew to include more than 300 people, are told by the historian Dorothy Spruill Redford in the amazing book *Somerset Homecoming.*

Somerset Place is an eerily lovely place to visit. The restored grounds and buildings,

including the Collins family's house, slave quarters, and several dependencies, are deafeningly quiet, and the huge cypress trees growing right up to the quarters and the mansion make the place feel almost prehistoric. Visitors are permitted to walk around the estate at their leisure.

Pettigrew State Park

On the banks of Lake Phelps, **Pettigrew State Park** (2252 Lakeshore Rd., Creswell, 252/797-4475, http://ncparks.gov, day use hours June-Aug. 8am-9pm, Mar.-May and Sept.-Oct. 8am-8pm, Nov.-Feb. 8am-6pm, free) preserves a weird ancient waterscape that's unlike anywhere else in the state. Archaeological studies reveal that there was a human presence here a staggering 10,000 years ago. The lake, which is five miles across, has yielded more than 30 ancient dugout canoes, some as old as 4,000 years and measuring more than 30 feet long. The natural surroundings are ancient too, encompassing some of eastern North Carolina's only remaining old-growth forests.

Visitors to Pettigrew State Park can camp at the family campground ($15), which has drive-in sites and access to restrooms and hot showers, or at primitive group campsites (from $9).

Sports and Recreation

Palmetto-Peartree Preserve (Pot Licker Rd./Loop Rd./Hwy. 1220, east of Columbia, 252/796-0723 or 919/967-2223, www.palmettopeartree.org, daily dawn-dusk, free) is a 10,000-acre natural area, wrapped in 14 miles of shoreline along the Albemarle Sound and Little Alligator Creek. Originally established as a sanctuary for the red cockaded woodpecker, this is a great location for bird-watching and spotting other wildlife, including the birds, alligators, wolves, bears, and bobcats; hiking, biking, and horseback riding along the old logging trails through the forest; and canoeing and kayaking. The preserve's excellent paddle trail passes by Hidden Lake, a secluded cypress-swamp blackwater lake. There is an overnight camping platform at the lake, which can be used in the daytime without a permit for bird-watching and picnicking. To stay overnight, arrange for a permit through the Roanoke River Partners (252/792-3790, www.roanokeriverpartners.org).

Once the southern edge of the Great Dismal Swamp, **Pocosin Lakes National Wildlife Refuge** (252/796-3004, www.fws.gov/pocosinlakes, daily dawn-dusk, free) is an important haven for many species of animals, including migratory waterfowl and reintroduced red wolves. Five important bodies of water lie within the refuge: Pungo Lake, New Lake, the 16,600-acre Lake Phelps, and stretches of the Scuppernong and Alligator Rivers. All of these areas are good spots for observing migratory waterfowl, but Pungo Lake is particularly special in the fall and winter, when snow geese and tundra swans visit in massive numbers—approaching 100,000—on their round-trip Arctic journeys. The refuge headquarters is at Walter B. Jones Sr. Center for the Sounds (U.S. 64, 6 miles south of Columbia).

Also east of Columbia on U.S. 64 is the **Alligator River National Wildlife Refuge** (between Columbia and Roanoke Island, 252/473-1131, http://alligatorriver.fws.gov, daily dawn-dusk, free). This large swath of woods and pocosin represents one of the most important wildlife habitats in the state, home to over 200 species of birds, as well as alligators, red wolves, and more black bears than almost anywhere in the coastal mid-Atlantic. In the 1980s, red wolves were introduced into the Alligator River Refuge as they became extinct in the wild elsewhere in their original range. During the summer months the Columbia-based **Red Wolf Coalition** (252/796-5600, http://redwolves.com) leads "howlings," nighttime expeditions into the refuge to hear the wolves' calling in the woods. Reservations are required, and participation usually costs $7, though it is free on certain occasions.

GETTING THERE AND AROUND

This remote corner of North Carolina is crossed by two major north-south routes, U.S. 17 and U.S. 168, both running south from Chesapeake, Virginia. U.S. 168 passes to the east, through Currituck, while U.S. 17 is the westerly route, closest to the Dismal Swamp and Elizabeth City, and passing through Edenton, Windsor, and Williamston. At Williamston, U.S. 17 meets U.S. 64, a major east-west route that leads to Plymouth, Creswell, and Columbia to the east.

Pamlico Sound

WASHINGTON, BATH, AND BELHAVEN

On the north side of the Pamlico River, as you head toward Mattamuskeet National Wildlife Refuge and the Outer Banks, the towns of Washington, Bath, and Belhaven offer short diversions into the nature and history of this region.

North Carolina Estuarium

The **North Carolina Estuarium** (223 E. Water St., Washington, 252/948-0000, www.partnershipforthesounds.org, Tues.-Sat. 10am-4pm, $3 adults, $2 children) is a museum about both the natural and cultural history of the

Tar-Pamlico River Basin. In addition to the exhibits, which include live native animals, historic artifacts, and much more, the Estuarium operates pontoon boat tours on the Pamlico River. River roving is free, but reservations are required.

Turnage Theater

Washington has a great performing arts facility in the restored early 20th-century **Turnage Theater** (150 W. Main St., Washington, 252/975-1711, www.turnagetheater.com). All sorts of performances take place at the Turnage throughout the year, including prominent artists from around the country. There are concerts of all kinds of music, productions by touring dance troupes and regional theater companies, and screenings of classic movies.

Moss House

Located in the historic district, a block from the river, is the **Moss House** (129 Van Norden St., Washington, 252/975-3967, www.the-mosshouse.com, $110-235). This 1902 house is a cozy bed-and-breakfast with airy guest rooms and delicious breakfasts. An easy walk from the Moss House is **Bill's Hot Dogs** (109 Gladden St., Washington, 252/946-3343, daily 8:30am-5pm), a longtime local favorite for a quick snack.

Goose Creek State Park

Goose Creek State Park (2190 Camp Leach Rd., 252/923-2191, http://ncparks.gov, daily 8am-dusk, free) is on the banks of the Pamlico, where Goose Creek empties into the river. It's an exotic environment of brackish marshes, freshwater swamps, and tall pine forests, home to a variety of wildlife, including bears, a multitude of bird species, and rather many snakes. More than eight miles of hiking trails, as well as boardwalks and paddle tails, traverse the hardwood swamp environment. Twelve primitive campsites ($13/day), with access to toilets and water, are available year-round, including one that is disabled-accessible.

Historic Bath

North Carolina's oldest town, Bath, was chartered in 1705. The town is so little changed that even today it is mostly contained within the original boundaries laid out by the explorer John Lawson. For its first 70 or so years, Bath enjoyed the spotlight as one of North Carolina's most important centers of trade and politics—home of governors, refuge from conflicts with Native Americans, frequent host to and victim of Blackbeard. Much as Brunswick Town, to the south, was made redundant by the growth of Wilmington, Bath faded into obscurity as the town of Washington grew in the years after the Revolutionary War. Today, almost all of Bath is designated as **Historic Bath**

(252/923-3971, www.bath.nchistoricsites.org, visitors center and tours Apr.-Oct. Mon.-Sat. 9am-5pm, Sun. 1pm-5pm, Nov.-Mar. Tues.-Sat. 10am-4pm, Sun. 1pm-4pm, $2 admission for Palmer-Marsh and Bonner Houses). Important sites on the tour of the village are the 1734 St. Thomas Church, the 1751 Palmer-Marsh House, the 1790 Van Der Veer House, the 1830 Bonner House, and, from time immemorial, a set of indelible hoofprints said to have been made by the devil's own horse.

While in Bath, drop in at the **Old Town Country Kitchen** (436 Carteret St., 252/923-1840, Fri.-Sat. 7am-8:30pm, Sun.-Tues. 7am-2pm, Wed.-Thurs. 7am-8pm, $10) for some country cooking and seafood. If you decide to stay the night, try the **Inn on Bath Creek** (116 S. Main St., 252/923-9571, www.innonbathcreek. com, 2-night minimum Apr.-Nov. Fri.-Sat., $130-225). This bed-and-breakfast, built on the site of the former Buzzard Hotel, fits in nicely with the old architecture of the historic town, but because it was built in 1999, it has modern conveniences to make your stay especially comfortable.

Belhaven

The name of **Belhaven Memorial Museum** (210 E. Main St., Belhaven, 252/943-6817, www.beaufort-county.com, Thurs.-Tues. 1pm-5pm, free) gives no hint as to what a very strange little institution this is. The museum houses the collection of Miss Eva—Eva Blount Way, who died in 1962 at the age of 92—surely one of the most accomplished collectors of oddities ever. The local paper wrote of her in 1951 that, "housewife, snake killer, curator, trapper, dramatic actress, philosopher, and preserver of all the riches of mankind, inadequately describes the most fascinating person you can imagine." Miss Eva kept among her earthly treasures a collection of pickled tumors (one weighs 10 pounds), a pickled one-eyed pig, a pickled two-headed kitten, cataracts (pickled), and three pickled human babies. It must have taken a very long time to carry everything over here, but Miss Eva's collection is now on public display, the core of the Belhaven Memorial Museum's collection.

© JIM MOREKIS

Mattamuskeet National Wildlife Refuge

Belhaven has an especially nice inn, the **Belhaven Water Street Bed and Breakfast** (567 E. Water St., 866/338-2825, www.belhavenwaterstreetbandb.com, $85-115). The guest rooms in this 100-year-old house face Pantego Creek and have their own fireplaces and private baths as well as wireless access.

◖ MATTAMUSKEET NATIONAL WILDLIFE REFUGE

Near the tiny town of Swan Quarter, the **Mattamuskeet National Wildlife Refuge** (Hwy. 94, between Swan Quarter and Englehard, 252/926-4021, www.fws.gov/mattamuskeet, daily dawn-dusk, free) preserves one of North Carolina's most remarkable natural features, as well as one of its most famous buildings. Lake Mattamuskeet, 18 miles long by 6 miles wide, is the state's largest natural lake, and being an average of 1.5 feet deep—five feet at its deepest point—it is a most unusual environment. The hundreds of thousands of waterfowl who rest here on

their seasonal rounds make this a world-famous location for bird-watching and wildlife photography.

Old-timers in the area have fond memories of dancing at the **Lodge at Lake Mattamuskeet,** one of eastern North Carolina's best-known buildings. The huge old building was constructed in 1915 and was, at the time, the world's largest pumping station, moving over one million gallons of water per minute. In 1934 it was bought by the federal government along with the wildlife sanctuary, and the Civilian Conservation Corps transformed it into the lodge that was a favorite gathering place for the next 40 years. The lodge is closed at the time of this writing, but is undergoing restoration for future public use.

Hiking and biking trails thread through the refuge, but camping is not permitted. Within the administration of the Mattamuskeet Refuge is the **Swan Quarter National Wildlife Refuge** (252/926-4021, www.fws.gov/swanquarter, daily dawn-dusk, free), located along the north shore of the Pamlico Sound, and mostly accessible only by water. This too is a gorgeous waterscape full of wildlife.

GETTING THERE AND AROUND

If you continue south on U.S. 17 from Williamston, the next major town you'll reach is Washington. From there you can turn east on U.S. 264 to reach Bath and Belhaven. Alternatively, you can reach U.S. 264 from the other direction, by taking Highway 94 at Columbia and crossing Lake Mattamuskeet.

There is one state ferry route in this region, at the far northwest corner, between **Currituck and Knotts Island** (877/287-7488, 45 minutes, free).

New Bern

New Bern's history is understandably a great draw, and that, coupled with its beautiful natural setting at the confluence of the Neuse and Trent Rivers, makes it one of North Carolina's prime spots for tourism and retirement living. Despite the considerable traffic it draws, it is still a small and enormously pleasant city.

One all-important note: how to say it. It's your choice of "NYEW-bern" or "NOO-bern"—and in some folks' accents it sounds almost like "neighbor"—but never "new-BERN."

New Bern is easy to access at the intersection of two major highways. U.S. 17 passes through New Bern going north to south, and U.S. 70 crosses east to west, with Beaufort and Morehead City to the east and Kinston to the west.

HISTORY

New Bern was settled in 1710 by a community of Swiss and German colonists. Despite early disasters, New Bern was on its feet again by the mid-18th century, at which time it was home to the colony's first newspaper and its first chartered academy. It also became North Carolina's capital in an era symbolized by the splendor of Tryon Palace, one of the most recognizable architectural landmarks in North Carolina.

SIGHTS
◖ Tryon Palace

Tryon Palace (610 Pollock St., 252/514-4956 or 252/514-4900, www.tryonpalace.org, Mon.-Sat. 9am-5pm, Sun. 1pm-5pm, last tour 4pm, gardens summer Mon.-Sat. 9am-7pm, Sun. 1pm-7pm, shop Mon.-Sat. 9:30am-5:30pm, Sun. 1pm-5:30pm, $20 adults, $10 grades 1-12, gardens and stables only $8 adults, $3 grades 1-12) is a rather remarkable feat of historic re-creation, a from-the-ground-up reconstruction of the 1770 colonial capitol and governor's mansion. Tryon Palace was a magnificent project the first time around too; Governor William Tryon bucked the preferences of Piedmont Carolinians, and had his and the colonial government's new home built here on the coastal plain. He hired English architect John Hawks to design the complex, what would become a Georgian house on an estate laid out in the Palladian style. The palace's first incarnation was a fairly short one. It stood for a scant 25 years before burning down in 1798, and as the by-now state of North Carolina had relocated its governmental operations to Raleigh, there was no need to rebuild the New Bern estate.

It continued, however, to live on in Carolinians' imaginations. In the early 20th century, a movement to rebuild Tryon Palace began. By the 1950s, both the funds and, incredibly, John Hawks' original drawings and plans had been secured, and over a period of seven years the palace was rebuilt. Tryon Palace is open for tours year-round, and it hosts many lectures and living history events throughout the year. One of the best times to visit is during the Christmas season, when not only is the estate beautifully decorated, but they celebrate **Jonkonnu,** a colonial African American

NEW BERN

Neuse River

HOWARD ST.
PASTEUR ST.
CRAVEN ST.
FRONT ST.

BERN ST.
JOHNSON ST.
JOHNSON ST.

QUEEN ST.
CHANGE ST.
LINDAN ST.

NEW ST.
NEW ST.

FIREMEN'S MUSEUM ★

BROAD ST. 17 70
COUNTRY BISCUIT RESTAURANT
ATTMORE-OLIVER HOUSE ▼
BROAD ST.

GEORGE ST.
BEAR TOWNE JAVA
HANCOCK ST.
MIDDLE ST.
CRAVEN ST.
HANNA HOUSE BED & BREAKFAST ●

AERIE B&B ●
MEADOWS INN ●

POLLOCK ST.
METCALF ST.
BIRTHPLACE OF PEPSI ★
NEW BERN AT WORKS ■
POLLOCK ST.
PERSIMMONS RESTAURANT ▼

CHURCH ALLEY
247 CRAVEN
HOWARD HOUSE B&B ●

BERN ST.
EDEN ST.
HANCOCK ST.
CAPTAIN RATTY'S SEAFOOD RESTAURANT ▼

☾ TRYON PALACE ★

TRENT ST.
TRYON PALACE DR.
SOUTH
FRONT ST.
TRENT RIVER COFFEE ▼
17

HARVEY MANSION ★

★ NEW BERN GRAND MARINA

Union Point

0   200 yds
0   200 m

Trent River
70
© AVALON TRAVEL

celebration that was once found throughout the Caribbean and Southeastern United States.

When you visit Tryon Palace, allow yourself plenty of time—a whole afternoon or even a full day. There are several buildings on the property where tours and activities are going on, the gardens are well worth seeing, and the surrounding neighborhood contains some wonderful old houses.

In 2010, in honor of New Bern's 300th anniversary, Tryon Palace opened its **North Carolina History Center,** an enormous new complex along the Trent River next to the Tryon Palace gardens, with galleries, a performance hall, outdoor interpretive areas, and more.

New Bern Firemen's Museum

The **New Bern Firemen's Museum** (408 Hancock St., 252/636-4087, www.newbernmuseums.com, Mon.-Sat. 10am-4pm, $5 adults, $2.50 children) is a fun little museum—an idyll for the gearhead with an antiquarian bent. The museum houses a collection of 19th- and early-20th-century fire wagons and trucks, and chronicles the lively and contentious history of firefighting in New Bern. The city was the first in North Carolina, and one of the first in the country, to charter a fire department. After the Civil War, three fire companies operated here, one of which was founded before the war, and one founded during the Yankee occupation. The third was a boys bucket brigade, a

© JIM MOREKIS

Tryon Palace

sort of training program for junior firefighters. During Reconstruction, every fire was occasion for a competition, as residents would gather around to see which company got to a blaze first—the good old boys (white Southerners) or the carpetbaggers (Northerners who moved south during Reconstruction for economic opportunities).

Attmore-Oliver House

The beautiful 1790 **Attmore-Oliver House** (510 Pollock St., 252/638-8558, www.new-bernhistorical.org, call for hours and tour schedule, $4 adults, free for students) is a nice historic house museum, with exhibits about New Bern's very significant Civil War history. It's also the headquarters of the New Bern Historical Society.

Birthplace of Pepsi

We often think of Coca-Cola as the quintessential Southern drink, but it was here in New Bern that Caleb Bradham, a drugstore owner, put together what he called Brad's Drink—later

Pepsi-Cola. Pepsi-Cola Bottling Company operates a soda fountain and gift shop at the location of Bradham's pharmacy, called the **Birthplace of Pepsi** (256 Middle St., 252/636-5898, www.pepsistore.com).

ENTERTAINMENT AND EVENTS

New Bern's historic Harvey Mansion has a cozy old-fashioned pub in its cellar, the **1797 Steamer Bar** (221 S. Front St., 252/635-3232). As one would gather from its name, the pub serves steamed seafood and other light fare. **Captain Ratty's Seafood Restaurant** (202-206 Middle St., 252/633-2088 or 800/633-5292, www.captainrattys.com) also has a bar that's a popular gathering spot for locals and visitors alike.

SHOPPING

New Bern is a great place to shop for antiques. The majority of the shops are on the 220-240 blocks of Middle Street. There are also periodic antiques shows (and even a salvaged antique

EARLY MENTAL INSTITUTIONS

Two of the state's most remarkable museums, both tiny and little-known, are located in Goldsboro and Kinston, about half an hour apart and an easy drive from Raleigh. They both display artifacts from the history of early mental institutions, from Cherry Hospital—formerly the state's Asylum for the Colored Insane—in Goldsboro, and the Caswell Center, a residential home for the developmentally disabled in Kinston. These museums are not for the faint of heart; amid lists of accomplishments and milestones of medicine are intimations of a tragic past, of suffering on an overwhelming scale and misguided early-20th-century attempts at progressive mental health care. Emblematic of these institutions' shared past is the fact that each museum has on display a cage, an early solution for controlling unruly patients.

Cherry Hospital (201 Stevens Mill Rd., Goldsboro, 919/731-3417, www.cherryhospital. org) is still a state-operated inpatient psychiatric hospital, located on the same grim, industrial-looking campus where the first patient was admitted in 1880. It was a segregated hospital, housing only African American patients, until 1965. The strikingly unselfconscious **Cherry Museum** (Mon.-Fri. 8am-5pm, donation) focuses mainly on the history of the staff and the evolution of medical treatment at the facility, but among the displays one catches fleeting glimpses of what life may have been like here for the early patients. A framed page in one display case lists "Some Supposed Causes of Insanity in the Early Years," and among them are "religion," "jealousy," "hard study," "business trouble," "love affair," "pregnancy," "masturbation," "la grippe," "blow on head," and, most curious, simply "trouble." In a time when the definition of insanity was so all-encompassing, and, compounding the terror, African Americans had little or no legal recourse to protect themselves from false charges or incarceration, one can only imagine how many of the "insane" here were in fact healthy, lucid people who had fallen on hard times or committed some infraction of segregation's etiquette. In the earliest days, "therapy" consisted of work—picking crops in the fields, laboring in the laundry, or making bricks by the ton in the brickyard (which

were then sold by the state for a profit). Clearly, such horrors as these are long behind us. They weren't confined to Cherry Hospital at the time, and certainly don't occur here today, but the grief of the tens of thousands of people who lived here in the early 1900s hangs heavy in the air.

To visit Cherry Museum, you must enter the campus of Cherry Hospital on Highway 581, near I-70 and U.S. 117, outside of Goldsboro; you'll see a sign on I-70. Once on campus, follow the signs to the museum. Once there, you must ring the doorbell and wait to be admitted.

Down the road in Kinston, about half an hour east, you'll find the **Caswell Center Museum and Visitors Center** (2415 W. Vernon Ave., Kinston, 252/208-3780, www. caswellcenter.org, Mon.-Fri. 8am-5pm and by appointment, donation). The Caswell Center admitted its first patients in 1914 as the Caswell School for the Feeble Minded. Like Cherry Hospital, the Caswell Center is still an active inpatient facility, and it is nothing like the bleak place documented in the museum's displays about the first years here. But this too is an eye-opening education in early attitudes toward mental health care. The Caswell Center's museum is more blunt in its presentation than the delicate Cherry Museum, confronting directly the sad facts of its history by exhibiting objects like the combination straightjacket-rompers that the earliest patients had to wear, and addressing the Depression-era overcrowding and lack of food. Though the Caswell Center's patients were all white until the era of integration, they were like the residents of the Asylum for the Colored Insane in that among their ranks were mentally healthy people—unwed mothers, people with physical disabilities, juvenile delinquents—who were crowded into dormitories with the patients who did suffer from mental disabilities. An articulate love letter written from one patient, clearly not disabled, to another hints at the bizarre contradictions of life in an early mental institution.

Both museums are free, but make a donation to help ensure that their amazing stories will continue to be told.

© JIM MOREKIS

Birthplace of Pepsi, New Bern

architectural hardware show) at the New Bern Convention Center. See www.visitnewbern.com for details.

Tryon Palace is a fun shopping spot for history buffs and home-and-garden fanciers. The historical site's **Museum Shop** (Jones House, Eden St. and Pollock St., 252/514-4932, Mon.-Sat. 9:30am-5:30pm, Sun. 1pm-5:30pm) has a nice variety of books about history and architecture as well as handicrafts and children's toy and games. The **Garden Shop** (610 Pollock St., 252/514-4932, Mon.-Sat. 10am-5pm, Sun. 1pm-5pm) sells special bulbs and plants, when in season, grown in Tryon Palace's own greenhouse. Off-season you can still find a nice variety of gardening tools and accessories. A Shop Pass is available at the Museum Shop; this allows you to visit the shops at Tryon Palace without paying the entrance fee.

SPORTS AND RECREATION

At New Bern's Sheraton Marina, **Barnacle Bob's Boat and Jet Ski Rentals** (100 Middle St., Dock F, 252/634-4100, www.

boatandjetskinewbern.com, daily 9am-7pm) rents one- and two-person Jet Skis ($65 per hour, half-hour $45) and 6- to 8-person pontoon boats ($65 per hour, 4 hours $220, 8 hours $420).

ACCOMMODATIONS

The **🄲 Aerie Bed and Breakfast** (509 Pollock St., 800/849-5553, www.aeriebedandbreakfast.com, $119-169) is the current incarnation of the 1880s Street-Ward residence. Its seven luxurious guest rooms are done up in Victorian furniture and earth-tone fabrics reflecting the house's earliest era. There is a lovely courtyard for guests to enjoy, and the inn is only one short block from Tryon Palace.

Also on Pollock Street, a few blocks away, are the **Harmony House Inn** (215 Pollock St., 800/636-3113, www.harmonyhouseinn.com, $99-175), the **Howard House Bed and Breakfast** (207 Pollock St., 252/514-6709, www.howardhousebnb.com, $89-149), and the **Meadows Inn** (212 Pollock St., 877/551-1776, www.meadowsinn-nc.com, $106-166). All three are appealing 19th-century houses decorated in the classic bed-and-breakfast style, and within easy walking distance to Tryon Palace and downtown.

Several motels can be found around New Bern as well, including **Holiday Inn Express** (3455 Martin Luther King Jr. Blvd., 877/863-4780, www.hiexpress.com, from $100), and **Hampton Inn** (200 Hotel Dr., 252/637-2111, www.hamptoninn.com, from $125).

Camping
New Bern's **KOA Campground** (1565 B St., 800/562-3341, www.newbernkoa.com, $30) is just on the other side of the Neuse River from town, located right on the riverbank. Choices include 20-, 30-, and 40-amp RV sites; "kamping kabins and lodges"; and tent sites. Pets are allowed, and there is a dog park on-site.

FOOD
Down-home food choices include the **Country Biscuit Restaurant** (809 Broad St., 252/638-5151, Mon.-Tues. 5am-2pm, Wed.-Fri. 5am-2pm and 4pm-9pm, Sat. 5am-9pm, $7-12), which is open for breakfast, and is popular for, not surprisingly, its biscuits. **Moore's Olde Tyme Barbeque** (3711 U.S.

17 S./Martin Luther King Jr. Blvd., 252/638-3937, www.mooresbarbeque.com, Mon.-Sat. 10am-8pm, $6-9) is a family business, in operation (at a series of different locations) since 1945. They roast and smoke their own barbecue in a pit on-site, burning wood that you'll see piled up by the shop. The menu is short and simple, featuring pork barbecue, chicken, shrimp, fish, hush puppies, fries, and slaw, and their prices are lower than many fast-food joints.

The **Trent River Coffee Company** (208 Craven St., 252/514-2030, www.trentrivercoffee.com, Mon.-Fri. 7:30am-5pm, Sat. 8am-5pm, Sun. 10am-5pm) is a casual coffee shop in a cool old downtown storefront, and the coffee is good. It's sometimes patronized by well-behaved local dogs that lie under the tables patiently while their owners read the newspaper. This is a nice meeting place, and a dark oasis in the summer heat. **Port City Java** (323 Middle St., 252/633-7900, www.portcityjava.com, Fri.-Sat. 7am-8pm, Sun. 7am-3pm, Mon.-Thurs. 7am-6:30pm) is an international chain, but it started in Wilmington, and has many locations on the North Carolina coast. The punch packed by Port City coffee is reliably good.

WILMINGTON AND THE CAPE FEAR REGION

The Cape Fear region has traditionally been part of the Caribbean-basin culture that stretches up through the south Atlantic coast of North America—a world that reflects English, Spanish, and French adaptation to the tropics and, above all, to the profoundly transformative influence of the African cultures brought to the New World by enslaved people. Wilmington is part of the sorority that includes Havana, Caracas, Port au Prince, Santo Domingo, New Orleans, Savannah, and Charleston, and the surrounding Cape Fear coast exhibits the richness of Afro-Caribbean culture in its architecture, cuisine, folklore, and speech.

The area between Wilmington and Lumberton in the state's southeast corner is a strange, exotic waterscape (more so than a landscape) of seductively eerie swamps and backwaters. In this little band of coastal counties straddling the state line, within a 100-mile radius of Wilmington, is the native habitat—the only one in the world—of the Venus flytrap, a ferocious little plant of rather ghastly beauty. It somehow seems like an appropriate mascot for these weird backwaters.

The greatest draw to this region, even more than colonial cobblestones and carnivorous plants, are the beaches of Brunswick, New Hanover, Pender, and Onslow Counties. Some of them, like Wrightsville and Topsail, are well known, and others remain comparatively secluded barrier island strands. In some ways the "Brunswick Islands," as visitors bureaus designate them, can be thought of as the northern edge of the famous Grand Strand area around Myrtle Beach, South Carolina. No part of this

© JIM MOREKIS

HIGHLIGHTS

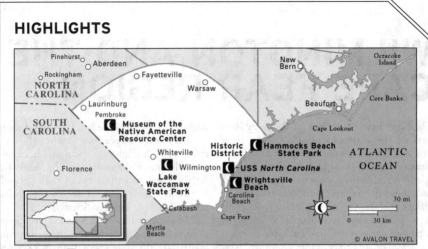

LOOK FOR **(** TO FIND RECOMMENDED SIGHTS, ACTIVITIES, DINING, AND LODGING.

(Wilmington's Historic District: North Carolina's largest 19th-century historic district is a gorgeous collection of antebellum and late Victorian townhouses and commercial buildings, including many beautiful Southern iterations of the Italianate craze that preceded the Civil War (page 83).

(Wrightsville Beach: North Carolina has many wonderful beaches, but few can compare with Wrightsville for its pretty strand, easy public access, clear waters, and overall beauty (page 85).

(USS *North Carolina*: This enormous gray battleship, veteran of the Pacific theater of World War II, is permanently berthed on the Cape Fear River and open for tours of its decks and fascinating, labyrinthine interior (page 86).

(Hammocks Beach State Park: Accessible only by boat, one of the wildest and least disturbed Atlantic coast beaches is a popular stopover for migrating waterfowl and turtles (page 95).

(Museum of the Native American Resource Center: This small but high-quality museum in Pembroke highlights the culture and artifacts of the local Lumbee people (page 102).

(Lake Waccamaw State Park: The central feature of this scenic area is a large example of a Carolina Bay, a unique geographical feature with a diverse surrounding ecosystem (page 103).

region could be mistaken for Myrtle Beach, though; even the beaches that are most liberally peppered with towel shops and miniature golf courses will seem positively bucolic in comparison.

HISTORY

The Cape Fear River, deep and wide, caught the attention of European explorers as early as 1524, when Giovanni de Verrazzano drifted by, and two years later, when Lucas Vásquez de Ayllón and his men (including, possibly, the first enslaved Africans brought to the present-day United States) walked around before proceeding to their appointment for shipwreck near Winyah Bay in South Carolina. Almost 150 years later, William Hilton and explorers from the Massachusetts Bay Colony visited.

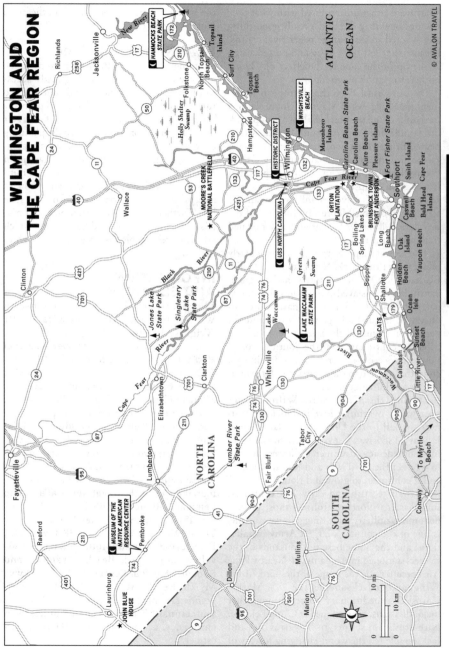

WILMINGTON AND
THE CAPE FEAR REGION

WILMINGTON

© AVALON TRAVEL

They were either unimpressed with what they saw or knew they'd found a really good thing and wanted to discourage other rival claims, because they left right away and posted a sign at the tip of the cape to the effect of, "Don't bother; the land's no good."

It wasn't until 1726 that European settlement took hold, when Maurice Moore claimed the banks of the river on behalf of a group of allied families holding a patent to the area. Moore platted Brunswick Town, and his brother Roger established his own personal domain at Orton. Brunswick was briefly an important port, but it was soon eclipsed by Wilmington, a new settlement up the river established by an upstart group of non-Moores. By the time of the Revolution, it was Wilmington that dominated trade along the river.

The Lower Cape Fear region, particularly present-day Brunswick, New Hanover, Duplin, Bladen, and Onslow Counties, had a significantly larger enslaved population than most parts of North Carolina. The naval stores industry demanded a large workforce, and the plantations south of the river were, to a large extent, a continuation of the South Carolina Lowcountry economy, growing rice and indigo, crops that also led to the amassing of large populations of human chattel.

During the Civil War, Wilmington's port was a swarming hive of blockade runners. Its fall to the Union at the late date of January 1865 was a severe blow to the sinking Confederacy. Commerce allowed the city to weather the Civil War and Reconstruction, and it continued to grow and flourish.

In the late 20th and early 21st centuries, southeastern North Carolina's most prominent role is military. Fort Bragg, in Fayetteville, is one of the country's largest Army installations, and the home base of thousands of the soldiers stationed in Afghanistan. Nearby Pope Air Force Base is the home of the 43rd Airlift Wing, and at Jacksonville, the U.S. Marine Corps' II Expeditionary Force, among other major divisions, are stationed at Camp Lejeune. Numerous museums in Fayetteville and Jacksonville tell the world-changing history of the military men and women of southeastern North Carolina.

PLANNING YOUR TIME

Wilmington is an easy drive from pretty much anywhere in this region, giving ready access to the beaches to the north and south. It's so full of sights and activities that you'll probably want to stay here, and give yourself a day or more just to explore the city. If you're planning on visiting the beaches south of Wilmington, you might also want to consider staying in Myrtle Beach, South Carolina, about 20 minutes' drive (with no traffic—in high season it's a very different story) on U.S. 17 from the state line. Farther inland, you'll find plenty of motels around Fayetteville and Lumberton, which are also a reasonable distance from Raleigh to make day trips.

INFORMATION AND SERVICES

The several area hospitals include two in Wilmington, **Cape Fear Hospital** (5301 Wrightsville Ave., 910/452-8100, www.nhhn.org) and the **New Hanover Regional Medical Center** (2132 S. 17th St., 910/343-7000, www.nhhn.org); two in Brunswick County, **Brunswick Community Hospital** (1 Medical Center Dr., Supply, 910/755-8121, www.brunswickcommunityhospital.com) and **Dosher Memorial Hospital** (924 N. Howe St., Southport, 910/457-3800, www.dosher.org); two in Onslow County, **Onslow Memorial Hospital** (317 Western Blvd., Jacksonville, 910/577-2345, www.onslowmemorial.org) and the **Naval Hospital at Camp Lejeune** (100 Brewster Blvd., Camp Lejeune, 910/451-1113); and Fayetteville's **Cape Fear Valley Medical System** (1638 Owen Dr., Fayetteville, 910/609-4000, www.capefearvalley.com). Myrtle Beach's **Grand Strand Regional Medical Center** (809 82nd Pkwy., Myrtle Beach, SC, 843/692-1000, www.grandstrandmed.com) is not too far from the southernmost Brunswick communities. In an emergency, of course, calling 911 is the safest bet.

Extensive travel and visitor information is available from local convention and visitors bureaus: the **Wilmington/Cape Fear Coast CVB** (23 N. 3rd St., Wilmington, 877/406-2356, www.cape-fear.nc.us, Mon.-Fri. 8:30am-5pm, Sat. 9am-4pm, Sun. 1pm-4pm), and the **Brunswick County Chamber of Commerce** (4948 Main St., Shallotte, 800/426-6644, www.brunswickcountychamber.org, Mon.-Fri. 8:30am-5pm).

Wilmington

In many cities, economic slumps have an unexpected benefit: historic preservation. With Wilmington's growth at a standstill in much of the 20th century, there was no need to replace the old buildings and neighborhoods. As a result, downtown Wilmington has remained a vast museum of beautiful architecture from its early days, and that historic appeal accounts for much of its popularity today as a destination.

Hollywood noticed the little city a couple of decades ago, and Wilmington has become one of the largest film and TV production sites east of Los Angeles. *Sleepy Hollow, Homeland,* and *Eastbound & Down* are just some of the series filmed here, and noteworthy movies filmed at least partly in Wilmington include *Forrest Gump, Iron Man 3, The Conjuring* and many more (though not, ironically, either version of *Cape Fear*). It's not unlikely that you'll happen on a film crew at work while strolling through the city.

SIGHTS
◖ Historic District
Wilmington is to 19th-century architecture what Asheville is to that of the early 20th century. Having been the state's most populous city until around 1910, when Charlotte and its Piedmont neighbors left the old port city in their wake, Wilmington's downtown reflects its glory days of commerce and high society. This is North Carolina's largest 19th-century historic district, a gorgeous collection of antebellum and late Victorian townhouses and commercial buildings, including many beautiful Southern iterations of the Italianate craze that preceded the Civil War.

The **Bellamy Mansion** (503 Market St., 910/251-3700, www.bellamymansion.org, tours hourly Tues.-Sat. 10am-5pm, Sun. 1pm-5pm, $10 adults, $4 under age 12) is a spectacular example of Wilmington's late-antebellum Italianate mansions. This enormous white porticoed house ranks among the loveliest Southern city houses of its era. Built by planter Dr. John Bellamy just before the outbreak of the Civil War, the house was commandeered by the Yankees after the fall of Fort Fisher, and a trip to Washington DC and a pardon granted personally by President Andrew Johnson, a fellow North Carolinian, were required before Bellamy could pry his home out of government hands. In addition to the mansion, another highly significant building stands on the property: the slave quarters. This confined but rather handsome two-story brick building is one of the few surviving examples in the country of urban slave dwellings. Extensive renovations are underway to restore the quarters to its early appearance.

The **Burgwin-Wright House** (224 Market St., 910/762-0570, www.burgwinwrighthouse.com, tours Feb.-Dec. Tues.-Sat. 10am-4pm, $10 adults, $5 under age 12) has an oddly similar history to that of the Bellamy Mansion, despite being nearly a century older. John Burgwin (the emphasis is on the second syllable), a planter and the treasurer of the North Carolina colony, built the house in 1770 on top of the city's early jail. Soon thereafter, Wilmington became a theater of war, and the enemy, as was so often the case, took over the finest dwelling in town as its headquarters. In this case, the occupier, who had a particularly fine eye for rebel digs, was General Cornwallis, then on the last leg of his campaign

WILMINGTON

before falling into George Washington's trap. The Burgwin-Wright House, like the Bellamy Mansion, is a vision of white-columned porticoes shaded by ancient magnolias, but the architectural style is a less ostentatious, though no less beautiful, 18th-century form, the mark of the wealthy merchant and planter class in the colonial South Atlantic and Caribbean world. Seven terraced sections of garden surround the house; they are filled with native plants and many original landscape features, making an intoxicating setting for an early spring stroll.

Yet another beautiful home in the historic district is the **Zebulon Latimer House** (126 S. 3rd St., 910/762-0492, www.latimerhouse. org, Mon.-Fri. 11am-1pm, Sat. 10am-3pm, $10

adults, $4 children). The Latimer House is several years older than the Bellamy Mansion, but in its day was a little more fashion-forward, architecturally speaking. Latimer, a merchant from Connecticut, preferred a more urban expression of the Italianate style, a blocky, flat-roofed design with cast-iron cornices and other details that hint at the coming decades of Victorian aesthetics. Also located on the grounds is a very interesting two-story brick slave dwelling. The Latimer House is the headquarters of the Lower Cape Fear Historical Society, whose archive of regional history is important to genealogists and history preservationists.

If you'd like to visit the Bellamy Mansion,

COURTESY OF WILMINGTON AND BEACHES CVB

Bellamy Mansion

Latimer House, and Burgwin-Wright House, be sure to buy a **three-house ticket** at the first house you visit. For $24, it will save you several bucks over what you'd pay were you to buy a ticket at each stop.

Wrightsville Beach

Wrightsville Beach, just outside of Wilmington, is easily one of the nicest beaches in the coastal Carolinas, which is a linear kingdom of beautiful strands. The beach is wide and easily accessible, visitor- and family-friendly, and simply beautiful. The water at Wrightsville often seems to be a brighter blue than one is accustomed to seeing this far north on the Atlantic coast, lending the feeling of a tropical beach. Wrightsville enjoys warm summertime water temperatures, a very wide strand, and lots of lodging and rental choices along the beach. Numerous public beach access points line Lumina Avenue, searchable at www.townof-wrightsvillebeach.com; some are wheelchair-accessible and some have showers or restrooms. The largest public parking lot, with 99 spaces,

is at Beach Access No. 4 (2398 Lumina Ave.); No. 36 (650 Lumina Ave.) also has a large lot. They all fill up on busy days, but if you press on from one access point to the next, you'll eventually find a spot.

Historic Sights Around Wilmington
MOORE'S CREEK NATIONAL BATTLEFIELD

Not surprisingly, given its importance as a maritime center, the environs of Wilmington have seen much military action over the last 300 years. About 20 miles northwest of Wilmington, outside the town of Currie, near Burgaw, is the **Moore's Creek National Battlefield** (40 Patriots Hall Dr., Currie, 910/283-5591, www.nps.gov/mocr, daily 9am-5pm except Thanksgiving Day, Dec. 25, and Jan. 1). The site commemorates the brief and bloody skirmish of February 1776 in which a Loyalist band of Scottish highlanders, kilted and piping, clashed with Patriot colonists. The revolutionaries fired on the Scotsmen with

© JIM MOREKIS

Wilmington waterfront

cannons as they crossed a bridge over Moore's Creek, which they'd previously booby-trapped, greasing it and removing planks. About 30 of the Loyalist soldiers died, some drowning after they were blown off the bridge. An important moment in the American Revolution, it was also a noteworthy occasion in Scottish military history as the last major broadsword charge in Scottish history, led by the last Scottish clan army.

USS *NORTH CAROLINA*
Docked in the Cape Fear River, across from the Wilmington waterfront at Eagles Island, is the startling gray colossus of the battleship **USS North Carolina** (Eagles Island, 910/251-5797, www.battleshipnc.com, Memorial Day-Labor Day daily 8am-8pm, Labor Day-Memorial Day daily 8am-5pm, $12 adults, $6 under age 13). This decommissioned World War II warship, which saw service at Guadalcanal, Iwo Jima, and many other important events in the Pacific theater, is a floating monument to the nearly 10,000 North Carolinians who died in World War II as well as a museum of what life was like in a floating metal city.

Tours are self-guided and include nine decks, the gun turrets and the bridge, crew quarters, the sick deck, and the Roll of Honor display of the names of North Carolina's war dead. Allow at least two hours to see it all. Visitors prone to claustrophobia might want to stay above deck; the passageways and quarters below are close, dark, and very deep. From the heart of the ship it can take quite a while to get back out, and on a busy day the crowds can make the space seem even more constricted. (Just imagine how it would have felt to be on this ship in the middle of the Pacific, with nearly 2,000 other sailors aboard.)

The battleship is also one of North Carolina's most famous haunted houses, as it were—allegedly home to several ghosts who have been seen and heard on many occasions. The ship has been featured on the Syfy Channel and on ghost-hunting television shows. Visit www.hauntednc.com to hear some chilling unexplained voices caught on tape.

© JIM MOREKIS

USS *North Carolina*

1pm-5pm, Memorial Day-Labor Day Mon.-Sat. 9am-5pm, Sun. 1pm-5pm, $7 adults, $6 students and seniors, $4 ages 3-17) has exhibits about the ecology of the Cape Fear and its human history. Special treats are exhibits about giant indigenous life forms, including the prehistoric ground sloth and Michael Jordan.

LOUISE WELLS CAMERON ART MUSEUM
The **Louise Wells Cameron Art Museum** (3201 S. 17th St., 910/395-5999, www.cameronartmuseum.com, Tues.-Wed. and Fri.-Sun. 10am-5pm, Thurs. 10am-8pm, $8 adults, $5 students, $3 ages 2-12) is one of the major art museums in North Carolina, a very modern gallery with a good permanent collection of art in many media, with a special emphasis on North Carolina artists. Masters represented include Mary Cassatt and Utagawa Hiroshige. Special exhibits change throughout the year.

WILMINGTON RAILROAD MUSEUM
The **Wilmington Railroad Museum** (505 Nutt St., 910/763-2634, www.wilmingtonrailroadmuseum.org, Apr.-Sept. Mon.-Sat. 10am-5pm, Sun. 1pm-5pm, Oct.-Mar. Mon.-Sat. 10am-5pm, $8.50 adults, $7.50 seniors and military, $4.50 ages 2-12) explores a crucial but now largely forgotten part of this city's history: its role as a railroad town. In 1840, Wilmington became the terminus for the world's longest continuous rail line, the Wilmington and Weldon Railroad. The Atlantic Coast Line Railroad (into which the W&W merged around 1900) kept its headquarters at Wilmington until the 1960s, when it moved its offices, employees, and a devastatingly large portion of the city's economy to Florida. All manner of railroad artifacts are on display in this great little museum, from timetables to locomotives. A classic iron horse, steam engine no. 250, sits on the track outside and has been beautifully restored.

OAKDALE CEMETERY
In the mid-19th century, as Wilmington was bursting at the seams with new residents, the city's old cemeteries were becoming overcrowded with former residents. **Oakdale Cemetery** (520 N. 15th St., 910/762-5682, www.oakdalecemetery.org, daily 8am-5pm) was founded some distance from downtown to ease the subterranean traffic jam. It was designed in the parklike style of graveyards popular at the time, and soon filled up with splendid funerary art—weeping angels, obelisks, willows—to set off the natural beauty of the place. (Oakdale's website has a primer on Victorian grave art symbolism.) It's a fascinating place for a quiet stroll.

Museums
CAPE FEAR MUSEUM OF HISTORY AND SCIENCE
The **Cape Fear Museum of History and Science** (814 Market St., 910/798-4370, www.capefearmuseum.com, Labor Day-Memorial Day Mon. and Wed.-Sat. 9am-5pm, Sun.

Gardens and Parks
AIRLIE GARDENS
Airlie Gardens (300 Airlie Rd., 910/798-7700, www.airliegardens.org, Mar. 20-Dec. daily

WILMINGTON

ANOLES OF CAROLINA

During your visit to the Wilmington area, you'll almost certainly see anoles. These are the tiny green lizards that skitter up and down trees and along railings—impossibly fast, beady-eyed little emerald beasts. Sometimes called "chameleons" by the locals, anoles can change color to camouflage themselves against their backgrounds. They also like to puff out their crescent-shaped dewlaps, the little scarlet pouches under their chins, when they're courting, fighting, or otherwise advertising their importance. Explorer John Lawson was quite

taken with them, as he describes in his 1709 *A New Voyage to Carolina:*

Green lizards are very harmless and beautiful, having a little Bladder under their Throat, which they fill with Wind, and evacuate the same at Pleasure. They are of a most glorious Green, and very tame. They resort to the Walls of Houses in the Summer Season, and stand gazing on a Man, without any Concern or Fear. There are several other Colours of these Lizards, but none so beautiful as the green ones are.

9am-5pm, longer hours in Apr.-May, $8 adults, $3 ages 6-12, no pets) is most famous for its countless azaleas, but this 100-year-old formal garden park has many remarkable features, including an oak tree believed to be nearly 500 years old, and the Minnie Evans Sculpture Garden and Bottle Chapel. Evans, a visionary African American artist whose mystical work is among the most prized "outsider art," was the gatekeeper here for 25 of her 95 years. Golf cart tours are available with 48 hours' notice for visitors who are not mobile enough to walk the gardens.

HALYBURTON PARK

A more natural landscape for hiking and biking is **Halyburton Park** (4099 S. 17th St., 910/341-7800, www.halyburtonpark.com, park daily dawn-dusk, nature center Tues.-Sat. 9am-5pm). The 58 acres of parkland, encircled by a 1.3-mile wheelchair-accessible trail and crisscrossed by interior trails, gives a beautiful glimpse of the environment of sandhills, Carolina bays (elliptical, often boggy depressions), and long-leaf pine and oak forest that used to make up so much of the natural landscape of this area.

ENTERTAINMENT AND EVENTS
Performing Arts

Thalian Hall (310 Chestnut St., 800/523-2820,

www.thalianhall.com) was built in the mid-1850s and today is the last standing theater designed by the prominent architect John Montague Trimble. It is still a major arts venue in the region, hosting performances of classical, jazz, bluegrass, and all sorts of other music. Its resident theater company is the **Thalian Association** (910/251-1788, www.thalian.org), which traces its roots back to 1788 and has been named the official community theater company of North Carolina.

Also making its home at Thalian Hall is **Big Dawg Productions** (http://bigdawgproductions.org). They put on a variety of plays and musicals of all genres throughout the year and host the **New Play Festival** of first-time productions by authors under age 18. Another Thalian company for nearly 25 years, the **Opera House Theatre Company** (910/762-4234, www.operahousetheatrecompany.net) has produced one varied season after another of big-name musicals and dramas, as well as the work of North Carolinian and Southern playwrights.

There's also a lot of theater going on outside the walls of Thalian Hall. One of the most critically acclaimed is **Red Barn Studio Theatre** (1122 S. 3rd St., 910/762-0955, www.redbarnstudiotheatre.com). Actress Linda Lavin of *Alice* fame and her husband, Steve Bakunas, moved to Wilmington several years ago and

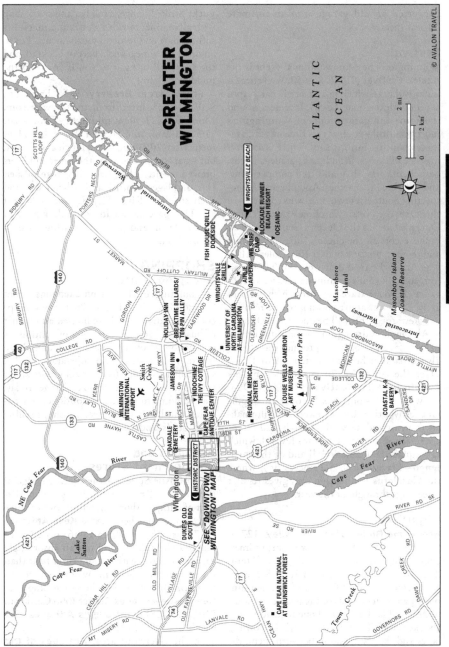

WILMINGTON

© AVALON TRAVEL

GREATER WILMINGTON

ATLANTIC OCEAN

2 mi

2 km

WRIGHTSVILLE BEACH

BLOCKADE RUNNER BEACH RESORT

OCEANIC

WE SURF CAMP

FISH HOUSE GRILL/DOCKSIDE

WRIGHTSVILLE GRILLE

AIRLIE GARDENS

UNIVERSITY OF NORTH CAROLINA AT WILMINGTON

BREAKTIME BILLARDS/EN PIN ALLEY

HOLIDAY INN

JAMESON INN

Smith Creek

WILMINGTON INTERNATIONAL AIRPORT

INDOCHINE/THE IVY COTTAGE

OAKDALE CEMETERY

CAPE FEAR ANTIQUE CENTER

REGIONAL MEDICAL CENTER

LOUISE WELLS CAMERON ART MUSEUM

Halyburton Park

Masonboro Island

Masonboro Island Coastal Reserve

COASTAL K-9 BAKERY

Wilmington

HISTORIC DISTRICT

DUKES OLD SOUTH BBQ

SEE "DOWNTOWN WILMINGTON" MAP

Lake Sutton

Cape Fear River

NE Cape Fear River

CAPE FEAR NATIONAL AT BRUNSWICK FOREST

Cape Fear River

Town Creek

Intracoastal Waterway

Masonboro Island Coastal Reserve

converted an old garage into an intimate 50-seat theater.

Festivals

Wilmington's best-known annual event is the **Azalea Festival** (910/794-4650, www.ncazaleafestival.org), which takes place in early April at venues throughout the city. It centers around the home and garden tours of Wilmington's most beautiful—and, at this time of year, azalea-festooned—historic sites. There is a dizzying slate of events, including a parade, a circus, gospel concerts, shag and step competitions, and even boxing matches. And like any self-respecting Southern town, it crowns royalty—in this case, the North Carolina Azalea Festival Queen as well as the Queen's Court; a slate of cadets escort all the queen's ladies in waiting, and there's a phalanx of over 100 Azalea Belles. The Azalea Festival draws over 300,000 visitors, so book your accommodations well in advance. If you're traveling through the area in early April but aren't coming to the festival, be forewarned, this will be one crowded town.

Although Wilmington has become a magnet for Hollywood film production, there's also a passion here for independent films. Over the course of 20 years, November's **Cucalorus Film Festival** (910/343-5995, www.cucalorus.org) has become an important festival that draws viewers and filmmakers from around the world. Roughly 100 films are screened during each year's festival, which takes place at Thalian Hall and at the small Jengo's Playhouse (815 Princess St.), where the Cucalorus Foundation also gives regular screenings throughout the year.

Nightlife

Breaktime Billiards/Ten Pin Alley (127 S. College Rd., 910/452-5455, www.breaktimetenpin.com, billiards and bowling daily 11am-2am, lounge Mon.-Fri. 6pm-2am, Sat.-Sun. 11am-2am) is a 30,000-square-foot entertainment palace. It consists of Breaktime Billiards, with 24 billiard tables and one regulation-size snooker table; Ten Pin Alley, with 24 bowling lanes and skee ball; and in between them, the Lucky Strike Lounge, a full bar and snack shop with all manner of video games and that hosts soft-tip dart and foosball tournaments. Put in an order for a meal and a beer or cocktail, and the staff will bring it to you if you're in the middle of a game.

Front Street Brewery (9 N. Front St., 910/251-1935, http://frontstreetbrewery.com, Mon.-Wed. 11:30am-midnight, Thurs.-Sat. 11:30am-2am, Sun. 11:30am-10pm, late-night menu from 10:30pm) serves lunch and dinner, but what is most special is their menu of beers brewed on-site. They serve their own pilsner, IPA, and lager, Scottish and Belgian ales, and their specialty River City Raspberry Wheat ale. The space has an attractive dark-paneled saloon decor, and plenty of seating areas to choose from.

SHOPPING
Shopping Centers

The buildings of **The Cotton Exchange** (Front St. and Grace St., 910/343-9896, www.shopcottonexchange.com) have housed all manner of businesses in over 150 years of continuous occupation: a flour and hominy mill, a Chinese laundry, a peanut cleaning operation (really), a "mariner's saloon" (we'll say no more about that), and, of course, a cotton exchange. Today, they're home to dozens of boutiques, restaurants, and lovely little specialty shops selling kites, beads, and spices.

Antiques and Consignment Stores

Along Castle Street, at the southern edge of the historic district, there is a growing district of antiques shops, all within two or three blocks of each other. **Castle Keep Antiques** (507 Castle St., 910/343-6046) occupies an old church building and has an absorbingly varied selection, with a more rural bent than the surrounding shops, many of which specialize in fine furniture. Also be sure to stop in at **New Castle Antiques Center** (606 Castle St., 910/341-7228) and **Maggy's Antiques** (511 Castle St., 910/343-5200).

In the riverfront area, **Antiques of Old**

Wilmington (25 S. Front St., 910/763-5188) and **Silk Road Antiques** (103 S. Front St., 910/343-1718) are within an easy walk of many restaurants and each other. An especially intriguing shop is **J. Robert Warren Antiques** (110 Orange St., 910/762-6077, www.jrobertwarrenantiques.com), which occupies an 1810 townhouse downtown. Warren specializes in fine and rare antiques from North Carolina, including furniture from the early masters, the work of colonial silversmiths, prints and paintings of early Carolinians and Carolina scenes, nautical hardware from old ships, and much more.

On Market Street headed away from downtown is **Cape Fear Antique Center** (1606 Market St., 910/763-1837, www.capefearantiquecenter.com), which carries fancy vintage home furnishings, from bedroom and dining room furniture to desks and armoires in beautiful tones of wood, as well as a nice selection of antique jewelry.

Books

Wilmington has quite a few nice bookstores, both retail and used. **McAllister & Solomon** (4402-1 Wrightsville Ave., 910/350-0189, www.mcallisterandsolomon.com) stocks over 20,000 used and rare books, a great treat for collectors to explore. **Two Sisters Bookery** (318 Nutt St., Cotton Exchange, 910/762-4444, www.twosistersbookery.com, Mon.-Sat. 10am-6pm, Sun. noon-6pm) is a nice little independent bookseller at the Cotton Exchange, with an inventory covering all genres and subject matters, and a calendar full of readings by favorite authors. Also excellent is **Pomegranate Books** (4418 Park Ave., 910/452-1107, www.pombooks.net, Mon.-Sat. 10am-6pm), which has a progressive bent and a wide selection of good reads.

Galleries and Art Studios

New Elements Gallery (216 N. Front St., 910/343-8997, www.newelementsgallery.com, Tues.-Sat. 11am-5:30pm) has been a leading institution in Wilmington's art scene since 1985. Featuring contemporary art in a wide variety of styles and media, New Elements has a special focus on artists from North Carolina and the wider Southeast.

An unusual retail art gallery is found between Wilmington and Wrightsville: The 23,000-square-foot **Racine Center for the Arts** (203 Racine Dr., 910/452-2073, www.galleryatracine.com) has, in addition to the sales gallery, art space for classes in pottery, stained glass, and other crafts, and operates the Firebird Paint Your Pottery and Art Studio. Visitors can show up at the Firebird without reservations and go right to work on their own pottery and mosaics with the help of staff.

Music

Finkelstein Music (6 S. Front St., 910/762-5662, www.finkelsteins.com) is a family business that has been at this site, a great old commercial building on a busy downtown corner, for over 100 years. It began as a dry goods store but gradually evolved into today's music store, which carries a great selection of guitars, electric basses, and percussion.

For Dogs

Coastal K-9 Bakery (5905 Carolina Beach Rd., Suite 9, 866/794-4014, www.coastalk-9bakery.com, Mon.-Sat. 10am-6pm, Sun. 1pm-5pm) sells fresh-baked gourmet dog treats, including various organic and hypoallergenic goodies, Carolina barbecue biscuits, liver brownies, and even vegetarian bacon bits.

SPORTS AND RECREATION
Masonboro Island

A half hour's boat ride from Wrightsville Beach is Masonboro Island, an undeveloped barrier island that is a favorite spot for birding, shelling, and camping. **Wrightsville Beach Scenic Tours** (910/200-4002, www.capefearnaturalist.com) operates the Wrightsville Water Taxi, which docks across the street from the Blockade Runner Hotel (275 Waynick Blvd.) and offers daily shuttle service ($20 round-trip) to the island in high season. The boat leaves the dock Monday-Saturday at 9am and returns at 3pm. Call ahead for reservations.

Surfing

Wrightsville Beach is a very popular destination for East Coast surfers and is home to several surfing schools. **Surf Camp** (530 Causeway Dr., 866/844-7873, www.wbsurfcamp.com) is probably the area's largest surfing instruction provider. They teach a staggering number of multiday camps; one-day courses; kids-only, teenagers-only, women-only, and whole-family offerings; and classes in safety as well as technique. **Crystal South Surf Camp** (Public Access No. 39, on the beach, 910/395-4431, www.crystalsouthsurfcamp.com) is a family-run operation that gives group and individual five-day instruction for all ages.

Spectator Sports

Wilmington has its own professional basketball team, in the Continental Basketball League. The **Wilmington Sea Dawgs** (910/791-6523, www.goseadawgs.com, $8 adults, $5 children) play downtown in the Schwartz Center at Cape Fear Community College (601 N. Front St.). In baseball, the **Wilmington Sharks** (910/343-5621, www.wilmingtonsharks.com, box seats $8, general admission $5), a Coastal Plains League team, play at the Legion Sports Complex (2131 Carolina Beach Rd.).

ACCOMMODATIONS
Under $150

Affordable options are plentiful, especially on Market Street a couple of miles from downtown. Wilmington's **Holiday Inn** (5032 Market St., 866/553-0169, www.wilmingtonhi.com, $65-135) is clean and comfortable, and just a few minutes' drive from the historic district. Nearby is the **Jameson Inn** (5102 Dunlea Court, 910/452-9828, www.jamesoninns.com, from $65), another fine choice. The Jameson Inn is a little hard to find, hidden behind other buildings. From Market Street, turn onto New Centre Drive, and look for the sign across the street from Target.

$150-300

Wilmington overflows with historic bed-and-breakfasts. **◖ Front Street Inn** (215 S. Front St., 800/336-8184, www.frontstreetinn.com, $139-239) is a tiny boutique hotel in the historic district, one block from the Cape Fear River and easy walking distance from the restaurants and shops at Market and Front Streets. The Inn occupies the old Salvation Army of the Carolinas building, an attractive brick city building with arched windows and bright, airy guest rooms. For comfortable and classy lodging in the heart of the historic district, the Front Street Inn is a best bet.

The **Wilmingtonian** (101 S. 2nd St., 910/343-1800, www.thewilmingtonian.com, $87-325) is a complex of five buildings, four of which are renovated historic structures, from the 1841 De Rosset House to a 1950s convent. The De Rosset House is an utterly fabulous Italianate mansion, one of the most recognizable buildings in Wilmington. For $325 ($250 off-season), you can stay in the Cupola Suite, a spectacular aerie with a panoramic view of the port. The **Rosehill Inn** (114 S. 3rd St., 800/815-0250, www.rosehill.com, $90-200) occupies a pretty 1848 residence three blocks from the river. The flowery high-B&B-style decor suits the house well, making for elegant but comfy quarters. The **Taylor House** (14 N. 7th St., 800/382-9982, www.taylorhousebb.com, $125-140) is an absolutely lovely 1905 home—rather subdued in design when compared to some of the architectural manifestos nearby, but in a very attractive way. The pretty, sunny guest rooms promise relaxation. The famous **◖Graystone Inn** (100 S. 3rd St., 888/763-4773, www.graystoneinn.com, $159-379) was built in the same year as the Taylor House, but its builder, the widow Elizabeth Bridgers, had a very different aesthetic. The splendor of the palace first known as the Bridger House reflects the fortune of Mrs. Bridgers' late husband, a former Confederate congressman and one of the most influential figures in Wilmington's days as a railroad center.

These are by no means the only excellent bed-and-breakfast inns in Wilmington; the city is full of them. Check in with the **Wilmington and Beaches Convention and Visitors Bureau** (www.wilmingtonandbeaches.com) for comprehensive listings.

A plush place to stay in the downtown area is the **Hilton Wilmington Riverside** (301 N. Water St., 888/324-8170, www.wilmingtonhilton.com, $180-200). Located right on the river, many of the guest rooms have a great view. The shops, restaurants, and galleries of the riverfront are right outside the front door, making this a great place to stay if you're planning to enjoy Wilmington's downtown.

FOOD
Continental
Caprice Bistro (10 Market St., 910/815-0810, www.capricebistro.com, Sun.-Thurs. 5pm-10pm, Fri.-Sat. 5pm-midnight, bar until 2am, entrées $13-22) is an absolutely wonderful little café and bar hosted by Thierry and Patricia Moity. The French cuisine here is delicious and the wine list is extensive. This is one of the best restaurants in town and well worth a visit.

Le Catalan French Café (224 S. Water St., 910/815-0200, www.lecatalan.com, fall-spring lunch and dinner Tues.-Sat. from 11:30am, summer Tues.-Sun. from 11:30am, $10-20) couldn't have a nicer location, on the Riverwalk in the old downtown. They serve wonderful classic French food—quiches and *feuilletés,* beef bourguignonne on winter Fridays, and a chocolate mousse for which they are famous. Their greatest draw, though, is the wine list (and the attached wine store). The proprietor, Pierre Penegre, is a Cordon Bleu-certified oenologist, and is frequently on hand to make recommendations.

Seafood
Wrightsville Beach's **Bridge Tender** (1414 Airlie Rd., Wilmington, 910/256-4519, www.thebridgetender.com, lunch daily 11:30am-2pm, dinner daily from 5pm, $20-35) has been in business for over 30 years and is an icon of the local restaurant scene. The atmosphere is simple and elegant, with a dockside view. Entrées focus on seafood and Angus beef, with an extensive à la carte menu from which you can create delicious combinations of your

favorite seafood and the Bridge Tender's special sauces. A sushi menu rounds out the appetizers, and a long wine list complements everything.

When you see a restaurant set in a really beautiful location, you dearly hope the food is as good as the view. Such is the case at Wrightsville's **Oceanic** (703 S. Lumina, Wrightsville Beach, 910/256-5551, www.oceanicrestaurant.com, Mon.-Sat. 11am-11pm, Sun. 10am-10pm, $10-27). The Wilmington *Star-News* has repeatedly voted it the Best Seafood Restaurant in Wilmington, and it receives similar word-of-mouth accolades right and left. It occupies a big old house right on the beach, with a wraparound porch and a pier. For an extra-special experience, ask for a table on the pier.

Southern and Barbecue
Right downtown at the Cotton Exchange, facing Front Street, is **The Basics** (319 Front St., 910/343-1050, www.thebasicswilmington.com, breakfast Mon.-Fri. 8am-11am, lunch Mon.-Fri. 11am-4pm, dinner daily from 5pm, brunch Sat.-Sun. 11am-4pm, $10-18). In a streamlined, simple setting, The Basics serves comfort food classics, Southern-style. Be sure to try the Coca-Cola cake, a surprisingly delicious Southern delicacy.

In business since 1984, [**Jackson's Big Oak Barbecue** (920 S. Kerr Ave., 910/799-1581, Mon.-Sat. 10:30am-8:45pm, under $8) is an old favorite. Their motto is, "We ain't fancy, but we sure are good." Good old vinegary eastern North Carolina-style pork barbecue is the main item, though you can pick from Brunswick stew, fried chicken, and a mess of country vegetables. You'll get hush puppies and corn sticks at the table, but it will be worth your while not to fill up too fast—the cobblers and banana pudding are great.

Eclectic American
Flaming Amy's Burrito Barn (4002 Oleander Dr., 910/799-2919, www.flamingamysburritobarn.com, daily 11am-10pm) is, in their own words, "Hot, fast, cheap, and easy." They've got a long menu with 20 specialty burritos

(Greek, Philly steak, Thai), eight fresh salsas, and bottled and on-tap beers. It's very inexpensive—you can eat well for under $10, drinks included. Frequent special promotions include Tattoo Tuesdays; if you show the cashier your tattoo (come on, we all know you've got one), you can take 10 percent off your meal.

Boca Bay (2025 Eastwood Rd., 910/256-1887, www.bocabayrestaurant.com, Mon.-Thurs. 5pm-10pm, Fri.-Sat. 5pm-11pm, brunch Sun. 9am-2pm, entrées $11-20) serves a tapas-style menu of sushi, stir fries, and heartier entrées, all very tasty. Vegetarian options are fairly limited, but you can cobble together a meal of tapas, salad, and sides.

Asian

Indochine, A Far East Café (7 Wayne Dr., at Market St., 910/251-9229, www.indochinewilmington.com, lunch Tues.-Thurs. 11am-2pm, Sat. 11am-3pm, dinner daily 5pm-10pm, $10-15) specializes in Thai and Vietnamese cuisine, has an extensive vegetarian menu, and has plenty of options for nonvegetarians as well. This restaurant is not downtown, but some distance out on Market Street; it's worth the drive. Try the vegetarian samosa egg rolls as an appetizer.

(**Double Happiness** (4403 Wrightsville Ave., 910/313-1088, daily lunch and dinner, $12-18) is a popular Chinese and Malaysian restaurant known for serving traditional dishes that are a refreshing departure from the standard canon of American Chinese restaurants. The setting is original too, without, as one local food critic wrote, "a buffet or glamour food photos over a hospital-white take-out counter." You can choose between regular booths and traditional floor seating. If you're lucky, you might be present when the chef decides to send around rice balls, a sweet dessert snack, for everyone on the house.

NORTH OF WILMINGTON
Topsail Island

In the manner of an old salt, Topsail is pronounced "Tops'l." The three towns on Topsail Island—Topsail Beach, North Topsail Beach, and Surf City—are popular beach communities; they're less commercial than some of their counterparts elsewhere along the coast, but still destinations for throngs of visitors in the summer months. A swing bridge gives access to the island at Surf City (the bridge opens around the beginning of each hour, so expect backups) and there is a high bridge between Sneads Ferry and North Topsail.

At Topsail Beach is the **Missiles and More Museum** (720 Channel Ave., 910/328-8663, www.missilesandmoremuseum.org, Memorial Day-Labor Day Mon.-Sat. 2pm-5pm, Labor Day-Memorial Day Mon.-Fri. 2pm-5pm, free). This little museum commemorates a rather peculiar chapter in the island's history: when it was used by the U.S. government for a project called Operation Bumblebee. During Operation Bumblebee, Topsail was a proving ground for missiles, and the work done here led to major advancements in missile technology and the development of a precursor of the ram jet engine used later in supersonic jet design. Exhibits include real warheads left over from the tests. Especially interesting to lovers of projectiles will be the 1940s color film of missile firings here at Topsail.

Jacksonville

Jacksonville is best known as the home of **Camp Lejeune,** a massive Marine installation that dates to 1941. Lejeune is the home base of the II Marine Expeditionary Force, and of MARSOC, the Marine Corps division of U.S. Special Operations Command. The nearly 250 square miles of the base include extensive beaches, where servicemen and women receive training in amphibious assault skills.

Camp Johnson, a satellite installation of Camp Lejeune, used to be known as Montford Point, and was the home of the famous African American Montford Point Marines. Their history, a crucial chapter in the integration of the United States Armed Forces, is paid tribute at the **Montford Point Marine Museum** (Bldg. 101, East Wing, Camp Gilbert Johnson,

910/450-1340, www.montfordpointmarines.
com, Tues.-Thurs. 11am-2pm and 4pm-7pm,
Sat. 11am-4pm, free).

◖ Hammocks Beach State Park

At the very appealing little fishing town of
Swansboro you'll find the mainland side
of **Hammocks Beach State Park** (1572
Hammocks Beach Rd., 910/326-4881, http://
ncparks.gov, Sept.-May daily 8am-6pm, June-
Aug. daily 8am-7pm, free). Most of the park
lies on the other side of a maze of marshes, on
Bear and Huggins Islands. These wild, totally
undeveloped islands are important havens for
migratory waterfowl and nesting loggerhead sea
turtles. Bear Island is 3.5 miles long and less
than a mile wide, surrounded by the Atlantic
Ocean, Intracoastal Waterway, Bogue and Bear
Inlets, and wild salt marshes. A great place to
swim, Bear Island has a bathhouse complex
with a snack bar, restrooms, and outdoor showers. Huggins Island, by contrast, is significantly
smaller, and covered in ecologically significant
maritime forest and lowland marshes. Two paddle trails, one just over 2.5 miles and the other
6 miles, weave through the marshes that surround the islands.

Camping is permitted on Bear Island, in
reserved and first-come sites near the beach
and inlet, with restrooms and showers available nearby.

A private boat or **passenger ferry** (910/326-
4881, $5 adults, $3 seniors and children) are
the only ways to reach the islands. The ferry's
schedule varies by days of the week and season:
in May and September Wednesday-Saturday
and in April and October Friday-Saturday, the
ferry departs from the mainland every half
hour 9:30am-4:30pm, and departs from the

island every hour 10am-5pm. Memorial Day-
Labor Day Monday-Tuesday, it departs from
the mainland every hour 9:30am-5:30pm,
and departs from the island every hour 10am-
6pm; Wednesday-Sunday it departs from the
mainland every half hour 9:30am-5:30pm,
and departs from the island every half hour
10am-6pm.

GETTING THERE AND AROUND

Wilmington is the eastern terminus of I-40,
more than 300 miles east of Asheville, approximately 120 miles east of Raleigh. The Cape
Fear region is also crossed by a major north-
south route, U.S. 17, the old Kings Highway of
colonial times. Wilmington is roughly equidis-
tant along U.S. 17 between Jacksonville to the
north and Myrtle Beach, South Carolina, to
the south; both cities are about an hour away.

Wilmington International Airport (ILM,
1740 Airport Blvd., 910/341-4125, www.fly-
ilm.com) serves the region with flights to East
Coast cities. For a wider selection of routes,
it may be worthwhile to consider flying into
Myrtle Beach or Raleigh and renting a car. If
driving to Wilmington from the Myrtle Beach
airport, add another 30 to 60 minutes to get
through Myrtle Beach traffic, particularly in
summer, as the airport there is on the southern
edge of town. If driving from Raleigh-Durham
International Airport, figure on the trip taking
at least 2.5 hours. There is no passenger train
service to Wilmington.

Wave Transit (910/343-0106, www.wave-
transit.com), Wilmington's public transportation system, operates buses throughout the
metropolitan area and trolleys in the historic
district. Fares are $4 round trip.

WILMINGTON

The Southern Coast

From the beaches of Brunswick and New Hanover County to the swampy, subtropical fringes of land behind the dunes, this little corner of the state is one of the most beautiful parts of North Carolina.

There are a string of beaches here, starting with Carolina Beach and Kure, just south of Wilmington, and descending through the "Brunswick Islands," as designated in tourist literature. Most of these beaches are low-key, quiet family beaches, largely lined with residential and rental properties. They're crowded in the summertime, of course, but are still much more laid back than Myrtle Beach, over the state line to the south, and even Wrightsville and some of the "Crystal Coast" beaches.

You'll see some distinctive wildlife here. The first you'll notice, more likely than not, is the ubiquitous green anole (called "chameleons" by many locals). These tiny lizards, normally a bright lime green, but able to fade to brown when camouflage is called for, are everywhere—skittering up porch columns and along balcony railings, peering at you around corners, hiding between the fronds of palmetto trees. The males put on a big show by puffing out their strawberry-colored dewlaps.

This is also the part of the state where the greatest populations of alligators live. Alligators are nonchalant creatures that rarely appear better than comatose, but are genuinely deadly if crossed. All along river and creek banks, bays, and swamps, you'll see their scaly hulks basking motionless in the sun. Keep small children and pets well clear of anywhere a gator might lurk.

In certain highly specialized environments—mainly in and around Carolina bays that offer both moistness and nutrient-poor soil—the Venus flytrap and other carnivorous plants thrive. To the average fly, these are more threatening than an alligator any day. The flytrap and some of its cousins are endangered, but in this region—and nowhere else in the world—you'll have plenty of opportunities to see them growing and gorging.

KURE BEACH

Kure is a two-syllable name: pronounced "KYU-ree" (as in Marie Curie, not "curry"). This is a small beach community, not an extravaganza of neon lights and shark-doored towel shops. Most of the buildings on the island are houses, both rental houses for vacationers and the homes of Kure Beach's year-round residents. The beach itself, like all North Carolina ocean beaches, is public.

Carolina Beach State Park

Just to the north of Kure is **Carolina Beach State Park** (1010 State Park Rd., off U.S. 421, Carolina Beach, 910/458-8206, http://ncparks. gov, Mar.-Apr., Sept.-Oct. 8am-8pm, May-Aug. 8am-10pm, Nov.-Feb. 8am-6pm, free). Of all the state parks in the coastal region, this may be the one with the greatest ecological diversity. Within its boundaries are coastal pine and oak forests, pocosins between the dunes, saltwater marshes, a 50-foot sand dune, and lime-sink ponds; of the lime-sink ponds, one is a deep cypress swamp, one is a natural garden of water lilies, and one an ephemeral pond that dries into a swampy field every year, an ideal home for the many carnivorous plants that live here. You'll see Venus flytraps and their ferocious cousins, but resist the urge to dig or pick them, or to tempt them with your fingertips. Sort of like stinging insects that die after delivering their payload, the flytraps' traps can wither and fall off once they're sprung.

The park has 83 drive-to and walk-in campsites ($20), each with a grill and a picnic table. Two are wheelchair accessible. Restrooms and hot showers are nearby.

Fort Fisher State Park

At the southern end of Kure Beach is **Fort Fisher State Park** (1000 Loggerhead Rd.,

COURTESY OF WILMINGTON AND BEACHES CVB

Carolina Beach State Park

off U.S. 421, 910/458-5798, http://ncparks. gov, June-Aug. daily 8am-9pm, Mar.-May and Sept.-Oct. daily 8am-8pm, Nov.-Feb. daily 8am-6pm, free). Fort Fisher has six miles of beautiful beach, a less crowded and commercial alternative to the other beaches of the area. A lifeguard is on duty from Memorial Day to Labor Day daily 10am-5:45pm. The park also includes a 1.1-mile hiking trail that winds through marshes and along the sound, ending at an observation deck where visitors can watch wildlife.

This is also a significant historic site. Fort Fisher was a Civil War earthwork stronghold designed to withstand massive assault. Modeled in part on the Crimean War's Tower of Malakoff, Fort Fisher's construction was an epic saga in itself, as hundreds of Confederate soldiers, enslaved African Americans, and conscripted indigenous Lumbee people were brought in to build what became the Confederacy's largest fort. After the fall of Norfolk in 1862, Wilmington became the most important open port in the South, a vital

harbor for blockade-runners and military vessels. Fisher held until nearly the end of the War. On December 24, 1864, U.S. general Benjamin "The Beast" Butler attacked the fort with 1,000 soldiers but was repulsed. A few weeks later, in January 1865, Fort Fisher was finally taken, but it required a Yankee force of 9,000 soldiers and 56 ships in what was to be the largest amphibious assault until World War II. Without its defenses at Fort Fisher, Wilmington soon fell, hastening the end of the war, which came only three months later. Thanks to the final assault by the Union forces and 150 subsequent years of winds, tides, and hurricanes, not a great deal of the massive earthworks survives. But the remains of this vitally important Civil War site are preserved in an oddly peaceful and pretty seaside park, which contains a restored gun emplacement and a visitors center with interpretive exhibits.

Also at Fort Fisher is a branch of the **North Carolina Aquarium** (910/458-8257, daily 9am-5pm, $8 adults, $7 seniors, $6 under age 17). Like its sisters at Roanoke and Pine Knoll

COURTESY OF WILMINGTON AND BEACHES CVB

WILMINGTON

North Carolina Aquarium at Fort Fisher

Shores, this is a beautiful aquarium that specializes in the native marine life of the North Carolina waters. It's also a center for marine biology and conservation efforts, assisting in the rescue and rehabilitation of sea turtles, marine mammals, freshwater reptiles, and other creatures of the coast. While at the aquarium, be sure to visit the albino alligator.

Accommodations

The beaches of the Carolinas used to be lined with boarding houses, the old-time choice in lodging for generations of middle-class travelers. They were sort of a precursor to today's bed-and-breakfasts, cozy family homes where visitors dined together with the hosts and were treated not so much like customers as houseguests—which is just what they were. Hurricane Hazel razed countless guesthouses when it pummeled the coast in 1954, ushering in the next epoch, that of the family motel. The **Beacon House** (715 Carolina Beach Ave. N., 877/232-2666, www.beaconhouseinnb-b.com, from $150 high season, breakfast not included,

some pets permitted in cottages with an extra fee) at Carolina Beach, just north of Kure, is a rare survival from that era. The early-1950s boarding house has the typical upstairs and downstairs porches and dark wood paneling indoors. (Nearby cottages are also rented by the Beacon House.) The price is much higher than it was in those days, but you'll be treated to a lodging experience from a long-gone era.

BALD HEAD ISLAND

Bald Head Island, an exclusive community where golf carts are the only traffic, is a two-mile, 20-minute ferry ride from Southport. More than 80 percent of the island is designated as a nature preserve, and at the southern tip stands "Old Baldy," the oldest lighthouse in North Carolina.

Sights

The **Bald Head Island Lighthouse** (910/457-5003, www.oldbaldy.org, spring-fall Tues.-Sat. 10am-4pm, Sun. 11am-4pm, call for winter hours, $5 adults, $3 children) was built in 1818, replacing an even earlier tower that was completed in 1795. Despite being the newcomer at Bald Head, the 109-foot lighthouse is the oldest such structure surviving in North Carolina. A visit to the lighthouse includes a stop next door at the **Smith Island Museum,** housed in the lighthouse keeper's home. The development of Smith Island (of which Bald Head is the terminus) allowed almost 17,000 acres to be set aside as an ecological preserve. The Old Baldy Foundation leads **historic tours** (910/457-5003, Tues.-Sat. 10:30am, $57, includes round-trip ferry) of Bald Head, departing from Island Ferry Landing, a short walk from the lighthouse.

Food

At Carolina Beach the **Shuckin' Shack** (6 N. Lake Park Blvd., 910/458-7380, www.pleasureislandoysterbar.com, Mon.-Sat. 11am-midnight, Sun. noon-midnight, $7-25) is a friendly little oyster bar that serves fresh local seafood, and oysters by the bucket. After a meal at the Shuckin' Shack, stop by **Britt's Donuts** (11

Boardwalk, 910/707-0755, www.carolina-beach.net, Mon.-Thurs. 8:30am-10:30pm, Fri. 4pm-midnight, Sat.-Sun. 8:30am-10:30pm, closed Oct.-Feb.). Britt's has been famous for its homemade doughnuts since opening its doors in 1939.

SOUTHPORT

One of North Carolina's prettiest towns, Southport is an 18th-century river town whose port was overtaken in importance by Wilmington's—and hence it has remained small and quiet. It was the Brunswick County seat until the late 1970s, when that job was outsourced to Bolivia (Bolivia, North Carolina, that is). It's a wonderfully charming place, with block upon block of beautiful historic houses and public buildings. The old cemetery is a gorgeous spot, and in it you'll find many tombstones that bear witness to the town's seafaring history—epitaphs for sea captains who died while visiting Smithville (Southport's original name), and stones carved with pictures of ships on rolling waves.

Sights

The **North Carolina Maritime Museum at Southport** (204 E. Moore St., 910/457-0003, www.ncmaritime.org, Tues.-Sat. 9am-5pm, $2 adults, $1 over age 62, free under age 16) is a smaller branch of the Maritime Museum at Beaufort, where you can learn about the seafaring history of the Carolina coast. Among the many topics of interest here is the life of pirate Stede Bonnet, whose girly surname belies his infamous life of crime. Bonnet, who spent much time in the Southport area, was by turns the pillaging buddy and bitter rival of Blackbeard. Other cool displays in the museum include a section of a 2,000-year-old, 54-inch-long Indian canoe, and the eight-foot jawbone of a whale.

Events

Southport hosts the state's best-known **Fourth of July Celebration** (910/457-6964, www.nc-4thofjuly.com), attended each year by up to 50,000 people. (That's approximately 20 times

the normal population of the town.) In addition to the requisite fireworks, food, and music, the festival features a special tribute to veterans, a flag retirement ceremony (that is, folks bring their old and worn-out flags), and a naturalization ceremony for new Americans.

Accommodations

Lois Jane's Riverview Inn (106 W. Bay St., 800/457-1152, www.loisjanes.com, $93-143, depending on season) is a Victorian waterfront home built by the innkeeper's grandfather. The guest rooms are comfortably furnished, bright and not froufrou, and the Queen Deluxe Street, a cottage behind the inn, has its own kitchen and separate entrance. The front porch of the inn gives a wonderful view of the harbor. Another affordable option is the **Inn at River Oaks** (512 N. Howe St., 910/457-1100, www.theinnatriveroaks.com, $65-135), a motel-style inn with very simple suites. The **Island Resort and Inn** (500 Ocean Dr., Oak Island, 910/278-5644, www.islandresortandinn.com, $75-190, depending on season) is a beachfront property with standard motel rooms and one- and two-bedroom apartment suites.

Food

The ◖ **Yacht Basin Provision Company** (130 Yacht Basin St., 910/457-0654, www.provisioncompany.com, Sun.-Thurs. 11am-4pm, Fri.-Sat. 11am-9pm, $10-20) is a Southport seafood joint with a super-casual atmosphere. Customers place their orders at the counter and serve themselves drinks (on the honor system), then seat themselves dockside to await the arrival of their chow. Most popular here are the conch fritters and grouper salad sandwich, but anything you order will be good.

OCEAN ISLE

Ocean Isle is the next-to-most-southerly beach in North Carolina, separated from South Carolina only by Bird Island and the town of Calabash. In October, Ocean Isle is the site of the **North Carolina Oyster Festival** (www.brunswickcountychamber.org), a huge event that's been happening for nearly 30 years. In addition to an oyster stew cook-off, surfing competition, and entertainment, this event features the North Carolina Oyster Shucking Competition. In the not-that-long-ago days when North Carolina's seafood industry was ascendant, workers—most often African American women—lined up on either side of long work tables in countless oyster houses along the coast and the creeks, and opened and cut out thousands of oysters a day. A complex occupational culture was at work in those rooms, one with its own vocabulary, stories, and songs. The speed at which these women worked was a source of collective and individual pride, and the fastest shuckers enjoyed quite a bit of prestige among their colleagues. The state shucking championship is the time when some of the best shuckers prove that although North Carolina may have changed around them, they haven't missed a beat.

SOUTH ALONG U.S. 17

U.S. 17 is an old colonial road—in fact, its original name, still used in some stretches, is the King's Highway. George Washington passed this way on his 1791 tour of the South, staying with the prominent planters of this area and leaving in his wake the proverbial legends about where he lay his head of an evening. Today, the King's Highway, following roughly its original course, is still the main thoroughfare through Brunswick County into South Carolina.

Brunswick Town and Fort Anderson

Near Orton is the **Brunswick Town/Fort Anderson State Historic Site** (8884 St. Philip's Rd. SE, Winnabow, 910/371-6613, www.ah.dcr.state.nc.us, Tues.-Sat. 9am-5pm, free), the site of what was a bustling little port town in the early and mid-1700s. In its brief life, Brunswick saw quite a bit of action. It was attacked in 1748 by a Spanish ship that, to residents' delight, blew up in the river. (One of that ship's cannons was dragged out of the river about 20 years ago and is on display here.) In 1765, the town's refusal to observe royal tax stamps was a successful precursor to the Boston

Tea Party eight years later. But by the end of the Revolutionary War, Brunswick Town was completely gone, burned by the British but having been made obsolete anyway by the growth of Wilmington. Today, nothing remains of the colonial port except for the lovely ruins of the 1754 **St. Philip's Anglican Church** and some building foundations uncovered by archaeologists. During the Civil War, Fort Anderson, sand earthworks that were part of the crucial defenses of the Cape Fear, was built on this site, protecting the blockade runners who came and went from Wilmington. A visitors center at the historic site tells the story of this surprisingly significant stretch of riverbank, and the grounds, with the town's foundations exposed and interpreted, are an intriguing vestige of a forgotten community.

Nature Preserves

The Nature Conservancy's **Green Swamp Preserve** (Hwy. 211, 5.5 miles north of Supply, 910/395-5000, www.nature.org, daily dawn-dusk, free) contains nearly 16,000 acres of some of North Carolina's most precious coastal ecosystems, the longleaf pine savanna and evergreen shrub pocosin. Hiking is allowed in the preserve, but the paths are primitive. It's important to stay on the trails and not explore in the wilds because this is an intensely fragile ecosystem. In this preserve are communities of rare carnivorous plants, including the monstrous little pink-mawed Venus flytrap, four kinds of pitcher plant, and sticky-fingered sundew. It's also a habitat for the rare red-cockaded woodpecker, which is partial to diseased old-growth longleaf pines as a place to call home.

The Nature Conservancy maintains another nature preserve nearby, the **Boiling Spring Lakes Preserve** (off Hwy. 87, Boiling Spring Lakes, trail begins at Community Center, 910/395-5000, www.nature.org, daily dawn-dusk, free), with a trail that begins at the Boiling Spring Lakes Community Center. Brunswick County contains the state's greatest concentration of rare plant species, and the most diverse plant communities anywhere on the East Coast north of Florida. This preserve is owned by the Plant Conservation Program and includes over half the acreage of the town of Boiling Spring Lakes. The ecosystem comprises Carolina bays, pocosins, and longleaf pine forests. Like the Green Swamp Preserve, many of the species here are dependent on periodic fires to propagate and survive. The Nature Conservancy does controlled burning at both sites to maintain this rare habitat.

Calabash and Vicinity

The once tiny fishing village of Calabash, just north of the South Carolina line, was founded in the early 18th century as Pea Landing, a shipping point for the bounteous local peanut crop. Calabashes, a kind of gourd, were used as dippers in the town supply of drinking water, and when the settlement was renamed in 1873, it was supposedly for that reason that it became Calabash.

In the early 1940s, a style of restaurant seafood was developed here that involves deep-frying lightly battered fish and shellfish. As the style caught on and more restaurants were built, the term "Calabash-style seafood" was born. Jimmy Durante was fond of dining in Calabash, and some people claim that it was in tribute to food here that he signed off on his shows saying, "Good night, Mrs. Calabash, wherever you are." Though Calabash seafood is now advertised at restaurants all over the country, this little town has more than enough restaurants of its own to handle the yearly onslaught of visitors in search of an authentic Calabash meal. Local favorite spots for seafood are the **Calabash Seafood Hut** (1125 River Rd., 910/579-6723, daily 11am-9pm, $10-28) and, right on the docks, **Dockside Seafood House** (9955 Nance St. SW, 910/579-6775, daily 4pm-9pm, $9-17).

Indigo Farms (1542 Hickman Rd. NW, 910/287-6794, www.indigofarmsmarket.com, Mon.-Sat. 8:30am-5:30pm, longer hours in warm months), three miles north of the South Carolina line in Calabash, is a superb farm market, selling all manner of produce, preserves, and baked goods. It also has corn mazes and farm activities in the fall, and is a training site for porcine contestants in the prestigious local NASPIG races.

Sunset Beach, the southernmost of the Brunswick County beaches, is a wonderfully small-time place, a cozy town that until 2008 could only be reached via a one-lane pontoon bridge. One of the area's most popular restaurants is located just on the inland side of the bridge to Sunset Beach: **Twin Lakes Seafood Restaurant** (102 Sunset Blvd., 910/579-6373, http://twinlakesseafood.com, daily 4:30pm-9:30pm, closed Nov.-Feb., $10-30) was built almost 40 years ago by Clarice and Ronnie Holden, both natives of the area. Clarice was born into a cooking family, the daughter of one of the founders of the Calabash restaurant tradition. Twin Lakes serves fresh locally caught seafood, a rarity in this time and place. In high season and on weekends, expect long lines.

GETTING THERE AND AROUND

The Brunswick County beaches, including Holden, Ocean Isle, and Sunset, are an easy drive on U.S. 17. The beaches and islands along the cape, due south of Wilmington, are not as close to U.S. 17. They can be reached by taking U.S. 76 south from Wilmington, or by ferry from Southport. The **Southport-Fort Fisher Ferry** (800/293-3779 or 800/368-8969) is popular as a sightseeing jaunt as well as a means simply to get across the river. It's a 30-minute crossing; most departures are 45 minutes apart, from Southport in summer daily 5:30am-7:45pm, winter daily 5:30am-6:15pm, and leaving Fort Fisher in summer daily 6:15am-8:30pm, winter daily 6:15am-7pm. For most vehicles the fare is $5, but if you're driving a rig that's more than 20 feet long, boat trailers and the like included, the price can be as high as $15. It's $1 for pedestrians, $2 for bicyclists, and $3 motorcyclists. Pets are permitted if leashed or in a vehicle, and there are restrooms on all ferries.

WILMINGTON

Points Inland from Wilmington

Moving inland from the Wilmington area, you first pass through a lush world of wetlands distinguished by the peculiar Carolina bays. Not necessarily bodies of water, as the name would suggest, the bays are actually ovoid depressions in the earth, of unknown and much debated origin. They are often water-filled, but by definition are fed by rainwater rather than creeks or groundwater. They create unique environments and are often surrounded by bay laurels (hence the name), and are guarded by a variety of carnivorous plants.

The next zone, bounded by the Waccamaw and Lumber Rivers, is largely farmland and small towns. This was for generations prime tobacco country, and that heritage is still very much evident in towns like Whiteville, where old tobacco warehouses line the railroad tracks. Culturally, this area—mostly in Columbus County, extending some distance into Robeson to the west and Brunswick to the east—is congruous with the three counties in South Carolina with which it shares a border—Horry, Marion, and Dillon.

The area around the Lumber River, especially in Robeson County, is the home of the indigenous Lumbee people, who have an amazing heritage of devotion to faith and family and steadfast resistance to oppression. If you turn on the radio while driving through this area, you'll likely find Lumbee gospel programming and get a sense of the cadences of Lumbee English.

At the edge of the region is Fayetteville. From its early days as the center of Cape Fear Scottish settlement to its current role as one of the most important military communities in the United States, Fayetteville has always been a significant North Carolina city.

ALONG U.S. 74

A little way inland from Calabash, the countryside is threaded by the Waccamaw River, a gorgeous, dark channel full of cypress knees and dangerous reptiles. (The name is pronounced "WAW-cuh-MAW," with slightly more emphasis on the first syllable than the third.) It winds its way down from Lake Waccamaw through a swampy little portion of North Carolina, crossing Horry County, South Carolina (unofficial motto: "The *H* is silent"), before joining the Pee Dee and Lumber Rivers to flow into Winyah Bay at the colonial port of Georgetown. Through the little toenail of North Carolina that the Waccamaw crosses, it parallels the much longer Lumber River, surrounding the very rural Columbus County and part of Robeson County in an environment of deep subtropical wetlands.

Sights
◖ MUSEUM OF THE NATIVE AMERICAN RESOURCE CENTER

Pembroke is the town around which much of the indigenous Lumbee community revolves, and at the center of life here is the University of North Carolina at Pembroke (UNCP). Founded in 1887 as the Indian Normal School, UNCP's population is now only about one-quarter Native American, but it's still an important site in the history North Carolina's indigenous people. The **Museum of the Native American Resource Center** (Old Main, UNCP, 910/521-6282, www.uncp.edu, Mon.-Sat. 8am-5pm, free) is on campus, occupying Old Main, a 1923 building that's a source of pride for the Pembroke community. The Resource Center has a small but very good collection of historical artifacts and contemporary art by Native Americans from across the country.

JOHN BLUE HOUSE
Laurinburg's **John Blue House** (13040 X-way Rd., Laurinburg, 910/276-2495, www.johnbluecottonfestival.com, Tues.-Sat. 10am-noon and 1pm-4pm, free) is a spectacle of Victorian design, a polygonal house built entirely of heart

THE LEGEND OF HENRY BERRY LOWRY

In some places, the Civil War didn't end the day General Lee surrendered, but smoldered on in terrible local violence. One such place was the indigenous Lumbee community of Robeson County, in the days of the famous Lowry Band.

Then as now, Lowry (also spelled Lowrie) was a prominent surname among the Lumbee people. During the Civil War, Allen Lowry led a band of men who hid out in the swamps, eluding conscription into the backbreaking corps of semi-slave labor that was forced to build earthworks to defend Wilmington. When the war ended, violence against the Lumbees continued, and the Lowry Band retaliated, attacking the plantations of their wartime pursuers. Allen Lowry and his oldest son were captured in 1865 and executed. Henry Berry Lowry, the youngest son, inherited the mantle of leadership.

For the next several years, long after the end of the Civil War, the Lowry Band was pursued relentlessly. Arrested and imprisoned, Lowry and his men escaped from prison in Lumberton and Wilmington. Between 1868 and 1872, the state and federal governments tried various ways to apprehend them—putting a bounty on Lowry's head, even sending in a federal artillery battalion. After an 11-month campaign of unsuccessful pursuit, the federal soldiers gave up. Soon afterward, the Lowry Band emerged from the swamps, raided Lumberton, and made off with a large amount of money. This was the end of the road for the Lowry Band, however, and one by one its members were killed in 1872—except, perhaps, Henry Berry. It's unknown whether he died, went back into hiding, or left the area altogether. As befits a legend, he seems simply to have disappeared.

Henry Berry Lowry is a source of fierce pride to modern Lumbee people, a symbol of the community's resistance and resilience. Every summer, members of the Lumbee community perform in the long-running outdoor drama *Strike at the Wind,* which tells the story of the Lowry Band. Another vivid retelling of the story is the 2001 novel *Nowhere Else on Earth* by Josephine Humphreys.

WILMINGTON

pine harvested from the surrounding property and done up like a wedding cake with endless decorative devices. John Blue, the builder and original owner, was an inventor of machinery used in the processing of cotton. A pre-Civil War cotton gin stands on the property and is used for educational demonstrations throughout the year. This is the site of the **John Blue Cotton Festival,** an October event that showcases not only the ingenuity of the home's famous resident and the process of ginning cotton, but also lots of local and regional musicians and other artists.

Sports and Recreation

Several beautiful state parks line the Waccamaw and Lumber Rivers.

Yogi Bear's Jellystone Park (626 Richard Wright Rd., 877/668-8586, www.taborcityjellystone.com, $30 tents, $120 cabins), formerly known as Daddy Joe's, is a popular campground with RV and tent spaces, rental cabins, and yurts. The facilities are clean and well maintained, and there are tons of children's activities on-site. Some of the camping is in wooded areas, but for the most part expect direct sun and plan accordingly.

In Fair Bluff is **River Bend Outfitters** (1206 Main St., 910/649-5998, www.whitevillenc.com/rbo), a canoe and kayak company that specializes in paddling and camping trips along the beautiful blackwater Lumber River.

🄲 LAKE WACCAMAW STATE PARK
Lake Waccamaw State Park (1866 State Park Dr., Lake Waccamaw, 910/646-4748, http://ncparks.gov, office daily 8am-5pm, park Nov.-Apr. daily 8am-6pm, Mar.-May and Sept.-Oct. daily 8am-8pm, June-Aug. daily 8am-9pm, free) encompasses the 9,000-acre Lake Waccamaw. The lake is technically a Carolina bay, a mysterious geological feature of

this region. Carolina bays are large, oval depressions in the ground, many of which are boggy and filled with water, but which are actually named because of the bay trees that typically grow in and around them. Lake Waccamaw has geological and hydrological characteristics that make it unique even within the odd category of Carolina bays. Because of its proximity to a large limestone deposit, the water is more neutral than its usually very acidic cousins and so supports a greater diversity of life. There are several aquatic creatures that live only here, with great names like the Waccamaw fatmucket and silverside (a mollusk and a fish, respectively). The park draws many boaters and paddlers, naturally, although the only available launches are outside the park. Primitive campsites are available in the park.

JONES LAKE STATE PARK
North of Whiteville on Highway 701 is Elizabethtown, location of **Jones Lake State Park** (4117 Hwy. 242, Elizabethtown, 910/588-4550, http://ncparks.gov, office Mon.-Fri. 8am-5pm, park Nov.-Feb. daily 8am-6pm, Mar.-May and Sept.-Oct. daily 8am-8pm, June-Aug. daily 8am-9pm). Visitors can go boating on Jones Lake, either in their own craft (no motors over 10 hp), or in canoes or paddleboats rented from the park ($5 per hour, $3 each additional hour). The lake is also great for swimming Memorial Day to Labor Day, with shallow, cool water and a sandy beach. There are a concession stand and a bathhouse at the beach. Camping is available in a wooded area, with drinking water and restrooms nearby. Visit the park's website for the rather complicated pricing system.

SINGLETARY LAKE STATE PARK
Singletary Lake State Park (6707 Hwy. 53 E., Kelly, 910/669-2928, http://ncparks.gov, daily 8am-5pm, free), north of Lake Waccamaw in Kelly, centers around one of the largest of the Carolina bays, the 572-acre Singletary Lake, which lies within the Bladen Lakes State Forest. There is no individual camping allowed, although there are facilities for large

groups—including the entrancingly named Camp Ipecac—which date from the Civilian Conservation Corps (CCC) era. There is a nice one-mile hiking trail, the CCC-Carolina Bay Loop Trail, and a 500-foot pier extending over the bay. Some of the cypress trees here are estimated to have been saplings when the first English colonists set foot on Roanoke Island.

LUMBER RIVER STATE PARK
Lumber River State Park (2819 Princess Ann Rd., Orrum, 910/628-4564, http://ncparks.gov, Mar.-May, Sept.-Oct. 8am-8pm, June-Aug. 8am-9pm, Nov.-Feb. 8am-6pm, free) has 115 miles of waterways, with numerous put-ins for canoes and kayaks. The river, referred to as the Lumber or Lumbee River, or, in areas farther upstream, Drowning Creek, traverses both the coastal plain region and the eastern edge of the Sandhills. Camping is available at unimproved walk-in and canoe-in sites.

Food
If you pass through Tabor City, don't neglect to have a meal at the **◖Todd House** (102 Live Oak St., 910/653-3778, www.todd-house.com, Mon.-Fri. 11am-8pm, Sun. 11am-3pm, $12), which has been serving fine country cooking since 1923. The Todds are one of the oldest families in the area along the state line, and the first in the restaurant business was Mary Todd, who took to cooking meals for visiting tobacco buyers. Through her daughter's time, and a couple of subsequent owners, the Todd House has continued to serve famously good barbecue, fried chicken, and other down-home specialties. The wonderful pies are available for purchase, so pick one up for the road.

There's a take-out counter in Whiteville that chowhounds will drive an hour out of their way to reach because it's said to have the best burgers anywhere around. Next to the railroad tracks, **Ward's Grill** (706 S. Madison St., 910/642-2004, Mon.-Tues. and Thurs. 7am-2pm, Wed. 7am-1pm, 1st 2 Sat. of the month 7am-noon, $8) has no seating, just a walk-up counter. Its burgers are famous, as are its chili dogs.

In Lumberton, try **Fuller's Old-Fashion BBQ** (3201 Roberts Ave., Lumberton, 910/738-8694, www.fullersbbq.com, Mon.-Sat. 11am-9pm, Sun. 11am-4pm, lunch buffet $7, dinner buffet $9.50). Fuller's has a great reputation for its barbecue, but it also makes all sorts of country specialties like chicken gizzards and chitterlings, and a special 12-layer cake.

Getting There and Around

This section of Southeastern North Carolina is bisected by I-95, the largest highway on the East Coast. I-95 passes just outside both Fayetteville and Lumberton. Major east-west routes include U.S. 74, which crosses the Cape Fear at Wilmington and proceeds through Lake Waccamaw and Whiteville to pass just south of Lumberton and Pembroke, going to Laurinburg. Highway 87 goes through Elizabethtown, where you can choose to branch off onto Highway 211 to Lumberton, or bear north on Highway 87 to Fayetteville.

FAYETTEVILLE

Fayetteville is North Carolina's sixth-largest city, and in its own quiet way has always been one of the state's most powerful engines of growth and change. In the early 1700s it became a hub for settlement by Scottish immigrants, who helped build it into a major commercial center. From the 1818 initiation of steamboat travel between Fayetteville and Wilmington along the Cape Fear—initially a voyage of six days!—to the building of the Plank Road, a huge boon to intrastate commerce, Fayetteville was well connected to commercial resources all through the Carolinas.

At a national level, Fayetteville serves as the location of two high-level military installations. Fort Bragg is the home of the XVIII Airborne Corps, the 82nd Airborne, the Delta Force, and the John F. Kennedy Special Warfare Center and School. As such, it's also the home of many widows and children of soldiers who have died in Iraq and Afghanistan. Pope Air Force Base is nearby, the home of the 43rd Airlift Wing and its Maintenance, Support, and Operations Groups.

Sights

The **Museum of the Cape Fear Regional Complex** (801 Arsenal Ave., 910/486-1330, www.ncdcr.gov/ncmcf, Tues.-Sat. 10am-5pm, Sun. 1pm-5pm, free) has three components, each telling different stories of Fayetteville's history. The museum itself has exhibits on the history and prehistory of the region, including its vital role in developing transportation in the state, as well as its centrality as a military center. There is an 1897 house museum, the Poe House, which belonged to Edgar Allen Poe—not Edgar Allan, the writer, but Edgar Allen, a brickyard owner. The third section is the 4.5-acre Arsenal Park, site of a federal arms magazine built in 1836, claimed by the Confederacy in 1861, and destroyed by General Sherman in 1865.

The **Airborne and Special Operations Museum** (100 Bragg Blvd., 910/643-2766, www.asomf.org, Fri.-Sat. 10am-5pm, Sun. noon-5pm, free) is an impressive facility that presents the history of Special Ops paratroopers, from the first jump in 1940 to the divisions' present-day roles abroad in peacekeeping missions and war. In the museum's theater you can watch an amazing film of what it looks like when a paratrooper makes the jump, and the 24-seat Pitch, Roll, and Yaw Vista-Dome Motion Simulator makes the experience even more exciting.

The **JFK Special Warfare Museum** (Bldg. D-2502, Ardennes St. and Marion St., Fort Bragg, 910/432-4272, www.jfkwebstore.com, Tues.-Sun. 11am-4pm, ID required) tells the story of further amazing facets of the U.S. military, including Special Ops and Psychological Ops. The museum focuses on the Vietnam War era, but chronicles unconventional warfare from colonial times to the present.

Going back farther in time, the **Fayetteville Independent Light Infantry Armory and Museum** (210 Burgess St., 910/433-1612, by appointment, free) displays artifacts from the history of the Light Infantry. The Fayetteville Independent Light Infantry (FILI) is still active, dedicated as North Carolina's official historic military command, a ceremonial duty.

WILMINGTON AND THE CAPE FEAR REGION

But in its active-duty days, which began in 1793, FILI had some exciting times, particularly during the Civil War. In addition to the military artifacts, this museum also exhibits a carriage in which the Marquis de Lafayette was shown around Fayetteville—the only one of the towns bearing his name that he actually visited.

The 79-acre **Cape Fear Botanical Garden** (536 N. Eastern Blvd., 910/486-0221, www.capefearbg.org, Mar.-mid-Dec. Mon.-Sat. 10am-5pm, Sun. noon-5pm, mid-Dec.-Feb. Mon.-Sat. 10am-5pm, $10 adults, $5 children) is one of the loveliest horticultural sites in North Carolina. The camellia and azalea gardens are spectacular sights in the early spring, but the variety of plantings and environments represented makes the whole park a delight. Along the banks of the Paw Paw River and Cross Creek, visitors will find dozens of garden environments, including lily gardens, hosta gardens, woods, a bog, and an 1880s farmhouse garden. Without a doubt, this is the prettiest place in Fayetteville.

Cross Creek Cemetery (North Cool Spring St. and Grove St., 800/255-8217, daily dawn-dusk) is an attractively sad spot, the resting place of many Scottish men and women who crossed the ocean to settle the Cape Fear. Though all kinds of people were buried here over the years, it is the oldest section that is most poignant, where one stone after another commemorates Mr. or Mrs. Mac-So-and-So, Late of Glasgow or Perth, Merchant in This Town.

Entertainment and Events

The **Cameo Theatre** (225 Hay St., 910/486-6633, www.cameoarthouse.com) is a cool old early-20th-century movie house, originally known as the New Dixie. Today it is "Fayetteville's alternative cinematic experience," a place for independent and art-house movies.

The **Cape Fear Regional Theatre** (1209 Hay St., 910/323-4233, www.cfrt.org) began in 1962 as a tiny company with a bunch of borrowed equipment. Today it is a major regional theater with a wide reputation. Putting on several major productions each season, with a specialty in popular musicals, it draws actors and directors from around the country, but maintains its heart here in the Fayetteville arts community.

Fayetteville's late-April **Dogwood Festival** features rock, pop, and beach music bands; a dog show; a recycled art show; a "hogs and rags spring rally"; and the selection and coronation of Miss, Teen Miss, Young Miss, and Junior Miss Dogwood Festival.

Accommodations and Food

Fayetteville's lodging options are mostly chain motels, a multitude of which can be found at I-95's Fayetteville exits. You'll generally find a pretty reasonable deal at the old standards, but if you'd like to stay somewhere with more personality, Wilmington and Raleigh are both easily accessible.

Likewise, the city's dining choices tend toward highway chains. There are some exceptions; the ◖ **Hilltop House** (1240 Fort Bragg Rd., 910/484-6699, www.hilltophousenc.com, lunch Mon.-Sat. 11am-2pm, dinner Mon.-Thurs. 5pm-9pm, Fri.-Sat. 5pm-10pm, brunch Sun. 10:30am-2:30pm, $15-25) serves hearty fare in an elegant setting, has complimentary wine tasting Tuesday evening, and was recognized in 2007 with a Wine Spectator Award for Excellence—not surprising, given that the Hilltop House has a 74-page wine list. More casual is the **Mash House** (4150 Sycamore Dairy Rd., 910/867-9223, www.themashhouse.com, Mon.-Thurs. 5pm-10pm, Fri. 5pm-11pm, Sat. noon-11pm, Sun. noon-9pm $8-16), which has a good variety of pizzas and sandwiches as well as heavier entrées and a selection of good homemade brews.

Information and Services

Cape Fear Valley Health Services (1638 Owen Dr., 910/615-4000, www.capefearvalley.com) is a large hospital complex with acute care services, a major cardiac care program, and everything else one would expect from a major regional hospital.

The website of the **Fayetteville Area Convention and Visitors Bureau** (www.visitfayettevillenc.com) is an excellent source of visitor information for this city. You'll find the basics as well as detailed driving tours, extensive historical information, and much more.

Getting There and Around

Fayetteville is a short hop off I-95. Fayetteville is also easily reached by Highway 24 via Jacksonville, Warsaw, and Clinton. **Fayetteville Regional Airport** (FAY, 400 Airport Rd., 910/433-1160, flyfay.ci.fayetteville.nc.us) has daily flights to Charlotte, Atlanta, and Washington DC on Delta and US Airways. The city is served by **Amtrak** (472 Hay St., 800/872-7245, www.amtrak.com, daily 10am-5:45pm and 10pm-5:45am) via the regional *Palmetto* and the New York-Miami *Silver Meteor* lines.

CENTRAL NORTH CAROLINA

The name Triangle, long used to describe the Raleigh-Durham-Chapel Hill area, referred originally to the three major universities here, the University of North Carolina (UNC) in Chapel Hill, Duke University in Durham, and North Carolina State University (NC State) in Raleigh. In satellite images, the Triangle is an unbroken sprawl of humanity. But Raleigh, Durham, and Chapel Hill are each very different places.

That said, there is a spirit that unites the communities of the Triangle. The concentration of colleges—there are over a dozen institutions of higher learning, including several prominent historically black universities—make for a highly educated population. By some counts, there are more PhDs per capita in the Triangle than anywhere else in the United States. The Triangle also has a deeply liberal bent, to the consternation and puzzlement of much of the rest of this red state. The Chapel Hill area is the epicenter of progressive politics in the area.

UNC's Creative Writing Program has a lot to do with the concentration of fine writers, but the whole region is full of talent and has been home to writers such as Thomas Wolfe, Charles Kuralt, and David Sedaris. The music scene is just as rich, with great symphonies and chamber groups, a century-old blues tradition, and probably more old-time string band musicians than anywhere outside the mountains. If you like alternative country, you'll find a live music scene that rivals those of Austin and Nashville.

© ISTOCKPHOTO.COM

HIGHLIGHTS

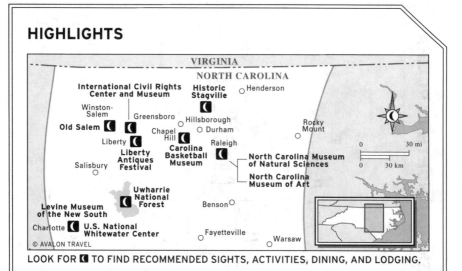

© AVALON TRAVEL

LOOK FOR ◖ TO FIND RECOMMENDED SIGHTS, ACTIVITIES, DINING, AND LODGING.

◖ **North Carolina Museum of Natural Sciences:** Get breathtakingly close to massive whale and dinosaur skeletons and discover the many ecosystems of the region (page 111).

◖ **North Carolina Museum of Art:** Amazingly varied collections encompass art from ancient Greece, Egypt, and the Americas as well as Judaica, pop art, and 18th- and 19th-century American and European masters (page 113).

◖ **Historic Stagville:** One of the South's largest enslaved populations lived and worked on this plantation. The story of their community is preserved here (page 119).

◖ **Carolina Basketball Museum:** The University of North Carolina's basketball program has one of the greatest, if not the greatest, collegiate athletic traditions in American sports. This new museum celebrates the pride of Chapel Hill (page 126).

◖ **Old Salem:** Craftspeople and historic interpreters bring this 18th- and 19th-century religious community to life in this beautiful restored Moravian village (page 131).

◖ **International Civil Rights Center and Museum:** Learn about the fight for integra-tion and justice in North Carolina, a lesser-known but crucial front in the civil rights movement (page 135).

◖ **Liberty Antiques Festival:** This bian-nual event is a favorite among antiques collec-tors throughout the Southeast. From the finest of antique Southern furniture to tobacco tags, enthusiasts of old stuff will find treasures here (page 142).

◖ **Uwharrie National Forest:** This out-cropping of low mountains is unfamiliar even to residents of the region. Hiding under the canopy of forest are miles of hiking trails, wil-derness campsites, and mysterious back roads (page 144).

◖ **Levine Museum of the New South:** This important museum tells the complicated and sometimes painful story of the post-Civil War South, and Charlotte in particular, in ways that are both respectful and innovative (page 149).

◖ **U.S. National Whitewater Center:** Home to the U.S. Olympic canoe and kayak teams, this facility is also designed for first-time paddlers and other adventure sports en-thusiasts (page 154).

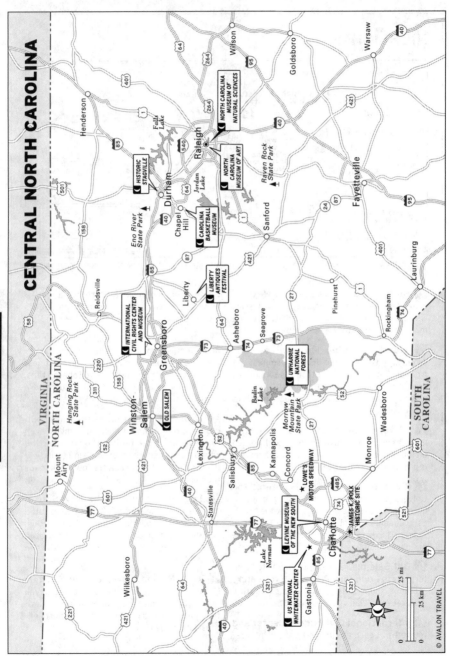

CENTRAL NORTH CAROLINA

CENTRAL NORTH CAROLINA

VIRGINIA
NORTH CAROLINA
SOUTH CAROLINA

Warsaw
Goldsboro
Wilson
Henderson
Falls Lake
Raleigh
Fayetteville
Laurinburg
Rockingham
Pinehurst
Sanford
Chapel Hill
Durham
Liberty
Asheboro
Seagrove
Greensboro
Reidsville
Winston-Salem
Lexington
Salisbury
Kannapolis
Concord
Monroe
Wadesboro
Statesville
Mount Airy
Wilkesboro
Gastonia
Charlotte
Lake Norman

Eno River State Park
Jordan Lake
Raven Rock State Park
Hanging Rock State Park
Badin Lake
Morrow Mountain State Park

NORTH CAROLINA MUSEUM OF NATURAL SCIENCES
HISTORIC STAGVILLE
NORTH CAROLINA MUSEUM OF ART
CAROLINA BASKETBALL MUSEUM
LIBERTY ANTIQUES FESTIVAL
INTERNATIONAL CIVIL RIGHTS CENTER AND MUSEUM
UWHARRIE NATIONAL FOREST
OLD SALEM
LOWE'S MOTOR SPEEDWAY
JAMES K. POLK HISTORIC SITE
LEVINE MUSEUM OF THE NEW SOUTH
US NATIONAL WHITEWATER CENTER

25 mi
25 km

© AVALON TRAVEL

PLANNING YOUR TIME

The ground covered in this chapter is best approached as three destinations for the purpose of setting out a practical itinerary. Raleigh calls for a full day, as it is large and flows in all directions. Durham and Chapel Hill are only nine miles apart, so together they are a base for the other region of this chapter.

If you decide to choose one town in the Triangle to stay at night while exploring the whole area during the day, Durham is the most centrally located of the three. That said, I-40 and U.S. 70 link the whole Triangle area quite efficiently, and there are few points in the Triangle that are more than half an hour's drive from any other destination.

Raleigh and Vicinity

Loyal watchers of *The Andy Griffith Show* know that when trouble came to Mayberry, it came from one of two places: Up North or Raleigh. But Raleigh is no hive of citified depravity. As the home of the state government and several universities, Raleigh is a spark that helps power the cultural engine of the rest of the state. North Carolina State University is here, as are two prominent historically black universities, Shaw and Saint Augustine's,

and two small women's colleges, Peace and Meredith.

SIGHTS
(North Carolina Museum of Natural Sciences

The **North Carolina Museum of Natural Sciences** (Bicentennial Plaza, 11 W. Jones St., 877/462-8724, www.naturalsciences.org, Mon.-Sat. 9am-5pm, Sun. noon-5pm, 1st Fri.

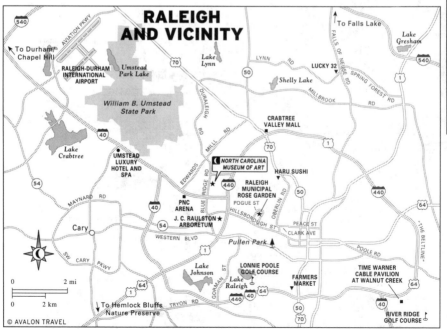

of the month 9am-9pm, free) hosts national traveling exhibitions and is home to excellent permanent exhibits. *Mountains to the Sea* is a re-creation of the regional environments of the state, populated with live and mounted animals and plants. *Stars of Prehistoric North Carolina* include the world's only publicly displayed skeleton of an *Acrocanthosaurus,* a 38-foot, 4.5-ton predatory dinosaur, and the remains of "Willo," a 66-million-year-old small vegetarian dinosaur, whose fossilized heart is a miraculous boon to paleontology. Visitors can also walk among hummingbirds and butterflies in the Living Conservatory, a top-floor tropical forest, and work among museum collections in the public Naturalist Center.

North Carolina Museum of History

Across Bicentennial Plaza is the **North Carolina Museum of History** (5 E. Edenton St., 919/807-7900, http://ncmuseumofhistory.org, Tues.-Sat. 9am-5pm, Sun. noon-5pm, free), where visitors learn about the history

© AVALON TRAVEL

of the state's exemplary military, from the Revolutionary War to Afghanistan; about the musicians and genres that make this state one of the wellsprings of American music; about the handicrafts, including pottery, textiles, and furniture, created by centuries of renowned artisans; and about medicine in North Carolina, from traditional African American root medicine and Native American herbs to the pharmaceuticals and technology that draw patients and researchers from around the world.

◀ North Carolina Museum of Art

The **North Carolina Museum of Art** (2110 Blue Ridge Rd., 919/839-6262, http://ncartmuseum.org, Tues.-Thurs. and Sat.-Sun. 10am-5pm, Fri. 10am-9pm, free) is just outside the Beltline. Its collections are of the highest quality and include masterpieces of art from all eras and regions of the world, from ancient Egyptian, Greek, Roman, and pre-Columbian American art to the work of Botticelli, Giotto, and Raphael; Monet; Copley, Cole, Homer, Eakins, and Chase; Georgia O'Keeffe and Thomas Hart Benton; and many more. The gallery is also home to one of the nation's two Jewish ceremonial art collections, and to collections of 19th- and 20th-century African art.

Historic Homes

The 1770s **Joel Lane Museum House** (St. Mary's St. and W. Hargett St., 919/833-3431, www.joellane.org, Wed.-Fri. 10am-2pm, tours 10am, 11am, noon, and 1pm, Sat. 1pm-4pm, tours 1pm, 2pm and 3pm, $8 adults, $7 seniors, $4 children) is Wake County's oldest extant home. Costumed docents lead tours of the house and period gardens.

The 1799 **Haywood Hall** (211 New Bern Place, 919/832-8357, Thurs. 10:30am-1:30pm, free) is another of Raleigh's oldest extant buildings. Built for the state's first elected treasurer and his family, the house and gardens are open to the public and feature a historic doll collection. Tours are available for a fee.

Mordecai Historic Park (Mimosa St. and Wake Forest Rd., 919/857-4364, www.raleighnc.gov/mordecai, grounds daily dawn-dusk, hourly house tours Tues.-Sat. 9am-4pm, Sun. 1pm-4pm, $5 adults, $3 seniors, $3 ages 7-17) includes a late-18th-century and early-19th-century plantation house, restored dependencies, and other buildings, including the birthplace of President Andrew Johnson.

Other Sights

The **North Carolina State Capitol** (1 E. Edenton St., 866/724-8687, www.ncstatecapitol.org, Mon.-Sat. 9am-5pm, free) and the **Executive Mansion** (200 N. Blount St., 919/807-7950) built in the 1830s and 1890s, respectively, are lovely examples of Victorian architecture. The Greek Revival capitol building has been restored to its antebellum appearance. Free guided tours last approximately 45 minutes. The Executive Mansion was described by FDR as possessing "the most beautiful governor's residence interior in America." Tours are available depending on state functions—it is still the home of the governor.

The **J.C. Raulston Arboretum** (4415 Beryl Rd., 919/515-3132, www.ncsu.edu/jcraulstonarboretum, Apr.-Oct. daily 8am-8pm, Nov.-Mar. daily 8am-5pm, free), across from Capitol City Lumber Company, is a free public garden focused on the development of ornamental plants suitable to the Southern climate, where one can visit highly specialized areas devoted to white flowers, roses, and border plants. The **Raleigh Municipal Rose Garden** (301 Pogue St., near NC State, free) is home to over 1,000 roses of 60 varieties. Carolina roses are blessed with an extra-long growing season, and the Municipal Rose Garden also features bulbs and other ornamental plants, so a visit to the garden is special at any time of year.

ENTERTAINMENT AND EVENTS
Performing Arts

The **North Carolina Symphony** (919/733-2750, www.ncsymphony.org), a full-time 65-member orchestra under the direction of conductors Grant Llewellyn and William Henry Curry, tours throughout the state and beyond. Its home venue in Raleigh is the

CENTRAL NORTH CAROLINA

wonderful Meymandi Concert Hall at Progress Energy Center (2 E. South St., 919/831-6060). The **North Carolina Opera** (919/792-3850, www.operanc.com) has its home stage at Memorial Auditorium, also in the Progress Energy Center. The opera's rehearsals, held at a nearby church, are sometimes open to the public—see their website for details.

The **Time Warner Cable Music Pavilion at Walnut Creek** (3801 Rock Quarry Rd., 919/831-6400, www.livenation.com/raleigh) is a top local music venue, attracting pop and country chart-toppers. The **Lincoln Theatre** (126 E. Cabarrus St., 919/821-4111, www.lincolntheatre.com, all ages, $2 surcharge under age 18) is another important local performing arts institution where major rock, blues, jazz, and other bands fill the schedule.

Nightlife

The best place to find out what's going on at Triangle-area clubs on any given night of the week is the *Independent Weekly* (www.indyweek.com), a free newspaper that's available at restaurants and shops throughout the region. By state law, establishments that serve liquor and make no more than 30 percent of their revenue from food must be private-membership clubs, but every club has ways of getting first-time visitors through the doors. Some clubs must be joined a few days in advance, while others accept applications with nominal dues at the door. Raleigh's popular nightspots are dance clubs, lots of live music venues, and gay clubs with great drag events.

The **Pour House Music Hall** (224 S. Blount St., 919/821-1120, www.the-pour-house.com) is a great venue with alternative-country, rock and roll, bluegrass, and all sorts of other bands on the schedule. Visitors must print the membership form from the website, fill it out, and bring it to the door with $1. For Irish ambience, visit **Tír Na Nóg Irish Pub and Restaurant** (218 S. Blount St., 919/833-7795, www.tirnanogirishpub.com) and the **Hibernian Restaurant and Bar** (311 Glenwood Ave., 919/833-2258, www.hibernianpub.com).

Legends (330 W. Hargett St., 919/831-8888, www.legends-club.com, daily 9pm-close) is one of the most popular gay and lesbian clubs in the state, a fun bar that is also ground zero for the area's pageant circuit. Call for membership details.

Fairs and Festivals

The 10-day **North Carolina State Fair** (1025 Blue Ridge Rd., 919/821-7400, www.ncstatefair.org), held each October, is the nation's largest agricultural fair, with an annual attendance of about 800,000. Plan on going back several times to take it all in. It has everything you might want in an agricultural fair: livestock and produce competitions, big-name bluegrass concerts, carnival rides, fighter jet flyovers, and lots of deep-fried food.

SHOPPING

Cameron Village (Oberlin Rd. between Hillsborough St. and Wade Ave.) was one of the earliest shopping centers in the Southeast, a planned commercial neighborhood built on the grounds of the old Cameron plantation in the late 1940s. The complex opened with three stores, but today there are dozens. It tends toward independent boutiques and high-end chains and is a fun place to splurge. Some of the notable shops are the **Seagrove Pottery** store (443-B Daniels St., 919/831-9696, www.seagrovepotterygallery.com, Mon.-Fri. 10am-6pm, Sun. 1pm-5pm) which sells, of course, pottery from Seagrove; **Uniquities** (450 Daniels St., 919/832-1234, www.uniquities.com, Mon.-Sat. 10am-7pm, Sun. 1pm-6pm), a great women's clothing boutique; and the **Junior League Bargain Box** (401 Woodburn Ave., 919/833-7587, Mon.-Sat. 10am-6pm), a nice thrift shop.

The 1914 **City Market** (214 E. Martin St., 919/821-8023, www.citymarketraleigh.com) complex is another collection of nifty little shops and restaurants in a historic setting. **Crabtree Valley Mall** (Glenwood Ave./U.S. 70 at I-440) is the main conventional shopping mall in Raleigh.

SCORING COLLEGE BASKETBALL TICKETS

If you're visiting the Triangle during college basketball season and are hoping to catch a game in person, don't count on being able to buy a ticket at the box office. In fact, count on not being able to. The 20,000-seat Dean Dome, UNC's Dean E. Smith Center, routinely sells out for men's in-conference games, and the RBC Centura Center, the NC State Wolfpack men's 20,000-seat home arena, often does as well. Duke plays at the comparatively quaint Cameron Indoor Stadium, and its 9,000 seats are the hardest of all to obtain. Tickets for women's games, which at UNC and NC State take place on the older, smaller courts, are much less difficult to come by, though Atlantic Coast Conference (ACC) games sometimes sell out, and the Duke-UNC women's games always do. The most prized and scarce treasure of all is a ticket to the Duke-UNC men's game. Unless a current student at one of the schools really, really likes you, or you're a major benefactor with a building named in your honor, your chances of paying face value for a ticket are slim to none.

During basketball season, tickets appear on eBay, Craigslist, and ticket-scalping search engines. Really good tickets will probably go on the auction block well in advance of the game and are fought over fiercely. If you wait until the day of a game, there's a chance of finding a seller who has just that day decided not to use his or her own tickets and wants to get rid of them fast. To obtain these, you've got to stay alert and act fast. Prices vary from game to game depending on the teams' respective records that season and the heat of the rivalry. For a minor out-of-conference game, such as are played early in the season—the Wolfpack versus the Flying Menace of Snickelfritz County Community College, let's say—you should be able to get a reasonably good ticket for $10-20 above face value and without much difficulty, if the game sells out at all. For a sold-out game between ACC teams, prices go up steeply. Expect to pay three or more times the face value for a good seat at an in-conference game of minor importance. For an important ACC game, the worst seats in the house could be over $100, and the good seats $200-300 and up. If you want to go to a UNC-Duke game, seats up in the rafters will be in the hundreds, and a good seat could easily set you back $1,000 or more.

Scalping is illegal in North Carolina; it's also pretty common. On game day, the scalpers are the people hanging around outside the arena, or on nearby street corners, holding signs that say "Need Tickets." Technically, they probably will buy tickets if you're selling, but "Need Tickets" is code for "I've got tickets." If you ask one of them if he has a ticket, he'll ask cagily what you're looking for. Draw your line in the sand—you want a really good ticket for not a lot of money. If you ask for courtside seats for $20 each, you'll only get laughter and lose your bargaining chips, but if you start not too far from the bounds of reason, he'll talk business. Be firm, and be willing to turn down a best offer. There's another scalper just a few steps away. If you don't mind missing the first few minutes of the game, you'll find that prices start going down at tip-off.

For the hard-core basketball fan, the research and haggling and dollars are a small price to pay for a chance to be present at an ACC game. There's nothing like watching your favorite team warm up, or seeing Crazy Towel Guy do his thing at Cameron Indoor Stadium, or being in the same room, albeit a large one, with 10,000 other people who know all the words to the team's fight song.

SPORTS AND RECREATION
Spectator Sports

North Carolina State University is the southern terminus of Tobacco Road, the zone of legendary college sports traditions in the Atlantic Coast Conference (ACC). Though the UNC-Duke rivalry may score more media attention, NC State's **Wolfpack athletics** (www.gopack. com) is nothing to sniff at. Men's basketball games take place at the 20,000-seat **RBC**

Center (1400 Edwards Mill Rd., 919/861-2300, www.rbccenter.com) and football is next door at **Carter-Finley Stadium** (4600 Trinity Rd., 919/865-1510). Women's basketball and other Wolfpack sporting events take place at **Reynolds Coliseum** (2411 Dunn Ave., 919/515-2100) and **Doak Field** (1081 Varsity Dr., 919/515-2100).

During hockey season, the RBC Center is home to the **Carolina Hurricanes** (http://hurricanes.nhl.com). North Carolina may seem an unlikely place for an NHL franchise, but the Canes proved themselves in the 2005-2006 season, beating the Edmonton Oilers to win the Stanley Cup. Tickets can be purchased in person at the Time Warner Cable Box Office inside the RBC Center (919/861-2323, no phone sales) or through Ticketmaster (www.ticketmaster.com).

Women's Roller Derby has made a national comeback, and the cities of the Carolinas are blessed with some bruisers. Raleigh-based **Carolina Rollergirls** (www.carolinarollergirls.com) is a Women's Flat Track Derby Association league that currently consists of three teams: the Debutante Brawlers, the Tai Chi-tahs, and the Trauma Queens. Derbies take place at Dorton Arena on the State Fairgrounds (1025 Blue Ridge Blvd., 919/821-7400). Tickets are available from Schoolkids Records (2712-100 Hillsborough St., 919/821-7766, www.schoolkidsrecords.com, Mon.-Sat. 10am-9pm, Sun. noon-7pm) in Raleigh and other enlightened establishments.

Outdoor Recreation

William B. Umstead State Park (8801 Glenwood Ave., 919/571-4170, http://ncparks.gov, May-Aug. 8am-9pm, Mar.-Apr., Sept.-Oct. 8am-8pm, Nov.-Feb. 8am-6pm, free), between Raleigh and Durham, offers 20 miles of hiking trails, boat rentals in season, and mountain bike trails. The deep forests and creek banks feature flora normally found at higher elevations, including mountain laurel, and are frequented by a variety of wildlife. The Crabtree Creek entrance,

where you'll find the visitors center, is 10 miles northwest of Raleigh off U.S. 70.

If your canoe or kayak is already strapped onto your car and all you need is a place to put in, try the **Neuse River Canoe Trail.** Over a stretch of 17 miles of the Neuse, you can choose from five different launches, beginning at the Falls Lake Dam. Visit www.raleighnc.gov for information on launch sites.

ACCOMMODATIONS

Raleigh is still catching up to other North Carolina cities when it comes to small nonchain hotels. There are dozens of chain motels around the city, concentrated near the airport and downtown, and at various exits off I-40 and U.S. 70. But for individualized service, your best choice in Raleigh is a bed-and-breakfast.

Raleigh's best-known B&B is the ◖ **Oakwood Inn** (411 N. Bloodworth St., 919/832-9712, www.oakwoodinnbb.com, from $140). Housed in the 1871 Raynor-Stronach House, it's listed on the National Register of Historic Places and is one of only four of the original 11 houses remaining in the historic Oakwood neighborhood. If you're hoping to attend a theater production while in Raleigh, the Oakwood can set you up with a special package, subject to availability. Innkeepers Gary and Doris Jurkiewicz have won a slew of awards for the inn's excellence and their hospitality.

Cameron Park Inn (211 Groveland Ave., 919/835-2171 or 888/257-2171, www.cameronparkinn.com, from $139) is a 1916 home in the Cameron Park historic district, located in the NC State-Cameron Village area. The wide porch and lush English garden are mellow retreats after a day in the city.

If you don't need to stay inside the city limits and are craving some pampering, ◖ **Umstead Luxury Hotel and Spa** (100 Woodland Pond, Cary, 866/877-4141, www.theumstead.com, from $299) in Cary shouldn't be missed. The Umstead's 14,000-square-foot spa has an incredible menu of services: 10 different specialized massages; many facial, manicure, and pedicure choices; milk, mineral, and aromatherapy baths; and a long list of body therapies and Asian body-care rituals. There's also a three-acre lake on the property, a 24-hour fitness center, and an outdoor heated pool. Guests have tee privileges at the Prestonwood Country Club, about 10 minutes away.

FOOD
Eclectic American

One of the most popular eateries in the Triangle since the 1970s, **(The Irregardless Café** (901 W. Morgan St., 919/833-8898, www.irregardless.com, lunch Tues.-Fri. 11:30am-2:30pm, dinner Tues.-Thurs. 5:30pm-10:30pm, Fri.-Sat. 5:30pm-10pm, brunch Sun. 10am-2pm, $15-25) began as a strictly vegetarian café, and has since expanded to include omnivorous fare—in fact, most of the entrées are now seafood and chicken dishes, but it still serves some good vegetarian and even vegan chow. From the long list of desserts, try the pear and almond caramelized tart and the vegan chocolate mocha raspberry cake.

Lilly's Pizza (1813 Glenwood Ave., 919/833-0226, www.lillyspizza.com, Sun.-Wed. 11am-10pm, Thurs. 11am-11pm, Fri.-Sat. 11am-midnight, under $10) is a locally owned, one-of-a-kind parlor that's been around for more than 15 years. They use lots of organic local ingredients, even in the homemade crusts. You can choose favorite ingredients for a custom pie, or have an equally tasty calzone, stromboli, or lasagna.

Asian

A popular sushi spot is **Haru Sushi** (2603-155 Glenwood Ave., 919/235-0589, www.harusushiusa.com, lunch Mon.-Fri. 11:30am-2:30pm, dinner Mon.-Fri. 5pm-10pm, Sat. 5pm-11pm, Sun. 5pm-9pm, $10-20), located in Glenwood Village. Also very good is **Sono** (319 Fayetteville St., Suite 101, 919/521-5328, www.sonoraleigh.com, lunch Mon.-Fri. 11am-2pm, dinner Sun.-Thurs. 5pm-10pm, Fri.-Sat. 5pm-11pm, $10-20), with many original sushi rolls as well as bento and noodle dishes.

Middle Eastern

Sitti (137 S. Wilmington St., 919/239-4070, www.sitti-raleigh.com, Mon.-Thurs. 11am-10pm, Fri.-Sat. 11am-midnight, $12-25) derives its name from the Lebanese affectionate nickname for grandmothers, and this Lebanese restaurant draws from the owner-chef's Lebanese family traditions. Chef Ghassan Jarrouj prepares old family recipes, as well as specialties he has developed over his 30-year career, which has included jobs as chef for three U.S. ambassadors in Lebanon. The menu includes kebabs and hearty stews as well as special chef's creations such as pan-seared sea bass.

Southern

Big Ed of **Big Ed's City Market Restaurant** (220 Wolfe St., 919/836-9909, Mon.-Fri. 7am-2pm, Sat. 7am-noon, lunch $10, cash only) has made some remarkable claims about his food over the years—asserting that a Big Ed's breakfast will make a tadpole slap a whale, and that the biscuits alone will empower a poodle to pull a freight train. The joint specializes in pork products—bacon, country ham, barbecue—and in-season regional vegetables. If you visit for breakfast, you'll be able to order the classic Southern breakfast: ham, grits, and biscuits with red-eye gravy.

Greek-American restaurateur families have had a strong influence on Southern cuisine for more than a century, often opening the first restaurants in small towns, and mastering the arts of frying chicken and boiling greens. Raleigh's **Mecca Restaurant** (13 E. Martin St., 919/832-5714, daily 7:30am-7pm) was opened in 1930 by the Dombalis family, and has become such a local institution—particularly a favorite of state government officials and workers—that when it celebrated its 75th anniversary, the whole city celebrated Mecca Restaurant Day. At the Mecca's lunch counter, you can order up most any Southern classic you can think of, including eastern North Carolina barbecue and fried trout as well as the popular hamburgers. There's also assorted Mediterranean fare.

Another such case is the Poniros family's **Roast Grill** (7 S. West St., 919/832-8292,

CENTRAL NORTH CAROLINA

www.roastgrill.com, Mon.-Sat. 11am-4pm, under $5), which has been serving hot dogs since 1940. You can get a hot dog blackened to your specifications, chili, a glass-bottle Coke or beer, pound cake, and baklava.

INFORMATION AND SERVICES

The main hospital in Raleigh is **WakeMed** (3000 New Bern Ave., 919/350-8900), though Rex Healthcare and Duke Health also operate hospitals here. If you have an emergency, call 911 and let the EMTs decide which one is closest. There is at least one 24-hour pharmacy, **CVS** (3914 Capital Blvd., 919/876-5600).

Visitor information can be found at the **Greater Raleigh Convention and Visitors Bureau** (Bank of America Plaza, 421 Fayetteville St., 800/849-8499, www.visitraleigh.com), at the **Capital Area Visitor Information Desk** in the lobby of the Museum of History (5 E. Edenton St., 866/724-8687), the **Greater Raleigh Chamber of Commerce** (800 S. Salisbury St., 919/664-7000, www.raleighchamber.org), and the state **Department of Tourism** (301 N. Wilmington St., 1st Fl., 800/847-4862, www.visitnc.com).

For international travelers, Raleigh-Durham International Airport contains **Travelex** (919/840-0366, Terminal A daily 7am-8pm, Terminal C daily 2:30pm-6pm) outlets.

GETTING THERE AND AROUND

I-40 and U.S. 70 are the main highways to and through town. The Raleigh Beltline, I-440, forms a loop around the city, with I-40, U.S. 70, and U.S. 64 radiating outward. I-40 is the quickest route to Chapel Hill, to the west, and east to I-95. I-40 and U.S. 70 are both good routes to Durham. U.S. 64 goes to Wilson, and on the other side of the city joins with U.S. 1 headed southeast toward Sanford and the Sandhills.

Raleigh-Durham International Airport (RDU, 2400 John Brantley Blvd, Morrisville, 919/840-2123, www.rdu.com) is one of the main airports in North Carolina, and the primary airport in the Triangle. It's located 15 minutes from Raleigh off I-40, and is a hub for major national airlines. There is a Raleigh **Amtrak Station** (320 W. Cabarrus St., 800/872-7245, www.amtrak.com) and a station in Cary (211 N. Academy St.).

Raleigh's **CAT System** (Capital Area Transit, 919/485-7433, www.gotriangle.org) runs buses all over the city, both inside and outside the Beltline, and links readily to other major transportation hubs. Many taxi and driver services are available, including **Yellow Cab** (919/875-1821), **Alliance Concierge** (919/815-6953), and **Blue Diamond Limousines and Sedans** (919/772-9595).

Durham

Home of Duke University and North Carolina Central University (NCCU), Durham is an exciting place. Major arts festivals bring tens of thousands of visitors to Durham every year. Duke University's famous Blue Devils are one of the nation's dominant basketball teams, and NCCU's Eagles are a football powerhouse. There's a great deal of literary activity too, with one of the best selections of bookstores in the region.

DUKE UNIVERSITY

Duke is often thought of as a sort of Southern Ivy League school, and the reputation is justly deserved, for its students are among the academic and athletic elite in the country. The architecture of the Duke campus—much of it designed by turn-of-the-century African American architect Julian Abele—is done up in dark Gothic stonework, and it really does feel like an island transported from some northeastern state. Originally called Trinity College and located in Randolph County, it came to Durham and became Duke University under the auspices of the Duke family, tobacco barons who were also responsible for the university's early policy of admitting women as students.

Duke's **Center for Documentary Studies** (1317 W. Pettigrew St., 919/660-3663, http:// documentarystudies.duke.edu, gallery Mon.- Thurs. 9am-9pm, Fri. 9am-7pm, Sat. 9am- 5pm) is an invaluable resource for artists, documentarians, and educators throughout the region as well as a fascinating place to visit.

The Nasher Museum of Art (2001 Campus Dr., 919/684-5135, www.nasher.duke.edu, Tues.-Wed. and Fri.-Sat. 10am-5pm, Thurs. 10am-9pm, Sun. noon-5pm, $5 adults, $4 seniors, $3 students, free under age 16) is home to extensive collections of ancient and medieval art, including one of the largest collections of pre-Columbian Latin American art in the United States. Adjoining the grounds of the Nasher are the **Sarah P. Duke Gardens** (919/684-3698, www.hr.duke.edu/dukegardens, daily 8am-dusk, free), 55 acres of some of the finest landscaping and horticultural arts to be seen in the Southeast.

Duke's History of Medicine Collections contains antique medical equipment and the nation's largest collection of miniature ivory mannequins. The Collections are closed until fall of 2015. In the lobby of the Mary Duke Biddle Music Building, on East Campus, is the **Eddy Collection of Music Instruments** (Mon.- Fri. 9am-4pm, free), over 500 instruments that date from the last three centuries.

NORTH CAROLINA CENTRAL UNIVERSITY

NCCU was founded in 1910, the first public liberal arts college for African Americans in the United States. Still a predominantly black institution, Central is one of the state's great universities and as important to the history and vitality of the city as Duke, its historically white and much larger neighbor.

The **North Carolina Central University Art Museum** (NCCU campus, Lawson St. between Fine Arts Bldg. and Music Bldg., 919/530-6211, www.nccu.edu/artmuseum, Tues.-Fri. 9am-4:30pm, Sun. 2pm-5pm, free) specializes in the work of 19th- and 20th-century African American artists. The collections include work by such prominent and varied masters as Romare Bearden, Jacob Lawrence, Henry Ossawa Tanner, and Minnie Evans.

Inside the William Jones Building on Central's campus is a display of the Durham **Woolworth lunch counter,** site of a 1960 sit-in attended by Martin Luther King Jr.

Historic Stagville

About 15 minutes north of downtown Durham, **Historic Stagville** (5828 Old Oxford Hwy., 919/620-0120, www.historicstagvillefoundation.org, Tues.-Sat. 10am-4pm, tours hourly 10am-3pm) preserves part of what was a staggeringly large plantation system. The Cameron-Bennehan family's holdings totaled nearly 30,000 acres in 1860, and the 900 enslaved African Americans who worked the land were one of the South's largest enslaved communities. Historic Stagville includes 71 acres of the original plantations, with several notable vernacular structures that include two-story timber-frame slave quarters, a massive hipped-roof barn built in 1860, and the late-18th-century Bennehan plantation house.

OTHER SIGHTS

A different side of 19th-century Durham life is presented at the **Duke Homestead and Tobacco Museum** (2828 Duke Homestead Rd., 919/477-5498, www.dukehomestead. nchistoricsites.org, Tues.-Sat. 9am-6pm, free), where the patriarch of Durham's tobacco industry, Washington Duke, began his career as a humble tobacco farmer. This was the beginning of North Carolina's rise to the top of the world tobacco market.

Bennett Place (4409 Bennett Memorial Rd., 919/383-4345, www.bennettplace.nchistoricsites.org, Tues.-Sat. 9am-5pm, free) is a historic site that commemorates the meeting of Confederate general Joseph Johnston and

CENTRAL NORTH CAROLINA

CENTRAL NORTH CAROLINA

Union general William Tecumseh Sherman in April 1865. In the last days of the Civil War, when Confederate president Jefferson Davis was fleeing south to Georgia and Abraham Lincoln was dead, Johnston and Sherman had a series of negotiations here that led to the surrender of all the Confederate forces in the Carolinas, Georgia, and Florida.

The **North Carolina Museum of Life and Science** (433 Murray Ave., 919/220-5429, www.ncmls.org, Tues.-Sat. 10am-5pm, Sun. noon-5pm, $14 adults, $11 over age 64 and active military, $10 ages 3-12), home of the Magic Wings Butterfly House and Bayer Crop Science Insectarium, is the perfect place for children who enjoy meeting strange bugs, climbing inside tornadoes, and taking a trip on a locomotive to see red wolves.

ENTERTAINMENT AND EVENTS

Full Frame Documentary Festival

April brings the **Full Frame Documentary Festival** (919/687-4100, www.fullframefest. org), which, before it had celebrated its 10th year, had already been identified by the *New*

York Times as the premier documentary film festival in the United States. Venues throughout downtown host screenings, workshops, panels, and soirees, where documentary fans and aspiring filmmakers can mingle with the glitterati of the genre.

Other Festivals

The **Grady Tate Jazz Festival** (www.nccu.edu) takes place in April at North Carolina Central University. North Carolina was home to such jazz legends as Thelonious Monk and John Coltrane, and Central has a widely respected jazz program, so it's only fitting that Durham should host this prestigious event.

For six weeks every summer, Durham is the site of the **American Dance Festival** (ADF, 919/684-6402, www.americandancefestival.org), an internationally known event where the world's best choreographers often premiere new work. Durhamites and the visitors who come from around the world to ADF are one step ahead of the audiences in New York.

One of the region's most popular music festivals is the **Festival for the Eno** (www.enoriver.org), which takes place every Fourth of July weekend. The festival is held on the banks of the Eno River, so you can listen to the performances from the comfort of your inner tube while floating on the river.

August's **North Carolina Gay and Lesbian Film Festival** (www.carolinatheater.org) is the second-largest such event in the Southeast. Approximately 10,000 visitors attend the festival every year to watch new work by up-and-coming LGBT filmmakers at Durham's Carolina Theater.

Nightlife

The **All People's Grill** (6122 Guess Rd., 919/620-9591, www.allpeoplesgrill.com) has been serving Southern soul food and great blues music for generations. While gobbling up on-the-money collard greens and fried chicken, you can hear some of the top blues artists of this region, many of them on the roster of the Music Maker Relief Foundation (www.musicmaker.org), a regional organization that promotes blues musicians to ensure that they are able to make a living playing and so carry on their art. Nowadays it's only open for special events, so check the All People's website for upcoming shows.

Bingo parlors dot the landscape, but Durham is one of the few places where you can be part of the craze that is **Drag Bingo** (www.dragbingo.com, $15 in advance, $17 at the door). Once a month, tickets go on sale—and sell out fast—for a bingo event to benefit area HIV/AIDS services. It's an incredibly fun scene—a mixture of gay and straight, folks in drag and in their usual attire, covetable prizes, a little bit of raunchy humor, and a lot of money going to a great cause.

SHOPPING
Malls and Shopping Districts

Brightleaf Square (Main St. and Gregson St., www.historicbrightleaf.com) occupies handsome circa-1900 warehouses of the American Tobacco Company, which are no longer hives of cigarette rollers but have evolved into the flagship of Durham's post-tobacco-industry revitalization. Over a dozen restaurants now occupy the old industrial bays, side-by-side with diverse and interesting retailers.

The **Streets at Southpoint** (Fayetteville St. at I-40, www.streetsatsouthpoint.com) is a traditional shopping mall with movie theaters and a food court. In addition to the usual anchor department stores and mall chains, Southpoint features a nice selection of upscale clothing shops and has one of only three Apple stores in North Carolina.

Books

The Regulator (720 9th St., 919/286-2700, www.regulatorbookshop.com, Mon.-Sat. 9am-9pm, Sun. 10am-6pm) is one of the Triangle area's favorite bookshops. It hosts readings by important authors from around the world and has a periodicals section that carries a nice and eccentric selection of literary journals and homemade zines.

The Know (2520 Fayetteville St., 919/682-7223) specializes in African American fiction and history as well as Afrocentric literature and philosophy. On Friday night the store bustles with jazz fans who come to hear Yusuf Salim, a legendary Durham pianist.

Wentworth and Leggett Rare Books and Prints (Brightleaf Square, 905 W. Main St., 919/688-5311, www.wentworthleggettbooks. com, Jan.-Oct. Mon.-Sat. 11am-7pm, call for hours Sun. and Nov.-Dec.) is an antiquarian dealer, also specializing in old prints, maps, postcards, and magazines.

SPORTS AND RECREATION
Hiking, Biking, and Water Sports
Durham is loaded with choices for hikers, joggers, and cyclists. The Eno River is surrounded by thousands of acres of parkland, much of which is marked for hiking. **Eno River State Park** (6101 Cole Mill. Rd., 919/383-1686, http://ncparks.gov, May-Aug. 8am-9pm, Mar.-Apr., Sept.-Oct., 8am-8pm, Nov.-Feb. 8am-6pm, free), northwest of Durham, offers hiking, canoeing (Class I-III rapids), and camping ($13) in the beautiful and wild river valley. See the Eno River Association website (www.enoriver.org) for information on more places and ways to enjoy the river. **Frog Hollow Canoe and Kayak** (919/949-4315, www.frog-hollowoutdoors.com, Wed.-Fri. 10am-6pm, Sat.-Sun. 9am-6:30pm, by reservation only) rents boats and guides tours. During the warm months, you have the leisurely option of **Wafting the Eno** (919/471-3802, www.wafter. org, $12, reservations required). These guided float trips take off from West Point Park daily at 10am and 3:30pm, and at 9pm when there's a full moon.

Spectator Sports
Thanks to the exploits of a demon and a smoke-snorting steer, Durham is probably even better known for its sports tradition than its history as a tobacco dynamo. The National Collegiate Athletic Association (NCAA) Division I **Duke Blue Devils** embody the gold standard in college basketball, and excel in many other sports. Their history is chronicled in the **Duke Sports Hall of Fame** (Towerview Rd., 919/613-7500),

inside Cameron Indoor Stadium. Coach Mike Krzyzewski—that's pronounced "shuh-SHEV-skee," but you can call him Coach K—has shepherded the men's basketball team since 1980, leading them to a phenomenal number of championships. His resemblance to the Duke mascot is equally phenomenal. Duke has turned out some of the greatest basketball players of the last 20 years, including Grant Hill, Christian Laettner, and J. J. Reddick. Not surprisingly, it is extremely difficult to come by Duke basketball tickets.

Duke students are famous for living in tents for months on end outside Cameron Indoor Stadium, waiting first to buy tickets and then to snag good standing-room spots in the courtside student section of the arena. If you're on campus in season, take a look at their tent city, known as Krzyzewskiville. (Beware: it's not for the Carolina-blue at heart. There are as many anti-Tar Heel banners in Krzyzewskiville as there are textbooks.) If you're lucky enough to get into a game, you'll have the treat—or trauma, depending on your loyalties—of seeing the "Cameron Crazies" in the flesh. These Duke fans, often half-naked and painted blue like Picts, are known far and wide for their creative, funny, and sometimes edgy chants and heckles.

The **Durham Bulls** (Durham Bulls Athletic Park, 409 Blackwell St., 919/956-2855, www. durhambulls.com)—yes, of "Bull Durham" fame—are one of the nation's most recognizable minor-league baseball teams. They are the Triple-A farm team for the Tampa Bay Devil Rays, so you're likely to see big-league players rehabbing from injury and rookies on the brink of making it big. The ballpark, designed by the architect who built Baltimore's Camden Yards, is comfortable and fun. A big wooden bull peers down from the end of the third-base line, and when a Bull hits a homer, the bull's eyes light up red, his tail flaps, and smoke billows from his nostrils.

ACCOMMODATIONS
The most upscale place to stay in Durham is the **Washington Duke Inn and Golf Club**

(3001 Cameron Blvd., 800/443-3853, www.washingtondukeinn.com, from $130). Located on the grounds of the Duke University Golf Course, on the Duke campus, the guest rooms and suites are sunny and plush, with the option of bunk beds for families traveling with kids. Babysitting services can be arranged by the concierge. Also convenient to the Duke campus, the **University Inn** (502 Elf St., 919/286-3817 or 800/313-3585, www.universityinnduke.com, from $70) is a basic motel, a good value in a good location.

Durham's most celebrated bed-and-breakfast is the **(Arrowhead Inn** (106 Mason Rd., 800/528-2207, http://arrowheadinn.com, from $135), a AAA Four Diamond awardee on a Revolutionary-era plantation about 15 minutes from downtown. All of the very luxurious guest rooms have their own fireplaces, and several have two-person whirlpools. On the inn's grounds are a garden cottage, with a whirlpool and two-person steam shower, and a rather fabulous log cabin with a sleeping loft and spa-like bath appointments.

The **Old North Durham Inn** (922 N. Mangum St., 919/683-1885, www.bbonline.com, from $110) is a pretty house on one of the old primary roads in the city. It's been cited by the Durham Historic Preservation Society for its excellent renovation. Guests receive free tickets to Durham Bulls games, and can look out their bedroom windows across the street at the home where much of *Bull Durham* was filmed.

FOOD
Eclectic American
(Watts Grocery (1116 Broad St., 919/416-5040, www.wattsgrocery.com, entrées $14-20), located in the Watts neighborhood of Durham, near the Duke campus, is the restaurant of Amy Tornquist, a master Southern chef. The menu features locally grown produce in season, North Carolina seafood, and local artisanal cheeses. The menu features many gourmet variations on classic North Carolina dishes and is bound to please any fan of Southern food.

The **(Cosmic Cantina** (1920 Perry St.,

919/286-1875, Mon. noon-4am, Tues.-Fri. 11am-3am, Sat. noon-4am, Sun. noon-midnight, under $10), a casual take-out-or-seat-yourself joint in the middle of the 9th Street neighborhood by the Duke campus, serves the best burritos you'll find just about anywhere. The friend who introduced me to it preaches that a first visit to the Cantina is a life-changing experience.

The award-winning restaurant **Nana's** (2514 University Dr., 919/493-8545, www.nanasdurham.com, Mon.-Sat. 5:30pm-10pm, $18-30) is presided over by chef Scott Howell, a North Carolina native. The fare is hearty but elegant, and the wine list has won *Wine Spectator*'s Award of Excellence. Vegetarian pickings are slim, but carnivores will be well satisfied.

Asian
The **(Thai Café** (2501 University Dr., 919/493-9794, www.thaicafenc.com, Mon.-Thurs. 11:30am-3pm, 5pm-10pm, Fri. 11:30am-3pm, 5pm-11pm, Sat. noon-11pm, Sun. noon-10pm, $10-20) is the sort of restaurant whose regulars might visit a dozen times before they'll try a second item on the menu, because whatever they tried on that first visit was so good they've been craving it ever since. The Thai Café serves all of the classic Thai restaurant dishes like pad thai, tom yum, and pad prik—all delicious—but the real masterpieces are the curries. You can choose among yellow, green, panang, and massaman with meat, seafood, tofu, or vegetables. One warning: "not spicy" at Thai Café means incredibly spicy. If you want mild food, you'll need to make a special point of it to the server.

Latin American
A new star of Durham's food scene is **Dos Perros** (200 N. Mangum St., 919/956-2750, http://dosperrosrestaurant.com, breakfast Mon.-Fri. 7:30am-10:30am, lunch Mon.-Fri. 11:30am-2:30pm, dinner Mon.-Sat. 5pm-10:30pm, entrées $10-18), located in the heart of downtown. Try the pork roasted in banana leaves or the spice-rubbed grouper. There are also good vegetarian entrées. **Cuban**

CAROLINA BREADS

The following catalog of Tar Heel taste in baked goods appeared in the 1955 *North Carolina Guide*.

Outside of baker's bread, Tar Heels like (in an ascending scale from plain to fancy) cornbread, ashcakes, hoecakes, johnnycakes, cracklin' bread, potato bread, soda biscuits, buttermilk biscuits, rolls, muffins, popovers that pop, buckwheat cakes, eggbread or batterbread (called "spoonbread" in Virginia), bland Sally Lunn and flaky beaten biscuits; the last two are company bread.

The 1955 list should be updated for the 21st century's multiethnic and multinational culinary culture in North Carolina to include tortillas (there are dozens of *tortillerías* around the state), *papadum*, roti, chapati, naan, baguettes, madeleines, biscotti, pita, bagels, challah, matzo, and *banh mi*.

Revolution (318 Blackwell St., 919/687-4300, www.thecubanrevolution.com, Fri.-Sat. 11am-2am, Sun.-Thurs. 11am-midnight, entrées $10-16) is another new arrival to Durham. Decorated with portraits of revolutionaries and trappings of circa-1959 Cuba, this restaurant serves classic Cuban dishes like ropa vieja and Cuban sandwiches as well as new inventions like the shrimp and maduro kebab. **Blue Corn** (716 9th St., 919/286-9600, www.bluecorncafedurham.com, Mon.-Thurs. 11:30am-9pm, Fri.-Sat. 11:30am-9:30pm, $12-15) is an award-winning pan-Latin restaurant. The menu includes Mexican favorites like fajitas and quesadillas, Cuban specialties like picadillo, and plenty of vegetarian choices.

Durham is busting out with wonderful Latin American restaurants and taco stands, more every year as the number of Latin American residents in the area swells. A local favorite is **La**

Vaquita (2700 Chapel Hill Rd., 919/402-0209, http://lavaquitanc.com, daily 10am-9:30pm, $5-10), a little building with an outdoor walk-up counter and a huge fiberglass cow on the roof. It's very authentic Mexican cuisine, with many kinds of tacos, stews, tamales, ribs, *barbacoa,* and lots more. Just a few blocks away is the **Azteca Grill** (1929 Chapel Hill Rd., 919/403-2527, daily 11am-9pm, $10), where the food is also great. Its highest recommendation comes from the clientele: At the lunch hour, the dining room fills with Latin American working men, clearly happy to find a taste of home in North Carolina.

European

Best known as a bakery and patisserie, **Guglhupf** (2706 Durham-Chapel Hill Blvd., 919/401-2600, www.guglhupf.com, breakfast Tues.-Fri. 8am-11am, lunch Tues.-Fri. 11am-4:30pm, dinner Tues.-Thurs. 5:30pm-9:30pm, Fri.-Sat. 5:30pm-10pm, brunch Sat. 8am-4:30pm, Sun. 9am-3pm, dessert Sun. 3pm-5pm, $10-20) is also a wonderful café. Guglhupf's founder is from southern Germany, and the menu is based on that cuisine, with forays into other continental and American styles. Even if you don't have time for a full sit-down meal, do stop in here for dessert, or to pick up a pastry or artisanal bread for the road.

INFORMATION AND SERVICES

Duke University Medical Center (2301 Erwin Rd., 919/416-3853) is the main hospital in Durham. **Durham Regional Hospital** (3643 N. Roxboro Rd., 919/470-4000) is also operated by Duke Health Systems. **Walgreens** (6405 Fayetteville St., 919/544-6430) has a 24-hour pharmacy.

Information for travelers is available from the **Durham Convention and Visitors Bureau** (101 E. Morgan St., 800/446-8604, www.durham-nc.com). The *Durham Herald-Sun* is the primary Durham-specific newspaper, though many people also read the Raleigh *News & Observer*. The *Independent* is a popular weekly cultural newspaper, available free throughout the region.

GETTING THERE AND AROUND

Information about the Triangle's extensive network of **buses and shuttles** can be found at www.ridetta.org. **Raleigh-Durham International Airport** (RDU, 2400 John Brantley Blvd, Morrisville, 919/840-2123, www.rdu.com) is 10-20 minutes from Durham, reachable by an easy cab or shuttle ride. **Amtrak** (400 W. Chapel Hill St., 800/872-7245, www.amtrak.com, daily 7am-9pm) has direct service to Durham on the *Carolinian* line, pulling in to the station in the heart of downtown.

Chapel Hill and Vicinity

The third corner of the Triangle is occupied by Chapel Hill. The University of North Carolina is the heart of the town, but the approximately 50,000 permanent residents, many of them former UNC students who grew so attached to Chapel Hill that they decided to stay, maintain a stimulating community in which the arts thrive. Singer James Taylor, blues guitarist Elizabeth Cotten, and the Squirrel Nut Zippers are among the many Chapel Hill area natives who have gone on to wider fame in the musical world.

The Chapel Hill area is the epicenter of progressive politics in North Carolina, most intensely concentrated in the emphatically left-wing little nearby town of Carrboro, which is so closely linked to Chapel Hill—it's difficult to tell exactly which block of Franklin Street and Main Street demarcates their respective city limits—that they're often treated as if they were one town. Carrboro was North Carolina's first municipality to elect an out gay mayor.

CENTRAL NORTH CAROLINA

© AVALON TRAVEL

CENTRAL NORTH CAROLINA

SIGHTS
University of North Carolina

The University of North Carolina campus, which dates to 1789, is made up of a couple of beautiful quads surrounded by many outlying complexes. Massive poplar trees on the quads make the campus an indulgently shady hideaway during the 100°F weather of a central Carolina summer. Elegantly unpretentious federal-style buildings were dorms and classrooms for 18th- and 19th-century scholars, and they're home to undergraduates today. Guided tours of the historic sites on campus depart from the UNC **Visitors Center** (250 E. Franklin St., 919/962-1630, www.unc.edu) Monday-Friday at 1:30pm. You can also pick up a brochure and walk through campus at your own pace.

The 1851 Old Playmakers Theater, at East Cameron Avenue in the middle of campus, was built by Alexander Jackson Davis, originally intended as a library and ballroom. In the 1920s the university converted the building to a theater.

At **Kenan Football Stadium** (Bell Tower Dr., off South Rd., 919/966-2575, www.tarheelblue.com), the **Charlie Justice Hall of Honors** chronicles the doughty deeds of UNC's football program. It's open Monday-Friday 8am-5pm and for three hours on home-game days until half an hour before kickoff.

The **Ackland Art Museum** (919/966-5736, www.ackland.org, Wed.-Sat. 10am-5pm, Sun. 1pm-5pm, free), at the heart of the UNC campus near the intersection of Franklin and Columbia Streets, has a very special collection of European sculpture and painting spanning centuries, and an acclaimed collection of Asian art. The **North Carolina Collection Gallery** (919/962-1172, www.lib.unc.edu, Mon.-Fri. 9am-5pm, Sat. 9am-1pm, Sun. 1pm-5pm, free), on the ground floor of Wilson Library, is a cozy museum that will capture the fancy of any Southern history enthusiast.

◖ Carolina Basketball Museum

While on campus, visit the **Carolina Basketball Museum** (Ernie Williamson Athletic Center, 450 Skipper Bowles Dr., www.tarheelblue.com, Mon.-Fri. 10am-4pm, closes 1 hour before weekday games, opens 3.5 hours before and closes 1 hour before weekend games, free), a new addition to the roster of campus attractions. This multimillion-dollar 8,000-square-foot hagiological shrine holds mementos from a century of Carolina basketball. On a reproduction of the Heels' court, footprints and even players' actual shoes mark the spots from which some of the program's most memorable baskets were launched. There's a lot of video and interactive content, but the item most likely to please the Tar Heel faithful, and inspire hoots of derision, is a letter from Duke coach Mike Krzyzewski to a high school player from Wilmington, expressing his regret that the young man had chosen to attend UNC rather than Duke. The addressee was famed basketball player Michael Jordan.

Other Museums

Across Franklin Street from the main quad is **Kidzu** (105 E. Franklin St., 919/933-1455, www.kidzuchildrensmuseum.org, Tues.-Sat. 10am-5pm, Sun. 1pm-5pm, $5), a children's museum that features imaginative interactive exhibits for kids to explore, as well as a fun gift shop.

Nostalgic College Spots

Every college town has a few emblematic hangouts—joints that would seem like no great shakes to the uninitiated, but that to generations of alumni are charged with nostalgia. At UNC, these icons are the **Carolina Coffee Shop** (138 E. Franklin St., 919/942-6875, Tues.-Thurs. 11am-9pm, Fri. 11am-10pm, Sat. 9am-10 pm, Sun. 9am-2pm) and **Sutton's Drug Store** (159 E. Franklin St., 919/942-5161). The Carolina Coffee Shop, a dark, soporific retreat, has been the site of thousands of first dates over the last 90 years. It's a place to have an afternoon breakfast if you've been up studying all night, or to inhale a sandwich before heading across Franklin to a movie at the Carolina Theater. At night, the liquor license kicks in and it becomes a busy bar. Across the street is Sutton's Drug Store, a good place to catch a glimpse of members of the basketball team, who often stop here between classes. An old-time small-town drugstore, Sutton's has a greasy-spoon burger-and-fries lunch counter, and a tiny prescription window at the back staffed by a benevolent druggist who knows everyone's name (and knew their parents too).

Weaver Street Market

Weaver Street Market (WSM, 101 E. Weaver St., 919/929-0010, www.weaverstreetmarket. coop, Mon.-Fri. 7:30am-9pm, Sat.-Sun. 8am-9pm) is the community hub of the politically liberal, artistically active, and often quite eccentric residents of Carrboro. WSM is an organic foods co-op with a small eating area—it's too plain to be called a café—inside and on the front lawn. On a pretty day, the lawn is jam-packed with families and college students eating locally grown food and listening to local bluegrass, old-time mountain, punk, or perhaps Hare Krishna musicians.

ENTERTAINMENT AND EVENTS
Movies

Like a good college town should, Chapel Hill has several movie theaters, including small theaters that show independent films. The **Varsity Theater** (123 E. Franklin St., 919/967-8665) is on the edge of campus, and the **Chelsea** (1129 Weaver Dairy Rd., 919/968-3005) and the **Movies at Timberlyne** (120 Banks Dr., 919/933-8600) are in the Timberlyne shopping center, up Highway 86 (Columbia Rd./Martin Luther King Jr. Dr.). The **Lumina Theater** (620 Market St., 919/932-9000, www.thelumina.com) is located in Southern Village, a development south of Chapel Hill on U.S. 15/501. The Lumina screens movies outdoors on summer evenings.

Nightlife
LIVE MUSIC

Chapel Hill-Carrboro is one of the best places in the Southeast to hear live music, and several small top-notch clubs here are legendary venues where major artists not only get their starts but

return to again and again. The best known is probably the **Cat's Cradle** (300 E. Main St., Carrboro, 919/967-9053, www.catscradle.com). The artists who play the Cat's Cradle are leading lights in rock and roll, Americana, alt-country, and world music, and the audiences come to hear the music, not to play pool and shoot the breeze. Shows sell out quickly, so check the website. **Local 506** (506 W. Franklin St., Chapel Hill, 919/942-5506, www.local506.com) and the **Cave** (452½ W. Franklin St., Chapel Hill, 919/968-9308, http://caverntavern.com, no advance tickets) are also important local venues, tending more toward pop, rock, and punk. Note that to attend shows at Local 506, you must first join the club; membership is only $3, but it has to be arranged at least three days in advance.

BEER AND WINE BARS

You have other options if you want to go out for a drink but haven't planned your barhopping three days in advance. The **West End Wine Bar** (450 W. Franklin St., Chapel Hill, 919/967-7599, www.westendwinebar.com, daily 5pm-2am) has a great rooftop patio, over 100 by-the-glass wines, and lots of "boutique beers." **He's Not Here** (112½ W. Franklin St., Chapel Hill, 919/942-7939, daily 1pm-2am) has been a hot spot since 1975. There's good live rock and roll with a low cover charge. **Caffe Driade** (1215-A E. Franklin St., Chapel Hill, 919/942-2333, www.caffedriade.com, Mon.-Thurs. 7am-11pm, Fri.-Sat. 7am-midnight, Sun. 7:30am-11pm), an elegant little coffee shop in the woods off East Franklin Street, serves wine and beer as well as caffeine and pastries, and in the warm months they have live outdoor music on Wednesday, Friday, and Saturday evenings.

SHOPPING
Malls and Shopping Districts

University Mall (Estes Dr. between Franklin St. and Fordham Blvd./U.S. 15/501) is gradually evolving from a small 1970s-style mall to a collection of fancy boutiques and commercial art galleries. There are still a few fast-food counters and a discount shoe outlet or two, but these shops are being replaced by upscale jewelry and lingerie stores. Stop in at **Cameron's** (919/942-5554, www.camerons-gallery.com) for pretty one-of-a-kind jewelry and funky stationery, as well as sushi-shaped wind-up toys, librarian action figures, and other comical doodads. University Mall is anchored at its southern terminus by **A Southern Season** (800/253-3663, www.southernseason.com, Mon.-Fri. 10am-9pm, Sun. 11am-6pm), probably the region's most famous specialty foods retailer. With a strong emphasis on local and regional delicacies, Southern Season has a spectacular variety of gourmet foods and fine cookware.

Books

Along Franklin Street, which becomes Carrboro's Main Street a few blocks west of campus, you'll find the usual college-town mix of textbook-exchanges, all-night convenience stores, and purveyors of sustainably crafted fair-trade bongs. There are also a handful of chichi women's clothing shops, trendy vintage-wear boutiques, and some great bookstores. Among the best in this last category is **The Book Shop** (400 W. Franklin St., 919/942-5178, www.bookshopinc.com, Mon.-Fri. 11am-9pm, Sat. 11am-6pm, Sun. 1pm-5pm), a wonderful used and rare book dealer, where you can find a $5 paperback classic or a $1,000 rare first edition. **Internationalist Books** (405 W. Franklin St., 919/942-1740, www.internationalistbooks. org, Mon.-Sat. 11am-8pm, Sun. 11am-6pm) is the area's best-known source for far-left-of-center political and philosophical literature and a hangout for progressive activists. **Nice Price Books** (100 Boyd St., Carrboro, 919/929-6222) sells good secondhand books and music, including a good selection of used vinyl.

SPORTS AND RECREATION
Botanical Gardens

UNC's **North Carolina Botanical Garden** (Old Mason Farm Rd., off U.S. 15/501/Hwy. 54, 919/962-0522, www.ncbg.unc.edu, Mon.-Fri. 8am-5pm, Sat. 9am-5pm, Sun. 1pm-5pm)

is the Southeast's largest botanical garden. The 800 acres contain beautiful hiking trails, a herb garden, an aquatic plant area, and a carnivorous plant garden. Back on campus, **Coker Arboretum** (E. Cameron St. and Raleigh St., daily dawn-dusk) is much smaller, but it's also a beautiful retreat. The five landscaped acres are most beautiful in springtime, when students will make detours on their way to class just to pass through the amazing 300-foot-long arbor of purple wisteria.

Spectator Sports

Tar Heel athletics (www.tarheelblue.com) are well loved in Chapel Hill. The pinnacle of UNC sports is the men's basketball team—six-time NCAA Champions, coached for many years by the legendary Dean Smith and now by fellow Hall of Famer Roy Williams, and college home court to Michael Jordan, James Worthy, Lennie Rosenbluth, and a dizzying number of other all-time-great basketball players. The men play at the Dean E. Smith Center on Skipper Bowles Road, a great glowing dome that seats more than 20,000. Carolina women's basketball is also of the highest caliber. Coached by Sylvia Hatchell, a member of the Women's Basketball Hall of Fame, the Tar Heel women play at historic Carmichael Auditorium in the heart of campus. (When the women play Duke at home, their biggest game of the year, they move over to the much larger Smith Center.) Coach Butch Davis leads the football team, whose home field is the 1927 Kenan Stadium. The baseball team plays at Boshamer Stadium, which, like the Smith Center and Kenan Stadium, is off Manning Drive in the southern part of campus, in the area of the Medical School. UNC excels in many other sports—soccer (Mia Hamm is an alumna), golf (Davis Love III), track (Marion Jones), among others.

Acquiring tickets to UNC athletic events ranges from impossible to quite easy, with men's basketball tickets at the most precious end of the spectrum, followed by football and women's basketball. For all other tickets, try your luck with the main ticket office (800/722-4335, www.tarheelblue.com). Craigslist (www.craigslist.org) and eBay (www.ebay.com) are often reliable sources as well.

ACCOMMODATIONS
Under $150
Chapel Hill has a handful of motels where guest rooms usually run $80-100. The **Days Inn** (1312 N. Fordham Blvd./U.S. 15/501, 919/929-3090, www.daysinn.com), **Holiday Inn** (1301 N. Fordham Blvd./U.S. 15/501, 919/929-2171, www.hichapelhill.com), and **Hampton Inn** (6121 Farrington Rd., 919/403-8700, www.hamptoninn.com) are all in convenient and safe neighborhoods. None is within walking distance of campus, but campus is only a very brief drive or bus ride (remember, buses are free here).

$150-300
One of the favorite inns in the state, the **Carolina Inn** (211 Pittsboro St., 800/962-8519, www.carolinainn.com, from $180) has been a landmark on the UNC campus since it first opened in 1924. It's the place where visiting dignitaries are hosted, where the most important faculty functions take place, where lucky couples get married, and where old alumni couples celebrate their milestone anniversaries. The Carolina Inn is located at the center of the UNC campus, between the original quads and the modern medical school complexes, and not far from the Dean Smith Center. Any special occasion related to the university will book the Carolina Inn far in advance—homecoming weekends, for example, and big basketball and football games. The Inn's restaurant, **Carolina CrossRoads** (919/918-2735, $20-30), serves three elegant meals a day, created by chef Jimmy Reale, a believer in creative cuisine from local ingredients. Afternoon tea (Mon.-Sat. 3pm, $18-28) at the Carolina Inn is a popular treat in Chapel Hill; reservations are recommended.

The **Franklin Hotel** (311 W. Franklin St., 866/831-5999, www.franklinhotelnc.com, from $200) is a boutique hotel with a great location on Franklin Street near where Chapel Hill and Carrboro blend together. The furnishings are elegant and the beds extremely comfortable. Guest rooms have great modern touches like flat-screen TVs and iPod docks.

The **Inn at Bingham School** (Hwy. 54 and Mebane Oaks Rd., near Saxapahaw, 800/566-5583, www.chapel-hill-inn.com, rooms $150, cottage $195) is a 200-year-old home, originally the residence of the headmaster of the preparatory academy that operated here in the 18th and 19th centuries. The house sits in a region of sweeping countryside, near the little town of Saxapahaw, about 20 minutes outside Chapel Hill. Innkeepers Francois and Christina Deprez are renowned hosts and chefs whose talents shine in this beautiful setting.

FOOD
Southern and Soul
Crook's Corner (610 W. Franklin St., 919/929-7643, www.crookscorner.com, dinner Tues.-Sun. 5:30pm, brunch Sun. 10:30am-2pm, $15-20), is one of the most influential restaurants in the South. It was the late Bill Eliot, its first chef, who put this restaurant on the culinary map with, among other brilliant creations, his now world-famous shrimp and grits recipe. Now led by chef Bill Smith, a native Tar Heel whose simple yet exquisite recipes—including watermelon and tomato salad, honeysuckle sorbet, and some of the best fried green tomatoes you'll ever find—Crook's Corner continues to be a great innovator in Southern cuisine.

Just a few blocks from Crook's Corner is another legendary Carolina chef's restaurant, **Mama Dip's Kitchen** (408 W. Rosemary St., 919/942-5837, www.mamadips.com, Mon.-Sat. 8am-9:30pm, Sun. 8am-9pm, $10-12). Proprietress Mildred Council, "Mama Dip" herself, has been cooking since she was nine years old, and if you grew up in the South, you'll recognize at first bite the comfort-food recipes of a Southern matriarch. Dip's is known for its good fried chicken and for its vegetables. In soul food, the vegetable sides are not an afterthought but an art in their own right. Vegetarians, be sure to ask your server which vegetable dishes are vegetarian; as is the old-time way, Dip's greens and beans sometimes conceal a zest of pork fatback.

Eclectic American

La Residence (202 W. Rosemary St., 919/967-2506, www.laresidencedining.com, Tues.-Sun. 6pm-9:30pm, late menu and bar daily 9:30pm-2am, $20-25) has been a Chapel Hill favorite, though in different locations, for nearly 35 years. La Residence has an elegant continental-inspired menu created by chef Stephen Amos and delicious desserts by pastry chef Jill Lazarus.

Carrboro's **Glasshalfull** (106 S. Greensboro St., Carrboro, 919/967-9784, http://glasshalfullcarrboro.com, lunch Mon.-Fri. 11:30am-2:30pm, dinner Mon.-Sat. 5pm-10pm, late menu Fri.-Sat. after 10pm, $10-30) is equal parts restaurant and wine bar. The menu of contemporary American fare makes use of local ingredients and offers vegetarians plenty of good choices.

A special treat for Triangle diners is **Sage** (Timberlyne Shopping Center, 1129 Weaver Dairy Rd., Chapel Hill, 919/968-9266, Mon.-Thurs. 11:30am-2:30pm, 5pm-9pm, Fri.-Sat. 11:30am-2:30pm, 5pm-10pm, around $20), a vegetarian and vegan restaurant that draws at least as many omnivores as hard-core veggies. The proprietress is originally from Iran, where she learned to cook, and Sage's beautiful dishes are a fusion of classic Persian cooking and modern vegetarian haute cuisine. Try the pomegranate soup and the appetizer platter in addition to the can't-miss entrées.

Asian

Lantern (423 W. Franklin St., 919/969-8846, http://lanternrestaurant.com, Mon.-Sat. 5:30pm-10pm, bar Mon.-Sat. until 2am, $15-25) was named one of America's top 50 restaurants by *Gourmet Magazine*. The pan-Asian menu draws from fresh locally raised meats and North Carolina-caught seafood. The meals may be exotic, but the ingredients are down-home.

Local Fare

The **Carrboro Farmers' Market** (301 W. Main St., http://carrborofarmersmarket.com, Sat. 7am-noon, Wed. 3:30pm-6:30pm) is a bustling, festive scene. The market features local organic produce in abundance as well as gorgeous cut flowers, artisanal cheeses, and charmingly cuckoo lawn art.

The Chapel Hill area is blessed with a local dairy, which supplies residents not only with old-fashioned bottled milk but with fantastic ice cream. To sample Mapleview Ice Cream, you have two choices beyond the freezer aisle of the grocery store. At the Carrboro **Mapleview Store** (100 E. Weaver St., 919/967-6842), you can pick up a cone or cup to eat while you listen to one of the free concerts on the lawn of Weaver Street Market, directly across the street. Alternatively, you might choose to make the scenic drive to the home store (3111 Dairyland Rd., 919/933-3600, www.mapleviewfarm.com, daily noon-10pm), out in the country toward Hillsborough, where you can linger over your ice cream on the front porch, surrounded by beautiful farmland of Orange County.

GETTING THERE AND AROUND

Chapel Hill can be reached via the major highways, I-40 and I-85, as well as by U.S. 15/501, from Durham to the east and Pittsboro to the southwest.

Winston-Salem

The village of Salem was established in the mid-18th century by the Unitas Fratrum, better known as the Moravians, a community of Protestants from Europe who migrated to the Americas and eventually into the hills of North Carolina.

The Winston part of Winston-Salem was founded as the seat of Forsyth County, and through the 19th and early 20th centuries it boomed as an industrial and trading hub, fed by what seemed for generations an endless stream of tobacco and textile money. Although the textile mills are nearly all gone in North Carolina, and the cigarette industry sputters along in fits and starts, Winston-Salem is still alive and well as a banking center and the home of Wake Forest University, Winston-Salem State University, and other important educational institutions.

SIGHTS
◖ Old Salem

Though nestled in the center of a modern city, **Old Salem** (900 Old Salem Rd., 888/653-7253, www.oldsalem.org, Tues.-Sat. 9:30am-4:30pm, Sun. 1pm-4:30pm, $23 adults, $11 children) was once a bustling independent village that was home to the industrious Moravians. That era is now recreated in the streets and homes of the old village, where costumed interpreters reconstruct the old Moravian ways and continue to make expertly crafted goods prized by fellow Carolinians.

Old Salem is also home to three museums, each a gem, and all housed in the Horton Museum Center. The **Museum of Early Southern Decorative Arts** (924 S. Main St., www.mesda.org, Tues.-Sat. 10am-4pm, Sun. 1pm-4pm, admission cost varies) recreates 24 period rooms and six galleries to display the furniture, paintings, fabrics, and other distinctive decorative arts of the old South, representing the years between 1670 and approximately 1850 in the Lowcountry, Chesapeake, and Backcountry regions.

Museums

Winston-Salem's multitude of museums represent art of many places and centuries. **The Southeastern Center for Contemporary Art** (750 Marguerite Dr., 336/725-1904, www.secca.org, Tues.-Wed. and Fri.-Sat. 10am-5pm, Thurs. 10am-8pm, Sun. 1pm-5pm, free) hosts changing exhibits of stimulating modern work in a variety of media. The **Reynolda House Museum of American Art** (2250 Reynolda Rd., 888/663-1149, www.reynoldahouse.org, Tues.-Sat. 9:30am-4:30pm, Sun. 1:30pm-4:30pm, last entry 4pm, $14 adults, free students and under age 18) has a distinguished collection of American masterpieces from colonial times through the present day. The **Diggs Gallery** (601 S. Martin Luther King Dr., 336/750-2458, www.wssu.edu, Tues.-Sat. 11am-5pm, free) at Winston-Salem State University has excellent permanent and changing exhibitions of work by African and African American artists, with a particular emphasis on North Carolina and the Southeast.

SciWorks, the Science and Environmental Museum of Forsyth County (400 W. Hanes Mill Rd., 336/767-6730, www.sciworks.org, Tues.-Fri. 10am-4pm, Sat. 10am-5pm, Sun. noon-5pm, $11 adults, $9 ages 3-19 and over age 62) was named one of the top 25 science museums by *Parents Magazine*. Here children can pet horseshoe crabs, play a floor piano with their feet, brush giant teeth, and learn about physics and biology.

A very different kind of gallery is the **Winston Cup Museum** (1355 N. Martin Luther King Dr., 336/724-4557, www.winstoncupmuseum.com, Tues.-Sat. 10am-5pm, $8 adults, $4 ages 5-12, free under age 5), which chronicles R. J. Reynolds' 33-year sponsorship of NASCAR. (There can be

CENTRAL NORTH CAROLINA

no more Carolinian combination than cigarettes and stock cars.) Here you'll see cars driven by Dale Senior and Dale Junior (as the Earnhardts are known in these parts), drivers' helmets, winners' checks, and other great racing memorabilia.

Historic Bethabara Park

In northern Winston-Salem, **Historic Bethabara Park** (2147 Bethabara Rd., 336/924-8191, www.bethabarapark.com, guided tours Apr.-Nov. Tues.-Fri. 10:30am-4:30pm, Sat.-Sun. 1:30pm-4:30pm, $4

adults, $1 children) explores an even earlier period of Moravian settlement than that of Salem. Bethabara was the first foothold of the Moravians in North Carolina. The 15 original settlers and the other Moravians who would soon join them constructed a sturdy, attractive little village in a very brief few years.

By the late 1760s the construction of Salem was underway, and the population of Bethabara gradually began to decline. The village mill and distillery remained in operation for some decades, but by the early 19th century Bethabara had become a small farming community, and

CENTRAL NORTH CAROLINA

Salem, to the south, became the Moravian metropolis.

Körner's Folly

Without a doubt, one of the most unforgettably strange places in North Carolina is **Körner's Folly** (413 S. Main St., 336/996-7922, www.kornersfolly.org, Thurs.-Sat. 10am-4pm, Sun. 1pm-4pm, $10 adults, $6 ages 5-16, free under age 5), located east of Winston-Salem in Kernersville. The seven-level house with 22 rooms of insanely ornate frippery and eccentric architectural contraptions fits all the requirements of the classic Victorian monstrosity. But it's no monstrosity, as it turns out; the peculiarities make it oddly, somewhat awkwardly, beautiful. In its late-1870s infancy, Körner's Folly was intended not as a home but a display of designer Jule Körner's architectural innovations, a house of showrooms for his clients to tour. Little by little it also became Körner's home.

ENTERTAINMENT AND EVENTS
Performing Arts

The **Piedmont Opera** (336/725-7101, www.piedmontopera.org, $15-70) is a 30-year-old company that presents several operas each season, with a special emphasis on classic Italian opera. Now more than 60 years old, the **Winston-Salem Symphony's** (336/725-1035, www.wssymphony.org, $15-60) performance schedule includes a variety of music, from baroque to pop.

Events

Starting at midnight and lasting into the early hours of Easter Sunday every year, **roving brass bands** play throughout the city, in a tradition that the Moravians of Salem practiced 200 years ago and that remains an important part of Easter worship. The bands' "rounds," as they're called, always begin with Bach's "Sleepers, Wake," a composition that was brand-new when the first Moravian band was organized in Saxony.

April brings the **RiverRun Film Festival** (336/724-1502, www.riverrunfilm.com), one of the largest film festivals in the Southeast. The festival is a great opportunity to see the work of both established and emerging filmmakers, and to attend workshops and panels about the art and business of moviemaking.

In June at the **North Carolina Wine Festival** (www.ncwinefestival.com), you can sample prize wines from dozens of vineyards across the state, from the sandy lowlands to steep mountainsides, and from the famously fertile Yadkin Valley, a short drive from Winston-Salem. The festival is held just outside the city in Clemmons, southwest of Winston-Salem on I-40.

The end of July and beginning of August is time for the **National Black Theater Festival** (336/723-2266, www.nbtf.org). The six-day gathering includes classic and modern dramas as well as poetry slams and many other events. It draws 60,000 visitors annually.

SHOPPING

The Downtown Arts District, referred to as **DADA** (www.dadaws.org), is a neighborhood of galleries and boutiques located downtown between 5th, 6th, and Trade Streets. There are over a dozen commercial galleries, including the **Piedmont Craftsmen** (601 N. Trade St., 336/725-1516, www.piedmontcraftsmen.org, Tues.-Fri. 10:30am-5pm, Sat. 10am-5pm), which has a beautiful showroom where you'll find the work of hundreds of North Carolina's finest studio potters, fiber artists, jewelry designers, and craftspeople who work in many other media. Several restaurants, bars, and coffee shops are located in DADA.

The **Reynolda Village Shops** (2201 Reynolda Rd., 336/758-5584, www.reynolda-village.com), near the historic Reynolda House and museum, is a cluster of specialty stores and boutiques full of unique jewelry, clothing, books, antiques, and more.

SPORTS AND RECREATION
Spectator Sports

Wake Forest University is the fourth school in the famous Tobacco Road athletic rivalry, and a worthy competitor to its nemeses in the Triangle: Duke, UNC, and NC State.

The jewels in the crown of **Demon Deacon Athletics** (888/758-3322, www.wfu.edu) are Wake's ACC Division I football and basketball teams. The hoops team made it into the second round of the NCAA tournament in 2010. The basketball program has produced such notables as Billy Packer, and the 5-foot-3 Muggsy Bogues, now both famous sports broadcasters, as well as Tim Duncan, Randolph Childress, and Chris Paul. Following the tragic sudden death of coach Skip Prosser in 2007, the basketball program embarked on a new era with coach Dino Gaudio at the helm. The women's field hockey team is consistently among the nation's elite, winning three consecutive NCAA championships in the early 2000s, and the golf program is the athletic alma mater of Arnold Palmer, Curtis Strange, Lanny Wadkins, Scott Hoch, and Jay Haas. As is the case at its Tobacco Road counterparts, obtaining a ticket to a Wake Forest football or basketball game can be quite difficult.

NASCAR
NASCAR racing at **Bowman Gray Stadium** (1250 S. Martin Luther King Dr., 336/723-1819, www.bowmangrayracing.com, gates 6pm, races 8pm, $10 adults, $2 ages 6-11, free under age 6) is not only a classic Carolina experience—weekly races have been run here for 50 years—but is also a less daunting experience than race events at the massive stadiums elsewhere in the state. Whereas Lowe's Speedway in Concord can accommodate over 200,000 spectators, Bowman Gray seats a cozy 17,000. It's inexpensive too, making this an ideal place for your first NASCAR event. Weekly races include modified, street stock, sportsman, and stadium stock events.

ACCOMMODATIONS
A cotton mill built in the 1830s, the building that's home to the (**Brookstown Inn** (200 Brookstown Ave., 336/725-1120, www.brookstowninn.com, from $90) has been renovated and transformed into a luxurious hotel, with beautiful exposed brick walls and wooden floors. Guests enjoy wine and cheese in the evenings, and milk and cookies at night. The Brookstown Inn is within walking distance of Old Salem.

(**Augustus T. Zevely Inn** (803 S. Main St., Old Salem, 800/928-9299, www.winston-salem-inn.com, from $95) is the only inn in Old Salem proper. The beautiful 1830s house is furnished in original and reproduction Moravian furniture, with special features peppered throughout, such as steam baths in some guest rooms, heated brick tile floors in others, and working cooking fireplaces. Every guest room has a view either of the old village or of the house's period gardens.

FOOD
Eclectic American
Bernardin's Fine Dining (373 Jonestown Rd., 336/768-9365, www.bernardinsfinedining.com, lunch Mon.-Fri., dinner Mon.-Sat., $19-32) is one of the most lauded restaurants in Winston. In fact, the Greensboro *News & Record* labeled it "the Triad's only five-star restaurant." Chef Freddy Lee honed his skills at several prominent Manhattan restaurants before moving south and opening Bernardin's with his brother Terry. Seafood and hearty cuts of beef and veal dominate the menu. The wine list is extensive, and the desserts alone are worth a visit.

Asian
Newly relocated to West Fourth Street, **Downtown Thai and Sushi** (202 W. 4th St., 336/777-1422, www.downtownthai.com, lunch Mon.-Fri. 11am-2pm, dinner Mon.-Thurs. 5pm-10pm, Fri.-Sat. 5pm-11pm, Sun. 5pm-10pm, $20-25) is an elegant pan-Asian restaurant, specializing in sushi and Thai favorites such as pad thai and curries.

Bakeries
Among the best-loved Moravian arts is that of baking, a tradition that is carried on by, among others, **Salem Baking Company** (224 S. Cherry St., 336/748-0230) and **Dewey's** (3121 Indiana Ave.; 2820 Reynolda Rd.; 262 Stratford Rd., 800/274-2994). At its Winston-Salem locations, and several shops elsewhere in the state,

you'll find heavenly Moravian cookies, a thin, spiced wafer that is one of this state's most popular exports around Christmastime. In business since 1930, Dewey's Bakery produces a long list of variations on the basic Moravian cookie, as well as cheese straws (another classic Southern snack), shortbread, and more.

INFORMATION AND SERVICES

Winston-Salem's main emergency hospital is **Wake Forest University Baptist Medical Center** (Medical Center Blvd., 336/716-2255, www1.wfubmc.edu), located off Business I-40 between Cloverdale and Hawthorne. **Carolina Veterinary Specialists** (1600 Hanes Mall Blvd., 336/896-0902, www.carolinavet.com), a 24-hour emergency veterinary hospital, is located off I-40 just west of U.S. 421.

The *Winston-Salem Journal* (www.journalnow.com) is the city's main newspaper.

The **Winston-Salem Visitors Center** (200 Brookstown Ave., 866/728-4200, www.visitwinstonsalem.com) has extensive travel information is available.

GETTING THERE AND AROUND

Winston-Salem is on I-40, North Carolina's largest east-west highway. It is about 20 minutes from Greensboro, about two hours from Raleigh, and about an hour and a half from Charlotte.

Piedmont Triad International Airport (GSO, 1000 A. Ted Johnson Pkwy., Greensboro, 336/665-5600, www.flyfrompti.com) is nearby on the northwest side of Greensboro. Winston's bus system, **WSTA** (336/727-2648, www.wstransit.com) is connected to that of Greensboro via Piedmont Area Regional Transit's **Express Bus** (336/662-0002, www.partnc.org).

Greensboro and Vicinity

Greensboro might be more densely packed with colleges and universities than any other city in North Carolina. It's the home of the University of North Carolina at Greensboro, North Carolina A&T, the small Quaker college Guilford, and Bennett, a historically African American women's college known as the "Vassar of the South." And that's just a few. Befitting its role as a college town many times over, Greensboro has hopping arts and music scenes and a creative, culturally engaged population.

SIGHTS
Historic Parks

When one thinks of Revolutionary War battles and campaigns, those that come first to mind are probably in the mid-Atlantic and New England states. In truth, much of the Revolution was fought in the South, and some of the major turning points occurred here in North Carolina. The **Guilford**

Courthouse National Military Park (2332 New Garden Rd., 336/288-1776, www.nps.gov/guco, visitors center Tues.-Sat. 8:30am-5pm, free) commemorates the battle of Guilford Courthouse, at which 1,900 British troops led by General Cornwallis routed 4,500 Patriots under General Nathaniel Greene. It proved only a pyrrhic victory, however, as Cornwallis's army was severely hobbled by the action. A 2.5-mile self-guided tour, which can be driven, hiked, or biked, stops at the essential spots on the battlefield.

International Civil Rights Center and Museum

Greensboro, the home of North Carolina A&T, a prominent historically black university, has played an important role in African American history. The **International Civil Rights Center and Museum** (134 S. Elm St., 800/748-7116, www.sitinmovement.org, Mon.-Thurs. 9am-6pm, Fri.-Sat. 9am-7pm,

GREENSBORO AND VICINITY

© AVALON TRAVEL

$10 adults, $8 students and seniors, $6 ages 6-12) is housed in Greensboro's old downtown Woolworth's building, the site of a famous 1960 lunch counter sit-in that lit a fire under North Carolina's civil rights movement. That whites-only counter is the touchstone for this museum's exploration of the civil rights movement. The four men who staged the sit-in—David Richmond, Franklin McCain, Jibreel Khazan, and Joseph McNeil—are honored on the A&T campus with the **A&T Four Statue** (1601 E. Market St.).

Museums

The **Natural Science Center of Greensboro** (4301 Lawndale Dr., 336/288-3769, www.natsci.org, daily 9am-5pm, Animal Discovery daily 10am-4pm, $12.50 adults, $11.50 ages 3-13, OmniSphere Theater shows $3-5) is a great place for kids and adults. Outside, the Animal Discovery displays live tigers, meerkats, alligators, and crocodiles, and other wild animals. Inside are the 22,000 square foot

Sciquarium, featuring sharks, stingrays, and otters, and the OmniSphere Theater, which projects 3-D digital shows on the domed planetarium ceiling.

For children under 10, the **Greensboro Children's Museum** (220 N. Church St., 336/574-2898, www.gcmuseum.com, Tues.-Thurs. 9am-5pm, Fri. 9am-8pm, Sat. 9am-5pm, Sun. 1pm-5pm, $8 adults and children, $7 seniors, $4 Fri. after 5pm) features a pretend town with a Main Street where children can shop for groceries, bake and deliver pizza, put on a play with costumes and props, learn how houses are built, and scale a rock-climbing wall.

The **Green Hill Center for North Carolina Art** (200 N. Davie St., 336/333-7460, www.greenhillcenter.org, Tues. and Thurs.-Sat. 10am-5pm, Wed. 10am-7pm, Sun. 2pm-5pm, $2 donation) presents exhibits of work by artists who are from or have close ties to North Carolina. Much attention is given to North Carolina's folk art traditions, and

International Civil Rights Center and Museum

© GREENSBORO, NC TRAVEL & TOURISM

deservedly so, but the state is also rich with practitioners of the formal studio arts. Some of the best of those artists are represented in this gallery.

ArtQuest (200 N. Davie St., 336/333-7460, www.greenhillcenter.org, Tues. and Thurs.-Sat. 12:30pm-5pm, Wed. 10am-7pm, Sun. 2pm-5pm, $5), an interactive children's museum in the Green Hill Center, teaches kids to appreciate the visual arts through hands-on studio experience.

The **Weatherspoon Art Museum** (Spring Garden St. and Tate St., 336/334-5770, http://weatherspoon.uncg.edu, Tues.-Wed. and Fri. 10am-5pm, Thurs. 10am-9pm, Sat.-Sun. 1pm-5pm, free), on the campus of UNC-Greensboro, has been dedicated to modern art since the early 1940s and has assembled a collection that includes work by Willem de Kooning, Andy Warhol, Cindy Sherman, and many other masters of 20th-century art. Theirs is the best collection of modern art in North Carolina, and one of the very best in the Southeast.

Blandwood Mansion

Blandwood Mansion (447 W. Washington St., 336/272-5003, www.blandwood.org, Feb.-Dec. Tues.-Sat. 11am-4pm, Sun. 2pm-5pm, $8 adults, $5 under age 12) was built in 1790 as a farmhouse, before the city itself was born. In the 1840s, its famous resident was Governor John Motley Morehead, the "Father of Modern North Carolina," one of the most important governors in this state's history because of his efforts to institute humane treatment of the mentally ill, prisoners, and children with disabilities as well as to modernize the state's schools. In 1844, Morehead engaged Alexander Jackson Davis, the architect largely responsible for the country's Gothic revival, to redo Blandwood. The result was the Italianate villa that stands today.

ENTERTAINMENT AND EVENTS
Nightlife

Greensboro is a college town several times over, so there's a lot of late-night mischief to enjoy.

CENTRAL NORTH CAROLINA

To Table 32

DOWNTOWN GREENSBORO

Green Hill Cemetery

NewBridge Bank Park

GREENSBORO GRASSHOPPERS

0   400 yds
0   400 m

UNDERCURRENT RESTAURANT

GREENSBORO CHILDREN'S MUSEUM

GREEN HILL CENTER FOR NORTH CAROLINA ART

NC A&T STATE UNIVERSITY

GREENSBORO COLLEGE

BLANDWOOD MANSION

CITY & GOVERNMENT CENTER

LIBERTY OAK RESTAURANT AND BAR

INTERNATIONAL CIVIL RIGHTS CENTER AND MUSEUM

GREENSBORO VISITORS CENTER

NATTY GREENE'S PUB

BENNETT COLLEGE

WEATHERSPOON ART GALLERY

TABLE 16

© AVALON TRAVEL

Popular pubs include **Natty Greene's Pub** (345 S. Elm St., 336/274-1373, www.nattygreenes. com, Mon.-Sat. 11am-2am, Sun. noon-midnight), and the cigar and drinks bar **Churchill's on Elm** (213 S. Elm St., 336/275-6367, www. churchillscigarlounge.com).

Warehouse 29 (1011 Arnold St., 336/333-9333) is a rather spectacular place, a hot spot for gay nightlife in this region for more than 15 years. In addition to great dancing, drinks, and shows—"from pageants and contests, to fan dances and go-go boys"—Warehouse 29 has a huge outdoor patio that features a sand volleyball court. A more low-key gay bar is **Club Q** (708 W. Market St., 336/272-2587, www.theqlounge.com, Mon.-Fri. from 4pm, Sat. from 9pm, Sun. from 7pm). It has a more traditional neighborhood-pub ambience and is a good place to catch up with friends over martinis.

Performing Arts

The **Greensboro Symphony Orchestra** (multiple venues, 336/335-5456, ext. 223, www. greensborosymphony.org) was born in the 1920s as a student orchestra at Greensboro

© GREENSBORO, NC TRAVEL & TOURISM

Blandwood Mansion

Women's College (now UNC Greensboro). It grew to be a beloved institution in the wider community of the city and became a highly successful regional orchestra. Today's incarnation is conducted by Azerbaijani violinist Dmitry Sitkovetsky. The **Greensboro Opera** (multiple venues, 336/273-9472, www.greensboroopera.org) has been turning out wonderful performances of classical and modern opera for more than 25 years. The **Greensboro Ballet** (multiple venues, 336/333-7480, www.greensboroballet.org) presents several major productions each season, starring both longtime professional dancers and highly talented up-and-coming students.

SHOPPING

Featured in a memorable early scene in the 2006 movie *Junebug,* **Replacements, Ltd.** (1089 Knox Rd., just off I-85 exit 132, between Greensboro and Burlington, 800/737-5223, www.replacements.com, daily 8am-10pm) is an incredible place to shop as well as simply to gawk. Replacements is five football fields' worth of retail and behind-the-scenes space dedicated to what is surely the world's largest collection of tableware and flatware. What began in the 1970s as a small china collection in a North Carolina state auditor's attic has grown so much that today it comprises an 11-million-piece inventory featuring 250,000 patterns.

SPORTS AND RECREATION
Spectator Sports

The **Greensboro Grasshoppers** (408 Bellemeade St., 336/268-2255, www.gsohoppers.com, premium seats $9, lawn $6, $2 less for children and seniors), a Single-A baseball affiliate of the Miami Marlins, play at First Horizon Park, a field that has been graced by all-star pitcher Dontrelle Willis and catcher Paul LoDuca.

For more than 50 years, central Carolinians have been enjoying the roar and burning rubber fumes of the race track experience at the **Piedmont Dragway** (6750 Holts Store Rd., Julian, 6 miles from I-85 exit 132,

336/449-7411, http://piedmontdragway.com, ticket prices vary), located between Greensboro and Burlington. All manner of wheeled motor vehicles tear around this 0.1-mile track, and you can catch an event almost any time of year.

Recreation

Greensboro's **Wet 'N Wild Emerald Point Water Park** (3910 S. Holden Rd., 336/852-9721, www.emeraldpointe.com, May-Sept., hours vary, $36) offers more water rides than one could try in a full weekend. In addition to the central attraction, the two-million-gallon Thunder Bay wave pool, which features 48-foot tsunami waves, there are five-story slides and riptide pools for the most intrepid swimmers, lazy rivers and shallow pools for those who prefer to relax, and many adventures in between.

ACCOMMODATIONS

The **Proximity Hotel** (704 Green Valley Rd., 336/379-8200, www.proximityhotel.com, from $159) is a remarkable venture. The designers of this high-style luxury boutique hotel have set out to create an example of green architectural practices, and are winning awards and high praise for their accomplishments, including the highest rating of "Eco-Getaways" in *Outside* magazine. Solar panels on the roof, huge windows (that really open, miracle of miracles!) in each guest room, recycled building materials, and many other green features mean that the Proximity reduces energy and water use by almost half over what would be expected of a comparable hotel. It's accomplished with no sacrifice in comfort or style. The hotel's interior is beautiful and chic, and the guest rooms are comfortable, brightly lit with natural light, and full of modern amenities.

The **O.Henry Hotel** (624 Green Valley Rd., 336/854-2000, www.ohenryhotel.com, from $239), named for the Greensboro-born author of "Gift of the Magi," is a 1920s-style luxury hotel. The oversize guest rooms feature nine-foot ceilings, neighbor-silencing double walls, comfy beds, terrazzo showers and huge bathtubs, and, like the Proximity, windows that open. The O.Henry's own checkered cab will carry you to and from the airport free of charge.

FOOD
Southern

Lucky 32 (1421 Westover Terrace, 336/370-0707, www.lucky32.com, Mon. 11:15am-9pm, Tues.-Thurs. 11:15am-10pm, Fri.-Sat. 11:15am-11pm, Sun. 10am-9pm, $11-27), just off Wendover Avenue, has been a Greensboro staple for 20 years. The menu features creative renditions of classic Southern fare. Standouts include chicken and dumplings, cornmeal-crusted catfish, and pulled pork on johnnycakes.

Stamey's Old Fashioned Barbecue (2206 High Point Rd., 336/299-9888, Mon.-Sat. 10am-9pm; 2812 Battleground Ave./U.S. 220, 336/288-9275, www.stameys.com, Mon.-Sat. 11am-9pm, under $10) has been around in one form or another for almost 70 years. The Lexington-style barbecue is pit-fired over hickory wood for as much as 10 hours—old-time quality that's kept customers coming back for generations.

Eclectic American

Table 16 (600 S. Elm St., 336/279-8525, www.table16restaurant.com, lunch Tues.-Fri. 11:30am-2pm, dinner Tues.-Fri. 5:30pm-9:30pm, $22-34) is considered by many to be one of Greensboro's best restaurants. The menu blends New World cuisines with European culinary disciplines, resulting in such creations as honeyed salmon and kumquats, tilefish and country ham, and striped bass with fried apples.

The **Liberty Oak Restaurant and Bar** (100-D W. Washington St., 336/273-7057, www.libertyoakrestaurant.com, Mon.-Thurs. 11am-10pm, Fri.-Sat. 11am-11pm, Sun. 10am-10pm, $10-27) is credited with having started a culinary revolution in Greensboro, a fad for casual restaurants serving New American gourmet cuisine. Specialties here include many seafood creations, duck confit, quail stuffed with andouille, and homemade red pepper and goat cheese ravioli.

European

The award-winning **Print Works Bistro** (702 Green Valley Rd., 336/379-0699, www.printworksbistro.com, lunch Mon.-Fri. 11:15am-4pm, dinner Sun.-Thurs. 4pm-10:30pm, Fri.-Sat. 4pm-11pm, brunch Sat.-Sun. 7:30am-4pm, $11-31) is located at the Proximity Hotel and shares its clean, green aesthetic. The menu here comprises French bistro fare, from escargot to grilled pork tenderloin and duck confit.

Adjacent to the O.Henry Hotel and in the same restaurant family as Print Works is **Green Valley Grill** (622 Green Valley Rd., 336/854-2015, www.greenvalleygrill.com, Mon.-Thurs. 11:15am-10:30pm, Fri.-Sat. 11:15am-11pm, Sun. 9am-10pm, $18-31). The menu spans many European traditions, featuring dishes from paella to Jägerschnitzel. Green Valley Grill's wine list wins *Wine Spectator*'s Award of Excellence every year, with over 100 choices, including 50 by-the-glass selections.

Asian

Greensboro has a long-established Vietnamese community and a wealth of Vietnamese restaurants. A favorite of local diners is **Saigon Cuisine Restaurant** (4205 High Point Rd., 336/294-9286, Mon.-Sat. 11am-2pm, 5pm-9pm), where some of the best dishes are the grilled pork over vermicelli and the flounder in basil sauce. **Van Loi** (3829-D High Point Rd., 336/855-5688, Wed.-Mon. 10am-10pm, $8) serves good *pho* and Vietnamese sandwiches.

INFORMATION AND SERVICES

The **Greensboro Visitors Center** (317 S. Greene St., 800/344-2282, www.greensboronc.org, Mon.-Fri. 8:30am-5:30pm, Sat. 9am-4pm, Sun. 1pm-4pm), downtown across from the Carolina Theater, is every day. Greensboro has several hospitals, the largest of which is **Moses H. Cone Memorial Hospital** (1200 N. Elm St., 336/832-7000, www.mosescone.com). Should your pet have an emergency, you can go to the **After Hours Veterinary Emergency Clinic** (5505 W. Friendly Ave., 336/851-1990, www.ahvec.com).

GETTING THERE AND AROUND

Greensboro is connected to North Carolina's other cities by two of the state's major highways, I-40 and I-85. It is connected to the rest of the world by **Piedmont Triad International Airport** (GSO, 1000 A. Ted Johnson Pkwy., Greensboro, 336/665-5600, www.flyfrompti.com). The city is also a stop on the **Amtrak** (236 E. Washington St., 800/872-7245, station daily 24 hours) *Piedmont* and *Carolinian* lines. Greensboro's local bus system, the **Greensboro Transit Authority** (336/335-6499, www.greensboro-nc.gov), is connected to its counterpart in Winston-Salem by Piedmont Area Regional Transit's **Express Bus** (336/662-0002, www.partnc.org).

LEXINGTON

The Piedmont town of Lexington is a veritable mecca for Southern chowhounds. Billing itself as the "Barbecue Capital of the World," Lexington is known as the epicenter of North Carolina's western barbecue tradition. Known locally as "honeymonk," Lexington barbecue comes from the pork shoulder, rather than whole-hog meat; also unlike in the east, the sauce usually has a dose of ketchup in it.

Foodies will argue endlessly about which barbecue purveyor in the Lexington area is the best, but an oft-cited favorite is **Lexington #1** (10 U.S. 29/70 S., 704/249-9814, Mon.-Sat. 10am-9:30pm, $8). In this friendly eatery, the barbecue is slow-cooked over wood coals. The hush puppies, a category of food that can inspire nearly as much partisan debate as barbecue, are also quite special. Also popular is **Stamey's** (524 S. Hwy. 150, 336/853-6426, www.stameys.com, Mon.-Sat. 10am-9pm, $7), which has been serving Lexingtonians since 1930. Stamey's barbecue is cooked over hickory coals for up to 10 hours before it reaches the table. Another top bet is **Speedy's** (1317 Winston Rd., 336/248-2410, http://speedysbqinc.com, Mon.-Sat. 10:30am-9pm, $8). Not only is the food here good and plentiful, but the waitstaff will bring it right to the curb for you, old-time drive-in style.

October is officially Barbecue Month here in Davidson County, and late in the month every year, up to 100,000 people descend on Lexington for the **Barbecue Festival** (336/956-1880, www.barbecuefestival.com). Stamey's, Speedy's, and a host of other local honeymonkeries provide the eats, while concerts, contests, and children's activities fill the city.

After a visit to one of Lexington's barbecue joints, make your way to **The Candy Factory** (15 N. Main St., 336/249-6770, www.thecandyfactory.net, Mon.-Thurs. 10am-5:30pm, Fri. 10am-7:30pm, Sat. 10am-4pm). A third-generation candy-making business, the Candy Factory is housed in a 1907 old-time hardware store, with beautiful creaky old floors. Barrels of candy line the shop.

The Sandhills

Far from most of North Carolina's major highways, the region known as the Sandhills, an exceptionally beautiful part of the state, is often forgotten by travelers and travel writers. These roads less traveled will carry you through placid countryside to a tiny town that seems inhabited almost entirely by artists, savannas traversed by elephants and zebras, and into some mysterious haunted mountains—and to towns called Whynot and Climax. The centerpiece of the Sandhills—indeed, the geographic center of North Carolina—is the tiny town of Seagrove (population approximately 250), where a distinctive style of folk pottery is approaching its third century of tradition and innovation. The Uwharrie Mountains, an outcropping of deep hills and dark forests, are nearby. Asheboro, the largest town in the Sandhills, with 20,000 residents, is home to the wild animals of the North Carolina Zoo, and to one of North Carolina's greatest achievements, Cheerwine.

ASHEBORO AND VICINITY
North Carolina Zoo
The **North Carolina Zoo** (Zoo Pkwy., 800/488-0444, www.nczoo.org, Apr.-Oct. daily 9am-5pm, Nov.-Mar. daily 9am-4pm, $12 adults, $10 college students and over age 62, $8 ages 2-12) sprawls over more than 500 acres of Purgatory Mountain, at the edge of the Uwharries. Animals that include elephants, zebras, polar bears, alligators, and many more live on large expanses of land planted and landscaped to approximate their native habitats. Over five miles

of hiking trails, with a parking lot at each end of the zoo, are the best way to see the animals. Trails are wheelchair-accessible, and for those who don't want to walk long distances, buses and trams run from exhibit to exhibit within the park (although you still have to leave the vehicle to see the animals). This acclaimed zoo is operated by the state of North Carolina.

Other Sights and Activities
At the **North Carolina Aviation Museum** (2222-G Pilots View Rd., 336/625-0170, www.ncairmuseumhalloffame.com, Thurs.-Sun. 11am-5pm, $10 adults, $5 students), World War II through Vietnam War-era fighter aircraft gleam in restored splendor. After touring the two hangars where the airplanes and other military memorabilia are housed, check out the gift shop, which is a model plane lover's dream.

The **Asheboro Copperheads** (McCrary Stadium, Southway Rd., off McCrary St., 336/460-7018, www.teamcopperhead.com), part of the Coastal Plain League, are a summer baseball team of college players from schools in North Carolina and throughout the South, whose alumni include at least two current big-league pitchers.

◖ Liberty Antiques Festival
Liberty, located between Asheboro and I-85, hosts a twice-yearly antiques fair that draws crowds from all over the Southeast. At the **Liberty Antiques Festival** (2855 Pike Farm Rd., Staley, just outside Liberty, 800/626-2672,

www.libertyantiquesfestival.com, $7), usually held over a three-day weekend in late April and again in late September, hundreds of vendors set up shop in a farm field, creating a huge outdoor antiques mall that offers many happy hours of browsing. There's huge variety among the dealers' wares, but overall the theme leans toward rustic Southern.

SEAGROVE

The little crossroads town of Seagrove is built over beds of clay that perfectly suited the needs of 18th- and 19th-century potters. Several families of potters settled in this region, and using the excellent red and gray clays so readily available, were soon supplying much of the rest of the region with jugs, crocks, plates, and other utilitarian wares. Within just a few miles of Seagrove's downtown, reaching into little nearby communities like Whynot and Westmoore, are the shops and studios of over 100 potters. The pottery made by all of these Seagrove artists is among the most collectible Southern folk art.

North Carolina Pottery Center

The **North Carolina Pottery Center** (233 East Ave., 336/873-8430, www.ncpotterycenter.com, Tues.-Sat. 10am-4pm, $2 adults, $1 high school students) is the ideal place to start your tour of Seagrove. Though the primary focus of the Pottery Center is to preserve and present the work of Seagrove-area potters, you'll also see representative work from the state's several other distinctive pottery traditions. The permanent exhibit and rotating shows introduce visitors to such late master artists as M. L. Owens, A. R. Cole, and Dorothy and Walter Auman, all in a beautiful, airy building designed to echo the lines of a barn. There's also a very nice little gift shop. On your way out the door, pick up a map of area potteries. There are dozens, each uniquely appealing, each representing a different facet of the tradition, and you'll need a map to help you choose which ones to sample.

Pottery Studios

Ben Owen Pottery (2199 Hwy. 705, 910/464-2261, www.benowenpottery.com), three miles south of the Pottery Center on Highway 705, "The Pottery Highway," is the studio and showroom of one of Seagrove's finest young potters. Ben Owen III learned the art from his grandfather, who was also a renowned area potter. Incorporating elements of Asian ceramics into his native Seagrove tradition, Owen has made a name for himself in the fine arts world. Much of his work is positively monumental, massive vases and jars, many glazed in the brilliant red for which the family is famous. A small museum attached to the shop shows some of his father's and grandfather's beautiful work.

David and Mary Farrell of **Westmoore Pottery** (4622 Busbee Rd., Westmoore, 910/464-3700, www.westmoorepottery.com, Mon.-Sat. 9am-5pm) specialize in recreating historical ceramics, primarily of North Carolina styles. Their work is so accurate that it appears in historic houses throughout the United States and has been featured in many movies, including *Amistad* and *Cold Mountain*.

Luck's Ware (1606 Adams Rd., Seagrove, 336/879-3261, Mon.-Fri. 9am-5pm) is the workshop of Sid Luck and his sons Matt and Jason, today's representatives of a generations-old family tradition. Sid fires (bakes) his pots in a groundhog kiln—an old-time Carolina form that has a long arched brick tunnel, part of which is usually subterranean.

Shopping

It's hard to imagine, but there is one shop in Seagrove with wares that rival the gleaming pottery in beauty. **Seagrove Orchids** (3451 Brower Mill Rd., 336/879-6677, www.seagroveorchids.com, Tues.-Sun. 10am-5pm and by appointment) is a wonderful place to visit even if your hobbies don't include exotic horticulture. There are over 220 kinds of orchids in the greenhouses here, from rare species to affordable plants good for beginners.

Accommodations

The **Duck Smith House** (465 N. Broad St., 888/869-9018, www.ducksmithhouse.com, $125), a farmhouse built in 1914, is the classic Southern bed-and-breakfast, with a large wraparound porch and a hearty country breakfast. The location is perfect for a weekend of shopping for pottery.

UWHARRIE MOUNTAINS

The Uwharrie Mountains are strange and beautiful, a range of hills covered in deep rocky woods and dotted with small quiet towns with names like Ether and Troy. Peaks of this range, one of the oldest in North America, once soared to 20,000 feet, but the millennia have worn them down until the highest mountain now stands at just over 1,000 feet. Lakes, hiking trails, and history are hidden in these mountains.

◖ Uwharrie National Forest

The trail system of the Uwharrie Forest has aptly been compared to a "mini-Appalachian Trail." Although the Uwharrie Mountains are significantly lower than the Blue Ridge Mountains and the Smokies, they do shelter delicate mountain ecosystems closely related to those of the Appalachians. Two major trails run through the park, the Uwharrie National Recreational Trail and the Dutchman's Creek Trail. Both begin 10 miles west of Troy, with parking at Highway 24/27. The 10-mile Dutchman's Creek trail loops with the 20-mile Uwharrie Trail, which ends 2 miles east of Ophir at Highway 1306. The hikes are somewhat strenuous—these are mountains, after all, though low ones—and they travel through pretty and sometimes spooky terrain—rocky woods with old homesites and graveyards, with some abandoned gold mines nearby.

Two large campgrounds are located near Badin Lake, at the western edge of the park. **Arrowhead Campground** (Forest Rd. 597B, off Mullinix Rd./Forest Rd. 1154, 910/576-6391, reservations 877/833-6777, www.recreation.gov, $9 with electricity, $6 without electricity) has 48 sites with picnic tables and tent pads, 33 of which have electrical hookups. The Arrowhead Campground is 0.5 miles from Badin Lake. **The Badin Lake Campground** (Forest Rd. 576, off Hwy. 109, 910/576-6391, reservations 877/444-6777, www.recreation.

gov, $8), which has 34 sites, is directly on the lake. Several smaller sites throughout the park are accessible for tent camping, and one, Canebrake Horse Camp near Badin Lake, is for folks traveling with their horses.

Morrow Mountain State Park

Located catty-corner to Badin and Albemarle, **Morrow Mountain State Park** (49104 Morrow Mountain Rd., Albemarle, 704/982-4402, http://ncparks.gov, May-Aug. 8am-9pm, Mar.-Apr., Sept.-Oct. 8am-8pm, Nov.-Feb. 8am-6pm, free) preserves one of the Uwharries' highest peaks, the 936-foot Morrow Mountain. Within the park, visitors can go boating on Lake Tillery or on the Pee Dee River, with rowboat and canoe rentals available in the spring and summer. More than 15 miles of trails snake up and down the mountains. Cabins are available for rent (summer $400 per week, off-season $80 per night, 2-night minimum). There are also over 100 campsites ($9-15) with water, restrooms, and showers nearby, but no electricity. Visitors can also check out the exhibit hall (daily 10am-5pm) to learn about the ecology and Native American heritage of the region.

INFORMATION AND SERVICES

Asheboro is the population center of Randolph County, where you'll find plenty of affordable chain motels and a fast-food jungle clustered along U.S. 64. This is also a center for area medical services. The **Asheboro/Randolph County Chamber of Commerce** (317 E. Dixie Dr., 336/626-2626, http://chamber.asheboro.com) can fix you up with all the logistical information you need as you venture into the Sandhills.

GETTING THERE AND AROUND

U.S. 220, which runs from Greensboro almost to the South Carolina border, is the only major artery in this region, which is served by no major airports or rail lines. The Charlotte, Greensboro, and Raleigh-Durham airports are all within one to two hours' drive.

Southern Pines and Pinehurst

Flip through the old postcards at any antiques shop in the Carolinas and you're likely to come across turn-of-the-20th-century images of the Southern Pines region of the North Carolina Sandhills. The area's development kicked into high gear in the 1890s, when Bostonian James Tufts constructed the Pinehurst Resort with money he made in the soda fountain industry. He commissioned Frederick Law Olmsted to design a village, which he named Pinehurst. The first hotel opened in 1895, followed by the Pinehurst golf course (now called Pinehurst No. 1) in 1898, and the Pinehurst No. 2 course in 1907. The area quickly became a haven for northern snowbirds. Postcards from that early era are clearly geared to a Yankee audience, portraying the early spring blossoms that cover the Sandhills while New York, Chicago, and Milwaukee are still buried in snow, or showing rustic cabins and rural African Americans driving ox-carts or playing the banjo—holdovers from the stereotypical Victorian notions of the old South, appealing to urbanites in search of a change of pace.

Today, this whole section of Moore County, anchored by the picturesque towns of Pinehurst and Southern Pines, is a sea of golf courses and still a magnet for snowbirds and "halfbacks" (Northerners who retired to Florida, found it too hot, and came halfway back, to North Carolina). Primarily known for golf, the Pinehurst area has hosted the U.S. Open, the U.S. Women's Open, and the USGA National Championship. The spring months are exceptionally pretty, and the weather is usually warm but not dangerously hot (as it is in summer), so from March to May, hotels and restaurants fill to the gills, and golf courses can book solid. The key to having a good golf vacation in the springtime is planning well in advance. Golf packages are key; by bundling lodging and greens fees, you can save cash and hassle.

SPORTS AND RECREATION
Golf

Given its background of Scottish settlement, it's no surprise that one of the most famous golf centers in the world is the Southern Pines, Pinehurst, and Aberdeen area, with more than 40 major courses. An epicenter of American golf for over 100 years, Pinehurst has been so influential in the development of the modern game that an entire format of play, the Pinehurst system—also called the Chapman system or American foursomes—was developed there.

The **Pinehurst Resort** (1 Carolina Vista Dr., Pinehurst, 800/487-4653, www.pinehurst.com) comprises eight major courses (called Pinehurst No. 1, No. 2, etc.), designed by some of the great golf course architects of the last century: Donald Ross, Ellis Maples, George and Tom Fazio, and Rees Jones. The circa-1907 Ross-designed Pinehurst No. 2 is considered the most important and has hosted numerous U.S. Open championships, including both the 2014 men's and women's championships. **Pine Needles** (Midland Rd., Southern Pines, 910/692-7111, www.pineneedles-midpines.com, greens fees $135-235) incorporates the Pine Needles (18 holes, par 71) and Mid-Pines (18 holes, par 72) courses, both Donald Ross creations. The **Talamore** (48 Talamore Dr., Southern Pines, 800/552-6292, www.talamoregolfresort.com, 18 holes, par 71, greens fees $60-130) was designed by Rees Jones. If you visit at the right time, you might be treated to the able caddying services of the Talamore llamas.

Other courses in the area were designed by Jack Nicklaus, Jack Nicklaus II, Dan Maples, Gary Player, and other leading lights of golf course architecture. Best of all, almost all of them are clustered within half an hour's drive or less from each other.

One of the most remarkable aspects of the Pinehurst golf scene, unlike some of the more vacation-oriented golfing centers of the country, is the prevalence of retired professionals, instructors, and skilled locals on the links. It makes for a more immersive and respectful golf experience, one with a certain addictive quality that keeps people coming back.

Your first stop online should be at the Pinehurst golf tourism website (www.homeofgolf.com). The Sandhills Golf Association website (www.sandhillsgolf.com) is another good source for golf-specific background and info. There are plenty of packages available and plenty of websites that offer them; among the best is www.villageofpinehurstgolf.com.

Other Activities

This area pulsates to the rhythm of the links, but there are a few sights not related to golf. In the town of Southern Pines is **Campbell House** (482 E. Connecticut Ave., www.mooreart.org, Mon.-Fri. 9am-5pm, free), headquarters of the Moore County Arts Council and host to several galleries of local and regional artists. For those who want a touch of history, visit the **Tufts Archives** (150 Cherokee Rd., www.tuftsarchives.org, Mon.-Fri. 9:30am-5pm, Sat. 9:30am-12:30pm) in Pinehurst. Enjoy the area's railroad history at **Union Station Railroad Museum** (100 E. Main St., 910/757-0161, www.townofaberdeen.net, by appointment only Mon.-Fri. 8am-5pm, free) at the circa-1900 depot in Aberdeen. Also in Aberdeen is the **Malcolm Blue Farm and Museum** (1177 Bethesda Rd., www.malcolmbluefarm.com, Fri.-Sat. 1pm-4pm, free), taking you back to a working farm environment from the early 1800s when the Sandhills area was settled.

Hiking and Walking

Weymouth Woods-Sandhills Nature Preserve (1024 Fort Bragg Rd., Southern Pines, 910/692-2167, http://ncparks.gov, Nov.-Feb. daily 8am-6pm, Mar.-Oct. daily 8am-8pm, free) comprises nearly 900 acres and is home to red-cockaded woodpeckers, fox squirrels, and other natives of the longleaf pine barrens. Most of the preserve is a limited-use area, but several trails, most one mile long or shorter, let visitors explore the woods and swamps.

Another nice spot for walking is the **Horticultural Garden** (3395 Airport Rd., Pinehurst, 910/695-3882, http://sandhillshorticulturalgardens.com, daily dawn-dusk, free) at Sandhills Community College. A full acre of the property is dedicated to a formal English garden, while other areas show off plants of the woodlands and wetlands.

ACCOMMODATIONS

A word to the wise: If you want to visit the Pinehurst area during a major tournament, you must book accommodations well in advance. When the U.S. Open is played in Pinehurst, as it often is, area hotel rooms are typically booked solid as the date approaches. Check the online calendar at www.vopnc.org to plan your dates.

Resorts

A separate entity from the town of Pinehurst, the **☚ Pinehurst Resort** (80 Carolina Vista Dr., Pinehurst, 800/487-4653, www.pinehurst.com), opened in 1895, is the world's second-largest golf resort. The resort is built around eight golf courses, including the famed Pinehurst Numbers 1, 2, 3, and 4, designed by Donald Ross. There are three inns to choose from. The **Carolina** (from $250), built in 1901 and listed in the National Register of Historic Places, is a grand hotel in the Edwardian style, with long piazzas and lush lawns. The 1895 **Holly Inn** (from $230) was the first hotel built at the resort, and is a smaller and cozier clublike inn. The third inn, the **Manor** (from $150), is the smallest and most laid-back of the accommodations here.

For beginning golfers, as well as experienced players, the **Pinehurst Golf Academy** (from $1,329) gives weekend and weeklong classes, taught on Pinehurst Nos. 1, 3, and 5, with a stay at the Carolina included in the course fee. Also on the grounds is the four-star **Spa at Pinehurst**, with a long menu of skin and body care therapies. The **Pinehurst Tennis Club** is regarded as a top tennis resort nationally, with a high-quality pro shop and adult tennis camps. Golf, spa, and tennis packages can significantly reduce the overall cost of a stay at the Pinehurst, although surcharges for amenities might still apply.

Inns

The **Pine Crest Inn** (Dogwood Rd., Pinehurst, 800/371-2545, www.pinecrestinnpinehurst.com, $70-120, plus 15 percent service charge) was owned for many years by Donald Ross, the golf course designer who helped make the Pinehurst Resort famous. Operated for the last 40 years by the Barrett family, the Pine Crest is a favorite for golfers and vacationers, and for local diners who come to the Pine Crest Inn Restaurant and Mr. B's Lounge.

The **Magnolia Inn** (Magnolia Rd. and Chinquapin Rd., Pinehurst, 800/526-5562, www.themagnoliainn.com, $75-190), built in 1896, sits in a great downtown location. Guests are just steps from local shopping and restaurants, and very close to the best area golfing. The **C Knollwood House** (1495 W. Connecticut Ave., Southern Pines, 910/692-9390, from $140) is one of the most popular inns in the area, a bed-and-breakfast located on the 15th green of the Mid Pines golf course. The elegant house, built in 1927 as a Philadelphia family's vacation home, has a beautiful sunroom and front porch overlooking the azalea-spangled yard.

FOOD

Some of the best places to dine in this area are at the Pinehurst Resort (800/487-4653). The **Carolina Dining Room** (Carolina Inn, 80 Carolina Vista Dr., Pinehurst, daily 6am-10am, 6:30pm-9pm, $36-37, dinner jacket required) is the resort's most formal dining room, serving fine chops and steaks presented with the

chef's suggestions for wine accompaniment. At the **1895 Grille** (Holly Inn, 80 Carolina Vista Dr., Pinehurst, Wed.-Sat. 6pm-9pm, $24-35), specialties feature savory grilled veal and steak, filet of grouper served over oyster risotto, and the signature cider-brined grilled pork chop with apple-pecan chutney. The **Tavern** (The Manor, 80 Carolina Vista Dr., Pinehurst, daily 11:30am-10pm, $16-27) serves lighter café fare, with entrée soups and sandwiches as well as an array of pasta dishes. Seven other restaurants, cafés, and tea shops are scattered throughout the Pinehurst Resort.

At the **Magnolia Inn** (Magnolia Rd. and Chinquapin Rd., Pinehurst, 800/526-5562, www.themagnoliainn.com, Tues.-Sat. 4:30pm-10pm, dining room $15-35, pub $6-12), the main dining room serves three-course meals with such specialties as lobster chimichanga, pork napoleon, fire-roasted pepper over grits, and the inn's special tomato bisque. At the pub, several of these specialties are served, along with sandwiches like the corned beef reuben panini, barbecue pork sandwich, and pub burger with the works.

GETTING THERE AND AROUND

Southern Pines and Pinehurst are most easily reached by U.S. 15/501 and U.S. 1, south from Chapel Hill and Raleigh, respectively, and can be reached easily from Fayetteville, just a short drive east. The region is also served by **Moore County Airport** (910/692-3212, www.moore-countyairport.com).

When you get here, it's a good idea to stop by the Pinehurst-Aberdeen **Convention and Visitors Bureau** (10677 U.S. 15/501, www.homeofgolf.com, 800/346-5632, Mon.-Fri. 9am-5pm) to stock up on timely information and brochures.

CENTRAL NORTH CAROLINA

Charlotte

There has only been one brief period, in Charlotte's earliest days, when it was not a boomtown. In the late 18th century it was a midsize county seat, but 1799 brought a taste of things to come when a child's creek-side discovery of a 17-pound lump of gold sparked a minor gold rush.

When the railroad came to the Carolina backcountry, Charlotte was first in line to get its ticket punched. Cotton farmers throughout the Carolina Piedmont carried their crops to Charlotte, and brokers funneled the raw cotton down the line to the port of Charleston. These early ties to South Carolina could arguably be the origin of the subtle but pervasive sense that Charlotte is only technically part of North Carolina.

Economically adventurous, Charlotte rebounded quickly after the Civil War, encouraging Northern and foreign investment and

© JIM MOREKIS

Charlotte's bustling downtown

businesspeople—again drawing the disapprobation of other North Carolinians, but laying the groundwork for greater prosperity. Textile mill money enriched the city throughout the early 20th century. In more recent years, Charlotte became the second-largest banking center of the United States after New York City. Bank of America, the now defunct Wachovia, and other locally based giants brought waves of newcomers to the Queen City.

Keep in mind that unlike most cities, Charlotte refers to its hopping city center area as Uptown.

SIGHTS
Art Museums and Installations
The **Mint Museum of Art** (2730 Randolph Rd., 704/337-2000, www.mintmuseum.org, Wed. 11am-9pm, Thurs.-Sat. 11am-6pm, Sun. 1pm-5pm, $10 adults, $8 seniors and college students, $5 ages 6-17) and the **Mint Museum Uptown** (220 N. Tryon St., 704/337-2000, www.mintmuseum.org, Wed. 11am-9pm, Thurs.-Sat. 11am-6pm, Sun. 1pm-5pm, $10 adults, $8 seniors and college students, $5 ages 6-17) are two of the state's premier art galleries. The Mint Museum of Art occupies an 1836 building that originally served as a branch of the federal mint during the height of North Carolina's brief but frenzied gold rush. Its collections include an array of art from many lands and eras. The Mint Museum Uptown, within the Levine Center, hosts the Craft + Design collection, focusing on studio craft with special attention to North Carolina artists, but also with a global sweep.

History Museums and Sites
The **Charlotte Museum of History** (3500 Shamrock Dr., 704/568-1774, www.charlottemuseum.org, Thurs.-Sat. 1pm-5pm, $7 adults, $5 students and seniors, $5 children) chronicles the origins of Charlotte in entertaining exhibits geared toward all ages; the 1774 **Hezekiah**

CENTRAL NORTH CAROLINA

birthplace of President James K. Polk

© JIM MOREKIS

Alexander Homesite, on the museum grounds, is the oldest structure in Mecklenburg County.

On a busy block of North Tryon Street just outside Uptown is **Historic Rosedale Plantation** (3427 N. Tryon St., 704/335-0325, www.historicrosedale.org, Thurs.-Sat. 1:30pm-3pm, $10), a graceful 1830s house. Twenty enslaved people worked the surrounding 911 acres, most of which are now hidden under strip malls and parking lots. Early plantation life is also represented at **Historic Latta Plantation** (5225 Sample Rd., Huntersville, 704/875-2312, www.lattaplantation.org, Tues.-Sat. 10am-5pm, Sun. 1pm-5pm, house tours on the hour, $7 adults, $6 students and over age 62, free under age 5), a circa-1800 cotton farm that presents living history events year-round to teach about life in the late 18th century and early-mid-19th century. It also sits alongside a 1,300-acre nature preserve, an important haven for migratory birds and the home of the Carolina Raptor Center. A farm of the same era is recreated at the **James K. Polk Historic Site** (12031 Lancaster Hwy.,

Pineville, 704/889-7145, www.nchistoricsites. org, Tues.-Sat. 9am-5pm, free), where the 11th president was born. Visitors can tour log buildings that date to the era of his childhood (but are not original to the site), and at the visitors center can learn about Polk and the often overlooked significance of his short but influential presidency.

Levine Museum of the New South

The **Levine Museum of the New South** (200 E. 7th St., 704/333-1887, www.museumofthenewsouth.org, Mon.-Sat. 10am-5pm, Sun. noon-5pm, $8 adults, $6 seniors, $5 children) tells the story—in its permanent exhibit called *Cotton Fields to Skyscrapers*—of the South's emergence from the devastation of the Civil War and the rancor of Reconstruction, through the postwar reign of King Cotton, and the lives of the tobacco and textile industries that for so long were the staples of North Carolina's economy. Interwoven are stories of segregation and the civil rights movement, and the waves

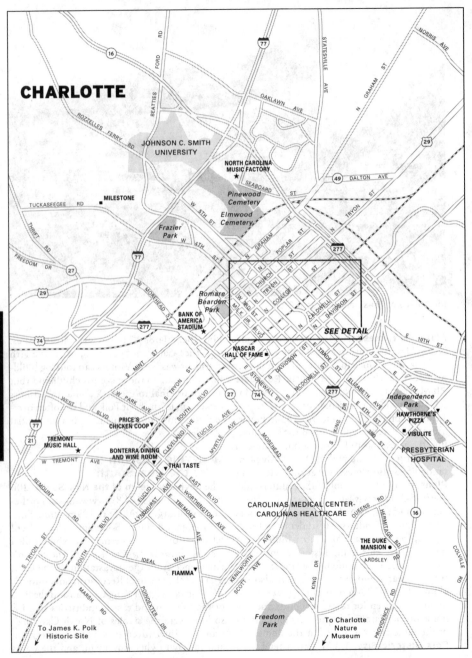

CHARLOTTE

JOHNSON C. SMITH UNIVERSITY

NORTH CAROLINA MUSIC FACTORY ★

MILESTONE ■

TUCKASEEGEE RD

Pinewood Cemetery

Elmwood Cemetery

Frazier Park

Romare Bearden Park

BANK OF AMERICA STADIUM ★

NASCAR HALL OF FAME ■

SEE DETAIL

Independence Park

HAWTHORNE'S PIZZA ▼

VISULITE ■

PRESBYTERIAN HOSPITAL

PRICE'S CHICKEN COOP ▼

TREMONT MUSIC HALL ★

BONTERRA DINING AND WINE ROOM ▼

THAI TASTE ▼

CAROLINAS MEDICAL CENTER- CAROLINAS HEALTHCARE

THE DUKE MANSION ●

FIAMMA ▼

Freedom Park

To James K. Polk Historic Site

To Charlotte Nature Museum

CENTRAL NORTH CAROLINA

© AVALON TRAVEL

CENTRAL NORTH CAROLINA

BEYOND BANKTOWN

Charlotteans and outsiders alike often refer to the Queen City as Banktown, a name meant to conjure images of spotless sidewalks and shining office towers, a nine-to-five corporate culture with little room for the arts or nonconformity. But there's a lot more to Charlotte than the Bank of America tower (sometimes called the Taj McColl, for former CEO Hugh McColl).

I happen to think that Uptown, with its sparkly skyscrapers and stampeding suits, is kind of cool–a little bit of Washington's K Street in a more tropical clime. But we do a disservice to Charlotte and to ourselves as travelers if we overlook the beautiful variety of people who live here. In addition to the suggestions you'll find in this chapter, explore these websites and pick up these publications while you're in Banktown to find out what's happening outside the tower's shadow.

- *Creative Loafing* (http://clclt.com), a free weekly that you can find all over the city, does a bang-up job of covering the arts, food, politics, and everything else that makes Charlotte hum. The website is as good a resource as the print edition.

- **Weird Charlotte** (www.weirdcharlotte. com)–motto "Keep Charlotte weird? Make Charlotte weird!"–is an online compendium of "current weirdness," "historic weirdness," "random acts of weirdness," and "weirdos" in this fine city.

of globalization and immigration that are defining today's new New South. Changing exhibits address head-on, often in daring ways, community, race, nationality, stereotyping, religion, and other fascinating and extremely complex issues of Southern life, past and present, in presentations that are engaging and thought-provoking.

Museums and Activity Centers for Kids

Discovery Place (301 N. Tryon St., 704/372-6261, www.discoveryplace.org, Mon.-Fri. 9am-4pm, Sat. 10am-6pm, Sun. noon-5pm, museum $12, museum plus IMAX $17) is an interactive museum with an indoor rainforest, an IMAX theater, preserved human body parts, and much more. Discovery Place also operates the **Charlotte Nature Museum** (1658 Sterling Rd., 704/372-6261, www.charlottenaturemuseum.org, Tues.-Fri. 9am-5pm, Sat. 10am-5pm, Sun. noon-5pm, $6) next to Freedom Park, which is home to live animals and a walk-through butterfly pavilion. **ImaginOn** (300 E. 7th St., 704/416-4600, www.imaginon.org, Tues.-Thurs. 10am-7pm, Fri.-Sat. 10am-5pm, Sun. 1pm-5pm) is a major Uptown arts complex for children and teens. It has theaters, libraries, a story lab, and a teen center.

ENTERTAINMENT AND EVENTS
Performing Arts

Among the city's several excellent theater companies are **Theatre Charlotte** (501 Queens Rd., 704/376-3777, www.theatrecharlotte.org), which has been in business since the 1920s; the **Actor's Theatre of Charlotte** (650 E. Stonewall St., 704/342-2251, www.actorstheatrecharlotte.org), a company specializing in contemporary dramas; the **Carolina Actors Studio Theatre** (1118 Clement Ave., 704/455-8542, www.nccast.com) for experiential art; and the **Children's Theatre of Charlotte** (704/973-2800, www.ctcharlotte.org), which has its home at ImaginOn.

The **Blumenthal Performing Arts Center** (130 North. Tryon St., 704/372-1000, www.blumenthalcenter.org) in Uptown is the home theater of the **Charlotte Symphony** (www.charlottesymphony.org), which has been in existence for nearly 80 years. These days it puts together seasons of baroque, romantic, and modern classical music, as well as a series of pops-style concerts with guest artists.

Almost 40 years old, the **North Carolina Dance Theater** (704/372-1000, www.ncdance.org) is another venerable institution in Charlotte's arts scene. They dance full-length classical ballets and modern works, and tour widely. **Opera Carolina** (704/372-1000, www.operacarolina.org), at 60 years old, is the leading opera company in the Carolinas. They produce four major operas each year, as well as an annual run of *Amahl and the Night Visitors* at Christmastime.

Festivals

Each May, race fans take over several blocks of Uptown for **Speed Street** (704/455-5555, www.600festival.com). For three days, entertainers, race-car drivers, and thousands of enthusiasts celebrate the area's auto racing industry. Autograph sessions throughout the festival bring participants in close contact with racing royalty.

Charlotte is an incredible city for foodies, and one way to learn the culinary ropes here in a short time is to come to the early-June **Taste of Charlotte** (704/262-9847, www.tasteofcharlotte.com). Dozens of area restaurants make samples of their art available, from haute European masterpieces to soul food favorites, plus plenty of international flavors from this wonderfully diverse community.

Charlotte's rapidly expanding population of recent immigrants has filled the city's entertainment calendar with dozens of festivals and holidays from around the world. June's Annual **Asian Festival** (704/540-6808) features dragon boat races on Ramsey Creek in Cornelius. Early September brings the **Yiasou Greek Festival** (704/334-4771, www.yiasoufestival.org), which celebrates one of the South's long-established Greek communities. October's **Latin American Festival** (704/531-3848, www.latinamericancoalition.org) celebrates the South's largest new immigrant group.

Nightlife

The **North Carolina Music Factory** (1000 Seaboard St., 704/987-0612, http://ncmusicfactory.com) is a huge complex of clubs and theaters on the northeast side of Uptown. Its venues range from the 5,000-seat Uptown Amphitheater to Butter, a new nightclub with top national DJs. Visit the website to find out about upcoming acts, and for a map of the factory; it helps to get your bearings before you go. **Tremont Music Hall** (400 W. Tremont Ave., 704/343-9494, www.tremontmusichall.com) has a capacity of more than 1,000 and hosts national acts in rock, punk, hardcore, ska, metal, and other styles. The smaller venue on the site, the Casbah, holds 325 and often hosts regional and local acts. The **Visulite** (1625 Elizabeth Ave., 704/358-9200, www.visulite.com) is another major venue, hosting major rock and roll, reggae, world music, and other bands.

The **Milestone** (3400 Tuckaseegee Rd., 704/398-0472, www.themilestoneclub.com) has been hosting underground and up-and-coming bands since 1969 and was a major landmark for punk music in the South in the 1980s. Artists who've made appearances in the club's history include R.E.M., Hasil Adkins, and Fugazi. Today's lineups are just as inspired. **Coyote Joe's** (4621 Wilkinson Blvd., 704/399-4946, www.coyote-joes.com) is a huge country dance hall and honky-tonk that hosts top Nashville artists. **Puckett's Farm Equipment** (2740 W. Sugar Creek Rd., 704/597-8230, www.puckettsfarm.com) is a smaller country juke joint with regular bluegrass and rockabilly shows.

The **Double Door Inn** (1218 Charlottetown Ave./Independence Blvd., 704/376-1446, http://doubledoorinn.com) calls itself "Charlotte's home of the blues." It has brought the glitterati of blues, roots, and roots-rock music to Charlotte for nearly four decades. The **Neighborhood Theatre** (511 E. 36th St., 704/358-9298, www.neighborhoodtheatre.com, all ages) in the NoDa (North Davidson) neighborhood is a place where artists already high on the charts, or new artists starting to make the climb to stardom, appear when they're in Charlotte. Visitors of all ages are admitted to most shows. NoDa also has a folk club, **The Muse** (3227 N. Davidson St., 704/376-3737, www.theeveningmuse.com,

Wed.-Thurs. 6pm-midnight, Fri.-Sat. 6pm-late). This is an intimate listening room, and music fans of all ages are admitted.

SPORTS AND RECREATION
Spectator Sports
The Carolinas' only National Basketball Association franchise, the **Charlotte Hornets** (333 E. Trade St., 704/262-2287, www.nba.com/hornets.com), play in the massive Time Warner Cable Arena in Uptown. The Hornets attract a statewide following by recruiting talent from the ranks of UNC Tar Heel basketball alums. Carolina legends Phil Ford and Buzz Peterson are part of the team's administration.

Charlotte is also home to the Carolinas' only National Football League team, the **Carolina Panthers** (9800 S. Mint St., 704/358-7800, www.panthers.com), who play at the Bank of America Stadium at the edge of Uptown. Fans, twirling their growl-towels, cheered them on to National Football Conference titles in 1996 and 2003.

The Boston White Sox Triple-A baseball affiliate is the **Charlotte Knights** (704/357-8071, www.charlotteknights.com), whose home field is just over the state line in Fort Mill, South Carolina. As with any AAA team, there's a good chance at any given game of seeing a major-leaguer rehabbing from injury or brushing up on his skills, or a young hotshot about to break into a big-league career.

Professional ECHL hockey team the **Charlotte Checkers** play at the Bobcats Arena. Ticket and schedule information are available from 704/342-4423 and www.gocheckers.com.

⟨ U.S. National Whitewater Center
The **U.S. National Whitewater Center** (820 Hawfield Rd., 704/391-3900, www.usnwc.org, daily 10am-5pm, passes $20-54, canopy tours $89), which opened in 2007, features "the world's only multichannel recirculating white-water river"—that is, a complex of artificial rapids—designed for training athletes at the Olympic level (it is the home of the U.S. Olympic canoe and kayak team), as well as first-time thrill-seekers. The center's 300 acres also feature mountain biking trails, a climbing center, and more.

ACCOMMODATIONS
When it comes to the languid elegance of the old South, ⟨ **The Duke Mansion** (400 Hermitage Rd., 704/714-4400, www.duke-mansion.com, from $179) is close kin to heaven. The circa-1915 mansion in Charlotte's lovely Myers Park neighborhood was home to North Carolina royalty, the Duke family, including the young Doris Duke. The downstairs foyer and gallery were clearly designed for entertaining high society, but the bedrooms—most restored to reflect the Duke family's tastes of around 1930—are simple and comfortable, and some of the en suite baths still have their original tubs and tiles. In a wonderful Southern tradition, most rooms open onto sleeping porches, which themselves are worth more than the price of the rooms. You'll receive first-rate service from all of the staff, and the culinary team will present you with a splendid breakfast.

The ⟨ **VanLandingham Estate** (2010 The Plaza, 704/334-8909 or 888/524-2020, www.vanlandinghamestate.com, from $140), built in 1913, provides a glimpse of the affluent infancy of the neighborhood known as Plaza-Midwood. A streetcar ran down the middle of The Plaza, and wealthy families established five- and six-acre estates in what was then a bucolic suburb. Plaza-Midwood now feels very close to the center of the city, and the lots have long since been subdivided, but it is still a charming enclave of early 20th-century craftsman-style bungalows. The VanLandingham is an architectural marriage of the best arts-and-crafts design elements and aesthetics individually tailored to the tastes of the builders, early textile magnates Ralph and Susie Harwood VanLandingham. The staff take good care of guests, the grounds are beautiful, and Uptown is only a few minutes away.

FOOD

Charlotte is the eatingest place. There are so many good new restaurants opening every week that it's hard to keep up, but for reviews of the newest restaurants (with lots of interesting cultural observation), check out Tricia Childress' column in *Creative Loafing* (free at many area businesses, http://charlotte.creativeloafing.com), and Helen Schwab's and Kathleen Purvis' food writing in the *Charlotte Observer* (www.charlotteobserver.com/restaurants).

Southern and Soul

Price's Chicken Coop (1614 Camden Rd., 704/333-9866, www.priceschickencoop.com, Tues.-Sat. 10am-6pm, under $10) is one of Charlotte's favorite chicken places, a takeout counter where you can buy a box of deep-fried chicken, perch, shrimp, or liver and gizzards. Another venerable fried chicken laboratory is the **Chicken Box Café** (3726 N. Tryon St., 704/332-2636, daily 11am-9pm, under $10).

Southeast Asian

Charlotte is a city of immigrants, with more arriving every year, and among the many benefits of growing diversity is an amazingly rich culinary environment. Asian cuisines are especially prominent, especially Vietnamese, Thai, and Malaysian restaurants.

Thai Taste (324 East Blvd., 704/332-0001, www.thaitastecharlotte.com, lunch Mon.-Fri. 11:30am-2:30pm, dinner Sun.-Thurs. 5pm-9pm, Fri.-Sat. 5pm-10:30pm, $10-18) has been a favorite for more than 20 years. The menu includes a variety of curries, noodle dishes, and stir-fries, including many vegetarian options.

Charlotte has quite a few Vietnamese restaurants, which are great fun to sample. Perhaps the best known is ◖ Lang Van (3019 Shamrock Dr., 704/531-9525, www.langvanrestaurant.com, Fri.-Sat. 11am-11pm, Sun.-Thurs. 11am-9:45pm, under $10). Lang Van has an incredibly long menu, with many *phos*, noodle soups, and vermicelli dishes. Like many Vietnamese restaurants, this is an ideal eatery for vegetarians. *Charlotte Observer* readers have voted Lang Van the area's top Asian restaurant multiple times.

Pizza

Everyone seems to like **Brooklyn South Pizza** (19400 Jetton Rd., Cornelius, 704/896-2928, Mon.-Wed. 11am-9pm, Thurs.-Sat. 11am-10pm, Sun. noon-9pm, $10-15) in Cornelius, north of the city. **Tony's Pizza** (14027 Conlan Circle, 704/541-8225; 1530 Overland Park, 704/688-6880, http://tonysbigpizza.com, Mon.-Fri. 11am-9:30pm, Sun. noon-8pm, $5-25), founded by two Italian-born, Brooklyn-raised friends, is another favorite. Also loudly lauded is **Hawthorne's Pizza** (1701 E. 7th St., 704/358-9339; 5814 Prosperity Church Rd., 704/875-8502; 4100 Carmel Rd., Suite A, 704/544-0299, http://hawthornespizza.com, Sun.-Thurs. 11am-midnight, Fri.-Sat. 11am-2am, $8-20).

Latin American

Charlotte has a large Latino population, and their imprint on the culinary landscape of the city adds a welcome dimension to the diversity of restaurants here. Most immediately noticeable are the wealth of small home-style taquerias. Many can be found along Central Avenue. Try **Taquería Linares** (4918 Central Ave., 704/535-6716, daily 11am-9pm, $7), **Taquería las Delicias** (5111 Central Ave., 704/537-5156, daily 11am-9pm, $7), and **Taquería la Única** (2801 Central Ave., 704/347-5115, daily 11am-9pm, $8). **Lempira** (5906 South Blvd., 704/552-1515, Mon.-Thurs. 8am-11pm, Fri.-Sat. 8am-midnight, $12) is an especially good Central American restaurant on South Boulevard. Delicious Latin American bakeries also are popping up all over, like **Panadería Salvadoreña** (4800 Central Ave., 704/568-9161) and **Taste of Colombia** (212 N. Polk St., Pineville, 704/889-5328).

European

The Plaza-Midwood neighborhood has lots of appealing eateries, and among the most popular is **Lulu's** (1911 Central Ave., 704/376-2242, www.luludinewine.com, Mon.-Thurs.

11am-10pm, Fri. 11am-11pm, Sun. 5pm-9pm, brunch Sun. 10am-3pm, under $30). The American and pan-European fare ranges from burgers and reuben sandwiches to choucroute (garlic sausage) and wild boar ragout.

Another special place is **Fiamma** (2418 Park Rd., 704/333-4363, daily 11:30am-3:30pm and 5pm-11pm, under $30), an Italian restaurant in the Dilworth neighborhood. For their spectacular menu, Fiamma has fresh fish flown in every day from Italy, and they make their pasta and pizza crust dough twice daily from scratch. Such dedication to quality can be tasted at first bite.

Indian

◀ **Woodlands** (7128-A Albemarle Rd., 704/569-9193, Mon.-Fri. 11:30am-3pm and 5pm-9:30pm, Sat.-Sun. 11:30am-10pm, $7-15) serves absolutely wonderful vegetarian southern Indian cuisine, offering nearly 20 different curries, *utthapam* (rice and lentil pancakes), Chinese-influenced rice and noodle dishes, and dozens of other components with which to assemble one of the best Indian meals you'll find in North Carolina.

Eclectic American

Among Charlotte's fanciest places to dine is **Bonterra Dining and Wine Room** (1829 Cleveland Ave. at E. Worthington Ave., 704/333-9463, http://bonterradining.com, $20-45). Bonterra, which has received both the Four Diamond Award from AAA and *Wine Spectator* Magazine's Award of Excellence, makes its home in an old Methodist church. House specialties include New York strip steak, veal chops, and fried lobster tail. Really, though, it's as much about wine here as food. The wine list features many dozens of fine wines from California, France, Australia, and even North Carolina. There are also many choices of single-malt scotch, port, and cognac.

INFORMATION AND SERVICES

Two Uptown (Charlotte's name for its downtown) locations serve as Charlotte **visitors**

centers: one at 330 South Tryon Street (704/339-6040, www.crva.com, Mon.-Fri. 8:30am-5pm, Sat. 9am-3pm), and the other in the lobby of the Levine Museum of the New South (200 E. 7th St., 704/331-2753, www.museumofthenewsouth.org, Mon.-Sat. 10am-5pm, Sun. noon-5pm). The Charlotte *Observer* publishes an excellent annual guide to the region, geared toward new residents and visitors, called *Living Here.* You can pick it up at many major destinations, or read it at www.charlotteobserver.com. Another comprehensive resource is www.visitcharlotte.com.

Carolinas Medical Center (1000 Blythe Blvd., 704/355-2000, www.carolinasmedicalcenter.org) is one of the largest hospitals in the Carolinas. Emergency vet clinics include **Carolina Veterinary Specialists** (2225 Township Rd., 704/588-7015 or 704/504-9608, www.carolinavet.com) and **Emergency Veterinary Clinic** (2440 Plantation Center Dr., Matthews, 704/844-6440).

GETTING THERE AND AROUND

Charlotte Douglas International Airport (CLT, 5501 Josh Birmingham Pkwy., 704/359-4013, www.charmeck.org) is the 10th-largest hub in the United States, with nonstop flights to and from over 120 destinations worldwide. Nearly 30 million passengers come through CLT each year. Charlotte's **Amtrak Station** (1914 N. Tryon St., 704/376-4416, www.amtrak.com) is a short cab ride from major Uptown hotels and attractions.

Charlotte's extensive and ever-expanding public transportation system provides affordable jaunts from place to place throughout the city. Some bus routes around the Center City and Uptown areas are free. The city has an ambitious light-rail system called **LYNX**, currently connecting Uptown to some southern neighborhoods and which will eventually give rapid access to and from Charlotte's many far-flung neighborhoods and suburbs. Routes and fares are posted at www.charmeck.org, or call 704/336-7433.

Vicinity of Charlotte

The number of NASCAR-related attractions and sites of interest to racing enthusiasts in general are too numerous to name, but you'll find a selection of the best listed among the attractions here.

Several of the state's special food traditions intersect near Charlotte. The fumes of Lexington barbecue waft over the entire Piedmont, causing an irresistible urge to mix ketchup into one's barbecue sauce. Serious aficionados of fried fish don't drive all the way to the coast to get their fix, but instead scout out inland fish camps on the back roads of Gaston and neighboring counties. Folks in country kitchens radiating out from Shelby and down from the foothills know that the best thing to do with those spare pig heads and organs lying around is to mash them up with cornmeal and serve them up as livermush. You'll see livermush sandwiches on the menu of many a little café in this region.

MOORESVILLE AND LAKE NORMAN

Mooresville is home to some of the state's—and the nation's—most important car racing facilities and attractions, as well as the home bases of more than 60 individual teams. There are several racing museums here, including the **North Carolina Auto Racing Hall of Fame** (Mooresville Visitor Center, 119 Knob Hill Rd., Mooresville, 704/663-5331, www.ncarhof.com, Mon.-Fri. 10am-5pm, Sat. 10am-3pm, $6 adults, $4 seniors and children). The **Memory Lane Motorsports Museum** (769 River Hwy., Mooresville, 704/662-3673, www.memorylaneautomuseum.com, daily 10am-5pm during race weeks, $10 adults, $6 ages 6-12, free under age 6) features the largest private collection of retired NASCAR automobiles and the world's largest collection of go-karts.

Major teams and racing companies are based here, and some operate facilities that are open to the public. **Dale Earnhardt Inc.** (1675 Coddle Creek Hwy./Hwy. 3, Mooresville, 704/334-9663, www.daleearnhardtinc.com, Mon.-Fri. 9am-5pm and Sat. 10am-4pm) has a showroom and a museum about the career of Dale Sr., a NASCAR legend. Teams' complexes are scattered throughout the area, including Dale Earnhardt Jr.'s **JR Motorsports** (349 Cayuga Dr., Mooresville, 704/799-4800, www.jrmotorsport.com), **Penske Racing** (200 Penske Way, Mooresville, 704/664-2300, www.penskeracing.com), and **Robert Yates Racing** (112 Byers Creek Rd., Mooresville, 704/662-9625, www.robertyatesracing.com).

Not to be missed either are the **NASCAR Technical Institute** (220 Byers Creek Rd., Mooresville, 877/201-2597, www.uti.edu), a formal training school for motorsports automotive technology, and **PIT Instruction and Training LLC** (156 Byers Creek Rd., Mooresville, 866/563-3566, www.5off5on.com), a pit-crew training school.

Sports and Recreation

If it's too hot to be around all that asphalt, there's plenty to do on the water. **Lake Norman State Park** (159 Inland Sea Lane, Troutman, 704/528-6350, http://ncparks.gov, May-Aug. 8am-9pm, Mar.-Apr., Sept.-Oct. 8am-8pm, Nov.-Feb. 8am-6pm, free) shelters the state's largest artificial lake, with boating, swimming, camping ($20), and more than six miles of biking and hiking trails.

CONCORD AND KANNAPOLIS

Cabarrus County, which wraps around the northeastern corner of Charlotte, is one of the phonetic zones that give newcomers and longtime North Carolinians alike the fits. Banish from your mind all thoughts of three-headed dogs and celebrated jumping frogs: it's "cuh-BA-russ," and the *a* is pronounced as in "hat." Kannapolis rhymes with the capital of Maryland.

CENTRAL NORTH CAROLINA

Lowe's Motor Speedway

Lowe's Motor Speedway (5555 Concord Pkwy. S., Concord, 800/455-3267, www.lowesmotorspeedway.com, tours nonevent days Mon.-Sat. 9:30am, 10:30am, 11:30am, 1:30pm, 2:30pm, 3:30pm, Sun. 1:30pm, 3:30pm, $5), on U.S. 29 south, is Concord's best-known attraction. The 167,000-seat arena with a 1.5-mile track hosts the NASCAR Nextel Cup as well as other NASCAR, Busch, and Craftsman Truck Series events. The Speedway is also home to the **Richard Petty Driving Experience,** where you can ride—or even drive—a 600-hp stock car at speeds up to 165 mph, as well as the **Xtreme Measures Teen Driving School,** where teenage drivers can spend two days learning safe driving skills in an exhilarating environment. Oddly enough, the Speedway's Smith Tower, on the second floor, hosts the **Carolinas Boxing Hall of Fame** (704/455-3200).

Racing Sights and Racing Schools

Not to be outdone by its neighbor Concord, Kannapolis honors racing and the life of its hometown star Dale Earnhardt Sr., with the **Dale Trail.** "Dale Senior" died at the age of 50 in an infamous last-lap crash at the 2001 Daytona 500, one of the tragedies in racing history that have most starkly illustrated the great danger to which drivers subject themselves. He is honored by a nine-foot bronze statue, a fan-financed granite monument, and huge murals, all at the **Dale Earnhardt Tribute** (Main St. and B. St.) in the middle of Cannon Village, a historic shopping district in Kannapolis.

ASHEVILLE AND THE BLUE RIDGE PARKWAY

One of the first impressions recorded by a visitor to North Carolina's Blue Ridge Mountains came in 1752, when Bishop Augustus Spangenberg came down from Pennsylvania in search of a prospective Southern home for the Moravian Church. He eventually found a welcoming spot near present-day Winston-Salem, but it's a wonder he didn't turn back when he first saw the Blue Ridge, a sight that filled him with dread. This man, who had crossed the Atlantic and tramped all over the American frontier, wrote in his diary, "We have reached here after a hard journey over very high, terrible mountains and cliffs. . . . When we reached the top we saw mountains to the right, to the left, before and behind us, rising like great waves in a storm."

The Blue Ridge is still pretty daunting, and indeed nearly impenetrable in parts, but times have changed, and the region attracts visitors and adventurers from all over the world for its blend of rustic scenery and authentic folk culture.

Nestled in a valley along the colorfully named French Broad River, Asheville—western North Carolina's largest city—is something of a paradox. An oasis of left-leaning, New Age-y thought in a generally very conservative area, Asheville boasts a large and influential creative community of artists, artisans, academics, and musicians of all types, from street buskers to classical performers (indeed, sometimes they're one and the same).

Begun in the 1930s as part of Franklin D. Roosevelt's Works Progress Administration, the Blue Ridge Parkway (BRP, www.blueridgeparkway.org) is 469 miles of road from

© JIM MOREKIS

HIGHLIGHTS

LOOK FOR **◖** TO FIND RECOMMENDED SIGHTS, ACTIVITIES, DINING, AND LODGING.

◖ *The Merry Go-Round* **Show:** Mount Airy is blessed with a rich musical tradition and a great small-town radio station, WPAQ. Its weekly *Merry Go-Round* show is broadcast in front of a live audience (page 163).

◖ MerleFest: For one long weekend in April, the best artists in American roots music are in North Wilkesboro, along with thousands of their fans (page 167).

◖ Grandfather Mountain: Take a gander at the surrounding UN-designated International Biosphere Reserve from the famous Mile-High Swinging Bridge—if you dare (page 173).

◖ Mount Mitchell: The tallest peak east of South Dakota was the subject of a scholarly feud in the mid-1800s. One of the feuders, Mitchell himself, is buried at the summit (page 176).

◖ Chimney Rock: A natural tower of stone growing out of a mountainside like a rhino's horn, Chimney Rock is the centerpiece of a large park with amazing hiking trails (page 181).

◖ Downtown Asheville Architecture: In the early 20th century, wealthy summer vaca-

tioners left their mark in Asheville's downtown, a district packed with art deco and beaux arts masterpieces (page 182).

◖ Biltmore Estate: This awe-inspiring palace of the Gilded Age hosts a collection of great little restaurants and shops, a winery, equestrian activities, and much more, all in a beautiful riverside setting (page 184).

◖ North Carolina Arboretum: One of the most beautiful collections of horticulture in the country is framed by the surrounding Pisgah National Forest (page 186).

◖ Folk Art Center: Learn about the master craftspeople of the Southern Appalachians and purchase gorgeous handmade items, including unique jewelry, traditional weaving and woodcarving, and fine-art furniture (page 187).

◖ Pisgah Ranger District: This 150,000-plus-acre section of the Pisgah National Forest encompasses the Cradle of Forestry Museum, Shining Rock Wilderness, Sliding Rock, Cold Mountain, and many other favorite outdoor destinations (page 200).

ASHEVILLE

ASHEVILLE AND THE BLUE RIDGE PARKWAY

VIRGINIA

KENTUCKY

NORTH CAROLINA

Cherokee National Forest

Pisgah National Forest

Nantahala National Forest

Cumberland Knob Recreation Area

Stone Mountain State Park

New River State Park

Mount Jefferson State Natural Area

Elk Knob State Park

Blue Ridge Pkwy

Lake James State Park

Linville Gorge

Mount Mitchell State Park

Chimney Rock Park

THE MERRY GO-ROUND SHOW

MERLEFEST

TRADITIONS POTTERY

GRANDFATHER MOUNTAIN

LINN COVE VIADUCT

LOST COVE OVERLOOK/ BROWN MOUNTAIN LIGHTS

LINVILLE CAVERNS

CROSSNORE SCHOOL

ORCHARD AT ALTAPASS

CHIMNEY ROCK

MOUNT MITCHELL

WNC NATURE CENTER

FOLK ART CENTER

BILTMORE ESTATE

BOTANICAL GARDENS

NORTH CAROLINA ARBORETUM

DOWNTOWN ASHEVILLE ARCHITECTURE

PISGAH RANGER DISTRICT

Mount Airy

Mocksville

Salisbury

Yadkinville

Wilkesboro

North Wilkesboro

Sparta

Statesville

Mooresville

Lincolnton

Gastonia

Charlotte

Granite Falls

Hickory

Shelby

Lenoir

Morganton

Blowing Rock

Boone

Linville

Marion

Rutherfordton

Hendersonville

Flat Rock

Saluda

Black Mountain

Burnsville

Asheville

Brevard

Waynesville

To Cashiers and Highlands

To Dillsboro

Johnson City

Erwin

Greeneville

Kingsport

Bristol

20 mi

20 km

ASHEVILLE

© AVALON TRAVEL

the North Carolina-Tennessee border into Virginia's Shenandoah Valley, the vast bulk of it in the Tarheel State. It's fun, accessible, tastefully done, and very scenic. The BRP took 50 years to complete—the last section was finished in 1987—and boasts 26 tunnels blasted out of the rock, 25 of them in North Carolina. Its complexion changes slightly as you wind your way farther north, but the twisty mountain driving at a maximum 45 mph is a constant.

Until the 20th century the farthest northwestern counties of North Carolina were so remote and so cut off from the rest of the state that they were known as the Lost Provinces. Gradually, improved roads and the BRP brought curious flatlanders up into the clouds, and the region evolved into a popular destination for vacationers. But stands of virgin forest are still hidden in remote coves, and places like the Linville Gorge dare the most accomplished outdoors enthusiasts.

On any given weekend in Mount Airy, and in many other mountain and foothills towns nearer to the heart of the Blue Ridge at the Virginia border, you can hear the old-time string band music that is as popular here today as it was in the days before the radio. Even if you've come to the mountains to ski or to eat at the gourmet restaurants in Boone and Blowing Rock, be sure to set aside a little time for the back roads.

PLANNING YOUR TIME

Always keep the weather in mind when driving in the mountains here and all along the BRP, not only snow and ice from fall to spring but frequent dense fog throughout the year. Conditions can be completely different from one moment to the next and from one mountain to the next. Don't hesitate to pull over and wait out the fog. It often lifts and dissipates quickly.

Driving the BRP, while most satisfying, takes longer than it may look on a map due to the low speed limit and the winding nature of the road. The heavily traveled stretch from Asheville to Boone, for example, will take about four hours.

Asheville, to the south, boasts by far the greatest number of amenities, but there are fine restaurants and B&B-style lodging all through the towns of western North Carolina. If you're planning on spending most of your time roaming the deep mountains around Mount Mitchell and Grandfather Mountain, the Linville area, and the Banner Elk and Beech Mountain areas, Boone is a convenient place to stay. Wilkesboro and Mount Airy are both at the edge of the mountains and easily accessible from the junction of I-77 and U.S. 421, a jumping-off point to almost any foothills location.

If you're planning on hitting several of the major attractions while you're in the mountains, the **Go Blue Ridge Card** (800/887-9103, www.goblueridgecard.com) might be a money-saver. Among the attractions in this chapter that the Go Blue Ridge Card will give you access to are Grandfather Mountain, the Orchard at Altapass, and Linville Caverns. It costs between $50 and $160, depending on where you go and how many days you want to use it. At participating attractions that charge admission, the card gets you in without having to buy tickets. At many shops and restaurants throughout the region, it'll get you a good discount.

INFORMATION AND SERVICES

The state Department of Transportation operates a real-time road conditions map (http://tims.ncdot.gov/tims). For current conditions along the Blue Ridge Parkway, you can check the recorded message at 828/298-0398.

Hospitals are located in most of the major towns in this region, but in case of an emergency, help might be delayed by weather, road conditions, or distance. In many areas—not just deep in the woods, but in populated areas as well—there may be no cell phone signal.

GETTING THERE AND AROUND

The Blue Ridge Parkway is especially enjoyable in that there is no cross traffic. The BRP is bridged over interstate highways, and it has separate side roads for every intersection.

Everything on the BRP is measured by milepost, with mile marker number 1 beginning in northwest Virginia, going all the way to number 469 at U.S. 441.

Along the BRP you'll be sharing the road with plenty of motorcyclists, drawn to the scenery and challenging roads. Always be aware of their presence, for their safety and for yours.

Mount Airy and the Virginia Border

MOUNT AIRY AND VICINITY
Sights
In downtown Mount Airy you'll notice 1960s police squad cars, business names that may seem oddly familiar, and cardboard cutouts of Barney Fife peering out from shop windows. Mount Airy is the hometown of Andy Griffith and a mecca for fans of *The Andy Griffith Show*. TAGSRWC (www.mayberry.com) is an intentionally obtuse acronym for The Andy Griffith Show Rerun Watchers Club, the show's international fan club whose hundreds of chapters have in-reference names like "Her First Husband Got Runned over by a Team of Hogs" (Texas) and "Anxiety Magnifies Fearsome Objects" (Alabama). The Surry Arts Council hosts the citywide **Mayberry Days,** an annual fall festival entering its second decade, in which TAGSRWC members, other fans, cast members, and impersonators of Mayberry characters come to town and have a big time getting haircuts at Floyd's Barbershop, riding in squad cars, and arresting each other.

For a one-of-a-kind view of Mount Airy, hop into a Mayberry squad car to tour all the major sights in town. **Mayberry Squad Car Tours** (625 S. Main St., 336/789-6743, www.tourmayberry.com) leave from "Wally's Service Station," and cost "$35 for a carload."

Finally, two roadside oddities in Mount Airy are not to be missed. At 594 North Andy Griffith Parkway/U.S. 52 stands the **Giant Milk Carton.** This 12-foot-tall metal milk carton now advertises Pet Milk, but since its creation in the 1940s it has also stood as an advertisement for Coble Dairy and Flavo-Rich Milk. At the intersection of U.S. 52 and Starlite Drive stands a **Great Big Man,** a very tall, friendly metal service station attendant. He is an old

friend to out-of-towners who come to Mount Airy for the fiddlers' convention every year, who remember to turn off the highway to get to Veterans Park when they see "The Big Man."

◖ *The Merry Go-Round* Show
Teamed up with WPAQ (AM 740), the Surry Arts Council hosts *The Merry Go-Round,* the country's third-longest-running live bluegrass and old-time music radio show. Come to the **Downtown Cinema Theater** (142 N. Main St., Mount Airy, 800/286-6193, www.surryarts.org) for the show (Sat. 11am-1:30pm), or show up as early as 9am toting an instrument if you'd like to join in the preshow jam session. It's one of the state's great small-town treats.

Other Entertainment and Events
When you visit Mount Airy or pass close, tune in to **WPAQ** (AM 740, also streaming online at www.wpaq740.com). For over 60 years, WPAQ has provided a venue for live local talent to perform old-time, bluegrass, and gospel music. Tune in for the live Saturday-morning *The Merry Go-Round* show, or any other day of the week, when you'll hear local call-in shows, old-style country preaching, and more music. Another local institution that has a great deal to do with the vitality of Mount Airy's musical traditions is the **Bluegrass and Old-Time Fiddlers Convention** (631 W. Lebanon St., 800/286-6193, www.mtairyfiddlersconvention.com), held for almost 40 years during the first full weekend in June at Veterans Memorial Park. Thousands of people come to the festival from around the world to play old-time and bluegrass music with their friends and compete in what is a very prestigious competition in this genre of music.

ASHEVILLE

CHANG AND ENG: SIAMESE TWINS

Andy Griffith may be Mount Airy's most famous living son, but in the middle of the 19th century, two of the most famous men in the world lived on a quiet farm in rural Surry County, just outside Mount Airy. Chang and Eng were born in Siam (now Thailand) in 1811, joined at the sternum by a cartilaginous band of flesh. Had they been born today, it probably would have been an easy operation to separate the brothers, but in 1811 they were lucky not to have been killed at birth. Beginning when they were teenagers, Chang and Eng toured the world, eventually becoming top draws at P. T. Barnum's shows.

During their travels through the United States, they took a shine to North Carolina, and when they burned out on show business, around age 30, they decided to settle in Wilkesboro. In North Carolina they adopted the last name of Bunker. Chang fell in love with a local girl named Addie Yates, and soon Eng took to courting her older sister Sally. The four married and moved in together, and raised a very large family—Eng and Sally had 11 children, and Chang and Addie had 10. Many of their descendants live in the area today.

In some ways Chang and Eng seemed like one person. When they first learned English, they referred to themselves as "I," and they were rarely observed to speak to each other, as if it was unnecessary. In one of countless medical experiments they underwent, an examining doctor tickled one brother, which caused the other brother to become angry. Yet in other ways they were very different, and inevitably this caused them great unhappiness. Chang was temperamental and vivid; Eng was reticent and contemplative. More dangerously, Chang liked to drink and Eng liked to gamble. Sometimes they had bitter arguments and, on a couple of occasions, fistfights. Perhaps it's best not to dwell too much on the Bunkers' conjugal relations, but their domestic arrangements required plenty of compromise. They divided their time between Chang and Addie's and Eng and Sally's houses, each brother being the other's houseguest half of the time.

In spite of the limitations that biology placed on them, the Bunkers became fairly conventional upper-middle-class farmers, owning slaves and sending two sons to fight in the Confederate Army. The War left them in dire financial straits, however, and in 1870 they sailed for Europe for another tour. On the voyage home, Chang had a severe stroke, from which he never fully recovered. He began to drink heavily, and his health declined. One January night in 1874, Eng awoke to find that Chang was dead. Within a few hours, Eng, who had been in excellent health, was also dead. An autopsy showed that Chang had died of a cerebral hemorrhage, but Eng's cause of death is still unknown. It's thought that he may have died of fright.

Chang and Eng Bunker, to whom we owe the existence of the phrase "Siamese twins," are buried at White Plains Baptist Church (506 Old Hwy. 601), south of Mount Airy.

The **Surry Arts Council** is one of the hubs of artistic activity in the Mount Airy-Surry County area. Located at the **Andy Griffith Theater** (218 Rockford St., 800/286-6193, www.surryarts.org), they sponsor and host many events throughout the year that showcase local talent in drama, visual arts, and especially music. On the third Saturday of the month, local and regional old-time and bluegrass bands perform in the **Voice of the Blue Ridge Series** ($10 adults, free under age 6).

Sports and Recreation

Mount Airy and its neighbors are foothills towns, and you have to drive some distance farther west before you start to climb the Blue Ridge. This is why the geographical anomaly of Pilot Mountain is so startling. The 1,400-foot mountain, with a prominent rocky knob at the top, kind of looks like a giant dog's head, or the UHF knob of an old TV set that you could use to turn on *The Andy Griffith Show.* The surrounding **Pilot Mountain State Park**

(792 Pilot Knob Park Rd., Pinnacle, 336/325-2355, http://ncparks.gov, mountain section May-Aug. 8am-9pm, Mar.-Apr., Sept.-Oct. 8am-8pm, Nov.-Feb. 8am-6pm, river section May-Aug. 8:30am-8pm, Mar.-Apr., Sept.-Oct. 8:30am-7pm, Nov.-Feb. 8:30am-5pm, free) is a beautiful place for hiking, swimming, rock climbing and rappelling (in designated areas), canoeing on the Yadkin River, and camping (Mar. 15-Nov. 30, $20, $15 over age 62) at 49 designated tent and trailer sites. Each site has a tent pad, a picnic table, and a grill as well as access to drinking water and hot showers.

A series of 400-foot rock faces, extending for two miles, are the most striking feature of **Hanging Rock State Park** (Hwy. 2015, 4 miles northwest of Danbury, 336/593-8480, http://ncparks.gov, Nov.-Feb. daily 8am-6pm, Mar. and Oct. daily 8am-7pm, Apr.-May and Sept. daily 8am-8pm, June-Aug. daily 8am-9pm, free). It's a great place for rock climbing and rappelling (which requires a permit and registration with park staff as well as a schedule that allows climbers to be finished and out of the park by closing time). You can also hike to waterfalls and beautiful overlooks, and swim in a nearby lake. Hanging Rock State Park has 73 tent and trailer campsites ($20), one of which is wheelchair-accessible. There are also two-bedroom, four-bed vacation cabins available for rent during the summer by the week (about $450) and off-season nightly ($88) for a minimum of two nights. Registration is best arranged at least a month in advance; contact the park office for application details.

Yadkin River Adventures (104 Old Rockford Rd., Rockford, 336/374-5318, www.yadkinriveradventures.com) offers rentals of canoes, kayaks, and sit-on-tops, and shuttle service for full- and half-day paddling adventures. The Class I Yadkin River is great for paddlers of all ages and experience levels, and it has some beautiful views of Pilot Mountain.

Balloon pilots Tony and Claire Colburn lead tours of the Yadkin Valley by hot-air balloon, weather permitting, any time of year. **Yadkin Valley Hot Air Balloon Adventures**

(336/922-7207, www.balloonadventure.net) requires special arrangements—contact the Colburns for fees and availability—and it's an amazing way to see the Carolina foothills.

Accommodations
UNDER $150
The Rockford Bed and Breakfast (4872 Rockford Rd., Dobson, 800/561-6652, www.rockfordbedandbreakfast.com, $120-140) is a beautiful mid-19th-century farmhouse south of Mount Airy in Dobson, convenient to many of the Yadkin Valley wineries.

In Mount Airy, try **Quality Inn** (2136 Rockford St., 336/789-2000, www.qualityinn.com, from $70), **Holiday Inn Express** (1320 Ems Dr., 336/719-1731, www.ichotels.group.com, from $80, pets allowed), and **Hampton Inn** (2029 Rockford St., 336/789-5999, www.hamptoninn.com, from $100).

$150-300
Pilot Knob Inn Bed and Breakfast (361 New Pilot Knob Lane, Pinnacle, 336/325-2502, www.pilotknobinn.com, $129-249) is unusual in that guests can stay not only in suites in the main lodge but in one of several restored, century-old tobacco barns on the property. Each one-bedroom barn-turned-cabin is well equipped with modern conveniences, including two-person hot tubs as well as wood-burning stone fireplaces. Children are not allowed; nor are pets, other than your horse, who can occupy a stall on the property for an additional $50 per night.

Food
The Snappy Lunch (125 N. Main St., 336/786-4931, www.thesnappylunch.com, Tues., Thurs., Sat. 5:45am-1:15pm, Mon., Wed., Fri. 5:45am-1:45pm, $4) is most famous for having been mentioned in *The Andy Griffith Show*. But having seated its first customer in 1923, the Snappy Lunch is much older than the show and older even than Andy himself. Pack your cholesterol drugs when you go to Mount Airy so that you can enjoy Snappy's signature pork chop sandwich.

ASHEVILLE

There are at least two sources for good, strong coffee in Mount Airy. My favorites are the **Good Life Café** (Main-Oak Emporium, N. Main St. and E. Oak St., 336/789-2404, www.mainoakemporium.com, Mon.-Sat. 10am-6pm, Sun. 1pm-5pm), downtown, and **Moby's Coffee** (2123 Rockford St./U.S. 601, Suite 200, 336/786-1222, Mon.-Thurs. 7am-10pm, Fri.-Sat. 7am-1pm).

CUMBERLAND KNOB

Up at the Virginia border at milepost 217 of the Blue Ridge Parkway is the **Cumberland Knob Recreation Area,** where construction of the BRP began in 1935. Today it remains a popular destination for hikers, who enjoy the fairly strenuous treks on and around the 2,860-foot-high Cumberland Knob. The most enjoyable hike, however, is down to little Gully Creek. If you don't want to hike, there's a nice picnic area.

STONE MOUNTAIN STATE PARK

In the town of Roaring Gap is **Stone Mountain State Park** (3042 Frank Pkwy., Roaring Gap, 336/957-8185, http://ncparks.gov, office daily 8am-5pm, park Nov.-Feb. daily 8am-6pm, Mar.-Apr. and Sept.-Oct. daily 8am-8pm, May-Aug. daily 8am-9pm, free). The centerpiece of the park, a designated National Natural Landmark, is the spectacular 600-foot smooth rock face of **Stone Mountain,** which though similar in shape and texture, isn't to be confused with the much larger granite outcropping of the same name outside Atlanta.

This is, of course, a popular spot for rock climbing and rappelling, but adventurous hikers can make the strenuous trek to the summit on foot to enjoy the amazing view. Along one of the hiking trails are the multiple restored log-and-stone buildings of the historic Hutcheson homestead.

The park recommends that only experienced climbers attempt the faces in the park. Be sure to register with the park office, and carefully read the park literature about climbing before setting out. Some very pleasant camping ($13-25) is available, both primitive backpack camping and family camping in sites near a washhouse with hot showers.

ASHEVILLE

view from Stone Mountain

© JIM MOREKIS

Accommodations

The camping is great in Stone Mountain State Park, but those requiring more creature comforts might want to head to the nearby town of Elkin, near I-77. The best of the chain accommodations in the area is the **Fairfield Inn & Suites** (628 CC Camp Rd., 866/576-5693, www.marriott.com, $105).

MOUNT JEFFERSON STATE NATURAL AREA

Mount Jefferson State Natural Area (SR 1152, Jefferson, 336/246-9653, http://ncparks. gov, May-Aug. 9am-8pm, Mar.-Apr., Sept.-Oct. 9am-7pm, Nov.-Feb. 9am-5pm, free) preserves a peak that was known long ago as Panther Mountain as well as a couple of less savory names. Mount Jefferson has a forbidding countenance, with outcroppings of black volcanic rock and, on the north slope, a stunted forest of wind-daunted aspen and maple. Hiking trails, ranging from gentle to strenuous, wend along the crests and up to the peak, through laurel thickets and virgin red oak forests.

New River State Park (park office on Wagoner Access Rd./Hwy. 1590, east of Jefferson, 336/982-2587, http://ncparks.gov, May-Aug. 8am-9pm, Mar.-Apr., Sept.-Oct. 8am-8pm, Nov.-Feb. 8am-6pm, free) threads along what is, despite the name, believed to be one of the oldest rivers in North America. The beautiful New is a very popular canoeing river, a gentle ride through some stunning countryside. Water is highest in May and June, lowest in August and September. Access points are all along the river. There are also many campsites, both canoe-in (no facilities, $13) and drive-to (with showers and restrooms, $25).

New River Outfitters (10725 U.S. 221 N., Jefferson, 800/982-9190, www.canoethenew.com) offers canoe runs, ranging from one hour to six days, and tubing trips along the New River. They operate from the old New River General Store, where you can buy mountain honey, hoop cheese, and local crafts. **Zaloo's Canoes** (3874 Hwy. 16 S., Jefferson, 800/535-4027, www.zaloos.com) is another long-established area outfitter that also offers canoe and raft trips.

Elk Knob State Park

The small, scenic New River town of Todd is a slow, winding 12 miles north of Boone. Newish **Elk Knob State Park** (5564 Meat Camp Rd., Todd, 828/297-7261, http://ncparks.gov, office daily 8am-5pm, park Nov.-Feb. daily 8am-6pm, Mar.-May and Sept.-Oct. daily 8am-8pm, June-Aug. daily 8am-9pm, free) is under development and currently offers three primitive campsites, but the big draw is the fact that it stays open during the winter, unlike many other state parks in the mountains, to enable visitors to enjoy cross-country skiing. Elk Knob, the second-highest peak in Watauga County at 5,520 feet, is a steep, strenuous hike along an old road leading to the summit. All facilities here are free of charge.

WILKESBORO AND NORTH WILKESBORO

❰ MerleFest

It began as a small folk festival more than 20 years ago, but **MerleFest** (www.merlefest.org, usually the last weekend in Apr.) has grown into one of the premier roots music events in the country. It was founded in honor of Merle Watson, the son of legendary guitarist Doc Watson. Merle, also a guitarist, passed away in 1985 in a tractor accident, cutting short an influential career. Doc Watson, who grew up in the nearby community of Deep Gap, continues to be the festival's ceremonial host, and nowadays he is joined by Merle's son Richard, who has also grown to be an expert guitarist. MerleFest draws thousands of visitors every year and many of the top-name performers in folk, country, and bluegrass music. It's quite expensive: $40-60 per day for general admission, $145-260 for multiday packages. Springtime in the mountains can be changeful; some years it's boiling hot and sunny at MerleFest, other times as damp and raw as winter, and sometimes it's both by turns. If you're traveling through the northern mountains during MerleFest, keep in mind that all the motels within an hour's drive of North Wilkesboro, and probably farther, will be booked solid, so be sure to put dibs on a room well in advance. Tenting and RV camping are available on the festival grounds.

Food

North Wilkesboro's **Brushy Mountain Smokehouse and Creamery** (201 Wilkesboro Blvd., 336/667-9464, www.brushymtnsmokehouseandcreamery.com, Mon., Wed., Thurs.-Sat. 11am-9pm, Sun. 11am-2pm) is famous for its pulled pork barbecue and country sides (biscuits, fried okra, baked apples), but it's also a great ice cream shop. The ice cream is made there, and they bake their own waffle cones, so it's as fresh as it can be. Fried apple pie, cobbler, and ice cream pie are all available by the slice as well as whole-hog.

Deep Mountains

There's something exciting about the ascent into the High Country—glimpses of a shadowy mountain range on the horizon; cows grazing in steep, rocky fields; hairpin turns in the road around dynamited stone faces; the popping sound in your ears as you reach the first mountain. Most travelers experience this part of North Carolina by winding along the Blue Ridge Parkway (BRP), making side-trips deeper into the mountains and peering down from the crest to the Piedmont below.

Boone is a fun and hip little city, the home of Appalachian State University, good antique shops and organic markets, and a rambunctious green counterculture. Blowing Rock and Linville were tony summertime roosts for wealthy folks early in the 20th century, and much of that elegance remains, both in the stylish bungalows left behind and in the modern spas and resorts found here today.

Venturing off the Parkway and into the deep mountains, visit the little settlements of Penland and Crossnore, as well as Bakersville and other towns in the Toe River Valley. Here you'll find a thriving colony of artists. Many of them came to this area to be part of the folk school at Penland, which in its quiet way has exerted a great deal of influence on modern American craft movements.

BOONE

Boone is the quintessential western North Carolina city, a blend of old and new, where proponents of homesteading and holistic living find a congenial habitat in the culture of rural Appalachia. It's also a college town, the home of Appalachian State University, and as such has an invigorating youthful verve.

Shopping

Several antiques shops in Boone make the downtown a great place for browsing. **Appalachian Antiques** (631 W. King St., 828/268-9988, summer Mon.-Sat. 10am-6pm, Sun. 11am-6pm, winter Mon.-Sat. 10am-5pm, Sun. noon-5pm) is one of the best and biggest.

Footsloggers (Depot St. and Howard St., 828/265-5111, www.footsloggers.com) has been selling gear for climbing, hiking, and camping for almost 40 years. At the Boone location (there's also a store in Blowing Rock) is a 40-foot climbing tower that simulates many conditions you might find climbing real rock faces.

There are several branches of the **Mast General Store** (Hwy. 194, Valle Crucis, 828/963-6511, www.mastgeneralstore.com, summer Mon.-Sat. 7am-6:30pm, Sun. noon-6pm, winter hours vary) in the Carolina High Country, but the original is in Valle Crucis, about 20 minutes west of Boone. Though it has been an attraction for more than 20 years now, its history as a community institution goes back generations, to the 1880s and before. When the Mast family owned it, the store had the reputation of carrying everything "from cradles to caskets," and today it still has an awfully varied inventory, with specialties in outdoor wear (Carhartt, Columbia, Teva), camping gear, and ever so much candy.

Sports and Recreation
ROCK CLIMBING
Rock Dimensions (131 Depot St., 828/265-3544, www.rockdimensions.com) is a guide service that leads rock climbs at gorgeous locations throughout western North Carolina and to parts of Tennessee and Virginia. Guides teach proper multipitch, top rope anchoring, and rappelling techniques and lead caving expeditions over the state lines.

SKIING
The Banner Elk area has some of the state's best ski slopes. **Sugar Mountain** (800/784-2768, www.skisugar.com) is North Carolina's largest winter resort, with 115 acres of ski slopes and 20 trails. In addition to skiing, activities on the 5,300-foot-high mountain include snow tubing, skating, snowshoeing, and, in the summertime, the Showdown at Sugar National Mountain Bike Series. They offer lessons in skiing and snowboarding for adults and children. Nearby **Ski Beech Mountain Resort** (1007 Beech Mountain Pkwy., Beech Mountain, 800/438-2093, www.beechmountainresort.com) peaks at 300 feet higher than Sugar Mountain and has 15 slopes and 10 lifts, as well as skating and snowboarding areas. **Hawksnest** (2058 Skyland Dr., Seven Devils, 800/822-4295, www.hawksnest-resort.com) is on a 4,800-foot mountain in Seven Devils with 12 slopes, many geared for beginners and intermediate skiers.

HIKING, RAFTING, AND CAVE TRIPS
Down the road from the Mast General Store in Valle Crucis, **River and Earth Adventures** (3618 Broadstone Rd., 866/411-7238, www.raftcavehike.com) leads all sorts of exciting trips on the water, in the woods, and in the area's deep caves. Rafting expeditions ($65-85 adults, $55-65 children) ride the Lower

Nolichucky (Class II-III), French Broad (Class III-IV), and Watauga (Class II-III) Rivers. Cave trips (year-round daily, $75 pp) meet at the Valle Crucis shop, from where you'll proceed to Elizabethton, Tennessee, about an hour away, for a day's spelunking in Worley's Cave. Guided hiking trips are also available, including all-day kids-only hikes (with adult guides, of course) to free up parents who'd like a day on their own.

High Mountain Expeditions (1380 Hwy. 105 S., Banner Elk, 800/262-9036, www.highmountainexpeditions.com), which also has a Boone location, leads rafting trips on the Watauga River (Class I-III) and the much more challenging Nolichucky River (Class III-IV). They also lead caving expeditions for adults and children, for which no experience is necessary.

Accommodations
UNDER $150
The **Smoketree Lodge** (11914 Hwy. 105 S., 800/422-1880, www.smoketree-lodge.com, from $75 high season, from $55 off-season) is another good choice; it's a large hotel with basic but comfortable guest rooms and efficiencies, a large rustic lobby, and a nice indoor pool and saunas.

The **Yonahlossee Resort** (Shulls Mill Rd., 800/962-1986, www.yonahlossee.com, from $109), between Boone and Blowing Rock, is a former girls' camp built in the 1920s. The resort has a big stone inn and studio cottages, a fitness center and a sauna, tennis courts with a pro shop, and a 75-foot indoor heated pool.

Among area motels, some good bets are **Fairfield Inn and Suites** (2060 Blowing Rock Rd., 828/268-0677, www.marriott.com, from $40), **Comfort Suites** (1184 Hwy. 105, 828/268-0099, www.choicehotels.com, from $100), **Holiday Inn Express** (1943 Blowing Rock Rd./U.S. 321 S., 828/264-2451, www.hiexpress.com, from $90), and **Best Western Blue Ridge Plaza** (840 E. King St., 828/266-1100, www.bestwesternboone.com, from $65).

ASHEVILLE

$150-300

The **Lovill House Inn** (404 Old Bristol Rd., 800/849-9466, www.lovillhouseinn.com, $149-219) is close to the Appalachian State campus, and it was in the parlor of this 1875 farmhouse that the papers were drawn up that led to the founding of the university. The inn sits on 11 evergreen-shaded acres and is a lovely place to relax and read.

Food

The menu at **Our Daily Bread** (627 W. King St., 828/264-0173, www.ourdailybreadboone. com, Mon.-Thurs. 11am-8pm, Fri.-Sat. 11am-10pm, Sun. noon-6pm) includes no fewer than 30 specialty sandwiches, from their bestselling Jamaican Turkey Sub ($6.50) to the Elvis Prezz (bananas and peanut butter, the King's favorite, $5). Try the Tempeh Reuben ($6.25), a daring mixture of flavors that features marinated tempeh, sauerkraut, Swiss cheese, and mustard on rye. Sounds outrageous, but it works. Our Daily Bread also makes a variety of fresh soups and chili (meat and veggie) every day.

Melanie's Food Fantasy (664 W. King St., 828/263-0300, www.melaniesfoodfantasy. com, Mon.-Sat. 8am-2:30pm, Sun. 8:30am-2:30pm) is worth a special trip to Boone. The breakfast menu is nothing short of spectacular, with its variety of wholegrain waffles, pancakes, and french toast ($4.25-8), all sorts of fancy omelets (try the spinach-garlic-provolone-Swiss, $6), and enough options to keep both carnivores and vegetarians full. Lunch at Melanie's is every bit as good.

The **Dan'l Boone Inn** (130 Hardin St., 828/264-8657, http://danlbooneinn.com, hours vary) serves old-time country food family-style. Despite the complicated pricing system (dinner $15 adults, $9 ages 9-11, $7 ages 6-8, $5 ages 4-5, free under age 4, breakfast $9 adults, $6 ages 9-11, $5 ages 6-8, $4 ages 4-5, free under age 4), the food is straightforward good. At breakfast you can feast on country ham and red-eye gravy, stewed apples, grits, and much more; at dinner there's fried chicken, country-style steak, ham biscuits, and lots of vegetable sides.

The **Gamekeeper Restaurant and Bar** (3005 Shull's Mill Rd., 828/963-7400, www. gamekeeper-nc.com, bar May-Oct. daily from 5pm, dinner May-Oct. Sun.-Fri. from 6pm, Sat. from 5:30pm, $20-50) is tucked away between Boone and Blowing Rock at the Yonahlossee Resort. This restaurant is making a stir as an innovator in high Southern fusion cuisine, with a menu that features appetizers like fried green tomatoes and fried okra, and entrées that include mountain trout, ostrich, wapiti, and buffalo. Don't miss the bourbon pudding and white Russian cheesecake—or the seemingly endless wine list ($20-215 per bottle).

BLOWING ROCK

The town of Blowing Rock, named for the nearby geological oddity, is an old rocking chair resort, graced by stately old houses that were built long ago by early-20th-century captains of industry. Today, cafés and galleries make this a very pleasant place to stroll for a few well-manicured touristy blocks, and the Blue Ridge Parkway gives easy access to the Moses Cone Manor and other notable local landmarks. The main street—called Main Street, of course—gets pretty crowded on summer weekends, the high season.

Sights

Blowing Rock (U.S. 321 S., 828/295-7111, www.theblowingrock.com, hours vary, $6 adults, $1 children), just outside the cute town of Blowing Rock, is a strange rock outcropping purported (by *Ripley's Believe It or Not*) to be the only place in the world where snow falls upward. Indeed, light objects (think handkerchiefs, leaves, hats) thrown off Blowing Rock—not allowed, by the way, to prevent the valley from filling up with too-heavy litter—do tend to come floating back up. The view from the rock is quite lovely.

The **Moses Cone Manor** (BRP milepost 294, 828/295-7938, Mar. 15-Nov. daily 9am-5pm, free) is a huge white mountain palace, the 1901 country home of North Carolina textile baron Moses Cone. After making his fortune,

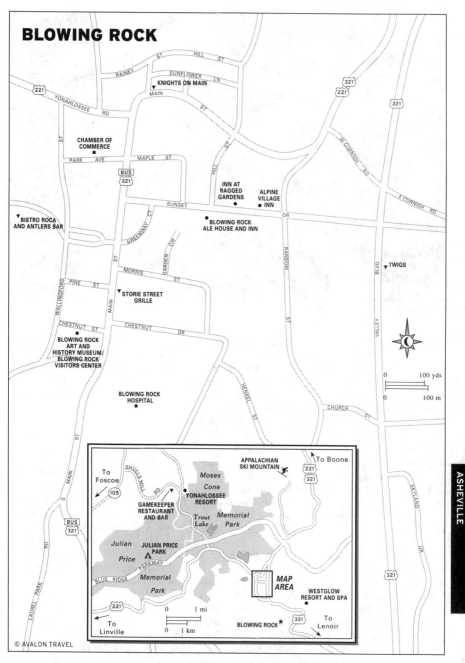

BLOWING ROCK

HILL ST
RAINEY ST
SUNFLOWER LN
221
YONAHLOSSEE RD
KNIGHTS ON MAIN
MAIN ST
321
321
321

CHAMBER OF COMMERCE
PARK AVE
MAPLE ST
BUS 321
W CORNISH RD
F CORNISH RD

INN AT RAGGED GARDENS
ALPINE VILLAGE INN
SUNSET
DR
▼ **BISTRO ROCA AND ANTLERS BAR**
GREENWAY CT
BLOWING ROCK ALE HOUSE AND INN
RANSOM ST
BLVD
▼ **TWIGS**

MORRIS ST
GARDEN CIR
PINE ST
WALLINGFORD
▼ **STORIE STREET GRILLE**
MAIN ST
VALLEY BLVD

CHESTNUT ST
CHESTNUT DR
BLOWING ROCK ART AND HISTORY MUSEUM/ BLOWING ROCK VISITORS CENTER
HENKEL ST

0   100 yds
0   100 m

BLOWING ROCK HOSPITAL
CHURCH ST

To Foscoe
SHULLS MILL RD
APPALACHIAN SKI MOUNTAIN
To Boone
221 321
105
Moses Cone
YONAHLOSSEE RESORT
GAMEKEEPER RESTAURANT AND BAR
Trout Lake
Memorial Park
SKYLAND DR
BUS 321
Julian Price
JULIAN PRICE PARK
Memorial Park
PARKWAY
321
BLUE RIDGE
LAUREL PARK RD
S MAIN ST
MAP AREA
WESTGLOW RESORT AND SPA
221
0   1 mi
0   1 km
To Linville
BLOWING ROCK ★
321
To Lenoir

© AVALON TRAVEL

ASHEVILLE

© JIM MOREKIS

charming downtown Blowing Rock

Cone became a leading philanthropist, and as you drive around the state, particularly in the northern Piedmont, you'll notice that his name still graces quite a few institutions. Flat Top Manor, as the mansion on the Parkway was called, is a wonderfully crafted house, white and ornate like a wedding cake. Appropriately, it is home to one of the **Southern Highland Craft Guild** (828/298-7928, www.southern-highlandguild.org) stores, a place to buy beautiful textiles, pottery, jewelry, furniture, dolls, and much more, handmade by some of the best craftspeople of the Appalachian Mountains. There are also extensive hiking and riding trails on the estate.

Accommodations
UNDER $150
Alpine Village Inn (297 Sunset Dr., 828/295-7206, www.alpine-village-inn.com, from $50) in downtown Blowing Rock has comfortable accommodations at a good price. The guest rooms are located in a main inn and in a motel-style wing. It's a convenient location

for checking out the shops and restaurants in town. Another good value is the **Cliff Dwellers Inn** (116 Lakeview Tr., 800/322-7380, www.cliffdwellers.com, from $70) with clean, simple guest rooms and a beautiful lakefront view.

$150-300
The lavish 1916 Greek Revival mansion of painter Elliott Daingerfield is now home to the **Westglow Resort and Spa** (224 Westglow Circle, 828/295-4463 or 800/562-0807, www.westglow.com, from $250, spa packages from $450). In addition to the cushy guest rooms, many of which have whirlpool tubs, private decks, and views of Grandfather Mountain, the menu of spa treatments and health services befits the elegance of the surroundings. All kinds of massage and body therapy are available, as well as fitness classes, cooking and makeup lessons, and a variety of seminars in emotional well-being. Taking advantage of the spa's wonderful location, visitors can also sign up for hiking, biking, snowshoeing, and camping trips.

The **Inn at Ragged Gardens** (203 Sunset

Dr., 877/972-4433, www.ragged-gardens.com, from $140) is a handsome, stylish turn-of-the-century vacation home, a stone-walled and chestnut-paneled manor. The plush guest rooms feature goose-down bedding, fireplaces, and, in most cases, balconies and whirlpool tubs.

CAMPING

The campground at **Julian Price Park** (BRP milepost 297, near Blowing Rock, 828/963-5911, www.recreation.gov, $16) is the largest on the Parkway, with a good selection of standard and tent-only nonelectric campsites. Pets are allowed, flush toilets and a telephone are accessible, and there's good hiking and boating nearby, with boat rentals available.

Food

Storie Street Grille (1167 Main St., 828/295-7075, www.storiestreetgrille.com, fall-spring Mon.-Sat. 11am-3pm and 5pm-9pm, later hours in summer, lunch $6-13, dinner $10-30) has a long lunch menu of sandwiches, quesadillas, and main-course salads. Try the pot-roast melt or the bacon, brie, and apple panini. For dinner there are many Italian choices, grilled steak and seafood, and intriguing twists on Southern snacks, like crab hush puppies and pork barbecue spring rolls. **Bistro Roca and Antlers Bar** (143 Wonderland Tr., 828/295-4008, http://bistroroca.com, Mon. and Wed.-Sat. 11:30am-10pm, brunch Sun. 11am-2:30pm, bar until midnight, $20-30) serves hearty and creative dishes like chicken and duck pot pie, roasted duck pizza, prosciutto and manchego pizza, and crab and crawfish cakes with gouda and grits. Also popular is **Twigs** (U.S. 321 Bypass, 828/295-5050, http://twigsbr.com, Tues.-Thurs. and Sun. 5:30pm-9:30pm, Fri.-Sat. 5:30pm-10pm, bar until 2am, $17-34), which has both a casual bar and a fancier dining room. Popular regional dishes like shrimp and grits and mountain trout appear on the menu alongside more unusual fare like sautéed boar sausage. There are 17 wines available by the glass, and another 133 by the bottle, featuring a wide selection of California wines as well as Australian, European, and Argentine choices.

SOUTH OF BLOWING ROCK
Grandfather Mountain

Grandfather Mountain (U.S. 221, 2 miles north of Linville, 800/468-7325, www.grandfather.com, summer daily 8am-7pm, spring and fall daily 8am-6pm, winter daily 8am-5pm, weather permitting, $18 adults, $15 over age 60, $8 under age 12), at a lofty 5,964 feet, is not the very highest mountain in North Carolina, but it is one of the most beautiful. The highest peak in the Blue Ridge Mountains (Mount Mitchell is in the Black Mountains), Grandfather is a United Nations-designated International Biosphere Reserve. Privately owned for decades although open to the public, Grandfather Mountain has remained a great expanse of deep forests and wildlife, with many hiking trails. The main attraction is the summit, and the **Mile High Swinging Bridge** (it's quite safe, but it is indeed a mile high and it swings in the breeze). The view from Grandfather Mountain is stunning, and the peak is easily accessible via the beautiful road that traces the skyward mile.

Linn Cove Viaduct

Wrapping around Grandfather Mountain is a "bridge over land," the marvel of engineering known as the Linn Cove Viaduct. This last section of the Blue Ridge Parkway to be completed, in 1987, was intended to minimize environmental damage to the mountain. The National Park Service operates the **Linn Cove Visitor Center** (daily 10am-5pm) at the south end of the 0.25-mile viaduct, around BRP milepost 304. An adjacent hiking trail goes beside and beneath the viaduct.

Linville Gorge

The deepest gorge in the United States, Linville Gorge is near Blue Ridge Parkway milepost 316 in a 12,000-acre federally designated wilderness area. Some of the hollers in this preserve are so remote that they still shelter virgin forests. **Linville Falls** (BRP milepost 316) is one

ASHEVILLE

SOUTH OF BLOWING ROCK

of the most photographed places in North Carolina, a spectacular series of cataracts that fall crashing into the gorge. It can be seen from several short trails that depart from the **Linville Falls Visitors Center** (milepost 316, Apr. 25-Nov. 2 and weekends in Apr. daily 9am-5pm). The National Park Service operates the **Linville Falls Campground** (828/765-7818, www.recreation.gov, $19) near the falls at BRP milepost 316.3. Tent and RV sites are mixed together, and water and flush toilets are available May to October.

Linville Gorge has some great climbing spots. They range in difficulty from Table Rock, parts of which are popular with beginning climbers and other parts of which should only be attempted by experts, to the extremely strenuous Hawksbill cliff face and Sitting Bear rock pillar. Speak to the folks at the visitors center or at **Fox Mountain Guides** (3228 Asheville Hwy., Pisgah Forest, 888/284-8433, www.foxmountainguides), a Hendersonville-area service that leads climbs in the gorge, to determine which of Linville Gorge's many climbing faces would be best suited to your skill level.

Linville Caverns

You just can't visit the Blue Ridge Mountains without visiting caverns. **Linville Caverns** (U.S. 221, between Linville and Marion, south of BRP milepost 317, 800/419-0540, www.linvillecaverns.com, Mar. and Nov. daily 9am-4:30pm, Apr.-May and Sept.-Oct. daily 9am-5pm, June-Aug. daily 9am-6pm, Dec.-Feb. Sat.-Sun. 9am-4:30pm, $8 adults, $7 seniors, $6 children) is one of the venerable underground attractions of the Southern mountains. The natural limestone caverns feature all sorts of strange rock formations, underground trout streams, the occasional roosting bat, and, of course, a gift shop.

Crossnore School

Since the early 1920s the master weavers of the **Crossnore Weaving Room** (Crossnore School, 100 D.A.R. Dr., Crossnore, 828/733-4305, www.crossnoreweavers.org) have produced beautiful textiles—afghans, rugs and runners, baby blankets, scarves, and more—which they've sold for the benefit of the Crossnore School. Founded in the 1910s for orphaned and disadvantaged children, the Crossnore School is today an actively operating children's home for western North Carolina kids who have no guardians—and for some local children who live with their families but whose educational needs are best served by the structure offered here. The fame of the weaving room is much more than a fund-raising program. The skills of the Crossnore Weavers are highly regarded among craftspeople throughout this region, and the sales gallery is an essential stop for the visitor interested in North Carolina's finest crafts.

Orchard at Altapass

At milepost 328 on the Blue Ridge Parkway, the **Orchard at Altapass** (888/765-9531, www.altapassorchard.com, Mon. and Wed.-Sat. 10am-6pm, Sun. noon-6pm, free) is much more than

© JIM MOREKIS
Linville Gorge

ASHEVILLE

an orchard, although it does produce apples in abundance. The land on which the orchard grows has been settled since the 1790s, when Charlie "Cove" McKinney and his large family lived here. McKinney had four wives—at the same time—who bore him 30 sons and a dozen daughters. Today, the Orchard at Altapass continues to turn out wonderful apples. It is also a favorite music venue in this region. On weekends, country, bluegrass, old-time, and gospel musicians along with artists of a variety of other styles perform at the Orchard.

Penland School of Crafts

In the 1920s, Lucy Morgan, a teacher at a local Episcopal school, and her brother embarked on a mission to help the women of the mountains gain some hand in their own economic well-being. Equipping several households in the Penland area with looms, they touched off a local cottage industry in weaving, which quickly centralized and grew into the Penland School, a center for craft instruction and production. Several "folk schools" sprouted in the southern Appalachians in this era, most of them the projects of idealistic Northerners wanting to aid the benighted mountaineers. The Penland School, however, has the distinction of being one of the few such institutions that was truly homegrown, as Morgan was herself a child of the rural Carolina highlands. Today, the **Penland School of Crafts** (off Penland Rd., Penland, 828/765-2359, www.penland.org) is an arts instruction center of international fame. More than 1,000 people, from beginners to professionals, enroll in Penland's one-, two-, and eight-week courses every year to learn about craft in many different media. While the studios are not open to visitors, tours are given April-December on Tuesday and Thursday (advance reservations required). The school operates a beautiful shop, the **Penland Gallery** (Conley Ridge Rd., 828/765-6211, www.penland.org, Tues.-Sat. 10am-5pm, Sun. noon-5pm), where the work of many of the school's instructors and students can be purchased.

Museum of North Carolina Minerals

Right off the BRP at the junction with Highway 226, just in time for some science education as well as perhaps a restroom stop, is the delightful little **Museum of North Carolina Minerals** (milepost 331, 828/765-2761, daily 9am-5pm, free). This small but well-curated museum highlights the geology and topography of the Tarheel State's portion of Appalachia, with a nod to the wealth of minerals and valuable gems extracted from the ground throughout its history.

Mount Mitchell

At 6,684 feet, **Mount Mitchell** (accessible from BRP milepost 355, near Burnsville) is the highest mountain east of South Dakota. It is the pinnacle of the Black Mountain range, a 15-mile-long, J-shaped ridge that was formerly considered to be one mountain. Now that the various peaks are designated as separate mountains, six of them are among the 10 highest in the eastern United States. Clingmans Dome, a mere 41 feet shorter, glares up at Mount Mitchell from the Tennessee border. **Mount Mitchell State Park** (BRP milepost 355, near Burnsville, 828/675-4611, http://ncparks.gov, May-Aug. 8am-9pm, Mar.-Apr., Sept.-Oct. 8am-8pm, Nov.-Feb. 8am-6pm, free) is not only a place to catch an amazing panoramic view—up to 85 miles in clear weather—but it also has an education center, restaurant, gift shop, and nine campsites (late Apr.-late Oct. $20, $15 over age 60, Nov.-Apr. $12).

Brown Mountain Lights

One of North Carolina's most enduring mysteries is that of the Brown Mountain Lights, glowing orbs that float in the air some evenings around Brown Mountain, at the Burke-Caldwell County line. According to the U.S. Geological Survey, the orbs may be a reflection of car and train headlights in the valley below. This theory would seem to ignore the fact that the lights have been seen since at least 1833, long before the first headlights shone in this valley. The Brown Mountain Lights are widely believed to be of supernatural origin, and no scientific explanation has yet been proffered that satisfactorily clears up the mystery. Ghost fanciers will be delighted to know that the Brown Mountain Lights can be observed by visitors from the Lost Cove overlook on the southeast side of the road, near milepost 310 on the Blue Ridge Parkway. Try a clear evening in the summer, right around dusk, and you might see them.

Lake James State Park
Lake James State Park (Hwy. 126, 5 miles northeast of Marion, 828/652-5047, http://ncparks.gov, May-Aug. 8am-9pm, Mar.-Apr., Sept.-Oct. 8am-8pm, Nov.-Feb. 8am-6pm, free) comprises a 6,500-acre lake and its 150 miles of shoreline. Lake James is artificial, created around 1920, but the graceful mountain setting among hemlocks and rhododendrons makes this a favorite natural area. The park rents canoes ($5 per hour), and campsites ($20) are open March 15 to November 30; restrooms, showers, and drinking water are available nearby.

Accommodations
Linville's **Eseeola Lodge** (175 Linville Ave., 800/742-6717, www.eseeola.com, from $400) has been in the business of luxury mountain vacations for more than 100 years. The first lodge was built in the 1890s, along with a nine-hole golf course. The original lodge burned and was replaced by the present lodge, and, in 1924 Donald Ross was engaged to build the championship golf course now known as the Linville Golf Club. Eseeola Lodge offers a complex but splendid array of lodging packages, with breakfast and dinner at the lodge's restaurant included and, depending on your predilections, tee times at the Linville Golf Club, spa services, and even croquet lessons. Greens fees for nonguests are $115 for the first round, $57.50 for same-day second rounds.

Scattered around a 92-acre private nature preserve in Marion, the six **Cottages at Spring House Farm** (219 Haynes Rd., Marion, 877/738-9798, www.springhousefarm.com, from $245) are quiet hideaways with ecoconscious comforts. The proprietors, who live in a historic farmhouse on the property, stock the cabin kitchens with fresh bread and eggs and local honey. Each cottage has an outdoor hot tub and access to pond-side gazebos and hiking trails.

Food
Famous Louise's Rockhouse Restaurant (23175 Rockhouse Lane, Linville Falls, near BRP milepost 321, 828/765-2702, daily 6am-8pm, $10), built in 1936 with stones taken from the Linville River, is not a large restaurant, but the dining room is spread out over three counties. The lines of Burke, McDowell, and Avery Counties meet on this exact spot, and customers, for reasons of loyalty or legality, often have preferences about where to take their repast. Famous Louise's is owned by a mother and daughter, and Louise, the mom, is a cook of some renown. The fare is traditional and homemade—the pimento cheese is mixed here, the cornbread and biscuits are whipped up from scratch, the pot roast stewed at a leisurely simmer. On your way out, pick up a jar or two of Louise's homemade berry jams, probably the best $3 souvenirs to be found in the mountains. You'll find them in Avery County.

GETTING THERE AND AROUND
There are no major airports in this region, but two are reasonably close: **Asheville Regional Airport** (AVL, 61 Terminal Dr., Fletcher, 828/684-2226, www.flyavl.com) and **Piedmont Triad International Airport** (GSO, 1000 A. Ted Johnson Pkwy., Greensboro, 336/665-5600, www.flyfrompti.com) in Greensboro. There is one major interstate highway, I-77, that runs north-south along the edge of the mountains west of Mount Airy. Two other major highways run along or just beyond the boundaries of the northern mountains: I-40 to the east and south, running between Winston-Salem and Asheville, and I-26 to the south and west, between Asheville and Johnson City, Tennessee. U.S. 321 and

ASHEVILLE

U.S. 421 are the main roads here, and U.S. 19 winds through the southwest edge of the area covered in this chapter.

While it's probably the most fun and scenic route, the Blue Ridge Parkway is not the most efficient if you're trying to cover a lot of ground fast. The maximum speed is 45 mph, and because of weather, traffic, and twists and turns, you can count on driving slower than that most of the time.

Watauga County, which includes the towns of Blowing Rock, Boone, Deep Gap, and Zionville, is served by **AppalCart bus routes** (828/264-2278, www.appalcart. com). Riders must make reservations to ride,

and the service is only available on weekdays, but the fares, which vary by route, are much cheaper than the gas it takes to get from place to place. AppalCart also runs routes to Charlotte, Winston-Salem, Hickory, Lenoir, and Wilkesboro, with fares ranging $10-50 round-trip. Another way to get to and from the area is via the **Mountaineer Express Bus** (336/662-0002 or 800/588-7787, www.partnc. org), which runs among Greensboro, Winston-Salem, Yadkinville, Wilkesboro, and Boone. The most expensive one-way trip (Greensboro-Boone) is only $10, and fares are half-price for students, wheelchair users, and passengers over age 60.

East of the Blue Ridge Parkway

As you wind your way along the Blue Ridge Parkway, to the east you'll find several worthwhile detours, all within a half hour's drive of the Parkway.

SOUTH ALONG U.S. 321
Sights
Traditions Pottery (4443 Bolick Rd., 3 miles south of Blowing Rock, 828/295-5099, www. traditionspottery.com) is a hotbed of Piedmont and Appalachian folk traditions. The Owen-Bolick-Calhoun families trace their roots as potters back through six generations in the sandhills community of Seagrove and here in Caldwell County. They have also become renowned old-time musicians and storytellers. Traditions Pottery is not only a place to buy beautiful ceramics with an impeccable folk pedigree, but also the location of the Jack Tales Festival in August (Glenn Bolick learned his storytelling from the great Ray Hicks of Beech Mountain, a National Heritage Award winner), as well as numerous music jams and kiln openings throughout the year.

The **Antique Vending Company Museum** (30 S. Main St., Granite Falls, 828/962-9783, www.antiquevending.com, call for tour times) is a collection of more than 1,000 early soda

machines (which North Carolinians are more likely to identify as "Coke machines," regardless of the brand of soft drink contained therein). The machines go back to the earliest days of automated cold drink dispensing, and include the only known remaining 1925 Icy-O Coca-Cola machine in the world.

The county seat of Caldwell County, Lenoir (pronounced "luh-NORE"), was named for General William Lenoir, a Revolutionary War hero and chronicler of the Battle of King's Mountain. **Fort Defiance** (1792 Fort Defiance Dr./Hwy. 268, Happy Valley, 828/758-1671, www.fortdefiancenc. org, Apr.-Oct. Thurs.-Sat. 10am-5pm, Sun. 1pm-5pm, Nov.-Mar. Sat. 10am-5pm, Sun. 1pm-5pm and by appointment, $6 adults, $4 children), his 1792 plantation house in Happy Valley, is beautifully restored and open to the public. Among its unusual charms are a 200-year-old oriental chestnut tree, an English boxwood garden of the same vintage, and the largest beech tree in the state.

The **Hickory Museum of Art** (243 3rd Ave. NE, Hickory, 828/327-8576, www.hickory-museumofart.org, Tues.-Sat. 10am-4pm, Sun. 1pm-4pm, free) was established in the early 1950s and was the first major museum of

THE REAL TOM DOOLEY

What is probably North Carolina's most famous murder case, the 1867 murder of a young Wilkes County woman named Laura Foster by her lover, Tom Dula, is known around the world because of a 1950s recording by the Kingston Trio. "The Ballad of Tom Dooley," as it has come to be known, was sung in the North Carolina mountains long before its emergence as a Folk Revival standard. Most notably, the Watauga County banjo player and ballad singer Frank Profitt kept the story alive through song. Even today, almost 150 years later, the intricacies of the Dula case are debated in this area by descendants of the principal players, and by neighbors who have grown up with the legend.

The story is a sordid one. Tom Dula was 18 years old when he enlisted in the Confederate Army, and by that time he had already been involved for several years in a romantic relationship with a woman named Ann Melton. Following the Civil War, much of which he spent as a prisoner at the notoriously ghastly Point Lookout prison in Maryland, Dula came home to Wilkes County, older but apparently no wiser. He picked up where he left off with Ann Melton, by then married to another man, and at the same time commenced living with another local woman, Laura Foster. (In one version of

the story, he was seeing yet a third woman, also a Melton.)

The subtleties of the motives and means that led to Laura Foster's death are still subjects of hot debate, but the facts are as follows. On May 25, 1866, Laura Foster set off from home riding her father's horse. The next day, the horse returned without her. After searchers had combed the woods and riverbanks for nearly a month, Laura Foster's body was finally discovered. She had been stabbed to death and buried in a shallow grave. When news got out that the body was found, Dula disappeared.

He was caught a few weeks later in Tennessee. Back in Wilkes County, Tom Dula and Ann Melton were indicted for murder. Officials moved the trial down the mountain to nearby Iredell County, where a jury found Dula guilty (Ann Melton was acquitted). After a series of appeals and an eventual overturning of the verdict by the state Supreme Court, a new trial was convened, and Dula was again convicted. He was hanged on May 1, 1868, in Statesville. Historians write that even before the hanging was carried out, people in the area were singing a song with the verse, "Hang your head, Tom Dula/ Hang your head and cry/ You killed poor Laura Foster/ And now you're bound to die."

American art in the Southeast. Its early partnership with the National Academy of Design in New York City gained it the nickname of the "Southern Outpost of the National Academy." The museum has an impressive permanent collection, with special emphases on American painting, outsider and folk art, North Carolina folk pottery, and American studio pottery and glass.

Festivals

Every Labor Day weekend, Caldwell County is home to the **Historic Happy Valley Old-Time Fiddlers' Convention** (828/726-0616, www.happyvalleyfiddlers.com), a laid-back event in a gorgeous location, the Jones Farm. The festival includes music competitions and concerts,

drawing some great traditional artists from all over the hills. There are also a rubber duck race, demonstrations by instrument makers, tours of Fort Defiance, and visits to the grave of Laura Foster, the 1867 victim of North Carolina's most famous murderer, Tom "Dooley"—who happened to be a fiddler. Participants and visitors can camp along the Yadkin River on the Jones Farm during the festival for $10 per night. No alcohol is allowed; pets are permitted as long as they're leashed.

The Catawba Valley is one of the important pockets of North Carolina folk pottery, with a tradition all its own dating back to the early 19th-century potter Daniel Seagle, and exemplified in modern times by the late Burlon Craig (one of the giants of Southern folk art)

ASHEVILLE

and contemporary master Kim Ellington. Hickory's annual **Catawba Valley Pottery and Antiques Festival** (Hickory Convention Center, late Mar., $6 adults, $2 children) brings together more than 100 potters and dealers in pottery and antiques. It's a great introduction to Southern folk pottery, and a danger zone if you're on a budget, because the wares sold here are most covetable.

Sports and Recreation

Between Hickory and Morganton, outside the town of Connelly Springs, is **South Mountain State Park** (3001 South Mountain Park Ave., Connelly Springs, 828/433-4772, http://ncparks.gov, office Mon.-Fri. 8am-5pm, park Nov.-Feb. daily 8am-6pm, Mar.-Apr. and Sept.-Oct. daily 8am-8pm, May-Aug. daily 8am-9pm, free). One of the state's most rugged recreational areas, South Mountain State Park rises to elevations of 3,000 feet. One trail follows the Jacob Fork River to the top of 80-foot High Shoals Falls. Another trail, 0.75 miles long, runs along the lower reaches of Jacob Fork, and is wheelchair accessible. There are 17 miles of strenuous mountain biking trails. Primitive and equestrian campsites ($13) are located in various spots throughout the park, from 0.5 miles to 5.5 miles away from the Jacob Fork parking area. Pit toilets are located nearby campsites, but all supplies and water must be packed in. Watch out for bears!

The **Hickory Crawdads** (2500 Clement Blvd. NW, Hickory, 828/322-3000, www.hickorycrawdads.com) are a Single-A baseball affiliate team of the Pittsburgh Pirates. The 2004 South Atlantic League Champions play at the modern Frans Stadium, where you may meet the mascot, Conrad—yes, Conrad—the Crawdad.

Food

If you're traveling between Lenoir and Hickory on a weekend, take a detour to the little community of Dudley Shoals, where you'll find **Sims Country BBQ** (6160 Petra Mill Rd., Dudley Shoals, 828/396-5811, www.simscountrybarbque.com, Fri.-Sat. 5pm-9pm, all-you-can-eat buffet $11). Sims is known not only for its all-you-can-eat Texas-style barbecue, which they pit-cook all day, but for live bluegrass music and clogging. It also hosts the annual Molasses Festival on the second Saturday in October, with bluegrass, dancing, and harvest-time activities.

BLACK MOUNTAIN
Sights

Black Mountain is a beautiful little town only a short distance from Asheville. Step into the **Swannanoa Valley Museum** (223 W. State St., 828/669-9566, www.swannanoavalleymuseum.org, Tues.-Sat. 10am-5pm, Sun. 2pm-5pm, free) to learn about the history of this area, from its prehistory, Cherokee settlement, and early industrialization through the close of the all-important Beacon Blanket Factory to today. Asheville is by no means the only interesting and significant part of Buncombe County; a lot has happened up in this neck of the woods. While you're here, stop in next door at the **Black Mountain Center for the Arts** (225 W. State St., 828/669-0930, www.blackmountainarts.org, Mon.-Fri. 10am-5pm, Sat. 1pm-4pm) to get a feel for what some of this region's many artists are up to.

East of Black Mountain, the **Mountain Gateway Museum** (102 Water St., Old Fort, 828/668-9259, http://ncmuseumofhistory.org, Mon.-Sat. 10am-5pm, Sun. noon-5pm, free) presents the cultural history of the North Carolina mountains from its earliest days, to the time before the Revolution, when Old Fort was the wild frontier, through the present day. The museum hosts events throughout the year, showcasing all manner of traditional arts from this region.

Entertainment and Events

Twice yearly, in the spring and fall, Black Mountain is the scene of the **Lake Eden Arts Festival** (828/686-8742, www.theleaf.com), better known as LEAF. Though based around the roots music of the world—and there are some amazing performers here every year—LEAF is also a festival of visual arts, poetry, food, and even the healing arts. LEAF is equal parts hippie festival and a delightful family-friendly atmosphere with an overlay of progressive thought and worldview. It takes place, appropriately, at Camp Rockmont, once the campus of Black Mountain College (377 Lake Eden Rd.).

NIGHTLIFE
Pisgah Brewing Company (150 Eastside Dr., 828/669-0190, http://pisgahbrewing.com, Mon.-Wed. 4pm-9pm, Thurs.-Sat. usually 2pm-midnight, Sun. 2pm-9pm) is both a brewpub and music venue, featuring an eclectic mix of bands, from roots music to rock. Pisgah was the Southeast's first certified organic brewery. Several beers are on tap all year, including pale ale, porter, stout, and a long list of seasonal brews that rotate throughout the year. Tours are given Saturday at 2pm and 3pm.

Shopping
Black Mountain Books (103 Cherry St., 828/669-8149, Mon.-Sat. 11am-5pm, Sun. 11am-3pm) specializes in rare and out-of-print titles, and is a great place to find unusual volumes on "North Carolina, Black Mountain College, the Southern Appalachians, nature, religion, and 18th- and 19th-century England and Scotland."

Down the road, stop in at **Chocolate Gems** (106 W. State St., 828/669-9105, www.chocgems.com) to see works of art of an entirely different flavor. This chocolatier makes all sorts of truffles and barks, and even chocolate sculptures, right on the premises.

Accommodations
The **Inn Around the Corner** (109 Church St., 800/393-6005, www.innaroundthecorner.com, no credit cards, $140-175) is a classic bed-and-breakfast in a lovely 1915 wooden house with a big front porch.

Food
A great local exponent of the farm-to-table movement is Black Mountain's **Blackbird Restaurant: A New American Tavern** (10 E. Market St., 828/669-5556, www.

theblackbirdrestaurant.com, Mon.-Sat. lunch 11am-2:30pm, bar 3pm-5:30pm, dinner 5:30pm-9:30pm, bar later, brunch Sun. 10am-2pm, $12-22). Blackbird brings fresh local ingredients to a Southern-inspired menu. They also have a long list of microbrews and California wines.

Over on Church Street you'll find the **Black Mountain Bakery** (102 Church St., 828/669-1626, Tues.-Sat. 8am-4pm), a little café where you can order a quick soup and sandwich as well as a dessert or cookie for the road.

CHIMNEY ROCK AND LAKE LURE
⊡ Chimney Rock
Chimney Rock Park (U.S. 64/74A, Chimney Rock, 800/277-9611, www.chimneyrockpark.com, hours vary, $15 adults, $7 ages 6-15) is home to some amazing rock formations. The star of the show, of course, is the Chimney Rock itself. Whether you climb the long series of steps to the top of this 315-foot tower of rock or take the elevator, you'll get there just the same, and the view is great. Also dazzling are the "Needle's Eye," the "Opera Box," and many more formations that visitors can explore.

The 400-foot **Hickory Nut Falls** can be reached by the Hickory Nut Falls Trail, a fairly leisurely 0.75-mile walk. An easy walk for children, the 0.6-mile Woodland Walk is dotted with animal sculptures and "journal entries" by Grady the Groundhog. The Skyline-Cliff Trail Loop is a good deal more strenuous, but this two-hour hike will carry you to some spectacular sights. (You may also recognize it from the 1992 film *The Last of the Mohicans*.) Chimney Rock's website (www.chimneyrockpark.com) has a nifty interactive trail map that will show you the lay of the land.

Needless to say, Chimney Rock Park is a mighty desirable location for rock climbing. By all means, give it a try—but remember that in this park, you must arrange your climb with **Fox Mountain Guides** (888/284-8433, www.foxmountainguides.com). They offer all sorts of instruction and guide services for climbers of all levels.

ASHEVILLE

Sports and Recreation

Lake Lure, a 720-acre highland lake, was created in the 1920s. Several local outfitters will guide you on or get you all prepared for a day on the lake or on area rivers. Try **Lake Lure Adventure Company** (442 Memorial Hwy., 828/625-8066), or, for a relaxed sightseeing tour on the lake, **Lake Lure Tours** (next to Lake Lure Town Marina, 877/386-4255, www.lakelure.com, daily 9am-6pm, twilight cruises 6pm-9pm, dinner cruises 6pm and 7pm, $10-40 adults, $6-16 under age 12), which offers dinner and sunset cruises as well as daytime jaunts.

Accommodations

The 1927 **Lake Lure Inn and Spa** (2771 Memorial Hwy., 888/434-4970, www.lakelure.com, from $109) is a grand old hotel that was one of the fashionable Southern resorts in its day. Franklin Roosevelt and Calvin Coolidge stayed here, and so did F. Scott Fitzgerald. The lobby is full of strange antiques that are the picture of obsolete opulence—such as a Baccarat chandelier much older than the hotel and a collection of upright disc music boxes (up to eight feet tall) that were all the rage before the invention of the phonograph. The Lake Lure Inn has been beautifully restored and equipped with two restaurants, a bar, and a spa.

Asheville

The steady year-round percolation of often offbeat ideas and art in the largest city in western North Carolina welcomes a sizeable contingent of visitors each year, visiting the massive Biltmore Estate and enjoying the city's adventurous cuisine and nightlife. It's all against a backdrop of rock-ribbed mountain conservatism, reflected in the many and varied churches that dominate social life outside the bohemian, organically-fed city center.

When the railroad finally came to town after the Civil War, Asheville became an important transportation hub, especially for the products of its burgeoning textile industry. Its dependence on the banking industry made it a casualty of the Great Depression, with the serendipitous side effect that much of its wonderful, often whimsical art deco architecture avoided the urban renewal that ruined so many cities in the post-World War II era.

Though Asheville's counterculture roots go back to the 1940s and nearby Black Mountain College, New Age and hippie culture first came to town in a big way in the 1960s, drawn by the climate, walkable downtown, and relative isolation of the surrounding mountains. Its strains are everywhere, from the regular drum circles held in city parks to the offbeat shops

to the political meetings advertised via leaflets stapled to power poles alongside the live band announcements.

SIGHTS
◖ Downtown Architecture

One of Asheville's chief charms is its striking architecture, which dates largely to the 1920s. Most famously, the Biltmore Estate and the surrounding developments brought together the illustrious minds of landscape architect Frederick Law Olmsted and architect Richard Morris Hunt, who were, in their day, two of the leading lights in American design, to create a palace and estate for George Washington Vanderbilt. The Montford neighborhood, contemporary to the Biltmore, is a striking mixture of ornate Queen Anne houses and craftsman-style bungalows. The Grove Park Inn was constructed in 1913, a huge, luxurious hotel fitted with rustic architectural devices to make vacationing New York nabobs feel like they were roughing it. Asheville's downtown features one of the largest concentrations of art deco buildings in the United States. The **Buncombe County Courthouse** (60 Court Plaza, dating from 1927-1929), the **Jackson Building** (22 S. Pack Square, 1923-1924), **First Baptist**

ASHEVILLE

ASHEVILLE

To Asheville Log Cabin Motor Court

VINNIE'S

To Navitat

UNIVERSITY OF NORTH CAROLINA, ASHEVILLE

GROVE PARK INN RESORT & SPA

Weaver Park

BOTANICAL GARDENS

ASHEVILLE ADVENTURE RENTALS

SEE "DOWNTOWN ASHEVILLE" MAP

To FOLK ART CENTER, Western North Carolina Nature Center, and Black Mountain

DOWNTOWN ARCHITECTURE

ASHEVILLE MUNICIPAL GOLF COURSE

THE GREY EAGLE TAVERN AND MUSIC HALL

Ashton Park

McCORMICK FIELD

RIVER ARTS DISTRICT

WEDGE BREWING COMPANY

BON PAUL AND SHARKEY'S HOSTEL OF ASHEVILLE

SUNNY POINT CAFÉ

BISCUIT HEAD

ANTIQUE TOBACCO BARN

ASHEVILLE GREEN COTTAGE

To NORTH CAROLINA ARBORETUM via Interstate 26

FIG

CORNER KITCHEN

BILTMORE VILLAGE

INN ON BILTMORE ESTATE

ANTLER HILL VILLAGE

BILTMORE WINERY

BILTMORE ESTATE

0   0.5 mi

0.5 km

© AVALON TRAVEL

Church (Oak St. and Woodfin St., 1925), the **S&W Cafeteria** (56 Patton Ave., 1929), the **Public Service Building** (89-93 Patton Ave., 1929), and the **Grove Arcade** (37 Battery Park Ave., 1926-1929) are just a few of the 1920s masterpieces in a city overflowing with important early 20th-century architecture.

◖ Biltmore Estate

The largest home in the United States, and still privately owned by the Vanderbilt family, the **Biltmore Estate** (1 Approach Rd., 800/411-3812, www.biltmore.com, check the website for hours, generally daily 9am-4:30pm, $59 adults, $29.50 children, discounts for advance online purchase) is the realized dream of George Washington Vanderbilt. Grandson of Gilded Age magnate Cornelius Vanderbilt, G. W. Vanderbilt, like many wealthy Northerners of his day, was first introduced to the North Carolina mountains when he came to Asheville for his health. So impressed was he with the beauty and the climate of this area that he amassed a 125,000-acre tract of land south

of Asheville on which to build his "country home." He engaged celebrity architect Richard Morris Hunt to build the mansion itself, and because the estate reminded them both of the Loire Valley, Hunt and Vanderbilt agreed that the house should be built in the style of a 16th-century château. No less illustrious was Vanderbilt's choice of landscape architect for Biltmore: The grounds would be designed by Frederick Law Olmsted, creator of New York City's Central Park. It's hard to imagine that Olmsted could find a grander commission than that of designing Central Park, but in the Biltmore Estate, he was given a canvas that was nine times larger than that dinky lot in Manhattan. While Biltmore Estate's original 125,000 acres are now greatly diminished—though a large part of that tract was fortunately transferred to the federal government and has become part of Pisgah National Forest—the gorgeously landscaped core of the property remains.

The mansion, constructed between 1888 and 1895, has over 250 rooms—three acres

ASHEVILLE

© BILTMORE ESTATE

Biltmore Estate

THOMAS WOLFE LOOKS HOMEWARD

Thomas Wolfe
Memorial

© JIM MOREKIS

A native son of Asheville, author Thomas Wolfe grew up in a boardinghouse that his mother ran, and which is operated today as the **Thomas Wolfe Memorial** (52 N. Market St., 828/253-8304, www.wolfememorial.com, Tues.-Sat. 9am-5pm, $5 adults, $2 students). He described the town of "Altamont" (Asheville) and its people so vividly in *Look Homeward, Angel* that the Asheville library refused to own it, and Wolfe himself avoided the town for almost eight years. In this passage, Wolfe describes the excitement of approaching Asheville as a traveler.

His destination was the little town of Altamont, twenty-four miles away beyond the rim of the great outer wall of the hills. As the horses strained slowly up the mountain road Oliver's spirit lifted a little. It was a gray-golden day in late October, bright and windy. There was a sharp bite and sparkle in the mountain air: the range soared above him, close, immense, clean, and barren. The trees rose gaunt and stark:

they were almost leafless. The sky was full of windy white rags of cloud; a thick blade of mist washed slowly around the rampart of a mountain.

Below him a mountain stream foamed down its rocky bed, and he could see little dots of men laying the track that would coil across the hill toward Altamont. Then the sweating team lipped the gulch of the mountain, and, among soaring and lordly ranges that melted away in purple mist, they began the slow descent toward the high plateau on which the town of Altamont was built.

In the haunting eternity of these mountains, rimmed in their enormous cup, he found sprawled out on its hundred hills and hollows a town of four thousand people.

There were lands. His heart lifted.

ASHEVILLE

ASHEVILLE

of floor space!—most of which are open to the public for gawking. The wonders inside the house are too numerous to list, but they include paintings by Renoir, Whistler, and Sargent; an amazing collection of European antiques, among them Napoleon's chess set; and room after room that show, in every inch of paneling, tiles, woodwork, and stonework, the work of the best craftspeople of the 1890s. Technologically, the house was a wonder in its day. It had electricity, central heat, elevators, and hot water. The bowling alley and basement swimming pool are reminiscent of Rich Manor, home of Richie Rich, and as it happens, the 1994 movie *Richie Rich* was indeed filmed here.

There is more than enough to do and see here to occupy a full weekend. The inn and restaurants are only the beginning. The **Biltmore Winery** operates in what was once the estate's dairy. Daily tours and tastings allow visitors to sample the award-winning wines. **River Bend Farm** recreates the working farm that supported the estate and its many workers. Blacksmiths, woodworkers, and other artisans work in the River Bend barn. The kitchen garden—backyard gardeners, just imagine this—is four acres.

The **Equestrian Center** gives lessons, and if you happen to travel with your own horse, the two of you can explore 80 miles of equestrian trails. Your horse can even have his or her own stall and board like a Vanderbilt steed. Visitors without the equestrian urge can also tour the estate by carriage, bike, raft, canoe, Segway, or, of course, on foot. Last but not least, you can zip around in a Land Rover after receiving expert training from Biltmore's own **Land Rover Experience Driving School.**

Admission to Biltmore varies by season; there is no charge for parking. Your ticket gets you in to the mansion itself, the gardens, the winery, and the farm. Some of the other features carry additional fees.

North Carolina Arboretum

The enormous **North Carolina Arboretum** (100 Frederick Law Olmsted Way, 828/665-2492, www.ncarboretum.org, Apr.-Oct. daily 8am-9pm, Nov.-Mar. daily 8am-7pm, greenhouse Mon.-Sat. 8am-2pm, parking $12) is considered by many to be one of the most beautiful such institutions in the country. The 434 natural and landscaped acres back onto the Pisgah National Forest, just off Blue Ridge Parkway milepost 393. Major collections include the National Native Azalea Repository, where you can see almost every species of azalea native to the United States, as well as several hybrids, and the very special Bonsai Collection, where staff horticulturists care for over 200 bonsais, many of their own creation. Bicycles and leashed dogs are permitted on many of the trails. Walking areas range from easy to fairly rugged.

For an unusual approach, sign up for one of the Arboretum's twice-daily **Segway Tours** (828/665-2492, Mon.-Sat. 10am and 2pm, $45 Mon.-Fri., $55 Sat.), for riders over age 14 and between 80 and 250 pounds. The price may seem steep, but there's a lot packed into these tours. First, you'll get 45 minutes of training on how to drive a Segway. Then for the next 2 to 2.5 hours, you'll glide all around the arboretum, stopping in beautiful spots throughout for photos and learning. The arboretum also has a very nice café, the **Savory Thyme Café** (Mon.-Sat. 10am-4pm, Sun. noon-5pm) and gift shop, the **Garden Trellis** (Mon.-Sat. 10am-5pm, Sun. noon-5pm).

Botanical Gardens

The **Botanical Gardens** (151 W. T. Weaver Blvd., adjacent to the UNC-Asheville campus, 828/252-5190, www.ashevillebotanicalgardens.org, daily dawn-dusk, free) is a 10-acre preserve for the region's increasingly threatened native plants. Laid out in 1960 for this purpose by landscape architect Doan Ogden, the gardens are an ecological haven. The many "rooms" are planted to reflect different environments of the mountains—the Wildflower Trail, the Heath Cove, the Fern and Moss Trail, and others. Spring blooms peak in mid-April, but the gardens are an absolutely lovely, visually rich place to visit any time of year. Because of its serious mission of plant preservation, neither dogs nor bicycles are allowed. Admission is free, but as the Gardens are entirely supported by donations, your contribution will have a real impact. On the first Saturday in May, the **Day in the Gardens** brings food and music to this normally placid park, and garden and nature enthusiasts from all around come to tour and to buy native plants for their home gardens. The gift shop is open mid-March-December Monday-Saturday 10am-4pm.

Western North Carolina Nature Center

Asheville—and western North Carolina generally—is very ecologically conscious. This concern is reflected in the **Western North Carolina Nature Center** (75 Gashes Creek Rd., 828/298-5600, www.wildwnc.org, daily 10am-5pm, $7 adults, $6 seniors, $3 ages 3-15, under age 16 must be accompanied by an adult). On the grounds of an old zoo—don't worry, it's not depressing—wild animals who are, for various reasons, unable to survive in the wild (they were injured, for example, or raised as pets and abandoned) live in wooded habitats where the public can view them. This is the place to see some of the mountains' rarest species, animals that most lifetime mountain residents have never seen: cougars, wolves, coyotes, bobcats, and even the elusive hellbender. What's a hellbender, you ask? Come to the Nature Center and find out.

Black Mountain College

Considering the history of Black Mountain College from a purely numerical standpoint, one might get the false impression that this little institution's brief, odd life was a flash in the pan. In its 23 years of operation, Black Mountain College had only 1,200 students, 55 of whom actually completed their degrees. But in fact, between 1933 and 1956, the unconventional school fired a shot heard round the world as an innovative model of education and community life.

The educational program was almost devoid of structure. Students had no set course schedule or requirements. They lived and farmed

with the faculty, and no sense of hierarchy was permitted to separate students and teachers. Most distinguished as a school of arts, Black Mountain College hired Josef Albers as its first art director, when the Bauhaus icon fled Nazi Germany. Willem de Kooning taught here for a time, as did Buckminster Fuller, who began his design of the geodesic dome while he was in residence. Albert Einstein and William Carlos Williams were among the roster of guest lecturers.

Black Mountain College closed in 1956, due in part to the prevailing antileftist climate of that decade. The **Black Mountain College Museum and Arts Center** (56 Broadway, 828/350-8484, www.blackmountaincollege.org, Wed.-Sat. noon-4pm) is located not in the town of Black Mountain but in downtown Asheville. It's both an exhibition space and a resource center dedicated to the history and spirit of the college.

◖ Folk Art Center

An essential sight near Asheville on the BRP is the **Folk Art Center** (BRP milepost 382, 828/298-7928, Jan.-Mar. daily 9am-5pm, Apr.-Dec. daily 9am-6pm). At this beautiful gallery, coupled with the oldest continuously operating craft shop in the United States, **Allanstand Craft Shop,** you'll find the work of members of the prestigious Southern Highland Craft Guild, a juried-membership organization that brings together many of the best artists in Appalachia. Though the folk arts are well represented here in the forms of beautiful pottery, baskets, weaving, and quilts, you'll also find the work of contemporary studio artists in an array of media, including gorgeous handcrafted furniture, clothing, jewelry, and toys. Bring your Christmas shopping list, even if it's April.

ENTERTAINMENT AND EVENTS

Everywhere you turn in this city, you'll stumble on musicians—on street corners, in cafés, on front porches. There are also formal music venues where, on any given weekend and many weeknights, you can hear rock, bluegrass,

DOWNTOWN ASHEVILLE

© AVALON TRAVEL

Appalachian, "Afrolachian," blues, honky-tonk, country, and mountain swing.

Bluegrass at The Fiddlin' Pig

The Fiddlin' Pig (28 Tunnel Rd., 828/251-1979, www.thefiddlinpig.com), a popular barbecue joint on U.S. 70, has live bluegrass music six nights a week. The host bands, the Whitewater Bluegrass Company and Balsam Range, are all-star locals whose fame spreads far beyond Asheville. The Pig has a good small

dance floor, shared by clogging teams and dancing customers. There's also a full bar, but the restaurant remains a very child-friendly environment.

Nightlife

The **Orange Peel Social Aid and Pleasure Club** (101 Biltmore Ave., 828/225-5851, www.theorangepeel.net) is another fabulous nightspot. Billed as "the nation's premiere live music hall and concert venue," they can back up that claim by boasting of performances by Bob Dylan, Sonic Youth, Smashing Pumpkins, Blondie, and many other artists of that caliber—as well as some of the best up-and-coming acts from Asheville and the Southeast. There's a great dance floor and a cool bar. A leading host of roots music is the **Grey Eagle Tavern and Music Hall** (185 Clingman Ave., 828/232-5800, www.thegreyeagle.com). A listening room-style venue rather than a bar or club—that is, folks come here when they want to hear music, not bar-hop—the Grey Eagle does provide good Louisiana-style eats at its **Twin Cousins Kitchen,** and plenty of good beers and wines. Another favorite is **Jack of the Woods** (95 Patton Ave., 828/252-5445,

BABE RUTH IN ASHEVILLE

One day in 1925, the New York Yankees baseball team was on its way to Asheville to play an exhibition game at **McCormick Field** (30 Buchanan Place, 828/258-0428). Babe Ruth was on the train, and he didn't feel well–a touch of flu, perhaps, or indigestion, and the bumpy rails of western North Carolina did him no good. Stepping off the train at Asheville, greeted by a rush of fans, he fainted and fell. Luckily, Ruth passed out next to the catcher, Steve O'Neill, who did his job and caught his bulky teammate before the famous mug hit the station's marble floor. Ruth was rushed off to the Battery Park Hotel, where he apparently made a full recovery. The newspapers failed to note that fact, though, and it was briefly reported that Ruth had died in Asheville–a story that caused no small consternation. All was well a few years later when, on April 8, 1931, Ruth returned to Asheville, and both he and Lou Gehrig hit home runs here at McCormick Field. This august ground is now the home field of the **Asheville Tourists** (30 Buchanan Place, 828/258-0428, www.theashevilletourists.com), the Class A farm team of the Colorado Rockies.

www.jackofthewood.com). The shows here, which start on Friday and Saturday at 9:30, tend toward progressive approaches to traditional music, from bluegrass and old-time Appalachian to Irish and folk. Local musicians gather regularly to jam. Sunday night starting at 5pm, Irish musicians play, while on Wednesday beginning at 9pm, old-time (Appalachian) musicians jam. The bluegrass jam is on Thursday night beginning at 10pm. This is a region of outstanding musicians, and Jack of the Woods is a good place to experience the area's musical traditions up-close.

Asheville is home to some excellent microbreweries, and to visit them in the company of enthusiastic experts, try the **Asheville Brews Cruise** (828/545-5181, www.brewscruise.com, $37, $70 per couple). Mark and Trish Lyons take you all around town in the Brews Cruise van to sample some homegrown beers. You'll visit the **Asheville Pizza and Brewing Company** (675 Merrimon Ave., 828/254-1281, www.ashevillepizza.com), where you can start off the evening with one of this pizzeria, microbrewery, and movie house's tasty IPA beers, and fortify yourself for the evening by filling up on good pizza. The **French Broad Brewery** (101 Fairview Rd., 828/277-0222, www.frenchbroadbrewery.com) is another popular local nightspot that has grown up around a first-rate beer-making operation, and here you can choose from a varied menu that includes signature pilsners, lagers, ales, and more while listening to some good live music. The third destination on the Cruise is the **Highland Brewing Company** (12 Old Charlotte Hwy., Suite H, 828/299-3370, www.highlandbrewing.com), Asheville's first microbrewery. They've been making beer and raking in awards for well over a decade, and on first sip you'll understand why they're one of the Southeast's favorite breweries.

Another good microbrewery is **Wedge Brewing Company** (125B Roberts St., 828/505-2792, www.wedgebrewing.com, Mon.-Fri. 4pm-10pm, Sat. 2pm-10pm, Sun. 2pm-9pm), located in an old warehouse in the River Arts

District. Wedge keeps seven brews on tap, including pale ales, pilsners, and a Russian imperial stout flavored with raspberries.

Ballet

Asheville's noteworthy ballet company, **Terpsicorps** (2 N. Pack Square, 828/252-4530, http://terpsicorps.org), performs for two brief but brilliant runs in the summer. Under the direction of North Carolinian dancer and choreographer Heather Malloy, Terpsicorps takes advantage of what is normally a slow season for other companies and hires some of the country's best dancers for a brief stint in Asheville. They have two productions each summer, and each usually has only a three-night run, so the tickets sell out fast.

Festivals

Twice yearly, in late July and late October, the Southern Highland Craft Guild hosts the **Craft Fair of the Southern Highlands** (U.S. Cellular Center, 87 Haywood St., www.southernhighlandguild.org, Thurs.-Sun. 10am-6pm, $6). Since 1948 this event has brought much-deserved attention to the Guild's more than 900 members, who live and work throughout the Appalachian Mountains. Hundreds of craftspeople participate in the Craft Fair, selling all sorts of handmade items.

Asheville's **Mountain Dance and Folk Festival** (www.folkheritage.org, 828/258-6101, ext. 345, daily $20 adults, $10 under age 12, three days $54 adults, $24 under age 12) is the nation's longest-running folk festival, an event founded in the 1920s by musician and folklorist Bascom Lamar Lunsford to celebrate the heritage of his native Carolina mountains. Musicians and dancers from western North Carolina perform at the downtown Diana Wortham Theater at Pack Place for three nights each summer. On Saturday nights at Martin Luther King Jr. Park, also downtown, many of the same artists can be heard in the city's **Shindig on the Green** concert series.

In October, a series of creepy and offbeat happenings take place in the monthlong festival called **Ashtoberfest** (www.ashtoberfest.com). Among the events are a horror film festival, a summit of horror writers, and—the pinnacle of Ashtoberfest—the Zombie Walk. Ashevillians (and a surprising number of out-of-towners) prepare for the Zombie Walk a month in advance by burying clothes in their yards. This way, when they dig them back up and don their zombie garb, they'll give off a properly fetid, sepulchral funk. On the appointed date, the zombies, in their grubby duds and nasty makeup, gather at a city cemetery, and all at once begin to lurch, in the top-heavy fashion of the zombies in *Night of the Living Dead*, in an undead shamble along the sidewalks of Asheville. The Zombie Walk ends as the ghouls gradually disappear into various pubs and parties downtown. Event dates and locations change each year, so take a look at Ashtoberfest's website.

SHOPPING
Antiques and Secondhand Goods

The best store in Asheville—of any kind—is the tiny curiosity shop **Not Your Average Antiques** (21 Page Ave., across from the Grove Arcade, 828/252-1333, www.notyouraverageantiques.com). This fine retailer trades almost exclusively in items that were coveted by 10-year-old boys between the years 1900 and 1960, approximately. Included in this bounty: tin robots and astronauts, ray guns, magician and circus posters, carousel animals, and cowboy accoutrements. Interspersed is some wonderful Southern folk art, birds made by area woodcarvers, and pottery from all over the state. You probably didn't realize until now that you needed a wind-up Buck Rogers toy from the 1930s—but you do.

It's an unusual sort of a town that has both the supply and demand necessary for a business like **Second Gear** (415-A Haywood Rd., 828/258-0757, www.secondgearwnc.com, Mon.-Fri. 10am-6pm, Sat. 10am-5pm). This consignment shop deals exclusively in secondhand outdoor equipment and clothes. It's a great place to find canoes and kayaks, tents, climbing gear, men's and women's outdoor

Malaprop's Bookstore and Café

© JIM MOREKIS

clothing and shoes, and many other items at very low prices.

Galleries

One of Asheville's best places to shop is the 1929 **Grove Arcade** (1 Page Ave., 828/252-7799, www.grovearcade.com). The expansive Tudor Revival fortress, ornately filigreed all around, inside and out, in ivory-glazed terra-cotta, was originally meant to be the base of a 14-story building, a skyscraper for that time and place. As it is, the Grove Arcade is rather like an exposition hall at an early World's Fair. There are some great little galleries and boutiques here, including **Mountain Made** (828/350-0307, www.mtnmade.com, Mon.-Sat. 10am-6pm, Sun. noon-5pm) and the **Grove Arcade ARTS & Heritage Gallery** (828/255-0775, www.grovearcade.com, Mon.-Sat. 10am-6pm, Sun. noon-5pm), both galleries of local artists' work; **Asheville Home Crafts** (828/350-7556, www.ashevillehome-crafts.com, Mon.-Sat. 10am-6pm, Sun. noon-6pm), which sells handmade quilts, dolls,

afghans, and knit garments; several cafés; and a chocolatier.

Books, Toys, and Crafts

One of the social hubs of this city is **Malaprop's Bookstore and Café** (55 Haywood St., 828/254-6734, www.malaprops.com, Mon.-Thurs. 8am-9pm, Fri.-Sat. 8am-10pm, Sun. 8am-7pm). The very good bookstore—progressive, with a deep selection on many subjects and a particular interest in regional literature—is joined to the requisite coffee bar, actually my favorite java joint in a town filled with great java joints. In addition to its appealing inventory, Malaprop's has a great atmosphere for hanging out. It's bright and comfortable, and as you sip your strong coffee you can watch the Ashevillians stroll down Haywood Street. The variety of people who live here is striking, and among the young and artistic, there's a great deal of creativity invested in clothes, hairstyles, tattoos, and jewelry.

Dancing Bear Toys (144 Tunnel Rd., 800/659-8697, www.dancingbeartoys.com, Mon.-Sat. 10am-7pm, Sun. noon-5pm) is located among the motels and chain restaurants out on U.S. 70 (Tunnel Rd.), but inside it has the ambience of a cozy village toyshop. Dancing Bear, which also has a location in Hendersonville, has toys for everyone, from babies to silly grown-ups—a fabulous selection of Playmobil figures and accessories, Lego, Brio, and other favorite lines of European toys; beautiful stuffed animals of all sizes; all sorts of educational kits and games; and comical doodads that would be a welcome find in an adult's or a child's stocking.

There are a lot of bead shops in North Carolina, but my two favorites are Carrboro's Original Ornament and Asheville's **Chevron Trading Post & Bead Company** (40 N. Lexington Ave., 828/236-2323, www.chevron-beads.com, Mon.-Sat. 10am-6pm). The millions of beads, in bowls and tubes and strands on every surface in the shop, are so irresistibly twinkly and colorful that even if you're not crafty you'll want to buy them by the basket just to hoard like a magpie. Best of all, Chevron

ASHEVILLE

Trading Post is the home of Rosie, a rotund orange and white cat who, if you're lucky, will help you shop.

ACCOMMODATIONS
Under $150

Bon Paul and Sharky's Hostel of Asheville (816 Haywood Rd., 828/350-9929, www.bonpaulandsharkys.com) is a pleasant old white house with a porch and porch swing, high-speed Internet access, and dorm-style bunks (in a shared room, women-only, or coed, $22). You can camp in the yard for $13, or rent the private room ($65) with a TV and queen-size bed. Dogs must stay in the outdoor kennels. The hostel offers pick-up service from the bus station ($8) or from the airport ($15). Bon Paul and Sharky, by the way, were goldfish.

The **Asheville ArtHaus Hostel** (16 Ravenscroft Dr., 828/225-3278, http://aahostel.com) is a private room-only hostel. The two-person rooms (one with a queen bed and one with two twins) are $50 per night, the three-person room (one queen and one twin) is $60, and the family room (one queen and two twins) is $70. Pets are not permitted. The website has a handy text-only page (linked from the main page) with walking directions and contact information for mobile browsers.

In the days before motels became the norm for budget lodging, the motor court or cottage court was a favorite overnight option for middle-class travelers. This style of lodging is almost a thing of the past, and the buildings themselves are disappearing steadily, but there are still some very cool examples scattered through the North Carolina mountains. Several in the Asheville area are still in business and in good repair, providing today's travelers with charmingly retro accommodations. **Asheville Log Cabin Motor Court** (330 Weaverville Hwy., 828/645-6546, www.cabinlodging.com, $55-250, 2-night minimum, pets allowed for a fee) was constructed around 1930 and appears in the 1958 Robert Mitchum movie *Thunder Road*. The cabins have cable TV and wireless Internet access but no phones. Some are air conditioned, but that's not usually a necessity at this elevation. Another great cabin court is the **Pines Cottages** (346 Weaverville Hwy., 888/818-6477, http://ashevillepines.com, $45-175, depending on season, up to 2 pets allowed for $15 per pet). Billed as "A nice place for nice people," it's also a friendly place for pets.

My own favorite is the quirky, kitschy **Mountaineer Inn** (155 Tunnel Rd., 828/254-5331, $50-70), run for decades by a Greek-American family. The conveniently located Mountaineer sports one of the most awesome old-school neon signs you'll see anywhere. They offer a humble free breakfast in the tiny lobby, where the TV is usually tuned to a satellite Greek station.

$150-300

If you've spent the day touring Biltmore House, viewing the incredible splendor in which a baron of the Gilded Age basked, it may be jarring to return to real life unless you're Richard Branson or the Queen of England. But you can soften the transition with a stay at the luxurious **Inn on Biltmore Estate** (800/411-3812, www.biltmore.com, $189-479). It's everything you'd wish for from a hotel in this location. The suites are beautifully furnished, the view is magnificent, and the lobby and dining room and library have the deluxe coziness of a turn-of-the-century lodge.

Over $300

The [**Grove Park Inn Resort & Spa** (290 Macon Ave., 800/438-5800, www.groveparkinn.com, $225-300) is the sort of place to which Asheville residents will bring their out-of-town houseguests when giving them a grand tour of the city, simply to walk into the lobby and ooh and ah. The massive stone building—constructed by a crew of 400 workers who had only mule teams and a single steam shovel to aid them—was erected in 1912 and 1913, the project of St. Louis millionaire E. W. Grove. He was the Grove behind Grove's Tasteless Chill Tonic, a medicinal syrup that outsold Coca-Cola in the 1890s. You may have seen it in antiques shops; on the label was a picture of a wincing baby, who looks more like he's just been given a dose of the tonic than that he needs one.

The opening of the Grove Park Inn was cause for such fanfare that William Jennings Bryan addressed the celebratory dinner party. In the coming years, at least eight U.S. presidents would be guests here, as would a glittering parade of early 20th-century big shots: Henry Ford, Thomas Edison, Eleanor Roosevelt, Harry Houdini, F. Scott Fitzgerald, Will Rogers, and George Gershwin. Even if you don't stay at the Grove Park while you are visiting Asheville, swing by just to see it. You can drive right up to the front door, and if you tell the valets that you just want to nip in and see the lobby, they'll probably be willing to watch your car for five minutes. (Don't forget to tip.) The lobby is quite amazing, like a cross between a Gilded Age hunting lodge and the great hall of a medieval castle. There are 14-foot fireplaces at each end, and the elevators are, believe it or not, inside the chimneys.

In addition to the spectacle of the lodge and its multiple restaurants, cafés, bars, and shops, guests have (for an additional charge) access to its world-famous spa. Day passes cost $55 for guests on weekdays, and $65 on weekends. Nonguests can purchase day passes Monday-Thursday. The pass gives access to the lounges, pools, waterfall, steam room, inhalation room, and outdoor whirlpool tub. The indoor pool is a truly nifty pirate's cove of a place, a subterranean stone room with vaulted skylights and tropical plants. For extra fees (ranging $75-500, with most around $200-300), guests can choose from a four-page menu of spa treatments: massage, facials, manicures, aromatherapy, body wraps, the works. For $60, you can have your aura photographed before and after the treatment, to gauge the depth of your relaxation.

If you do happen to be Richard Branson or the Queen of England, and simply need a mountain getaway, consider the Inn's **Cottage on Biltmore Estate** (800/411-3812, www.biltmore.com, call for rates). This historic two-room cottage was designed by Richard

Howland Hunt, the son of the mansion's designer, Richard Morris Hunt. Your own personal butler and chef come with the digs.

FOOD
Eclectic American

Though only a few years old, **Early Girl Eatery** (8 Wall St., 828/259-9292, www.earlygirleatery.com, Mon.-Fri. 7:30am-3pm, Tues.-Thurs. 5pm-9pm, Sat.-Sun. 5pm-10pm, brunch Sat.-Sun. 9am-3pm, $10-15) has caused a stir among area locavores. More than half of the vegetables, meat, and fish that go into Early Girl was raised or caught within 20 miles of the restaurant. The menu is very accommodating of Asheville's large vegetarian and vegan contingent, but nonveg diners can feast on pan-fried trout with green tomato-blackberry sauce, squash casserole, and hush puppies, or pan-seared duck with roasted shallots, sweet potato fritters, and sautéed greens—and many other delicious New Southern creations.

A few doors down, **Laughing Seed Café** (40 Wall St., 828/252-3445, www.laughingseed.com, Mon. and Wed.-Thurs. 11:30am-9pm, Fri.-Sat. 11:30am-10pm, Sun. 10am-9pm, under $20) achieves what vegetarian restaurants always aim for but are seldom able to achieve—their food is so good, and so widely praised, that a legion of nonvegetarians have become loyal fans and customers. The restaurant describes its style as "international vegetarian cuisine," and it draws on Latin American, Thai, Indian, and other cuisines of the world to create hearty and addictively flavorful dishes.

Say you've been at the Grey Eagle or the Orange Peel, and the show has just let out. It's the middle of the night. You and your friends are not ready for the night to end, but you've got to refuel with some good food in order to keep going. The lights are on at **Rosetta's Kitchen** (111 Broadway Ave., 828/232-0738, www.rosettaskitchen.com, Mon.-Thurs. 11am-11pm, Fri.-Sun. 11am-3pm, $5-11), and the stove is hot. There's so much to recommend this place. First off, the food is good. It's all vegetarian, mostly vegan, and made with local produce in season. It's open late on weekends, 10pm-3am.

© JIM MOREKIS

Laughing Seed Café

ASHEVILLE

They compost every scrap of organic material that makes its way back to the kitchen, they recycle hundreds of pounds of trash, and make sure their used vegetable oil goes to power bio-diesel cars. It's Asheville all over.

A few years ago, husband and wife Jacob and Alicia Sessoms, and their friend Matthew Dawes, who met as students at Warren Wilson College in nearby Swannanoa, realized their longtime dream of founding a restaurant. They established **Table** (48 College St., 828/254-8980, http://tableasheville.com, lunch Mon. and Wed.-Sat. 11am-2:30pm, dinner Mon. and Wed.-Sat. 5:30pm-10pm, brunch Sun. 10:30am-2pm, $13-27), to critical acclaim. Using ingredients like locally caught bass and mountain-raised pork and lamb, chefs Jacob and Matthew have created a menu that takes full advantage to the culinary riches of western North Carolina.

The Market Place (20 Wall St., 828/252-4162, www.marketplace-restaurant.com, Mon.-Thurs. 5:30pm-10pm, Fri.-Sat. 5:30pm-11pm, entrées $16-30) has graced downtown Asheville

for 30 years. This local favorite constructs an elegant menu from ingredients raised or caught within 100 miles of the restaurant. Try the sweet potato ravioli, or the locally caught trout with roasted corn and black bean cakes.

West Asheville's **Sunny Point Café** (626 Haywood Rd., 828/252-0055, www.sunny-pointcafe.com, Sun.-Mon. 8:30am-2:30pm, Tues.-Sat. 8:30am-9pm) serves three meals most days, but is so famous for its brunch that a line sometimes forms outside the door. The breakfast menu here is so popular that it is served at any time of day, even though the lunch and dinner menus are well worth a trip as well. This is a great bet for vegetarians—the meatless options are imaginative and beautifully created. On Wednesday, Sunny Point offers $2 pints of microbrews, and on Saturday, bottles of wine normally priced over $20 are half price.

BILTMORE VILLAGE

In one of the historic cottages of Biltmore Village is the **C Corner Kitchen** (3 Boston

Way, 828/274-2439, www.thecornerkitchen. com, breakfast Mon.-Sat. 7:30am-11am, brunch Sun. 9am-3pm, lunch Mon.-Sat. 11:30am-3pm, dinner daily 5pm). Head chef Joe Scully, first in his class at the Culinary Institute of America, counts among his illustrious former gigs the Waldorf Astoria and the United Nations (where he served as executive chef). The elegant menu combines home-style and haute most harmoniously, and includes heavenly appetizers (most around $9) like almond-fried brie, served over a bed of greens (in the winter) with pear and apple conserve and a red-wine reduction; and entrées like the blackberry ketchup pork chop, which comes with sweet potatoes and fried green tomatoes ($21); and sweet potato salad with chow-chow (a Southern specialty relish) and a fried green tomato napoleon ($18). For lunch you can choose from a nice selection of classic sandwiches, or order the Ploughman's Lunch ($9)—a cup of soup, a small salad, two cheeses, and either country-style terrine or roasted portabella mushroom. Also tempting at lunch are the fried-oyster salad, apple-poached salmon, and sesame catfish ($9 and $10). The long wine list features many Napa Valley, French, and Italian wines, including several fine champagnes and sparkling whites and rosés. Prices range $9-120 by the bottle, and the wines under $20 per bottle are available for $6 by the glass. The cozy, cheerful dining room of this Victorian cottage opens into the kitchen, where guests can see every step of their meal's preparation while chatting with the staff.

Also excellent in Biltmore Village is **fig** (18 Brook St., 828/277-0889, www.figbistro.com, lunch daily 11:30am-3pm, dinner Mon.-Sat. 5:30pm-9pm, Sun. 10am-2pm, $12-27). Chef William Klein worked at fine restaurants in France and San Francisco before returning to western North Carolina, where his career began. Here at fig he has created an elegant bistro menu, including classic French desserts.

BILTMORE ESTATE

There are no fewer than nine places to eat on the Biltmore Estate (800/411-3812, www.

biltmore.com, estate admission required to visit restaurants). The **Dining Room** (daily 5:30pm-9:30pm, reservations required) is an elegant restaurant, led by chef Richard Boyer, featuring estate-raised Angus beef, mountain trout, and Biltmore wines. Evening dress and reservations are suggested. At the **Biltmore Bistro** (daily 11am-9pm), chef Edwin French creates a fabulous gourmet menu from the Biltmore's own kitchen garden, locally raised heirloom crops, meat and seafood delicacies, and artisanal cheeses and breads. The dining room of the **Deerpark Restaurant** (Jan.-Mar. 14 Fri. 5pm-8pm, Sat.-Sun. 10am-3pm, Mar. 15-Dec. Mon.-Sat. 11am-3pm, Sun. 10am-3pm, buffet dinner Nov.-Dec. daily from 5pm) is a former barn designed by architect Richard Morris Hunt, now renovated to an airy splendor with walls of windows. Here, chef Angela Guiffreda creates hearty and homey meals based on Appalachian cuisine. Like the Deerpark, the **Stable Café** (lunch daily 11am-4pm, dinner daily from 5pm) is former livestock housing, and guests can sit in booths that were once horse stalls. This is a meat-eater's paradise, where you can order estate-raised Angus beef, pork barbecue with chef Don Spear's famous special sauce, and lots of other tasty dishes. The **Arbor Grill** (Mon.-Thurs. noon-7pm, Fri.-Sat. noon-8pm) is an alfresco café next to the winery, featuring live music on weekends. In the stable area near the mansion, both the **Bake Shop** and **Ice Cream Café** serve fresh treats. The **Creamery Grill** is the place for sandwiches and hand-dipped ice cream, and the **Conservatory Café** will keep the children happy with hot dogs and soft drinks.

Indian

◖ **Mela** (70 Lexington Ave., 828/225-8880, www.melaasheville.com, daily 11:30am-2:30pm and 5:30pm-9:30pm) is one of the best Indian restaurants in North Carolina. The elaborate menu offers dozens of choices, combining cuisines of both Northern and Southern India, with great meat, seafood, and vegetable dishes. The restaurant is dark and elegant, but the prices are surprisingly low. While the entrées are mostly in the $10-15 range, you can put together a great patchwork meal of appetizers, which start at $2, soup, and roti. Don't miss the samosas.

A new local favorite is **Chai Pani** (22 Battery Park Ave., 828/254-4003, www.chaipani.net, Mon.-Thurs. 11:30am-9pm, Fri.-Sat. 5:30pm-10pm, Sun. noon-9pm, under $10). "Chai pani" means "tea and water," a phrase that refers to a snack or a small gift. This restaurant is inspired by Indian street food vendors, and serves casual and affordable specialties from all over India.

Latin American

Ask an Asheville resident for restaurant recommendations, and chances are **◖ Salsa's** (6 Patton Ave., 828/252-9805, www.salsas-asheville.com, Mon.-Thurs. 11:30am-2:30pm and 5:30pm-9pm, Fri. 11:30am-2:30pm and 5:30pm-10pm, Sat. noon-3pm and 5:30pm-10pm, Sun. noon-3pm and 5:30pm-9pm, $10-20) will be one of the first names intoned. It's definitely my favorite restaurant in town. Salsa's pan-Latin concoctions, from their famous fish burritos to exquisite cocktails, keep this tiny little café jam-packed with locals and with visitors who drive to Asheville just for a special meal. The flavors here are essentially earthy and hearty, but always topped with a refreshing touch of Caribbean lightness, courtesy largely of chef Hector Diaz's genius with various fruit-infused salsas, influenced by the cuisine of his Puerto Rico home.

Also delicious is **Limones** (13 Eagle St., 828/252-2327, http://limonesrestaurant.com, daily 10am-5pm, brunch Sun. 10:30am-2:30pm). Chef Hugo Ramirez, a native of Mexico City, combines his backgrounds in Mexican and French-inspired Californian cuisine to create a special menu.

European

Chef Michael Baudouin grew up in France's Rhône Valley, the son of a winemaker and an excellent cook. He brings his culinary heritage to Asheville at his restaurant **Bouchon** (62 N. Lexington Ave., 828/350-1140, http://

ashevillebouchon.com, daily from 5pm, small plates $5-13, large plates $10-20). Bouchon's "French comfort food" ranges from classics like rabbit in a Dijon mustard sauce and boeuf bourguignon to chicken thighs simmered in local apple cider. Delicious vegetarian options are available.

Zambra (85 Walnut St., 828/232-1060, www.zambratapas.com, dinner daily from 5pm, $10-20) combines cuisines of the Western Mediterranean-Spanish, Gypsy, and North African with fresh North Carolina ingredients. Specials change nightly and often feature North Carolina seafood. The long tapas menu has many choices for vegetarians.

Vinnie's (641 Merrimon Ave., 828/253-1077, www.vinniesitalian.com, Sun.-Mon. and Wed.-Thurs. 5pm-9:30pm, Fri.-Sat. 5pm-10:30pm, $10-20), on Merrimon Avenue downtown, is a good and reasonably priced Italian eatery. Pasta and pizza, heroes and calzone are offered in abundance, along with heartier veal and chicken dishes, lasagna, and eggplant parmigiana.

Chocolate

French Broad Chocolates (10 S. Lexington Ave., 828/252-4181, http://frenchbroad-chocolates.com, Sun.-Thurs. 11am-11pm, Fri.-Sat. 11am-midnight) describes itself as "a sacred space for chocophiles." This mellow café serves a menu that celebrates chocolate, featuring French Broad Chocolates' own artisanal truffles, brownies, and pastries as well as sipping chocolates and floats. If by some freak of nature you don't care for chocolate, you can sample Pisgah Brewing Company beers, and nonchocolate desserts like pecan tart and butter cake. French Broad Chocolates is open early and late, perfect for an afternoon snack or a special dessert after a night on the town.

INFORMATION AND SERVICES

The **Asheville Visitors Center** (36 Montford Ave., off I-240 exit 4C, 828/258-6129), can set you up with all the maps, brochures, and recommendations you could need. Other sources are www.exploreasheville.com and www.ashevillechamber.org.

Mission Hospital (509 Biltmore Ave.; 428 Biltmore Ave., 828/213-1948 or 828/213-4063, www.missionhospitals.org) in Asheville has two campuses and two emergency departments.

GETTING THERE AND AROUND

Asheville lies spread-eagled at the crossroads of I-40, North Carolina's primary east-west highway, and I-26, a roughly north-south artery through the Southern highlands. Splitting the difference, U.S. 19 runs at a diagonal, deep into the Smokies in one direction and into the northern Blue Ridge in the other.

Asheville has an extensive public bus system, connecting most major points in the metropolitan area, including the airport, with downtown. Buses run Monday-Saturday 6am-11:30pm and cost $1 ($0.50 seniors). Visit www.ashevillenc.gov for routes and schedules.

Asheville Regional Airport (AVL, 61 Terminal Dr., Fletcher, 828/684-2226, www.flyavl.com) is a bit of a jog from the city, located to the south in Fletcher. It's an easy 20-minute drive on I-26.

MADISON COUNTY

North of Asheville, Madison County is a world unto itself: wild mountain terrain with a handful of small peculiar towns whose reputation in the rest of the state is that of tough independence. Madison is revered by lovers of traditional balladry because a group of families—including Chandlers, Wallins, Nortons, and their kin—have committed to disc and tape over the course of the last half century some of the finest and most powerful renditions of the ancient ballads brought to the mountains by its first English and Celtic settlers. A new generation of singers is emerging today, with a core group of young women reared in the tradition who have inherited the remarkable voices, memories, and sense of stewardship for which their ancestors are honored.

Entertainment and Events

Mars Hill, a tiny college town, is a center of mountain culture thanks to Mars Hill College. The **Bascom Lamar Lunsford "Minstrel of the Appalachians" Festival** (828/689-1571, www.mhc.edu, $10 adults, $5 children), usually in early September, is a 50-year-old annual gathering of some of the best mountain musicians, dancers, and craftspeople from this hotbed of folk traditions. Mars Hill College is also the home of the **Southern Appalachian Repertory Theatre** (Owen Theatre, 44 College St., 828/689-1239, http://sartplays.org), a highly regarded ensemble presenting a range of contemporary drama, musicals, and family productions. SART's stage is in the Owen Theater, a great-looking old Baptist Church on the Mars Hill campus.

Sports and Recreation

On a 4,700-foot mountaintop above Mars Hill, the **Wolf Ski Resort** (578 Valley View Circle, 800/817-4111, www.skiwolfridgenc.com) has more than 80 acres of prime skiing and snowboarding slopes. It is also the home of the Snow Sports School, which offers private and group lessons for all ages of beginning and intermediate winter sports enthusiasts. There are multiple lifts, two lodges for relaxing, and multiple hearty dining options. The attached **Scenic Wolf Resort** offers year-round cabin accommodations ($240-290), a huge indoor heated pool, and numerous recreational activities.

Sandy Bottom Trail Rides (1459 Caney Fork Rd., Marshall, 800/959-3513, www.sandybottomtrailrides.net, rides depart daily 10am, noon, 2pm, and 4pm), based at a 100-year-old family farm, leads horseback treks deep into the forest on one- to four-hour expeditions to an early 19th-century garnet mine. They'll also carry you in style in a horse-drawn buggy, if you prefer.

There are plenty of white-water rafting opportunities up here along with several guide companies to choose from. **Huck Finn River Adventures** (158 Bridge St., Hot Springs, 877/520-4658, www.huckfinnrafting.com) runs guided and unguided white-water rafting and float trips as well as overnight paddles.

French Broad Rafting Expeditions (U.S. 25/70, Marshall, 800/570-7238, www.frenchbroadrafting.com) can get you equipped and ready for a guided or unguided rafting trip on the French Broad River, which has both whitewater and calm sections to choose from.

Accommodations and Food

Defying that worn-out stereotype of mountain isolation, Madison County has for centuries been a destination for vacationers because of its natural hot springs. Going back at least to the mid-18th century—and, according to tradition, long before the first nonnative settlers arrived—the springs have had a reputation for curative powers. A succession of grand hotels operated at Hot Springs, all long since burned down.

Modern visitors can still take the waters. **Hot Springs Resort and Spa** (U.S. 25/70, at the entrance to the town of Hot Springs, 828/622-7676, www.nchotsprings.com, suites $150-200, cabins $50-150, camping $50-60) is a much simpler affair than the old hotels here, not a luxury destination but a place where you can lodge or camp for the night and soak in the famous 100°F water.

The **Mountain Magnolia Inn** (204 Lawson St., Mars Hill, 828/622-3543 or 800/914-9306, www.mountainmagnoliainn.com, $95-268) provides lodging in an ornate 1868 home and in nearby creek-side cabins. The inn's dining room is a nice gourmet restaurant that features locally raised organic produce, meats, cheeses, and wines.

Southern Blue Ridge and Foothills

The mountains of Polk, Rutherford, and Henderson Counties, south of Asheville, have an air of enchantment to them. There are some quantifiable symptoms of this peculiarity. For one, Polk County has its own climate. Called the Thermal Belt, the meteorological pocket formed on this sheltered slope of the Blue Ridge has distinctly milder summers and winters than the surrounding areas. In the 19th century it became a favorite summering spot for the Charleston elite and other Southerners of the plantation class. Some lovely old houses and inns remain as vestiges of this genteel past.

BREVARD

Brevard is the pleasant seat of the improbably named Transylvania County. As you might expect, Halloween is a big deal in this town. Brevard is also known for sheltering a population of rather startling white squirrels. The local legend about their origin goes that their ancestors escaped from an overturned circus truck in Florida in 1940, and made their way to Brevard as pets. More likely, say researchers, is that they came from an exotic pet breeder in Florida and were acquired by a Brevard area

family that way. In any case, the white squirrels escaped into the wild of Transylvania County, and you'll probably see their descendants in the area when you visit.

Entertainment and Events

The **Brevard Music Center** (349 Andante Lane, 828/862-2100, www.brevardmusic.org) has attracted the highest caliber of young musicians for more than 70 years for intensive summer-long classical music instruction. Throughout the summer, Brevard Music Center students as well as visiting soloists of international fame put on a world-class concert series in the summer, performing works by the likes of Tchaikovsky and Gilbert and Sullivan.

Shopping

A center for a very different sort of music is **Celestial Mountain Music** (16 W. Main St., 828/884-3575, www.celestialmtnmusic.com). This nice little shop carries, among the usual wares of a good music store, two lines of very special locally made instruments. Cedar Mountain Banjos, of the open-backed, old-time variety, are beautifully crafted and ring clear

SOUTHERN BLUE RIDGE AND FOOTHILLS

ASHEVILLE

NORTH CAROLINA

SOUTH CAROLINA

TENNESSEE

GEORGIA

Great Smoky Mountains National Park

Pisgah National Forest

Pisgah National Forest

Gorges State Park

FOLK ART CENTER
WESTERN NORTH CAROLINA NATURE CENTER
BILTMORE ESTATE
DOWNTOWN ARCHITECTURE
CHIMNEY ROCK
NORTH CAROLINA ARBORETUM
CARL SANDBURG HOME NATIONAL HISTORIC SITE
CRADLE OF FORESTRY
PISGAH RANGER DISTRICT
END OF THE BLUE RIDGE PARKWAY
NAVITAT
WOLF LAUREL

Marion
Little Switzerland
Mt Mitchell State Park
Black Mountain
Weaverville
Mars Hill
Marshall
Asheville
Canton
Mt Pisgah
Waynesville
Richland Balsam
Maggie Valley
Cherokee
Cullowhee
Sylva
Dillsboro
Bryson City
Franklin
Waterville
Lake Lure
Chimney Rock
Hendersonville
Flat Rock
Rutherfordton
Columbus
Tryon
Saluda
Looking Glass Falls
Sliding Rock
Brevard
Lake Toxaway
Sapphire
Cashiers
Highlands
Whitewater Falls
Dry Falls
Bridal Veil Falls
Gneiss

Blue Ridge Parkway
French Broad River

10 mi
10 km

© AVALON TRAVEL

and pretty. The work of local fiddle builder Lyle Reedy is also sold at Celestial Mountain Music.

Sports and Recreation

About 10 miles south of Brevard, **Dupont State Forest** (U.S. 276, 828/877-6527, www.dupontforest.com, daily dawn-dusk, free) has more than 90 miles of hiking trails covering 10,000 acres. Some of Transylvania County's beautiful waterfalls are located within the forest and accessible on foot (most trails in the forest are moderate or strenuous) or, with special permits and advance reservation for people with disabilities only, by vehicle. Visitors should use caution, wear brightly colored clothing, and leave their bearskin capes at home from September through the end of the year, when hikers share the woods with hunters.

◖ PISGAH RANGER DISTRICT

Just to the north of Brevard in the town of Pisgah Forest is the main entrance to the **Pisgah Ranger District** (off U.S. 276, 828/877-3265, www.cs.unca.edu, park hours daily dawn-dusk, office hours Mon.-Fri. 8am-5pm, free) of the Pisgah National Forest. The forest covers half a million acres, a large swath of western North Carolina, but this 157,000-acre ranger district encompasses many of the forest's favorite attractions. A good topographical map of the ranger district is available from National Geographic (Map 780, $10, sold at Cradle of Forestry store and at www.cradleofforestry.com). In the ranger district are more than 275 miles of hiking trails and several campgrounds, the most easily accessible of which is **Davidson River Campground,** 1.5 miles from the Brevard entrance (877/444-6777, www.recreation.gov, year-round, $10), with restrooms and showers.

The **Shining Rock Wilderness** and the **Middle Prong Wilderness,** which join Shining Rock at the southwest, are a rugged terrain that rises from 3,200 feet elevation at its lowest point along the West Pigeon River to a towering 6,400 feet at Richmond Balsam. **Cold Mountain,** made famous by the book and

movie of the same name, is a real peak located within the Shining Rock Wilderness. These mountains are steep and the forests dense, and what trails there are have no signage. This is a popular area among experienced backwoods trekkers but is not recommended for casual visits as it is exceedingly easy to get lost here. It's recommended that at a minimum, you should be adept at using both a compass and a topo map before venturing into these wilderness areas.

Not to be confused with Shining Rock, **Sliding Rock** is an easily accessible waterfall and swimming spot with a parking lot, a bathhouse, and lifeguards (on duty Memorial Day-Labor Day daily 10am-6pm). You can actually ride down the 60-foot waterfall, a smooth rock face (not so smooth that you shouldn't wear sturdy britches) over which 11,000 gallons of water rush every minute into the chilly swimming hole below.

The **Cradle of Forestry** (U.S. 276, Pisgah Forest, 828/877-3130, www.cradleofforestry.com, mid-Apr.-early Nov. daily 9am-5pm, $5 adults, free under age 16) is a museum and activity complex commemorating the rise of the forestry profession in the United States, which originated here at a turn-of-the-century training school in the forests once owned by George Washington Vanderbilt, master of the Biltmore Estate in Asheville. Plow days and living history days throughout the year give an interesting glimpse into this region's old-time methods of farming and frontier living. Self-guided trails lead through the woods to many interesting locations of this campus of the nation's first school of forestry.

HENDERSONVILLE

An easy drive from Asheville, Hendersonville is a comfortable small city with a walkable downtown filled with boutiques and cafés. It's also the heart of North Carolina's apple industry. Hundreds of orchards cover the hillsides of Henderson County, and all along the highway, long packinghouses bustle in the late summer as they process more than three million tons of apples. There are also many shops and produce stands run by members of old orchard-owning families, where you can buy apples singly or by the bushel, along with cider, preserves, and many other apple products.

Sights

One of North Carolina's cool small transportation museums is located at the Hendersonville Airport. The **Western North Carolina Air Museum** (Hendersonville Airport, off U.S. 176/Spartanburg Hwy., 828/698-2482, www.wncairmuseum.com, Apr.-Oct. Sat. 10am-5pm, Wed. and Sun. noon-5pm, Nov.-Mar. Wed. and Sat.-Sun. noon-5pm, free) houses a collection of more than a dozen historic small aircraft, both originals and reproductions. Most are from the 1930s and 1940s, though some are even older, and they're all wonderfully fun contraptions to visit.

Shopping

Hendersonville's downtown **Curb Market** (221 N. Church St. at 2nd Ave., 828/692-8012, www.curbmarket.com, Apr.-Dec. Tues., Thurs., and Sat. 8am-2pm, Jan.-Mar. Tues. and Sat. 8am-2pm) has been operating since 1924. Here you can buy fresh locally grown fruits, vegetables, and flowers; fresh-baked cakes, pies, and breads; jams, jellies, and pickles made in local home kitchens; and the work of local woodcarvers, weavers, and other craftspeople.

While in the Hendersonville area, keep an eye out for brightly colored, folk painting-adorned packages of **Immaculate Baking Company** (www.immaculatebaking.com) cookies. Besides making totally delicious cookies, this Hendersonville-based company helps support the work of visionary "outsider" artists throughout the South.

FLAT ROCK
Sights

Just south of Hendersonville is the historic village of Flat Rock. Founded in the early 19th century as a vacation spot for the Charleston plantation gentry, Flat Rock retains a delicate, cultured ambience created so many years ago. Many artists and writers have lived in this area, most famously Carl Sandburg, whose house, Connemara, is preserved as the **Carl Sandburg Home National Historic Site** (81 Carl Sandburg Lane, Flat Rock, 828/693-4178, www.nps.gov/carl, daily 9am-5pm, house tour $5 adults, $3 over age 61, free under age 16). Here Sandburg and his family lived for more than 20 years, during which time he wrote, won the Pulitzer Prize for *Complete Poems*, and no doubt observed bemusedly as his wife and daughters raised champion dairy goats. (A herd of goats lives on the grounds today.) Half-hour tours take visitors through the house to see many of the Sandburgs' own belongings. There is a bookstore in the house, and more than five miles of trails through the property.

Entertainment and Events

Another literary landmark in the village is the **Flat Rock Playhouse** (2661 Greenville Hwy., Flat Rock, 866/732-8008, www.flatrockplayhouse.org). Now the state theater of North Carolina, the Flat Rock Playhouse's history dates to 1940, when a roving theater company called the Vagabonds wandered down from New York and converted an old gristmill here in the village into a stage. They now have a 10-month season, drawing more than 90,000 patrons yearly.

SALUDA AND VICINITY

Just east and south of Hendersonville, bordering South Carolina, Polk County is home to several interesting little towns, most notably Tryon and Saluda, and a lot of beautiful mountain countryside. In Saluda you'll find a tiny downtown, laid out along the old Norfolk Southern Railway tracks. The tracks at Saluda are the top of the steepest standard gauge mainline railroad grade in the United States.

Entertainment and Events

For one weekend every July, Saluda busts at the seams with visitors to the **Coon Dog Day Festival** (800/440-7848, www.saluda.com). Hundreds of beautifully trained dogs from all over the region come to town to show off in

ASHEVILLE

a parade and trials, while the humans have a street fair and 5K race.

Shopping

Six miles southeast of Columbus, potters Claude and Elaine Graves have been making distinctive pottery for 35 years at **Little Mountain Pottery** (6372 Peniel Rd., www.crowsounds.com). The Graves's work draws on North Carolina's folk traditions in ceramics, but it's quite different from much of the pottery made in this area in that it also draws inspiration from the ceramics of North Africa, the Canary Islands, Spain, and Mexico. Don't miss Claude's wonderful portraits of influential North Carolina potters, arranged in an outdoor gallery along the walls of his barns and kiln.

Sports and Recreation

The equestrian life plays a growing role in Polk and the surrounding counties of North Carolina's southern mountains. The **Foothills Equestrian Nature Center** (3381 Hunting Country Rd., Tryon, 828/859-9021, www.fence.org), known as FENCE, occupies 380 beautiful acres along the border with South Carolina. The equestrian center has stables for 200 horses and two lighted show rings. FENCE hosts cross-country, three-day, A-rated hunter and jumper, dressage, and many other equestrian events throughout the year. The annual Block House Steeplechase has been held in Tryon for 60 years, and FENCE has hosted the event for 20 of those years. FENCE also offers regular hikes and bird-watching excursions on its beautiful property.

Food

For such a tiny town, there are an awful lot of eating places in Saluda. Just stand in the middle of Main Street and look around; there are several choices, and you won't go wrong at any of them. The **Whistlestop Café** (173 Main St., 828/749-3310, Thurs.-Mon. 11am-5pm, $7) serves good hearty meals and strong coffee in its tiny dining room. The apple pound cake is perfect. **Wildflour Bakery** (173 E. Main, 828/749-9224, www.saluda.com, Wed.-Sat. 8am-3pm, Sun. 10am-2pm) stone-grinds wheat, with which it makes absolutely delicious breads, every single morning. Breakfast and lunch are served here, making this a great place to fill up before a day of kayaking or hiking.

HIGHLANDS AND VICINITY
Waterfalls

This country is blessed with some beautiful waterfalls, some of which are easily visited. **Whitewater Falls** (Hwy. 281, on the state line, south of Highlands, daily dawn-dusk, $2 per vehicle), at over 400 feet, is reported to be the highest waterfall east of the Rockies. An upper-level viewing spot is at the end of a wheelchair-accessible paved trail, while a flight of more than 150 steps leads to the base of the falls. A much smaller but still very beautiful waterfall is **Silver Run Falls** (Hwy. 107, 4 miles south of Cashiers), reached by a short trail from a roadside pull-off. **Bridal Veil Falls** (U.S. 64, 2.5 miles west of Highlands) flows over a little track of road, right off of U.S. 64. You'll see a sign from the main road where you can turn off and actually drive behind the waterfall, or park and walk behind it. Another falls that you can walk through is **Dry Falls** (U.S. 64, between Highlands and Franklin, daily dawn-dusk, $2 per vehicle), reached by a small trail off the highway, curving right into and behind the 75-foot waterfall.

Sports and Recreation

North Carolina's newest state park, **Gorges State Park** (Hwy. 281 S., Sapphire, 828/966-9099, http://ncparks.gov, May-Aug. 8am-9pm, Mar.-Apr., Sept.-Oct. 8am-8pm, Nov.-Feb. 8am-6pm, free) is a lush mountain rainforest, receiving 80 inches of rain a year. The steep terrain rises 2,000 feet in four miles, creating a series of rocky waterfalls and challenging trails. The park is so new that facilities are still under development, but currently primitive camping ($9) is permitted in designated areas.

relaxation, Highlands style

Accommodations and Food

The 3,500-foot-high town of Cashiers ("CASH-ers") is home to the **High Hampton Inn and Country Club** (1525 Hwy. 107 S., 800/334-2551, www.highhamptoninn.com, from $100, 3-night minimum), a popular resort for generations of North Carolinians. This was originally the home of Confederate general Wade Hampton, the dashing Charlestonian cavalryman. The lodge, a big old 1930s wooden chalet with huge, cozy fireplaces in the lobby, is surrounded by 1,400 acres of lakeside woodlands, with an 18-hole golf course, a good restaurant that serves buffet-style (dinner jacket requested in the evening), clay tennis courts, and a fitness center that features a climbing tower.

INFORMATION AND SERVICES

In addition to Asheville's **Mission Hospital** (509 Biltmore Ave.; 428 Biltmore Ave., 828/213-1948 or 828/213-4063, www.missionhospitals.org), there are several regional hospitals with emergency or urgent care departments. **Park Ridge Hospital** (77 Airport Rd., Arden, 828/651-0098, www.parkridgehospital.org), located between Asheville and Hendersonville, has urgent care (Mon.-Fri. 8am-7pm, Sat.-Sun. 11am-6pm). Hendersonville also has **Pardee Hospital** (800 N. Justice St., Hendersonville, 828/696-4270, www.pardeehospital.org). In Brevard, the main hospital is **Transylvania Community Hospital** (90 Hospital Dr., Brevard, 828/883-5243, www.tchospital.org), and in Rutherfordton it's **Rutherford Hospital** (288 S. Ridgecrest Ave., Rutherfordton, 828/286-5000, www.rutherfordhosp.org).

Maps and guides are available at the **Hendersonville and Flat Rock Visitors Information Center** (201 S. Main St., Hendersonville, 800/828-4244, www.historichendersonville.com), and at the **Transylvania County Tourism Development Authority** (35 W. Main St., Brevard, 800/648-4523, www.visitwaterfalls.com).

GETTING THERE AND AROUND

The Brevard-Hendersonville area is an easy drive from Asheville, with Hendersonville less than half an hour down I-26, and Brevard a short jog west from there on U.S. 64. To reach Tryon and Rutherfordton, follow U.S. 74 south and east from Hendersonville. **Asheville Regional Airport** (AVL, 61 Terminal Dr., Fletcher, 828/684-2226, www.flyavl.com), south of Asheville, is very convenient to this region.

ASHEVILLE

Waynesville and Vicinity

Over toward Asheville and the Balsam Range, the town of Waynesville is an artistic community where crafts galleries and studios line the downtown. In nearby Cullowhee, Western Carolina University is one of the mountain region's leading academic institutions, as well as the location of the wonderful Mountain Heritage Center museum and Mountain Heritage Day festival.

WAYNESVILLE
Waynesville's downtown can keep a gallery-hopper or shopper happy for hours. Main Street is packed with studio artists' galleries, cafés and coffee shops, and a variety of boutiques.

Shopping
Blue Ridge Books & News (152 S. Main St., 828/456-6000, www.brbooks-news.com, Mon.-Sat. 8am-8pm, Sun. 8am-5pm) is a very nice bookstore, with specialties in books of regional interest and cups of good coffee. **Good Ol' Days Cigars** (46 N. Main St./145 Wall St., 828/456-2898, www.goodoldayscigars. com, Mon.-Thurs. 10am-6pm, Fri.-Sat. 10am-7pm) offers a large selection of fine tobacco and smoking products—cigars, of course, as well as pipes, loose tobacco, rolling papers, and much more—and a TV lounge in which you can enjoy them.

One of the several locations of **Mast General Store** (63 N. Main St., 828/452-2101, www. mastgeneralstore.com, summer Mon.-Sat. 10am-6pm, Sun. noon-5pm, winter hours vary) is here in Waynesville. While the stores are perhaps best known among vacationers for making children clamor—they carry over 500 varieties of candy, many kept in big wooden barrels, old-time dry-goods-store style—they have an even larger selection of outdoor-focused merchandise for adults.

Galleries
Waynesville's galleries are many and varied, although the overarching aesthetic is one of studio art with inspiration in the environmental and folk arts. **Twigs and Leaves** (98 N. Main St., 828/456-1940, www.twigsandleaves.com, Mon.-Sat. 10am-5:30pm, Sun. 1pm-4pm) carries splendid art furniture that is both fanciful and functional, pottery of many hand-thrown and hand-built varieties, jewelry, paintings, fabric hangings, mobiles, and many other beautiful and unusual items inspired by nature.

Textures on Main (142 N. Main St., 828/452-0058, www.texturesonmain.com, Mon.-Sat. 10am-6pm, Sun. noon-5pm) is a gallery showcasing the work of John and Suzanne Gernandt, furniture and fabric artists, respectively, and several other partners. Suzanne's fabric art is often abstract and features beautiful, deeply saturated colors. John's furniture and that of his fellow designers whose work is carried by Textures cover a stunning array of sensibilities—Jonathan Adler's hyper-mod pieces, Robin Bruce's gorgeous, understated upholstery, and Gernandt's own dazzling cabinetry, which has the grace of Shaker carpentry and the slightest hint of a Tim Burton-style offbeat aesthetic.

Studio Thirty Three (33 Pidgeon St., 828/456-3443, www.studio33jewelry.com) carries the work of a very small and select group of fine jewelers from western North Carolina. Their retail and custom inventory consists of spectacular handcrafted pieces in a variety of styles and an array of precious stones and metals. This is a must-see gallery if you are engaged or have another special occasion coming up.

Accommodations
UNDER $150
Up on the Blue Ridge Parkway above Waynesville, and quite close to Asheville, is one of my favorite inns in all of North Carolina. The **(** **Pisgah Inn** (BRP milepost 410, 828/235-8228, www.pisgahinn.com, late Mar.-early Nov., from $100) is much like Skyland

and Big Meadows on Virginia's Skyline Drive, with motel-style accommodations surrounding an old lodge with a large family-style dining room and a Parkway gift shop. The inn sits on a nearly 5,000-foot-high mountaintop, so the view is sensational. Trails surround the Pisgah like the spokes of a wheel, leading to short, pretty strolls and challenging day-long hikes. The restaurant, open for breakfast, lunch, and dinner (daily 7:30am-10:30am, 11:30am-4pm, and 5pm-9pm), has a mesmerizing view and an appetizing and varied menu ($5-25) of both country and fancy meals. The guest rooms are simple but comfortable, each with its own balcony and rocking chairs overlooking the valley, and TV but no telephones.

Waynesville also has quite a selection of luxury inns. The **Andon-Reid Inn** (92 Daisey Ave., 800/293-6190, www.andonreidinn.com, from $115, no pets, guests under 16 not encouraged) is a handsome turn-of-the-century house close to downtown, with five tranquil rooms, each with its own fireplace, and a sumptuous four-course breakfast menu that might include sweet-potato pecan pancakes and pork tenderloin, homemade cornbread with honey butter, and many more treats.

$150-300

Outside of Waynesville in the community of Balsam, the **C Balsam Mountain Inn** (68 Seven Springs Dr., Balsam, 800/224-9498, www.balsaminn.com, $139-219, dogs and cats permitted with prior approval) has stood watch for a century. It's a haunting, and haunted, location—an imposing old wooden hotel with huge double porches overlooking, in the foreground, a rather spooky little railroad platform, and, in the background, the beautiful ridges of Jackson and Haywood Counties. The interior has barely changed since the earliest days, paneled in white horizontal bead board throughout, with 10-foot-wide hallways said to have been designed to accommodate steamer trunks. The one telephone is at the front desk, and there are no TVs, so plan to go hiking or to sit on the porch before dining in the downstairs restaurant, and then curl up and read in

the library. (There is, paradoxically, fast Wi-Fi.) Among the inn's ghosts is a woman in a blue dress. She is said to originate in room 205, but comes and goes elsewhere on the second floor.

The **Inn at Iris Meadows** (304 Love Lane, 888/466-4747, www.irismeadows.com, from $225, dogs permitted with advance notice, children discouraged) is another splendid house, on a hillside surrounded by lush trees and gardens. Shepherd-mix Scratch and gray tabby-cat Zephyrus help run the place, and are added attractions themselves.

OVER $300

For tip-top luxury, try **The Swag** (2300 Swag Rd., 800/789-7672, www.theswag.com, $430-750). Superb guest rooms and cabins of rustic wood and stone each have a steam shower, and several have saunas, wet bars, and cathedral ceilings. The inn is at 5,000 feet elevation, at the very edge of the Great Smoky Mountains National Park.

Food

A popular spot is **Bogart's** (303 S. Main St., 828/452-1313, Sun.-Thurs. 11am-9pm, Fri.-Sat. 11am-10pm, $10-20), which is locally famous for its filet mignon. If you're just passing through town and need a jolt of really strong, good coffee, visit **Panacea** (66 Commerce St., 828/452-6200, Mon.-Fri. 7am-5pm, Sat. 8am-5pm, under $5) in the funky Frog Level neighborhood downhill from downtown.

SYLVA

The small town of Sylva, southwest of Waynesville, is crowned by the pretty Jackson County Courthouse, an Italianate building with an ornate cupola, and kept under wistful watch by the requisite courthouse-square Confederate monument.

Sights

South of Sylva, the mysterious **Judaculla Rock** (off Caney Fork Rd.) has puzzled folks for centuries. The soapstone boulder is covered in petroglyphs, estimated to be at least 500 years old. The figures and symbols and squiggles were clearly made by people and are significant, but as of yet not understood. The soft rock is greatly eroded, and the images are not as clear as they were in earlier generations, but many can still be discerned. To reach the rock, drive south on Highway 107 eight miles past the intersection with Sylva's U.S. 23 Business. Make a left on Caney Fork Road/Highway 1737, and drive 2.5 miles to a gravel road. Turn left, and in just under 0.5 miles, you'll see the rock on the right and a parking area on the left.

Shopping

Sylva's City Lights Bookstore (3 E. Jackson St., 828/586-9499, www.citylightsnc.com, Mon.-Sat. 9am-9pm) is hardly a knockoff of the monumental beat establishment in San Francisco with which it shares its name. Instead, it's a first-rate small-town bookstore, with a stock that has the novelty sought by vacationers and the depth to make regulars of the local patrons. In addition to the sections you'll find in any other good bookstore, at City Lights there is an excellent selection of books of regional interest, including folklore, nature, recreation guides, history, fiction, and poetry by Appalachian and Southern authors.

Food

The North Carolina mountains are blessed with a booming organic foods movement, and you'll find eco-aware eateries throughout the area.

Lulu's Café (612 W. Main St., 828/587-5858, www.lulusonmain.com, summer Mon.-Sat. 11:30am-9pm, winter Mon.-Sat. 11:30am-8pm, $12-15) is one of the most acclaimed restaurants of the North Carolina mountains. The menu is American gourmet at its heart, with splashes of Mediterranean and Nuevo Latino specialties. Try the walnut-spinach ravioli or the raspberry rum pork loin. There are plenty of vegetarian options.

A more casual option is **Nick and Nate's Pizza** (556 W. Main, 828/586-3000, Mon. and Wed.-Sat. 11:30am-9pm, Sun. noon-9pm, lunch $6-8, dinner $8-15), where the dough is

handmade, the toppings are fresh, and the beer is from fine microbreweries.

Also, try **Annie's Naturally** (506 W. Main St., 828/586-9096, www.anniesnaturallybakery.com, breakfast, lunch, and snacks Tues.-Fri. 7am-5pm, Sat. 8am-5pm), a bakery and sandwich shop owned by Joe and Annie Ritota. Joe is a fourth-generation professional baker from an old Italian American family known for its skill in the kitchen. The breads, cookies, and pastries are baked on-site in the Ritotas' old-time way. **Soul Infusion** (628 E. Main St., 828/586-1717, www.soulinfusion.com, warm weather Tues.-Thurs. 11am-10pm, Fri. noon-midnight, Sat. 5pm-midnight, off-season Tues.-Thurs. 11am-9pm, $5-16), between Sylva Tire and UPS, is a cozy hippie-gourmet teahouse in an old house on Main Street. Here you can get very good burritos, sandwiches, pizza, wraps, and choose from several dozen kinds of loose-leaf tea, and even more selections of bottled beer. On weekends and some weeknights, local blues, folk, reggae, and experimental musicians put on a show. Seize the opportunity to hear some of the talent in this incredibly musical region.

DILLSBORO

Next door to Sylva is Dillsboro, a river town of rafters and crafters. **Dogwood Crafters** (90 Webster St., 828/586-2248), in operation for more than 30 years, is a gallery and co-op that represents approximately 100 local artisans. While the shop carries some of the ubiquitous country-whimsical stuff, mixed in is the work of some very traditional Blue Ridge weavers, potters, carvers, and other expert artisans, and the shop is well worth visiting for that reason.

Sports and Recreation

Dillsboro River Company (18 Macktown Rd., 866/586-3797, www.northcarolinarafting.com, open after May 20 daily 10:30am-6pm, rentals $10-30, guided trips $20-35), across the river from downtown Dillsboro, will set you afloat on the Tuckaseegee River, a comparatively warm river with stretches of Class II rapids. (It's pronounced "tuck-a-SEE-jee," but often simply referred to as "the Tuck.") They rent rafts, "ducks," and inflatable and sit-on-top kayaks. If you'd like to hire a river rat, guides will be happy to lead you on tours twice daily, and for an extra fee you can share a boat with the guide. There are minimum weight restrictions for these watercraft, so if you are traveling with children, call ahead and ask if the guides think your young'uns are ready for the Tuckaseegee.

Accommodations

Of the many historic inns in this region, one of the oldest is Dillsboro's **Jarrett House** (100 Haywood St., 800/972-5623, www.jarretthouse.com, $80-95, includes breakfast). The 1880s three-story lodge was built to serve passengers on the railroad, and today it is once again a busy rail stop, now for the Great Smoky Mountains Railroad's excursion trains. The guest rooms are furnished in old-fashioned furniture, and while they have air conditioning and private baths, the only TV is in the lobby. The Hartbarger family, keepers of this inn for over 30 years, are serious about giving their guests a chance for what they call "honest loafing"—real recuperative peace and quiet.

Food

The 🅒 **Jarrett House** (100 Haywood St., 800/972-5623, www.jarretthouse.com) is also famous for its dining room (daily 11:30am-2:30pm and 4:30pm-7:30pm, under $15), an extravaganza of country cooking based around the staples of country ham and red-eye gravy. You can also order many other mountain specialties, like fried catfish, fried chicken, sweet tea, biscuits, and for dessert the daily cobbler or vinegar pie (it's good). There's not much for vegetarians, but if you like heavy Southern fare, you'll think you're in heaven.

CULLOWHEE

The unincorporated village of Cullowhee (pronounced "CULL-uh-wee"), located on Highway 107 between Sylva and Cashiers, is the home of Western Carolina University (WCU). The university's **Mountain Heritage Center** (lobby of the H. F. Robinson Administration Bldg., WCU campus, 1 University Way, 828/227-7129, www.wcu.edu, Nov.-May Mon.-Fri. 8am-5pm, June-Oct. Mon.-Fri. 8am-5pm, Sun. 2pm-5pm, free) is a small museum with a great collection that will fascinate anyone interested in Appalachian history. The permanent exhibit, *Migration of the Scotch-Irish People,* is full of artifacts like a 19th-century covered wagon, wonderful photographs, and homemade quilts, linens, musical instruments, and more. The Mountain Heritage Center also hosts two traveling exhibits at a time in addition to the permanent installation, and the annual **Mountain Heritage Day** festival (late Sept.), which brings together many of western North Carolina's best and most authentic traditional musicians and artisans in a free festival that draws up to 25,000 visitors.

GETTING THERE AND AROUND

Waynesville is easily reached from Asheville by heading west on I-40, and then taking either U.S. 23 or U.S. 74. The Blue Ridge Parkway also passes a little to the south of the town near Balsam. Sylva is southwest of Waynesville on U.S. 23, and from there, Cullowhee is an easy drive down Highway 107.

ASHEVILLE

GREAT SMOKY MOUNTAINS

When the Atlanta Olympic Park bomber, Eric Rudolph, was on the lam in the Smokies in 1996, there was a commonly held opinion among western North Carolinians that he would never be found. No doubt people watching the news from living rooms around the country were mystified that a man couldn't be tracked down in this relatively small geographical area, a few sparsely populated counties largely made up of federal land. But after driving a little way into the high country south and west of Asheville, one can easily imagine that hundreds of people could hide in this wilderness and that the outside world wouldn't notice so much as a rustling leaf.

In fact, exactly that occurred in the 1830s, although under very different circumstances, when President Van Buren gave the final go-ahead to start the removal of the Cherokee people on the Trail of Tears. Several extended Cherokee families took to the deep mountains, and these resisters who refused to leave their homeland—choosing instead to brave months of living in fear, exposed to the elements—are the ancestors of many of today's Eastern Band of the Cherokee.

The ancient Cherokee culture has been rooted in the Smokies for thousands of years, from the early days described in their mythology, when the Ani-gituhwa-gi shared these mountains with witches and fairies, and birds and leeches as big as bears. The darkest hour came in the 19th century, when the Cherokee nation was rent apart by forced exile to Oklahoma. But between those who stayed and hid out in the mountains, and those who

© 123RF.COM

HIGHLIGHTS

◖ Museum of the Cherokee Indian:
The Cherokee people have lived in the Smoky
Mountains for thousands of years, and this excellent museum tells unforgettable tales of
their history (page 213).

◖ Qualla Arts and Crafts Mutual:
Ancient craft traditions still thrive among
Cherokee artists in western North Carolina.
At the Qualla Mutual, visitors can learn about
and purchase the work of today's masters
(page 213).

◖ Cades Cove: The most visited spot in the
Great Smoky Mountains National Park is a formerly bustling mountain village that is witness
to the depth of history in the Southern highlands (page 218).

◖ Clingmans Dome: From this third-highest peak in the eastern United States, set in a
dramatic alpine environment, you'll find an as-
tounding view of up to 100 miles on a clear day
(page 219).

◖ Nantahala River Gorge: So steep that in
some places the water is only brushed by sunlight at high noon, this gorge is an unbeatable
place for white-water rafting (page 225).

◖ John C. Campbell Folk School: For
nearly a century, the Folk School has been a
leading light in promoting American craft her-

itage and nurturing new generations of artists
(page 228).

**LOOK FOR ◖ TO FIND RECOMMENDED
SIGHTS, ACTIVITIES, DINING, AND
LODGING.**

walked home from Oklahoma to rebuild their
lives in their ancestral home, the Cherokee people regained strength—and today the seat of
the Eastern Band is here in far western North
Carolina on the land known as the Qualla
Boundary.

PLANNING YOUR TIME
Many people plan their visits to the Smokies
to coincide with what's blooming or blaz-
ing on the mountainsides. Spring wildflowers begin to bloom in late March, and peak in
mid- to late April. Azaleas, mountain laurels,

and rhododendrons are the showiest blooms of
the summer, and they begin to bloom at the
lower elevations first, and then higher up in
the mountains. Flame azaleas peak in different areas between April and July, mountain
laurels in May and June, and rhododendrons
in June and July. The fall colors appear in the
opposite sequence, appearing first at the peaks
in early October, and gradually moving down
the mountains until, in mid- to late October
and early November, trees in the lower elevations change. Factors including summer heat
and rainfall, or lack thereof, can throw these

GREAT SMOKY MOUNTAINS

GREAT SMOKY MOUNTAINS

© AVALON TRAVEL

schedules off a bit, but if you call Great Smoky Mountains National Park or check regional websites, you can find out how the season is progressing.

The Newfound Gap Road bisects the national park across the middle, from Cherokee in the southeast, where it meets the southern end of the Blue Ridge Parkway, to Gatlinburg at the northwest. For a brief visit to the park, Gatlinburg is the entry point that gives easiest access to short loop roads. For a longer visit, Gatlinburg and Cherokee are good places to find a motel, and the Elkmont and Smokemont campsites are centrally located front-country camping areas where you can sleep in the woods but have your car with you for daytime driving. While you can certainly cross the park in an afternoon and see some sights, the more time you can devote to your visit, the better. Many visitors spend a week or more at a time in the Great Smoky Mountain National Park. Campground stays are limited to one week at a time May 15-October 31, and two weeks November 1-May 14.

Maggie Valley

Maggie Valley is a family vacation town from the era of the nuclear family in their wood-paneled station wagon, the kids in the back seat eating Lik-M-Aid and wearing plastic Indian headdresses. Coming down the mountain toward Maggie Valley, you'll pass an overlook, which, on a morning when the mountains around Soco Gap are looped with fog, is surely one of the most beautiful vistas in the state. Drink in your fill, because you're headed into a different world. You'll know it when you pass the hand-lettered sign that says, "Have your picture made with a real moonshine still and a real moonshiner and his truck for a donation of $3; use your own camera."

SIGHTS AND ENTERTAINMENT

The most famous attraction in Maggie Valley is **Ghost Town in the Sky** (16 Fie Top Rd., 828/926-1140, www.ghosttowninthesky.com, May-Sept. Fri.-Sun. 9am-7pm, Oct. Fri.-Sun. 10am-5pm, weather permitting, $25 adults, $15 children), an Old West theme park where the good guys and bad guys shoot it out daily for your viewing pleasure. That's in addition to the rides—which include a 98-foot free-fall tower and a mountainside roller coaster—and bluegrass and gospel concerts. After a brief hiatus from operation, the Ghost Town reopened with a new attraction: zip lines ($45 pp).

Bluegrass music and clogging are a big deal in this town. The great bluegrass banjo player Raymond Fairchild is a Maggie native, and after his 50-year touring and recording career, he and his wife, Shirley, are now the hosts of the **Maggie Valley Opry House** (3605 Soco Rd., 828/648-7941, www.raymondfairchild. com, May-Oct. daily 8pm, about $12). In season, you can find bluegrass and country music concerts and clogging exhibitions every night.

In a state with countless attractions for automotive enthusiasts, Maggie Valley's **Wheels Through Time Museum** (62 Vintage Lane, 828/926-6266, www.wheelsthroughtime.com, Mar.-Dec. Thurs.-Mon. 9am-5pm, $12 adults, $10 over age 65, $6 ages 5-12, free under age 4) stands out as one of the most fun. A dazzling collection of nearly 300 vintage motorcycles are on display, including a 1908 Indian, a 1914 Harley Davidson, military motorcycles from both World Wars, and some gorgeous post-war machines. This collection, which dates mostly to before 1950, is maintained in working order—almost every one of the bikes is revved up from time to time, and the museum's founder has been known to take a spin on one of the treasures.

SPORTS AND RECREATION

Maggie Valley's **Cataloochee Ski Area** (1080 Ski Lodge Rd., off U.S. 19, 800/768-0285, slopes report 800/768-3588, www.cataloochee.com, lift tickets $20-60, equipment rentals $15-30) has slopes geared to every level of skier and snowboarder. Classes and private lessons are taught for all ages. At the nearby **Tube World** (U.S. 19, next to Ski Area, 800/768-0285, www.tubemaggievalley.com, $25 per session, must be over 42 inches tall, "Wee Bowl" area for smaller visitors $5 per session, call ahead for Wee Bowl, Thanksgiving-mid-Mar.), you can zip down the mountain on inner tubes.

ACCOMMODATIONS

The main drag through Maggie Valley (Soco Rd./U.S. 19) is lined with motels, including some of the familiar national brands. Among the pleasant private motels are the **Valley Inn** (236 Soco Rd., 800/948-6880, www.thevalleyinn.com, from $39 off-season, rates vary in high season, call for specifics during your target dates), and **Jonathan Creek Inn and Villas**

(4324 Soco Rd., 800/577-7812, www.jonathancreekinn.com, from about $90). The latter has creek-side guest rooms with screen porches.

FOOD

J. Arthurs Restaurant (2843 Soco Rd., 828/926-1817, www.jarthurs.com, Wed.-Sat. 4:30pm-9pm, Sun. noon-8pm, $15-25) is a popular spot locally for steaks, which are the house specialty. The restaurant also has a variety of seafood and pasta dishes, but very little by way of vegetarian meals. Visit the website for a printable coupon.

GETTING THERE AND AROUND

U.S. 19 is the main thoroughfare in these parts, leading from Asheville to the Great Smoky Mountains National Park. Maggie is also a reasonably short jog off I-40 via exits 20, 24, and 27.

Cherokee and the Qualla Boundary

The town of Cherokee is a mixture of seemingly contradictory forces: tradition and commerce, nature and development. Cherokee is the civic center of the Eastern Band of the Cherokee, a people who have lived in these mountains for many centuries and whose history, art, government, and language are very much alive. It is the seat of the Qualla (pronounced "KWA-lah," like the marsupial but with just two syllables) Boundary, which is not precisely a reservation, but a large tract of land owned and governed by the Cherokee people. Institutions like the Museum of the Cherokee Indian and the Qualla Arts and Crafts Mutual provide a rock-solid foundation for the Eastern Band of the Cherokee's cultural life. Take a look at the road signs as you drive around here. That beautiful, Asiatic-looking lettering below the English road names is the Cherokee language, in the written form famously created by Sequoyah in 1821. That language, once dying

away with the Cherokee elders, is now taught to the community's youth; there are even plans for a Cherokee-language immersion school on the Qualla Boundary.

On the other hand, much of Cherokee's main drag is a classic old-timey tourist district. Here you'll find the "Indian" souvenirs—factory-made moccasins, plastic tomahawks, the works—so familiar to gift shop-goers across the country. In its own retro way, this side of Cherokee can actually be kind of charming, if you have a soft spot for the mid-20th century family vacation aesthetic, the world of fudge counters and garish motel signs. (There are some incredible examples of the latter in Cherokee. Keep an eye out for the Princess, Warrior, and Chief Motels, each featuring a larger-than-life figure from the imaginary world of Hollywood and comic-book Indians.)

Enjoy this facet of Cherokee for what it's worth, but dig deeper—don't take this for the real Cherokee. The Cherokee are a people with thousands of years of history, much of which you can learn about here.

SIGHTS
◖ Museum of the Cherokee Indian

Make a visit to the **Museum of the Cherokee Indian** (589 Tsali Blvd., 828/497-3481, www.cherokeemuseum.org, daily 9am-5pm, $10 adults, $6 ages 6-13, free under age 6). Founded in 1948 and originally housed in a log cabin, this is now a widely acclaimed modern museum and community cultural locus. In the exhibits that trace the long history of the Cherokee people, you may notice the disconcertingly realistic mannequins. Local members of the community volunteered to be models for these mannequins, allowing casts to be made of their faces and bodies so that the figures would not reflect an outsider's notion of what a Native American should look like, but rather the real people whose ancestors this museum honors. The Museum of the Cherokee Indian traces their history from the Paleo-Indian period, when the ancestral Cherokees were hunter-gatherers, through the ancient civilization into recorded history. A great deal of this exhibit area focuses on the 18th and 19th centuries, times when many tragedies befell the Cherokee as a result of the European invasion of their homeland. It was also a time of great cultural advancement, which included the development of Sequoyah's syllabary. The terrible Trail of Tears began near here, along the North Carolina-Georgia border. A small contingent of Cherokees remained in the Smokies at the time of the Trail of Tears, successfully eluding, and then negotiating with, the U.S. military, who were trying to send all of the Cherokee to Oklahoma. Those who lived out in the woods, along with other Cherokees who were able to return home from Oklahoma, are the ancestors of today's Eastern Band, and their history is truly remarkable.

◖ Qualla Arts and Crafts Mutual

Catty-corner to the museum is the **Qualla Arts and Crafts Mutual** (645 Tsali Blvd., 828/497-3103, www.visitcherokeenc.com, Mon.-Fri. 9am-5pm), a community arts co-op. Local artists sell their work here, and the gallery's high standards and, of course, the Cherokees' thousands of years of artistry, make for a collection of very special pottery, baskets, masks, and other traditional art. As hard as it is to survive as an artist in Manhattan, artists in such rural areas as this have an exponentially more difficult go of it, trying to support themselves through the sale of their art, while at the same time maintaining the integrity of their vision and creativity. The Qualla co-op does a great service to this community in providing a year-round market for the work of traditional Cherokee artists, whose stewardship of and innovation in traditional arts are so important.

ENTERTAINMENT AND EVENTS

Of the several outdoor dramas for which North Carolina is known, among the longest running is Cherokee's *Unto These Hills* (Mountainside Theater, 688 Drama Rd., 866/554-4557, www.visitcherokeenc.com, summer Mon.-Sat. 8pm, $9.40-$29.40). For 60 summers, Cherokee actors have told the story of their nation's history, from ancient times through the Trail of Tears. Recently updated by Kiowa playwright Hanay Geiogomah, in consultation with the Cherokee people, the drama is now called *Unto These Hills: A Retelling.*

ACCOMMODATIONS

The Eastern Band of the Cherokee operates **Harrah's Cherokee Casino and Hotel** (777 Casino Dr., 828/497-7777, www.harrahs.com, from $60). This full-bore Vegas-style casino with two towers of guest rooms has more than 3,000 games, mostly digital slots, with some digital table games run by croupiers. There's also a 1,500-seat theater that hosts major country artists throughout the year.

Cherokee has many motels, including **Holiday Inn** (37 Tsalagi Rd., 828/497-9181, www.holidayinn.com, from about $50), and **Econo Lodge** (20 River Rd./U.S. 19, 828/497-4575, www.econolodge.com, from about $80, pets allowed).

GETTING THERE AND AROUND

Cherokee is located on a particularly pretty, winding section of U.S. 19, between Maggie Valley and Bryson City. Just north of Cherokee is the southern terminus of the Blue Ridge Parkway.

Great Smoky Mountains National Park

An environment like no other, the Great Smoky Mountains National Park (GSMNP) comprises over 800 square miles of high, cloud-ringed peaks and genuine rainforests. Tens of thousands of species of plants and animals live in the national park—80 different kinds of reptiles and amphibians alone (the park is sometimes called the Salamander Capital of the World), 200 species of birds, and more than 50 mammal species, from mice to mountain lions. The organization Discover Life in America (www.dlia.org) has for several years been conducting an All Taxa Biodiversity Inventory—that is, a census of all nonmicrobial life forms—in the GSMNP, and as of early 2010 had discovered more than 900 species of plants and animals hitherto unknown to science. The deep wilderness of the Great Smoky Mountains National Park is also a wonderful refuge for today's outdoors enthusiast, while the easy accessibility of ravishing scenery makes this the most visited national park in the United States.

VISITING THE PARK
Weather Considerations

To get a sense of the variability of the weather in the GSMNP, keep in mind that elevation ranges from under 1,000 feet to over 6,600 feet. A low-lying area like that around Gatlinburg, Tennessee, is not a whole lot cooler than Raleigh in the summertime, with an average high of 88°F in July. For only three months of the year (Dec.-Feb.) does Gatlinburg have average lows under freezing, and then only by a few degrees. The opposite extreme is illustrated by Clingmans Dome, the highest elevation in the park. There the average high temperature is

only 65°F in July—and only in June, July, and August can you be sure that it won't snow. If ever there were a place for layered clothing, this is it. No matter what season the calendar tells you it is, be on the safe side and pack clothing for the other three as well. Keep these extremes in mind, too, in terms of safety; a snowstorm can bring two feet of snow to high elevations, and it's not at all unusual that the weather will be balmy at the foot of the mountain and icy at the top. At times, the temperature here has fallen to -20°F. Roads can be closed in the winter if the weather gets bad or restricted to vehicles with snow chains or four-wheel drive. Drive very slowly when it's icy. Leave plenty of room between you and the next car, and shift to a lower gear when going down slippery slopes. You can find out current conditions by calling the park (865/436-1200, ext. 630).

Seasonal Considerations

The most crowded times in the park are from mid-June to mid-August, and all of October. Traffic is most likely to be heavy on the Cades Cove Loop Road and Newfound Gap Road. Several roads in the park are closed in the wintertime, though the dates vary. Among these are Balsam Mountain, Clingmans Dome, Little Greenbrier, Rich Mountain, and Round Bottom Roads and Roaring Fork Motor Nature Trail.

Safety

Sometimes even the most experienced outdoorsmen and women have emergencies. Whether going into the backcountry by yourself or with others, make sure that someone

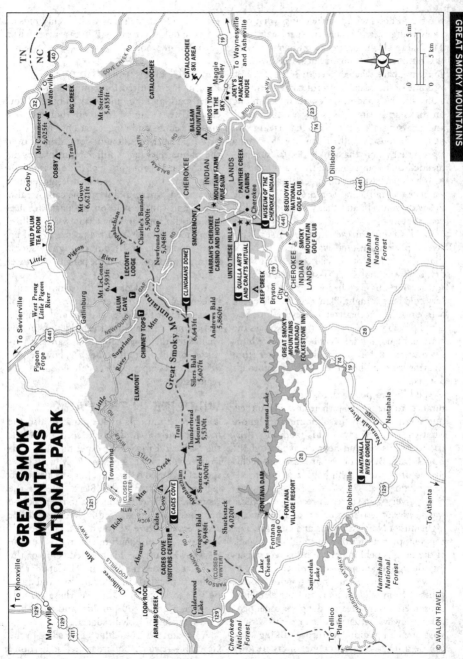

GREAT SMOKY MOUNTAINS NATIONAL PARK

TN
NC

To Knoxville
To Sevierville

Maryville

Chilhowee Mtn

Look Rock

Abrams Creek

Cades Cove Visitors Center

Townsend

Cades Cove (CLOSED IN WINTER)

Cades Cove

Gregory Bald 4,948ft

Shuckstack 4,020ft

Spence Field 4,900ft

Thunderhead Mountain 5,530ft

Elkmont

Chimney Tops

Newfound Gap 5,048ft

Charlie's Bunion 5,900ft

Mt Guyot 6,621ft

Mt Cammerer 5,025ft

Cosby

Big Creek

Mt Sterling 5,835ft

Cataloochee

Waterville

Cataloochee Ski Area

Ghost Town In The Sky

Maggie Valley

To Waynesville and Asheville

Joey's Pancake House

Balsam Mountain

Cherokee Indian Lands

Mountain Farm Museum

Smokemont

Museum of the Cherokee Indian

Cherokee

Harrah's Cherokee Casino and Hotel

Panther Creek Cabins

Sequoyah National Golf Club

Dillsboro

Unto These Hills

Qualla Arts and Crafts Mutual

Smoky Mountain Golf Club

Cherokee Indian Lands

Deep Creek

Bryson City

Great Smoky Mountains Railroad/Folkstone Inn

Fontana Dam

Fontana Lake

Fontana Village Resort

Fontana Village

Lake Cheoah

Robbinsville

Nantahala River Gorge

Nantahala River

Nantahala National Forest

To Atlanta

Santeetlah Lake

Nantahala National Forest

Cherokee National Forest

To Tellico Plains

Clingmans Dome 6,643ft

Andrews Bald 5,860ft

Silers Bald 5,607ft

LeConte Lodge

Mt LeConte 6,593ft

Alum Cave

Gatlinburg

Pigeon Forge

Wild Plum Tea Room

Little Pigeon River

West Prong Little Pigeon River

Pigeon River

Little River

Appalachian Trail

© AVALON TRAVEL

5 mi
5 km

you trust knows where you're going, what your likely route is, and when to expect you back. The National Park Service recommends leaving this number with someone at home, to call if you're not back when expected: 865/436-1230.

Some of the basic safety rules may seem obvious, but it's good to review them. Climbing on rocks and waterfalls is always dangerous, and crossing a deep or flooded stream can be treacherous as well. If you have to cross a stream that's more than ankle-deep, it's recommended that you unbuckle the waist strap on your backpack (so you don't get pinned underwater if you fall), that you use a hiking stick to steady yourself, and that you wear nonslippery shoes.

Cold is a concern, even in the summer. Wear layers, pack additional warm duds (warmer than you think you'll need), and try to stay dry. It may be shorts-and-T-shirt weather when you set out, but even in the summer it can be very cold here at night. Plan well, double-check before setting out that you have everything you could possibly need on your trek, and, says the National Park Service, "eat before you're hungry and rest before you're tired." Water from streams must be boiled or filtered before it's potable.

Wildlife can pose hazards here. Despite assurances to the contrary, there are still panthers (mountain lions) in these mountains. Ignore what the officials say in this (and only this) regard; locals see and hear them throughout Appalachia. But panthers are rare and reclusive, as are coyotes, wild hogs, and other resident tough guys.

On a very grim note, in recent years there was a series of terrible murders of hikers in the highlands of North Carolina and Georgia. The apparent perpetrator of some, and possibly all, of the cases is behind bars. It bears remembering, though, that one is very vulnerable out in the woods. You might know how to protect yourself from wild animals and the elements, but sometimes the greatest danger is other people. It's always better to hike or camp with at least one companion. A sturdy walking stick can be a lifesaver, and pepper spray, readily available and cheap in many different kinds of stores, should always be within easy reach when you're in the woods.

Permits and Regulations

Permits are required for camping in the national park and are quite easy to obtain. You can register at any of the more than a dozen visitors centers and ranger stations. This must be done in person, though, not online or over the phone. Fishing requires permits as well, which can be bought at outfitters and bait shops in nearby towns. Strict rules governing how, when, where, and what one can fish also apply, and can be read on the park website. Other rules apply to interaction with wildlife. Don't feed animals, and make sure to seal up your foodstuffs to discourage night visitors. Firearms are forbidden in the park as, of course, is hunting.

Your dog is welcome in the park, but only in certain areas. To prevent transmission of diseases to or from the wildlife, and to avoid disrupting or frightening the resident fauna, as well as for their own safety, dogs are not permitted on hiking trails. They are, however, allowed to accompany you at campgrounds and picnic sites.

WILDLIFE IN THE PARK

The largest animals in the park are also the most recently arrived. In the spring of 2001, the National Park Service experimentally reintroduced **elk** to the Great Smoky Mountains, a species that used to live here but was hunted to regional extinction in the 18th century. In the years since their reintroduction to the park, the herd has reproduced steadily, boding well for a successful future. If you hear a strange bellowing in the early autumn, it may be a male elk showing off for his beloved. One of the best places to see the elk is in the Cataloochee Valley, particularly in fields at dawn and dusk. Be sure to keep your distance; these animals can weigh up to 700 pounds, and the males have some formidable headgear.

An estimated 1,600 **black bears** live in the GSMNP—two per square mile—so it's quite

© 123RF.COM

elk in Cataloochee Valley

possible that you'll encounter one. Though they are a wonder to see, bears, which in this park weigh 100-400 pounds as adults, do pose a real risk to humans—and we to them—so it's important to be very aware of how we interact with them. It is illegal to come within 50 yards (150 feet) of a bear or elk, and those who knowingly get closer can be arrested. It sounds like a cliché, but the recommended procedure is this: If you see a bear, back away slowly. The National Park Service recommends that if the bear follows, you should stand your ground. If it keeps coming toward you persistently and looks menacing (and how could a bear persistently coming toward you not look menacing?), make yourself big and scary. Stand on a rock to look taller, or close to anyone else present, to show the bear that it's outnumbered. If it keeps coming closer, make a lot of noise and chuck things at it (rocks or sticks, that is; a bag of marshmallows or the fish you were just grilling would scarcely be deterrents). Should a bear actually attack you, the National Park Service

recommends that you "fight back aggressively with any available object."

The best course of action is simply to avoid them and hope that any sightings you have will be from a safe distance. When camping, lock your food in the trunk of your car, if possible—or hoist it into a tree too high off the ground for a bear to reach it on its hind legs, and at a long enough length of rope from the nearest branch that one can't reach it by climbing the tree. Bears may approach in picnic areas. For goodness sake, don't feed them, no matter how winsome they look! "Habitual panhandler bears" (this is a real term) have been proven to die sooner than those that are afraid of humans, as they are more likely to be hit by cars, swallow indigestible food packaging, become easy targets for hunters, or even, if they are too problematic, be captured and euthanized.

Bears are hardly the only huge, ferocious animals in the park. Believe it or not, there are hundreds of snorting, tusky **wild hogs** here, descendants of a herd that escaped from a hunting preserve in Murphy in the 1910s. There are coyotes, wolves, and bobcats, and, though extremely rare, there are mountain lions (often called "panthers" or "painters" in this region) as well.

Of the many natural miracles in this park, one of the most astonishing is the light show put on for a couple of weeks each year by synchronous fireflies. Of the park's 14 species of firefly, only one, *Photinus carolinus,* flashes in this manner. While the average back yard's worth of fireflies twinkles like Christmas lights, synchronous fireflies, as their name implies, are capable of flashing in unison, by the hundreds or thousands. The sight is so amazing that, during the peak flashing period (usually in June), the park organizes nighttime expeditions to the best viewing spots.

If you go hiking in the backcountry, you might well see a snake. It's unlikely that you'll encounter a poisonous one, as there are only two kinds of vipers here—rattlesnakes and copperheads—that pose a danger to humans. There has never been a death from snakebite in the park, as far as anyone knows, but to be on the safe side, watch where you step or put your hands; it wouldn't do to be first on that list. But snakes are shy, so don't worry too much.

SIGHTS
Mountain Farm Museum
The area that is now the Great Smoky Mountains National Park was once dotted with towns and farms, communities that were displaced for the establishment of the park. The **Mountain Farm Museum** (U.S. 441, 2 miles north of Cherokee, 828/497-1900), next to the Oconaluftee Visitors Center, recreates a mountain fastness of the late 19th and early 20th centuries. On the site of what was the Enloe family's farm, on the banks of the Oconaluftee River, a collection of historic buildings are preserved, some original to the site and others moved from elsewhere in the Smokies. The Davis House, a circa-1900 log house, is remarkable in that it is constructed from enormous chestnut timbers, a wood not available in this region for several generations (since the chestnut blight of the 1930s). A large

cantilevered barn is constructed to allow wagons to be driven straight through, with stalls and haylofts to the sides. A variety of other dependencies—a meat house, a chicken house, an apple house, a corncrib, a gear shed, a blacksmith shop, and a springhouse—give a notion of what a plethora of homesteading skills were necessary for a mountain farm like this to prosper. Demonstrations are held here throughout the year, as well as two festivals, one a harvest festival and the other a commemoration of women's work in mountain farm life.

◖ Cades Cove
On the Tennessee side of the park, an 11-mile one-way loop road traverses Cades Cove, a historic settlement dating to the late 18th century. Originally part of the Cherokee Nation, the land was ceded to the United States in 1819. The population grew through the 19th century until it was a busy town of several hundred people. The village is preserved today as it appeared around 1900, with homes, churches, barns, and a working gristmill, but minus the people—a mountain counterpart to Cape Lookout National Seashore's Portsmouth Village. Because of the cove's scenic beauty and abundance of wildlife, this is the most popular part of the nation's most visited national park. The loop road through Cades Cove takes about an hour to drive when visitors are sparse. On crowded days—in the peak summer and fall seasons, and most weekends—it can take several hours to cover the 11 miles.

The **Cades Cove Visitors Center** (Dec.-Jan. daily 9am-4:30pm, Feb. and Nov. daily 9am-5pm, Mar. and Sept.-Oct. daily 9am-6pm, Apr.-Aug. daily 9am-7pm) is located at about the halfway point on the Cades Cove Loop. It has a bookstore, exhibits on Southern mountain culture, and seasonal ranger programs. At the southwestern side of the park, Cades Cove is most easily reached from the Laurel Creek Road inside the park, which links up to Route 73 near Townsend, Tennessee. Cades Cove Loop road begins and ends at Laurel Creek Road, but there are two outlets toward the western end—Forge Creek Road and Rich

the gristmill in Cades Cove

Mountain Road—that both lead out of the park, one-way, and are closed in wintertime.

Cataloochee

Cataloochee in North Carolina was an even larger village than Cades Cove. Several important historic buildings from this extremely remote apple-growing town are standing and can be toured, including Palmer Chapel, the settlement's only church house, which was served by once-monthly visits by circuit riding Methodist preachers. Cataloochee is also a prime spot for watching the park's elk, reintroduced in 2001 and prospering. Look for them in the open fields around sunrise and twilight. The Cataloochee area is at the far northeastern edge of the park, and it's a reasonably direct drive from I-40 via the Cove Creek Road. The National Park Service also recommends a more adventurous route for those with plenty of time and immunity to car sickness (it's a twisty road): Highway 32 from Cosby, Tennessee. Whichever way you go, part of the route will be on a gravel road. The park sells an auto tour booklet at the visitors centers, which will help guide you through Cataloochee. Several houses, a school, churches, and barns are open to the public.

(Clingmans Dome

At 6,643 feet, Clingmans Dome is the third-highest mountain in the eastern United States, and the highest in the Great Smoky Mountains. A flying saucer-like observation tower at the end of a long, steep walkway gives 360-degree views of the surrounding mountains, and on a clear day, that view can be as far as 100 miles. More often, though, it's misty up here in the clouds, and Clingmans Dome receives so much precipitation that its woods are actually a coniferous rainforest. The road to the summit is closed December 1-March 31, but the observation tower remains open for those willing to make the hike. To get to Clingmans Dome, turn off Newfound Gap Road 0.1 miles south of Newfound Gap, and then take Clingmans Dome Road (closed in winter), which leads seven miles to the parking lot. The peak is view from the observation deck of Clingmans Dome

right near the center of the park, due north as the crow flies (though not directly accessible) from Bryson City.

Fontana Dam

At the southeastern edge of the park, Fontana Dam, 11,000 acres of water, is an artificial impoundment of the Little Tennessee River. This largest dam east of the Rockies was built in the 1940s, a stupendous wall of concrete the height of a 50-story skyscraper. It caused the river to flood back through little mountain towns, vestiges of which can be seen every five years when the water level is lowered for dam inspection. The **visitors center** (Hwy. 28, Fontana Dam, 828/498-2234 or 800/467-1388, May-Nov. daily 9am-7pm, free) is well worth a visit, and the Appalachian Trail goes right along the top of the dam.

SPORTS AND RECREATION

The Great Smoky Mountains National Park covers over half a million acres, and within that expanse are more than 800 miles of hiking trails, ranging from easy walks around major attractions to strenuous wilderness paths suited to the most experienced backpackers. A section of the Appalachian Trail goes through the park, crossing the Fontana Dam. There are dozens of books available about hiking in the Smokies, available at bookstores and outfitters throughout the region, as well as online. The park staffs a **Backcountry Information Office** (865/436-1297, daily 9am-noon), and the knowledgeable folks who work there are a good first resource when planning a hiking trip. The park website (www.nps.gov/grsm) has some downloadable maps to give you a general sense of the lay of the land. The Great Smoky Mountains Association website (www.smokiesinformation. org) has a good online bookstore where you can find many books about hiking in the park.

Hiking

The Great Smoky Mountains National Park contains hundreds of miles of hiking trails, ranging from family-friendly loop trails to strenuous wilderness treks. Following are a sampling of hikes in the park. Before embarking on any of these trails, obtain a park map, and have a word with a park ranger to ascertain trail conditions and gauge whether it's well suited to your hiking skills.

A quick and easy foray into the woods is the **Spruce-Fir Trail,** off Clingmans Dome Road, a walk of just over 0.3 miles. Almost flat, and mostly following a wooden boardwalk, this is the ideal trail if you've been traveling in the car all day and simply want to stretch your legs and experience a bit of easily-accessible forest atmosphere.

A longer but also fairly easy walk is the **Oconaluftee River Trail,** which begins behind the Oconaluftee Visitor Center. This path, which is gravel-covered, follows the river and goes through part of the Mountain Farm Museum grounds. Unlike nearly all other trails in the GSMNP, dogs and bicycles are allowed on this one.

The **Alum Cave Trail** has a trailhead off Newfound Gap Road. A 4.4-mile round-trip will carry you past some amazing views and interesting geological features, culminating at the Alum Cave, from which Epsom salts and saltpeter were mined beginning in the 1830s. The moderately strenuous couple of miles to Alum Cave represent the first leg of what becomes a much more difficult, treacherous hike, the 11 miles to the top of Mount LeConte.

The **Boogerman Trail** is a loop trail off the Cove Creek Road in the Cataloochee section of the park. This is a moderately strenuous, 7.5-mile round trip that takes two to three hours to complete. You'll pass old-growth trees, streams and cascades, and several old homesites, including that of "Boogerman" himself, an early resident named Robert Palmer.

As if the mountains and valleys, flora and fauna, and close-enough-to-touch clouds weren't wonder enough, the GSMNP has literally hundreds of waterfalls. Several of the most popular and most beautiful are accessible from major trails.

Close to Bryson City, 25-foot **Indian Creek Falls** is a moderately difficult hike of less than two miles round-trip, and it's a two-for-one

deal, as the path also goes by Tom Branch Falls. Crossing Deep Creek on bridges and logs and going by old homesites, this is an especially interesting hike. The Deep Creek-Indian Creek Trailhead is at the end of Deep Creek Road in Bryson City. It gets very crowded in nice weather, particularly because this is a popular area for tubing, and this makes parking quite difficult. Restrooms are available at the picnic area. Also accessible from the Indian Creek Trailhead is the path to 90-foot **Juney Whank Falls.** The hike to Juney Whank Falls is shorter but more difficult than that to Indian Creek Falls. Since it shares the same trailhead, you can expect to find the same crowds and parking difficulties as for the trail to Indian Creek Falls.

Mingo Falls, a beautiful 120-foot plume, is just outside the park, on the Qualla Boundary (Cherokee land). It can be seen from the Pigeon Creek Trail, which begins in the Mingo Falls Campground, off Big Cove Road south of Cherokee. The hike is very short, less than 0.5 miles round-trip, but is fairly strenuous.

Some longer hikes on the Tennessee side of

Mingo Falls

© 123RF.COM

the line lead to equally beautiful falls. **Rainbow Falls** is 80 feet high, and is as much a cloud of mist as it is a cataract—so much so that, when the sun hits it just right, you can see a rainbow. In the winter, it sometimes freezes solid, an amazing sight. The Rainbow Falls Trail near Gatlinburg is difficult, and is almost 5.5 miles round-trip. It ascends about 1,500 vertical feet and is very rocky most of the way, but it provides some great views, both of the falls and of Gatlinburg. Parking is available on Cherokee Orchard Road in Gatlinburg, but it fills up pretty quickly; you may need to pay to park a little farther from the trailhead.

The tallest waterfall, 100-foot **Ramsey Cascades,** is also the most difficult to reach. Those able to make a strenuous eight-mile round-trip hike are richly rewarded with a journey through old-growth hardwood forests and along fast-moving rivers. The pool at the bottom of the falls is a great place to glimpse some of the creatures that make GSMNP the "Salamander Capital of the World."

It is never safe to climb on waterfalls, and quite a few people in the park have died doing that, so it's best to admire the cascading water from the trails. Ramsey Cascades is particularly dangerous. The parking area for the Ramsey Cascades Trail is off Greenbrier Road, a few miles southeast of Gatlinburg. The nearest portable toilets are at the picnic area on Greenbrier Road.

Maps and guides to the waterfalls are available at many locations in the park.

Horseback Riding

Three commercial stables in the park offer "rental" horses on a by-the-hour basis (about $20 per hour). **Smokemont** (828/497-2373) is located in North Carolina near Cherokee. Two are in Tennessee: **Smoky Mountain** (865/436-5634, www.smokymountainridingstables.com) and **Cades Cove** (10018 Campground Dr., Townsend, 865/448-6286, http://discovercadescove.com).

Cycling

The **Cades Cove Store** (near Cades Cove Campground, 865/448-9034) rents bicycles in the summer and fall. From the second week in May to the second-to-last Saturday in September, the park closes off the loop road through Caves Cove on Wednesday and Saturday mornings, from sunrise until 10am, so that cyclists and hikers can enjoy the cove without having to worry about vehicular traffic.

Field Schools

Two Tennessee-based organizations affiliated with the GSMNP offer ways to get to know the park even better. The **Smoky Mountain Field School** (http://smfs.utk.edu) teaches workshops and leads excursions to educate participants in a wide array of fields related to the Smokies. One-day classes focus on the history and cultural heritage of the park, the lives of some of the park's most interesting animals, folk medicine and cooking of the southern Appalachians, and much more. Instructors also lead one-day and overnight hikes into the heart of the park.

The **Great Smoky Mountains Institute at Tremont** (9275 Tremont Road, Townsend, TN, 865/448-6709, www.gsmit.org) teaches students of all ages about the ecology of the region, wilderness rescue and survival skills, and even nature photography. Many of the classes and guided trips are part of Elderhostel events, kids' camps, or teacher-training institutes; however, there are also rich opportunities for unaffiliated learners.

ACCOMMODATIONS

There is only one inn in the entire 500,000-acre park, and it's a highly unusual one. **◖ LeConte Lodge** (865/429-5704, www.lecontelodge.com, cabin beds $64 adults, $53 children, lodges $512-768, meals $33 adults, $23.50 children, cash or check only, no pets), built in the 1920s, is at an elevation of nearly 6,600 feet, and is accessible only on foot after a hike of several hours. The lodge is supplied by thrice-weekly llama train. There are flush toilets, but no showers. Nor is there electricity at the lodge, and though kerosene heaters will keep you toasty, remember that even in the summertime, temperatures can fall into the

30s at night. It's an amazing place, and enough people are willing to make the necessary trek to stay here that reservations are often required very far in advance.

Luckily for those who don't want to camp or to hike to a rustic lodge, there are countless motels just outside the GSMNP. Reservations are always a good idea, especially in the summer and in leaf season, but you'll not want for choices in Cherokee, Maggie Valley, Bryson City, Pigeon Forge, Gatlinburg, Sevierville, and other neighboring communities. In addition to the many chain motels, affordable mom-and-pop motels also dot this landscape in abundance. A good choice is **Johnson's Inn** (242 Bishop Lane, Gatlinburg, 800/842-1930, www.johnsonsinn.com, $49-104, depending on season).

Camping

The GSMNP has many locations for camping, fees for which range $12-20. Campers can stay up to three nights at campsites, but only one night at a time in shelters. There are 10 front-country (car-accessible) campgrounds, each of which has cold running water and flush toilets in the restrooms, but no showers or power and water hookups. Most of these sites are first-come, first-served, but between May 15 and October 15, sites at the Elkmont, Smokemont, Cades Cove, and Cosby campgrounds can be reserved online (www.recreation.gov) or by calling 877/444-6777.

Within North Carolina, from northeast to southwest, the first campground is **Big Creek,** near I-40, at an elevation of 1,700 feet. This walk-in, tenting-only campsite features the beautifully soporific sound of rushing water from the nearby creek. It's open from spring to the beginning of November. The **Cataloochee** Campground, also reasonably close to I-40, is at 2,610 feet elevation and is also open from spring to the beginning of November.

The highest campground in the park, Balsam Mountain Campground, sits at a lofty 5,300 feet elevation and is a short drive from the terminus of the Blue Ridge Parkway. It's open only mid-May through late September

and is less likely to be crowded than many of the other campgrounds. **Smokemont,** open year-round, is the closest to Cherokee, and sits at 2,198 feet elevation. **Deep Creek,** at 1,800 feet, is closest to Bryson City and is open spring through early November.

In Tennessee, again from northeast to southwest, **Cosby** campground, at 2,459 feet elevation, open spring through early November, is closest to the town of Cosby and is not far from I-40. **Elkmont,** at 2,150 feet elevation on the Little River, open spring through the beginning of November, is the closest campsite to the Gatlinburg entrance to the park.

The **Cades Cove** campground, located off the loop road at Cades Cove, at an elevation of 2,610 feet, is open year-round. Close to Cades Cove and to each other as the crow flies, though a considerable drive apart, are the southwestern-most Tennessee campsites, **Abrams Creek,** at 1,125 feet elevation, open spring through early November, and Big Creek, at 1,700 feet, open spring through early November.

Backcountry camping is abundant. It is only allowed at designated sites and shelters, and a permit is required, but the permits are free and can be obtained at any of 15 different visitors centers and campground offices throughout the park. There are also five drive-in horse camps ($20-25) and seven group campgrounds ($35-65). A map of the available campsites is downloadable at www.nps.gov/grsm/planyourvisit. Before camping at the GSMNP, be sure to familiarize yourself with the park's backcountry regulations and etiquette, available online and at locations in the park.

FOOD

Unless you're staying at the LeConte Lodge or have packed a picnic or provisions, you'll have to leave the park for meals. The easiest way is simply to drive into Bryson City, Cherokee, or Gatlinburg, all right on the edge of the park. In Gatlinburg, try the **Smoky Mountain Brewery** (1004 Parkway, Suite 501, 865/436-4200, www.smoky-mtn-brewery.com, daily 11:30am-1am, under $20), a popular brewpub and restaurant. The **Wild Plum Tea Room** (555

Buckhorn Rd., 865/436-3808, daily 11am-3pm, under $10) is a nice spot for soup and sandwiches, homemade desserts, and the signature wild plum muffins served with every entrée. The formal restaurant of the **Buckhorn Inn** (2140 Tudor Mountain Rd., 866/941-0460, www.buckhorninn.com, dinner seating at 7pm, breakfast daily 8am-9:30am, $30 prix fixe, reservations required) has a different beautiful multicourse set menu every day of the week. Vegetarian meals can be prepared with advance notice.

INFORMATION AND SERVICES

The national park's official website is www.nps.gov/grsm. Much visitor information can be found to help you plan your trip at the websites of **Smoky Mountain Host** (www.visitsmokies.org) and the **Blue Ridge National Heritage Area** (www.blueridgeheritage.com). Detailed touring suggestions for sites associated with local history and heritage can be found at the **North Carolina Folklife Institute** (www.ncfolk.org), and in *Cherokee Heritage Trails,* an excellent guidebook that can be purchased at either website.

Area hospitals include those in Bryson City, Sylva, and Clyde, as well as a little farther afield in Asheville and in Knoxville and Maryville, Tennessee.

GETTING THERE AND AROUND

The closest commercial airport to the Smokies is **Asheville Regional Airport** (AVL, 61 Terminal Dr., Fletcher, 828/684-2226, www.flyavl.com) in Fletcher; the **Gatlinburg-Pigeon Forge Airport** (GKT, 1255 Airport Rd., Sevierville, 865/453-6136), over the state line in Tennessee, is used by private planes has no commercial passenger flights. Amtrak doesn't run anywhere in this area, but the closest stations, both hours away, are in Gastonia, near Charlotte, and in Spartanburg, South Carolina. Unless you're hiking through on the Appalachian Trail, the best way to get around the Smokies is by car. U.S. 19 and U.S. 23 stretch down from Asheville to the Georgia line, while U.S. 64, which stretches from Murphy to Manteo, snakes along the southern edge of the Smokies. Cresting the northern edge is I-40, running between Asheville and Knoxville.

Bryson City and the Nantahala Forest

Mossy gorges, misty riverbanks, and cloud-ringed mountain peaks make the Nantahala region feel like a setting for fairy tales and conjuration. Cherokee mythology tells of a witch, Spearfinger, known to have frequented the Nantahala Gorge, which was also the abode of a monstrous snake and, of all things, an inchworm so large that it could span the top of the gorge and block out the light of the sun. Today, the Nantahala River, running through the narrow gorge, has become a favorite white-water rafting run.

Nearby Bryson City is an aqua-centric river town, one whose proximity to great white-water rapids makes it a favorite haunt for rafters and kayakers and their ilk. If you approach Bryson

City from the north on U.S. 19, you're in for a strange sight: The banks of the Tuckaseegee River are shored up with crushed cars. Look closely and you may recognize the fenders of trusty warhorses of your childhood.

SIGHTS

The **Great Smoky Mountain Railroad** (Bryson City and Dillsboro depots, 800/872-4681, www.gsmr.com, from $30 adults, $16 children) is one of the best and most fun ways to see the Smokies. On historic trains, the GSMR carries sightseers on excursions, from two to several hours long, through some of the most beautiful scenery in the region. Trips between Dillsboro and Bryson City (with a layover at each end for shopping and dining) follow the banks of the Tuckaseegee River, while round-trips from Bryson City follow the Little Tennessee and Nantahala Rivers deep into the Nantahala Gorge, and the Fontana Trestle Excursion crosses over the top of the Fontana Dam just at sunset. Many other excursions are offered, including gourmet dining and wine and beer tasting trips, *Thomas the Tank Engine* and *Little Engine That Could* themed trips for kids, and runs to and from river rafting outfitters.

SPORTS AND RECREATION
(Nantahala River Gorge
The stunningly beautiful Nantahala River Gorge, just outside Bryson City in the Nantahala National Forest, supports scores of river guide companies, many clustered west along U.S. 19. "Nantahala" is said to mean "Land of the Noonday Sun," and there are indeed parts of this gorge where the sheer rock walls above the river are so steep that sunlight only hits the water at the noon hour. Eight miles of the Nantahala River flow through the gorge, over Class II and III rapids. The nearby Ocoee River is also a favorite of rafters, and the Cheoah River, on the occasions of controlled releases, has some of the South's most famous and difficult Class III and IV runs.

Outfitters and Tours
Endless River Adventures (14157 U.S. 19 W., near Bryson City, 800/224-7238, www. endlessriveradventures.com) gives white-water and flat-water kayaking instruction, rentals, and guided trips on the Nantahala, Ocoee, and Cheoah Rivers. They'll be able to suggest a run suited to your skill level. In addition to river guide services, **Wildwater Rafting** (10345 U.S. 19 W., 12 miles west of Bryson City, 800/451-9972, www.wildwaterrafting.com) leads **Wildwater Jeep Tours** ($40-90 adults, $25-70 children), half-day and full-day jeep excursions on back roads and through wilderness and to waterfalls and old mountain settlements.

Because some of these rapids can be quite dangerous, be sure to call ahead and speak to a guide if you have any doubts as to your readiness. If rafting with children, check the company's weight and age restrictions beforehand.

ACCOMMODATIONS
The (**Folkestone Inn** (101 Folkestone Rd., 888/812-3385, www.folkestoneinn.com, from $80) is one of the region's outstanding bed-and-breakfasts, a roomy 1920s farmhouse expanded and renovated into a charming and tranquil inn. Each guest room has a balcony or porch. Baked treats at breakfast include shortcake, kuchen, cobblers, and other delicacies.

An 85-year-old hotel on the National Register of Historic Places, the **Fryemont Inn** (245 Fryemont St., Bryson City, 800/845-4879, www.fryemontinn.com, spring-fall, from $125, including meals) has a cozy, rustic feel, with chestnut-paneled guest rooms and an inviting lobby with an enormous stone fireplace.

Some river outfitters offer lodging, which can be a very cheap way to pass the night if you don't mind roughing it. The **Rolling Thunder River Company** (10160 U.S. 19 W., near Bryson City, 800/408-7238, www.rollingthunderriverco.com, no alcohol permitted) operates a large bunkhouse, with beds ($8-12) available for its rafting customers. The **Nantahala Motel** at Carolina Outfitters has very simple guest rooms with private baths (from $40). Many of the outfitters also offer camping on their properties.

Way back in the forest by Fontana Lake, the **Fontana Village Resort** (Hwy. 28, Fontana Dam, 800/849-2258, www.fontanavillage.com, from $60) was originally built as housing for the workers doing construction on the dam, a massive World War II-era undertaking that created a whole town out here in the woods. Renovated into a comfortable resort, Fontana Village features a lodge, cabins, camping (from $25) and, for the more adventurous lodger, houseboats. Houseboats are a tradition on the lake, and the two that are rented by Fontana Village make for a most memorable vacation.

Camping
For a look at the range of camping options

available in the Nantahala National Forest, visit www.fs.usda.gov/nfsnc. Among the nicest is **Standing Indian Campground** (90 Sloan Rd., Franklin, 828/524-6441, Apr.-Nov., $16). Standing Indian has a nice diversity of campsites to choose from, from flat, grassy areas to cozy mountainside nooks. Drinking water, hot showers, flush toilets, and a phone are all available on-site, and leashed pets are permitted. At 3,400 feet elevation, the campground is close to the Appalachian Trail.

GETTING THERE AND AROUND

Bryson City can be reached via U.S. 19, if you're coming south from Maggie Valley and Cherokee. U.S. 74 also passes very close by, an easy route from the east or west.

Robbinsville and the Valley Towns

Another region at the heart of Cherokee life, both past and present, is found between Robbinsville and the Georgia state line. Near Robbinsville, the area known as Snowbird is one of the most traditional Cherokee communities, where the Cherokee language is still spoken as a first language, and the old crafts and folkways are alive as well. Here also is the grave of Junaluska, one of the Eastern Band's most prominent ancestors.

The town of Murphy is closely linked with the great tragedy of Cherokee history, the Trail of Tears. About 16,000 Cherokee people, including children, the elderly, and the infirm, were arrested and made to leave their homes and farms in North Carolina, Georgia, and Tennessee. They were brought here to Fort Butler, where they began their forced march to Oklahoma. The names of these people, many of whom died along the way, are inscribed in Cherokee on a memorial at the L&N Depot in Murphy.

In addition to the places of historic significance to Cherokee culture, this farthest southwest corner of North Carolina has other compelling sights. Brasstown, a tiny village on the Georgia line, is the home of the John C. Campbell Folk School, an artists colony nearly a century old, where visitors can stroll among studios and along trails, and stop in to a gallery shop with some of the most beautiful crafts you'll find in the region. Back up toward Robbinsville, the relentlessly scenic Cherohala Skyway crosses 36 miles of the Cherokee and Nantahala National Forests. This road is a major destination for motorcyclists and sports-car drivers as well as day-trippers and vacationers.

ROBBINSVILLE

The whole southwestern corner of North Carolina is rich with Cherokee history and culture, and the Robbinsville area has some of the deepest roots and sites of greatest significance to the modern and historical generations of the Cherokee people. In little towns and crossroads a few miles outside Robbinsville, several hundred people known as the Snowbird community keep alive some of the Cherokee's oldest ways. The Cherokee language is spoken here—it is still some residents' first language—and some of the Eastern Band's most admired basket makers, potters, and other artists continue to make and teach their traditional arts.

Sights

Outside Robbinsville in the ancient Stecoah Valley, an imposing old rock schoolhouse, built in 1930 and used as a school until the mid-1990s, has been reborn as the **Stecoah Valley Center** (121 Schoolhouse Rd., Stecoah, 828/479-3364, www.stecoahvalleycenter. com). This is the home of a weaver's guild, a native plants preservation group, a concert series, several festivals, and a great **gallery shop** (828/497-3098, May-Mar. Mon.-Fri. 10am-5pm, Apr. Mon.-Sat. 10am-5pm) of local

JUNALUSKA'S LEGACY TO THE CHEROKEE

Among the most important figures in the history of the Eastern Band of the Cherokee is Junaluska, who was born in 1776 near Dillard, Georgia. During the wars against the Creek people (1812-1814), the Cherokee fought alongside the U.S. military, and it's said that young Junaluska saved the life of Andrew Jackson at the battle of Horse Shoe Bend in Alabama.

Almost 20 years later, Andrew Jackson, now president, thanked the Cherokee by signing the Indian Removal Act, which ordered that they and four other major Southern nations be forced off their lands and marched to the new Indian Territory of Oklahoma. Junaluska traveled all the way to Washington to try to convince Jackson to change his mind, but his plea fell on deaf ears.

Junaluska was one of about 16,000 members of the Cherokee Nation who were made to walk the thousand miles to Oklahoma. In Tennessee, he led an attempted escape but was captured and made the rest of the march in manacles and leg irons. In 1841 he was finally able to leave Oklahoma and made the 17-day trip by horseback all the way back to North Carolina. Supposedly Junaluska once said, "If I had known what Andrew Jackson would do to the Cherokees, I would have killed him myself that day at Horse Shoe Bend."

He spent his later years in Cherokee County, on land that was given to him by the state of North Carolina. He and his third wife, Nicie, are buried at Robbinsville, at what is now the Junaluska Memorial and Museum. A marker was commissioned in 1910 by the Daughters of the American Revolution, and during the dedication ceremony, a eulogy was delivered in the Cherokee language by the Reverend Armstrong Cornsilk:

He was a good man. He was a good friend. He was a good friend in his home and everywhere. He would ask the hungry man to eat. He would ask the cold one to warm by his fire. He would ask the tired one to rest, and he would give a good place to sleep. Juno's home was a good home for others.

He was a smart man. He made his mind think good. He was very brave. He was not afraid...

I hope we shall all meet Junaluska in heaven [pointing upward] and all be happy there together.

artisans' work. Concerts in the Appalachian Evening summer series, featuring area musicians, are preceded by community suppers of traditional mountain cuisine.

On Robbinsville's Main Street is the **Junaluska Memorial** (Main St., about 0.5 miles north of the Graham County Courthouse, 828/479-4727, Mon.-Sat. 9am-4pm). Here Junaluska and his third wife, Nicie, are buried. The marker was dedicated in 1910 by the Daughters of the American Revolution. The gravesite is maintained by the Friends of Junaluska, who also operate the **Heritage Center** (www.lakejunaluska.com) on the same site. At the museum you'll find ancient artifacts from life in Cheoah thousands of years ago.

There are also contemporary Cherokee crafts on display, and outside you can walk a path that highlights the medicinal plants used for generations in this area.

Fourteen miles outside Robbinsville, down a winding country road, **Yellow Branch Pottery and Cheese** (136 Yellow Branch Circle, Robbinsville, 828/479-6710, www.yellowbranch.com, Tues.-Sat. noon-5pm, or by appointment) is a beautifully rustic spot for an afternoon's excursion. Bruce DeGroot, Karen Mickler, and their herd of jersey cows produce prize-winning artisanal cheeses and graceful, functional pottery. (The cows don't actually help with the pottery.) Visitors are welcome at their farm and shop.

Entertainment and Events

Every year in late May on the Saturday of Memorial Day Weekend, the Snowbird Cherokee host the **Fading Voices Festival** (www.cherokeeheritagetrail.org) in Robbinsville. The festival features a mound-building ceremony, and all of the usual festival attractions—music, dancing, storytelling, crafts, and lots of food—but in the deeply traditional forms carried on by the Snowbird community.

Sports and Recreation

The **Joyce Kilmer Memorial Forest** (Joyce Kilmer Rd., off Hwy. 143, west of Robbinsville, 828/479-6431, www.westernncattractions.com, daily dawn-dusk, free) is one of the largest remaining tracts of virgin forest in the eastern United States, where 450-year-old tulip polar trees have grown to 100 feet tall and 20 feet around. The two-mile loop (or two one-mile loops) makes for an easy hike through a remarkable forest.

Accommodations

The **Snowbird Mountain Lodge** (4633 Santeetlah Rd., 11 miles west of Robbinsville, 800/941-9290, www.snowbirdlodge.com, from $180) was built in the early 1940s, a rustic chestnut-and-stone inn atop a 3,000-foot mountain. The view is exquisite, and the lodge is perfectly situated between the Cherohala Skyway, Lake Santeetlah, and the Joyce Kilmer Forest. Guests enjoy a full breakfast, picnic lunch, and four-course supper created from seasonal local specialties. Another pleasant place to stay near Robbinsville is the **Tapoco Lodge Resort** (14981 Tapoco Rd., 15 miles north of Robbinsville, 800/822-5083, www.tapocolodge.com, Apr.-Nov., from $109 private bath, $75 shared bath). Built in 1930, the lodge is on the National Register of Historic Places and has the feel of an old-time hotel. Guest rooms in the main lodge and surrounding cabins are simple but comfortable, and the resort overlooks the Cheoah River, a legendary run for rafters several times each year when stored water is released to form crazy-fast rapids.

HAYESVILLE AND BRASSTOWN

Between Hayesville and Brasstown, you can get a really good sense of the art that has come out of this region over the years. These two small towns are along the Georgia border on U.S. 64.

◖ John C. Campbell Folk School

One of North Carolina's most remarkable cultural institutions, the **John C. Campbell Folk School** (1 Folk School Rd., Brasstown, 800/365-5724, www.folkschool.org) was born of the unusual honeymoon of unusual newlyweds from up North who traveled through Appalachia 100 years ago to educate themselves about Southern highland culture. John C. and Olive Dame Campbell, like other notable Northern liberals in their day, directed their humanitarian impulses toward the education and economic betterment of Southern mountaineers. John Campbell died a decade later, but Olive, joining forces with her friend Marguerite Butler, set out to establish a "folk school" in the Southern mountains that she and John had visited. She was inspired by the model of the Danish *folkehojskole*, workshops that preserved and taught traditional arts as a means of fostering economic self-determination and personal pride in rural communities. Brasstown, North Carolina, was chosen as the site for this grand experiment, and in 1925, the John C. Campbell Folk School opened its doors.

Today, thousands of artists travel every year to this uncommonly lovely remote valley, the site of an ancient Cherokee village. In week-long and weekend-long classes, students of all ages and skill levels learn about traditional arts native to this region, such as pottery, weaving, dyeing, storytelling, and chair caning, as well as contemporary and exotic crafts, such as photography, kaleidoscope making, bookmaking, and paper marbling. By all means, visit the website or order a catalog, and see if any of the hundreds of courses offered every year strike your fancy. But even if you're passing through the area on a shorter visit, the Folk School welcomes you to explore the

COURTESY OF JOHN C. CAMPBELL FOLK SCHOOL

John C. Campbell Folk School

campus. Visitors are sincerely asked to help preserve the quiet atmosphere of learning and concentration when peering at artists' studios, but you can have an up-close look at some of their marvelous wares in the school's **Craft Shop** (bottom floor of Olive Dame Campbell Dining Hall, Mon.-Sat. 8am-5pm, Sun. 1pm-5pm), one of the nicest such shops in western North Carolina. Exhibits about the school's history, and historic examples of the work of local artists of past generations, are on display at the **History Center**, next to Keith House. There are several nature trails on campus that thread through this lovely valley. Be sure to visit the 0.25-mile **Rivercane Walk**, which features outdoor sculpture by some of the greatest living artists of the Eastern Band of the Cherokee. In the evenings you'll often find concerts by traditional musicians or community square, contra, and English country dances. A visit to the John C. Campbell Folk School, whether as a student or a traveler, is an exceptional opportunity to immerse yourself in a great creative tradition.

Clay County Historical and Arts Council Museum

Hayesville's Old Clay County Jail, built in 1912, is now home to the **Clay County Historical and Arts Council Museum** (21 Davis Loop, Hayesville, 828/389-6814, June-Aug. daily 10am-4pm, call for hours off-season). This is a small and extremely interesting museum with varied collections, including the medical instruments of an early country doctor, an original jail cell (with a file hidden by a long-ago prisoner, discovered during renovations), an old moonshine still, a collection of beautiful Cherokee masks, and a remarkable crazy quilt embroidered with strange and charming illustrations.

Food

Across from the courthouse in Hayesville, the **Café on the Square** (Mon.-Thurs. 6am-10pm, Fri.-Sat. 6am-11pm, under $10) is a spot to nip in for a good cup of coffee and a pastry as you set off on a mountain adventure.

GETTING THERE AND AROUND

This is the southwesternmost corner of North Carolina, in some places as close to Atlanta as to Asheville. Robbinsville is located on U.S. 129, southwest of Bryson City. Hayesville and Brasstown are easily reached from U.S. 64, which closely parallels the Georgia border.

MYRTLE BEACH AND THE GRAND STRAND

The West has Las Vegas, Florida has Orlando, and South Carolina has Myrtle Beach. There's no Bellagio Resort or Magic Kingdom here, but Myrtle Beach remains the number-one travel destination in the state, with even more visitors than Charleston. Unlike Charleston, you'll find little history here. With several theme parks, 100 golf courses, 50 miniature golf courses, over 2,000 restaurants—not to mention miles of beautiful shoreline—Myrtle Beach is built for all-out vacation enjoyment.

The hot, hazy height of the summer also marks the busy season on the Strand. Its long main drag, Kings Highway (a.k.a. Business U.S. 17), is packed full of families on the go eager for more swimming, more shopping, more eating, and just plain more.

While to many people the name Myrtle Beach conjures an image of tacky, downscale people doing tacky, downscale things, that's an outmoded stereotype. Tacky is certainly still in vogue here, but an influx of higher-quality development, both in accommodations and entertainment value, has lifted the bar significantly. Rather than slumming in a beat-up motel, quaffing PBR on the beach, and loading up on $2 T-shirts like in the "good old days," a typical Myrtle Beach vacation now involves a stay in a large condo apartment with flat-screen TVs, a full kitchen, and a sumptuous palmetto-lined pool; dining at the House of Blues; having drinks at the Hard Rock Café; stops at high-profile attractions like Ripley's Aquarium; and shopping at trendy retailers like Anthropologie and Abercrombie & Fitch.

The Grand Strand on which Myrtle Beach

© 123RF.COM

MYRTLE BEACH

HIGHLIGHTS

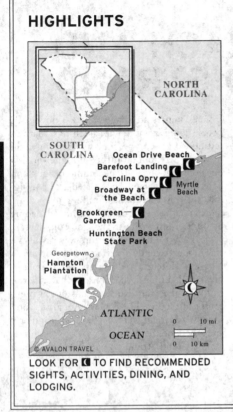

© AVALON TRAVEL

LOOK FOR ◖ TO FIND RECOMMENDED SIGHTS, ACTIVITIES, DINING, AND LODGING.

◖ **Broadway at the Beach:** You'll find good cheesy fun along with tons of interesting shops, theme restaurants, and, of course, miniature golf (page 235).

◖ **Barefoot Landing:** North Myrtle Beach's answer to Broadway at the Beach, with the Alabama Theatre and the House of Blues nearby (page 239).

◖ **Ocean Drive Beach:** The still-beating, still-shuffling heart of the Grand Strand is also the center of shag dancing culture (page 241).

◖ **Carolina Opry:** This popular show offers corny but quality family entertainment in an intimate, friendly setting (page 243).

◖ **Brookgreen Gardens:** Enjoy the country's largest collection of outdoor sculptures, set amid a fine collection of formal gardens (page 263).

◖ **Huntington Beach State Park:** The scenic beach combines with one-of-a-kind Atalaya Castle to make a unique getaway (page 264).

◖ **Hampton Plantation:** This historic Georgian mansion on the scenic Wambaw Creek inspired a South Carolina poet laureate to give it to the state for posterity (page 271).

sits—a long, sandy peninsula stretching 60 miles from Winyah Bay to the North Carolina border—has also been a vacation playground for generations of South Carolinians. Unlike Hilton Head, where New York and Midwestern accents are more common than Lowcountry drawls, Myrtle Beach and the Grand Strand remain largely homegrown passions, with many visitors living within a few hours' drive. Despite the steady increase of money and high-dollar development in the area, its strongly regional nature works to your advantage in that prices are generally lower than in Vegas or Orlando.

To the south of Myrtle proper lies the understated, affluent, and relaxing Pawleys Island, with nearby Murrells Inlet and its great seafood restaurants. Unique, eclectic Brookgreen Gardens hosts the largest collection of outdoor sculpture in the country, with one-of-a-kind Huntington Beach State Park literally right across the street.

Even farther south, in the northern quarter of the Lowcountry proper, you'll find a totally different scene: the remnants of the Carolina rice culture in quaint old Georgetown, and the haunting antebellum mansions at Hampton Plantation and Hopsewee Plantation.

HISTORY

The Grand Strand was once the happy hunting and shellfish-gathering grounds of the Waccamaw people, whose legacy is still felt

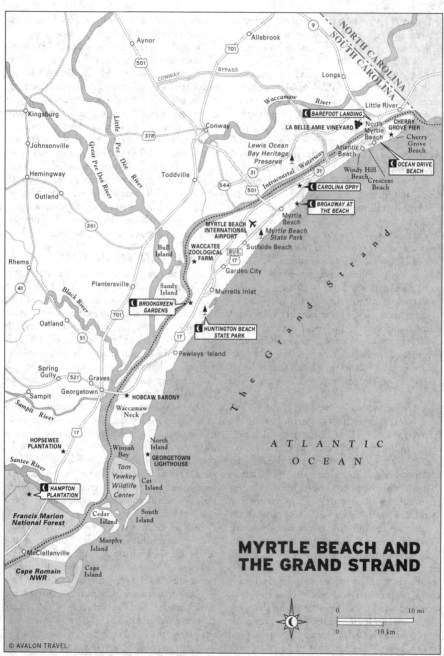

MYRTLE BEACH

MYRTLE BEACH AND THE GRAND STRAND

© AVALON TRAVEL

today in the name of the dominant river in the region and the Strand's main drag itself, Kings Highway, which is actually built on an old Native American trail.

The southern portion of the Strand, especially Georgetown and Pawleys Island, rapidly became home to a number of rice plantations soon after the area was colonized. However, the area now known as Myrtle Beach didn't share in the wealth since its soil and topography weren't conducive to the plantation system. Indeed, the northern portion of the Grand Strand was largely uninhabited during colonial times, and hurricane damage prevented much development through the first half of the 19th century.

That changed after the Civil War with the boom of nearby Conway to the west, now the seat of Horry County (pronounced "OR-ee"). As Conway's lumber and export economy grew, a railroad spur was built to bring in lumber from the coast, much of which was owned by a single firm, the Conway Lumber Company. Lumber company employees began using the rail lines to take vacation time on the Strand, in effect becoming the first of millions of tourists to the area. At this time it was simply called "New Town," in contrast to Conway's "Old Town."

In the second half of the 19th century, Civil War veteran Franklin G. Burroughs, of the Burroughs and Collins Company, which supplied lumber and turpentine to Conway business interests, sought to expand the tourism profitability of the coastal area. He died in 1897, but his heirs continued his dream, inaugurated by the opening of the Seaside Inn in 1901. The first bona fide resort came in the 1920s with the building of the Arcady resort, which included the first golf course in the area.

In 1938 Burroughs's widow, Adeline, known locally as "Miss Addie," was credited with giving the town its modern name, after the locally abundant wax myrtle shrub. During this time, locals on the Strand originated the shagging subculture, built around the dance of the same name and celebrated at numerous pavilions and "beach clubs." The building of Myrtle Beach

Air Force Base in 1940—now closed—brought further growth and jobs to the area.

Tourism, especially, grew apace here until Hurricane Hazel virtually wiped the slate clean in 1954. In typical Carolinian fashion, residents and landowners made lemonade out of lemons, using the hurricane's devastation as an excuse to build even bigger resort developments, including a plethora of golf courses.

Since then, the Strand has grown to encompass about 250,000 permanent residents, with about 10 million visitors on top of that each year. A huge influx of money in the 1990s led to a higher-dollar form of development on the coast, sadly leading to the demolition of many of the old beach pavilions in favor of new attractions and massive condo high-rises.

PLANNING YOUR TIME

The most important thing to remember is that the Grand Strand is *long*—60 miles from one end to the other. This has real-world effects that need to be taken into account. For example, while the separate municipality of North Myrtle Beach (actually a fairly recent aggregation of several small beachside communities) may sound like it is right next door to Myrtle Beach proper, getting from one to the other can take half an hour even in light traffic.

Due to this geographical stretching, as well as to all the attractions, it is impossible to cover this area in a single day, and even two days is a ridiculously short amount of time. That's probably the main reason many folks indulge in a weekly rental. Not only does it give you enough time to see everything, it enables you to relax, slow down, and enjoy the beaches and the general laid-back attitude.

In May, Memorial Day weekend and Bike Week have traditionally signaled the beginning of the tourism season in Myrtle Beach. The busy season exactly corresponds with the hottest months of the year, July and August. This is when crowds are at their peak, restaurants are most crowded, and the two spurs of U.S. 17 are at their most gridlocked.

Springtime in Myrtle Beach is quite nice, but keep in mind that water temperatures are still chilly through April. There is almost always one last cold snap in March that augurs the spring.

Personally, I recommend hitting Myrtle Beach just as the busy season wanes, right after Labor Day. Rooms are significantly cheaper, but most everything is still fully open and adequately staffed, with the added benefit of the biggest crush of visitors being absent.

Winter on the Grand Strand is very slow, as befitting this very seasonal locale. Many restaurants, especially down the Strand near Murrells Inlet, close entirely through February.

ORIENTATION

Don't get too hung up on place names around here. This part of the Strand comprises several different municipalities, from Surfside Beach to the south up to Little River near the North Carolina border, but for all intents and purposes it's one big place all its own. As a general rule, development (read: money) is moving more quickly to the North Myrtle Beach area rather than the older Myrtle Beach proper to the south.

North Myrtle is actually a recent aggregation of several historic beachfront communities: Windy Hill, Crescent Beach, Cherry Grove, and Ocean Drive. You'll see numerous signs announcing the entrance or exit into or out of these communities, but keep in mind you're still technically in North Myrtle Beach.

The Grand Strand grid is based on a system of east-west avenues beginning just north of Myrtle Beach State Park. Confusingly, these are separated into "North" and "South" avenues. Perhaps even more confusing, North Myrtle Beach also uses its own distinct north-and-south avenue system, also for roads running east-west. Got it? It goes like this: Myrtle Beach starts with 29th Avenue South at the Myrtle Beach International Airport and goes up to 1st Avenue South just past Family Kingdom Amusement Park. From here, the avenues are labeled as "North" from 1st Avenue North up to 82nd Avenue North, which concludes Myrtle Beach proper. North Myrtle Beach begins at 48th Avenue South near Barefoot Landing and goes up to Main Street (the center of the shag culture). It continues with 1st Avenue North, goes up to 24th Avenue North (Cherry Grove Beach), and finally concludes at 61st Avenue North, near the North Carolina state line.

Sights

◖ BROADWAY AT THE BEACH

Love it or hate it, **Broadway at the Beach** (1325 Celebrity Circle, 800/386-4662, www. broadwayatthebeach.com, summer daily 10am-11pm, winter daily 10am-6pm), between 21st and 29th Avenues, is one of Myrtle's biggest and flashiest attractions—which is saying a lot. First opened over 15 years ago and added onto significantly since then, this collection of three hotels, over two dozen restaurants, about 50 shops, and a dozen kid-oriented activities sprawls over 350 acres with several other major attractions, restaurants, and clubs (such as the Hard Rock Café and Planet Hollywood) on its periphery.

Just like the Magic Kingdom that many of Myrtle's attractions seek to emulate, Broadway at the Beach has at its center a large lagoon, around which everything else is situated. Needless to say, there's also a massive parking lot. Activity goes on all day and well into the wee hours, with the weekly Tuesday-night fireworks a big draw. While there's plenty to do, what with the great shops, tasty treats, and fun piped-in music following you everywhere, it's also fun just to walk around.

The main complaint about Broadway at the Beach has to do with the price of the various attractions within the park, some of which are fairly small-scale. Indeed, the quality of the attractions within Broadway at the Beach varies, and much depends on what floats your boat,

MYRTLE BEACH

© JIM MOREKIS

Broadway at the Beach

but you can still find plenty to enjoy as long as you know the scoop ahead of time. Here's a quick guide to the specific attractions.

The biggest new attraction at Broadway—and it's really big—is **Wonderworks** (1313 Celebrity Circle, 843/626-9962, www.wonderworksonline.com, Sun.-Thurs. 10am-8pm, Fri.-Sat. 10am-9pm, $23 adults, $15 children). You can't miss it—look for the thing that looks exactly like a massive, life-size, crumbling, upside-down creepy mansion. Inside you'll find a wide and quite varied assortment of interactive experiences designed to let you know what it's like to be upside down, or on a bed of nails, or in a hurricane, or freezing after the *Titanic* sank, and things of that nature. Think Ripley's Believe It or Not updated for a modern age, complete with laser tag.

Harry Potter fans will likely enjoy **MagiQuest** (1185 Celebrity Circle, 843/913-9460, www.magiquest.com, daily 10am-9:30pm, $26-40), which takes you on a 90-minute journey to find clues that lead to hidden treasure. Folks of an older generation will find it a surprisingly high-tech experience for something dealing with the ancient arts of wizardry—including an orientation session and the programmable wands that are indispensable to the quest. But don't worry; the young ones will get it.

MagiQuest has a certain addictive quality, and many people opt to go back for more (additional quests cost less) after their usually confusing, full-price first experience. Note that there's an intro game you can play online, which might help you get acquainted. Like many attractions at Myrtle Beach, this one can get very crowded, which is certain to impede the quality of your experience (Whose wand uncovered the clue? Who knows?). Try to go right when it opens.

Similarly medieval—and right nearby—is **Medieval Times** (2904 Fantasy Way, 843/236-4635, www.medievaltimes.com, $51 adults, $31 ages 3-12), a combination dinner theater and medieval tournament reenactment.

Now that almost all of the old-fashioned amusement parks at Myrtle Beach are gone,

MYRTLE BEACH

Wonderworks

victims of "modernization," you can find a facsimile of sorts at **Pavilion Nostalgia Park** (843/913-9400, www.pavilionnostalgiapark. com, summer daily 11am-11pm, hours vary in other seasons, rides $3 each), which seeks to simulate the days of Myrtle gone by.

Of course, nowhere in Myrtle is really complete without miniature golf, and Broadway at the Beach's version is **Dragon's Lair Fantasy Golf** (1197 Celebrity Circle, 843/913-9301, $9), with two medieval-themed 18-hole courses boasting a fire-breathing dragon.

Ripley's Aquarium

If you've been to Boston's New England Aquarium, don't expect something similar at **Ripley's Aquarium** (1110 Celebrity Circle, 800/734-8888, www.ripleysaquarium.com, Sun.-Thurs. 9am-9pm, Fri.-Sat. 9am-10pm, $22 adults, $11 ages 6-11, $4 ages 2-5, free under age 2) at Broadway at the Beach. This is a smaller but quite delightful aquarium built primarily for entertainment purposes rather than education. Calming music plays throughout,

MYRTLE BEACH

© JIM MOREKIS

Ripley's Aquarium

and a moving sidewalk takes you around and under a huge main tank filled with various marine creatures. There's even the requisite sting-ray-petting touch tank.

You'll no doubt see the garish billboards for the aquarium up and down U.S. 17, featuring massive sharks baring rows of scary teeth. But don't expect an over-the-top shark exhibit—the truth is that most of the sharks in the aquarium are smaller and much more peaceful.

NASCAR SpeedPark

Just outside Broadway at the Beach you'll find the **NASCAR SpeedPark** (1820 21st Ave. N., 843/918-8725, www.nascarspeedpark.com, summer daily 10am-11pm, shorter hours in other seasons, from $24), where can you speed around at 50 mph in a fairly decent replica of an actual NASCAR track. Because there are several different tracks to choose from, based on age and difficulty, there's something here for adults and kids alike.

The serious track, Thunder Road, is open only to drivers age 16 and over; it allows drivers to get into half-size versions of Nextel Cup cars. Pint-size drivers 48, 40, and 36 inches tall can take part in racing on the Champions, Qualifier, and Kiddie Speedway courses, respectively. As if all that's not enough, there are water-based racing courses and, this being Myrtle Beach, NASCAR-themed miniature golf.

If you're worried about metal-shearing, flame-spewing, multiple-car pileups like in a real NASCAR race, don't. Safety is a paramount concern at this national chain of parks, and the likelihood of an accident at the SpeedPark is far less than on crowded U.S. 17, a stone's throw away.

Myrtle Waves Water Park

Billed as South Carolina's largest water park, **Myrtle Waves Water Park** (U.S. 17 Bypass and 10th Ave. N., 843/913-9260, www.myrtlewaves.com, summer daily 10am-6pm, hours vary in other seasons, $25 age 7 and over, $23 ages 3-6, free under age 3) is right across the street from Broadway at the Beach, covers 20

© JIM MOREKIS

Skywheel

you through the more commercial areas of the beachfront area but to provide easy pedestrian beach access. One section provides a nice peaceful walking experience amid the dune-scape.

Unveiled in 2010, the Boardwalk has been a very important improvement in civic life and morale in the wake of the loss of the old pavilion nearby, now mostly a grassy field.

Skywheel

You can't miss spotting the new **Skywheel** (1110 N. Ocean Blvd., 843/839-9200, http://myrtlebeachskywheel.com, summer daily noon-midnight, $13 adults, $9 children), a huge Ferris wheel dominating the skyline at the new Boardwalk. The cars are family-size, fully enclosed, and offer a great view of the ocean and surrounding area during the approximately 10-minute, three-rotation trip.

◖ BAREFOOT LANDING

Before the arrival of Broadway at the Beach was the Strand's original high-concept retail and dining complex, **Barefoot Landing** (4898 U.S. 17 S., 843/272-8349, www.bflanding.com, hours vary). It's less flashy on the surface and certainly more tasteful, but trust me, it's just as commercial.

The centerpiece of the two-decade-old entertainment and shopping complex is **The Alabama Theatre** (4750 U.S. 17 S., 843/272-5758, www.alabama-theatre.com, ticket prices vary), a project of the famed country-and-western band of the same name, who despite their eponymous roots actually got their start gigging in juke joints in the Grand Strand. A stone's throw away is the **House of Blues** (4640 U.S. 17 S., 843/272-3000, www.hob.com), bringing in name acts on an almost nightly basis as well as diners to its excellent restaurant. On some nights you can pose for a picture with a real live tiger cub on your lap at **T.I.G.E.R.S. Preservation Station** (843/361-4552, www.tigerfriends.com, hours vary). Shopping is mostly the name of the game here, though.

acres, and features all kinds of safe fun "rides," such as the Ocean in Motion Wave Pool, the Layzee River, and the Saturation Station, wherein a huge water volcano absolutely soaks everybody in proximity every five minutes or so. That's just to name a few.

As you would expect, there are plenty of lifeguards on hand at all the rides. Food is plentiful if unremarkable, and there are shaded areas for the less adventurous to chill while the kids splash around. With one admission price covering all rides all day, this is one of the better deals in Myrtle Beach, which has more than its share of confusingly (and occasionally exorbitantly) priced attractions.

MYRTLE BEACH BOARDWALK AND PROMENADE

The new pride of old Myrtle, the **Boardwalk** (www.visitmyrtlebeach.com, daily 24 hours, free) is a fun, meandering 1.2-mile jaunt from 2nd Avenue Pier to the 14th Avenue Pier. Built in three different and distinct sections, the point of the Boardwalk is not only to take

Alligator Adventure

One of the most popular attractions within

MYRTLE BEACH

Barefoot Landing is Alligator Adventure (www.alligatoradventure.com, $18 adults, $13 ages 4-12, free under age 4). They have hundreds of alligators, yes, but also plenty of turtles, tortoises, snakes, and birds. The otters are a big hit as well. The highlight, though, comes during the daily alligator feedings, when you get a chance to see the real power and barely controlled aggression of these magnificent indigenous beasts. Keep in mind that due to the cold-blooded reptiles' dormant winter nature, the feedings are not held in the colder months.

CHILDREN'S MUSEUM OF SOUTH CAROLINA

A less-expensive form of entertainment with an added educational component at Myrtle is the **Children's Museum of South Carolina** (2501 N. Kings Hwy., 843/946-9469, www.cmsckids.org, summer Mon.-Sat. 9am-4pm, Sun. noon-5pm, $8). This facility tries hard to compete with the splashier attractions in town but still manages to keep a reasonably strong educational focus with programs like "Crime Lab Chemistry," "World of Art," and "Space Adventures."

FAMILY KINGDOM AMUSEMENT AND WATER PARK

For a taste of old-time beachfront amusement park fun, try the **Family Kingdom** (300 4th Ave. S., 843/626-3471, www.family-kingdom.com, free admission, cost of rides varies) overlooking the Atlantic Ocean. It boasts several good old-school rides, such as the Sling Shot, the Yo-Yo, and everyone's favorite, the wooden Swamp Fox roller coaster with a crazy 110-foot free fall. The attached Water Park, though not a match to the one at Broadway at the Beach, is a lot of fun, with the requisite slides and a long "lazy river" floating ride.

As Family Kingdom's marketing is quick to point out, one of the big attractions here is the fact that you can look out over the beach itself. I think one of the best things is that there is no admission charge—you pay by the ride (although all-inclusive wristbands are available

starting at $27). This means parents and grandparents without the stomach for the rides don't have to pay through the nose just to chauffeur the little ones who do.

RIPLEY'S BELIEVE IT OR NOT!

Distinct in all but name from Ripley's Aquarium at Broadway at the Beach, this combo attraction down in the older area of Myrtle Beach—but very close to the brand-new Boardwalk—features several separate, though more or less adjacent, offerings from the venerable Ripley's franchise.

The **Ripley's Believe It or Not! Odditorium** (901 N. Ocean Blvd., 843/448-2331, www.ripleys.com, Sun.-Thurs. 10am-10pm, Fri.-Sat. 10am-11pm, $15 adults, $10 ages 6-11, free under age 6) is your typical Ripley's repository of strange artifacts from around the world, updated with video and computer graphics for the new generation.

Ripley's Haunted Adventure (915 N. Ocean Blvd., 843/448-2331, www.ripleys.com, Sun.-Thurs. noon-10pm, Fri.-Sat. noon-11pm, $15 adults, $10 ages 6-11, free under age 6) is a sort of scaled-down version of Disney's famous Haunted House ride, with live actors scaring you through three floors.

Ripley's Moving Theater (917 N. Ocean Blvd., 843/448-2331, www.ripleys.com, Sun.-Thurs. 10am-10pm, Fri.-Sat. 10am-11pm, $15 adults, $10 ages 6-11, free under age 6) is a combined ride and movie theater featuring two motion-oriented films screened on a self-contained human conveyor belt, with a sort of kinetic IMAX effect.

WACCATEE ZOOLOGICAL FARM

The closest thing to a bona fide zoo in Myrtle is **Waccatee Zoological Farm** (8500 Enterprise Rd., 843/650-8500, www.waccateezoo.com, daily 10am-5pm, $9 adults, $4 ages 1-12). A humble affair by comparison to the state's premier zoo in Columbia, Waccatee is a totally private venture on 500 acres of land about 15 minutes' drive out of town. There are buffalo, zebras, kangaroos, and emus, many of which the kids will enjoy feeding for a few bucks per bag.

Animal activists be forewarned: Many of the animals are kept in enclosed spaces, and there is a noticeable lack of professionally trained staff.

◖ OCEAN DRIVE BEACH

Less an actual place than a state of mind, the "OD" up in North Myrtle Beach is notable for its role in spawning one of America's great musical genres, beach music. Don't confuse beach music with the Beach Boys or Dick Dale—that's surf music. Beach music, simply put, is music to dance the shag to. Think the Drifters, the Platters, and the Swingin' Medallions.

To experience the OD, go to the intersection of Ocean Boulevard and Main Street and take in the vibe. There's still major shag action going on up here, specifically at several clubs specializing in the genre. If you don't want to shag, don't worry—this is still a charming, laid-back area that's a lot of fun simply to stroll around and enjoy a hot dog or ice cream cone.

CHERRY GROVE PIER

One of the few grand old pavilions left on the Southeast coast, North Myrtle's **Cherry Grove Pier** (3500 N. Ocean Blvd., 843/249-1625, www.cherrygrovepier.com, Sun.-Thurs. 6am-midnight, Fri.-Sat. 6am-2am, free) was built in the 1950s. Despite remodeling in the late 1990s, it still retains that nostalgic feel, with anglers casting into the waters and kids eating ice cream cones. There's a neat two-story observation deck, and on a clear day you can see North Carolina.

Unusually, this is a privately owned pier. It's particularly popular with anglers, who have their state licensing needs covered by the pier. Get bait or rent a fishing rod ($20 per day plus refundable $50 deposit) at the **Tackle and Gift Shop** (843/249-1625). They'll also sell you a crab net to cast off the pier ($6, licenses and permits included).

LA BELLE AMIE VINEYARD

The only vineyard on the Strand, the peaceful and scenic **La Belle Amie Vineyard** (1120 St. Joseph Rd., 843/399-9463, www.labelleamie.com, Mon.-Sat. 10am-6pm) in Little River is owned by two sisters, Vicki Weigle and June Bayman, who are descended from this old tobacco plantation's owners (in French the vineyard's name means "beautiful friend," but it's also a play on the family name, Bellamy). You can purchase wine for your own enjoyment or for gifts, or you can just visit the tasting room (Mon.-Sat. 10am-5:30pm), where a mere $5 pp gets you a sampling of any five wines. Coupons for discounted purchase are available at the tasting room.

TOURS

The number of tours offered in Myrtle Beach is nothing compared to Charleston, this being much more of a "doing" place than a "seeing" place. The most fun and comprehensive tour in the area is **Coastal Safari Jeep Tours** (843/497-5330, www.carolinasafari.com, $38 adults, $20 children), which takes you on a guided tour in a super-size jeep (holding 12-14 people). You'll go well off the commercial path to see such sights on the Waccamaw Neck as old plantations, Civil War sites, and slave cabins as well as hear lots of ghost stories. They'll pick you up at most area hotels.

Entertainment and Events

NIGHTLIFE

Any discussion of Myrtle Beach nightlife must begin with a nod to **The Bowery** (110 9th Ave. N., 843/626-3445, www.thebowerybar.com, daily 11am-2am), a country-and-western and Southern-rock spot right off the beach, which has survived several hurricanes since opening in 1944. Its roadhouse-style decor hasn't changed a whole lot since then, other than some cheesy marketing to play up its role in history as the place where the country band Alabama got its start playing for tips in 1973 under the name Wildcountry. They were still playing gigs here when their first hit, "Tennessee River," hit the charts in 1980.

Bands usually crank up here around 9pm, and there is a nominal cover charge. There's only one type of draft beer served at The Bowery, at $2.50 per mug, and there is no real dance floor to speak of. If the proud display of Confederate flags doesn't bother you, it's usually a lot of fun.

Once overlooking the now-razed historic Myrtle Beach Pavilion, as of this writing The Bowery is fronted by an empty lot that will presumably be filled by a more modern attraction; if history is any guide, The Bowery will probably outlive it as well. Right next door is The Bowery's "sister bar," **Duffy's** (110 9th Ave. N., 843/626-3445, daily 11am-2am), owned by the same folks and with a similarly down-home vibe, except without the live music.

For a more upscale if definitely less personal and unique experience, Broadway at the Beach hosts the high-profile (some say overrated) national clubs **Planet Hollywood** (2915 Hollywood Dr., 843/448-7827, www.planethollywood.com, hours vary by season) and the **Hard Rock Café** (1322 Celebrity Circle,

The Bowery

© JIM MOREKIS

843/946-0007, www.hardrock.com, Mon.-Sun. 11am-midnight).

You don't have to be a Parrothead to enjoy **Jimmy Buffett's Margaritaville** (1114 Celebrity Circle, 843/448-5455, www.margaritaville.com, daily 11am-midnight) at Broadway at the Beach, actually a pretty enjoyable experience considering it's a national chain. The eponymous margaritas are, of course, the beverage highlight, but they also serve Jimmy's signature LandShark Lager on tap for beer lovers.

In addition to its attached live performance space, the **House of Blues** (4640 U.S. 17, 843/272-3000, www.hob.com) at Barefoot Landing features a hopping bar in its dining area, situated amid a plethora of folk art reminiscent of the Mississippi Delta. Most nights feature live entertainment on a small stage starting at about 10pm.

SHAG DANCING

North Myrtle Beach is the nexus of that Carolina-based dance known as the shag. There are several clubs in town that have made a name for themselves as the unofficial "shag clubs" of South Carolina. The two main ones are **Duck's** (229 Main St., 843/249-3858, www.ducksatoceandrive.com) and **Fat Harold's** (210 Main St., 843/249-5779, www.fatharolds.com). There's also **The Pirate's Cove** (205 Main St., 843/249-8942).

Another fondly regarded spot is the **OD Pavilion** (91 S. Ocean Blvd., 843/280-0715), a.k.a. the Sunset Grill or "Pam's Palace," on the same site as the old Roberts Pavilion that was destroyed by 1954's Hurricane Hazel. Legend has it this was where the shag was born. Also in North Myrtle, the **Ocean Drive Beach Club** (100 S. Ocean Blvd., 843/249-6460), a.k.a. "the OD Lounge," inside the Ocean Drive Beach and Golf Resort, specializes in shag dancing most days after 4pm. The resort is a focal point of local shag conventions and is even home to the **Shaggers Hall of Fame.** Also inside the Ocean Drive Resort is another popular shag club, **The Spanish Galleon** (100 N. Ocean Blvd., 843/249-1047), a.k.a. "The Galleon."

Key local shag events, which are quite well attended, include the **National Shag Dance Championships** (www.shagnationals.com, Jan.-Mar.), the **Spring Safari** (www.shagdance.com, Apr.), and the **Fall Migration** (www.shagdance.com, mid-Sept.).

THE ARTS
(Carolina Opry

Nothing can duplicate the experience of the Grand Ole Opry in Nashville, but don't snicker at Myrtle's **Carolina Opry** (8901-A Business U.S. 17, 800/843-6779, www.thecarolinaopry.com, showtimes and ticket prices vary). Since 1986 this well-respected stage show, begun by legendary promoter Calvin Gilmore, has packed 'em in at the Grand Strand. It is a hoot for country music fans and city slickers alike.

The main focus is the regular Opry show, done in the classic, free-wheeling, fast-moving variety format known to generations of old-school country fans from the original Opry. Some of the humor is corny, and the brief but open displays of patriotic and faith-based music aren't necessarily for everyone and might be slightly confusing given the emphasis on sexy and accomplished female dancers. But there's no arguing the high energy and vocal and instrumental abilities of these very professional singers, instrumentalists, and dancers, who gamely take on hits through the generations ranging from bluegrass to Motown, pop, and modern country.

The Carolina Opry augments its regular music, comedy, and dance show with a seasonal Christmas special, which is extremely popular and sells out even faster than the regular shows, often six or more months in advance. There is generally one other bit of specialty programming each year, such as the recent *Good Vibrations* pop hits revue.

The 2,200-seat Carolina Opry theater, while no match for Nashville's classic Ryman Auditorium, is pretty classy for a venue only built in 1992.

Legends in Concert

Way down in Surfside Beach, where the big

MYRTLE BEACH

MYRTLE BEACH

THE STORY OF THE SHAG

© JIM MOREKIS

Judy's House of Oldies

In South Carolina, the shag is neither a type of rug nor what Austin Powers does in his spare time. It's a dance—a smooth, laid-back, happy dance done to that equally smooth, laid-back, happy kind of rhythm-and-blues called beach music (not to be confused with surf music such as the Beach Boys). The boys twirl the girls while their feet kick and slide around with a minimum of upper-body movement—the better to stay cool in the Carolina heat.

Descended from the Charleston, another indigenous Palmetto State dance, the shag originated on the Strand sometime in the 1930s, when the popular Collegiate Shag was slowed down to the subgenre now called the Carolina Shag. While shag scholars differ as to the exact spawning ground, there's a consensus that North Myrtle Beach's Ocean Drive, or "OD" in local patois, became the home of the modern shag sometime in the mid-1940s.

Legend has it that the real shag was born when white teenagers, "jumping the Jim Crow rope" by watching dancers at black nightclubs in the segregated South, brought those moves back to the beach and added their own twists.

Indeed, while the shag has always been primarily practiced by white people, many of the leading beach music bands were (and still are) African American.

By the mid-late 1950s, the shag, often called simply "the basic" or "the fas' dance," was all the rage with the Strand's young people, who gathered at beachfront pavilions and in local juke joints called beach clubs, courting each other to the sounds of early beach music greats like the Drifters, the Clovers, and Maurice Williams and the Zodiacs. This is the time period most fondly remembered by today's shaggers, a time of penny loafers (no socks!), poodle skirts, and 45-rpm records, when the sea breeze was the only air-conditioning.

The shag is practiced today by a graying but devoted cadre of older fans, with a vanguard of younger practitioners keeping the art form alive. A coterie of North Myrtle clubs specializes in the dance, while the area hosts several large-scale gatherings of shag aficionados each year.

To immerse yourself in shag culture, head on up to Ocean Drive Beach in North Myrtle at the intersection of Ocean Boulevard and Main Street and look down at the platters in the sidewalk marking the **Shaggers Walk of Fame.** Walk a couple of blocks up to the corner of Main Street and Hillside Drive and visit the mecca of beach music stores, **Judy's House of Oldies** (300 Main St., 843/249-8649, www.judyshouseofoldies.com, Mon.-Sat. 9am-6pm). They also sell instructional DVDs.

To get a taste of the dance itself, stop by the **OD Pavilion** (91 S. Ocean Blvd., 843/280-0715), **Duck's** (229 Main St., 843/249-3858, www.ducksatoceandrive.com), or **Fat Harolds** (210 Main St., 843/249-5779, www.fatharolds.com), or visit **The Spanish Galleon** (100 N. Ocean Blvd., 843/249-1047) inside the Ocean Drive Beach Resort. If you're interested, don't be shy; shaggers are notoriously gregarious and eager to show off their stock-in-trade. It's easy to learn, it's family-friendly, and there will be no shortage of pleasant young-at-heart shaggers around who will be happy to teach you the steps.

© JIM MOREKIS

MYRTLE BEACH

Carolina Opry

buildup on the Strand begins, you'll find **Legends in Concert** (301 Business U.S. 17, 843/238-7827, www.legendsinconcert.com, prices vary), a popular rotating show of celebrity impersonators from Elvis to Barbra Streisand. As cheesy as that sounds, the resemblances can be quite uncanny, and the shows are quite entertaining.

House of Blues

Besides being a great place for dinner, on the other side of the restaurant is the stage for the **House of Blues** (4640 U.S. 17 S., 843/272-3000, www.hob.com, prices vary) at Barefoot Landing in North Myrtle Beach. They bring some pretty happening names in R&B, straight blues, and rock-and-roll to this fun venue dedicated to preserving old-school music and live performance.

Medieval Times

Oh, come on—what's not to like about bountiful feasts, juggling jesters, skillful falconers, fetching maidens, and brave jousting knights? At **Medieval Times** (2904 Fantasy Way, 843/236-4635, www.medievaltimes. com, $51 adults, $31 under age 13) you'll get all that and more. The kitsch quotient is high at this Renaissance Faire on steroids, a live-action story line featuring plenty of stage combat, music, and a steady stream of culinary items for your enjoyment (and yes, there's a full bar for those of drinking age). But there's an honest-to-goodness educational element as well: You'll be eating everything with your hands—no utensils in the 11th century—and most of the action and history is roughly authentic. The price may seem high at first glance, but keep in mind you're getting a hearty full dinner plus a two-hour stage show.

Pirate's Voyage

Sharing a parking lot with the Carolina Opry is **Pirate's Voyage** (8901-B N. Kings Hwy., 843/497-9700, www.piratesvoyage.com, $42 adults, $22 ages 4-11), the newest entertainment attraction to hit Myrtle Beach. Affiliated with Dolly Parton's entertainment empire—her

© JIM MOREKIS

MYRTLE BEACH

House of Blues at Barefoot Landing

"Dixie Stampede" originally occupied this building—Pirate's Voyage takes you on a rollicking two-hour trip into the world of buccaneers, with fighting, lost treasure, dancing, acrobatics, mermaids, and assorted high-seas drama, all with photographers on hand to document your experience . . . for a price, me hearties. Like Medieval Times, this is essentially dinner theater with three shows a day in the high season of late summer, offering a variety of suitably swashbuckling menu items like chicken, pork, and fried shrimp. OK, so you don't come here for the food.

The Alabama Theatre

The **Alabama Theatre** (4750 U.S. 17, 843/272-5758, www.alabama-theatre.com, ticket prices vary) at Barefoot Landing in North Myrtle Beach focuses on the long-running song-and-dance revue *One: The Show* as well as big-name acts who may be past their prime but are still able to fill seats, such as the Oakridge Boys, George Jones, Kenny Rogers, and, of course, the eponymous troubadours Alabama, who got

their big break while playing at Myrtle Beach. It's not all country, though—Motown and beach music acts like the Temptations and the Platters are often featured as well. As with the Carolina Opry, Barefoot Landing has its own Christmas special, and as with the Opry's offering, this one sells out well in advance.

Palace Theatre

The **Palace Theatre** (1420 Celebrity Circle, 800/905-4228, www.palacetheatremyrtlebeach.com, ticket prices vary) at Broadway at the Beach offers a variety of toned-down Vegas-style entertainment. The most recent show was *Le Grande Cirque,* a family-friendly version of the kind of show made famous by Cirque du Soleil.

CINEMA

At Broadway on the Beach, there's a multiplex, Carmike's **Broadway Cinema 16** (843/445-1600, www.carmike.com). Other movie theaters include the **Cinemark** (2100 Coastal Grand Circle, 843/839-3221, www.cinemark.com) at the Coastal Grand Mall and the massive new **Grand 14 at the Market Common** (4002 Deville St., 843/282-0550) at the multiuse Market Common, actually a repurposed Air Force base.

FESTIVALS AND EVENTS

Interestingly, most events in Myrtle Beach don't happen during the three-month high season of June-August, mostly because it's so darn hot that all anyone wants to do is get in the water.

Winter

The Grand Strand is the birthplace of the dance called the shag, and each winter for the last 25 years the **National Shag Dance Championships** (2000 N. Kings Hwy., 843/497-7369, www.shagnationals.com, from $15 per night) have been the pinnacle of the art form. Beginning with preliminaries in January, contestants in five age ranges compete for a variety of awards, culminating in the finals the first week in March. The level of professionalism might amaze you—for such a lazy-looking dance, these are serious competitors.

Spring

You might not automatically associate our colder neighbor to the north with Myrtle Beach, but **Canadian American Days** (various venues, www.myrtlebeachinfo.com, free), or "Can Am," brings tens of thousands of visitors of both nationalities to sites all over the Strand each March to enjoy a variety of musical and cultural events. Always on top of marketing opportunities, the Myrtle Beach Chamber of Commerce makes sure this happens during Ontario's spring holidays to ensure maximum north-of-the-border attendance. While most of the events have little or nothing to do with Canada itself, this is basically a great excuse for Canucks to get some Carolina sunshine.

The **Spring Games and Kite Flying Contest** (843/448-7881, free) brings an exciting array of airborne craft to the Strand in front of Broadway on the Beach on an April weekend as the springtime winds peak.

Also in April is the area's second-largest shag event, the **Society of Stranders Spring Safari** (www.shagdance.com). Several clubs in North Myrtle Beach participate in hosting shag dancers from all over for a week of, well, shagging.

The biggest single event in Myrtle Beach happens in May with the **Spring Bike Rally** (various venues, www.myrtlebeachbikeweek.com, free), always known simply as "Bike Week." In this nearly 70-year-old event, over 250,000 Harley-Davidson riders and their entourages gather to cruise around the place,

MOTORCYCLE MADNESS

Growling engines? Spinning tires? Patriotic colors? Polished chrome? Bikini car washes? Erotic bull-riding contests? That is the spectacle known as Myrtle Beach Bike Week, one of the largest gatherings of Harley-Davidson enthusiasts on the East Coast and one of the oldest, at about 65 years.

The event has historically happened each May on the weekend before Memorial Day weekend, bringing over 250,000 motorcyclists and their entourages to town for 10 days of riding, bragging, and carousing. South Carolina's lack of a helmet law is a particular draw to these freedom-cherishing motorcyclists. A few days later, on Memorial Day weekend, there's another bike rally, this one simply called Black Bike Week. Nearly as large as the regular Bike Week, the focus is on African American riders and their machines.

Contrary to stereotype, there's not much of an increase in crime during either Bike Week. Regardless, they are widely known as a particularly bad time to bring families to the area, and therein lies the controversy. Joining other municipalities around the nation in discouraging motorcycle rallies, the city of Myrtle Beach has enacted tough measures to force the bike rallies to leave town and make the area more family-friendly during that time. Most controversial among recent measures was a municipal helmet law, enforceable only within Myrtle Beach city limits, that was later struck down by the South Carolina Supreme Court. Other, still-standing measures include stringent noise ordinances designed to include the roaring, rattling tailpipes of pretty much every Harley ever made. The separate municipality of North Myrtle Beach, however, has made it clear that bikers are welcome there even if they're non grata a few miles to the south.

As of now, it seems that the rallies will remain on the Strand rather than gun their collective throttle and head elsewhere, as they occasionally threaten to do when relations with local municipalities and police departments get too tense. The upshot for the nonmotorcyclist visitor? Bikers are somewhat less of a factor than in years past, and certainly local police are taking them more seriously. But the time around Memorial Day is still as crowded as ever.

admire each other's custom rides, and generally party their patooties off. While the typical Harley dude these days is getting on in years and is probably a mild-mannered store manager in regular life, young or old they all do their best to let their hair down at this festive event. Dozens of related events go on throughout the week at venues all over the Strand, from tough-man contests to "foxy boxing" matches to wet T-shirt contests. You get the picture—it's not for the politically correct or for young children.

Summer

Right after the Spring Bike Rally is the **Atlantic Beach Bikefest** (various venues), on Memorial Day weekend, much more commonly referred to as "Black Bike Week." This event started in the 1980s and is spiritually based in Atlantic Beach, formerly the area's "black beach" during the days of segregation. It sees over 200,000 African American motorcycle enthusiasts gather in Myrtle Beach for a similar menu of partying, bikini contests, cruising, and the like. While the existence of separate events often reminds some people of the state's unfortunate history of segregation, supporters of both Bike Week and Black Bike Week insist it's not a big deal, and that bikers of either race are welcome at either event.

Kicking off with a festive parade, the 50-year-old **Sun Fun Festival** (various venues, www.grandstrandevents.com), generally held the weekend after Memorial Day weekend,

signals the real beginning of the summer season with bikini contests, Jet Ski races, parades, air shows, and concerts galore.

The **City of Myrtle Beach Independence Day Celebration** (www.cityofmyrtlebeach.com, free) each July 4 weekend is when the largest number of visitors is in Myrtle Beach. It's fun, it's hot, there's fireworks aplenty, and boy, is it crowded.

Fall

For a week in mid-September, North Myrtle Beach hosts one of the world's largest shag dancing celebrations, the **Society of Stranders Fall Migration** (www.shagdance.com, free). Head up to the intersection of Ocean Drive and Main Street to hear the sounds of this unique genre, and party with the shaggers at various local clubs. If you don't know the steps, don't worry—instructors are usually on hand.

There's another, smaller Harley riders' rally the first week in October, the **Fall Motorcycle Rally** (various venues, www.myrtlebeachbikeweek.com, free).

Thanksgiving Day weekend, when the beaches are much less crowded and the hotels much cheaper, is the **South Carolina Bluegrass Festival** (2101 N. Oak St., 706/864-7203, www.aandabluegrass.com, $30 adults, $20 ages 6-13, free under age 6), a delightful and well-attended event at the Myrtle Beach Convention Center, celebrating the Appalachian music tradition in a coastal setting with some of the biggest names in the genre.

Shopping

Shopping on the Grand Strand is strongly destination-oriented. You tend to find shops of similar price points and merchandise types clustered together in convenient locations: Upscale shops are in one place and discount and outlet stores in another. Here's a rundown of the main retail areas on the Strand with some of the standout shops.

BROADWAY AT THE BEACH

The sprawling **Broadway at the Beach** (U.S. 17 Bypass and 21st Ave. N., www.broadwayatthebeach.com, hours vary) complex has scads of stores, some of which are quite interesting and rise well beyond tourist schlock. There are maps and directories of the site available at various kiosks around the area.

One of my favorite shops is **Retroactive** (843/916-1218, www.shopretroactive.com), a shop specializing in '70s and '80s styles and kitsch, with some of the best (and wittiest) pop-culture T-shirts I've seen. The owners are frank about their continuing obsession with '80s hair bands. Another awesome T-shirt and trinket shop that the kids and teens will particularly enjoy is **Stupid Factory** (843/448-1100). There are lots of mediocre sports apparel stores out there, but **Sports Fanatics** (843/445-2585) has an amazing collection of jerseys, shirts, and lids, primarily focused on pro teams. The kids—and those with a sweet tooth—will go crazy in the aptly named **It'SUGAR** (843/916-1300, www.itsugar.com), a store dedicated to just about any kind of candy and candy-themed merchandise you can think of, from modern brands to retro favorites. If the packaged or bulk varieties don't float your boat, you can design your own massive chocolate bar. And, of course, this being Myrtle Beach, there's a **Harley Davidson** (843/293-5555) gift store with Hog-oriented merch galore.

The bottom line on Broadway at the Beach, though, is that it's made for walking around and browsing. Just bring your walking shoes—the place is huge—and keep in mind that there's not a lot of shade.

BAREFOOT LANDING

There are over 100 shops at **Barefoot Landing** (4898 U.S. 17 S., 843/272-8349, www.bfland-ing.com, hours vary) in North Myrtle Beach—as well as one cool old-fashioned carousel—but perhaps the most unique spot is **T.I.G.E.R.S. Preservation Station** (843/361-4552, www.tigerfriends.com, hours vary), where you get the opportunity to have your picture taken with a live tiger or lion cub. This is the fund-raising arm of a local organization for conservation of the big cats as well as gorillas and monkeys, so the service isn't cheap. Portraits begin at about $60 to pose with a single critter and go up from there depending on the number of animals you want to pose with. However, you don't pay per person, so the whole family can get in the shot for the same price as a child. It may sound like a lot of money, but this is truly a once-in-a-life-time experience. An attendant takes the animal of your choice out of a spacious holding area, places it on your lap, and a photographer takes the shot. Sometimes you can hold a milk bottle to the cub's mouth. If you don't want to spring for a photo, you can just watch the frolicking (or more often, slumbering) cubs up close from behind a transparent wall. They're unbelievably cute, as you can imagine.

Just relocated to the Strand from their grape yards in Chester, South Carolina, is **Carolina Vineyards Winery** (843/361-9181, www.caro-linavineyards.com). Buy wine as a gift, or taste any seven of their labels for only $3.

There are magic shops, and then there are *magic shops*. **Conley's House of Magic** (843/272-4227, http://conleyshouseofmagic. com) is definitely the latter. Packed in this relatively small space is just about every legendary trick and trick deck known to the magician's art, along with a cool variety of magic books teaching you, in deadly serious fashion, the innermost secrets of the trade. **Toys & Co.** (843/663-0748, www.toysandco.com) carries a wide range of toys and games, with an emphasis on way-cool European-style brands you won't see at the local Wal-Mart.

THE MARKET COMMON

One of the most hotly anticipated and cutting-edge things to hit Myrtle Beach in years, **The Market Common** (4017 Deville St., www.mar-ketcommonmb.com, hours vary) is an ambi-tious residential-retail mixed-use development opened for business on the site of the decom-missioned Myrtle Beach Air Force Base. While its location near the Myrtle Beach International Airport means it's not exactly amid the sun-and-fun action (possibly a good thing, depend-ing on the season), the very pedestrian-friendly development style and tasteful shops might provide a refreshing change of pace.

There are three dozen (and counting) stores, including Anthropologie, Williams-Sonoma, Copper Penny, Chico's, Brooks Brothers,

Fossil, Banana Republic, Barnes & Noble, and Jake and Company ("Life Is Good"). There are plenty of restaurants, including Ultimate California Pizza and P. F. Chang's, and a large multiplex movie theater.

For those interested in how the sprawling old base was closed in the 1990s and repurposed so completely, there's interpretive signage all around the pedestrian mall and along the roadways leading to it. At the Market Common's entrance is Warbird Park, a well-done veterans memorial featuring an Air Force A-10 attack aircraft, an F-100 Super Sabre, and a Corsair II.

MALLS

The premier mall in the area is **Coastal Grand Mall** (2000 Coastal Grand Circle, 843/839-9100, www.coastalgrand.com, Mon.-Sat. 10am-9pm, Sun. noon-6pm) at the U.S. 17 Bypass and U.S. 501. It's anchored by Belk, J. C. Penney, Sears, Dillard's, and Dick's Sporting Goods.

Your basic meat-and-potatoes mall, **Myrtle Beach Mall** (10177 N. Kings Hwy., 843/272-4040, http://shopmyrtlebeachmall.com, Mon.-Sat. 10am-9pm, Sun. noon-6pm) is anchored by Belk, J. C. Penney, and Bass Pro Shops.

DISCOUNT BEACHWEAR

Literally dozens of cavernous, tacky, deep-discount T-shirt-and-towel type places are spread up and down Kings Highway like mushrooms after a rain. The vast majority of them belong to one of several well-established chains: **Eagles Beachwear** (www.eaglesbeachwear.

net), **Whales** (www.whalesnauticalgifts.com), **Wing's Beachwear** (www.wingsbeachwear.com), and **Bargain Beachwear** (www.bargain-beachwear.com). These are the kinds of places to get assorted bric-a-brac and items for your beach visit. The quality isn't that bad, and the prices are uniformly low.

OUTLET MALLS

There are two massive **Tanger Outlets** (www.tangeroutlet.com) at Myrtle Beach: **Tanger Outlet North** (10835 Kings Rd., 843/449-0491), off Kings Road/U.S. 17, and **Tanger Outlet South** (4635 Factory Stores Blvd., 843/236-5100), off U.S. 501. Both offer over 100 factory outlet stores of almost every imaginable segment, from Fossil to Disney, OshKosh B'Gosh to Timberland. Full food courts are available, and many folks easily spend an entire day here.

For years, busloads of hard-core shoppers from throughout the South have taken organized trips to the Grand Strand specifically to shop at **Waccamaw Factory Shoppes** (3071 Waccamaw Blvd., 843/236-8200). Their passion hasn't abated, as new generations of shopaholics get the fever to come here and browse the often deeply discounted offerings at row after row of outlet stores. There are actually two locations, the Factory Shoppes themselves and the nearby **Waccamaw Pottery** (3200 Pottery Dr., 843/236-6152). Bring your walking shoes (or buy some new ones at one of the many shoe stores), but don't worry about getting from one mall to the other—there's a free shuttle.

Sports and Recreation

Myrtle Beach's middle name might as well be recreation. While some of the local variety tends toward overkill—I personally loathe Jet Skis, for example—there's no denying that if it involves outdoor activity, it's probably offered here. For general info, visit www.grandstrandevents.com. For municipal recreation info, visit www.cityofmyrtlebeach.com.

ON THE WATER
Beaches

The center of activity is on the Strand itself: miles of user-friendly beaches. They're not the most beautiful in the world, but they're nice enough, and access is certainly no problem. In Myrtle Beach and North Myrtle Beach, you'll find clearly designated public access points off

Ocean Boulevard, some with parking and some without. Both municipalities run well-marked public parking lots at various points, some of which are free during the off-season.

Dog owners will be pleased to know that May 15-September 15, dogs are allowed on the beach before 9am and after 5pm. September 15-May 15, dogs are allowed on the beach at any time of day.

Restrict your swimming to within 150 feet of shore. Surfside Beach to the south is a no-smoking beach with access points at 16th Avenue North, 6th Avenue North, 3rd Avenue North, Surfside Pier, 3rd Avenue South, 4th Avenue South, 13th Avenue South, and Melody Lane.

Surfing

There's a steady, if low-key, surf scene in Myrtle Beach despite the fact that the surfing is not really that good and the sport is restricted to certain areas of the beach during the busy summer season. The rules are a little complicated. In Myrtle Beach proper, surfing is only allowed April 15-September 15 daily 10am-5pm in the following zones:

- 29th Avenue South to the southern city limits

- 37th Avenue North to 47th Avenue North

- 62nd Avenue North to 68th Avenue North

- 82nd Avenue North to northern city limits

Up in North Myrtle Beach, surfers must stay in the following zones May 15-September 15 daily 9am-4pm:

- Cherry Grove Pier

- 6th Avenue North

- 13th Avenue South

- 28th Avenue South

- 38th Avenue South

Down at Surfside Beach, surfing is restricted to the following zones, year-round daily 10am-5pm:

- 12th Avenue North to 14th Avenue North

- Melody Lane to 13th Avenue South

The oldest surf shop in the area, south of Myrtle in Garden City Beach, is the **Village Surf Shoppe** (500 Atlantic Ave., 843/651-6396, www.villagesurf.com), which has catered to the Strand's growing surf scene since 1969. Nearly as old is the **Surf City Surf Shop** (1758 U.S. 17 S., 843/272-1090; 3001 N. Kings Hwy., 843/626-5412, www.surfcitysurfshop.com) franchise in Myrtle proper.

Diving

Diving is popular on the Strand. As with fishing, many trips depart from Little River just above North Myrtle Beach. Offshore features include many historic wrecks, including the post-Civil War wreck of the USS *Sherman* offshore of Little River, and artificial reefs such as the famed "Barracuda Alley," teeming with marine life, off Myrtle Beach.

Coastal Scuba (1901 U.S. 17 S., 843/361-3323, www.coastalscuba.com) in North Myrtle is a large operator, offering several different dive tours.

Parasailing, Windsurfing, and Jet Skis

Ocean Watersports (405 S. Ocean Blvd., 843/445-7777, www.parasailmyrtlebeach.com) takes groups of up to six people on well-supervised, well-equipped parasailing adventures (about $50 pp), with tandem and triple flights available. Observers can go out on the boat for about $20. They also rent Jet Skis and offer "banana boat" rides ($15) in which a long—yes, banana-shaped—raft, straddled by several riders, is towed by a boat up and down the beach.

Downwind Watersports (2915 S. Ocean

MYRTLE BEACH

Blvd., 843/448-7245, www.downwindsails-myrtlebeach.com) has similar offerings, with the addition of good old-fashioned sailboat lessons and rentals ($16). Parasailing is about $65 pp single ride, banana boats are $16 for 20 minutes, and Jet Ski rentals about $100 per hour.

Farther up the Strand in North Myrtle, between Cherry Grove Beach and Little River, you'll find **Thomas Outdoors Watersports** (2200 Little River Neck Rd., 843/280-2448, www.mbjetski.com), which rents kayaks in addition to Jet Skis and pontoon boats. They offer several Jet Ski tours ($75-125), including a dolphin-watching trip, as well as all-day kayak rental ($45 pp).

Fishing

Most fishing on the Strand is saltwater, with charters, most based in Little River, taking anglers well into Atlantic waters. Tuna, wahoo, mackerel, and dolphin (not the mammal!) are big in the hot months, while snapper and grouper are caught year-round but are best in the colder months.

A good operator up in Little River is **Longway Fishing Charters** (843/249-7813, www.longwaycharters.com), which specializes in offshore fishing. Another in the same area is **Capt. Smiley's Inshore Fishing** (843/361-7445, www.captainsmileyfishingcharters.com). **Fish Hook Charters** (2200 Little River Neck Rd., 843/283-7692, www.fishhookcharters.com) takes a 34-foot boat out from North Myrtle Beach.

For surf fishing on the beach, you do not need a license of any type. All other types of fishing require a valid South Carolina fishing license, available for a nominal fee online (http://dnr.sc.gov) or at any tackle shop and most grocery stores.

Cruises

Except in the winter months, there are plenty of places to cruise in the Strand, from Little River down to Murrells Inlet, from the Waccamaw River to the Intracoastal Waterway. The **Great American Riverboat Company** (8496 Enterprise Rd., 843/650-6600, www.

mbriverboat.com) offers sightseeing and dinner cruises along the Intracoastal Waterway. **Island Song Charters** (4374 Landing Rd., 843/467-7088, www.sailingmyrtlebeach.com) out of Little River takes you on sunset and dolphin cruises on the 32-foot sailboat *Island Song*.

Up in North Myrtle, **Getaway Adventures** (843/663-1100, www.myrtlebeachboatcruises.com) specializes in dolphin tours. Also in North Myrtle, **Thomas Outdoors Watersports** (2200 Little River Neck Rd., 843/280-2448, www.mbjetski.com) runs dolphin cruises.

ON LAND
Golf

The Grand Strand in general, and Myrtle Beach in particular, is world golf central. There are over 120 courses in this comparatively small area, and if golfers can't find something they like here, they need to sell their clubs. While the number of truly great courses is few—the best courses are farther down the Strand near Pawleys Island—the quality overall is still quite high.

A great bonus is affordability. Partially because of dramatically increased competition due to the glut of courses, and partially because of savvy regional marketing, greens fees here are significantly lower than you might expect, in many cases under $100. For even more savings, finding a golf-lodging package deal in Myrtle Beach is like finding sand on the beach—almost too easy. Check with your hotel to see if they offer any golf packages. At any time of year, some good one-stop shops on the Internet are at www.mbn.com and www.myrtlebeachgolf.com.

Some highlights of area golf include the Davis Love III-designed course at **Barefoot Resort** (4980 Barefoot Resort Ridge Rd., 843/390-3200, www.barefootgolf.com, $105-185) in North Myrtle, maybe the best in the Strand outside Pawleys Island. Or would that be the Greg Norman course, or the Tom Fazio course, or the Pete Dye course, all also at Barefoot? You get the picture.

Also up near North Myrtle is a favorite with visitors and locals alike, the challenging **Glen**

Dornoch Golf Club (4840 Glen Dornoch Way, 800/717-8784, www.glensgolfgroup.com, from $100), on 260 beautiful acres. Affiliated with Glen Dornoch are the 27 holes at Little River's **Heather Glen** (4650 Heather Glen Way, 800/868-4536, www.glensgolfgroup.com, $130), which are divided into Red, White, and Blue courses. They combine for what's consistently rated one of the best public courses in the United States.

And no list of area golf is complete without a nod to **Myrtle Beach National** (4900 National Dr., 843/347-4298, www.mbn.com, from $80). With three distinct courses—King's North, West, and South Creek, with its South Carolina-shaped sand trap at hole 3—the National is one of the state's legendary courses, not to mention a heck of a deal.

Miniature Golf

Don't scoff—miniature golf, or "putt-putt" to an older generation, is a big deal in Myrtle Beach. If you thought there were a lot of regular golf courses here, the 50 miniature golf courses

will also blow your mind. Sadly, almost all of the classic old-school miniature golf courses are no more, victims of the demand for increased production values and modernized gimmick holes. But here are some of the standouts, including the best of the North Myrtle courses as well.

The most garishly wonderful course is the completely over-the-top **Mount Atlanticus Minotaur Goff** (707 N. Kings Hwy., 843/444-1008, www.mountatlanticus.com, $10 for 18 holes) down near the older section of Myrtle. And yes, that's how it's spelled—get it? Legend has it that this one course cost $3 million to build. Literally the stuff of dreams—or maybe hallucinations—this sprawling course mixes the mythological with the nautical to wonderful effect. You don't actually encounter the Minotaur until the bonus 19th hole, a fiendish water trap. If you get a hole in one, you get free golf here for life.

Hawaiian Rumble (3210 U.S. 17, 843/458-2585, www.prominigolf.com) in North Myrtle is not only a heck of a fun, attractive course,

© JIM MOREKIS

Mount Atlanticus Minotaur Goff

MYRTLE BEACH

it's also the headquarters of the official training center for the U.S. Professional Miniature Golf Association (the folks who generally get a hole in one on every hole). The Rumble's sister course is **Hawaiian Village** (4205 U.S. 17, 843/361-9629, www.prominigolf.com) in North Myrtle, which is also the home of serious professional miniature golf competitions.

For a bit of retro action, try **Rainbow Falls** (9550 Kings Hwy., 843/497-2557). It's not as garish as some of the newer courses, but fans of old-school putt-putt will love it.

While at Broadway at the Beach, you might want to try the popular medieval-themed **Dragon's Lair** (1197 Celebrity Circle, 843/913-9301, hours vary by season). Yep, it has a 30-foot fire-breathing dragon, Sir Alfred, that you have to make your way around. While the dinosaur craze has cooled somewhat, the golf at **Jurassic Golf** (445 29th Ave., 843/448-2116), festooned with dozens of velociraptors and the like, certainly has stayed hot. There is a similarly themed site in North Myrtle, the new **Dinosaur Adventure** (700 7th Ave., 843/272-8041).

Tennis

There are over 200 tennis courts in the Myrtle Beach area. The main municipal site is the **Myrtle Beach Tennis Center** (3302 Robert Grissom Pkwy., 843/918-2440, www.myrtlebeachtennis.com, $2 pp per hour), which has 10 courts, 8 of them lighted. The city also runs six lighted courts at **Midway Park** (U.S. 17 and 19th Ave. S.).

The privately owned **Kingston Plantation** (843/497-2444, www.kingstonplantation.com) specializes in tennis vacations, and you don't even have to be a guest. They have a pro on staff and offer lessons. Down in Pawleys Island, the **Litchfield Beach and Golf Resort** (14276 Ocean Hwy., 866/538-0187, www.litchfieldbeach.com) has two dozen nice courts.

Cycling

In Myrtle Beach, when they say "biker," they mean a Harley dude. Bicycling—or safe bicycling, anyway—is largely limited to fat-tire riding along the beach and easy pedaling through the quiet residential neighborhoods near Little River. There is a bike lane on North Ocean Boulevard from about 29th Avenue North to about 82nd Avenue North. Riding on the sidewalk is strictly prohibited.

As for bike rentals, a good operator is **Beach Bike Shop** (711 Broadway St., 843/448-5335, www.beachbikeshop.com). In North Myrtle, try **Wheel Fun Rentals** (91 S. Ocean Blvd., 843/280-7900, www.wheelfunrentals.com).

Horseback Riding

A horse ride along the surf is a nearly iconic image of South Carolina, combining two of the state's chief pursuits: equestrian sports and hanging out on the beach. A great way to enjoy a horseback ride along the Grand Strand without having to bring your own equine is to check out **Horseback Riding of Myrtle Beach** (843/294-1712, www.myrtlebeachhorserides.com). They offer a variety of group rides, each with a guide, going to nature-preserve or beach locales. While they'll take you out any day of the week, advance reservations are required. Ninety minutes on a nature preserve costs about $50 pp, while a 90-minute ride on the beach is about $75 pp.

You can go horseback riding on Myrtle Beach from the third Saturday in November until the end of February, with these conditions: You must access the beach from Myrtle Beach State Park, you cannot ride over sand dunes in any way, and you must clean up after your horse.

SPECTATOR SPORTS

Playing April-early September in a large new stadium near Broadway at the Beach are the **Myrtle Beach Pelicans** (1251 21st Ave. N., 843/918-6000, www.myrtlebeachpelicans.com, $8-11), a single-A affiliate of the Texas Rangers.

NASCAR fans already know of the **Myrtle Beach Speedway** (455 Hospitality Lane, www.myrtlebeachspeedway.com, $12, free under age 10) off U.S. 501, one of the more vintage tracks in the country, dating back to 1958 (it was actually a dirt track well into the 1970s). Currently the main draws are the NASCAR Whelen All-American Series races (Apr.-Nov. Sat. 7:30pm).

Other spectator sports in the area tend to revolve around the Chanticleer teams of **Coastal Carolina University** (132 Chanticleer Dr. W.,

843/347-8499, www.goccusports.com) just inland from Myrtle Beach in Conway. They play football in the Big South Conference. By the way, *chanticleer* is an old name for a rooster, and in this case is a self-conscious derivative of the mascot of the University of South Carolina, the gamecock.

Accommodations

There is no dearth of lodging in the Myrtle Beach area, from the typical high-rise "resorts" (think condos on steroids) to chain hotels, vacation villas, house rentals, and camping. Because of the plethora of options, prices are generally reasonable, and competition to provide more and more on-site amenities—free breakfasts, "lazy river" pools, washers and dryers, hot tubs, poolside grills, and so on—has only increased. You are the beneficiary, so you might as well take advantage of it.

Note that the stated price range may be very broad because so many Myrtle Beach lodgings offer several room options, from one-bed guest rooms to full three-bedroom suites. Here are a few general tips to consider when booking a room:

- The larger suites are generally "condo apartments," meaning they're privately owned. While they're usually immaculately clean for your arrival, it means that housekeeping is minimal and you won't get lots of complimentary goodies whenever you call the front desk.

- The entire Myrtle Beach area is undergoing growth, and that includes the accommodations. This means that many properties have older sections and newer ones. Ask beforehand which section you're being booked in.

- Check www.myrtlebeachhotels.com for last-minute deals and specials at 11 well-run local resorts.

- By the end of September, prices drop dramatically.

- Almost all area lodgings, especially the high-rises, feature on-site pools galore; lounge chairs and tables are at a premium and go very quickly during high season when the sun's out.

- Always keep in mind that summer is the high season here, unlike the rest of South Carolina, and guest rooms, especially at beachfront places, get snapped up very early.

UNDER $150

For 75 years, **❰ Driftwood on the Oceanfront** (1600 N. Ocean Blvd., 843/448-1544, www.driftwoodlodge.com, $100-120) has been a favorite place to stay. Upgraded over the years, but not *too* upgraded, this low five-story 90-room complex is family-owned and takes pride in delivering personalized service that is simply impossible to attain in the larger high-rises nearby. As you'd expect, the guest rooms and suites are a bit on the small side by modern Myrtle Beach standards—with none of the increasingly popular three-bedroom suites available—but most everyone is impressed by the value.

Probably the best-regarded bed-and-breakfast in Myrtle Beach (yes, there are a precious few) is the **❰ Serendipity Inn** (407 71st Ave. N., 843/449-5268, www.serendipityinn.com, $90-150). A short walk from the beach but sometimes seemingly light years away from the typical Myrtle sprawl, this 15-room gem features a simple but elegant pool, an attractive courtyard, and sumptuous guest rooms. The full breakfast is simple but hearty. There's free Wi-Fi throughout the property.

If you're looking for a basic, inexpensive, one-bed hotel experience on the beach, ask for a room at the new oceanfront section of the **Best Western Grand Strand Inn and Suites** (1804 S. Ocean Blvd., 843/448-1461, $80-140), a smallish but clean and attentively run chain hotel. The property's other buildings are significantly older and are located across busy Ocean Boulevard, and the walk across the street to the beach can be difficult, especially if you have small kids. That said, this is a great value and a quality property.

If water park-style entertainment is your thing, try **Dunes Village Resort** (5200 N. Ocean Blvd., 877/828-2237, www.dunesvillage.com, $140-300), also one of the better values in Myrtle. Its huge indoor water park has copious waterslides, including several for adults, and various other aquatic diversions. The buildings themselves—the property comprises two high-rise towers—are new and well-equipped, although since this is a time-share-style property, housekeeping is minimal.

$150-300

My favorite place to stay at Myrtle Beach is the ◖ **Island Vista Oceanfront Resort** (6000 N. Ocean Blvd., 888/733-7581, www.islandvista.com). While not the flashiest or heaviest in amenities by any means, Island Vista's location in a quiet residential area overlooking a mile of the Strand's best and least-traveled beach makes it a standout alternative to the often crowded and logistically challenging environment you'll find in the more built-up high-rise blocks farther south on the beach. In the high season you'll be paying about $300 for a one-bedroom suite, but the prices on the spacious and very well-equipped two- and three-bedroom suites are competitive. They have the usual multiple-pool option, including an indoor heated pool area. A big plus is the fact that the in-house fine-dining restaurant, the **Cypress Room,** is a definite cut above most area hotel kitchens.

Consistently one of the best-regarded properties in Myrtle proper, the **Hampton Inn & Suites Oceanfront** (1803 S. Ocean Blvd., 843/946-6400, www.hamptoninnoceanfront.com, $169-259) has been made even better by a recent and thorough upgrade. This is a classic beachfront high-rise (not to be confused with the Hampton Inn at Broadway at the Beach), clean inside and out, with elegant tasteful guest rooms in various sizes (yes, flat-screen TVs were part of the makeover). Guest rooms range from typical one-bed, one-bath hotel-style rooms to larger condo-style suites with a fridge.

Situated more toward North Myrtle and hence closer to those attractions, the **Sea Watch Resort** (161 Sea Watch Blvd., $171-395) is a good choice for those who want the full-on condo high-rise Myrtle Beach experience but not necessarily the crowds that usually go with it. The guest rooms are clean and well-equipped, and by edging north a little on the beach, you can actually spread out and enjoy some breathing room.

An oldie but a goodie, the beachfront **Carolina Winds** (200 76th Ave. N., 843/497-5648, www.carolinawinds.com, $150-300) remains one of the better overall condo-style vacation spots in Myrtle. Unlike many of the newer monolithic high-rises, Carolina Winds almost has a retro Miami Beach feel to it, both in architecture and attitude. A two-night minimum stay is required during the high season.

One of the better-quality stays for the price in Myrtle is the **Roxanne Towers** (1604 N. Ocean Blvd., 843/839-1016, www.theroxanne.com, $150-250). Known for attentive service, this is a busy property in a busy area. Parking is historically something of a problem. Keep in mind that room size is capped at two bedrooms, so there are none of the sprawling three-bedroom suites that many other local places have.

For a quality stay in the heart of Myrtle's beach bustle, go for the **Sandy Beach Resort** (201 S. Ocean Blvd., 800/844-6534, www.beachtrips.com, $200-300). The guest rooms are top-notch, and the service is professional. As is the case with many local properties, there is a newer section, the Palmetto Tower, and an "old" section, the venerable Magnolia Tower. There are one-, two-, and three-bedroom units available, the latter a particularly good value.

Considered one of the major remaining centers of the shag subculture on the Strand, the **Ocean Drive Beach and Golf Resort** (98 N. Ocean Blvd., $200-350) up in North Myrtle Beach hosts many events surrounding the notable regional dance, including the Shaggers Hall of Fame. Its on-site lounge, **The Spanish Galleon,** specializes in beach music. It's also just a great place to stay, with amenities such as a "lazy river," a whirlpool, full galley-style kitchens, and, of course, extreme proximity to the beach. A remodel in 2007 has made it even plusher inside and out.

Also up in North Myrtle is the new **◖ Tilghman Beach and Golf Resort** (1819 Ocean Blvd., 843/280-0913, www.tilghman-resort.com, $200-350), owned by the same company as the Ocean Drive Beach Resort. It's not directly on the beach, but since the buildings in front of it are pretty low, you can still get awesome ocean views. Even the views from the back of the building aren't bad, since they overlook a golf course. But you don't have to be a duffer to enjoy the Tilghman—the pool scene is great, the balconies are roomy, and the suites are huge and well enough equipped (a flat-screen TV in every room) to make you feel right at home.

VACATION RENTALS

There are hundreds, probably thousands, of privately rented condo-style lodgings at Myrtle Beach, in all shapes and forms. Most, however, do a great job of catering to what vacationers here really seem to want: space, convenience, and a working kitchen. All rental agencies basically work with the same listings, so looking for and finding a rental is easier than you might think.

Some of the key brokers are **Myrtle Beach Vacation Rentals** (800/845-0833, www.mb-vacationrentals.com), **Beach Vacations** (866/453-4818, www.beachvacationsmb.com), **Barefoot Vacations** (800/845-0837, www.

barefootvacations.info), **Elliott Realty and Beach Rentals** (www.elliottrealty.com), and **Atlantic Dunes Vacation Rentals** (866/544-2568, www.atlanticdunesvacations.com).

CAMPING

Myrtle Beach is not where you go for a pristine quiet camping experience. For that, I suggest Huntington State Park down near Murrells Inlet. However, there is plenty of camping, almost all of it heavily RV-oriented, if you want it. For more info, visit www.campmyrtlebeach.com.

The closest thing to a real live campground is good old **Myrtle Beach State Park** (4401 S. Kings Hwy., 843/238-5325, www.southcarolinaparks.com, daily 6am-10pm, $4 adults, $1.50 ages 6-15, free under age 6), which despite being only a short drive from the rest of the beachfront sprawl is still a fairly relaxing place to stay, complete with its own scenic fishing pier (daily fishing fee $4.50). There's even a nature center with a little aquarium and exhibits.

The charming and educational atmosphere is largely due to the fact that this is one of the 17 Civilian Conservation Corps parks, built during the Great Depression. There are four cabins ($54-125) available, all fully furnished and about 200 yards from the beach. The main campground is about 300 yards from the beach and comprises 300 sites with electricity and water ($23-25) and a 45-site tent and overflow campground ($17-19), which is only open during the summer high season.

The **Myrtle Beach KOA** (613 6th Ave. S., 800/562-7790, www.myrtlebeachkoa.com), though not at all cheap ($40-50 even for tenters), offers the usual safe, dependable amenities of that well-known chain, including rental "kabins" and activities for kids.

Willow Tree RV Resort and Campground (520 Southern Sights Dr., 843/756-4334, www.willowtreervr.com) is set inland on a well-wooded 300-acre tract with large sites well away from the sprawl and offers lakeside fishing and bike trails. In the summer high season, basic sites are $50-82, and the one- and two-bedroom cabins range $120-190.

Food

There are about 2,000 restaurants in the Myrtle Beach area, not counting hotel room service and buffets. You can find any dining option that floats your boat at almost any price level. Seafood, of course, is big and is heartily recommended. But there are steak houses, rib joints, pizza places, and vegetarian restaurants galore as well. We can only explore a small fraction here, but following is a breakdown of some of the more unique and tasty experiences on this bustling part of the Grand Strand.

BREAKFAST

Pancakes are big on the Strand, with many flapjack places open daily 24 hours to accommodate partiers and night owls. A prime purveyor of pancakes is **Harry's Breakfast Pancakes** (2306 N. Kings Hwy., 843/448-8013, www.harryspancake.com, daily 5:30am-2pm, $4-10). They're not open all day, but there's enough time to enjoy their fluffy stacks and rich omelets.

BARBECUE, BURGERS, AND STEAKS

The best barbecue in town—and a delightfully low-key experience in this often too-flashy area—is at ☾ **Little Pigs Barbecue** (6102 Frontage Rd., 843/692-9774, Mon.-Sat. 11am-8pm, $8-12). This is a local-heavy place dealing in no-frills pulled pork, piled high at the counter and reasonably priced with a selection of sauces. The lack of atmosphere *is* the atmosphere, and they prefer to let the barbecue (and the hushpuppies and onion rings) do the talking.

Since opening 20 years ago, ☾ **Thoroughbreds** (9706 N. Kings Hwy., 843/497-2636, www.thoroughbredsrestaurant.com, Sun.-Thurs. 5pm-10pm, Fri.-Sat. 5pm-11pm, $20), on the old Restaurant Row, has been considered the premier fine-dining place in Myrtle Beach, dealing in the kind of wood-heavy, clubby, Old World-meets-New World ambience you'd expect to see in Palm Beach, Florida. That said, the prices are definitely more Myrtle Beach; you can easily have a romantic dinner for two for under $100. The menu is a carnivore's delight: Beef includes the signature prime rib, a great steak au poivre, and a nod to cowboy machismo, the 22-ounce bone-in rib eye.

The new darling of the steak-loving set is **Rioz Brazilian Steakhouse** (2920 Hollywood Dr., 843/839-0777, www.rioz.com, daily 4pm-10pm, $20-40). It's not cheap—the recommended 15-item meat sampler is about $35 pp—but then again, an experience this awesome shouldn't be cheap (a big plus is that kids under age 7 eat for free). The meats are fresh and vibrant, slow-cooked over a wood fire in the simple but succulent style typical of the gaucho *churrascaria* tradition. The service is widely considered to be the best in the area. But the biggest surprise may turn out to be the salad and seafood bar, which even has sushi.

There is no dearth of places to nosh at Barefoot Landing, but meat lovers (not to mention golfers) will probably enjoy **Greg Norman's Australian Grille** (4930 Kings Hwy. S., 843/361-0000, www.gregnormanaustraliangrille.com, lunch daily 11am-3pm, dinner daily 5pm-10pm, $20-30), which, despite the chain-sounding name, is the only restaurant of its kind. It's the place to enjoy a cocktail by the lake and a premium entrée like the lobster-crusted swordfish.

I normally shy away from mentioning national chain-type places, but I'll make an exception for Myrtle Beach, where you expect things to be a little cheesy. **Jimmy Buffett's Margaritaville** (1114 Celebrity Circle, 843/448-5455, www.margaritavillemyrtlebeach.com, Sun.-Thurs. 11am-10pm, Fri.-Sat. 11am-midnight, $13-22) at Broadway at the Beach is widely regarded as the best single location of the national chain. The signature

Cheeseburger in Paradise is the obvious big hit. You get a lot of entertainment for your money as well, with balloon-twisting performers coming to your table and a bizarre whirling "hurricane" that acts up in the main dining area every now and then. As you'd expect, the margaritas are good, if expensive.

Many locals insist the better burger is at another Buffett-owned chain, the succinctly titled **Cheeseburger in Paradise** (7211 N. Kings Hwy., 843/497-3891, www.cheeseburgerinparadise.com, Sun.-Thurs. 11:30am-11pm, Fri.-Sat. 11:30am-midnight, $10-15), which offers a range of burgers on the menu with sweet potato chips on the side, all served up in a less flashy but still very boisterous atmosphere than the flagship restaurant.

CLASSIC SOUTHERN

If you've got a hankering for some spicy Cajun-creole food, go no farther than **The House of Blues** (4640 U.S. 17 S., 843/272-3000, www.hob.com, Mon.-Fri. 4pm-9pm, Sat. 8am-9pm, Sun. 9am-2pm and 3pm-9pm, $10-25) at Barefoot Landing in North Myrtle Beach. With 17 similarly themed locations around North America, this particular venue deals in the same kind of retro Delta vibe, with specially commissioned folk art festooning the walls and live music cranking up at about 9pm. At your table, a gregarious server will walk you through the limited but intense menu, which includes such tasty bits as Buffalo Tenders (actually boneless chicken wings in a perfectly spicy sauce) and a couple of excellent jambalaya-type dishes. All portions are enormous and richly spiced. It's a loud, clanging room, so keep in mind that this is less a romantic experience than an exuberant earthy one.

A special experience at House of Blues is the weekly Gospel Brunch (Sun. 9am-2pm, $20 adults, $10 ages 6-12), an opportunity not only to enjoy some tasty Southern-style brunch treats like cheese grits, jambalaya, and catfish tenders but to enjoy some really rather outstanding gospel entertainment at the same time. The Gospel Brunch is served in seatings, and reservations are recommended.

CONTINENTAL

In Myrtle Beach it can be difficult to find a good meal that's not fried or smothered or both. For a highbrow change of pace, try **The Library** (1212 N. Kings Hwy., 843/448-4527, www.thelibraryrestaurantsc.com, Mon.-Sat. 5pm-10pm, $20-50), which is hands-down the most romantic dining experience in Myrtle proper. It's not cheap, but then again, nothing about this place is pedestrian, from the very attentive European-style service to the savvy wine list and the signature dishes (many of them prepared tableside), like she-crab soup, Caesar salads, Steak Diane, and the ultimate splurge, steak and lobster.

Like art? Like food? Try the **Collector's Café** (7726 N. Kings Hwy., 843/449-9370, www.collectorscafeandgallery.com, $10-20), which, as the name implies, is a combined gallery and dining space. Don't be daunted by the strip mall setting—inside is a totally different ball game with a trendy open kitchen and plush, eclectic furniture awaiting you amid the original artwork. As for the menu, you may as well go for what's widely regarded as the best single dish, the scallop cakes. Make sure you save room for dessert.

ITALIAN

The best-regarded Italian place in Myrtle Beach—though it could just as easily go in the *Steaks* category, since that's its specialty—is **Angelo's** (2011 S. Kings Hwy., 843/626-2800, www.angelosteakandpasta.com, Sun.-Thurs. 4pm-8:30pm, Fri.-Sat. 4pm-9pm, $12-25). The signature dishes are intriguingly spiced cuts of steak (request beforehand if you don't want them seasoned), cooked medium and under for an exquisite tenderness. You can get spaghetti as a side with the steaks, or just go with the classic baked potato. Don't forget to check out the Italian buffet, including lasagna, Italian sausage, chicken cacciatore, ravioli, and, of course, pizza.

SEAFOOD

The grandest old Calabash seafood joint in town, **Original Benjamin's** (9593 N. Kings

Hwy., 843/449-0821, daily 3:30pm-10pm, buffet $25 adults, $12 children) on the old Restaurant Row is one of the more unique dining experiences in Myrtle Beach. With themed rooms overlooking the Intracoastal Waterway, including the concisely named Bus Room—yes, it has an old school bus in it—you'll find yourself in the mood to devour copious amounts of fresh seafood at its humongous 170-item buffet line.

Closer to Broadway on the Beach, try **George's** (1401 29th Ave. N., 843/916-2278, www.captaingeorges.com, Mon.-Sat. 3pm-10pm, Sun. noon-9pm, buffet $31, $16 ages 5-12). Despite the usual kitschy nautical decor, this is the kind of place even locals will admit going to for the enormous seafood buffet, widely considered a cut above the norm.

With old reliables like crab cakes and sea scallops as well as signature house dishes like pecan-encrusted grouper and stuffed flounder, you can't go wrong at **The Sea Captain's House** (3002 N. Ocean Blvd., 843/448-8082, daily 6am-10:30am, 11:30am-2:30pm, and 5pm-10pm, $10-20), one of Myrtle Beach's better seafood restaurants. This opinion is widely held, however, so prepare to wait—often up to two hours. Luckily, you can sip a cocktail and gaze out over the Atlantic Ocean as you do so. Old hands will tell you it's not as good as back in the day, but it's still a cut above.

When you're at Ocean Drive Beach up in North Myrtle, check out another venerable old name, the **Duffy Street Seafood Shack** (202 Main St., 843/281-9840, www.duffyst.com, daily noon-10pm, $10). This is a humble unkempt roadside affair dealing in the kind of down-home treats Myrtle Beach seems to love ("pigskin" shrimp, fried pickles, and the like). Overall, it's a good place to get a tasty bite and soak in the flavor of this Cherry Grove neighborhood at the heart of the old shag culture.

Information and Services

The main visitors center for Myrtle Beach is the **Myrtle Beach Area Chamber of Commerce and Visitor Center** (1200 N. Oak St., 843/626-7444, www.visitmybeach.com, Mon.-Fri. 8:30am-5pm, Sat. 10am-2pm). There's an **Airport Welcome Center** (1180 Jetport Rd., 843/626-7444) as well, and a visitors center in North Myrtle Beach, the **North Myrtle Beach Chamber of Commerce and Convention & Visitors Bureau** (270 U.S. 17 N., 843/281-2662, www.northmyrtlebeachchamber.com).

The main health care facility in the Myrtle Beach area is **Grand Strand Regional Medical Center** (809 82nd Pkwy., 843/692-1000, www.grandstrandmed.com). Myrtle Beach is served by the **Myrtle Beach Police Department** (1101 N. Oak St., 843/918-1382, www.cityofmyrtlebeach.com). The separate municipality of North Myrtle Beach is served by the **North Myrtle Beach Police Department** (843/280-5555, www.nmb.us).

Getting There and Around

GETTING THERE

The Myrtle Beach area is served by the fast-growing **Myrtle Beach International Airport** (MYR, 1100 Jetport Rd., 843/448-1589, www.flymyrtlebeach.com), which hosts Delta, Northwest, Southern Skyways, Spirit, US Airways, and United.

Unusually for South Carolina, a state that is exceptionally well-served by the interstate highway system, the main route into the area is the smaller U.S. 17, which runs north-south, with a parallel business spur, from Georgetown up to the North Carolina border. The approach from the west is by U.S. 501, called Black Skimmer Trail as it approaches Myrtle Beach.

The local **Greyhound Bus Terminal** (511 7th Ave. N., 843/231-2222) is in "downtown" Myrtle Beach.

GETTING AROUND

In practice, the Myrtle Beach municipalities blend and blur into each other in one long sprawl parallel to the main north-south route, U.S. 17. However, always keep this in mind: Just south of Murrells Inlet, U.S. 17 divides into two distinct portions. There's the U.S. 17 Bypass, which continues to the west of much of the coastal growth, and there's Business U.S. 17, also known as Kings Highway, the main drag along which most key attractions and places of interest are located.

The other key north-south route, Ocean Boulevard, runs along the beach. This is a two-lane road that can get pretty congested in the summer.

Thankfully, area planners have provided a great safety valve for some of this often horrendous traffic. Highway 31, the Carolina Bays Parkway, begins inland from Myrtle Beach at about 16th Avenue. This wide new highway roughly parallels the Intracoastal Waterway and takes you on a straight shot, with a 65 mph speed limit, all the way to Highway 22 (the Conway Bypass) or all the way to Highway 9 at Cherry Grove Beach, the farthest extent of North Myrtle Beach. The bottom line is that if time is of the essence, you should use Highway 31 whenever possible.

Rental Car, Taxi, and Bus

You will need a vehicle to make the most of this area. Rental cars are available at the airport. Rental options outside the airport include **Enterprise** (1377 U.S. 501, 843/626-4277; 3401 U.S. 17 S., 843/361-4410, www.enterprise.com), **Hertz** (851 Jason Blvd., 843/839-9530, www.hertz.com), and the unique **Rent-a-Wreck** (901 3rd Ave. S., 843/626-9393).

Taxi service on the Strand is plentiful but fairly expensive. Look in the local Yellow Pages for full listings; a couple of good services are **Yellow Cab** (917 Oak St., 843/448-5555) and **Beach Checker Cab** (843/272-6212) in North Myrtle.

The area is served by the **Coastal Rapid Public Transit Authority** (1418 3rd Ave., 843/248-7277), which runs several bus routes up and down the Strand. Ask at a visitors center or call for a schedule.

Bicycle

Bicyclists in Myrtle Beach can take advantage of some completed segments of the South Carolina portion of the **East Coast Greenway** (www.greenway.org), which, generally speaking, is Ocean Boulevard. You can actually ride Ocean Boulevard all the way from 82nd Avenue North down to the southern city limit.

In North Myrtle Beach, from Sea Mountain Highway in Cherry Grove, you can bike Ocean Boulevard clear down to 46th Avenue South, with a detour from 28th to 33rd Avenues. A right on 46th Avenue South takes you to Barefoot Landing. And, of course, for a scenic ride, you can pedal on the beach itself for miles. But remember: Bicycling on the sidewalk is strictly prohibited.

As for bike rentals, try **Beach Bike Shop** (711 Broadway St., 843/448-5335, www.beach-bikeshop.com). In North Myrtle, try **Wheel Fun Rentals** (91 S. Ocean Blvd., 843/280-7900, www.wheelfunrentals.com).

Points Inland

CONWAY

A nice day trip west of Myrtle Beach—and a nice change from that area's intense development—is to the charming town of Conway, just northwest of Myrtle Beach on U.S. 501 and the Waccamaw River. Founded in 1733 with the name Kingston, it originally marked the frontier of the colony. It was later renamed Conwayborough, soon shortened to Conway, in honor of local leader Robert Conway, and now serves as the seat of Horry County.

Conway's heyday was during Reconstruction, when it became a major trade center for timber products and naval stores from the interior. The railroad came through town in 1887 (later being extended to Myrtle Beach), and most remaining buildings date from this period or later. The most notable Conway native is perhaps an unexpected name: William Gibson, originator of the cyberpunk genre of science fiction, was born here in 1948.

Conway is small and easily explored. Make your first stop at the **Conway Visitors Center** (903 3rd Ave., 843/248-1700, www.cityofconway.com, Mon.-Fri. 9am-5pm), where you can pick up maps. It also offers guided tours ($2 pp) that depart from City Hall (3rd Ave. and Main St.); call for a schedule. You can also visit the **Conway Chamber of Commerce** (203 Main St.) for maps and information.

Sights

Conway's chief attraction is the 850-foot **Riverwalk** (843/248-2273, www.conwaysc-chamber.com, daily dawn-dusk) along the blackwater Waccamaw River, a calming location with shops and restaurants nearby. Waterborne tours on the *Kingston Lady* leave from the Conway Marina at the end of the Riverwalk.

Another key stop is the **Horry County Museum** (428 Main St., 843/248-1542, www.horrycountymuseum.org, Tues.-Sat. 9am-4pm, free), which tells the story of this rather large South Carolina county from prehistory to the present. It holds an annual Quilt Gala in February, which features some great regional examples of the art.

Across from the campus of Coastal Carolina University is the circa-1972 Traveler's Chapel, a.k.a. **The Littlest Church in South Carolina** (U.S. 501 and Cox Ferry Rd.). At 12 by 24 feet, it seats no more than a dozen people. Weddings are held here throughout the year. Admission is free, but donations are accepted.

Accommodations

The best stay in town is at the four-star **Cypress Inn** (16 Elm St., 843/248-8199, www.acypressinn.com, $145-235), a beautiful and well-appointed 12-room B&B right on the Waccamaw River.

LEWIS OCEAN BAY HERITAGE PRESERVE

The humongous (over 9,000 acres) **Lewis Ocean Bay Heritage Preserve** (803/734-3886, www.dnr.sc.gov, daily dawn-dusk, free) is one of the more impressive phenomena in the Palmetto State, from a naturalist's viewpoint, made all the more special by its location a short drive from heavily developed Myrtle Beach. Managed by the state, it contains an amazing 23 Carolina bays, by far the largest concentration in South Carolina. These elliptical depressions, scattered throughout the Carolinas and all oriented in a northwest-southeast direction, are typified by a cypress-tupelo bog environment. The nearby Highway 31 is named the Carolina Bays Parkway in a nod to its neighbors. As if that weren't enough, the preserve boasts other unique aspects as well. It has the largest concentration of Venus flytraps in the state, and it is also said to be the only place in eastern South Carolina where black bears still live in the wild.

To get here from Myrtle Beach, take U.S. 501 north to Highway 90 and head east. After about seven miles, turn east on the unpaved International Drive across from the Wild Horse subdivision. After about 1.5 miles on International Drive, veer left onto Old Kingston Road. The preserve is shortly ahead on both sides of the road; park along the shoulder.

The Lower Grand Strand

Tiny Pawleys Island (year-round population about 200) likes to call itself "America's first resort" because of its early role, in the late 1700s, as a place for planters to go with their families to escape the mosquito-infested rice and cotton fields. It's still a vacation getaway and still has a certain elite understatement, an attitude the locals call "arrogantly shabby." While you can visit casually, most people who enjoy the famous Pawleys Island beaches do so from one of the many vacation rental properties. Shabby arrogance does have its upside, however—there is a ban on further commercial development in the community, allowing Pawleys to remain slow and peaceful. For generations, Pawleys was famous for its cypress cottages, many on stilts. Sadly, 1989's Hurricane Hugo destroyed a great many of these iconic structures—27 out of 29 on the south end alone, most of which have been replaced by far less aesthetically pleasing homes.

Directly adjacent to Pawleys, Litchfield Beach offers similar low-key enjoyment along with a world-class golf resort. Murrells Inlet is chiefly known for a single block of seafood restaurants on its eponymous waterway.

SIGHTS
◖ Brookgreen Gardens
One of the most unique—and unlikely—sights in the developed Grand Strand area is bucolic **Brookgreen Gardens** (1931 Brookgreen Dr., 843/235-6000, www.brookgreen.org, May-Mar. daily 9:30am-5pm, Apr. daily 9:30am-8pm, $14 adults, $7 ages 6-12, free under age 6), directly across U.S. 17 from Huntington Beach State Park. Once one of several massive contiguous plantations in the Pawleys Island area, the modern Brookgreen is a result of the charity and passion of Archer Milton Huntington and his wife, Anna. Quite the sculptor in her own right, Anna Huntington saw to it that Brookgreen's 9,000 acres would host by far the largest single collection of

© SONJA WALLEN

Brookgreen Gardens

MYRTLE BEACH

outdoor sculpture in the United States. To learn more, visit the on-site **Carroll A. Campbell Jr. Center for American Sculpture,** which offers seminars and workshops throughout the year.

On the other end of the grounds opposite the gardens is the **E. Craig Wall Jr. Lowcountry Nature Center,** which includes a small enclosed cypress swamp with a boardwalk, herons and egrets, and a delightful river otter exhibit.

To add an extra layer of enjoyment to your visit, you can explore this massive preserve much more deeply by taking one of several tours offered on Brookgreen's pontoon boat ($7 adults, $4 children, on top of regular admission); check the website for a schedule.

◖ Huntington Beach State Park

Right across the street from Brookgreen is **Huntington Beach State Park** (16148 Ocean Hwy., 843/237-4440, www.southcarolinaparks.com, daily 6am-10pm, $5 adults, $3 ages 6-15, free under age 6), probably the best of South Carolina's state parks not built by the Civilian Conservation Corps. Once a part of the same vast parcel of land owned by Archer Huntington and his wife, Anna, the state has leased it from the trustees of their estate since the 1960s.

You can tour the "castle" on the beach, **Atalaya,** former home of the Huntingtons and now the yearly site of the Atalaya Arts and Crafts Festival. This evocative Moorish-style National Historic Landmark is open to the public for free guided tours (Memorial Day-Sept. daily noon-1pm, Oct. Tues.-Sat. noon-2pm, Sun.-Mon. noon-1pm). You can stroll three miles of beach, view birds and wildlife from several boardwalks into the marsh, hike several nature trails, and visit the well-done **Environmental Education Center** (843/235-8755, Tues.-Sun. 10am-5pm), which features a saltwater touch tank and a baby alligator.

Pawleys Island Historic District

Although many of the island's homes were leveled by Hurricane Hugo, the **Pawleys Island Historic District** (843/237-1698, www.townofpawleysisland.com), in the central portion of the island, still has a dozen contributing structures, almost all on Myrtle Avenue. Among them are the **Weston House** (506 Myrtle Ave.), or Pelican Inn, and the **Ward House** (520 Myrtle Ave.), or Liberty Lodge. As you view the structures, many with their own historic markers, note the architecture. Because these were intended to be lived in May-November, they resemble open and airy Caribbean homes, with extensive porches and plenty of windows.

EVENTS

The highlight of the lower Grand Strand calendar is the annual **Atalaya Arts and Crafts Festival** (www.atalayafestival.com, $6 adults, free under age 16), which takes place on the grounds of Huntington Beach State Park each September. There's music, food, and about 100 vendors who show their art and wares within the exotic Atalaya home. Admission to the park is free during the festival.

Also in September is the **Pawleys Island**

© JIM MOREKIS

Weston House in the Pawleys Island Historic District

THE LOWER GRAND STRAND **265**

Festival of Music and Art (www.pawleys-music.com, prices vary), which happens outdoors, across U.S. 17 under the stars in Brookgreen Gardens, with a few performances at nearby Litchfield Plantation.

A main event in Murrells Inlet is the annual **Fourth of July Boat Parade** (843/651-0900, free), which celebrates American independence with a patriotically themed procession of all kinds of streamer- and flag-bedecked watercraft down the inlet. It begins at about 6pm and ends, of course, with a big fireworks display.

Another big deal in Murrells Inlet is the annual **Blessing of the Inlet** (843/651-5099, www.belinumc.org), always held the first Saturday in May and sponsored by a local Methodist church. Enjoy food vendors, goods baked by local women, and a great family atmosphere.

SHOPPING

The shopping scene revolves around the famous Pawleys Island hammock, a beautiful and practical bit of local handiwork sold primarily at the **Hammock Shops Village** (10880 Ocean Hwy., 843/237-8448, Mon.-Sat. 10am-6pm, Sun. 1pm-5pm). To purchase a Pawleys Island hammock, go to **The Original Hammock Shop** (843/237-9122, www.thehammockshop.com), housed in a century-old cottage. Next door is the affiliated **Hammock Shop General Store,** which, as the name implies, sells a variety of other goods such as beachwear, books, and a notable style of local fudge. The actual hammocks are handcrafted in the shed next door, the way they have been since 1889.

SPORTS AND RECREATION
Beaches

First, the good news: The beaches are pristine and beautiful. The bad news: Public access is very limited. Simply put, that means the best way to enjoy the beach is to rent one of the many private beach homes for a week or so. Although it's only a short distance from Myrtle Beach, the beaches at Pawleys and vicinity are infinitely more peaceful and easygoing.

Beach access with parking at Pawleys Island includes a fairly large lot at the south end of the island and parking areas off Atlantic Avenue at Hazard, 1st, Pearce, 2nd, and 3rd Streets, and Shell Road.

Kayaking and Canoeing

The Waccamaw River and associated inlets and creeks are peaceful and scenic places to kayak, with plenty of bird-watching opportunities to boot. For a two-hour guided tour of the area salt marsh, reserve a spot on the kayak trips sponsored by the **Environmental Education Center** (Huntington Beach State Park, 843/235-8755, office Tues.-Sun. 10am-5pm, $30 pp). Call for tour days and times. Or you can put in yourself at Oyster Landing, about one mile from the entrance to the state park.

Golf

Home to some of the best links in the Carolinas, the lower part of the Grand Strand recently organized its courses under the umbrella moniker **Waccamaw Golf Trail** (www.waccamawgolftrail.com), chiefly for marketing purposes. No matter, the courses are still as superb as ever, if generally pricier than their counterparts up the coast.

The best course in the area, and one of the best in the country, is the **Caledonia Golf and Fish Club** (369 Caledonia Dr., 843/237-3675, www.fishclub.com, $195). While the course itself is almost ridiculously young—it opened in 1995—this masterpiece is built, as so many area courses are, on the grounds of a former rice plantation. The clubhouse, in fact, dates from before the Civil War. Packages (800/449-4005, www.myrtlebeachcondorentals.com) are available. Affiliated with Caledonia is the fine **True Blue Golf Club** (900 Blue Stem Dr., 843/235-0900, www.fishclub.com, $100), considered perhaps the most challenging single course on the Strand.

Another excellent Pawleys course is the **Litchfield Country Club** (U.S. 17 and Magnolia Dr., 843/237-3411, www.litchcc.com, $60), one of the Grand Strand's oldest.

MYRTLE BEACH

The facilities are self-consciously dated—this is a country club, after all—setting it apart from the flashier, newer courses sprouting like mushrooms farther up the Strand. It's a deceptive course that's short on yards but heavy on doglegs.

The Jack Nicklaus-designed **Pawleys Plantation Golf and Country Club** (70 Tanglewood Dr., 843/237-6100, www.pawleysplantation.com, $150) has set a tough example for the last 20 years. The front nine is a traditional layout, while the back nine melts into the marsh.

ACCOMMODATIONS
Under $150
Similarly named but not to be confused with Litchfield Plantation is the nearby **Litchfield Beach and Golf Resort** (14276 Ocean Hwy., 866/538-0187, www.litchfieldbeach.com, $100-170). In typical Grand Strand fashion, this property delivers a lot of service for a surprisingly low price and offers a wide range of lodging choices, from a basic room at the Seaside Inn on the low end to four-bedroom villas ($230). A regular free shuttle takes you to the beach. There are also lots of water activities right on the premises, including a ubiquitous "lazy river" tube course.

$150-300
The premier B&B-style lodging on the entire Grand Strand is (**Litchfield Plantation** (Kings River Rd., 843/237-9121, www.litchfieldplantation.com, $230-275) on Pawleys Island, built, as you've probably come to expect by now, on an old plantation. There is a host of lodging choices, all of them absolutely splendid. The Plantation House has four sumptuous suites, all impeccably decorated. The humbly named Guest House—actually an old mansion—has six bedrooms, and the entire second floor is an executive suite. Lastly, the newer outparcel Villas contain an assortment of two- and three-bedroom suites.

Vacation Rentals
Many who enjoy the Pawleys area do so using a vacation rental as a home base rather than a traditional hotel or B&B. **Pawleys Island Realty** (88 N. Causeway Rd., 800/937-7352, www.pawleysislandrealty.com) can hook you up.

Camping
At **Huntington Beach State Park** (16148 Ocean Hwy., 843/237-4440, www.southcarolinaparks.com, daily 6am-10pm, $5 adults, $3 ages 6-15, free under age 6), the beach is beautiful, there are trails and an education center, and the bird-watching is known as some of the best on the East Coast. While there are 131 RV-suitable sites ($23-28), tenters should go to one of the six walk-in tent sites ($17-19).

FOOD
Breakfast and Brunch
The high-end strip mall setting isn't the most romantic, but by broad consensus the best breakfast on the entire Strand is at **Applewood House of Pancakes** (14361 Ocean Hwy., 843/979-1022, daily 6am-2pm, $5-10) in Pawleys. Eggs benedict, specialty omelets, crepes, waffles, and pancakes abound in this roomy, unpretentious dining room. Do it; you won't regret it.

Seafood
Murrells Inlet has several good places clustered together along the marsh on U.S. 17. The best is (**Lee's Inlet Kitchen** (4460 Business U.S. 17, 843/651-2881, www.leesinletkitchen.com, Mar.-Nov. Mon.-Sat. 4:30pm-10pm, $20-40), which is the only original Murrells Inlet joint still in the original family—in this case the Lee family, who started the place in the mid-1940s. The seafood is simply but delectably prepared (your choice of fried or broiled). They close down December-February.

Along similar lines is **Flo's Place Restaurant** (3797 Business U.S. 17, 843/651-7222, www.flosplace.com, daily 11am-10pm, $15-25). Flo is sadly no longer with us, but her place still eschews schlock for a more humble, down-home feel. Everything is fresh, hot, and tasty, from the fried green tomatoes

to the crab cakes and the alligator nuggets—yes, it's real alligator meat. But the signature dish is the legendary Dunkin' Pot—a kettle filled with oysters, clams, shrimp, potatoes, sausage, and shellfish, topped with snow crab legs.

On the other end of the spectrum style-wise is **Divine Fish House** (3993 Business U.S. 17, 843/651-5800, www.divinefishhouse.com, daily 5pm-10pm, $20-33), which offers more adventurous high-end cuisine like the fine San Antonio Salmon (smothered with pepper-jack cheese and bacon) and the Asian-flavored Banana Leaf Mangrove Grouper.

INFORMATION AND SERVICES

On Pawleys Island is the **Georgetown County Visitors Bureau** (95-A Centermarsh Lane, 843/235-6595, www.visitgeorgetowncountysc.com). The **Myrtle Beach Area Chamber of Commerce** (3401 U.S. 17, 843/651-1010, www.visitmybeach.com) and the new **Waccamaw Community Hospital** (4070 U.S. 17 Bypass, 843/652-1000, www.georgetownhospitalsystem.org) are in Murrells Inlet. Pawleys Island is served by the **Pawleys Island Police Department** (321 Myrtle Ave., 843/237-3008, www.townofpawleysisland.com).

Georgetown and Vicinity

Think of Georgetown as Beaufort's lesser-known cousin. Like Beaufort, it's an hour away from Charleston, it boasts a tidy historic downtown, and it was once a major center of Lowcountry plantation culture. However, Georgetown gets significantly less attention and less traffic. Certainly the fact that the entrance to town is dominated by the sprawling, ominous-looking Georgetown Steel mill on one side of the road and the massive International Paper plant on the other has something to do with it. Making matters worse was a huge fire in September 2013, which destroyed nearly an entire downtown block of historic waterfront buildings.

There are several enjoyable and educational places a short way north of Georgetown on U.S. 17, chief among them Hobcaw Barony, former playground of the rich turned environmental education center, and Hampton Plantation, a well-preserved look back into antebellum elegance and rice-culture history.

HISTORY

The third-oldest city in South Carolina, after Charleston and Beaufort, Georgetown was founded in 1729 on a four- by eight-block grid, most of which still exists today, complete with original street names. The Revolutionary War hero Francis Marion, the "Swamp Fox," was born in nearby Berkeley County and conducted operations in and around the area during the entire war.

While Charleston-area plantations get most of the attention, the truth is that by 1840 about 150 rice plantations on the Sampit and Little Pee Dee Rivers were producing half of the entire national output of the staple crop. After the Civil War, the collapse of the slave-based economy (at its height, 90 percent of Georgetown's population were enslaved) meant the collapse of the rice economy as well.

In 1905, Bernard Baruch—native South Carolinian, Wall Street mover and shaker, and adviser to presidents—came to town, purchasing Hobcaw Barony, a former plantation. It became his winter residence and hunting ground, and his legacy of conservation lives on there today in an education center on the site.

On the national level Georgetown is perhaps best known for being the hometown of comedian Chris Rock; although he moved away long ago, many members of his family continue to live here.

SIGHTS

Kaminski House

The city of Georgetown owns and operates

MYRTLE BEACH

GEORGETOWN

© AVALON TRAVEL

the historic **Kaminski House** (1003 Front St., 843/546-7706, www.cogsc.com, Mon.-Sat. 9am-5pm, $7 adults, $3 ages 6-12, free under age 6). Built in 1769, it was home to several city mayors. It is furnished with a particularly exquisite selection of 18th- and 19th-century antiques. The grounds are beautiful as well, overlooking the Sampit River and lined with Spanish moss-covered oaks. The only way to see the inside of the house is to take the free 45-minute guided tour departing every hour on the hour Monday-Saturday 10am-4pm and Sunday 1pm-4pm; call ahead to confirm tour times.

Rice Museum

The succinctly named **Rice Museum** (633 Front St., 843/546-7423, www.ricemuseum. org, Mon.-Sat. 10am-4:30pm, $7 adults, $3 ages 6-21, free under age 6) is a look back at the all-important staple crop and its massive effects

on Georgetown, which at one point accounted for half of the country's rice production.

There are actually two parts of the museum: The Old Market building, often simply called "The Town Clock" because of its 1842 timepiece, hosts the bulk of the archival information on the impact of rice growing on the region's history and economy; the adjacent Kaminski Hardware Building includes a 17-minute video on the rice industry, a good Gullah-Geechee cultural exhibit, and a gift shop. Most visitors to the Rice Museum take a one-hour guided tour, included in the price of admission.

South Carolina Maritime Museum

As the Palmetto State's second-largest port, Georgetown has more than its share of nautical history. Check it out at the burgeoning little **South Carolina Maritime Museum** (729 Front St., 843/520-0111, www.scmaritimemuseum. org, Mon.-Sat. 11am-5pm, free). The 2013

MYRTLE BEACH

© JIM MOREKIS

Georgetown's historic district

downtown fire caused a bit of damage to the building, but the museum is still humming. It sponsors the fun Wooden Boat Show each October on the waterfront.

Georgetown County Museum

For a more complete look at various aspects of local history, check out the **Georgetown County Museum** (632 Prince St., 843/545-7020, Tues.-Fri. 10am-5pm, Sat. 10am-3pm, $4 adults, $2 ages 6-18, free under age 6). The highlight is a recently discovered letter written by Revolutionary War hero Francis Marion.

Prince George Winyah Episcopal Church

It has seen better days—the British partially burned it during the Revolutionary War—but **Prince George Winyah Episcopal Church** (301 Broad St., 843/546-4358, www.pgwinyah.org, Mon.-Fri. 11:30am-4:30pm, services Sun. 8am, 9am, and 11am) is still a fine example of the Anglican tradition of the Lowcountry rice culture. First built in 1750 out of ballast stones

(the parish itself dates from substantially earlier, 1721), the sanctuary features classic box pews, expert stained glass, and ornate woodwork on the inside. The bell tower dates from 1824.

Hopsewee Plantation

Beautiful in an understated way, **Hopsewee Plantation** (494 Hopsewee Rd., 843/546-7891, www.hopsewee.com, Feb.-Nov. Tues.-Fri. 10am-4pm, Sat. 11am-4pm, Dec.-Jan. by appointment only, $17.50 adults, $10.50 ages 12-17, $7.50 ages 5-11), on the Santee River 12 miles south of Georgetown, was the birthplace of Thomas Lynch Jr., one of South Carolina's signers of the Declaration of Independence. Some key archaeological work is going on at the former slave village on this old indigo plantation; you can visit two of the original slave cabins on the tour. While not as grand as many other Lowcountry plantation homes, the 1740 main house is a masterpiece of colonial architecture, and all the more impressive because it's very nearly original, with the black cypress exterior largely intact. The focus here is on

THE SWAMP FOX AND THE COMING OF GUERRILLA WARFARE

I have it from good authority, that this great soldier, at his birth, was not larger than a New England lobster, and might easily enough have been put into a quart pot.

> Peter Horry, who fought with Francis Marion

Short, bowlegged, and moody, Francis Marion was as far away from the template of the dashing war hero as his tactics were from the storybook exploits of military literature. The father of modern guerrilla warfare was born an unimpressively small and sickly baby, the youngest of seven, somewhere in Berkeley County, South Carolina, in 1732 to hardworking French Huguenot parents. Soon his family would move near Georgetown on the coast, and the teenage Marion became enamored with the sea. While his infatuation with maritime life lasted exactly one voyage—a whale rammed and sank his ship—a taste for adventure remained.

During the French and Indian War, Marion fought local Cherokee people, and revisionist historians would later revile the enthusiasm he showed in this venture. But Marion's own words show a more conflicted character, as shown by his reaction to an order to burn Cherokees out of their homes.

> Some of our men seemed to enjoy this cruel work, laughing very heartily at the curling flames, as they mounted loud crackling over the tops of the huts. But to me it appeared a shocking sight. *Poor creatures!* thought I, we surely need not grudge you such miserable habitations.

While the irregular tactics Marion learned fighting the Cherokee would come in handy during the Revolutionary War, his first experience in that conflict was in more textbook engagements, such as the defenses of Fort Moultrie and Fort Sullivan and the siege of Savannah. But with the fall of Charleston in 1780, a vengeful Marion and his ragged band of volunteer fighters—who, unusually for the time, included African Americans—vanished into the bogs of the Pee Dee and took up a different way of warfare: ambush and retreat, harass and vanish. In a foreshadowing of the revolutionary movements of the 20th century, "Marion's Men" provisioned themselves with food and supplies from a sympathetic local populace, offering receipts for reimbursement after the war.

Astride small agile mounts called Marsh Tackies, descendants of horses originally left by the Spanish, the Patriots rode where bigger British cavalry horses balked. Marion's nocturnal cunning and his superior intelligence network frustrated the British army and their Loyalist supporters to no end, leading to his nickname, "The Swamp Fox."

British Colonel Banastre Tarleton, himself known as "The Butcher" for atrocities on civilians, was dispatched to neutralize Marion. The savage cat-and-mouse game between the two formed the basis for the storyline of Mel Gibson's *The Patriot* (Gibson's character was reportedly a composite of Marion and several other South Carolina irregulars). Filmed entirely in South Carolina—including at Middleton Plantation, Cypress Gardens, and Historic Brattonsville—*The Patriot* is far from an exact chronicle, but it does accurately portray the nature of the war in the Southern theater, in which quarter was rarely asked or given, and little distinction was made between combatant and civilian.

While certainly the most famous, the Swamp Fox was merely first among equals in a veritable menagerie of hit-and-run fighters. Thomas Sumter, a Virginian by birth, became known as "The Carolina Gamecock" for his ferocity on the battlefield. Andrew Pickens, "The Wizard Owl," and his militiamen played a key role in the Battle of Cowpens in the Upstate.

After the war, Marion served in elected office, married, and settled down at his Pine Bluff Plantation, now submerged under the lake that bears his name. He died in 1795 at the age of 63, peaceful at last.

© JIM MOREKIS

Hampton Plantation

preservation, not restoration. There's a fairly active calendar of events throughout the year, including sweetgrass basket-weaving classes in the basement. Check the website for info on specific events.

Hampton Plantation

Tucked away three miles off U.S. 17 on the South Santee River is **Hampton Plantation State Historic Site** (1950 Rutledge Rd., 843/546-9361, www.southcarolinaparks. com, grounds daily 9am-5pm, free, house tours Sat.-Tues. 1pm, 2pm, and 3pm, $7.50 adults, $3.50 ages 6-15). This Georgian gem, one of the grandest of the antebellum Lowcountry homes, hosted George Washington in 1791. It was also the home of South Carolina poet laureate Archibald Rutledge, who sold it to the state in 1971. Because it's now a state-run project, admission fees are significantly lower than at most of the private plantation homes in the area. The imposing antebellum main house, circa 1735, is magnificent both inside and out. If

you want to skip the house tour, visiting the grounds is free. A two-mile nature trail takes you around one of the original rice fields on Wambaw Creek.

St. James-Santee Episcopal Church

This redbrick church doesn't look that old, but the sanctuary of **St. James-Santee Episcopal Church** (Old Georgetown Rd., 843/887-4386), south of Georgetown near Hampton Plantation State Historic Site, dates from before the Revolutionary War. This building dates from 1768, but the St. James-Santee parish it serves was actually the second in the colony after St. Michael's in Charleston. The parish was notable for incorporating large numbers of French Huguenots. The interior is nearly as Spartan as the exterior, featuring the rare sight of old-fashioned family pews. While the brick was imported from Britain, the columns are made of cypress. Today, only one official service is held each year in the old brick church, during Easter.

McClellanville

The almost unbearably cute little fishing village of McClellanville is nestled among the woods of Francis Marion National Forest and is known mostly for the annual **Lowcountry Shrimp Festival and Blessing of the Fleet** (http://lowcountryshrimpfestival.com), held on the waterfront in early May. This is the place to go for any kind of delectable fresh shrimp dish you might want, from fried shrimp to shrimp kebabs and shrimp tacos. The event culminates with the colorful and touching Blessing of the Fleet ceremony.

Hobcaw Barony

Once a plantation, then a winter home for a Wall Street investor, **Hobcaw Barony** (22 Hobcaw Rd., 843/546-4623, www.hobcaw-barony.org, hours and prices vary) is now an environmental education center. Hobcaw entered its modern period when 11 of the former plantations were purchased en masse in 1905 by Wall Street investor Bernard Baruch, a South Carolina native who wanted a winter residence to escape the brutal Manhattan winters. Presidents and prime ministers came to hunt and relax on its nearly 18,000 acres. Fifty years later, Baruch died, and his progressive-minded daughter Belle took over, immediately wanting to open the grounds to universities for scientific research.

Still privately owned by the Belle W. Baruch Foundation, much of Hobcaw Barony is open only to researchers, but the **Hobcaw Barony Discovery Center** (843/546-4623, www.hobcawbarony.org, Mon.-Fri. 9am-5pm, free) has various exhibits on local history and culture, including Native American artifacts and a modest but fun aquarium with a touch tank. To experience the rest of Hobcaw Barony, you must take one of the various themed guided tours (call for days and times). The basic Hobcaw tour ($20) takes you on a three-hour van ride all around the grounds, including the main Hobcaw House, historic stables, and the old slave quarters, with an emphasis on the natural as well as human history of the area. Other special tours include Birding on the Barony

($30), Christmas in the Quarters ($20), and a catch-and-release fly-fishing tour ($250) of local waters.

Georgetown Lighthouse

While you can't access the state-owned **Georgetown Lighthouse,** you can indeed take a trip to the beach on North Island, where the lighthouse stands. The 1811 structure, repaired after heavy damage in the Civil War, is still an active beacon, now entirely automated.

North Island was part of lands bequeathed to the state by former Boston Red Sox owner Tom Yawkey; North Island is now part of a wildlife preserve bearing Yawkey's name. In 2001, the Georgetown Lighthouse, on the National Register of Historic Places, was added to the preserve.

Tours and Cruises

One of the most sought-after tour tickets in the Georgetown area is for the annual **Plantation Home Tour** (843/545-8291). Sponsored by the Episcopal Church Women of Prince George Winyah Parish, this event, generally happening the first week in April, brings visitors onto many local private antebellum estates that are not open to the public at any other time. Each ticket is for either the Friday or Saturday tour, both of which feature a different set of homes. Tickets include tea at the Winyah Indigo Society Hall each afternoon.

For a standard downtown tour, get on one of the blue-and-white trams of **Swamp Fox Historic District Tours** (1001 Front St., 843/527-6469, $10 pp) which leave daily on the hour starting at 10am near the Harborwalk.

The best walking tour of Georgetown is **Miss Nell's Tours** (843/546-3975, Tues. and Thurs. 10:30am and 2:30pm, other times by appointment, $7-24 depending on length of tour). Leaving from the Harborwalk Bookstore (723 Front St.), Miss Nell, who's been doing this for over 20 years, takes you on a delightful trek through Georgetown's charming downtown waterfront.

One of the more interesting local waterborne tours is on board the *Jolly Rover* and *Carolina*

Rover (735 Front St., 843/546-8822, www. rovertours.com, Mon.-Sat., times and prices vary). The *Jolly Rover* is an honest-to-goodness tall ship that takes you on a two-hour tour of beautiful Winyah Bay and the Intracoastal Waterway, all with a crew in period dress. The *Carolina Rover* takes you on a three-hour eco-tour to nearby North Island, site of the historic Georgetown Lighthouse. You can't tour the lighthouse itself, but you can get pretty darn close to it on this tour.

ENTERTAINMENT AND EVENTS

The **Winyah Bay Heritage Festival** (632 Prince St., 843/833-9919, www.winyahbay. org, free) happens each January at various venues and benefits the local historical society. The focus is on wooden decoys and waterfowl paintings, similar to Charleston's well-known Southeast Wildlife Exposition.

Each October brings the delightful **Wooden Boat Show** (843/545-0015, www. woodenboatshow.com, free) to the waterfront, a 20-year-old celebration of, you guessed it, wooden boats. These aren't toys but the real thing—sleek, classic, and beautiful in the water. There are kid's activities, canoe-making demonstrations, a boat contest, and the highlight, a boatbuilding challenge involving two teams working to build a skiff in four hours.

SPORTS AND RECREATION
Kayaking and Canoeing

Kayakers and canoeists will find a lot to do in the Georgetown area, the confluence of five rivers and the Atlantic Ocean. A good trip for more advanced paddlers is to go out **Winyah Bay** to undeveloped North Island. With advance permission from the state's Department of Natural Resources (803/734-3888), you can camp here. Any paddling in Winyah Bay is pleasant, whether you camp or not.

Another long trip is on the nine-mile black-water **Wambaw Creek Wilderness Canoe Trail** in the Francis Marion National Forest, which takes you through some beautiful cypress

MYRTLE BEACH

the Georgetown waterfront

© JIM MOREKIS

BROAD STREET TO WALL STREET: THE STORY OF BERNARD BARUCH

Bernard Baruch grew up in Camden before purchasing Hobcaw Barony

He became one of the country's most influential men and a world-famous adviser to presidents during both world wars, but Bernard Baruch never strayed far in spirit from his South Carolina home.

Born to German-Jewish parents in the town of Camden, near Columbia, Baruch was born a mere five years after the end of the Civil War. Ironically, his father emigrated from Prussia to avoid the draft, but soon after arriving in the United States, he found himself a surgeon on Robert E. Lee's staff.

and tupelo habitats. Launch sites are at the Wambaw Creek Boat Ramp and a bridge landing. Other good trips in the national forest are on the Santee River and Echaw Creek.

For rentals and guided tours, contact **Nature Adventures Outfitters** (800/673-0679), which runs daylong paddles (about $85 pp), and **Black River Outdoors Center and Expeditions** (21 Garden Ave., 843/546-4840, www.blackriveroutdoors.com), which runs a good half-day tour ($55 adults, $35 under age 13). For those who want to explore the intricate matrix of creeks and tidal canals that made

up the Georgetown rice plantation empire, a guided tour is essential.

Occasional kayak ecotours leave from the **Hobcaw Barony Discovery Center** (22 Hobcaw Rd., 843/546-4623, www.hobcawbarony.org, Mon.-Fri. 9am-5pm, $50) under the auspices of the **North Inlet Winyah Bay National Estuarine Research Reserve** (843/546-6219, www.northinlet.sc.edu).

Hiking

The **Francis Marion National Forest** (www.fs.fed.us) hosts a number of great hiking

Educated in New York City, Baruch gained a love of finance and a taste for the high life. By age 30 he had become so wealthy playing the market that he was able to buy a seat on the New York Stock Exchange. It was during this phase of his life that he purchased the 18,000-acre Hobcaw Barony near Georgetown, a conglomeration of several former rice plantations that became his hunting retreat, a hallowed place of solitude where no phones were allowed.

Baruch's prowess in the realm of high finance led him to a post as adviser to President Woodrow Wilson; perhaps influencing the selection was the whopping $50,000 contribution Baruch gave to Wilson's 1914 campaign, an enormous sum for that time. Required to divest his funds and give up his stock-exchange seat, Baruch turned his aggressive financier's mind to a larger playing field. A sort of economic czar for the Wilson administration, he would play a key role in mobilizing American industry for the war effort, turning what had been a largely agrarian rural society into a modern manufacturing juggernaut.

Under President Franklin D. Roosevelt, Baruch was a key member of the New Deal's National Recovery Administration and favored a centralized (some said heavy-handed) approach to organizing the national economy.

While this served him well during the New Deal and World War II, his often idealistic approach—which envisioned a key role of the United States as an enforcer of nuclear non-proliferation—fell out of favor with the Truman administration's realpolitik. Still, Baruch would leave his mark on the postwar era as well: He was the first to coin the phrase *Cold War*, in a speech in 1947.

Indeed, Baruch was always a colorful and succinct communicator, no doubt a legacy of his Southern boyhood. He is said to have originated the witticism "If all you have is a hammer, everything looks like a nail." Other great one-liners of his include "Millions saw the apple fall, but only Newton asked why," and "Old age is always 15 years older than I am."

Baruch died in New York City in June 1965, but he spent all of that May down in South Carolina at Hobcaw Barony. By that time his daughter Belle had purchased most of Hobcaw; she would eventually deed it to a foundation in her name, administered by the University of South Carolina and Clemson University.

Baruch's boyhood home in Camden is no more, but it is commemorated with a marker on Broad Street. You can also enjoy the beauty and tranquility of **Hobcaw Barony** (22 Hobcaw Rd., 843/546-4623, www.hobcawbarony.org, hours and prices vary) for yourself.

opportunities, chief among them the Swamp Fox passage of the **Palmetto Trail** (www.palmettoconservation.org). This 47-mile route winds through longleaf pine forests, cypress swamps, bottomland hardwood swamps, and various bogs, much of the way along an old logging rail bed. The main entrance to the trail is near Steed Creek Road off U.S. 17; the entrance is clearly marked on the west side of the highway.

Another way to access the Swamp Fox passage is at **Buck Hall Recreation Area** (843/887-3257) on the Intracoastal Waterway. This actually marks the trailhead of the Awendaw Connector of that part of the Palmetto Trail, a more maritime environment. Another trailhead from which to explore Francis Marion hiking trails is farther down U.S. 17 at the **Sewee Visitor Center** (5821 U.S. 17, 843/928-3368, www.fws.gov/seweecenter, Tues.-Sat. 9am-5pm).

Golf

The closest really good links to Georgetown are the courses of the **Waccamaw Golf Trail** (www.waccamawgolftrail.com), a short drive north on U.S. 17. The best public course close to Georgetown is the **Wedgefield Plantation Golf Club** (129 Clubhouse Lane, 843/546-8587, www.wedgefield.com, $69), on the grounds of an old rice plantation on the Black River about four miles west of town.

ACCOMMODATIONS
Under $150
Close to the historic district is **Quality Inn & Suites** (210 Church St., 843/546-5656, www.qualityinn.com, $90-140), which has an outdoor pool and an included breakfast. On the north side of town on U.S. 17 you'll find the **Hampton Inn Georgetown-Marina** (420 Marina Dr., 843/545-5000, www.hamptoninn.com, $140-170), which also offers a pool and complimentary breakfast.

$150-300
By far the most impressive lodging near Georgetown—and indeed among the most impressive in the Southeast—is **€ Mansfield Plantation** (1776 Mansfield Rd., 843/546-6961, www.mansfieldplantation.com, $150-200), a bona fide antebellum estate dating from a 1718 king's grant. It is so evocative and so authentic that Mel Gibson shot part of his film *The Patriot* here, and renovation was recently completed on a historic slave chapel and cabin. As is typical of the Georgetown area, you will find the prices almost ridiculously low for this unique experience on this historic 1,000-acre tract, with gardens, trails, and free use of bicycles. You can stay in one of nine guest rooms situated in three guesthouses on the grounds, each within easy walking distance of the public areas in the main house, which include a 16-seat dining room.

With the closing of two longtime favorite B&Bs, the Dupre House and the Harbour House Inn, it's left to another B&B, the **Keith House Inn** (1012 Front St., 843/485-4324, www.thekeithhouseinn.com, $149-169), to carry on the tradition. Its four second-floor suites, with balconies, are each differently themed. The public areas are wonderfully and whimsically furnished.

FOOD
Don't be fooled by Georgetown's small size—there's often a wait for tables at the better restaurants.

Breakfast and Brunch
The *Southern Living*-recommended **Thomas Cafe** (703 Front St., 843/546-7776, www.thomascafe.net, Mon.-Fri. 7am-2pm, Sat. 7am-1pm, $5-9) offers awesome omelets and pancakes in addition to more Lowcountry-flavored lunch dishes like crab-cake sandwiches and fried green tomatoes.

Classic Southern
Georgetown's best-known fine-dining establishment is **The Rice Paddy** (732 Front St., 843/546-2021, www.ricepaddyrestaurant.com, lunch Mon.-Sat. 11:30am-2pm, dinner Mon.-Sat. 6pm-10pm, $20-30), with the name implying not an Asian menu but rather a nod to the town's Lowcountry culture. The seafood is strong, but they do a mean veal scaloppine and rack of lamb as well. Reservations are strongly recommended.

Coffee, Tea, and Sweets
A perennial favorite is **€ Kudzu Bakery** (120 King St., 843/546-1847, Mon.-Fri. 9am-5:30pm, Sat. 9am-2pm), renowned for its fresh-baked goodies such as delectable breakfast muffins, velvety chocolate cakes, and seasonal pies with fresh ingredients like strawberries, peaches, and pecans.

Seafood
Find the best shrimp and grits in town at **The River Room** (801 Front St., 843/527-4110, www.riverroomgeorgetown.com, Mon.-Sat. 11:30am-2:30pm and 5pm-10pm, $15-25), which combines a gourmet attitude in the kitchen with a casual attitude on the floor. However, dishes like the herb-encrusted grouper or the signature crab cakes taste like fine dining all the way. Reservations are not accepted, and dress is casual. Literally right on the waterfront, the dining room in this former hardware store extends 50 feet over the

Sampit River, adjacent to a public dock where many diners arrive by boat. There's even a large aquarium inside to complete the atmosphere.

INFORMATION AND SERVICES

In the historic waterfront area, you'll find the **Georgetown County Chamber of Commerce and Visitor Center** (531 Front St., 843/546-8436, www.georgetownchamber.com). **Georgetown Memorial Hospital** (606 Black River Rd., 843/527-7000, www.georgetown-hospitalsystem.org) is the main medical center in the area; this 131-bed institution is in the middle of a proposed expansion and relocation. If you need law enforcement help, call the **Georgetown Police** (2222 Highmarket St., 843/545-4300, www.cityofgeorgetownsc.com). In emergencies call 911.

GETTING THERE AND AROUND

Georgetown is at the extreme southern tip of the Grand Strand, accessible by U.S. 17 from the east and south and U.S. 521 (called Highmarket St. in town) from the west. Very centrally located for a tour of the coast, it's about an hour north of Charleston and slightly less than an hour from Myrtle Beach.

Although there's no public transportation in Georgetown, its small size makes touring fairly simple. Metered parking is available downtown.

MYRTLE BEACH

CHARLESTON

Charleston made news in 2011 when it unseated San Francisco for the first time ever in the annual *Condé Nast Traveler* Reader's Choice award for "Top U.S. City." That giant-killing win was quite a coup for this smallish, old-fashioned city in the Deep South. But the most revealing Charleston award is its perennial ranking at the top of the late Marjabelle Young Stewart's annual list for "Most Mannerly City in America." (Charleston has won the award so many times that Stewart's successor at the Charleston School of Protocol and Etiquette, Cindy Grosso, has retired the city from the competition.) This is a city that takes civic harmony so seriously that it boasts the country's only "Livability Court," a binding legal proceeding that meets regularly to enforce local quality-of-life ordinances.

To some eyes, Charleston's hospitable nature has bordered on licentiousness. From its earliest days, the city gained a reputation for vice. (The city's nickname, "The Holy City," derives from the skyline's abundance of church steeples rather than any excess of piety among its citizens.) The old drinking clubs are gone, and the yearly bacchanal of Race Week—in which personal fortunes were won or lost in seconds—is but a distant memory. But that hedonistic legacy is alive and well today in Charleston; the city is full of lovers of strong drink and serious foodies, with every weekend night finding downtown packed with partiers, diners, and show-goers.

Don't mistake the Holy City's charm and joie de vivre for weakness, however. That would be a mistake, for within Charleston's velvet glove

© SOPHIA MOREKIS

HIGHLIGHTS

LOOK FOR ◖ TO FIND RECOMMENDED SIGHTS, ACTIVITIES, DINING, AND LODGING.

◖ **The Battery:** Tranquil surroundings combine with beautiful views of Charleston Harbor, key historical points in the Civil War, and amazing mansions (page 284).

◖ **Rainbow Row:** Painted in warm pastels, these old merchant homes near the cobblestoned waterfront take you on a journey to Charleston's antebellum heyday (page 286).

◖ **Fort Sumter:** Take the ferry to this historic place where the Civil War began, and take in the gorgeous views along the way (page 291).

◖ **St. Philip's Episcopal Church:** A sublimely beautiful sanctuary and two historic graveyards await you in the heart of the evocative French Quarter (page 292).

◖ **Aiken-Rhett House:** There are certainly more ostentatious house museums in Charleston, but none that provide such a virtually intact glimpse into real antebellum life (page 302).

◖ **Drayton Hall:** Don't miss Charleston's oldest surviving plantation home and one of the country's best examples of professional historic preservation (page 305).

◖ **Middleton Place:** Wander one of the world's most beautifully landscaped gardens (page 306).

◖ **CSS *Hunley*:** Ensconced for public viewing in its special preservation tank, the first submarine to sink a ship in battle is a moving example of bravery and sacrifice (page 308).

has always been an iron fist. This is where the colonists scored their first clear victory over the British during the Revolutionary War (another Charleston first). This is the place where the Civil War began, and which stoically endured one of the longest sieges in modern warfare during that conflict. This is the city that survived the East Coast's worst earthquake in 1886 and one of its worst hurricanes a century later.

While many visitors come to see the Charleston of Rhett Butler and Pat Conroy—finding it and then some, of course—they leave impressed by the diversity of Charlestonian life. It's a surprisingly cosmopolitan mix of students, professionals, and longtime inhabitants—who discuss the finer points of Civil War history as if it were last year, party on Saturday night like there's no tomorrow, and

CHARLESTON AND VICINITY

MAGNOLIA PLANTATION AND GARDENS

CHARLESTON INTERNATIONAL AIRPORT

NURSERY RD

To MIDDLETON PLACE and The Inn at Middleton Place

DRAYTON HALL

Hanahan

REMOUNT RD

Goose Creek

642

26
52
78

526

AVIATION ACCESS RD

DORCHESTER ACCESS RD

MONTAGUE AVE

RIVERS AVE

RHETT AVE

North Charleston

NORTH CHARLESTON AND AMERICAN LAFRANCE FIRE MUSEUM AND EDUCATIONAL CENTER

CHARLESTON NAVY YARD

NAVY YARD AT NOISETTE

526

61

ASHLEY RIVER RD

DORCHESTER RD

MONTAGUE AVE

Ashley River

DORCHESTER AVE

NOISETTE BLVD

SPRUILL AVE

CSS HUNLEY

642

7

52
78

Cooper River

Clouter Creek

Daniel Island

0   1 mi
0   1 km

526

61

SAM RITTENBERG BLVD

OLD TOWN RD

171

7

West Ashley

CHARLES TOWNE LANDING

Duck Island

Ashley River

26

MAGNOLIA CEMETERY

Wando River

17

SAVANNAH HWY

ST ANDREWS BLVD

61

171

THE CITADEL

Hampton Park

JOSEPH P. RILEY JR. BALLPARK

KING ST

MORRISON DR

MEETING ST

Town Creek

Drum Island

Mount Pleasant

To Wild Dunes Resort and KOA at Mt Pleasant

Stono River

Wappoo Creek

THE COBURG COW

Wappoo Creek

CALHOUN ST

E BAY ST

17

COLEMAN BLVD

61

CITY MARINA

FERRY TO FORT SUMTER

PATRIOTS POINT RD

PATRIOTS POINT

700

MAY BANK HWY

171

30

BROAD

ST

PATRIOTS POINT RD

703

James Island

HARBOR VIEW RD

Sullivan's Island

RIVERLAND DR

CENTRAL PARK RD

James Creek

FOLLY BEACH RD

SEE CHARLESTON MAPS

Charleston Harbor

JAMES ISLAND COUNTY PARK

To Holiday Inn Follow Beach Oceanfront

To FORT SUMTER

© AVALON TRAVEL

CHARLESTON

go to church on Sunday morning dressed in their finest.

But don't be deceived by these history-minded people. Under the carefully honed tradition and the ever-present ancestor worship, Charleston possesses a vitality of vision that is irrepressibly practical and forward-looking.

HISTORY

Unlike so many of England's colonies in America that were based on freedom from religious persecution, Carolina was strictly a commercial venture from the beginning. The tenure of the Lords Proprietors—the eight English aristocrats who literally owned the colony—began in 1670 when the *Carolina* finished its journey to Albemarle Creek on the west bank of the Ashley River.

Those first colonists would set up a small fortification called Charles Towne, named for Charles II, the first monarch of the Restoration. In a year they'd be joined by colonists from the prosperous but overcrowded British colony of Barbados, who brought a Caribbean sensibility that exists in Charleston to this day.

Finding the first Charles Towne not very fertile and vulnerable to attack from Native Americans and the Spanish, they moved to the peninsula and down to "Oyster Point," what Charlestonians now call White Point Gardens. Just above Oyster Point they set up a walled town, bounded by modern-day Water Street to the south (then a marshy creek, as the name indicates), Meeting Street to the west, Cumberland Street to the north, and the Cooper River on the east.

Growing prosperous as a trading center for deerskin from the great American interior, Charles Towne came into its own after two nearly concurrent events in the early 1700s: the decisive victory of a combined force of Carolinians and Native American allies against the fierce Yamasee people, and the final eradication of the pirate threat in the deaths of Blackbeard and Stede Bonnet.

Flushed with a new spirit of independence, Charles Towne threw off the control of the anemic, disengaged Lords Proprietors, tore down the old defensive walls, and was reborn as an outward-looking, expansive, and increasingly cosmopolitan city that came to be called Charleston. With safety from hostile incursion came the time of the great rice and indigo plantations. Springing up all along the Ashley River soon after the introduction of the crops, they turned the labor and expertise of imported enslaved Africans into enormous profit for their owners. However, the planters preferred the pleasures and sea breezes of Charleston, and gradually summer homes became year-round residences.

It was during this colonial era that the indelible Charlestonian character was stamped: a hedonistic aristocracy combining a love of carousing with a love of the arts; a code of chivalry meant both to reflect a genteel spirit and reinforce the social order; and, ominously, an ever-increasing reliance on slave labor.

As the storm clouds of civil war gathered in the early 1800s, the majority of Charleston's population was of African descent, and the city was the main importation point for the transatlantic slave trade. The worst fears of white Charlestonians seemed confirmed during the alleged plot by slave leader Denmark Vesey in the early 1820s to start a rebellion. The Lowcountry's reliance on slave labor put it front and center in the coming national confrontation over abolition, which came to a head literally and figuratively in the bombardment of Fort Sumter in Charleston Harbor in April 1861.

By war's end, not only did the city lay in ruins—mostly from a disastrous fire in 1861, as well as from a 545-day Union siege—so did its way of life. Pillaged by Northern troops and freed slaves, the great plantations along the Ashley River became the sites of the first strip-mining in the United States, as poverty-stricken owners scraped away the layer of phosphate under the topsoil to sell—perhaps with a certain poetic justice—as fertilizer.

The Holy City didn't really wake up until the great "Charleston Renaissance" of the 1920s and 1930s, when the city rediscovered art, literature, and music in the form of jazz

NOT JUST A MATTER OF BLUE AND GRAY

While the Charleston area is best-known for its pivotal role in the Civil War, this is a drastic oversimplification. South Carolina may have been the "cradle of secession," but it also lost more men in the fight for American independence than any other colony. Here are some military history highlights from other eras:

In Charleston, go to **The Citadel** and enjoy the colorful weekly parade of cadets, the fabled "long gray line," most Fridays at 3pm. In Mount Pleasant, eat lunch in the mess hall of the **USS Yorktown** at the **Patriot's Point Naval Museum.** Visit historic **Middleton Place,** home of one of the signers of the Declaration of Independence and where some scenes from Mel Gibson's The Patriot were filmed.

Further out of town at Santee National Wildlife Refuge on Lake Marion, see the remains of **Fort Watson**—itself built directly atop an ancient Native American mound–which the great Francis Marion himself successfully took from the British during the Revolutionary War. Climb to the top of the mound to enjoy the view.

Down in the Lowcountry, a visit to the **Tuskegee Airmen Memorial** in charming little Walterboro reveals a little-known chapter of World War II history. For an interesting combination of old and new, on Parris Island you can tour the iconic **Marine Corps Recruit Depot Parris Island** with its associated museum, and also see one of the oldest European archaeological sites in the United States, **Charlesfort,** located on what's now a golf course.

And, of course, a more lengthy jaunt deep into the Upstate takes you to **Cowpens National Battlefield,** site of one of the pivotal engagements of the Revolutionary War.

and the world-famous Charleston dance. This was also the time that the world rediscovered Charleston. In the 1920s George Gershwin read local author DuBose Heyward's novel *Porgy* and decided to write a score around the story. Along with lyrics by Ira Gershwin, the three men's collaboration became the first American opera, *Porgy and Bess,* which debuted in New York in 1935. It was also during this time that a new appreciation for Charleston's history sprang up, as the local Preservation Society spearheaded the nation's first historic preservation ordinance.

World War II brought the same economic boom that came to much of the South then, most notably with an expansion of the Navy Yard and the addition of a military air base. By the 1950s, the automobile suburb and a thirst for "progress" claimed so many historic buildings that the inevitable backlash came with the formation of the Historic Charleston Foundation, which continues to lead the fight to keep intact the Holy City's architectural legacy.

Civil rights came to Charleston in earnest with a landmark suit to integrate the Charleston Municipal Golf Course in 1960. The biggest battle, however, would be the 100-day strike in 1969 against the Medical University of South Carolina, then, as now, a large employer of African Americans.

Charleston's next great renaissance—still ongoing today—came with the redevelopment of downtown and the fostering of the tourism industry under the nearly 40-year tenure of Mayor Joe Riley, during which so much of the current visitor-friendly infrastructure became part of daily life here. Today, Charleston is completing the transition away from a military and manufacturing base and attracting professionals and artists to town.

PLANNING YOUR TIME

Even if you're just going to confine yourself to the peninsula, I can't imagine spending less than two nights. You'll want half a day for shopping on King Street and a full day for seeing various attractions and museums. Keep in mind that one of Charleston's key sights, Fort Sumter, will take almost half a day to see once you factor in ticketing and boarding time for the ferry out to the fort and back; plan accordingly.

If you have a car, there are several great places to visit off the peninsula—especially the plantations along the Ashley River. You can visit all of them in a single day if you get an early start.

The real issue for most visitors boils down to two questions: How much do you want to spend on accommodations, and in which part of town do you want to stay? Lodging is generally not cheap in Charleston, but because the price differential is not that much between staying on the peninsula and staying on the outskirts, I recommend the peninsula. You'll pay more, but not *that* much more, with the bonus of probably being able to walk to most places you want to see—which, after all, is the best way to enjoy the city.

ORIENTATION

Charleston occupies a peninsula bordered by the Ashley River to the west and the Cooper River to the east, which "come together to form the Atlantic Ocean," according to the haughty phrase once taught to generations of Charleston schoolchildren.

The peninsula is ringed by islands, many of which have become heavily populated suburbs. Clockwise from the top of the peninsula they are: Daniel Island, Mount Pleasant, Isle of Palms, Sullivan's Island, Morris Island, Folly Island, and James Island. The resort island of Kiawah and the much less-developed Edisto Island are farther south down the coast.

North Charleston is not only a separate municipality; it's also a different state of mind. A sprawling combination of malls, light industry, and low-income housing, it also boasts some of the more cutting-edge urban redesign activity in the area.

Parking is at a premium in downtown Charleston. Luckily the city has many reasonably priced parking garages, which I recommend that you use. But cars should only be used when you have to. Charleston is best enjoyed on foot, both because of its small size and the cozy, meandering nature of its old streets, designed not for cars and tour buses but for boots, horseshoes, and carriage wheels.

Charleston is made up of many small neighborhoods, many of them quite old. The boundaries are confusing, so your best bet is simply to look at the street signs (signage in general is excellent in Charleston). If you're in a historic neighborhood, such as the French Quarter or Ansonborough, a smaller sign above the street name will indicate that.

Other key terms you'll hear are "the Crosstown," the portion of U.S. 17 that goes across the peninsula; "Savannah Highway," the portion of U.S. 17 that traverses "West Ashley," which is the suburb across the Ashley River; "East Cooper," the area across the Cooper River that includes Mount Pleasant, Isle of Palms, and Daniel and Sullivan's Islands; and "the Neck," up where the peninsula narrows. These are the terms that locals use, and hence what you'll see in this guide.

CHARLESTON

Sights

Though most key sights in Charleston do indeed have some tie to the city's rich history, house museums are only a subset of the attractions here. Charleston's sights are excellently integrated into its built environment, and often the enjoyment of nearby gardens or a lapping river is part of the fun.

SOUTH OF BROAD

As one of the oldest streets in Charleston, the east-west thoroughfare of Broad Street is not only a physical landmark, it's a mental one as well. The first area of the Charleston peninsula to be settled, the area south of Broad Street—often shortened to the mischievous acronym "SOB" by local wags—features older homes, meandering streets (many of them built on "made land" filling in former wharfs), and a distinctly genteel, laid-back feel.

As you'd expect, it also features more affluent residents, sometimes irreverently referred to as "SOB snobs." This heavily residential area has no nightlife to speak of and gets almost eerily quiet after hours, but rest assured that plenty of people live here.

While I highly recommend just wandering among these narrow streets and marveling at the lovingly restored old homes, keep in mind that almost everything down here is in private hands. Don't wander into a garden or take photos into a window unless you're invited to do so (and given Charleston's legendary hospitality, that can happen).

◖ The Battery

For many, **The Battery** (E. Battery St. and Murray Blvd., 843/724-7321, daily 24 hours, free) is the single most iconic Charleston spot, drenched in history and boasting dramatic views. A look to the south gives you the sweeping expanse of the Cooper River, with views of Fort Sumter, Castle Pinckney, Sullivan's Island, and, off to the north, the old carrier *Yorktown* moored at Mount Pleasant. A landward look

gives you a view of the adjoining, peaceful **White Point Gardens,** the sumptuous mansions of the Battery, and a beguiling peek behind them into some of the oldest neighborhoods in Charleston. But if you had been one of the first European visitors to this tip of the peninsula about 400 years ago, you'd have seen how it got its first name, Oyster Point: This entire area was once home to an enormous outcropping of oysters.

Once the bustling (and sometimes seedy) heart of Charleston's maritime activity, the Battery was where pirate Stede Bonnet and 21 of his men were hanged in 1718. As you might imagine, the area got its name for hosting cannons during the War of 1812, with the current distinctive seawall structure built in the 1850s.

Contrary to popular belief, no guns fired from here on Fort Sumter, as they would have been out of range. However, many thankfully inoperable cannons, mortars, and piles of shot still reside here, much to the delight of kids of all ages. This is where Charlestonians gathered in a giddy, party-like atmosphere to watch the shelling of Fort Sumter in 1861, blissfully ignorant of the horrors to come. A short time later the North would return the favor, as the Battery and all of Charleston up to Broad Street would bear the brunt of shelling during the long siege of the city (the rest was out of reach of Union guns).

Look for the three-story private residence where East Battery curves northward. You won't be taking any tours of it, but you should be aware that it's the **DeSaussure House** (1 E. Battery St.), best known in Charleston history for hosting rowdy, celebratory crowds on the roof and the piazzas to watch the 34-hour shelling of Fort Sumter in 1861.

Edmondston-Alston House

The most noteworthy single attraction on the Battery is the 1825 **Edmondston-Alston House** (21 E. Battery St., 843/722-7171,

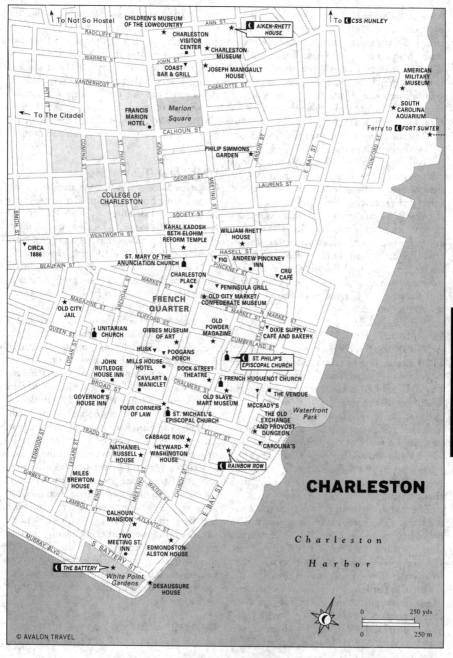

CHARLESTON

To Not So Hostel

CHILDREN'S MUSEUM
OF THE LOWCOUNTRY

ANN ST.

★ ◖ AIKEN-RHETT
HOUSE

To ◖ CSS HUNLEY

RADCLIFFE ST.

CHARLESTON
VISITOR
CENTER

★ CHARLESTON
MUSEUM

WARREN ST.

JOHN ST.

▼ COAST
BAR & GRILL

★ JOSEPH MANIGAULT
HOUSE

VANDERHOST ST.

CHARLOTTE ST.

AMERICAN
MILITARY
MUSEUM

PITT ST.

← To The Citadel

FRANCIS
MARION
HOTEL ●

Marion
Square

★ SOUTH
CAROLINA
AQUARIUM

CALHOUN ST.

Ferry to ◖ FORT SUMTER
★ ┄┄┄┄

COMING ST.

ST. PHILIP ST.

KING ST.

PHILIP SIMMONS
GARDEN ★

ANSON ST.

E. BAY ST.

CONCORD ST.

GEORGE ST.

MEETING ST.

LAURENS ST.

COLLEGE OF
CHARLESTON

SMITH'S ST.

SOCIETY ST.

WENTWORTH ST.

KAHAL KADOSH
BETH ELOHIM
REFORM TEMPLE

WILLIAM RHETT
HOUSE

▼ CIRCA
1886

ST. MARY OF THE
ANUNCIATION CHURCH 🏛

HASELL ST.

▼ FIG ANDREW PINCKNEY
INN

BEAUFAIN ST.

PINCKNEY ST.

CRU
▼ CAFÉ

MARKET ST.

CHARLESTON
PLACE

ARCHDALE ST.

▼ PENINSULA GRILL

MAGAZINE ST.

FRENCH
QUARTER

CLIFFORD ST.

★ OLD CITY MARKET/
CONFEDERATE MUSEUM

S. MARKET ST.

N. MARKET ST.

OLD CITY
JAIL ●

QUEEN ST.

🏛 UNITARIAN
CHURCH

GIBBES MUSEUM
OF ART

OLD
POWDER
MAGAZINE

▼ DIXIE SUPPLY
CAFÉ AND BAKERY

LOGAN ST.

HUSK ▼

▼ POOGANS
PORCH

CUMBERLAND ST.

JOHN
RUTLEDGE
HOUSE INN ●

MILLS HOUSE
HOTEL ●

DOCK STREET
THEATRE ★

🏛 ST. PHILIP'S
EPISCOPAL CHURCH

CAVLART &
MANICLET ■

CHALMERS ST.

★ FRENCH HUGUENOT CHURCH

BROAD ST.

GOVERNOR'S
HOUSE INN ●

FOUR CORNERS
OF LAW

OLD SLAVE
MART MUSEUM ★

MCCRADY'S

▼ THE VENDUE

🏛 ST. MICHAEL'S
EPISCOPAL CHURCH

ELLIOT ST.

THE OLD
EXCHANGE
AND PROVOST
★ DUNGEON

Waterfront
Park

TRADD ST.

CABBAGE ROW ★

▼ CAROLINA'S

LENWOOD ST.

LEGARE ST.

NATHANIEL
RUSSELL ★
HOUSE

HEYWARD-
WASHINGTON
HOUSE

KING ST.

MEETING ST.

WATER ST.

CHURCH ST.

◖ RAINBOW ROW ★

GIBBES ST.

MILES
BREWTON
HOUSE ●

LAMBOLL ST.

CALHOUN
MANSION ●

ATLANTIC ST.

E. BAY ST.

CHARLESTON

MURRAY BLVD.

TWO
MEETING ST.
INN ●

S. BATTERY ST.

★
EDMONDSTON-
ALSTON HOUSE

Charleston

◖ THE BATTERY ★

*White Point
Gardens*

★ DESAUSSURE
HOUSE

Harbor

0   250 yds
0   250 m

© AVALON TRAVEL

CHARLESTON

www.middletonplace.org, Tues.-Sat. 10am-4:30pm, Sun.-Mon. 1:30pm-4:30pm, $12 adults, $8 students), the only Battery home open to the public for tours. This is one of the most unique and well-preserved historic homes in the United States, thanks to the ongoing efforts of the Alston family, who acquired the house from shipping merchant Charles Edmondston for $15,500 after the Panic of 1837 and who still live on the third floor (tours only visit the first two stories).

Over 90 percent of the home's furnishings are original items from the Alston era. The Edmondston-Alston House has withstood storms, fires, earthquakes, and Yankee shelling, due in no small part to its sturdy construction; its masonry walls are two bricks thick, and it features both interior and exterior shutters. Originally built in the federal style, second owner Charles Alston added several Greek Revival elements, notably the parapet, balcony, and piazza, where General Beauregard watched the attack on Fort Sumter.

◖ Rainbow Row

At 79-107 East Bay Street, between Tradd and Elliot Streets, is one of the most photographed sights in the United States: colorful **Rainbow Row.** The reason for its name becomes obvious when you see the array of pastel-colored mansions, all facing the Cooper River. The bright, historically accurate colors—nine of them, to be exact—are one of the many vestiges you'll see around town of Charleston's Caribbean heritage, a legacy of the English settlers from the colony of Barbados who were among the city's first citizens.

The homes are unusually old for this fire-, hurricane-, and earthquake-ravaged city, with most dating from 1730 to 1750. As you admire Rainbow Row from across East Battery, keep in mind you're actually walking on what used to be water. These houses were originally right on the Cooper River, their lower stories serving as storefronts on the wharf. The street was created later on top of landfill, or "made land" as it's called locally. The restoration projects on Rainbow Row directly inspired the creation of

the Charleston Preservation Society, the first such group in the United States.

Continue walking up the High Battery past Rainbow Row and find Water Street. This aptly named little avenue was in fact a creek in the early days, acting as the southern border of the original walled city. The large brick building on the seaward side housing the Historic Charleston Foundation sits on the site of the old Granville bastion, a key defensive point in the wall.

Nathaniel Russell House

Considered one of Charleston's grandest homes despite being built by an outsider from Rhode Island, the **Nathaniel Russell House** (51 Meeting St., 843/724-8481, www.historic-charleston.org, Mon.-Sat. 10am-5pm, Sun. 2pm-5pm, last tour 4:30pm, $10 adults, $5 children) is now a National Historic Landmark and one of the country's best examples of neoclassicism. Built in 1808 for the then-princely sum of $80,000 by Nathaniel Russell, a.k.a. "King of the Yankees," the home is furnished as accurately as possible to represent not only the lifestyle of the Russell family but the 18 African American servants who shared the premises. As with fine antebellum homes throughout coastal South Carolina and Georgia, the use of faux finishing is prevalent throughout, mimicking surfaces such as marble, wood, and lapis lazuli.

When you visit, keep in mind that you're in the epicenter of not only Charleston's historic preservation movement but perhaps the nation's as well. In 1955 the Nathaniel Russell House was the first major project of the Historic Charleston Foundation, which raised $65,000 to purchase it. Two years later, admission fees from the house would support Historic Charleston's groundbreaking revolving fund for preservation, the prototype for many such successful programs. For an extra $6, you can gain admission to the Aiken-Rhett House farther uptown, also administered by the Historic Charleston Foundation.

Calhoun Mansion

The single largest of Charleston's surviving

KNOW YOUR CHARLESTON HOUSES

Charleston's homes boast not only a long pedigree but an interesting and unique one as well. Here are the basics of local architecture:

Single House: A legacy of the early Barbadians among the first settlers here, the Charleston single house is named for the fact that it's a single room wide. The phrase refers to layout, not style, which can range from Georgian to federal to Greek Revival, or a combination. Furnished with full-length piazzas, or long verandas, on the south side to take advantage of southerly breezes, the single house is perhaps the nation's first sustainable house design. The house is lengthwise on the lot, with the entrance on the side of the house. This means the "backyard" is actually the side yard. They're everywhere in Charleston, but Church Street has great examples, including 90, 92, and 94 Church Street, and the oldest single house in town, the 1730 Robert Brewton House (71 Church St.).

Double House: This layout is two rooms wide with a central hallway and a porched facade facing the street. Double houses often had separate carriage houses. The Aiken-Rhett and Heyward-Washington houses are good examples.

Charleston Green: This uniquely Charlestonian color—extremely dark green that looks pitch black in low light—has its roots in the aftermath of the Civil War. The federal government distributed surplus black paint to contribute to reconstruction of the ravaged peninsula, but Charlestonians were too proud (and tasteful) to use as-is. So they added a tiny bit of yellow to each gallon, producing Charleston green.

Earthquake Bolt: Structural damage after the 1886 earthquake was so extensive that many buildings were retrofitted with one or more long iron rods running wall to wall to keep the house stable. The rod was capped at both ends by a "gib plate," often disguised with a decorative element such as a lion's head, an S or X shape, or other design. Earthquake bolts can be seen all over town, but notable examples are at 235 Meeting Street, 198 East Bay Street, 407 King Street, and 51 East Battery (a rare star design); 190 East Bay Street is unusual for having both an X and an S plate on the same building.

Joggling Board: This long (10-15 feet) flexible plank of cypress, palm, or pine with a handle at each end served various recreational purposes for early Charlestonians. As babies, they might be bounced to sleep. As small children, they might use it as a trampoline. Later it was a method of courtship, whereby a couple would start out at opposite ends and bounce until they met in the middle.

Carolopolis Award: For over 50 years, the Preservation Society of Charleston has handed out these little black badges, to be mounted near the doorway of the winning home, to local homeowners who have renovated historic properties downtown. On the award you'll see "Carolopolis," the Latinized name of the city; "Condita AD 1670," the Latin word for founding with the date of Charleston's inception; and another date referring to when the award was given.

Ironwork: Before the mid-19th century, wrought iron was a widely used ornament. Charleston's best-known blacksmith, the late Philip Simmons, made a life's work of continuing the ancient craft of working in wrought iron, and his masterpieces are visible throughout the city, most notably at the Philip Simmons Garden (91 Anson St.), a gate for the Visitors Center (375 Meeting St.), and the Philip Simmons Children's Garden at Josiah Smith Tennent House (Blake St. and East Bay St.). Chevaux-de-frise are iron bars on top of a wall through which project some particularly menacing spikes. They became popular after the Denmark Vesey slave revolt conspiracy of 1822. The best example is on the wall of the Miles Brewton House (27 King St.).

grand homes, the 1876 **Calhoun Mansion** (16 Meeting St., 843/722-8205, www.calhounmansion.net, tours daily 11am-5pm, $15) boasts 35 opulent rooms (with 23 fireplaces!) in a striking Italianate design taking up a whopping 24,000 square feet. The grounds feature some charming garden spaces. A 90-minute "grand tour" is available for $75 pp; call for an appointment. Though the interiors at this privately run house are packed with antiques and furnishings, be aware that not all of them are accurate or period.

Miles Brewton House

A short distance from the Nathaniel Russell House but much less viewed by visitors, the circa-1769 **Miles Brewton House** (27 King St.), now a private residence, is maybe the best example of Georgian-Palladian architecture in the world. The almost medieval wrought-iron fencing, or chevaux-de-frise, was added in 1822 after rumors of a slave uprising spread through town. This imposing double house was the site of not one but two headquarters of occupying armies, British general Clinton during the Revolutionary War and the federal garrison after the end of the Civil War. The great Susan Pringle Frost, principal founder of the Charleston Preservation Society and a Brewton descendant, grew up here.

Heyward-Washington House

The **Heyward-Washington House** (87 Church St., 843/722-0354, www.charlestonmuseum.org, Mon.-Sat. 10am-5pm, Sun. 1pm-5pm, $10 adults, $5 children, combo tickets to Charleston Museum and Manigault House available) takes the regional practice of naming a historic home for the two most significant names in its pedigree to its logical extreme. Built in 1772 by the father of Declaration of Independence signer Thomas Heyward Jr., the house also hosted George Washington in 1791. It's now owned and operated by the Charleston Museum. The main attraction at the Heyward-Washington House is its masterful woodwork, exemplified by the cabinetry of legendary Charleston carpenter Thomas Elfe.

Look for his signature, a figure eight with four diamonds.

Cabbage Row

You know these addresses, 89-91 Church Street, better as "Catfish Row" in Gershwin's opera *Porgy and Bess* (itself based on the book *Porgy* by the great Charleston author DuBose Heyward, who lived at 76 Church St.). Today, the **Cabbage Row** complex—which once housed 10 families—next to the Heyward-Washington House is upgraded from years past, but the row still has the humble appeal of the tenement housing it once was. The house nearby at 94 Church Street was where John C. Calhoun and others drew up the infamous Nullification Acts that eventually led to the South's secession.

St. Michael's Episcopal Church

The oldest church in South Carolina, **St. Michael's Episcopal Church** (71 Broad St., 843/723-0603, services Sun. 8am and 10:30am, tours available after services) is actually the second sanctuary on this spot. The first church was made out of black cypress and was called St. Philip's, or "the English Church," which was later rebuilt on Church Street. Although the designer is not known, we do know that work on this sanctuary in the style of Christopher Wren began in 1752 as a response to the overflowing congregation at the rebuilt St. Philips, and it didn't finish until 1761. Other than a small addition on the southeast corner in 1883, the St. Michael's you see today is virtually unchanged, including the massive pulpit, outsized in the style of the time. Services here over the years hosted such luminaries as Marquis de Lafayette, George Washington, and Robert E. Lee, the latter two of whom are known to have sat in the "governor's pew." Two signers of the U.S. Constitution, John Rutledge and Charles Cotesworth Pinckney, are buried in the sanctuary. St. Michael's offers informal, free guided tours to visitors after Sunday services; contact the greeter for more information.

Four Corners of Law

No guidebook is complete without a mention of the famous intersection of Broad and Meeting Streets, named **Four Corners of Law** for its confluence of federal law (the Post Office building), state law (the state courthouse), municipal law (City Hall), and God's law (St. Michael's Episcopal Church). That's all well and good, but no matter what the tour guides may tell you, the phrase "Four Corners of Law" was actually popularized by *Ripley's Believe It or Not!* Still, there's no doubt that this intersection has been key to Charleston from the beginning. Meeting Street was laid out around 1672 and takes its name from the White Meeting House of early Dissenters, meaning non-Anglicans. Broad Street was also referred to as Cooper Street in the early days. Right in the middle of the street once stood the very first statue in the United States, a figure of William Pitt erected in 1766.

WATERFRONT

Charleston's waterfront is a place where tourism, history, and industry coexist in a largely seamless fashion. Another of the successful—if at one time controversial—developments spearheaded by Mayor Joe Riley, the centerpiece of the harbor area as far as visitors are concerned is Waterfront Park up toward the High Battery. Farther up the Cooper River is Aquarium Wharf, where you'll find the South Carolina Aquarium, the American Military Museum, the Fort Sumter Visitor Education Exhibit, and the dock where you take the various harbor ferries, whether to Fort Sumter or just a calming ride on the Cooper River.

The Old Exchange and Provost Dungeon

It's far from glamorous, but nonetheless the **Old Exchange and Provost Dungeon** (122 East Bay St., 843/727-2165, www.oldexchange.com, daily 9am-5pm, $7 adults, $3.50 children and students) at the intersection of East Bay and Meeting Streets is known as one of the three most historically significant colonial buildings in the United States, along with Philadelphia's Independence Hall and Boston's Faneuil Hall. This is actually the old Royal Exchange and Custom House, with the cellar serving as a British prison, all built in 1771 over a portion of the old 1698 fortification wall. Three of Charleston's four signers of the Declaration of Independence did time downstairs for sedition against the crown. Fans of kitsch will get a hoot out of the animatronic Hall of the Presidents-style figures. Kids might especially get a scary kick out of the basement dungeon, where the infamous pirate Stede Bonnet was imprisoned in 1718 before being hanged with his crew on the Battery.

Waterfront Park

Situated on Concord Street roughly between Exchange Street and Vendue Range, **Waterfront Park** (843/724-7327, daily dawn-dusk, free) was, like many waterfront locales in Charleston, built on what used to be marsh and water. This particularly massive chunk of "made land" juts about a football field's length farther out than the old waterline. Visitors and locals alike enjoy the relaxing vista of Charleston Harbor, often from the many swinging benches arranged in an unusual front-to-back, single-file pattern all down the pier. Children will enjoy the large "Vendue" wading fountain at the Park's entrance off Vendue Range, while a bit farther south is the large and quite artful Pineapple Fountain with its surrounding wading pool.

South Carolina Aquarium

If you've been to the more expansive aquariums in Monterey or Boston, you might be disappointed at the breadth of offerings at the **South Carolina Aquarium** (100 Aquarium Wharf, 843/720-1990, www.scaquarium.org, Mar.-Aug. daily 9am-5pm, Sept.-Feb. daily 9am-4pm, $24.95, $14.95 children, combo tickets with Fort Sumter tour available). But nonetheless, it's clean and well done and is a great place for the whole family to have some fun while getting educated about the rich aquatic life off the coast and throughout this small but ecologically diverse state.

CHARLESTON

THE GREAT CHARLESTON EARTHQUAKE

The Charleston peninsula is bordered by three faults, almost like a picture frame: the Woodstock Fault above North Charleston, the Charleston Fault running along the east bank of the Cooper River, and the Ashley Fault to the west of the Ashley River. On August 31, 1886, one of them buckled, causing one of the most damaging earthquakes ever to hit the United States.

The earthquake of 1886 was actually signaled by several foreshocks earlier that week. Residents of the nearby town of Summerville, South Carolina, 20 miles up the Ashley River, felt a small earthquake after midnight on Friday, August 27. Most slept through it. But soon after dawn a larger shock came, complete with a loud bang, causing many to run outside their houses. That Saturday afternoon another tremor hit Summerville, breaking windows and throwing a bed against a wall in one home. Still, Charlestonians remained unconcerned. Then, that Tuesday at 9:50pm came the big one. With an epicenter somewhere near the Middleton Place plantation, the Charleston earthquake is estimated to have measured about 7 on the Richter scale. Tremors were felt across half the country, with the ground shaking in Chicago and a church damaged in Indianapolis. A dam 120 miles away in Aiken, South Carolina, immediately gave way, washing a train right off the tracks. Cracks opened up parallel to the Ashley River, with part of the riverbank falling into the water. Thousands of chimneys all over the state either fell or were rendered useless. A Charleston minister at his summer home in Asheville, North Carolina, described a noise like the sound of wheels driving straight up the mountain, followed by the sound of many railroad cars going by. A moment later, one corner of his house lifted off the ground and slammed back down again. The quake brought a series of "sand blows," a particularly disturbing phenomenon in which craters open up and spew sand and water up into the air like a small volcano. In Charleston's case, some of the craters were 20 feet wide, shooting debris another 20 feet into the air. The whole event lasted less than a minute.

In crowded Charleston, the damage was horrific: over 2,000 buildings destroyed, a quarter of the city's value gone, 27 killed immediately and almost 100 more to die from injuries and disease. Because of the large numbers of newly homeless, tent cities sprang up in every available park and green space. The American Red Cross's first field mission soon brought some relief, but the scarcity of food, and especially fresh water, made life difficult for everyone.

Almost every surviving building had experienced structural damage, in some cases severe, so a way had to be found to stabilize them. This led to the widespread use of the "earthquake bolt" now seen throughout older Charleston homes. Essentially acting as very long rods with a washer on each end, the idea of the earthquake bolt is simple: Poke a long iron rod through two walls that need stabilizing, and cap the ends. Charleston being Charleston, of course, the end caps were often decorated with a pattern or symbol.

The seismic activity of the earthquake was so intense that more than 300 aftershocks occurred in the 35 years after the event. In fact, geologists think that most seismic events measured in the region today—including a large event in December 2008, also centering near Summerville—are probably also aftershocks.

Earthquake bolts are a common sight in downtown Charleston.

© JIM MOREKIS

When you enter you're greeted with the 15,000-gallon Carolina Seas tank, with placid nurse sharks and vicious-looking moray eels. Other exhibits highlight the five key South Carolina ecosystems: beach, salt marsh, coastal plain, piedmont, and mountain forest. Another neat display is the Touch Tank, a hands-on collection of invertebrates found along the coast, such as sea urchins and horseshoe crabs. The pièce de résistance is the three-story Great Ocean Tank with literally hundreds of deeper-water marine creatures, including sharks, puffer fish, and sea turtles.

American Military Museum

Slightly out of place thematically with the Aquarium, the **American Military Museum** (360 Concord St., 843/577-7000, www.americanmilitarymuseum.org, Mon.-Sat. 10am-6pm, Sun. 1pm-5pm, $9 adults, $6 students) is one of those under-the-radar types of small museums that can be unexpectedly enriching. Certainly its location near the embarkation point for the Fort Sumter ferry hasn't hurt its profile. It's heavy on uniforms, with a wide range all the way from the Revolution to the modern day.

C Fort Sumter

This is it: the place that brought about the beginning of the Civil War, a Troy for modern times. Though many historians insist the war would have happened regardless of President Lincoln's decision to keep **Fort Sumter** (843/883-3123, www.nps.gov/fosu, hours vary, free) in federal hands, nonetheless the stated casus belli was Major Robert Anderson's refusal to surrender the fort when requested to do so in the early morning hours of April 12, 1861. A few hours later came the first shot of the war, fired from Fort Johnson by Confederate Captain George James. Notorious secessionist Edmund Ruffin gets credit for firing the first shot in anger, only moments after James's signal shell, from a battery at Cummings Point. The first return shot from Fort Sumter was fired by none other than Captain Abner Doubleday, the father of baseball. The first death of the Civil

War also happened at Fort Sumter, not from the Confederate bombardment but on the day after. U.S. Army Private Daniel Hough died when the cannon he was loading, to be fired as part of a 100-gun surrender salute to the Stars and Stripes, exploded prematurely. Today, the battered but still-standing Fort Sumter remains astride the entrance to Charleston Harbor on an artificial 70,000-ton sandbar.

As you might expect, you can only visit by boat, specifically the approved concessionaire **Fort Sumter Tours** (843/881-7337, www.fortsumtertours.com, $17 adults, $10 ages 6-11, $15 seniors). Once at the fort, there's no charge for admission. Ferries leave from Liberty Square at Aquarium Wharf on the peninsula three times a day during the high season (Apr.-Oct.); call or check the website for times. Make sure to arrive about 30 minutes before the ferry departs. You can also get to Fort Sumter by ferry from Patriot's Point at Mount Pleasant through the same concessionaire.

Budget at least 2.5 hours for the whole trip, including an hour at Fort Sumter. At Liberty Square on the peninsula is the **Fort Sumter Visitor Education Center** (340 Concord St., www.nps.gov/fosu/index.htm, daily 8:30am-5pm, free), so you can learn more about where you're about to go. Once there, you can be enlightened by the regular ranger talks on the fort's history and construction (generally at 11am and 2:30pm), take in the interpretive exhibits throughout the site, and enjoy the view of the spires of the Holy City from afar. If you want to skip Sumter, you can still take an enjoyable 90-minute ferry ride around the harbor and past the fort on the affiliated **SpiritLine Cruises** (800/789-3678, www.spiritlinecruises.com, $17 adults, $10 ages 6-11).

Some visitors are disappointed to find many of the fort's gun embrasures bricked over. This was done during the Spanish-American War, when the old fort was turned into an earthwork.

FRENCH QUARTER

Unlike the New Orleans version, Charleston's French Quarter is Protestant in origin and

© SOPHIA MOREKIS

Fort Sumter

flavor. Historically this area was indeed the main place of commerce for the city's population of French Huguenots, primarily a merchant class who fled religious persecution in their native country. Today, the five-block area—roughly bounded by East Bay, Market Street, Meeting Street, and Broad Street—contains some of Charleston's most historic buildings, its most evocative old churches and graveyards, and its most tasteful art galleries.

(St. Philip's Episcopal Church

With a pedigree dating back to the colony's fledgling years, **St. Philip's Episcopal Church** (142 Church St., 843/722-7734, www.stphilipschurchsc.org, sanctuary Mon.-Fri. 10am-noon and 2pm-4pm, services Sun. 8:15am) is the oldest Anglican congregation south of Virginia. The first St. Philip's was built in 1680 at the corner of Meeting Street and Broad Street, the present site of St. Michael's Episcopal Church. That first St. Philip's was damaged by a hurricane in 1710, and the city fathers approved the building of a new sanctuary on Church Street.

However, that building was nearly destroyed by yet another hurricane during construction. Alas, that St. Philip's burned to the ground in 1835. Construction immediately began on a replacement, and it's that building you see today. Heavily damaged by Hurricane Hugo in 1989, a $4.5 million renovation kept the church usable. So, to recap: St. Philip's was originally on the site of the present St. Michael's. And while St. Philip's is the oldest congregation in South Carolina, St. Michael's has the oldest physical church building in the state. Are we clear?

South Carolina's great statesman John C. Calhoun—who ironically despised Charlestonians for what he saw as their loose morals—was originally buried across Church Street in the former "stranger's churchyard," or West Cemetery, after his death in 1850. But near the end of the Civil War, Calhoun's body was moved to an unmarked grave closer to the sanctuary in an attempt to hide its location from Union troops, who it was feared would go out of their way to wreak vengeance on the tomb of one of slavery's staunchest advocates.

MARY CHESNUT'S DIARY

I have always kept a journal after a fashion of my own, with dates and a line of poetry or prose, mere quotations, which I understood and no one else, and I have kept letters and extracts from the papers. From today forward I will tell the story in my own way.

Mary Boykin Chesnut

Mary Boykin Chesnut's seminal Civil War diary—originally titled *A Diary From Dixie* and first published in 1905—provides an extraordinary eyewitness account of antebellum life in Charleston. By turns wise and witty, fiery and flirtatious, Chesnut's writing is a gripping, politically savvy, and dryly humorous chronicle of a life lived close to the innermost circles of Confederate decision-makers. Her husband, James Chesnut Jr., was a U.S. Senator until South Carolina seceded from the Union, whereupon he became a key aide to Confederate President Jefferson Davis and a general in the Confederate Army.

The diary runs from February 1861—three months before the firing on Fort Sumter, which she witnessed—to August 1865, after the Confederate surrender. Along the way the diary shifts to and from various locales, including Montgomery, Alabama; Richmond, Virginia; Columbia, South Carolina; and, of course, Charleston, which she held in high regard:

On the Battery with the Rutledges, Captain Hartstein was introduced to me. He has done some heroic things—brought home some ships and is a man of mark. Afterward he sent me a beautiful bouquet, not half so beautiful, however, as Mr. Robert Gourdin's, which already occupied the place of honor on my center table. What a dear, delightful place is Charleston!

Chesnut was a Southern patriot, and some of her observations are wildly politically incorrect by today's standards. But while supportive of slavery and suspicious of the motives of abolitionists—"People in those places expect more virtue from a plantation African than they can insure in practise among themselves with all their own high moral surroundings," she says of white Northern abolitionists—she does allow for a few nuanced looks at the lives of African Americans in the South, as in this observation about her own house servants after the fall of Fort Sumter:

You could not tell that they even heard the awful roar going on in the bay, though it has been dinning in their ears night and day. People talk before them as if they were chairs and tables. They make no sign. Are they stolidly stupid? or wiser than we are; silent and strong, biding their time?

While the diary begins on a confident note regarding the South's chances in the war, as the news from the battlefield gets worse we see how Southerners cope with the sure knowledge that they will lose:

I know how it feels to die. I have felt it again and again. For instance, some one calls out, "Albert Sidney Johnston is killed." My heart stands still. I feel no more. I am, for so many seconds, so many minutes, I know not how long, utterly without sensation of any kind—dead; and then, there is that great throb, that keen agony of physical pain, and the works are wound up again. The ticking of the clock begins, and I take up the burden of life once more.

Southern historian C. Vann Woodward compiled an annotated edition of the Chesnut diary in 1981, *Mary Chesnut's Civil War*, which won a Pulitzer Prize the following year. Her words came to even wider national exposure due to extensive quotations from her diary in Ken Burns's PBS miniseries *The Civil War*.

CHARLESTON

In 1880, with Reconstruction in full swing, the state legislature directed and funded the building of the current large memorial in the West Cemetery.

French Huguenot Church

One of the oldest congregations in town, the **French Huguenot Church** (44 Queen St., 843/722-4385, www.frenchhuguenotchurch. org, liturgy Sun. 10:30am) also has the distinction of being the only remaining independent Huguenot church in the country. Founded around 1681 by French Calvinists, the church had about 450 congregants by 1700. The first church was built on this site in 1687, and became known as the "Church of Tides" because at that time the Cooper River lapped at its property line. This sanctuary was deliberately destroyed as a firebreak during the great conflagration of 1796. The church was replaced in 1800, but that building was in turn demolished in favor of the picturesque, stucco-coated Gothic Revival sanctuary you see today, which was completed in 1845 and subsequently survived Union shelling and the 1886 earthquake.

Sunday services are conducted in English now, but a single annual service in French is still celebrated in April.

Dock Street Theatre

Fresh from an extensive multiyear renovation project, the **Dock Street Theatre** (135 Church St., 843/720-3968), right down the street from the Huguenot Church, is where any thespian or lover of the stage must pay homage to this incarnation of the first theater built in the western hemisphere. In a distressingly familiar Charleston story, the original 1736 Dock Street Theatre burned down. A second theater opened on the same site in 1754. That building was in turn demolished for a grander edifice in 1773, which, you guessed it, also burned down. The current building dates from 1809, when the Planter's Hotel was built near the site of the original Dock Street Theatre. To mark the theater's centennial, the hotel added a stage facility in 1835, and it's that building you see today. In addition to a very active and well-regarded annual season from the resident Charleston Stage Company, the 464-seat venue has hosted

the restored Dock Street Theatre, one of America's oldest playhouses

© JIM MOREKIS

CHARLESTON

FRENCH HUGUENOTS

French Huguenot Church

A visitor can't spend a few hours in Charleston without coming across the many French-sounding names so prevalent in the region. Some are common surnames, such as Ravenel, Manigault ("MAN-i-go"), Gaillard, Laurens, or Huger ("huge-EE"). Some are street or place names, such as Mazyck or Legare ("le-GREE"). Unlike the predominantly French Catholic presence in Louisiana and coastal Alabama, the Gallic influence in Charleston was strictly of the Calvinist Protestant variety. Known as Huguenots, these French immigrants—refugees from an increasingly intolerant Roman Catholic regime in their mother country—were numerous enough in the settlement by the 1690s that they were granted full citizenship and property rights if they swore allegiance to the British crown.

The Huguenot's quick rise in Charleston was due to two factors. Unlike other colonies, Carolina never put much of a premium on religious conformity, a trait that exists to this day despite the area's overall conservatism. And unlike many who fled European monarchies to come to the New World, the French Huguenots were far from poverty-stricken. Most had to buy their own journeys across the Atlantic and arrived already well educated and skilled in one or more useful trades. In Charleston's early days, they were mostly farmers or tar burners (makers of tar and pitch for maritime use). In later times their pragmatism and work ethic would lead them to higher positions in local society, such as lawyers, judges, and politicians. One of the wealthiest Charlestonians of all, the merchant Gabriel Manigault, was by some accounts the richest person in the American colonies during the early 1700s. South Carolina's most famous French Huguenot of all was Francis Marion, the "Swamp Fox" of Revolutionary War fame. Born on the Santee River, Marion grew up in Georgetown and is now interred near Moncks Corner.

During the 18th century a number of charitable aid organizations sprang up to serve various local groups, mostly along ethnoreligious lines. The wealthiest and most influential of them all was the South Carolina Society, founded in 1737 and first called "The Two Bit Club" because of the original weekly dues. The society still meets today at its building at 72 Meeting Street, designed in 1804 by none other than Manigault's grandson, also named Gabriel, who was Charleston's most celebrated amateur architect. Another aid organization, the **Huguenot Society of Carolina** (138 Logan St., 843/723-3235, www.huguenotsociety.org, Mon.-Fri. 9am-2pm), was established in 1885. Their library is a great research tool for anyone interested in French Protestant history and genealogy.

To this day, the spiritual home of Charleston's Huguenots is the same as always: the French Huguenot Church on Church Street, one of the earliest congregations in the city. Though many of the old ways have gone, the church still holds one liturgy a year (in April) in French.

© SOPHIA MOREKIS

umpteen events of the Spoleto Festival over the past three decades and continues to do so since its renovation.

Old Powder Magazine

The **Old Powder Magazine** (79 Cumberland St., 843/722-9350, www.powdermag.org, Mon.-Sat. 10am-4pm, Sun. 1pm-4pm, $2 adults, $1 children) may be small, but the 1713 edifice is the oldest public building in South Carolina. As the name indicates, this was where the city's gunpowder was stored during the Revolution. It was opened to the public as an attraction in 1997. Now directly across the street from a huge parking garage, the site has continuing funding issues, so occasionally the hours for tours can be erratic. Inside, you'll see displays, a section of the original brick, and an exposed earthquake rod. Right next door is the privately owned, circa-1709 **Trott's Cottage,** the first brick dwelling in Charleston.

Old Slave Mart Museum

Slave auctions became big business in the South after 1808, when the United States banned the importation of slaves, thus increasing both price and demand. But in the 1850s, public auctions in Charleston were put to a stop when city leaders discovered that visitors from European nations—all of which had banned slavery years before—were horrified at the practice. The slave trade was moved indoors to "marts" near the Cooper River waterfront, where the sales could be conducted out of the public eye. The last remaining such structure is the **Old Slave Mart Museum** (6 Chalmers St., 843/958-6467, www.charlestoncity.info, Mon.-Sat. 9am-5pm, $7 adults, $5 children, free under age 6). The last auction was held in November 1863. After the war the Slave Mart became a tenement, and then in 1938 an African American history museum. The city of Charleston opened it as a museum in late 2007. There are two main areas: the orientation area, where visitors learn about the transatlantic slave trade and the architectural history of the building itself; and the main exhibit area, where visitors can see documents, tools, and displays recreating what

Old Slave Mart Museum

happened inside during this sordid chapter in local history and celebrating the resilience of the area's African American population.

NORTH OF BROAD

This tourist-heavy part of town is sometimes called the Market area because of its proximity to the Old City Market. We'll start east at the border of the French Quarter on Meeting Street and work our way west and north toward Francis Marion Square.

Circular Congregational Church

Services were originally held on the site of the **Circular Congregational Church** (150 Meeting St., 843/577-6400, www.circular-church.org, services fall-spring Sun. 11am, summer Sun. 10:15am, tours Mon.-Fri. 10:30am) beginning in 1681 for a polyglot mix of Congregationalists, Presbyterians, and Huguenots. For that reason it was often called the Church of Dissenters (*Dissenter* being the common term at the time for anyone not an Anglican). As with many structures in town, the 1886 earthquake necessitated a rebuild, and the current edifice dates from 1891. Look for the adjacent meetinghouse, which gave the street its name; a green-friendly addition houses the congregation's Christian outreach, has geothermal heating and cooling, and boasts Charleston's only vegetative roof.

Gibbes Museum of Art

The **Gibbes Museum of Art** (135 Meeting St., 843/722-2706, www.gibbesmuseum.org, Tues.-Sat. 10am-5pm, Sun. 1pm-5pm, $9 adults, $7 students, $5 ages 6-12) is one of those rare Southern museums that manages a good blend of the modern and the traditional, the local and the international. Beginning in 1905 as the Gibbes Art Gallery—the final wish of James Shoolbred Gibbes, who willed $100,000 for its construction—the complex has grown through the years in size and influence. The influential Gibbes Art School in the early 20th century formed a close association with the Woodstock School in New York, bringing important ties and prestige to the

fledgling institution. Georgia O'Keeffe, who taught college for a time in Columbia, South Carolina, brought an exhibit here in 1955.

Unitarian Church

In a town filled with cool old church cemeteries, the coolest belongs to the **Unitarian Church** (4 Archdale St., 843/723-4617, www.charlestonuu.org, services Sun. 11am, free tours Fri.-Sat. 10am-1pm). As a nod to the beauty and power of nature, vegetation and shrubbery in the cemetery have been allowed to take their natural course (walkways excepted). The church itself—the second-oldest such edifice in Charleston and the oldest Unitarian sanctuary in the South—is pretty nice too. Begun in 1776 because of overcrowding at the Circular Congregational Church, the brand-new building saw rough usage by British troops during the Revolutionary War. In 1787 the church was repaired, though it was not officially chartered as a Unitarian church until 1839. An extensive modernization happened in 1852, during which the current English Perpendicular Gothic Revival walls were installed, along with the beautiful stained-glass windows. The church was spared in the fire of 1861. Sadly, the 1886 earthquake toppled the original tower.

Old City Market

Part kitschy tourist trap, part glimpse into the old South, part community gathering place, **Old City Market** (Meeting St. and Market St., 843/973-7236, daily 6am-11:30pm) was originally built on Daniel's Creek—claimed from the marsh in the early 1800s. One of City Market's early features was a colony of vultures who hung around for scraps of meat from butcher stalls. Sensing that the carrion eaters would keep the area cleaner than any human could, city officials not only allowed the buzzards to hang around, they were protected by law, becoming known as "Charleston eagles" in tongue-in-cheek local jargon. No matter what anyone tries to tell you, Charleston's City Market never hosted a single slave auction. A recent multimillion-dollar renovation has prettified the bulk of City Market into a

CHARLESTON

THE NEW CHARLESTON GREEN

Most people know "Charleston green" as a unique local color, the result of adding a few drops of yellow to post-Civil War surplus black paint. But these days the phrase might refer to all the environmentally friendly development in Charleston, which you might find surprising considering the city's location in one of the most conservative states in the country's most conservative region.

The most obvious example is the ambitious Navy Yard redevelopment, which seeks to repurpose the closed-down facility. That project is part of a larger civic vision to reimagine the entire 3,000-acre historic Noisette community of North Charleston, with an accompanying wetlands protection conservancy. From its inception in 1902 at the command of President Theodore Roosevelt through the end of the Cold War, the Charleston Navy Yard was one of the city's biggest employers. Closed down in 1995 as part of a national base realignment plan, locals feared the worst. But a 340-acre section, the **Navy Yard at Noisette** (www.navyyardsc.com), now hosts an intriguing mix of green-friendly design firms, small nonprofits, and commercial maritime companies. The activity centers on the restoration of three huge former naval warehouses at 7, 10, and 11 Storehouse Row. Nearby, on the way to where the CSS *Hunley* is currently being restored, is the big Powerhouse, once the electrical station for the whole yard and now envisioned as the center of a future entertainment and retail district. In the meantime, the Navy Yard's no-frills retro look is so realistic that it has played host to scenes in the Lifetime TV series *Army Wives*. But the largest Navy Yard development is still to come. Clemson University—with the help of a massive federal grant, the largest in the school's history—will oversee one of the world's largest wind turbine research facilities, to be built in Building 69. The project is expected to create hundreds of local jobs.

Also in North Charleston, local retail chain Half Moon Outfitters has a green-friendly warehouse facility in an old Piggly Wiggly grocery store. The first Leadership in Energy and Environmental Design (LEED) Platinum-certified building in South Carolina, the warehouse features solar panels, rainwater reservoirs, and locally harvested or salvaged interiors. There's also the LEED-certified North Charleston Elementary School as well as North Charleston's adoption of a "dark skies" ordinance to cut down on light pollution. On the peninsula, the historic meetinghouse of the Circular Congregation Church, which gave Meeting Street its name, has a green addition with geothermal heating and cooling, rainwater cisterns, and Charleston's first vegetative roof.

In addition to walking the historic byways of the Old Village of Mount Pleasant, architecture and design buffs might also want to check out the 243-acre **I'On** (www.ionvillage.com) "neo-traditional" planned community, a successful model for this type of pedestrian-friendly New Urbanist development. On adjacent Daniel Island, the developers of that island's 4,000-acre planned residential community have been certified as an "Audubon Cooperative Sanctuary" for using wildlife-friendly techniques on its golf and recreational grounds. Even ultra-upscale Kiawah Island has gone green in something other than golf—the fabled Kiawah bobcats are making a comeback, thanks to the efforts of the Kiawah Conservancy.

Why has Charleston proven so adept at moving forward? Locals chalk it up to two things: affluent, well-connected Charlestonians who want to maintain the area's quality of life, and the forward-thinking leadership of Mayor Joe Riley in Charleston and Mayor Keith Summey in North Charleston. For many Charlestonians, however, the green movement manifests in simpler things: the pedestrian and bike lanes on the new Ravenel Bridge over the Cooper River, the thriving city recycling program, or the Sustainable Seafood Initiative, a partnership of local restaurants, universities, and conservation groups that brings the freshest, most environmentally responsible dishes to your table when you dine out in Charleston.

© JIM MOREKIS
the restored Old City Market

excellent prototypical example of a Charleston single house easily from the street and read the nearby historical marker.

St. Mary of the Annunciation Church

The oldest Roman Catholic church in the Carolinas and Georgia, **St. Mary of the Annunciation** (89 Hasell St., 843/722-7696, www.catholic-doc.org/saintmarys, mass Sun. 9:30am) traces its roots to 1789, when the Irish priest Matthew Ryan was sent to begin the first Catholic parish in the colony. The original church was destroyed in the great Charleston fire of 1838, and the present sanctuary dates from immediately thereafter. While it did receive a direct hit from a Union shell during the siege of Charleston in the Civil War—taking out the organ—the handsome Greek Revival edifice has survived in fine form the 1886 earthquake, the great hurricane of 1893, and 1989's Hurricane Hugo. You can tour the interior most weekdays 9:30am-3:30pm.

Kahal Kadosh Beth Elohim Reform Temple

The birthplace of Reform Judaism in the United States and the oldest continuously active synagogue in the nation is **Kahal Kadosh Beth Elohim Reform Temple** (90 Hasell St., 843/723-1090, www.kkbe.org, services Sat. 11am, tours Mon.-Fri. 10am-noon, Sun. 10am-4pm). The congregation—Kahal Kadosh means "holy community" in Hebrew—was founded in 1749, with the current temple dating from 1840 and built in the Greek Revival style so popular at the time. The temple's Reform roots came about indirectly because of the great fire of 1838. In rebuilding, some congregants wanted to introduce musical instruments into the temple—previously a no-no—in the form of an organ. The Orthodox contingent lost the debate, and so the new building became the first home of Reform Judaism in the country. Technically speaking, because the Holocaust destroyed all Reform temples in Europe, this is actually the oldest existing Reform synagogue in the world.

more big-city air-conditioned pedestrian shopping mall. It's not as shabbily charming as it once was, but certainly offers a more comfortable stroll during the warmer months.

Confederate Museum

Located on the second floor of City Market's iconic main building, Market Hall on Meeting Street, the small but spirited **Confederate Museum** (188 Meeting St., 843/723-1541, Tues.-Sat. 11am-3:30pm, $5 adults, $3 children, cash only) hosts an interesting collection of Civil War memorabilia, with an emphasis on the military side, and is also the local headquarters of the United Daughters of the Confederacy. Perhaps its best contribution, however, is its research library.

William Rhett House

The oldest standing residence in Charleston is the circa-1713 **William Rhett House** (54 Hasell St.), which once belonged to the colonel who captured the pirate Stede Bonnet. It's now a private residence, but you can admire this

CHARLESTON

Old City Jail

If you made a movie called *Dracula Meets the Lord of the Rings,* the **Old City Jail** (21 Magazine St., 843/577-5245) might make a great set. Built in 1802 on a lot set aside for public use since 1680, the edifice was indeed the Charleston County lockup until 1939. Some of the last pirates were jailed here in 1822 while awaiting hanging, as was slave rebellion leader Denmark Vesey. (As a response to the aborted Vesey uprising, Charleston for a while required that all black sailors in port be detained at the jail.) During the Civil War, prisoners of both armies were held here at various times.

The Old City Jail currently houses the American College of the Building Arts. Unless you're a student there, the only way to tour the Old Jail is through **Bulldog Tours** (40 N. Market St., 843/722-8687, www.bulldogtours. com). Their Haunted Jail Tour ($20 adults, $10 children) starts daily at 7pm, 8pm, 9pm, and 10pm; meet at the jail.

UPPER KING AREA

For many visitors, the area around King Street north of Calhoun Street is the most happening area of Charleston, and not only because its proximity to the Visitors Center makes it the first part of town many see up close. On some days—Saturdays when the Farmers Market is open, for instance—this bustling, active area of town seems a galaxy away from the quiet grace of the older South of the Broad area. Its closeness to the beautiful College of Charleston campus means there's never a shortage of young people around to patronize the area's restaurants and bars and to add a youthful feel. And its closeness to the city's main shopping district, King Street, means there's never a shortage of happy shoppers toting bags of new merchandise.

Marion Square

While The Citadel moved lock, stock, and barrel almost a century ago, the college's old home, the South Carolina State Arsenal, still overlooks 6.5-acre **Francis Marion Square** (between King St. and Meeting St. at Calhoun St., 843/965-4104), a reminder of the former glory days when this was the institute's parade ground, the "Citadel Green" (the old Citadel is now a hotel). Marion Square is named for the "Swamp Fox" himself, Revolutionary War hero and father of modern guerrilla warfare Francis Marion, for whom the hotel at the square's southwest corner is also named. The newest feature of Marion Square is the Holocaust Memorial on Calhoun Street. However, the dominant monument is the towering memorial to John C. Calhoun. Marion Square hosts many events, including the Farmers Market every Saturday mid-April-late December, the Food and Wine Festival, and, of course, some Spoleto events.

College of Charleston

The oldest college in South Carolina and the first municipal college in the country, the **College of Charleston** (66 George St., 843/805-5507, www.cofc.edu) boasts a fair share of history in addition to the way its 12,000-plus students bring a modern, youthful touch to so many of the city's public activities. The oldest building on this gorgeous campus, the Bishop Robert Smith House, dates from the year of the College's founding, 1770, and is now the president's house; find it on Glebe Street between Wentworth and George. The large Greek Revival building dominating the College's old quad off George and St. Philip's Streets is the magnificent Randolph Hall (1828), the oldest functioning college classroom in the country and now host to the president's office. The huge circular feature directly in front of it is "The Cistern," a historic reservoir that's a popular place for students to sit in the grass and enjoy the sun filtering through the live oaks. If you have an iPhone or iPod Touch, you can download a neat self-guided tour, complete with video, from the Apple iTunes App Store (www.apple.com, free).

The **Halsey Institute of Contemporary Art** (54 St. Philip St., 843/953-5680, www. halsey.cofc.edu, Mon.-Sat. 11am-4pm, free) focuses on modern visual art and also offers film

© JIM MOREKIS

replica of the CSS *Hunley*, outside the Charleston Museum

screenings and lectures. The groundbreaking **Avery Research Center for African American History and Culture** (843/953-7609, www.cofc.edu/avery, Mon.-Fri. 10am-5pm, Sat. noon-5pm, free) features rotating exhibits from its permanent archive collection.

Charleston Museum

The **Charleston Museum** (360 Meeting St., 843/722-2996, www.charlestonmuseum.org, Mon.-Sat. 9am-5pm, Sun. 1pm-5pm, $10 adults, $5 children, combo tickets to Heyward-Washington and Manigault Houses available) is currently housed in a noticeably modern building, but make no mistake: This is the nation's oldest museum, founded in 1773. For a long time this was the only place to get a glimpse of the CSS *Hunley,* albeit just a fanciful replica. (Now you can see the real thing at its conservation site in North Charleston, and it's even smaller than the replica would indicate.) Much of the Charleston Museum's collection focuses on aspects of everyday life of Charlestonians, from the aristocracy to slaves,

including items such as utensils, clothing, and furniture. There are quirks as well, such as the Egyptian mummy and the fine lady's fan made out of turkey feathers.

Joseph Manigault House

Owned and operated by the nearby Charleston Museum, the **Joseph Manigault House** (350 Meeting St., 843/723-2926, www.charlestonmuseum.org, Mon.-Sat. 10am-5pm, Sun. 1pm-5pm, last tour 4:30pm, $10 adults, $5 children, combo tickets to Charleston Museum and Heyward-Washington House available) is sometimes called the "Huguenot House." Its splendor is a good reminder of the fact that the French Protestants were far from poverty-stricken, unlike so many groups who came to America fleeing persecution. This circa-1803 National Historic Landmark was designed by wealthy merchant and investor Gabriel Manigault for his brother, Joseph, a rice planter of local repute and fortune. The three-story brick town house is a great example of Adams, or federal, architecture. Each December, the

the Aiken-Rhett House stables

© JIM MOREKIS

Manigault House offers visitors a special treat, as the Garden Club of Charleston decorates it in period seasonal fashion, using only flowers that would have been used in the 19th century.

◖ Aiken-Rhett House

A comparatively recent acquisition of the Historic Charleston Foundation, the poignant **Aiken-Rhett House** (48 Elizabeth St., 843/723-1159, www.historiccharleston.org, Mon.-Sat. 10am-5pm, Sun 2pm-5pm, last tour 4:15pm, $10 adults, $5 children) shows another side of that organization's mission. Whereas the Historic Charleston-run Nathaniel Russell House seeks to recreate a specific point in time, work at the Aiken-Rhett House emphasizes conservation and research. Built in 1818 and expanded by South Carolina Governor William Aiken Jr., after whom we know the house today, parts of this huge, rambling, almost Dickensian house remained sealed from 1918 until 1975 when the family relinquished the property to the Charleston Museum, providing historians with a unique opportunity to

study original documents from that period. As you walk the halls, staircases, and rooms—seeing the remains of original wallpaper and the various fixtures added through the years—you can really feel the impact of the people who lived within these walls and get a great sense of the full sweep of Charleston history. While the docents are very helpful, the main way to enjoy the Aiken-Rhett House is by way of a self-guided MP3-player audio tour—unique in Charleston.

Children's Museum of the Lowcountry

Recognizing that historic homes and Civil War memorabilia aren't enough to keep a family with young children in town for long, the city established the **Children's Museum of the Lowcountry** (25 Ann St., 843/853-8962, www. explorecml.org, Tues.-Sat. 9am-5pm, Sun. 1pm-5pm, $7, free under age 1) in 2005 specifically to give families with kids ages 3 months to 12 years a reason to spend more time (and money) downtown. A wide variety of hands-on

© JIM MOREKIS

ironwork at the Philip Simmons Garden

activities—such as a 30-foot shrimp boat replica and a medieval castle—stretch the definition of *museum* to its limit.

Philip Simmons Garden

Charleston's most beloved artisan is the late Philip Simmons. Born on nearby Daniel Island in 1912, Simmons went through an apprenticeship to become one of the most sought-after decorative ironworkers in the United States. In 1982 the National Endowment for the Arts awarded him its National Heritage Fellowship. His work is on display at the National Museum of American History, the Smithsonian Institution, and the Museum of International Folk Art in Santa Fe, New Mexico, among many other places. In 1989 the congregation at Simmons's **St. John's Reformed Episcopal Church** (91 Anson St., 843/722-4241, www.st-johnsre.org) voted to make the church garden a commemoration of the life and work of this legendary African American artisan, who died in 2009 at age 97. Completed in two phases, the Bell Garden and the Heart Garden, the project

is a delightful blend of Simmons's signature graceful, sinuous style and fragrant flowers.

HAMPTON PARK AREA

Expansive Hampton Park is a favorite recreation spot for Charlestonians. The surrounding area near the east bank of the Ashley River has some of the earliest suburbs of Charleston, now in various states of restoration and hosting a diverse range of residents. Hampton Park is bordered by streets all around, which can be fairly heavily trafficked because this is the main way to get to The Citadel. But in the spring the park streets are closed to vehicles Saturday morning 8am-noon so neighborhood people, especially those with young children, can enjoy themselves without worrying about the traffic.

The Citadel

Although for many its spiritual and historic center will always be at the old state Arsenal in Marion Square, **The Citadel** (171 Moultrie St., 843/953-3294, www.citadel.edu, grounds daily 8am-6pm) has been at this 300-acre site farther up the peninsula along the Ashley River since 1922 and shows no signs of leaving. Getting there is a little tricky, in that the entrance to the college is situated behind beautiful Hampton Park off Rutledge Avenue, a main north-south artery on the western portion of the peninsula. The Citadel (technically its full name is The Citadel, The Military College of South Carolina) has entered popular consciousness through the works of graduate Pat Conroy, especially his novel *Lords of Discipline,* starring a thinly disguised "Carolina Military Institute."

There's lots for visitors to see, including **The Citadel Museum** (843/953-6779, daily noon-5pm, free), on your right just as you enter campus, and the "Citadel Murals" in the Daniel Library. Ringing vast Summerall Field—the huge open space where you enter campus—are the many castle-like cadet barracks. If you peek inside their gates, you'll see the distinctive checkerboard pattern on which the cadets line up. All around the field itself are various military items, such as a Sherman tank and an F-4 Phantom jet. The most interesting single experience for visitors to The Citadel is the colorful Friday afternoon dress parade on Summerall Field, in which cadets pass for review in full dress uniform (the fabled "long gray line") accompanied by a marching band and pipers. Often called "the best free show in Charleston," the parade happens almost every Friday at 3:45pm during the school year; you might want to consult the website before your visit to confirm. Arrive well in advance to avoid parking problems.

Joseph P. Riley Jr. Ballpark
When you hear Charlestonians talk about "The Joe," they're referring to **Joseph P. Riley Jr. Ballpark** (360 Fishburne St., 843/577-3647, www.riverdogs.com), a charming minor-league baseball stadium that's home of the Charleston River Dogs, a New York Yankees affiliate playing April-August in the venerable South Atlantic League. It's also another part of the civic legacy of longtime Mayor Joe Riley, in this case in partnership with the adjacent Citadel. Inspired by the retro design of Baltimore's Camden Yards, The Joe opened in 1997 to rave reviews from locals and baseball connoisseurs all over the nation. From downtown, get here by taking Broad Street west until it turns into Lockwood Drive. Follow that north until you get to Brittlebank Park and The Joe, right next to The Citadel.

WEST ASHLEY
Ironically, Charleston's first postwar automobile suburb also has roots back to the first days of the colony's settlement and was the site of some of the antebellum era's grandest plantations. As the cost of housing on the peninsula continues to rise, this area on the west bank of the Ashley River is experiencing a newfound cachet today for hipsters and young families alike. For most visitors, though, the biggest draws are the ancient plantations and historic sites along the west bank of the river: Charles Towne Landing, Drayton Hall, Magnolia Plantation, and Middleton Place, farthest north. Getting to this area from Charleston proper is easy. Take U.S. 17 ("the Crosstown") west across the Ashley River to the junction with Highway 61 and take a right (north) onto Highway 61; veer right to get on Highway 7 for Charles Towne Landing, or stay left on Highway 61 for the plantations.

Charles Towne Landing
Any look at West Ashley must begin where everything began, with the 600-acre historic site **Charles Towne Landing** (1500 Old Towne Rd., 843/852-4200, www.charlestowne.org, daily 9am-5pm, $7.50 adults, $3.50 students, free under age 6). This is where Charleston's original settlers first arrived from Barbados and camped in 1670, remaining only a few years before eventually moving to the more defensible peninsula where the Holy City now resides. The *Adventure,* a beautiful and fully seaworthy replica of a settlers' ship, is the main highlight, docked creek-side on the far side of the long and well-done exploration trail through the site. You can get on board, and a helpful ranger will explain aspects of the ship as well as the original settlement. Another highlight

© JIM MOREKIS

aboard the *Adventure* at Charles Towne Landing

is the archaeological remnant of the original palisade wall (there's a reconstructed palisade to show what it looked like). Ranger-guided programs are available Wednesday-Friday at 10am; call ahead for reservations.

A new audio tour has been instituted, where you can rent an MP3 player ($5), but the self-guided approach works just fine, and you can get a nice map from the front desk to help you around. The outdoor highlights of Charles Towne Landing are obvious, but don't miss the fantastic exhibits inside the visitors center, which are particularly well done and give a comprehensive and informative look back at the time of the original settlers.

◖ Drayton Hall

A mecca for historic preservationists all over the country, **Drayton Hall** (3380 Ashley River Rd., 843/769-2600, www.draytonhall.org, daily 9am-4pm, $20 adults, $10 ages 12-18, $6 ages 6-11, grounds only $10) is remarkable not only for its pedigree but for the way in which it has been preserved. This stately redbrick Georgian-Palladian building, the oldest plantation home in the country that is open to the public, has been literally historically preserved—as in no electricity, heat, or running water. Since its construction in 1738 by John Drayton, son of Magnolia Plantation founder Thomas, Drayton Hall has survived almost completely intact through the ups and downs of Lowcountry history. Drayton died while fleeing the British in 1779; subsequently his house served as the headquarters of British general Clinton and later General Cornwallis. During the Civil War, Drayton Hall escaped the depredations of the conquering Union Army, one of only three area plantation homes to survive.

Visitors expecting the more typical approach to house museums, i.e. subjective renovation with period furnishings that may or may not have any connection with the actual house, might be disappointed. But for others the experience at Drayton Hall is quietly exhilarating, almost in a Zen-like way. Planes are routed around the house so that no rattles will endanger its structural integrity. There's no furniture to speak of, only bare rooms, decorated with original paint, no matter how little remains. It can be jarring at first, but after you get into it, you might wonder why anyone does things any differently.

Guided tours are offered punctually at the top of the hour, except for the last tour of the day, which starts on the half-hour. A separate 45-minute program is "Connections: From Africa to America," which chronicles the diaspora of the enslaved people who originally worked this plantation, from their capture to their eventual freedom. "Connections" is presented at 11:15am, 1:15pm, and 3:15pm.

Magnolia Plantation and Gardens

A different legacy of the Drayton family is **Magnolia Plantation and Gardens** (3550 Ashley Rd., 843/571-1266, www.magnoliaplantation.com, Mar.-Oct. daily 9am-4:30pm, call for winter hours, $15 adults, $10 children, free under age 6). It claims not only the first garden in the United States, dating back to the 1680s, but also the first public garden, dating to 1872. There's a slightly kitschy feel here, a contrast to the quiet dignity of Drayton Hall.

The original plantation home was burned during the Civil War—either by Union troops or freed slaves—so one of the Draytons barged a colonial-era summer house from Summerville, South Carolina, down the Ashley River to this site and built the modern Magnolia Plantation around it specifically as an attraction. Magnolia's reputation became so exalted that at one point Baedeker's travel guides listed it as one of the three main attractions in America, alongside the Grand Canyon and Niagara Falls. While spring remains the best—and also the most crowded—time to come, a huge variety of camellias blooms in early winter, a time marked by a yearly Winter Camellia Festival. House tours, the 45-minute Nature Train tour, the 45-minute Nature Boat tour, and a visit to the Audubon Swamp Garden run about $8 pp extra for each offering.

◖ Middleton Place

Not only the first landscaped garden in the

United States but still one of the most magnificent in the world, **Middleton Place** (4300 Ashley River Rd., 843/556-6020, www.middletonplace.org, daily 9am-5pm, $28 adults, $15 students, $10 children, guided house tour $15 extra) is a sublime combination of history and sheer natural beauty. Nestled along a quiet bend in the Ashley River, the grounds contain a historic restored home, working stables, and 60 acres of breathtaking gardens, all manicured to perfection. In 1741 the plantation became the family seat of the Middletons, one of the most notable surnames in U.S. history. As the Civil War wound down, in February 1865, the 56th New York Volunteers burned the main house and destroyed the gardens, leaving only the circa-1755 guest wing, which today is the Middleton Place House Museum. The great earthquake of 1886 added insult to injury by wrecking the Butterfly Lakes. It wasn't until 1916 that renovation began. In 1971 Middleton Place was named a National Historic Landmark.

All that's left of the great house are the remains of the foundation, still majestic in ruin. Today, visitors can tour the excellently restored **Middleton Place House Museum** (4300 Ashley River Rd., 843/556-6020, www.middletonplace.org, guided tours Mon. 1:30pm-4:30pm, Tues.-Sun. 10am-4:30pm, $15)—actually the only remaining "flanker" building—and see furniture, silverware, china, and books belonging to the Middletons along with family portraits.

At the Plantation Stableyards, costumed craftspeople still work using historically authentic tools and methods, surrounded by a happy family of domestic animals. The newest addition to the Stableyards is a pair of magnificent male water buffalo. Meet the fellas daily 9am-5pm. For an extra $18 pp you can take a 45-minute carriage ride through the bamboo forest to an abandoned rice field. Rides start daily around 10am and run every hour or so, weather permitting.

The 53-room **Inn at Middleton Place,** besides being a wholly gratifying lodging

© JIM MOREKIS

Middleton Place

experience, is also a quite self-conscious and largely successful experiment. Its bold Frank Lloyd Wright-influenced modern design, comprising four units joined by walkways, is modern. But both inside and outside it manages to blend quite well with the surrounding fields, trees, and riverbanks. The Inn also offers kayak tours and instruction—a particularly nice way to enjoy the grounds from the waters of the Ashley—and features its own organic garden and labyrinth, intriguing modern counterpoints to the formal gardens of the plantation itself.

They still grow the exquisite Carolina Gold rice in a field at Middleton Place, harvested in the old style each September. You can sample some of it in many dishes at the **Middleton Place Restaurant** (843/556-6020, www.middletonplace.org, lunch daily 11am-3pm, dinner Tues.-Thurs. 6pm-8pm, Fri.-Sat. 6pm-9pm, Sun. 6pm-8pm, $15-25). Hint: You can tour the gardens for free if you arrive for a dinner reservation at 5:30pm or later.

The Coburg Cow

The entire stretch of U.S. 17 (Savannah Hwy.) heading into Charleston from the west is redolent of a particularly Southern brand of retro Americana. The chief example is the famous **Coburg Cow,** a large, rotating dairy cow accompanied by a bottle of chocolate milk. The current installation dates from 1959, though a version of it was on this site as far back as the early 1930s when this area was open countryside. During Hurricane Hugo the Coburg Cow was moved to a safe location. In 2001 the attached dairy closed down, and the city threatened to have the cow moved or demolished. But community outcry preserved the delightful landmark, which is visible today on the south side of U.S. 17 in the 900 block. You can't miss it—it's a big cow on the side of the road!

NORTH CHARLESTON

For years synonymous with crime, blight, and sprawl, North Charleston—actually a separate municipality—was for the longest time considered a necessary evil by most Charlestonians, who generally ventured there only to shop at a mall or see a show at its concert venue, the Coliseum. But as the cost of real estate continues to rise on the peninsula in Charleston proper, more and more artists and young professionals are choosing to live here. This is where to go if you want to see the raised submarine CSS *Hunley,* now in a research area on the grounds of the old Navy Yard.

Magnolia Cemetery

Although not technically in North Charleston, historic **Magnolia Cemetery** (70 Cunnington Ave., 843/722-8638, Sept.-May daily 8am-5pm, June-Aug. daily 8am-6pm) is on the way, well north of the downtown tourist district in the area called "The Neck." This historic burial ground is a stirring site for its natural beauty and ornate memorials as well as for its historic aspects. Here are buried the crewmen who died aboard the CSS *Hunley,* reinterred after their retrieval from Charleston Harbor. In all, over 2,000 Civil War dead are buried here, including five Confederate generals and 84 rebels who fell at Gettysburg and were moved here.

❰ CSS *Hunley*

For the longest time, the only glimpse of the ill-fated Confederate submarine was a not-quite-accurate replica outside the Charleston Museum. But after maritime novelist and adventurer Clive Cussler and his team finally found the *Hunley* in 1995 off Sullivan's Island, the tantalizing dream became a reality: We'd finally find out what it looked like, and perhaps even be lucky enough to bring it to the surface. That moment came on August 8, 2000, when a team comprising the nonprofit **Friends of the Hunley** (Warren Lasch Conservation Center, 1250 Supply St., Bldg. 255, 866/866-9938, www.hunley.org, Sat. 10am-5pm, Sun. noon-5pm, $12, free under age 5), the federal government, and private partners successfully implemented a plan to safely raise the vessel. It was recently moved to its new home in the old Navy Yard. You can now view the sub in a 90,000-gallon conservation tank on the grounds of the old Navy Yard, see the life-size

model from the TNT movie *The Hunley,* and look at artifacts such as the "lucky" gold piece of the commander. You can even see facial reconstructions of some of the eight sailors who died on board the sub that fateful February day in 1864, when it mysteriously sank right after successfully destroying the USS *Housatonic* with the torpedo attached to its bow. Reserve tickets ahead of time. (The remains of the crew lie in Magnolia Cemetery, where they were buried in 2004 with full military honors.) To get to the Warren Lasch Center from Charleston, take I-26 north to exit 216B. Take a left onto Spruill Avenue and a right onto McMillan Avenue. Once in the Navy Yard, take a right on Hobson Avenue, and after about one mile take a left onto Supply Street. The Lasch Center is the low white building on the left.

Fire Museum

It's got a mouthful of a name, but the **North Charleston and American LaFrance Fire Museum and Educational Center** (4975 Centre Pointe Dr., 843/740-5550, www.legacyofheroes.org, Mon.-Sat. 10am-5pm, Sun. 1pm-5pm, last admission 4pm, $6 adults, free under age 14), right next to the huge Tanger Outlet Mall, does what it does with a lot of chutzpah—which is fitting considering that it pays tribute to firefighters and the tools of their dangerous trade. The museum, which opened in 2007 and shares a huge 25,000-square-foot space with the North Charleston Convention and Visitors Bureau, is primarily dedicated to maintaining and increasing its collection of antique American LaFrance firefighting vehicles and equipment. The 18 fire engines here date from 1857 to 1969. The museum's exhibits have taken on greater poignancy in the wake of the tragic loss of nine Charleston firefighters killed trying to extinguish a warehouse blaze on U.S. 17 in summer 2007—one of the largest single losses of life for a U.S. firefighting department.

EAST COOPER

The main destination in this area on the east bank of the Cooper River is the island of Mount Pleasant, primarily known as a peaceful,

RAISING THE *HUNLEY*

The amazing, unlikely raising of the Confederate submarine CSS *Hunley* from the muck of Charleston harbor sounds like the plot of an adventure novel—which makes sense considering that the major player is an adventure novelist. For 15 years, the undersea diver and best-selling author Clive Cussler looked for the final resting place of the *Hunley*. The sub was mysteriously lost at sea after sinking the USS *Housatonic* on February 17, 1864, with the high-explosive "torpedo" mounted on a long spar on its bow. It marked the first time a sub ever sank a ship in battle.

For over a century before Cussler, treasure-seekers had searched for the sub, with P. T. Barnum even offering $100,000 to the first person to find it. But on May 3, 1995, a magnetometer operated by Cussler and his group, the National Underwater Marine Agency, discovered the *Hunley*'s final resting place—in 30 feet of water and under 3 feet of sediment about four miles off Sullivan's Island at the mouth of the harbor. Using a specially designed truss to lift the entire sub, a 19-person dive crew and a team of archaeologists began a process that would result in raising the vessel on August 8, 2000. But before the sub could be brought up, a dilemma had to be solved: For 136 years the saltwater of the Atlantic had permeated its metallic skin. Exposure to air would rapidly disintegrate the entire thing. So the conservation team, with input from the U.S. Navy, came up with a plan to keep the vessel submerged in a special solution indefinitely at the specially constructed **Warren Lasch Conservation Center** (1250 Supply St., Bldg. 255, 866/866-9938, www.

hunley.org, Sat. 10am-5pm, Sun. noon-5pm, $12, free under age 5) in the old Navy Yard while research and conservation was performed on it piece by piece.

And that's how you see the *Hunley* today, submerged in its special conservation tank, still largely covered in sediment. Upon seeing the almost unbelievably tiny, cramped vessel—much smaller than most experts imagined it would be—visitors are often visibly moved at the bravery and sacrifice of the nine-man Confederate crew, who no doubt would have known that the *Hunley*'s two previous crews had drowned at sea in training accidents. Theirs was, in effect, a suicide mission. That the crew surely realized this only makes the modern visitor's experience even more poignant.

The Warren Lasch Center, operated under the auspices of Clemson University, is only open to the public on weekends. Archaeology continues apace during the week—inch by painstaking inch, muck and tiny artifacts removed millimeter by millimeter. The process is so thorough that archaeologists have even identified an individual eyelash from one of the crewmembers. Other interesting artifacts include a three-fold wallet with a leather strap, owner unknown; seven canteens; and a wooden cask in one of the ballast tanks, maybe used to hold water or liquor or even used as a chamber pot.

The very first order of business once the sub was brought up, however, was properly burying those brave sailors. In 2004, Charleston came to a stop as a ceremonial funeral procession took the remains of the nine to historic Magnolia Cemetery, where they were buried with full military honors.

fairly affluent suburb of Charleston—a role it has played for about 300 years now. Although few old-timers (called "hungry necks" in local lingo) remain, Mount Pleasant does have several key attractions well worth visiting—the old words of former Charleston mayor John Grace notwithstanding: "Mount Pleasant is neither a mount, nor is it pleasant." Through Mount Pleasant is also the only land route to

access Sullivan's Island, Isle of Palms, and historic Fort Moultrie. Shem Creek, which bisects Mount Pleasant, was once the center of the local shrimping industry.

Patriots Point Naval and Maritime Museum

Directly across Charleston Harbor from the old city lies the **Patriots Point Naval and**

the USS *Yorktown* at Patriots Point

Maritime Museum (40 Patriots Point Rd., 843/884-2727, www.patriotspoint.org, daily 9am-6:30pm, $18 adults, $11 ages 6-11, free for active-duty military) complex, one of the first chapters in Charleston's tourism renaissance. The project began in 1975 with what is still its main attraction, the World War II aircraft carrier **USS *Yorktown*,** named in honor of the carrier lost at the Battle of Midway. Much of "The Fighting Lady" is open to the public, and kids and nautical buffs will thrill to walk the decks and explore the many stations below deck on this massive 900-foot vessel, a veritable floating city. You can even have a full meal in the CPO Mess Hall just like the crew once did (except you'll have to pay $8.50 pp). And if you really want to get up close and personal, try the Navy Flight Simulator for a small additional fee. The *Yorktown* flight deck (the top of the ship) and the hangar deck (right below) are packed with authentic warplanes, not only from World War II but from subsequent conflicts the ship participated in.

Other ships moored beside the *Yorktown*

and open for tours are the Coast Guard cutter USCG *Ingham,* the submarine USS *Clamagore,* and the destroyer USS *Laffey,* which survived being hit by three Japanese bombs and five kamikaze attacks—all within an hour.

A big plus is the free 90-minute guided tour. If you really want to make a family history day out of it, you can also hop on the ferry from Patriots Point to Fort Sumter and back.

Boone Hall Plantation

Visitors who've also been to Savannah's Wormsloe Plantation will see the similarity in the majestic, live oak-lined entrance avenue to **Boone Hall Plantation** (1235 Long Point Rd., 843/884-4371, www.boonehallplantation.com, mid-Mar.-Labor Day Mon.-Sat. 8:30am-6:30pm, Sun. noon-5pm, Labor Day-Nov. Mon.-Sat. 9am-5pm, Sun. 1pm-4pm, Dec.-mid-Mar. Mon.-Sat. 9am-5pm, Sun. noon-5pm, $20 adults, $10 children). But this site is about half a century older, dating back to a grant to Major John Boone in the 1680s (the oaks of the entranceway were planted in

1743). Boone Hall takes the phrase "living history" to its extreme, as it's not only an active agricultural facility but lets visitors go on "u-pick" walks through its fields, which boast succulent strawberries, peaches, tomatoes, and even pumpkins in October—as well as free hayrides. While Boone Hall's most genuine historic buildings include the big Cotton Gin House (1853) and the 1750 Smokehouse, to me the most poignant and educational structures by far are the nine humble brick slave cabins from the 1790s, expertly restored and most fitted with interpretive displays. In all, three different tours are available: a 30-minute house tour, a tour of "Slave Street," and a garden tour.

Charles Pinckney National Historic Site

This is one of my favorite sights in Charleston, for its uplifting, well-explored subject matter as well as its tastefully maintained house and grounds. Though "Constitution Charlie's" old Snee Farm is down to only 28 acres from its original magnificent 700, the **Charles Pinckney National Historic Site** (1240 Long Point Rd., 843/881-5516, www.nps.gov/chpi, daily 9am-5pm, free) that encompasses it is still an important repository of local and national history. Sometimes called "the forgotten founder," Charles Pinckney was not only a hero of the American Revolution and a notable early abolitionist but one of the main authors of the U.S. Constitution. His great aunt Eliza Lucas Pinckney was the first woman agriculturalist in the United States, responsible for opening up the indigo trade. Her son Charles Cotesworth Pinckney was one of the signers of the Constitution. President George Washington slept and had breakfast under a nearby oak tree in 1791 while touring the South. No matter what anyone tells you, no one is buried underneath the tombstone in the grove of oak trees bearing the name of Constitution Charlie's father, Colonel Charles Pinckney. The marker incorrectly states the elder Pinckney's age, so it was put here only as a monument. A memorial to the colonel is in the churchyard of the 1840s-era Christ Church, about one mile down Long Point Road.

Isle of Palms

This primarily residential area of about 5,000 people received the state's first "Blue Wave" designation from the Clean Beaches Council for its well-managed and preserved beaches. Like adjacent Sullivan's Island, there are pockets of great wealth here, but also a laid-back, windswept beach-town vibe. You get here from Mount Pleasant by taking the Isle of Palms Connector off U.S. 17 (Johnnie Dodds/Chuck Dawley Blvd.). Aside from just enjoying the whole scene, the main self-contained attraction here is **Isle of Palms County Park** (14th Ave., 843/886-3863, www.ccprc.com, May-Labor Day daily 9am-7pm, Mar.-Apr. and Sept.-Oct. daily 10am-6pm, Nov.-Feb. daily 10am-5pm, $7 per vehicle, free for pedestrians and cyclists), with its oceanfront beach, complete with umbrella rental, a volleyball court, a playground, and lifeguards. Get here by taking the Isle of Palms Connector (Hwy. 517) from Mount Pleasant, going through the light at Palm Boulevard, and taking the next left at the gate. The island's other claim to fame is the excellent (and surprisingly affordable) **Wild Dunes Resort** (5757 Palm Blvd., 888/778-1876, www.wilddunes.com), with its two Fazio golf courses and 17 clay tennis courts. Breach Inlet, between Isle of Palms and Sullivan's Island, is where the Confederate sub *Hunley* sortied to do battle with the USS *Housatonic*. During 1989's Hurricane Hugo, the entire island was submerged.

Sullivan's Island

Part funky beach town, part ritzy getaway, Sullivan's Island has a certain timeless quality. While much of it was rebuilt after Hurricane Hugo's devastation, plenty of local character remains, as evidenced by some cool little bars in its tiny "business district" on the main drag of Middle Street. There's a ton of history on Sullivan's, but you can also just while the day away on the quiet, windswept beach on the Atlantic, or ride a bike all over the island and back. Unless you have a boat, you can only get here from Mount Pleasant. From U.S. 17, follow the signs for Highway 703 and Sullivan's Island. Cross the Ben Sawyer Bridge, and then turn right onto Middle Street; continue for about 1.5 miles.

FORT MOULTRIE
While Fort Sumter gets the vast bulk of the media, the older **Fort Moultrie** (1214 Middle St., 843/883-3123, www.nps.gov/fosu, daily 9am-5pm, $3 adults, free under age 16) on Sullivan's Island actually has a much more sweeping history. Major Robert Anderson's detachment at Fort Sumter at the opening of the Civil War was actually the Fort Moultrie garrison, reassigned to Sumter because Moultrie was thought too vulnerable from the landward side. Moultrie's first incarnation, a perimeter of felled palm trees, didn't even have a name when it was unsuccessfully attacked by the British in the summer of 1776, the first victory by the colonists in the Revolutionary War. The redcoat cannonballs bounced off those soft, flexible trunks, and thus was born South Carolina's nickname, "The Palmetto State."

In 1809 a brick fort was built here; it soon gained notoriety as the place where the great chief Osceola was detained soon after his capture, posing for the famous portrait by George Catlin. His captors got more than they bargained for when they jokingly asked the old guerrilla soldier for a rendition of the Seminole battle cry. According to accounts, Osceola's realistic performance scared some bystanders half to death. The chief died here in 1838, and his modest grave site is still on-site, in front of the fort on the landward side. Other famous people to have trod on Sullivan's Island include Edgar Allan Poe, who was inspired by Sullivan's lonely, evocative environment to write *The Gold Bug* and other works. There's a Gold Bug Avenue and a Poe Avenue.

Moultrie's main Civil War role was as a target for Union shot during the long siege of Charleston. It was pounded so hard and for so long that its walls fell below a nearby sand hill and were finally unable to be hit anymore.

A full military upgrade happened in the late 1800s, extending over most of Sullivan's Island (some private owners have even bought some of the old batteries and converted them into homes). It's the series of later forts that you'll visit on your trip to the Moultrie site, which is technically part of the Fort Sumter National Monument and administered by the National Park Service.

Most of the outdoor tours are self-guided, but ranger programs typically happen Memorial Day-Labor Day daily at 11am and 2:30pm. There's a bookstore and visitors center across the street, offering a 20-minute video on the hour and half-hour 9am-4:30pm. Keep in mind there's no regular ferry to Fort Sumter from Fort Moultrie; the closest ferry to Sumter leaves from Patriots Point on Mount Pleasant.

BENCH BY THE ROAD
Scholars say that about half of all African Americans alive today had an ancestor who once set foot on Sullivan's Island. As the first point of entry for at least half of all slaves imported to the United States, the island's "pest houses" acted as quarantine areas so enslaved people could be checked for communicable diseases before going to auction in Charleston proper. But few people seem to know this. In a 1989 magazine interview, African American author and Nobel laureate Toni Morrison said about historic sites concerning slavery, "There is no suitable memorial, or plaque, or wreath or wall, or park or skyscraper lobby. There's no 300-foot tower, there's no small bench by the road." In 2008, that last item became a reality, as the first of several planned "benches by the road" was installed on Sullivan's Island to mark the sacrifice of enslaved African Americans. It's a simple black steel bench, with an attached marker and a nearby plaque. The Bench by the Road is at the Fort Moultrie visitors center.

FOLLY BEACH
A large percentage of the town of Folly Beach was destroyed by Hurricane Hugo in 1989, and erosion since then has increased and hit the beach itself pretty hard. All that said, enough

of Folly's funky charm is left to make it worth visiting. Called "The Edge of America" during its heyday from the 1930s through the 1950s as a swinging resort getaway, Folly Beach is now a slightly beaten but enjoyable little getaway on this barrier island. Folly's main claim to larger historic fame is playing host to George Gershwin, who stayed at a cottage on West Arctic Avenue to write the score for *Porgy and Bess,* set across the harbor in downtown Charleston. (Ironically, Gershwin's opera couldn't be performed in its original setting until 1970 because of segregationist Jim Crow laws.) Original *Porgy* author DuBose Heyward stayed around the corner at a summer cottage on West Ashley Avenue that he dubbed "Follywood."

Called Folly Road until it gets to the beach, Center Street is the main drag here, dividing the beach into east and west. In this area you'll find the **Folly Beach Fishing Pier** (101 E. Arctic Ave., 843/588-3474, Apr.-Oct. daily 6am-11pm, Nov. and Mar. daily 7am-7pm, Dec.-Feb. daily 8am-5pm, parking $7, fishing $8), which replaced the grand old wooden pier-and-pavilion structure that tragically burned down in 1960.

Back in the day, restaurants, bars, and amusement areas with rides lined the way up to the old pavilion. The new fishing pier, while not as grand as the old one, is worth visiting—a massive, well-built edifice jutting more than 1,000 feet into the Atlantic with a large diamond-shaped pavilion at the end. To get to Folly Beach from Charleston, go west on Calhoun Street and take the James Island Connector. Take a left on Folly Road (Hwy. 171), which becomes Center Street on into Folly Beach.

At the far east end of Folly Island, about 300 yards offshore, you'll see the **Morris Island Lighthouse,** an 1876 beacon that was once surrounded by lush green landscape, now completely surrounded by water as the land has eroded around it. Now privately owned, there's an extensive effort to save and preserve the lighthouse (www.savethelight.org). There's also an effort to keep high-dollar

condo development off beautiful bird-friendly Morris Island itself (www.morrisisland.org). To get here while there's still something left to enjoy, take East Ashley Street until it dead-ends. Park in the lot and take a 0.25-mile walk to the beach.

TOURS

Because of the city's small, fairly centralized layout, the best way to experience Charleston is on foot—either yours or via hooves of equine nature. Thankfully, there's a wide variety of walking and carriage tours for you to choose from. The sheer number and breadth of tour options in Charleston is beyond the scope of this section. For a full selection of available tours, visit the **Charleston Visitor Reception and Transportation Center** (375 Meeting St., 800/774-0006, www.charlestoncvb.com, Mon.-Fri. 8:30am-5pm), where they have entire walls of brochures for all the latest tours, with local tourism experts on-site. Here are some notable highlights.

Walking Tours

If you find yourself walking around downtown soon after dark, you'll almost invariably come across a walking tour in progress, with a small cluster of people gathered around a tour guide. There are too many walking tours to list them all, but here are the best.

For more than 10 years, **Ed Grimball's Walking Tours** (306 Yates Ave., 843/762-0056, www.edgrimballtours.com, $16 adults, $8 children) has run two-hour tours on Friday-Saturday mornings, courtesy of the knowledgeable and still-sprightly Ed himself, a native Charlestonian. All of Ed's walks start from the big Pineapple Fountain in Waterfront Park, and reservations are a must. **Original Charleston Walks** (45 Broad St., 800/729-3420, www.charlestonwalks.com, daily 8:30am-9:30pm, $18.50 adults, $10.50 children) has received much national TV exposure. They leave from the corner of Market and State Streets and have a full slate of tours, including a popular adults-only pub crawl. **Charleston Strolls Walk with History** (843/766-2080, www.

DOIN' THE CHARLESTON

It has been called the biggest song and dance craze of the 20th century. It first entered the American public consciousness via New York City in a 1923 Harlem musical called *Runnin' Wild*, but the roots of the dance soon to be known as the Charleston were indeed in the Holy City. No one is quite sure of the day and date, but local lore assures us that members of Charleston's legendary Jenkins Orphanage Band were the first to start dancing that crazy "Geechie step," a development that soon became part of the band's act. The Jenkins Orphanage was started in 1891 by the African American Baptist minister Reverend D. J. Jenkins and was originally housed in the Old Marine Hospital at 20 Franklin Street (which you can see today, although it's not open to the public). To raise money, Reverend Jenkins acquired donated instruments and started a band comprising talented orphans from the house. The orphans traveled as far away as London, where they were a hit with the locals but not with the constabulary, who unceremoniously fined them for stop-ping traffic. A Charleston attorney who happened to be in London at the time, Augustine Smyth, paid their way back home, becoming a lifelong supporter of the orphanage in the process.

From then on, playing in donated old Cita-del uniforms, the Jenkins Orphanage Band frequently took its act on the road. They played at the St. Louis and Buffalo exposi-tions, and even at President Taft's inaugura-tion. They also frequently played in New York, and it was there that African American pianist and composer James P. Johnson heard the Charlestonians play and dance to their Gullah rhythms, considered exotic at the time. John-son would incorporate what he heard into the tune "Charleston," one of many songs in the revue *Runnin' Wild*. The catchy song and its accompanying loose-limbed dance seemed tailor-made for the Roaring '20s and its lib-erated, hedonistic spirit. Before long the Charleston had swept the nation, becoming a staple of jazz clubs and speakeasies across the country, and indeed, the world.

charlestonstrolls.com, $18 adults, $10 children) is another popular tour good for a historical overview and tidbits. They have three daily embarkation points: Charleston Place (9:30am), the Days Inn (9:40am), and the Mills House (10am). **Architectural Walking Tours** (173 Meeting St., 800/931-7761, www.architectur-alwalkingtoursofcharleston.com, $20) offers an 18th-century tour Monday and Wednesday-Saturday at 10am and a 19th-century tour at 2pm, which are geared more toward historic preservation. They leave from the Meeting Street Inn (173 Meeting St.). A relatively new special interest tour is **Charleston Art Tours** (53 Broad St., 843/860-3327, www.charleston-arttours.com, $49). The brainchild of local artists Karen Hagan and Martha Sharp, this tour is led by a professional artist guide and includes refreshments and a gift bag from one of the featured galleries. The Fine Art Tour ($50) runs 2pm-4pm and leaves from 27½ State Street. They also run a Charleston Renaissance tour (Tues.-Sat. 10am, $55), which includes a visit to the Gibbes Museum of Art, and a "Gibbes Museum Plus" tour (Thurs. and Sat. 1:30pm).

Ghost tours are very popular in Charleston. **Bulldog Tours** (40 N. Market St., 843/722-8687, www.bulldogtours.com) has exclusive access to the Old City Jail, which features prominently in most of their tours. Their most popular tour, the Haunted Jail Tour ($18 adults, $10 children) leaves daily at 7pm, 8pm, 9pm, and 10pm; meet at the Old City Jail (21 Magazine St.). The Ghosts and Dungeons tour ($18) leaves March-November Tuesday-Saturday at 7pm and 9pm from 40 North Market Street. Other tours include the Ghosts and Graveyard Tour (daily 7:30pm and 9:30pm, $18) and the adults-only Dark Side of Charleston (daily 8pm and 10pm, $18).

Tour Charleston (184 East Bay St., 843/723-1670, www.tourcharleston.com, $18) offers two paranormal tours: Ghosts of Charleston I, which leaves daily at 5:30pm, 7:30pm, and 9:30pm from Waterfront Park, and Ghosts of Charleston II, which leaves daily at 7pm and 9pm from Marion Square.

Carriage Tours
The city strictly regulates the treatment and up-keep of carriage horses and mules, so there's not a heck of a lot of difference in service or price among the various tour companies. Typically, rides take 1-1.5 hours and hover around $20 per adult, about half that per child. Tours sometimes book up early, so call ahead. The oldest service in town is **Palmetto Carriage Works** (40 N. Market St., 843/723-8145, www.carriagetour.com), which offers free parking at its "red barn" base near City Market. Another popular tour is **Old South Carriage Company** (14 Anson St., 843/723-9712, www.oldsouthcarriage.com) with its Confederate-clad drivers. **Carolina Polo & Carriage Company** (16 Hayne St., 843/577-6767, www.cpcc.com) leaves from several spots, including the Doubletree Hotel and their Hayne Street stables.

Motorized Tours
Leaving from Charleston Visitor Reception and Transportation Center (375 Meeting St.), **Adventure Sightseeing** (843/762-0088, www.touringcharleston.com, $20 adults, $11 children) offers several comfortable 1.5-2 hour rides, including the only motorized tour to the Citadel area. Tour times are daily at 9:30am, 10am, 10:30am, 10:45am, 11:30am, 12:20pm, 1:30pm, and 2:45pm. You can make a day of it with **Charleston's Finest Historic Tours** (843/577-3311, www.historictoursofcharleston.com, $19 adults, $9.50 children), which has a basic two-hour city tour daily at 10:30am and offers some much longer tours to outlying plantations. They offer free downtown pickup from most lodgings. The old faithful **Gray Line of Charleston** (843/722-4444, www.graylineofcharleston.com, $20 adults, $12 children) offers a 90-minute tour departing from the visitors center every 30 minutes March-November daily 9:30am-3pm (hotel pickup by reservation). The last tour leaves at 2pm during the off-season.

African American History Tours
Charleston is rich in African American history, and a couple of operators specializing in this area are worth mentioning: Al Miller's **Sites & Insights Tours** (843/762-0051, www.sitesandinsightstours.com, $13-18) has several packages, including a Black History and Porgy & Bess Tour as well as a good combo city and island tour, all departing from the visitors center. Alphonso Brown's **Gullah Tours** (843/763-7551, www.gullahtours.com, $18), featuring stories told in the Gullah dialect, all leave from the African American Art Gallery (43 John St.) near the visitors center, Monday-Friday at 11am and 1pm, and Saturday at 11am, 1pm, and 3pm.

Water Tours
The best all-around tour of Charleston Harbor is the 90-minute ride offered by **SpiritLine Cruises** (800/789-3678, www.spiritlinecruises.com, $17 adults, $10 ages 6-11), which leaves from either Aquarium Wharf or Patriots Point. Allow about 30 minutes for ticketing and boarding. They also have a three-hour dinner cruise in the evening leaving from Patriots Point (about $50 pp) and a cruise to Fort Sumter. **Sandlapper Water Tours** (843/849-8687, www.sandlappertours.com, $20-27) offers many types of evening and dolphin cruises on a 45-foot catamaran. They also offer Charleston's only waterborne ghost tour. Most of their tours leave from the Maritime Center near East Bay and Calhoun Streets.

Ecotours
This aspect of Charleston's tourism scene is very well represented. The best operators include: **Barrier Island Eco Tours** (50 41st Ave., 843/886-5000, www.nature-tours.com, from $38), taking you up to the Cape Romain Refuge out of Isle of Palms; **Coastal Expeditions** (514-B Mill St., 843/884-7684,

www.coastalexpeditions.com, prices vary), with a base on Shem Creek in Mount Pleasant, offering several different-length sea kayak adventures; and **PaddleFish Kayaking**

(843/330-9777, www.paddlefishkayaking.com, from $45), offering several kinds of kayaking tours (no experience necessary) from downtown, Kiawah Island, and Seabrook Island.

Entertainment and Events

Charleston practically invented the idea of diversion and culture in the United States, so it's no surprise that there's plenty to do here, from museums to festivals and a brisk nightlife scene.

NIGHTLIFE

Unlike the locals-versus-tourists divide you find so often in other destination cities, in Charleston it's nothing for a couple of visitors to find themselves at a table next to four or five college students enjoying themselves in true Charlestonian fashion: loudly and with lots of good food and strong drink nearby. Indeed, the Holy City is downright ecumenical in its partying. The smokiest dives also have some of the best brunches. The toniest restaurants also have some of the most hopping bar scenes. Tourist hot spots written up in all the guidebooks also have their share of local regulars. Bars close in Charleston at 2am. At the retail level, all hard-liquor sales stop at 7pm, with none at all on Sunday. You can buy beer and wine in grocery stores 24-7.

Pubs and Bars

In a nod to the city's perpetual focus on well-prepared food, it's difficult to find a Charleston watering hole that *doesn't* offer really good food in addition to a well-stocked bar. One of Charleston's favorite neighborhood spots is **Moe's Crosstown Tavern** (714 Rutledge Ave., 843/722-3287, daily 11am-2am) at Rutledge Avenue and Francis Street in the Wagener Terrace/Hampton Square area.

Nipping on Moe's heels for best pub food in town is **A.C.'s Bar and Grill** (467 King St., 843/577-6742, daily 11am-2am). Though this dark, quirky watering hole might seem out of

place in the increasingly tony Upper King area, this only adds to its appeal. A.C.'s at its best is all things to all people: Charleston's favorite late-night bar, a great place to get a burger basket, and also one of the best (and certainly most unlikely) Sunday brunches in town, featuring chicken and waffles.

The Guinness flows freely at **Tommy Condon's Irish Pub** (160 Church St., 843/577-3818, www.tommycondons.com, Sun.-Thurs. 11am-2am, dinner until 10pm, Fri.-Sat. 11am-2am, dinner until 11pm)—after the obligatory and traditional slow-pour, that is—as do the patriotic Irish songs performed live most nights. You have three sections to choose from in this large, low building right near City Market: the big outdoor deck, the cozy pub itself, and the back dining room with classic wainscoting.

If it's a nice day out, a good place to relax and enjoy happy hour outside is **Vickery's Bar and Grill** (15 Beaufain St., 843/577-5300, www.vickerysbarandgrill.com, Mon.-Sat. 11:30am-2am, Sun. 11am-1am, kitchen closes 1am), actually part of a small regional chain based in Atlanta. Start with the oyster bisque, and maybe try the turkey and brie sandwich or crab cakes for your entrée.

Because of its commercial nature, Broad Street can get quiet when the sun goes down and the office workers disperse back to the burbs. But a warm little oasis can be found a few steps off Broad Street in the **Blind Tiger** (36-38 Broad St., 843/577-0088, daily 11:30am-2am, kitchen closes Mon.-Thurs. 10pm, Fri.-Sun. 9pm), which takes its name from the local Prohibition-era nickname for a speakeasy. Wood panels, Guinness and Bass on tap, and some good bar-food items make

Poe's Tavern on Sullivan's Island

© JIM MOREKIS

this a good stop off the beaten path if you find yourself in the area. A patio out back often features live music.

Located not too far over the Ashley River on U.S. 17, Charleston institution **Gene's Haufbrau** (17 Savannah Hwy., 843/225-4363, www.geneshaufbrau.com, daily 11:30am-2am) is worth making a special trip into West Ashley. Boasting the largest beer selection in Charleston—from the Butte Creek Organic Ale from California to a can of PBR—Gene's also claims to be the oldest bar in town, established in 1952.

Though Sullivan's Island has a lot of high-dollar homes, it still has friendly watering holes like **Dunleavy's Pub** (2213-B Middle St., 843/883-9646, Sun.-Thurs. 11:30am-1am, Fri.-Sat. 11:30am-2am). Inside is a great bar festooned with memorabilia, or you can enjoy a patio table. The other Sullivan's watering hole of note is **Poe's Tavern** (2210 Middle St., 843/883-0083, daily 11am-2am, kitchen closes 10pm) across the street, a nod to Edgar Allan Poe and his service on the island as a clerk

in the U.S. Army. It's a lively, mostly-locals scene, set within a fun but suitably dark interior (though you might opt for one of the outdoor tables on the raised patio). Simply put, no trip to Sullivan's is complete without a stop at one (or possibly both) of these two local landmarks, each within a stone's throw of the other.

If you're in Folly Beach, enjoy the great views and the great cocktails at **Blu Restaurant and Bar** (1 Center St., 843/588-6658, www.blufollybeach.com, $10-20) inside the Holiday Inn Folly Beach Oceanfront. There's nothing like a Spiked Lemonade on a hot Charleston day at the beach. Another notable Folly Beach watering hole is the **Sand Dollar Social Club** (7 Center St., 843/588-9498, Sun.-Fri. noon-1am, Sat. noon-2am), the kind of cash-only, mostly local, and thoroughly enjoyable dive you often find in little beach towns. You have to pony up for a "membership" to this private club, but it's only a buck. There's a catch, though: You can't get in until your 24-hour "waiting period" is over.

If you find yourself up in North Charleston,

by all means stop by **Madra Rua Irish Pub** (1034 E. Montague Ave., 843/554-2522, daily 11am-1am), an authentic watering hole with a better-than-average pub food menu that's also a great place to watch a soccer game.

Live Music

Charleston's music scene is best described as hit-and-miss. There's no distinct "Charleston sound" to speak of (especially now that the heyday of Hootie and the Blowfish is long past), and there's no one place where you're assured of finding a great band any night of the week. The scene is currently in even more of a state of flux because the city's best-regarded live rock club, Cumberland's on King Street, closed in 2007 after 15 years in business. The best place to find up-to-date music listings is the local free weekly *Charleston City Paper* (www.charleston-citypaper.com).

These days the hippest music spot in town is out on James Island at **The Pour House** (1977 Maybank Hwy., 843/571-4343, www.charlestonpourhouse.com, 9pm-2am on nights with music scheduled, call for info), where the local characters are sometimes just as entertaining as the acts onstage. The venerable **Music Farm** (32 Ann St., 843/722-8904, www.musicfarm.com) on Upper King isn't much to look at from the outside, but inside the cavernous space has played host to all sorts of bands over the past two decades. Recent concerts have included G. Love and Special Sauce, Third Eye Blind, Galactic, Modest Mouse, and Drive-By Truckers.

A great jazz place and a very good restaurant to boot is **Mercato** (102 N. Market St., 843/722-6393, www.mercatocharleston.com, bar daily 4pm-2am, late-night food menu until 1am). Italian in menu and feel, the live jazz and R&B (Wed.-Sat.) at this establishment— owned by the same company that owns the five-star Peninsula Grill—is definitely all-American. The late kitchen hours are a great bonus.

Lounges

Across the street from Gene's Haufbrau, the retro-chic **Voodoo Lounge** (15 Magnolia Lane, 843/769-0228, Mon.-Fri. 4pm-2am, Sat.-Sun. 5:30pm-2am, kitchen until 1am) is another very popular West Ashley hangout. It has a wide selection of trendy cocktails and killer gourmet tacos.

The aptly named **Rooftop Bar and Restaurant** (23 Vendue Range, 843/723-0485, Tues.-Sat. 6pm-2am) at the Library Restaurant in The Vendue is a very popular waterfront happy-hour spot from which to enjoy the sunset over the Charleston skyline. It's also a hot late-night hangout with a respectable menu.

Located in a 200-year-old building and suitably right above a cigar store, **Club Habana** (177 Meeting St., 843/853-5900, Mon.-Sat. 5pm-1am, Sun. 6pm-midnight) is the perfect place to sink down into a big couch, warm yourself by the fireplace, sip a martini (or port, or single-malt scotch), and enjoy a good smoke in the dim light. Probably the last, best vestige of the cigar-bar trend in Charleston, Club Habana remains popular. You get your cigars downstairs in Tinderbox Internationale, which features a range of rare "Legal Cuban" smokes, rolled from preembargo tobacco that has been warehoused for decades in Tampa, Florida.

Dance Clubs

The **Trio Club** (139 Calhoun St., 843/965-5333, Thurs.-Sat. 9pm-2am), right off Marion Square, is a favorite place to make the scene. There's a relaxing outdoor area with piped-in music, an intimate sofa-filled upstairs bar for dancing and chilling, and the dark candlelit downstairs with frequent live music. Without a doubt Charleston's best dance club is **Club Pantheon** (28 Ann St., 843/577-2582, Fri.-Sun. 10pm-2am).

Gay and Lesbian

Charleston is very tolerant by typical Deep South standards, and this tolerance extends to gays and lesbians as well. Most gay- and lesbian-oriented nightlife centers in the Upper King area. Charleston's hottest and hippest dance spot of any type, gay or straight, is **Club Pantheon** (28 Ann St., 843/577-2582,

Fri.-Sun. 10pm-2am) on Upper King on the lower level of the parking garage across from the visitors center (375 Meeting St.). Pantheon is not cheap—cover charges are routinely well over $10—but it's worth it for the great DJs, the dancing, and the people-watching, not to mention the drag cabaret on Friday and Sunday nights. Just down the street from Club Pantheon—and owned by the same people—is a totally different kind of gay bar, **Dudley's** (42 Ann St., 843/577-6779, daily 4pm-2am). Mellower and more appropriate for conversation or a friendly game of pool, Dudley is a nice contrast to the thumping Pantheon a few doors down.

CHARLESTON NATIVES

In addition to the long list of historic figures, some notable modern personalities born in Charleston or closely associated with the city include:

- Counterculture artist Shepard Fairey, who designed the iconic "Hope" campaign poster for Barack Obama
- Actress Mabel King (*The Wiz*)
- Actress-model Lauren Hutton
- Author Nancy Friday
- Actor Thomas Gibson (*Criminal Minds*)
- Author-lyricist DuBose Heyward
- Author Josephine Humphreys
- Author Sue Monk Kidd (*The Secret Life of Bees*)
- Actress Vanessa Minnillo (attended high school)
- Actor Will Patton (*Remember the Titans*)
- Author Alexandra Ripley
- Musician Darius Rucker (singer for Hootie & the Blowfish, now a solo country artist)
- Comedian Andy Dick
- Comedian Stephen Colbert

Though **Vickery's Bar and Grill** (15 Beaufain St., 843/577-5300, www.vickerysbarandgrill.com, Mon.-Sat. 11:30am-2am, Sun. 11am-1am, kitchen closes 1am) does not market itself as a gay and lesbian establishment, it has nonetheless become quite popular with that population—not least because of the good reputation its parent tavern in Atlanta has with that city's large and influential gay community.

PERFORMING ARTS
Theater
Unlike the more puritanical (literally) colonies farther up the American coast, Charleston was from the beginning an arts-friendly settlement. The first theatrical production in the western hemisphere happened in Charleston in January 1735, when a nomadic troupe rented a space at Church and Broad Streets to perform Thomas Otway's *The Orphan.* The play's success led to the building of the Dock Street Theatre on what is now Queen Street. On February 12, 1736, it hosted its first production, *The Recruiting Officer,* a popular play for actresses of the time because it calls for some female characters to wear tight-fitting British army uniforms. Live theater became a staple of Charleston social life, with notable thespians including both Edwin and Junius Booth (brothers of Lincoln's assassin, John Wilkes) and Edgar Allan Poe's mother, Eliza, performing here. Several high-quality troupes continue to keep that proud old tradition alive, chief among them being **Charleston Stage** (843/577-7183, www.charlestonstage.com), the resident company of the Dock Street Theatre.

The city's most unusual players are **The Have Nots!** (843/853-6687, www.thehavenots.com), with a total ensemble of 35 comedians who typically perform their brand of edgy improv every Friday night at Theatre 99 (280 Meeting St.). The players of **PURE Theatre** (843/723-4444, www.puretheatre.org) perform at the Circular Congregation Church's Lance Hall (150 Meeting St.). Their shows emphasize compelling, mature drama, beautifully performed. **The Footlight Players** (843/722-4487, www.footlightplayers.net) are the oldest continuously

STEPHEN COLBERT, NATIVE SON

A purist would insist that Charlestonians are born, not made. While it's true that comedian Stephen Colbert was actually born in Washington DC, he did spend much of his young life in the Charleston suburb of James Island and downtown on Meeting Street, attending the Porter-Gaud School. And regardless of his literal birthplace, few would dispute that Colbert is the best-known Charlestonian in American pop culture today.

While it's commonly assumed that Colbert's surname is a link to Charleston's French Huguenot heritage, the truth is that it's really an Irish name. To further burst the carefully crafted bubble of Colbert's faux on-air persona, his father, a vice president at Charleston's Medical University of South Carolina, adopted the current French pronunciation himself—historically his family pronounced the *t*.

All that being said, Colbert returns quite often to Charleston. In 2012 he hosted a mock political rally at the College of Charleston, allegedly on behalf of Citizens United, the controversial Supreme Court ruling on political contributions.

He also represents his hometown to the world at large. In 2011, he personally accepted the Conde Nast Traveler Reader's Choice Award for favorite U.S. city on behalf of Charleston, poking fun at the "Rice-a-Roni eating bastards" who reside in traditional winner San Francisco.

The comedian's life isn't without tragedy. His father and two of his brothers perished in an airplane accident in 1974. And in 2013 he did something quite rare, breaking character on his show The Colbert Report to acknowledge the passing of his 91-year-old mother Lorna, who lived in Charleston all her life, raising Stephen and his 10 siblings.

In 2014, Comedy Central announced that the finale of Colbert's eponymous show was imminent—long-time Late Show host David Letterman had announced plans for retirement, and Colbert was hired as his successor.

active company in town (since 1931), and perform in their space at 20 Queen Street.

Music

The forerunner to the **Charleston Symphony Orchestra** (CSO, 843/554-6060, www.charlestonsymphony.com) performed for the first time on December 28, 1936, at the Hibernian Hall on Meeting Street. During that first season the CSO accompanied *The Recruiting Officer,* the inaugural show at the renovated Dock Street Theatre. For seven decades, the CSO continued to provide world-class orchestral music, gaining "Metropolitan" status in the 1970s, when they accompanied the first-ever local performance of *Porgy and Bess,* which despite its Charleston setting couldn't be performed locally before then due to segregation laws. Due to financial difficulty, the CSO cancelled its 2010-2011 season. They are making quite the comeback of late, however, and I suggest checking the website for upcoming concerts.

The separate group **Chamber Music Charleston** (843/763-4941, www.chambermusiccharleston.org), which relies on many core CSO musicians, continues to perform around town, including at Piccolo Spoleto. They play a wide variety of picturesque historic venues, including the Old Exchange (120 East Bay St.), the Calhoun Mansion (16 Meeting St.), and the Footlight Players Theatre (20 Queen St.).

Dance

The premier company in town is the 20-year-old **Charleston Ballet Theatre** (477 King St., 843/723-7334, www.charlestonballet.org). Its 18 full-time dancers perform a great mix of classics, modern pieces, and, of course, a yuletide *Nutcracker* at the Gaillard Municipal Auditorium. Most performances are at the Sottile Theatre (44 George St., just off King St.) and in the Black Box Theatre at their home office on Upper King Street.

CINEMA

The most interesting art house and indie venue in town is currently **The Terrace** (1956 Maybank Hwy., 843/762-9494, www.terrace-theater.com), and not only because they offer beer and wine, which you can enjoy at your seat. Shows before 5pm are $7. It's west of Charleston on James Island; get there by taking U.S. 17 west from Charleston and go south on Highway 171, then take a right on Maybank Highway (Hwy. 700).

For a generic but good multiplex experience, go over to Mount Pleasant to the **Palmetto Grande** (1319 Theater Dr., 843/216-8696).

FESTIVALS AND EVENTS

Charleston is a festival-mad city, especially in the spring and early fall. And new festivals are being added every year, further enhancing the hedonistic flavor of this city that has also mastered the art of hospitality. Here's a look through the calendar at all the key festivals in the area.

January

Held on a Sunday in late January at historic Boone Hall Plantation on Mount Pleasant, the **Lowcountry Oyster Festival** (www.charlestonlowcountry.com, 11am-5pm, $8, food additional) features literally truckloads of the sweet shellfish for your enjoyment. Gates open at 10:30am, and there's plenty of parking. Oysters are sold by the bucket and served with crackers and cocktail sauce. Bring your own shucking knife or glove, or buy them on-site.

February

One of the more unique events in town is the **Southeastern Wildlife Exposition** (various venues, 843/723-1748, www.sewe.com, $12.50 per day, $30 for 3 days, free under age 13). For the last quarter century, the Wildlife Expo has brought together hundreds of artists and exhibitors to showcase just about any kind of naturally themed art you can think of, in over a dozen galleries and venues all over downtown. Kids will enjoy the live animals on hand as well.

March

Generally straddling late February and the first days of March, the four-day **Charleston Food & Wine Festival** (www.charlestonfoodandwine.com, various venues and admission) is a glorious celebration of one of the Holy City's premier draws: its amazing culinary community. While the emphasis is on Lowcountry gurus like Donald Barickman of Magnolia's and Robert Carter of the Peninsula Grill, guest chefs from as far away as New York, New Orleans, and Los Angeles routinely come to show off their skills. Oenophiles, especially of domestic wines, will be in heaven as well. Tickets aren't cheap—an all-event pass is over $500 pp—but then again, this is one of the nation's great food cities, so you might find it worth every penny.

Immediately before the Festival of Houses and Gardens is the **Charleston International Antiques Show** (40 East Bay St., 843/722-3405, www.historiccharleston.org, admission varies), held at Historic Charleston's headquarters at the Missroon House on the High Battery. It features over 30 of the nation's best-regarded dealers and offers lectures and tours.

Mid-March-April, the perennial favorite **Festival of Houses and Gardens** (843/722-3405, www.historiccharleston.org, admission varies) is sponsored by the Historic Charleston Foundation and is held at the very peak of the spring blooming season for maximum effect. In all, the Festival goes into a dozen historic neighborhoods to see about 150 homes. Each day sees a different three-hour tour of a different area, at about $45 pp. This is a fantastic opportunity to peek inside some amazing old privately owned properties that are inaccessible to visitors at all other times. A highlight is a big oyster roast and picnic at Drayton Hall.

One of Charleston's newest and most fun events, the five-night **Charleston Fashion Week** (www.fashionweek.charlestonmag.com, admission varies) is sponsored by *Charleston* magazine and benefits a local women's charity. Mimicking New York's Fashion Week events under tenting in Bryant Park, Charleston's version features runway action under big tents in Marion Square—and, yes, past guests have included former contestants on *Project Runway*.

April

The annual **Cooper River Bridge Run** (www. bridgerun.com) happens the first Saturday in April (unless that's Easter weekend, in which case it runs the week before) and features a six-mile jaunt across the massive new Arthur Ravenel Bridge over the Cooper River, the longest cable span in the western hemisphere. It's not for those with a fear of heights, but it's still one of Charleston's best-attended events—with well over 30,000 participants. The whole crazy idea started when Dr. Marcus Newberry of the Medical University of South Carolina in Charleston was inspired by an office fitness trail in his native state of Ohio to do something similar in Charleston to promote fitness. Participants can walk the course if they choose, and many do. Signaled with the traditional cannon shot, the race still begins in Mount Pleasant and ends downtown, but over the years the course has changed to accommodate growth—not only in the event itself but in the city. Auto traffic, of course, is rerouted from the night before the race.

From 1973 to 2000—except for 1976, when it was in Florida—the **Family Circle Cup** (161 Seven Farms Dr., Daniel Island, 843/856-7900, www.familycirclecup.com, admission varies) was held at Sea Pines Plantation on Hilton Head Island. But in 2001 the popular Tier 1 Women's tennis tournament moved to Daniel Island's brand-new Family Circle Tennis Center, specifically built for the event through a partnership of *Family Circle* magazine and the city of Charleston. (The Tennis Center is also open to the public and hosts many community events as well.)

Mount Pleasant is the home of Charleston's shrimping fleet, and each April sees all the boats parade by the Alhambra Hall and Park for the **Blessing of the Fleet** (843/884-8517, www. townofmountpleasant.com). Family events and lots and lots of seafood are also on tap.

May

One of Charleston's newest annual events is the **Charleston International Film Festival** (843/817-1617, www.charlestoniff.com, various venues and prices). Despite being a relative latecomer to the film-festival circuit, the event is pulled off with Charleston's usual aplomb.

Indisputably Charleston's single biggest and most important event, **Spoleto Festival USA** (843/579-3100, www.spoletousa.org, admission varies) has come a long way since it was a sparkle in the eye of the late Gian Carlo Menotti three decades ago. Though Spoleto long ago broke ties with its founder, his vision remains indelibly stamped on the event from start to finish. There's plenty of music, to be sure, in genres that include orchestral, opera, jazz, and avant-garde, but you'll find something in every other performing art, such as dance, drama, and spoken word, in traditions from Western to African to Southeast Asian. For 17 days from Memorial Day weekend through early June, Charleston hops and hums nearly 24 hours a day to the energy of this vibrant, cutting-edge, yet accessible artistic celebration, which dominates everything and every conversation for those three weeks. Events happen in historic venues and churches all over downtown and as far as Middleton Place, which hosts the grand finale under the stars. If you want to come to Charleston during Spoleto—and everyone should, at least once—book your accommodations and your tickets far in advance. Tickets usually go on sale in early January for that summer's festival.

As if all the hubbub around Spoleto didn't give you enough to do, there's also **Piccolo Spoleto** (843/724-7305, www.piccolospoleto. com, various venues and admission), literally "little Spoleto," running concurrently. The intent of Piccolo Spoleto—begun just a couple of years after the larger festival came to town and run by the city's Office of Cultural Affairs—is to give local and regional performers a time to shine, sharing some of that larger spotlight on the national and international performers at the main event. Of particular interest to visiting families will be Piccolo's children's events,

A MAN, A PLAN: SPOLETO!

Sadly, Gian Carlo Menotti is no longer with us, having died in 2007 at the age of 95. But the overwhelming success of the composer's brainchild and labor of love, **Spoleto Festival USA,** lives on, enriching the cultural and social life of Charleston and serving as the city's chief calling card to the world at large.

Menotti began writing music at age seven in his native Italy. As a young man he moved to Philadelphia to study music, where he shared classes—and lifelong connections—with Leonard Bernstein and Samuel Barber. His first full-length opera, *The Consul,* would garner him the Pulitzer Prize, as would 1955's *The Saint of Bleecker Street.* But by far Menotti's best-known work is the beloved Christmas opera *Amahl and the Night Visitors,* composed especially for NBC television in 1951. At the height of his fame in 1958, the charismatic and mercurial genius—fluent and witty in five languages—founded the "Festival of Two Worlds" in Spoleto, Italy, specifically as a forum for young American artists in Europe. But it wasn't until nearly two decades later, in 1977, that Menotti was able to make his long-imagined dream of an American counterpart a reality.

Attracted to Charleston because of its longstanding support of the arts, its undeniable good taste, and its small size—ensuring that his festival would always be the number-one activity in town while it was going on—Menotti worked closely with the man who was to become the other key part of the equation: Charleston Mayor Joe Riley, then in his first term in office. Since then, the city has built on Spoleto's success by founding its own local version, **Piccolo Spoleto**—literally, "little Spoleto"—which focuses exclusively on local and regional talent.

Things haven't always gone smoothly. Menotti and the stateside festival parted ways in 1993, when he took over the Rome Opera. Making matters more uneasy, the Italian festival—run by Menotti's longtime partner (and later adopted son) Chip—also became estranged from what was intended to be its soul mate in South Carolina. (Chip was later replaced by the Italian Culture Ministry.) But perhaps this kind of creative tension is what Menotti intended all along. Indeed, each spring brings a Spoleto USA that seems to thrive on the inherent conflict between the festival's often cutting-edge offerings and the very traditional city that hosts it. Unlike so many of the increasingly generic arts "festivals" across the nation, Spoleto still challenges its audiences, just as Menotti intended it to. Depending on the critic and the audience member, that modern opera debut you see may be groundbreaking or gratuitous. The drama you check out may be exhilarating or tiresome.

Still, the crowds keep coming, attracted just as much to Charleston's many charms as to the art itself. Each year, a total of about 500,000 people attend both Spoleto and Piccolo Spoleto. Nearly one-third of the attendees are Charleston residents—the final proof that when it comes to supporting the arts, Charleston puts its money where its mouth is.

a good counter to some of the decidedly more adult fare at Spoleto USA.

June

Technically part of Piccolo Spoleto but gathering its own following, the **Sweetgrass Cultural Arts Festival** (www.sweetgrassfestival.org) is held the first week in June in Mount Pleasant at the Laing Middle School (2213 U.S. 17 N.). The event celebrates the traditional sweetgrass basket-making skills of African Americans in the historical Christ Church Parish area of Mount Pleasant. If you want to buy some sweetgrass baskets made by the world's foremost experts in the field, this would be the time.

The free, weekend-long, outdoor **Charleston Harbor Fest** (www.charlestonharborfest.org, free) at the Maritime Center on the waterfront is without a doubt one of the coolest events in town for the whole family. You can see and tour working tall ships, and watch master boatbuilders at work building new ones. There are free sailboat rides into the harbor, and the U.S. Navy provides displays. As if all that weren't enough, you get to witness the start of the 777-mile annual Charleston-to-Bermuda race.

July

Each year over 30,000 people come to see the **Patriots Point Fourth of July Blast** (866/831-1720), featuring a hefty barrage of fireworks shot off the deck of the USS *Yorktown* moored on the Cooper River in the Patriots Point complex. Food, live entertainment, and kids' activities are also featured.

September

From late September into the first week of October, the city-sponsored **MOJA Arts Festival** (843/724-7305, www.mojafestival. com, various venues and admission) highlights the cultural contributions of African Americans and people from the Caribbean with dance, visual art, poetry, cuisine, crafts, and music in genres that include gospel, jazz, reggae, and classical. In existence since 1984, MOJA's name comes from the Swahili word for "one," and its incredibly diverse range of offerings in so many media have made it one of the Southeast's premier events. Highlights include a Reggae Block Party and the always-fun Caribbean Parade. Some events are ticketed, while others, such as the kids' activities and many of the dance and film events, are free.

October

Another great food event in this great food city, on a weekend in October, the **Taste of Charleston** (1235 Long Point Rd., 843/577-4030, www.charlestonrestaurantassociation. com, 11am-5pm, $12) is held at Boone Hall Plantation in Mount Pleasant and sponsored by the Greater Charleston Restaurant Association. Over 50 area chefs and restaurants come together so you can sample their wares, including a wine and food pairing, with proceeds going to charity.

November

Plantation Days at Middleton Place (4300 Ashley River Rd., 843/556-6020, www. middletonplace.org, daily 9am-5pm, last tour 4:30pm, guided tour $10) happen each Saturday in November, giving visitors a chance to wander the grounds and see artisans at work practicing authentic crafts, as they would have done in antebellum days, with a special emphasis on the contributions of African Americans. A special treat comes on Thanksgiving, when a full meal is offered on the grounds at the Middleton Place restaurant (843/556-6020, www.middletonplace.org, reservations strongly recommended).

Though the **Battle of Secessionville** actually took place in June 1862 much farther south, November is the time the battle is reenacted at Boone Plantation (1235 Long Point Rd., 843/884-4371, www.boonehallplantation. com, $17.50 adults, $7.50 children) on Mount Pleasant. Call for specific dates and times.

December

A yuletide in the Holy City is an experience you'll never forget, as the **Christmas in Charleston** (843/724-3705, www.charlestoncity.info) events clustered around the first week of the month prove. The festivities begin with lighting the city's 60-foot Tree of Lights in Marion Square, followed by a parade of brightly lit boats from Mount Pleasant all the way around Charleston up the Ashley River. The key event is the Sunday Christmas Parade through downtown.

Shopping

For a relatively small city, Charleston has an impressive amount of big-name, big-city stores to go along with its charming one-of-a-kind locally owned shops. I've never known anyone to leave Charleston without bundles of good stuff.

KING STREET

Without a doubt, King Street is by far the main shopping thoroughfare in the area. It's unique not only for the fact that so many national name stores are lined up so close to each other but because there are so many great restaurants of so many different types scattered in and among the retail outlets, ideally positioned for when you need to take a break to rest and refuel. Though I don't necessarily recommend doing so—Charleston has so much more to offer—a visitor could easily spend an entire weekend doing nothing but shopping, eating, and carousing up and down King Street from early morning to the wee hours of the following morning. King Street has three distinct areas with three distinct types of merchandise: Lower King is primarily top-of-the-line antiques stores (most are closed Sunday, so plan your trip accordingly); Middle King is where you'll find upscale name-brand outlets such as Banana Republic and American Apparel as well as some excellent shoe stores; and Upper King, north of Calhoun Street, is where you'll find funky housewares shops, generally locally owned.

Antiques

A relatively new addition to Lower King's cluster of antiques shops, **Alexandra AD** (156 King St., 843/722-4897, Mon.-Sat. 10am-5pm) features great chandeliers, lamps, and fabrics. As the name implies, **English Patina** (179 King St., 843/853-0380, Mon.-Sat. 10am-5pm) specializes in European furniture, brought to its

© JIM MOREKIS

Shopping on King Street never disappoints.

CHARLESTON

MAYOR JOE'S LEGACY

Few cities anywhere have been as greatly influenced by one mayor as Charleston has by Joseph P. "Joe" Riley, reelected in November 2011 to his 10th four-year term (he swears this will be his last). "Mayor Joe," or just "Joe," as he's usually called, is not only responsible for instigating the vast majority of redevelopment in the city, he continues to set the bar for its award-winning tourism industry—always a key component in his long-term plans.

Riley won his first mayoral race at the age of 32, the second Irish American mayor of the city. The first was John Grace, elected in 1911 and eventually defeated by the allegedly anti-Catholic Thomas P. Stoney. Legend has it that soon after winning his first mayoral election in 1975, Riley was handed an old envelope written decades before by the Bishop of Charleston, addressed to "The Next Irish Mayor." Inside was a note with a simple message: "Get the Stoneys."

The well-regarded lawyer, Citadel grad, and former member of the state legislature had a clear vision for his administration: It would bring unprecedented numbers of women and minorities into city government, rejuvenate then-seedy King Street, and enlarge the city's tax base by annexing surrounding areas (during Riley's tenure the city has grown from 16.7 square miles to over 100). But in order to make any of that happen, one thing had to happen first—Charleston's epidemic street crime had to be brought under control. Enter a vital partner in Riley's effort to remake Charleston: Chief of Police Reuben Greenberg. From 1982 to 2005, Greenberg—who intrigued locals and the national media not only for his dominant personality but because he was that comparative rarity, an African American Jew—turned old ideas of law enforcement in Charleston upside down through his introduction of "community

policing." Charleston cops would have to have a college degree. Graffiti would not be tolerated. And for the first time in recent memory, they would have to walk beats instead of stay in their cars. With Greenberg's help, Riley was able to keep together the unusual coalition of predominantly white business and corporate interests and African American voters that brought him into office in the first place.

It hasn't all been rosy. Riley was put on the spot in 2007 after the tragic deaths of the "Charleston 9" firefighters, an episode which seemed to expose serious policy and equipment flaws in the city's fire department. And he's often been accused of being too easily infatuated with high-dollar development projects instead of paying attention to the needs of regular Charlestonians, such as perennial flooding problems.

Here's only a partial list of the major projects and events Mayor Joe has made happen in Charleston that visitors are likely to enjoy:

· Charleston Maritime Center

· Charleston Place

· Children's Museum of the Lowcountry

· Hampton Park rehabilitation

· King Street-Market Street retail district

· Mayor Joseph P. Riley Ballpark (named after the mayor at the insistence of city council, over his objections)

· MOJA Arts Festival

· Piccolo Spoleto

· The South Carolina Aquarium

· Spoleto USA

· Waterfront Park

· West Ashley Bikeway and Greenway

big James Island warehouse three times a year in shipping containers. Since 1929, **George C. Birlant & Co.** (191 King St., 843/722-3842, Mon.-Sat. 9am-5:30pm) has been importing 18th- and 19th-century furniture, silver, china, and crystal, and also deals in the famous "Charleston Battery Bench." On the 200 block, **A'riga IV** (204 King St., 843/577-3075, Mon.-Sat. 10:30am-4:30pm) deals in a quirky mix of 19th-century decorative arts, including rare apothecary items. **Carlton Daily Antiques** (208 King St., 843/853-2299,

Mon.-Sat. 10am-5:30pm) intrigues with its unusual focus on art deco and modernist pieces and furnishings.

Art Galleries
Ever since native son Joseph Allen Smith began one of the country's first art collections in Charleston in the late 1700s, the Holy City has been fertile ground for visual artists. For most visitors, the center of visual arts activity is in the French Quarter between South Market and Tradd Streets. Thirty galleries reside here within short walking distance, including: **Charleston Renaissance Gallery** (103 Church St., 843/723-0025, www.fineartsouth. com, Mon.-Sat. 10am-5pm), specializing in 19th- and 20th-century oils and sculpture, featuring artists from the American South, including some splendid pieces from the Charleston Renaissance; the city-funded **City Gallery at Waterfront** (34 Prioleau St., 843/958-6484, Tues.-Fri. 11am-6pm, Sat.-Sun. noon-5pm); the **Pink House Gallery** (17 Chalmers St., 843/723-3608, http://pinkhousegallery.tripod.com, Mon.-Sat. 10am-5pm), in the oldest tavern building in the South, circa 1694; **Helena Fox Fine Art** (106-A Church St., 843/723-0073, www.helenafoxfineart.com, Mon.-Sat. 10am-5pm), dealing in 20th-century representational art; the **Anne Worsham Richardson Birds Eye View Gallery** (119-A Church St., 843/723-1276, www.anneworshamrichardson.com, Mon.-Sat. 10am-5pm), home of South Carolina's official painter of the state flower and state bird; and the more modern-oriented **Robert Lange Studios** (2 Queen St., 843/805-8052, www.robertlangestudios.com, daily 11am-5pm). The best way to experience the area is to go on one of the popular and free **French Quarter ArtWalks** (843/724-3424, www.frenchquarterarts.com), held the first Friday of March, May, October, and December 5pm-8pm and featuring lots of wine, food, and, of course, art. You can download a map at the website.

One of the most important single venues, the nonprofit **Redux Contemporary Art Center** (136 St. Philip St., 843/722-0697, www.reduxstudios.org, Tues.-Thurs. noon-8pm, Fri.-Sat. noon-5pm) features modernistic work in a variety of media, including illustration, video installation, blueprints, performance art, and graffiti. Outreach is hugely important to this venture and includes lecture series, classes, workshops, and internships. For a more modern take from local artists, check out the **Sylvan Gallery** (171 King St., 843/722-2172, www. thesylvangallery.com, Mon.-Fri. 9am-5pm, Sat. 10am-5pm, Sun. 11am-4pm), which specializes in 20th- and 21st-century art and sculpture. Right up the street and incorporating works from the estate of Charleston legend Elizabeth O'Neill Verner is **Ann Long Fine Art** (177 King St., 843/577-0447, www.annlongfineart.com, Mon.-Sat. 11am-5pm), which seeks to combine the painterly aesthetic of the Old World with the edgy vision of the New. Farther up King and specializing in original Audubon prints and antique botanical prints is **The Audubon Gallery** (190 King St., 843/853-1100, www. audubonart.com, Mon.-Sat. 10am-5pm), the sister store of the Joel Oppenheimer Gallery in Chicago. In the Upper King area is **Gallery Chuma** (43 John St., 843/722-7568, www.gallerychuma.com, Mon.-Sat. 10am-6pm), which specializes in the art of the Gullah people of the South Carolina coast. They do lots of cultural and educational events about Gullah culture as well as display art on the subject.

Books and Music
It's easy to overlook at the far southern end of retail development on King Street, but the excellent **Preservation Society of Charleston Book and Gift Shop** (147 King St., 843/722-4630, Mon.-Sat. 10am-5pm) is perhaps the best place in town to pick up books on Charleston lore and history as well as locally themed gift items. The charming **Pauline Books and Media** (243 King St., 843/577-0175, Mon.-Sat. 10am-6pm) is run by the Daughters of Saint Paul and carries Christian books, Bibles, rosaries, and images from a Roman Catholic perspective. Housed in an extremely long and narrow storefront on Upper King, Jonathan Sanchez's funky and friendly **Blue Bicycle**

Books (420 King St., 843/722-2666, www.bluebicyclebooks.com, Mon.-Sat. 10am-6pm, Sun. 1pm-6pm) deals primarily in used books and has a particularly nice stock of local and regional books, art books, and fiction.

Clothes

Cynics may scoff at the proliferation of high-end national retail chains on Middle King, but rarely will a shopper find so many so conveniently located, and in such a pleasant environment. The biggies are: **The Gap** (269 King St., 843/577-2498), **Banana Republic** (247 King St., 843/722-6681), **J.Crew** (264 King St., 843/534-1640), **American Apparel** (348 King St., 843/853-7220), and a massive **Forever 21** (211 King St., 843/937-5087).

For a locally owned clothing shop, try the innovative **Worthwhile** (268 King St., 843/723-4418, www.shopworthwhile.com, Mon.-Sat. 10am-6pm, Sun. noon-5pm), which has lots of organic fashion. Big companies' losses are your gain at **Oops!** (326 King St., 843/722-7768, Mon.-Fri. 10am-6pm, Sat. 10am-7pm, Sun. noon-6pm), which buys factory mistakes and discontinued lines from major brands at a discount, passing along the savings to you. The range here tends toward colorful and preppy. If hats are your thing, make sure you visit **Magar Hatworks** (57 Cannon St., 843/577-7740, leighmagar@aol.com, www.magarhatworks.com), where Leigh Magar makes and sells her whimsical, all-natural hats, some of which she designs for Barneys New York. Another notable locally owned clothing store on King Street is the classy **Berlins Men's and Women's** (114-120 King St., 843/722-1665, Mon.-Sat. 9:30am-6pm), dating from 1883.

Health and Beauty

The Euro-style window display of **Stella Nova** (292 King St., 843/722-9797, Mon.-Sat. 10am-7pm, Sun. 1pm-5pm) beckons at the corner of King and Society Streets. Inside this locally owned cosmetics store and studio, you'll find a wide selection of high-end makeup and beauty products. There's also a **Stella Nova Day Spa**

(78 Society St., 843/723-0909, Mon.-Sat. 9am-6pm, Sun. noon-5pm).

Inside the Francis Marion Hotel near Marion Square is **Spa Adagio** (387 King St., 843/577-2444, Mon.-Sat. 10am-7pm, Sun. by appointment only), offering massage, waxing, and skin and nail care. On Upper King you'll find **Allure Salon** (415 King St., 843/722-8689, Tues. and Thurs. 10am-7pm, Wed. and Fri. 9am-5pm, Sat. 10am-3pm) for stylish haircuts.

Home, Garden, and Sporting Goods

With retail locations in Charleston and Savannah and a new cutting-edge, green-friendly warehouse in North Charleston, **Half Moon Outfitters** (280 King St., 843/853-0990, www.halfmoonoutfitters.com, Mon.-Sat. 10am-7pm, Sun. noon-6pm) is something of a local legend. Here you can find not only top-of-the-line camping and outdoor gear and good tips on local recreation but some really stylish outdoorsy apparel as well. A couple of good home and garden stores are worth mentioning on Upper King: **Charleston Gardens** (650 King St., 866/469-0118, www.charleston-gardens.com, Mon.-Sat. 9am-5pm) for furniture and accessories, and **Haute Design Studio** (489 King St., 843/577-9886, www.hautedesign.com, Mon.-Fri. 9am-5:30pm) for upper-end furnishings with an edgy feel.

Jewelry

Joint Venture Estate Jewelers (185 King St., 843/722-6730, www.jventure.com, Mon.-Sat. 10am-5:30pm) specializes in antique, vintage, and modern estate jewelry as well as pre-owned watches, including Rolex, Patek Philippe, and Cartier. Since 1919, **Croghan's Jewel Box** (308 King St., 843/723-3594, www.croghansjewelbox.com, Mon.-Fri. 9:30am-5:30pm, Sat. 10am-5pm) has offered amazing locally crafted diamonds, silver, and designer pieces to generations of Charlestonians. An expansion in the late 1990s tripled the size of the historic location. **Art Jewelry by Mikhail Smolkin** (312 King

CHARLESTON

St., 843/722-3634, www.fineartjewelry.com, Mon.-Sat. 10am-5pm) features one-of-a-kind pieces by this St. Petersburg, Russia, native.

Shoes
Rangoni of Florence (270 King St., 843/577-9554, Mon.-Sat. 9:30am-6pm, Sun. 12:30pm-5:30pm) imports the best women's shoes from Italy, with a few men's designs as well. **Copper Penny Shooz** (317 King St., 843/723-3838, Mon.-Sat. 10am-7pm, Sun. noon-6pm) combines hip and upscale fashion. Funky and fun **Phillips Shoes** (320 King St., 843/965-5270, Mon.-Sat. 10am-6pm) deals in Dansko for men, women, and kids (don't miss the awesome painting above the register of Elvis fitting a customer). **Mephisto** (322 King St., 843/722-4666, www.mepcomfort.com, Mon.-Sat. 10am-6pm) deals in that incredibly comfortable, durable brand. A famous locally owed place for footwear is **Bob Ellis Shoe Store** (332 King St., 843/722-2515, www.bobellisshoes.com, Mon.-Sat. 10am-6pm), which has served Charleston's elite with high-end shoes since 1950.

CHARLESTON PLACE
Charleston Place (130 Market St., 843/722-4900, www.charlestonplaceshops.com, Mon.-Wed. 10am-6pm, Thurs.-Sat. 10am-8pm, Sun. noon-5pm), a combined retail-hotel development begun to much controversy in the late 1970s, was the first big downtown redevelopment project of Mayor Riley's tenure. While naysayers said people would never come downtown to shop for boutique items, Riley proved them wrong, and 30 years later The Shops at Charleston Place and the Riviera (the entire complex has itself been renovated through the years) remains a big shopping draw for locals and visitors alike. Highlights inside the large, stylish space include Gucci, Talbots, Louis Vuitton, Yves Delorme, Everything But Water, and Godiva.

NORTH OF BROAD
In addition to the myriad of tourist-oriented shops in the Old City Market itself, there are a few gems in the surrounding area that also appeal to locals. For years dominated by a flea market vibe, **Old City Market** (Meeting St. and Market St., 843/973-7236, daily 6am-11:30pm) was recently upgraded and is now chockablock with boutique retail all along its lengthy interior. The more humble crafts tables are toward the back. If you must have one of the handcrafted sweetgrass baskets, try out your haggling skills—the prices have wiggle room built in.

Women come from throughout the region to shop at the incredible consignment store **The Trunk Show** (281 Meeting St., 843/722-0442, Mon.-Sat. 10am-6pm). You can find one-of-a-kind vintage and designer wear and accessories. Some finds are bargains, some not so much, but there's no denying the quality and breadth of the offerings. For a more budget-conscious and countercultural vintage shop, walk a few feet next door to **Factor Five** (283 Meeting St., 843/965-5559), which has retro clothes, rare CDs, and assorted paraphernalia. **Indigo** (4 Vendue Range, 800/549-2513, Sun.-Thurs. 10am-6pm, Fri.-Sat. 10am-7pm), a favorite home accessories store, has plenty of one-of-a-kind pieces, many of them by regional artists and rustic in flavor, almost like outsider art. Affiliated with the hip local restaurant chain Maverick Kitchens, **Charleston Cooks!** (194 East Bay St., 843/722-1212, www.charlestoncooks.com, Mon.-Sat. 10am-9pm, Sun. 11am-6pm) has an almost overwhelming array of gourmet items and kitchenware, and even offers cooking classes.

OFF THE PENINSULA
Though the best shopping is in Charleston proper, there are some noteworthy independent stores in the surrounding areas. Mount Pleasant boasts a fun antiques and auction spot, **Page's Thieves Market** (1460 Ben Sawyer Blvd., 843/884-9672, www.pagesthievesmarket.com, Mon.-Fri. 9am-5:30pm, Sat. 9am-5pm). The biggest music store in the region is **The Guitar Center** (7620 Rivers Ave., 843/572-9063, Mon.-Fri. 11am-7pm, Sat. 10am-7pm, Sun. noon-6pm) in North

Charleston across from Northwood Mall. With just about everything a musician might want or need, it's part of a chain that has been around since the late 1950s, but the Charleston location is relatively new. Probably Charleston's best-regarded home goods store is the nationally recognized **ESD, Elizabeth Stuart Design** (422 Savannah Hwy./U.S. 17, 843/225-6282, www.esdcharleston.com, Mon.-Sat. 10am-6pm), with a wide range of antique and new furnishings, art, lighting, jewelry, and more.

SHOPPING CENTERS

The newest and most pleasant mall in the area is the retro-themed, pedestrian-friendly **Mount Pleasant Towne Center** (1600 Palmetto Grande Dr., 843/216-9900, www.mtpleasant-townecentre.com, Mon.-Sat. 10am-9pm, Sun. noon-6pm), which opened in 1999 to serve the growing population of East Cooper residents tired of having to cross a bridge to get to a big mall. In addition to national chains, you'll find

a few cool local stores here, like Stella Nova spa and day salon, Shooz by Copper Penny, and the men's store Jos. A. Banks.

You'll find the **Northwoods Mall** (2150 Northwoods Blvd., North Charleston, 843/797-3060, www.shopnorthwoodsmall.com, Mon.-Sat. 10am-9pm, Sun. noon-6pm) up in North Charleston. Anchor stores include Dillard's, Belk, Sears, and J. C. Penney. North Charleston also hosts the **Tanger Outlet** (4840 Tanger Outlet Blvd., 843/529-3095, www.tangeroutlet.com, Mon.-Sat. 10am-9pm, Sun. 11am-6pm). Get factory-priced bargains from stores such as Adidas, Banana Republic, Brooks Brothers, CorningWare, Old Navy, Timberland, and more.

The somewhat decrepit **Citadel Mall** (2070 Sam Rittenberg Blvd., 843/766-8511, www.shopcitadel-mall.com, Mon.-Sat. 10am-9pm, Sun. noon-6pm) is in West Ashley (and curiously not at all close to the actual Citadel college). Anchors here are Dillard's, Parisian, Target, Belk, and Sears.

Sports and Recreation

Because of the generally great weather in Charleston, helped immensely by the steady, soft sea breeze, outdoor activities are always popular and available. Though it's not much of a spectator sports town, there are plenty of things to do on your own, such as golf, tennis, walking, hiking, boating, and fishing.

ON THE WATER
Beaches
In addition to the charming town of Folly Beach itself, there's the modest county-run **Folly Beach County Park** (1100 W. Ashley Ave., Folly Beach, 843/588-2426, www.ccprc.com, May-Feb. daily 10am-dusk, Mar.-Apr. daily 9am-dusk, $7 per vehicle, free for pedestrians and cyclists) at the far west end of Folly Island. It has a picnic area, restrooms, outdoor showers, and beach chair and umbrella rentals. Get here by taking Highway 171 (Folly Rd.)

until it turns into Center Street, and then take a right on West Ashley Avenue.

On Isle of Palms you'll find **Isle of Palms County Park** (14th Ave., Isle of Palms, 843/886-3863, www.ccprc.com, fall-spring daily 10am-dusk, summer daily 9am-dusk, $5 per vehicle, free for pedestrians and cyclists), which has restrooms, showers, a picnic area, a beach volleyball area, and beach chair and umbrella rentals. Get there by taking the Isle of Palms Connector (Hwy. 517) to the island, go through the light at Palm Boulevard, and take the next left at the park gate. There's good public beach access near the Pavilion Shoppes on Ocean Boulevard, accessed via J C Long Boulevard.

On the west end of Kiawah Island to the south of Charleston is **Kiawah Island Beachwalker Park** (843/768-2395, www.ccprc.com, Mar.-Apr. and Oct. Sat.-Sun. only

10am-6pm, May-Aug. daily 9am-7pm, Sept. daily 10am-6pm, Nov.-Feb. closed, $7 per vehicle, free for pedestrians and cyclists), the only public facility on this mostly private resort island. It has restrooms, showers, a picnic area with grills, and beach chair and umbrella rentals. Get there from downtown by taking Lockwood Avenue onto the Highway 30 Connector bridge over the Ashley River. Turn right onto Folly Road, then take a left onto Maybank Highway. After about 20 minutes you'll take another left onto Bohicket Road, which leads you to Kiawah in 14 miles. Turn left from Bohicket Road onto the Kiawah Island Parkway. Just before the security gate, turn right on Beachwalker Drive and follow the signs to the park.

For a totally go-it-alone type of beach day, go to the three-mile-long beach on the Atlantic Ocean at **Sullivan's Island.** There are no facilities, no lifeguards, strong offshore currents, and no parking lots on this residential island (park on the side of the street). There's also a lot of dog-walking on this beach, since no leash is required November-February. Get here from downtown by crossing the Ravenel Bridge over the Cooper River and bearing right onto Coleman Boulevard, which turns into Ben Sawyer Boulevard. Take the Ben Sawyer Bridge onto Sullivan's Island. Beach access is plentiful and marked.

Kayaking

An excellent outfit for guided kayak tours is **Coastal Expeditions** (654 Serotina Court, 843/881-4582, www.coastalexpeditions.com), which also runs the only approved ferry service to the Cape Romain National Wildlife Refuge. They'll rent you a kayak for roughly $50 per day. Coastal Expeditions also sells an outstanding kayaking, boating, and fishing map of the area (about $12). **Barrier Island Eco Tours** (50 41st Ave., 843/886-5000, www.nature-tours.com) takes you up to the Cape Romain refuge out of Isle of Palms. **PaddleFish Kayaking** (843/330-9777, www.paddlefishkayaking.com) offers several kinds of kayaking tours (no experience necessary) and is quite accommodating

in terms of scheduling them. Another good tour operator is **Nature Adventures Outfitters** (1900 Iron Swamp Rd., McClellanville, 800/673-0679) out of Awendaw Island. Closer to town, many kayakers put in at the **Shem Creek Marina** (526 Mill St., 843/884-3211, www.shemcreekmarina.com) or the public **Shem Creek Landing** in Mount Pleasant. From here it's a safe, easy paddle—sometimes with appearances by dolphins or manatees—to the Intracoastal Waterway. Some kayakers like to go from Shem Creek straight out into Charleston Harbor to **Crab Bank Heritage Preserve,** a prime birding island. Another good place to put in is at **Isle of Palms Marina** (50 41st Ave., 843/886-0209) behind the Wild Dunes Resort on Morgan Creek, which empties into the Intracoastal Waterway. Local company **Half Moon Outfitters** (280 King St., 843/853-0990; 425 Coleman Blvd., 843/881-9472, www.halfmoonoutfitters.com, Mon.-Sat. 10am-7pm, Sun. noon-6pm) sponsors an annual six-mile Giant Kayak Race at Isle of Palms Marina in late October, benefiting the Coastal Conservation League.

Behind Folly Beach is an extensive network of waterways, including lots of areas that are great for camping and fishing. The Folly River Landing is just over the bridge to the island. On Folly Island, a good tour operator and rental house is **OceanAir Sea Kayak** (520 Folly Rd., 800/698-8718, www.seakayaksc.com).

Fishing and Boating

For casual fishing off a pier, try the well-equipped new **Folly Beach Fishing Pier** (101 E. Arctic Ave., Folly Beach, 843/588-3474, parking $5, fishing $8, rod rentals available) on Folly Beach, or the **North Charleston Riverfront Park** (843/745-1087, www.northcharleston.org, daily dawn-dusk) along the Cooper River on the grounds of the old Navy Yard. Get onto the Navy Yard grounds by taking I-26 north to exit 216B. Take a left onto Spruill Avenue and a right onto McMillan Avenue.

Key local marinas include **Shem Creek Marina** (526 Mill St., 843/884-3211, www.shemcreekmarina.com), **Charleston Harbor**

Marina (24 Patriots Point Rd., 843/284-7062, www.charlestonharbormarina.com), **Charleston City Marina** (17 Lockwood Dr., 843/722-4968), **Charleston Maritime Center** (10 Wharfside St., 843/853-3625, www.cmcevents.com), and the **Cooper River Marina** (1010 Juneau Ave., 843/554-0790, www.ccprc.com).

Good fishing charter outfits include **Barrier Island Eco Tours** (50 41st Ave., 843/886-5000, www.nature-tours.com, about $80) out of Isle of Palms; **Bohicket Boat Adventure & Tour Co.** (2789 Cherry Point Rd., 843/559-3525, www.bohicketboat.com) out of the Edisto River; and **Reel Fish Finder Charters** (315 Yellow Jasmine Court, Moncks Corner, 843/697-2081). Captain James picks up clients at many different marinas in the area. For a list of all public landings in Charleston County, go to www.ccprc.com.

Water Parks

During the summer months, Charleston County operates three water parks, though none are on the peninsula: **Splash Island Waterpark** (444 Needlerush Pkwy., Mount Pleasant, 843/884-0832); **Whirlin' Waters Adventure Waterpark** (University Blvd., North Charleston, 843/572-7275); and **Splash Zone Waterpark at James Island County Park** (871 Riverland Dr., 843/795-7275), on James Island west of town. Admission runs about $10 pp. Go to www.ccprc.com for more information.

ON LAND
Golf

The country's first golf course was constructed in Charleston in 1786. The term "greens fee" is alleged to have evolved from the maintenance fees charged to members of the South Carolina Golf Club and Harleston Green in what's now downtown Charleston. So, as you'd expect, there's some great golfing in the area, generally on the outlying islands. Here are some of the highlights; fees are averages and subject to season and time of day.

The folks at the nonprofit **Charleston Golf, Inc.** (423 King St., 843/958-3629, www.

charlestongolfguide.com) are your best one-stop resource for tee times and packages. The main public course is the 18-hole **Charleston Municipal Golf Course** (2110 Maybank Hwy., 843/795-6517, www.charlestoncity.info, $40). To get here from the peninsula, take U.S. 17 south over the Ashley River, take Highway 171 (Folly Rd.) south, and then take a right onto Maybank Highway. Probably the most renowned area facilities are at the acclaimed **Kiawah Island Golf Resort** (12 Kiawah Beach Dr., Kiawah Island, 800/654-2924, www.kiawahgolf.com), about 20 miles from Charleston. The resort has five courses in all, the best-known of which is the **Kiawah Island Ocean Course**. These are public courses, but be aware that tee times are limited for golfers who aren't guests at the resort.

Two excellent resort-style public courses are at **Wild Dunes Resort Golf** (5757 Palm Blvd., Isle of Palms, 888/845-8932, www.wilddunes.com, $165) on Isle of Palms. The 18-hole **Patriots Point Links** (1 Patriots Point Rd., Mount Pleasant, 843/881-0042, www.patriotspointlinks.com, $100) on the Charleston Harbor right over the Ravenel Bridge is one of the most convenient courses in the area, and it boasts some phenomenal views.

Tennis

Tennis fans are in for a treat at the new **Family Circle Tennis Center** (161 Seven Farms Dr., 800/677-2293, www.familycirclecup.com, Mon.-Thurs. 8am-8pm, Fri. 8am-7pm, Sat. 8am-5pm, Sun. 9am-5pm, $15 per hour) on Daniel Island. This multimillion-dollar facility is owned by the city of Charleston and was built in 2001 specifically to host the annual Family Circle Cup women's competition, which was previously held in Hilton Head for many years. But it's also open to the public year-round (except when the Cup is on) with 17 courts.

The best resort tennis activity is at the **Kiawah Island Golf Resort** (12 Kiawah Beach Dr., Kiawah Island, 800/654-2924, www.kiawahgolf.com), with a total of 28 courts. There are four free, public, city-funded facilities on the peninsula: **Moultrie Playground** (Broad St. and Ashley Ave., 843/769-8258, www.charlestoncity.info, 6 lighted hard courts), **Jack Adams Tennis Center** (290 Congress St., 6 lighted hard courts), **Hazel Parker Playground** (70 East Bay St., on the Cooper River, 1 hard court), and **Corrine Jones Playground** (Marlowe St. and Peachtree St., 2 hard courts). Over in West Ashley, the city also runs the public **Charleston Tennis Center** (19 Farmfield Rd., 843/769-8258, www.charlestoncity.info, 15 lighted courts).

Hiking and Biking

Early risers will especially enjoy the beauty of dawn breaking over the Cooper River as they walk or jog along the Battery or a little farther north at Waterfront Park. Charleston-area beaches are perfect for a leisurely bike ride on the sand. Sullivan's Island is a particular favorite, and you might be surprised at how long you can ride in one direction on these beaches. Those desiring a more demanding use of their legs can walk or ride their bike in the dedicated pedestrian and bike lane on the massive **Arthur Ravenel Jr. Bridge** over the Cooper River, the longest cable-stayed bridge in the western hemisphere. There's public parking on both sides of the bridge, on the Charleston side off Meeting Street and on the Mount Pleasant side on the road to Patriots Point. **Bike the Bridge Rentals** (360 Concord St., 843/853-2453, www.bikethebridgerentals.com) offers self-guided tours over the Ravenel Bridge and back on a Raleigh Comfort bike, and also rents road bikes for lengthier excursions. In West Ashley, there's an urban walking and biking trail, the **West Ashley Greenway,** built on a former rail bed. The 10-mile trail runs parallel to U.S. 17 and passes parks, schools, and the Clemson Experimental Farm, ending near John Island. To get to the trailhead from downtown, drive west on U.S. 17. About 0.5 miles after you cross the bridge, turn left onto Folly Road (Hwy. 171). At the second light, turn right into South Windermere Shopping Center; the trail is behind the center on the right.

The most ambitious trail in South Carolina is the **Palmetto Trail** (www.palmettoconservation.org), begun in 1997 and eventually covering 425 miles from the Atlantic to the Appalachians. The coastal terminus near Charleston, the seven-mile Awendaw Passage through the Francis Marion National Forest, begins at the trailhead at the Buck Hall Recreational Area (843/887-3257, $5 vehicle fee), which has parking and restroom facilities. Get there by taking U.S. 17 north from Charleston about 20 miles and through the Francis Marion National Forest and then Awendaw. Take a right onto Buck Hall Landing Road.

Another good nature hike outside town is on the eight miles of scenic and educational trails at **Caw Caw Interpretive Center** (5200 Savannah Hwy., Ravenel, 843/889-8898, www.ccprc.com, Wed.-Fri. 9am-3pm, Sat.-Sun. 9am-5pm, $1) on an old rice plantation.

One of the best outfitters in town is **Half Moon Outfitters** (280 King St., 843/853-0990, www.halfmoonoutfitters.com, Mon.-Sat. 10am-7pm, Sun. noon-6pm). They have a Mount Pleasant location (425 Coleman Blvd., 843/881-9472) as well, and it has better parking.

Bird-Watching

Right in Charleston Harbor is the little **Crab Bank Heritage Preserve** (803/734-3886), where thousands of migratory birds can be seen, depending on the season. October-April you can either kayak there yourself or take a charter with **Nature Adventures Outfitters** (1900 Iron Swamp Rd., Awendaw Island, 800/673-0679). On James Island southwest of Charleston is **Legare Farms** (2620 Hanscombe Point Rd., 843/559-0763, www.legarefarms.com), which holds migratory bird walks ($6 adults, $3 children) in the fall each Saturday at 8:30am.

SPECTATOR SPORTS
Charleston River Dogs

A New York Yankees farm team playing in the South Atlantic League, the **Charleston**

CHARLESTON

River Dogs (www.riverdogs.com, $5 general admission) play April-August at Joseph P. Riley Jr. Park, a.k.a. "The Joe" (360 Fishburne St.). The park is great, and there are a lot of fun promotions to keep things interesting should the play on the field be less than stimulating (as minor league ball often can be). Because of the intimate, retro design of the park, there are no bad seats, so you might as well save a few bucks and go for the general admission ticket. From downtown, get to The Joe by taking Broad Street west until it turns into Lockwood Drive. Follow that north until you get to Brittlebank Park and The Joe, next to the Citadel. Expect to pay $3-5 for parking.

Family Circle Cup

Moved to Daniel Island in 2001 from its longtime home in Hilton Head, the prestigious Family Circle Cup women's tennis tournament is held each April at the **Family Circle Tennis Center** (161 Seven Farms Dr., Daniel Island, 843/856-7900, www.familycirclecup.com, admission varies). Almost 100,000 people attend the multiple-week event. Individual session tickets go on sale the preceding January.

Charleston Battery

The professional A-League soccer team **Charleston Battery** (843/971-4625, www.charlestonbattery.com, about $10) plays April-July at Blackbaud Stadium (1990 Daniel Island Dr.) on Daniel Island, north of Charleston. To get here from downtown, take I-26 north and then I-526 to Mount Pleasant. Take exit 23A, Clements Ferry Road, and then a left on St. Thomas Island Drive. Blackbaud Stadium is about one mile along on the left.

South Carolina Stingrays

The ECHL professional ice hockey team the **South Carolina Stingrays** (843/744-2248, www.stingrayshockey.com, $15) get a good crowd out to their rink at the North Charleston Coliseum (5001 Coliseum Dr., North Charleston), playing October-April.

Citadel Bulldogs

The Citadel (171 Moultrie St., 843/953-3294, www.citadelsports.com) plays Southern Conference football home games at Johnson-Hagood Stadium, next to the campus on the Ashley River near Hampton Park. The basketball team plays home games at McAlister Field House on campus. The school's ice hockey team skates home games at the Carolina Ice Palace (7665 Northwoods Blvd., North Charleston).

Accommodations

As one of the country's key national and international destination cities, Charleston has a very well-developed infrastructure for housing visitors—a task made much easier by the city's longstanding tradition of hospitality. Because the bar is set so high, few visitors experience a truly bad stay in town. Hotels and bed-and-breakfasts are generally well maintained and have a high level of service, ranging from very good to excellent. There's a 12.5 percent tax on hotel rooms in Charleston.

SOUTH OF BROAD
$150-300

On the south side of Broad Street is a great old Charleston lodging, ◖**Governor's House Inn** (117 Broad St., 843/720-2070, www.governorshouse.com, $285-585). This circa-1760 building, a National Historic Landmark, is associated with Edward Rutledge, a signer of the Declaration of Independence. Though most of its 11 guest rooms—all with four-poster beds, period furnishings, and high ceilings—go for around $300, some of the smaller guest rooms can be had for closer to $200 in the off-season.

The nine guest rooms of 🌙 **Two Meeting Street Inn** (2 Meeting St., 843/723-7322, www.twomeetingstreet.com, $220-435) down by the Battery are individually appointed, with themes like "The Music Room" and the "The Spell Room." The decor in this 1892 Queen Anne bed-and-breakfast is very traditional, with lots of floral patterns and hunt club-style pieces and artwork. It's considered by many to be the most romantic lodging in town, and you won't soon forget the experience of sitting on the veranda enjoying the sights, sounds, and breezes. Three of the guest rooms—the Canton, Granite, and Roberts—can be had for not much over $200.

WATERFRONT AND FRENCH QUARTER
$150-300

About as close to the Cooper River as a hotel gets, the **Harbourview Inn** (2 Vendue Range, 843/853-8439, www.harbourviewcharleston. com, $259) comprises a "historic wing" and a larger, newer, but still tastefully done main building. For the best of those eponymous harbor views, try to get a room on the third floor or you might have some obstructions. It's the little touches that keep guests happy here, with wine, cheese, coffee, tea, and cookies galore and an emphasis on smiling, personalized service. The guest rooms are quite spacious, with big baths and 14-foot ceilings. You can take your complimentary breakfast—good but not great—in your room or eat it on the nice rooftop terrace.

Over $300

The guest rooms and the thoroughly hospitable service are the focus at the nearby 🌙 **The Vendue** (19 Vendue Range, 800/845-7900, www.thevendue.com, $300-450), just off a $5 million renovation and expansion. All guest rooms are sumptuously appointed in that boutique style, with lots of warm, rich fabrics, unique pieces, and high-end bath amenities.

That said, the public spaces are cool as well, the renovation being particularly focused on featuring quality art and essentially creating one huge exhibition space. The inn gets a lot of traffic in the evenings because of the popular and hopping Rooftop Bar, which has amazing views.

Another great place in this part of town is the **French Quarter Inn** (166 Church St., 843/722-1900, www.fqicharleston.com, $359). The decor in the 50 surprisingly spacious guest rooms is suitably high-period French, with low-style noncanopied beds and crisp fresh linens. Many guest rooms feature fireplaces, whirlpool baths, and private balconies. One of Charleston's hottest restaurants, Tristan, is on the ground floor. You're treated to champagne on your arrival, and goodies are available all day, with wine and cheese served every night at 5pm.

NORTH OF BROAD
$150-300

It calls itself a boutique hotel, perhaps because each room is totally different and sumptuously appointed. But the charming 🌙 **Andrew Pinckney Inn** (199 Church St., 843/937-8800, www.andrewpinckneyinn.com, $200-290) is very nearly in a class by itself in Charleston not only for its great rates but for its casual West Indies-style decor, charming courtyard, gorgeous three-story atrium, and rooftop terrace on which you can enjoy your complimentary (and delicious) breakfast. For the money and the amenities, it's possibly the single best lodging package in town.

If you plan on some serious shopping, you might want to stay right on the city's main shopping thoroughfare at the **Kings Courtyard Inn** (198 King St., 866/720-2949, www.kingscourtyardinn.com, $240-270). This 1853 Greek Revival building houses a lot more guest rooms—more than 40—than meets the eye, and it can get a little crowded at times. Still, its charming courtyard and awesome location on King Street are big bonuses, as is the convenient but cramped parking lot right next door (about

$12 per day, a bargain for this part of town), with free in-and-out privileges.

Although it is a newer building by Charleston standards, the **Mills House Hotel** (115 Meeting St., 843/577-2400, www.mills-house.com, $285-380) boasts an important pedigree and still tries hard to maintain the old tradition of impeccable Southern service at this historic location. An extensive round of renovations completed in 2007 has been well received. Dating to 1853, the first incarnation was a grand edifice that hosted luminaries such as Robert E. Lee. Through the years, fire and restoration wrought their changes, and the modern version basically dates from an extensive renovation in the 1970s. Because of its healthy banquet and event schedule—much of it centering on the very good restaurant and lounge inside—the Mills House isn't the place to go for peace and quiet. Rather, this Holiday Inn-affiliated property is where you go to feel the bustle of downtown Charleston and to be conveniently close to its main sightseeing and shopping attractions. Some of the upper floors of this seven-story building offer spectacular views.

Over $300

Considered Charleston's premier hotel, **(Charleston Place** (205 Meeting St., 843/722-4900, www.charlestonplace.com, $419-590) maintains a surprisingly high level of service and decor considering its massive 440-room size. Now owned by the London-based Orient-Express Hotels, Charleston Place is routinely rated as one of the best hotels in North America by *Condé Nast Traveler* and other publications. The guest rooms aren't especially large, but they are well appointed, featuring Italian marble baths, high-speed Internet, and voice messaging—and, of course, there's a pool available. A series of suite offerings—Junior, Junior Executive, Parlor, and the 800-square-foot Senior—feature enlarged living areas and multiple TVs and phones. A Manager's Suite on the Private Club level up top comprises 1,200 square feet of total luxury that will set you back at least $1,600 per night. It's the additional

offerings that make Charleston Place closer to a lifestyle decision than a lodging decision. The on-site spa (843/937-8522) offers all kinds of massages, including couples and "mommy to be" sessions. Diners and tipplers have three fine options to choose from: the famous **Charleston Grill** (843/577-4522, dinner daily from 6pm) for fine dining; the breakfast, lunch, and brunch hot spot **Palmetto Cafe** (843/722-4900, breakfast daily 6:30am-11am, lunch daily 11:30am-3pm); and the **Thoroughbred Club** (daily 11am-midnight) for cocktails and afternoon tea.

On the north side of Broad Street, the magnificent **(John Rutledge House Inn** (116 Broad St., 843/723-7999, www.johnrutledgehouseinn.com, $300-442) is very close to the old South of Broad neighborhood not only in geography but in feel. Known as "America's most historic inn," the Rutledge House boasts a fine old pedigree indeed: Built for Constitution signer John Rutledge in 1763, it's one of only 15 homes belonging to the original signers to survive. George Washington breakfasted here with Mrs. Rutledge in 1791. The interior is stunning: Italian marble fireplaces, original plaster moldings, and masterful ironwork abound in the public spaces. The inn's 19 guest rooms are divided among the original mansion and two carriage houses. All have antique furnishings and canopy beds, and some suites have fireplaces and whirlpool baths. A friendly and knowledgeable concierge will give you all kinds of tips and make reservations for you.

Affiliated with the Kings Courtyard—and right next door, in fact—is the smaller, cozier **Fulton Lane Inn** (202 King St., 866/720-2940, www.fultonlaneinn.com, $300), with its lobby entrance on tiny Fulton Lane between the two inns. Small, simple guest rooms—some with fireplaces—have comfortable beds and spacious baths. This is the kind of place for active people who plan to spend most of their days out and about but want a cozy place to come back to at night. You mark down your continental breakfast order at night, leave it on your doorknob, and it shows up at the *exact* time you requested

© JIM MOREKIS
John Rutledge House Inn

the next morning. Then when you're ready to shop and walk, just go down the stairs and take the exit right out onto busy King Street. Also nice is the $12-per-day parking with free in-and-out privileges.

UPPER KING AREA
Under $150
Stretching the bounds of the "Upper King" definition, we come to the **Ashley Inn** (201 Ashley Ave., 843/723-1848, www.charleston-sc-inns.com, $100-125) well northwest of Marion Square, almost in the Citadel area. Although it's too far to walk from here to almost any historic attraction in Charleston, the Ashley Inn does provide free bikes to its guests as well as free off-street parking, a particularly nice touch. It also deserves a special mention not only because of the romantic, well-appointed nature of its six guest rooms, suite, and carriage house but for its outstanding breakfasts. You get to pick a main dish, such as Carolina sausage pie, stuffed waffles, or cheese blintzes.

$150-300
In a renovated 1924 building overlooking beautiful Marion Square, the **Francis Marion Hotel** (387 King St., 843/722-0600, www.francismarioncharleston.com, $200-300) offers quality accommodations in the hippest, most bustling area of the peninsula—but be aware that it's quite a walk down to the Battery from here. The guest rooms are plush and big, though the baths can be cramped. The hotel's parking garage costs a reasonable $12 per day, with valet parking available until about 8pm. A Starbucks in the lobby pleases many a guest on their way out or in. Most rooms hover around $300, but some are a real steal.

HAMPTON PARK AREA
Under $150
Charleston's least-expensive lodging is also its most unique, the **Not So Hostel** (156 Spring St., 843/722-8383, www.notsohostel.com, $21 dorm, $60 private). The already-reasonable prices also include a make-your-own bagel breakfast, off-street parking, bikes, high-speed Internet access in the common room, and even an airport, train, and bus shuttle. The inn actually comprises three 1840s Charleston single houses, all with the obligatory piazzas to catch the breeze. (However, unlike some hostels, there's air-conditioning in all the rooms.) Because the free bike usage makes up for its off-the-beaten-path location, a stay at the Not So Hostel is a fantastic way to enjoy the Holy City on a budget, while having the opportunity to meet cool people from all over the world who are also staying here. One caveat: While they offer private rooms in addition to dorm-style accommodations, keep in mind this is still a hostel, despite the Charleston-style hospitality and perks. In other words, if there's a problem at 3am, you may not be able to get anyone to help you in a hurry.

WEST ASHLEY
$150-300
Looking like Frank Lloyd Wright parachuted into a 300-year-old plantation and got to work, **The Inn at Middleton Place** (4290 Ashley

CHARLESTON

River Rd., 843/556-0500, www.theinnatmiddle-tonplace.com, $215-285) is one of Charleston's most unique lodgings—and not only because it's on the grounds of the historic and beautiful Middleton Place Plantation. The four connected buildings, comprising over 50 guest rooms, are modern yet deliberately blend in with the forested, neutral-colored surroundings. The spacious guest rooms have that same woody minimalism, with excellent fireplaces, spacious Euro-style baths, and huge floor-to-ceiling windows overlooking the grounds and the river. Guests also have full access to the rest of the gorgeous Middleton grounds. The only downside is that you're a lengthy drive from the peninsula and all its attractions, restaurants, and nightlife. While those who need constant stimulation will be disappointed in the deep quietude here, nature-lovers and those in search of peace and quiet will find this almost paradise. And don't worry about food—the excellent Middleton Place Restaurant is open for lunch and dinner.

ISLE OF PALMS
$150-300
One of the more accessible and enjoyable resort-type stays in the Charleston area is on the Isle of Palms at **Wild Dunes Resort** (5757 Palm Blvd., 888/778-1876, www.wilddunes. com, $254-320). This is the place to go for relaxing, beach-oriented vacation fun, either in a traditional hotel room, a house, or a villa. Bustling Mount Pleasant is only a couple of minutes away, and Charleston proper not much farther.

FOLLY BEACH
$150-300
The upbeat but still cozy renovation of the **Holiday Inn Folly Beach Oceanfront** (1 Center St., 843/588-6464, $250-270) has locals raving. If you're going to stay on Folly Beach, this hotel—with its combination of attentive staff and great oceanfront views—is the place to be.

Food

If you count the premier food cities in the United States on one hand, Charleston has to be one of the fingers. Its long history of good taste and livability combines with an affluent and sophisticated population to attract some of the brightest chefs and restaurateurs in the country. Kitchens here eschew fickle trends, instead emphasizing quality, professionalism, and most of all, freshness of ingredients. In a sort of Southern Zen, the typical Charleston chef seems to take pride in making a melt-in-your-mouth masterpiece out of the culinary commonplace—in not fixing what ain't broke, as they say down here. (I've heard Charleston's cuisine described as "competent classics," which also isn't far off the mark.) Unlike Savannah, its more drink-oriented neighbor to the south, even Charleston's bars have great food. So don't assume you have to make reservations at a formal restaurant to fully enjoy the cuisine here. An entire volume could easily be written about

Charleston restaurants, but here's a baseline from which to start your epicurean odyssey.

SOUTH OF BROAD
Classic Southern
The only bona fide restaurant in the quiet old South of Broad area is also one of Charleston's best and oldest: **Ⓒ Carolina's** (10 Exchange St., 843/724-3800, Sun.-Thurs. 5pm-10pm, Fri.-Sat. 5pm-11pm, $18-30). There's a new chef in town, Jeremiah Bacon, a Charleston native who spent the last seven years honing his craft in New York City. His Lowcountry take on European classics includes grilled salmon with potato gnocchi, tagliatelle with Lowcountry prosciutto, and pan-roasted diver scallops, with as many fresh ingredients as possible from the nearby Kensington Plantation. A tried-and-true favorite that predates Bacon's tenure, however, is Perdita's *fruit de mer*—a recipe that goes back to the restaurant's 1950s

predecessor, Perdita's, which is commonly regarded as Charleston's first fine-dining restaurant. If you can get the whole table to agree, try the $49-pp Perdita's four-course tasting menu (wine flights extra). A recent renovation of this Revolutionary War-era building—once the legendary Sailor's Tavern—hasn't negatively affected the romantic ambience of the three themed areas: Perdita's Room (the oldest dining area), the Sidewalk Room, and the Bar Room. Free valet parking is a nice plus.

French

If you find yourself in lodging near the Broad Street area—or if you just love crepes—you will want to acquaint yourself with the **Queen Street Grocery** (133 Queen St., 843/723-4121, www.queenstreetgrocerycafe.com, Mon.-Sat. 8am-8:30pm, kitchen Mon.-Sat. 10am-5pm, Sun. 11am-3pm, $7-10). The kind of place frequented almost exclusively by locals, this corner store is where you can load up on light groceries, beer, wine, and cigarettes—as well as some of the tastiest made-to-order crepes this side of France.

WATERFRONT
New Southern

Few restaurants in Charleston inspire such impassioned vocal advocates as **⟨ McCrady's** (2 Unity Alley, 843/577-0025, www.mccradysrestaurant.com, Sun.-Thurs. 5:30pm-10pm, Fri.-Sat. 5:30pm-11pm, $28-40). Housed in one of Charleston's oldest tavern buildings (circa 1788), McCrady's is also known as Charleston's best-kept secret, since despite its high quality it has managed to avoid the siege of tourists common at many local fine-dining spots. But their loss can be your gain as you enjoy the prodigious talents of chef Sean Brock, whose *sous vide,* or vacuum cooking, is spoken of in hushed tones by his clientele. McCrady's is not the place to gorge on usual Lowcountry fare. Portions here are small and dynamic, based on a rotating seasonal menu. Many diners find the seven-course Chef's Tasting ($90), in which you get whatever floats chef Brock's boat that night, a near-religious experience. For an extra

$75, master sommelier Clint Sloan provides paired wine selections. Or you can just go with a three-course ($45) or four-course ($60) dinner where you pick your courses. You may read complaints in online reviews about the prices at McCrady's. Let me set the record straight: (a) They're not really that high at all when you break them down per item, and (b) the perfect blending of flavors you will enjoy with any dish on the menu is worth every penny and then some. Quite simply, McCrady's is a world-class restaurant that, were it in just about any other city in the world, would actually set you back quite a bit more. Just go.

While not as flashy as some other local chefs, Craig Deihl has, over the past decade, brought **Cypress** (167 East Bay St., 843/727-0111, www.magnolias-blossom-cypress.com, Sun.-Thurs. 5:30pm-10pm, Fri.-Sat. 5:30pm-11pm, $20-40) to the forefront of the local foodie movement. From aged beef from a local farm to sustainably caught wreckfish, the menu reflects a deep commitment to locavore sensibilities. Any meat or seafood entrée is a can't-lose proposition here. They also offer table-side service of chateaubriand or rack of lamb for two.

FRENCH QUARTER
New Southern

With an art deco-style vibe that's a refreshing change from the usual Charleston restaurant decor, **Tristan** (55 Market St., 843/534-2155, www.tristandining.com, Mon.-Thurs. 11:30am-10pm, Fri.-Sat. 11:30am-11pm, Sun. 11am-10pm, $18-32) inside the French Quarter Inn draws raves for its globally influenced cuisine. At last count, the copious wine list boasted over 400 labels. The real scene here is for the à la carte Sunday brunch, with crab cake benedicts, corned beef hash, frittatas, live jazz, and Bloody Marys galore. Save room for the ridiculously good fried chocolate doughnut dessert.

NORTH OF BROAD
Breakfast and Brunch

You can sit inside the crowded, noisy diner, or outside literally in the parking lot of a strip mall; either way you're doing the right thing

CHARLESTON

at (**Dixie Supply Cafe and Bakery** (62 State St., 843/722-5650, www.dixiecafecharleston. com, daily 8am-2:30pm, $8-10), certainly one of the humblest but no doubt tastiest places in Charleston and perhaps the entire South. Dixie Supply has gained a certain amount of cachet lately with the filming of a *Diners, Drive-ins and Dives* episode, but don't let the trendiness keep you away. What you get at this simple old-school eatery is some of the best comfort food you'll ever taste, with a focus on breakfast and brunch items. A case could be made that their signature Tomato Pie—melted cheese over a perfect tomato slice with a delicious crust on the bottom, served with a hunk of sweet potato cornbread—is the single best dish in Charleston. However, you could make the same case for their Shrimp 'n' Grits or, for that matter their "stuffed" french toast. You place your order at the front counter, the cooks a few feet away. When your plate is ready, they call you, and you just come up and get your food and take it back to your table. It can get crowded, but just brave the

© JIM MOREKIS

the veranda at Husk restaurant

lines and go. And while they do take plastic, they appreciate cash.

Classic Southern

Walk through the gaslit courtyard of the Planter's Inn at Market and Meeting Streets into the stately yet surprisingly intimate dining room of the (**Peninsula Grill** (112 N. Market St., 843/723-0700, www.peninsulagrill.com, daily from 5:30pm, $28-35) and begin an epicurean journey you'll not soon forget. Known far and wide for impeccable service as well as the mastery of chef Robert Carter, Peninsula Grill is perhaps Charleston's quintessential purveyor of high-style Lowcountry cuisine and the odds-on favorite as best restaurant in town. From the lobster skillet cake and crab cake appetizer to the bourbon-grilled jumbo shrimp to the benne-crusted rack of lamb to sides like wild mushroom grits and hoppin' John, the menu reads like a "greatest hits" of regional cooking. Choose from 20 wines by the glass or from over 300 bottles. Four stars from the Mobil Travel Club, four diamonds from AAA, and countless other accolades have come this restaurant's way. Needless to say, reservations are strongly recommended.

Named for a now-deceased beloved dog who once greeted guests, **Poogan's Porch** (72 Queen St., 843/577-2337, www.poogansporch. com, lunch Mon.-Fri. 11:30am-2:30pm, dinner daily 5pm-9:30pm, brunch Sat.-Sun. 9am-3pm, $12-20) is the prototype of a classic Charleston restaurant: a lovingly restored old home, professional but unpretentious service, great fried green tomatoes, and rich, calorie-laden Lowcountry classics. I can't decide which entrée I like best, the crab cakes or the shrimp and grits. Some swear that even the biscuits at Poogan's—flaky, fresh-baked, and moist—are better than some entrées around town, although that's a stretch. Brunch is the big thing here, a bustling affair with big portions, Bloody Marys, mimosas, and soft sunlight bathing what were, after all, living and dining rooms where people once lived.

Executive chef Sean Brock of McCrady's fame already has a healthy reputation as one of Charleston's—indeed, the country's—leading purveyors of the farm-to-table fine dining aesthetic, and one with a particularly Southern panache. He cements that reputation with the opening of ◖ Husk (76 Queen St., 843/577-2500, www.huskrestaurant.com, lunch Mon.-Sat. 11:30am-2pm, dinner Sun.-Thurs. 5:30pm-10pm, Fri.-Sat. 5:30pm-11pm, brunch Sun. 10am-2:30pm, $25), voted "Best New Restaurant in the U.S." by *Bon Appétit* magazine soon after its 2011 opening. While the hype is a little overdone, Husk is still firmly in the top tier of local restaurants. Upon entering the cleanly restored interior of the multi-story historic home this once was, you'll see a blackboard with the origins of the day's ingredients—the farms and their location, never more than a day's drive away. Understandably, the spare, focused menu—"If it doesn't come from the South, it's not coming through the door," Brock says of his ingredients—is constantly changing with the seasons. On a recent lunch visit my party enjoyed two types of catfish (a fried catfish BLT on Texas toast and a lightly cornmeal-dusted broiled catfish with local vegetables), Husk's signature cheeseburger, and—wait for it—lamb barbecue. We finished with a sweet potato pie dessert to die for. The emphasis on the freshest of ingredients means a subtle, unpretentious palette of flavors. Unlike many of today's trendy chefs, Brock doesn't overseason the food, so you taste it the way nature intended. Husk is literally right next door to Poogan's Porch, and as with Poogan's, reservations are recommended.

For many visitors to Charleston, there comes a point when they just get tired of stuffing themselves with seafood. If you find yourself in that situation, the perfect antidote is ◖ High Cotton (199 East Bay St., 843/724-3815, www.mavericksouthernkitchens.com, Mon.-Thurs. 5:30pm-10pm, Fri. 5:30pm-11pm, Sat. 11:30am-2:30pm and 5:30pm-11pm, Sun. 10am-2pm and 5:30pm-10pm, $20-44), a meat-lovers paradise offering some of the best steaks in town as well as a creative menu of assorted lamb and pork dishes. Chef Anthony Gray places heavy emphasis on using fresh local ingredients, both veggies and game, and the rotating menu always reflects that. None of this comes particularly cheap, but splurges rarely do. In the woody (and popular) bar area there's usually a solo live pianist or sax player after 6pm.

The long lines at Wentworth and Meeting Streets across from the fire station are waiting to follow Rachael Ray's lead and get into **Jestine's Kitchen** (251 Meeting St., 843/722-7224, Tues.-Thurs. 11am-9:30pm, Fri.-Sat. 11am-10pm, $8-15) to enjoy a simple, Southern take on such meat-and-three comfort food classics as meatloaf, pecan-fried fish, and fried green tomatoes. Most of the recipes are handed down from the restaurant's namesake, Jestine Matthews, the African American woman who raised owner Dana Berlin.

French

On the north side of Broad Street itself you'll find **Gaulart & Maliclet** (98 Broad St., 843/577-9797, www.fastandfrench.org, Mon. 8am-4pm, Tues.-Thurs. 8am-10pm, Fri.-Sat. 8am-10:30pm, $12-15), subtitled "Fast and French." This is a gourmet bistro with a strong takeout component. Prices are especially reasonable for this area of town, with great lunch specials under $10 and Thursday-night "fondue for two" coming in at just over $20.

Mediterranean

One of the most romantic restaurants in Charleston—which is saying a lot—**Il Cortile del Re** (193A King St., 843/853-1888, Mon.-Sat. 5pm-10:30pm, $18-30) is amid the antiques stores on Lower King. Thankfully the Italian owners don't overdo the old-country sentimentality, either in atmosphere or in menu. Sure, the tablecloths are white and the interior is warm, dark, and decorated with opera prints. But the piped-in music is long on cool jazz and short on over-the-top tenors, and the skinny wine bar in the front room is a favorite destination all its own. Portions here manage to be simultaneously large and light, as in the overtopped mussel plate in a delightfully thin and spicy tomato sauce, or the big spinach salad with goat cheese croutons sprinkled with a subtle vinaigrette. The entrées emphasize the Tuscan countryside, focusing both on slow-roasted meats and sublime takes on traditional pasta dishes. My favorite is the perfect roasted lamb in a dark juniper and rosemary sauce, served on a bed of what are likely to be the best mashed potatoes in the world. Save room for the gelato dessert, served swimming in a pool of dark espresso.

Literally right around the corner from Il Cortile del Re is the other in Charleston's one-two Italian punch, **Fulton Five** (5 Fulton St., 843/853-5555, Mon.-Sat. from 5:30pm, $15-32). The cuisine of northern Italy comes alive in this bustling, dimly lit room, from the *bresaola* salad of spinach and thin dried beef to the caper-encrusted tuna on a bed of sweet pea risotto. It's not cheap, and the portions aren't necessarily the largest, but with these tasty, non-tomato-based dishes and this romantic, gusto-filled atmosphere, you'll be satiated with life itself.

New Southern

Don't be put off by the initials of **Slightly North of Broad** (192 East Bay St., 843/723-3424, www.mavericksouthernkitchens.com, lunch Mon.-Fri. 11:30am-3pm, dinner daily 5:30pm-11pm, $15-35). Its acronym, "SNOB," is an ironic play on the often pejorative reference to the insular South of Broad neighborhood. This hot spot, routinely voted best restaurant in town in such contests, is anything but snobby. Hopping with happy foodies for lunch and dinner, the fun is enhanced by the long, open kitchen with its own counter area. The dynamic but comforting menu here is practically a bible of the new wave of Lowcountry cuisine, with dishes like beef tenderloin, jumbo lump crab cakes, grilled barbecue tuna—and, of course, the sinful Wednesday-night dinner special: deviled crab-stuffed flounder. An interesting twist at SNOB is the selection of "medium plates," meaning dishes a little more generous than an appetizer but with the same adventurous spirit.

Just across the street from Hyman's Seafood

is that establishment's diametrical opposite, the intimate bistro and stylish bar ◖ **FIG** (232 Meeting St., 843/805-5900, www.eatatfig.com, Mon.-Thurs. 6pm-11pm, Fri.-Sat. 6pm-midnight, $20-25)—but the two do share one key thing: a passion for fresh, simple ingredients. While Hyman's packs in the tourists, FIG—short for "Food Is Good"—attracts young professional scenesters as well as the diehard foodies. Chef Mike Lata won James Beard's Best Chef of the Southeast award in 2009. FIG is one of Charleston's great champions of the Sustainable Seafood Initiative, and the kitchen staff strives to work as closely as possible with local farmers and anglers in determining its seasonal menu.

Inside the plush Charleston Place Hotel you'll find ◖ **Charleston Grill** (224 King St., 843/577-4522, www.charlestongrill.com, dinner daily from 6pm, $27-50), one of the city's favorite (and priciest) fine-dining spots for locals and visitors alike. Veteran executive chef Bob Waggoner was recently replaced by his longtime sous chef Michelle Weaver, but the menu still specializes in French-influenced Lowcountry cuisine like a niçoise vegetable tart. There are a lot of great fusion dishes as well, such as the tuna and *hamachi* sashimi topped with pomegranate molasses and lemongrass oil. Reservations are a must.

A new hit with local foodies, **Cru Café** (18 Pinckney St., 843/534-2434, lunch Tues.-Sat. 11am-3pm, dinner Tues.-Thurs. 5pm-10pm, Fri.-Sat. 5pm-11pm, $20-24) boasts an adventurous menu within a traditional-looking Charleston single house, with a choice of interior or exterior seating. Sample entrées include Poblano and Mozzarella Fried Chicken and Seared Maple Leaf Duck Breast.

Seafood

Hyman's Seafood (215 Meeting St., 843/723-6000, www.hymanseafood.com, Mon.-Thurs. 11am-9pm, Fri.-Sun. 11am-11pm, $14-25) is thought by many locals to border on a tourist trap. That said, this is a genuine tradition—rest assured that some member of the same family that began Hyman's in 1890 will be on the premises any time it's open for business. To keep things manageable, Hyman's offers the same menu and prices for both lunch and dinner. After asking for some complimentary fresh boiled peanuts in lieu of bread, start with the Carolina Delight, a delicious appetizer (also available as an entrée) involving a lightly fried cake of grits topped with your choice of delectable seafood, or maybe a half dozen oysters from the Half Shell oyster bar. In any case, definitely try the she-crab soup, some of the best you'll find anywhere. As for entrées, the ubiquitous Lowcountry crispy scored flounder is always a good bet. Alas, this establishment, popular with locals and visitors as well as the occasional movie star, doesn't take reservations, so budget your time accordingly. Lunch crowds are generally lighter, although that's a relative term.

UPPER KING AREA
Asian
There's usually a long wait to get a table at the great Thai place **Basil** (460 King St., 843/724-3490, www.basilthairestaurant.com, lunch Mon.-Thurs. 11:30am-2:30pm, dinner Mon.-Thurs. 5pm-10:30pm, Fri.-Sat. 5pm-11pm, Sun. 5pm-10pm, $15-23) on Upper King, since they don't take reservations. But Basil also has one of the hippest, most happening bar scenes in the area, so you won't necessarily mind. (Tip: Basil calls your cell phone when your table is ready, so a lot of people go across the street to Chai's to have a drink while they wait.) Basil is a long, loud room with big open windows for people-watching. But most of the action takes place inside, as revelers down cosmos and diners enjoy fresh, succulent takes on Thai classics like cashew chicken and pad thai, all cooked by Asian chefs. The signature dish, as you might imagine, is the basil duck.

Seafood
Many say the cashew-encrusted seared rare tuna on a bed of crabmeat and buckwheat noodles at **COAST Bar and Grill** (39D John St., 843/722-8838, www.coastbarandgrill. com, daily from 5:30pm, $18-30) is the single best dish in Charleston. I wouldn't go that far,

but it's certainly up there. COAST makes the most of its loud, hip former warehouse setting. While the fun-loving decor in the dining room will suck you in, what keeps you happy is what goes on in the kitchen—specifically on its one-of-a-kind hickory-and-oak grill, which cooks up some of the freshest seafood in town. The raw bar is also satisfying, with a particularly nice take on and selection of seviche. Getting here is a little tricky: find Rue de Jean on John Street and then duck about 100 feet down the alley beside it.

COLLEGE OF CHARLESTON AREA
New Southern
Focusing on purely seasonal offerings that never stay on the menu longer than three months, **Circa 1886** (149 Wentworth St., 843/853-7828, www.circa1886.com, Mon.-Sat. 5:30pm-9:30pm, $23-32) combines the best Old World tradition of Charleston with the vibrancy of its more adventurous kitchens. The restaurant—surprisingly little-known despite its four-star Mobil rating—is located in the former carriage house of the grand Wentworth Mansion B&B just west of the main College of Charleston campus. It is now the playground of chef Marc Collins, who delivers entrées like a robust beef au poivre and a shrimp-and-crab stuffed flounder, to name two recent offerings. The service here is impeccable and friendly, the ambience classy and warm, and the wine list impressive. Be sure to check the daily prix fixe offerings; those can be some great deals.

HAMPTON PARK AREA
Classic Southern
Moe's Crosstown Tavern (714 Rutledge Ave., 843/722-3287, Mon.-Sat. 11am-midnight, bar until 2am, $10-15) is not only one of the classic Southern dives but has one of the best kitchens on this side of town, known for hand-cut fries, great wings, and, most of all, excellent burgers. On Tuesday, the burgers are half price at happy hour—one of Charleston's best deals.

With a motto like "Grits are good for you," you know what you're in store for at **Hominy**

CHARLESTON

LOWCOUNTRY LOCAVORES

It might seem strange that a Deep South city founded in 1670 would be on the country's cutting edge of the sustainable food movement, but that's the case with Charleston. Perhaps more seamlessly than any other community in the United States, Charleston has managed to merge its own indigenous and abiding culinary tradition with the "new" idea that you should grow your food as naturally as possible and purchase it as close to home as you can. From bacon to snapper to sweet potatoes, the typical Charleston dish of today is much like it was before the days of processed factory food and back to its soulful Southern roots.

Spurred in part by an influx of trained chefs after the establishment of the Spoleto Festival in the 1970s, the locavore movement in Charleston came about less from market demand than from the efforts of a diehard cadre of epicureans committed to sustainability and the principles of community-supported agriculture (CSA). Spearheaded by visionaries like the James Beard Award-winning Mike Lata of the bistro FIG and McCrady's Sean Brock, a multitude of sustainable food initiatives have sprung up in Charleston and the Lowcountry, such as the South Carolina Aquarium's Sustainable Seafood Initiative (http://scaquarium.org), partnering with local restaurants to assure a sustainable wild-caught harvest; Certified South Carolina (www.certifiedsc.com), guaranteeing that the food you eat was grown in the Palmetto State; a local chapter of the Slow Food Movement (http://slowfoodcharleston.org); and Cypress Artisan Meat Share (www.magnolias-blossom-cypress.com), in which a group of highly regarded restaurants makes their fine locally sourced meats available to the public.

The list of Holy City restaurants relying almost exclusively on local and sustainable sources is too long to replicate in this space, but here are a few notable examples:

- Husk (76 Queen St., 843/577-2500, www.huskrestaurant.com)
- McCrady's (2 Unity Alley, 843/577-0025, www.mccradysrestaurant.com)
- Cypress (167 East Bay St., 843/727-0111, www.magnolias-blossom-cypress.com)
- Charleston Grill (224 King St., 843/577-4522, www.charlestongrill.com)
- High Cotton (199 East Bay St., 843/724-3815, www.mavericksouthernkitchens.com)
- FIG (232 Meeting St., 843/805-5900, www.eatatfig.com)
- Al Di La (25 Magnolia Rd., 843/571-2321)
- Queen Street Grocery (133 Queen St., 843/723-4121)
- Carolina's (10 Exchange St., 843/724-3800)
- Middleton Place Restaurant (4300 Ashley River Rd., 843/556-6020, www.middletonplace.org)
- Circa 1886 (149 Wentworth St., 843/853-7828, www.circa1886.com)
- COAST Bar and Grill (39D John St., 843/722-8838, www.coastbarandgrill.com)
- Cru Café (18 Pinckney St., 843/534-2434, www.crucafe.com)
- Hominy Grill (207 Rutledge Ave., 912/937-0930, www.hominygrill.com)
- Il Cortile del Re (193A King St., 843/853-1888, www.ilcortiledelre.com)
- Peninsula Grill (112 N. Market St., 843/723-0700, www.peninsulagrill.com)
- Tristan (55 Market St., 843/534-2155, www.tristandining.com)

Charleston is a center of the locally-sourced food movement.

Grill (207 Rutledge Ave., 912/937-0930, breakfast Mon.-Fri. 7:30am-11:30am, lunch and dinner daily 11:30am-8:30pm, brunch Sat.-Sun. 9am-3pm, $10-20), set in a renovated barbershop at Rutledge Avenue and Cannon Street near the Medical University of South Carolina. Primarily revered for his Sunday brunch, chef Robert Stehling has fun—almost mischievously so—breathing new life into American and Southern classics. Because this is largely a locals' place, you can impress your friends back home by saying you had the rare pleasure of the Hominy's sautéed shad roe with bacon and mushrooms—when the shad are running, that is.

Italian

A new rave of Charleston foodies is the Tuscan-inspired fare of chef Ken Vedrinski at ◖ **Trattoria Lucca** (41 Bogard St., 843/973-3323, www.trattorialuccadining.com, Tues.-Thurs. 6pm-10pm, Fri.-Sat. 6pm-11pm, Sun. 5pm-8pm, $20-23). The menu is simple but perfectly focused, featuring handmade pasta and signature items like the pork chop or the fresh cheese plate. You'll be surprised at how much food your money gets you here. Sunday evening sees a family-style prix fixe communal dinner.

WEST ASHLEY
American

The kitchen at **Gene's Haufbrau** (17 Savannah Hwy., 843/225-4363, www.geneshaufbrau.com, daily 11:30am-1am, $6-10) complements its fairly typical bar-food menu with some good wraps. Start with the "Drunken Trio" (beer-battered cheese sticks, mushrooms, and onion rings) and follow with a portobello wrap or a good old-fashioned crawfish po'boy. One of the best meals for the money in town is Gene's rotating $7 blue plate special, offered Monday-Friday 11:30am-4:30pm. The late-night kitchen hours, until 1am, are a big plus.

Barbecue

For connoisseurs, **Bessinger's** (1602 Savannah Hwy., 843/556-1354, www.bessingersbbq.com) is worth the trip over to West Ashley for its Carolina-style mustard-based wizardry. There are two scenes at Bessinger's, the sit-down Southern buffet (Thurs. 5pm-8pm, Fri.-Sat. 5pm-9pm, Sun. noon-8pm, $11.50 adults, $6 children)—Friday is fried catfish night—and the Sandwich Shop (Mon.-Sat. 10:30am-9:30pm, $6.35 for a "Big Joe" basket) for quick takeout. In old-school tradition, Bessinger's is a dry joint that doesn't sell alcohol. (To clarify: Bessinger's in Charleston was founded by the brother of Maurice Bessinger, who started the Columbia-based "Maurice's Gourmet BBQ" chain, famous for its ultra-right-wing neo-Confederate sensibilities. You may safely patronize Bessinger's in Charleston without worrying that you are supporting anything you may have objections to.)

However, another West Ashley joint, ◖**Fiery Ron's Home Team BBQ** (1205 Ashley River Rd., 843/225-7427, www.hometeambbq.com, Mon.-Sat. 11am-9pm, Sun. 11:30am-9pm, $7-20) is even better than Bessinger's. I cannot say enough about both the pulled pork and the ribs, which rank with the best I've had anywhere in the country. Even the sides are amazing here, including perfect collards and tasty mac-and-cheese. Chef Madison Ruckel provides an array of table-side sauces, including hot sauce, indigenous South Carolina mustard sauce, and his own "Alabama white," a light and delicious mayonnaise-based sauce. As if that weren't enough, the owners' close ties to the regional jam-band community means there's great live blues and indie rock most nights after 10pm (Thursday is bluegrass night) to spice up the bar action, which goes until 2am.

Classic Southern

Tucked away on the grounds of the Middleton Place Plantation is the romantic **Middleton Place Restaurant** (843/556-6020, www.middletonplace.org, lunch daily 11am-3pm, dinner Tues.-Thurs. 6pm-8pm, Fri.-Sat. 6pm-9pm, Sun. 6pm-8pm, $15-25). Theirs is a respectful take on traditional plantation fare like hoppin' John, gumbo, she-crab soup, and collards. The special annual Thanksgiving buffet is a real treat. Reservations are required for dinner. A nice plus is being able to wander the gorgeous landscaped gardens before dusk if you arrive at 5:30pm or later with a dinner reservation.

Mediterranean

Anything on this northern Italian-themed menu is good, but the risotto—a legacy of original chef John Marshall—is the specialty dish at **Al Di La** (25 Magnolia Rd., 843/571-2321, www.aldilarestaurant.com, Tues.-Sat. 6pm-10pm, $13-20), a very popular West Ashley fine dining spot. Reservations are recommended.

New Southern

One of the more unassuming advocates of farm-to-table dining, **C Glass Onion** (1219 Savannah Hwy., 843/225-1717, www.ilovetheglassonion.com, Mon.-Thurs. 11am-9pm, Fri. 11am-10pm, Sat. 4pm-10pm, brunch Sat. 10am-3pm, $15) is also in an unassuming location, on U.S. 17 (Savannah Hwy.) on the western approaches to town. That said, their food is right in the thick of the sustainable food movement, and is also incredibly tasty to boot (not to mention more parking than downtown). The interior says "diner," and indeed the emphasis here is on Southern soul and comfort food classics. A recent trip saw a duck leg with pork belly as a special entrée, and a chicken and andouille gumbo that was zesty without being overspiced, thick without being pasty. There are occasional "all-you-can-eat quail" nights, and every Tuesday is Fried Chicken Dinner night, offering what many insist is the best fried chicken in Charleston. The Glass Onion also boasts a good variety of specialty craft brews to wash it all down with. Another plus: In this town full of Sunday brunches, Glass Onion's specialty is a Saturday brunch!

MOUNT PLEASANT

Most restaurant action in Mount Pleasant centers on the picturesque shrimping village of Shem Creek, which is dotted on both banks with bars and restaurants, most dealing in fresh local seafood. As with Murrells Inlet up the coast, some spots on Shem Creek border on tourist traps. Don't be afraid to go where the lines aren't.

Seafood

A well-regarded spot on Shem Creek is **Water's Edge** (1407 Shrimp Boat Lane, 843/884-4074, daily 11am-11pm, $20-30), which consistently takes home a *Wine Spectator* Award of Excellence for its great selection of vintages. Native Charlestonian Jimmy Purcell concentrates on fresh seafood with a slightly more upscale flair than many Shem Creek places.

Right down the road from Water's Edge is another popular spot, especially for a younger crowd: **Vickery's Shem Creek Bar and Grill** (1313 Shrimp Boat Lane, 843/884-4440, daily 11:30am-1am, $11-16). With a similar menu to its partner location on the peninsula, this Vickery's has the pleasant added bonus of a beautiful view overlooking the Creek. You'll get more of the Vickery's Cuban flair here, with a great black bean soup and an awesome Cuban sandwich.

If you find yourself thirsty and hungry in Mount Pleasant after dark, you might want to stop in the **Reddrum Gastropub** (803 Coleman Blvd., 843/849-0313, www.reddrumrestaurant.com, Mon.-Tues. 5:30pm-9pm, Wed.-Sat. 5:30pm-10pm, $15), so named because the food here is just as important as the drink. While you're likely to need reservations for the dining room, where you can enjoy Lowcountry-Tex-Mex fusion-style cuisine with a typically Mount Pleasant-like emphasis on seafood, the bar scene is very hopping and fun, with live music every Wednesday-Thursday night.

Vegetarian

For a vegetarian-friendly change of pace from seafood, go to the **Mustard Seed** (1026 Chuck Dawley Blvd., 843/849-0050, Mon.-Sat. 11am-2:30pm and 5pm-9:30pm, $14-18). The pad thai is probably the best thing on New York-trained chef Sal Parco's creative and dynamic menu, but you might also get a kick out of the sweet potato ravioli.

For a real change of pace, try **The Sprout Cafe** (629 Johnnie Dodds Blvd., 843/849-8554, www.thehealthysprout.com, Mon.-Fri. 6am-8pm, Sat. 9am-3pm, Sun. 11am-3pm, $3-10) on U.S. 17. Dealing totally in raw foods, the obvious emphasis here is on health and freshness of ingredients. You might be surprised at the inventiveness of their breakfast-through-dinner seasonal menu—memorably described by the staff as "grab and go"—which might include a tasty crepe topped with a pear-and-nut puree and maple syrup, or a raw squash and zucchini "pasta" dish topped with walnut "meatballs."

SULLIVAN'S ISLAND

A new location of **(Fiery Ron's Home Team BBQ** (2209 Middle St., 843/883-3131, www.hometeambbq.com, kitchen Mon.-Sat. 11am-11pm, Sun. 11:30am-11pm, $8-14) provides the same incredible melt-in-your-mouth pork and ribs made famous by the original West Ashley location. For a friendly bite and an adult beverage or two, go straight to **Poe's Tavern** (2210 Middle St., 843/883-0083, daily 11am-2am, kitchen until 10pm), a nod to Edgar Allan Poe's stint at nearby Fort Moultrie.

FOLLY BEACH
Breakfast and Brunch

The closest thing to a taste of old Folly is the **Lost Dog Café** (106 W. Huron St., 843/588-9669, daily 6:30am-3pm, $5-7), so named for its bulletin board stacked with alerts about lost pets, pets for adoption, and newborns for sale or giveaway. They open early, the better to offer a tasty, healthy breakfast to the surfing crowd. It's a great place to pick up a quick, inexpensive, and tasty meal while you're near the beach.

Mexican

Taco Boy (15 Center St., 843/588-9761, Sun.-Thurs. 11am-10pm, Fri.-Sat. 11am-11pm, $5-15) is a fun place to get a fish taco, have a margarita, and take a walk on the nearby beach afterward. Though no one is under any illusions that this is an authentic Mexican restaurant, the fresh guacamole is particularly rave-worthy, and there's a good selection of tequilas and beers *hecho en México,* with the bar staying open until 2am on weekends.

Seafood

Fans of the legendary **(Bowens Island Restaurant** (1870 Bowens Island Rd., 843/795-2757, Tues.-Sat. 5pm-10pm, $5-15, cash only), on James Island just before you get to Folly, went into mourning when it burned to the ground in 2006. But you can't keep a good oysterman down, and owner Robert Barber rebuilt. Regulars insist that this institution, which began in the 1940s as a fishing camp, remains as old-school as ever. A universe removed from the Lexus-and-khaki scene downtown, Bowens Island isn't the place for the uptight. This is the place to go when you want shovels of oysters literally thrown onto your table, freshly steamed and delicious and all-you-can-eat. The fried shrimp, flounder, and hush puppies are incredible too. The understated setting—a nondescript building with little to no signage—only adds to the authenticity of the whole experience. To get there from the peninsula, take Calhoun Street west onto the James Island Connector (Hwy. 30). Take exit 3 onto Highway 171 south and look for Bowens Island Road on the right. The restaurant is on the left in a short while, after passing by several ritzy McMansions that in no way resemble the restaurant you're about to experience.

NORTH CHARLESTON

If you have a hankering for pizza in North Charleston, don't miss **EVO Pizzeria** (1075 E. Montague Ave., 843/225-1796, www.evo-pizza.com, lunch Tues.-Fri. 11am-2:30pm, dinner Tues.-Fri. 5pm-10pm, Sat. 6pm-10pm, $10-15) in the Olde North Charleston area at Park Circle. They specialize in a small but rich menu of unusual gourmet pizza toppings, like pistachio pesto.

COFFEE, TEA, AND SWEETS

By common consensus, the best java joint in Charleston is **Kudu Coffee** (4 Vanderhorst Ave., 843/853-7186, Mon.-Sat. 6:30am-7pm, Sun. 9am-6pm) in the Upper King area. A kudu is an African antelope, and the Africa theme extends to the beans, which all have an African pedigree. Poetry readings and occasional live music add to the mix. A lot of green-friendly, left-of-center community activism goes on here as well; a recent discussion group was titled "How to Survive the Bible Belt but Still Find God." The adjacent African art store is owned by the coffeehouse.

If you find yourself needing a quick pick-me-up while shopping on King Street, avoid the lines at the two Starbucks on the avenue and instead turn east on Market Street and duck inside **City Lights Coffeehouse** (141 Market St., 843/853-7067, Mon.-Thurs. 7am-9pm, Fri.-Sat. 7am-10pm, Sun. 8am-6pm). The sweet goodies are delectable in this cozy little Euro-style place, and the Counter Culture organic coffee is to die for. If you're really lucky, they'll have some of their Ethiopian Sidamo brewed.

A unique Charleston phenomenon on Upper King by Marion Square is the aptly named **Cupcake** (433 King St., 843/853-8181, www.freshcupcakes.com, Mon.-Sat. 10am-7pm). Their eponymous specialty compels Charlestonians to form lines onto the sidewalk, waiting to enjoy one or more of the 30 flavors of little cakes. Routinely voted as having the best desserts in the city, the cakes alone at **Kaminsky's** (78 N. Market St., 843/853-8270, daily noon-2am) are worth the trip to the City Market area. The fresh fruit torte, the red velvet, and the "Mountain of Chocolate" are the three best sellers. There's also a Mount Pleasant location (1028 Johnnie Dodds Blvd., 843/971-7437).

MARKETS AND GROCERIES

A fun and favorite local fixture April to mid-December, the **Charleston Farmers Market** (843/724-7309, www.charlestoncity.info, Sat. 8am-2pm) rings beautiful Marion Square with stalls of local produce, street eats, local arts and crafts, and kids' activities. Running April-October, East Cooper has its own version in the **Mount Pleasant Farmers Market** (843/884-8517, http://townofmountpleasant.com, Tues. 3pm-dusk) at the Moultrie Middle School on Coleman Boulevard.

For organic groceries or a quick healthy bite while you're in Mount Pleasant, check out **Whole Foods** (923 Houston Northcutt Blvd., 843/971-7240, daily 8am-9pm). The biggest and best supermarket near the downtown area is the regional chain **Harris Teeter** (290 East Bay St., 843/722-6821, daily 24 hours). There are other Harris Teeter stores in Mount Pleasant (920 Houston Northcutt Blvd. and 620 Long Point Rd., 843/881-4448) and Folly Beach (675 Folly Rd., 843/406-8977). For a charming grocery shopping experience, try **King Street Grocery** (435 King St., 843/958-8004, daily 8am-midnight) on Upper King. If you're down closer to the Battery, go to the delightful **Queen Street Grocery** (133 Queen St., 843/723-4121, Mon.-Sat. 8am-8:30pm, kitchen Mon.-Sat. 10am-5pm, Sun. 11am-3pm). Need groceries at 4am on Folly Beach? Go to **Bert's Market** (202 E. Ashley Ave., 843/588-9449, daily 24 hours).

Information and Services

VISITORS CENTERS

I highly recommend a stop at the **Charleston Visitor Reception and Transportation Center** (375 Meeting St., 800/774-0006, www.charlestoncvb.com, Mon.-Fri. 8:30am-5pm). Housed in a modern building with an inviting, open design, the center has several high-tech interactive exhibits, including an amazing model of the city under glass. Wall after wall of well-stocked, well-organized brochures will keep you informed on everything a visitor would ever want to know about or see in the city. A particularly welcoming touch is the inclusion of the work of local artists all around the center. I recommend using the attached parking garage not only for your stop at the Center but also anytime you want to see the many sights this part of town has to offer, such as the Charleston Museum, the Manigault and Aiken-Rhett Houses, and the Children's

Museum. The big selling point at the center is the friendliness of the smiling and courteous staff, who welcome you in true Charleston fashion and are there to book rooms and tours and find tickets for shows and attractions. If for no other reason, you should go to the center to take advantage of the great deal offered by the **Charleston Heritage Passport** (www.heritagefederation.org), which gives you 40 percent off admission to all of Charleston's key historic homes, the Charleston Museum, and the two awesome plantation sites on the Ashley River: Drayton Hall and Middleton Place. You can get the Heritage Passport *only* at the Charleston Visitor Reception and Transportation Center on Meeting Street.

Other area visitors centers include the **Mt. Pleasant-Isle of Palms Visitors Center** (99 Harry M. Hallman Jr. Blvd., 800/774-0006, daily 9am-5pm) and the new **North Charleston Visitors Center** (4975B Centre Pointe Dr., 843/853-8000, Mon.-Sat. 10am-5pm).

HOSPITALS
If there's a silver lining in getting sick or injured in Charleston, it's that there are plenty of high-quality medical facilities available. The premier institution is the **Medical University of South Carolina** (171 Ashley Ave., 843/792-2300, www.muschealth.com) in the northwest part of the peninsula. Two notable facilities are near each other downtown: **Roper Hospital** (316 Calhoun St., 843/402-2273, www.roperhospital.com) and **Charleston Memorial Hospital** (326 Calhoun St., 843/792-2300). In Mount Pleasant there's **East Cooper Regional Medical Center** (1200 Johnnie Dodds Blvd., www.eastcoopermedctr.com). In West Ashley there's **Bon Secours St. Francis Hospital** (2095 Henry Tecklenburg Ave., 843/402-2273, www.ropersaintfrancis.com).

POLICE
For nonemergencies in Charleston, West Ashley, and James Island, contact the **Charleston Police Department** (843/577-7434, www.charlestoncity.info). You can also contact the police department in Mount Pleasant (843/884-4176). North Charleston is a separate municipality with its own police department (843/308-4718, www.northcharleston.org). Of course, for emergencies always call **911**.

GAY AND LESBIAN RESOURCES
Contrary to many media portrayals of the region, Charleston is quite open to gays and lesbians, who play a major role in arts, culture, and business. As with any other place in the South, however, it's generally expected that people—straights as well—will keep personal matters and politics to themselves in public settings. A key local advocacy group is the **Alliance for Full Acceptance** (29 Leinbach Dr., Suite D-3, 843/883-0343, www.affa-sc.org). The **Lowcountry Gay and Lesbian Alliance** (843/720-8088) holds a potluck the last Sunday of each month. For the most up-to-date happenings, try the Gay Charleston blog (http://gaycharleston.ccpblogs.com), part of the *Charleston City Paper.*

CHARLESTON

Getting There and Around

BY AIR

Way up in North Charleston is **Charleston International Airport** (CHS, 5500 International Blvd., 843/767-1100, www.chs-airport.com), served by AirTran (www.airtran.com), American Airlines (www.aa.com), Delta (www.delta.com), JetBlue (www.jetblue.com), Southwest (www.southwest.com), United (www.ual.com), and US Airways (www.us-airways.com). As in most cities, taxi service from the airport is regulated. This translates to about $30 for two people from the airport to Charleston Place downtown.

BY CAR

There are two main routes into Charleston: I-26 from the west-northwest (which dead-ends downtown) and U.S. 17 from the west (called Savannah Highway when it gets close to Charleston proper), which continues on over the Ravenel Bridge into Mount Pleasant and beyond. There's a fairly new perimeter highway, I-526 (Mark Clark Expressway), which loops around the city from West Ashley to North Charleston to Daniel Island and into Mount Pleasant. It's accessible both from I-26 and U.S. 17. Keep in mind that I-95, while certainly a gateway to the region, is actually a good ways out of Charleston, about 30 miles west of the city.

Car Rentals

Charleston International Airport has rental kiosks for **Avis** (843/767-7031), **Budget** (843/767-7051), **Dollar** (843/767-1130), **Enterprise** (843/767-1109), **Hertz** (843/767-4550), **National** (843/767-3078), and **Thrifty** (843/647-4389). There are a couple of rental locations downtown: **Budget** (390 Meeting St., 843/577-5195) and **Enterprise** (398 Meeting St., 843/723-6215). **Hertz** has a location in West Ashley (3025 Ashley Town Center Dr., 843/573-2147), as does **Enterprise** (2004 Savannah Hwy., 843/556-7889).

BY BUS

Public transportation by **Charleston Area Regional Transit Authority** (CARTA, 843/724-7420, www.ridecarta.com) is a convenient and inexpensive way to enjoy Charleston without the more structured nature of an organized tour. There's a wide variety of routes, but most visitors will limit their acquaintance to the tidy, trolley-like **DASH** (Downtown Area Shuttle) buses run by CARTA primarily for visitors. Each ride is $1.75 pp ($0.85 seniors). The best deal is the $6 one-day pass, which you get at the Charleston Visitors Center (375 Meeting St.). Keep in mind that DASH only stops at designated places. DASH has three routes: the 210, which runs a northerly circuit from the Aquarium to the College of Charleston; the 211, running up and down the parallel Meeting and King Streets from Marion Square down to the Battery; and the 212 Market/Waterfront shuttle from the Aquarium area down to Waterfront Park.

BY TAXI

The South is generally not big on taxis, and Charleston is no exception. The best bet is simply to call rather than try to flag one down. Charleston's most fun service is **Charleston Black Cabs** (843/216-2627, www.charleston-blackcabcompany.com), using Americanized versions of the classic British taxi. A one-way ride anywhere on the peninsula below the bridges is about $10 pp, and rates go up from there. They're very popular, so call as far ahead as you can or try to get one at their stand at Charleston Place. Two other good services are **Safety Cab** (843/722-4066) and **Yellow Cab** (843/577-6565).

You can also try a human-powered taxi service from **Charleston Rickshaw** (843/723-5685). A cheerful (and energetic) young cyclist will pull you and a friend to most points on the lower peninsula for about $10-15. Call 'em or find one by City Market. They work late on Friday and Saturday nights too.

PARKING

As you'll quickly see, parking is at a premium in downtown Charleston. An exception seems to be the large number of free spaces all along the Battery, but unless you're an exceptionally strong walker, that's too far south to use as a reliable base from which to explore the whole peninsula. Most metered parking downtown is on and around Calhoun Street, Meeting Street, King Street, Market Street, and East Bay Street. That may not sound like a lot, but it constitutes the bulk of the area that most visitors visit. Most meters have three-hour limits, but you'll come across some as short as 30 minutes. Technically you're not supposed to "feed the meter" in Charleston, as city personnel put little chalk marks on your tires to make sure people aren't overstaying their welcome. Metered parking is free daily 6pm-6am and all day Sunday. On Saturday, expect to pay.

The city has several conveniently located and comparatively inexpensive parking garages. I strongly suggest that you make use of them. They're located at: The Aquarium, Camden and Exchange Streets, Charleston Place, Concord and Cumberland Streets, East Bay and Prioleau Streets, Marion Square, Gaillard Auditorium, Liberty and St. Philip Streets, Majestic Square, the Charleston Visitor Reception and Transportation Center, and Wentworth Street. There are several private parking garages as well, primarily clustered in the City Market area. They're convenient, but many have parking spaces that are often too small for some vehicles. The city's website (www.charlestoncity.info) has a good interactive map of parking.

Greater Charleston

Although one could easily spend a lifetime enjoying the history and attractions of Charleston itself, there are many unique experiences to be had in the less-developed areas surrounding the city. Generally there are two types of vibes: isolated close-knit communities with little overt development (although that's changing), or private resort-style communities amid stunning natural beauty.

SUMMERVILLE AND VICINITY

The Dorchester County town of Summerville, population 30,000, is gaining a reputation as a friendly, scenic, and upscale suburb north of Charleston. Summerville is about 30 minutes from downtown Charleston; take I-26 north.

Sights

Due to its longstanding popularity as a getaway for wealthy planters and then as a spa town, Summerville boasts a whopping 700 buildings on the National Register of Historic Places. For a walking tour of the historic district, download the map at www.visitsummerville.com or pick up a hard copy at the **Summerville Visitors Center** (402 N. Main St., 843/873-8535). Alas, the grand old Pine Forest Inn, perhaps the greatest of all Summerville landmarks, Winter White House for presidents William Taft and Theodore Roosevelt, was torn down after World War II, a victim of the Florida vacation craze. Much visitor activity in Summerville centers on **Azalea Park** (S. Main St. and W. 5th St. S., daily dusk-dawn, free), rather obviously named for its most scenic inhabitants. Several fun yearly events take place here, most notably the **Flowertown Festival** (www.flowertownfestival.com, free) each April, a three-day affair heralding the coming of spring and the blooming of the flowers. One of the biggest festivals in South Carolina, 250,000 people usually attend. Another event, **Sculpture in the South** (www.sculptureinthesouth.com),

CHARLESTON

© AVALON TRAVEL

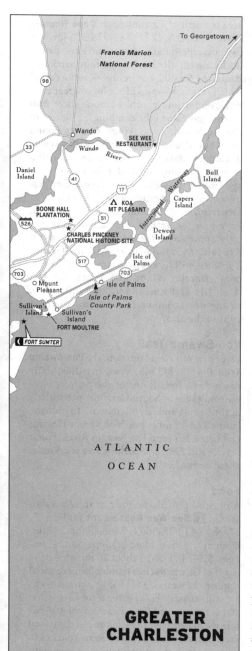

in May, takes advantage of the extensive public sculpture in the park.

To learn more about Summerville's interesting history, go just off Main Street to the **Summerville-Dorchester Museum** (100 E. Doty Ave., 843/875-9666, www.summervilledorchestermuseum.org, Mon.-Sat. 9am-2pm, donation). Located in the former town police station, the museum has a wealth of good exhibits and boasts a new curator, Chris Ohm, with wide local experience, including at Middleton Place and with the CSS *Hunley* project in North Charleston.

Just south of Summerville on the way back to Charleston is the interesting **Colonial Dorchester State Historic Site** (300 State Park Rd., 843/873-1740, www.southcarolinaparks.com, daily 9am-6pm, $2 adults, free under age 16), chronicling a virtually unknown segment of Carolina history. It turns out a contingent of Massachusetts Puritans ("Congregationalists" in the parlance of the time) were given special dispensation in 1697 to form a settlement of their own specifically to enhance commercial activity on the Ashley River, which they did in fine form. Today, little is left of old Dorchester except the tabby walls of the 1757 fort overlooking the Ashley. Don't miss the unspectacular but still historically vital remains of the wooden wharf on the walking trail along the river, once the epicenter of a thriving port.

Accommodations and Food

The renowned **Woodlands Resort & Inn** (125 Parsons Rd., 843/875-2600, $325-650) is one of a handful of inns in United States with a five-star rating both for lodging and dining. Its 18 guest rooms within the 1906 great house are decorated in a mix of old-fashioned plantation high-style and contemporary designer aesthetics, with modern, luxurious baths. There's also a freestanding guest cottage ($850) that seeks to replicate a hunting-lodge type of vibe. As you'd expect, there's a full day spa on the premises; a one-hour massage, the most basic offering, will run you $110. Within Woodlands is its award-winning world-class restaurant, simply called **The Dining Room** (Mon.-Sat. 11am-2pm

CHARLESTON

CHARLESTON

and 6pm-9pm, brunch Sun. 11:30am-2pm, $25-40). It will come as no surprise to find out that the 900-entry wine list and somme-lier are collectively awesome, as are the des-serts. Jackets are required, and reservations are strongly advised.

In Summerville proper, try **Mustard Seed** (101 N. Main St., 843/821-7101, lunch Mon.-Sat. 11am-2:30pm, dinner Mon.-Thurs. 5pm-9pm, Fri.-Sat. 5pm-10pm, $8-10), a health-food restaurant that doesn't skimp on the taste. For a more down-home-style pancakes-and-sandwich place that's popular with the locals at all hours of the day, try **Flowertown Restaurant** (120 E. 5th N. St., 843/871-3202, daily 24 hours, $8).

Another popular local landmark is **Guerin's Pharmacy** (140 S. Main St., 843/873-2531, Mon.-Fri. 9am-6pm, Sat. 9am-5pm), which claims to be the state's oldest pharmacy. Complete with an old-fashioned soda fountain, they offer malted milk shakes and lemonade.

AWENDAW AND POINTS NORTH

This area just north of Charleston along U.S. 17—named for the Sewee Indian village orig-inally located here, and known to the world chiefly as the place where Hurricane Hugo made landfall in 1989—is seeing some new growth, but still hews to its primarily rural, nature-loving roots.

Sewee Visitor and Environmental Education Center

Twenty miles north of Charleston you'll find the **Sewee Visitor and Environmental Education Center** (5821 U.S. 17, 843/928-3368, www.fws.gov/seweecenter, Tues.-Sat. 9am-5pm, free). Besides being a gateway of sorts for the almost entirely aquatic Cape Romain National Wildlife Refuge, Sewee is primarily known for its popula-tion of rare red wolves, who were part of a unique release program on nearby Bull Island begun in the late 1970s.

Cape Romain National Wildlife Refuge

One of the best natural experiences in the

area is north of Charleston at **Cape Romain NWR** (5801 U.S. 17 N., 843/928-3264, www.fws.gov/caperomain, year-round daily dawn-dusk). Essentially comprising four barrier is-lands, the 66,000-acre refuge—almost all of which is marsh—provides a lot of great pad-dling opportunities, chief among them **Bull Island** (no overnight camping). Slightly to the south within the refuge, **Capers Island Heritage Preserve** (843/953-9300, www.dnr.sc.gov, daily dawn-dusk, free) is still a popular camping locale despite heavy dam-age from 1989's Hurricane Hugo. Get per-mits in advance by calling the South Carolina Department of Natural Resources. You can kayak to the refuge yourself or take the only approved ferry service from **Coastal Expeditions** (514B Mill St., Mount Pleasant, 843/881-4582, www.coastalexpeditions.com). **Barrier Island Eco Tours** (50 41st Ave., Isle of Palms, 843/886-5000, www.nature-tours.com) on Isle of Palms also runs trips to the area.

I'on Swamp Trail

Once part of a rice plantation, the **I'on Swamp Trail** (843/928-3368, www.fs.fed.us, daily dawn-dusk, free) is one of the premier bird-watching sites in South Carolina, particularly during spring and fall migrations. To get here, head about 15 miles north of Mount Pleasant and take a left onto I'on Swamp Road (Forest Service Rd. 228). The parking area is 2.5 miles ahead on the left.

Food

A must-stop roadside diner in the Awendaw area is **¢ See Wee Restaurant** (4808 U.S. 17 N., 843/928-3609, Mon.-Thurs. 11am-8:30pm, Fri.-Sat. 11am-9:30pm, Sun. 11am-8pm, $10-23), located about 20 minutes' drive north of Charleston in a humble former general store on the west side of U.S. 17 (the restrooms are still outside). Folks come from Charleston and as far away as Myrtle Beach to enjoy signa-ture menu items like the grouper and the unreal she-crab soup, considered by some epicures to be the best in the world; you can't miss with any of their seafood entrées. Occasionally the crowds can get thick, but rest assured it's worth any wait.

POINTS WEST AND SOUTHWEST
Caw Caw Interpretive Center

Just west of Charleston on U.S. 17 you'll find the unique **Caw Caw Interpretive Center** (5200 Savannah Hwy., Ravenel, 843/889-8898, www.ccprc.com, Wed.-Sun. 9am-5pm, $1), a treasure trove for history buffs and naturalists wanting to learn more about the old rice culture of the South. With a particular emphasis on the expertise of those who worked on the rice plantations using techniques they brought with them from Africa, the county-run facility comprises 650 acres of land on an actual former rice plantation built on a cypress swamp, eight miles of interpretive trails, an educational center with exhibits, and a wildlife sanctuary with seven different habitats. Most Wednesday and Saturday mornings, guided bird walks are held at 8:30am ($5 pp). You can put in your own canoe for $10 October-April on Saturday-Sunday. Bikes and dogs aren't allowed on the grounds.

Johns Island

The outlying community of Johns Island is where you'll find **Angel Oak Park** (3688 Angel Oak Rd., Mon.-Sat. 9am-5pm, Sun. 1pm-5pm), home of a massive live oak, 65 feet in circumference, that's well over 1,000 years old and commonly considered the oldest tree east of the Mississippi River. The tree and the park are owned by the city of Charleston, and the grounds are often used for weddings and special events. Get here from Charleston by taking U.S. 17 over the Ashley River, then Highway 171 to Maybank Highway. Take a left onto Bohicket Road near the Piggly Wiggly, and then look for signs on the right.

Here is also where you'll find **Legare Farms** (2620 Hanscombe Point Rd., 843/559-0763, www.legarefarms.com), open to the public for various activities, including its annual pumpkin patch in October, its "sweet corn" festival

in June, and bird walks (Sat. 8:30am, $6 adults, $3 children) in fall.

If you find your tummy growling on Johns Island, don't miss ◖ **Fat Hen** (3140 Maybank Hwy., 843/559-9090, Tues.-Sat. 11:30am-3pm and 5:30pm-10pm, Sun. 10am-3pm, $15-20), a self-styled "country French bistro" begun by a couple of old Charleston restaurant hands. The fried oysters are a particular specialty. There's also a bar menu for late-night hours (10pm-2am).

If barbecue is more your thing, head straight to ◖ **JB's Smokeshack** (3406 Maybank Hwy., 843/557-0426, www.jbssmokeshack.com, Wed.-Sat. 11am-8:30pm, $8), one of the best 'cue joints in the Lowcountry. They offer a buffet for $8.88 pp ($5 under age 11), or you can opt for a barbecue plate, including hash, rice, and two sides. In a nice twist, the plates include a three-meat option: pork, chicken, ribs, or brisket.

Wadmalaw Island

Like Johns Island, Wadmalaw Island is one of those lazy, scenic areas gradually becoming subsumed within Charleston's growth. That said, there's plenty of meandering, laid-back beauty to enjoy, and a couple of interesting sights.

Currently owned by the R. C. Bigelow Tea corporation, the **Charleston Tea Plantation** (6617 Maybank Hwy., 843/559-0383, www.charlestonteaplantation.com, Mon.-Sat. 10am-4pm, Sun. noon-4pm, free) is no cute living history exhibit: It's a big, working tea plantation—the only one in the United States—with acre after acre of *Camellia sinensis* being worked by modern farm machinery. Visitors get to see a sample of how the tea is made, "from the field to the cup." Factory tours are free, and a trolley tour of the "Back 40" is $10. To get here from Charleston, take the Ashley River Bridge, stay left to Folly Road (Hwy. 171), turn right onto Maybank Highway for 18 miles, and look for the sign on the left.

The muscadine grape is the only varietal

CHARLESTON

that dependably grows in South Carolina. That said, the state has several good wineries, among them Wadmalaw's own **Irvin House Vineyard** (6775 Bears Bluff Rd., 843/559-6867, www.charlestonwine.com, Thurs.-Sat. 10am-5pm), the Charleston area's only vineyard. Jim Irvin, a Kentucky boy, and his wife, Anne, a Johns Island native, make several varieties of muscadine wine here, with tastings and a gift shop. They also give free tours of the 50-acre grounds every Saturday at 2pm. There's a Grape-stomping Festival at the end of each August ($5 per car). Also on the Irvin Vineyard grounds you'll find **Firefly Distillery** (6775 Bears Bluff Rd., 843/559-6867, www.fireflyvodka.com), home of their signature Firefly Sweet Tea Vodka. They offer tastings (Feb.-Dec. Wed.-Sat. 11am-5pm, $6 per tasting). To get here from Charleston, go west on Maybank Highway about 10 miles to Bears Bluff Road, veering right. The vineyard entrance is on the left after about eight miles.

Kiawah Island

Only one facility for the public exists on beautiful Kiawah Island, the **Kiawah Island Beachwalker Park** (843/768-2395, www.

ccprc.com, Mar.-Apr. and Sept. daily 10am-6pm, May-Labor Day daily 9am-7pm, Oct. Mon.-Fri. 9am-5pm, Sat.-Sun. 10am-6pm, Nov.-Feb. daily 10am-5pm, $7 per vehicle, free for pedestrians and cyclists). Get here from downtown Charleston by taking Lockwood Drive onto the Highway 30 Connector bridge over the Ashley River. Turn right onto Folly Road, then a left onto Maybank Highway. After about 20 minutes, take a left onto Bohicket Road, which leads to Kiawah in 14 miles. Turn left from Bohicket Road onto the Kiawah Island Parkway. Just before the security gate, turn right on Beachwalker Drive and follow the signs to the park.

The island's other main attraction is the **Kiawah Island Golf Resort** (12 Kiawah Beach Dr., 800/654-2924, www.kiawah-golf.com), which is a key location for PGA tournaments. Several smaller private, family-friendly resorts exist on Kiawah, with fully furnished homes and villas and every amenity you could ask for and then some, giving you full access to the island's 10 miles of beautiful beach. Go to www.explorekiawah.com for a full range of options or call 800/877-0837.

HILTON HEAD AND THE LOWCOUNTRY

The Lowcountry embodies many of the South's most noteworthy qualities: an emphasis on manners, a constant look back into the past, and a slow and leisurely pace (embodied in the joking but largely accurate nickname "Slowcountry").

History hangs in the humid air where first the Spanish came to interrupt the indigenous peoples' ancient reverie, then the French, followed by the English. Although time, erosion, and development have erased most traces of these occupants, you can almost hear their ghosts in the rustle of the branches in a sudden sea breeze, or in the piercing call of a heron over the marsh.

Between Beaufort and Charleston is the huge ACE (Ashepoo, Combahee, Edisto) Basin, a beautiful and important estuary and a national model for good conservation practices. In all, the defining characteristic of the Lowcountry is its liquid nature—not only literally, in the creeks and waterways that dominate every vista and the seafood cooked in all manner of ways, but figuratively too, in the slow but deep quality of life here. While the archetypal South has been marketed in any number of ways to the rest of the world, here you get a sense that this is the real thing—timeless, endlessly alluring, but somehow very familiar.

South of Beaufort is the East Coast Marine Recruit Depot of Parris Island. East of Beaufort is the center of Gullah culture, St. Helena Island, and the scenic gem of Hunting Island. To the south is the scenic but entirely developed golf and tennis mecca Hilton Head Island, and Hilton Head's close neighbor but diametrical

© JIM MOREKIS

HIGHLIGHTS

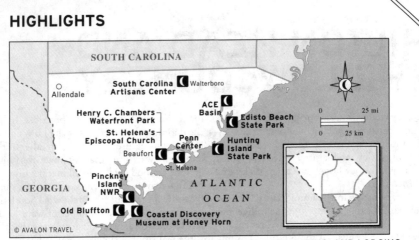

LOOK FOR **C** TO FIND RECOMMENDED SIGHTS, ACTIVITIES, DINING, AND LODGING.

C Henry C. Chambers Waterfront Park: Walk the dog or while away the time on a porch swing at this clean and inviting gathering place on the serene Beaufort River (page 362).

C St. Helena's Episcopal Church: To walk through this Beaufort sanctuary and its walled graveyard is to walk through Lowcountry history (page 363).

C Penn Center: Not only the center of modern Gullah culture and education, this is a key site in the history of the civil rights movement as well (page 371).

C Hunting Island State Park: One of the most peaceful natural getaways on the East Coast is only minutes away from the more civilized temptations of Beaufort (page 374).

C ACE Basin: Spend a lifetime learning your way around this massive, marshy estuary—or just a few hours soaking in its lush beauty (page 375).

C Edisto Beach State Park: Relax at this quiet, friendly, and relatively undeveloped Sea Island, a mecca for shell collectors (page 378).

C Pinckney Island National Wildlife Refuge: This well-maintained sanctuary is a major birding location and a great getaway from nearby Hilton Head (page 380).

C Coastal Discovery Museum at Honey Horn: This beautifully repurposed plantation house and spacious grounds are a great way to learn about Hilton Head history, both human and natural (page 382).

C Old Bluffton: Gossipy and gorgeous by turns, this charming village on the May River centers on a thriving artists colony (page 394).

C South Carolina Artisans Center: Visual artists and fine craftspeople from all over the state contribute work to this high-quality collective in Walterboro (page 398).

HILTON HEAD

HILTON HEAD AND THE LOWCOUNTRY

© AVALON TRAVEL

HILTON HEAD

opposite in every other way, Daufuskie Island, another important Gullah center. Nestled between is the close-knit and gossipy little village of Bluffton on the gossamer May River.

PLANNING YOUR TIME

A commonsense game plan is to use centrally located Beaufort as a home base. Take at least half a day of leisure to walk all over Beaufort. Another full day should go to St. Helena's Penn Center and on to Hunting Island. If you're in the mood for a road trip, dedicate a full day to tour the surrounding area to the north and northeast, with a jaunt to the ACE Basin National Wildlife Refuge. While the New York accents fly fast and furious on Hilton Head Island, that's no reason for you to rush. Plan on at least half a day just to enjoy the fine broad beaches alone. I recommend another half day to tour the island itself, maybe including a stop in Sea Pines for a late lunch or dinner.

Beaufort

Sandwiched halfway between the prouder, louder cities of Charleston and Savannah, Beaufort is in many ways a more authentic slice of life from the past than either of those two. Long a staple of movie crews seeking to portray some archetypal aspect of the old South (*The Prince of Tides, The Great Santini, Forrest Gump*) or just to film beautiful scenery for its own sake (*Jungle Book, Last Dance*), Beaufort—pronounced "BYOO-fert," by the way, not "BO-fort"—features many well-preserved examples of Southern architecture, most all of them in idyllic family-friendly neighborhoods.

While you'll run into plenty of charming and gracious locals during your time here, you might be surprised at the number of transplanted Northerners. That's due not only to the high volume of retirees who've moved to the area but the active presence of three major U.S. Navy facilities: the Marine Corps Air Station Beaufort, the Marine Corps Recruit Depot on nearby Parris Island, and the Beaufort Naval Hospital. Many is the time a former sailor or Marine has decided to put down roots in the area after being stationed here, the most famous example being author Pat Conroy's father, a.k.a. "The Great Santini."

HISTORY

This was the site of the second landing by the Spanish on the North American continent, the expedition of Captain Pedro de Salazar in 1514

(Ponce de León's more famous landing at St. Augustine was but a year earlier). A Spanish slaver made a brief stop in 1521, long enough to name the area Santa Elena. Port Royal Sound didn't get its modern name until the first serious attempt at a permanent settlement, Jean Ribault's exploration in 1562. Though ultimately disastrous, Ribault's base of Charlesfort was the first French settlement in America.

After the French faded, the Spaniards came, but attacks by Native Americans and Francis Drake's attack on St. Augustine forced the Spanish to abandon the area in 1587. Within the next generation, British indigo planters had established a firm presence, chief among them John "Tuscarora Jack" Barnwell and Thomas Nairn. These men would go on to found the town of Beaufort, named for the Duke of Beaufort, and it was chartered in 1711 as part of the original Carolina colony. In 1776, Beaufort planter Thomas Heyward Jr. signed the Declaration of Independence. After independence, Lowcountry planters turned to cotton as the main cash crop, since England had been their prime customer for indigo. The gambit paid off, and Beaufort soon became one of the wealthiest towns in the new nation. Only seven months after secessionists fired on Fort Sumter in nearby Charleston, a Union fleet sailed into Port Royal and occupied the Lowcountry for the duration of the war.

© AVALON TRAVEL

Gradually developing their own distinct dialect and culture, much of it linked to their West African roots, isolated Lowcountry African Americans became known as the Gullah. Evolving from an effort by abolitionist missionaries early in the Civil War, in 1864 the Penn School was formed on St. Helena Island specifically to teach the children of the Gullah communities. Now known as the Penn Center, the facility has been a beacon for the study of this aspect of African American culture ever since.

ORIENTATION

Don't be discouraged by the big-box sprawl that assaults you on the approaches to Beaufort on Boundary Street, lined with the usual discount megastores, fast-food outlets, and budget motels. After you make the big 90-degree bend where Boundary turns into Carteret Street—known locally as the "Bellamy Curve"—it's like entering a whole new world of slow-paced, Spanish moss-lined avenues, friendly people, gentle breezes, and inviting storefronts. While you can make your way to downtown by taking Carteret Street all the way to Bay Street—don't continue over the big bridge unless you want to go straight to Lady's Island and St. Helena Island—I suggest availing yourself of one of the "Downtown Access" signs before you get that far. Because Carteret Street is the only way to that bridge, it can get backed up at rush hour. By taking a quick right and then a left all the way to Bay Street, you can come into town from the other, quieter end, with your first glimpse of downtown proper being its timelessly beguiling views of the Beaufort River.

Unlike Charleston or Savannah, any visitor in reasonably good shape can walk the entire length and breadth of Beaufort's 300-acre downtown with little trouble. In fact, that's by far the best way to experience it.

HILTON HEAD

PAT CONROY'S LOWCOUNTRY

I was always your best subject, son.
Your career took a nose dive after
The Great Santini came out.

Colonel Donald Conroy, to his son Pat

Although born in Georgia, no other person is as closely associated with the South Carolina Lowcountry as author Pat Conroy. After moving around as a child in a military family, he began high school in Beaufort. His painful teen years there formed the basis of his first novel, a brutal portrait of his domineering Marine pilot father, Colonel Donald Conroy, a.k.a. Colonel Bull Meecham of *The Great Santini* (1976). Many scenes from the 1979 film adaptation were filmed at the famous Tidalholm, the Edgar Fripp House (1 Laurens St.) in Beaufort. (The house was also front and center in *The Big Chill*.)

Conroy's pattern of thinly veiled autobiography actually began with his first book, the self-published *The Boo*, a tribute to a teacher at The Citadel in Charleston while Conroy was still a student there. His second work, *The Water is Wide* (1972), is a chronicle of his experiences teaching in a one-room African American school on Daufuskie Island. Though ostensibly a straightforward first-person journalistic effort, Conroy changed the location to the fictional Yamacraw Island, supposedly to protect Daufuskie's fragile culture from curious outsiders. The 1974 film adaptation starring Jon Voight was titled *Conrack* after the way his students mispronounced his name. You can visit that same one-room school today on Daufuskie. Known as the Mary Field School, the building is now a local community center.

Conroy also wrote the foreword to the cookbook *Gullah Home Cooking the Daufuskie Way: Smokin' Joe Butter Beans, Ol' 'Fuskie Fried Crab Rice, Sticky-Bush Blackberry Dumpling,* *and Other Sea Island Favorites* by Daufuskie native and current Savannah resident Sallie Ann Robinson. Conroy would go on to publish in 1980 *The Lords of Discipline*, a reading of his real-life experience with the often-savage environment faced by cadets at The Citadel–though Conroy would change the name, calling it the Carolina Military Institute. Still, when it came time to make a film adaptation in 1983, The Citadel refused to allow it to be shot there, so the "Carolina Military Institute" was filmed in England instead.

For many of his fans, Conroy's *The Prince of Tides* is his ultimate homage to the Lowcountry. Surely, the 1991 film version starring Barbra Streisand and Nick Nolte–shot on location and awash in gorgeous shots of the Beaufort River marsh–did much to implant an idyllic image of the area with audiences around the world. According to local legend, Streisand originally didn't intend to make the film in Beaufort, but a behind-the-scenes lobbying effort allegedly coordinated by Conroy himself, and including a stay at the Rhett House Inn, convinced her.

The Bay Street Inn (601 Bay St.) in Beaufort was seen in the film, as was the football field at the old Beaufort High School. The beach scenes were shot on nearby Fripp Island. Interestingly, some scenes set in a Manhattan apartment were actually shot within the old Beaufort Arsenal (713 Craven St.), now a visitors center. Similarly, the Beaufort Naval Hospital doubled as New York's Bellevue.

Despite the many personal tribulations he faced in the area, Conroy has never given up on the Lowcountry and still makes his home here with his family on Fripp Island. As for the "Great Santini" himself, you can visit the final resting place of Colonel Conroy in the Beaufort National Cemetery–Section 62, Grave 182.

SIGHTS
◖ Henry C. Chambers Waterfront Park

A tastefully designed, well-maintained, and user-friendly mix of walkways, bandstands, and patios, **Henry C. Chambers Waterfront Park** (843/525-7054, www.cityofbeaufort.org, daily 24 hours) is a favorite gathering place for locals and visitors alike, beckoning one and all with its open green space and wonderful

Henry C. Chambers Waterfront Park on the Beaufort River

marsh-front views. Kids will especially enjoy the park not only because there's so much room to run around but for the charming playground at the east end near the bridge, complete with a jungle gym in the form of a Victorian home. The clean, well-appointed public restrooms are a particularly welcome feature.

John Mark Verdier House Museum

A smallish but stately federalist building on the busiest downtown corner, the **Verdier House Museum** (801 Bay St., 843/379-6335, www.historicbeaufort.org, tours on the half-hour Mon.-Sat. 10:30am-3:30pm, $5) is the only historic Beaufort home open to regular tours. Built in 1805 for the wealthy planter John Mark Verdier, its main claim to fame was acting as the Union headquarters during the long occupation of Beaufort during the Civil War and hosting Revolutionary War hero the Marquis de Lafayette, who stayed at the Verdier House on his 1825 U.S. tour.

Beaufort Arsenal and Visitors Center

The imposing yellow-gray tabby facade of the 1852 **Beaufort Arsenal** (713 Craven St.) once housed the Beaufort Museum, which sadly closed due to financial issues. The historic building currently houses the relocated offices of the **Beaufort Chamber of Commerce and Convention and Visitors Bureau** (843/986-5400, www.beaufortsc.org, daily 9am-5:30pm), and you can find plenty of visitor information and gifts inside; there are also public restrooms.

◖ St. Helena's Episcopal Church

Nestled within a low brick wall surrounding this historic church and cemetery, **St. Helena's Episcopal Church** (505 Church St., 843/522-1712, Tues.-Fri. 10am-4pm, Sat. 10am-1pm) has witnessed some of Beaufort's most compelling tales. Built in 1724, this was the parish church of Thomas Heyward, one of South Carolina's signers of the Declaration of Independence. John "Tuscarora Jack"

© JIM MOREKIS

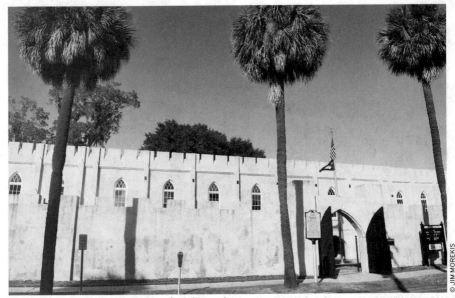

© JIM MOREKIS

the visitors center, in the old Beaufort Arsenal

Barnwell, one of Beaufort's founders, is buried on the grounds.

The balcony upstairs was intended for black parishioners; as was typical throughout the region before the Civil War, both races attended the same church services. After the entire congregation fled with the Union occupation, Federal troops decked over the second floor and used St. Helena's as a hospital.

Tabernacle Baptist Church

Built in 1845, the handsome **Tabernacle Baptist Church** (911 Craven St., 843/524-0376) had a congregation of over 3,000 before the Civil War. Slaves made up most of the congregation, and during the war freed slaves purchased the church. A congregant was the war hero Robert Smalls, who kidnapped the Confederate steamer he was forced to serve on and delivered it to Union forces. He is buried in the church cemetery and has a nice memorial dedicated to him facing the street.

Beaufort National Cemetery

Begun by order of Abraham Lincoln in 1863, **Beaufort National Cemetery** (1601 Boundary St., daily 8am-sunset) is one of the few cemeteries containing the graves of both Union and Confederate troops. National Cemetery is where 19 soldiers of the all-black Massachusetts 54th and 55th Infantries were reinterred after being found on Folly Island near Charleston. Also buried here is "The Great Santini" himself, novelist Pat Conroy's father, Donald.

A Walking Tour of Beaufort Homes

Here's a walking tour of some of Beaufort's fine historic homes in private hands. You won't be taking any tours of the interiors, but these homes are part of the legacy of the area and are locally valued as such. Be sure to respect the privacy of the inhabitants by keeping the noise level down and not trespassing on private property to take photos.

© JIM MOREKIS

Lewis Reeve Sams House

- **Thomas Fuller House:** Begin at the corner of Harrington and Bay Streets and view the 1796 Thomas Fuller House (1211 Bay St.), one of the oldest in Beaufort and even more unique in that much of the building material is tabby (hence the home's other name, the Tabby Manse).

- **Milton Maxcy House:** Walk east on Bay Street one block and take a left on Church Street; walk up to the corner of Church and Craven Streets. Otherwise known as the Secession House (113 Craven St.), this 1813 home was built on a tabby foundation dating from 1743. In 1860, when it was the residence of attorney Edmund Rhett, the first Ordinance of Secession was signed here, and the rest, as they say, is history.

- **Lewis Reeve Sams House:** Pick up the walking tour on the other side of the historic district, at the foot of the bridge in the old neighborhood simply called "The Point." The beautiful Lewis Reeve Sams House (601 Bay St.) at the corner of Bay and New Streets, with its double-decker veranda, dates from 1852 and like many Beaufort mansions served as a Union hospital during the Civil War.

- **Berners Barnwell Sams House:** Continue up New Street, where shortly ahead on the left you'll find the 1818 Berners Barnwell Sams House (310 New St.), which served as the African American hospital during the Union occupation. Harriet Tubman of Underground Railroad fame worked here for a time as a nurse.

- **Joseph Johnson House:** Continue up New Street and take a right on Craven Street. Cross East Street to find the 1850 Joseph Johnson House (411 Craven St.), with the massive live oak in the front yard. Legend has it that when the Yankees occupied Hilton Head, Mr. Johnson buried his valuables under an outhouse. After the war he returned to find his

HILTON HEAD

home for sale due to unpaid back taxes. He dug up his valuables, paid the taxes, and resumed living in the home. You might recognize the home from the film *Forces of Nature.*

• **Marshlands:** Backtrack to East Street, walk north to Federal Street, and go to the end. Built by James R. Verdier, Marshlands (501 Pinckney St.) was used as a hospital during the Civil War, as many Beaufort homes were, and is now a National Historic Landmark. It was the setting of Francis Griswold's 1931 novel *A Sea Island Lady.*

• **The Oaks:** Walk up to King Street and take a right. Soon after you pass a large open park on the left, King Street dead-ends at the Short Street. The Oaks (100 Laurens St.) at this corner was owned by the Hamilton family, who lost a son who served with General Wade Hampton's cavalry in the Civil War. After the conflict, the family couldn't afford the back taxes, and neighbors paid the debts and returned the deed to the Hamiltons.

• **Edgar Fripp House:** Continue east on Laurens Street toward the water to find this handsome Lowcountry mansion, sometimes called Tidalholm (1 Laurens St.). Built in 1856 by the wealthy planter for whom nearby Fripp Island is named, this house was a key setting in *The Big Chill* and *The Great Santini.*

• **Francis Hext House:** Go back to Short Street, walk north to Hancock Street, and take a left. A short way ahead on the right, the handsome red-roofed estate known as Riverview (207 Hancock St.) is one of the oldest structures in Beaufort; it was built in 1720.

• **Robert Smalls House:** Continue west on Hancock Street, take a short left on East Street, and then a quick right on Prince Street. The 1834 Robert Smalls House (511 Prince St.) was the birthplace of Robert Smalls, a former slave and Beaufort native who stole the Confederate ship *Planter* from

Charleston Harbor while serving as helmsman and delivered it to Union troops in Hilton Head. Smalls and a few compatriots commandeered the ship while the officers were at a party at Fort Sumter. Smalls used the bounty for the act of bravery to buy his boyhood home. After the war, Smalls was a longtime U.S. Congressman.

Organized Tours

Colorful character Jon Sharp runs the popular **Jon Sharp's Walking History Tour** (843/575-5775, www.jonswalkinghistory.com, Tues.-Sat. 11am, $20), taking a break during the summer months. The two-hour jaunt begins and ends at the Downtown Marina and takes you all through the downtown area. **The Spirit of Old Beaufort** (103 West St. Extension, 843/525-0459, www.thespiritofoldbeaufort.com, Mon.-Sat. 10:30am, 2pm, and 7pm, $13 adults, $8 children) runs a year-round series of good walking tours, roughly two hours long, with guides usually in period dress. If you don't want to walk, you can hire one of their guides to join you in your own vehicle (from $50).

As you might expect, few things could be more Lowcountry than an easygoing carriage ride through the historic neighborhoods. **Southurn Rose Buggy Tours** (843/524-2900, www.southurnrose.com, daily 10am-5pm, $18 adults, $7 children)—yes, that's how they spell it—offers 50-minute narrated carriage rides of the entire Old Point, including movie locations, embarking and disembarking near the Downtown Marina about every 40 minutes.

An important specialty bus tour in the area is **Gullah-N-Geechie Man Tours** (843/838-7516, www.gullahngeechietours.net, $20 adults, $18 children), focusing on the rich Gullah history and culture of the St. Helena Island area, including the historic Penn Center. Call for pickup information.

ENTERTAINMENT AND EVENTS
Performing Arts

Beaufort's fine arts scene is small but professional in outlook. Most performances are based in the nice new Performing Arts Center on the oak-lined campus of the University of South Carolina Beaufort (USCB, 801 Carteret St., 843/521-4100). A prime mover of the local performing arts scene is **Beaufort Performing Arts Inc.** (www.uscb.edu), formed by a mayoral task force in 2003 specifically to encourage arts and cultural development within the area. Ticket prices typically range $12-40.

Perhaps surprisingly for such a small place, Beaufort boasts its own full orchestra, the **Beaufort Orchestra** (1106 Carteret St., 843/986-5400, www.beaufortorchestra.org), which plays in the Performing Arts Center.

Cinema

One of only two functional drive-ins in the state, the **Highway 21 Drive In** (55 Parker Dr., 843/846-4500, www.hwy21drivein.com) has two screens, great sound, and awesome concessions that include Angus beef hamburgers. All you need to provide is the car and the company.

Festivals and Events

Surprisingly for a town so prominent in so many films, Beaufort didn't have its own film festival until 2007. The **Beaufort Film Festival** (843/986-5400, www.beaufortfilmfestival.com) is held in February. It's small in scale—the inaugural festival was only two days, at a now-defunct theater—but boasts a diverse range of high-quality, cutting-edge entries, including shorts and animation.

Now over 20 years old, the **Gullah Festival of South Carolina** celebrates Gullah history and culture on Memorial Day weekend at various locations throughout town, mostly focusing on Waterfront Park.

By far the biggest single event on the local festival calendar is the over 50-year-old **Beaufort Water Festival** (www.bftwaterfestival.com), held over two weeks in June or July each year, centering on the Waterfront Park area. One of the most eclectic and idiosyncratic events of its kind in a region already known for quirky hyperlocal festivals, the signature events are the Saturday-morning two-hour Grand Parade and a blessing and parade of the shrimp fleet on the closing Sunday.

Fall in the Lowcountry means shrimping season, and early October brings the **Beaufort Shrimp Festival** (www.beaufortsc.org). Highlights include an evening concert with specially lighted shrimp boats docked along the river, a 5K run over the Woods Memorial Bridge, and a more laid-back 5K walk through the historic district. Various cooking competitions are held, obviously centering around the versatile crustaceans that are the raison d'être of the shrimp fleet.

St. Helena Island hosts the three-day **Penn Center Heritage Days** (www.penncenter.com) each November, without a doubt the Beaufort area's second-biggest celebration after the Water Festival. Focusing on Gullah culture, history, and delicious food, Heritage Days does a great job of combining fun with education.

SHOPPING

My favorite shop in Beaufort is **The Bay Street Trading Company** (808 Bay St., 843/524-2000, www.baystreettrading.com, Mon.-Fri. 10am-5:30pm, Sat. 10am-5pm, Sun. noon-5pm), sometimes known simply as "The Book Shop," which has a friendly staff and the best collection of Lowcountry-themed books I've seen in one place.

Across the street, the recently renovated Old Bay Marketplace, with a facade so bright red you can't miss it, hosts a few cute shops, most notably the stylish **Lulu Burgess** (917 Bay St., 843/524-5858, Mon.-Sat. 10am-6pm, Sun. noon-5pm), an eclectic store that brings a rich, quirky sense of humor to its otherwise tasteful assortment of gift items for the whole family.

A unique gift item, as well as something you can enjoy on your own travels, can be found at **Lowcountry Winery** (705 Bay St., 843/379-3010, Mon.-Sat. 10am-5pm). They host tastings daily in the tasting room (because of state law, they must charge a fee for the tasting, but it's only $1 pp).

HILTON HEAD

Art Galleries

My favorite gallery in town is **The Gallery** (802 Bay St., 843/470-9994, www.thegallery-beaufort.com, Mon.-Sat. 11am-5pm). Deanna Bowdish brings in the most cutting-edge regional contemporary artists in a large, friendly, loftlike space. A complete art experience blending the traditional with the cutting-edge is at the **I. Pinckney Simons Art Gallery** (711 Bay St., 843/379-4774, www.ipinckneysimons-gallery.com, Tues.-Fri. 11am-5pm, Sat. 11am-3pm), which is pronounced "Simmons" despite the spelling.

Right on the water is a fun local favorite, the **Longo Gallery** (103 Charles St., 843/522-8933, Mon.-Sat. 11am-5pm). Owners Suzanne and Eric Longo provide a whimsical assortment of less traditional art than you might find in the more touristy waterfront area. Take Charles Street as it works its way toward the waterfront, and the gallery is right behind a storefront on the corner of Charles and Bay Streets.

You'll find perhaps the area's best-known gallery over the bridge on St. Helena Island. Known regionally as one of the best places to find Gullah folk art, **Red Piano Too** (870 Sea Island Pkwy., 843/838-2241, www.redpi-anotoo.com, Mon.-Sat. 10am-5pm) is on the corner before you turn onto the road to the historic Penn Center. Over 150 artists from a diverse range of traditions and styles are represented in this charming little 1940 building with the red tin awning.

SPORTS AND RECREATION

Beaufort County comprises over 60 islands, so it's no surprise that nearly all recreation in the area revolves around the water, which dominates so many aspects of life in the Lowcountry. The closer to the ocean you get, the more it's a salt marsh environment. But as you explore more inland, in the sprawling ACE Basin, you'll encounter primarily blackwater.

Kayaking

The Lowcountry is tailor-made for kayaking. Most kayakers put in at the public landings in nearby Port Royal (1 Port Royal Landing Dr., 843/525-6664) or Lady's Island (73 Sea Island Pkwy., 843/522-0430), across the river from

Red Piano Too gallery on St. Helena Island deals in Gullah art.

© JIM MOREKIS

downtown Beaufort. If you don't feel comfortable with your navigation skills, it's a good idea to contact Kim and David at **Beaufort Kayak Tours** (843/525-0810, www.beaufortkayaktours.com), who rent kayaks and can guide you on a number of excellent tours of all three key areas. They charge about $40 for adults and $30 for children for a two-hour trip. A tour with Beaufort Kayak Tours is also the best (and nearly the only) way to access the historically significant ruins of the early British tabby Fort Frederick, now located on the grounds of the Beaufort Naval Hospital and inaccessible by car.

Fishing and Boating

Key marinas in the area are the **Downtown Marina** (1006 Bay St., 843/524-4422) in Beaufort, the **Lady's Island Marina** (73 Sea Island Pkwy., 843/522-0430), and the **Port Royal Landing Marina** (1 Port Royal Landing Dr., 843/525-6664). Hunting Island has a popular 1,000-foot fishing pier at the south end. A good local fishing charter service is Captain Josh Utsey's **Lowcountry Guide Service** (843/812-4919, www.beaufortscfishing.com). **Captain Ed Hardee** (843/441-6880) offers good inshore charters.

The ACE Basin is a very popular fishing, crabbing, and shrimping area. It has about two dozen public boat ramps, with colorful names like Cuckold's Creek and Steamboat Landing. There's a useful map of them all at www.ace-basin.net, or look for the brown signs along the highway.

Hiking and Biking

Despite the Lowcountry's, well, lowness, biking opportunities abound. It might not get your heart rate up like a ride in the Rockies, but the area lends itself to laid-back two-wheeled enjoyment. Many local B&Bs provide bikes free for guests, and you can rent your own just across the river from Beaufort in Lady's Island at **Lowcountry Bikes** (102 Sea Island Pkwy., 843/524-9585, Mon.-Tues. and Thurs.-Fri. 10am-6pm, Wed. 10am-1pm, Sat. 10am-3pm, about $5 per hour). They can also hook you up with some good routes around the area.

ACCOMMODATIONS

Beaufort's historic district is blessed with an abundance of high-quality accommodations that blend well with their surroundings. There are plenty of budget-minded chain places, some of them acceptable, in the sprawl of Boundary Street outside of downtown, but here are some suggestions within bicycling distance of the Historic District. (That's not a hypothetical, as most inns offer free bicycles to use as you please during your stay.)

Under $150

The **Best Western Sea Island Inn** (1015 Bay St., 843/522-2090, www.bestwestern.com, $135-170) is a good value for those for whom the B&B experience is not paramount. Anchoring the southern end of the historic district in a tasteful low brick building, the Best Western offers decent service, basic amenities, and surprisingly attractive rates for the location on Beaufort's busiest street.

$150-300

Any list of upscale Beaufort lodging must highlight the **(Beaufort Inn** (809 Port Republic St., 843/379-4667, www.beaufortinn.com, $152-425), consistently voted one of the best B&Bs in the nation. It's sort of a hybrid in that it comprises not only the 1897 historic central home but also a cluster of freestanding historical cottages, each with a charming little porch and rocking chairs. Within or outside the main building, each suite has a character all its own, whether it's the 1,500-square-foot Loft Apartment or one of the cozier Choice Rooms with a queen bed.

The 18-room, circa-1820 **Rhett House Inn** (1009 Craven St., 843/524-9030, www.rhetthouseinn.com, $175-320) is the local vacation getaway for the stars. Such arts and entertainment luminaries as Robert Redford, Julia Roberts, Ben Affleck, Barbra Streisand, Dennis Quaid, and Demi Moore have all stayed here at one time or another.

There's nothing like enjoying the view of the Beaufort River from the expansive porches of the **(Cuthbert House Inn** (1203 Bay St.,

HILTON HEAD

843/521-1315, www.cuthberthouseinn.com, $205-250). This grand old circa-1790 federal mansion was once the home of the wealthy Cuthbert family of rice and indigo planters. General Sherman spent a night here in 1865. Some of the king rooms have fireplaces and claw-foot tubs. Of course you get a full Southern breakfast, in addition to sunset hors d'oeuvres on the veranda.

While a stay at a B&B is the classic way to enjoy Beaufort, many travelers swear by the new **City Loft Hotel** (301 Carteret St., 843/379-5638, www.cityflofthotel.com, $200). Housed in a former motel, City Loft is a total modernist makeover, gleaming from stem to stern with chrome and various art deco touches.

FOOD
Breakfast and Brunch
One of the best breakfasts I've had anywhere was a humble two-egg plate for five bucks at Beaufort's most popular morning hangout, **◖ Blackstone's Café** (205 Scott St., 843/524-4330, Mon.-Sat. 7:30am-2:30pm, Sun. 7:30am-2pm, under $10), complete with tasty hash browns, a comparative rarity in this part of the country, where grits rule as the breakfast starch of choice.

Burgers and Sandwiches
Another lunch favorite is **Magnolia Bakery Café** (703 Congress St., 843/524-1961, Mon.-Sat. 9am-5pm, under $10). Lump crab cakes are a specialty item, but you can't go wrong with any of the lunch sandwiches. Vegetarian diners are particularly well taken care of with a large selection of black-bean burger plates. As the name indicates, the range of desserts here is tantalizing, with the added bonus of a serious espresso bar.

New Southern
The stylishly appointed **Wren Bistro, Bar and Market** (210 Carteret St., 843/524-9463, Mon.-Sat. 11am-10pm, $15-25) is known for any of its chicken dishes. While the food is great, the interior is particularly well done, simultaneously warm and classy. As seems to be

typical of Beaufort, the lunches are as good as the dinners.

Seafood
The hottest dinner table in town is at the **◖ Saltus River Grill** (802 Bay St., 843/379-3474, Sun.-Thurs. 5pm-9pm, Fri.-Sat. 5pm-10pm, $10-39), famous throughout the state for its raw bar menu. Other specialties include she-crab bisque, lump crab cakes, and the ubiquitous shrimp and grits. The Saltus River Grill is more upscale in feel and in price than most Lowcountry places, with a very see-and-be-seen attitude and a hopping bar. Reservations are recommended.

The short and focused menu at **Plum's** (904½ Bay St., 843/525-1946, lunch daily 11am-4pm, dinner daily 5pm-10pm, bar until 2am, $15-25) keys in on entrées highlighting local ingredients, such as the shrimp penne *al'amatriciana* and fresh black mussel pasta. Because of the outstanding microbrew selection, Plum's is a big nightlife hangout as well; be aware that after 10pm, when food service ends but the bar remains open, it's no longer smoke-free.

An up-and-comer downtown is **Breakwater Restaurant & Bar** (203 Carteret St., 843/379-0052, www.breakwatersc.com, dinner Thurs.-Sat. 6pm-9:30pm, bar until 2am, $10-20). The concise menu makes up in good taste what it lacks in comprehensiveness, with an emphasis on seafood, of course.

Steaks
Luther's Rare & Well Done (910 Bay St., 843/521-1888, daily 10am-midnight, from $8) on the waterfront is the kind of meat-lover's place where even the french onion soup has a morsel of rib eye in it. While the patented succulent rubbed steaks are a no-brainer here, the handcrafted specialty pizzas are also quite popular. Housed in a historic pharmacy building, Luther's is also a great place for late eats after many other places in this quiet town have rolled up the sidewalk. A limited menu of appetizers and bar food to nosh on at the inviting and popular bar is available after 10pm.

HILTON HEAD

Tapas

Right around the corner from Breakwater is **Emily's** (906 Port Republic St., 843/522-1866, www.emilysrestaurantandtapasbar.com, dinner Mon.-Sat. 4pm-10pm, bar until 2am, $10-20), a very popular fine dining spot that specializes in a more traditional brand of rich, tasty tapas and is known for its active bar scene.

INFORMATION AND SERVICES

The **Beaufort Visitors Information Center** (713 Craven St., 843/986-5400, www.beaufortsc.org, daily 9am-5:30pm), the headquarters of the Beaufort Chamber of Commerce and Convention and Visitors Bureau, has relocated from its old Carteret Street location and can now be found within the Beaufort Arsenal, once home to the now-closed Beaufort Museum.

GETTING THERE AND AROUND

While the Marines can fly their F-18s directly into Beaufort Naval Air Station, you won't have that luxury. The closest major airport to Beaufort is the **Savannah/Hilton Head International Airport** (SAV, 400 Airways Ave., 912/964-0514, www.savannahairport.com) off I-95 outside Savannah. If you're not going into Savannah for any reason, the easiest route to the Beaufort area from the airport is to take I-95's exit 8, and from there to take U.S. 278 east to Highway 170.

Alternately, you could fly into the **Charleston International Airport** (CHS, 5500 International Blvd., www.chs-airport.com), but because that facility is on the far north side of Charleston, it actually might take you longer to get to Beaufort. From the Charleston Airport the best route south to Beaufort is U.S. 17 south, exiting onto U.S. 21 at Gardens Corner and then into Beaufort.

If you're coming into the region by car, I-95 will be your likely primary route, with your main point of entry being exit 8 off I-95 connecting to U.S. 278 east to Highway 170.

There's no public transportation in Beaufort,

but that's OK—the historic section is quite small and can be traversed in an afternoon. A favorite mode of transportation is by bicycle, often complimentary to bed-and-breakfast guests. Rent one at **Lowcountry Bikes** (102 Sea Island Pkwy., 843/524-9585, Mon.-Tues. and Thurs.-Fri. 10am-6pm, Wed. 10am-1pm, Sat. 10am-3pm, about $5 per hour) in Lady's Island, just over the bridge.

OUTSIDE BEAUFORT

The areas outside tourist-traveled Beaufort can take you even farther back into sepia-toned Americana, into a time of sharecropper homesteads, sturdy oystermen, and an altogether variable and subjective sense of time.

◖ Penn Center

By going across the Richard V. Woods Memorial Bridge over the Beaufort River on the Sea Island Parkway (which turns into U.S. 21), you'll pass through Lady's Island and reach St. Helena Island. Known to old-timers as Frogmore, the area took back its old Spanish-derived place name in the 1980s. Today, St. Helena Island is most famous for the **Penn Center** (16 Martin Luther King Jr. Dr., 843/838-2474, www.penncenter.com, Mon.-Sat. 11am-4pm, $4 adults, $2 seniors and children), the spiritual home of Gullah culture and history. When you visit here among the live oaks and humble but well-preserved buildings, you'll instantly see why Martin Luther King Jr. chose this as one of his major retreat and planning sites during the civil rights era. The dream began as early as 1862, when a group of abolitionist Quakers from Philadelphia came during the Union occupation with the goal of teaching recently freed slave children. In the late 1960s, the Southern Christian Leadership Conference used the school as a retreat and planning site.

The 50-acre campus is part of the Penn School Historic District, a National Historic Landmark comprising 19 buildings, most of key historical significance. The Retreat House was intended for Dr. King to continue his strategy meetings, but he was assassinated before being able to stay there. The museum and bookshop are housed in the Cope Building, now called the York W. Bailey Museum, situated right along MLK Jr. Drive.

To get to the Penn Center from Beaufort, proceed over the bridge until you get to St. Helena Island. Take a right onto MLK Jr. Drive when you see the Red Piano Too Art Gallery. The Penn Center is a few hundred yards down on the right. If you drive past the Penn Center and continue a few hundred yards down MLK Jr. Drive, look for the ancient tabby ruins on the left side of the road. This is the **Chapel of Ease,** the remnant of a 1740 church destroyed by forest fire in the late 1800s.

Fort Fremont Preserve

Military historians and sightseers of a particularly adventurous type will want to drive several miles past the Penn Center on St. Helena Island to visit **Fort Fremont** (Lands End Rd., www.fortfremont.org, daily 9am-dusk, free). Two artillery batteries remain of this Spanish-American War-era coastal defense fort (an adjacent private residence is actually the old Army hospital.) The big guns are long gone, but the concrete emplacements—along with many very dark tunnels and small rooms—are still here. Bring a flashlight and be warned that there are no facilities of any kind, including lights and guardrails.

Old Sheldon Church Ruins

A short ways north of Beaufort are the poignantly desolate ruins of the once-magnificent **Old Sheldon Church** (Old Sheldon Church Rd., off U.S. 17 just past Gardens Corner, daily dawn-dusk, free). One of the first Greek Revival structures in the United States, the house of worship held its first service in 1757. The sanctuary was first burned by the British in 1779. After being rebuilt in 1826, the sanctuary survived until General Sherman's arrival in 1865, whereupon Union troops razed it once more. Nothing remains now but these towering walls and columns, made of red brick instead of the tabby often seen in similar ruins on the coast. It's now owned by the nearby St. Helena's Episcopal Church in Beaufort, which

Old Sheldon Church ruins

© JIM MOREKIS

holds outdoor services here the second Sunday after Easter.

Oyotunji Village

Continuing north of the Sheldon Church a short way, the more adventurous can find a quirky Lowcountry attraction, **Oyotunji Village** (56 Bryant Lane, 843/846-8900, www.oyotunji.org, daily 11am-dusk, $10). Built in 1970 by self-proclaimed "King" Ofuntola Oseijeman Adelabu Adefunmi I, a former used car dealer with an interesting past, Oyotunji claims to be North America's only authentic African village, and also claims to be a separate kingdom and not a part of the United States—though I'm sure the State Department begs to differ.

Parris Island

Though more commonly known as the home of the legendary **Marine Corps Recruit Depot Parris Island** (283 Blvd. de France, 843/228-3650, www.mcrdpi.usmc.mil, free), the island is also of historic significance as the site of some of the earliest European presence in the New World. Today, it's where all female U.S. Marine recruits and all male recruits east of the Mississippi River go through the grueling 13-week boot camp. Almost every Friday during the year marks the graduation of a company of newly minted Marines. That's why you might notice an influx of visitors to the area each Thursday, a.k.a. "Family Day," with the requisite amount of celebration on Friday after that morning's ceremony.

Unlike many military facilities in the post-9/11 era, Parris Island still hosts plenty of visitors. Just check in with the sentry at the gate and show your valid driver's license, car registration, and proof of insurance. Rental car drivers must show a copy of the rental agreement. On your way to the Depot proper, there are a couple of beautiful picnic areas. Once inside, stop first at the **Douglas Visitor Center** (Bldg. 283, Blvd. de France, 843/228-3650, Mon. 7:30am-noon, Tues.-Wed. 7:30am-4:30pm, Thurs. 6:30am-7pm, Fri. 7:30am-3pm), a great place to find maps and information. As you go

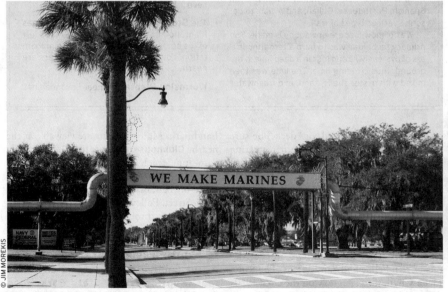

© JIM MOREKIS

HILTON HEAD

You don't have to be a U.S. Marine to get something out of a trip to Parris Island.

THE LOST ART OF TABBY

Let's clear up a couple of misconceptions about tabby, that unique construction technique combining oyster shells, lime, water, and sand found along the South Carolina and Georgia coast.

First, it did not originate with Native Americans. The confusion is due to the fact that the indigenous population left behind many middens, or trash heaps, of oyster shells. While these middens indeed provided the bulk of the shells for tabby buildings to come, Native Americans had little else to do with it.

Second, although the Spanish were responsible for the first use of tabby in the Americas, contrary to lore almost all remaining tabby in the area dates from later English settlement. The British first fell in love with tabby after the siege of Spanish-held St. Augustine, Florida, and quickly began building with it in their colonies to the north.

Scholars are divided as to whether tabby was invented by West Africans or its use spread to Africa from Spain and Portugal, circuitously coming to the United States through the knowledge of imported slaves. The origin of the word itself is also unclear, as similar words exist in Spanish, Portuguese, Gullah, and Arabic to describe various types of wall.

We do know for sure how tabby is made: The primary technique was to burn alternating layers of oyster shells and logs in a deep hole in the ground, thus creating lime. The lime was then mixed with oyster shells, sand, and freshwater and poured into wooden molds, or "forms," to dry and then be used as building blocks, much like large bricks. Tabby walls were usually plastered with stucco. Tabby is remarkably strong and resilient, able to survive the hurricanes that often batter the area. It also stays cool in the summer and is insect-resistant, two enormous advantages down here.

Following are some great examples of true tabby you can see today on the South Carolina and Georgia coasts, from north to south:

- **Dorchester State Historic Site** in Summerville, north of Charleston, contains a well-preserved tabby fort.

- Several younger tabby buildings still exist in downtown Beaufort: the **Barnwell-Gough House** (705 Washington St.); the Thomas Fuller House, or **"Tabby Manse"** (1211 Bay St.); and the **Saltus House** (800 block of Bay St.), perhaps the tallest surviving tabby structure.

- The **Chapel of Ease** on St. Helena Island dates from the 1740s. If someone tells you General Sherman burned it down, don't believe it; the culprit was a forest fire.

- The **Stoney-Baynard Ruins** in Sea Pines Plantation on Hilton Head are all that's left of the home of the old Braddock's Point Plantation. Foundations of a slave quarters are nearby.

- **Wormsloe Plantation** near Savannah has

by the big parade ground, or "deck," be sure to check out the beautiful sculpture recreating the famous photo of Marines raising the flag on Iwo Jima. A short ways ahead is the **Parris Island Museum** (Bldg. 111, 111 Panama St., 843/228-2951, www.parrisislandmuseum.com, daily 10am-4:30pm, free).

The Spanish built Santa Elena directly on top of the original French settlement, Charlesfort. They then built two other settlements, San Felipe and San Marcos. The Santa Elena-Charlesfort site, now on the circa-1950s depot golf course, is now a National Historic Landmark. Many artifacts are viewable at the nearby **Clubhouse-Interpretive Center** (daily 7am-5pm, free). You can take a self-guided tour; to get to the site from the museum, continue on Panama Street and take a right on Cuba Street. Follow the signs to the golf course and continue through the main parking lot of the course.

🄲 Hunting Island State Park

A true family-friendly outdoor adventure spot, **Hunting Island State Park** (2555 Sea Island Pkwy., 866/345-7275, www.

the remains of Noble Jones's fortification of the Skidaway Narrows.

- **St. Cyprian's Episcopal Church** in Darien is one of the largest tabby structures still in use.

- **Fort Frederica** on St. Simons Island has not only the remains of a tabby fort but many foundations of tabby houses in the surrounding settlement.

- The remarkably intact walls of the **Horton-DuBignon House** on Jekyll Island, Georgia, date from 1738, and the house was occupied into the 1850s.

© JIM MOREKIS

the Chapel of Ease on St. Helena Island

huntingisland.com, winter daily 6am-6pm, during daylight saving time daily 6am-9pm, $5 adults, $3 children) has something for everyone—kids, parents, and newlyweds. Yet it still retains a certain sense of lush wildness—so much so that it doubled as Vietnam in the movie *Forrest Gump*.

At the north end past the campground is the island's main landmark, the historic **Hunting Island Light,** which dates from 1875. While the 167-step trek to the top (donation $2 pp) is strenuous, the view is stunning. At the south end of the island is a marsh walk, nature trail, and a fishing pier complete with a cute little nature center.

Getting to Hunting Island couldn't be easier—just take the Sea Island Parkway (U.S. 21) about 20 minutes beyond Beaufort and you'll run right into it.

◖ ACE Basin

Occupying pretty much the entire area between Beaufort and Charleston, the ACE Basin—the acronym signifies its role as the collective estuary of the Ashepoo, Combahee, and Edisto Rivers—is one of the most enriching natural

HILTON HEAD

the Grove Plantation House at the Ernest F. Hollings ACE Basin National Wildlife Refuge

© JIM MOREKIS

HILTON HEAD

experiences the country has to offer. The ACE Basin is so big that it is actually divided into several parts for management purposes under the umbrella of the ACE Basin Project (www.acebasin.net).

About 12,000 acres of the ACE Basin Project form the **Ernest F. Hollings ACE Basin National Wildlife Refuge** (8675 Willtown Rd., 843/889-3084, www.fws.gov/acebasin, grounds year-round daily dawn-dusk, office Mon.-Fri. 7:30am-4pm, free), run by the U.S. Fish and Wildlife Service. The historic 1828 **Grove Plantation House** is in this portion of the basin and houses the refuge's headquarters. Sometimes featured on local tours of homes, it's one of only three antebellum homes left in the ACE Basin. Surrounded by lush, ancient oak trees, it's really a sight in and of itself.

This section of the Refuge, the **Edisto Unit,** is almost entirely composed of paddies from the area's role as a rice plantation before the Civil War. To get to the Edisto Unit of the Hollings ACE Basin National Wildlife Refuge, take U.S. 17 to Highway 174 (going all the way down this route takes you to Edisto Island) and turn right onto Willtown Road. The unpaved entrance road is about two miles ahead on the left. There are restrooms and a few picnic tables.

You can also visit the two parts of the **Combahee Unit** of the refuge, which offers a similar scene of trails among impounded wetlands along the Combahee River, with parking; it's farther west near Yemassee. Get here by taking a left off U.S. 17 onto Highway 33. The larger portion of the Combahee Unit is soon after the turnoff, and the smaller, more northerly portion is about five miles up the road.

About 135,000 acres of the entire ACE Basin falls under the protection of the South Carolina Department of Natural Resources (DNR) as part of the **National Estuarine Research Reserve System** (www.nerrs.noaa.gov/acebasin). The DNR also runs two Wildlife Management Areas (WMAs), **Donnelly WMA** (843/844-8957, www.dnr.sc.gov, year-round Mon.-Sat. 8am-5pm) and **Bear Island WMA** (843/844-8957, www.dnr.sc.gov, Feb. 1-Oct. 14 Mon.-Sat. dawn-dusk), both of which provide rich opportunities for birding and wildlife observation.

Recreation
KAYAKING
You can put in at the ramp at the **Lady's Island Marina** (73 Sea Island Pkwy., 843/522-0430) just across the bridge from Beaufort. **Hunting Island State Park** (2555 Sea Island Pkwy., 866/345-7275, www.huntingisland.com, winter daily 6am-6pm, during daylight saving time daily 6am-9pm, $5 adults, $3 children) has a wonderful inlet that is very popular with kayakers.

A good service for rental and knowledgeable guided tours of the ACE Basin is **Outpost Moe's** (843/844-2514, www.geocities.ws/outpostmoe), where the basic 2.5-hour tour costs $40 pp, and an all-day extravaganza through the basin is $80. Moe's provides lunch for most of its tours. Another premier local outfitter for ACE Basin tours is **Carolina Heritage Outfitters** (U.S. 15, Canadys, 843/563-5051, www.canoesc.com), which focuses on the Edisto River trail. In addition to guided tours ($30) and rentals, you can camp overnight in their cute tree houses ($125) along the kayak routes. They load you up with your gear and drive you 22 miles upriver; then you paddle downriver to the tree house for the evening. The next day, you paddle yourself the rest of the way downriver back to home base.

To have a drier experience of the ACE Basin from the deck of a larger vessel, try **ACE Basin Tours** (1 Coosaw River Dr., Beaufort, 843/521-3099, www.acebasintours.com, Mar.-Nov. Wed. and Sat. 10am, $35 adults, $15 children), which will take you on a three-hour tour in the 40-passenger *Dixie Lady*. To get to their dock, take Carteret Street over the bridge to St. Helena Island, and then take a left on Highway 802 east (Sam's Point Rd.). Continue until you cross Lucy Point Creek; the ACE Basin Tours marina is on the immediate left after you cross the bridge.

The state of South Carolina has conveniently gathered some of the best self-guided kayak trips at www.acebasin.net/canoe.html.

GOLF
Golf is much bigger in Hilton Head than in the Beaufort area, but here are some local highlights. The best-regarded public course in the area, and indeed one of the best military courses in the world, is **Legends at Parris Island** (Bldg. 299, Parris Island, 843/228-2240, www.mccssc.com, $30). Call in advance for a tee time.

Another popular public course is **South Carolina National Golf Club** (8 Waveland Ave., Cat Island, 843/524-0300, www.scnational. com, $70). Get to secluded Cat Island by taking the Sea Island Parkway onto Lady's Island and continuing south as it turns into Lady's Island Drive. Turn onto Island Causeway and continue for about three miles.

CAMPING
Hunting Island State Park (2555 Sea Island Pkwy., 866/345-7275, www.huntingisland. com, winter daily 6am-6pm, during daylight saving time daily 6am-9pm, $5 adults, $3 children, $25 campsites, $87-172 cabins) has 200 campsites on the north end of the island, with individual water and electric hookups. Most are available by reservation only, but 20 are available on a first-come, first-served basis. (There used to be plenty of cabins for rent, but beach erosion has sadly made the ones near the water uninhabitable. One cabin near the lighthouse is still available for rent.)

Another neat place to camp is **Tuck in De Wood** (22 Tuc In De Wood Lane, St. Helena, 843/838-2267, $25), a very well-maintained 74-site private campground just past the Penn Center on St. Helena Island.

HILTON HEAD

Edisto Island

One of the last truly unspoiled places in the Lowcountry, Edisto Island has been highly regarded as a getaway spot since the Edisto people first started coming here for shellfish. In fact, locals swear that the island was settled by English-speaking colonists even before Charleston was settled in 1670. Now this barrier island, for the moment unthreatened by the encroachment of planned communities and private resorts so endemic to the Carolina coast, is a nice getaway for area residents in addition to being a great—if a little isolated—place to live for its 800 or so full-time residents, who operate on "Edisto Time," with a *mañana* philosophy (i.e., it'll get done when it gets done) that results in a mellow pace of life out in these parts.

◖ EDISTO BEACH STATE PARK

Edisto Beach State Park (8377 State Cabin Rd., 843/869-2156, www.southcarolinaparks. com, Nov.-mid-Mar. daily 8am-6pm, mid-Mar.-Oct. daily 6am-10pm, $4 adults, $1.50 children, free under age 6) is one of the world's foremost destinations for shell collectors. Largely because of fresh loads of silt from the adjacent ACE Basin, there are always new specimens, many of them fossils, washing ashore. The park stretches almost three miles and features the state's longest system of fully accessible hiking and biking trails, including one leading to the 4,000-year-old shell midden, now much eroded from past millennia. The new and particularly well-done **Interpretive Center** (Tues.-Sat. 9am-4pm) has plenty of interesting exhibits about the nature and history of the park as well as the surrounding ACE Basin.

OTHER SIGHTS

The **Edisto Museum** (8123 Chisolm Plantation Rd., 843/869-1954, www.edistomuseum.org, Tues.-Sat. 11am-4pm, $4 adults, $2 children, free under age 10), a project of the Edisto Island Historic Preservation Society, is in the middle of a major expansion that will incorporate a nearby slave cabin. Its well-done exhibits of local lore and history are complemented by a gift shop. The Edisto Museum is before you get to the main part of the island, off Highway 174.

Opened in 1999 by local snake hunters the Clamp brothers, the **Edisto Island Serpentarium** (1374 Hwy. 174, 843/869-1171, www.edistoserpentarium.com, hours vary, $14.95 adults, $10.95 ages 4-12, free under age 3) is educational and fun, taking you up close and personal with a variety of reptilian creatures native to the area. They usually close Labor Day-April 30.

TOURS

Edisto has many beautiful plantation homes, relics of the island's longtime role as host to cotton plantations. While all are in private hands and therefore off limits to the public, an exception is offered through **Edisto Island Tours & T'ings** (843/869-9092, $20 adults, $10 under age 13). You'll take a van tour around Edisto's beautiful churches and old plantations.

SPORTS AND RECREATION

As the largest river of the ACE (Ashepoo, Combahee, Edisto) Basin complex, the Edisto River figures large in the lifestyle of residents and visitors. A good public landing is at Steamboat Creek off Highway 174 on the way down to the island. Take Steamboat Landing Road (Hwy. 968) from Highway 174 near the James Edwards School. Live Oak Landing is farther up Big Bay Creek near the Interpretive Center at the State Park. The **Edisto Marina** (3702 Docksite Rd., 843/869-3504) is on the far west side of the island.

Captain Ron Elliott of **Edisto Island Tours** (843/869-1937) offers various ecotours and fishing trips as well as canoe and kayak rentals for about $25 per day. A typical kayak tour runs about $35 pp for a 1.5- to 2-hour trip, and he offers a "beachcombing" trip for $15 pp. **Ugly Ducklin'** (843/869-1580) offers creek and in-shore fishing charters. You can get gear as well as reserve boat and kayak tours of the entire area, including into the ACE Basin, at **Edisto Watersports & Tackle** (3731 Docksite Rd., 843/869-0663, www.edistowatersports.com). Their guided tours run about $30 pp, with a two-hour rental running about $20.

Riding a bike on Edisto Beach and all around the island is a great relaxing way to get some exercise and enjoy its scenic, laid-back beauty. The best place to rent a bike—or a kayak or canoe, for that matter—is **Island Bikes and Outfitters** (140 Jungle Rd., 843/869-4444, Mon.-Sat. 9am-4pm). Bike rentals run about $16 per day; single kayaks are about $60 per day.

ACCOMMODATIONS AND FOOD

A great thing about Edisto Island is the total absence of ugly chain lodging or beachfront condo development. My recommended option is staying at the **Edisto Beach State Park** (843/869-2156, www.southcarolinaparks.com, $25 tent sites, $75-100 cabins) itself, either at a campsite on the Atlantic side or in a marsh-front cabin on the northern edge. During high season (Apr.-Nov.), there's a minimum weeklong stay in the cabins; during the off-season, the minimum stay is two days. You can book cabins up to 11 months in advance.

If you want something a little more plush, there are rental homes galore on Edisto Island. Because of the aforementioned lack of hotels, this is the most popular option for most vacationers here—indeed, it's just about the only option. Contact **Edisto Sales and Rentals Realty** (1405 Palmetto Blvd., 800/868-5398, www.edistorealty.com).

One of the all-time great barbecue places in South Carolina is on Edisto, **◖ Po Pigs Bo-B-Q** (2410 Hwy. 174, 843/869-9003, Wed.-Sat. 11:30am-9pm, $4-10) on the way into town. This is the real thing, the full pig cooked in all its many ways: white meat, dark meat, cracklin's, and hash, served in the local style of "all you care to eat." Unlike many barbecue spots, they do serve beer and wine.

The legendary **◖ Old Post Office** (1442 Hwy. 174, 843/869-2339, www.theoldpostofficerestaurant.com, Tues.-Sun. 5:30pm-10pm, $20), a Lowcountry-style fine-dining spot, kept a devoted clientele for 20 years. It recently reopened with a bang and thankfully kept its old-school mystique intact. Specialties include fine crab cakes drizzled with mousseline sauce, the pecan-encrusted Veal Edistonian, and a Carolina rib eye topped with a pimiento cheese sauce.

Hilton Head Island

Literally the prototype of the modern planned resort community, Hilton Head Island is also a case study in how a landscape can change when money is introduced. From Reconstruction until the post-World War II era, the island consisted almost entirely of African Americans with deep roots in the area. In the mid-1950s Hilton Head began its transformation into an almost all-white, upscale golf, tennis, and shopping mecca populated largely by Northern transplants and retirees. As you can imagine, the flavor here is now quite different from surrounding areas of the Lowcountry, to say the least, with an emphasis on material excellence, top prices, get-it-done-yesterday punctuality, and the attendant aggressive traffic.

One of the unsung positive aspects of modern Hilton Head is its dedication to sustainable living. With the support of voters, the town routinely buys large tracts of land to preserve as open space. Hilton Head was the first municipality in the country to mandate the burying of all power lines, and one of the first to regularly use covenants and deed restrictions. All new development must conform to rigid guidelines on setbacks and tree canopy. It has one of the most comprehensive signage ordinances in the country as well, which means no garish commercial displays will disrupt your views of the night sky. If those are "elite" values, then certainly we might do well in making them more mainstream.

HISTORY

The second-largest barrier island on the East Coast was named in 1663 by adventurer Sir William Hilton, who thoughtfully named the island—with its notable headland or "Head"—after himself. Later it gained fame as the first location of the legendary "Sea Island Cotton," a long-grain variety that, following its introduction in 1790 by William Elliott II of the Myrtle Bank Plantation, would soon be the dominant version of the cash crop.

Nearby Bluffton was settled by planters from Hilton Head Island and the surrounding area in the early 1800s as a summer retreat. Though Charleston likes to claim the label today, Bluffton was actually the genuine "cradle of secession." Indeed, locals still joke that the town motto is "Divided We Stand."

Though it seems unlikely given the island's modern demographics, Hilton Head was almost entirely African American through much of the 20th century. When Union troops occupied the island at the outbreak of the Civil War, freed and escaped slaves flocked to the island, and most of the dwindling number of African Americans on the island today are descendants of this original Gullah population.

In the 1950s the Fraser family bought 19,000 of the island's 25,000 acres with the intent to continue forestry on them. But in 1956—not at all coincidentally the same year the first bridge to the island was built—Charles Fraser convinced his father to sell him the southern tip. Fraser's brainchild and decades-long labor of love—some said his obsession—Sea Pines Plantation was the prototype of the golf-oriented resort community so common today on both U.S. coasts. Fraser himself was killed in a

boating accident in 2002 and is buried under the famous Liberty Oak in Harbour Town.

ORIENTATION

Hilton Head Islanders have long referred to their island as the "shoe" and speak of driving to the toe or going to the heel. If you take a look at a map, you'll see why: Hilton Head bears an uncanny resemblance to a running shoe pointed toward the southwest, with the aptly named Broad Creek forming a near facsimile of the Nike "swoosh" symbol. Running the length and circumference of the shoe is the main drag, U.S. 278 Business (William Hilton Pkwy.), which crosses onto Hilton Head right at the "tongue" of the shoe, a relatively undeveloped area. The new Cross Island Parkway toll route (U.S. 278), beginning up toward the ankle as you first get on the island, is a quicker route straight to the toe near Sea Pines. While it is technically the business spur, when locals say "278" they're talking about the William Hilton Parkway. It takes you along the entire sole of the shoe, including the beaches, and on down to the toe, where you'll find a confusing, crazy British-style traffic circle called Sea Pines Circle. It's also the site of the Harbour Town Marina and the island's oldest planned development, Sea Pines Plantation.

While making your way around the island, always keep in mind that the bulk of it consists of private developments, and local law enforcement frowns on people who aimlessly wander among the condos and villas.

SIGHTS

Contrary to what many think, there are things to do on Hilton Head that don't involve swinging a club at a little white ball or shopping for designer labels but instead celebrate the area's history and natural setting. Following are some of those attractions, arranged in geographical order from where you first access the island.

◖ Pinckney Island National Wildlife Refuge

Actually consisting of many islands and hammocks, **Pinckney Island NWR** (912/652-4415,

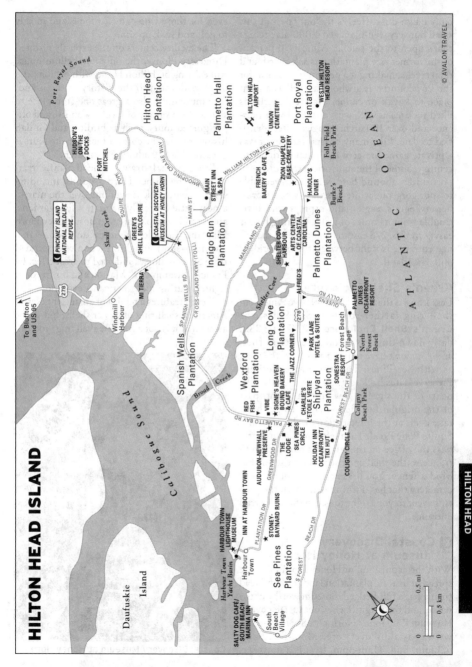

HILTON HEAD ISLAND

© AVALON TRAVEL

HILTON HEAD

daily dawn-dusk, free) is the only part of this small but very well-managed 4,000-acre refuge that's open to the public. Almost 70 percent of the former rice plantation is salt marsh and tidal creeks, making it a perfect microcosm for the Lowcountry as a whole, as well as a great place to kayak or canoe. Native Americans liked the area as well, with a 10,000-year presence and over 100 archaeological sites identified to date. Like many coastal refuges, it was a private game preserve for much of the 20th century. Some of the state's richest birding opportunities abound here, with observers able to spot gorgeous white ibis, rare wood storks, herons, egrets, eagles, and ospreys with little trouble from its miles of trails. Getting here is easy: On U.S. 278 east to Hilton Head, the refuge entrance is right between the two bridges onto the island.

Green's Shell Enclosure

Less known than the larger Native American shell ring farther south at Sea Pines, the **Green's Shell Enclosure** (803/734-3886, daily dawn-dusk) is certainly easier to find, and you don't have to pay $5 to enter the area, as with Sea Pines. This three-acre Heritage Preserve dates back to at least the 1300s. The heart of the site is a low embankment, part of the original fortified village. To get here, take a left at the intersection of U.S. 278 and Squire Pope Road. Turn left into Greens Park, pass the office on the left, and park. The entrance to the shell enclosure is on the left behind a fence. You'll see a small community cemetery that has nothing to do with the shell ring; veer to your right to get to the short trail entrance.

◖ Coastal Discovery Museum at Honey Horn

With the acquisition of Honey Horn's 70-acre spread of historic plantation land, Hilton Head finally has a full-fledged museum worthy of the name, and the magnificent **Coastal Discovery Museum** (70 Honey Horn Dr., 843/689-6767, www.coastaldiscovery.org, Mon.-Sat. 9am-4:30pm, Sun. 11am-3pm, free) is a must-see,

even for those who came to the island mostly to golf and soak up sun.

The facility centers on the expertly restored Discovery House, the only antebellum house still existing on Hilton Head, with exhibits and displays devoted to the history of the island. The museum is also a great one-stop place to sign up for a variety of specialty on-site and off-site guided tours, such as birding and Gullah history tours. The cost for most on-site tours is a reasonable $10 adults, $5 children.

But the real draw is the 0.5-mile trail through the Honey Horn grounds, including several boardwalk viewpoints over the marsh, a neat little butterfly habitat, a few gardens, and a stable and pasture that host Honey Horn May and Tadpole, the museum's two Marsh Tackies—short, tough little ponies descended from Spanish horses and used to great effect by Francis "Swamp Fox" Marion and his freedom fighters during the American Revolution. The trail even features a replica of an ancient Native American shell ring of oyster shells, but do be aware that it is not a genuine shell ring (you can

Coastal Discovery Museum at Honey Horn

find the real thing at Green's Shell Enclosure a bit farther west on Highway 278 and in Sea Pines at the south end of the island).

While a glance at a map and area signage might convince you that you must pay the $1.25 toll on the Cross Island Parkway to get to Honey Horn, that isn't so. The exit to Honey Horn on the Parkway is actually before you get to the toll plaza, therefore access is free.

Union Cemetery

A modest but key aspect of African American history on Hilton Head is at **Union Cemetery** (Union Cemetery Rd.), a small burial ground featuring several graves of black Union Army troops (you can tell by the designation "USCI" on the tombstone, for "United States Colored Infantry"). Also of interest are the charming, hand-carved cement tombstones of nonveterans. To get here, turn north off William Hilton Parkway onto Union Cemetery Road. The cemetery is a short way ahead on the left. There is no signage or site interpretation.

Zion Chapel of Ease Cemetery

More like one of the gloriously desolate scenes common to the rest of the Lowcountry, this little cemetery in full view of the William Hilton Parkway at Folly Field Road is all that remains of one of the "Chapels of Ease," a string of chapels set up in the 1700s. The **Zion Chapel of Ease Cemetery** (daily dawn-dusk, free) is said to be haunted by the ghost of William Baynard, whose final resting place is in a mausoleum on the site (the remains of his ancestral home are farther south at Sea Pines Plantation).

Audubon-Newhall Preserve

Plant lovers shouldn't miss this small but very well-maintained 50-acre wooded tract in the south-central part of the island, on Palmetto Bay Road between the Cross Island Parkway and Sea Pines circle. Almost all plant life, even that in the water, is helpfully marked and identified. The **Audubon-Newhall Preserve** (year-round dawn-dusk, free) is open to the public, but you can't camp here. For more

information, call the Hilton Head Audubon Society (843/842-9246).

Sea Pines Plantation

This private residential resort development at the extreme west end of the island—first on Hilton Head and the prototype of every other such development in the country—hosts several attractions that collectively are well worth the $5 per vehicle "road use" fee, which you pay at the main entrance gate.

HARBOUR TOWN

It's not particularly historic and not all that natural, but Harbour Town is still pretty cool. The dominant element is the squat, colorful **Harbour Town Lighthouse Museum** (149 Lighthouse Rd., 843/671-2810, www.harbourtownlighthouse.com, daily 10am-dusk, $3), which has never really helped a ship navigate its way near the island. The 90-foot structure was built in 1970 purely to give visitors a little atmosphere, and that it does, as kids especially love climbing the stairs to the top ($2 pp) and looking out over the island's expanse.

STONEY-BAYNARD RUINS

The tabby **Stoney-Baynard Ruins** (Plantation Dr., dawn-dusk, free) in a residential neighborhood are what remains of the circa-1790 central building of the old Braddock's Point Plantation, first owned by Patriot and raconteur Captain "Saucy Jack" Stoney and then the Baynard family. Active during the island's heyday as a cotton center, the plantation was destroyed after the Civil War. Two other foundations are nearby, one for slave quarters and one whose use is still unknown. Note that there is a $5 fee to enter Sea Pines.

SEA PINES FOREST PRESERVE

The **Sea Pines Forest Preserve** (175 Greenwood Dr., 843/363-4530, free) is set amid the Sea Pines Plantation golf resort development, but you don't need a bag of clubs to enjoy this 600-acre preserve, which is built on the site of an old rice plantation (dikes and logging trails are still visible). Here you can ride

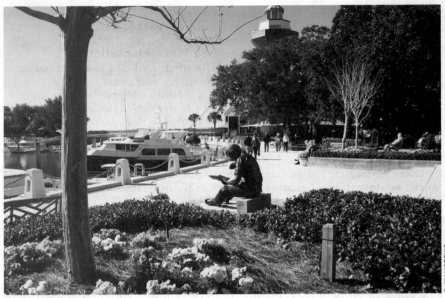

© JIM MOREKIS

Harbour Town

HILTON HEAD

a horse, fish, or just take a walk on the eight miles of trails (dawn-dusk) and enjoy the natural beauty around you. No cycling is allowed on the trails, however.

In addition to the Native American shell ring farther north off Squire Pope Road, the Sea Pines Forest Preserve also boasts a shell ring set within a canopy of tall pines. Scientists date the ring itself to about 1450 BC, although human habitation on the island goes as far back as 8000 BC.

Tours and Cruises

Most guided tours on Hilton Head focus on the water. **Harbour Town Cruises** (843/363-9023, www.vagabondcruise.com, $29.95-59.95) offers several sightseeing tours as well as excursions to Daufuskie and Savannah. They also offer a tour on a former America's Cup racing yacht.

Dolphin tours are extremely popular on Hilton Head, and there is no shortage of operators. **Dolphin Watch Nature Cruises** (843/785-4558, $25 adults, $10 children) departs from Shelter Cove, as does **Lowcountry Nature Tours** (843/683-0187, www.lowcountrynature-tours.com, $40 adults, $35 children, free under age 3). The *Gypsy* (843/363-2900, www.bite-mybait.com, $15 adults, $7 children) sails out of South Beach Marina, taking you all around peaceful Calibogue Sound. Two dolphin tours are based on Broad Creek, the large body of water that almost bisects the island through the middle. Captain Jim runs **Island Explorer Tours** (843/785-2100, www.dolphintourshil-tonhead.com, 2-hour tour $45 pp) from a dock behind the old Oyster Factory on Marshland Road. Not to be outdone, Captain Dave leads tours at **Dolphin Discoveries** (843/681-1911, 2-hour tour $40 adults, $30 under age 13), leaving out of Simmons Landing next to the Broad Creek Marina on Marshland Road. **Outside Hilton Head** (843/686-6996, www.outsidehiltonhead.com) runs a variety of water ecotours and dolphin tours as well as a guided day-trip excursion to Daufuskie, complete with golf cart rental.

There is a notable land-based tour by **Gullah Heritage Trail Tours** (leaves from Coastal

Discovery Museum at Honey Horn, 843/681-7066, www.gullahheritage.com, $32 adults, $15 children) delving into the island's rich, if poorly preserved, African American history, from slavery through the time of the freedmen.

ENTERTAINMENT AND EVENTS
Nightlife

The best-quality live entertainment on the island is at **The Jazz Corner** (1000 William Hilton Pkwy., 843/842-8620, www.thejazzcorner.com, dinner daily 6pm-9pm, late-night menu daily after 9pm), which brings in the best names in the country—and outstanding regulars like Bob Masteller and Howard Paul—to perform in this space in the unlikely setting of a boutique mall, the Village at Wexford. The dinners are actually quite good, but the attraction is definitely the music. Reservations are recommended. Live music starts daily around 7pm.

For years islanders have jokingly referred to the "Barmuda Triangle," an area named for the preponderance of bars within walking distance of Sea Pines Circle. While some of the names have changed over the years, the longtime anchor of the Barmuda Triangle is the **Tiki Hut** (1 S. Forest Beach Dr., 843/785-5126, Sun.-Thurs. 11am-8pm, Fri.-Sat. 11am-10pm, bar until 2am), actually part of the Holiday Inn Oceanfront Hotel at the entrance to Sea Pines. This popular watering hole is the only beachfront bar on the island, which technically makes it the only place you can legally drink alcohol on a Hilton Head beach. Another Barmuda Triangle staple is **Hilton Head Brewing Company** (7 Greenwood Dr., 843/785-3900, daily 11am-2am), the only brewpub on the island and indeed South Carolina's first microbrewery since Prohibition. It offers a wide range of handcrafted brews, from a Blueberry Wheat to a Mocha Porter. Another longtime Triangle fave is **The Lodge** (7 Greenwood Dr., 843/842-8966, www.hiltonheadlodge.com, daily 11:30am-midnight). After the martini and cigar craze waned, this popular spot successfully remade itself into a beer-centric place

with 36 rotating taps. They still mix a mean martini, though. Also nearby is **Murphy's Irish Pub** (81 Pope Ave., 843/842-3448, Mon. 5pm-10pm, Tues.-Thurs. 3pm-midnight, Fri.-Sat. noon-4am, Sun. 11am-10pm), where the name pretty much says it all (unlike most pubs with made-up Irish names, this one's actually run by a guy named Murphy). There is great bangers and mash in this frequent rugby players' hangout.

Despite its location in the upscale strip mall of the Village at Wexford, the **British Open Pub** (1000 William Hilton Pkwy./Hwy. 278, 843/686-6736, daily 11am-10pm) offers a fairly convincing English vibe with, as the name suggests, a heavy golf theme. The fish-and-chips and shepherd's pie are both magnificent.

Inside Sea Pines is the **Quarterdeck Lounge and Patio** (843/842-1999, www.seapines.com, Sun.-Thurs. 5:30pm-10pm, Fri.-Sat. 5:30pm-midnight) at the base of the Harbour Town Lighthouse. This is where the party's at after a long day on the fairways during the Heritage golf tournament. Within Sea Pines at the South Beach marina is also where you'll find **The Salty Dog Cafe** (232 S. Sea Pines Dr., 843/671-2233, www.saltydog.com, lunch daily 11am-3pm, dinner daily 5pm-10pm, bar daily until 2am), one of the area's most popular institutions (some might even call it a tourist trap) and something akin to an island empire, with popular T-shirts, a gift shop, books, and an ice cream shop, all overlooking the marina. My suggestion, however, is to make the short walk to the affiliated **Wreck of the Salty Dog** (843/671-7327, daily until 2am) where the marsh views are better and the atmosphere not quite so tacky.

There's only one bona fide gay club on Hilton Head, **Vibe** (32 Palmetto Bay Rd., 843/341-6933, www.vibehhi.com, Mon.-Fri. 8pm-3am, Sat. 8pm-2am). Wednesday is karaoke night, and Thursday brings an amateur drag revue.

Performing Arts

Because so many residents migrated here from art-savvy metropolitan areas in the Northeast,

Hilton Head maintains a very high standard of top-quality entertainment. Much of the activity centers on the multimillion-dollar **Arts Center of Coastal Carolina** (14 Shelter Cove Lane, 843/842-2787, www.artshhi.com), which hosts touring shows, resident companies, musical concerts, dance performances, and visual arts exhibits.

Now over a quarter-century old and under the direction of maestro John Morris Russell, the **Hilton Head Symphony Orchestra** (843/842-2055, www.hhso.org) performs a year-round season of masterworks and pops programs at various venues, primarily the First Presbyterian Church (540 William Hilton Pkwy./Hwy. 278). They also take their show on the road with several concerts in Bluffton and even perform several "Symphony Under the Stars" programs at Shelter Cove. **Chamber Music Hilton Head** (www.cmhh.org) performs throughout the year with selections ranging from Brahms to Smetana at All Saints Episcopal Church (3001 Meeting St.).

Cinema

There's an art house on Hilton Head, the charming **Coligny Theatre** (843/686-3500, www.colignytheatre.com) in the Coligny Plaza shopping center before you get to Sea Pines. For years this was the only movie theater for miles around, but it has reincarnated as a primarily indie film venue. Look for the entertaining murals by local artist Ralph Sutton. Showtimes are Monday 11:30am and 4pm, Tuesday and Friday 11:30am, 4pm, and 7pm, Wednesday-Thursday and Saturday-Sunday 4pm and 7pm.

Festivals and Events

Late February-early March brings the **Hilton Head Wine and Food Festival** (www.hilton-headhospitality.org), culminating in what they call "The East Coast's Largest Outdoor Public Tasting and Auction," which is generally held at the Coastal Discovery Museum at Honey Horn. Some events charge admission.

Hilton Head's premier event is the **RBC Heritage Classic Golf Tournament**

(843/671-2248, http://theheritagegolfsc.com), held each April (usually the week after the Master's) at the Harbour Town Golf Links on Sea Pines Plantation. Formerly known as the Verizon Heritage Classic, the event is South Carolina's only PGA Tour event and brings thousands of visitors to town yearly.

A fun and fondly anticipated yearly event is the **Kiwanis Club Chili Cookoff** (www.hilton-headkiwanis.org), held each October at Honey Horn on the south end. A low admission price gets you all the chili you can eat plus free antacids. All funds go to charity, and all excess chili goes to a local food bank.

Every November brings Hilton Head's second-largest event, the **Hilton Head Concours d'Elegance & Motoring Festival** (www.hhi-concours.com), a multiday event bringing together vintage car clubs from throughout the nation and culminating in a prestigious "Best of Show" competition. It started as a fund-raiser for the Hilton Head Symphony, but now people come from all over the country to see these fine vintage cars in a beautiful setting.

SHOPPING

As you'd expect, Hilton Head is a shopper's delight, with an emphasis on upscale stores and prices to match. Keep in mind that hours may be shortened in the off-season (Nov.-Mar.). Here's a rundown of the main island shopping areas in the order you'll encounter them as you enter the island.

Shelter Cove

As of this writing, the Mall at Shelter Cove is being completely repurposed, with plans for boutique retail centered around a Belk anchor store. The other two shopping entities at this shopping area on Broad Creek right off the William Hilton Parkway are the **Plaza at Shelter Cove** and the dockside **Shelter Cove Harbour.** The most interesting store at the Plaza is the flagship location of **Outside Hilton Head** (843/686-6996, www.outsidehiltonhead.com, Mon.-Sat. 10am-5:30pm, Sun. 11am-5:30pm), a complete outdoor outfitter with a thoroughly knowledgeable staff. Whatever outdoor gear you need and whatever tour you want to take, they can most likely hook you up. Shelter Cove Harbour hosts a few cute shops hewing to its overall nautical-vacation theme, such as the clothing stores **Camp Hilton Head** (843/842-3666, Mon.-Sat. 10am-9pm, Sun. noon-5pm) and the marine supplier **Ship's Store** (843/842-7001, Mon.-Sat. 7:30am-5pm, Sun. 7:30am-4pm).

Village at Wexford

Easily my favorite place to shop on Hilton Head, this well-shaded shopping center on William Hilton Parkway (Hwy. 278) hosts plenty of well-tended shops, including the foodie equipment store **Le Cookery** (843/785-7171, Mon.-Sat. 10am-6pm), the Lily Pulitzer signature women's store **S. M. Bradford Co.** (843/686-6161, Mon.-Sat. 10am-6pm) and the aromatic **Scents of Hilton Head** (843/842-7866, Mon.-Fri. 10am-6pm, Sat. 10am-5pm).

My favorite shop on all Hilton Head is at Wexford, **The Oilerie** (843/681-2722, www.oilerie.com, Mon.-Sat. 10am-7pm, Sun. noon-5pm). This franchise provides free samples of all its high-quality Italian olive oils and vinegars. After you taste around awhile, you pick what you want and the friendly staff bottles it for you in souvenir-quality glassware. They also have a selection of spices, soaps, and other goodies.

Coligny Circle

This is the closest Hilton Head comes to funkier beach towns like Tybee Island or Folly Beach, although it doesn't really come that close. You'll find dozens of delightful and somewhat quirky stores here, many keeping long hours in the summer, like the self-explanatory **Coligny Kite & Flag Co.** (843/785-5483, Mon.-Sat. 10am-9pm, Sun. 11am-6pm), the hippie-fashion **Loose Lucy's** (843/785-8093, Mon.-Sat. 10am-6pm, Sun. 11am-5pm), and the Caribbean-flavored **Jamaican Me Crazy** (843/785-9006, daily 10am-10pm). Kids will love both **The Shell Shop** (843/785-4900, Mon.-Sat. 10am-9pm, Sun. noon-9pm) and

Black Market Minerals (843/785-7090, Mon.-Sat. 10am-10pm, Sun. 11am-8pm).

Harbour Town

The Shoppes at Harbour Town (www.seapines.com) are a collection of about 20 mostly boutique stores along Lighthouse Road in Sea Pines Plantation. At **Planet Hilton Head** (843/363-5177, www.planethiltonhead.com, daily 10am-9pm) you'll find some cute, eclectic gifts and home goods. Other clothing highlights include **Knickers Men's Store** (843/671-2291, daily 10am-9pm) and **Radiance** (843/363-5176, Mon.-Tue. 10am-5pm, Wed.-Sat. 10am-9pm, Sun. 11am-9pm), a very cute and fashion-forward women's store.

The **Top of the Lighthouse Shoppe** (843/671-2810, www.harbourtownlighthouse.com, daily 10am-9pm) is where many a climbing visitor has been coaxed to part with some of their disposable income. And, of course, as you'd expect being near the legendary Harbour Town links, there's the **Harbour Town Pro Shop** (843/671-4485), routinely voted one of the best pro shops in the nation.

South Beach Marina

On South Sea Pines Drive at the Marina you'll find several worthwhile shops, including a good ship's store and all-around grocery dealer **South Beach General Store** (843/671-6784, daily 8am-10pm). I like to stop in the **Blue Water Bait and Tackle** (843/671-3060, daily 7am-8pm) and check out the cool nautical stuff. They can also hook you up with a variety of kayak trips and fishing charters. And, of course, right on the water there's the ever-popular **Salty Dog Cafe** (843/671-2233, www.saltydog.com, lunch daily 11am-3pm, dinner daily 5pm-10pm), whose ubiquitous T-shirts seem to adorn every other person on the island.

Art Galleries

Despite the abundant wealth apparent in some quarters here, there's no freestanding art museum in the area, that role being filled by independent galleries. A good representative example is **Morris & Whiteside Galleries**

HILTON HEAD

(220 Cordillo Pkwy., 843/842-4433, www. morris-whiteside.com, Mon.-Fri. 9am-5pm, Sat. 10am-4pm), located in the historic Red Piano Art Gallery building, which features a variety of paintings and sculpture, heavy on landscapes but also showing some fine figurative work. The nonprofit **Art League of Hilton Head** (14 Shelter Cove Lane, 843/681-5060, Mon.-Sat. 10am-6pm) is located in the Walter Greer Art Gallery within the Arts Center of Coastal Carolina and displays work by member artists in all media. The **Nash Gallery** (13 Harbourside Lane, 843/785-6424, Mon.-Fri. 10am-9pm, Sat. 10am-8pm, Sun. 11am-5pm) in Shelter Cove Harbour deals more in North American craft styles. Hilton Head art isn't exactly known for its avant-garde nature, but you can find some whimsical stuff at **Picture This** (78D Arrow Rd., 843/842-5299, Mon.-Fri. 9:30am-5:30pm, Sat. 9:30am-12:30pm), including a selection of Gullah craft items. A wide range of regional painters, sculptors, and glass artists is featured at **Endangered Arts** (841 William Hilton Pkwy., 843/785-5075, www.endangeredarts.com).

SPORTS AND RECREATION
Beaches
First, the good news: Hilton Head Island has 12 miles of some of the most beautiful, safe beaches you'll find anywhere. The bad news is that there are only a few ways to gain access, generally at locations referred to as "beach parks." Don't just drive into a residential neighborhood and think you'll be able to park and find your way to the beach; for better or worse, Hilton Head is not set up for that kind of casual access.

Driessen Beach Park has 207 long-term parking spaces, costing $0.25 for 30 minutes. There's free parking but fewer spaces at the Coligny Beach Park entrance and at Fish Haul Creek Park. Also, there are 22 metered spaces at Alder Lane Beach Access, 51 at Folly Field Beach Park, and 13 at Burkes Beach Road. Most other beach parks are for permit parking only. Clean, well-maintained public restrooms are available at all the beach parks. You can find

beach information at 843/342-4580 and www. hiltonheadislandsc.gov. Beach Park hours vary: Coligny Beach Park is open daily 24 hours; all other beach parks are open March-September daily 6am-8pm and October-February daily 6am-5pm.

Alcohol is strictly prohibited on Hilton Head's beaches. There are lifeguards on all the beaches during the summer, but be aware that the worst undertow is on the northern stretches. Also remember to leave the sand dollars where they are; their population is dwindling due to souvenir hunting.

Kayaking
Kayakers will enjoy Hilton Head Island, which offers several gorgeous routes, including Calibogue Sound to the south and west and Port Royal Sound to the north. For particularly good views of life on the salt marsh, try Broad Creek, which nearly bisects Hilton Head Island, and Skull Creek, which separates Hilton Head from the natural beauty of Pinckney Island. Broad Creek Marina is a good place to put in. There are also two public landings, Haigh Landing and Buckingham Landing, on Mackay Creek at the entrance to the island, one on either side of the bridge.

If you want a guided tour, there are plenty of great kayak tour outfits to choose from in the area. Chief among them is certainly **Outside Hilton Head** (32 Shelter Cove Lane, 800/686-6996, www.outsidehiltonhead.com). They offer a wide range of guided trips, including "The Outback," in which you're first boated to a private island and then taken on a tour of tidal creeks, and five- or seven-hour "Ultimate Lowcountry Day" trips to Daufuskie, Bluffton, or Bull Creek. Other good places to book a tour or just rent a kayak are **Water-Dog Outfitters** (Broad Creek Marina, 843/686-3554) and **Kayak Hilton Head** (Broad Creek Marina, 843/684-1910). Leaving out of the Harbour Town Yacht Basin is **H2O Sports** (843/671-4386, www.h2osportsonline.com), which offers 90-minute guided kayak tours ($30) and rents kayaks for about $20 per hour. Within Palmetto Dunes Oceanfront Resort (4 Queens

Folly Rd., 800/827-3006, www.palmettodunes. com) is **Palmetto Dunes Outfitters** (843/785-2449, www.pdoutfitters.com, daily 9am-5pm), which rents kayaks and canoes and offers lessons on the resort's 11-mile lagoon.

Fishing and Boating

As you'd expect, anglers and boaters love the Hilton Head-Bluffton area, which offers all kinds of saltwater, freshwater, and fly-fishing opportunities. Captain Brian Vaughn runs **Off the Hook Charters** (68 Helmsman Way, 843/298-4376, www.offthehookcharters.com), which offers fully licensed half-day trips ($400). **Miss Carolina Sportfishing** (168 Palmetto Bay Rd., 843/298-2628, www.misscarolinafishing. com) offers deep-sea action at a little over $100 per hour. Captain Dave Fleming of **Mighty Mako Sport Fishing Charters** (164 Palmetto Bay Rd., 843/785-6028, www.mightymako. com) can take you saltwater fishing, both backwater and near-shore, on the 25-foot *Mighty Mako* for about $400 for a half-day. If you're at the South Beach Marina area of Sea Pines Plantation, head into **Blue Water Bait and Tackle** (843/671-3060) and see if they can hook you up with a trip.

Public landings in the Hilton Head area include the Marshland Road Boat Landing and the Broad Creek Boat Ramp under the Charles Fraser Bridge, and the Haigh Landing on Mackay Creek.

Hiking and Biking

Although the very flat terrain is not challenging, Hilton Head provides some scenic and relaxing cycling opportunities. Thanks to wise planning and foresight, the island has an extensive award-winning 50-mile network of biking trails that does a great job of keeping cyclists out of traffic. A big plus is the long bike path paralleling the William Hilton Parkway, enabling cyclists to use that key artery without braving its traffic. There is even an underground bike path beneath the Parkway to facilitate crossing that busy road. In addition, there are also routes along Pope Avenue as well as North and South Forest Beach Drive. Go to

www.hiltonheadisland.org/biking to download a map of the entire island bike path network.

Palmetto Dunes Oceanfront Resort (4 Queens Folly Rd., 800/827-3006, www.palmettodunes.com) has a particularly nice 25-mile network of bike paths that all link up to the island's larger framework. Within the resort is **Palmetto Dunes Outfitters** (843/785-2449, www.pdoutfitters.com, daily 9am-5pm), which will rent you any type of bike you might need. Sea Pines Plantation also has an extensive 17-mile network of bike trails; you can pick up a map at most information kiosks within the plantation.

But the best bike path on Hilton Head is the simplest of all, where no one will ask you where you're staying that night: the beach. For a few hours before and after low tide, the beach effectively becomes a 12-mile bike path around most of the island, and a pleasant morning or afternoon ride may well prove to be the highlight of your trip.

There's a plethora of bike rental facilities on Hilton Head with competitive rates. Be sure to ask if they offer free pickup and delivery. Try **Hilton Head Bicycle Company** (112 Arrow Rd., 843/686-6888, daily 9am-5pm, $16/day).

Hikers will particularly enjoy Pinckney Island National Wildlife Refuge, which takes you through several key Lowcountry ecosystems, from maritime forest to salt marsh. Other peaceful, if nonchallenging, trails are at the Audubon-Newhall Preserve.

Horseback Riding

Within the Sea Pines Forest Preserve is **Lawton Stables** (190 Greenwood Dr., 843/671-2586, www.lawtonstableshhi.com), which features pony rides, a small animal farm, and guided horseback rides through the preserve. You don't need any riding experience, but you do need reservations.

Bird-Watching

The premier birding locale in the area is the **Pinckney Island National Wildlife Refuge** (U.S. 278 east, just before Hilton Head, 912/652-4415, www.fws.gov, free). You can see bald eagles, ibis, wood storks, painted buntings, and many more species. Birding is best in spring and fall. The refuge has several freshwater ponds that serve as wading bird rookeries. During migratory season, so many beautiful birds make such a ruckus that you'll think you've wandered onto an Animal Planet shoot.

Golf

Hilton Head is one of the world's great golf centers, with no less than 23 courses, and one could easily write a book about nothing but that. This, however, is not that book. Perhaps contrary to what you might expect, most courses on the island are public, and some are downright affordable. All courses are 18 holes unless otherwise described; greens fees are averages and vary with season and tee time.

The best-regarded course, with prices to match, is **Harbour Town Golf Links** (Sea Pines Plantation, 843/363-4485, www.seapines.com, $239). It's on the island's south end at Sea Pines and is the home of the annual RBC Heritage Classic, far and away the island's number-one tourist draw.

There are two Arthur Hills-designed courses on the island, **Arthur Hills at Palmetto Dunes Resort** (843/785-1140, www.palmettodunes.com, $125) and **Arthur Hills at Palmetto Hall** (Palmetto Hall Plantation, 843/689-4100, www.palmettohallgolf.com, $130), both of which now offer the use of Segway vehicles on the fairways. The reasonably priced **Barony Course** at Port Royal Plantation (843/686-8801, www.portroyalgolfclub.com, $98) also boasts some of the toughest greens on the island. Another challenging and affordable course is the **George Fazio** at Palmetto Dunes Resort (843/785-1130, www.palmettodunes.com, $105).

Hilton Head National Golf Club (60 Hilton Head National Dr., 843/842-5900, www.golf-hiltonheadnational.com), which is actually on the mainland just before you cross the bridge to Hilton Head, is still highly rated for both condition and service, despite recently losing nine holes to a road-widening project. *Golf Week* has named it one of the country's best golf courses.

The 18-hole course is public and greens fees are below $100.

It's a good idea to book tee times through the **Golf Island Call Center** (888/465-3475, www.golfisland.com), which can also hook you up with good packages.

Tennis

One of the top tennis destinations in the country, Hilton Head has over 20 tennis clubs, some of which offer court time to the public (walk-on rates vary; call for information). They are: **Palmetto Dunes Tennis Center** (Palmetto Dunes Resort, 843/785-1152, www.palmetto-dunes.com, $30 per hour), **Port Royal Racquet Club** (Port Royal Plantation, 843/686-8803, www.portroyalgolfclub.com, $25 per hour), **Sea Pines Racquet Club** (Sea Pines Plantation, 843/363-4495, www.seapines.com, $25 per hour), **South Beach Racquet Club** (Sea Pines Plantation, 843/671-2215, www.seapines.com, $25 per hour), and **Shipyard Racquet Club** (Shipyard Plantation, 843/686-8804, $25 per hour).

Free first-come, first-served play is available at the following public courts, maintained by the Island Recreation Association (www.islandreccenter.org): **Chaplin Community Park** (Singleton Beach Rd., 4 courts, lighted), **Cordillo Courts** (Cordillo Pkwy., 4 courts, lighted), **Fairfield Square** (Adrianna Lane, 2 courts), **Hilton Head High School** (School Rd., 6 courts), and **Hilton Head Middle School** (Wilborn Rd., 4 courts).

ACCOMMODATIONS

Generally speaking, accommodations on Hilton Head are often surprisingly affordable given their overall high quality and the breadth of their amenities.

Under $150

You can't beat the price at **Park Lane Hotel and Suites** (12 Park Lane, 843/686-5700, www.hiltonheadparklanehotel.com, $130). This is your basic suite-type hotel (formerly a Residence Inn) with kitchens, laundry, a pool, and a tennis court. The allure here is the price, hard to find anywhere these days at a resort location. For a nonrefundable fee, you can bring your pet. The one drawback is that the beach is a good distance away. The hotel does offer a free shuttle, however, so it would be wise to take advantage of that and avoid the usual beach parking hassles. As you'd expect given the price, rooms here tend to go quickly; reserve early.

$150-300

By Hilton Head standards, the ▌**Main Street Inn & Spa** (2200 Main St., 800/471-3001, www.mainstreetinn.com, $160-210) can be considered a bargain stay, and with high quality to boot. With its Old World touches, sumptuous appointments, charming atmosphere, and attentive service, this 33-room inn and attached spa on the grounds of Hilton Head Plantation seem like they would be more at home in Charleston than Hilton Head. The inn serves a great full breakfast—not continental—daily 7:30am-10:30am.

Another good place for the price is the **South Beach Marina Inn** (232 S. Sea Pines Dr., 843/671-6498, www.sbinn.com, $186) in Sea Pines. Located near the famous Salty Dog Cafe and outfitted in a similar nautical theme, the inn not only has some pretty large guest rooms for the price, it offers a great view of the marina and has a very friendly feel. As with all Sea Pines accommodations, staying on the plantation means you don't have to wait in line with other visitors to pay the $5-per-day "road fee." Sea Pines also offers a free trolley to get around the plantation.

One of Hilton Head's favorite hotels for beach lovers is the **Holiday Inn Oceanfront** (1 S. Forest Beach Dr., 843/785-5126, www.hihiltonhead.com, $200), home of the famed Tiki Hut bar on the beach. Staff turnover is less frequent here than at other local accommodations, and while it's no Ritz-Carlton and occasionally shows signs of wear, it's a good value on a bustling area of the island.

One of the better resort-type places for those who prefer the putter and the racquet to the Frisbee and the surfboard is the **Inn at Harbour Town** (7 Lighthouse Lane, 843/363-8100,

www.seapines.com, $199) in Sea Pines. The big draw here is the impeccable service, delivered by a staff of "butlers" in kilts, mostly Europeans who take the venerable trade quite seriously. While it's not on the beach, you can take advantage of the free Sea Pines Trolley every 20 minutes.

Recently rated the number-one family resort in the United States by *Travel + Leisure*, the well-run ▌**Palmetto Dunes Oceanfront Resort** (4 Queens Folly Rd., 800/827-3006, www.palmettodunes.com, $150-300) offers something for everybody in terms of lodging. There are small, cozy condos by the beach or larger villas overlooking the golf course and pretty much everything in between. The prices are perhaps disarmingly affordable considering the relative luxury and copious recreational amenities, which include 25 miles of very well-done bike trails, 11 miles of kayak and canoe trails, and, of course, three sets of signature links. As with most developments of this type on Hilton Head, most of the condos are privately owned, and therefore each has its particular set of guidelines and cleaning schedules.

A little farther down the island you'll find the **Sonesta Resort Hilton Head Island** (130 Shipyard Dr., 843/842-2400, www.sonesta.com/hiltonheadisland, $160-200), which styles itself as Hilton Head's only green-certified accommodations. The guest rooms are indeed state-of-the-art, and the expansive shaded grounds near the beach are great for relaxation. No on-site golf here, but immediately adjacent is a well-regarded tennis facility with 20 courts.

Another good resort-style experience heavy on the golf is on the grounds of the Port Royal Plantation on the island's north side, **The Westin Resort Hilton Head Island** (2 Grasslawn Ave., 843/681-4000, www.westin.com/hiltonhead, from $200), which hosts three PGA-caliber links. The beach is also but a short walk away. This AAA four diamond-winning Westin offers a mix of suites and larger villas.

Vacation Rentals

Many visitors to Hilton Head choose to rent a home or villa for an extended stay, and there is no scarcity of availability. Try **Resort Rentals of Hilton Head** (www.hhivacations.com) or **Destination Vacation** (www.destinationvacationhhi.com).

FOOD

Because of the cosmopolitan nature of the population, with so many transplants from the northeastern United States and Europe, there is uniformly high quality in Hilton Head restaurants. And because of another demographic quirk of the area, its large percentage of senior citizens, you can also find some great deals by looking for some of the common "early bird" dinner specials, usually starting around 5pm.

Breakfast and Brunch

There are a couple of great diner-style places on the island. Though known more for its hamburgers and Philly cheesesteaks, **Harold's Diner** (641 William Hilton Pkwy., 843/842-9292, Mon.-Sat. 7am-3pm, $4-6) has great pancakes as well as its trademark brand of sarcastic service. Unpretentious and authentic in a place where those two adjectives are rarely used, it has been said of Harold's that "the lack of atmosphere *is* the atmosphere." The place is small, popular, and reservations are not taken.

If you need a bite in the Coligny Plaza area, go to **Skillets** (1 N. Forest Beach Dr., 843/785-3131, www.skilletscafe.com, breakfast daily 7am-5pm, dinner daily 5pm-9pm, $5-23) in Coligny Plaza. Their eponymous stock-in-trade is a layered breakfast dish of sautéed ingredients served in a porcelain skillet, like the "Kitchen Sink" (pancakes ringed with potatoes, sausage, and bacon, topped with two poached eggs).

A great all-day breakfast place with a twist is **Signe's Heaven Bound Bakery & Café** (93 Arrow Rd., 843/785-9118, www.signesbakery. com, Mon.-Fri. 8am-4pm, Sat. 9am-2pm, $5-10). Breakfast is tasty dishes like frittatas and breakfast polenta, while the twist is the extensive artisanal bakery, with delicious specialties like the signature key lime pound cake. You'll be surprised at the quality of the food for the low prices. Expect a wait during peak periods.

A fairly well-kept local secret is the **French Bakery and Courtyard Cafe** (430 William Hilton Pkwy./U.S. 278, 843/342-5420, www.frenchbakeryhiltonhead.com, Mon.-Sat. 8:30am-4pm, $5). Set inside the Pineland Station shopping center and with nice open-air seating, French Bakery offers a full range of fresh-baked goods like quiches, croissants, paninis, artisanal breads, cakes, and gourmet pastries.

German

I'm pretty sure you didn't come all the way to South Carolina to eat traditional German food, but while you're here...check out **Alfred's** (807 William Hilton Pkwy./Hwy. 278, 843/341-3117, www.alfredsofhiltonhead. com, $20-30), one of the more unique spots on Hilton Head and a big favorite with the locals. Expect a wait. Bratwurst, veal cordon bleu, and of course wiener schnitzel are all standouts. I recommend the German Mix Platter ($25), which features a brat, some sauerbraten, and a schnitzel.

Mediterranean

For upscale Italian, try **Bistro Mezzaluna** (55 New Orleans Rd., 843/842-5011, daily 5pm-9:30pm, $15-30). Known far and wide for its osso buco as well as its impeccable service, there's also a great little bar for cocktails before or after dinner.

Mexican

There are a couple of excellent and authentic Mexican restaurants on the island. Just off the William Hilton Parkway near the island's entrance is **Mi Tierra** (160 Fairfield Square, 843/342-3409, lunch daily 11am-4pm, dinner Mon.-Fri. 4pm-9pm, Sat.-Sun. 4pm-10pm, $3-15). You'll find lots of traditional seafood dishes, like seviche, octopus, shrimp, and oysters. On Monday there is often a real mariachi band.

Middle Eastern

Hard to describe but well worth the visit, **Daniel's Restaurant and Lounge** (2 N. Forest Beach Dr., 843/341-9379, http://

danielshhi.com, daily 4pm-2am, tapas $10-12) combines elements of a traditional Middle Eastern eatery, an upscale tapas place, a beach spot, and a swank bar scene to create one of the more memorable food-and-beverage experiences on the island. Add in the fact that the prices are actually quite accessible and you've got a must-visit. Their "big small plates," meaning larger-portion tapas, run about $10-12 per plate. While they market their Middle Eastern flavor with plates like the cinnamon lamb kebab, their tapas have a cosmopolitan feel and range from a Caribbean salmon steak to chicken pesto sliders.

Seafood

Not to be confused with Charley's Crab House next door to Hudson's, seafood lovers will enjoy the experience down near Sea Pines at (**Charlie's L'Etoile Verte** (8 New Orleans Rd., 843/785-9277, http://charliesgreenstar. com, lunch Tues.-Sat. 11:30am-2pm, dinner Mon.-Sat. 5:30pm-10pm, $25-40), which is considered by many connoisseurs to be Hilton Head's single best restaurant. The emphasis here is on "French country kitchen" cuisine—think Provence, not Paris. In keeping, each day's menu is concocted from scratch and handwritten. Listen to these recent entrées and feel your mouth water: flounder sauté meunière, grilled wild coho salmon with basil pesto, and breast of duck in a raspberry demi-glace. Get the picture? Of course, you'll want to start with the escargot and leeks vol-au-vent, the house pâté, or even some pan-roasted Bluffton oysters. Reservations are essential.

A longtime Hilton Head favorite is **Red Fish** (8 Archer Rd., 843/686-3388, www. redfishofhiltonhead.com, lunch Mon.-Sat. 11:30am-2pm, dinner daily beginning with early-bird specials at 5pm, $20-37). Strongly Caribbean in decor as well as the menu, with romanticism and panache to match, this is a great place for couples. The creative but accessible menu by executive chef Sean Walsh incorporates unique spices, fruits, and vegetables for a fresh, zesty palette. Reservations are essential.

Fresh seafood lovers will enjoy one of Hilton Head's staples, the huge **Hudson's on the Docks** (1 Hudson Rd., 843/681-2772, www. hudsonsonthedocks.com, lunch daily 11am-4pm, dinner daily from 5pm, $14-23) on Skull Creek just off Squire Pope Road on the less-developed north side. Much of the catch—though not all of it, by any means—comes directly off the boats you'll see dockside. Try the stuffed shrimp filled with crabmeat. Leave room for one of the homemade desserts crafted by Ms. Bessie, a 30-year veteran employee of Hudson's.

INFORMATION AND SERVICES

The best place to get information on Hilton Head, book a room, or secure a tee time is just as you come onto the island at the **Hilton Head Island Chamber of Commerce Welcome Center** (100 William Hilton Pkwy., 843/785-3673, www.hiltonheadisland.org, daily 9am-6pm).

GETTING THERE AND AROUND

A few years back, the **Savannah International Airport** (SAV, 400 Airways Ave., Savannah, 912/964-0514, www.savannahairport.com) added Hilton Head to its name specifically to identify itself with that lucrative market. It has been a success, and this facility remains the closest large airport to Hilton Head Island and Bluffton. From the airport, go north on I-95 into South Carolina, and take exit 8 onto U.S. 278 east. There is a local regional airport as well, the **Hilton Head Island Airport** (HXD, 120 Beach City Rd., 843/689-5400, www. bcgov.net). While very attractive and convenient, keep in mind that it only hosts propeller-driven commuter planes because of the runway length and concerns about noise.

If you're entering the area by car, the best route is exit 8 off I-95 onto U.S. 278, which takes you by Bluffton and right into Hilton Head. Near Bluffton, U.S. 278 is called Fording Island Road, and on Hilton Head proper it becomes the William Hilton Parkway business route. Technically, U.S. 278 turns into the new Cross Island Parkway, but when most locals say "278" they're almost always referring to the William Hilton Parkway.

Other than taxi services, there is no public transportation to speak of in the Lowcountry, unless you want to count the free shuttle around Sea Pines Plantation. Taxi services include **Yellow Cab** (843/686-6666), **Island Taxi** (843/683-6363), and **Ferguson Transportation** (843/842-8088).

Bluffton and Daufuskie Island

Just outside Hilton Head are two of the Lowcountry's true gems, Bluffton and Daufuskie Island. While Bluffton's outskirts have been taken over by the same gated community and upscale strip-mall sprawl spreading throughout the coast, at its core is a delightfully charming little community on the quiet May River, now called Old Bluffton, where you'd swear you just entered a time warp.

Daufuskie Island still maintains much of its age-old isolated, timeless personality, and the island—still accessible only by boat—is still one of the spiritual centers of the Gullah culture and lifestyle.

◖ OLD BLUFFTON

Similar to Beaufort, but even quieter and smaller, historic Bluffton is an idyllic village on the banks of the serene and well-preserved May River. Bluffton was the original hotbed of secession, with Charleston diarist Mary Chesnut famously referring to the town as "the center spot of the fire eaters." While its outskirts (so-called "Greater Bluffton") are now a haven for planned communities hoping to mimic some aspect of Bluffton's historic patina, the town center itself remains an authentic look at old South Carolina. Retro cuts both ways, however, and Bluffton has been a notorious speed trap for generations. Always obey the speed limit. During their Civil War occupation, Union troops repaid the favor of those original Bluffton secessionists, which is why only nine homes in Bluffton are of antebellum vintage; the rest were torched in a search for Confederate guerrillas.

The center of tourist activity focuses on the **Old Bluffton Historic District,** several blocks of 1800s-vintage buildings clustered between the parallel Boundary and Calhoun Streets (old-timers sometimes call this "the original square mile"). Many of the buildings are private residences, but most have been converted into art studios and antiques stores.

Heyward House Historic Center

The **Heyward House Historic Center** (70 Boundary St., 843/757-6293, www.heyward-house.org, Mon.-Fri. 10am-5pm, Sat. 10am-4pm, tours $5 adults, $2 students) is not only open to tours but serves as Bluffton's visitors center. Built in 1840 as a summer home for the owner of Moreland Plantation, John Cole, the house was later owned by George Cuthbert Heyward, grandson of Declaration of Independence signer Thomas Heyward. (Remarkably, it stayed in the family until the 1990s.) Of note are the intact slave quarters on the grounds.

The Heyward House also sponsors walking tours of the historic district (843/757-6293, $15, by appointment only). Download your own walking-tour map at www.heywardhouse. org.

Church of the Cross

Don't fail to go all the way to the end of Calhoun Street, as it dead-ends on a high bluff on the May River at the Bluffton Public Dock. Overlooking this peaceful marsh-front vista is the photogenic **Church of the Cross** (110 Calhoun St., 843/757-2661, www.the-churchofthecross.net, free tours Mon.-Sat. 10am-2pm). The current sanctuary was built in 1854 and is one of only two local churches

HILTON HEAD

not burned in the Civil War, but the parish itself began in 1767, with the first services on this spot held in the late 1830s. While the church looks as if it were made of cypress, interestingly it's actually constructed of heart pine.

Bluffton Oyster Company

You might want to get a gander at the state's last remaining working oyster house, the **Bluffton Oyster Company** (63 Wharf St., 843/757-4010, www.blufftonoyster.com, Mon.-Sat. 9am-5:30pm), and possibly purchase some of their maritime bounty. Larry and Tina Toomer continue to oversee the oyster harvesting-and-shucking family enterprise, which has roots going back to the early 1900s.

SHOPPING

Bluffton's eccentric little art studios, most clustered in a two-block stretch on Calhoun Street, are by far its main shopping draw. Named for the Lowcountry phenomenon you find in the marsh at low tide among the fiddler crabs, Bluffton's **Pluff Mudd Art** (27 Calhoun St.,

843/757-5551, Mon.-Sat. 10am-5:30pm) is a cooperative of 16 great young painters and photographers from throughout the area. The **Guild of Bluffton Artists** (20 Calhoun St., 843/757-5590, Mon.-Sat. 10am-4:30pm) features works from many local artists, as does the outstanding **Society of Bluffton Artists** (48 Boundary St., 843/757-6586). For cool, custom handcrafted pottery, try **Preston Pottery and Gallery** (10 Church St., 843/757-3084). Another great Bluffton place is the hard-to-define **Eggs'n'tricities** (71 Calhoun St., 843/757-3446). The name pretty much says it all for this fun and eclectic vintage, junk, jewelry, and folk art store.

If you want to score some fresh local seafood for your own culinary adventure, the no-brainer choice is the **Bluffton Oyster Company** (63 Wharf St., 843/757-4010, Mon.-Sat. 9am-5:30pm), the state's only active oyster facility. They also have shrimp, crab, clams, and fish, nearly all of it from the nearly pristine May River on whose banks it sits.

For a much more commercially intense

Bluffton's Calhoun Street hosts many offbeat galleries.

© JIM MOREKIS

HILTON HEAD

experience, head just outside town on U.S. 278 on the way to Hilton Head to find the dual **Tanger Outlet Centers** (1414 Fording Island Rd., 843/837-4339, Mon.-Sat. 10am-9pm, Sun. 11am-6pm), an outlet-shopper's paradise with virtually every major brand represented.

SPORTS AND RECREATION

A key kayaking outfitter in Bluffton is **Native Guide Kayak Tours** (8 2nd St., 843/757-5411, www.nativeguidetours.com), which features tours of the May and New Rivers led by native Ben Turner. Another good outfit is **Swamp Girls Kayak Tours** (843/784-2249, www.swampgirls.com), the labor of love of Sue Chapman and Linda Etchells.

To put in your own kayak or canoe on the scenic, well-preserved May River, go to the **Alljoy Landing** at the eastern terminus of Alljoy Road along the river. Or try the dock at the end of Calhoun Street near the Church of the Holy Cross. There's also a rough put-in area at the Bluffton Oyster Company (63 Wharf St.), which has a public park adjacent to it. For fishing, public landings include the dock on Calhoun Street, Alljoy Landing, and Bluffton Oyster Company.

The closest public golf courses to Bluffton are the Arnold Palmer-designed **Crescent Pointe Golf Club** (1 Crescent Pointe Dr., 888/292-7778, www.crescentpointegolf.com, $90) and the nine-hole **Old Carolina Golf Club** (89 Old Carolina Rd., 888/785-7274, www.oldcarolinagolf.com, $26), certainly one of the best golf deals in the region.

ACCOMMODATIONS
Under $150

A quality bargain stay right between Bluffton and Hilton Head is the **Holiday Inn Express Bluffton** (35 Bluffton Rd., 843/757-2002, www.ichotelsgroup.com, $120), on U.S. 278 as you make the run onto Hilton Head proper. It's not close to the beach or to Old Town Bluffton, so you'll definitely be using your car, but its central location will appeal to those who want to keep their options open.

Over $300

For an ultra-upscale spa and golf resort environment near Bluffton, the clear pick is the **Inn at Palmetto Bluff** (476 Mt. Pelia Rd., 843/706-6500, www.palmettobluffresort.com, $650-900) just across the May River. This Auberge property was picked recently as the number-two U.S. resort by *Condé Nast Traveler* magazine. Lodging is dispersed among a series of cottages and "village home" rentals. There are three top-flight dining options on the grounds: the fine dining **River House Restaurant** (843/706-6542, breakfast daily 7am-11am, lunch or "porch" menu daily 11am-10pm, dinner daily 6pm-10pm, $30-40); the **May River Grill** (Tues.-Sat. 11am-4pm, $9-13) at the golf clubhouse; and the casual **Buffalo's** (843/706-6630, Sun.-Tues. 11:30am-5pm, Wed.-Sat. 11:30am-9pm, $10-15).

FOOD
Breakfast and Brunch

No discussion of Bluffton cuisine is complete without the famous **Squat 'n' Gobble** (1231 May River Rd., 843/757-4242, daily 24 hours), a local phenomenon not to be confused with a similarly named chain of eateries in California. Long a site of gossiping and politicking as well as, um, squatting and gobbling, this humble diner on the May River Road is an indelible part of the local consciousness. They specialize in the usual "American" menu of eggs, bacon, hamburgers, hot dogs, and fries.

French

Most dining in Bluffton is pretty casual, but you'll get the white-tablecloth treatment at **Claude & Uli's Signature Bistro** (1533 Fording Island Rd., 843/837-3336, lunch Mon.-Fri. 11:30am-2:30pm, dinner Mon.-Sat. from 5pm, $18-25) just outside of town in Moss Village. Chef Claude does a great veal cordon bleu as well as a number of fine seafood entrées, such as an almond-crusted tilapia and an excellent seafood pasta. Don't miss their specialty soufflé for dessert, which you should order with dinner as it takes almost half an hour to bake.

WHO ARE THE GULLAH?

A language, a culture, and a people with a shared history, Gullah is more than that—it's also a state of mind. Simply put, the Gullah are African Americans of the Sea Islands of South Carolina and Georgia. (In Georgia, the term *Geechee*, from the nearby Ogeechee River, is more or less interchangeable.) Protected from outside influence by the isolation of this coastal region after the Civil War, Gullah culture is the closest living cousin to the West African traditions of their ancestors imported as slaves.

While you might hear that *Gullah* is a corruption of "Angola," some linguists think it simply means "people" in a West African language. In any case, the Gullah speak what is known as a creole language, meaning one derived from several sources. Gullah combines elements of Elizabethan English, Jamaican patois, and several West African dialects; for example *goober* (peanut) comes from *n'guba* in the Kongo language. Another creole element is a word with multiple uses, for example Gullah's *shum* could mean "see them," "see him," "see her," or "see it" in either past or present tense, depending on context. Several white writers in the 1900s published collections of Gullah folk tales, but for the most part the Gullah tongue was simply considered broken English. That changed with the publication of Lorenzo Dow Turner's groundbreaking *Africanisms in the Gullah Dialect* in 1949. Turner traced elements of the language to Sierra Leone in West Africa and more than 300 Gullah words directly to Africa.

Gullah is typically spoken very rapidly, which of course only adds to its impenetrability to the outsider. Gullah also relies on colorful turns of phrase. *"E tru mout"* ("He true

mouth") means the speaker is referring to someone who doesn't lie. *"Ie een crack muh teet"* ("I didn't even crack my teeth") means "I kept quiet." A forgetful Gullah speaker might say, *"Mah head leab me"* ("My head left me").

Gullah music, as practiced by the world-famous Hallelujah Singers of St. Helena Island, also uses many distinctly African techniques, such as call and response (the folk hymn "Michael Row the Boat Ashore" is a good example). The most famous Americans with Gullah roots are boxer Joe Frazier (Beaufort), hip-hop star Jazzy Jay (Beaufort), NFL great Jim Brown (St. Simons Island, Georgia), and Supreme Court Justice Clarence Thomas (Pin Point, Georgia, near Savannah).

Upscale development continues to claim more and more traditional Gullah areas, generally by pricing them out through rapidly increasing property values. Today, the major pockets of living Gullah culture in South Carolina are in Beaufort, St. Helena Island, Daufuskie Island, Edisto Island, and a northern section of Hilton Head Island.

The old ways are not as prevalent as they were, but several key institutions are keeping alive the spirit of Gullah: the **Penn Center** (16 Martin Luther King Dr., St. Helena, 843/838-2474, www.penncenter.com, Mon.-Sat. 11am-4pm, $4 adults, $2 seniors and children) on St. Helena Island near Beaufort; the **Avery Research Center** (66 George St., Charleston, 843/953-7609, www.cofc.edu/avery, Mon.-Fri. 10am-5pm, Sat. noon-5pm) at the College of Charleston; and **Geechee Kunda** (622 Ways Temple Rd., Riceboro, Georgia, 912/884-4440, www.geecheekunda.com) near Midway off U.S. 17.

Mexican

My favorite restaurant in Bluffton by far is a near-copy of an equally fine Mexican restaurant in Hilton Head, ℂ **Mi Tierra** (101 Mellichamp Center, 843/757-7200, lunch daily 11am-4pm, dinner Mon.-Fri. 4pm-9pm, Sat.-Sun. 4pm-10pm, $3-15). They have very high-quality Tex-Mex-style food in a fun atmosphere at great

prices. Another highly regarded Mexican place in Bluffton is **Amigo's Café Y Cantina** (133 Towne Dr., 843/815-8226, Mon.-Sat. 11am-9pm, $8).

DAUFUSKIE ISLAND

Sitting between Savannah and Hilton Head Island and accessible only by water, Daufuskie

HILTON HEAD

Island has about 500 full-time residents, most of whom ride around on golf carts or bikes (there's only one paved road, Haig Point Road, and cars are a rare sight). Once the home of rice and indigo plantations and rich oyster beds—the latter destroyed by pollution and overharvesting—the two upscale residential resort communities on the island, begun in the 1980s, give a clue as to where the future lies, although the recent global economic downturn slowed development to a standstill.

The area of prime interest to visitors is the unincorporated western portion, or **Historic District,** the old stomping grounds of Pat Conroy during his stint as a teacher of resident African American children. His old two-room schoolhouse of *The Water Is Wide* fame, the **Mary Field School,** is still here, as is the adjacent 140-year-old **Union Baptist Church,** but Daufuskie students now have a surprisingly modern new facility (middle school students are still ferried to mainland schools every day). Farther north on Haig Point Road is the new **Billie Burn Museum,** housed in the old Mt. Carmel Church and named after the island's resident historian. On the southern end you'll find the **Bloody Point Lighthouse,** named for the vicious battle fought nearby during the Yamasee War of 1815 (the light was actually moved a 0.5 miles inland in the early 1900s). Other areas of interest throughout the island include Native American sites, tabby ruins, the old Baptist Church, and a couple of cemeteries.

The **Melrose Beach Golf Club** (55 Ave. of the Oaks, 888/851-4971, www.melroseonthebeach.com) is back in operation, an iteration of the long-troubled Melrose golf resort that recently went through an extended bankruptcy. While not everything is back up and running, you can play golf on the Jack Nicklaus-designed course; call the club to schedule a tee time. Lodging is not available as of this writing.

For overnight stays, you can rent a humble cabin at **Freeport Marina** (843/785-8242, rates vary). For the freshest island seafood, check out the **Old Daufuskie Crab Company** (Freeport Marina, 843/785-6652, daily 11:30am-9pm, $7-22).

A public ferry between Daufuskie and Hilton Head is **Calibogue Cruises** (843/342-8687). It brings you in on the landward side of the island, and from there you can take shuttles or rent golf carts or bikes.

Points Inland

It's very likely that at some point you'll find yourself traveling inland from Beaufort, given that area's proximity to I-95. While generally more known for offering interstate drivers a bite to eat and a place to rest their heads, there are several spots worth checking out in their own right, especially Walterboro and the Savannah National Wildlife Refuge.

WALTERBORO
The very picture of the slow, moss-drenched Lowcountry town—indeed, the municipal logo is the silhouette of a live oak tree—Walterboro is a delightful artsy oasis. Right off I-95, Walterboro serves as a gateway of sorts to the Lowcountry, and the cheap commercial sprawl on the interstate shows it. But don't be put off by this ugliness—once you get into town it's as charming as they come, with roots dating back to 1783 and offering the added bonus of being one of the best antiquing locales in South Carolina. Convenient and walkable, the two-block Arts and Antiques District on Washington Street centers on over a dozen antiques and collectible stores, interspersed with gift shops and eateries.

Sights
(SOUTH CAROLINA ARTISANS CENTER
If you're in town, don't miss the **South Carolina Artisans Center** (334 Wichman St.,

HILTON HEAD

© JIM MOREKIS

the South Carolina Artisans Center in Walterboro

843/549-0011, www.scartisanscenter.com, Mon.-Sat. 9am-5pm, Sun. 1pm-5pm, free), an expansive and vibrant collection of the best work of local and regional painters, sculptors, jewelers, and other craftspeople, for sale and for enjoyment. Imagine a big-city folk art gallery, except without the pretension, and you get the idea. The Artisans Center hosts numerous receptions, and every third Saturday of the month they hold live artist demonstrations 11am-3pm.

MUSEUMS

Walterboro boasts three museums. The newly relocated and upgraded **Colleton Museum** (506 E. Washington St., 843/549-2303, www.cm-fm.org, Tues. noon-6pm, Wed.-Fri. 10am-5pm, Sat. 10am-2pm, free) is one of the best examples of a small town museum you're likely to find anywhere. Adjacent is the Farmers Market (May-Oct. Tues. 2pm-6pm, Sat. 10am-2pm).

The **Bedon-Lucas House Museum** (205 Church St., 843/549-9633, Thurs.-Sat. 1pm-4pm, $3 adults, free under age 8) was built by a local planter in 1820. An example of the local style of "high house," built off the ground to escape mosquitoes and catch the breeze, the house today is a nice mix of period furnishings and unadorned simplicity.

The **Slave Relic Museum** (208 Carn St., 843/549-9130, www.slaverelics.org, Mon.-Thurs. 9:30am-5pm, Sat. 10am-3pm, $6 adults, $5 children) houses the area Center for Research and Preservation of the African American Culture. It features artifacts, photos, and documents detailing the Atlantic passage, the lives of enslaved people, and the Underground Railroad.

TUSKEGEE AIRMEN MEMORIAL

Yes, the Tuskegee Airmen of World War II fame were from Alabama, not South Carolina. But a contingent trained in Walterboro, at the site of the present-day Lowcountry Regional Airport (537 Aviation Way, 843/549-2549) a short way south of downtown on U.S. 17. Today, on a publicly accessible, low-security

HILTON HEAD

TUSKEGEE AIRMEN IN WALTERBORO

© JIM MOREKIS

Tuskegee Airmen Memorial

In a state where all too often African American history is studied in the context of slavery, a refreshing change is the tale of the Tuskegee Airmen, one of the most lauded American military units of World War II. Though named for their origins at Alabama's Tuskegee Institute, the pilots of the famed 332nd Fighter Group actually completed final training in South Carolina at Walterboro Army Airfield, where the regional airport now sits.

The U.S. military was segregated during World War II, with African Americans mostly relegated to support roles. An interesting exception was the case of the 332nd, formed in 1941 as the 99th Pursuit Squadron by an act of Congress and the only all-black flying unit in the American military at the time. For the most part flying P-47 Thunderbolts and P-51 Mustangs, the pilots of the 332nd had one of the toughest missions of the war: escorting bombers over the skies of Germany and protecting them from Luftwaffe fighters. Though initially viewed with skepticism, the Tuskegee Airmen wasted no time in proving their mettle.

In fact, it wasn't long before U.S. bomber crews—who were, needless to say, all white—specifically requested that they be escorted by the airmen, who were given the nickname "Red-tail Angels" because of the distinctive markings of their aircraft. While legend has it that the 332nd never lost a bomber, this claim has been debunked. But as Tuskegee Airman Bill Holloman said, "The Tuskegee story is about pilots who rose above adversity and discrimination and opened a door once closed to black America, not about whether their record is perfect." The 332nd's reputation for aggressiveness in air combat was so widely known that the Germans also had a nickname for them—*Schwartze Vogelmenschen,* or "Black Birdmen."

Today, Walterboro honors the Tuskegee Airmen with a monument on the grounds of the Lowcountry Regional Airport, on U.S. 17 just northeast of town. In an easily accessible part of the airport grounds, the monument features a bronze statue and several interpretive exhibits. Another place to catch up on Tuskegee Airmen history is at the **Colleton Museum** (506 E. Washington St., 843/549-2303, www.colletonmuseum.com, Tues. noon-6pm, Wed.-Fri. 10am-5pm, Sat. 10am-noon, free), which has a permanent exhibit on the pilots and their history in the Walterboro area.

Walterboro Army Airfield's contribution to the war effort was not limited to the Tuskegee Airmen. Seven of the famed Doolittle Raiders were trained here, there was a compound for holding German prisoners of war, and it was also the site of the U.S. military's largest camouflage school.

HILTON HEAD

area of the airport stands the **Tuskegee Airmen Memorial,** an outdoor monument to these brave flyers. There's a bronze statue and several interpretive exhibits.

GREAT SWAMP SANCTUARY
A short way out of town in the other direction is the **Great Swamp Sanctuary** (www.thegreatswamp.org, daily dawn-dusk, free), a still-developing ecotourism project focusing on the Lowcountry environment. Located in one of the few braided-creek habitats accessible to the public, the 842-acre Sanctuary has three miles of walking and biking trails, some along the path of the old Charleston-Savannah stagecoach route. Kayakers and canoeists can paddle along over two miles of winding creeks. There are three entry points to the Great Swamp Sanctuary, all off Jefferies Boulevard. In west-to-east order from I-95: north onto Beach Road, north onto Detreville Street (this is considered the main entrance), and west onto Washington Street.

SAVANNAH NATIONAL WILDLIFE REFUGE
Roughly equally divided between Georgia and South Carolina, the sprawling 30,000-acre **Savannah NWR** (912/652-4415, www.fws.gov/savannah, daily dawn-dusk, free) is a premier bird-watching and nature-observing locale in the Southeast. The system of dikes and paddy fields once used to grow rice now helps make this an attractive stopover for migrating birds. Bird-watching is best October-April. While you can kayak on your own on miles of creeks, you can also call **Swamp Girls Kayak Tours** (843/784-2249, www.swampgirls.com), who work out of nearby Hardeeville, for a guided tour. To get here, take exit 5 off I-95 onto U.S. 17. Go south to U.S. 170 and look for the Laurel Hill Wildlife Drive. Be sure to stop by the brand-new visitors center.

HILTON HEAD

COLUMBIA AND THE MIDLANDS

Between the living movie set that is the Lowcountry and the more dramatic landscape of the Upstate, the Midlands—flat and crisscrossed with interstate highways—sometimes seem plain by comparison. But the Midlands have long been something of an honest broker between the Lowcountry and the Upcountry, from Columbia's original role as compromise state capital to the region's default mode as a cultural buffer zone between the insouciant coast and the staunch mountains.

In addition to great fishing, throughout the region there's an abundance of outdoor activity, including some of the best white-water rafting in the South near Columbia and the altogether unique Congaree National Park, home to some of the most ancient old-growth forest on the planet.

PLANNING YOUR TIME

Columbia is an easy city to get around in. Reserve half a day for the Riverbanks Zoo and a minimum of another half day for the other major sights. Two days will allow you to see more of the city, including a night out in the Vista and an evening in Five Points.

Because of the physical breadth of the Midlands, one day is not nearly enough to enjoy the rest of the region outside Columbia. Reserve half a day alone for Congaree National Park. If you only have a day or a day and a half, choose between two areas: the Pee Dee or Santee Cooper.

© JIM MOREKIS

HIGHLIGHTS

LOOK FOR ◖ TO FIND RECOMMENDED SIGHTS, ACTIVITIES, DINING, AND LODGING.

◖ **South Carolina State House:** The resilient and grand state capitol features gorgeous grounds and interesting monuments (page 407).

◖ **South Carolina State Museum:** Learn all about the Palmetto State in an excellently restored warehouse in the Congaree Vista (page 408).

◖ **University of South Carolina:** The quietly elegant Horseshoe area is a slice of history at one of the South's oldest universities (page 408).

◖ **Riverbanks Zoo and Garden:** One of the country's best all-around zoos has a dynamic educational and conservation component as well as a beautiful botanical garden (page 410).

◖ **Congaree National Park:** This park features an ancient cypress swamp with what may be the tallest old-growth canopy remaining on earth (page 416).

◖ **Woods Bay State Natural Area:** This very well-preserved Carolina bay features a canoe trail and scenic boardwalk (page 420).

◖ **Edisto Memorial Gardens:** The pride of Orangeburg showcases thousands of varieties of roses (page 423).

◖ **Aiken Winter Colony:** See the cozy, historic cottages of the wealthy Northerners who put Aiken on the map (page 427).

◖ **Carolina Bay Nature Preserve:** This scenic and accessible Carolina bay features a good walking trail all around its circumference (page 429).

COLUMBIA

Columbia

Columbia's broad, inviting avenues—a necessity of the rebuilding after General Sherman's torching, now considered a civic signature—are a welcome break from the winding, often-cramped streets of Charleston and the predictable Main Streets of dozens of South Carolina hamlets. And while it seems that almost every little burg you drive through in this state has its own little private college—certainly not an unattractive trait—Columbia has the big enchilada, the University of South Carolina, which brings with it that comparatively rare thing in the Palmetto State: a genuine, honest-to-goodness college-town vibe, as opposed to just a town with a college.

The first planned capital in the United States and only the second planned city in the nation (after Savannah, Georgia), Columbia was born in compromise. Shortly after the Revolution and statehood, South Carolina was in need of a state capital. However, generations of resentment by Upcountry farmers toward their wealthier counterparts in the Lowcountry meant the capital would likely be nowhere near the slave-tended fiefdoms of Charleston. Therefore it was decided to locate the new capital as close as possible to the geographic center of the Palmetto State. The name of the new city would reflect the symbol of the new nation, a feminine figure who was the Uncle Sam of her day.

For reasons still unknown to history, though long debated, General William T. Sherman took a big left turn into South Carolina upon ending his March to the Sea at Savannah. The wrath that could have been Charleston's was visited on Columbia in February 1865. A third of the city went up in flames, with over 300 acres and nearly 1,400 buildings destroyed.

SIGHTS

While the "must-see" picks are limited here to specific attractions, any local will tell you that no trip to Columbia is complete without stops at Five Points and the Congaree Vista (more often "the Vista"), both downtown.

Robert Mills House

Not the oldest but certainly the most architecturally significant of the three antebellum homes to survive Sherman's torching, the **Robert Mills House** (1616 Blanding St., 803/252-7742, www.historiccolumbia.org, Tues.-Sat. 10am-3pm, Sun. 1pm-4pm, $8 adults, $6 children, free under age 6) is named for its designer, whose impressive oeuvre includes the Washington Monument. A seminary began holding classes here in 1831, and Woodrow Wilson's father and uncle, both Presbyterian ministers, were on the faculty. The interior hosts a range of furniture and decorative arts, including examples of American Federal, English Regency, and French Empire styles. You can get a combo ticket (803/252-7742, $15 adults, $9 children) at the Mills House for all the Foundation's house museums, including the Hampton-Preston Mansion and the Mann-Simon Cottage. The last tour at each house begins Tuesday-Saturday at 3pm and Sunday at 4pm.

Hampton-Preston Mansion

Across the street from the Mills House is the 1818 **Hampton-Preston Mansion** (1615 Blanding St., 803/252-7742, www.historic-columbia.org, Tues.-Sat. 10am-3pm, Sun. 1pm-4pm, $8 adults, $6 children, free under age 6). This classic example of an elite planter's domicile was built for cotton merchant Ainsley Hall, who also had the Mills House built several years later, but soon ended up in the hands of an even wealthier planter, Wade Hampton, who at his death in 1835 was widely held to be the richest man in the United States. The mansion served as a Union Army headquarters during the Civil War occupation of Columbia. Tickets are purchased at the Robert Mills House. You can also buy a combo ticket

COLUMBIA

COLUMBIA

To Little Pigs and Fort Jackson

MILLWOOD AVE

BENEDICT COLLEGE

HARDEN ST

LAURENS ST

GREGG ST

BARNWELL ST

HENDERSON ST

PICKENS ST

INN AT CLAUSSENS

VILLAGE IDIOT

FIVE POINTS

DEVINE ST

JAKE'S BAR & GRILL

PUB ON SANTEE

DRIP

GOATFEATHERS

YESTERDAYS

SALUDA AVE

BLOSSOM ST

WOODROW WILSON FAMILY HOME

HAMPTON-PRESTON MANSION

BLANDING ST

ROBERT MILLS HOUSE

BULL ST

MANN-SIMON COTTAGE

To Modjeska Montieth Simkins House

MARION ST

SUMTER ST

MAIN ST

ASSEMBLY ST

COLUMBIA MUSEUM OF ART

LADY ST

GERVAIS ST

INN AT USC

McKISSICK MUSEUM

USC MELTON MEMORIAL OBSERVATORY

UNIVERSITY OF SOUTH CAROLINA

PENDLETON ST

TRINITY EPISCOPAL CATHEDRAL

SOUTH CAROLINIANA LIBRARY

SENATE ST

THE HORSESHOE

COURTYARD BY MARRIOTT DOWNTOWN AT USC

COLLEGE ST

GREENE ST

DEVINE ST

ASSEMBLY ST

BLOSSOM ST

WHALEY ST

W MAIN ST

HEYWARD ST

To Williams-Brice Stadium

SOUTH CAROLINA STATE HOUSE

BLUE MARLIN

HAMPTON INN DOWNTOWN

PARK ST

LINCOLN ST

GADSDEN ST

GERVAIS & VINE

GOVERNOR'S MANSION AND GARDENS

Finlay Park

Memorial Park

WASHINGTON ST

TAYLOR ST

HAMPTON ST

PULASKI ST

WAYNE ST

HUGER ST

ELMWOOD AVE

CALHOUN ST

RICHLAND ST

LINCOLN ST

LAUREL ST

SOUTH CAROLINA STATE MUSEUM

EDVENTURE

JARVIS KLAWAMA BLVD

Riverfront Park

Congaree River

To RIVERBANKS ZOO AND GARDEN

© AVALON TRAVEL

400 yds

400 m

0

0

(803/252-7742, $15 adults, $9 children) at the Mills House for all the Foundation's house museums, including the Robert Mills House and Mann-Simon Cottage. The last tour at each house begins Tuesday-Saturday at 3pm and Sunday at 4pm.

Woodrow Wilson Family Home

The Wilson family arrived in Columbia from Augusta, Georgia, during Reconstruction. Woodrow Wilson, who went by the name Tommy at the time, was 14 years old. The Wilsons only stayed in the house for a couple of years. Structural issues closed the **Woodrow Wilson Family Home** (1705 Hampton St., 803/252-7742, www.historiccolumbia.org, Tue.-Sat. 10am-3pm, Sun. 1pm-4pm, $8 adults, $6 children) to the public in 2005; luckily, it reopened for tours in early 2014. Historically, the key object in the collection is the bed in which the president was born in 1856 in Staunton, Virginia.

Mann-Simon Cottage

Born into slavery near Charleston in 1799, Celia Mann somehow escaped servitude and made her way to Columbia to work as a midwife. By 1844 she was living in the **Mann-Simon Cottage** (1403 Richland St., 803/252-7742, www.historiccolumbia.org, Tues.-Sat. 10am-3pm, Sun. 1pm-4pm, $8 adults, $6 children, free under age 6), one of a precious handful of antebellum homes in South Carolina owned by free blacks. Admission tickets are purchased at the Robert Mills House. You can also buy a combo ticket (803/252-7742, $15 adults, $9) at the Mills House for all the Foundation's house museums, including the Hampton-Preston Mansion and the Robert Mills House. The last tour at each house begins Tuesday-Saturday at 3pm and Sunday at 4pm.

◖ South Carolina State House

South Carolina is a pretty small state, both in area and in population. But the **South Carolina State House** (1101 Gervais St., 803/734-2430, www.discoversouthcarolina.com, www.scstatehouse.gov, grounds daily dawn-dusk, free),

whose grounds cover nearly 20 acres, is one of the grandest state capitols in the nation. Free guided tours of the entire capitol are available Monday-Saturday and the first Sunday of the month.

One of the most satisfying things to do on a nice day in Columbia is stroll the expansive grounds of the State House. It's pleasant and relaxing, and interesting as well—the various tributes and monuments, many of them somewhat politically incorrect, are a lively and evolving chronicle of the state's history and quirky politics. Below is a walking tour of the highlights.

Start at the entrance on Gervais Street, at the controversial **Confederate Monument.** At one time, the rebel Stars and Bars flew over the State House. However, after negative media attention in the 1990s and a threatened national boycott, the Confederate battle flag was moved to fly alongside this 1879 monument instead.

The **Strom Thurmond Monument** is another controversial memorial on the grounds. Though the statue depicts the longtime senator and conservative icon at the ripe young age of 60, the late Thurmond himself attended the unveiling in 1999, when he was 97. Most interestingly—and ironically, given Thurmond's long support of segregation and opposition to civil rights—the list of his children was amended to include a mixed-race daughter he had out of wedlock, Essie Mae Washington-Williams, now 87.

On the west side of the State House you will see brass stars marking six **Union cannonball hits** on the State House during the bombardment before General Sherman took the city. The imposing **George Washington Statue** at the capitol's front steps is sculpted of bronze on a granite base, and is Washington's exact height: six feet, two inches tall. If you're here after hours, you may notice joggers running up and down the front steps, Rocky-style.

Trinity Episcopal Cathedral

The beautiful buffed-brick **Trinity Episcopal Cathedral** (1100 Sumter St., 803/771-7300, www.trinitysc.org), near the State House, is a fine example of Gothic Revival church architecture, and a recent renovation has made it even more attractive. Its congregation has roots back to the very first backcountry Episcopalian church in the state, around 1812. The current sanctuary hosts deceased luminaries in the attached cemetery, including five governors of South Carolina and three Confederate generals (and one who was both: Wade Hampton III). Good construction and benevolent wind patterns (and divine intervention?) saved the church from Yankee fires in 1865.

(South Carolina State Museum

The mother lode of all history of the Palmetto State, the **South Carolina State Museum** (301 Gervais St., 803/898-4921, www.scmuseum.org, Labor Day-Memorial Day Tues. 10am-8pm, Wed.-Fri. 10am-5pm, Sat. 10am-6pm, Sun. 1pm-5pm, Memorial Day-Labor Day Mon. and Wed.-Fri. 10am-5pm, Tues. 10am-8pm, Sat. 10am-6pm, Sun. 1pm-5pm, $7 adults, $5 children, free under age 3) occupies the 1893 Columbia Mill textile building. There are over 70,000 artifacts in its growing collection, with the highlights being the detailed and vibrant exhibits on particular segments of the human history of South Carolina. As you'd expect, the Civil War exhibit is particularly vivid, but that is by no means the only high point.

Housed within the State Museum complex is the small but well-tended **South Carolina Relic Room & Military Museum** (301 Gervais St., 803/737-8095, www.crr.sc.gov, Tues.-Sat. 10am-5pm, 1st Sun. of the month 1pm-5pm, $5 adults, $2 youth, free under age 12, $1 1st Sun. of the month), which maintains an interesting collection of artifacts and memorabilia highlighting the state's significant contributions to American military history, with a strong focus on the Civil War era. A combo ticket ($9) provides admission to both the State Museum and the Relic Room.

EdVenture

The new-fangled children's museum **EdVenture** (211 Gervais St., 803/779-3100, www.edventure.org, Tues.-Sat. 9am-5pm, Sun. noon-5pm, $11.50), within the State Museum complex but in a separate building, was built specifically for those ages 12 and under. In it are over 350 hands-on exhibits, mostly concentrating on science and nature. A highlight is "Eddie," a 40-foot-tall schoolboy within whose simulated innards kids can climb and slide on.

Columbia Museum of Art

The small but well-done **Columbia Museum of Art** (Main St. and Hampton St., 803/799-2810, www.columbiamuseum.org, Tues.-Fri. 11am-5pm, Sat. 10am-5pm, Sun. noon-5pm, $12 adults, $5 children, free under age 5) is in a suitably modern-looking building, erected in 1998. The highlight of its permanent collection is the Samuel H. Kress Collection on the upper floor, including some wonderful Renaissance and baroque pieces. The most notable single works here are Botticelli's matchless *Nativity* and Claude Monet's *The Seine at Giverny.* Occasionally hours and admission cost are different during special exhibits; check the website for details.

(University of South Carolina

Columbia isn't just the state capital; it's a college town as well. The **University of South Carolina** (USC, 803/777-0169, www.sc.edu) hosts nearly 30,000 students at its main campus in Columbia, although apparently only a few attend during summer, which is dead compared to the busy fall and spring.

On Sumter Street at College Street you'll find the wrought iron gates opening onto **The Horseshoe,** the oldest and most beautiful part of campus. The grand **McKissick Museum** (816 Bull St., 803/777-7251, www.cas.sc.edu, Mon.-Fri. 8:30am-5pm, Sat. 11am-3pm, free), a New Deal-era public works project, houses USC's many collections and has diverse exhibits on public life and history in the state. There are two galleries on the second floor, a natural history component on the third floor, and a small collection of Baruch silver within the Visitors Center on the first floor.

The key building to note during your

WALTER EDGAR'S JOURNAL

He's originally from Alabama, but you could call University of South Carolina professor Walter Edgar the modern voice of the Palmetto State. From the rich diversity of barbecue to the inner workings of the poultry business and the charms of beach music, Edgar covers the gamut of South Carolina culture and experience on his popular weekly radio show *Walter Edgar's Journal*, airing on South Carolina public radio stations throughout the state.

Currently director of the USC Institute of Southern Studies, the Vietnam vet and certified barbecue contest judge explains the show like this: "On the *Journal* we look at current events in a broader perspective, trying to provide context that is often missing in the mainstream media." More specifically, Edgar devotes each one-hour show to a single guest, usually a South Carolinian—by birth or by choice—with a unique perspective on some aspect of state culture, business, arts, or folkways. By the time the interview ends, you not only have a much deeper understanding of the topic of the show but of the interviewee as well. And because of Edgar's unique way of tying strands of his own vast knowledge and experience into every interview, he'll also leave you with a deeper understanding of South Carolina itself.

In these days of media saturation, a public radio show might sound like a rather insignificant perch from which to influence an entire state. But remember that South Carolina is a small, close-knit place, a state of Main Street towns rather than impersonal metro areas. During any given show, many listeners in Edgar's audience will know his guests on a personal basis. And by the end of the show, the rest of the listeners will feel as if they did.

Listen to *Walter Edgar's Journal* Friday at noon on South Carolina public radio, with a repeat Sunday at 8pm. Hear podcasts of previous editions at www.scetv.org.

walking tour of the Horseshoe is one near the Sumter Street entrance, the **South Caroliniana Library** (910 Sumter St., 803/777-3131, www.sc.edu, Mon.-Fri. 8:30am-5pm, Sat. 9am-1pm, free). Designed by renowned American architect Robert Mills, who also designed Columbia's premier house museum, the Caroliniana is the first freestanding college library in the country (two fireproof wings were added in 1927). The library has one of the most significant collections on Southern history anywhere, with a particularly distinguished reading room full of stately busts and Harry Potter-esque alcoves. It's open to the public; all you need is a photo ID. Keep in mind that it's open only when classes are in session.

The **USC Melton Memorial Observatory** (803/777-4180, www.physics.sc.edu, free), on campus right off Greene Street, hosts public viewing sessions of the night sky (Apr.-Sept. Mon. 9:30pm-11:30pm, Oct.-Mar. Mon. 8pm-10pm) on clear evenings.

To learn more about USC and campus life, visit its excellent **Visitors Center** (1500 Pendleton St., 803/777-0169, www.sc.edu/visitorcenter, Mon.-Fri. 8:30am-5pm, Sat. 11am-3pm) within the McKissick Museum building. Public parking is adjacent to the building. They hold regular free walking tours of the campus, led by specially trained University Ambassadors. The tours last over two hours, so wear your walking shoes.

Governor's Mansion and Gardens

Not to be confused with the home of the Palmetto State's legislative branch at the State House, the executive branch is headquartered at the **Governor's Mansion and Gardens** (800 Richland St., 803/737-1710, www.scgovernorsmansion.org, gardens Mon.-Fri. 9am-5pm, free). Built in 1855 as the Arsenal Military Academy, the building, which now houses the governor and family, survived the burning of the city in 1865 and hosted its first chief executive in 1869. The six rooms of the Mansion open to the public contain an impressive

COLUMBIA

collection of furnishings and artwork from various eras. Call to set up a free tour.

(Riverbanks Zoo and Garden

One of the nation's best, if underrated, zoos and South Carolina's most popular single attraction, **Riverbanks Zoo and Garden** (500 Wildlife Pkwy., 803/779-8717, www.riverbanks.org, fall-winter daily 9am-5pm, spring-summer Mon.-Fri. 9am-5pm, Sat.-Sun. 9am-6pm, $11.75 adults, $9.25 children, free under age 2) is a fairly unique combo site. Not only do you get a crackerjack zoo, with nearly 400 species represented and an extensive environmental and educational component, but there's a beautiful and well-done botanical garden as well.

The 20,000-square-foot **Aquarium Reptile Complex** is a stunning and vibrantly colorful collection of reptiles, fish, amphibians, and invertebrates. Another particularly outstanding collection is the **Birdhouse,** which actually comprises three separate avian habitats. The zoo is only part of the picture, however. Take

© SOPHIA MOREKIS

the botanical garden at Riverbanks Zoo

a free regular tram from the zoo grounds to the 70-acre **botanical garden,** one of the most extensive in the South. The tram drops you at a nice little visitors center run by Clemson University. Go early or late in the day to see the animals at their best. Regardless of the heat, Riverbanks begins attracting heavy crowds just before lunchtime. Riverbanks couldn't be easier to get to; it's just off I-26 at the Greystone Boulevard exit.

ENTERTAINMENT AND EVENTS

Columbia is a fun town with plenty of nightlife, especially when USC is in session. In addition to its cultural offerings, there are two main areas to remember for entertainment, dining, and shopping: Five Points, the intersection of Harden and Greene Streets and Saluda Avenue; and the Vista (sometimes called the Congaree Vista), a more recently restored area closer to downtown amid the old mill buildings.

Nightlife

As you'd expect, nightlife here is plentiful, boisterous, and centers around the college scene, especially in Five Points. The Vista appeals to visitors as well as trendy and well-heeled locals. There's no smoking in all bars, restaurants, and public places in Columbia.

Any discussion of nightlife in Columbia, and specifically in Five Points, should begin with **Jake's Bar & Grill** (2112 Devine St., 803/252-5253, Mon.-Thurs. 4pm-2am, Fri. 3pm-2am, Sat.-Sun. noon-2am). Formerly called Rockafella's, it often hosted Hootie and the Blowfish when they were getting their start, and it remains the quintessential Five Points neighborhood joint despite its new name. The beer list is long, and the outdoor deck is a great place to chill on a nice night. Speaking of Hootie and the Blowfish, the space where they first played in Five Points is at **Pub on Santee** (733 Santee St., 803/256-4292), back when it was called Monterrey Jack's.

Not to be outdone is **Five Points Pub** (2020 Devine St., 803/253-7888, Mon. and Sat. 8pm-2am, Tues.-Fri. 5pm-2am). With

© JIM MOREKIS

Five Points is the birthplace of Hootie and the Blowfish.

one entrance on Devine Street and another on Santee Avenue, this cavernous space might confuse you into thinking it is two establishments. This is the place to go for live music, good company, and passable bar food. The closest thing to a Five Points-style dive in the Vista is **The Whig** (1200 Main St., 803/931-8852, daily 4pm-2am, kitchen until 10pm), a bohemian-slacker joint with what's generally considered the best jukebox in town. The main gay and lesbian bar in town is **PTs 1109** (1101 Harden St., 803/758-6090, www.pts1109.com, Mon.-Sat. 8pm-close). They have various drag and cabaret shows with varying cover charges.

Performing Arts

The nearly half-century-old **South Carolina Philharmonic** (721 Lady St., 803/771-7937, www.scphilharmonic.com) plays most of its classical music concerts at the **Koger Center for the Arts** (1051 Greene St., 803/777-7500, www.koger.sc.edu) under the baton of Morihiko Nakahara.

Columbia City Ballet (www.columbiacity-ballet.com), a professional troupe, generally dances at the Koger Center for the Arts. They offer one of the more eclectic seasons you'll find outside New York, with a ballet about Dracula every Halloween, and even a ballet chronicling the history of Hootie and the Blowfish. Of course, there's an annual holiday *Nutcracker* as well.

The **South Carolina Shakespeare Company** (803/787-2273, www.shakespearesc.org, $12 adults, free under age 12) holds vibrant outdoor performances of the Bard's work each fall at the amphitheater in Finlay Park downtown.

Cinema

The place to see indie film in Columbia is at **The Nickelodeon** (937 Main St., 803/254-3433, www.nickelodeon.org, $7.50) downtown next to the USC campus. Run by the nonprofit Columbia Film Society, a year's membership costs $35 and gets you discounted admission. They hold various tiny film festivals throughout the year, including the "Indie

Grits" festival (Apr.), a Native American festival (Nov.), a Latin festival (Sept.-Oct.), an African American festival (Jan.-Feb.), and a Jewish festival (Mar.-Apr.).

SHOPPING

Other than malls, the main shopping area in Columbia is at Five Points. The Vista also has a growing range of good stores.

Antiques

As with much of South Carolina, the capital has some good antiques action. The largest antiques malls near Columbia proper are in the Vista: **City Market Antiques Mall** (707 Gervais St., 803/799-7722, Tues.-Sat. 10am-5pm, Sun. 2pm-5pm), with over 65 dealers; and the massive **Columbia Antique Mall** (602 Huger St., 803/765-1584, Mon.-Sat. 10:30am-5:30pm, Sun. 1:30pm-5:30pm).

Over the river, West Columbia has a sort of antiques colony of its own, at **763 Meeting Street Antique Mall** (763 Meeting St., 803/796-1516, Mon.-Sat. 10am-5:30pm, Sun. 1:30pm-5:30pm), **Antiques on Meeting** (614 Meeting St., 803/791-0008, Mon.-Sat. 10:30am-5:30pm), and **Marketplace on Meeting** (550 Meeting St., 803/794-1000, Mon.-Fri. 10am-3pm).

Art Galleries

The acclaimed **Blue Sky Gallery** (733 Saluda Ave., 803/779-4242, www.blueskyart.com, by appointment) in Five Points is the place where you'll find original work from none other than Blue Sky himself, a.k.a. Warren Edward Johnson, a nationally renowned local artist who specializes in murals and folk art. Call for an appointment. The Vista hosts a number of great galleries in the restored old warehouse spaces, including the modern-tinged **if** (1223 Lincoln St., 803/238-2351, Mon.-Fri. 11am-7pm, Sat. 11am-5pm) and the eclectic **Gallery at DuPre** (807 Gervais St., 803/546-1143).

Clothes

Sid Nancy (733 Saluda Ave., 803/779-6454,

Mon.-Fri. noon-8pm, Sat. 11am-7pm, Sun. 1pm-3pm) in Five Points, as the name might indicate, is an awesome vintage and thrift store with a definite cutting-edge postpunk appeal. Adjacent is the excellent consignment shop **Revente** (737 Saluda Ave., 803/256-3076), which tends to cater to the upper end of the scale, though with some great bargains if your timing is right.

A couple of streets over, **Natural Vibrations** (719 Harden St., 803/771-4144, Mon.-Sat. 11am-6pm, Sun. 1pm-6pm) deals on the Rasta end of the scale, with hemp products, T-shirts, and various reggae-related merch.

Music

Serious vinyl junkies should head straight to Five Points to check out **Papa Jazz** (2014 Greene St., 803/256-0096, www.papajazz.com, Mon.-Sat. 10am-7pm, Sun. 1pm-6pm). Besides the eponymous genre, they deal in used vinyl of all types, including rare funk records and the occasional punk gem. It's a tiny store packed to the gills with music, but it has been a Columbia tradition for over 25 years.

Farmers Markets

The granddaddy of them all is **Columbia State Farmers Market** (1001 Bluff Rd., 803/737-4664, Mon.-Sat. 6am-9pm, Sun. 1pm-6pm), in operation at a 50-acre site with a 100,000-square-foot drive-through building. This state-operated facility, one of three in South Carolina, has 500 stalls, 100 wholesale outlets, about 40 retail outlets, and even its own U.S. Post Office location.

Downtown, the **Trinity Episcopal Church Farmers Market** (1100 Sumter St., 803/771-7300, Sun. 8:30am-noon) sells local produce each Sunday in the warm seasons. In the Vista you'll find the **All-Local Farmers Market** (www.stateplate.org), held every second Saturday of the month 8am-noon on the patio of the popular local restaurant Gervais & Vine (620A Gervais St.) and every fourth Saturday at Rosewood Market (2803 Rosewood Dr.).

SPORTS AND RECREATION

Kayaking, Canoeing, and Rafting

Because of its position at the confluence of the Saluda, Broad, and Congaree Rivers and the presence of Lake Murray nearby, Columbia is a haven for water-based pastimes. Generally speaking, most put-in spots are in West Columbia, using the large Gervais Street Bridge from downtown as a major landmark. The **Three Rivers Greenway** (www.riveralliance.org, daily dawn-dusk, free) joins several different hiking and biking paths as well as providing numerous river access points.

A great place to put in on the Saluda River is **Saluda Shoals Park** (5605 Bush River Rd., 803/731-5208, www.icrc.net, daily dawn-dusk, $4 per vehicle), a 350-acre park on the Saluda River outside of town with a good launch ramp. They offer periodic guided kayak trips; call for details.

There are several good outfitters in town for rental, purchase, or guided tours. **Adventure Carolina** (1107 State St., 803/796-4505, www.adventurecarolina.com) runs several trips on all area rivers, including a quick and easy selection of three-hour, three-mile paddles (about $50 pp). They also rent anything you might need. **River Runner Outdoor Center** (905 Gervais St., 803/771-0353, www.riverrunner.us, Mon.-Sat. 10am-6pm) is the designated outfitter for Saluda Shoals Park but will rent for any trip at about $40 per day.

Fishing and Boating

Columbia is fishing crazy, and fishing around here mostly means **Lake Murray** (www.scjewel.com). This 50,000-acre lake boasts 650 miles of shoreline. Lake Murray was used for bombing practice in World War II; in fact, the island in the middle now called Lunch Island is still known to generations of Columbians as "Bomb Island." Whatever you call it, it's still home to thousands of purple martins who stop over each year.

To rent boats on Lake Murray, go to www.lakemurraycountry.com. The easiest access point for the lake is from **Dreher Island** State Recreation Area (3677 State Park Rd., 803/364-4152, www.southcarolinaparks.com, daily dawn-dusk, $2, free under age 16).

Hiking and Biking

The premier walking and biking site in Columbia is the excellent **Three Rivers Greenway** (803/765-2200, www.riveralliance.org, daily dawn-dusk, free), actually an umbrella project comprising three separate river walks on the banks of the Congaree and Broad Rivers, most directly connected. There are lighted and paved trails, boardwalks, and overlooks all along the nearly nine-mile collective Greenway. All paths are accessible to people with disabilities; you can even take baby strollers along with no problem. Plenty of designated public parking is available at all entrances to the Three Rivers Greenway.

On the other side of the rivers in West Columbia and the suburb of Cayce are the **West Columbia Riverwalk** (from town, cross over the Gervais St. Bridge, take a left on Alexander Rd., and you'll see the amphitheater and parking lot on the left) and the **Cayce Riverwalk** (take Blossom St. over the river, a left onto Axtell Dr./Jessamine St., and the entrance is on the left).

Spectator Sports

Spectator sports in Columbia essentially begin and end with **University of South Carolina athletics** (www.gamecocksonline.cstv.com). As part of the Southeastern Conference, the Gamecocks play football at **Williams-Brice Stadium** (1127 George Rogers Blvd., 803/254-2950), basketball at the **Colonial Center** (801 Lincoln St., 803/576-9200), and baseball at a new field on Williams Street. Good luck getting tickets, especially for home football games; regardless of how the 'Cocks are doing on the gridiron, their games are always attended by fiercely passionate, sold-out crowds.

ACCOMMODATIONS

Columbia has plenty of lodging but is somewhat underserved in terms of quality accommodations for travelers and business-people. This is slowly changing, however. These are the best picks close to major attractions.

Under $150

Perhaps the most beloved stay in Columbia is the ◖ **Inn at USC** (1619 Pendleton St., 866/455-4753, www.innatusc.com, $145), a real hidden gem right on campus. A particular emphasis is placed on a certain clubby collegiality. A plus is the complimentary cooked-to-order breakfast in the Palmetto Room.

The **Courtyard by Marriott Downtown at USC** (630 Assembly St., 803/799-7800, www.marriott.com, $120-125) puts you a short walk from several performing arts facilities, the State House, and the Vista. There's a small and somewhat windy roof-top pool.

There aren't many bed-and-breakfasts in Columbia—thanks to General Sherman, the stock of nostalgic old homes is small—but one well-regarded B&B is the **1425 Inn** (1425 Richland St., 803/252-7225, www.the1425inn.com, $130-150). Formerly the Richland Inn, this property has had a slight but still tasteful makeover since a management change. However, its tradition of Southern hospitality has stayed intact, with its five guest rooms sumptuously appointed and the breakfasts hot and delicious.

$150-300

It's hard to beat the ◖ **Hampton Inn Downtown** (822 Gervais St., 803/231-2000, www.hamptoninncolumbia.com, $159) for its combination of location and service. Right in the Vista and close by the State House, this property has the usual high standards associated with the Hampton brand, along with the usual price premium. The only problematic thing about this property is its continuing tight parking issue.

Housed in a former bakery building, the **Inn at Claussen's** (2003 Greene St., 803/765-0440, www.theinnatclaussens.com, $150-200) is the premier lodging in Five Points proper.

FOOD

Columbia may not be challenging Charleston on the food front anytime soon, but a growing number of very tasty establishments have sprung up in the Five Points and Vista districts to go along with other longtime favorites in town. And if you're a barbecue fan, you're definitely in luck.

American

Columbians swear by the pimento cheese-burgers and the pimento cheese fries at **Rockaway's** (2719 Rosewood Dr., 803/256-1075, daily 11am-11pm, $8), an under-the-radar locals-only type place in a nondescript building on the south side of the USC campus. For a brewpub, **Hunter Gatherer Brewery** (900 Main St., 803/748-0540, Tues.-Sat. 4pm-midnight, $10) has an excellent kitchen, and many locals insist the best burger in town is actually here.

Asian

For a ridiculously hip night out with some ridiculously tasty Pacific Rim cuisine, go straight to **SakiTumi** (831 Gervais St., 803/931-0700, www.sakitumigrill.com, Mon.-Wed. 4:30pm-10pm, Thurs.-Sat. 4:30pm-midnight, $12-18) in the Vista. Any tuna sushi or sashimi is the way to go; they bring in whole tuna loins, cut to order on the spot.

Barbecue and Ribs

While his neo-Confederate politics are an acquired taste, **Maurice's Gourmet Barbecue** (1600 Charleston Hwy., 803/796-0220, www.mauricesbbq.com, Sun.-Thurs. 10am-10pm, Fri.-Sat. 10am-11pm, $7-12) in West Columbia is the real thing: mustard-based Carolina pulled pork, and lots of it. Maurice's barbecue is the traditional Midlands variety, in a yellow mustard sauce.

While Maurice gets way more press, many locals insist the totally nonpartisan ◖ **Little Pigs** (4927 Alpine Rd., 803/788-8238, www.littlepigs.biz, Wed. 11am-2pm, Thurs.-Sat. 11am-9pm, $8) outside downtown near Fort Jackson has much better 'cue, despite not cooking with wood (a sticky issue with connoisseurs). This is all-you-can-eat buffet-style dining in a simple setting, with the focus purely on the pig itself—literally, since you can see it all right there in the buffet line.

Classic Southern

Not Columbia's best restaurant, but certainly its best-known, **(Yesterday's** (2030 Devine St., 803/799-0196, www.yesterdayssc. com, Sun.-Thurs. 11:30am-midnight, Fri.-Sat. 11:30am-1am, $6-12), in the heart of Five Points, is as close to a Southern institution as the city offers. This simple, always-crowded diner has a menu perfect for a Southern game-day meal for the whole family: "Confederate fried" steak, special-recipe fried chicken, fried catfish, and, of course, the signature meatloaf. Yes, meatloaf. They also have all kinds of sandwiches, including wraps, burgers, clubs, and Southwestern chicken.

Coffee, Tea, and Sweets

Probably the best cuppa joe in Columbia is at **Drip** (729 Saluda Ave., 803/661-9545, www. dripcoffeecolumbia.com, Mon.-Sat. 7am-6pm, Sun. 8am-6pm) in the heart of Five Points, which, as the name implies, specializes in the hot newish trend of pour-over drip coffee. There is also wine and beer.

A favorite, if quirky, spot in the Vista is **Nonnah's** (930 Gervais St., 803/779-9599, Mon.-Fri. 11:30am-2pm and 5pm-10pm, Sat. 6pm-midnight), an eatery better known for its bar scene and for its great desserts.

Mediterranean and Middle Eastern

Generally considered one of the best restaurants in Columbia and certainly the most romantic, **(Gervais & Vine** (620A Gervais St., 803/799-8463, www.gervine.com, Mon.-Sat. 4:30pm-close, $8-10) specializes in Spanish-style tapas. An extensive vibrant menu of both hot and cold tapas awaits, including seared pork tenderloin with cucumber-melon salsa and lavender honey, and marinated manchego cheese with thyme and garlic.

New Southern

A longtime favorite with locals, visitors, and the college crowd alike, the **Blue Marlin** (1200 Lincoln St., 803/799-3838, www.bluemarlincolumbia.com, lunch Mon.-Fri. 11:30am-2:30pm, dinner Mon.-Thurs. 5pm-10pm, Fri. 5pm-11pm, Sat. 4pm-11pm, Sun. 11:30am-9pm, $16-25) in the Vista is known for its mix of Lowcountry and New Orleans-style entrées, like the oyster and shrimp Bienville, seafood gumbo, and shrimp and grits. Each table gets a community-style bowl of collard greens.

My favorite restaurant in Five Points is **(Goatfeathers** (2107 Devine St., 803/256-3325, Mon.-Sat. 5:30pm-10pm, $10-22). This dark, stylish place has acquired a reputation as something of a hipster hangout, but the food is incredible. Look to the specials board, where you will find treats like delectable bacon and scallops or a unique take on salmon. The bar stays open until 2am on weekends.

Vegetarian

The premier vegan and vegetarian spot in Columbia is **Blue Cactus Café** (2002 Greene St., 803/929-0782, Tues.-Fri. 11am-3pm and 5pm-9pm, Sat. noon-9pm, $7-10). While the veggie burrito is to die for, carnivores will be pleased at the various spicy meat dishes offered, especially in Southwestern and Korean cuisine.

INFORMATION AND SERVICES
Visitors Centers

The main visitors center in the area is the **Columbia Regional Visitors Center** (1101 Lincoln St., 803/545-0000, Mon.-Fri. 8am-6pm, Sat. 10am-4pm, Sun. 1pm-5pm, www. columbiacvb.com) on the upper floor of the Convention Center in the Vista. The Lake Murray area has its own, the **Capital City/Lake Murray Country Visitors Center** (2184 North Lake Dr., Irmo, 800/725-3935, www. scjewel.com, Mon.-Fri. 9am-5pm, Sat. 10am-4pm, Sun. 1pm-5pm), northwest of town near the lake. The university runs an excellent visitors center as well, the **University of South Carolina Visitors Center** (816 Bull St.,

803/777-0169, www.sc.edu/visitor, Mon.-Fri. 8:30am-5pm, Sat. 11am-3pm) in the historic McKissick Museum at the USC Horseshoe. Visitor parking is available at the corner of Pendleton and Bull Streets.

GETTING THERE

Columbia is served by **Columbia Metropolitan Airport** (CAE, 3000 Aviation Way, www.columbiaairport.com), southwest of town, which hosts American, Delta, United, and US Airways.

If you're driving, three interstate highways—I-20, I-26, and I-77—intersect near the city. Signage is plentiful and accurate from all three.

Amtrak (850 Pulaski St., 803/252-8246 or 800/872-7245, www.amtrak.com) has a station downtown with daily New York-Miami *Silver Star* trains. There's a **Greyhound** bus station

(2015 Gervais St., 803/256-6465, www.greyhound.com, daily 24 hours) downtown as well.

GETTING AROUND

The airport has numerous **rental car** kiosks, including Alamo, Avis, Budget, Hertz, and Thrifty. In town you'll find an abundance of Enterprise (www.enterprise.com) locations; several Hertz locations, including one downtown (508 Gervais St., 803/252-2561, www.hertz.com); and a Budget location downtown (408 Blossom St., 803/779-3707, www.budget.com).

The **Central Midlands Regional Transit Authority** (803/255-7100, www.gocmrta.com) is the city's public transportation system. Buses run throughout the area, including a full schedule of downtown routes. Single trips are $1.50, or you can purchase a 10-ride pass for $10.

Outside Columbia

⬛ CONGAREE NATIONAL PARK

Set on a pristine tract of land close to Columbia's sprawl but seemingly a galaxy away, **Congaree National Park** (100 National Park Rd., 803/776-4396, www.nps.gov/cosw, daily dawn-dusk, free) contains the most ancient stands of old-growth cypress left in the world. Adjacent to the **Harry Hampton Visitors Center** (daily 8:30am-5pm), which has a great gift shop in addition to good educational exhibits, you'll embark on a system of elevated boardwalks and trails, 20 miles in total, that takes you into and through a good portion of Congaree's 22,000 acres. A well-done self-guided tour brochure explains the fascinating aspects of this unique environment, almost unknown today.

You'll see cypresses towering over 130 feet into the air (Congaree is said to have the tallest forest canopy on earth, taller than the boreal forests of Canada and the Himalayas). You'll see unbelievably massive loblolly pines. You can kayak the Cedar Creek, or take one of the free

guided canoe tours every Saturday and Sunday, with canoes provided. And serious hikers will enjoy the expansive series of trails that go even deeper into the wilderness than the standard boardwalk loop. If you're really into it, you can even primitive camp here for free; get a permit from the visitors center.

CAMDEN

Archaeologists now think the great and influential Native American town of Cofitachequi, which gained fame when Spanish explorer Hernando De Soto made contact with the Creek people, was headquartered nearby. Notably, Camden was the home of Mary Boykin Chesnut, famed Civil War diarist. Today, Camden is a major equestrian center, nicknamed the "Steeplechase Capital of the World."

Historic Camden Revolutionary War Site

Unlike most historic battlefields in the state, the **Historic Camden Revolutionary War**

COLUMBIA

© JIM MOREKIS

the cypress swamp at Congaree National Park

Site (803/432-9841, www.historic-camden. net, Tues.-Sat. 10am-5pm, Sun. 2pm-5pm, free) commemorates a British victory. The 107-acre "outdoor museum" includes the town site of Camden, the oldest inland city in South Carolina. Sprinkled around the grounds are a variety of restored historic buildings. You can choose self-guided tours or an assortment of guided tours, such as the full guided tour (Tues.-Fri. 10:30am and 3pm, Sat. 10:30am and 1:30pm, Sun. 2:30pm-4pm, $5 adults, $3 ages 6-17, free under age 6), including a tour of the Kershaw-Cornwallis headquarters mansion.

One caveat: This is not the actual battle site, which is several miles away and largely uninterpreted. To get to the actual battlefield, go north from Historic Camden about seven miles on U.S. 521, then take a left onto Flat Rock Road. The marker commemorating the battle is about two miles up on the right.

Springdale Race Course

Northwest of town is the nearly 100-year-old **Springdale Race Course** (200 Knights Hills Rd., 803/432-6513), which also hosts the town's two biggest steeplechase events. At the entrance to the track you'll find the **National Steeplechase Museum** (803/432-6513, www. nationalsteeplechasemuseum.org, Sept.-May Wed.-Sat. 10am-4pm, other times by appointment, free), containing a well-managed and exhaustive collection of vintage photos, artifacts, trophies, racing colors, and archival records. Get to Springdale Race Course by taking U.S. 521 (Broad St.) north through Camden, and then turn left onto Knights Hill Road. The track is a little way up on the right.

EVENTS

The key events in Camden are three important equestrian events at the Springdale Race Course. The **Carolina Cup** (www.carolina-cup.org, $30-45) steeplechase happens on a Saturday in late March and brings almost 70,000 attendees to the events. The smaller **Colonial Cup** (www.carolina-cup.org, $20-25) steeplechase takes place on a Sunday in mid-November. The events are a lot of fun,

COLUMBIA

with tailgating and beautiful spring and fall fashions, not to mention the great equestrian action on the track. (Gambling on any horse sport is illegal in South Carolina.) While prime parking spots at Springdale go for $200 and up, there is $10 general admission parking available. The third major equestrian event involves polo, specifically the **Camden Polo Cup** (803/425-7676, adults $10, children $5) the first weekend in May, which raises funds for the Fine Arts Center downtown.

Accommodations and Food
There are several great B&Bs in town, chief among them the outstanding **Bloomsbury Inn** (1707 Lyttleton St., 803/432-5858, www.bloomsburyinn.com, $150-180), widely rated one of the best in the United States. The 1849 property itself is of great historical importance as the onetime home of James and Mary Chesnut, he a Confederate general and she a famous wartime diarist.

The best-regarded eating spot in the Camden area is actually a short drive outside Camden in Boykin, a historic little hamlet just south of town on U.S. 521, past I-20. **The Mill Pond Steakhouse** (84 Boykin Mill Rd., 803/424-0261, www.themillpondsteakhouse.com, Tues.-Sat. 5pm-10pm, $20-40) serves awesome high-end connoisseur-style steaks and Southern classics like crab cakes and shrimp and grits.

SUMTER
The main attraction in Sumter is **Swan Lake Iris Gardens** (822 W. Liberty St.,

803/436-2640, www.sumter-sc.com, daily 7:30am-dusk, free), begun in 1927 as the labor of love of regional business titan and amateur botanist Hamilton Carr Bland. The best time to come is May-June, when the irises are in bloom. Around the last weekend in May is the **Iris Festival,** a four-day event.

The center of civic and cultural life in town is the **Sumter Opera House** (21 N. Main St., 803/436-2640), which in addition to hosting multiple performances also hosts city hall. There's a regular schedule of Friday-night events at the Opera House throughout the month, including films and live performances, all reasonably priced.

INFORMATION AND SERVICES
Visitors Centers
Congaree National Park has the excellent **Harry Hampton Visitors Center** (daily 8:30am-5pm), which has extensive educational exhibits. In Camden, the old courthouse downtown hosts the **Kershaw County Chamber of Commerce and Visitors Center** (607 S. Broad St., 800/968-4037, www.camden-sc.org, Mon.-Fri. 9am-5pm, Sat. 11am-4pm, Sun. 1:30pm-5pm), where you can get brochures and information on self-guided walking tours. In Newberry, check out the **Newberry Visitors Center** (1109 Main St., 803/276-4274, www.newberrycounty.org, Mon.-Fri. 9am-5pm, Sat. 10am-2pm) downtown. In Sumter, visit the **Sumter Convention and Visitors Bureau** (822 W. Liberty St., 803/436-2640, www.sumtertourism.com, Mon.-Fri. 8:30am-5pm).

The Pee Dee

Named for the Pee Dee River running through it, this region in the extreme northeast of the state—always called "the Pee Dee," not just "Pee Dee"—is largely off the tourism radar. That's a shame, because it offers a particularly relaxing, rolling landscape and a plethora of charming small towns. Though Florence is by far the major city in the region—largely due to its location straddling the region's interstate highways—it has very little to offer. Where possible, stay off the beaten path to explore the region further.

Cheraw Historic District

The beguiling little town of Cheraw on the Pee Dee River is my favorite place in the Pee Dee and one of the Palmetto State's great, but underrated, gems. How gemlike? To tour some of its historic buildings, you simply sign out the keys at the little visitors center. Only in South Carolina, folks. Primarily known today as the birthplace of jazz great Dizzy Gillespie, Cheraw—pronounced "chuh-RAW"—was actually one of the first settlements in the state, dating from the 1730s.

The **Cheraw Visitors Bureau** (221 Market St., 843/537-8425, Mon.-Fri. 9am-5pm, www.cheraw.com) inside the Chamber of Commerce building puts out an excellent walking-tour map; call or go by to get one. You can even make appointments to tour sites on the weekend, but make sure to call ahead.

A natural first stop is the place where Cheraw's favorite son grew up, the **Dizzy Gillespie Home Site Park** (300 block of Huger St., dawn-dusk, free). Get here by taking Huger Street a couple of blocks north of Market Street as you come into town. A particularly cool aspect of the park is the chrome fence along Huger Street, illustrating several bars from Gillespie's biggest hit, "Salt Peanuts." (No statue of Dizzy? No worries. There's a nice one a few blocks farther into town.) The premier event in Cheraw, as you'd expect, given

its favorite son, is the **South Carolina Jazz Festival** (various venues, 843/537-8420, www.scjazzfestival.com, $20 per day) each autumn.

Sand Hills State Forest

The vast and unusual **Sand Hills State Forest** (16218 U.S. 1, 843/498-6478, www.state.sc.us, office daily 8am-4:30pm, free) comprises 46,000 acres of recreational opportunities. The rare red-cockaded woodpecker calls the forest home, and there are a copious variety of fish in the forest's 13 ponds. The eponymous sand hills are vestiges of sand deposits made millions of years ago. Horseback riding on the trails is encouraged, but you need a permit in advance ($5 per day). There are also several campsites ($10-15).

Carolina Sandhills National Wildlife Refuge

Established in 1939, **Carolina Sandhills NWR** (23734 U.S. 1, 843/335-8401, www.fws.gov/carolinasandhills, daily dawn-dusk, free) is one of the last, best places to find the once-ubiquitous longleaf pine and wiregrass habitat, home of the endangered red-cockaded woodpecker. Several well-maintained hiking trails allow you to fully explore and observe this rare ecosystem, and a handful of lakes are available for fishing, and a state fishing license (www.dnr.sc.gov) is required.

Darlington Raceway

Darlington Raceway (1301 Harry Byrd Hwy./U.S. 52, 843/395-8499, www.darlingtonraceway.com, dates vary, $35-150) is the granddad of all NASCAR tracks, the first ever to host a major race. While it's not as plush as the ritzier raceways built to accommodate the sport's push to gentrify its ranks, this is still an impressive sight right on U.S. 52. Racing fans can celebrate the "return" of the NASCAR Sprint Cup Series Southern 500, now held the Saturday before Mother's Day. If you're not in

COLUMBIA

© JIM MOREKIS

Dizzy Gillespie Home Site Park, in Cheraw

town that weekend, you can call ahead for tours (Mon.-Fri., $5 pp). Sharing a parking area is the **Darlington Raceway Stock Car Museum** (1301 Harry Byrd Hwy./U.S. 52, 843/395-8862, www.darlingtonraceway.com, Mon.-Fri. 10am-5pm, Sat. 10am-4pm, Sun. 11am-4pm, $5 adults, free under age 13).

◖ Woods Bay State Natural Area
Woods Bay State Natural Area (11020 Woods Bay Rd., 843/659-4445, www.southcarolinaparks.com, daily 9am-6pm, free) is one of the largest remaining Carolina bays, a unique and somewhat mysterious geological phenomenon. These elliptical depressions, scattered throughout the Carolinas and all oriented in a northwest-southeast direction, are typified by a cypress-tupelo bog environment. A nature trail goes around the circumference of the bay. Fishing is permitted in its waters with a valid state fishing license (www.dnr.sc.gov). Although the signage is good, it can still be tricky getting here. The quickest route is I-95 exit 146, but if you're coming from Florence,

take U.S. 52 (Irby St.) through the city and take a right on U.S. 301 south of town. When you get to Olanta, start looking for the brown signs for Woods Bay. To get back on I-95, take a left onto Woods Bay Road and continue on to little Shiloh. I-95 is a short distance away.

Heritage Preserves
Just on the other side of I-95 from Woods Bay State Natural Area, near the town of Lynchburg, are two adjacent heritage preserves devoted to a unique and rapidly diminishing ecosystem.

The **Longleaf Pine Heritage Preserve** (803/734-3886, www.dnr.sc.gov, daily dawn-dusk, free) is an echo of what was once the dominant habitat throughout the Southeast, featuring a very different and more aesthetically pleasing species of pine than the typical slash pine monoculture that replaced it to feed the pulp and paper industry. Bird-watchers can find the endangered red-cockaded woodpecker here. Get to the Longleaf Pine Heritage Preserve from I-95 exit 141. Take Highway 53 south to Three Mile Branch Road, and take a

COLUMBIA

© JIM MOREKIS

Darlington Raceway

right. Continue to Road S-31-101. Take a right, and the preserve entrance is close by, a couple of miles ahead.

The **Lynchburg Savanna Heritage Preserve** (803/734-3886, www.dnr.sc.gov, daily dawn-dusk, free) also features the longleaf pine habitat, and a whopping 10 species of carnivorous plants. To get to Lynchburg Savannah Heritage Preserve from Longleaf Pine Heritage Preserve, continue east on County Road 101 and take a left on Highway 53. Continue past Atkins and take a left onto Road S-31-327. The preserve is about five miles ahead on the right.

Lynches River

A 54-mile stretch of **Lynches River** (www.dnr.sc.gov) was named an official state Scenic River in 1994. This heavily forested, virtually pristine section of the blackwater river was named for Declaration of Independence signer Thomas Lynch. There are two great ways to enjoy the Lynches River: **Lee State Natural Area** (487 Loop Rd., 803/428-5307, www.southcarolinaparks.com, daily 9am-9pm, free), a Civilian Conservation Corps-era state park conveniently right off I-20 at exit 123, and **Lynches River County Park** (1110 Ben Gause Rd., 843/389-2785, www.florenceco.org, daily dawn-dusk, free), farther downstream near Florence. Canoe and kayak rental is available at Lynches River County Park (843/667-0920, about $30 per day); call for rental information. In addition, both sites offer hiking trails. You can camp at Lee State Natural Area, which has 25 sites ($12-13) with electricity and water.

SOUTH OF THE BORDER

For generations, travelers along I-95 were treated to billboards for hundreds of miles with a stereotyped Mexican named Pedro with a penchant for puns ("chile today, hot tamale") lazily exhorting people to visit **South of the Border** (I-95 and U.S. 301/501, 843/774-2411, www.thesouthoftheborder.com, daily 24 hours, free). Begun in 1950 by Al Schafer as a beer stand servicing a dry North Carolina county just across the state line—"south of the border," get it?—the entertainment empire near Dillon gradually grew to encompass motels, restaurants (Mexican and otherwise), gas stations, RV campgrounds, fireworks stands, sprawling gift shops, and even an adult entertainment store, the Dirty Old Man's Shop. At one point, South of the Border, which covers nearly 150 acres, had its own police and fire departments.

A changing world and vastly increased entertainment options mean that South of the Border is but a shadow of its former self. Schafer gradually became South Carolina's reclusive, eccentric version of Howard Hughes, dying in 2001 at age 87. Employees no longer wear "Pedro" nametags. The borderline racist content of the billboards was watered down for a more evolved world in 1997 ("These baby boomers do not have a sense of humor," Schafer said at the time).

The main landmark is the 75-foot sombrero-clad Pedro himself, between whose massive legs you can drive your car. He sports a new neon paint scheme to fit the new times. While a mere $0.50 gets you a trip to the top to view the surrounding countryside, unfortunately the elevator breaks down a lot, and you won't be allowed up at all on a windy day.

While its best days are clearly behind it, South of the Border retains its off-the-chart kitsch quotient and is still a welcome respite from that particular stretch of mind- and body-numbing boredom along I-95. There are over 300 guest rooms at the **South of the Border Motor Inn** ($55-75), which might surprise you with the comparatively high quality of the rooms given the bargain rates.

Strange-but-true fact: Former Federal Reserve Chairperson Ben Bernanke once worked here when he was a teenager.

GETTING THERE AND AROUND
By Air
The airport serving the Pee Dee is **Florence Regional Airport** (FLO, 2100 Terminal Dr., 843/669-5001, www.florencescairport.com), which hosts Delta and US Airways. However, most travelers drive to the Pee Dee or arrive at larger airports in the region such as Greenville, Charleston, or Charlotte.

By Car
Interstate highways I-95 and I-20 intersect in the Pee Dee, and they are by far the dominant arteries. Other major highways include U.S. 1 from Camden to Cheraw; U.S. 301, which largely parallels I-95 to the east; and U.S. 52 from Cheraw through Darlington to Florence.

Florence Regional Airport has several **car rental** kiosks, including Hertz, Budget, and Avis. There's an Enterprise location (213 S. Coit St., 843/317-6857) downtown. Hartsville has a couple of locations, including Hertz (1 N. 2nd St., 843/662-7930) and Enterprise (826 N. 5th St., 843/857-9088).

By Train
Two cities in the Pee Dee have **Amtrak** (www.amtrak.com) passenger train stations with daily New York City-Miami *Silver Meteor* trains: Florence (807 E. Day St.) and Dillon (100 N. Railroad Ave.), near the North Carolina border.

By Bus
Greyhound (www.greyhound.com) has bus stations in Florence (611 S. Irby St., 843/662-8407) and in Sumter (129 S. Harvin St., 803/775-3849).

The Santee Cooper Region

As primordial as Lakes Marion and Moultrie seem to be, they're actually artificial. Both are byproducts of a New Deal-era hydroelectric project under the auspices of the Santee Cooper Authority, named after the two rivers impounded to form the lakes. One of the largest public works projects in history, the Santee Cooper project was so expansive that eventually the entire region would be known by the same name. While today Santee Cooper is a sports enthusiast's paradise, if all you want is a taste of life here, it's an easy enough visit, since I-95 makes transportation a breeze.

◖ Edisto Memorial Gardens

The main attraction in Orangeburg is **Edisto Memorial Gardens** (200 Riverside Dr., 800/545-6153, www.orangeburg.sc.us/gardens, daily dawn-dusk, free). The keynotes are the vast fields of heirloom roses in a dazzling variety of colors, which you'll be able to see approximately April-November, with May being the best month. You can't pick the roses, but you can just about get lost wandering among the rows. A scenic duck pond provides a relaxing backdrop.

The key event of the year is the **Festival of Roses** (803/534-6821, www.festivalofroses. com, free), held, fittingly, the weekend before Mother's Day. About 30,000 people attend this weekend-long event, which culminates in a Parade of Roses downtown, with a special float carrying the Queen of Roses.

Food in Orangeburg largely begins and ends with ◖ **Duke's Barbecue,** the legacy of the legendary Earl Duke. There are two locations, one uptown (789 Chestnut St., 803/534-9418, call for hours, $8) and one downtown (1298 Whitman St., 803/534-2916, call for hours, $8). In both cases, you get freshly cooked

© JIM MOREKIS

outdoor sculpture at Edisto Memorial Gardens

pulled pork served all-you-can-eat buffet-style with a local version of the indigenous mustard-based sauce.

LAKES MARION AND MOULTRIE

Wild-looking Lake Marion on the Santee River, known for its plethora of striped bass, is the largest and northernmost of the two, covering over 100,000 acres. More manicured Lake Moultrie on the Cooper River covers about 60,000 acres and is known for its massive catfish; blue cats over 40 pounds are not uncommon, and some over 50 pounds have been caught. There are numerous marinas, public landings, and fish camps all around the circumference of both lakes.

Santee National Wildlife Refuge

Located an easy jaunt off I-95, **Santee NWR** (2125 Fort Watson Rd., 803/478-2217, www.fws.gov/santee, daily dawn-dusk, free) actually comprises several federally run locations on the eastern shore of Lake Marion. The well-done **visitors center** (Tues.-Fri. 8am-4pm, 1st, 2nd, and 3rd Sat. of the month 8am-4pm) is at the main Bluff Unit of the refuge, with a nice overlook of the lake and an easy walk down to the sandy shore. A very short drive away is the site of Fort Watson, built by the British on a 3,000-year-old Indian mound. Francis Marion caused the British surrender of Fort Watson in 1781. Each October sees a Revolutionary War encampment on-site in honor of the victory.

Pinopolis Dam

The tallest single-step lock in North America and the second tallest in the world, the Pinopolis Dam at the south end of Lake Moultrie separates the impounded lake from the Cooper River. If you're in a boat or kayak, it's a whopping 75-foot, half-hour drop from the lake to the 1940s-era Tailrace Canal, a short trip on which takes you to the river. For a guided kayak tour that includes a jaunt through the lock, contact **Blackwater Adventures** (843/761-1850, www.blackwateradventure.com, about $50).

Francis Beidler Forest

The **Francis Beidler Forest** (336 Sanctuary Rd., Harleyville, 843/462-2150, www.sc.audubon.org, Tues.-Sun. 9am-5pm, $8 adults, $4 ages 6-18, free under age 6) is jointly owned by the Nature Conservancy and the Audubon Society to conserve this rare and special 15,000-acre habitat in the blackwater Four Holes Swamp. A 1,800-acre section of the forest contains some of the largest and most ancient old-growth stands of bald cypress and tupelo trees in the world. To get here from Charleston, take I-26 west out of town to exit 187. Make a left onto Highway 27 south to U.S. 78, where you turn right. Veer right on U.S. 178, and then take a right on Francis Beidler Forest Road. To get to the visitors center, veer right onto Mims Road after a few miles.

Sports and Recreation
ON THE WATER

A good way for the casual traveler to enjoy the lakes is at **Santee State Park** (251 State Park Rd., 803/854-2408, www.southcarolinaparks.com, Mon.-Sun. 6am-10pm, $2 adults, free under age 16) on Lake Marion near the town of Santee. A nature-based boat tour of the lake (Wed. and Fri.-Sun., call for times) run by Fish Eagle Tours (803/854-4005) departs from the Tackle Shop. The park also has two boat ramps.

An easy way to fish is on the old bridge over Lake Marion, parallel to I-95 and now used as a fishing pier. Serious anglers, however, gravitate toward the many fish camps and marinas all around the huge circumference of the lakes. Some are quite plush by semirural standards, featuring cabins, lighted fishing piers, and attached restaurants. Notable examples are **Randolph's Landing** (122 Randolph's Landing Way, 803/478-2152, www.randolphs-landing.com), up at the Santee Dam; **Cooper's Landing** (1526 Gordon Rd., 803/478-2549), just off I-95; and **Harry's Heart of the Lakes** (320 Harry's Camp Circle, 843/351-4561, www.harrysfishcamp.net), at the southern tip of Lake Marion.

All fishing on the lakes for those over age 16

requires a valid South Carolina fishing license, available at any tackle shop, online (www.dnr. sc.gov), or by phone (888/434-7472). A seven-day nonresident license is $11. A total of 40 game fish can be kept any one day, with no more than 10 black bass, 5 striped bass, and only 1 catfish over 36 inches long.

Kayakers can put in at many spots on the lakes, including Santee State Park. Of particular interest is the **Berkeley County Blueways** (843/719-4146, www.berkeleyblueways.com), 175 miles of paddling trails from lower Lake Marion all the way southeast to Francis Marion National Forest. **Blackwater Adventures** (843/761-1850, www.blackwateradventure. com) and **Nature Adventures** (843/928-3316, www.natureadventuresoutfitters.com) offer various kayak and canoe tours along with rentals.

An outstanding recreation guide is available at www.santeecoopercountry.org.

ON LAND
There are three courses of note on Lake Marion around the town of Santee: **Santee Cooper Country Club** (630 Santee Dr., 803/854-2467, www.santeecoopergolf.com, $30-60), the area's first; **Lake Marion Golf Course** (9069 Old Hwy. 6, 803/854-2554, www.santeecoopergolf.com, $27-51), built in 1979; and **Santee National Golf Club** (8638 Old Hwy. 6, 803/854-3531, www.santeenational.com, $40-60). **Wyboo Golf Club** (1 Warrens Way, 803/478-7899, www.wyboogolfclub.com, $40-50), a Tom Jackson design near Manning (take I-95 exit 119), is consistently rated one of the top 10 public courses in South Carolina. There are tons of golf packages available in the area; call the Santee Cooper Country commission (800/227-8510) for more info.

Accommodations
There's a plethora of fishing-related lodging and RV-style camping all around the lakes—about two dozen places in all, the vast majority on Lake Marion. For a comprehensive look, go to www.santeecoopercountry.org. A lot of folks opt for vacation rentals on the lakes; go

to www.lakemarionvacation.com for more information.

A fun place to stay near the lakes is **Santee State Park** (251 State Park Rd., 803/854-2408, www.southcarolinaparks.com). Ten well-furnished cabins are situated on a long pier over Lake Marion, with another 20 cabins on the lake itself. While all are two-bedroom, sleeping a maximum of six, they run $80-120, depending on size. Call or go to the website well in advance to reserve a cabin. There are also 158 lakeside campsites ($16-18).

Elloree has had quite a bit of national press for its picturesque qualities. While the exterior of the 1906 **Elloree Bed and Breakfast** (660 W. Hampton St., 803/897-2225, www. elloreebandb.com) doesn't provide the best architectural example in town, its guest rooms are particularly well-appointed.

Food
Any discussion of great food in South Carolina must include C **Sweatman's Bar-b-que** (1313 Gemini Dr., 803/492-7543, Fri.-Sat. 11:30am-9:30pm, $8-15, cash only), outside the town of Holly Hill on the western side of the lakes. People drive 2 or 3 hours, literally from the other side of the state, just to eat here on a weekend. They cook their pork the old-fashioned way: the proverbial whole hog, slow-cooked over wood in a blockhouse out back. The result is served buffet-style, in two types: the dry white portion, the "inside meat," and the glazed outer portion, "the outside meat." Don't miss the "cracklin's," crunchy fried pig-skin. You get your choice of sauces, either the indigenous mustard sauce or vinegar-based. You also get the requisite serving of the staple South Carolina hash, some coleslaw and rice, and, of course, sweet tea.

Sweatman's closes for most of August, and they only take cash. To get here, take I-95 exit 90 and then head east on U.S. 176, which becomes Main Street in Holly Hill. Turn left onto Highway 453 and head north for a few miles, and Sweatman's is on the right. When in Holly Hill looking for the turn, keep in mind that Highway 453 is not contiguous through town.

© JIM MOREKIS

Sweatman's Bar-b-que, near Holly Hill

You're looking for the spur of Highway 453 that begins on the west side of the railroad tracks.

Sweatman's has only one serious competitor in the area, and that's **◀ McCabe's Bar-B-Que** (480 N. Brooks St., 803/435-2833, Thurs.-Sat. 5:30pm-9pm, $10) on the eastern side of Lake Marion in the town of Manning. The pork is finely pulled, and the sauce is the tangy, kicky Pee Dee-style pepper-and-vinegar variety. Served with that distinctive hash side dish and sliced tomatoes, this plate is often considered the equal of Sweatman's.

MONCKS CORNER

The town of Moncks Corner, seat of Berkeley County, is at the southern tip of Lake Moultrie at the headwaters of the Cooper River; it is a gateway of sorts to the greater Charleston area.

Mepkin Abbey

The burg of Moncks Corner is actually named for a person, not a vocation, but nonetheless that's where you'll find a fully active, practicing Trappist monastery, **Mepkin Abbey** (1098 Mepkin Abbey Rd., 843/761-8509, www.mepkinabbey.org, Tues.-Fri. 9am-4:30pm, Sat. 9am-4pm, Sun. 1pm-4pm, free), notable for the fact that it's not only open to visitors but welcomes them. The focal point of natural beauty is the **Mepkin Abbey Botanical Garden** (Tues.-Sun.), a 3,200-acre tract with a camellia garden. Tours of the abbey itself are usually given Tuesday-Sunday at 11:30am and 3pm.

Cypress Gardens

Nature lovers can also enjoy **Cypress Gardens** (3030 Cypress Gardens Rd., 843/553-0515, www.cypressgardens.info, daily 9am-5pm, last admission 4pm, $10 adults, $5 ages 6-12), one of the first nature preserves in the Lowcountry. There are millions of flowers, including azaleas, daffodils, camellias, wisteria, dogwoods, roses, lotuses, and more. The old paddy system was made navigable for small boats—today they're glass-bottomed—to meander among the tall cypress trees. The Butterfly House is a 2,500-square-foot building packed full of butterflies, caterpillars, turtles, and birds.

INFORMATION AND SERVICES

The centrally located visitors center for Santee Cooper is the **Santee Cooper Country Visitor Information Center** (9302 Old Hwy. 6, Santee, 803/854-2131, www.santeecoopercountry.org) in the town of Santee, right off I-95.

GETTING THERE AND AROUND

I-95 goes directly through Santee Cooper, making it one of the more accessible parts of South Carolina. U.S. 301 is another key route, cutting through the region and serving Orangeburg before briefly joining I-95 and crossing Lake Marion to Manning. U.S. 17 is the main road to Moncks Corner.

A car is a must in Santee Cooper, unless you're planning on simply boating to the lakes from the Intracoastal Waterway, which is theoretically possible. Rental cars are available in Orangeburg from **Enterprise** (1624 Saint Matthews Rd., 803/534-0143, www.enterprise.com) and **Hertz** (907 Chestnut St., 803/534-0447, www.hertz.com).

Aiken

There are towns with horses, and then there are horse towns. Aiken is the latter. How can you tell the difference? Let's put it this way: Horses have the right of way over cars within Aiken city limits. Indeed, roads in Aiken's Horse District are intentionally kept unpaved so as not to cause stress to tender equine hooves.

Several Kentucky Derby winners have Aiken roots, including Pleasant Colony (1981), Swale (1984), and Sea Hero (1993). Thoroughbred racing, polo, steeplechase, fox hunting—virtually the entire history of equestrian activity in the country—is here in one form or another.

HISTORY

In the early 1800s, William Aiken, president of the South Carolina Canal and Railroad Company, commissioned the construction of a railroad from Charleston on the coast to Hamburg on the Savannah River. Work began on the railroad in 1830, with the town of Aiken, named after the company president, laid out in 1834. After the Civil War, Aiken recovered quickly as wealthy Northerners established the famous Winter Colony.

SIGHTS

Aiken manages a good mix of horse-related attractions and those having nothing to do with our fast four-legged friends. The majority of attractions in town, whether horsey or not, make the most of Aiken's scenic easygoing natural beauty and optimistic all-American atmosphere.

(Winter Colony

The old homes of the wealthy Northerners who really put Aiken on the map are almost all privately owned. But a drive or a walk through the **Winter Colony Historic Districts** (www.nationalregister.sc.gov), which are three nationally recognized areas, will give you a good idea not only of their wealth but of their taste as well. Major sectors include the area just west of the intersection of Richland Avenue and Laurens Street; Highland Park Drive near the railroad tracks; the Hitchcock Woods-Hopelands-Rye Patch area off Whiskey Road, south of downtown; and the matchless oak-lined canopy along Boundary Street. Key estates—all private—in the Winter Colony include **Let's Pretend, Joye Cottage,** and **Sandhurst.** The best way to tour the historic areas of Aiken, including the Winter Colony, is to join the city's tour (803/642-7631, www.cityofaikensc.gov, Sat. 10am, $15) leaving from the new Visitors Center and Train Museum (406 Park Ave.) downtown.

You'll often hear the phrase **Horse District** in Aiken. This is actually an informal name

COLUMBIA

© JIM MOREKIS

equine statue in downtown Aiken

for the residential area within the Winter Colony near two vintage racetracks, the Aiken Mile Track (Banks Mill Rd.) and the Aiken Training Track (538 Two Notch Rd.). Keep in mind that during the warmer months there are precious few horses to see—most will be racing or training up North (this is, after all, a winter colony).

Aiken Railroad Depot

The newest attraction in town is the Aiken Railroad Depot, also called the **Visitors Center and Train Museum** (406 Park Ave., 803/293-7846, www.aikenrailroaddepot.com, Wed.-Fri. 10am-5pm, Sat. 10am-2pm, free). Based in the old 1899 Southern Railway Depot, this beautifully restored facility now centers around nine HO-gauge model train dioramas depicting stops on the historic railroad.

Aiken County Historical Museum

For a good look at area history, housed within a beautiful historic building, check out the **Aiken County Historical Museum** (433 Newberry St., 803/642-2015, http://aikencounty.net, Tues.-Sat. 10am-5pm, Sun. 2pm-5pm, free). While the exhibits are OK, you might honestly be more impressed by the 32-room great house itself, called Banksia (after a variety of rose).

Hopelands Gardens

The exquisitely done outdoor arboretum called **Hopelands Gardens** (1700 Whiskey Rd., 803/642-7631, daily 10am-dusk, free) is, like many sights in Aiken, a legacy of transplanted Northern wealth. Monday nights in May-August bring free outdoor evening concerts. To get here from downtown, just head south on Chesterfield Street, which shortly turns into Whiskey Road.

Thoroughbred Racing Hall of Fame and Museum

Set in the restored old Iselin carriage house in a corner of Hopelands Gardens is the **Thoroughbred Racing Hall of Fame and Museum** (1700 Whiskey Rd., 803/642-7631, http://aikenracinghalloffame.com, Sept.-May

AIKEN

To Augusta and
USC/Aiken

NEW MOON CAFE
ST. THADDEUS
EPISCOPAL CHURCH
CAFE RIO
BLANCO
HOTEL AIKEN
THE ALLEY
AIKEN
BREWING
COMPANY
THE
WILLCOX
AIKEN RAILROAD DEPOT/
VISITORS CENTER
& TRAIN MUSEUM
WINTER COLONY
AIKEN COUNTY
HISTORICAL MUSEUM
JOYE
COTTAGE
LET'S
PRETEND
COKER
SPRING
THOROUGHBRED RACING
HALL OF FAME AND MUSEUM/
HOPELANDS GARDENS
To Montmorenci
Hitchcock
Woods
RYE PATCH
WHITNEY POLO
FIELD & TRACK
AIKEN TRAINING
TRACK
AIKEN
MILE TRACK
0   400 yds
0   400 m
To CAROLINA BAY
NATURE PRESERVE
STEEPLECHASE
TRACK
© AVALON TRAVEL

Tues.-Fri. and Sun. 2pm-5pm, Sat. 10am-5pm, June-Aug. Sat. 10am-5pm, Sun. 2pm-5pm, free). Downstairs is the actual Hall of Fame, a suitably clubby-looking collection of actual racing silks from famous horses that have trod local tracks. Upstairs is a rambling series of rooms devoted to Aiken's long and distinguished polo and steeplechase history.

Carolina Bay Nature Preserve

The **Carolina Bay Nature Preserve** (Whiskey Rd. and Price Ave., daily dawn-dusk, free) is one of the few sights in town not associated with rich people, horses, or both. This particular specimen is a great example of a restored Carolina bay, with some indigenous flora reintroduced, including a wildflower meadow. To get here, take Whiskey Road well south of Hopeland Gardens until you get to Price Avenue, where you turn east; the preserve parking area is shortly ahead on the left.

COLUMBIA

© JIM MOREKIS

Carolina Bay Nature Preserve

Hitchcock Woods

Once the fox hunting grounds of Thomas Hitchcock, New Yorker and avid sportsman, **Hitchcock Woods** (South Boundary Rd. and Whiskey Rd., 803/642-0528, www.hitchcockwoods.org, daily dawn-dusk, free) is now considered the largest urban forest preserve in the country at a whopping 2,000 acres. It's a great place to hike and stroll, though oddly—given that any number of horse-related activities is allowed—no bicycling is allowed. There are seven main entrances, each with a kiosk that has maps to the woods; or go to the website for a printable, delightfully *Lord of the Rings*-like map. The closest entrance to downtown is on South Boundary Road west of Laurens Street. Another is on Coker Spring Road just west of the spring.

Tours

The key tour in Aiken is provided by the city (803/642-7631, www.cityofaikensc.gov, Sat. 10am, $15) leaving from the new Visitors Center and Train Museum (406 Park Ave.) downtown. Lasting about two hours, it takes you by trolley to all significant areas of town, including through the Winter Colony, with a stop for a walk through Hopelands Gardens. Call for reservations or information.

ENTERTAINMENT AND EVENTS
Equestrian Events

The center of the polo universe in Aiken is **Whitney Field** (Mead Ave.), a historic site that has the distinction of being the oldest polo field in continuous service in the United States. Regular games of the Aiken Polo Club (www.aikenpoloclub.org, Sun. 3pm, $5) happen each Sunday during the season. Tournaments occur throughout the two playing seasons; go to the website for dates and times.

By far the main equestrian event in Aiken happens each March with the **Aiken Triple Crown,** which actually comprises three weeks of activities. The Aiken Trials (www.aikentrainingtrack.com, $10), a race, happens at the Aiken Training Track the first week. The

Aiken Steeplechase (www.aikensteeplechase. com, $15) happens during the second week at Ford Conger Field. Polo (www.aikenpoloclub. org, $10) finishes the event in the third week at Whitney Field.

Another key event, with even more aristocratic overtones, happens just after the Triple Crown, when Hitchcock Woods hosts the **Aiken Horse Show** (www.aikenhorseshow.org, $10 per vehicle).

October-March is fox-hunting season, and Hitchcock Woods is the usual site of the hunts, or "drags," sponsored by the largest club in town, **Aiken Hounds** (803/643-3724, www.aiken-hounds.com). The public is invited to watch their regular hunts (Tues. 2pm and Sat. 9am), all leaving from the Memorial Gate within Hitchcock Woods. The season opens Thanksgiving Day at 11am with a hunt, before which the hounds are blessed by an Episcopal priest.

GETTING TO THE FIELDS
To get to **Whitney Field** from downtown, turn south on Chesterfield Street, which becomes Whiskey Road. Go one mile and turn left onto Mead Avenue. The entrance to Whitney Field is shortly ahead on your right. To get to the **Aiken Training Track** from downtown, turn south on Chesterfield Street, which becomes Whiskey Road. Take a left onto Grace Avenue and then a right on Two Notch Road; the track is shortly ahead on the left. **Ford Conger Field** is at the intersection of Audubon Drive and Powderhouse Road, south of downtown.

SHOPPING
There are at least half a dozen antiques shops downtown, many with Sunday hours—a nice change from a lot of sleepy South Carolina towns. The most notable examples are **Aiken Antique Mall** (112 Laurens St., 803/648-6700, Mon.-Sat. 10am-6pm, Sun. 1:30pm-6pm), **Aiken Antiques and Auction** (1060A Park Ave., 803/642-0107, Mon.-Sat. 9am-6pm, Sun. 1:30pm-6pm), and **Swan Antique Mall** (321 Richland Ave., 803/643-9922, Mon.-Sat. 10am-5:30pm, Sun. 1pm-5pm). **The Iron Pony**

(210 York St., 803/642-5004, Wed.-Sat. 11am-5pm) is set in an antebellum home.

If you like paintings of horses, boy, are you in luck. **Equine Divine** (135 Laurens St., 803/642-9772, www.equinedivineonline.com, Mon.-Sat. 10am-5pm) deals in plenty of equestrian-related artwork and doodads, and it even stays open an hour later during polo season. **Jackson Gallery** (300 Park Ave., 803/648-7397, by appointment) features high-end horse sculpture.

SPORTS AND RECREATION
Natural Areas
The 1,000-acre **Aiken State Natural Area** (1145 State Park Rd., 803/649-2857, www. southcarolinaparks.com, daily 9am-dusk, $2 adults, free under age 16) is right on the blackwater South Edisto River about 15 miles east of town. You can canoe or kayak (rentals $15 per day), fish on any of four spring-fed lakes (state fishing license required), enjoy some great bird-watching, and hike on the Jungle Nature trail, a two-mile loop through various habitats. RV and tent camping is available ($12-13).

A wholly unique natural site south of town is the **Aiken Gopher Tortoise Heritage Preserve** (www.dnr.sc.gov, daily dawn-dusk, free), 1,500 acres devoted to the northernmost habitat of the endangered gopher tortoise. Over 16 miles of trails take you through the heart of the preserve, but bicycles are not allowed, and there are no facilities. To get here, drive south from Aiken on U.S. 78 for 12 miles to Windsor. Take a left onto Spring Branch Road, which turns into unpaved Windsor Road after 1.5 miles.

Equestrian
As you'd expect, there are plenty of riding facilities in Aiken, ranging from spectacularly well-equipped to merely very well-equipped. Most are open by appointment only. One of the largest is **Black Forest Equestrian Center** (4343 Banks Mill Rd., 803/644-6644, www.black-forestfarm.com), which has four arenas and 12 miles of trails. Another is **Jumping Branch Farm** (179 Fox Pond Rd., 803/642-3484, www.

jbfarm.com). For trail riding, try **Fox Hollow Stable** (803/640-6202).

ACCOMMODATIONS

The most important thing to remember about staying in Aiken is that all lodging is at a premium during the week of the Masters golf tournament, held each year in early April in nearby Augusta, Georgia.

Under $150

For an interesting and remarkably inexpensive stay right downtown, try the **Hotel Aiken** (235 Richland Ave., 803/648-4265, www.hotelaiken.com, $65-100), a historic property built in 1898 at the height of the Winter Colony's glory. Renovated in 2001, it still retains a certain well-worn patina. However, this isn't where to go for peace and quiet: The hotel's two attached bars, the clubby **Polo Tavern** and the ritzy **One Hundred Laurens**, are centers of downtown nightlife. In fact, things get so noisy that the guest rooms directly over the bar area are discounted.

$150-300

For a truly grand historic hotel experience downtown, try ◖ **The Willcox** (100 Colleton Ave., 877/648-2200, www.thewillcox.com, $185-425), which once hosted Franklin D. Roosevelt as well as a host of well-heeled visitors during Aiken's Winter Colony glory days.

FOOD

Good dining options are scattered throughout the central downtown area, with several in "The Alley," a short lane off Laurens Street.

American

The **Aiken Brewing Company** (140 Laurens St., 803/502-0707, www.aikenbrewingcompany.com, Mon.-Sat. 11am-2am, $10) is a popular restaurant and microbrewery at the entrance to the Alley. While it is best known for its surprisingly wide selection of hand-crafted brews, it also offers above-average bar food, such as quesadillas and beer-battered (of course) chicken tenders and wings.

Coffee and Treats

For a cup of joe, some hipster attitude, and a light wrap, sandwich, or sweet treat, go to ◖ **New Moon Cafe** (116 Laurens St., 803/643-7088, http://newmoondowntown.com, Mon.-Fri. 8am-5pm, Sat.-Sun. 9am-2pm, $5), certainly the closest thing to an alternative place in this preppy town, although note the weird hours.

Cuban

◖ **Cafe Rio Blanco** (148 Laurens St., 803/643-7075, Mon.-Wed. 11:30am-6:30pm, Thurs.-Sat. 11:30am-7:30pm, $7-10) offers a full and fresh Cuban buffet, daily specials, tasty Cuban sandwiches, and, of course, delectable (and sweet!) Cuban coffee with flan for dessert. When he's in the mood, the chef riffs Latin jazz on his sax in the kitchen.

INFORMATION AND SERVICES

The main **Aiken Visitors Center** (113 Laurens St., 803/642-7557, www.aikenis.com) has moved and is now inside the historic Holley Building. The **Visitors Center and Train Museum** (406 Park Ave., 803/293-7846, www.aikenrailroaddepot.com) also features good visitor info.

GETTING THERE

Aiken is very accessible either from I-20 just to the north or directly from Augusta, Georgia, via U.S. 78, which is called Jefferson Davis Highway in Augusta and becomes Richland Avenue in downtown Aiken.

The closest airport to Aiken is the small **Augusta Regional Airport** (AGS, 1501 Aviation Way, 706/798-3236, http://ags.skyharbors.com) in Georgia, hosting carriers Delta Connection and US Airways Express. Indeed, when in Aiken it's important to remember that the much larger Augusta is a short drive away and is for all intents and purposes considered a part of the local economy.

In Aiken, there's a **Greyhound bus station** (153 Pendleton St., 803/648-6894, www.greyhound.com).

Outside Aiken

While Aiken is the main tourism draw in the South Carolina horse country, take some time to check out some of the beguiling towns dotting the countryside around it, in particular Edgefield and Blackville. All of them have their own distinct personality, but all share the innate grace prevalent in this historic region in the watershed of the mighty Savannah River.

NORTH OF AIKEN
Edgefield

On U.S. 25 between Greenwood and Aiken is proud little Edgefield, which for some reason was the hometown of no fewer than 10 governors of South Carolina. The most famous is Strom Thurmond, later a U.S. senator, a well-done modernist statue of whom dominates the charming and attractive town square. The other thing Edgefield is known for is being the epicenter of the beautiful, unique, and utilitarian art form called Edgefield pottery.

OLD EDGEFIELD POTTERY

The main purveyor of the most famous indigenous art form is **Old Edgefield Pottery** (230 Simkins St., 803/637-2060, Tues.-Sat. 10am-6pm, donation) in a small freestanding building right off the main square down Potter's Alley. This is not a retail store per se but rather the real workshop of master potter Stephen Ferrell, with some truly amazing specimens of pottery in various states of completion.

FRESHWATER COAST DISCOVERY CENTER

On the state's "Discovery Corridor," the Joanne T. Rainsford Region 2 Discovery Center, sometimes called the **Freshwater Coast Discovery Center** (405 Main St., 803/734-0767, www.sc-heritagecorridor.org, Tues.-Sat. 10am-5pm, free), features exhibits about the history of Edgefield and the surrounding area. This is also a good place to get brochures and tips about refining your visit.

OAKLEY PARK MUSEUM

A few blocks south of the square, behind a gated drive, is the **Oakley Park Museum** (300 Columbia Rd., 803/637-4027, Wed.-Fri. 10am-4pm or by appointment, nominal fee), home of Confederate general Martin W. Gary. The stately mansion is now operated by the local Daughters of the Confederacy as a museum and self-professed "shrine" to the Red Shirts, a paramilitary group of the Reconstruction era.

TEN GOVERNORS RAILS TO TRAILS

Continue south to find a much more innocent pleasure, the **Ten Governors Rails to Trails** (803/637-4014, daily dawn-dusk, free), a one-mile passage that incorporates an old train trestle over U.S. 25. It's a relaxing and scenic way to get some exercise or let the kids (and dogs) blow off some steam. Park in the lot south of the intersection of Main and Mims Streets.

NATIONAL WILD TURKEY FEDERATION

Just outside Edgefield on U.S. 25 is the **National Wild Turkey Federation Visitor Center and Museum** (770 Augusta Rd., 803/637-3106, www.nwtf.org, Mon.-Fri. 8:30am-5pm, free). No, it's not dedicated to the beloved Kentucky bourbon; it's the national headquarters of the society dedicated to the study and conservation of one of South Carolina's great game birds and Benjamin Franklin's unsuccessful choice for our national symbol. The campus includes the 60,000-square-foot Wild Turkey Center, a wild turkey museum (including the world's largest box call, a gift shop called the Turkey Shoppe, natch), and a 125-acre outdoor education center. In front of the complex you'll find a huge bronze turkey, sculpted by Cody Houston.

Monetta

About 30 minutes north of Aiken en route to Columbia on U.S. 1 is tiny Monetta, known for hosting one of only two working drive-in theaters in South Carolina (the other is

COLUMBIA

© AVALON TRAVEL

OUTSIDE AIKEN

To Lake Thurmond

To Edgefield

To Monetta

To Columbia

Savannah Bluffs Heritage Preserve

North Augusta

Eureka

Wagener

Salley

North

Augusta

Beech Island

REDCLIFFE PLANTATION STATE HISTORIC SITE

HOPELANDS GARDENS

WINTER COLONY

Aiken

Hitchcock Woods

CAROLINA BAY NATURE PRESERVE

Montmorenci

Aiken State Park

South Fork Edisto River

Windsor

Williston

New Ellenton

U.S. DEPARTMENT OF ENERGY SAVANNAH RIVER SITE

Blackville

GOD'S ACRE HEALING SPRINGS

Barnwell State Park

Barnwell

CHURCH OF THE HOLY APOSTLES

Salkehatchie River

Denmark

To Rivers Bridge State Historic Site and Ehrhardt

SOUTH CAROLINA

GEORGIA

Savannah River

Waynesboro

10 mi

10 km

EDGEFIELD POTTERY

© JIM MOREKIS

Edgefield pottery has become a hot commodity.

Currently one of the hottest-selling categories of folk art in the world, Edgefield pottery embodies the ideal of elegant simplicity and the effortless grace of functional art. Named for the old Edgefield District along the banks of the mighty Savannah River (now split into Aiken and Edgefield Counties), Edgefield pottery began around 1810 on the plantation of Dr. Abner Landrum. He had his African American slave potters take the excellent clay from this area along the mighty Savannah River, throw it on the wheel, fire it in a kiln, and glaze the resulting stoneware with versatile and attractive alkaline glazes. It sounds simple to us, but it was groundbreaking at the time, a period when toxic lead-based glazes were commonplace. The only other known use of alkaline pottery glaze was in China about 2,000 years ago.

Generally speaking, Edgefield pottery dates from the early 1800s through the early 20th century. While both white and African American potters made it, the bulk of it was made by African American potters on plantations. Some key potters made many thousands of pieces dur-

ing their lifetimes, but not to sell: This pottery was always intended for heavy use. While the identity of most of the potters is lost to history, we know some by name, including "Dave the Slave," subject of the best-selling book *Carolina Clay*. As you'd expect, signed pieces of Edgefield pottery fetch the highest prices, as do examples bearing decorations—typically swirly designs with rough human figures.

Unlike much vintage pottery, Edgefield pottery can still be used in your kitchen with no harmful side effects because of its safe alkaline glaze. A great place to pick up some amazing examples—from as low as $35 up to several thousand dollars—is **Past Times** (165 S. Mechanic St., 864/654-5985, Tues.-Sat. 11am-5pm) in Pendleton, near Clemson. In Edgefield, visit **Old Edgefield Pottery** (230 Simkins St., 803/637-2060, Tues.-Sat. 10am-6pm, donation) just off the town square. Artist-in-residence Stephen Ferrell is nationally known for the beautiful and historically authentic work he does in this rough-hewn little studio.

COLUMBIA

© JIM MOREKIS

Church of the Holy Apostles, in Barnwell

near Beaufort). A real blast from the past, the **Monetta Drive-In** (5822 Columbia Hwy., 803/685-7949, www.thebigmo.com, Mar.-Nov., $7 adults, $4 children, free under age 4), a.k.a. "The Big Mo," shows current releases, with audio tracks broadcast over two FM frequencies. Gates open at 6:30pm, with the flicks starting about 7:30pm. It's cash only for admission, but plastic is accepted for concessions. Get to The Big Mo by taking U.S. 1 about a mile north of Monetta.

EAST AND SOUTH OF AIKEN
Barnwell
Chiefly known to the world as the birthplace of music legend James Brown, Barnwell was once a powerhouse in state politics, and it still serves as the government seat of Barnwell County. The town's signature landmark is the **Barnwell Sundial** (141 Main St., www.barnwellcounty. sc.gov), billed as the world's only freestanding vertical sundial. You can't miss it; it sits next to the traffic circle in front of the imposing county courthouse.

CHURCH OF THE HOLY APOSTLES
A few blocks away is the hauntingly beautiful **Church of the Holy Apostles** (228 Hagood Ave., 803/259-3477, www.holyapostlesbarn-well.org), built in the 1850s of cypress from local swamps, with heart-pine pews. General Sherman wanted Barnwell burned to the ground because it was named for a leading secessionist. While most of the town was indeed burned, about a dozen antebellum homes and all the churches survived more or less intact. A deserter from Sherman's army, James Bolen, ordered a bell made for the church when he noticed it didn't have one. Today, it is rung once for each apostle except Judas.

Blackville
There's not much going on in little Blackville, a tidy hamlet that began as a stop on the old Charleston-Hamburg rail line. Now it's known chiefly for its Mennonite presence—a fairly recent addition from the 1970s—and its legendary springs.

GOD'S ACRE HEALING SPRINGS
Yes, the man upstairs himself is listed on county records as property owner of **God's Acre Healing Springs** (Healing Springs Rd., daily dawn-dusk, free), since its last mortal owner, L. P. Boylston, bequeathed it to Him in 1944. Low, burbling, and tree-lined, with several open spigots installed on its banks, the Healing Springs attracts locals who bring their own jugs to fill up with water and take home for kitchen and bathing use. The Healing Springs are just north of Blackville on Highway 3 (adhere to the speed limit religiously—no pun intended). Follow the signs for the Healing Springs Baptist Church and take a right onto Healing Springs Road. In the church parking lot you'll see signs to lead you about 100 yards to the springs, where you can drive up and park.

Rivers Bridge State Historic Site
It might shock you to know that in the entire state there is only one preserved battlefield from the Civil War. It is at the **Rivers Bridge**

COLUMBIA

THE IRISH TRAVELERS

We know that the clan of nomads called the Irish Travelers arrived in South Carolina sometime in the mid-1800s. But before that, their past is murkier. Some scholars say the Travelers were refugees from Cromwell's pillage of Ireland in the 1600s. Others say they fled the Irish Potato Famine in the 1800s. The Travelers themselves claim to descend from wandering tinkers, or tin sellers, of medieval times. But the locals around North Augusta simply call them "Gypsies."

Whatever their origin, the Irish Travelers are one of the most interesting sociological phenomena in South Carolina. Numbering about 3,000, the community supports itself mostly by spending much of the year traveling around the Southeast doing odd jobs and day labor. When among non-Travelers—whom they call "country people"—they've been known to speak a quirky dialect, vaguely related to Gaelic, called "the Cant" or "Shelta." As with carnie lingo, the Cant isn't taught to anyone outside the Traveler family. So what are the Travelers hiding? Law-enforcement officials around the country say that in many cases, the "odd jobs" the Travelers do for unsuspecting clients—roofing and driveway painting, for example—are elaborate scams.

The Traveler lifestyle is a fascinating, often disturbing glimpse into an age gone by. Children are sometimes taken out of school after eighth grade—the legal limit—in order to take them on the road and teach them the trade. To maintain privacy, many Travelers marry only other Travelers, often in arranged marriages at ages as young as 12 (although that practice seems to be dying out). Years of intermarriage mean there are only a handful of Traveler surnames, chief among them Carroll, Gorman, Riley, and Sherlock.

South Carolina hosts the bulk of Travelers in the United States, with North Augusta hosting the largest single group in the country. In fact, they have their own subdivision, called Murphy Village after the priest who made the community possible in the 1960s. Contrary to any mental images you may have, many Travelers drive new upscale cars and big shiny pickup trucks. Murphy Village is chockablock with spacious new McMansions, many of which boast large Madonna statues in the front yard.

You literally can't miss Murphy Village. It's on both sides of U.S. 25 on the border of Edgefield County and Aiken County. Just look for the statuary and the big nice houses. Many of the McMansions have their windows covered with butcher paper and sit side-by-side with well-maintained double-wide trailers. Local lore has it that the big houses are part of the dowry of Traveler daughters, intended for the long-engaged couple to move into when they come of age. Another version has it that the paper is to keep *haints* (evil spirits) out of the houses while they're unoccupied.

While the Travelers are not particularly welcoming of curiosity-seekers driving through their community, they'll cause you no harm. In fact, unless you're here in the winter, it's rare to come into contact with the Travelers at all. In the warmer months many are out on the road, doing their thing.

State Historic Site (325 State Park Rd., 803/267-3675, www.southcarolinaparks.com, Thurs.-Mon. 9am-6pm, free), a small but well-managed facility just south of the little town of Ehrhardt. In February 1865 a ragtag group of Confederates held out for two days against a larger contingent of General Sherman's mighty army.

Food
In Blackville, by all means stop at ◖Miller's

Bread Basket (438 Main St., 803/284-3117, Tues. and Thurs.-Fri. 11am-5pm, Wed. and Sat. 11am-3pm, $5-10) on the town's main drag. The women who cook and serve the food wear the traditional simple dresses particular to this strand of the church known as Beachy Mennonites (think less-strict Amish). Load up on the simple but tasty Dutch-influenced Southern buffet, but don't neglect to buy a loaf or two of their famous fresh-baked Mennonite bread.

COLUMBIA AND THE MIDLANDS

COLUMBIA

South of Aiken, the town of New Ellenton, known as "South Carolina's Atomic City," hosts one of the best barbecue joints in the South: **(Carolina Bar-B-Que** (109 Main St., 803/652-2919, Thurs.-Sat. 11am-8pm, $7.50). Within its suitably Spartan locale you'll find a delectable buffet of smoked pulled pork with two sauces available as well as the requisite sides of hash, cracklin's, and hush puppies.

WEST OF AIKEN
Redcliffe Plantation State Historic Site

Beech Island's most famous citizen was South Carolina governor and U.S. Senator James Hammond, who in 1857 began the construction of his grand Greek Revival home, now part of **Redcliffe Plantation State Historic Site** (181 Redcliffe Rd., 803/827-1473, www.southcarolinaparks.com, Thurs.-Mon. 9am-5pm, free). Once a plantation with nearly 1,000 African American slaves working here—Hammond, after all, was the man who famously declared "Cotton is king" on the floor of the Senate—Redcliffe was donated to the state in 1973 by a descendant, *Time* magazine editor John Shaw Billings. You can tour the extensively restored and appointed house (Thurs.-Mon. 1pm, 2pm, 3pm, $4 pp). In addition, there is a 1.5-mile nature trail with great bird-watching through Redcliffe's hardwood forest.

GREENVILLE AND THE UPSTATE

Conservative in culture and worldview, the Upstate—you'll also hear it called the Upcountry—is the fastest-growing region of South Carolina. As such, it's becoming much more diverse each passing year, but the area's hospitality and small-town values remain largely intact.

You don't read about it much in the history books, but the Upstate was the most pivotal theater of the American Revolution, in which groups of Upcountry militia and Loyalist Tories savagely battled back and forth while the uniformed regular armies in New England were at a stalemate. (Filmed entirely in South Carolina, Mel Gibson's film *The Patriot,* though much embellished, does a good job of encapsulating this turbulent period.)

By far the region's main metro area, Greenville is rapidly outpacing its reputation for conservatism. It does so through a devotion to smart urban redevelopment and a forward-looking business sense that has allowed it to move beyond the old mill-based economy that long ago moved offshore.

In the northernmost part of the state, along the fringes of the Blue Ridge Mountains, you'll find stunning natural beauty and plenty of outdoor recreation, all at prices much lower than in the heavily visited havens across the border in more trendy North Carolina.

PLANNING YOUR TIME

You can spend as much or as little time in the Upstate as you want. For the full flavor, you'll need at least three days and two

© JIM MOREKIS

GREENVILLE

HIGHLIGHTS

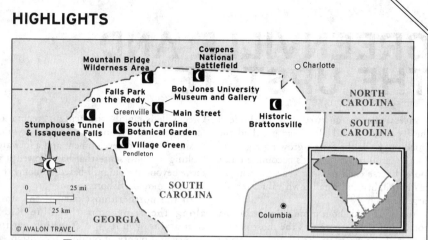

LOOK FOR ◖ TO FIND RECOMMENDED SIGHTS, ACTIVITIES, DINING, AND LODGING.

◖ **Falls Park on the Reedy:** This rolling green oasis is in excellently restored downtown Greenville (page 443).

◖ **Greenville's Main Street:** A nationally renowned example of great walkable urban redesign (page 443).

◖ **Bob Jones University Museum and Gallery:** The largest single collection of religious-themed fine art in North America is housed here (page 444).

◖ **Cowpens National Battlefield:** This interpretive site commemorates a key Patriot victory in the American Revolution (page 451).

◖ **Stumphouse Tunnel and Issaqueena Falls:** This fun twofer features a tunnel with a unique history and a scenic waterfall (page 455).

◖ **Mountain Bridge Wilderness Area:** The wildest area of the Upstate combines Jones Gap State Park with Caesars Head State Park (page 457).

◖ **South Carolina Botanical Garden:** The state's official gardens are on the scenic campus of Clemson University (page 459).

◖ **Pendleton Village Green:** This historic hamlet has a delightful central square (page 461).

◖ **Historic Brattonsville:** Living history and educational fun for the whole family can be found at this restored Upcountry village (page 464).

GREENVILLE

SOUTH CAROLINA

NORTH CAROLINA

GEORGIA

**GREENVILLE AND
THE UPSTATE**

© AVALON TRAVEL

nights. Remember to budget time to explore Greenville's Main Street. For a more focused stay—say, one devoted to hiking or fishing along the Cherokee Foothills Scenic Highway (Hwy. 11)—a couple of nights, or perhaps even one, will do.

Greenville

Greenville, South Carolina, might be the coolest city you've never heard of. There are plenty of well-scrubbed megachurches here, but the only crusade most residents seem to be on is spreading the word that their city is not populated by backward Bible-thumping bigots, but rather is a rapidly growing and increasingly wealthy city nestled in the scenic foothills of the Appalachians.

Early settler Richard Pearis began a plantation around 1770 in what's now downtown Greenville, at East Court and South Main Streets. Well regarded by his Cherokee neighbors, Pearis built up his possessions to include a trading post, stables, a dairy, and a sawmill at what's now Greenville's main visitor attraction, Falls Park on the Reedy River.

By the turn of the 20th century, textile mills began to thrive in the area, and by 1917 Greenville began promoting itself as the "Textile Center of the South." After World War II, that slogan was expanded to "Textile Center of the World." In the 1960s, however, as far-sighted community and business leaders began to see the coming decline of the U.S. textile industry, Greenville began pursuing a more diversified economy, concentrating on increasing foreign investment.

SIGHTS
◖ Falls Park on the Reedy
In a fun quirk of fate, Greenville's most historic spot, the place it began, is also its coolest visitor attraction. **Falls Park on the Reedy** (864/232-2273, www.greatergreenville.com, daily dawn-dusk, free), a rambling, manicured, eclectic outdoor experience along the Reedy River, is where Richard Pearis, the first nonnative settler

up this way, set up his trading post and grist mill in 1768 on what was then Cherokee land. The scenic **Reedy River Falls** themselves powered Pearis's mill and literally helped spawn the city you see today. While the Pearis Mill is long gone, you can still see some ruins of the later Vardry and McBee mills from the early 1800s on the riverbank.

◖ Greenville's Main Street
This renovated area—one of the most well-done I've seen in the country—runs roughly from the Hyatt Regency Hotel slightly downhill to the newest restored area, the West End. Along the way you will enjoy quality stores, cafés, and restaurants of all descriptions, all under a particularly well-crafted and shady tree canopy. Buildings of note along Main Street include the old **Greenville County Courthouse** (130 S. Main St.), which served as a courthouse 1918-1950; the **Chamber of Commerce Building** (130 S. Main St.), built in 1925 and one of the first skyscrapers in Greenville; the way-cool **First National Bank Building** (102 S. Main St.),

GREENVILLE

© JIM MOREKIS
Falls Park on the Reedy

Greenville's only major art deco structure; and, of course, the grand old **Poinsett Hotel** (120 S. Main St.), one of Greenville's original skyscrapers, built in 1925 at the then-enormous cost of $1.5 million, now a Westin property.

Shoeless Joe Jackson Museum
With memorabilia from the life and career of Greenville's favorite native son, the **Shoeless Joe Jackson Museum** (356 Field St., 864/235-6280, www.shoelessjoejackson. org, Sat. 10am-4pm and Greenville Drive home game nights, free) suitably sits adjacent to the new Fluor Field minor-league ballpark in the historic West End. The house, formerly the home of Joe and his family, was moved to this site from 119 East Wilborn Street in 2008, and it currently houses a variety of photos and artifacts, all in a cozy loving setting. Parking next to the museum is free except on Greenville Drive game days.

◀ Bob Jones University Museum and Gallery
Though Bob Jones University gained national notoriety during the 2000 presidential election for its unfortunate stance on interracial dating, you have to give credit where it's due: A fair-minded person has to say that Bob Jones U. deserves national praise for the outstanding collection of religious art at the **Bob Jones University Museum and Gallery** (1700 Wade Hampton Blvd., 864/770-1331, www.bjumg. org, Tues.-Sun. 2pm-5pm, $5 adults, $3 students, free ages 6-12). Indeed, the museum calls itself "Greenville's best-kept secret." The largest single array of such artwork in the western hemisphere, this museum contradicts the idea that Bob Jones U. is a backward collection of bigoted malcontents.

The main gallery at the museum, and the highlight for most visitors, is the Old Masters collection. It includes work by Botticelli, Rubens, and Anthony van Dyck, but don't overlook the often stunning works by lesser-known artists such as the starkly beautiful *Crucifix* by the 14th-century Italian painter Francesco di Vannuccio.

Note the unusually truncated hours of the gallery—it's open only three hours each afternoon Tuesday-Sunday—and plan accordingly. There's a much smaller downtown satellite, the **Museum and Gallery at Heritage Green** (Buncombe St., 864/770-1331, www.bjumg. org, Tues.-Sat. 10am-5pm, Sun. 2pm-5pm, $5 adults, $4 students, free under age 12). Get a combo ticket ($8 adults, $4.50 students and children) to see both collections the same day.

Greenville County Museum of Art
The **Greenville County Museum of Art** (420 College St., 864/271-7570, www.greenvillemuseum.org, Tues.-Wed. and Fri.-Sat. 11am-5pm, Thurs. 11am-8pm, Sun. 1pm-5pm, free) is located in a nice space on the "Heritage Green" downtown at the corner of Academy and College Streets. The feather in their cap is the resident collection, always on display, of 32 of what Andrew Wyeth himself called his best watercolors. They also have an eclectic collection of American contemporary artists such as Josef Albers, Jasper Johns, Andy Warhol, Edward Hopper, and Romare Bearden.

Upcountry History Museum
Also at Heritage Green is a much newer facility, the **Upcountry History Museum** (540 Buncombe St., 864/467-3100, www.upcountryhistory.org, Tues.-Sat. 10am-5pm, Sun. 1pm-5pm, $5 adults, $3 ages 4-12, free under age 4).

Greenville Zoo
The smallish **Greenville Zoo** (150 Cleveland Park Dr., 864/467-4300, www.greenvillezoo.com, daily 10am-4:30pm, $8.75 adults, $5.50 children, free under age 4) is good for an hour or so of fun if you're in the downtown area. It comprises 10 acres tucked into verdant Cleveland Park.

TOURS
Carriage rides (864/369-1411, Fri.-Sat. 6pm-11pm) are available downtown. For more detailed guided tours, check out **Greenville History Tours** (864/567-3940, www.greenvillehistorytours.

THE STORY OF SHOELESS JOE

With the possible exception of another controversial man with the same surname—civil rights leader Jesse Jackson—Greenville's most famous native son is Joseph Jefferson "Shoeless Joe" Jackson, one of a handful of baseball players whose name is mentioned in the same breath as Babe Ruth (who eagerly took hitting tips from the South Carolinian, in fact). Baseball purists remember him for his powerful natural swing and his claim on the third-highest career batting average at .356. But to much of the general public, he's best known for his role in the Black Sox gambling scandal, which he seems to have actually had little to do with.

Born in next-door Pickens County in 1888 (or 1889, some scholars believe), Jackson began working in a textile mill while still a young child, and had no formal education. In those days each mill fielded its own team, and "textile ball" was a popular local pastime for mill workers and area spectators alike. Jackson soon became a standout on the Brandon Mill nine, gaining his nickname when, during a game in nearby Anderson, he took the batter's box in his socks because his new cleats were aggravating a bad blister. After he then swatted a triple, a frustrated fan of the opposing team called Jackson a "shoeless son of a gun," and the name stuck—along with an unfortunate image of a clueless Southern bumpkin.

In 1908 Jackson went on to play minor league ball for the Greenville Spinners. He was soon signed for a short stint with the Philadelphia Athletics, an unproductive relationship that soon had him moonlighting around the South Atlantic League with the Savannah minor-league team. Settling into life in the big leagues, he went on to a five-year run with the Cleveland Indians, chalking up a .408 batting average his rookie season. The gangly left-fielder signed with the Chicago White Sox in 1915, and he still holds the career triples and batting average records for that team.

Jackson's aw-shucks persona would come back to haunt him during the 1919 Black Sox scandal, when the White Sox were accused of throwing that year's World Series. Although he had by far the best performance of both teams during the series, his output dipped notably in the games the White Sox lost. The Chicago papers had a field day savaging the Southerner when under oath he admitted he'd participated. Modern scholarship has shown, however, that an unscrupulous lawyer manipulated him into making the admission. Years later, his teammates admitted he was at none of the meetings where the fix was discussed.

While the jury acquitted Jackson, baseball commissioner Kenesaw Mountain Landis banned him from the sport anyway. A hangdog Jackson returned to the familiar South, opening up a successful dry-cleaning business back in Savannah. He also quietly managed and played on several Georgia semipro and "outlaw" teams. He moved back to Greenville with his wife in 1933, continuing to play and manage. For the rest of his life Jackson proclaimed his innocence, though he fatalistically accepted his tarnished place in history. While working at a Greenville liquor store he owned late in life, none other than the great Ty Cobb and sportswriter Grantland Rice came in. According to Rice, after Cobb paid for his bottle, he asked Jackson, "Don't you know me, Joe?" Jackson said, "Sure, I know you, Ty, but I wasn't sure you wanted to speak to me. A lot of them don't."

Jackson died of a heart attack in 1951 and is buried in Woodlawn Memorial Park in Greenville, section 5, plot 333. You can find a striking bronze statue of Shoeless Joe in downtown Greenville in the West End on Main Street. The **Shoeless Joe Jackson Museum** (356 Field St., 864/235-6280, www.shoelessjoejackson. org, Sat. 10am-4pm and Greenville Drive home game nights, free) is adjacent to the new ballpark in the historic West End. Once the Jackson family home, the structure was moved from 119 East Wilborn Street to this location. Another effort to honor him is the dedication of **Shoeless Joe Jackson Memorial Park** (406 West Ave., 864/288-6470, daily dawn-dusk, free), farther out on the West End on the site of an old ball field where the man himself once played.

Today, Jackson's legacy is in a bit of a renaissance, and you can find out more about the advocacy effort to get him into the Baseball Hall of Fame at www.blackbetsy.com, a website bearing the nickname of his favorite bat.

com, $12, culinary tour $39), which offers several options.

ENTERTAINMENT AND EVENTS
Nightlife
Since native son Edwin McCain's heyday in the late 1990s, there has been no Greenville music "scene" per se, but the center of live music is **The Handlebar** (304 E. Stone Ave., 864/233-6173, www.handlebar-online.com, ticket prices vary), a little way north of downtown. Subtitled "A Listening Room," the Handlebar markets itself specifically as an intimate space that's friendly for musicians and audiences alike.

In the restored West End across from Falls Park is **Chicora Alley** (608 S. Main St., 864/232-4100, www.chicoraalley.com, Tues.-Sat. 5pm-2am, Sun.-Mon. 5pm-midnight), a great place to grab a bite, have a brew, and listen to reggae or jazz.

Performing Arts
One might not rank the **Greenville Symphony Orchestra** (GSO, 200 S. Main St., 864/232-0344, www.greenvillesymphony.org) among the world's greatest ensembles, but it is an impressive group nonetheless and is the city's performing arts crown jewel. The GSO now plays most of its concerts at the modern and beautiful Peace Center Concert Hall on the banks of the Reedy River.

My favorite Greenville event—and perhaps the most surprising one to outsiders who assume the city is populated by clueless hayseeds—is the summer-long **Upstate Shakespeare Festival** (Falls Park, S. Main St., 864/787-4016, www.upstateshakespearefestival.org, performances May-Aug. Thurs.-Sun. 7pm, free). The festival brings two complete productions by the Bard in the rolling Falls Park.

SHOPPING
For all practical purposes, shopping in Greenville comes in two forms: on Main Street and off. Don't neglect the restored West End section of Main Street.

Main Street
The most unique shopping experience on Main Street is at the **Mast General Store** (111 N. Main St., 864/235-1883, Mon.-Thurs. 10am-6pm, Fri.-Sat. 10am-9pm, Sun. noon-5pm), a branch of a North Carolina-based regional chain. This hard-to-define and sprawling store, restored to a 1920s vibe, has camping gear, outdoor clothing, preppy clothes, local books, maps, gifts, and an entire candy section in the back.

Paying homage to one of the area's largest employers is **Michelin on Main** (550 S. Main St., 864/241-4450), which contains every kind of Michelin-branded thing you can imagine. The funky **Christopher Park Gallery** (608-A S. Main St., 864/232-6744, www.chickenmanart.com) in the West End has a variety of outsider paintings and sculptures and locally crafted jewelry. On the other end of Main is the **Mary Praytor Gallery** (26 S. Main St., 864/235-1800, www.themarypraytorgallery.com, Tues.-Sat. 10am-5pm), which features eclectic folk art and contemporary paintings from regional artists.

SPORTS AND RECREATION
While most serious outdoor activity in the Upstate is in the region to the north, there are still plenty of delightful recreation opportunities in and around Greenville, especially for families with children.

Parks
Falls Park on the Reedy (601 S. Main St., 864/467-4350, www.fallspark.com, daily 24 hours, free) is a great place downtown to relax, exercise, get some sun, or simply just enjoy the greenery.

Paris Mountain State Park (2401 State Park Rd., 864/244-5565, www.southcarolinaparks.com, daily 8am-sunset, $2 adults, free under age 16), is an absolutely charming Civilian Conservation Corps-built state park. There are 39 sites, 13 of which are dedicated tent sites ($14-15). There are also five primitive sites ($10-12) on the North Lake trail. To get to Paris Mountain State Park, take the North

Pleasantburg Drive/Highway 291 exit from I-385. Go north on Piney Mountain Road, take a right onto State Park Road, and continue on to the park entrance.

Spectator Sports

If you ask the typical Greenville resident what is the most important sports event in the area, they'll say Clemson football. But technically speaking, a more pertinent spectator pastime in Greenville comes courtesy of the **Greenville Drive** (945 S. Main St., 864/240-4528, www.greenvilledrive.com, box seats $8), an affiliate of the Boston Red Sox playing in the South Atlantic League. They play in the retro-style Fluor Field in the historic West End, built in 2005 as a nearly exact facsimile of Boston's Fenway Park.

ACCOMMODATIONS

Visitors to Greenville will be pleasantly surprised at the low rates for lodging compared to other American metropolitan areas, a surprise made even more pleasant by the generally high standards.

Under $150

The best accommodations value in Greenville, the **Drury Inn and Suites** (10 Carolina Point Pkwy., 800/378-7946, www.druryhotels.com, $96-175) has excellent facilities, classy decor, prompt, attentive service, and most rooms under $150.

The best and most popular B&B in town is **Pettigru Place** (302 Pettigru St., 864/242-4529, www.pettigruplace.com, $115-195), and not only because of its proximity to scenic Cleveland Park and being a 20-minute walk from Main Street's activity. Pettigru's five guest rooms are decorated tastefully along particular themes.

$150-300

The only four-diamond hotel in Greenville and easily its most pedigreed, the **Westin Poinsett** (120 South Main St., 864/421-9700, www.starwoodhotels.com, $185-245) isn't for those who insist on a brand-new building. This

is a historic inn built in 1925, and the elegantly simple guest rooms and decor reflect this. The staff is professional and friendly, and you can't beat the location—right on top of the old town center on bustling Main Street.

Anchoring the east end of Main Street's revitalization is the **Hyatt Regency Greenville** (220 N. Main St., 864/235-1234, www.greenvillehyatt.com, $159-259), which is somewhat dated in its monolithic style, typical of the chain. When people downtown talk about going "up near the Hyatt," this is what they're referencing.

FOOD
Barbecue

Don't be put off by the nondescript exterior and small dining room at **Henry's Smokehouse** (240 Wade Hampton Blvd., 864/232-7774, www.henryssmokehouse.com, call for hours, $4-10). This is one of the best, if not the best, Upstate barbecue joints and a true Greenville tradition, even though they have taken on some trappings of Midlands 'cue cooking, offering a mustard-based sauce. If the mustard sauce is too much of an acquired taste for you, they also offer the indigenous upcountry tomato-based sauce as well.

Just about as good as Henry's is **Smokin' Stokes** (1622 Augusta St., 864/242-9716, www.smokinstokes.com, call for hours, $7-10), a similarly humble location offering a lot of taste for the buck. Their signature sauce is made from Cheerwine, a regional cherry-flavored soda.

Classic Southern

Like its older sister location in Charleston, **High Cotton** (550 S. Main St., 864/335-4200, www.mavericksouthernkitchens.com, daily 5:30pm-10pm, Sun. jazz brunch 10am-2pm, $20-40) deals in robust, no-nonsense takes on Southern and American classics. Meats and game are a particular specialty. Reservations are recommended.

The word *quaint* seems to be applied quite often to dining at **Mary's Restaurant at Falls Cottage** (615 S. Main St., 864/298-0005, www.fallscottage.com, Tues.-Sat. 11am-2pm, Sun. 10am-2pm, prix fixe dinner $22-33), and rightly so for an experience in this daintily restored little cottage scenically overlooking Falls Park. Breakfast buffet, lunches, and brunches are popular here, and the dinner menu is a range of prix fixe offerings. Reservations are strongly recommended.

New Southern

Housed in an old cigar factory, **Devereaux's** (25 E. Court St., 864/241-3030, www.devereauxsdining.com, Tues.-Sun. from 6pm, $20-40) is the kind of place where out-of-town executives or locals looking for a special night out dine. You can go one of three ways: either the usual à la carte selections, such as a bourbon pork loin or a seared black grouper; the five-course tasting menu ($75 pp, wine flights $25); or the 10-course Chef's Ultimate Tasting Menu (price varies).

A trendier pick is **American Grocery** (732 S. Main St., 864/232-7665, www.americangr.com, Tues.-Sat. 6pm-10pm, $15-25), which is not a grocery store at all but an upscale advocate for *very* locally sourced organic and all-natural meats and produce.

INFORMATION AND SERVICES

The main visitors center in Greenville is the **Greenville Downtown Visitor Center** (206 S. Main St., 864/233-0461, www.greenvillecvb.com, Mon.-Fri. 8:30am-5pm). Another one close by is the **Greenville Convention and Visitors Bureau** (631 S. Main St., 864/421-0000, www.greenvillecvb.com, Mon.-Fri. 8:30am-5pm), which has brochures and maps only.

GETTING THERE AND AROUND
By Air

This rapidly growing metro area is served by the **Greenville-Spartanburg International Airport** (GSP, www.gspairport.com), the busiest in the state, at I-85 exit 57. Airlines here include American, Delta, Northwest, United, and US Airways.

By Train

Trains stop at the **Greenville Amtrak Station** (1120 W. Washington St., 864/255-4221, www.amtrak.com), with daily service in each direction on the New Orleans-New York City *Crescent.*

By Car

The main routes into Greenville are I-85 as well as I-185, which enters the city from the west side and becomes Mills Avenue, and then shortly becomes Church Street. From there, most attractions of interest are to the west (on your left) as you drive into town. Signage is generally excellent in Greenville.

A spur off I-85 called I-385 enters Greenville from the east and runs by the airport. Keep in mind, however, that this is a toll road. There really is no need to use it unless you are coming in and out of the airport. Laurens Road (U.S. 276) on the other side of the airport leads into town in virtually the same place.

By Bus

Greenlink (864/467-5000, www.ridegreenlink.com) is an all-biodiesel fleet with various routes throughout Greenville County. Each ride is $1.25 and transfers are $0.50. Children under age 6 ride free.

Spartanburg

A half hour's drive from Greenville, it's tempting to think of Spartanburg as a miniature version of the same thing. They're quite often mentioned literally in the same breath, as when people speak of the Greenville-Spartanburg metro area. But Spartanburg definitely has a vibe all its own. Not as enveloped in new construction as Greenville or as thick with newer residents, it retains its small-town attitude while hosting a growing contingent of progressive thinkers.

Spanish explorer Juan Pardo came through in 1567 and etched his name on "The Pardo Stone," now in a local museum. One of the Revolutionary War's key engagements took place at nearby Cowpens, where a combined force of colonial militia and Continental Army soldiers soundly defeated a British contingent of redcoats and Loyalists. In the 19th century, with a break during the Civil War, Spartanburg, along with Greenville, grew in importance as major textile centers. It was during this time that Spartanburg got its nickname, "Hub City."

SIGHTS
Morgan Square
The best place to start your explorations in Spartanburg is downtown at **Morgan Square** (daily 24 hours), the center of the city's efforts to transform into a model of pedestrian-friendly downtown redevelopment. Nicely restored in an effort begun in 2005 to upgrade the downtown area, nearby is a throwback to Spartanburg's rail heyday, the **Magnolia Street Train Depot** (Magnolia St. and Morgan Ave.), which now hosts the local Amtrak station, the Visitors Bureau, and the Hub City Farmer's Market (Sat. 8am-noon).

Seay House
Vernacular architecture buffs will enjoy viewing the oldest building still standing in Spartanburg, the **Seay House** (106 Darby Rd., 864/596-3501, by appointment Apr.-Oct. the 3rd weekend of the month Sat. 11am-5pm, Sun. 2pm-5pm, donation), built by farmer Kinsman Seay around 1800. Take Crescent Drive off John B. White Boulevard, and then a left onto Darby Road.

Hatcher Garden and Woodland Preserve
The delightful **Hatcher Garden and Woodland Preserve** (832 John B. White Sr. Blvd., 864/574-7724, www.hatchergarden.org, daily dawn-dusk, free) was the labor of love of Harold and Josephine Hatcher, who in 1969 began planting over 10,000 trees and flowering bushes to realize their vision of a community garden. Now an expertly and lovingly tended 10-acre public garden, the site boasts gorgeous flower displays, little ponds, and tastefully arranged viewing platforms.

Walnut Grove Plantation
The most notable historic structure in the Spartanburg area is the **Walnut Grove Plantation** (1200 Otts Shoals Rd., Roebuck, 864/576-6546, Apr.-Oct. Tues.-Sat. 11am-5pm, Sun. 2pm-5pm, Nov.-Mar. Sat. 11am-5pm, $6 adults, $3 children, free under age 6), outside of town in little Roebuck. It was built in 1765 on land granted by King George III to the family of planter Charles Moore; the most famous resident was their daughter Margaret Kathryn "Kate" Moore (later Barry), the local heroine who warned of the approach of the British on the eve of the pivotal Battle of Cowpens. About 500 yards west of the main house is the Moore family cemetery.

BMW Zentrum
Although it's technically located in Greer, right next door, Spartanburg tends to claim the **BMW Zentrum** (1400 Hwy. 101 S., Greer, 888/868-7269, Mon.-Fri. 9:30am-5:30pm, free admission, guided factory tours $5 adults, $3.50

GREENVILLE

© JIM MOREKIS

Morgan Square in downtown Spartanburg

students, advance tour reservations required) as its own. Currently the only place outside Germany where BMWs are manufactured, the Zentrum is an interesting hybrid exhibit combining a factory and a museum.

There are two basic experiences: the sleek, crescent-shaped Zentrum Museum, where you'll explore the history of the Bavarian Motor Works, see some fine historical autos and motorcycles, and witness some experimental models; and the BMW factory, where guided tours take you inside the intriguing high-tech process whereby these modern machines are made. No high heels or open-toe shoes are allowed on the factory tours, and you have to be 12 or older to take part.

Spartanburg Museum of Art

The aggressively local **Spartanburg Museum of Art** (200 E. St. John St., 864/948-5364, www.spartanburgartmuseum.org, Tues.-Wed. and Fri.-Sat. 10am-5pm, Thurs. 10am-8pm, $5 adults, $3 students and ages 4-17, free under age 4, first Thurs. of the month free)

began with the acquisition of *The Girl with Red Hair* by Robert Henri in 1907. Since then, the Museum has acquired over 400 pieces of art and sculpture for its permanent collection, which mostly focuses on regional artists. It's housed in the big Chapman Cultural Center downtown.

Spartanburg Regional Museum of History

In the same building as the Museum of Art is the **Spartanburg Regional Museum of History** (200 E. St. John St., 864/596-3501, Tues.-Wed. and Fri.-Sat. 10am-5pm, Thurs. 10am-8pm, Sun. 1pm-5pm, $5 adults, $3 students and ages 4-17, free under age 4, first Thurs. of the month free), run by the Spartanburg County Historical Association and housed in the big Chapman Cultural Center downtown. Perhaps the single most historically important item in the collection is the Pardo Stone, a boulder supposedly bearing graffiti from the first Spanish explorer to come through the Upstate, Juan Pardo.

GREENVILLE

© JIM MOREKIS

Cowpens National Battlefield

🏛 Cowpens National Battlefield

In historical terms the most significant sight in the Spartanburg area is **Cowpens National Battlefield** (4001 Chesnee Hwy., 864/461-2828, www.nps.gov/cowp, daily 9am-5pm, free). Fought literally in an old cattle pasture, hence the name, the once-dreaded British cavalry colonel Banastre Tarleton was driven from the field by a combined force of General Daniel Morgan's continentals and local militia (Morgan is memorialized with a park bearing his name in nearby downtown Spartanburg). From that point on, the British remained on the defensive for the rest of the war.

The 1.3-mile **Battlefield Trail** includes exhibits, the 1856 Washington Light Infantry Monument, and the Green River Road, along which the battle was fought. If you want to stay in your car, take the 3.8-mile **Auto Loop Road,** which includes exhibits and parking areas with short trails to the Green River Road, an 1818 log cabin, and a picnic area. Also at Cowpens you'll find a trailhead for the **Overmountain Victory National Historic**

Trail (864/936-3477, www.nps.gov/ovvi), which goes all the way to Virginia.

From April to October you can take advantage of free one-hour guided walks of the battlefield (Sat. 9:30am, Sun. 1:30pm). Each year on the weekend closest to January 17, the anniversary of the battle, the park celebrates with various demonstrations of period weaponry and a cool living-history encampment.

Poinsett Bridge

The oldest bridge in the state is the beautiful little 14-foot **Poinsett Bridge** (Callahan Mountain Rd., Lyman), built around 1820 by Joel T. Poinsett, city father of Greenville and the man for whom the poinsettia is named. Get there by taking U.S. 25 north past its intersection with Highway 11 and turn right onto Old Highway 25. Take a right onto Callahan Road.

ENTERTAINMENT AND EVENTS
Nightlife

On Morgan Square you can't miss the

HOW SOUTH CAROLINA SAVED AMERICA

To read most history books, you'd think the Revolutionary War took place almost entirely in Boston. But South Carolina was the location of the conflict's fiercest fighting, suffering the most men killed of all 13 colonies. Savage and personal, the fighting here usually involved not uniformed regulars but Patriot and Tory militia.

In a span of 90 days, Upstate South Carolina hosted two of the most important Patriot victories of the war, Kings Mountain and Cowpens. Sent to pacify the backcountry's independent-minded Scots-Irish colonists, British major Patrick Ferguson led 1,000 Tory militiamen to a stronghold at the base of Kings Mountain on the border of the Carolinas. On October 7, 1780, an equal number of Appalachian militiamen assaulted the position using tactics they'd learned fighting Native Americans. Rather than marching as a unit and shooting en masse as a European army would, each militiaman fired at will as he attacked, hiding behind rocks to reload. Another trick the colonists learned from the indigenous people was the demoralizing effect of a high-pitched whoop as they attacked.

The battle seesawed for an hour. The end came when Ferguson, attempting to rally his men, was riddled with eight bullets. As the Tory line collapsed, colonists initially sounded the cry "Tarleton's Quarter!," an ironic reference to the brutal British colonel Banastre Tarleton, infamous for murdering prisoners. But cooler heads prevailed, and 700 Loyalists were taken prisoner.

By January 1781 many Kings Mountain veterans had joined General Daniel Morgan, who chose a large cattle-grazing area—literally, the "cow pens"—outside modern-day Spartanburg to make a stand. Learning from the debacle at Camden, Morgan picked a wide-open battlefield with no place for potentially panicking militiamen to run and hide. To further bolster the colonists, he posted regular Continental Army troops behind them.

Thinking the retreating militiamen were panicking, Tarleton's men advanced into a firestorm of bullets. Sending militiamen out on both wings, Morgan surrounded the British in a classic double envelopment, studied by military leaders to this day.

In a very real way, Cowpens led directly to American victory in the war. With the exception of his stronghold at Charleston, General Cornwallis wrote off South Carolina and moved his troops into North Carolina instead. A series of engagements led to his retreat up the Virginia coast to Yorktown, where, bottled up by Washington's army and the French fleet, he was forced to surrender.

You can visit both battle sites today, at **Kings Mountain National Military Park** (2625 Park Rd., 803/222-3209, www.nps.gov/kimo, Labor Day-Memorial Day daily 9am-5pm, Memorial Day-Labor Day daily 9am-6pm, free) near Blacksburg and **Cowpens National Battlefield** (4001 Chesnee Hwy., 864/461-2828, www.nps.gov/cowp, daily 9am-5pm, free) near Gaffney.

popular, cavernous **Delaney's Irish Pub** (117 W. Main St., 864/583-3100, Mon.-Sat. 11am-2am, Sun. 3pm-2am). They have a great selection of beer on tap and in the bottle as well as a very good menu of pub food. Dating from 1938, the **Nu-Way Restaurant and Lounge** (373 E. Kennedy St., 864/582-9685) is Spartanburg's version of every town's lovable old dive. This is the place to go for that ironically hip night out on the town.

Performing Arts

Some vibrant stuff goes on downtown at the **Hub-Bub** (149 S. Daniel Morgan Ave., Suite 2, 864/582-0056, www.hub-bub.com, admission varies). Housed in a former Nash Rambler dealership, Hub-Bub hosts over 100 evenings a year of concerts, film, art exhibits, plays, and workshops, almost all of it with a countercultural edge for this conservative area.

The very definition of a "multiuse" venue,

the beautiful new **Chapman Cultural Center** (200 E. St. John St., 864/542-2787, www.chapmanculturalcenter.org, admission varies) next to Barnet Park has a 500-seat theater that hosts performances by several local theater groups as well as Ballet Spartanburg. It also houses the city's two main museums, the Spartanburg County Museum of Art and the Spartanburg Regional History Museum.

SHOPPING

My favorite shop in Spartanburg is the nonprofit **Hub City Bookshop** (186 W. Main St., 864/577-9349, www.hubcity.org, Mon.-Thurs. 10am-7pm, Fri.-Sat. 10am-9pm), which has a great selection of new and used tomes and also serves as the central meeting point for the Hub City Writers Project and houses the Hub City Press. There's also an attached coffee shop.

SPORTS AND RECREATION
Hiking and Biking

Spartanburg is becoming a mecca of sorts for bicyclists. The city is the launching point for the **Assault on Mt. Mitchell** (www.freewheelers.info) each May, an amateur race over 100 miles long taking participants from Spartanburg to Mt. Mitchell, North Carolina, highest point east of the Mississippi River.

The main recreation area close to Spartanburg is **Croft State Natural Area** (450 Croft State Park Rd., 864/585-1283, www.southcarolinaparks.com, daily 7am-9pm, $2 adults, free under age 16), which offers 12 miles of biking and hiking trails within its massive acreage, once a U.S. Army training ground. As the Palmetto Trail nears completion, a section is expected to join Croft with the rest of the trail.

ACCOMMODATIONS
Under $150

The first and still best-regarded B&B in Spartanburg is the award-winning **◖ Inn on Main** (319 E. Main St., 864/585-5001, www.innonmain-spartanburg.com, $95-155). Located in a historic 1904 building right on the main drag, Inn on Main offers six distinctive,

exquisitely furnished suites that wouldn't be out of place in one of the classic B&Bs in Charleston or Beaufort (and at about half the price). The beds alone, some of which are genuine antiques, will wow you. Of course, you get the requisite full Southern breakfast served in a clubby setting typical of the inn's common areas. Keep in mind they discourage kids under age 12.

As far as hotels in Spartanburg, your best bet is the **Spartanburg Marriott at Renaissance Park** (299 N. Church St., 864/596-1211, www.spartanburgmarriott.com, $109-179). This spacious (240 rooms) new facility is smoke-free and within walking distance of the downtown area.

FOOD
Asian

A good Thai place, right downtown on Morgan Square, is **Lime Leaf** (101 E. Main St., 864/542-2171, www.limeleaf101.com, Mon.-Fri. 11:30am-3pm and 5pm-10pm, Sat. 5pm-11pm, $9-15). For a sushi fix, check out **Wasabi** (1529 John B. White Sr. Blvd., 864/576-8998, Tues.-Sat. 11:30am-2:30pm and 5pm-10pm, $5-10).

Classic Southern

No visit to Spartanburg is complete without a visit to the **Beacon Drive-In** (255 John B. White Blvd., 864/585-9387, www.beacondrivein.com, Mon.-Sat. 6:30am-10pm, $5-7). As is the case with many surviving greasy spoon-type places with retro allure, the media hype now surrounding the Beacon doesn't quite match up to the food, which is really very simple when you get down to it. The signature offering is the Chili Cheese A-Plenty, which sounds like a chili dog but is actually a burger topped with chili and cheese ("A-Plenty" means you get a huge mound of fries and onion rings tossed on top).

Coffee, Tea, and Sweets

The most happening coffee and sweet-treat shop in town is **◖ The Coffee Bar** (188-A W.

GREENVILLE

Main St., 864/582-1227, www.littlerivercoffeebar.com), located in the historic Masonic Temple downtown and directly adjacent to the Hub City Bookshop and the nonprofit goings-on there.

Pizza
There's a continuing rivalry over who has the best pizza in Spartanburg: **Venus Pie Pizza** (400 E. Main St., 864/582-4200, Mon.-Tues. 11:30am-9pm, Wed. 11:30am-9:30pm, Thurs.-Fri. 11:30am-10:30pm, Sat. 11:30am-10pm, $6-12) or **The Mellow Mushroom** (464 E. Main St., 864/582-5495, Mon.-Thurs. 11am-10pm, Fri.-Sat. 11am-midnight, Sun. noon-9pm, $7-14) down the block. The former is a totally local venture, while the latter is a regional chain.

GETTING THERE AND AROUND
While Spartanburg does have its own small municipal airport, **Spartanburg Downtown Memorial Airport** (SPA, 500 Ammons Rd., 864/574-8552, www.cityofspartanburg.org), it has no commercial flights, and most visitors fly into the area at the much larger **Greenville-Spartanburg International Airport** (GSP, 2000 GSP Dr., 864/877-7426, www.gspairport.com), a short distance west of town along I-85. Another option is **Charlotte-Douglas International Airport** (CLT, 5501 Josh Birmingham Pkwy., 704/359-4000, www.clt.com) 70 miles east in nearby North Carolina.

Amtrak (290 Magnolia St., 800/872-7245, www.amtrak.com) has a station downtown, with daily service in each direction on the New Orleans-New York City *Crescent*. There's also a **Greyhound bus station** (100 N. Liberty St., www.greyhound.com).

Public transportation by bus in Spartanburg is offered by **Spartanburg Area Regional Transit Agency (SPARTA)** (100 N. Liberty St., 864/562-4287, www.spartabus.com). Fares run $1.25 per trip, and eight interlocking routes take you all over town, including the mall area.

Along the Blue Ridge

While the landscape is not as stark as north of the border, the Blue Ridge in South Carolina has the dual advantages of being both more easily accessible and much less expensive than the increasingly upscale area of the North Carolina mountains.

ELLICOTT ROCK WILDERNESS AREA
With roots in a scenic area designated in the 1960s, one of the oldest trails in the Southeast is the **Ellicott Rock Wilderness Area** (864/638-9568, www.fs.fed.us, daily year-round, free), which has acreage in three states. It takes you through the Chattooga River gorge in the Sumter National Forest, with about half the trail in North Carolina and a small portion in Georgia. Ellicott Rock itself, once inaccurately considered the meeting point of the three states, is actually in North Carolina. You can reach it on one of the trails in the wilderness area.

Get here by taking Forest Road 708 (Burrells Ford Rd.) west of Highway 107. There's a parking area near the Burrells Ford campground, and it's a short hike to the Chattooga River. Since the Chattooga River became designated a Wild and Scenic River, you can no longer drive your car all the way into **Burrell's Ford Campground** in the Sumter National Forest. But if you don't mind hiking a short distance, you'll be happy to be away from the RV crowd. As you'd expect, this is a no-frills campground, with a hand-pumped well and minimal toilet facilities.

OCONEE STATE PARK
One of the gems of the Civilian Conservation Corps era in South Carolina, **Oconee State Park** (624 State Park Rd., Mountain Rest,

864/638-5353, www.southcarolinaparks. com, during daylight saving time daily 7am-9pm, other seasons Sun.-Thurs. 7am-7pm, Fri.-Sat. 7am-9pm, $2 adults, free under age 16), a few miles north of Walhalla, is also one of the Upstate's most popular campgrounds. Its two lakes are picturesque, with paddleboat and johnboat rentals available ($10 per day). There's a good network of trails onsite, including the beginning of the Foothills Trail.

◖ STUMPHOUSE TUNNEL AND ISSAQUEENA FALLS

This combo free attraction, a neat place to bring the family, is overseen by the nearby town of Walhalla as part of a conservation agreement among the town, local landowners, and a few nonprofit groups. You'll find it clearly marked on the east side of Highway 28 several miles north of Walhalla.

The **Stumphouse Tunnel** (864/638-4343, daily 8am-5pm, free) is a cool (literally) and possibly slightly frightening experience that kids will either really enjoy or be really petrified of. You won't know until you get them here, so it's worth checking out.

In the early 1800s somebody hatched a plan to run a railroad from Charleston to the Midwest, to be known as the Blue Ridge Rail Line. The line was built from Charleston to nearby Pendleton, but one big problem remained: Stumphouse Mountain was in the way. Residing in a hastily formed rough-and-rowdy burg called, suitably enough, Tunneltown, 1,500 workers managed to dig about 1,600 feet of the planned mile-long tunnel when funds ran out. Then the Civil War started, and thus ended the Blue Ridge Line.

The 25-foot-high tunnel stayed empty until the 1940s, when Clemson University professor Paul Miller discovered that the tunnel's interior stayed a consistent 56°F with 85 percent humidity year-round, making it a perfect natural cooler to store and age the signature Clemson blue cheese. The school in fact aged its cheese in the Stumphouse Tunnel for years until they were able to duplicate those conditions on

GREENVILLE

© JIM MOREKIS

Stumphouse Tunnel, near Walhalla

GREENVILLE

THE LEGEND OF ISSAQUEENA FALLS

Issaqueena Falls

Oconee County lore says that sometime in the late 1700s, Cherokee maiden Issaqueena fell in love with an English trader named Allan Francis. When the local Cherokee planned an attack on an English outpost, Issaqueena got on her pony and took a 96-mile ride to warn them, which fittingly ended at the English fort at Ninety Six. She stayed by her man, beginning a family with

© JIM MOREKIS

him back at Stumphouse Mountain where she had grown up.

But one day a group of Cherokee staged a kidnapping attempt on Issaqueena. She ran from them, but they eventually caught up to her at the 200-foot waterfall at the base of the mountain. Legend has it that Issaqueena pretended to fling herself to her death over the falls but actually hid under a ledge until her pursuers left. Another version has it that she hid under the falls because the Cherokee supposedly thought evil spirits dwelled in waterfalls.

So is the story true? In the frontier memoirs of Ann Matthews, we read about an Indian woman: Because she "disliked very much to think that the white women who had been so good to her in giving her clothes and bread and butter in trading parties would be killed, she became determined to let them know their danger, she started after night, when all was still, and walked 96 miles in twenty-four hours spreading news as she went." Other accounts confirm this story. Some recent scholars, however, doubt her existence at all, citing a curious abundance of highly romantic and elaborately embellished tales from the Victorian era about comely Indian maidens falling in love with white settlers.

If she did exist, however, perhaps the best clue to Issaqueena's psychology has as much to do with lineage as with love. Legend says that Issaqueena was actually one of the Choctaw people kidnapped by the Cherokee, and her given name at birth was Cateechee.

campus. Today, a walk in the tunnel—about 500 feet of it is still open—is like a scary, albeit very low-budget, thrill ride.

A short walking distance from Stumphouse Tunnel is another charming attraction, **Issaqueena Falls** (864/638-4343, daily 8am-5pm, free). It's a popular place to visit and admire the water's forceful path down over the rocks, many of which you can climb out on if you're feeling adventurous (be warned: the rock gets very slippery in places).

OCONEE STATION STATE HISTORIC SITE

Not to be confused with nearby Oconee State Park, **Oconee Station State Historic Site** (500 Oconee Station Rd., 864/638-0079, www.southcarolinaparks.com, daily 9am-6pm, free) is a much smaller park with no camping facilities, geared toward the enjoyment of two historic sites within it as well as a popular and easily accessible waterfall. The main structure is **Oconee Station** (Sat.-Sun. 1pm-5pm, free), a reconstructed late-1700s blockhouse (fort), used to defend what was then the frontier. Get here by taking Highway 11 (Cherokee Foothills Scenic Byway) north of West Union and Walhalla a few miles and following the signs.

DEVIL'S FORK STATE PARK

Devil's Fork State Park (161 Holcombe Circle, 864/944-2639, www.southcarolinaparks.com, spring-summer daily 7am-9pm, winter Sat.-Thurs. 7am-6pm, Fri. 7am-8pm, $2 adults, free under age 16) is one of the easier and more picturesque modern, non-Civilian Conservation Corps South Carolina state parks. Its claim to fame is being the only public access to Lake Jocassee, which despite its artificial nature is pretty picturesque.

KEOWEE-TOXAWAY STATE NATURAL AREA

At the halfway point between the two ends of the Cherokee Foothills Scenic Byway (Hwy. 11) lies **Keowee-Toxaway State Natural Area** (108 Residence Dr., Sunset, 864/868-2605, www.southcarolinaparks.com, during daylight saving time daily 7am-9pm, other seasons Sat.-Thurs. 9am-6pm, Fri. 9am-8pm, free). This is one of the state's newer and smaller campgrounds, built in the 1970s on 1,000 acres of land donated by Duke Power, which is also responsible for the existence of Lake Keowee, on which the site resides and under which are the remains of an ancient Cherokee town.

Don't miss the **Cherokee Heritage Interpretive Center** (daily 11am-noon and 4pm-5pm, free) on-site. While the story ends with the tragic chapter of the Trail of Tears, you'll come away with a new appreciation for the majesty and culture of the Cherokee people, whom 19th-century settlers considered one of the "Five Civilized Tribes."

TABLE ROCK STATE PARK

A very popular state park with the casual RV crowd as well as with serious hikers is **Table Rock State Park** (158 E. Ellison Lane, 864/878-9813, www.southcarolinaparks.com, during daylight saving time Sun.-Thurs.

7am-7pm, Fri.-Sat. 7am-9pm, other seasons Sun.-Thurs. 7am-9pm, Fri.-Sat. 7am-10pm, $2 adults, free under age 16), just off Highway 11, the Cherokee Foothills Scenic Byway. With two lakes, well-appointed cabins, tent and RV sites, and some exceptional examples of Civilian Conservation Corps handiwork, there is plenty to do and see. But perhaps the key element is Table Rock itself, dominating the northern sky-scape and compelling hikers like a large magnet. Serving as the eastern trailhead for the 76-mile-long Foothills Trail, the park provides access to several strenuous but ultimately rewarding journeys.

Just off the Cherokee Foothills Scenic Highway is **The Inn at Table Rock** (117 Hiawatha Tr., 864/878-0078, www.theinnattablerock.com, $129-179). This six-room historic Victorian offers a bucolic, sumptuous setting on four acres, with some nice views of Table Rock and the Blue Ridge to the north. Keep in mind they discourage guests under age 18.

◖ MOUNTAIN BRIDGE WILDERNESS AREA

By far the most wild and wooly nature experience in the Upstate is at **Mountain Bridge Wilderness Area** (8155 Geer Hwy./U.S. 276, Cleveland, 864/836-6115, www.southcarolinaparks.com, spring-summer daily 9am-9pm, fall-winter daily 9am-6pm, $2 adults, free under age 16) just shy of the border with North Carolina. Technically speaking, this site actually comprises two well-known parks, **Caesars Head State Park** and **Jones Gap State Park,** but these are very atypical South Carolina state parks, so don't be fooled by the designation.

The only way to stay here is truly primitive camping—no water, no tent pad, no electricity, and certainly no showers or restrooms nearby. On the Middle Saluda River through the area, anglers find some great trout fishing; a valid state fishing license is required (www.dnr.sc.gov).

The focal point of the area is the hike to Caesars Head, a fancifully shaped 3,622-foot-tall rock outcropping along the Blue Ridge Escarpment. The other major

WATERFALLS OF THE UPSTATE

Because of South Carolina's location on the Blue Ridge Escarpment—the so-called "Blue Wall" marking the sudden end of the Appalachians—it contains dozens of waterfalls, from grand to humble. While there are plenty of brochures and websites out there guiding you to the locations of South Carolina's waterfalls, keep in mind that some falls are significantly more difficult to get to than others, especially if there has been a recent rain to turn the old logging roads into muck. Also remember that some of the more remote falls require strenuous, if enjoyable, hikes.

Here is a sampling of some of the more accessible falls in the Upstate. For more info, go to www.alleneasler.com/waterfalls.html or www.sctrails.net.

- At 420 feet, **Raven Cliff Falls** are the highest in South Carolina, and by some measures, the highest in the eastern United States. Get here by way of a fairly easy 4.4-mile round-trip hike out of Caesars Head State Park in the Mountain Bridge Wilderness Area. There's a parking area off U.S. 276.

- Table Rock State Park has several smaller falls on its network of trails, with most on the two-mile **Carrick Creek** loop.

- **Issaqueena Falls** just north of Walhalla on Highway 28 comes with its own legend of a love-struck Cherokee princess. The parking area is near the head of the falls, and there's a nice trail down the falls with a scenic overlook.

- **Spoon Auger Falls** up near the Chattooga River in the northwest corner of the state has a 40-foot drop. It's a short hike out of the Burrells Ford Campground parking area. To get here from Walhalla, take Highway 107 north 17 miles to Forest Road 708 (Burrells Ford Rd.). The parking lot is three miles ahead.

- The comically misnamed **Hidden Falls** are easily found within Oconee State Park. Get to this 40-foot cascade by taking the two-mile yellow-blazed Hidden Falls Trail.

- Just up the road on Highway 11 are the 60-foot **Station Cove Falls,** easily found on a short trail within the Oconee Station State Historic Site.

- The picturesque 30-foot **Reedy Branch Falls** are very easy to get to. From Westminster, take U.S. 76 about 15 miles north and look for a pull-off on the left after you pass Chattooga Ridge Road on the right. The falls are about a 300-yard walk from the road.

- Perhaps the easiest cascade to find—and one of the more enjoyable—is 30-foot **Chau-Ram Falls** in Oconee County's Chau-Ram County Park. (The name derives from the Chauga River and Ramsey Creek.) Drive west of Westminster on U.S. 76 for about three miles; the park entrance is on the left. Unlike most local waterfalls, this one has a nice campground nearby.

landmark—besides the stark Escarpment—is the 420-foot **Raven Cliff Falls,** one of the most stunning cataracts in the state. It greets you at the end of a strenuous two-mile hike, with a suspension bridge available for your scenic vertigo-inducing pleasure.

Campers will find 24 primitive trail-side sites ($8-20), 18 of which have fire rings and 6 of which allow no fires. You must have a permit in advance to camp in the Mountain Bridge Wilderness; call 866/345-7275 or go to the website.

GETTING AROUND

Getting around is quite easy. The main route is Highway 11, the Cherokee Foothills Scenic Byway, running roughly east-west along the base of the Blue Ridge. Other key routes are U.S. 76 in the northwest corner, which takes you from Westminster up to the Chattooga River and into Georgia; Highway 28, which links Highway 11 and U.S. 76 through the cute town of Walhalla; and U.S. 276, a spur from Highway 11 to the Caesars Head area.

Clemson and Vicinity

There's no mistaking you're in Clemson when you hit College Avenue and see the big orange paw prints leading the way to campus. Like any great American college town, the home of the Clemson University Tigers is vocally proud of their local sports teams and has few boundaries in terms of letting everyone know it. If you're the type to scoff at the Southern passion for college football—or if you're a fan of their archrival, the University of South Carolina—you might not enjoy Clemson very much. Also, if you don't like the color orange: There's lots of orange here.

Sights

With the key exception of the Old Stone Church, the following attractions are all on the Clemson University campus, which welcomes visitors. Catch a campus tour at the **Clemson University Visitors Center** (109 Daniel Dr., 864/656-4789, www.clemson.edu) most days at 9:45am and 1:45pm.

JOHN C. CALHOUN HOME

The ancestral home of the great South Carolina statesman and subsequently his daughter and Thomas Clemson, the **John C. Calhoun Home** (101 Fort Hill St., 864/656-2475, www.clemson.edu, Mon.-Sat. 10am-noon and 1pm-4:30pm, Sun. 2pm-4:30pm, $5 adults, $2 ages 6-12, free under age 6) is the spiritual center of Clemson. Also known as Fort Hill, the Greek Revival mansion, a National Historic Landmark, is essentially all that remains of the original plantation.

◖ SOUTH CAROLINA BOTANICAL GARDEN

The official botanical garden of the Palmetto State since 1992, the **South Carolina Botanical**

GREENVILLE

© JIM MOREKIS

South Carolina Botanical Garden

Garden (150 Discovery Lane, 864/656-3405, www.clemson.edu, daily dawn-dusk, free) takes up the entire southeastern tip of the Clemson campus and is a delightful place to stroll, relax, and take in the aromas of the tens of thousands of types of plants, flowers, and herbs planted on the site's 300 acres. There are 70 acres of display gardens, including the impressive camellia garden, a dwarf conifer garden, a hosta garden, and a butterfly garden. A 40-acre arboretum and nearly 100 acres of woodlands with walking trails completes the outdoor package. The best times to visit are spring and fall; in the summer there are significantly fewer flowering plants, and the heat can be stifling.

Within the grounds of the Botanical Garden is the **Bob Campbell Geology Museum** (140 Discovery Lane, 864/656-4600, http://virtual.clemson.edu/groups/geomuseum, Wed.-Sat. 10am-5pm, Sun. 1pm-5pm, closed home football Sat., $3 adults, $2 children), which has its roots in a small rock collection in the Clemson geology department.

Sometimes called the Huguenot House, the fabulously old **Hanover House** (South Carolina Botanical Garden, 864/656-2475, www.clemson.edu, Sat. 10am-noon and 1pm-5pm, Sun. 2pm-5pm, free) is on the grounds of the South Carolina Botanical Garden. A relic of the French Huguenot presence in the Lowcountry, this charming, circa-1716 cypress-built house is said to be the only surviving example of French Huguenot architecture in the United States.

Entertainment and Events

Like everything else in Clemson, local entertainment here moves with the ebb and flow of student life—especially during football season.

NIGHTLIFE

The most famous college bar in Clemson is **The Esso Club** (129 Old Greenville Hwy., 864/654-5120, www.theessoclub.com), on the edge of campus. As the name indicates, it's in an old gas station, built in 1933 on what was then the main road to Atlanta. Sometime in the 1940s, beer began to be sold on-site, in addition to bait, tackle, fishing licenses, and gasoline. You

could actually fill up your car until the mid-1980s, when it became a full-time bar and tavern.

The other key watering hole in town is the **Tiger Town Tavern** (368 College Ave., 864/654-5901, www.tigertowntavern.com), a.k.a. Triple T's. Upstairs is Top of Tiger Town Tavern, a "private club"—meaning for a few bucks a year its members can drink there on Sunday. You can too if you come as a current member's guest and pony up.

Sports and Recreation
SPECTATOR SPORTS

Clemson University plays about seven Saturday home football games during the regular season, August-November. During this time, everything in town focuses on the game, to the exclusion of all else except basic bodily functions. Many attractions in town are closed on home football Saturdays. The games are played in **Clemson Memorial Stadium** (Centennial Blvd., 864/656-2118, http://clemsontigers.cstv.com), a.k.a. "Death Valley," at the western edge of campus. You can buy advance tickets to a Clemson University home game at the school's official ticket site (http://clemsontigers.cstv.com) or by calling the school directly at 800/253-6766.

GOLF

Golfers will enjoy the **John E. Walker Sr. Golf Course** (864/656-0236, www.clemson.edu, call for greens fees), an 18-hole Nathan DeVictor-designed course that is the stomping grounds of the Clemson University golf team, who were national champs in 2003. The course is fully open to the public as well as students and alumni, but you must have a reserved tee time to play.

Accommodations

There are several nice places to stay in Clemson, but don't stay near Tiger Boulevard unless you enjoy the sound of trains—there are busy railroad tracks that cut through town in that area. Also keep in mind that rates here skyrocket on home-game weekends.

Not near the train tracks and right next to the campus's Walker Golf Course—and like that facility, completely open to the public—is the **James F. Martin Inn** (100 Madren Center Dr., 864/654-9020, www.clemson.edu, $100). Many of its 89 guest rooms overlook Lake Hartwell. There's an outdoor pool, tennis courts, Wi-Fi, and included continental breakfast.

The circa-1837 **Sleepy Hollow Bed and Breakfast** (220 Issaqueena Tr., 864/207-1540, www.sleepyhollow.ws, $100-175) is reportedly the site of the first introduction of Percheron horses and Jersey cows to South Carolina, in addition to what's purported to be the state's largest white oak tree out back. A full breakfast is offered on weekends and a continental breakfast during the week.

Food

Don't miss a stop by the Hendrix Student Center on campus, where you'll find 🄲 **'55 Exchange** (864/656-2155, www.clemson.edu/

historic Farmers Society Hall on Pendleton's Village Green

© JIM MOREKIS

icecream, Aug.-May Mon.-Fri. 11:30am-6pm, Sat.-Sun. 1pm-6pm, June-July Mon.-Thurs. 11:30am-8pm, Fri. 11:30am-6pm, Sat.-Sun. 1pm-6pm, $4-10). They have what I believe to be the best ice cream and milk shakes on the planet, courtesy of the Clemson University Dairy Sciences Department. Totally open to the public, this little corner shop features rich, robust ice cream in the old style.

Considered the finest of fine dining in Clemson, **Pixie & Bill's** (1058 Tiger Blvd., 864/654-1210, www.tigergourmet.com, lunch Mon.-Fri. 11:30am-1:30pm, dinner Mon.-Sat. 5:30pm-9:30pm, $18-26) is a favorite of students and visiting alumni alike. It ain't cheap, but any meat dish is good, especially the signature prime rib au jus.

PENDLETON

Right next door to Clemson and basically contiguous with it, the significantly older Pendleton is one of the most impossibly cute small towns you'll ever see. Founded in 1790, Pendleton's origin came over a century after Charleston's founding, but you'll find this Upstate town oddly familiar if you've been to that great Lowcountry city: Most of the finer buildings in Pendleton were built by Lowcountry planters who kept summer homes here.

Sights
🄲 VILLAGE GREEN

Pendleton's main claim to fame is its central **Village Green** (125 E. Queen St., 864/646-3782, www.pendleton-district.org). Now surrounded by cute shops and cafés, it's the center of the area of Pendleton that's on the National Register of Historic Places—over 50 buildings in town date from before 1850. The focal point is the circa-1828 **Farmers Society Hall** (255 Old Depot Rd., 864/646-8161) in the center of the green. Built on the site of the old courthouse, it is the oldest farmers hall in continuous use in the nation. Perhaps oddly, it currently houses a restaurant.

On the other end of the green from the Farmers Hall is the old **Guard House**

GREENVILLE

(Mon.-Fri. 9am-4:30pm), now a combined visitors center and magistrate's office. Just off the Green, the circa-1850 **Hunter's Store** (E. Queen St.) was once one of the main mercantile stores in the entire Upstate. Now it hosts the **Pendleton District Historical, Recreational, and Tourism Commission** (864/646-3782, Mon.-Fri. 9am-4:30pm, Sat. 10am-3pm).

ASHTABULA

Stately **Ashtabula** (444 Hwy. 88, 864/646-7249, www.pendletonhistoricfoundation.org, Thurs.-Sun. 1pm-4pm, $6 adults, $2 children), pronounced "ash-ta-BYEW-la," was built in the 1820s by Charleston's well-connected Lewis Ladson Gibbes. He was a descendant of the first English settler in South Carolina, Dr. Henry Woodward, and married Maria Henrietta Drayton, daughter of Dr. Charles Drayton of Drayton Hall fame, and Esther Middleton, of the magnificent Middleton Place and sister of Arthur Middleton, who signed the Declaration of Independence.

WOODBURN PLANTATION

Another magnificent home with historical roots is **Woodburn Plantation** (328 U.S. 76, 864/646-7249, www.pendletonhistoricfoundation.org, Fri. 2:30pm-5pm, $6 adults, $2 children). Like Ashtabula, it is a very short drive from Pendleton, although on the other side of town. And like Ashtabula, this four-story house with high ceilings, spacious verandas, and great cross-ventilation was owned as a summer home

by Lowcountry planter and statesman Charles Cotesworth Pinckney.

HISTORIC TOURS

Try **Historic Pendleton District Tours** (125 E. Queen St., 864/646-3782), inside the historic Hunter's Store building, which also houses the **Pendleton District Historical, Recreational, and Tourism Commission** (864/646-3782, Mon.-Fri. 9am-4:30pm, Sat. 10am-3pm); they can hook you up with materials to take your own self-guided tour.

Shopping

Antiques buffs will find themselves in heaven in Pendleton, with several good stores ringing the Village Green. Keep in mind that store hours are not always religiously observed. The best is **Past Times** (165 S. Mechanic St., 864/654-5985, Tues.-Sat. 11am-5pm), which boasts the largest collection of vintage Edgefield pottery in the nation. Colonial and Shaker furniture is the specialty of **The Renaissance Man** (130 S. Mechanic St., 864/646-8862).

Accommodations and Food

The premier bed-and-breakfast in Pendleton is the seven-room **Liberty Hall Inn** (621 S. Mechanic St., 864/646-7500, $159). Within the inn is (**Brandini's Cuisine at Liberty Hall Inn** (621 S. Mechanic St., 864/646-7500, lunch Tues.-Sat. 11am-2pm, dinner Tues.-Sat. 5pm-9pm, Sun. brunch 11am-2pm, dinner entrées $18-30), which specializes in Italian delicacies.

Ninety Six District

In the early 1700s, this region—or in colonial parlance, "district"—was named after the key trading post on the edge of what was then the rugged frontier. Ninety Six was thought, erroneously, to be 96 miles from the nearest big Cherokee settlement in Keowee.

ABBEVILLE

Founded in 1758 by a group of French Huguenots—who named it after their city back in the old country—pretty little Abbeville saw both the birth and the death of the Confederacy. In November 1860, on Secession Hill, the first meeting to discuss South Carolina's departure from the union was held. Five years later, Jefferson Davis dissolved the Confederacy in the Burt-Stark Mansion off the town square. Abbeville is also the birthplace of the polarizing statesman John C. Calhoun, author of the states' rights movement.

Sights
ABBEVILLE OPERA HOUSE

The town's main claim to fame these days is the 1908 **Abbeville Opera House** (Town Square, 864/366-2157, www.theabbevilleoperahouse. com), an elegant gem from the heyday of traveling theater. Now beautifully restored, it still hosts plenty of stage productions. Right next door, in front of the adjacent courthouse, is a monument to Thomas Howie, the "Major of Saint-Lô." Howie was a hero of the Normandy invasion during World War II and was killed in France trying to take the town of Saint-Lô. Howie was reportedly an inspiration for Tom Hanks's character, John Miller, in *Saving Private Ryan*.

BURT-STARK MANSION

Abbeville's other key attraction is the **Burt-Stark Mansion** (400 N. Main St., 864/366-0166, www.burt-stark.com, Fri.-Sat. 1:30pm-4:30pm, $10), where President Jefferson Davis uttered the simple words, "All

is indeed lost," and committed the last official act of his office—dissolving the Confederacy. Admission includes an hour-long tour.

TRINITY EPISCOPAL CHURCH

Tucked off the town square is the graceful **Trinity Episcopal Church** (Church St., daily 9am-5pm, free), now in a state of romantic decay. Outside, you can't miss the 125-foot spire or the salmon-colored stucco exterior. The chancel window, originally made in England and delivered to Charleston by a blockade-runner, was transported here in the middle of the Civil War.

Accommodations and Food

The best-known lodging in town is on the town square, the historic **Belmont Inn** (104 E. Pickens St., 864/459-9625, www.belmontinn. net, $75), where you have access not only to a nice tavern but to the hotel's Heritage Dining Room ($10-20). They offer some attractive combo packages with play tickets at the Opera House directly across the street.

There are two Mennonite-run restaurants in town, **Yoder's Dutch Kitchen** (809 E. Greenwood St., 864/366-5556, Wed.-Sat. 11am-2:30pm and Fri.-Sat. 5pm-8:30pm, $5-10) and **Dutch Oven** (108 N. Main St., 864/366-5513, www.dutchovenrestaurant.com, breakfast Tues. and Sat. 6:30am-10:30am, lunch Mon.-Fri. 10:30am-2:30pm, dinner Thurs.-Fri. 4:30pm-8:30pm, $5-10). Both are excellent and affordable, although the menu tends more toward simple Southern favorites.

NINETY SIX NATIONAL HISTORIC SITE

Virtually from the time of its founding in the mid-1700s, the trading post called Ninety Six—in the mistaken belief that it was 96 miles from the Cherokee town at Keowee—was a center of conflict. Its history is recalled at the

1,000-acre **Ninety Six National Historic Site** (1103 Hwy. 248, 864/543-4068, www.nps.gov/nisi, daily dawn-dusk, visitors center daily 9am-5pm, free). The redoubt is well preserved, and archaeological discoveries continue. There are also several nature trails, including a portion of the old Cherokee trail; get a map of them all from the visitors center.

Old English District

In the early days of the Revolution, this area was considered safe ground for British soldiers and settlers due to the Loyalist sentiments of the local population. All that changed due to the heavy-handed occupation by the redcoats. With Loyalists in shorter supply than promised, the British soon found themselves on the run, especially after key defeats at Cowpens and Kings Mountain.

KINGS MOUNTAIN NATIONAL MILITARY PARK

Nestled against the North Carolina border (the actual town of Kings Mountain is in the Tar Heel State) is **Kings Mountain National Military Park** (2625 Park Rd., 803/222-3209, www.nps.gov/kimo, Labor Day-Memorial Day daily 9am-5pm, Memorial Day-Labor Day daily 9am-6pm, free). The site marks the battle of October 7, 1780, when American militia defeated a band of Loyalists. Kings Mountain is the end point of the **Overmountain Victory National Historic Trail** (864/936-3477, www.nps.gov/ovvi), marking the route of the militia forces through the Carolinas.

KINGS MOUNTAIN STATE PARK

Not to be confused with the adjacent National Military Park of the same name, **Kings Mountain State Park** (1277 Park Rd., Blacksburg, 803/222-3209, www.southcarolinaparks.com, during daylight saving time daily 7am-8pm, other seasons daily 8am-6pm, $2 adults, free under age 16) offers plenty to do amid the picturesque setting of one of the classic South Carolina state parks built in the 1930s by the Civilian Conservation Corps. There are miles of good trails, two fishing lakes with boat rentals ($20 per day), and a living-history farm. The park has a whopping 115 RV and gravel tent sites with electricity and water ($16-18) and 10 primitive campsites with no water or electricity ($12-13).

◖ HISTORIC BRATTONSVILLE

Near the town of McConnells, **Historic Brattonsville** (1444 Brattonsville Rd., 803/684-2327, www.chmuseums.org, Tue.-Sat. 10am-5pm, Sun. 1pm-5pm, $6 adults, $3 ages 4-17, free under age 4) includes the site of the Revolutionary War Battle of Huck's Defeat, a pivotal victory of Patriot militia over the Tories. But the chief allure of this 775-acre site is the impressive grouping of more than 30 well-restored historic structures (although not all are open to the public), including the circa-1840 visitors center, a reconstruction of a backwoods log cabin, and a mid-1800s milk barn and hog pen. The crown jewel is the 1766 **William Bratton House,** probably the oldest building in this part of the state and where some scenes in Mel Gibson's *The Patriot* were filmed.

ROCK HILL AND VICINITY
York

Located in what was originally the Yorkville Female Academy, the **McCelvey Center** (212 E. Jefferson St.) is a Smithsonian-sponsored component of the state's Culture & Heritage Museums. Today it hosts the **Historical Center of York County** (803/684-3948, www.chmuseums.org, Mon.-Sat. 10am-4pm, free) as well as a 560-seat theater. Another important facet of the McCelvey Center is the **Southern Revolutionary War Institute** (803/684-3948), devoted to the study of the underreported

GREENVILLE

© JIM MOREKIS

Historic Brattonsville

Southern theater of the American Revolution. If you're hungry or thirsty when in York, go no farther than **The Coal Yard Restaurant and Lounge** (105 Garner St., 803/684-9653, Wed.-Sat. 4pm-midnight, $6-25), a fun place with good American cuisine.

Museum of York County

On the outskirts of Rock Hill is another of the Culture & Heritage Museums, the **Museum of York County** (4621 Mt. Gallant Rd., 803/329-2121, http://chmuseums.org, Tues.-Sat. 10am-5pm, Sun. 1pm-5pm, $5 adults, $3 students, free under age 5). The **Settlemyre Planetarium** (www.chmuseums.org, show-times vary, $5 adults, $3 ages 4-17, free under age 4) displays the night sky on the darkened interior of its large dome. Shows are generally Saturday at 11am, 2pm, and 3pm and Sunday at 2pm and 3pm, but check the website for details. Getting here can be tricky. Take Liberty Street (Hwy. 161) east of York, veering left to stay on Highway 161 (at that point called Old York Rd.). Continue past the intersection with

Highway 274 (Hands Mill Rd.), and the museum is two miles ahead on the right.

Downtown Rock Hill

The city's main historic claim to fame is the "Friendship Nine," a group of African Americans—eight of whom were students at Friendship Junior College in town—who staged a nonviolent "counter strike" in February 1961 to protest segregation. While McCrory's is no more, the historic spot on Main Street is now the home of **Old Town Bistro** (135 E. Main St., 803/327-9222, www.rholdtownbistro.com, Mon.-Fri. 10:30am-10pm, Sat.-Sun. 7am-10pm, $6-10), a cute diner-style restaurant based on the old McCrory's layout, including the counter.

Rock Hill Blackjacks Heritage Preserve

One of the last remaining prairie habitats in South Carolina, the **Rock Hill Blackjacks Heritage Preserve** (803/734-3886, www.dnr.sc.gov, daily dawn-dusk, free) gets its name from the blackjack oaks that predominate here, forming what's technically known as a montmorillonite forest. There are no facilities, and bow hunting does go on in the fall. To get here from downtown Rock Hill, take Main Street east to Albright Road. Take a right and then a left onto Blackmon Street. The Preserve's parking area is ahead on the left.

Carowinds

On a totally separate note is **Carowinds** (Ave. of the Carolinas, 800/888-4386, www.carowinds.com, summer daily, spring and fall Sat.-Sun., hours vary, admission varies). If you need a break from history, this is surely the place: a theme park that prides itself not on reenactments but on a whole bunch of outstanding roller-coaster rides sprinkled with a number of well-known pop-culture figures, arranged in a series of subparks. Carowinds is about 15 minutes north of Rock Hill and about the same distance south of Charlotte, North Carolina. Take I-77 to exit 90.

Catawba Reservation

The main attraction on the 640-acre reservation, home to about 300 people, is the **Catawba Cultural Center** (1536 Tom Steven Rd., 803/328-2427, www.ccppcrafts.com), the best place to explore the fascinating and unique world of Catawba pottery. Unlike other pottery traditions, the Catawba don't use a pottery wheel or glazes. They use favorite objects or whatever is at hand to shape the clay, which is dug from the banks of the Catawba River.

ANDREW JACKSON STATE PARK

Andrew Jackson State Park (196 Andrew Jackson Park Rd., 803/285-3344, www. southcarolinaparks.com, during daylight saving time daily 9am-9pm, other seasons daily 8am-6pm, $2 adults, free under age 16) is devoted not only to the great outdoors but also to the 7th president of the United States, born near this site. There is a museum detailing Jackson's boyhood, with occasional

reenactments. Don't miss the equestrian statue of Jackson sculpted by Anna Hyatt Huntington, responsible for many of the sculptures at Myrtle Beach's Brookgreen Gardens. The park has five pull-through RV campsites and 20 gravel sites for RVs and tents ($12-13) with electricity and water. You can fish at the 18-acre lake.

LANDSFORD CANAL STATE PARK

The popular **Landsford Canal State Park** (2051 Park Dr., Catawba, 803/789-5800, www.southcarolinaparks.com, daily 9am-6pm, $2 adults, free under age 16) chronicles the time when an active canal system made the Catawba River commercially navigable, from 1820 to 1835. This area is home to the largest population of Rocky Shoals spider lilies in the world. The plant blooms spectacularly in late May-early June.

MUSGROVE MILL STATE HISTORIC SITE

In August 1780, north of the modern-day town of Clinton, a force of Patriot militia clashed with a larger body of Tories. You can learn more about the battle at the **Musgrove Mill State Historic Site** (398 State Park Rd., 864/938-0100, www.southcarolinaparks.com, daily 9am-6pm, free), which has a good interpretive center (Mon.-Fri. 1pm-5pm, Sat.-Sun. 10am-5pm). At the site you can also put your kayak in on the Enoree River.

ROSE HILL PLANTATION STATE PARK

Just south of Union at the edge of the Sumter National Forest is **Rose Hill Plantation State Park** (2677 Sardis Rd., 864/427-5966, www. southcarolinaparks.com, daily 9am-6pm, free), the former homestead of the "Secession Governor," William H. Gist. The central attraction is the magnificent home along with its outbuildings and beautiful gardens. A tour of the house ($4 adults, $3 ages 6-16) runs every hour on the hour 1pm-4pm.

INFORMATION AND SERVICES

The main clearinghouse for information is the **Old English District Visitors Center** (201 N. Main St., Richburg, 803/789-7076, www.sctravel.net). For Rock Hill and York County, check out the **Rock Hill/York County Convention and Visitors Bureau** (452 S. Anderson Rd., Rock Hill, 803/329-5200, www.visityorkcounty.com).

GETTING THERE AND AROUND

Two major airports border the region: **Greenville-Spartanburg International Airport** (GSP, 864/877-7426, www.gspairport.com), along I-85 between Greenville and Spartanburg, and **Charlotte Douglas International Airport** (CLT, 704/359-4910, www.charmeck.org), over the border in North Carolina.

GREENVILLE

ATLANTA

It's a sprawling metropolis made up of friendly, bucolic neighborhoods. It's a concrete jungle sprinkled with lush green space. It's a center of dyed-in-the-wool Southern arts and culture filled to the brim with transplants from elsewhere. It's in the middle of the Bible Belt but is legendary, even notorious, for its nightlife. All these things are true in their own ways, and there's no use trying to sort them out. Indeed, the only constant in Atlanta life is change.

To the rest of Georgia, Atlanta is often an object of derision, both for its role as state capital as well as for its traffic and rampant growth. Atlanta is far and away the most commercially important city in the Southeast. Love it or hate it, everyone knows the city is a vast and vigorous economic engine that has almost single-handedly catapulted Georgia into the top nine most populous states.

Befitting a city that literally rose from the ashes of the Civil War, you can be anything you want here without worrying too much about who or what came before. Unlike some of the more rigidly stratified cities in the South, with historic social and economic divides, "the city too busy to hate" just wants to know what you're doing right now. This isn't always good—as Atlantans themselves will frankly admit, they've done a horrible job preserving their history—but sometimes it can be almost as refreshing as an ice-cold "Coke-Cola" on a summer day.

© SEAN PAVONE/123RF.COM

HIGHLIGHTS

LOOK FOR ((TO FIND RECOMMENDED SIGHTS, ACTIVITIES, DINING, AND LODGING.

((**Georgia Aquarium:** The largest single aquarium tank in the world is the centerpiece of this major tourist attraction (page 474).

((**Martin Luther King Jr. National Historic Site:** This stirring and expansive tribute to the civil rights leader contains many historically significant buildings, such as his birth home (page 476).

((**Zoo Atlanta:** A world-class gorilla habitat and two charming pandas are among the highlights (page 478).

((**High Museum of Art:** The multistory modern building contains a plethora of American arts and crafts, from folk art to high art, with some Old Masters mixed in as well (page 481).

((**Fox Theatre:** This ornate, Moorish-themed venue remains in constant use. It's Midtown's most cherished locale (page 483).

((**Michael C. Carlos Museum:** This small but significant museum hosts intriguing Egyptian and Greek artifacts in an intimate setting (page 485).

((**Atlanta History Center and Swan House:** View the excellent Civil War exhibit and tour the magnificent, one-of-a-kind Swan House (page 486).

((**Decatur:** This small city adjacent to Atlanta has one of the nation's most happening foodie and café scenes, all within a couple of blocks (page 520).

HISTORY

The words "Atlanta" and "history" rarely seem to occupy the same sentence, but the truth is that Atlanta's history is more interesting than it's generally given credit. While Georgia's first city, Savannah, was founded over a century before Atlanta, in typical spirit once Atlanta got going, it moved fast.

In 1837, after the cruel mass removal of Creek and Cherokee people and the subsequent influx of white settlers, the Western & Atlantic Railroad chose a spot just east of the Chattahoochee River as the southern end of a track into Tennessee. The little town that emerged around the zero milepost was simply called Terminus. In 1843 its name was changed to Marthasville, in honor of the daughter of former Governor Wilson Lumpkin, a major railroad booster.

A scant two years later the name was changed again to its modern version. There are conflicting stories: One theory says Atlanta is a feminine version of "Atlantic" and a nod to its first railroad line. Another much more

ATLANTA

To Chateau de Saigon

To Stone Mountain, Lake Lanier and Gainesville

ATLANTA

EMORY

UNIVERSITY

★ CENTERS FOR DISEASE CONTROL MUSEUM

CLIFTON RD

N DRUID HILLS RD

42

BUFORD HWY

85

E ROXBORO RD

LAVISTA RD

236

JOHNSON RD

ROCK SPRINGS RD

E MORNINGSIDE DR

Lenox

LENOX RD

LENOX SQUARE

MANDARIN ORIENTAL ●

400 (TOLL)

SIDNEY MARCUS BLVD

CHESHIRE BRIDGE RD

PIEDMONT AVE

Buckhead

141

PIEDMONT RD

▼ BONE'S

237

Lindbergh Center

85

Ansley Park

BUCKHEAD THEATRE ▼ Buckhead

PHARR RD

BUCKHEAD AVE NE

E PACES FERRY RD NE

ROSWELL RD

CAFÉ AGORA ▼

19   9

ST. REGIS ATLANTA

PEACHTREE RD

LINDBERGH DR

SLATON DR

ANDREW DR

◀ ATLANTA HISTORY CENTER

◀ SWAN HOUSE

W PACES FERRY RD

GOVERNOR'S MANSION ★

ANDREW RD

Creek

19   9

PEACHTREE RD

WILLIAM BREMAN JEWISH HERITAGE MUSEUM ★

AMTRAK STATION

CENTER FOR PUPPETRY ARTS ★

Lower Buckhead

COLLIER RD

W WESLEY RD

PEACHTREE BATTLE AVE

BOBBY JONES GOLF COURSE

Peachtree

75

NORTHSIDE DR

To Marietta

41   3

HOWELL MILL RD

ATLANTA

© AVALON TRAVEL

romantic version says it was renamed in honor of Martha Lumpkin's middle name, Atalanta, itself an homage to a Greek goddess.

Despite its modern association with the Confederacy, largely due to *Gone with the Wind,* business-oriented Atlanta was far less enamored with the idea of secession than most of the South. The Civil War initially provided an enormous economic boost to Atlanta, which rapidly became one of the Confederacy's largest industrial centers.

After a lengthy bombardment and General William T. Sherman's outmaneuvering of Confederate general Albert Hood, Atlanta fell to Union troops on September 2, 1864. The 4,000 remaining citizens who hadn't already fled the siege were ordered to evacuate, and thus the stage was set for the beginning of the notoriety of General Sherman. On November 15, a massive fire swept the city: It originated in the planned destruction of industrial and manufacturing areas, but through the carelessness of Union troops quickly spread to residential areas. Most of the city was burned to the ground and all its rail lines were destroyed. The fall of Atlanta mortally crippled the Confederate war effort, secured the reelection of Abraham Lincoln (which had been very much in doubt), and kicked off Sherman's "March to the Sea," which would conclude in Savannah that Christmas.

The railroad again came to Atlanta's rescue. Only a few months after the war's end, all five of its main lines were up and running, kept busy transporting materials and people to rebuild the city. The new spirit of rebirth was so contagious, in fact, that in 1868 Georgia politicos decided to move the state capital from Milledgeville—so symbolic of the old South—to Atlanta, its new commercial powerhouse.

Though segregation was very much in effect, Atlanta quickly became not only the birthplace of a large black middle class but the home of four institutions of higher learning for African Americans: Morris Brown College, Clark College, Morehouse College, and Spelman College, all of which joined existing white institutions such as Georgia Tech, Oglethorpe University, Agnes Scott College, and Emory University.

Auburn Avenue became the city's center of African American culture and commerce, with "Daddy King," Martin Luther King Sr., in the pulpit at Ebenezer Baptist Church. The "roar" in the Roaring Twenties in Atlanta came from its burgeoning airfield, soon to be named for its chief advocate, city councilman and mayor William Hartsfield.

Also in the 1920s, a humble local newspaper reporter named Margaret Mitchell, sidelined by an ankle injury, wrote *Gone with the Wind,* another of Atlanta's great exports. The premiere of the film came in 1939 with a star-studded gala; in a precursor to Atlanta's reputation as a racially enlightened Southern city, costar Hattie McDaniel became the first-ever African American Oscar winner.

The 1960s, in particular, gave proof of Atlanta's new nickname, "the city too busy to hate," actually coined by Hartsfield as mayor. His successor, Ivan Allen Jr., himself the son of an Atlanta mayor, formed a close partnership with local black civil rights leaders, chief among them Martin Luther King Jr., in order to promote fair housing and equal opportunity in the workplace as well as send a signal to the private sector at large that Atlanta was a great place to do business. In 1969, with the election of the city's first African American mayor, Maynard Jackson, Atlanta proper had become a majority-black city. Three years later, Atlantan Andrew Young was elected Georgia's first black Congressman since Reconstruction.

In 1971 the airport was renamed Hartsfield Atlanta International Airport and within a decade was the world's busiest (Maynard Jackson's name was added in 2003). By the middle of the decade Atlanta was America's third-busiest convention center. Those trends continued through the go-go 1980s and well into the 1990s.

Though unfortunately remembered most for the terrorist bombing that took place, the 1996 Summer Olympics in Atlanta was actually a successful staging overall and resulted in several important infrastructure improvements, chiefly Turner Field, athlete dorms that became housing for Georgia Tech and Georgia State University, and, of course, Centennial Olympic Park, site of the bombing and currently the hub of several major attractions.

PLANNING YOUR TIME

Atlanta is fun for a day or for several days, and there's always something to do any day of the week. Shoppers, be sure to carve out time to enjoy the city's many shopping opportunities, whether they be in the Lenox and Phipps malls in Buckhead or the little shops in Virginia-Highland and Decatur.

If you're driving a car, at some point you will be faced with Atlanta's heavy traffic. Weekday morning and afternoon rush hours are ridiculous; try to make plans to be as near your destination as possible before getting caught up in them. That said, for the most part traveling around Atlanta is a pleasure and not unusually time-consuming.

Afternoons in July and August are uncomfortably hot, so plan accordingly, especially if visiting an outdoor site like Stone Mountain. Zoo Atlanta is well worth a visit, but if the weather's hot, go right when it opens before the animals seek refuge from the heat.

NEIGHBORHOODS

Despite its ever-growing size, Atlanta remains a city of neighborhoods, and neighborhoods within neighborhoods, each with a separate character and feel. The specific geography is an inexact and debatable science, but here's an overview:

Downtown: This is the beating commercial and political heart of Atlanta as well as its most socioeconomically challenged area. Neighborhoods within Downtown include **Sweet Auburn, Fairlie-Poplar,** up-and-coming **Old Fourth Ward,** and **So-No** (South of North Ave.).

Five Points: Not to be confused with Little Five Points, this downtown area adjacent to Underground Atlanta is literally the city center. During the first days of settlement, the intersection of Peachtree, Decatur, and Marietta Streets with Edgewood Avenue was chosen as the central point around which all development would radiate.

Grant Park: This verdant Victorian area southeast of Downtown hosts Zoo Atlanta, the Cyclorama, and Oakland Cemetery. Up-and-coming **Cabbagetown** is adjacent.

Midtown: The culture-rich area between Downtown and Buckhead includes the Georgia Tech campus as well as the Margaret Mitchell House and the Fox Theatre.

Inman Park: This rejuvenated, gentrified Queen Anne garden suburb was Atlanta's first planned neighborhood.

Little Five Points: The gateway to East Atlanta at the intersection of Moreland and Euclid Streets is also the center of Atlanta's bohemian culture.

Atlantic Station: This planned New Urbanist development opened in 2005 and lies west of Midtown on the other side of I-75/85.

Westside: This increasingly trendy light industrial area just west of Downtown offers some of the best up-and-coming restaurants in the city.

West End: Not to be confused with the Westside, the West End is Atlanta's oldest historic district.

Buckhead: The traditional home of Atlanta's "old money" was not long ago also the center of Atlanta nightlife. Things have changed, and it's returning to its roots as a shopping and residential center.

Virginia-Highland: Atlanta's first streetcar suburb boasts charming craftsman bungalows and remains one of its liveliest and most livable neighborhoods. "Highland" is always singular.

Poncey-Highland: This subset of Virginia-Highland contains the Jimmy Carter Library and includes a large stretch of bustling Ponce De Leon Avenue.

Druid Hills: This residential area adjacent to Virginia-Highland is primarily known as the home of Emory University and the Fernbank Natural History Museum.

Decatur: Not an Atlanta neighborhood but an entirely separate city and the DeKalb County seat, fun, foodie-oriented Decatur is, however, directly connected to Atlanta by its own MARTA station.

Sights

DOWNTOWN
Centennial Olympic Park
For some reason the world seems to have forgotten that Atlanta hosted an actual summer Olympics in 1996. Perhaps the memory of the domestic terrorist attack that happened during the games has overshadowed the competition itself. In any case, after a 1998 rehab to accommodate regular daily use, **Centennial Olympic Park** (265 Park Ave., 404/222-7275, www.centennialpark.com, daily 7am-11pm, free) remains a well-maintained 21 acres of friendly green space adjoining the Pemberton Place attractions of the Georgia Aquarium and the World of Coca-Cola, amid a sea of downtown skyscrapers. Kids can splash and cool off in the colorful Fountain of Rings, which boasts over 250 water jets and provides numerous special light shows, with the streams going as high as 30 feet.

As for the bombing near the north end of the park committed by Eric Rudolph (for which the late Richard Jewell was unjustly tried and convicted by the media), it's commemorated by the Quilt of Remembrance, in honor of the 111 people injured and the lone fatality, Alice Hawthorne.

C Georgia Aquarium
If you compare the **Georgia Aquarium** (225 Baker St. NW, 404/581-4000, www.georgiaaquarium.org, Sun.-Fri. 10am-5pm, Sat. 9am-6pm, admission varies) with premier research-educational aquariums around the country, you might be disappointed. The main purpose of this aquarium is to entertain, and it's quite good at that. Completed in 2005 and largely funded by Home Depot mogul Bernie Marcus, the Georgia Aquarium anchors one corner of Centennial Olympic Park and is already one of the state's primary tourist destinations (so don't expect a relaxing jaunt).

The focal point is the huge Ocean Voyager exhibit, the largest single aquarium tank in the world at 6.3 million gallons. You observe the hundreds of species inside during a walk through a 100-foot viewing tunnel around which the tank is formed. For an even more up-close experience, the Georgia Explorer area has touch-pools with horseshoe crabs, stingrays, and other coastal creatures.

While the Georgia Aquarium is worth visiting, your experience will be enhanced by arriving as early in the day as you can to avoid peak crowds and the attendant onslaught of large baby strollers. (Also keep in mind that your tickets are for a specific entry time.) Two MARTA rapid transit stations are near the Aquarium: the CNN-Georgia World Congress Center station and Peachtree Center station.

World of Coca-Cola
If you want to immerse yourself in Atlanta's number-one export, or if you really just love the taste, don't miss the over-the-top **World of Coca-Cola** (121 Baker St. NW, 404/676-5151, www.worldofcoca-cola.com, daily, hours vary, $16 adults, $12 children). Essentially one long, cheerful commercial for the iconic Georgia creation (including a mandatory six-minute video prior to entering the exhibits), World of Coca-Cola is a quick, fun experience that is perhaps Atlanta's number-one guilty pleasure. Think Disney with syrup. After the video, you get free rein to examine Coca-Cola memorabilia, watch endless loops of historic Coca-Cola commercials, and the unquestionable highlight: taste dozens of samples of Coca-Cola products from six continents to your heart's content. Of course, there's a gift shop featuring every imaginable Coke-themed product you can imagine. Cheesy? Commercial? Yes and yes. But also good clean fun that the whole family will enjoy and a refreshing break from the Georgia heat.

Imagine It! The Children's Museum of Atlanta
The now-prime territory across the street

DOWNTOWN ATLANTA

ATLANTA

© AVALON TRAVEL

A "COKE-COLA" AND A SMILE

In the years after the Civil War, Atlanta was a boomtown, with its forward-looking business community using the city's destruction as a reason to rebuild bigger and better. By 1868, Atlanta was the new capital of Georgia, and a year later a former Confederate officer and druggist from Columbus, Georgia, moved here seeking opportunity.

John Pemberton was interested in the growing market for health tonics and hit upon a recipe using kola nut and coca leaf extracts. The first version was "French Wine Cola," but one of Pemberton's partners came up with "Coca-Cola," and the world's premier brand name was born.

Twenty years later Asa Griggs Candler bought Pemberton's company and had two great ideas. First was the idea of selling the product—the ingredients of which were secret, as they are to this day—in syrup form, to be carbonated right at the soda fountain. The second was franchising bottling rights nationwide, which catapulted Coca-Cola to prominence and created a number of family fortunes.

When the Woodruff family acquired Coca-Cola in 1919, president Robert Woodruff set his sights on global expansion. During World War II, in a brilliant blend of patriotism and business savvy, he promised a five-cent bottle to every U.S. serviceman no matter where they were stationed. It was not only a step toward expanding into 200 countries; by gaining the label of "wartime production" Coca-Cola could circumvent the rationing of sugar, its syrup's main ingredient!

There've been missteps along the way, chiefly the "New Coke" debacle, humorously chronicled at the **World of Coca-Cola** (121 Baker St. NW, 404/676-5151, www.worldofcoca-cola.com, daily, hours vary, $16 adults, $12 children), where you can sample a room full of Coke products. The company got in trouble when it was revealed that its Dasani bottled water was just purified City of Atlanta tap water. While the company maintains the product never contained actual cocaine (the drug wasn't made illegal until 1906), many analysts say it likely contained very minimal traces through the 1920s.

While the company is called Coca-Cola, Atlantans often ask to drink a "Coke-Cola."

Coca-Cola's philanthropic legacy is felt in Atlanta today at the Robert Woodruff Memorial Arts Center, Emory University, and the Centers for Disease Control and Prevention, among many others. Individually, the late Robert Woodruff's acts of philanthropy changed the face of the state, but exactly how much we may never know; most of his gifts are reckoned to be anonymous.

---

from Centennial Olympic Park is where the city chose to build its entry into the burgeoning kids museum category. **Imagine It! The Children's Museum of Atlanta** (275 Centennial Olympic Park Dr., 404/659-5437, www.childrensmuseumatlanta.org, Mon.-Fri. 10am-4pm, Sat.-Sun. 10am-5pm, $12.75) opened in 2003 and is a pioneer in the "museum without walls" concept. Unlike many other children's museums, which seem to have one eye on what parents expect, the focus here is on the power of play. There's a splash space, a farm space, a crawl space, and even a place where they just get to paint the walls.

◖ Martin Luther King Jr. National Historic Site

Easily one of the most expansive urban National Park Service-administered sites, the **Martin Luther King Jr. National Historic Site** (450 Auburn Ave., 404/331-5190, www.nps.gov, Memorial Day-Labor Day daily 9am-6pm, Labor Day-Memorial Day daily 9am-5pm, free) isn't only a moving elegy to the great Atlantan but an overview of the most crucial epoch of the civil rights movement itself. The facility, itself part of an even larger National Preservation District, comprises several wide-ranging features, all within a single block of historic (and historically African American) Auburn Avenue:

© JIM MOREKIS

Historic Ebenezer Baptist Church in "Sweet Auburn"

the **Visitors Center** (450 Auburn Ave.); the restored original sanctuary of **Historic Ebenezer Baptist Church** (corner of Auburn Ave. and Jackson St., www.historicebenezer.org); the **King Center for Nonviolent Social Change** (449 Auburn Ave.), directly across the street, and where King and his wife are buried; the heavily-visited **King Birth Home** (501 Auburn Ave.); and the nearby **Fire Station Number 6**, which played a key role in the desegregation of Atlanta's fire department.

Most visitors save time to pay their respects at the tomb of Dr. King and his wife, Coretta Scott King, at the King Center, situated at the end of a beautiful reflective pool and marked by an eternal flame (Dr. King was originally interred at Southview Cemetery). The King Center's other publicly accessible component is the Freedom Hall and its associated exhibits. But obviously there is much more to the entire site and you should reserve a fair amount of time to take it all in, especially if you're going on one of the guided tours, such as the popular

Birth Home tour (make sure to arrive early to book space).

A good bit more emotional in content than the typical education-heavy federally preserved site, the Visitors Center focuses a great deal on the sacrifice of King and his family, with an entire room devoted to a display of the humble wagon that served as his hearse following his assassination in 1968.

Even more moving than King's tomb is the experience within the church where he preached, Ebenezer Baptist, now called the Historic Sanctuary to differentiate itself from the megachurch across the street (the Horizon Sanctuary). This is a particularly exciting aspect in that it was only fully restored and opened to the public in 2001, with more restoration pending. (The historic sanctuary was the site of a lesser-known tragic incident in 1974, when King's mother, "Mama King," was shot and killed while playing the organ right before a church service by a man with no known motive. Three other people were also shot.)

Little "M. L.," as he was known as a child, was baptized in the church while his father, "Daddy King," acted as pastor. Of course, Martin Luther King Jr. would go on to become a pastor at Ebenezer himself, first as co-pastor along with his father in 1960 and then as full pastor in 1968. The sanctuary is kept as it would have looked during that time, with a continuous loop of King speeches and sermons.

A visit to the King birth home is also quite touching in that you really get a taste of life on Auburn Avenue in the 1930s, which, while segregated, at that time lacked the more modern type of urban blight that unfortunately is endemic along most of the street today. Within, the family rooms are preserved in a slice-of-life manner, with games and clothes strewn around the children's rooms, for example, instead of the more typical bare-bones aspect of many house museums. While most pieces are period and not actually King family items, the dishes in the kitchen are indeed relics of their time here. (Photography in the house is prohibited by request of the King family.)

As I mentioned, the free tour of the Birth

Home is quite popular, but there are no advance reservations. To secure a spot, you need to show up early the same day of the tour and book your space, preferably right at 9am when they open. If you arrive later in the day, you'll almost certainly be out of luck. However, as park rangers are quick to point out, there's a well-done video in the Visitors Center that gives you an extensive virtual tour.

CNN Studio Tour

Cable news may not be the ground-breaking novelty it once was, but the **CNN Studio Tour** (1 CNN Center, 404/827-2300, www.cnn. com, daily 9am-5pm, $15 adults, $12 children) offers an opportunity to see how the world's first 24-hour cable news channel operates, as well as to get a glimpse further inside two other landmark Ted Turner enterprises, Turner Network Television (TNT) and Turner Broadcasting Systems (TBS). If you'd like, you can take a crack at anchoring your own "show" with the option to buy the demo tape! The walking tours, departing every 10 minutes, are 55 minutes long and sell out very quickly, so book ahead. There are daily elevator-assisted tours at 10:30am, 1:30pm, and 3:30pm. The CNN Tour is one of the featured attractions in the Atlanta CityPASS (www.citypass.com, five attractions for $69).

State Capitol

Known colloquially as "The Gold Dome" for its shiny gilded top (among other less charitable, more descriptive names), the circa-1889 **Georgia State Capitol** (206 Washington St. SW, 404/330-6150, Mon.-Fri. 8am-5pm) is where the Peach State's often ugly sausage-making of laws happens. The state legislature, officially called the General Assembly, only meets for about 40 days each winter. But despite that brief annual meeting (or because of it?), Georgia has gained a reputation as one of the most corrupt states in the union. Until very recently, rural legislators routinely ate so many roasted peanuts during extended sessions that the floors would be covered with shells.

To learn more about the history of the General Assembly and see various historical and political artifacts, you can get a brochure and take a self-guided tour of the **Capitol Museum** (www.libs.uga.edu, Mon.-Fri. 8am-5pm, free). A free iPhone app is also available at the website. The grounds, while not the equal of the gorgeous State House grounds one state over in Columbia, South Carolina, are attractively maintained and feature various statuary, including a tribute to a group of African American legislators who were briefly kicked out of the capitol during Reconstruction.

APEX Museum

Another place to learn about Georgia black history is at the **APEX Museum** (135 Auburn Ave., 404/523-2739, www.apexmuseum.org, Tues.-Sat. 10am-5pm, $6 adults, $5 children), short for African American Panoramic Experience. APEX centers on three permanent exhibits: "Africa: The Untold Story," which chronicles humanity's rise in the African continent on to the trans-Atlantic slave trade; "Sweet Auburn: Street of Pride"; and "The Georgia Negro," based on W. E. B. Dubois's historic exhibit from the 1900 Paris Expo documenting black middle-class life in Georgia.

Atlanta-Fulton Public Library

The **Atlanta-Fulton Public Library** (1 Margaret Mitchell Square, 404/730-1700, www.afplweb.com, Mon.-Thurs. 9am-8pm, Fri.-Sat. 9am-6pm, Sun. 2pm-6pm, free) or "Central Library," by far the largest public library branch in the city, was designed and completed in 1980 by Marcel Breuer, noted German expressionist of the Bauhaus school. The fifth floor hosts the small but interesting Margaret Mitchell exhibit (including the typewriter on which she wrote *Gone with the Wind*), a genealogy collection, and a history collection on Atlanta and Georgia.

GRANT PARK
◖ Zoo Atlanta

There are larger zoos and there are more significant zoos. But few combine size with educational enjoyment as well as **Zoo Atlanta**

(800 Cherokee Ave. SE, 404/624-9453, www. zooatlanta.org, daily 9:30am-5:30pm, $21 adults, $16 ages 3-11), the pride of Grant Park. Primates are the prime specialty of Zoo Atlanta, and their expansive open gorilla habitat isn't only very enjoyable, it's a center of global gorilla research (Dian Fossey was a key collaborator). Venerable old Willie B., a silverback gorilla, lived at the zoo from 1961 until his death in 2000, but his garrulous image remains a symbol of Zoo Atlanta, especially since the zoo's significant upgrade and renovation in the late 1980s.

While there's a strong emphasis on crowd favorites from the African plains, like gorillas, elephants, giraffes, zebras, and a lion who sleeps 23 hours a day, the other key attraction at Zoo Atlanta is its pair of delightful giant pandas, Lun Lun and Yang Yang. Despite the sumptuous, specially built pagoda in which they cavort for your enjoyment, the pandas are actually the property of China (a return date is pending).

As with any zoo in the South, you'll want to get here as early in the day as possible to catch the animals before the heat drives them into shade and sleep (not to mention avoiding the crush of deluxe double-wide baby strollers when the crowd starts hitting at about 11am). Getting to Grant Park early will also help you get a parking space in the smallish zoo lot.

Atlanta Cyclorama

Back in the days before TV or even movies, a main form of popular entertainment was the "cyclorama," or circular painting wrapping 360 degrees around the viewer. Commonplace in the Victorian era, there are only three left intact in the country. The grandest by far is the **Atlanta Cyclorama** (800 Cherokee Ave., 404/658-7625, www.atlantacyclorama.org, Tues.-Sat. 9:15am-4:30pm, adults $10, children $8), an old-school over-the-top depiction of the Battle of Atlanta and the circumstances surrounding it.

Comprising a massive oil painting supplemented in the foreground by meticulously detailed figures of Civil War soldiers and functionaries, the Cyclorama is an immersive

© JIM MOREKIS

Zoo Atlanta

© JIM MOREKIS

Atlanta Cyclorama

experience with some things in common with modern 3-D film screenings. The difference here, other than the no-electricity part, is that you sit on a rotating platform in the center of the Cyclorama building while narration describes the various events you're witnessing of the 1864 engagement that ushered in Sherman's "March to the Sea." Guided tours happen every hour on the half-hour (except 12:30pm).

Funding is a continual challenge, and a new generation of demanding visitors and their tech-savvy progeny might find it a little rough around the edges. That said, for those with an appreciation for nostalgia, the Cyclorama is a delightfully charming and quirky piece of Atlanta history and an irreplaceable slice of Americana.

Oakland Cemetery

While not as ornately Victorian in its embellishments as, say, Savannah's Bonaventure Cemetery, Atlanta's **Oakland Cemetery** (248 Oakland Ave., www.oaklandcemetery.com,

daily 8am-8pm, free) is nonetheless a visually compelling and strangely relaxing location filled with history. The three most famous perpetual denizens are legendary golfer Bobby Jones, Atlanta's first African American mayor, Maynard Jackson, and, of course, iconic writer Margaret Mitchell. (There are lots of Mitchells buried in Oakland Cemetery, but technically the author of *Gone with the Wind* is not buried as a Mitchell; she was married to John Marsh when she died and her tombstone here bears that surname.)

The visitors center on-site offers tour information, and, perhaps oddly, cemetery-themed souvenirs. Cemetery-sponsored guided tours are available Saturday and Sunday at 10am, 2pm, and 4pm, no reservations required and all leaving from the visitors center. Weekday tours are available by appointment. There are also Saturday evening "Twilight Tours" leaving at 6:30pm. Those might seemingly be intended to cash in on the ghost story-paranormal craze, but actually they tend to focus on interesting areas of real-life local history.

MIDTOWN
◀ High Museum of Art

It bills itself as the most important art museum in the Southeast, and while that may be somewhat arguable, there's no doubt that the **High Museum of Art** (1280 Peachtree St. NE, 404/733-4400, www.high.org, $19.50 adults, $12 ages 6-17) is a crucial element of Atlanta cultural life and represents a significant collection of American art in its own right. The building itself, a gleaming white modernist structure not dissimilar in look and feel to New York's Guggenheim (here you also take a winding staircase up through the exhibits), seems strangely at home in posh Midtown, despite its architecture having absolutely nothing to do with any other building in the area. A major reason for the High's physical harmony with its neighborhood has to do with being set back within a well-maintained urban green space.

Once inside the cavernous interior, you'd be excused for briefly thinking that no amount of art could ever fill the space adequately. Indeed, you should take a few minutes to study the somewhat confusing layout of the three separate buildings (all linked by a sky bridge) that make up the High.

The vast bulk of the museum's noteworthy permanent collection occupies three floors in the Stent wing, expertly arranged in viewing areas that help split up the huge square footage into manageable chunks.

There is a smallish collection of European art, including works by Édouard Manet, Albrecht Dürer, and Giovanni Bellini, but the High's claim to fame is its gathering of work by American artists and craftspeople (not all of them Southern by any means). Don't miss the Folk Art collection upstairs, with a significant representation of work by noted Georgia outsider artist Howard Finster.

Margaret Mitchell House and Museum

Perhaps more accurately called Margaret Mitchell's apartment, this charmingly restored "Dump," as the great author and her husband John Marsh affectionately referred to it, takes you back in time to that 10-year span in the 1920s and 1930s when Mitchell wrote *Gone with the Wind* while recovering from a nasty ankle injury.

The furnishings at the **Margaret Mitchell House and Museum** (990 Peachtree St., 404/249-7015, www.margaretmitchellhouse.com, Mon.-Sat. 10am-5:30pm, Sun. noon-5:30pm, $13 adults, $8.50 children) aren't even close to original, since the three-story 1899 building, converted to an apartment in 1919, was severely blighted in the late 1970s, vandalized and essentially open to the elements. Indeed, it was slated for demolition until a cadre of local residents and donors teamed up to save the house in the late 1980s. Mayor Andrew Young was instrumental in making sure the building suffered no further abuse.

However, the Dump's tribulations still weren't over. After renovations had begun, two separate fires struck, one in 1994 and another in 1996. Finally, in May 1997, the house was open to the public.

Using Mitchell's own journal notes, restorationists furnished the tiny one-bedroom second-story apartment as closely as they could to what they thought was authentic when the building housed the Crescent Apartments, with the Marshes in apartment number 1. Your experience is by guided tour, leaving every half-hour and meeting in the cute and well-stocked gift shop. While the house opens at 10am, the first tour of the day doesn't begin until 10:30am. A charming tour guide will walk you through a small set of displays about Mitchell's young life and burgeoning journalism career before escorting you into the actual apartment.

Be sure to check out the small but interesting exhibit on the filming of *Gone with the Wind* in the restored building across the courtyard. With a particular emphasis on the cast and crew's interaction with the city of Atlanta, the exhibit also features the original huge portrait of Vivien Leigh as Scarlett O'Hara that is seen in the film.

A combo ticket ($22 adults, $12 children) with admission to the Mitchell House and the

© JIM MOREKIS

Margaret Mitchell House and Museum

Atlanta History Center is available at either location or online.

The Fed Museum

Directly across the street from the Margaret Mitchell House, though utterly different in look and purpose, is the Atlanta Monetary Museum, more commonly called **The Fed Museum** (1000 Peachtree St., www.frbatlanta.org, Mon.-Fri. 9am-4pm, free). Within the hulking Federal Reserve Bank of Atlanta building, the Fed Museum offers not only some surprisingly interesting exhibits on the history of money, from barter to modern times, but some amazing behind-the-scenes looks at enormous amounts of cash being counted, sorted, and bundled in various ways. It doesn't take long to visit, but in all this is one of the best free, fun, and informative hours you'll spend in Atlanta.

Atlanta Botanical Garden

If you love orchids, you'll go nuts for the **Atlanta Botanical Garden** (1345 Piedmont Ave., 404/876-5859, www.atlantabotanical-garden.org, Nov.-Mar. Tues.-Sun. 9am-5pm, Apr.-Oct. Tues.-Wed. and Fri.-Sun. 9am-7pm, Thurs. 9am-10pm, $19 adults, $13 children, parking $2 per hour). The centerpiece of this gorgeous 30-acre gem right beside Piedmont Park is the **Dorothy Chapman Fuqua Conservatory,** which specializes in rainforest habitat. Within the Conservatory you'll find the pièce de résistance, the **Fuqua Orchid Center,** which bills itself as the largest collection of orchid species in the United States. It features a special section devoted purely to mountain-habitat orchids as well as a massive display of tropical rainforest species.

The sprawling grounds are a collection of themed gardens, including a Japanese garden, a rose garden, a working organic herb garden, and a children's garden with sculptures and exhibits. A good way to enjoy it, albeit in the dark, is during one of the frequent Concert in the Garden series. Past performers have included Merle Haggard, Aaron Neville, and Neko Case.

MARGARET MITCHELL'S LEGACY

She was less than five feet tall, but she changed the world. Her novel *Gone with the Wind* would become one of the world's most printed books and inspire one of cinema's most popular films.

Margaret Mitchell was a reporter for the *Atlanta Journal-Constitution* when she had to quit due to a nagging ankle injury. Her husband John, anxious to give her something to do while confined to the ramshackle apartment on Peachtree Street they called "The Dump," urged her to write a book.

It took nearly 10 years to write, but once published in 1936, *Gone with the Wind* took the world by storm. A scant three years later the blockbuster film premiered at Atlanta's now-demolished Loew's Grand Theatre, with a crowd of one million gathered to see the greatest stars of the day. Generally shy, Mitchell spoke briefly at the premiere.

Coming from a long line of Atlantans, she was well equipped to write the ultimate tale of the old South. Her grandfather told her stories about serving in the Confederate army. Like her heroine Scarlett O'Hara, Mitchell was rebellious: During the Roaring Twenties, "Peggy," as she styled herself, adopted the Flapper look and lifestyle, at one point calling herself an "unscrupulous flirt."

At age 22, she married an abusive alcoholic. The best man at her wedding, John Marsh, would become her second husband. They were together when she was killed at age 48, hit by a speeding car just a few blocks from her house.

The best place to experience her legacy is at "The Dump" itself, the **Margaret Mitchell House and Museum** (990 Margaret St., 404/249-7015, www.margaretmitchellhouse. com, Mon.-Sat. 10am-5:30pm, Sun. noon-5:30pm, $13 adults, $8.50 children). The typewriter she used to write *Gone with the Wind*, however, is at a special Mitchell exhibit on the fifth floor of the **Atlanta-Fulton Public Library** (1 Margaret Mitchell Square, 404/730-1700, www.afplweb.com, Mon.-Thurs. 9am-8pm, Fri.-Sat. 9am-6pm, Sun. 2pm-6pm, free). Down Peachtree Street, you can visit the Georgian Terrace Hotel, where Clark Gable and Vivien Leigh stayed during the premiere. Up in Marietta you can visit the Gone with the Wind Museum: Scarlett on the Square.

For a kitschy look at the Battle of Atlanta in *Gone with the Wind*, visit the **Cyclorama** (800 Cherokee Ave., 404/658-7625, www.atlanta-cyclorama.org, Tues.-Sat. 9:15am-4:30pm, $10 adults, $8 children) in Grant Park. The author is buried in nearby **Oakland Cemetery** (248 Oakland Ave., www.oaklandcemetery.com, daily 8am-8pm, free). But don't look for the name "Mitchell"; she lies next to her husband, John Marsh, and bears his name.

◖ Fox Theatre

Truly one of the all-time classic vintage venues, the **Fox Theatre** (660 Peachtree St. NE, 404/881-2100, www.foxtheatre.org) is without question Atlanta's most beloved landmark and a priceless piece of Americana. Its rococo Moorish-Egyptian theme, complete with a faux minaret and stylized hieroglyphics, is a nod to its original incarnation, never realized, of being a Shriners temple. When completed in 1929 it was as a movie theater in a popular chain developed by William Fox. The 4,600-seat "Arabian courtyard" auditorium, including nearly 100 crystal stars, did not actually host the world premiere of *Gone with the Wind* in 1939, but the Fox Theatre was the only theater in Atlanta at the time that allowed both white and black patrons. The "Colored" box office window is still here, at the back entrance.

Over 300 performances a year are held at "the Fabulous Fox" these days, from traveling Broadway shows to musical performances to, yes, movies—today usually shown on a state-of-the-art new digital projector. However, the audience sing-alongs that occasionally precede the features are shown on the original 1929 projector.

The grand Egyptian Ballroom, designed after a temple for Pharaoh Ramses II (the mezzanine ladies lounge has a replica of King Tut's throne), continues to host large gala events and dances. The Fox also features its original pipe organ, nicknamed "Mighty Mo," occasionally played during special performances such as Atlanta Ballet's annual *Nutcracker.*

A community effort resulted in the Fox's entry on the National Register of Historic Places, and National Landmark status in 1976. There's an entire Fox Theatre Historic District now, including the Fox, the Georgian Terrace hotel, across the street, the Ponce De Leon Apartments, and the Cox-Carlton hotel, now Hotel Indigo.

Jimmy Carter Library and Museum

First, to clear up any confusion: The **Jimmy Carter Library and Museum** (441 Freedom Pkwy., 404/865-7100, www.jimmycarterlibrary.gov, Mon.-Sat. 9am-4:45pm, Sun. noon-4:45pm, library Mon.-Fri. 8:30am-4:30pm, $8 adults, free under age 17) is on the grounds of the globally renowned **Carter Center,** but they're not the same entity.

The nonprofit Carter Center pursues the former president's goals of international cooperation, free and fair elections, and human rights, and isn't usually open to the public. Since 1986 the public component has belonged to the Museum and Library, which houses not only about 27 million of the president's papers and records but exhibits of his life and work both in the White House and after. Highlights include a life-size Oval Office replica, furnished as if it were still 1974, and Carter's Nobel Peace Prize. A $10 million renovation was completed in 2009. (If you're looking for political memorabilia from Carter's campaigns, you might be disappointed; most of that is in various buildings in the Jimmy Carter National Historic District in his hometown of Plains, Georgia, a couple of hours south.)

The spacious boulevard called Freedom Parkway links the Carter Center to the Martin Luther King Jr. National Historic Site, and indeed the two sites are only about five minutes apart by car. The president and his wife,

Rosalynn, both maintain offices at the Carter Center and can occasionally be seen coming and going. The grounds are particularly nice and are free and open to the public whether or not you enter the museum building.

William Breman Jewish Heritage Museum

The **William Breman Jewish Heritage Museum** (1440 Spring St., 678/222-3700, www.thebreman.org, Mon.-Thurs. 10am-5pm, Fri. 10am-3pm, Sun. 1pm-5pm, $12 adults, $6 children), often just called the Breman, aspires to chronicle and honor the whole of the Jewish experience in Atlanta since antebellum times, but with a nod to greater events such as the Holocaust and aspects of social justice. The Breman is also the caretaker of a significant archive and library of letters and documents detailing Jewish history and regional genealogy. The Cuba Archives and Genealogy Center catalogs Jewish life in Georgia and Alabama.

Museum of Design Atlanta

It bills itself as the only museum in the South devoted purely to design. In any event, **Museum of Design Atlanta** (MODA, 1315 Peachtree St. NE, 404/979-6455, www.museumofdesign.org, Tues.-Sat. 10am-5pm, Sun. noon-5pm, $10 adults, $5 students and children) is 5,000 square feet of display space devoted to a constantly shifting array of exhibits, focusing on some aspect of modern design; there are no permanent displays. It's a fun visit in a hip environment. On the last Thursday evening of the month the museum stays open until 8pm and admission includes a cocktail. MODA is near the Woodruff Arts Center, and the nearby Arts Center MARTA transit station is very convenient. However, MODA has no parking lot; you're urged to pay to park at the LAZ lot (1337 Peachtree St.).

DRUID HILLS
Fernbank Museum of Natural History

Since opening in the early 1990s, the **Fernbank**

Museum of Natural History (767 Clifton Rd. NE, 404/929-6300, www.fernbankmuseum. org, Mon.-Sat. 10am-5pm, Sun. noon-5pm, $17.50 adults, $15.50 children) in Druid Hills has become a staple of the Atlanta cultural scene as well as a regular stop for local schoolchildren. While now a separate entity, the museum is an offshoot of the nearby Fernbank Science Center, a project of the DeKalb County Public Schools.

The main permanent exhibit at Fernbank and by far the most attention-demanding is the "Giants of the Mesozoic" display of massive, life-size dinosaur sculptures, including a 120-foot *Argentinosaurus,* the largest dinosaur known to science. Another permanent exhibit is "A Walk Through Time in Georgia," which tells the story of the Peach State in geological and biological terms. For many visitors, though, the highlight is the 300-seat IMAX Theater, which hosts a steady schedule of beautifully shot nature films. Every Friday evening sees another edition of "Martinis and IMAX," featuring a

Michael C. Carlos Museum

movie, finger food, and access to a cash bar for one low admission cost.

The **Fernbank Science Center** (156 Heaton Park Dr., 678/874-7102, http://fsc.fernbank. edu, Mon.-Wed. 9am-5pm, Thurs.-Fri. 9am-9pm, Sat. 10am-5pm, free), though a separate facility, has a cool observatory with frequent planetarium shows (Thurs.-Fri. 9am-10:30pm).

Michael C. Carlos Museum

One of the most enriching small museums I've found anywhere, the **Michael C. Carlos Museum** (571 S. Kilgo Circle NE, 404/727-4282, www.carlos.emory.edu, Tues.-Fri. 10am-4pm, Sat. 10am-5pm, Sun. noon-5pm, $8 adults, $6 children) on the Emory University quadrangle is one of Atlanta's hidden gems. The comparatively young age of the museum building itself, built in 1985 and majorly upgraded in 1993, is matched by its dynamic, intimate approach to its subject matter, primarily Greco-Roman, pre-Columbian, and Egyptian antiquities.

The collections, some of which date from an early collegiate collection in the Victorian era, are small, but their presentation is extremely well-curated and annotated, as befitting a university-affiliated institution. You can get up close and personal with just about everything, including the priceless sculptures.

These days the centerpiece of the Carlos is its extremely well preserved collection of Egyptian funerary artifacts (interestingly, many were acquired from a curiosity museum in upstate New York). You enter the Egyptian section on a dramatically lighted, gradual ramp bearing a huge stylized map of the Nile River. Inside the hall are several mummies, most bearing incredibly vivid, unrestored, and unretouched paint from thousands of years ago. If mummies aren't your thing, the topmost floor has an impressive collection of African folk masks and crafts and the museum has a vibrant collection of pre-Columbian Native American antiquities.

The museum is near the main entrance to the Emory campus off the traffic circle at Oxford and Decatur Roads. Parking is available in a nearby parking garage.

Centers for Disease Control Museum

Possibly Atlanta's most offbeat museum and perhaps its most interesting is the **David J. Sencer Centers for Disease Control Museum** (1600 Clifton Rd. NE, 404/639-0830, www.cdc.gov, Mon.-Fri. 9am-5pm, free), located on the world-famous campus of the crucial public health research institution. Until recently called "Global Odyssey of Health," the CDC Museum is a bit less clinical in nature than you might expect, the emphasis being on vibrant multimedia. Ongoing exhibits include a "Global Symphony," a 100-foot-long chronicle of the fight against diseases like polio and HIV/AIDS; "The Story of CDC," a history of the CDC and the evolution of its role; and the massive sculpture *Messengers.* Indeed, at the museum's rotating exhibits, you're just as likely to see cutting-edge art dealing with sociopolitical topics as you are anything of an overtly medical nature.

BUCKHEAD
◖ Atlanta History Center and Swan House

The **Atlanta History Center** (130 W. Paces Ferry Rd., 404/814-4000, www.atlantahistorycenter.com, Mon.-Sat. 10am-5:30pm, Sun. 1pm-4pm, $16.50 adults, $11 children) is a well-run, sharp city museum with a huge added bonus: the historic and beautifully restored **Swan House** (tours Mon.-Sat. 11am-4pm, Sun. 1pm-4pm), one of the finest house museums in the South. The History Center itself offers a multitude of well-curated exhibits, including the obligatory city history section (try to catch one of the free guided docent tours for much more information than the exhibits show).

The History Center purchased the nearby historic Swan House directly from Mrs. Inman, heir to the Inman fortune (and whose son is the namesake for nearby Inman Park), exactly as she left it. What this means to visitors is that they have an opportunity to tour this magnificent, 14,000-square-foot, elegantly and

historic Swan House in Buckhead

© JIM MOREKIS

ATLANTA

charmingly appointed mansion stocked almost completely with original furnishings. This is almost unheard of in the house museum world, which generally depends on approximating furnishings by period and almost never has the luxury of featuring original items.

Designed by Philip Trammell Shutze, the multistory Swan House dates from "only" 1928, but looks and feels significantly older thanks to the tastes of the owners, Edward and Emily Inman. Edward made his fortune as a cotton middleman. You'll get a distinct *Downton Abbey* vibe as you take your guided tour from room to room and note how marvelously clubby and cozy the house feels despite its swank opulence.

The Atlanta History Center also operates the Margaret Mitchell House, and you can purchase a combo ticket ($22 adults, $12 children) from either place. The center is also one of several attractions featured in the Atlanta CityPASS package ticket (www.citypass.com, $69).

Governor's Mansion

The official residence of the chief executive of the Peach State, the **Governor's Mansion** (391 W. Paces Ferry Rd. NW, http://mansion.georgia.gov, tours Tues.-Thurs. 10am-11:30am, free) is not to be confused with the much larger and more ornate State Capitol or "Gold Dome" downtown. This handsomely appointed, 30-room Greek Revival home in Buckhead is open for free tours for a short window each week. Keep in mind it's not exactly historic, given that it was only built in 1967.

WEST END
The Wren's Nest

Generations of Americans have enjoyed the folktales of Uncle Remus and Brer Rabbit, the brainchildren of the great Joel Chandler Harris. The memory of the author and his creations is preserved at Harris's West End home, **The Wren's Nest** (1050 Ralph David Abernathy Blvd., 404/753-7735, www.wrensnestonline.com, Tues.-Sat. 10:30am-2:30pm, $8 adults, $5 children), including many original furnishings. Atlanta's oldest house museum, the Wren's Nest's preservation was encouraged in the early 20th century by Andrew Carnegie and President Theodore Roosevelt.

Harris, also known as a vigorous and progressive editor at the *Atlanta Journal-Constitution,* lived in this Queen Anne house from 1881 to 1908, during which time he wrote many of his most famous tales gathered in the global best-seller *Uncle Remus: His Songs and His Sayings.* A particular highlight is storytelling time each Saturday at 1pm, courtesy of the "Wren's Nest Ramblers," the resident group of African American storytellers who bring Harris's tales to life. (Those who want to further their Brer Rabbit experience can drive a couple of hours south to Eatonton, Georgia, and visit Harris's birthplace at the Uncle Remus Museum.)

Six Flags over Georgia

A favorite day-trip destination of generations of Georgians, **Six Flags over Georgia** (275 Riverside Pkwy. SW, 770/739-3400, www.sixflags.com, $57, $40 children under 48 inches tall, free under age 2, parking $20) is known to thrill seekers the world over for its vast assortment of roller coasters. Many are authentically wooden and structured for maximum speed in the old-school way, while the newer variety emphasize the modern focus on heavy G-force and twists and turns. The 100-acre park features no less than 37 "thrill rides" ranging from the mild kiddie ride Tweetie's Tree House (Six Flags has an extensive licensing agreement with Warner Bros. movie and cartoon characters; Batman and Superman feature prominently here) to the monster world-class "hypercoaster," Goliath, opened in 2006. Of course, you can still ride that vintage classic, The Great American Scream Machine.

It's not cheap, and it can get pretty crowded. Your best bet for a slightly thinner crowd is to come on weekdays during summer as well as April-May and September-October.

UNIVERSITIES AND COLLEGES
Georgia Tech

Anchoring a large portion of downtown and midtown Atlanta, the **Georgia Institute of Technology** (North Ave., 404/894-2000, www.gatech.edu), always simply called "Georgia Tech" or even just "Tech," is one of the nation's oldest, largest, and best engineering schools. Founded in 1885 specifically as an effort to reboot the South's industrial efforts in the wake of the Civil War, it is one of the few premier engineering-research schools in the United States that is a fully public institution.

By far the most interesting portion of campus for visitors is the nine-acre "Old Campus" or Hill District, the original Tech campus and site of a dozen of its oldest and most picturesque buildings. A highlight is Tech Tower, named for its large, lighted "Tech" signage on each of its four sides. For decades students competed to "steal the T" as part of a traditional prank; however, the practice is much frowned upon today. Other important sights on "The Hill" include the YMCA building, funded by tycoon John D. Rockefeller and now the alumni offices; the old Andrew Carnegie school library, now the president's office; and Lyman Hall, first of many Tech chemistry buildings.

The Georgia Tech Yellow Jackets play football at Bobby Dodd Stadium at Historic Grant Field. While improved since its early days, Grant Field is the oldest major university gridiron in the United States, built in 1905. As skyscrapers have sprung up around it, the view from a typical Jacket home game is quite different from the bucolic setting of the typical college football stadium.

Don't be surprised to hear an old-fashioned steam whistle while walking around the Tech campus. An old school tradition, the whistle blows five minutes before the top of each hour during regular class times.

Emory University

A private university occupying 630 acres in the verdant, quiet Druid Hills residential area in northeast Atlanta, **Emory University** (1615 Pierce Dr. NE, 404/727-6123, www.emory.edu) hasn't been in town the entire time; it was founded in 1836 in Oxford, Georgia. However, in 1915 a land grant by Asa Griggs Candler, then-president of Coca-Cola, enabled the school to move to the state capital, beginning a long association with the locally based soft-drink giant. In 1979, another Coca-Cola president, Robert W. Woodruff, donated over $100 million in Coke stock to Emory, the largest-ever gift to a university up to that time. In 1994 the Emory business school was renamed for Roberto Goizueta, yet another Coca-Cola president and college benefactor.

However, you'll find very few commercial nods to Coca-Cola on Emory's understated, wooded campus. Despite Emory's old-fashioned roots as a Methodist institution, it is on the leading edge of design, with over two million square feet of building space LEED-certified to state-of-the-art sustainability and conservation standards. By far the main attraction for visitors is the **Michael C. Carlos Museum** (571 S. Kilgo Circle, 404/727-4282, www.carlos.emory.edu, Tues.-Fri. 10am-4pm, Sat. 10am-5pm, Sun. noon-5pm, $8 adults, $6 children), an excellently designed and curated museum devoted to Egyptian, Greco-Roman, and ancient Native American artifacts.

Historically Black Colleges and Universities

Perhaps nowhere else is Atlanta's importance to African American history as clear as in the presence of several of the country's oldest and most influential historically black colleges and universities (HBCUs), all nearby to each other in southwest Atlanta and since 1929 gathered in a consortium called the Atlanta University Center.

All member institutions share the **Robert W. Woodruff Library** (111 James P. Brawley Dr. SW, 404/978-2067, www.auctr.edu), whose main claim to fame these days is as the new home of an expansive collection of papers from Martin Luther King Jr., purchased from the King estate in 2006 and deeded to King's alma mater, Morehouse College. The papers are available for public research use.

The first higher education institution in the United States established especially for African Americans to attain graduate degrees was Atlanta College, founded in conjunction with the Freedmens Bureau in the months immediately following the Civil War. A few years later, Clark College was founded to grant undergraduate degrees. In 1929 both merged to form **Clark Atlanta University** (223 James P. Brawley Dr., 404/880-8000, www.cau.edu), which today has about 4,000 students and maintains its Methodist affiliation. It's one of only four HBCUs with full research institution status. Famed author and civil rights activist W. E. B. Du Bois was a longtime sociology professor here.

Easily the best known of Atlanta's HBCUs, however, are **Morehouse College** (830 Westview Dr., 404/681-2800, www.morehouse.edu) and **Spelman College** (350 Spelman Lane, 404/681-3643, www.spelman.edu). While technically unaffiliated, they're often mentioned in the same breath not only because of their academic excellence but because of their unique nature; Morehouse is an all-men's school, while Spelman is all women. Between them they account for an amazing variety of high-profile alumni, including Martin Luther King Jr. and his daughters, filmmaker Spike Lee, actor Samuel L. Jackson, authors Alice Walker and Tina McElroy Ansa, and Atlanta's first black mayor, Maynard Jackson.

The **Spelman College Museum of Fine Art** (350 Spelman Lane, 404/681-3643, www.spelman.edu, Tues.-Fri. 10am-4pm, Sat. noon-4pm, $3 donation) is in the Cosby Academic Center and is devoted purely to artwork by female artists covering the African diaspora.

Morris Brown College (643 MLK Jr. Dr., 404/739-1010, www.morrisbrown.edu) has the distinction of being the first African American college self-funded entirely by African Americans, almost all of them formerly enslaved. However, Morris Brown lost accreditation in 2002 after a financial scandal. No longer technically a member of the Atlanta University Center organization, Morris Brown currently has fewer than 100 students and faces a very uncertain future.

Georgia State University

Despite its heavily urban, occasionally sketchy setting downtown and its notoriously unattractive "concrete campus," **Georgia State University** (30 Courtland St., 404/413-2000, www.gsu.edu) is actually not as young as you'd think, with roots dating back to 1913. It's not as small as you'd think either; its enrollment is second largest in the state, behind only the enormous University of Georgia in Athens. Of prime interest to visitors is the school-run **Rialto Center for the Arts** (80 Forsyth St., 404/413-9849, www.rialtocenter.org) in the Fairlie-Poplar district, hosting most performances of Georgia State's esteemed music department.

Entertainment and Events

NIGHTLIFE
Live Music

"Died and gone to heaven" takes on new meaning at the downtown club **Masquerade** (695 North Ave. NE, 404/577-8178, www.masqueradeatlanta.com), certainly one of the South's most venerable live music venues, bringing in name acts (Matisyahu, Grouplove, Gwar) as well as on-fire metal-indie bands (Lazer/Wulf, Bad Books) and the occasional mixed martial arts fight to its rambling, castle-like space, a former mill. Most touring bands play upstairs on the third level, named "Heaven." The grungier and more local acts tend to play, you guessed it, in "Hell." (And yes, there's a "Purgatory" as well). Outside is its **Music Park,** basically a huge open space where the occasional rowdy outdoor show will be held (Alabama Shakes, North Mississippi Allstars). A rite of passage for generations of Atlantans and Southern music fans, the Masquerade is loud, dark, divey, and can get very crowded. But two possible bonuses are that, unlike most Atlanta clubs, Masquerade does host all-ages shows, and no smoking is ever allowed in the building.

The main rock-and-roll bar in happening Little Five Points is **The Star Community Bar** (437 Moreland Ave., www.starbaratlanta.com, Thurs.-Sun. 4pm-3am), more colloquially just called "Star Bar" and known far and wide as a Southern hipster mecca and live-music joint. It also boasts one of the coolest Elvis shrines outside of Memphis, upstairs in a special "vault."

The premier bigger-name live-music venue in Little Five Points is **Variety Playhouse** (1099 Euclid Ave. NE, 404/524-7354, www.variety-playhouse.com), a former movie theater converted into a concert space, with a mix of assigned seating and a dance floor up front near the stage. They do have beer and wine, but the best way to enjoy a night out at Variety Playhouse is to sample food and drink elsewhere in this lively entertainment district

before (and after!) the show. Unlike most nightspots in Atlanta, no smoking is allowed here.

The best blues joint in Atlanta proper and easily one of the more authentic dive bars in town as well, **Northside Tavern** (1058 Howell Mill Rd., 404/874-8745, www.northsidetavern.com, daily noon-3am) features live blues and jazz seven nights a week and has a beat-up interior to match that crushing schedule.

One of Atlanta's most iconic live-music hubs, **Blind Willie's** (828 N. Highland Ave., 404/873-2583, www.blindwilliesblues.com) brings the blues (and some jazz) six nights a week in the hip Virginia-Highland neighborhood.

Renowned as a late-night party place and metal club for the last 20 years, **The Highlander** (931 Monroe Circle, 404/872-0060, www.thehighlanderatlanta.com, Mon.-Sat. 11am-3am, Sun. 12:30pm-midnight) in Midtown has experienced a renewed popularity in the wake of an episode of *Diners, Drive-ins, and Dives* on the Food Channel. The focus food-wise is on the delectable burgers, which some call the best in Atlanta.

One of Atlanta's premier live-music clubs, East Atlanta's **The Earl** (488 Flat Shoals Ave., 404/522-3950, www.badearl.com) also boasts some of its best burgers (the Guacamole Burger is a fave rave, and don't forget the sweet-potato fries). The acts tend toward the indie or heavy side, and are generally bands on their way up to better things; in short, a great place to catch great bands in an intimate venue while you still can.

Like great, loud music? Love unicorns? Then **The Drunken Unicorn** (736 Ponce de Leon Ave., no phone, www.thedrunkenunicorn.net) in Poncey-Highland is for you. In classic rock bar style, it's basically a dark dungeon with a smallish stage and a really good sound system. The focus is on the bands—metal, punk, indie, basically anything not mainstream—and cheap and flowing beer. They're directly underneath **Friends on Ponce** (736 Ponce de Leon Ave.,

404/817-3820, www.friendsonponce-atl.com), a neighborhood gay bar.

No ATL pub crawl is complete without a visit to **Smith's Olde Bar** (1578 Piedmont Ave., 404/875-1522, www.smithsoldebar.com, Mon.-Sat. noon-3am, Sun. noon-midnight)— or "SOB," get it?—in the Piedmont Park-Morningside area just northeast of Midtown. Combine an Irish pub with a blues-rock club with a pool hall with a sports bar, but with a more open-minded attitude in this gay-friendly area of town, and you have a fairly complete nightlife experience.

Dive Bars

In a city that already has its share of quirky one-of-a-kind bars and clubs, the **Clermont Lounge** (789 Ponce de Leon Ave., 404/874-4783, www.clermontlounge.net, Mon.-Sat. 1pm-3am) in Virginia-Highland is perhaps the quirkiest and most unique. Originally a 1960s hotel bar in a hotel that has since shut down, the Clermont is a combination strip club-hipster dive with kitsch cachet to burn (movie stars can often be seen slumming here while in town). The vibe isn't so much classic gentlemen's club as it is sheer spectacle, with the generally over-the-hill but spirited topless dancers being an assortment of ages and body types. The booze is plentiful and cheap, the ubiquitous PBR running a buck apiece most nights, the company interesting and varied, and the burlesque entertainment . . . well, it is what it is.

No look at Atlanta nightlife is complete without a look at **Sister Louisa's Church of the Living Room & Ping Pong Emporium** (466 Edgewood Ave., 404/522-8275, www.sisterlouisaschurch.com, Mon.-Sat. 5pm-3am, Sun. 5pm-midnight), which, amazingly, is exactly what the name implies—except "Sister Louisa" is actually a guy, specifically Grant Henry, a former priest who turned in his robes for, well, different robes, and now serves libations and has painted some interesting quasi-religious themed artwork for the walls as well. There's even an "organ karaoke" night on Wednesday, which is exactly what it sounds like. As for the Ping-Pong, yes, there's one table upstairs. The

main show at "Church," as everyone calls it, is the clientele itself, a mix of über-hipsters, freaks, those of vague gender, and, of course, lookie-loos in search of the wild side of Atlanta life.

You'll find **El Bar** (939 Ponce de Leon Ave., 404/881-6040, Wed.-Sat. 10pm-3am) right behind and sort of underneath the El Azteca restaurant in Virginia-Highland, and if you like crazy nights, a combination of hip-hop and club music, and excellent and creative drink specials (the house specialty is a shot of tequila with a Miller High Life), you will have lots of *amor* for El Bar. It's cozy and crowded late on weekend nights, but that's how they roll.

Taverns and Pubs

The very personification of the neighborhood bar and grill, **Manuel's Tavern** (602 N. Highland Ave., 404/525-3447, www.manuelstavern.com, Tues.-Sat. 11am-2am, Sun.-Mon. 11am-midnight) is nearly as well known for its food as its spirits and convivial atmosphere. Older generations knew "Mannie's" as where Atlanta's old-school power structure let their hair down and exchanged scuttlebutt. Manuel's remains a Poncey-Highland must-visit for the beer connoisseur and comfort-food maven alike.

Virginia-Highland's favorite bar is **The Righteous Room** (1051 Ponce de Leon Ave., 404/874-0939, Mon.-Thurs. 11:30am-2am, Fri. 11:30am-3am, Sat. noon-3am, Sun. noon-2am), which also gets most everyone's vote for best bar food in Atlanta. The burgers in particular deserve the raves they get, but the menu is surprisingly extensive, with good veggie selections and even a salmon quesadilla.

Yes, the name's a joke: **Euclid Avenue Yacht Club** (1136 Euclid Ave. NE, 404/688-2582, www.theeayc.com, Mon.-Thurs. 3pm-2am, Fri.-Sat. noon-3am, Sun. noon-midnight) has nothing to do with boats of any kind. But this staple of the Little Five Points (L5P) bar scene does have something of a clubby atmosphere in the sense that it's really more of an old-school neighborhood blue-collar bar than some of the more hipster-oriented dives that have sprung up in L5P over the past few years.

ATLANTA

Nightclubs and Dancing

For a cover in the $5-10 range, you can go underground, literally, and dance all night to the DJs spinning old-school hip-hop and dance-pop at the epicenter of the ATL serious club scene, **MJQ** (736 Ponce de Leon Ave., 404/870-0575, Mon.-Wed. 10pm-4am, Thurs.-Fri. 11pm-4am, Sat. 11pm-3am), situated in the same complex as the also-popular Drunken Unicorn.

Probably Atlanta's premier gay dance club, **The Jungle Club** (215 Faulkner Rd. NE, 404/844-8800, www.jungleclubatlanta.com, daily 5pm-3am) is also one of the more serious purveyors of straight-up house music and its subvariants, often bringing in world-class DJs for a long night of partying until dawn.

Atlanta's go-to spot for authentic Latin and salsa dancing—actually, the DJs spin everything from reggaeton to merengue—**La Rumba II** (4300 Buford Hwy., 678/789-2888, www.larumba2.com, Thurs.-Sun. 10pm-4am) is the latest incarnation of a local Latino favorite.

If you're looking for the classic multilevel high-dollar hip-hop club, dance, and Red Bull-and-vodka scene, with all that that implies, go straight to **Compound** (1008 Brady Ave., 404/898-1702, www.compoundatl.com, Thurs.-Sat. 9pm-3am) and hope you look good enough to make it in.

PERFORMING ARTS

Because of its size, wealth, and population of affluent transplants from all areas of the country and the rest of the world, Atlanta offers a huge variety of fine arts performance and takes its place among the country's leading cultural centers.

Venues

Without question Atlanta's leading overall cultural venue is the **Robert W. Woodruff Memorial Arts Center** (1280 Peachtree St. NE, 404/733-4200, www.woodruffcenter.org). You'd be forgiven for thinking the *memorial* in the name refers to legendary philanthropist Woodruff, who provided much of the funding for its construction. The memorializing

in question, however, refers to the tragic 1962 airplane crash in Paris that claimed the lives of eight Atlanta art community movers and shakers, leading to the establishment of the Arts Center in 1968. This attractive 12-acre campus, around which Midtown has built a reputation as a leading arts center, includes 1,800-seat Symphony Hall, home of the Atlanta Symphony Orchestra, and the High Museum of Art, which comprises several buildings.

One of the country's great historic venues, the 4,600-seat **Fox Theatre** (660 Peachtree St. NE, 404/881-2100, box office 855/285-8499, www.foxtheatre.org) continues to host a full slate of productions, generally touring road shows and benefit performances. Its charmingly over-the-top design makes it worth seeing even if you're not attending a show here.

For many years it was known to Atlanta music fans as The Roxy, anchor of the Buckhead nightlife scene and host to some of the greatest names in rock and roll. Today, the fully restored and renamed, circa-1930 **Buckhead Theatre** (3110 Roswell Rd., 404/843-2825, www.thebuckheadtheatre.com) continues to host some of the biggest names in indie music as well as the occasional theatrical production.

The fairly new **Verizon Wireless Amphitheatre** (2200 Encore Pkwy., 404/733-5010, www.vzwamp.com), one of many bearing that name throughout the United States, is in the northern suburb of Alpharetta and hosts some of the biggest names in music in its 12,000-seat setting.

Verdant **Piedmont Park** (1320 Monroe Dr., 404/875-7275, www.piedmontpark.org) in Midtown hosts some of Atlanta's most popular live shows, often free ones, such as Music Midtown and the Pride Fest. Nearby **Atlanta Botanical Garden** (1345 Piedmont Ave. NE, 404/876-5859, www.atlantabotanicalgarden.org) also hosts a well-received concert series during the summer. Buckhead's answer to Piedmont Park, the amphitheater at **Chastain Park** (4469 Stella Dr., 404/233-2227, http://chastainseries.com) is also a popular place to see a live show during the summer.

ATLANTA

For years, The Omni was a premier local sports and entertainment venue. In 1999 that decaying cavern was demolished, and on that site now sits the 18,000-seat **Philips Arena** (1 Philips Dr., 404/878-3000, www.philipsarena. com) adjoining the CNN Center. (Local resident Elton John played its inaugural show.) "The Phil" is home of the Atlanta Hawks basketball team and is considered the third-busiest concert facility in the United States.

Atlanta's newest large-scale venue, **Cobb Energy Performing Arts Centre** (2800 Cobb Galleria Pkwy., 770/916-2800, www.cobbenergycentre.com), is situated right at the intersection of I-75 and the I-285 Perimeter just northwest of town.

Music and Dance

Long considered the leading orchestra of the Southeast and one of the best in the country, the nearly 70-year-old **Atlanta Symphony Orchestra** (1280 Peachtree St. NE, 404/733-5000, www.atlantasymphony.org) performs under the baton of conductor and music director Robert Spano, whose vision includes championing new works by up-and-coming conductors. The affiliated **Atlanta Symphony Chorus** is an award-winning entity in its own right and is one of the world's leading groups of its kind. The Atlanta Symphony Orchestra (ASO) performs at least 200 concerts a year, most at the Atlanta Symphony Center in the Woodruff Memorial Arts Center on Peachtree Street. But they can frequently be seen at huge outdoor shows as well, at places like Verizon Wireless Amphitheatre and Chastain Park.

Since its inception in the 1970s, the **Atlanta Chamber Players** (www.atlantachamberplayers.com) has relied on a core group from the ASO to perform intimate small-scale concerts from the chamber repertoire. They play a wide variety of venues, including the High Museum of Art, college campuses, and local churches.

The first dedicated baroque ensemble in the Southeast, the **Atlanta Baroque Orchestra** (770/557-7582, www.atlantabaroque.org) is under the direction of Julie Andrijeski and makes its home base well outside the Perimeter

in the northern suburb of Roswell, playing mostly at the Roswell Presbyterian Church.

Once the Marietta Symphony, then the Cobb Symphony, and now the **Georgia Symphony Orchestra** (770/429-7016, www.georgiasymphony.org), this all-professional group performs at various venues just north of Atlanta, with its main base at the Bailey Center at Kennesaw State University. Recent concerts included Mahler's Symphony No. 1 and a pops program featuring the music of Radiohead.

The **Georgia State University Symphony Orchestra** (404/413-5900, www.music.gsu. edu) is entirely affiliated with Georgia State University, which has a sprawling campus downtown. Its music department is excellent, and audiences at their performances are the beneficiaries. They typically play at the Rialto Center for the Arts in Fairlie-Poplar.

The highly regarded **Atlanta Opera** (404/881-8801, www.atlantaopera.org) has had to move locations a lot over the years to accommodate growing crowds, from the Woodruff Center to the Fox Theatre to the Civic Center, and now to the huge, plush new Cobb Energy Performing Arts Centre (2800 Cobb Galleria Pkwy.) in northwest Atlanta at I-75 and I-285. The 2012 season included *Carmen, La Traviata,* and *The Italian Girl in Algiers*.

The smaller **Capitol City Opera** (678/301-8013, www.ccityopera.org) concentrates more on light opera, such as *Cosi Fan Tutte,* and operates in close affiliation with Oglethorpe University. Capitol City generally performs at the university's Conant Performing Arts Center.

Closing in on the century mark, the **Atlanta Ballet** (404/873-5811, www.atlantaballet.com) has a long and storied history, but it's not hidebound by any means. These days it's as known for its innovation as for its tradition, regularly performing work by new choreographers. The Atlanta Ballet juggles three main performance venues, the massive new Cobb Energy Performing Arts Centre (2800 Cobb Galleria Pkwy.), the Fox Theatre (660 Peachtree St. NE), and the Gwinnett Performing Arts Center (6500 Sugarloaf Pkwy.), east of town.

ATLANTA

Billing itself as the nation's only fully integrated dance company, **Full Radius Dance** (404/724-9663, www.fullradiusdance.org) incorporates dancers with disabilities into its calendar of original choreography, with wheelchairs and dancers moving together in rhythm. Most of their shows are at 7 Stages (1105 Euclid Ave. NE) in Little Five Points.

Theater

The "establishment" company in Atlanta is **Alliance Theatre** (404/733-4650, www.alliancetheatre.org), performing primarily at the Woodruff Memorial Arts Center (1280 Peachtree St. NE) in Midtown. Since its founding in 1968, Alliance has served not only as the city's premier theater company but also as a developing ground for theatrical acting and directing talent from all over the Southeast.

The 30-year-old **Horizon Theatre** (1083 Austin Ave., 404/584-7450, www.horizontheatre.com) performs in an intimate space in Little Five Points, but don't let the small size of the room fool you: This is a fully professional theater presenting important work through the course of its five-show main season, and it's probably Atlanta's favorite theater company.

Since 1988, **Actor's Express** (887 W. Marietta St., 404/607-7469, www.actors-express.com) has provided Atlanta audiences with an enriching alternative to the usual chestnut offerings, with just enough familiarity to keep a high profile. They currently perform in the historic restored space of the King Plow Art Center just west of Downtown proper.

Atlanta's most politically vibrant theater, **7 Stages** (1105 Euclid Ave. NE, 404/523-7647, www.7stages.org) operates in its own space in the heart of Little Five Points, and appropriate to its bohemian location, provides a steady season of compelling, often controversial performances.

The professional **Theatrical Outfit** (84 Luckie St., 678/528-1500, www.theatricaloutfit.org), Atlanta's third-oldest theater group, now operates out of the first LEED-certified theater building in the United States, the new Balzer Theatre at Herren's in Midtown. It's

actually on the site of the old Herren's, the first restaurant in Atlanta to voluntarily desegregate. Theatrical Outfit focuses heavily on developing Atlanta-area writers, directors, and actors.

The **Center for Puppetry Arts** (1404 Spring St. NW, 404/873-3089, www.puppet.org) is the largest U.S. group dedicated to the art form. It not only hosts a regular season of performances at its space in Midtown, but there is a puppetry museum on-site, which includes a Jim Henson Wing, memorializing the Muppets founder (and ribbon-cutter of the center itself, back in 1978).

The improv gurus at **Dad's Garage** (280 Elizabeth St. NE, 404/523-3141, www.dadsgarage.com) near Inman Park specialize in staging bawdy original scripts and also feature a heavy weekly schedule of improv, some of it themed and quite long-running. The audience gets to drink beer and wine throughout the shows; this is not for kids.

In both look and feel, the **New American Shakespeare Tavern** (499 Peachtree St. NE, 404/874-5299, www.shakespearetavern.com) is intended to closely replicate the Elizabethan play-going experience, right down to the Globe Theatre-inspired facade of the building itself in the SoNo district on Peachtree Street. This beloved project of the Atlanta Shakespeare Company seeks to break down the barriers that sometimes make the enjoyment of the Bard's work a rather stuffy experience.

The company **Georgia Shakespeare** (4484 Peachtree Rd. NE, 404/504-1473, www.gashakespeare.org) puts on a full season of the Bard within the confines of host institution Oglethorpe University. While the shows are within a theater venue, many people opt for a pre-show picnic on the scenic grounds just outside.

CINEMA

In addition to a plethora of the usual generic multiplexes, Atlanta offers several unique moviegoing experiences. The oldest operating movie theater in Atlanta is the **Plaza Theatre** (1049 Ponce De Leon Ave., 404/873-1939, www.plazaatlanta.com) in Midtown. It delivers a steady diet of kitschy classics and pulp

WHAT HAPPENED TO BUCKHEAD?

Back in the 1980s and 1990s, Buckhead was a nationally renowned party central, specifically in the several-block entertainment area known as Buckhead Village. It was jammed with bars and live music venues that stayed hopping every night until 4am and attracted everybody from college students to yuppies to visiting CEOs. Here's how it happened, and how it all went away:

A gradual downturn through the 1970s convinced city officials to lift minimum parking requirements for nightclubs in order to encourage development. That it did, and soon the village was chockablock with popular watering holes and hordes of partiers pub-crawling between them, an atmosphere that was likened to "Mardi Gras every night." The 1980s were the glory days, with the Roxy Theatre (now the restored Buckhead Theatre) hosting some of the hottest bands on a weekly basis. By the mid-1990s, however, the village had over 100 liquor licenses, gangsta rap was more popular than rock and roll, and the crowds and cruising became more unruly.

Everything came to a head one Sunday in January 2000 when the Super Bowl was being played in Atlanta. Two people were shot and killed at a club called Cobalt in a high-profile case involving National Football League player Ray Lewis, who was implicated in the killings. Though Lewis was later acquitted, the PR damage was done. Another multiple shooting a couple of years later involving the rapper P. Diddy's entourage sealed Buckhead Village's fate. Residents persuaded the city to make last call at 2:30am and to tighten up on liquor licenses.

Partying gradually followed the path of least resistance to other areas of town. Developer Ben Carter began buying up the village's nine acres to make way for his massive and ambitious Buckhead Atlanta multiuse planned development. In 2007, acknowledging the imminent demise of the village's old character, a Bye Bye Buckhead party was held that attracted thousands. Soon nearly all the clubs were bulldozed, just in time for the 2008 economic collapse. The last of the old bars to close was Fado's Irish Pub.

In 2011 the OliverMcMillan company took over the stalled development. As of this writing, their cranes work slowly over the desolate urban stretch.

ATLANTA

fiction-style movies, with frequent midnight screenings of *The Rocky Horror Picture Show*.

For a flavor of high-quality Los Angeles-style cinema, head to Landmark Theatres' **Midtown Art Cinema** (931 Monroe Dr., 404/879-0160, www.landmarktheatres.com), generally considered the best new-release theater in the city and with the best atmosphere.

There are two IMAX theaters in Atlanta: the Fernbank Museum of Natural History's **Rankin M. Smith IMAX Theater** (767 Clifton Rd., 404/929-6400, www.fernbankmuseum.org), which shows science and nature-related films; and **Regal Atlantic Station Stadium 16 & IMAX** (261 19th St., 404/347-9894, www.imax.com), which offers various IMAX-formatted films in addition to a wide variety of non-IMAX new releases.

FESTIVALS
January

Understandably, a huge focus in his hometown is the **Martin Luther King Jr. Birthday Celebration** (404/526-8900, www.thekingcenter.org). The civil rights leader's birthday is a national holiday marked with a variety of events, most centering in or around the MLK Jr. National Historic Site (www.nps.gov) in Downtown. The keynote event is the annual March (www.mlkmarchaaar.org) down Auburn Avenue from Peachtree Street to Jackson Street. Ebenezer Baptist Church typically hosts an annual memorial service, and the MLK Jr. Birth Home often holds an open house. While the Atlanta Symphony Orchestra has generally played a memorial concert at King's alma mater, Morehouse College, in recent years they've begun playing the concert at Atlanta Symphony Hall on Peachtree Street.

March

Since 1976 the **Atlanta Film Festival** (678/929-8103, www.atlantafilmfestival.com) has brought Academy Award-qualifying indie and first-run films to town. Its main venue these days is the Landmark Midtown Art Cinema (931 Monroe Dr. NE, 404/879-0408, www.landmarktheatres.com).

April

For 75 years Atlantans have gathered in Piedmont Park for the annual **Dogwood Festival** (Piedmont Park, 404/817-6642, www.dogwood.org). While the focus is obviously on the blooming dogwoods, the festival itself is largely an open-air arts-and-crafts market featuring vendors from all over the Southeast, plus, of course, lots of food and music.

It's not often that a neighborhood festival is recommended for out-of-town visitors, but that's the case with the always fun and festive **Inman Park Festival** (www.inmanparkfestival.org), which happens the last weekend in April. Set in Atlanta's first planned neighborhood and now one of its most vibrant and up-and-coming, the festival features music, an eccentric and fun Saturday parade, and a popular tour of homes on Friday. Of course, the area's many awesome new restaurants are open, often with extended hours. It's a festival of a neighborhood artfully reclaimed from blight, and the overall sense of optimism pervades.

May

The city's premier foodie event is the **Atlanta Food & Wine Festival** (404/474-7330, www.atlfoodandwinefestival.com). Perhaps strangely, given Atlanta's long association with high-profile chefs, it's a comparatively young event, having started in 2006. Eateries and eaters, both highfalutin and lowbrow, come together for this popular Midtown event. The typical host venue is the Loews Atlanta Hotel (11th St. and Peachtree St.), with booths including the popular Tasting Tents radiating out a couple of blocks. Extensive evening events happen at various establishments around town, and there are frequent classes, seminars, and demonstrations as well. Tiered ticketing provides various levels of access, from the basic one-event ticket at $65 to an all-inclusive weekend pass for $500.

The **Atlanta Jazz Festival** (404/546-6820, www.atlantafestivals.com) is one of the largest free jazz fests in the country. Location and timing of the festival have bounced around over the years, but the current incarnation in Piedmont Park over the Memorial Day Weekend seems to be a real crowd-pleaser.

June

If you're in Atlanta in June, it seems a shame to miss the **Virginia-Highland Summer Fest** (http://vahi.org), which offers the chance to enjoy the full measure of fun in one of the city's most popular and vibrant neighborhoods.

July

Stone Mountain Fourth of July (1000 Robert E. Lee Blvd., Stone Mountain, 770/498-5690, www.stonemountainpark.com, parking $10) celebrations are always hugely well attended and feature a variety of events, culminating, of course, in a big fireworks display launched from areas at the top and bottom of Stone Mountain itself. Immediately before the fireworks, which are actually done on two consecutive nights, is a special laser show. I strongly advise getting here early as parking places and good spots on the lawn from which to observe the fireworks fill up fast.

A large section of Midtown shuts down for the annual **Peachtree Road Race** (404/231-9064, www.peachtreeroadrace.org), happening each Fourth of July, rain or shine. Even MARTA adjusts its schedule, starting trains at 5am that day to accommodate the lack of automobile traffic and the rush of runners and observers. The six-mile course starts in Buckhead and winds down Peachtree to take 10th Street to the finish in Piedmont Park, where an assortment of food, drink, and fun awaits. The foot race starts at 7:30am, with a wheelchair race beginning at 6:45am.

The **Chattahoochee River Summer Splash** (678/538-1200, www.nps.gov) in late July offers a festive opportunity for a six-mile float down the Chattahoochee River National Recreation Area.

The **National Black Arts Festival** (404/730-7315, http://nbaf.org) focuses on the African American cultural experience, including music, theater, literature, and film. The main weekend event centers on activities at Centennial Olympic Park, but satellite events happen at venues all around, including a gallery crawl and multiple jazz concerts.

September

Definitely not to be confused with Underground Atlanta, the **Atlanta Underground Film Festival** (1200 Foster St., www.auff.org) hosts edgy short films curated from national submissions. The venue, the Goat Farm Arts Center, is a restored warehouse and multiuse performing arts hub for Atlanta's more cutting-edge arts community.

Easily Atlanta's most highly regarded single music event, **Music Midtown** (www.music-midtown.com) in Piedmont Park still offers a stunning variety of top-name artists despite the economic downturn having taken a toll on its attendance in recent years. What used to be a three-day event is now down to two, but the 2012 edition featured Foo Fighters, Pearl Jam, the Avett Brothers, and local hero Ludacris. Not too shabby.

October

The South's largest such event and one of the oldest Pride festivals in the United States, the over-40-year-old **Atlanta Pride** (404/382-7588, www.atlantapride.org) attracts huge crowds to Piedmont Park and satellite venues over the course of an October weekend, timed to mark National Coming Out Day. Entertainment is top notch, with past performers including Nicki Minaj and the Indigo Girls. And, of course, the main event is the Pride Parade down Peachtree Street to Piedmont Park on Saturday and its spinoff parades, the Dyke March and the Trans March.

Technically separate from Atlanta Pride but happening concurrently, **Out on Film** (404/296-3807, www.outonfilm.org) has been screening gay- and lesbian-oriented fare for a quarter century. Currently based at the Landmark Midtown Art Cinema (931 Monroe Dr. NE, 404/879-0408, www.landmarktheatres.com), the festival also offers extensive Q&As with filmmakers and a host of special events.

The **Little Five Points Halloween** (404/230-2884, www.l5phalloween.com) celebration is everything you'd expect from this hipster-bohemian area. Let's just say it's probably not for small children.

Atlanta has a large and influential Greek-American community, and the annual **Atlanta Greek Festival** (404/633-5870, www.atlantagreekfestival.org) packs in the crowds for a taste of souvlaki, baklava, and other goodies. There is, of course, music and dancing as well. It happens at the grounds of the Greek Orthodox Cathedral of the Annunciation (2500 Clairmont Rd. NE) in North Druid Hills.

ATLANTA

Shopping

Atlanta is the Southeastern mecca of shopping. Every possible chain and boutique brand is represented, along with a vibrant independent retail community. Mall shoppers won't be disappointed either; Atlanta has some of the nation's oldest, all substantially renovated since their early days.

Atlanta's key shopping districts are the Buckhead-Perimeter area north of Downtown; Midtown (including Virginia-Highland, Little Five Points, and Atlantic Station); and Downtown.

ANTIQUES

Easily Atlanta's most beloved antiques-vintage store, **Paris on Ponce** (716 Ponce de Leon Ave., 404/249-9965, www.parisonponce.com, Mon.-Sat. 11am-6pm, Sun. noon-6pm), in Virginia-Highland, is, as the name implies, redolent of old Europe and full of unique furniture and assorted decorative items, all with a certain whimsical and quirky allure that treads the line between classic and kitsch.

The **Miami Circle Design District** (www.miamicircleshops.com) in Buckhead is commonly considered the headquarters of the hard-core Atlanta antiquing community, and indeed of the entire Southeast. Located in a large cul-de-sac, it comprises about 80 antiques shops, home goods stores, and art galleries; the enormity of its offerings is obviously beyond our scope here, but a few highlights are the ornate home goods of **Burroughs Wellington** (631 Miami Circle, 404/264-1616, www.burroughswellington. com, Mon.-Sat. 10am-5pm); the fabrics and furniture of **Curran Designers** (737 Miami Circle, 404/237-4246, www.curran-aat. com, Mon.-Sat. 10am-5:30pm); the classic Euro stylings at **Foxglove Antiques** (699 Miami Circle, 404/233-0222, www.foxglove-antiques.com, Mon.-Sat. 10am-5pm); and the unique Chinese offerings at **Mandarin Antiques** (700 Miami Circle, 404/467-1727,

www.mandarinantiquesinc.com, Mon.-Fri. 10am-5:30pm, Sat. 10am-5pm).

Another antiques center in Buckhead is the **West Village** (www.westvillagega.com), a loose collection of quaint and quirky antiques and home goods merchants within the triangle formed by East Andrews Drive, Roswell Road, and West Paces Ferry Road.

Up near the Perimeter, in the town of Chamblee, is the perennially popular **Chamblee Antique Row** (3519 Broad St., 770/458-6316, www.antiquerow.com), a retail district comprising nearly two dozen clothing and antiques stores, plus a few restaurants. Charming and pedestrian-friendly, it's a quick three blocks from the Chamblee MARTA station.

ART GALLERIES

While you're taking in the more traditional exhibits at the High Museum, you might want to extend your Midtown art crawl to **Atlanta Contemporary Art Center** (535 Means St., 404/688-1970, www.thecontemporary.org, Tues.-Sat. 11am-5pm, Sun. noon-5pm), a nonprofit cooperative established in 1973 and in its current space since 1989, dedicated to the work of new Atlanta artists.

A massive converted warehouse hosting about 300 individual studios and performing arts spaces, **Goat Farm Arts Center** (1200 Foster St.), on the west edge of Midtown, is one of Atlanta's most unique cultural spaces. It has two indoor performance spaces and three outdoor stages, all hosting experimental or indie-style work. The Goat Farm is performance- and exhibition-based, and doesn't really have regular hours. You can visit anytime, and the on-site coffee shop is open daily 10:30am-7pm.

An important part of the burgeoning art scene in the Atlantic Station area, **Sandler Hudson Gallery** (1009 Marietta St., 404/817-3300, www.sandlerhudson. com, Tues.-Fri. 10am-5pm, Sat. noon-5pm)

ATLANTA

focuses on contemporary Southern artists. In addition to its display space there's a sculpture area on the roof.

A key arts anchor in the up-and-coming Castleberry Hill area, **Besharat Gallery** (175 Peters St., 404/524-4781, www.besharatgallery.com, Fri.-Sat. 11am-6pm) and its companion space **Besharat Contemporary** (163 Peters St., 404/577-3660, www.besharatcontemporary.com, Tues.-Sat. 10am-5pm) together are one of the most balanced visual arts experiences in the city, blending a respect for craft and tradition with a real commitment to showcasing more modern sensibilities. Nearby is **Zucot Gallery** (100 Centennial Olympic Park Dr., 404/380-1040, www.zucotgallery.com, Tues.-Fri. 3pm-9pm, Sat. noon-10pm), which keeps things fresh in its compellingly minimalist space by completely changing out the entire exhibit every two months or so.

Since 1997, **Young Blood Gallery and Boutique** (636 N. Highland Ave., 404/254-4127, www.youngbloodgallery.com, Tues.-Sat. noon-8pm, Sun. noon-6pm) has been a key part of the renaissance of the Virginia-Highland area as well as a leading exponent of the Atlanta underground arts and music scene. Their offerings tend toward the bold, modern, and vibrant, with a strong nod toward sequential art.

BOOKS

Atlanta has several unique and independent bookstores, though sadly the most notable of them, the gay- and lesbian-oriented Outwrite Books, closed in 2012.

It's not affiliated with Georgia Tech, but it is near campus, and those of a math and science bent will enjoy the quirky, over half-century-old **Engineer's Bookstore** (748 Marietta St., 404/221-1669, www.engrbookstore.com, Mon-Fri. 9am-5:30pm, Sat. 10am-2pm), which is exactly what the name indicates: a haven for technically oriented tomes.

Since 1989, Inman Park has been home to **A Cappella Books** (208 Haralson Ave., 404/681-5128, www.acappellabooks.com, Mon.-Sat. 11am-7pm, Sun. noon-6pm), which deals in new, used, and rare volumes and features a remarkably well-informed, engaged staff.

Bound to Be Read Books (481 Flat Shoals Ave., 404/522-0877, www.boundtobereadbooks.com, Tues.-Thurs. 11am-9pm, Fri.-Sat. 11am-10pm, Sun. 1pm-6pm), an East Atlanta staple, has a very wide assortment, from fiction to technical books to gay and lesbian studies and literature.

The Green Room Actors Lounge (25 Bennett St., 404/351-4736, www.thegreenroomatl.com, Wed. noon-9pm, Thurs. noon-6pm, Fri. noon-11pm, Sat. 1pm-midnight) combines racks of books on acting, directing, and other aspects of show business with a stocked bar in a tony atmosphere. This is a favorite hangout of Atlanta's sizable theater community.

CLOTHES AND FASHION

The funky **Little Five Points** (L5P) neighborhood is a major thrift-vintage-counterculture shopping destination. The closest thing to an anchor store is **Junkman's Daughter** (464 Moreland Ave., 404/577-3188, www.thejunkmansdaughter.com, Mon.-Fri. 11am-7pm, Sat. 11am-8pm, Sun. noon-7pm), a combination vintage-novelty-tchotchke store and quasi-tourist trap. My favorite vintage shop in L5P is **Stefan's Vintage** (1160 Euclid Ave., 404/688-4929, www.stefansvintageclothing.com, Mon.-Sat. 11am-7pm, Sun. noon-6pm), the oldest store of its kind in Atlanta and where you can score some remarkable wearable finds.

In the **Peachtree Battle** (2341 Peachtree Rd., www.branchprop.com) shopping center in Buckhead, a sort of deluxe strip mall setting, you'll find fun locally-owned stores such as the **Frolic Boutique** (2385 Peachtree Rd., 404/846-8002, www.frolicboutique.com, Mon.-Sat. 11am-6pm) and **Mint Julep** (2353 Peachtree Rd., 404/814-9155, www.mintjulepga.com, Mon.-Sat. 10am-6pm, Sun. 1pm-5pm), Atlanta's Lilly Pulitzer outlet.

The vibrant and friendly Virginia-Highland neighborhood offers a charming array of largely independent locally owned stores, often with a twist, such as the vintage store **Mooncake** (1019

Virginia Ave., 404/892-8043, Mon.-Sat. 11am-7pm), which hosts frequent trunk shows, and the original location of **Bill Hallman** (792 N. Highland Ave., 404/876-6055, www.billhallman.com, Mon.-Sat. 11am-8pm, Sun. noon-7pm), which features a sleek take on both men's and women's up-to-the-moment fashions.

GROCERIES AND MARKETS

In addition to an endless variety of typical chain grocery stores, Atlanta has three locations of **Whole Foods** (www.wholefoodsmarket.com): in Buckhead (77 W. Paces Ferry Rd., 404/324-4100, Mon.-Sat. 7:30am-10pm, Sun. 9am-9pm); in Midtown (650 Ponce de Leon Ave., 404/853-1681, daily 8am-10pm); and in the suburb of Sandy Springs (5930 Roswell Rd., 404/236-0810, Mon.-Sat. 7am-10pm, Sun. 8:30am-9pm).

The best overall health foods market in Atlanta is in Little Five Points, **Sevananda Natural Foods Market** (467 Moreland Ave., 404/681-2831, www.sevanandacoop.com, daily 8am-10pm). This member-owned organic foods cooperative has been around since the dawn of the health food movement in the early 1970s and offers not only tons of fresh produce and a deli, but every vitamin and health supplement you might want.

Specialty retailer **Trader Joe's** (www.traderjoes.com) has several Atlanta locations, chief among them the Midtown location (931 Monroe Dr., 404/815-9210, daily 8am-10pm) and the Buckhead location (3183 Peachtree Rd., 404/842-0907, daily 8am-9pm).

The metro Atlanta area is blessed with a wide variety of farmers markets. Each Saturday from April through mid-December in Midtown you'll find the **Peachtree Road Farmers Market** (2744 Peachtree Rd., www.peachtreeroadfarmersmarket.com, Apr.-mid-Dec. Sat. 9am-noon), on the grounds of the Cathedral of St. Philip. It is one of the largest in the metro area. The most diverse farmers market is up in Doraville at the **Buford Highway Farmers Market** (5600 Buford Hwy., 770/455-0770, www.aofwc.com, daily 8am-10pm), which takes full advantage of the many cultural groups present in the area to provide a stunning array of produce and goods you're unlikely to find elsewhere. The **Grant Park Farmers Market** (600 Cherokee Ave., www.grantparkmarket.org, Apr.-Dec. Sun. 9:30am-1:30pm) is open April through December.

Downtown near the Martin Luther King Jr. Historic Site you'll find the indoor **Sweet Auburn Curb Market** (Edgewood Ave. and Jessie Hill Pkwy., 404/659-1665, www.sweetauburncurbmarket.com, Mon.-Sat. 8am-6pm), whose roots go back to the 1920s when it was called the Municipal Market and was a center of the local black community.

HOME GOODS

Chief among Atlanta's home goods offerings is one of the few **IKEA** (441 16th St., 404/745-4532, www.ikea.com, daily 10am-9pm) locations in the Deep South. You'll find it and its signature Swedish meatballs on the west side of town.

Virginia-Highland is definitely the main neighborhood for fun home goods shopping. Don't miss the quirky attraction of **Richards Variety** (931 Monroe Dr., 404/879-9877, www.richardsvarietystore.com, Mon.-Sat. 10am-8pm, Sun. noon-6pm), a half-century-old staple featuring unusual novelties, toys, costumes, and other assorted party supplies.

Into recycling and sustainable living? Hit the **Re-Inspiration Store** (591 N. Highland Ave., 404/352-1971, www.reinspirationstore.com, Mon.-Thurs. 11am-6pm, Fri.-Sat. 10am-6pm, Sun. noon-5pm), right across from the iconic Manuel's Tavern. You'll find funky items and gifts made from repurposed things like spark plugs, pop tops, and shell casings.

Also in Virginia-Highland you'll find the charming and unique **Indie-pendent** (1052 St. Charles Ave., 404/313-0004, www.theindiependent.com, Thurs.-Sat. 11am-5pm, Sun. 1pm-5pm), a hip and happening collection of DIY-style regionally handcrafted kitchen, home, and garden goods along with jewelry and art.

MALLS

Atlanta's premier mall and one of the nation's oldest, having opened in 1959, is **Lenox Square** (3393 Peachtree Rd. NE, 404/233-6767, www. simon.com, Mon.-Sat. 10am-9pm, Sun. noon-6pm) in Buckhead, with about 250 stores on four levels. Of course, the current incarnation bears no resemblance whatsoever to the Eisenhower administration version. Anchor stores are Macy's, Bloomingdale's, and Neiman Marcus, and there's a massive Forever 21 as well as an Apple retail location. This being Buckhead, there are also many high-dollar boutique outlets of note: Façonnable, Nicole Miller, Bulgari, Fendi, Cartier, Burberry, and Prada, to name but a few. There's a convenient MARTA stop.

Close to Lenox Square and owned by the same investment group is **Phipps Plaza** (3500 Peachtree Rd. NE, 404/262-0992, www. simon.com, Mon.-Sat. 10am-9pm, Sun. noon-5:30pm), an even more upscale Buckhead mall. Its anchors are Saks Fifth Avenue, Nordstrom, and Belk, with an impressive list of boutiques that include Armani, Valentino, Jimmy Choo, Versace, and Tiffany.

The simply and aptly named **Perimeter Mall** (4400 Ashford Dunwoody Rd., 770/394-4270, www.perimetermall.com, Mon.-Sat. 10am-9pm, Sun. noon-7pm) was the first such project along the I-285 corridor north of Atlanta proper in the satellite city of Dunwoody (it's served by the Dunwoody MARTA station). Current anchors are Von Maur, Dillard's, Macy's, and Nordstrom, and there's an Apple retail store.

Way outside the Perimeter in Buford, Georgia, about 30 miles from Downtown Atlanta, is the massive **Mall of Georgia** (3333 Buford Dr., Buford, 678/482-8788, www. mallofgeorgia.com, Mon.-Sat. 10am-9pm, Sun. noon-6pm). It has over 200 stores on three levels, including anchors Belk, Dillard's, JCPenney, Macy's, Nordstrom, Dick's Sporting Goods, and Havertys, plus an Apple retail store.

A totally reclaimed light industrial area turned mixed-use, **Atlantic Station** (1380 Atlantic Dr., 404/733-1221, www. atlanticstation.com, Mon.-Sat. 10am-9pm, Sun. noon-7pm) offers an outdoor pedestrian-style mall featuring H&M, Z Gallerie, and more familiar chain stores such as Banana Republic, American Eagle, and Nine West. Atlantic Station occasionally hosts traveling exhibits, such as a recent stop by a show of artifacts from the *Titanic*.

About halfway between Atlanta and Macon off I-75 you'll find the sprawling **Tanger Outlet Center** (1000 Tanger Dr., Locust Grove, 770/957-5310, www.tangeroutlet.com, Mon.-Sat. 9am-9pm, Sun. 11am-7pm), which has bargain outlets ranging from J.Crew to Lucky Brand to Skechers.

As the name implies, **Underground Atlanta** (50 Upper Alabama St., 404/523-2311, www. underground-atlanta.com, Mon.-Thurs. 10am-8pm, Fri.-Sat. 10am-9pm, Sun. noon-6pm) is an underground mall, legacy of an urban layer built up in the 1920s over previously existing rail lines. It has gone through several incarnations over the last half century, as the city tries to keep it afloat as a viable entertainment and shopping destination (a recent effort involved extending bar closing times to 4am). Sketchy and long removed from its heyday in the 1980s, Underground Atlanta today is an idea that sounds cooler than it really is; even the shops are mostly downscale here in an area of town that, frankly, is not Atlanta's safest or most welcoming. There will be many signs and ads urging you to visit, but I advise against it.

MUSIC AND RECORDS

In Little Five Points you'll find a couple of neat indie record stores. **Criminal Records** (1154 Euclid Ave., 404/215-9511, www.criminalatl. com, Mon.-Sat. 11am-9pm, Sun. noon-7pm) not only has an outstanding selection of happening music, they often host record release parties with live entertainment by the hottest regional bands.

Wax 'n' Facts (432 Moreland Ave., 404/525-2275, www.waxnfacts.com, Mon.-Sat. 11am-8pm, Sun. noon-6pm), in business since 1976, has an awesome vinyl collection and also hosts performances.

ATLANTA

OUTDOOR OUTFITTERS

Huge outdoor retailer **REI** (www.rei.com) has two locations in the metro area: one near Druid Hills (1800 Northeast Expressway, 404/633-6508, Mon.-Sat. 10am-9pm, Sun. 11am-6pm) and the other on the Perimeter (1165 Perimeter Center, 770/901-9200, Mon.-Sat. 10am-9pm, Sun. 11am-6pm).

Regional chain **Half Moon Outfitters** (1034 Highland Ave., 404/249-7921, www.halfmoonoutfitters.com, Mon-Fri. 10am-7pm, Sat. 10am-8pm, Sun. 11am-6pm) has a friendly location in Virginia-Highland, selling clothing in addition to gear. In Buckhead, go to **High Country Outfitters** (3906 Roswell Rd., 404/814-0999, www.highcountryoutfitters.com, Mon.-Fri. 10am-8pm, Sat. 10am-6pm, Sun. noon-6pm), serving Atlanta since 1975. For those wanting trendy adventurous outerwear, head to the retail store of **North Face** (35A W. Paces Ferry Rd., 404/467-0119, www.thenorthface.com, Mon.-Sat. 10am-8pm, Sun. 11am-6pm) in Buckhead.

Sports and Recreation

Atlanta's generally moderate weather and fairly mild winters mean residents spend a lot of time outdoors, a nice break from the city's legendary congestion. Generally considered an awful spectator sports town, Atlanta is better oriented to those of the more active persuasion, and it has plenty of parks and facilities to accommodate them.

PARKS

For a city known for its well-used superhighways, Atlanta has a surprisingly large amount of green space, and it is heavily used and admired by residents.

First landscaped in 1904, **Piedmont Park** (1320 Monroe Dr., 404/875-7275, www.piedmontpark.org, daily 6am-11pm) in Midtown is the most popular public park, not to mention the most conveniently located. Two major expansions, one in 2008 and one in 2011, brought its area to 190 acres and added a bathhouse-pool area. In addition to miles of jogging and biking paths, there's a boccie court and an off-leash dog park. A legacy of Atlanta's Victorian era expansion, Piedmont Park includes some areas of the old Civil War battlefield. It has hosted much sports history as well, being the home of the Atlanta Crackers pro baseball team and, during the leather helmet era, the home of the great University of Georgia and Georgia Tech football rivalry.

Chastain Park (Lake Forest Dr. and Powers Ferry Rd., www.chastainpark.org, daily dawn-dusk) in Buckhead is actually Atlanta's largest park at nearly 300 acres. It includes a popular amphitheater, a pool, a golf course, a new tennis center, and lots of jogging and biking opportunities.

Atlanta's oldest park is **Grant Park** (bounded by Boulevard SE, Atlanta Ave., Cherokee Ave., Sydney St., Park Ave., and Berne St.), where you'll find Zoo Atlanta and the Cyclorama. It fell into neglect until the 1990s and is sort of playing catch-up with the other city parks. It is currently under the stewardship of the Grant Park Conservancy (404/521-0938, www.gp-conservancy.org), which offers walking tours exploring the rich Victorian history of the park and surrounding neighborhood of the same name.

Downtown has the 200-acre, six-mile-long **Freedom Park** (North Ave. and Moreland Ave., www.freedompark.org, daily dawn-dusk) linear green space between the Martin Luther King Jr. National Historic Site and the Jimmy Carter Library. It is best known in local lore as the former civic battleground of the "Freeway Revolt," a successful grassroots effort in the 1970s to stop the massive proposed Stone Mountain Freeway from paving over the entire area. (You may have noticed by now that most Atlanta politics revolve around roads of some type.)

An ambitious, evolving, ongoing project, the **Atlanta BeltLine** (http://beltline.org) seeks to connect virtually nearly 50 neighborhoods throughout the entire metro area to a nearly 40-mile network of multiuse trails loosely based on old rail lines, with at least five MARTA public transit stops along the way. The first phase of the Beltline to open is the Eastside Trail, which connects Piedmont Park, Inman Park, and the Old Fourth Ward; it is probably the most germane to visitors.

RUNNING, WALKING, AND BIKING

Piedmont Park (1320 Monroe Dr., 404/875-7275, www.piedmontpark.org, daily 6am-11pm) has three basic footpaths (no bicycles allowed): the Active Oval, the Lake Loop, and the Park Loop; they interlock for a customized experience. Cycling is only allowed on the main roadway through the park and the meadow paths at 10th Street. **Chastain Park** (www.chastainpark.org) has two freshly renovated 5K loops and a 3K loop. Park at Powers Ferry Road near the amphitheater.

Atlanta has a robust running community, with a roster of marathons, triathlons, 5Ks and 10Ks. Though it's a fairly short race, the city's marquee runner's event is the **Peachtree Road Race** (404/231-9064, www.peachtreeroadrace.org), a very popular six-mile course down the city's main street each Fourth of July morning, ending in Piedmont Park. Other key events on the running calendar include the **ATL 20K Relay and 10K** on Labor Day weekend, the **Allstate Half-Marathon** in October, and the **Atlanta-Chattanooga-Atlanta Relay** in October. Go to http://rungeorgia.com for more info.

The moderately hilly terrain of the Georgia Piedmont makes it good bicycling territory. There's a bike path from Piedmont Avenue downtown all the way to Stone Mountain. Within **Stone Mountain Park** (1000 Robert E. Lee Blvd., 770/498-5690, www.stonemountainpark.com, daily 10am-10pm, $10 admission) are a lot of opportunities as well. The **Atlanta BeltLine** (http://beltline.org) offers multiuse trails all around metro Atlanta, with a completed course connecting Piedmont Park, Inman Park, and the Old Fourth Ward. See www.atlantabike.org for more info.

There's an actual velodrome in the Atlanta area, **Dick Lane Velodrome** (1889 Lexington Ave., 404/769-0012, www.dicklanevelodrome.com) in East Point, one of only a few dozen such facilities in the United States. Races are every Saturday night.

RAFTING AND BOATING

White-water rafting in the ATL? Most definitely. **"Shootin' the Hootch,"** or rafting down the Chattahoochee, has been a rite of passage for environmentalists and partying college students alike for decades. A 50-mile stretch of the river is managed by the National Park Service as the **Chattahoochee River National Recreation Area** (www.nps.gov). Several private companies are authorized to offer tube and raft rental; the two recommended options are **Chattahoochee Outfitters** (203 Azalea Dr., 770/650-1008, Apr.-Nov. daily, Dec.-Mar. Fri.-Sun.), which leaves from the northern suburb of Roswell, and **High Country Outfitters** (3906B Roswell Rd., 404/814-0999, www.highcountryoutfitters.com, Mon.-Fri. 10am-8pm, Sat. 10am-6pm, Sun. noon-6pm), which puts in at two locations (Johnson Ferry and Powers Island). Keep in mind that generally speaking, children under age 5 aren't allowed to "shoot the Hootch" at all for safety reasons. Of course you can opt to put your own vessel into the Hootch.

SWIMMING

Piedmont Park sports a new **Aquatic Center** (404/875-7275, www.piedmontpark.org, summer Mon.-Fri. 10am-5pm, Sat.-Sun. noon-5pm, $4 adults, $2 children). The **Grant Park Pool** (625 Park Ave. SE, 404/622-3041, $4 adults, $2 children) has weekend hours during the summer. The **Candler Park Pool** (1500 McLendon Ave. NE, 404/373-4349, $4 adults, $2 children) is operated by the City of Atlanta.

ATLANTA

ATLANTA

GOLF

Two public courses of note are in Buckhead. The 18-hole public **Bobby Jones Golf Course** (384 Woodward Way, 404/355-1009, www.bobbyjonesgc.com, $30-45) has been around since 1932 and sits atop part of the old Battle of Peachtree Creek site. The suitably named Peachtree Battle Creek winds amid five holes. **North Fulton Municipal Golf Course** (216 W. Wieuca Rd. NW, 404/255-0723, www.americangolf.com, $40) is in Chastain Park and gets very crowded.

TENNIS

The **Sharon J. Lester Tennis Center** (400 Park Dr., 404/853-3461, www.utatennis.com, Mon.-Thurs. 9am-10pm, Fri. 9am-9pm, Sat.-Sun. 9am-6pm) at Piedmont Park offers 12 lighted hard courts. The **Chastain Park Tennis Center** (110 W. Wieuca Rd. NW, 404/255-3210, www.utatennis.com, Mon.-Thurs. 9am-9pm, Fri. 9am-1pm and 3pm-7pm, Sat. 9am-7pm, Sun. 11am-7pm) is a brand-new EarthCraft building with nine lighted hard courts.

SPECTATOR SPORTS

The Major League Baseball **Atlanta Braves** (Turner Field, 755 Hank Aaron Dr. SE, www.atlanta.braves.mlb.com) play at Turner Field, a.k.a. "The Ted," and are quite popular by Atlanta standards. But you can usually score tickets ($30-80) since the games rarely sell out, with average attendance hovering around 30,000. A day at The Ted is an iconic Atlanta experience, both because of the ballpark's own charms (including above-average food) as well as the fact that Braves fans tend to be very well behaved. Unlike many metropolitan ballparks, there are plenty of pay-parking areas within a quick walk for about $10 per car. The closest MARTA stop is Five Points Station, which isn't close to the stadium at all, but every game day special Braves shuttles run from Underground Atlanta right across from Five Points directly to Turner Field and back again. The Braves shuttle is free with a MARTA transfer ticket; alternatively you can buy a Breeze card ($5.50) at Underground

Atlanta. Shuttles begin 90 minutes before game time.

Enjoy The Ted while you can: In 2017 the Braves intend to move to a not-yet-built stadium in suburban Cobb County.

The National Football League **Atlanta Falcons** (1 Georgia Dome Dr., 404/223-8444, www.atlantafalcons.com) play at the Georgia Dome, just down the road from Turner Field. There is a Georgia Dome MARTA stop, but the Vine City Station is about as close. Tickets range $60-180. The Falcons have an interactive site at http://vsv.falcons.com, which is specially designed to help with seating and parking issues.

The National Basketball Association **Atlanta Hawks** (1 Philips Dr., 404/878-3000, www.nba.com, www.philipsarena.com) play in the newish Philips Arena, next to the CNN Center Downtown. While the team is much better these days than in some eras past, the games almost never sell out, and single-game tickets are quite affordable considering the upscale experience in "The Phil" (even the restrooms are nice). There's a Philips Arena MARTA Station right here, so transportation and parking are no excuses not to go.

The **Atlanta Silverbacks** (3200 Silverbacks Way, 404/969-4900, www.atlantasilverbacks.com) play professional soccer at the second-tier level in the North American Soccer League. Their home pitch is the soccer-specific Silverbacks Park in Chamblee, just outside town, which once hosted an Adidas commercial shoot that featured David Beckham.

Atlanta has had two professional ice hockey teams in the past, the Atlanta Flames (which departed for Calgary in 1980) and the Atlanta Thrashers (which moved to Winnipeg in 2011). Currently the only pro action on the ice is from the **Gwinnett Gladiators** (Arena at Gwinnett Center, 6400 Sugarloaf Pkwy., 770/497-5100, www.gwinnettgladiators.com), who play in Duluth.

Autumn in the South means college football. Like most Georgians, Atlanta mostly roots for the Georgia Bulldogs in Athens, but in town, the hottest ticket is for **Georgia Tech** (www.

ramblinwreck.com) home football games. The Yellow Jackets play Downtown at Bobby Dodd Stadium at Historic Grant Field (North Ave. and Techwood Dr.) on the corner of campus (the Yellow Jackets' chief rivals, the Georgia Bulldogs, jokingly refer to Tech as the "North Avenue Trade School").

For years Georgia State University was primarily known as an urban commuter school, but the addition of a high-level football program in 2010 immediately made the **Georgia State Panthers** (1 Georgia Dome Dr., www.georgiastatesports.com) a high-profile enterprise. They play in the Georgia Dome.

Accommodations

As a major commercial center, convention location, and home to the world's busiest airport, Atlanta understandably offers a truly mind-boggling number of hotel rooms. As you might expect, there is a huge range in quality, from world-class to miserable. One local plus, however, is that because of the massive volume of lodging, prices are often surprisingly reasonable; but always be sure to inquire beforehand about common and typically poorly publicized surcharges, such as for parking and Internet access.

Hartsfield-Jackson International Airport is virtually a city of its own, with an extensive lodging infrastructure to match—there are at least 60 hotels in the immediate area. Prices are a bit lower than in more desirable areas of town, but the service is typically much poorer as well, not to mention the high stress level of most guests, either rushing to catch a plane or dead-tired from flying all day.

Because of Atlanta's size and the fact that there's not a huge price variation throughout the city, these accommodations are organized by area first and then by price.

DOWNTOWN
$150-300
Fresh off a $65 million renovation, one of downtown's oldest premier properties is now one of the plushest. Built in the late 1960s and virtually the harbinger of Atlanta's boom period, the ◖ **Hyatt Regency** (265 Peachtree St. NE, 404/577-1234, www.atlantaregency.hyatt.com, $190-230) offers all the crisp professionalism of that chain with a modernist minimalism.

The renovated rooms are geared to tourists as well as business travelers and conventioneers, with all the in-room amenities everyone demands these days, along with the usual crisp professionalism of the Hyatt chain. Designed by noted Atlanta architect John Portman (a nearby street is named after him), the Hyatt's atrium is something of an architectural legend in its own right: The ultrafast glass elevators were the first of their kind in Atlanta and still offer a thrill for guests of all ages. When first built, the 24-story Hyatt was considered very tall and featured a revolving restaurant at the top, which subsequently closed as much taller skyscrapers rose all around it. The Hyatt now offers two good dining options on the ground floor. The attractions of Centennial Olympic Park, such as the Georgia Aquarium and the World of Coca-Cola, are a short walk away.

It's no longer the tallest hotel in the world, as it briefly was when first built in 1976, but the 73-story **Westin Peachtree Plaza** (210 Peachtree St. NE, 404/659-1400, www.starwood.com, from $250) still offers stunning views, not the least of which can be found at its famous revolving rooftop restaurant, the Sun Dial (daily lunch and dinner, $20). Each of the nearly 1,100 guest rooms in this John Portman-designed edifice (he also designed the Hyatt Regency and the nearby Marriott Marquis) feature floor-to-ceiling windows. While taller than Portman's Hyatt, the Westin looks very similar and is often mistaken for it. The rooms aren't large, but they are well equipped and tastefully furnished.

One of the better Downtown stays and

ATLANTA

ATLANTA

© JIM MOREKIS

the Hyatt Regency, downtown

probably the best stay for any Georgia Tech-oriented visit is the **Hampton Inn Atlanta-Georgia Tech** (244 North Ave. NW, 404/881-0881, www.hamptoninn.com, $160). Situated literally on the edge of Tech's sprawling urban campus, the Hampton Inn is also quite convenient to the Centennial Olympic Park attractions like the Georgia Aquarium and the World of Coca-Cola. Be aware, however, that as with many Downtown hotels, parking is valet-only and not cheap.

If it's access to the Centennial Olympic Park area you're looking for, look no further than the **Embassy Suites Hotel** (267 Marietta St., 404/223-2300, www.embassysuites.com, $180-300), literally adjacent and within a stone's throw of the Georgia Aquarium (ask about package deals). The pool area actually overlooks the well-maintained park, which is a nice touch.

Over $300

Now run by the Marriott chain, Atlanta's first entry into the boutique hotel market was **Glenn**

Hotel (110 Marietta St., 404/521-2250, www.glennhotel.com, from $300). The main attraction of this property in the renovated Fairlie-Poplar district is the use of "personal hosts," that is, butlers, who are on call for you daily 24 hours. There's a popular rooftop bar, the SkyLounge, which is definitely worth a visit for the scintillating views as well as the signature cocktails. The in-house restaurant, Glenn's Kitchen, is a cut above most hotel offering and specializes in New Southern cuisine.

MIDTOWN
$150-300

Perhaps surprisingly, Atlanta is actually behind the curve in the boutique hotel trend. One of the newest and most charming is the **C Artmore** (1302 W. Peachtree St., 404/876-6100, www.artmorehotel.com, around $150), an independently owned delight in Midtown. This restored 1925 Spanish Mediterranean, with an art deco look inside and out, offers a little taste of Beverly Hills in this older area of Atlanta, but without the exorbitant rates. Unlike most boutique hotels, the guest rooms are quite, well, roomy. While the breakfast is called continental, it's likely one of the most extensive and well-prepared continental breakfasts you'll find. While not particularly suitable for business travelers, this is a fantastic and, for Atlanta, inexpensive choice for a romantic getaway or a fun-loving family stay.

While occasionally overlooked because of its location across the street from the Fox Theatre and right next to the equally historic (and huge) Georgian Terrace Hotel, **Hotel Indigo** (683 Peachtree St., 404/874-9200, www.hotelindigo.com, $175) offers one of Atlanta's few real boutique-hotel experiences. Like most boutique hotels, the emphasis is on quality rather than size, and the Indigo's guest rooms and baths are pretty small. Pet-friendly and personable, the Indigo is a nice break from the occasionally impersonal level of service at Atlanta's bigger chain hotels.

Atlanta doesn't have much history left, but the **Georgian Terrace Hotel** (659 Peachtree St. NE, 866/845-7551, www.thegeorgianterrace.

© JIM MOREKIS

Georgian Terrace Hotel

com, $175-350) is still here. This grand 1911 beaux arts masterpiece hosted Clark Gable, Vivien Leigh, and other *Gone with the Wind* cast members for the film's premiere, and the Georgian Terrace still retains that old Hollywood appeal. Contrary to popular opinion, the film's premiere didn't take place across the street at the Fox Theatre; nonetheless it's thrilling to have that ornate historic venue to gaze on, and of course to visit for a show. Other famous guests at the Georgian Terrace have included F. Scott Fitzgerald, Walt Disney, President Calvin Coolidge, and Arthur Murray, who literally began his dance instruction career in the hotel's ballroom. While the guest rooms have of course been renovated since then, most recently in 2009 (there's actually an entire new section built in 1991, originally as condos), keep in mind this is a historic property with the usual eccentricities, including slow elevators and guest rooms that vary widely in size and orientation. A bustling restaurant of fair-to-middling quality, Livingston's, spills out onto the roomy patio

area along Peachtree Street. And, two words: rooftop pool!

BUCKHEAD
Over $300
Atlanta's premier luxury-spa hotel, the **Mandarin Oriental** (3376 Peachtree St. NE, 404/995-7500, www.mandarinoriental. com) is an oasis of calm in busy Buckhead, but with every bit of the swank expected in that tony area. The emphasis at the Mandarin is on pampering guests to the nth degree, from the plush and spacious guest rooms to the luxurious baths to the state-of-the-art high-def plasma TVs artfully arranged throughout. There are several tiers of rooms, from the "budget" two-person King ($325) up to the incredible Mandarin Suite ($7,000). The level of relaxed attentiveness and confident professionalism of the staff is something of a local legend.

Buckhead's other premier luxury-spa lodging, the Starwood property **St. Regis Atlanta** (88 W. Paces Ferry Rd., 404/563-7900, www.stregis.com, $450-700), is particularly recommended for those for whom a swank old-school hotel pool experience is a must (it's open daily 24 hours!). The guest rooms are world-class as well, with a level of taste and furnishing that seems almost too good to be true. The extremely high level of customer service is vectored through butlers, who seemingly exist to serve your every whim at any hour of the day, providing everything from ice (no loud vending machines) to wakeup calls. As at the Mandarin, there's an ultra-exclusive penthouse suite, the Empire.

PERIMETER
Under $150
For a stay up near "the Perimeter," a.k.a. I-285 north of Buckhead, you'll do no better than ◖ **Holiday Inn Perimeter/Dunwoody** (4386 Chamblee-Dunwoody Rd., 770/457-6363, www.holidayinn.com, under $150), one of the more well-appointed and professionally staffed examples of that hotel chain, at incredibly low prices for Atlanta. They have state-of-the-art guest room renovations (including the trendy Keurig one-cup coffeemakers) and a hotel bar that's clearly a step above the usual.

$150-300
Another good stay in the clean and safe (if overly commercial) Perimeter area is the **Sheraton Atlanta Perimeter** (800 Hammond Dr., 404/564-3000, www.sheratonperimeter.com, under $200). While it's clearly designed more for the business traveler in mind, the hotel boasts an attentive staff and guest rooms that are well appointed and cleanly maintained.

BED-AND-BREAKFASTS AND HOSTELS
Under $150
For a quiet experience more typical of Southern B&Bs, try **Sugar Magnolia Bed and Breakfast** (804 Edgewood Ave., 404/222-0226, www.sugarmagnoliabb.com, under $150) in peaceful Inman Park, which still manages to be plenty close to a lot of key attractions. There are four

guest rooms, all at quite reasonable rates, in this historic property, including the extravagant Royal Suite, which features a king bed in a curtained alcove and a whirlpool tub.

Atlanta doesn't offer much in the way of hostels. In fact, as of this writing there's only one, the 85-bed Atlanta **International Hostel** (223 Ponce de Leon Ave., 404/875-9449, www.atlantahostel.com, under $30), offering stable, safe accommodations in a restored Victorian. There's free continental breakfast every day, free parking, a pool table, and an assortment of cute pets. Wi-Fi, however, is an added daily cost. The Midtown location on bustling, fun Ponce de Leon Avenue near the Fox Theatre and locally renowned Mary Mac's Tea Room is not the world's safest locale, but is primed for access to dining and nightlife as well as for public transportation (only four blocks from the North Avenue MARTA station).

$150-300
Atlanta has precious few true B&Bs, but a good one is **Virginia Highland Bed & Breakfast** (630 Orme Circle, 404/892-2735, www.virginiahighlandbb.com, $119-219), which capitalizes on the obvious charms of its namesake neighborhood with sumptuous beds and a much more private, intimate setting than you'll get at one of the many hundreds of hotels in the rest of the city. There are four guest rooms; the largest is the garden apartment, which sleeps four with two bedrooms and two baths.

The five-suite eco-friendly **Stonehurst Place** (923 Piedmont Ave., 404/881-0722, www.stonehurstplace.com, $160-400) offers a top-of-the-line B&B experience in Midtown. The guest rooms, including the art on the walls, are impeccably furnished with a good mix of old-school traditional taste and cutting-edge amenities like iPod-iPhone docking stations. It's even pet-friendly. The breakfasts are to die for, with unique but still comfort-oriented dishes such as a green chili egg puff and goat cheese phyllo bites.

Food

Atlanta isn't known as one of the nation's great food towns, but it's getting there. A remarkable resurgence of foodie culture with a typically Atlantan overlay of Southern charm is happening across town, particularly in Midtown, on the Westside, in Virginia-Highland, and in the Cabbagetown-Grant Park area.

DOWNTOWN
American
No other restaurant qualifies for the title of "Atlanta institution" more than **The Varsity** (61 North Ave. NW, 404/881-1706, www.the-varsity.com, Sun.-Thurs. 10am-11:30pm, Fri.-Sat. 10am-12:30am, $5), which since 1928 has fed generations of budget-conscious Georgia Tech students and is one of the last surviving quirky Southern fast-food diners. The cavernous space, largest drive-in restaurant in the world, they say, is daunting enough, but the counter experience is really what amps up your adrenaline. In decidedly non-Southern fashion, the grimly determined counter staff, like something out of a *Seinfeld* episode, demand to know, "What'll you have?" You'll quickly stammer something off the greasy-spoon style menu, probably a chili-cheese dog and onion rings washed down with their signature orange drink. (And don't forget Coca-Cola. The downtown Varsity is allegedly the world's largest single sales point of the iconic Georgia drink.) There are several satellite Varsities throughout Georgia now, as far afield as Athens and Dawsonville, but this original location on North Avenue astride I-75 is the one and only, in this author's opinion.

If you're as hooked on bison burgers as I am, you'll take comfort in the presence of **Ted's Montana Grill** (133 Luckie St., 404/521-9796, www.tedsmontanagrill.com, Sun.-Thurs. 11am-10pm, Fri.-Sat. 11am-11pm, $15) in Fairlie-Poplar. Atlanta icon Ted Turner opened the now-national chain in 2002 with restaurateur George McKerrow Jr. This is the original flagship location, and it still serves as a reminder of Turner's pioneering, hugely important work in bringing back the American buffalo population of the West. The payoff, of course, is delicious bison meat served up in a variety of dishes at the restaurant. If buffalo is a little too adventurous for you, there's also a good selection of classic seafood, beef, and poultry dishes. Ted's work doesn't stop with ranching, however; his place is 99 percent plastic-free. Even the straws are recyclable paper. There are now several other locations in the metro area, including a Midtown edition (1874 Peachtree St., 404/355-3897).

If you're staying in one of the large swank hotels in or near Peachtree Center close to Centennial Olympic Park and you don't particularly feel like eating in the hotel but also don't want to go too far, take a stroll to **Max Lager's** (320 Peachtree St., 404/525-4400, www.maxlagers.com, Mon.-Sat. 11:30am-11pm, Sun. 4pm-11pm, $15). At the oldest brewpub in the city, you can enjoy a pint of one of their very good handcrafted beers and a tasty dinner cooked in their signature wood-fired grill (my favorite is the bison burger, but any of the salmon dishes are also recommended).

New Southern
Surely one of the most unique dining experiences in Atlanta, ◖ **Lunacy Black Market** (231 Mitchell St. SW, 404/736-6164, www.lunacyblackmarket.com, Wed.-Sat. 6pm-10pm, $20) combines haute cuisine with the comfort of a living room, at almost unbelievably low prices. This small-plate restaurant does most everything differently, down to the menus, which are written in marker on cardboard. You're seated in one of a variety of homey areas of the lengthy dining room, at a big comfy sofa or at a cleared-off corner of the wine table. Once there, you order to your heart's content from the cardboard menu. Perhaps the al dente Asian-themed collards, the perfect

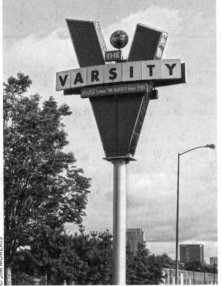

© JIM MOREKIS

The Varsity drive-in

tomato-mozzarella plate, or the mouth-watering braised beef? All those fresh, dynamic, but perfectly married flavors would be satisfying enough, but when you take a gander at the prices, generally under $4 per plate, you'll think you've died and gone to foodie heaven. To be fair, these small plates are *small*. But I've gotten away with a great dinner for two with wine for under $40. The food is so good I almost felt guilty about paying so little.

GRANT PARK
Brunch

Though it comes across as a venerable institution, **Ria's Bluebird** (421 Memorial Dr., 404/521-3737, daily 8am-3pm, $15), near Grant Park, is actually a fairly new place. Hipsters and preppies alike pack the place for their large, delicious breakfasts and brunches, served by a cadre of inked servers who are nicer than they might appear. All of the omelets are great, and they're very good about offering a range of veggie options (two words: tempeh reuben). There's almost always a line to get in.

Coffee and Sweets

Known all over town for their dark arts with a French press, making espresso, and raising latte foam-pulling to a fine art, the folks at **Octane Coffee** (437 Memorial Dr., 404/815-9886, http://octanecoffee.com, Mon. 7am-6pm, Tues.-Fri. 7am-midnight, Sat. 8am-midnight, Sun. 8am-10pm) take coffee seriously. They take painting seriously too, and the main Grant Park location (there's another on the Westside) features local artists all over the walls on steady rotation. The vibe is crisp and ultramodern rather than cozy and quirky, with hipsters and mover-shaker types alike enjoying the range of java, chai, and yes, craft brews.

Greek

If you gotta get your gyro on, go no farther than ☾ **Nick's To-Go** (240 Martin Luther King Jr. Blvd., 404/521-2220, www.nicksfood. com, Mon.-Fri. 11am-7:30pm, Sat. noon-7pm, $7), a local food icon and one of the best little Greek joints I've found stateside. It's not much to look at: a nearly windowless cinderblock building with faded blue paint in a less-than-upscale part of town, catty-corner to the popular Daddy D'z BBQ Joynt. Sometimes you'll order from Nick himself, who's well known to many local politicos who come here from the nearby state capitol for a quick lunch. But the food—authentic, perfectly spiced, and made to order with fresh ingredients—is more than worth the eyesore. This is one of the few places left where you can get an honest-to-Athena lamb gyro (other meats are available). The souvlaki is also a specialty. Even if all you want is a hearty Greek salad, you're assured of crisp lettuce and juicy tomatoes. As the name implies, the food is all technically to-go (you pick up at a window facing the parking lot), but there are a couple of picnic tables on-site.

Seafood

Yep, it's called **Six Feet Under Pub and Fish House** (437 Memorial Dr., 404/525-6664, www.sixfeetunderatlanta.com, Mon.-Thurs. 11am-1am, Fri.-Sat. 11am-2am, Sun. 11am-midnight, $15) because it's right across the street from historic Oakland Cemetery. In fact, from a perch on the third floor deck, you can count the headstones. The menu at this multi-level wood-paneled gastropub leans heavily to the seafood side, with some great raw bar stuff and fried oysters and shrimp and the like. It's not a microbrewery, but craft-artisanal beers are a big part of the experience, with frequent brew-related events and contests. There's a second location on the Westside (interestingly, the first restaurant in town to use wind power), but the cemetery location is the original.

Look for the full parking lot at the corner of Memorial Drive and Martin Luther King Jr. Drive and you've found **Daddy D'z BBQ Joynt** (264 Memorial Dr., 404/222-0206, www.daddydz.com, Sun.-Thurs. 11am-10:30pm, Fri.-Sat. 11am-midnight, Sun. noon-9:30pm, $12), generally considered one of the city's best barbecue restaurants. Atlanta isn't considered a 'cue capital—too many Northern transplants, you see—but Daddy's is certainly the real thing, especially when it comes to their signature ribs ($25 for a full slab). Portions are enormous and generally come with Texas toast. The sides, such as Brunswick stew and cornbread, are nearly as well regarded as the meats. They also offer an interesting appetizer, the "Que Wrap," consisting of pulled pork wrapped in fried dough.

MIDTOWN
Classic Southern
The closest thing Atlanta has to Paula Deen's Lady & Sons in Savannah, in both menu and media hype if not in the sheer volume of butter, is **Mary Mac's Tea Room** (224 Ponce de Leon Ave., 404/876-1800, www.marymacs.com, daily 11am-9pm, $20). On Ponce just down from the Georgian Terrace Hotel, Mary Mac's has packed in visitors and locals alike for 60 years with its range of Deep South specialties, some served "family style," like baked chicken, meatloaf, and grilled liver and onions. They have seafood as well, mostly of the tried-and-true fried variety. And yes, there's a fried green tomato appetizer.

At the other end of the price scale and with

status as the best inexpensive joint in Atlanta, **Eats** (600 Ponce de Leon Ave., 404/888-9149, www.eatsonponce.com, daily 11am-10pm, $5) lives up (or down?) to its name in gloriously humble fashion. The specialty is the excellent jerk chicken, served in heaping portions (not on Friday, though, when you get jerk tilapia). Barbecue and lemon pepper flavors are available for the spice-averse. How inexpensive? The meat and three-veggie combo plate, and we're talking very large servings here, runs a paltry $4.75. Because of the inclusive hours, you see a large slice of Atlanta life come in and out of these doors on one of Atlanta's most interesting thoroughfares.

While the name implies a trendy celeb-centered focus (please say I don't have to tell you who Gladys Knight is), the truth is that **Gladys Knight and Ron Winan's Chicken and Waffles** (529 Peachtree St., 404/874-9393, Mon.-Thurs. 11am-11pm, Fri.-Sat. 11am-4am, Sun. 11am-8pm, $10-15) represents an old Harlem tradition come South: A late-night hybrid dinner-breakfast to close out your evening of partying. So on weekends the kitchen stays open till 4am, serving up their eponymous chicken and waffles as well as other staple Southern comfort foods such as fried green tomatoes, fried catfish, chicken wings, and . . . collard green spring rolls? Yep.

New Southern
If you're looking for a cool place for drinks or a meal near Piedmont, perhaps before a concert, look no further than **Einstein's** (1077 Juniper St., 404/876-7925, www.metrocafes.com, Mon.-Thurs. 11am-11pm, Fri. 11am-midnight, Sat. 9am-midnight, Sun. 9am-11pm, $15). With plenty of indoor and outdoor seating, a large and very friendly staff, great signature drinks, excellent burgers, and a solid small-plates menu, they've pretty much got all your social needs covered. The location, a block off Peachtree Street and another block or so to the park, cannot be topped and is one of Atlanta's favorite see-and-be-seen locales, especially at Sunday brunch. This restaurant should not be confused with Einstein's Bagels.

ATLANTA

What's that you say? You want a great taqueria with Korean flair and flavor? That would be **Takorea** (818 Juniper St., 404/532-1944, www.mytakorea.com, Mon.-Thurs. 11:30am-10pm, Fri.-Sat. 11:30am-11pm, Sun. noon-10pm, $10), a concept restaurant that has actually managed to make the concept work. Chef Tomas Lee combined both of his culinary loves into this unique Midtown spot, which has a surprisingly sleek and sexy interior for a self-described "street food" joint. They also have a very interesting cocktail list, including a specialty martini made with a distinctive Korean liquor called *soju*.

Chef Ryan Smith has worked in some of Atlanta's finest restaurants, and now he's running his own kitchen at **(Empire State South** (999 Peachtree St. NE, 404/541-1105, www.empirestatesouth.com, Mon.-Thurs. 7am-10pm, Fri. 7am-11pm, Sat.-Sun. 10:30am-11pm, $25-35) in Midtown right on Peachtree Street, across the street from Margaret Mitchell's house. Empire State is somewhat unusual among the city's better restaurants in two ways: (1) The menu is extremely pared down; and (2) it offers breakfast on weekdays in addition to lunch and dinner. Did I mention the boccie ball courtyard? The morning meal is a simple yet versatile menu of Southern biscuits and New York bagels (get it? Empire State?), while the lunch menu focuses on high-quality sandwiches and one or two more savory dishes, such as a great pork belly. Dinner is a more heavy-hitting affair, with a full range of delicious, quirky appetizers like farm egg and octopus sausage (!) and entrées like Georgia trout and rib eye for two.

INMAN PARK AND LITTLE FIVE POINTS
Breakfast and Brunch

A beloved metro chain with nine Atlanta franchises to choose from, **Flying Biscuit Cafe** (1655 McLendon Ave., 404/687-8888, www.flyingbiscuit.com, daily 7am-10pm, $10) began in Candler Park near Little Five Points as an organic-friendly culinary project funded by Indigo Girls member and native Atlantan

boccie ball courtyard at Empire State South

© JIM MOREKIS

Emily Saliers. While not every location offers a dinner menu, all are best known for their delicious and cost-effective brunches served all day, which emphasize various specialty omelets such as the Piedmont with tasty chicken sausage. Even their namesake biscuits and gravy features an egg on top. That said, Flying Biscuit is also a big hit with the vegan crowd, offering a range of items. Cozy and often crowded, expect a wait at peak periods at all locations.

Coffee and Sweets
Atlanta has its share of good-to-great coffeehouses, but my favorite is **Inman Perk** (240 N. Highland Ave., 404/678/705-4545, www.inmanperkcoffee.com, Mon.-Thurs. 6am-11pm, Fri. 6am-10pm, Sat. 7am-10pm, Sun. 8am-11pm) in, yes, Inman Park. In keeping with some of the New Urbanist vibe you often see throughout Atlanta's up-and-coming neighborhoods, Inman Perk's exterior is resolutely modernist, even Bauhaus. Inside it's a little more like a typical coffeehouse, with a large amount of seating and good Wi-Fi. Not only is the coffee several cuts above a Starbucks or even the usual locally owned java joint, they boast a wide selection of teas as well. And if you prefer alcohol to caffeine, they have a good menu of craft beers and interesting wines as well.

Italian
Upscale Italian is the name of the game at Inman Park, with the one-two combination of **Sotto Sotto** (313 N. Highland Ave., 404/523-6678, www.urestaurants.net, Mon.-Thurs. 5:30pm-11pm, Fri.-Sat. 5:30pm-midnight, Sun. 5:30pm-10pm, $18-40) and its adjacent sibling **Fritti** (309 N. Highland Ave., 404/880-9559, www.urestaurants.net, Mon.-Thurs. 11:30am-11pm, Fri.-Sat. 11:30am-midnight, Sun. 12:30pm-10pm, $10-20). Sotto Sotto specializes in Tuscan cuisine, which is quite a bit different from the tomato-dominated stereotype of Italian food (though they do have a killer lasagna). Here you'll find succulent shellfish, delicate risotto, homemade pasta from scratch, and a very extensive wine list, all presented with top-notch service. Fritti is where

you go for wood-fired pizza in the trendy thin-crust genre from farther south in Italy's boot. Typical offerings are the gorgonzola, pineapple, and balsamic vinegar pizza and the Funghi di Bosco with white truffle oil and portobello mushrooms.

Steaks and Burgers
Small plates, big plates, cold plates, "second mortgage plates," **Rathbun's** (112 Krog St., 404/524-8280, www.rathbunsrestaurant.com, Mon.-Thurs. 5:30pm-10pm, Fri.-Sat. 5:30pm-11pm, $18-40) has it all. The new toast of the ATL foodie scene—exec chefs Kevin and Kent Rathbun beat Bobby Flay in an episode of *Iron Chef America*—this aspirational enterprise in Inman Park seeks to inject an almost ridiculous amount of innovation and flavor explosion across a wide-ranging menu. Where else can you find a hot smoked-salmon tostada, a 22-ounce bone-in rib eye, char-grilled octopus, roasted bone marrow, elk, duck breast with Thai risotto, and eggplant steak fries all in one place? And that's just a sampling of the rotating offerings. This is not to be confused with Rathbun's Steakhouse, owned by the same restaurant group.

As much tourist attraction as awesome burger spot, **Vortex** (438 Moreland Ave., 404/688-1828, www.thevortexbarandgrill.com, Sun.-Thurs. 11am-midnight, Fri.-Sat. 11am-2am, $10) dominates one approach to Little Five Points with its iconic zombie monster entrance. After walking through the skull's demonic open mouth, you sit down in a rather boisterous atmosphere and enjoy some of the larger, better burgers in town, with attitude to spare. The catch: Because this is specifically a "smoking allowed inside" restaurant, by law no one under 18 is permitted inside. There's a second version in Midtown.

BUCKHEAD
Classic Southern
A "diner" pretty much in name only—it's not cheap, and it offers valet parking—**Buckhead Diner** (3075 Piedmont Rd. NE, 404/262-3336, www.buckheadrestaurants.com, Mon.-Sat.

11am-midnight, Sun. 10am-10pm, $15-25) is primarily known as a place where celebrities can get a bite to eat in an atmosphere that is neither problematic for them nor exclusive from the rest of us. What this means in practice is you will get a mighty fine yet simply envisioned comfort-food meal, perhaps the signature roast beef sandwich with an opener of pimento cheese fritters, and maybe spot someone like Jane Fonda a few tables over. Overall, Buckhead Diner is one of those true Atlanta experiences, from the signed photos of movie stars on the wall to the long-serving staff decked out in old-school white coats.

Mediterranean

The crispiest, tastiest, fluffiest, most melt-in-your-mouth falafel I've had anywhere is at **Cafe Agora** (262 E. Paces Ferry Rd., 404/949-0900, www.cafeagora.com, Mon.-Thurs. 11am-10pm, Fri.-Sat. 11am-4am, Sun. 11am-9pm, $7-12), a Buckhead staple that specializes in freshly cooked, authentic Greek-Turkish cuisine made by the owners themselves using Old World recipes. They also deal a mean gyro and have a full range of homemade hummus, tabbouleh, dolmades, and baba ghanoush. You can't go wrong with anything on the menu. And on weekends it's all served till 4am! A new storefront location, smaller but just as good, has opened in Midtown (92 Peachtree Place NE, 404/253-2997, Mon.-Sat. 10am-10pm), literally just around the corner from the Margaret Mitchell House.

Steaks

Widely considered one of the best steak-houses in the United States, **[€** **Bone's** (3130 Piedmont Rd. NE, 404/237-2663, www.bones-restaurant.com, Mon.-Fri. 11:30am-2:30pm and 5:30pm-10pm, Sat.-Sun. 5:30pm-10pm, $30-50) is a throwback to the time when corporate movers-and-shakers gathered for three-martini lunches and enormous slabs of expertly seared beef. Some of that still goes on, of course, but in a changing world, Bone's has gained slightly more feminine appeal over the years, while still retaining that flavor of clubby

nostalgia. Even waiting for your table at the bar is an old-school experience in and of itself. There are actually some great seafood dishes on the menu, such as the crab-stuffed trout and the signature lobster bisque, but obviously the steaks are the draw here. All are amazing, but I call your attention to the two dry-aged items on the beef menu: a bone-in rib eye and a porterhouse for two. Needless to say, this isn't a particularly vegetarian-friendly restaurant.

Vietnamese

The best Vietnamese food in Buckhead is at **[€** **Chateau de Saigon** (4300 Buford Hwy. NE, 404/929-0034, www.chateaudesaigon. com, Sun.-Mon. and Wed.-Thurs. 11am-10pm, Fri.-Sat. 11am-11pm, $10-25). The menu is quite extensive, and you'll find all the usual fare, including *pho, bun,* fried rice entrées, and spring rolls. But don't stop there. There are some real gems here, including "shaken beef" filet mignon; "hot pots," where raw ingredients are cooked tableside; "sizzling fish," also cooked while you watch; and an entire page of clay pot offerings. There's even an entire sub-menu of tofu dishes.

VIRGINIA-HIGHLAND
Breakfast and Brunch

A Virginia-Highland brunch staple, **Murphy's** (997 Virginia Ave., 404/872-0904, www. murphys-atlanta-restaurant.com, Mon.-Thurs. 11am-10pm, Fri. 11am-11pm, Sat. 8am-11pm, Sun. 8am-10pm, $20) nearly always has a wait on Sunday, but most will say it's worth it. Crab cake benedict and shrimp and grits are particular faves, and the smoked salmon is highly recommended for fans of that delicacy. Every table gets a basket of delicious muffins and biscuits with jam.

While they did indeed start out chiefly as purveyors of sweet treats, **Highland Bakery** (655 Highland Ave. NE, 404/586-0772, www.highlandbakery.com, Mon.-Fri. 7am-4pm, Sat.-Sun. 8am-4pm, $4-12) in nearby Old Fourth Ward has expanded its menu far beyond muffins and the like. Nowadays it's better known for its delectable breakfast and brunch offerings, from ricotta pancakes to fried chicken benedict. The combination of down-home comfort food and the assortment of hipster servers has attracted a devoted following that has spread out to Highland Bakery's two subsequent locations, one in Midtown and one in Buckhead.

Italian

The Virginia-Highland neighborhood is picture-perfect for a relaxing lunch or dinner, and a great place to get just that is at one of the area's most beloved restaurants, **◖ La Tavola** (992 Virginia Ave., 404/873-5430, www.latavola-trattoria.com, Mon.-Thurs. 5:30pm-10pm, Fri.-Sat. 5:30pm-11pm, Sun. 11am-3pm and 5:30pm-10pm, $15-25). As the name implies, this is essentially an old-school trattoria with just enough bistro-style, open-kitchen atmosphere to keep a trendy edge. Northern Italian specialties such as risotto and mussels are the order of the day here, along with delights such as delicious prosciutto and perfect crusty bread. There's a full antipasti menu and a delightful assortment of Italian desserts such as tiramisu, panna cotta, and crostata. In all, it's a great place for a low-key romantic experience.

Seafood

A raw bar may not be the first thing that comes to mind when you think of Atlanta, but **◖ Fontaine's Oyster House** (1026 N. Highland Ave., 404/872-0869, www.nnnw-corp.com, Mon. 11:30am-1am, Tues. 4pm-2:30am, Wed.-Sat. 11:30am-2:30am, Sun. noon-midnight) is easily the best shellfish joint in town, as well as just a fun place to hang out into the wee hours, with the bar staying open past the usual kitchen closing time of midnight on weekends (11pm during the week). You can sit at a booth or at the bar to enjoy the range of fresh seafood. Gulf oysters, raw or steamed, will run you about $10 per dozen, and "specialty" oysters about twice that. They offer several roasted-oyster options as well. A lot of folks just split one of the combination platters, running around $40, which provide a sampling of boiled shrimp, snow crab legs, oysters,

and mussels. In keeping with the vaguely New Orleans-Cajun approach to the menu, their po'boys are amazing: You get your choice of oyster, shrimp, scallops, catfish, or crawfish.

DRUID HILLS
Ethiopian

Did someone say Ethiopian cuisine? Yes, Atlanta has it, along with a fairly large Ethiopian population, and the best place for it is **Desta Ethiopian Kitchen** (3086 Briarcliff Rd. NE, 404/929-0011, www.destaethiopiankitchen.com, Mon.-Thurs. 9am-midnight, Fri.-Sun. 9am-1am, $10-15). You eat Ethiopian food with thin, tasty bread rather than utensils, and your friendly server will provide plenty of it. The cuisine ranges from tasty stews to split-pea soup and expertly prepared tilapia.

PERIMETER
Chinese

North of Buckhead just outside the Perimeter is the closest thing to a classic Chinatown spot, **Canton Cooks** (5984 Roswell Rd. NE, 404/250-0515, Thurs.-Tues. 11am-2:30am, $10-15), offering delicacies such as fried fish maw, Peking spare ribs, fried squid, and, of course, General Tso's chicken. Possibly the best Chinese restaurant in the city, this humble spot is in a strip mall near a Whole Foods in the northern Atlanta suburb of Sandy Springs and is a favorite of that area's burgeoning Chinese population.

WESTSIDE
Italian

One of Atlanta's more full-immersion dining experiences is at **◖ Antico Pizza Napoletana** (1093 Hemphill Ave. NW, 404/724-2333, www.anticoatl.com, Mon.-Sat. 11:30am "until they run out of dough," about 11pm or midnight, pizza $20), where you'll find Old World authentic Naples-via-Brooklyn pizza in a hot, loud environment seemingly tailor-made for enjoying a big tasty pie. It's not all a bed of roses: The wait is usually quite long, they're closed on Sunday, and you can only add one topping to the pie of your choice. That's right: only one ingredient, no exceptions. But the thing is, all the major ingredients (prosciutto, pecorino, soppressata, etc.) come directly from Italy, and the pies are exactly as you would find them in Naples. Each pizza feeds a lot of people.

You'll never set foot in an Olive Garden again after a visit to **Osteria del Figo** (1210 Howell Mill Rd., 404/351-3700, www.figo-pasta.com, Mon.-Thurs. 11:30am-9:30pm, Fri. 11:30am-10pm, Sat. noon-10pm, Sun. noon-9:30pm, $12), a unique pasta restaurant that matches flavor with value. Though overshadowed in the local culinary scene by the five-star Bacchanalia across the parking lot, Figo, part of a citywide chain of similar pasta places, is no slouch, offering a wide-ranging menu of pastas, regional Italian sauces (tomato-based and cream-based), and specialty melt-in-your-mouth meatballs. You place your order and pay for it first, then sit down in the well-appointed dining room, where you're served by the waitstaff. There's a bit of a learning curve involved because of the menu's sheer size and frankly daunting plethora of custom combinations, but the counter staff is knowledgeable and can help match the sauce with the pasta.

New Southern

The most sought-after table in Atlanta is within the hallowed confines of ☾ **Bacchanalia** (1198 Howell Mill Rd., 404/365-0410, www.starprovisions.com, Mon.-Sat. from 6pm, $25-35, five-course prix fixe $85), a Southeastern mecca of so-called New American cuisine that continues to top most of the foodie lists for the city. Through their Star Provisions cooperative-conglomerate (you actually enter the restaurant through the retail arm), chef-owners Anne Quatrano and Clifford Harrison concentrate on sourcing all foods organically, locally, and regionally, many from their own Summerland Farm and associated abattoir. The menu centers on a five-course prix fixe that includes a cold appetizer, fish, entrée, cheese course, and dessert (*amuse-bouche* generally comes around as well). Typical dishes include a delectable slow roast porchetta, a perfect red snapper, the signature crab fritter, and yes, foie gras. You can order à la carte from the bar area. Don't expect to walk in and get a table; reservations fill up months in advance. Directly next door, chef David Carson runs the kitchen at **Quinones at Bacchanalia** (1198 Howell Mill Rd., 404/365-0410, www.starprovisions.com, Mon.-Sat. from 6pm), a smaller, more Southern-tinged dining room that also relies on the tried-and-true five-course prix fixe.

Information and Services

HOSPITALS

The main trauma center in Atlanta and in the entire Southeast is **Grady Memorial Hospital** (80 Jesse Hill Jr. Dr., 404/616-1000, www.grady-health.org). If you're in a serious accident while near Atlanta this is definitely the place to go.

Other important facilities include **Piedmont Atlanta Hospital** (1968 Peachtree Rd., 404/605-5000, www.piedmonthospital.org), north of Downtown, part of a metro-wide hospital chain; and **St. Joseph's Hospital** (5665 Peachtree Dunwoody Rd., 678/843-7001, www.stjosephsatlanta.org), even farther north at the Perimeter.

MEDIA
Newspapers

The newspaper of record in Atlanta is the venerable *Atlanta Journal-Constitution* (www.ajc.com). Famous alumni include Margaret Mitchell and Henry Grady.

But for complete arts and entertainment listings, in addition to a good amount of counterculture politics, you'll want to check out *Creative Loafing* (www.clatl.com), the city's longtime alt-weekly, which by some reckonings actually has the higher circulation of the two.

While the iconic gay paper *The Southern*

ATL LINGO

- AJC: nickname for the city's daily newspaper of record, the *Atlanta Journal-Constitution*.

- The ATL: hip-hop slang for Atlanta.

- Brookwood Split: the spot south of Buckhead where I-75 and I-85 separate north of the Connector.

- The Connector: that portion of I-75 and I-85 that passes directly through the center of Downtown.

- Dirty South: subgenre of hip-hop produced in the ATL.

- Grady: shorthand for the hulking Downtown presence of Grady Memorial Hospital, the South's premier trauma center. The Connector goes around it at the "Grady Curve."

- The Hootch: the Chattahoochee River. One "shoots the Hootch," that is, rides a white-water raft or tubes downstream. The Chattahoochee is also a key source of drinking water for Atlanta.

- Hotlanta: Using this nickname for Atlanta will mark you as a tourist or a generally lame person. Avoid it at all costs.

- L5P: acronym for Little Five Points.

- Peachtree: generally refers to Peachtree Street, the historic north-south main avenue through the heart of Atlanta. Do not confuse it with the 70 other roads in Atlanta bearing some variant of "Peachtree." Mov-ers and shakers all wanted a prestigious address on Peachtree Street. If they couldn't have that, nearby streets were named to feature the word, for example, Peachtree Circle, Peachtree Lane, and so on. Adding to the confusion is the fact that Peachtree Street becomes Peachtree Road in Buckhead. While Georgia is the Peach State, local folklore says Peachtree is probably a corruption of "pitch tree," a pine tree used for sap.

- The Perimeter: the vast swath of I-285 encircling the city and the demarcation between Atlanta proper and its fast-growing suburbs. Rush-hour traffic jams are the stuff of nightmares, with the northern portion, or "Top End," the most congested.

- Ponce: what locals call Ponce de Leon Avenue. The most upscale area during Atlanta's Victorian heyday, this sinuous and now occasionally seamy street is a center of dining and nightlife. If you insist on the full name, avoid Spanish inflection and say "LEE-on."

- Spaghetti Junction: the sprawling 14-bridge cloverleaf that includes the intersection of "The Perimeter" (I-285) and I-85 and handles over 250,000 vehicles a day.

- The Ted: nickname for Turner Field, home of the Atlanta Braves major league baseball team through 2017, when they move to the northern suburb of Cobb County. This is not to be confused with the nearby Georgia Dome, home of the Atlanta Falcons.

Voice is sadly no more, Atlanta's sizeable LGBT community is served by *Project Q Atlanta* (www.projectqatlanta.com) and by *Edge* (www.edgeatlanta.com).

Radio

Traffic reports are very important in Atlanta, and many locals tune to **WSB** (750 AM and 95.5 FM). **SiriusXM** also has Atlanta traffic at channel 134.

The Atlanta radio dial is full of options, but one of the more unique is the Georgia Tech student-run station, **WREK** (91.1 FM). The local Georgia Public Broadcasting public radio station is **WABE** (90.1 FM).

LIBRARIES

The main branch of the **Atlanta-Fulton Public Library System** (1 Margaret Mitchell Square, 404/730-1700, www.afplweb.com, Mon.-Thurs. 9am-8pm, Fri.-Sat. 9am-6pm, Sun. 2pm-6pm) frequently hosts exhibits, and its most notable standing exhibit is the Margaret Mitchell room on the fifth floor.

The major universities also have worthy

libraries: the vast **Georgia Tech Library** (704 Cherry St., 404/894-4500, www.library.gatech. edu, Mon.-Thurs. 7:30am-10pm, Fri. 7:30am-6pm, Sat. 9am-6pm, Sun. noon-10pm) and the **Georgia State University Library** (100 Decatur St., 404/413-2820, www.library.gsu. edu, Mon.-Fri. 8:30am-5:15pm), which is open to nonstudents.

Getting There and Around

BY CAR

Often to the chagrin of residents, Atlanta is a major nexus of interstate highways, and that's how most drivers enter and leave. Major thoroughfares are north-south arteries **I-75** and **I-85,** which actually combine into a single road through Downtown, separating a little south of Buckhead (from there I-75 heads into Chattanooga, Tennessee, and I-85 into Greenville, South Carolina). Northeast on I-85 is the infamous **"Spaghetti Junction,"** a vast collection of interchanges and one portion of highway with an incredible 18 lanes.

I-285, called **"The Perimeter"** by locals, and in portions labeled the "Atlanta Bypass," forms a vast circle around the metro area and serves primarily as a commuter avenue. It carries 250,000 vehicles a day at speeds ranging from blindingly fast to a barely perceptible crawl. Traffic is much worse at the **"Top End"** of the Perimeter, north of Atlanta near the city's most populous suburbs. New variable speed limit signs have been installed in portions of the Top End to adjust the speed limit from a max of 65 mph to lower limits to account for congestion and delays. Nonetheless, try to avoid it during rush hour if at all possible.

I-20 runs east-west along the bottom of the Atlanta metro area, its eastern end passing through Augusta and its western end going into Alabama. It's called Ralph David Abernathy Parkway near Downtown.

A key non-interstate route is **Highway 78,** called Stone Mountain Parkway east of the city and Ponce de Leon Avenue in town.

With Atlanta's heavy traffic and frequent accident and road construction delays, monitoring traffic conditions is a full-time job that's never dull. Local radio station **WSB** (95.5 FM and 750 AM) generally has the most frequent and up-to-date reports. **SiriusXM** also has a good satellite station covering DC-Baltimore-Atlanta traffic at channel 134.

On-street metered parking is available in increments of a half-hour and 1-4 hours. Parking enforcement in Atlanta is extremely aggressive. While meter enforcement times vary depending on the zone, most in the visitor-frequented areas are enforced Monday-Saturday 7am-10pm. As of this writing there's talk of 24-hour meter enforcement. There are many dozens of parking garages and public and private parking lots at various costs; an excellent resource with interactive mapping is www.atlantadowntown.com.

BY AIR

Hartsfield-Jackson Atlanta International Airport (ATL, 6000 North Terminal Pkwy., 404/530-6600, www.atlanta-airport.com) is the world's busiest, serving nearly 100 million passengers a year. Situated seven miles south of Atlanta proper astride Fulton and Clayton Counties, Hartsfield-Jackson is Georgia's largest employer and is in many ways a city unto itself. In one spot, I-75/85 actually goes under one of the runways.

Its flagship airline is Delta, whose hub here is the largest in the world, making up 60 percent of the airport's traffic. In all, about two dozen airlines fly in and out; domestic highlights include Southwest, AirTran, American, United, and US Airways, with international highlights including Air France, British Airways, KLM, Korean Air, and Lufthansa.

The massive **Hartsfield-Jackson Rental Car Center** opened in 2009 and houses 10 airport rental agencies, with room for more. Though freestanding, it is fully integrated with the airport by a people-moving transportation system, the ATL Skytrain, as well as its own access highway. The airport's transit system is the Plane Train, which provides full transport from terminal to terminal, including the new Maynard Jackson International Terminal, which opened in 2012.

Parking at the domestic terminal is in two tiers. The four-level Daily Parking area ($3 per hour, $16 per day) is closest to the terminal and provides a large amount of covered spots. The open-air Economy lots ($3 per hour, $12 per day) are the cheapest, and have a free shuttle that runs daily 8am-midnight.

There is an international shuttle connector (daily 24 hours, free) to link up international passengers with both the rental car center and the domestic terminal, where the MARTA station is located. The airport MARTA rapid transit station is on the north side of the airport near the baggage claim area. Unlike some metro transit systems that use a rotating fare system, all rides on MARTA, regardless of distance, are $2.50 one-way, including to and from Hartsfield-Jackson.

Various taxi services operate out of Hartsfield-Jackson, and the fare from the airport to Downtown will run you about $40.

MARTA PUBLIC TRANSIT

Atlanta's main public transit entity is **MARTA** (Metropolitan Atlanta Rapid Transit Authority, www.itsmarta.com, $2.50 one-way). While often the butt of jokes locally and certainly not on par with more expansive transit systems such as New York City's or San Francisco's, MARTA is a very handy and extremely cost-effective way to avoid the snarling traffic jams prevalent throughout Atlanta. There are two main components: the rapid transit trains and the extended bus system.

The train system layout is very simple: The two north-south lines, Gold and Red, go from Hartsfield-Jackson International Airport in the south and split in Buckhead, the Red Line

going to Sandy Springs and the Gold Line to Doraville. The main east-west route is the Blue Line, spanning the diameter of the I-285 Perimeter, with a shorter Green Line serving Downtown. There's only one transfer station: Five Points in Downtown.

There are nearly 40 MARTA train stops, with one convenient to just about every notable destination. Generally speaking, trains run about every 15-20 minutes Monday-Friday 5am-1am, Saturday-Sunday and most holidays 6am-1am. There is full access for riders with disabilities, and bicycles are accommodated on trains and buses anytime. One-way fares are $2.50 regardless of the length of the trip, which makes MARTA a remarkable bargain compared to other big-city transit systems. The best option is to purchase a reloadable BreezeCard at any MARTA station, which you just tap to a card reader to board.

Bus routes are fully integrated into MARTA. You can transfer to a bus line for free for one-way trips finished within three hours. The free transfer is automatically activated when used at the airport. Tap the card on the fare box on the bus.

The MARTA website features a handy downloadable *Rookie's Guide,* which is worth a quick look.

BY BUS AND TRAIN

The Atlanta **Amtrak** (1688 Peachtree St., 404/881-3060, www.amtrak.com) train station is smack-dab Downtown.

Atlanta has two **Greyhound** bus stations to get in and out of town: one in Downtown (232 Forsyth St., 404/584-1728, www.greyhound.com) and another at Hartsfield-Jackson International Airport (404/765-9598, www.greyhound.com).

TAXI SERVICE

While not a taxi-centric town, there are plenty of cab companies. Try **Atlanta Checker Cab** (404/351-1111, www.atlantacheckercab.com) or **Atlanta Lenox Taxi Company** (404/872-2600, www.atlantalenoxtaxi.com).

Greater Atlanta

The idea of Greater Atlanta might seem funny, or at least redundant, to those who live in Atlanta, considering the city's notorious sprawl. But there are indeed several separate municipalities worth visiting, which, though largely subsumed within the metro area, still have managed to retain their individual identity. One of Georgia's most popular attractions, Stone Mountain, is just east of town, as is the happening little city of Decatur. North of Atlanta are Marietta and Gainesville, the latter a gateway to North Georgia. And southeast of Atlanta is the unique and well-preserved natural getaway of Arabia Mountain.

◖ DECATUR

Decatur is that rarest of birds: a place with a true small-town vibe directly adjacent to a massive metro area. Despite its proximity to the city, when you're here, you feel like you're away from Atlanta's sometimes oppressive sprawl.

Decatur has had that feel from the beginning. Technically older than Atlanta, Decatur dates back to 1822. Citizens didn't want the rampant growth that would come with a major rail terminal, so they refused; the settlement that would later be Atlanta was founded a bit west in 1837.

Today, Decatur (www.visitdecaturgeorgia.com) is known for the success of its downtown revitalization, which has resulted in one of the most vibrant café, restaurant, and shopping scenes in the South. It's also one of the most assertively progressive little cities in the region, a trait that showed itself with the recent grassroots effort against a new Walmart.

Waffle House Museum

The national chain boasts over 1,600 locations today, but the very first Waffle House was in little old Decatur, founded in 1955 when neighbors Joe Roger and Tom Forkner went into business together. The **Waffle House Museum** (2719 E. College Ave., 770/326-7086, www.

wafflehouse.com, by appointment, free) contains memorabilia from back in the day. Aside from a few annual open houses, it's only open by appointment, so call ahead and check the website.

Nightlife and Food

The draw in Decatur, other than its beautiful, modernist town square, is its compelling food and nightlife, and the two pursuits are deeply intertwined here. Many of its hottest nightspots offer great food in addition to world-class craft beer selections, and many other venues offer frequent live music.

It's fittingly Decatur-ish that its most famous nightspot, **Eddie's Attic** (515 N. McDonough St., 404/377-4976, www.eddiesattic.com, daily from 5pm) is located literally right next door to City Hall. One of the most influential folk-acoustic venues in the South, Eddie's upstairs performance space is where the Indigo Girls got their start. Other big names who honed their craft at Eddie's include Sugarland, John Mayer, Michelle Malone, Shawn Mullins and, believe it or not, Justin Bieber. Mayer, Mullins, and Sugarland's Jennifer Nettles are all past winners of Eddie's semiannual songwriting contest. The main listening room isn't the place to get rowdy, or even to spend quality time with your smartphone; you're expected to pay attention to the performers. Mondays are standard open mike nights, and the quality is top-notch. For a louder good time, there is rooftop patio seating.

With a name taken from Shakespeare, **Cakes & Ale** (155 Sycamore St., 404/377-7994, www.cakesandalerestaurant.com, Tues.-Thurs. 6pm-11pm, kitchen closes 10pm, Fri.-Sat. 5:30pm-midnight, kitchen closes 10:30pm) recently moved into a larger space closer to the city center, the better to accommodate the crowds that come to enjoy their adventurous American farm-to-table style cuisine of Napa-trained lead chef Billy Allin, formerly of another great (and sadly now defunct) local spot, Watershed. The

ATLANTA

© AVALON TRAVEL

menus change too frequently to cover it here, but a recent dinner included an oyster sampler, chicory salad, and a great halibut. The attached bakery is known for its actual cakes.

For an Irish pub atmosphere with that thing that most Irish pubs lack, really good food, try **The Marlay House** (426 W. Ponce de Leon Ave., 404/270-9950, www.themarlayhouse. com, Mon.-Thurs. 11:30am-10:30pm, bar until midnight, Fri. 11:30am-11:30pm, bar until 2am, Sat. 10:30am-11:30pm, bar until 2am, Sun. 10:30am-10:30pm, bar until midnight, $15), known to old-timers as former home of The Grange. They are known for their righteous roast and Yorkshire pudding. Of course, they have a great beer-on-tap selection and pride themselves on pouring a pint of Guinness just as you would get it in Dublin. Most nights there is live traditional Irish music.

An intriguing and beguiling mix of neighborhood bar, signature cocktail joint, craft brew headquarters, and farm-to-table restaurant, **Leon's Full Service** (131 E. Ponce de Leon Ave., 404/687-0500, www.

leonsfullservice.com, Mon. 5pm-1am, Tues.-Thurs. 11:30am-1am, Fri.-Sat. 11:30am-2am, Sun. 11:30am-1am, kitchen closes 1 hour earlier, $15-20) lives up to its name. The range of old school specialty cocktails, hovering around $10, is inspiring; check out the seasonal offerings. The main plate menu is small but finely honed; try the grilled flatiron steak or the veggie loaf. In any case, don't miss out on the "pub frites," with your choice of two sauces, such as goat cheese fondue or horseradish mayo.

The first spot to really put Decatur's downtown renaissance on the map, **Brick Store Pub** (125 E. Court Square, 404/687-0990, www. brickstorepub.com, Mon. 11am-1am, Tues.-Sat. 11am-2am, Sun. noon-1am, $10) continues to offer a unique selection of amped-up yet affordable comfort food and pub fare, such as "Shepherd's Daughter's Pie," a great Cornish game hen, and an Italian-themed pierogi. The beer list includes a raft of great Belgians served in a dedicated space upstairs.

An outrageously popular tapas place, **Iberian**

Leon's Full Service in Decatur

© JIM MOREKIS

Pig (121 Sycamore St., 404/371-8800, www. iberianpigatl.com, Mon.-Thurs. 5pm-10pm, Fri.-Sat. 3pm-11pm, Sun. 5pm-9pm, tapas $5-15) offers great small plates and, as the name suggests, a remarkable variety of authentic Spanish pork dishes in a boisterous atmosphere. The best deal is the charcuterie sampler; don't miss the rare and incredible *jamón ibérico.*

For a more budget conscious, but still very gratifying, experience, **Raging Burrito and Taco** (141 Sycamore St., 404/377-3311, www. ragingburrito.com, Sun.-Thurs. 11am-10pm, Fri.-Sat. 11am-midnight, $7-10) offers fat and fresh Tex-Mex burritos and tasty tacos and quesadillas in a sports bar atmosphere. Their hot sauce is outstanding.

For a real Italian wood-oven pizza experience, head to **No. 246** (129 E. Ponce de Leon Ave., 678/399-8246, www.no246.com, Mon.-Thurs. 11am-3pm and 5pm-10pm, Fri.-Sat. 11am-3pm and 5pm-11pm, Sun. 11am-3pm and 5pm-9pm, $12-24). They also offer a pasta and gnocchi menu and a special chicken scaloppine for two.

For continental-quality dining, get a table at **Café Alsace** (121 E. Ponce de Leon Ave., 404/373-5622, www.cafealsace.net, Tues.-Fri. 11:30am-2:15pm and 6pm-10pm, Sat. 6pm-10pm, Sun. 10am-2pm, $25). As the name tells you, this is French cuisine with a Germanic feel, including spaetzle and *choucroute garnie,* a sauerkraut-sausage combo.

There are several coffeehouses in Decatur, but my favorite is **Java Monkey** (425 Church St., 404/378-5002, www.javamonkeydecatur. com, Mon.-Fri. 6:30am-midnight). They have tasty goodies in addition to great coffee, and every Tuesday night they host a surprisingly dynamic open-mike night for musicians.

Decatur has two great farmers market options, chief among them **Your Dekalb Farmers Market** (3000 E. Ponce de Leon Ave., www. dekalbfarmersmarket.com, daily 9am-9pm), an enormous collection of goods and produce not only from regional sources but literally from around the world. **The Decatur Farmers Market** (163 Clairemont Ave., Wed. 4pm-7pm; 498 N. McDonough St., Sat. 9am-1pm, www.

decaturfarmersmarket.com) is a more modest and typical collection of locally sourced organic produce.

Shopping

Decatur hosts numerous boutique-style retail establishments, including über-trendy **Squash Blossom** (113 E. Court Square, 404/373-1864, www.squashblossomboutique.com, Mon. 11am-7pm, Tues.-Thurs. 11am-8pm, Fri. 11am-9pm, Sat. 10am-9pm, Sun. 11am-6pm), a great place for hip women's apparel and accessories from companies like Free People, Michael Stars, and Echo. There's fun and fresh **World of Collage** (114 E. Ponce de Leon Ave., 404/377-1280, www.worldofcollage.com, Mon.-Sat. 11am-9pm, Sun. noon-6pm), which actually has little to do with collage and is a boutique with hard-to-find designers like Desigual and Johnny Was. For a slightly more mature take but still a lot of color, browse **Boutique Karma** (145 Sycamore St., 404/373-7533, www.boutique-karma.com, Mon.-Sat. 10:30am-7:30pm, Sun. 12:30pm-6pm).

Their branch in Athens, Georgia, is much more famous, but only two years after that one opened in 1976, another branch of **Wuxtry Records** (2096 N. Decatur Rd., 404/329-0020, www.wuxtry-records.com, Mon.-Sat. 11am-8pm, Sun. noon-6pm) opened in Decatur. Like its sister store, it's a gathering place for local musicians and hipsters alike.

The local arts and crafts scene is well represented at two cooperative galleries: **Wild Oats and Billy Goats** (112 E. Ponce de Leon Ave., 404/378-4088, www.wildoatsandbillygoats. com, Wed.-Fri. 11am-6pm, Sat. 11am-7pm, Sun. 1pm-5pm) and **HomeGrown Decatur** (412 Church St., 404/373-1147, www.home-growndecatur.com, Mon.-Sat. 10am-9pm, Sun. noon-8pm).

One of the most unique shops in town is **Houndstooth Road** (316 Church St., 404/220-8957, www.h2rd.com, Wed.-Sat. noon-7pm, Sun. noon-5pm, Tues. by appointment), a high-end Euro-style bicycle retailer, which also offers a range of clothing and accessories for the upwardly mobile cyclist.

Getting There and Around

Getting to Decatur from Atlanta proper couldn't be easier. The dedicated Decatur MARTA station is literally yards away from the town center, something that was quite controversial at first. Conversely, you can just drive east on Ponce de Leon Avenue from the heart of Atlanta's midtown on Peachtree Street, and end up directly in downtown Decatur. Once in Decatur, a car isn't necessary at all. It's very walkable, with almost every place you might want to visit within a couple of blocks.

STONE MOUNTAIN

Stone Mountain is both an iconic feature of the Atlanta landscape, literally, and a fairly cheesy tourist destination. In any case, it's certainly unique. The massive outcropping itself is incredible and geologically fascinating, a nearly 1,700-foot dome of quartz and granite five miles around at the base. The bas-relief sculpture on the north side of Stone Mountain, of Confederate general Robert E. Lee flanked by General Stonewall Jackson and Confederate president Jefferson Davis, all on horseback, is also an impressive work, regardless of what you may think of the implied message. The nightly narrated 45-minute laser shows, included with basic admission, have been a staple of the scene for generations at **Stone Mountain Park** (1000 Robert E. Lee Blvd., 770/498-5690, www.stonemountainpark.com, daily 10am-10pm, $10 admission, other attractions extra).

What is distinctly less unique about Stone Mountain is the theme park that has been built up around it since a major "upgrade" in the 1990s. A cynic might say that the Confederates in the rock have themselves become an afterthought, playing second, third, and fourth fiddles to the associated rides and seasonal attractions (extra ticket required) that have blossomed literally in the mountain's shadow, including an actual locomotive train that takes you, Magic Kingdom-style, around the park's periphery.

The Confederates on the rock look down on Memorial Hall, where you enter for the laser shows. Adjacent to Memorial Hall is where you hop on the Skyride tram to and from the top of the mountain (extra ticket required), which, I must say, is worth the price. Closer to the mountain are individual interpretive memorials to each state of the Confederacy, detailing their involvement and sacrifice in the Civil War. At the horses' feet lies a large reflective pool complete with fountains.

While summer brings a steady crowd, Christmastime is a really big deal at Stone Mountain Park, with a festival-of-lights style cordoned-off area with a show (extra charge) and even a fake "snow mountain" between Memorial Hall and the mountain. Perhaps understandably, the associated Confederate history museum has been shunted off to one side of the park, where you can park and take a hiking trail to the top of the mountain if you're so inclined.

Your $10 basic entrance fee also entitles you to the use of various picnic areas and walking-biking trails within the park's vast expanse. There are over 400 tent and RV camping sites ($45-60) available within the park, as well as the attached Stone Mountain Inn ($170-200) and Evergreen Marriott Conference Resort ($190-230).

Getting There and Around

When most folks talk about Stone Mountain, they're talking about the outcropping and theme park, not the separate small municipality. In any case, the best way to get to either is to take one of three routes east of Atlanta: Stone Mountain Parkway/U.S. 78, Ponce de Leon Avenue, or Memorial Drive. There is no MARTA train service to Stone Mountain, but you can take a MARTA bus from the Kensington Station.

MARIETTA

One of the largest entities in the Atlanta metro area, Marietta (www.mariettasquare.com) is the Cobb County seat, with well over 50,000 residents within its city limits alone. Sadly it has even less remaining antebellum history than Atlanta, given that General Sherman's troops left only four buildings intact during their torching of Marietta in 1864. A major battle was fought at nearby Kennesaw Mountain, now a National Park Service-preserved national battlefield. During World War II, the city and Cobb County got a boost with the construction of the enormous Bell airplane factory (later Lockheed Martin), which produced B-29 bombers by the thousands for the strategic bombing campaign on Japan. Cultural life in Marietta today revolves around the charming town square.

Gone with the Wind Museum: Scarlett on the Square

Marietta doesn't play a role in Margaret Mitchell's novel, but the city does host one of the few *Gone with the Wind* museums outside Atlanta proper. The **Gone with the Wind Museum** (18 Whitlock Ave., 770/794-5576, www.gwtwmarietta.com, Mon.-Sat. 10am-5pm, $7 adults, $6 children), also called "Scarlett on the Square," set within a restored 1875 cotton warehouse, offers a modest collection of memorabilia, mostly from the movie, most notably the honeymoon gown worn by Vivien Leigh in the film.

Marietta Museum of History

The **Marietta Museum of History** (1 Depot St., 770/794-5710, www.mariettahistory.org, Mon.-Sat. 10am-4pm, $5 adults, $3 children) is on the second floor of the 1845 Kennesaw House, one of a handful of antebellum structures left in town. There are displays on Native Americans, the Gold Rush, and of course the localized aspects of the Civil War. A relatively new and separate **Aviation Wing** (S. Cobb Dr. and Atlanta Rd. SE, 770/794-5710, www.mariettahistory.org, Thurs.-Sat. 10am-3pm) is on 15 acres of land and has vintage airplane displays focusing on Marietta's considerable contribution to the World War II production effort.

Marietta/Cobb Museum of Art

Dedicated purely to American art, mostly from the 19th and 20th centuries, the **Marietta/Cobb Museum of Art** (30 Atlanta

St., 770/528-1444, www.mariettacobbartmuseum.org, Tues.-Fri. 11am-5pm, Sat. 11am-4pm, Sun. 1pm-4pm, $8 adults, $5 children) is housed in Marietta's first post office. They host frequent community-oriented art instruction workshops, such as plein air and figure drawing.

Kennesaw Mountain National Battlefield Park

In June 1864, General Sherman's advance on Atlanta was temporarily stopped by Confederate troops, and artillery dug in along the top of Kennesaw Mountain outside of Marietta. The 3,000-acre **Kennesaw Mountain National Battlefield Park** (900 Kennesaw Mountain Dr., 770/427-4686, www.nps.gov, daily 8:30am-5pm, free) preserves and interprets the vast battleground. There are four self-guided driving-tour stops and an incredible 18 miles of hiking trails (no bikes) throughout the battlefield area, all interpreted. Go the website for info on a cell phone audio tour.

Marietta Confederate Cemetery

Over 3,000 Confederate veterans, including many killed in the Battle of Kennesaw Mountain, are laid to rest in **Marietta Confederate Cemetery** (395 Powder Springs St., 770/794-5606, www.mariettaga.gov, daily 8:30am-dusk, free), the largest Confederate cemetery south of Richmond, Virginia, the Confederate capital. The graveyard was founded in 1863 when a local woman donated land on her plantation to bury 20 soldiers who died in a train wreck.

The Big Chicken

For generations of Atlantans, the main attraction in "May-retta" has been what is universally called **The Big Chicken** (U.S. 41 and Hwy. 120). It's actually a vintage Kentucky Fried Chicken franchise started in 1956. The seven-story, 56-foot-tall chicken was designed by a Georgia Tech architecture student and erected in 1963. Severe storm damage in 1993 nearly caused it to be demolished, but it was saved by a public outcry, which included

STONE MOUNTAIN STORIES

© JIM MOREKIS

Stone Mountain carvings

"Let freedom ring from Stone Mountain of Georgia..."

When Dr. Martin Luther King Jr. included those famous words in his 1963 "I Have a Dream" speech, it wasn't a nod to the huge carving of three Confederate figures on the face of the granite outcropping, the largest bas-relief sculpture in the world. Commissioned in 1916, the carving wasn't actually completed until 1972, several years after King's assassination.

King was almost certainly referring to the fact—not generally mentioned in the Atlanta area today—that the modern incarnation of the Ku Klux Klan was founded in November 1915 on the summit of Stone Mountain. Those "Knights of Mary Phagan," as the hooded group called itself, burned a cross and took an oath administered by the grandson of the first KKK Grand Wizard, Confederate general Nathan Bedford Forrest. Also present that night was Sam Venable, owner of Stone Mountain, who would oversee efforts by various sculptors to finish the carving, one of which was Gutzon Borglum of Mount Rushmore fame, all the while allowing the KKK to hold meetings here. Frustrated by a 30-year hiatus in the carving, the state of Georgia finally purchased Stone Mountain from Venable in 1958 for $1 million.

Today, the carving of Confederate generals Robert E. Lee and Stonewall Jackson and Confederate president Jefferson Davis forms the central attraction of **Stone Mountain Park** (1000 Robert E. Lee Blvd., 770/498-5690, www.stonemountainpark.com, daily 10am-10pm, $10 admission, other attractions extra), one of Georgia's biggest tourist draws and a place where the KKK most certainly is not welcome anymore.

Truthfully, the most interesting history on Stone Mountain's summit happened long before the Civil War, when Creek and later Cherokee people held ceremonies up here. In the early 1800s, when it was called Rock Mountain, the summit was a frequent destination for daylong horseback trips. Contrary to what you might think, Stone Mountain was actually heavily quarried for granite throughout the history of nonnative settlement of the area. Stone Mountain rock is in the U.S. Capitol in Washington DC and was offered for use in the new Martin Luther King Jr. Memorial, but it was turned down in favor of granite from China.

Air Force pilots who use the Big Chicken as a navigation point while landing at a nearby base.

Accommodations and Food

Marietta's most beloved spot is the **ⓒ Marietta Diner** (306 Cobb Pkwy. S., 770/423-9390, www.mariettadiner.com, daily 24 hours, $15), a 24-hour meet-and-eat place known to generations of locals. It's getting a good amount of national buzz these days for its well-crafted menu of Southern comfort food (with a few twists, like kebabs and Romanian steak), all served in massive portions. Yes, they serve breakfast all day.

There's no shortage of good eats around Marietta's downtown square (www.eaton-thesquare.com), but your best bets include the unusual but delicious Tex-Mex-Asian fusion of **Taqueria Tsunami** (70 S. Park Square, 678/324-7491, www.taqueriatsunami.com, Mon.-Thurs. 11am-9pm, Fri.-Sat. 11am-10pm, Sun. 10:30am-9pm, $12-20); the Thai-Japanese blend at **Thaicoon & Sushi** (34 Mill St., 678/766-0641, www.thaicoonmarietta.com, Mon.-Thurs. 11:30am-2:30pm and 5pm-10pm, Fri. 11:30am-2:30pm and 5pm-11pm, Sat. 5pm-11pm, Sun. 5pm-10pm, $12-18); and the hearty pizzeria **Marietta Pizza Company** (3 Whitlock Ave., 770/419-0900, www.mariettapizza.com, Mon.-Thurs. 11am-10pm, Fri.-Sat. 11am-11pm, Sun. 12:30pm-10pm, $15), which offers a focused and well-conceived menu, including great subs and a gluten-free crust.

A favorite location to fuel up before or after a Kennesaw Mountain hike is **Mountain Biscuits** (1718 Old Hwy. 41, 770/419-3311, Mon.-Fri. 6am-2pm, Sat. 7am-2pm, $10), where all the namesake baked items are enormous, made from scratch, and served with delicious gravy and tasty country ham and eggs.

There are plenty of chain hotels in Cobb County, but for a more unique stay try the **Stanley House Bed & Breakfast** (236 Church St., 770/426-1881, www.thestanleyhouse.com, $125), housed in a beautiful Victorian a short walk from the main town square.

Getting There and Around

Unfortunately MARTA doesn't go directly to Marietta, but you can take a MARTA rapid transit train to the Holmes Station and then take a Cobb Community Transit bus (http://dot.cobbcountyga.gov) to where you need to go. MARTA and Cobb Community Transit are both $2.50. By car from Atlanta, take I-75 north to exit 265; take a left on the North Marietta Parkway (Hwy. 120).

LAKE LANIER

As the prime reservoir on the Chattahoochee River, Lake Lanier is the main drinking water source for Atlanta. It's also one of the most popular recreation spots in the metro area, a fact driven not only by its proximity to the big city but by its sheer size: nearly 700 miles of shoreline. Rowing events in the 1996 Olympics were held here. The nearest city to Lake Lanier is Gainesville, known chiefly as the home of Confederate general James Longstreet and more recently as the "Poultry Capital of the World" for the large number of chicken processing plants on its outskirts, as well as being the alleged birthplace of Southern fried chicken.

The U.S. Army Corps of Engineers operates Lake Lanier and also runs over 70 recreation and boat access areas, over 40 of which are operated directly by the corps with the rest leased out to various other government entities. In addition to the ubiquitous boat ramps, there are eight marinas.

Periodic draught in the region has also led to frequently low water levels. While there are over 100 boat ramp lanes in theory, in practice a percentage are often closed due to low water levels. The lowest level recorded since the lake's construction in the 1950s was during the severe drought of 2007.

By far the most upscale and comprehensive lodging on the lake is **ⓒ Lake Lanier Islands Resort** (7000 Lanier Islands Pkwy., 770/945-8787, www.lakelanierislands.com, $200-600). In addition to a variety of guest rooms, suites, lake houses, and villas, it has its own **golf course** (greens fees start at $50),

Canopy Zip-Line Tours ($200 full day, $30 "express"), a boat landing, an Equestrian Center (rides from $35), and even its own water park, LanierWorld ($35 adults, $20 children, lower after dark). Other amenities and activities include miniature golf, tennis, and volleyball. The main Legacy Lodge building features frequent live entertainment. Business travelers have use of the attached conference center. For those who want a more laid-back or luxurious vibe, there is a campground and hiking trails, and of course a full-service spa. While the intent is to provide anything and everything for the whole family with full lake access, interestingly there are no pet-friendly facilities at the resort. You don't have to be a registered guest to enjoy many of the à la carte amenities; the $10 gate fee (which guests also have to pay) entitles you to entrance and parking.

The Corps of Engineers operates several reservable campgrounds (www.recreation.gov, $30) on Lake Lanier with nearly 500 campsites: Bald Ridge Creek; Bolding Mill; Duckett Mill; Old Federal; Sawnee; and Van Pugh South Campground. Keep in mind they are seasonal, mostly due to lower water levels in the winter; check the website in advance. While there are many islands strewn throughout the lake and accessible by boat, you're not supposed to camp on them.

GAINESVILLE

Gainesville is chiefly known for two things: Its supposed status as "Poultry Capital of the World," a nod to the many chicken processing plants in the area; and as the home of Confederate general James Longstreet, Robert E. Lee's second-in-command. Despite his Confederate bona fides, Longstreet was quick to embrace northern Reconstruction policies after the Civil War, even becoming an active Republican during a time when that was considered borderline traitorous for a white Southerner. Get to Gainesville from Atlanta via I-85 north; take I-985/Lanier Parkway into town.

Piedmont Hotel

Opened by General James Longstreet in 1876,

over the years the Piedmont Hotel (827 Maple St., 770/539-9005, www.longstreetsociety.org, Tues.-Sat. 10am-4pm, free) has been reduced to only the ground floor of its former three-story opulence. It's a museum of sorts now and home to the Longstreet Society (www.longstreetsociety.org), dedicated to preserving the memory of the general. They have a good Longstreet-oriented walking tour at the website, which includes the hotel itself. President Woodrow Wilson's daughter Jesse was born in one of the rooms. Longtime *Atlanta Journal-Constitution* editor Henry Grady was a frequent guest, as was Joel Chandler Harris of "Uncle Remus" fame. Local lore has it that what we now know as Southern fried chicken was first cooked in the Piedmont's kitchen.

Alta Vista Cemetery

General James Longstreet was laid to rest in Alta Vista Cemetery (1080 Jesse Jewell Pkwy.). Well-wishers often leave cigars at his gravesite, an homage to the general's favorite vice. You'll also find the graves of many other Confederate veterans, a Space Shuttle astronaut, and Daniel Boone, though not *that* Daniel Boone. The cemetery's name means "high view" in Spanish, and the scenic hilltop location certainly provides that. Download a walking tour at www.gainesville.org.

Northeast Georgia History Center

The little Northeast Georgia History Center (322 Academy St., 770/297-5900, Tues.-Sat. 10am-4pm, $5 adults, $3 children) has some modest exhibits from the Gainesville area's history, which includes Northeast Georgia Sports Hall of Fame and the restored circa-1780 log cabin of Chief White Path of the Cherokee people. There's also a little Freedom Garden dedicated to veterans.

ARABIA MOUNTAIN NATIONAL HERITAGE AREA

Two wonderful areas of pristine nature right outside the concrete jungle of Atlanta are Panola Mountain State Park (2600 Hwy.

155, 770/389-7801, www.gastateparks.org, daily 7am-dusk, parking $5), near the suburban town of Stockbridge, and **Davidson-Arabia Nature Preserve** (3787 Klondike Rd., 770/492-5231, www.arabiaalliance.org, daily dawn-dusk, free) near Lithonia. Both areas are part of the Arabia Mountain National Heritage Area, administered by a cooperative partnership of local groups, and both are centered on enormous granite outcroppings similar to the larger Stone Mountain but without the attendant development.

Panola Mountain is known for its rich and rare botanical treasure, such as yellow daisies and Diamorpha. Because of its fragile ecosystem, hiking is allowed only through guided tours (depart from the park's nature center, generally Wed. and Fri.-Sun. 8am, $7 pp). Hikers have full use of Davidson-Arabia, with trails accessible from Klondike Road or by trailheads on the paved, 20-mile Rockdale River-Panola Mountain PATH Trail, which is open to bicycles and leashed dogs.

Panola Mountain and Arabia Mountain are both easily accessible from Atlanta by taking I-20 east. For Panola Mountain, get off at exit 68 and take Highway 155. For Arabia Mountain get off at Klondike Road, exit 74.

SENOIA

At the very edge of metro Atlanta—about 25 miles south—is Senoia (pronounced "seh-NOY"), better known to fans of the cable TV series *The Walking Dead* as Woodbury. In fact, shooting of the incredibly popular show is so integral to the economy of this 3,000-person burg that several buildings on Main Street, purpose-built for the show, simply bear the name of the fictional town, such as Woodbury Town Hall. Main Street itself is often closed for weeks during shooting, with on-camera lawns left unmowed in suitably apocalyptic style.

The unofficial hub of town activity is **Senoia Coffee & Café** (1 Main St., 770/599-8000, http://senoiacoffeeandcafe.com, Mon.-Thurs. 6:30am-3pm, Fri. 6:30am-9pm, Sat. 7:30am-9pm), also known as the Woodbury Coffee House from the show. Have a cup of Zombie Dark java and maybe overhear chatter from "Walker Stalkers"—admittedly obsessive fans—while the crew is in town filming.

For pub-style eats and entertainment, go to **Southern Ground Social Club** (18 Main St., 770/727-9014, www.southerngroundsocialclub.com, Tues.-Sat. 11am-2am, $15), owned by native son and country star Zac Brown. The limited menu is tasty; try the fried green tomato BLT. As you'd expect, most nights feature live music.

ATLANTA

NORTH GEORGIA

The southern tip of the Appalachian Mountain chain pushes into the northern portion of Georgia like a boot heel. Though crisscrossed by gorges, rivers, creeks, and hollows, North Georgia is a distinctly accessible mountainous area, more logistically forgiving than many areas farther into the Blue Ridge, but with a similar culture of self-sufficiency.

The northeastern portion of Georgia between the great coastal plain to the south and the mountainous regions of the far north has been a hotbed of activity from the earliest days of the colony. Today, exurban Atlanta has encroached on its western edge.

PLANNING YOUR TIME

It's theoretically possible to barnstorm through North Georgia in a day or two by car, just seeing the highlights. The northeast section has more sights and more and better roads; that said, in the summer those two-lane roads, especially in the Helen area, can get pretty crowded with vacationers.

The Piedmont hosts the state's largest university, in Athens. It can easily be experienced by car with a minimum of travel time. Using Athens as a base, you can take a fun day-trip circle route to Madison, Greensboro, Washington, and back.

© JIM MOREKIS

HIGHLIGHTS

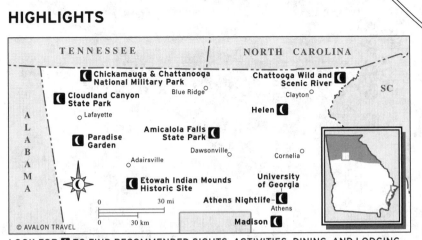

© AVALON TRAVEL

LOOK FOR 🌙 TO FIND RECOMMENDED SIGHTS, ACTIVITIES, DINING, AND LODGING.

🌙 **Chattooga Wild and Scenic River:** Take a raft ride on the Carolina border down through *Deliverance* country (page 534).

🌙 **Helen:** A little cheesy and a lot of fun, this "Alpine village" recreates *The Sound of Music* experience, but with beer (page 537).

🌙 **Amicalola Falls State Park:** View the tallest waterfall east of the Mississippi River, near where the Appalachian Trail begins (page 539).

🌙 **Etowah Indian Mounds Historic Site:** Climb to the top of an ancient Native American temple mound at this excellently preserved site and museum (page 547).

🌙 **Chickamauga & Chattanooga National Military Park:** Take in the huge battlefield where the Confederacy won its last major victory (page 548).

🌙 **Paradise Garden:** Immerse yourself in the eccentric, prolific vision of iconic folk artist Howard Finster (page 550).

🌙 **Cloudland Canyon State Park:** Dotted with caves, this fascinating geological feature offers jaw-dropping views and great hiking and spelunking (page 551).

🌙 **University of Georgia:** The nation's oldest chartered university is on a beautiful shaded campus full of historic buildings (page 552).

🌙 **Athens Nightlife:** The legacy of the B-52s and R.E.M. live on in this college town's robust live music scene (page 556).

🌙 **Madison:** One of the most charming and well-preserved old Southern towns is chock-full of eclectic and interesting architecture (page 561).

NORTH GEORGIA

NORTH GEORGIA

Sumter National Forest

Greenwood

Edgefield

Savannah River

Augusta

25

Harlem

278

1

25 mi

25 km

SOUTH CAROLINA

Greenville

Anderson

Clemson

CHATTOOGA WILD AND SCENIC RIVER

Chattooga River

Tallulah Gorge State Park

Black Rock Mountain State Park

Dillard

Clayton

123

Toccoa

Sautee Nacoochee

Clarkesville

HELEN

Hiawassee

Brasstown Bald

Unicoi State Park

Blairsville

Vogel State Park

75

Dahlonega

Springer Mountain

AMICALOLA FALLS STATE PARK

Chattahoochee National Forest

Nantahala National Forest

Appalachian Trail

Ellijay

Cohutta Mountains

Chatsworth

53

CHIEF VANN HOUSE HISTORIC SITE

NEW ECHOTA HISTORIC SITE

Dalton

76

Tunnel Hill

TENNESSEE

Chattanooga

75

CHICKAMAUGA & CHATTANOOGA NATIONAL MILITARY PARK

LaFayette

Johns Mountain

PARADISE GARDEN

Summerville

Lookout Mountain

CLOUDLAND CANYON STATE PARK

Trenton

ALABAMA

Talladega National Forest

Cedartown

Carrollton

Rome

Cartersville

411

ETOWAH INDIAN MOUNDS HISTORIC SITE

Allatoona Lake

5

75

278

20

LaGrange

85

Senoia

16

Hampton

41

19

75

Stockbridge

Conyers

Covington

Social Circle

20

ATLANTA

85

19

23

Lake Hartwell

Gainesville

Lake Sidney Lanier

Smithgall Woods State Park

129

UNIVERSITY OF GEORGIA

Athens

NIGHTLIFE

11

MADISON

278

Oconee National Forest

Lake Oconee

129

22

Milledgeville

GEORGIA

16

Greensboro

Crawfordville

Washington

Greenwood

78

72

Elberton

Royston

Victoria Bryant State Park

Lake Hartwell

85

29

Lake Russell

Clarks Hill Lake

Sumter National Forest

© AVALON TRAVEL

Rabun County

In the northeast corner of the state on the border of the Carolinas, the Rabun County area (www.gamountains.com) is one of the most visited portions of North Georgia. It's where you'll find some of the state's most scenic vistas.

Rabun hit the global map in the 1890s, when the high Tallulah Falls Railway was constructed along the Tallulah Gorge, the deepest east of the Mississippi River. The Railway brought vacationers to various Victorian-style mountain resorts, and the area served as the scenic location for several movies, including *The Great Locomotive Chase* and the Burt Reynolds film *Deliverance.*

CLAYTON

The Rabun County seat is Clayton (www. downtownclaytonga.org), a diverse little mountain town with rustic charm to spare but still a full slate of offerings for the more sophisticated traveler to this very conservative part of the country.

The **Rabun County Welcome Center** (232 U.S. 441, 706/782-4812, www.gamountains. com) is a good first stop. For a quick look at local history, go to the museum and research library at the **Rabun County Historical Society** (81 North Church St., Mon. 10am-2pm, Wed. 12:30pm-4:30pm, Fri. 10am-2pm) near the county courthouse.

My favorite restaurant in this part of North Georgia is **C** **Zeppelin's** (88 Main St., 706/212-0101, www.zeppelinspastahouse.com, Mon.-Thurs. 11:30am-9pm, Fri.-Sat. 11am-10pm, Sun. 11am-9pm, $12). A menu of perfectly crispy flatbread pizzas (about $15 and big enough for two) is their main claim to fame,

© AVALON TRAVEL

NORTH GEORGIA

© JIM MOREKIS

on the whitewater on the Chattooga River

but their burgers are incredible as well, including a bison option.

A short drive north of Clayton is **Tomlin's Barbecue** (5030 U.S. 441, 706/982-1750, www.tomlinbbq.com, May-Oct. Fri.-Sun. 10:30am-4:30pm, $7), set in a little red cabin adjacent to the Osage Farms Produce Market. They offer some sublime smoked pulled pork and a distinctive vinegar sauce.

Foxfire Museum & Heritage Center

For nearly 50 years, the *Foxfire* book and magazine series has chronicled and preserved the dwindling folkways of the southern Appalachians in North Georgia. The Foxfire organization funds and runs the **Foxfire Museum & Heritage Center** (Black Mountain Pkwy., 706/746-5828, www.foxfire.org, Mon.-Sat. 8:30am-4:30pm, $6 over age 10, $3 ages 7-10, free under age 6) in Mountain City, a few minutes north of Clayton. This collection of vernacular log buildings just off U.S. 441 contains a wealth of authentic displays

and equipment portraying the daily life of mountain people in this area. Each October in downtown Clayton is the **Foxfire Mountaineer Festival** (www.foxfire.org).

Dillard

North of Clayton and Mountain City near the North Carolina border, the first settlement in the area is named after the founding family, whose legacy continues at **The Dillard House** (1158 Franklin St., 800/541-0671, www.dillardhouse.com, restaurant daily 7am-10:30am and 11:30am-8pm, $15-25), a grand bed-and-breakfast-style inn with a variety of guest rooms and cottages. You don't have to be a guest to enjoy a nice meal here: The family-style community restaurant on-site features down-home Southern comfort food and plenty of it.

◖ CHATTOOGA WILD AND SCENIC RIVER

If you've seen the 1972 film *Deliverance,* you've seen the Chattooga River (www.rivers.gov), the South's best white-water rafting

© AVALON TRAVEL

GEORGIA

Chattahoochee
National Forest

To Clayton

Chattooga
River Trail

Bartram Trail

SOUTHEASTERN
EXPEDITIONS
RAFTING
OUTPOST

28

SECTION 1

884

EARL'S FORD RD

EARL'S FORD

SECTION 2

DICK'S CREEK RD

SECTION 3

721

193

196

Mountain Rest

Sumter
National
Forest

River

0   1 mi

0   1 km

SECTION 4

76

BULL SLUICE
OVERLOOK

NANTAHALA OUTDOOR
CENTER RAFTING
OUTPOST

WILDWATER LTD
RAFTING OUTPOST

Long Creek

CHATTOOGA
WHITEWATER
OUTFITTERS

SOUTH
CAROLINA

Chattooga

Tugaloo
Lake

CHATTOOGA WILD AND SCENIC RIVER

locale (in the movie it bore the fictional name "Cahulawassee"). The Chattooga River forms part of the Georgia–South Carolina border. If you're white-water rafting, you'll likely be putting in farther upstream, but the easiest way to get to the Chattooga is to take U.S. 76 until you just cross the Chattooga River Bridge into South Carolina. On the Carolina side is a sizeable parking area, unfortunately with subpar restroom facilities. You can park in Georgia if you'd like, but there's a $2 parking fee and fewer spaces.

Bull Sluice Falls is a popular thrill-seeking point for rafters and kayakers at the end of Section III of the river, with a 14-foot drop when the river is at full level (Bull Sluice also had a starring role in *Deliverance*). Bull Sluice is also a popular free place for area families to enjoy a dip in the cool water with the roaring sounds of the sluice.

For recreational purposes the Chattooga is divided into four sections. Section I is primarily for anglers. Section II begins at Highway 28

and ends at Earl's Ford, where there's a 0.25-mile hike to reach vehicles. This is a great little seven-mile run for families, tubers, and novice rafters. The real action begins at Section III, a 14-mile run from Earl's Ford to the U.S. 76 bridge, with a 0.25-mile walk to put in. Beginning with Warwoman Rapid, you'll get a lot of Class II, III, and IV rapids, including the final Class IV-V rapid at Bull Sluice, which concludes Section III. In all, Section III will take 6-8 hours from beginning to end. The most challenging ride is Section IV, from the U.S. 76 bridge to the river's end at Lake Tugaloo.

For serious rafting, the starting points are upriver on the South Carolina side. The main professional rafting tour company on the river is **Nantahala Outdoor Center** (888/905-7238, www.noc.com, prices vary). Expect to pay at least $85 pp, more during the high season in the summer. While walk-ins are welcome, I recommend reserving your trip in advance. Another popular Chattooga rafting guide is **Wildwater Rafting** (800/451-9972, www.wildwaterrafting.com, prices vary).

The prime independent outfitter is **Chattooga Whitewater Outfitters** (14239 U.S. 76, Long Creek, 864/647-9083, www.chattoogawhitewatershop.com). If you find yourself craving some carbs after a day of whitewater rafting on the Chattooga, check out the pizza joint **Humble Pie** (14239 U.S. 76, Long Creek, 864/647-9083, www.chattoogawhitewatershop.com, Tues.-Sun. 3pm-10pm, $10), within and owned by Chattooga Whitewater Outfitters.

BLACK ROCK MOUNTAIN STATE PARK

The highest state park in Georgia and one of the most enjoyable, **Black Rock Mountain State Park** (3085 Black Rock Mountain Pkwy., 706/746-2141, www.gastateparks.org, Mar.-Nov. daily 7am-10pm, parking $5, campsites $25-28, walk-in campsites $15, cottages $125-145) attracts particularly large crowds during leaf-turning season in the fall. The visitors center at the summit of the mountain is a

NORTH GEORGIA

© JIM MOREKIS

scenic views at Black Rock Mountain State Park

popular place for its relaxing views. Campers will find 44 tent and RV sites, 10 cottages, and a dozen walk-in campsites.

MOCCASIN CREEK STATE PARK

Moccasin Creek State Park (3655 Hwy. 197, 706/947-3194, www.gastateparks.org, Mar.-Nov. daily 7am-10pm, parking $5, campsites $25), nestled up against quiet, pretty Lake Burton, is focused on boating and fishing. Camping is a little snug here, with tent and RV gravel sites fairly close together. But it's a fine place for water recreation, with docks, a boat ramp, and a fishing pier open only to disabled people, seniors, and children.

Wildcat Creek

Just around the corner from Lake Burton is the access road to the hidden gem of **Wildcat Creek** (Forest Rd. 26, www.fs.usda.gov, campsites $10, first come, first served, no

water) in Chattahoochee-Oconee National Forest. You'll find outstanding fishing in the creek stocked with rainbow trout. Lining Wildcat Creek are two primitive campgrounds run by the U.S. Forest Service. Hikers can access the Appalachian Trail from this route as well. A sturdy 4WD vehicle is strongly recommended.

TALLULAH GORGE STATE PARK

Tallulah Gorge State Park (338 Jane Hurt Yarn Dr., 706/754-7981, www.gastateparks. org, daily 8am-dusk, parking $5) has been one of the state's most visited parks since its inception in the 1990s. It contains the eponymous and iconic Tallulah Falls as well as a vast area on either side of the deepest gorge (1,000 feet) in the eastern United States.

Your first stop is the **Jane Hurt Yarn Interpretive Center** (daily 8am-5pm), a combined visitors center and museum. This is where you get your free permit to hike to the floor of the gorge (only permit holders can go all the way to the bottom, and only 100 permits are given out each day; get here as early as you can).

For the less adventurous or those with less time, a simple walk along the north rim includes several viewing points. You may choose to go down the 531-step staircase and across a suspension walking bridge to the bottom of the gorge (you'll need a permit to actually walk onto the rocky bottom). Along the way you'll see the old iron towers used to stage Karl Wallenda's famous tightrope walk across the gorge in 1970. The most adventurous hikers can take the long trek from there to **Bridal Veil Falls,** where the only swimming in the park is allowed. At 600 feet, the second-tallest waterfall in the state is **Caledonia Cascade,** sometimes called Cascade Falls, near the beginning of Tallulah gorge. You can see it from the hiking trail around the rim.

The trail system within the park is extensive. Lodging within the park includes 50 tent and RV sites and three backcountry shelters ($15).

NORTH GEORGIA

Helen and Vicinity

The area around Helen is picturesque, easily accessible, and offers plenty of visitor amenities. No wonder, then, that it's an extremely popular summer and fall vacation spot, especially for day-trippers from metro Atlanta.

◧ HELEN

For generations of Georgians, the word "Helen" has either meant a fun place to get away in the mountains, a hilariously cheesy living theme park, or a combination of both. Situated in a neat little valley at the headwaters of the Chattahoochee River, this once-decrepit former logging town was literally rebuilt from scratch in the late 1960s specifically to mimic a stereotypical German-Swiss mountain village. Local regulations require that every structure conform to the classic Alpine look that feels familiar to most people from *The Sound of Music.*

© JIM MOREKIS

in the "Alpine village" of Helen

The highlight of the year is the annual **Oktoberfest** (706/878-1908, www.helen-chamber.com, $8 Mon.-Fri., $9 Sat., free Sun.) centering around the town's Festhalle (1074 Edelweiss Strasse). Unlike many towns that hold similar events, Oktoberfest in Helen is no mere long weekend: It lasts from mid-September through the end of October. In true German style, the Festhalle is filled with rows of long tables for you to enjoy your beer and brats and listen to oompah music.

Sights

Charlemagne's Kingdom (8808 N. Main St., 706/878-2200, www.georgiamodelrailroad.com, Thurs.-Tues. 10am-5pm, $5) is the labor of love of a German couple who, over the course of the last two decades, have built an entirely self-contained little part of Germany traversed by an extensive model railroad, featuring over 400 feet of indoor track.

Sixteen bears are the attraction at the **Black Forest Bear Park** (8160 S. Main St., 706/878-7043, www.blackforestbearpark.com, Sun.-Fri. 10am-6pm, Sat. 10am-7pm, $5), right downtown. An extra buck buys you a tray of apples and bread to feed them. While the bears are obviously well fed and will do tricks for snacks, their living conditions aren't exactly state-of-the-art and might offend not only animal rights activists but a goodly portion of visitors. On the plus side, all the bears, including a grizzly, are rescues.

Accommodations and Food

Quality chain lodging in Helen is scarce, but you can try the entirely Alpine-themed **Hampton Inn** (147 Unicoi St., 706/878-3310, www.hamptoninn.com, $100) or the **Country Inn & Suites** (877 Edelweiss Strasse, 706/878-9000, www.countryinns.com, $110-150) for a cut above the typical chain experience. For a

NORTH GEORGIA

romantic, and yes, German-themed getaway, head to **Black Forest Bed & Breakfast** (8902 N. Main St., 706/878-3995, www.blackforest-vacationrentals.com, $135-250).

The oldest German restaurant in Helen, the iconic **Old Heidelberg** (8660 N. Main St., 706/878-3273, spring-fall daily 11:30am-9pm, $20) calls itself the "most photographed building in Georgia." The menu has an entire page of schnitzel (about $20) and another for sausage dishes ($15). Conveniently across the street from the town's Festhalle, (**Bodensee** (64 Munichstrasse, 706/878-1026, spring-fall daily 11:30am-8pm, $15) is serves a mean jaeger schnitzel along with all the other staples.

SAUTEE NACOOCHEE

Directly adjacent to Helen is the more tasteful little community of Sautee Nacoochee. The **Folk Pottery Museum of Northeast Georgia** (283 Hwy. 255, 706/878-3300, www.folkpotterymuseum.com, Mon.-Sat. 10am-5pm, Sun. 1pm-5pm, $5 adults, $2 children), is within the Sautee Nacoochee Cultural Center. For the classic old-school country store experience, including the famous resident kitty "Wampus Cat," head to the **Old Sautee Store** (2315 Hwy. 17, 706/878-2281, www.oldsauteestore.com, Mon.-Sat. 10am-5:30pm, Sun. noon-5:30pm). **Sautee Nacoochee Vineyards** (1299 Hwy. 17, 706/878-1056, www.sauteenacoocheevineyards.com, Mon.-Sat. noon-6pm) features a tasting room and deck overlooking the foothills.

(**Lucille's Mountain Top Inn & Spa** (964 Rabun Rd., 706/878-5055, www.lucillesmountaintopinn.com, $200) is a far cry from Helen's tourism boom and offers a great place to get away from it all. The views from the balconies are stunning and the spa facilities are easily some of the best in the area. If you need a break from all things German, head directly to (**Nacoochee Village Tavern & Pizzeria** (7275 S. Main St., 706/878-0199, www.villagetavernpizza.com, Mon.-Thurs.

noon-10pm, Fri.-Sat. noon-11pm, Sun. 1pm-10pm, $15), known for wood-firing some of the best pizza in North Georgia.

RAVEN CLIFF FALLS

Situated within the massive **Raven Cliffs Wilderness Area** (www.fs.usda.gov), itself a major trout-fishing and hiking mecca, Raven Cliff Falls on Dodd Creek is one of North Georgia's most popular cascades despite being a relatively strenuous five-mile round-trip hike. The falls, with a total drop of 400 feet, are present in several sections along the hike. There is walk-in camping, but it's not particularly recommended due to the crowds. To get here, take Highway 75 north from Helen about a 1.5 miles and turn left onto Highway 356. From there go about 2.5 miles to the Richard B. Russell Scenic Highway, then turn right and go 3 miles to the well-marked trailhead and parking area.

SMITHGALL WOODS STATE PARK

With a focus on education, **Smithgall Woods State Park** (61 Tsalaki Tr., 706/878-3087, www.gastateparks.org, visitors center daily 8am-5pm, parking $5) is a delightful gem a bit north of Helen. The rustically attractive main visitors center (daily 8am-5pm) contains displays on flora and fauna, with the highlight being the nearby raptor aviary, where rescued birds of prey live under care. There is no camping at Smithgall Woods per se, but there are five reservable and perhaps surprisingly upscale cottages ($150-500).

UNICOI STATE PARK

Unicoi State Park and Lodge (1788 Hwy. 356, 706/878-2201, www.gastateparks.org, parking $5, tents and RVs $29-35, walk-in campsites $25, cottages $80-100) offers something for everyone on a sprawling 1,000 acres within a few miles of Helen. There are nearly 100 camping spaces for tents and RVs and a couple dozen walk-in tent sites, a vast array of charming cottages in various multilevel clusters, and the associated 100-room lodge (800/573-9659, $75-100).

Anna Ruby Falls

Although it is within Unicoi State Park, **Anna Ruby Falls** (www.fs.usda.gov, daily 9am-6pm, entry gate closes 5pm, $3) is run by the U.S. Forest Service and requires a separate admission. However, it's worth the nominal fee, not only for the perfectly situated twin falls themselves—uniting to form Smith Creek at the bottom, which itself empties into Unicoi Lake and, much later, eventually to the Gulf of Mexico—but for the relaxing, scenic walk from the parking area and visitors center to the falls. While Unicoi and the falls both have separate admission, if all you're going to do is visit the falls, the state park will waive the entrance fee.

CLARKESVILLE

The seat of Habersham County, Clarkesville is primarily known for its tidy downtown shopping area and one of the premier B&B's in the state: **(Glen-Ella Springs Inn** (1789 Bear Gap Rd., 706/754-7295, www.glenella.com, $150-275). Set in a restored yet still rustic-feeling 1800s building on a scenic 12 acres, Glen-Ella's 16 guest rooms all boast covered porches with rocking chairs. The attached restaurant (daily 6pm-10pm, $25) is considered one of Georgia's best, and it's open to nonguests.

A few miles north of Clarkesville on Highway 197 is the venerable and charming pottery makers' collective **Mark of the Potter** (9982 Hwy. 197 N., 706/947-3440, www.markofthepotter.com, daily 10am-6pm), set within the restored Watts gristmill.

The Appalachian Trail

Following the lead of the country's first conservationist president, Theodore Roosevelt, the first stirrings of the concept of a national "super-trail" began making the rounds in the early 1920s. Work soon began on what was then called "America's Footpath."

By 1937 the entire Appalachian Trail was finished on both ends, from Georgia to Maine. However, almost immediately a hurricane did heavy damage to the path, and Skyline Drive was extended to the Blue Ridge Parkway in the 1940s, which destroyed a 120-mile-long section of the trail.

Renewed interest in the trail came in the postwar years. The designation of the Appalachian Trail, or "AT" as it's often known, as a National Scenic Trail in 1968 cemented its status as a national treasure under federal protection.

(AMICALOLA FALLS STATE PARK

Home of the tallest cascade east of the Mississippi River, **Amicalola Falls State Park** (418 Amicalola Falls State Park Rd., 706/265-8888, www.gastateparks.org, daily 7am-10pm, visitors center daily 8:30am-5pm, parking $5) also happens to be a main gateway to the Appalachian Trail. It's an extremely popular park, especially during leaf-viewing season in the fall. The magnificent 730-foot falls are one of the "Seven Natural Wonders of Georgia" and are worth the crowds.

Lodging at Amicalola (www.galodges.com) includes the **Amicalola Falls Lodge** (from $150) near the top of the falls. You can also opt to stay in one of 14 rustic cottages. However, the most unique lodging at Amicalola is the **(Len Foote Hike Inn** (www.hike-inn.com, $100-140), an eco-friendly hiker's lodge that's a five-mile trek

THE APPALACHIAN TRAIL

from the main park area. Run by a nonprofit, the inn has a staff that lives on-site. The 20 guest rooms are really only intended for sleeping, but the communal areas are charmingly appointed. From Hike Inn, it is another mile to reach the AT.

There are a total of 12 miles of trails in the park, with the most popular and famous being the 8.5-mile **Southern Terminus Approach Trail** from the falls to Springer Mountain, the bottom tip of the AT.

SPRINGER MOUNTAIN

Reached by the Southern Terminus Approach Trail from Amicalola Falls, Springer Mountain, the springboard of the south-north traverse of the Appalachian Trail, is nearly 4,000 feet in elevation and about 2,100 miles from the trail's other end in Maine. A day-use parking area below on Forest Road 42 allows you to take a hike up and around on top; many AT hikers begin here instead of at Amicalola Falls, cutting almost nine miles off the total trip.

Georgia's section of the AT (www.appalachiantrail.org) is 76 miles long, from Springer Mountain to Bly Gap and on into North Carolina. At its highest point in Georgia, Blood Mountain, the AT is 4,460 feet above sea level; its low spot is Dicks Creek Gap at 2,675 feet. White rectangular blazes mark the trail, and turns are marked with double blazes.

Blairsville and Brasstown Bald

The largest town in north central Georgia, but still pretty small, Blairsville is a good base of operations from which to enjoy the Union County-Brasstown Bald area.

BLAIRSVILLE
Sights

Blairsville (www.visitblairsvillega.com) has done a particularly nice job restoring the

historic 1899 **Union County Courthouse** (1 Town Square, 706/745-5493, www.unioncountyhistory.org, Mon.-Sat. 10am-4pm, $2 adults, $1 children), which now hosts a modest local history museum and a variety of concerts.

The country's largest single O-gauge model train display, **Misty Mountain Model Railroad** (4381 Misty Mountain Lane, 706/745-9819, www.mistymountainmodelrailroad.com,

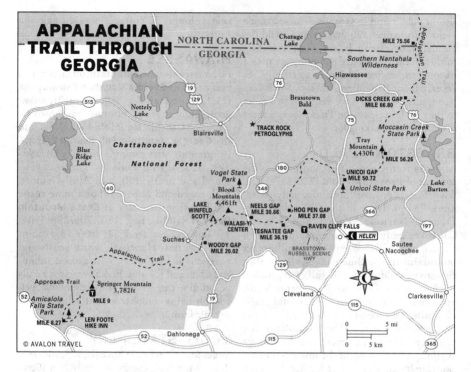

tours Mon., Wed., Fri., Sat. 2pm, $5 pp) features 14 trains on a mile of track with a variety of bridges and tunnels. The display simulates various portions of North Georgia topography, including the Tallulah Gorge.

Former Disney model-maker Art Millican used his experience to make **Sleepy Hollow Enterprises** (4339 Young Harris Hwy., 706/379-9622, www.whimsicalfairygarden. com, Mon.-Sat. 9:30am-4:30pm, free), a collection of fairies, hobbits, and the like gamboling in their own eccentric habitat.

Accommodations and Food

People love the rocker on the front porch at **Granny's Cabin** (55 Old Beech Rd., 727/585-3132, www.grannyscabin.net, $95) about five miles out of Blairsville. It's all about relaxation here in this two-bedroom, two-bath cabin. Pets are not allowed. **Your Home in the Woods Bed & Breakfast** (2830 Timber Lane,

706/745-9337, www.yourhomeinthewoods. com, $80-100) near Blairsville is a getaway nestled up against a woodsy hillside with three guest rooms to choose from.

☾   Dan's Grill (305 Murphy Hwy., 706/745-0013, Tues.-Thurs. 10am-8pm, Fri.-Sat. 10am-9pm, Sun. 11am-4pm, $10) has an unusual specialty for this area: Cuban food. And Dan makes a killer Cuban sandwich, great plantains, succulent flank steaks, and even tasty Cuban tamales. Get some outstanding pulled pork or ribs at **Jim's Smokin' Que** (4971 Gainesville Hwy./Hwy. 129, 706/835-7427, www.jimssmokinque.com, Thurs.-Sat. 11am-8pm, $8-12).

TRACK ROCK PETROGLYPHS

Track Rock Gap (Track Rock Gap Rd., 706/745-6928, www.fs.usda.gov, daily dawn-dusk, free) with its ancient Native American rock carvings, or petroglyphs, is the only such

NORTH GEORGIA

site on public land in Georgia. The soapstone rocks feature over 100 depictions of wildlife, animal tracks, symbols, and footprints. Get to this recently renovated site complete with a historic marker from Blairsville by taking U.S. 76 east about five miles. At Track Rock Gap Road, turn right and drive for about two miles to the gap. Drive past the Track Rocks a short distance to the parking lot.

BRASSTOWN BALD

At 4,784 feet, Georgia's highest point is the summit of **Brasstown Bald** (770/297-3000, www.fs.usda.gov, visitors center daily 10am-4pm, $3 pp). Deep in the Chattahoochee-Oconee National Forest and historic Cherokee country, the mountain is called Enotah by the Cherokee people. Unlike other mountains in the Blue Ridge called balds, Brasstown Bald is actually full of vegetation to the summit. On clear days, theoretically, you can see four states from the nostalgically charming and well-built observation deck: Georgia, Tennessee, and both Carolinas. You can even occasionally make out the Atlanta skyline. (The very top of the tower is for fire-spotting by the U.S. Forest Service, however, and is off-limits to visitors.)

Hike up from the parking area, about one mile round-trip, or wait for the frequent but seasonal shuttle buses ($3) to chug you up the winding path to the top. The visitors center underneath the observation tower has a number of interesting exhibits. Pack a lunch—the views from the picnic area are awesome.

The upscale lodging of note in the area is the fantastic ◖ **Brasstown Valley Resort and Spa** (6321 U.S. 76, 706/379-9900, www.brasstownvalley.com, $200) on a lush and scenic 500 acres near the town of Young Harris. There are 102 guest rooms in the central lodge, 32 cottages, and a single spa suite.

HIAWASSEE

Hiawassee (www.mountaintopga.com) is known for its **Georgia Mountain Fairgrounds** (1311 Music Hall Rd., 706/896-4191, www.georgiamountainfairgrounds.com), which hosts the **Georgia Mountain Fair** (July) and the **Georgia Mountain Fall Festival** (Oct.). Fairgrounds offer camping as well (706/896-4191, $21-34) with nearly 100 sites open year-round and nearly 200 open April-October, both paved and unpaved. For a more rustic brush with nature stay at **Enota Mountain Retreat** (1000 Hwy. 180, 706/896-7504, www.enota.com, tents $25, RVs $35, cabins $110-165) near Hiawassee, which boasts four waterfalls on its 60 acres. With a motel, cabins, and a tent and RV area, Enota combines a truly beautiful setting with no-frills, communal, pet-friendly living complete with attached 10-acre organic farm.

VOGEL STATE PARK

Vogel State Park (405 State Rt. 129, 706/745-2628, www.gastateparks.org, daily 7am-10pm, parking $5) is one of Georgia's oldest and most beloved. There's plenty of hiking with lots to see, including a peaceful 22-acre lake (no motorized watercraft allowed), complete with a little beachfront area, and the small but wonderful **Trahlyta Falls**. There's a 13-mile backcountry trail, and you can access the Appalachian Trail from the park as well. Perhaps the most unique aspect is the museum dedicated to the Civilian Conservation Corps (CCC), which constructed Vogel (along with many other Southern state parks) in the 1930s. This is also one of the better Georgia parks for camping, with roomy, woodsy sites.

Dahlonega

Epicenter of one of the first gold rushes in the United States, Dahlonega (www.dahlonega.org) still retains a fitting frontier vibe. Most everything in town revolves around either the town's literally golden history or the student life of North Georgia College and State University, the distinctive gold-leaf steeple of its administration building dominating the skyline. However, "purple gold" is making a big impact on the area these days in the form of a burgeoning wine region. The highlight of the Dahlonega calendar is the **Gold Rush Days** (www.dahlonegajaycees.com) festival every October, which features food, fun, and music in the square.

SIGHTS
Dahlonega Gold Museum State Historic Site

The **Dahlonega Gold Museum State Historic Site** (1 Public Square, 706/864-2257, www.gastateparks.org, Mon.-Sat. 9am-5pm, Sun. 10am-5pm, $6 adults, $3.50 children) is in the old 1836 Courthouse building, itself of great significance as the oldest surviving courthouse in Georgia. The museum commemorates and explains the phenomenon of the Georgia gold rush and Dahlonega's role in it. Don't miss the excellent short film upstairs documenting the gold rush with oral history from Georgians who worked the mines, many still open well into the 20th century. The seats in the theater are the courthouse's original courtroom benches.

Crisson Gold Mine

The only remaining working gold mine in Georgia is the **Crisson Gold Mine** (2736 Morrison Moore Pkwy., 706/864-6363, www.crissongoldmine.com, daily 10am-6pm, cost varies). You can pan for gold or just shop for

© JIM MOREKIS

Dahlonega Gold Museum State Historic Site

GOLD IN THEM THAR HILLS

An accident of geology put one of the world's largest, most accessible, and purest veins of gold in North Georgia, a diagonal swath running northeast to southwest with its epicenter in Lumpkin County. Millions of years after being formed it would spur one of the first gold rushes in the United States.

Georgia gold is legendary for its extraordinary purity: in some places as high as 98 percent (most miners are happy with 80 percent). While the quality was certainly part of its allure, most of the draw was its easy abundance. Indeed, local legend has it that a hunter began the rush in 1828 by literally tripping over a huge nugget.

The earliest method was placer mining (pronounced "plasser"), which involves sorting through alluvial deposits by an open-pit technique or by the old familiar "panning for gold." However, within a few years the most easily accessible gold in North Georgia had been discovered. Mining techniques became much more invasive, including hydraulic mining—essentially erasing entire mountainsides with very powerful hoses—or the classic dynamite-in-the-shaft method.

Above and below ground, the mines were everywhere, and the environmental devastation they caused can be seen to this day. The human devastation included the brutal removal of Native Americans and the Trail of Tears.

The sheer volume of gold extracted from these Appalachian foothills was so impressive that the U.S. Mint decided it would be more efficient to build a new branch in Dahlonega in 1838; it stayed open until the Civil War. You can see examples of the remarkably brilliant coins made at the Dahlonega Mint at the **Dahlonega Gold Museum State Historic Site** (1 Public Square, 706/864-2257, www. gastateparks.org, Mon.-Sat. 9am-5pm, Sun. 10am-5pm, $6 adults, $3.50 children) in the main square. Technically, Dahlonega wasn't the country's first gold rush town; that distinction belongs to nearby Auraria, which soon went extinct, with hardly a trace of the town remaining today.

As for the guy who first said, "There's gold in them thar hills," he was U.S. Mint chief assayer M.F. Stephenson, and what he really said was "There's millions in it." Ironically he wasn't trying to kick off the Georgia gold rush; he was trying to convince prospectors to stay in Dahlonega instead of going to California, where another, and eventually much more famous, gold rush had just begun in 1849.

jewelry made from gold that is still mined onsite for the souvenir market. You can also opt to buy their ore by the bucket and take it home with you to see if you get lucky. Those who purchase six buckets of ore can use the mine's own tools for a really authentic experience. Tours are given of the old stamp mill on the grounds.

Consolidated Gold Mines

It's not a working mine anymore, but **Consolidated Gold Mines** (185 Consolidated Gold Mine Rd., 706/864-8473, daily 10am-5pm, $15 adult, $9 children) is the actual site of what was once one of the largest gold processing plants in the world, only open for about 10 years at the turn of the 20th century. Some of the old mine shafts, including the legendary

"Glory Hole," have been excavated and restored for public tours, 200 feet underground, by knowledgeable guides.

WINERIES

The Dahlonega area has made quite a name for itself over the past 10-15 years or so as a regional wine center. The wine business is seasonal, however, so the wineries often take an extended hiatus from public visitation during the winter.

Wolf Mountain Vineyards (180 Wolf Mountain Tr., 706/867-9862, www.wolfmountainvineyards.com, tastings Thurs.-Sat. noon-5pm, Sun. 12:30pm-5pm, from $10) has rapidly established itself as Georgia's leading winemaker. **Frogtown Cellars** (700 Ridge

Point Dr., 706/865-0687, www.frogtown-wine.com, Mon.-Fri. noon-5pm, Sat. noon-6pm, Sun. 12:30pm-5pm, tastings from $15) has 42 acres on the outskirts of Dahlonega and a satellite tasting room in Helen (7601 S. Main St., daily). **Montaluce Estates** (946 Via Monteluce, 706/867-4060, www.montaluce.com, Tues.-Sat. 11am-5pm, Sun. noon-5pm) boasts a state-of-the-art upscale facility. The first Dahlonega winery of the modern era is **Three Sisters Vineyards** (439 Vineyard Way, 706/865-9463, www.threesistersvineyards.com, Thurs.-Sat. 11am-5pm, Sun. 1pm-5pm, tastings $5-30). **Blackstock Winery's** (5400 Town Creek Rd., 706/219-2789, www.bsvw.com, Mon.-Sat. 10am-6pm, Sun. 12:30pm-6pm) specializes in tasty reds.

ACCOMMODATIONS AND FOOD

Mountain Laurel Creek Inn & Spa (202 Talmer Grizzle Rd., 706/867-8134, www.mountainlaurelcreek.com, rooms $150-200, cottage $220) offers six guest rooms and the freestanding Dancing Bear Cottage, all in a well-maintained scenic foothills setting. Children are not allowed.

The signature shepherd's pie at ⟨ **Shenanigan's Irish Pub** (87 N. Chestatee St., 706/482-0114, www.theshenaniganspub.com, Mon.-Thurs. 11am-10pm, Fri.-Sat. 11am-midnight, Sun. noon-7pm, $10) is just what the doctor ordered to warm you up from the inside on a brisk day in the foothills.

For a more classically Southern, family-style dining experience, try ⟨ **Smith House Dining Inn and Country Store** (84 S. Chestatee St., 706/867-7000, www.smithhouse.com, Tues.-Thurs. 11am-3pm, Fri. 11am-3pm and 3:30pm-8pm, Sat.-Sun. 11am-8pm, $20).

The Crimson Moon Cafe (24 N. Park St., 706/864-3982, www.thecrimsonmoon.com, Wed.-Thurs. 10am-9pm, Fri.-Sat. 8am-10:30pm, Sun. 8am-9:30pm, $12-15) specializes in live music of the Americana and roots-folk variety, and is a popular nightspot on the square.

Cohutta Mountains

The central portion of North Georgia is dominated by the Cohutta Mountain range, which though technically not part of the Blue Ridge is for most purposes contiguous with it. The area is less populated than the Blue Ridge portion just to the east and almost completely dominated by the enormous Cohutta Wilderness Area.

ELLIJAY

For most of the year not much goes on in tiny, cute Ellijay, but it boasts one of Georgia's most popular annual festivals: the **Georgia Apple Festival** (www.georgiaapplefestival.org). Happening over two weekends each October, the Apple Festival celebrates the harvest of this area's chief crop—over 600,000 bushels a year—with food and arts and crafts booths and vendors. For a scenic look at the farms where the apples are grown, take a drive down "Apple Alley," Highway 52. Many farms are open in the autumn harvest season for tours, hayrides, and pick-your-own apples.

About 20 miles north of Ellijay is the popular and versatile **Fort Mountain State Park** (181 Fort Mountain Park Rd., 706/422-1932, www.gastateparks.org, parking $5, campsites $25-28, cottages $125-145), within the Chattahoochee National Forest and adjacent to the Cohutta Wilderness. Fourteen miles of hiking opportunities through the forest abound and are particularly scenic and gratifying. However, the specialty here is 27 miles of mountain biking trails.

COHUTTA WILDERNESS AREA

The most heavily used in the region, the **Cohutta Wilderness Area** (706/695-6736,

NORTH GEORGIA

www.georgiawildlife.com, free) includes 36,000 acres in Georgia and another 1,000 acres in Tennessee. It has about 100 miles of hiking trails of various skill levels, running through some very beautiful and extremely interesting country. Anglers come from all over to fly-fish on the numerous rivers cutting through.

While camping without a permit is allowed anywhere in Cohutta except directly on trails, usage regulations severely limit campfires; consult the website or call ahead.

There are several ways into Cohutta. To get to the southeast trailhead via Ellijay, travel west from town on Highway 52 for 9.5 miles to Forest Road 18. Turn right after the sign for Lake Conasauga Recreation Area; in about 1.5 miles the road becomes unpaved. At the fork, bear left over a one-lane bridge; at 3.5 miles, turn right onto Forest Road 68. In another mile is a picnic area, and in another mile a check station. At six miles you can take a right onto Forest Road 64, which takes you to the Conasauga River Trail, actually the bed of an old logging railroad.

Cartersville to the Tennessee Border

Conveniently located roughly along I-75 from northwestern metro Atlanta up to the Tennessee border at Chattanooga are several areas of historic and educational significance. Here they are listed in geographical order northward from Atlanta.

CARTERSVILLE

Benefiting from its proximity to the Atlanta metro area, Cartersville is a fairly bustling old railroad town with an active town square and several notable attractions.

Booth Western Art Museum

North Georgia isn't where you'd expect to find a huge shiny new museum dedicated to cowboy and Native American art, but you'll find that and more at the 120,000-square-foot limestone **Booth Western Art Museum** (501 Museum Dr., 770/387-1300, www.boothmuseum.org, Tues.-Wed. and Fri.-Sat. 10am-5pm, Thurs. 10am-8pm, Sun. 1pm-5pm, $10 adults, $7 students, free under age 12), which claims to be Georgia's biggest museum other than the High in Atlanta. While the highlight for many is the permanent and succinctly named Cowboy Gallery, the entire multistory edifice does a good job of inclusivity, with artwork by and about Native Americans, African Americans, and women.

Tellus Science Museum

The **Tellus Science Museum** (100 Tellus Dr., 770/606-5700, www.tellusmuseumorg, daily 10am-5pm, $14 adults, $10 children, planetarium shows $3.50) focuses on astronomy and geology, with mineral and fossil exhibits galore. The building is constructed around a central observatory, open during monthly special events (check the website). The all-digital planetarium provides frequent shows at additional cost.

Rose Lawn House Museum

A short walk from the town square is **Rose Lawn House Museum** (224 W. Cherokee Ave., 770/387-5162, www.roselawnmuseum.com, Tues.-Fri. 10am-noon and 1pm-5pm, $5 adults, $2 children), former home of influential 19th-century evangelist Samuel Porter Jones. The museum features period furnishings and serves as a home for memorabilia of another famous Bartow County native, Rebecca Latimer Felton, the first woman to serve in the U.S. Senate.

Food

Tasty dining options downtown include **Appalachian Grill** (14 E. Church St., 770/607-5357, Mon.-Thurs. 11am-9pm, Fri. 11am-10pm, Sat. noon-10pm, $15) with its signature trout dishes and combo platters, and

NORTH GEORGIA

© JIM MOREKIS

The Etowah Indian Mounds are particularly well-preserved.

Jefferson's (28 W. Main St., 770/334-2069, www.jeffersonsrestaurant.com, Mon.-Wed. 11am-10pm, Thurs.-Sat. 11am-11pm, Sun. 11:30am-10pm, $10), known for its wings and oysters.

☙ ETOWAH INDIAN MOUNDS HISTORIC SITE

The **Etowah Indian Mounds Historic Site** (813 Indian Mounds Rd., 770/387-3747, www. gastateparks.org, Wed.-Sat. 9am-5pm, $5), outside Cartersville, is the most intact Mound Builder site in the Southeast. On this 54 acres was one of the most influential communities of the Mississippian culture from about AD 1000 to 1500. Its six masterfully constructed earthen mounds are in surprisingly good shape today, with full access to the top, providing a beautiful panorama of the surrounding area and the other mounds.

The small but well-curated visitors center has a nice museum with some stunning artifacts retrieved from the site. Bring a picnic lunch and enjoy the tranquil serenity of the shaded picnic area on the banks of the Etowah River directly beside the mound site.

NEW ECHOTA HISTORICAL SITE

The beneficiary of a recent upgrade and renovation, **New Echota Historical Site** (1211 Chatsworth Hwy., 706/624-1321, www. gastateparks.org, Thurs.-Sat. 9am-5pm, $6.50 adults, $4.50 children) outside Calhoun has an especially bittersweet nature, serving both as capital of the Cherokee Nation 1825-1838 and as the place where the Trail of Tears began. Today there are a dozen original and reconstructed period buildings. The visitors center plays a 17-minute film about the history of the site and hosts a Cherokee Research Library.

CHIEF VANN HOUSE HISTORIC SITE

A short drive east of Dalton is the **Chief Vann House Historic Site** (82 Hwy. 225 N., 706/695-2598, www.gastateparks.org, Thurs.-Sat. 9am-5pm, $6 adults, $3.50 children),

NORTH GEORGIA

Chickamauga battlefield

© JIM MOREKIS

the best-preserved remaining house of the Cherokee nation.

TUNNEL HILL

The chief attraction in this little mountain town is the **Historic Western & Atlantic Railroad Tunnel** (215 Clisby Austin Dr., 706/876-1571, www.tunnelhillheritagecenter. com, Mon.-Sat. 9am-5pm, $7 adults, $5 children), part of the first railroad through the Appalachians. For a few minutes in 1862 it hosted part of the Great Locomotive Chase. The tunnel can be toured at the top of each hour.

◀ CHICKAMAUGA & CHATTANOOGA NATIONAL MILITARY PARK

Directly south of Ft. Oglethorpe on Highway 1 (or off I-75's exit 350) is the **Chickamauga & Chattanooga National Military Park** (3370 LaFayette Rd., www.nps.gov, visitors center daily 8:30am-5pm, grounds daily dawn-dusk, free), preserving and interpreting one of the last

major Confederate victories of the Civil War. The focus is primarily on the savage fighting around Chickamauga in September 1863.

There's a small and well-done visitors center and museum with a 20-minute video explaining the rather complicated action of the battle. The main draw is the seven-mile walking tour over the battlefield, culminating in a trip up an observation tower to view the entire area. There are interpretive maps, or you can dial a number on your cell phone to listen to an audio tour (get the number from the rangers at the visitors center). While no real artifacts from the battle remain on the grounds, other than at the museum, the park has attempted to recreate the conflict by strategically positioned artillery batteries, with color-coded informational markers (red for rebels, blue for Yankees).

Just across the border in Tennessee, you can also visit the **Lookout Mountain Battlefield** (110 Point Park Rd., 423/821-7786, visitors center summer daily 9am-6pm, fall-spring daily 9am-5pm), also expertly administered by the National Park Service.

Ridge and Valley Country

The northwestern portion of Georgia is geologically and culturally somewhat different from the rest of North Georgia. It's often called the Ridge and Valley Country, an area to the west of the Cartersville-Great Smoky Fault and a clear differentiation from the Blue Ridge Mountains to the east. Rome is by far its biggest city.

ROME

Named for the great Italian capital, like its namesake, Rome, Georgia, was built on seven hills. In front of **City Hall** (601 Broad St.) is a statue of Romulus and Remus nursing from a wolf, a nod to the creation story of the European city. A gift to the city from Italian dictator Benito Mussolini in 1929, the statue was taken down to prevent vandalism during World War II and put back in the 1950s. Today, Rome is a center of regional higher education, health care, and manufacturing. You might first want to check out the **Rome-Floyd County Visitors Center** (402 Civic Center Dr., 800/444-1834, www.romegeorgia.org).

Berry College

Rome's chief claim to fame is big and beautiful **Berry College** (2277 Martha Berry Hwy., 706/232-374, www.berry.edu), a liberal arts school on an expansive campus, the largest contiguous college campus in the world. Founder Martha Berry was the daughter of a wealthy area planter and was struck by the profound lack of educational opportunities for most young people in these hardscrabble foothills. She began an impromptu Sunday school at her home, which eventually expanded to a family log cabin, still on campus today. Much of the campus land is administered by the state as hunting and conservation areas; other parts are open to the public for walking and biking.

The highlight is the **Oak Hill & The Martha Berry Museum** (24 Veterans Memorial Hwy., 706/368-6789, www.berry.edu, Mon.-Sat. 10am-5pm, tours 10am-3:30pm every 30 minutes, $5 adults, $3 children), Berry's Greek Revival home where you can learn much more about the school's history.

Clocktower Museum

Downtown Rome's most famous sight is the 1872 **Clocktower** (East 2nd St., Mon.-Fri. 9am-3pm, free), a massive clock atop the 100-foot old city water tower. There's a small museum inside, and visitors can climb to the top.

Chieftains Museum and Major Ridge Home

One of the key remaining sites along the Trail of Tears, the **Chieftains Museum** (501 Riverside Pkwy., 706/291-9494, www.chieftainsmuseum.org, Fri.-Sat. 1pm-5pm, $5 adults, $3 children) is within the home of Major Ridge, who gathered a band of Cherokee people to fight alongside colonists during the American Revolution. Out of gratitude, Andrew Jackson gave him the rank of major, which Ridge would adopt as his first name. However, by the 1830s, pressure on the Cherokee to give up their lands was so intense he felt compelled to sign the controversial Treaty of New Echota, which resulted in the Trail of Tears.

Myrtle Hill Cemetery

Scenic **Myrtle Hill Cemetery** (Branham Ave. and S. Broad St., daily dawn-dusk, free) is set on a six-tiered terraced hill, one of Rome's seven signature hills, and provides beautiful views. The most controversial monument is the one to Confederate general Nathan Bedford Forrest, founder of the Ku Klux Klan.

Accommodations and Food

The premier lodging in Rome is the **C Claremont House** (906 E. 2nd Ave., 706/291-0900, www.theclaremonthouse.net, $150-170), set in an absolutely stunning high Victorian masterpiece of a building. There are

NORTH GEORGIA

© JIM MOREKIS

Howard Finster's Paradise Garden in Summerville

NORTH GEORGIA

four charming guest rooms with 14-foot ceilings and canopy beds.

A couple of good places to get a bite right downtown are **Harvest Moon Cafe** (234 Broad St., 706/292-0099, www.myharvestmooncafe.com, Mon. 11am-2:30pm, Tues.-Thurs. 11am-9pm, Fri.-Sat. 11am-10pm, $15), with good steaks, salmon, and catfish, and **Jefferson's** (340 Broad St., 706/378-0222, www.jeffersonsrestaurant.com, Mon.-Wed. 11am-10pm, Thurs.-Sat. 11am-11pm, Sun. 11:30am-10pm, $10), a regional chain famous for its wings and oysters.

NEAR ROME
Paradise Garden

You'd be forgiven for thinking that the late, great Georgia folk artist Howard Finster lived in Athens, Georgia, on the other side of the state. His collaborations on album-cover art for the iconic Athens band R.E.M. and later with the Talking Heads put Finster on the global map. He became known not only as one of the South's greatest and certainly

hippest outsider artists but as a classic Southern showman-raconteur.

Finster's memory lives on in Athens, but the best place to view his fertile, almost feverish imagination in action is at **Paradise Garden** (200 N. Lewis St., 706/808-0800, www.paradisegardenfoundation.org, Wed.-Sun. 10am-4pm, Sun. 1pm-4pm, donation), his Summerville studio on a swampy four acres of land off a side street. Like the world's most eccentric theme park, Finster's drawing, painting, and craftwork cover just about every foot of available space on every structure. Here, you fully understand the provenance of the phrase, "one man's junk is another man's treasure." Each May the town park at Summerville hosts **Finster Fest,** an expansive celebration not only of Finster's work but of regional folk artists from all around.

To get to the Garden, head north through Summerville on U.S. 27. Take a right on Rena Street, looking for the signs, and then a right onto North Lewis Street. You can't miss it!

If you need a bite to eat while you're in

Summerville, head straight for the delectable fried catfish at **Jim's Family Restaurant** (6 Lyerly St., 706/857-2123, daily 8am-8pm, $10). Camp for the night at little **James H. "Sloppy" Floyd State Park** (2800 Sloppy Floyd Lake Rd., 706/857-0826, www.gastateparks.org, parking $5, campsites $25-28, cottages $135-145), one of Georgia's smaller yet still picturesque parks.

TAG CORNER

The extreme northwestern tip of Georgia, sometimes called "TAG corner," an acronym referring to its position astride the borders of Tennessee, Alabama, and Georgia, is yet another geological substratum. Part of the Cumberland Plateau, it's a flat-topped highland area, one of whose dominant features is limestone. Long story short, this means lots of caves.

Lookout Mountain

By far the main geological feature of the area is Lookout Mountain, part of the Cumberland Plateau. Most of the 84-mile-long mountain is in Tennessee, including the remnants of a key Civil War battlefield and the popular Raccoon Mountain and Ruby Falls caves.

The East Coast's premier hang gliding location is **Lookout Mountain Flight Park and Training Center** (7201 Scenic Hwy., 800/688-5637, www.hanglide.com, Thurs.-Tues. 9am-6pm). Under the tutelage of certified staff, hang gliding enthusiasts launch from 1,340-foot McCarty's Bluff into the wild blue yonder off Lookout Mountain.

Cloudland Canyon State Park

Lookout Mountain's most dramatic feature is the 1,000-foot canyon at Sitton's Gulch, renamed Cloudland Canyon in the 1930s during the park's construction by the Civilian Conservation Corps. **Cloudland Canyon State Park** (122 Cloudland Canyon Park Rd., 706/657-4050, www.gastateparks.org, daily 7am-10pm, parking $5, backcountry trails $3 pp, campsites $25-28) is quite simply one of the most striking of all Southern state parks.

Its steep sandstone walls are the remnants of a 200-million-year-old shoreline. From the various lookout points along the West Rim Loop Trail skirting the edge of the main picnic area and parking lot along the canyon's edge, you can also see the entrances to some of the canyon's many limestone caves.

In all, the rim trail is about five miles in length and gives you overlook opportunities into three canyon gorges. There is another five-mile network of backcountry trails, along which primitive camping is permitted, a particularly recommended option for those so inclined. You can hike to the bottom of the canyon via some steep but well-maintained and staircase-augmented trails. There are another 72 tent and RV sites divided between the east and west rims, and 16 cottages along the west rim, two of which are dog-friendly.

For a small fee the park hosts frequent and fun guided hikes, at beginner and advanced levels, throughout the canyon and also into some of its many incredible caves; check the website for dates and times. The **Georgia Girl Guides** (www.georgiagirlguides.com) run many of them, as does the **Georgia Conservancy** (www.georgiaconservancy.org) and **Canyon Climbers Club** (www.gastateparks.org, $10), which you can join at Cloudland Canyon or at three other Georgia state parks with similar geology: Amicalola Falls, Tallulah Gorge, and Providence Canyon.

Pigeon Mountain

Adjoining the larger Lookout Mountain, Pigeon Mountain, close to LaFayette, Georgia, was named for the massive flocks of now-extinct passenger pigeons that once made their home here. It's particularly rich spelunking ground and also boasts many rare species of plants and salamanders. Most of the mountain is overseen by the Georgia Department of Natural Resources as the **Crockford-Pigeon Mountain Wildlife Management Area** (706/295-6041, www.georgiawildlife.com). The newly created Georgia Outdoor Recreation Pass (GORP, $3.50 for 3 days) is required to use the area; those with valid hunting and fishing licenses are exempt. To get here from Lafayette, take Highway 193 west for three miles to Chamberlain Road, then turn left and go another three miles to Rocky Lane Road, then turn right. The check station is about 0.25 miles ahead.

One of the most fun things noncavers can do in the area is hike **Rocktown Trail,** named for its 150 acres of whimsical, all-natural sandstone-and-iron formations, some with boulders three stories tall. To get to Rocktown from U.S. 27 in LaFayette, head west 3 miles on Highway 193 to Chamberlain Road, turn left and go another 3.5 miles, then turn right at the "Crockford-Pigeon Mountain WMA" sign. Pass the Department of Natural Resources check station and go straight; where the gravel road forks, veer right and then take the next gravel road on your left about 1.5 miles later.

From there, it's another 0.5 miles or so to the trailhead.

Johns Mountain

On 25,000 acres within the Chattahoochee National Forest, the **Johns Mountain Wildlife Management Area** (706/695-6736, www.fs.usda.gov) is a popular recreational area. A particularly popular area here is called **The Pocket** (camping Apr.-Oct., $10) because it lies between the ridges of the Horn and Hill Mountains. From Dalton, head south until you get to Highway 136, then head west until you hit Pocket Road. Take a left and continue; the Pocket will be on your left. Continue on Pocket Road to find Lake Marvin, around which you'll find plenty of free camping, not to mention fishing on the lake itself.

Athens

Home to the University of Georgia, Athens is a heady and often quirky mix of culture, partying, football, and progressive thought in an otherwise conservative area. What really makes Athens stand out, and clearly puts it head and shoulders above most college towns, is the fabled "Athens scene," a musical ethos that for the past 30 years has virtually defined, and in some cases directly authored, the sound of American indie rock and roll.

The Athens music and arts scene exists in an interesting creative tension with the other important side of local life, the University of Georgia Bulldogs, a perennially powerful team with a passionately devoted fan base who turn out by the many thousands on home-game Saturday, decked out in the school colors of red and black, to cheer on "them Dawgs."

A forward-thinking state legislature in 1785 made a bold step to endow a "college or seminary of learning," essentially giving birth to the idea of state-supported higher education in the United States. The surrounding town, created in 1806, was to be called Athens to channel

the spirit of the great artistic, literary, and scientific accomplishments of the ancient Greeks. Athens's most famous resident in the antebellum era was Henry W. Grady, who would go on to be a seminal editor of the *Atlanta Journal-Constitution* and founder of the University of Georgia school of journalism, which bears his name to this day.

SIGHTS
Church-Waddel-Brumby House

The main Athens visitors center is within the restored **Church-Waddel-Brumby House** (280 E. Dougherty St., 706/353-1820, www.athenswelcomecenter.com, Mon.-Sat. 10am-5pm, Sun. noon-5pm, free), a circa-1820 house museum alleged to be the oldest residence in the city.

◆ University of Georgia

As befitting its deep roots in the Deep South, the **University of Georgia** (www.uga.edu), "Georgia" or UGA in common parlance, boasts not only a devotion to tradition, but a

NORTH GEORGIA

large (over 600 acres) and scenic campus that is worth exploring whether you're affiliated with the university or not. You can take free student-guided tours leaving from the visitors center on South Campus or download a walking tour map (http://visit.uga.edu). Here's a quick look at the highlights:

Every visit to UGA should begin with the famous **Arch** at the old North Campus entrance on Broad Street. Old Bulldog etiquette demands that underclass students only walk around the Arch, not under it. As you walk through the Arch you'll see the Greek Revival **Hunter Holmes Academic Building,** actually two antebellum buildings combined in the early 20th century. In 2001 it was renamed to honor the first two African American students admitted to UGA: Hamilton Holmes and Charlayne Hunter-Gault (later a renowned broadcast journalist), who began classes in 1961.

Facing each other across the shady North Campus quad are twin debating

NORTH GEORGIA

UNIVERSITY OF GEORGIA

© AVALON TRAVEL

society headquarters **Demosthenes Hall** and **Phi Kappa Hall,** the latter of which housed Union troops after the Civil War. Right beside Demosthenes Hall is the 1832 **Chapel,** where students once attended services three days a week. These days, students take turns ringing the old chapel bell, now in a small tower nearby, until midnight after every Georgia football victory.

South of the Chapel and off to the right you'll run across verdant little **Herty Field,** where the Bulldogs played their first football game in 1892 (beating Mercer University 50-0) under the direction of Georgia's first coach, Charles Herty, also a chemist of national repute. A parking lot actually occupied this rectangle from the 1940s to 1999, when the hallowed athletic ground was reclaimed as relaxing green space for casual enjoyment.

Two buildings down from Phi Kappa Hall across the quad is the **Administration Building,** currently the university president's office. The small building adjacent is **Old College,** the oldest building on campus. The 1806 structure was based on Connecticut Hall at Yale University. Confederate vice president Alexander H. Stephens lived here during his time as a student at UGA.

The imposing building ahead is the Ila Dunlap Little Library, usually just called the **Main Library.** Its Hargrett Rare Book and Manuscript Library includes a copy of the original Confederate Constitution and some papers of Margaret Mitchell.

Continue down Sanford Drive, and impossible to miss is enormous **Sanford Stadium,** where the Bulldogs play home games "between the hedges" growing all along the sidelines.

At the extreme tip of South Campus at College Station Road is the **UGA Visitors Center** (Four Towers Building, 706/542-0842, http://visit.uga.edu), where the student-led campus tours begin.

State Botanical Garden

The tastefully landscaped and interpreted **State Botanical Garden** (2450 S. Milledge Ave., 706/542-1244, www.botgarden.uga.edu, visitors center Tues.-Sat. 9:30am-4:30pm, Sun. 11:30am-4:30pm, grounds daily 8am-dusk, donation), operated by UGA, eschews over-the-top displays of flora for a highly interesting and educational approach to the botanical arts. You enter through the Conservatory, which has a nice tropical plant and orchid display. Just outside, arrayed around an inviting quad, is a series of geographically themed gardens.

Georgia Museum of Art

Once on old North Campus, the **Georgia Museum of Art** (90 Carlton St., 706/542-4662, www.georgiamuseum.org, Tues.-Wed. and Fri.-Sat. 10am-5pm, Thurs. 10am-9pm, Sun. 1pm-5pm, donation) is now in a purpose-built modern space on the East Campus. Run by the university, it is the state's official art museum. It hosts a wide variety of rotating exhibits, and its own collections are surprisingly

The Arch is the introduction to the scenic UGA campus.

in 1978. The Police played here on their first U.S. tour and the B-52's forged their reputation after a legendary show here. After a bad fire in 2009, a community reinvestment effort led to a total repair of the venue, and only two years later it was up and running again. A fun rooftop bar, added during the renovation, is a great bonus.

City Hall and the Double-Barreled Cannon

Athens boasts an attractive **City Hall** (301 College Ave.). The double-barreled cannon on the northeast corner of the City Hall lot was built in Athens in 1862 as a Confederate "secret weapon." The idea was that the two cannonballs would be connected by an eight-foot chain, and when fired the resulting spinning anti-personnel weapon would cause much damage. It didn't work so well in test firings, however, and was never used in combat.

T. R. R. Cobb House

Lawyer and Confederate officer Thomas Reade Rootes Cobb is a key figure in Athens history, but interestingly the Greek Revival **T. R. R. Cobb House** (175 Hill St., 706/369-3513, www.trrcobbhouse.org, Tues.-Sat. 10am-4pm, $2) was at Stone Mountain Park near Atlanta for 20 years. It has since been returned to this site, about a block from the original location where it was first built in 1834. The ground floor is expertly restored to antebellum furnishings. The second floor is more of a museum format.

Taylor-Grady House

Named for its two most notable owners, Confederate officer and Irish native Robert Taylor and *Atlanta Journal-Constitution* editor and UGA journalism school founder Henry W. Grady, the **Taylor-Grady House** (634 Prince Ave., 706/549-8688, www.taylorgradyhouse.com, Mon., Wed., and Fri. 9am-3pm, Tues. and Thurs. 9am-1pm, $3) was built in 1844 as a summer home for Taylor and his family. It's now a house museum.

eclectic, ranging from home-grown folk art by Howard Finster to Georgia O'Keeffe to the Kress Collection of Italian Renaissance works. Note the late hours on Thursday.

Butts-Mehre Heritage Hall Sports Museum

For fans of "the Dawgs," the **Butts-Mehre Heritage Hall Sports Museum** (1 Selig Circle, www.georgiadogs.com, Mon.-Fri. 8am-5pm, free) is a must-see. Football takes center stage, including the two Heisman Trophies won by UGA players Frank Sinkwich and Herschel Walker, and the National Championship trophy won by the Dawgs in 1980 during Walker's tenure.

Georgia Theatre

With a foundation dating from 1889, the circa-1935 **Georgia Theatre** (215 N. Lumpkin St., 706/850-7670, www.georgiatheatre.com) has hosted many bands of note over the past 30-plus years since its restoration as a music venue

© JIM MOREKIS

© JIM MOREKIS

the legendary 40 Watt Club

ENTERTAINMENT AND EVENTS
❰ Athens Nightlife

In a matter of great local pride, the University of Georgia is usually at or near the top of the annual lists of best party schools in the country. Indeed, urban legend maintains that Athens has the highest number of bars per capita in the United States.

First among equals, the legendary **40 Watt Club** (285 W. Washington St., 706/549-7871, www.40watt.com, open show nights only) has been at the forefront of the Athens music scene since 1978, when it was cofounded by Curtis Crowe, drummer with local legends Pylon (it's now owned by the ex-wife of R.E.M. guitarist Peter Buck). It's the CBGB of the South, but unlike that NYC club, it's still open for business, albeit in its fifth location. Unlike the sweaty, cramped vibe of some earlier 40 Watts, the current space is a good bit larger than previous locations, the cavernous space broken up by artfully placed couches around the perimeter.

Despite its swank name, **Manhattan Cafe** (337 N. Hull St., 706/369-9767, Mon.-Sat. 4pm-2am) is one of Athens's most humbly charming bars, a cross between a dive, a hipster bar, and a Prohibition-era speakeasy. The house cocktail is a refreshing blend of Maker's Mark and spicy Blenheim Ginger Ale. **Little Kings** (223 W. Hancock St., 706/369-3144, Mon.-Sat. 7pm-2am) is a go-to for high-profile indie acts; local legend Pylon chose it to kick off a reunion tour.

If you're into concerts where even the band wears earplugs, **Caledonia Lounge** (256 W. Clayton St., 706/549-5577, www.caledonialounge.com, Mon.-Sat. 5pm-2am) is the place for you. Narrow little **Flicker Theatre and Bar** (263 W. Washington St., 706/546-0039, www.flickertheatreandbar.com, Mon.-Fri. 4pm-2am, Sat. 1pm-2am) is a favorite meet-up spot and also features occasional singer-songwriter music in a house-party atmosphere.

Small and sweaty, **Go Bar** (195 Prince Ave., 706/546-5609, Mon.-Sat. 9pm-2am), next to the popular restaurant The Grit in a block

PARTY OUT OF BOUNDS

Athens is renowned for its contributions to rock and roll, spawning names such as R.E.M., the B-52's, Widespread Panic, and Pylon, among many others. An entertaining 1987 documentary chronicling the scene, *Athens, GA: Inside/Out,* is now available on DVD. Here's a brief tour of venues that played a role in forming Athens's rock-and-roll legacy. Go to www.visitathensga.com for a full version courtesy of alt-weekly *The Flagpole.*

- **40 Watt Club:** Named because its first incarnation was lit by a single lightbulb, Athens's most legendary club has hosted every major name in local rock history. It's had several locations, in this order: second floor of 171 College Avenue (above The Grill); second floor of 100 College Avenue (above Starbucks); 382 East Broad Street (now university offices), and 285 West Washington Street, where it is now.

- **Georgia Theatre:** 215 North Lumpkin Avenue. The century-old venue reopened after a 2009 fire; The Police played here on their first U.S. tour.

- **"Murmur" Railroad Trestle:** 270 South Poplar Street. The railroad trestle on the back cover of R.E.M.'s "Murmur" album was recently restored through a community effort. Park at the lot near Dudley Park around the corner.

- **140 East Washington Street:** This was once the Uptown Lounge, which in the 1980s hosted The Pixies, Jane's Addiction, R.E.M., and Black Flag. Now it's home to Copper Creek Brewing Co.

- **St. Mary's Steeple:** An Episcopal church was here until it was demolished in 1990, leaving only this steeple. R.E.M. rehearsed and played their first concert here, a birthday party for a friend in April 1980. It's now surrounded by condos but easily accessible from the street.

- **312 East Broad Street:** The "Frigidaire" building was built in the 1880s as the Athens Opera House. For 10 years beginning in 1997, Tasty World operated here and hosted acts such as The Shins and Kings of Leon.

- **260 North Jackson Street:** Now Jackson Street Books, it was record store Wax Jr. Facts in the early 1980s, managed by Pylon bassist Michael Lachowski, who now owns a local design firm.

- **Wuxtry Records:** 197 East Clayton Street. R.E.M.'s Peter Buck once worked here, among many other local musicians. It's been in business since 1975.

restored and owned by R.E.M.'s Michael Stipe, is a popular spot to dance and enjoy live music. **New Earth Music Hall** (227 W. Dougherty St., 706/543-8283, www.newearthmusichall.com, Mon.-Sat. 9pm-2am) combines a hippie vibe with a rave-scene aesthetic, specializing in jam band shows.

Another great way to enjoy the local music scene is at **AthFest** (www.athfest.com). Happening every June in a blocked-off portion of downtown, this music festival features plenty of free live outdoor concerts, film screenings, arts and crafts displays, and product and food booths. The core experience, however, involves the ticketed bracelets ($17-20) which allow you to club-crawl.

SHOPPING

Before he became a rock star, R.E.M.'s Peter Buck once managed **Wuxtry Records** (197 E. Clayton St., 706/369-9428, www.wuxtry-records.com, Mon.-Fri. 10am-7pm, Sat. 11am-7pm, Sun. noon-6pm), and it remains one of the Southeast's best (and quirkiest) sources for vintage vinyl and hard-to-get recordings. Go upstairs to their even more eccentric cousin store **Bizarro Wuxtry Comics, Toys & Records** (197 E. Clayton St., 706/353-7938, Mon.-Fri. 10am-7pm, Sat. 11am-7pm, Sun. noon-6pm), which has an extensive collection of alternative zines as well as shirts and offbeat items.

Every great rock-and-roll town needs a great

music store, and here that would be **Chick Music** (240 W. Clayton St., 706/546-8742, www.chickmusic.net, Mon.-Fri. 9am-6pm, Sat. 10am-6pm), a 70-year-old Athens institution that has sold and rented instruments, amps, strings, and every other musical accessory to local luminaries.

The best bookstore in town for the past 25 years has been **Jackson Street Books** (260 N. Jackson St., 706/546-0245, Mon.-Sat. 11am-6pm, Sun. noon-4pm), which deals in plenty of good-condition used and rare volumes.

SPORTS AND RECREATION

The premier overall outdoor activity in Athens is the new **North Oconee River Greenway** (70 Sunset Dr., www.athensclarkecounty.com, daily dawn-dusk), a well-done project that has reclaimed much of the north bank of the Oconee, once the home of a thriving mill industry. Four miles of multilevel walk, jog, and bike trails, including one along the river, meander through the peaceful wooded bank. Interpretive signage explains the rich heritage of the river's industry.

Needless to say, the premier spectator sport in Athens involves the **Georgia Bulldogs football team** (www.georgiadogs.com, tickets from $55). They play in enormous Sanford Stadium on UGA's South Campus. The Dawgs are a huge deal around here, and for most big games, tickets are hard to come by, though there are often tickets for sale by enterprising individuals on game day. For less competitive games, check online. The home court of the Dawgs men's and women's **basketball team** (www.georgiadogs.com) is venerable Stegeman Coliseum (100 Smith St.). The baseball-playing **Diamond Dawgs** (www.georgiadogs.com) play at Foley Field. The UGA **women's soccer team** (www.georgiadogs.com) consistently plays at the highest level of NCAA competition, and you can watch their games for free at their specially built soccer stadium. Ten-time national champs, the women's gymnastics team the **Gym Dogs** (www.georgiadogs.com) compete at Stegeman Coliseum (100 Smith St.).

ACCOMMODATIONS

If you're coming to Athens on a graduation weekend or on one of the autumn Saturdays the Bulldogs play here, book your room well in advance or you'll be out of luck. Prices listed are for non-football nights; they double (or triple!) for football weekends.

Under $150

My favorite place to stay in Athens is the ◖ **UGA Hotel at the Georgia Center** (1197 S. Lumpkin St., 800/884-1381, www.georgia-center.uga.edu, $90-200). While constructed to serve as a lodging center for university-based conventions and for alumni, anyone can book a room. The location on campus is unbeatable and the 200 guest rooms and various public spaces are top-notch. Forget about staying here on a football weekend unless you've booked well in advance.

Athens has one B&B of note: **The Colonels** (3890 Barnett Shoals Rd., 706/559-9595, www.thecolonels.net, $115-200), a classic renovated seven-room antebellum farmhouse on historic Angel Oak Farm run by, yes, "Colonels" Marc and Beth. The breakfasts are magnificent. The location is about a 10-minute drive from downtown, but very convenient to the State Botanical Garden.

If you're looking for a total downtown base camp, the choice is **Hilton Garden Inn** (390 E. Washington St., 706/353-6800, www.hiltongardeninn3.hilton.com, $120), which couldn't be more centrally located. It's not the best hotel in town but it surpasses most standards. The only catch is a $10 parking fee for the separate deck, but that beats the impossible task of finding convenient on-street parking downtown.

$150-300

The newest addition, and Athens's first entry in the boutique category, is ◖ **Hotel Indigo** (500 College Ave., 706/546-0430, www.hotelindigoathens.com, $145-235). Its swank decor, frequent generous receptions, LEED-certified green attitude, and downtown location make it a no-brainer.

FOOD
Burgers and Barbecue

One of Athens's great food traditions, (**The Grill** (171 College Ave., 706/543-4770, www. thegrillathensga.com, daily 24 hours, breakfast daily midnight-noon, $7) is open 24-7 right on the town's most traveled block, so there's no excuse not to check it out. They serve traditional diner food in a 1950s retro decor. Upstairs is where the first incarnation of local music venue 40 Watt Club opened in the late 1970s.

Generally considered the best barbecue in town, **Harry's Pig Shop** (2425 Jefferson Rd., 706/612-9219, www.harryspigshop.com, daily 11am-9pm, $8), outside downtown, offers a few creative menu items in addition to their regular succulent pulled pork, such as a barbecue quesadilla and tenderloin or tofu sliders.

Coffeehouses

An expanding local chain, (**Jittery Joe's** (www.jitteryjoes.com) has several locations around town, and all of them offer a delicious variety of expertly roasted beans. The main "tasting room" location (780 E. Broad St., 706/227-2161, Mon.-Fri. 7am-6pm, Sat.-Sun. 8am-6pm), just east of the main downtown area, is a nice getaway inside a rustic former warehouse. There's a smaller location farther into downtown (297 E. Broad St., 706/613-7449, Mon.-Fri. 6:30am-midnight, Sat.-Sun. 7:30am-midnight) and one south of downtown in the Five Points neighborhood (1230 S. Milledge Ave., 706/208-1979, Mon.-Fri. 6:30am-midnight, Sat.-Sun. 7:30am-midnight), along with several others around town.

Walker's Pub & Coffee (128 College Ave., 706/543-1433, www.walkerscoffee.com, Mon.-Sat. 7am-2am, Sun. 7am-9pm), ironically a couple of doors down from a Starbucks, is, as the name indicates, a hybrid spot: During the day, it's a lounge-worthy coffeehouse, with big roomy wooden booths, and after about 10pm, it turns into a full-service bar.

Organic and Vegetarian

The kind of vegetarian and vegan place that even a carnivore could love, (**The Grit** (199 Prince Ave., 706/543-6592, www.thegrit.com, Mon.-Fri. 11am-10pm, Sat.-Sun. 10am-3pm and 5pm-10pm, $10) offers fresh, lovingly prepared, and extremely affordable meatless delicacies. Most are locally sourced, such as the grilled seitan steak, scintillating noodle bowls, and the signature must-try black bean chili.

A combination of natural food mecca and fine-dining date spot, (**The National** (232 W. Hancock St., 706/549-3450, www.thenationalrestaurant.com, Mon.-Thurs. 11am-3pm and 5pm-10pm, Fri.-Sat. 11am-3pm and 5pm-11pm, Sun. 5pm-10pm, $15-25) has perhaps the most tightly focused rotating menu in the city, all changing with the seasons. A recent visit featured pan-roasted North Carolina trout and a grilled hanger steak with marinated roasted peppers. There are always great veggie and vegan options. Or you could just content yourself with two or three starters, the "pizzettes" being particularly good choices. On Sunday-Tuesday nights they offer a combo dinner and a movie deal with the Cine BarCafe theater right next door.

Pizza

As the often-long line at both locations indicates, the most popular pizza place in town is **Transmetropolitan,** almost always just called "Transmet." There's a downtown location (145 E. Clayton St., 706/613-8773, daily 11am-11pm, pizza $10) and a location northwest of downtown (1550 Oglethorpe Ave., 706/549-5112, daily 11am-11pm, pizza $10). The vibe is combination college pizza joint, hipster bar, and sports bar. Any of the signature pizzas are great and affordable, with some adventurous options including, yes, the Hungry Sasquatch.

INFORMATION AND SERVICES
Hospitals

The main hospital in town is **Athens Regional Medical Center** (1199 Prince Ave., 706/475-7000, www.athenshealth.org), with a Level II emergency room. Their **Regional FirstCare Clinic** (485 Hwy. 29 N.) offers walk-in service for nonemergencies. **St.**

The Grit, a vegetarian foodie's paradise

© JIM MOREKIS

NORTH GEORGIA

Mary's Hospital (1230 Baxter St., 706/389-3000, www.stmarysathens.com) is the official health care provider of UGA athletics and has an emergency room.

Media

The newspaper of record in Athens is the *Athens Banner-Herald* (www.onlineathens.com). However, a more popular media outlet and certainly the one to consult for music and entertainment is the *Flagpole* (www.flagpole.com), the independent alt-weekly. Now weekly, *The Red and Black* (www.redandblack.com) is run by University of Georgia students, most of them in the journalism school. It is independent from the school administration, however.

The most unique radio station in town is the student-staffed and university-run **WUOG** (90.5 FM), which airs the usual eclectic and quirky blend of indie college rock, Americana, blues, and jazz. The local Georgia Public Broadcasting station is **WUGA** (91.7 FM and 97.9FM), which also broadcasts from campus.

Libraries

At the university, the **Walter J. Brown Media Archives and Peabody Awards Collection** (Waddell St., www.libs.uga.edu) is the only public archive in the state devoted to audiovisual material. The Peabody Awards, sponsored by the Henry W. Grady School of Journalism, are given for excellence in broadcasting. Also in the Russell Building is the **Hargrett Rare Book & Manuscript Library** (www.libs.uga.edu), with six million historical documents, over 100,000 rare books, and over 1,000 historical maps. And, of course, the **Main Library** at UGA (www.libs.uga.edu) offers a copious selection of liberal arts and humanities volumes, collections, and periodicals.

GETTING THERE AND AROUND
By Car

The main route to Athens from Atlanta is U.S. 78, the old "Atlanta Highway." It turns into Broad Street when you reach town. The main route into Athens from the south is U.S. 441, which runs into the Athens Perimeter (Hwy. 10), often called "The Loop" or the "Ten Loop," before you hit town.

By Air
Athens's airport is **Ben Epps Airport** (AHN, 1010 Ben Epps Dr., www.athensclarkecounty. com). As of this writing the only airline operating there is **GeorgiaSkies** (www.flygeorgiaskies. com), which runs flights to and from Atlanta's Hartsfield-Jackson International Airport.

Public Transit
The Athens city and county government runs a good bus system called simply **The Bus** (www. athenstransit.com, $1.60 per ride, free for UGA students). The Bus runs a UGA football shuttle ($5 round-trip, purchase ticket at airport) on home game Saturdays from Ben Epps Airport to the Arch on North Campus.

Also free to UGA students, the university runs a very comprehensive and active **Campus Transit System** (www.transit.uga. edu), from early morning well into the evening and technically limited to student use. Weekend service sees more limited hours, with no service at all on home football Saturdays in the fall.

Madison and Vicinity

About 30 minutes south of Athens, this charming and well-kept little burg, named for founding father James Madison, routinely tops travel magazines' lists of best small town in the country and provides location sets for movies seeking old South authenticity. Visitor traffic in Madison (www.madisonga.org) is steady, driven not only by the nostalgically picturesque town itself but also by an upscale real estate boom on nearby Lake Oconee.

Madison likes to market itself as "the town Sherman refused to burn." While technically true—Madison was the home of Unionist senator Joshua Hill, a friend of Sherman's brother—there are plenty of Georgia towns that Union troops spared from the torch. In any case, Madison is well worth a visit, not only to see its eclectic historic district but to enjoy its trim, pleasant vibe.

◖ MADISON
The best way to enjoy Madison's sizeable historic district is to pick up the official walking tour brochure at the **Madison Visitors Center** (115 E. Jefferson St., 706/342-4454, www. madisonga.org, Mon.-Fri. 9:30am-4pm, Sat. 10am-5pm, Sun. 1pm-4pm), itself inside the 1887 old firehouse and original city hall. You can easily spend a solid hour or two walking the perimeter of downtown, enjoying the occasionally quirky mix of antebellum and late-19th-century architecture.

Highlights include the magnificent 1811 Greek Revival **Heritage Hall** (277 S. Main St., 706/342-9627, www.friendsofheritagehall.org, Mon.-Sat. 11am-4pm, Sun. 1:30pm-4:30pm, $7 adults, $3 children), now home of the Morgan County Historical Society and open for tours daily. Other homes of aesthetic and historical significance, now private residences, are the Queen Anne gingerbread-style **Hunter House** (580 S. Main St.) and the **Joshua Hill Home** (485 Old Post Rd.), home of the senator credited with saving Madison from General Sherman's fires. The **Rogers House and Rose Cottage** (179 E. Jefferson St., 706/343-1090, Mon.-Sat. 10am-4:30pm, Sun. 1:30pm-4:30pm, $5 adults, $3 children) are Madison's two house museums, side-by-side and adorably hard to resist from the outside. The former is a rarely seen Piedmont Plain cottage from the early 1800s, charmingly restored, and the latter is the restored home of Adeline Rose, who built the home after being emancipated from slavery.

The **Madison Museum of Art** (300 Hancock St., 706/485-4530, mmofa.org, call for hours, donation) has a small but intriguing collection of work by European and regional artists. The

NORTH GEORGIA

Morgan County African American Museum (154 Academy St., 706/342-9191, www.mcaam.org, Tues.-Sat. 10am-4pm, $5) is actually more of an arts and crafts co-op focusing on African American artists and culture. It features several small but well-curated collections in an adorable 1895 cottage.

Shopping

There are several good antiques stores near each other in the town center, making for a great afternoon of browsing. Some highlights are three stores owned by the same folks and within shouting distance of each other: sprawling, fascinating **J&K Fleas An'Tiques** (184 S. Main St., 706/342-3009, www.j-and-k-enterprises.com, Mon.-Fri. 10:30am-5:30pm, Sat. 10:30am-6pm, Sun. 1pm-5:30pm), **J&K Antiques Etc.** (159 S. Main St., 706/752-0009, www.j-and-k-enterprises.com, Mon.-Sat. 10:30am-5:30pm), and the consignment shop **Just Out of the Kloset** (179 S. Main St., 706/752-1960, www.j-and-k-enterprises.com, Tues.-Sat. 10:30am-5:30pm).

Accommodations and Food

The small and plush boutique hotel **James Madison Inn** (260 W. Washington St., 706/342-7040, www.jamesmadisoninn.com, $190-220) is right off the big town park and offers full concierge service. The guest rooms are remarkably well appointed, both in terms of decor and technological compatibility. Book early; these rooms are in high demand. The ◖ **Farmhouse Inn** (1051 Meadow Lane, 706/342-7933, www.thefarmhouseinn.com, rooms $100-170, farmhouse $400-500) offers a delightful getaway-style experience in a charmingly rustic (but not too rustic) farm setting on 100 green and glorious acres outside of town.

Madison's fine dining spot is ◖ **Town 220** (220 W. Washington St., 706/752-1445, www.town220.com, Tues.-Thurs. 11am-2:30pm and 5pm-9pm, Fri.-Sat. 11am-2:30pm and 5pm-10pm, $15-30), just behind the James Madison Inn, featuring chef Fransisco De La Torre's hip take on fusion-style cuisine. Your best bet for casual dining is **Madison Chop House Grille** (202 S. Main St., 706/342-9009, daily 7am-10am and 11:30am-9:30pm, $10-15), on the main drag, for killer burgers and fresh salads.

Information and Services

The **Madison Visitors Center** (115 E. Jefferson St., 706/342-4454, www.madisonga.org, Mon.-Fri. 9:30am-4pm, Sat. 10am-5pm, Sun. 1pm-4pm) is the place to go for brochures and information.

Getting There and Around

Madison is conveniently located just north of I-20. However, a popular way to get into town is U.S. 278, which becomes the unavoidable Main Street as it passes through town. There is no public transportation in Madison, but the town is one of the most walkable you'll find.

EAST ALONG I-20
Lake Oconee

Second largest body of water in the state, Lake Oconee benefits from a gated-community boom and robust recreational tourism, including an internationally ranked Ritz-Carlton resort. Most residents live "behind the gates," as locals refer to the plethora of exclusive upscale communities. A good first stop for general visitor information is the **Lake Oconee Welcome Center** (5820 Lake Oconee Pkwy., Mon.-Fri. noon-8pm, Sat. 10am-5pm).

By far the premier property on Lake Oconee is the ◖ **Ritz-Carlton Lodge, Reynolds Plantation** (1 Lake Oconee Tr., 706/467-0600, www.ritzcarlton.com, $260-450), one of the nation's top resorts. While more casual in approach than other properties in the brand, the level of attentiveness is everything you'd expect, with a nice retro feel to the buildings themselves. While technically closed to everyone but guests, you can generally get on the grounds if you are dining at one of the facilities. You can book an upscale golf package (starting around $300 per night) at **Reynolds Plantation** (800/800-5250, www.reynoldsplantation.com), which offers 99 holes of golf on five world-class

NORTH GEORGIA

"I WILL MAKE GEORGIA HOWL"

Scorched-earth campaigns have been a part of war for centuries. But the first formal targeting of civilian infrastructure in modern times was **General William T. Sherman**'s infamous **"March to the Sea"** from Atlanta to Savannah during the Civil War. It took little more than a month, but by the time Sherman "gave" Savannah to President Abraham Lincoln as a Christmas present in December 1864, the March would enter Southern mythology as one of the war's most bitter memories, with Sherman himself regarded as satanic.

To keep the Confederates guessing, Sherman originally split his forces, 60,000 strong, into two wings deep in enemy territory with no supply lines, a daring, some said foolhardy, move that defied conventional military theory. The right wing headed toward Macon, while the left wing, farther north, headed to Augusta. Ironically, Sherman himself rode with a bodyguard unit made up entirely of Southerners, the Unionist 1st Alabama Cavalry Regiment.

Sherman's goal wasn't to starve Georgians into submission, but to break their will to resist and destroy confidence in the Confederate Army, to "make Georgia howl," as he told his boss, General Ulysses S. Grant. Sherman wanted his soldiers to feed on the move with local supplies. Foraging Union troops were called "bummers," and their behavior ranged from professional to atrocious. The destruction Sherman intended was for anything Confederates might use for military purposes: mills, manufacturing, bridges, and especially railroads, the tracks heated intensely and twisted into "Sherman's neckties."

So how much destruction did Sherman actually cause? If you travel today in the footsteps of his army, from Madison to Milledgeville, from Forsyth to Swainsboro, you'll see plenty of antebellum structures still standing, used as bed-and-breakfasts, law offices, and private homes. Contrary to reputation, the March's swath of destruction was actually quite narrow. (South Carolina, however, as the cradle of secession, would feel Northern vengeance intensely.)

Also contrary to opinion, Sherman never saw emancipating slaves as a chief goal. As crowds of freed slaves began following his army, Sherman just saw more mouths to feed: In his own orders, "Negroes who are able-bodied and can be of service to the several columns may be taken along, but each army commander will bear in mind that the question of supplies is a very important one and that his first duty is to see to them who bear arms."

public courses, including the Plantation Course and the Jack Nicklaus-designed Great Waters.

There are fishing and hunting opportunities galore in the well-stocked lake and in the portions of **Oconee National Forest** (www.fs.usda. gov) that border it.

Greensboro

Named for Revolutionary War hero Nathanael Greene, little Greensboro (www.visitlakeo-conee.com) isn't as energetically marketed as Madison but offers much of the same friendly confidence. The highlight, as far as I'm concerned, is the historic 1807 **Old Gaol** (E. Greene St., 706/453-7592), oldest jail still standing in Georgia. This sturdy, two-story little fortress has actual dungeons inside and includes an ominous hanging area with a trapdoor, complete with hangman's noose. You have to get the key from the nice folks around the corner at the **Greensboro Chamber of Commerce** (111 N. Main St., 706/453-7592, www.greeneccoc. org, Mon.-Sat. 10am-5pm) on the main drag.

For a closer look at local history, a stone's throw from the Old Gaol you'll find the **Greene County Historical Society Museum** (201 E. Greene St., 706/453-7592, Sat. 11am-2pm), a small collection of exhibits on local history. Get a bite to eat a few doors down at **Yesterday Cafe** (114 N. Main St., 706/453-0800, Mon.-Tues. 11am-3pm, Wed.-Sat. 11am-9pm, $10), where the house specialty is an Angus rib eye.

WEST ALONG I-20
Social Circle
There's not much to see in tiny Social Circle, but folks come from miles around to enjoy fried chicken, fried green tomatoes, fried catfish, peanut butter pie, lemon pie, and many other hearty Southern delicacies at the sumptuous all-you-can-eat buffet in the Greek Revival **(Blue Willow Inn** (294 N. Cherokee Rd., 770/464-2131, www.bluewillowinn.com, lunch Mon.-Fri. 11:30am-2:30pm, $15, Sat. 11:30am-2:30pm, $19, dinner Tues.-Thurs. 5pm-8pm, $17, Fri. 5pm-9pm, $24, Sat. 4:30pm-9pm, $24, Sun. 11am-7pm, $20).

Covington
If you ever watched *Sweet Home Alabama, The Dukes of Hazzard, In the Heat of the Night* with Carroll O'Connor, or *The Vampire Diaries,* you've seen Covington. Stop by the **Visitors Center** (2101 Clark St., 770/787-3868, www.gocovington.com, Mon.-Fri. 10am-5pm, Sat. 10am-4pm), which can hook you up with some good self-guided walking tour information of the various film and TV locations downtown.

Augusta

Yes, this is the home of the affluently aloof Augusta National Golf Club, which has refused to admit U.S. presidents on more than one occasion. But this is also where you'll find Tobacco Road, as in the actual Tobacco Road of Erskine Caldwell's eponymous novel about hardscrabble life in the old South during the Great Depression. There it is, right there, on the outskirts of town when you come in on U.S. 25.

SIGHTS
Augusta Riverwalk
There are few better places to enjoy the natural vistas of the river than the **Augusta Riverwalk** (daily dawn-dusk, free), which stretches for about five city blocks, from 6th to 10th Streets.

In order to better negotiate the steepness of the bluff, the Riverwalk actually comprises two bricked walkways. Access the upper level by ramps at the ends of 10th Street, 8th Street Plaza, and 6th Street; get to the lower level via RiverWalk Marina (5th St.), 8th Street Plaza, the Jessye Norman Amphitheatre, and 10th Street Plaza (in front of the Marriott and where the Morris Museum of Art is located).

Morris Museum of Art
The **Morris Museum of Art** (1 10th St., 706/724-7501, http://themorris.org, Tues.-Sat. 10am-5pm, Sun. noon-5pm, $5 adults, $3 children) has quickly become one of the most important second-tier art museums in the South. The core of its all-Southern collections is the life's gatherings of Robert P. Coggins, whose collection was acquired by the nascent Morris board in the late 1980s.

Augusta Museum of History
Standouts among the well-curated exhibits at the **Augusta Museum of History** (560 Reynolds St., 706/722-8454, www.augustamuseum.org, Thurs.-Sat. 10am-5pm, Sun. 1pm-5pm, $4 adults, $3 children) include the Civil War section, the exhibit of Savannah River Edgefield Pottery, including works by the renowned Dave "The Slave" Drake, and an homage to Augusta's golf heritage. Railroad buffs will be thrilled to know that the largest room of this restored mill warehouse contains essentially an entire train on its own track.

James Brown Statue
It took a while, but a bronze commemoration of the Godfather of Soul in his hometown was erected in 2005 in the median of Broad Street between 8th and 9th Streets, within sight of the Imperial Theatre where Brown rehearsed and performed, and a block from the portion of 9th

Street renamed James Brown Boulevard, where he shined shoes as a child.

The **James Brown Cam,** installed by the Augusta Arts Council, enables you to dial a number on your cell phone and have a picture taken for download later.

Laney-Walker Historic District

The old African American business district is commemorated today in the Laney-Walker Historic District north of Laney-Walker Boulevard (formerly Gwinnett St.), bounded on the west by Phillips and Harrison Streets and on the east by 7th and Twiggs Streets (Twiggs St. was the boyhood neighborhood of James Brown).

The most notable renovation is the formerly black-owned **Penny Savings Bank** (1114 James Brown Blvd.). The key attraction in Laney-Walker is the **Lucy Craft Laney Museum of Black History** (1116 Phillips St., 706/724-3546, www.lucycraftlaneymuseum.com, Tues.-Fri. 9am-5pm, Sat. 10am-4pm, $5 adults, $2

children). Ms. Laney herself, whose former home hosts the museum named for her, was one of the first black educators in the South.

Meadow Garden

Smack-dab in a somewhat incongruous location (a rehabilitative hospital campus), **Meadow Garden** (1320 Independence Dr., 706/724-4174, www.historicmeadowgarden. org, Mon.-Fri. 9am-4pm, last tour 3:30pm, Sat. by appointment, $4 adults, $1 children) is the preserved home site of George Walton, one of Georgia's three signers of the Declaration of Independence and the youngest of any who signed that august document, at the ripe old age of 26.

Augusta Canal National Heritage Area

Fairly unique among American canals in that it wasn't built for commercial transportation but for hydromechanical power, the Augusta Canal is the South's only industrial canal in

James Brown's statue by Dr. John Savage on Broad Street

© JIM MOREKIS

continuous use. Built in 1845, the Canal played a major role in Augusta's prominence before, during, and after the Civil War. By the 1990s a special authority had been created to oversee its preservation.

It isn't the only place to see the lengthy historic waterway, Georgia's first National Heritage Area, but the **Augusta Canal Interpretive Center** (1450 Greene St., 706/823-0440, www.augustacanal.com, Apr.-Nov. Mon.-Sat. 9:30am-5:30pm, Sun. 1pm-5:30pm, Dec.-Mar. Tues.-Sat. 9am-5:30pm, $6 adults, $4 children, free with $12.50-25 boat tour) at the well-restored Enterprise Mill building is the only place to see related exhibits and artifacts and take boat tours on it.

The headgate area is best explored at **Savannah Rapids Park** (3300 Evans to Locks Rd., 706/868-3349, www.columbiacountyga.gov, daily dawn-dusk, free) in the next county over. Launch your own canoe or kayak from a low point along the bank at the launch dock at Petersburg Boat Dock at the headgate.

You can rent a canoe or kayak at **Broadway Tackle & Canoe Rentals** (1730 Broad St., 706/738-8848, www.broadwaytackle.com). The old towpath runs alongside this entire section and can be walked or biked. Get a free self-guided tour map at the Interpretive Center.

Woodrow Wilson Boyhood Home

A native of Virginia, the future president led a peripatetic life before occupying the White House, never staying in one place for very long. Apparently the **Woodrow Wilson Boyhood Home** (419 7th St., 706/722-9828, www.wilsonboyhoodhome.org, Tues.-Sat. 10am-5pm, tours on the hour, $5 adults, $3 students) is the place where he stayed the longest, a 10-year stint from 1860 to 1870 while his father was pastor of the local First Presbyterian Church and before the family's move to Columbia, South Carolina (which boasts a Wilson home of its own). The 14 rooms are furnished with period pieces, including about a dozen originals that the Wilsons owned and used.

Tours and Information

The main city tour is the **Historic Trolley Tour** (560 Reynolds St., 706/724-4067, $12) on board the Lady Liberty trolley. You'll see the Canal, the Wilson home, several historic homes, and more. It leaves from the Augusta Museum of History each Saturday at 1:30pm, is roughly two hours, and they ask for 24-hour advance reservations. Admission to the Museum is included with the price of the tour. In the atrium of the Augusta Museum of History is the **Augusta Visitors Center** (560 Reynolds St., 706/724-4067, Mon.-Sat. 10am-5pm, Sun. 1pm-5pm) and gift shop.

Entertainment and Nightlife

The circa-1918 **Imperial Theatre** (749 Broad St., 706/722-8341, www.imperialtheatre.com) is where James Brown often rehearsed with his notoriously micromanaged bands prior to going on tour. These days it hosts a full calendar of various musicals and film screenings.

The most hallowed nightspot in Augusta is **The Soul Bar** (984 Broad St., 706/724-8880, www.soulbar.com, Mon.-Sat. 4pm-3am), a cavernous and charming old-school rock-punk-hipster dive just down from the Imperial Theatre and well known for hosting local musicians, including James Brown's band, even not long before the singer's death.

The larger **Sky City** (1157 Broad St., 706/945-1270, www.skycityaugusta.com, Mon.-Sat. 6pm-3am), down the road, is where to go for bigger-name touring acts such as Drive-By Truckers and Justin Townes Earle.

If only an Irish pub will do, head straight for **Tipsey McStumble's** (214 7th St., 706/955-8507, Mon.-Sat. 11:30am-3am), reportedly on the site of Augusta's first strip club. The current staff respects that spirit in that the women wear naughty Catholic schoolgirl outfits.

Festivals

Augusta's premier event is **The Masters** (www.themasters.com) golf tournament, which takes place each year on the first full weekend in May. While tickets to the actual weekend competition are notoriously hard to come by, tickets to the qualifying rounds during the week are actually not so hard to score. Lucky members of the general public can score tickets to the Masters through a lottery system (apply at the website) nearly a full year ahead. Augusta's other event of note is the **Westobou Festival** (www.westoboufestival.com, ticket prices vary), which takes place the first week in October at various downtown venues and features a ton of regional and national performing and artistic talent.

SHOPPING

Head straight to **Artists Row** (www.artistsrowaugusta.com), a delightful consortium of galleries within restored Victorian storefronts, many complete with lofts and wrought-iron balconies, clustered in and around the 1000 block of Broad Street. One of Broad Street's most classically Augustan establishments is the kitschy antique and bric-a-brac nostalgia market called **Merry's Trash & Treasures** (1236 Broad St., 706/722-3244, www.merrystrashandtreasures.com, Mon.-Fri. 9am-5:30pm,

Sat. 9am-5pm). Forty years of history and 25,000 square feet of display space mean you can get a lot here among the various furniture and home goods offerings.

SPORTS AND RECREATION
Spectator Sports

The minor league **Augusta GreenJackets** (www.milb.com), a single-A farm team of the San Francisco Giants, play at Lake Olmstead Stadium (78 Milledge Rd.). The great and infamous Ty Cobb, who was born near town, once played ball in Augusta. The **Augusta RiverHawks** (www.augustariverhawks.pointstreaksites.com) minor-league ice hockey team skates at James Brown Arena, as part of the Southern Professional Hockey League.

Golf

If you're a member of **Augusta National Golf Club** (www.masters.com) or an invitee of a member, and hence eligible to play here, you already know who you are. Even to members, it's open for play only a few weeks out of the year. Area public courses include the renovated links-style **Augusta Municipal** (2023 Highland Ave., 706/731-9344, www.thepatchaugusta.com, greens fees $20), a.k.a. "The Patch," and a very good state park course over the Savannah River in South Carolina, **Hickory Knob State Resort Park** (1591 Resort Dr., McCormick, SC, 864/391-1764, www.hickoryknobresort.com, greens fees $30-35).

ACCOMMODATIONS AND FOOD

With few exceptions, the Augusta hotel scene is dominated by national chains. Keep in mind that during Masters week in early April, accommodations in Augusta and the surrounding area are not only extremely difficult to obtain at the last minute, they are extraordinarily expensive. Augusta's premier accommodations option is the **(Partridge Inn** (2110 Walton Way, 706/737-8888, www.partridgeinn.com, $130-150). This highly hotel and attached spa in a century-old building features 144 guest rooms. For maximum ease of access to the

Riverwalk and downtown sights, go straight to the **Augusta Marriott at the Convention Center** (2 10th St., 706/722-8900, www.marriott.com, $150).

Most Augustans will tell you the best barbecue in town is at **Sconyer's** (2250 Sconyers Way, 706/790-5411, www.sconyersbar-b-que.com, Thurs.-Sat. 10am-10pm, $10). The hickory-smoked 'cue is delicious, with a tangy sauce a cut above the usual too-sweet variety you'll find in other parts of Georgia. You can get a beer here, not a given with most authentic barbecue joints in the Bible Belt. 【 **Boll Weevil Cafe & Sweetery** (10 9th St., 706/722-7772, http://thebollweevil.com, daily 11am-9pm, $20) is Augusta's newish nod to traditional, classic Southern cuisine. The best hush puppies—those addictive fried cornmeal fritters renowned throughout the South—I've ever had were at **T's Restaurant** (3416 Mike Padgett Hwy., 706/798-4145, www.tsrestaurant.com, Tues.-Thurs. 11am-9pm, Fri. 11am-10pm, Sat. 4:30pm-10pm, $10). This 60-year-old family concern also specializes in fried catfish.

GETTING THERE AND AROUND

Augusta is very conveniently located near east-west I-20. A loop highway, I-520, circles the city. Keep in mind that just north of the Savannah River is North Augusta, South Carolina, part of the greater Augusta metro area.

The city is served by **Augusta Regional Airport** (AGS, 1501 Aviation Way, 706/798-3236, www.flyags.com), which hosts flights by Delta and US Airways Express.

Greyhound (1128 Greene St., 706/722-6411, www.greyhound.com) offers bus service into and out of town. As for public transit, the city runs **Augusta Public Transit** (www.augustaga.gov, $1.25 per ride), with frequent bus routes around town.

OUTSIDE AUGUSTA
Harlem

Named after the famous neighborhood in New York City, Harlem was the birthplace in 1892 of Oliver Hardy, of the famed Laurel and

Harlem's Laurel & Hardy Museum

© JIM MOREKIS

Hardy comedy team. He wasn't here long, but Harlem really plays it up.

The main stop is the **Laurel & Hardy Museum** (250 N. Louisville St., 706/556-0401, www.harlemga.org, Tues.-Sat. 10am-4pm, free) on the main road, where the man's youth and life and times are celebrated in an exhibit and video. Old-timey cars and costumes abound the first weekend of each October as the entire town celebrates their native son's legacy at the **Oliver Hardy Festival** (http://harlemga. org), which brings as many as 30,000 people to this town that is normally home to fewer than 2,000 residents.

Washington

The first city in America named after George Washington (the nation's capital didn't bear his name until nearly 20 years later), stately Washington is also possibly the resting place of the legendary missing Confederate gold! In addition to the mythical lost treasure, the city figures large in Southern symbolism as onetime home of Alexander H. Stephens, vice president of the Confederacy, and as the place where Jefferson Davis convened the last meeting of his cabinet on May 5, 1865.

SIGHTS
Robert Toombs House
A hugely influential figure in U.S. and Georgia politics, Robert Toombs was a staunch Unionist for most of his political career (though also a slave-owning planter) who morphed into the state's most vocal advocate of secession. The **Robert Toombs House** (216 E. Robert Toombs Ave., 706/678-2226, www. gastateparks.org, Tues.-Sat. 9am-5pm, tours 10am-4pm, $5 adults, $3 children) brings his life, well, to life with guided tours in this antebellum Greek Revival mansion.

Washington Historical Museum
Run by the Washington-Wilkes Historical Foundation, the **Washington Historical Museum** (308 E. Robert Toombs Ave., 706/678-5001, www.historyofwilkes.org, Tues.-Sat. 10am-5pm, $3) is particularly interesting to Civil War buffs, chiefly because Wilkes County was so well connected at that time.

Tours
The delightful **"Miss Fanny"** (706/318-3128, http://missfanny.com, $20), whose real name is Elaine, gives very entertaining and informative tours that cover dozens of key homes and usually include a few invitations to come inside. And yes, you'll no doubt hear about the lost Confederate gold.

PRACTICALITIES
The well-restored 17-room **Fitzpatrick Hotel** (16 W. Square, 706/678-5900, www.thefitzpatrickhotel.com, $120-225) is oriented to weekend guests, so if you'd like to stay on a weekday, give them a call well ahead of time. The premier B&B in town is the circa-1828 **Washington Plantation Bed & Breakfast** (15 Lexington Ave., 877/405-9956, www.washingtonplantation.com, $160-230), known for its gourmet breakfasts and beautiful seven-acre grounds.

You don't have to look too hard for the best place to eat in town. The **Washington Jockey Club** (5 E. Square, 706/678-1672, www.washingtonjockeyclub.com, Wed.-Thurs. 5pm-9:30pm, Fri.-Sat. 11am-2pm and 5pm-9:30pm, $10-30) is right on the courthouse square. Signature entrées are the pecan chicken and the shrimp and grits. There's also a full-service bar, pretty much the only watering hole in this sleepy town.

The **Washington-Wilkes Chamber of Commerce** (22 W. Square, 706/678-5111, www.washingtonwilkes.org, Mon.-Fri. 10am-4pm),

NORTH GEORGIA

right on the main courthouse square, is where to get brochures and other information.

SOUTH OF WASHINGTON
Crawfordville

Crawfordville was the birthplace of Alexander H. Stephens, vice president of the Confederacy. These days its handsomely restored block of downtown serves as the frequent backdrop of movies. Stephens's home, **Liberty Hall** (456 Alexander St., 706/456-2602, www.gastateparks.org, Fri.-Sun. 9am-5pm), is preserved as a house museum and is on the grounds of nearby **A. H. Stephens Historic Park** (456 Alexander St., 706/456-2602, www.gastateparks.org, parking $5, campsites $24, cottages $115-125), a state-run site with a campground, cottages, a couple of cute little fishing lakes, and 12 miles of equestrian trails (horse campsites are available for roughly the same price as the regular ones).

Savannah River Lakes

The mighty Savannah River forms the border of Georgia and South Carolina, and since the 1950s the U.S. Army Corps of Engineers has controlled its flow. Dams make lakes, and millions come to frolic on three of them on the Savannah River each year; from north to south, they are Lake Hartwell, Lake Russell, and Clark's Hill-Lake Thurmond.

For a general overview, go to www. sas.usace.army.mil. Lakes Hartwell and Thurmond have **campgrounds** (877/444-6777, www.ReserveUSA.com) operated by the Corps. The general websites for reservations and info on Georgia and South Carolina state parks are www.gastateparks.org and www.discoversouthcarolina.com. Many recreation areas and campgrounds close in the off-season, after Labor Day, though most boat ramps stay open all year. Drought conditions can also affect water levels on Lakes Hartwell and Thurmond (Lake Russell is kept near full at all times). Check the corps websites for up-to-date info.

LAKE HARTWELL

Of the three lakes, northernmost Lake Hartwell (www.sas.usace.army.mil), named after Revolutionary war heroine Nancy Hart, has the most upscale feel and is focused more on private docks and private vacation rentals. For full information, stop by the **Hartwell Dam, Lake Office & Visitor Center** (5625 Anderson Hwy., Hartwell, 706/856-0300, year-round Mon.-Fri. 8am-4:30pm, summer Sat.-Sun. 9am-5:30pm, fall-spring Sat.-Sun. 8am-4:30pm).

Optimized for serious anglers, **Tugaloo State Park** (1763 Tugaloo State Park Rd., 706/356-4362, www.gastateparks.org, office daily 8am-5pm, RV and tent sites $23-30, primitive campsites $15, cottages $135) has one of the biggest boat ramps in the area. There are over 100 RV and tent sites, 5 primitive campsites, and 20 cottages.

Hart Outdoor Recreation Area (330 Hart Park Rd., 706/213-2045, http://gastateparks.org, campsites $19-26, walk-in campsites $19) is a good base of operations for fishing, and also offers self-registration seasonal camping with nice views of the lake (62 sites), as well as 16 walk-in campsites. The boat ramp is open year-round.

Royston

Nestled near the South Carolina line, Royston's main contribution to history is as the hometown of baseball legend Ty Cobb, the "Georgia Peach," whose impressive and often controversial career is memorialized at the **Ty Cobb Museum** (461 Cook St., 706/245-1825, www.tycobbmuseum.org, Mon.-Fri. 9am-5pm, Sat. 10am-4pm, $5 adults, $3 children). The museum is actually inside the Ty Cobb Healthcare Center, a philanthropic legacy of Cobb himself, an astute investor who amassed a large personal fortune.

If you're in the area on a weekend, head straight to **⟨C⟩ Vanna's Country Barbecue** (Hwy. 17 S., 706/246-0952, Fri.-Sat. 11am-9pm, Sun. 11am-3pm, $5) to get a bite in "beautiful downtown Vanna," a bit south of Royston. While the pulled pork is delectably soft and the Brunswick stew most excellent, I'd head straight for their legendary ribs.

Victoria Bryant State Park

Commonly known as one of the best lesser-known state parks in Georgia, **Victoria Bryant State Park** (1105 Bryant Park Rd., 706/245-6270, www.gastateparks.org, parking $5, campsites $25-28) has a nice creek that runs through the camping area, with 27 tent and RV sites. The highlight is the selection of eight raised-platform tenting sites. The adjacent **Highland Walk Golf Course** (706/245-6770, http://georgiagolf.com, daily from 8am) offers 18 holes.

LAKE RUSSELL

Named after long-serving Georgia Senator Richard B. Russell Jr., Lake Russell (www.sas.usace.army.mil) is the youngest of the three lakes. Because it was built after the Water Projects Act of 1974, private development on its shores is prohibited. For more information, stop by the **Russell Dam & Lake Office & Visitors Center** (4144 Russell Dam Dr., 706/213-3400, Mon.-Fri. 8am-4:30pm, Sat.-Sun. 8am-4pm).

Along Lake Russell is one of the gems in the Georgia state park system, **Richard B. Russell State Park** (2650 Russell State Park Rd., 706/213-2045, www.gastateparks.org, parking $5, tent and RV sites $25-28, cottages $130-140). It is home to the 18-hole **Arrowhead Pointe Golf Course** ($45-50) as well as a well-regarded disc golf course. There are only 28 RV and tent sites and no primitive sites, but there are 20 very nice lakefront cottages, two of which are dog-friendly ($40 per dog, maximum two).

CLARK'S HILL LAKE

Clark's Hill Lake is technically called Lake Strom Thurmond (www.sas.usace.army.mil); in 1988 Congress renamed it in honor of the controversial long-serving South Carolina politician. Georgia politicians refused to honor the change, and on Georgia maps it's still called Clark's Hill. It is the oldest of the three Army Corps of Engineers lakes on the Savannah River, and its 70,000 acres make it the largest such project east of the Mississippi. For more info, go across the border into South Carolina and visit the **Thurmond Lake Office & Visitors Center** (510 Clarks Hill Hwy., Clarks Hill, SC, 864/333-1147, daily 8am-4:30pm).

A great way to enjoy the lake with the family is **Elijah Clark State Park** (2959 McCormick Hwy., 706/359-3458, www.gastateparks.org, parking $5, tent and RV sites $25, walk-in campsites $15, Pioneer campground $35, cottages $120). There are 165 RV and tent sites, 10 walk-in tent sites, the Pioneer campground, and 20 lakefront cottages, two of which are dog-friendly ($40 per dog, maximum two).

Bass anglers should head straight to **Mistletoe State Park** (3725 Mistletoe Rd., 706/541-0321, www.gastateparks.org, parking $5, tent and RV sites $25, walk-in campsites $15, backcountry sites $10, cottages $140).

For a more barebones stay, try **Bobby Brown Outdoor State Recreation Area** (2509 Bobby Brown State Park, 706/359-3458, www.gastateparks.org, parking $5, campsites $25). It has a seasonal self-registration campground (61 sites), a year-round boat ramp, and two miles of trails. It's built near the circa-1790 dead town of Petersburg, and if water levels are low you can occasionally see some of the old foundations.

Elberton

The town of Elberton prides itself on being the "Granite Capital of the World." Fittingly, its chief attraction is made of granite as well, specifically the **Georgia Guidestones** (Guidestones Rd.) off Highway 77 north of town, known as "America's Stonehenge" because of the vague resemblance of the 19-foot-tall stones to the

Druid monument. The Guidestones, erected in 1980, feature an assortment of New-Agey exhortations in 12 languages, including four ancient tongues.

A more classic bit of Elberton history can be found at the **Nancy Hart Cabin** (off River Rd., daily dawn-dusk), a replica of the home of the colonist woman who, according to legend, singlehandedly captured a war party of Tories who accosted her and her family.

NORTH GEORGIA

MIDDLE AND SOUTH GEORGIA

Middle Georgia is full of surprises. Besides being the home of the Allman Brothers and Otis Redding, Macon also has one of the most beautifully ornate cathedrals you'll see outside Europe. Columbus is where the inventor of Coca-Cola was born. President Franklin Roosevelt was inspired by the healing properties of Warm Springs to found the March of Dimes. The nation's first state park was at Indian Springs. And polite Milledgeville once housed the largest insane asylum on the planet.

South Georgia is the least populous part of the state and unquestionably the hottest during the summer. One might be tempted to ask, "Why go to South Georgia?" Where else can you find an entire town devoted almost entirely to celebrating the life and times of a president born there, as is the case with Plains and native son Jimmy Carter? Where else can you find a swamp the size of Delaware, filled with blackwater that is as clean as what comes out of your tap at home, as is the case with the Okefenokee? Where else can you walk in the footsteps of Civil War POWs and visit a stirring national museum devoted to the memory of American POWs from all wars, as you can at Andersonville?

PLANNING YOUR TIME

Driving around Middle Georgia can be a bit time-consuming given the large east-west distances involved. Visiting the fairly nearby cities of Macon and Milledgeville can be done in a day each. To fully enjoy the scenic and invigorating area in the Pine Mountain-Warm Springs-Columbus area, I suggest slowing

© BRIAN LASENBY/123RF.COM

MIDDLE AND SOUTH GEORGIA

SOUTH CAROLINA

ANDALUSIA

Milledgeville

Waynesboro

Louisville

Allendale

Magnolia Springs State Park

Millen

Sylvania

441

Ohoopee Dunes Natural Area

80

Swainsboro

301

Statesboro

16

441
319

80

Eastman

Vidalia

VIDALIA ONION MUSEUM

Claxton

16

McRae

280

25
301

Savannah

1

Glennville

Hazlehurst

341

Hinesville

129

95

221

Fitzgerald

319

Ocilla

Alma

Jesup

Douglas

341

82

301

Darian

ATLANTIC OCEAN

Nashville

Waycross

Brunswick

Homerville

84

OKEFENOKEE NATIONAL WILDLIFE REFUGE

221

Folkston

Valdosta

441

129

95

0   25 mi

0   25 km

75

FLORIDA

Jacksonville

10

© AVALON TRAVEL

HIGHLIGHTS

◖ Allman Brothers Band Museum at the Big House: One of the country's favorite bands has a lovingly curated collection of unique memorabilia (page 582).

◖ Andalusia: Visit the farm where the great Flannery O'Connor authored most of her classic Southern Gothic novels and short stories (page 588).

◖ FDR's Little White House: A bittersweet look into the life of a pioneering figure is enriched with amazing memorabilia from his transformative presidency (page 591).

◖ National Infantry Museum and Soldier Center: A stirring look at the exploits of the American fighting soldier comes with state-of-the-art technology (page 595).

◖ Jimmy Carter Boyhood Farm: Take a nostalgic and insightful look into the Depression-era experiences of the Georgia-born president just outside his hometown of Plains (page 604).

◖ National Prisoner of War Museum: The site of the notorious Andersonville Civil War POW camp also hosts a deeply affecting exploration of cruelty and bravery during wartime (page 605).

LOOK FOR ◖ TO FIND RECOMMENDED SIGHTS, ACTIVITIES, DINING, AND LODGING.

◖ Hay House: One of the South's grandest house museums is also fascinatingly individualistic (page 577).

◖ Ocmulgee National Monument: Tour the enormous mounds, which are remnants of a once-glorious Native American civilization (page 581).

◖ Providence Canyon State Outdoor Recreation Area: This geological feature of high white walls and a deep floor, surprisingly developed by human impact, has been called "Georgia's Grand Canyon" (page 607).

◖ Okefenokee National Wildlife Refuge: Visit a vast and wholly fascinating natural feature the likes of which can't be found anywhere else on the planet (page 613).

down your pace and spending more than just a quick pass-through for the day.

Time management is a real challenge in South Georgia, a truly vast swath of land that, though served by an excellent road system, is simply too big to traverse quickly. While theoretically you could hit all the major sights in a three-day weekend, realistically, unless you have four or five days to spare, you will have to prioritize.

Basically, there are three routes of particular interest in South Georgia. The area occasionally called "Presidential pathways" includes sites related to Jimmy Carter as well as the Andersonville POW camp and museum and the Kolomoki Mounds and Providence Canyon sights. Then there's the southern band along the Florida border, with

Thomasville as the main stop; and finally, the huge Okefenokee Swamp, taking up virtually the entire southeastern corner of Georgia. The Okefenokee is something of a special case, as you can easily spend several days exploring it or simply confine it to a day trip.

Macon

It's fitting that Macon is pretty much dead center in the middle of Georgia, since in many ways it's the archetypal Georgia town: laid-back, churchified, heavy on fried food, built by the railroad, surrounded by seemingly endless farmland, and a center of cross-pollinating musical traditions.

SIGHTS

⬮ Hay House

Easily one of the most splendid and splendidly restored antebellum mansions in the South, the **Hay House** (934 Georgia Ave., 478/742-8155, www.georgiatrust.org, Sept.-Dec. and Mar.-June Tues.-Sat. 10am-4pm, Sun. 1pm-4pm, Jan.-Feb. and July-Aug. Tues.-Sat. 10am-4pm, last tour 3pm, $9 adults, $5 students) in the stately Intown neighborhood is worthy of a tour. Built in the Italian Renaissance Revival style and completed a scant five years before the outbreak of the Civil War, the Hay House was built by William Butler Johnston. It passed into the hands of insurance magnate Parks Lee Hay during the 1920s. The magnificent abode stayed in the Hay family until 1977, when it was given to the Georgia Trust for Historic Preservation.

Touring the multiple, often overlapping levels of the 18,000-plus-square-foot Hay House today brings to mind less a classic Southern mansion than a film set, perhaps even Shangri-La from *Citizen Kane*. However, the taste level is still remarkably high and consistent throughout, from the incredible plasterwork to the extensive faux finishes, which actually cost more in their day than the real materials they imitated.

For purposes of authenticity, the Hay House to this day lacks modern air-conditioning. It does get warm in the summertime, but tour patrons are given a fan to wave in front of their faces while inside.

St. Joseph Catholic Church

Oddly for this rigidly Baptist region, one of the most beautiful and ornate Roman Catholic churches pretty much anywhere is right in Macon's Historic Intown neighborhood. **St. Joseph Catholic Church** (830 Poplar St., 478/745-1631, www.stjosephmacon.com, office Mon.-Fri. 9:30am-4:30pm) was completed at the turn of the 20th century, though it harks back to a much older tradition of grand European cathedrals.

Inside you'll find over 60 stained glass windows, most crafted in Bavaria (southern Germany). While most of the decorative marble is Italian in origin, the columns are made of Georgia marble. At the top of the church's left tower, as you face the sanctuary from Poplar Street, you'll see three huge bronze bells, named Jesus, Mary, and Joseph. You can hear them rung daily at 6am, noon, and 6pm.

Sidney Lanier Cottage

Just around the corner from St. Joseph, the **Sidney Lanier Cottage** (935 High St., 478/743-3851, Mon.-Sat. 10am-4pm, last tour 3:30pm, $5 adults, $3 children) is where that great man of letters was born in 1842; this was actually his grandparents' home at the time. While he didn't live in this house most of his life, he did spend much of his time in the Macon area. He volunteered for

MACON

To Milledgeville

To Savannah

To Gray and Clinton

OCMULGEE NATIONAL MONUMENT

Central Park

Walker Lakes

FINCHER'S

SEE "DOWNTOWN MACON" MAP

HAY HOUSE

Rose Hill Cemetery

Riverside Cemetery

Ocmulgee River

MERCER UNIVERSITY

ASH ST

7TH ST

To Museum of Aviation, Perry, and Valdosta

BROADWAY

HOUSTON AVE

MILLERFIELD RD

INGLESIDE AVE

FOREST AVE

VINEVILLE AVE

ALLMAN BROTHERS BAND MUSEUM AT THE BIG HOUSE

PIERCE AVE

RIVERSIDE DR

To Comfort Inn and Suites

VINEVILLE AVE

NAPIER AVE

AVE

HILTON GARDEN INN

MERCER UNIVERSITY DR

MONTPELIER AVE

ANTHONY RD

RD

EISENHOWER PKWY

WILLIAMSON RD

PIO NONO AVE

MUSEUM OF ARTS AND SCIENCES

MUMFORD RD

FORSYTH RD

TUCKER RD

AYERS

LOG CABIN DR

MERCER

UNIVERSITY DR

BLOOMFIELD DR

BLOOMFIELD RD

CHAMBERS RD

EXIT 1

To Lake Tobesofkee

EXIT 2

EXIT 3

FOSTER RD

COLUMBUS RD

To Columbus

1 mi

1 km

0

0

© AVALON TRAVEL

MID. AND SOUTH GEORGIA

© JIM MOREKIS

the magnificent Hay House

the Confederate Army at the outbreak of the Civil War, eventually catching consumption as a prisoner of war at a Maryland camp.

Cannonball House

While General Sherman and his troops left Macon alone, an exchange of artillery fire led to some random shells hitting and embedding themselves into the antebellum **Cannonball House** (856 Mulberry St., 478/745-5982, www.cannonballhouse.org, Jan.-Feb. Mon.-Fri. 11am-last tour at 4:15pm, Sat. 10am-last tour at 4:15pm, Mar.-Dec. Mon.-Sat. 10am-last tour at 4:15pm, $6 adults, $3 students, free under age 4). Tours last 45 minutes and include the main house, with its furnishings and Civil War memorabilia, and the historically notable two-story brick kitchen building with servants quarters.

Grand Opera House

The 1,000-seat **Grand Opera House** (651 Mulberry St., 478/301-5470, www.thegrand-macon.com, Mon.-Fri. 10am-5pm, showtimes

vary), built in 1883, represents the height of Macon's opulent Victorian heyday. While Reconstruction and its aftermath were difficult throughout the South, Macon fared noticeably better than most Southern cities, and "The Grand" is proof.

Museum District

While not all offerings have worked out—the Georgia Music Hall of Fame was forced to close in 2011—Macon does boast its own fledgling museum district in a walkable, renovated section of downtown.

MUSEUM OF ARTS AND SCIENCES

Billing itself as Georgia's largest general-purpose museum, the **Museum of Arts and Sciences** (4182 Forsyth Rd., 478/477-3232, www.masmacon.org, Tues.-Sat. 10am-5pm, Sun. 1pm-5pm, $10 adults, $7 students, $5 ages 2-17) features a wide range of natural history exhibits and regionally oriented historical artifacts.

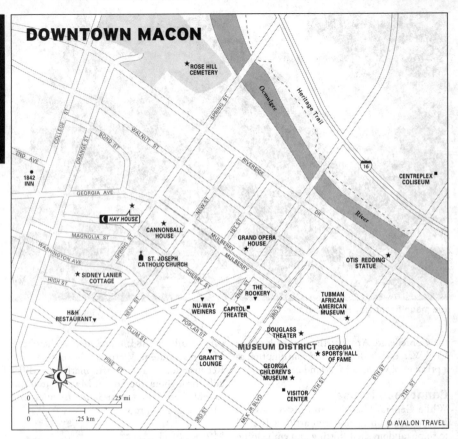

GEORGIA CHILDREN'S MUSEUM

Four floors of enriching, educational children's activities, some still under development, are the attraction in this handsome building in the heart of downtown, which also includes a decent café for the refreshment of the adults. Highlights of the **Georgia Children's Museum** (382 Cherry St., 478/755-9539, www.georgiachildrensmuseum.com, Tues.-Sat. 10am-5pm, $4) include a hands-on TV studio and an exhibit on the indigenous Creek people.

GEORGIA SPORTS HALL OF FAME

Georgia has a rich sports legacy that's celebrated at the **Georgia Sports Hall of Fame**

(301 Cherry St., 478/752-1585, www.gshf.com, Tues.-Sat. 9am-5pm, $8 adults, $3.50 children). Fans of the Atlanta Braves and the state's premier college football program at the University of Georgia will be particularly pleased with the memorabilia.

TUBMAN AFRICAN AMERICAN MUSEUM

Actually more of an art and art-history destination than strictly a historical museum, the **Tubman African American Museum** (340 Walnut St., 478/743-8544, www.tubmanmuseum.com, Tues.-Fri. 9am-5pm, Sat. 11am-5pm, $8 adults, $4 children) explores the African American experience and culture.

ON THE CHITLIN CIRCUIT

In the days of racial segregation, there was even a color line for music. Thus began the legendary "Chitlin Circuit" of African American entertainers playing to black audiences, with Macon as a key stop.

While an actual chitlin is an ingredient in Southern food, specifically fried pig intestine, or "chitterling," the chitlin circuit is best exemplified by four enormously influential Georgia artists: **Ray Charles, James Brown,** and two who grew up blocks apart in Macon's Pleasant Hill neighborhood, **Little Richard** and **Otis Redding.**

Richard "Little Richard" Penniman is considered in some circles the real father of rock and roll, emulated by white artists such as Elvis Presley and Jerry Lee Lewis. Little Richard wrote "Long Tall Sally" while working as a dishwasher at Ann's **Tic-Toc Room** (408 Broadway, now Martin Luther King Jr. Blvd.) about a waitress there. It's now a swank bar, but it's still the Tic-Toc Room, and a plaque outside explains the history of the building. A stone's throw away is the restored circa-1921 **Douglass Theatre** (355 Martin Luther King Jr. Blvd.), a major chitlin circuit venue that continues to host a full calendar of shows. Contrary to what many assume, the venue isn't named after early abolitionist Frederick Douglass but rather local black entrepreneur Charles Henry Douglass.

Otis Redding, though born in nearby Dawson, came of age in Macon. It's said that he won so many teen talent shows at the Douglass that he was eventually barred from competing. He sang at the Baptist church (850 Armory Dr.), where his father was pastor.

Redding nearly single-handedly brought chitlin circuit R&B to a white counterculture audience with his short but electrifying headlining appearance at the Monterey Pop Festival in 1967. Redding died in a plane crash only six months later, but his memory lives on at Macon's **Gateway Park,** where he is memorialized with a statue and plaza.

◀ Ocmulgee National Monument

There are a couple of sites elsewhere with somewhat better-preserved Native American mounds, but none quite so extensive as the sprawling and entirely fascinating **Ocmulgee National Monument** (1207 Emery Hwy., 478/752-8257, www.nps.gov, daily 9am-5pm, free). To early white settlers of the region they were simply called the "Old Fields," but to the Mississippian people that lived here from about 900 to 1650, it was a bustling center of activity, from the enormous temple mound (from the top you can see most of downtown Macon) to the intimate and striking Earth Lodge, which, though completely restored, boasts the only original and unchanged lodge floor in North America.

Begin and end your visit at the charming art deco visitors center. Inside you'll find an extensive series of displays illustrating not only artifacts from the area, but the scope of Native American life in the region covering at least 17,000 years. From the visitors center you take the trails through the actual mounds, which may not look like much more than grassy knolls until you fully digest the significance of this site, which some scholars say at its peak was more populous than modern-day Macon.

Perhaps the most amazing offering at the monument is actually some distance away from the rest of the mounds at the younger Lamar Mound. Built around 1350 during a later incarnation of the Mississippian culture, the Lamar site is the only known example of a spiral mound in North America. It is accessible only when the water level in the Ocmulgee River is low, and only by a Ranger-led tour that is held frequently throughout the year. Call ahead or check with the ranger at the visitors center.

Otis Redding Statue

Just as you cross the bridge over the Ocmulgee River from downtown into east Macon, on your left you'll see Gateway Park and the beginning of the Ocmulgee Heritage Trail. The key landmark here, however, is the small but well-done memorial plaza to the late great Otis Redding, Macon native and beloved R&B-soul musician who influenced an entire generation before dying in a plane crash at the age of 26. A nice touch is the buried, vandalism-proof speakers surrounding the statue, which play a steady 24-hour diet of Redding songs.

Rose Hill Cemetery

One of two adjacent historic cemeteries along Riverside Drive, **Rose Hill Cemetery** (1071 Riverside Dr., 478/751-9119, www.historicrosehillcemetery.org, daily dawn-dusk, free) is generally of more interest to visitors. This is where Duane Allman and Berry Oakley are buried side by side; they died in separate motorcycle accidents about a year and three blocks apart. Allman Brothers fans can also see the poignant graves of "Little Martha" Ellis and Elizabeth Reed, both of whom inspired band tunes.

Perhaps the most striking non-Allmans feature at Rose Hill is Soldiers Square, the extensive burial plot of over 600 Confederate Civil War casualties and veterans, which you'll find down the steepest hill near the railroad tracks. This is one of the few places in the United States where the official flag of the Confederate States of America, the familiar battle flag emblem set against an all-white background, still waves 24 hours a day on public land.

Riverside Cemetery

While adjacent Rose Hill Cemetery tends to get more attention, **Riverside Cemetery** (1301 Riverside Dr., 478/742-5328, www.riversidecemetery.com, daily dawn-dusk, free) is much more walkable. Notable sites include the poignant Babyland (a late-19th-century plot where small children are buried) and the grave of Charles Reb Messenburg, who, at his request, was buried standing up.

◖ Allman Brothers Band Museum at the Big House

If you're any kind of a fan of the Allman Brothers Band, or if the idea of vintage tube amps, beautiful guitars, well-used drums, handwritten set lists, and flamboyant 1970s outfits gets you excited, head straight to the wonderfully done **Allman Brothers Band Museum at the Big House** (2321 Vineville Ave., 478/741-5551, www.thebighousemuseum.com, Thurs.-Sun. 11am-6pm, $8 adults, $4 children). The rambling Tudor mansion, or "Big House," a very short drive northwest of downtown, where the band lived as an extended community from 1970 to 1973, and where many of their iconic hits were written, has been beautifully and tastefully restored. In some cases the intent is to replicate rooms where the Allmans and friends hung out; others create light-filled and joyously celebratory display areas for the enormous volume of Allman-related memorabilia and vintage instruments.

Make sure you get the printed guide to the museum, which corresponds to numbers posted throughout the rooms. An audio tour (no extra cost) guides you through the stops, or you can follow the numbers on your own.

Tours and Information

Easily the most unique tour in town is **Lights on Macon** (www.lightsonmacon.com), a free, self-guided, illuminated nighttime walking tour available every night of the year. A neighborhood of historic Intown Macon leaves its lights on every night so tour-goers can view at their leisure. Download the tour guide from the website or get the brochure at the **Downtown Macon Visitor Information Center** (450 Martin Luther King Jr. Blvd., 478/743-3401, www.maconga.org, Mon.-Fri. 9am-5pm, Sat. 10am-4pm). Begin your tour at one of two iconic Macon locations, the Hay House (934 Georgia Ave.) or 1842 Inn (353 College St.). Download a handy free daytime walking tour of downtown Macon at www.maconwalkingtours.com.

ENTERTAINMENT AND EVENTS
Nightlife

The premier rock club in town and a key part of Georgia's music history is **Grant's Lounge** (576 Poplar St., 478/746-9191, www.

© JIM MOREKIS

Allman Brothers Band Museum at the Big House

grantslounge.com, Mon.-Sat. noon-2am), the "original home of Southern rock," which still hosts regular live music after over four decades of nourishing the budding careers of Southern names like Lynyrd Skynyrd, Tom Petty, and the Marshall Tucker Band.

For another neat bit of Southern music history, have a cocktail at the **Tic-Toc Room** (408 Broadway, 478/744-0123, Mon.-Sat. 5pm-2am). It's more of a martini bar and swank café these days, but in the days before integration it was a key venue on the "Chitlin Circuit" of African American entertainment; James Brown, Little Richard, and Otis Redding all performed here. (Little Richard also worked here, and it's said he wrote "Long Tall Sally" about a coworker.)

Festivals

Without question Macon's premier event is the "pinkest party on earth," the **Cherry Blossom Festival** (www.cherryblossom.com, Mar.), which takes place in mid- to late March to take advantage of the annual blossoming of the city's estimated 300,000-plus Yoshino cherry trees, which are not indigenous but were imported from Japan. Events are varied, from a Bed Race to nightly concerts to, of course, the Cherry Blossom Parade, and take place at various venues, including Cherry Street downtown, Central City Park (Willie Smokie Glover Dr.), Mercer University, and Wesleyan College. A free trolley takes festivalgoers from spot to spot. While some events and concerts are ticketed, the majority are free and open to the public.

Easily the most unique event in the area is the **Ocmulgee Indian Celebration** (www.nps. gov, Sept.), which takes place on the grounds of the National Park Service-operated Ocmulgee National Monument and celebrates the heritage and culture of the descendants of the Creek people, who built the enormous mound complex here.

ACCOMMODATIONS
Under $150

Due to its very central location at the confluence of three interstate highways (I-75, I-475,

ALLMAN BROTHERS TOUR

Though their family roots are actually in north Florida, perhaps no other musical name is so associated with Macon and middle Georgia as the Allman Brothers Band. Far ahead of their time musically in their sinuous and rhythmic blend of rock, blues, soul, and even country, they were also one of the first true multiracial bands.

Duane and Gregg Allman grew up as competing siblings, with Duane's fiery personality and virtuosic slide guitar work driving their early success. Touring with what would become a close-knit bunch of friends in various incarnations through the mid- to late 1960s, the whole bunch ended up in Macon as the Allman Brothers Band. With the 1969 release of their eponymous debut album, nothing in the rock world, or in Macon, for that matter, was ever the same.

The city is chock-full of Allman sites that have inspired pilgrimages for decades. The band had various residences, including **309 College Street** and **315 College Street,** which was on the cover of the band's first album. The most famous was the "Big House," a large Tudor rented by bassist Berry Oakley and his wife, Linda, and memorialized today in the **Allman Brothers Band Museum at the Big House** (2321 Vineville Ave., 478/741-5551, www.thebighousemuseum.com, Thurs.-

Sun. 11am-6pm, $8 adults, $4 children), which opened in 2010.

Alas, the Allmans heyday was short-lived. In October 1971 Duane perished in a motorcycle crash at **Hillcrest Avenue and Bartlett Street.** Barely a year later, Oakley died in another motorcycle crash at **Napier and Inverness Avenues.** Both were only 24. Both are buried side by side at **Rose Hill Cemetery.** At Rose Hill you can also see two gravesites that inspired Allman songs, "Little Martha" Ellis and Elizabeth Napier Reed. The Bond tomb at Rose Hill was on the back cover of the band's debut record.

Not all is gloom and doom, however. Down the road from the Big House you can have the best fried chicken and collard greens for miles around at **H & H Restaurant** (807 Forsyth St., 478/742-9810, www.mamalouise.com, Mon.-Sat. 6:30am-4pm, $12), where the band frequently ate and which features much Allmans memorabilia.

While in Macon, the band's label was **Capricorn Record** (535 D.T. Walton Sr. Way/ Cotton Ave.), which, though now in other hands, still retains the old signage and exterior. The actual Capricorn studios were at **536 Martin Luther King Jr. Boulevard;** that exterior can be seen on the *Allman Brothers Band at Fillmore East* album.

---

and I-16), Macon offers a vast range of budget chain accommodations that tend to group in large clusters.

The I-75 cluster is just north of downtown, about a five-minute drive. I'd recommend the **Comfort Inn & Suites** (3935 Arkwright Rd., 478/757-8688, www.comfortinn.com, $75-100) or the pet-friendly **Candlewood Suites** (3957 River Place Dr., 478/254-3531, www.ichotelsgroup.com, $75-100). The densest cluster is off I-475 on the western edge of Macon, with downtown about 10 minutes away. Try **Comfort Inn West** (4951 Eisenhower Pkwy., 478/788-5500, www.comfortinn.com, $75-100), with renovated guest rooms, or the

pet-friendly **Sleep Inn West** (140 Plantation Inn Dr., 478/476-8111, www.sleepinn.com, $75-100).

A good budget choice a bit closer to downtown is the **Hilton Garden Inn** (1220 Stadium Dr., 478/741-5527, www.hilton.com, $130) adjacent to the tranquil Mercer University campus.

$150-300

By far the premier lodging in Macon is the **1842 Inn** (353 College St., 478/741-1842, www.1842inn.com, $140-255), and I urge you to make every effort to secure a room if you're planning to visit the city. It's in a particularly striking Greek Revival building that was once the home of a mayor, with "opulent" a fair description of its interior. Ten of the inn's 19 guest rooms are in the main building, which boasts a classic wraparound veranda with 17 columns. There's a separate Victorian Cottage, which was actually moved onto this parcel of land in the 1980s and has nine guest rooms.

FOOD

Because of Macon's central location near several interstate highways, pretty much every type of fast-food and chain restaurant you can think of has an outpost in town. Instead, here are some of the more unique and recommended local and regional offerings.

American

With an active bar scene to go along with its well-received menu, **C The Rookery Restaurant & Bar** (543 Cherry St., 478/746-8658, www.rookerymacon.com, Mon. 11am-3pm, Tues.-Thurs. 11am-9:30pm, Fri.-Sat. 11am-10pm, Sun. 11:30am-9pm, $8-15) is a great all-purpose stop in the most happening area of Macon's restored downtown, with history back to 1976. Specialties include Betsy's Grilled Pimento Cheese, a Southern delicacy, and a range of great burgers, all half a pound and all named after famous Georgians, from the Allman Brothers (Swiss cheese and mushrooms) to Jerry Reed (pepper jack cheese and jalapeños) to Jimmy Carter (peanut butter and bacon).

Perhaps the most unique restaurant in Macon is **Nu-Way Weiners** (430 Cotton Ave., 478/743-1368, www.nu-wayweiners.com, Mon.-Fri. 6am-7pm, Sat. 7am-6pm, $2-4), which has grown to nine locations in its nearly 100-year history. At all of them you'll find the same inexpensive menu of hot dogs built around Nu-Way's "secret" chili topping.

Barbecue

In operation for 75 years, **Fincher's** (891 Gray Hwy., 478/743-5866, www.finchers-bbqga.net, $5) is one of two longtime local 'cue joints considered the city's best, and it's

the most out of the ordinary. The sauce is sharper and tangier than the usual Georgia variety, a variant of the North Carolina vinegar-based sauce, along with Tarheel-style coleslaw topping. There's another location at 3947 Houston Avenue.

Soul Food

Allman Brothers fans will know **C H & H Restaurant** (807 Forsyth St., 478/742-9810, www.mamalouise.com, Mon.-Sat. 6:30am-4pm, $12) as the band's favorite hangout in Macon, but "Mama Louise" Hudson's place is also one of the best soul food diners anywhere. It's very informal: When you're ready to leave, you come back behind the counter and pay the cook, who also runs the register. The menu is as simple as it has been for the last 50 years; you pick a meat (go with the fried chicken) and three veggies, such as perfect collard greens and their signature squash. The walls are covered with memorabilia of Southern rock, particularly the Allman Brothers, who were taken under Mama Louise's wing during their early days as starving artists.

SOUTH OF MACON
Museum of Aviation

There's one very worthwhile reason to visit the town of Warner Robins, 14 miles south of Macon, and that's the excellent **Museum of Aviation** (Russell Pkwy., 478/926-6870, www.museumofaviation.org, daily 9am-5pm, free) on the massive Robins Air Force Base. Comprising several very large buildings with roughly outlined chronological themes, the core collection of the museum is its impressive array of many, many dozens of military aircraft from all eras of American aviation. Airplane buffs of all ages will go nuts seeing these beauties up close, from World War II classics like the P-51 Mustang to the host of Cold War and Vietnam War era jets to the starkly elegant U-2 and SR-71 spy planes. A nice plus with the museum is that, despite being on a military installation, it's in an area where you don't have to go through the usual checkpoints for your driver's license and proof of car insurance.

INFORMATION AND SERVICES

The centrally located **Downtown Macon Visitor Information Center** (450 Martin Luther King Jr. Blvd., 478/743-3401, www.maconga.org, Mon.-Sat. 9am-5pm, Sat. 10am-4pm) is in the offices of the local Convention and Visitors Bureau and is a must-stop. For those who prefer a visitors center off the interstate highway, go to the I-75 **Southbound Rest Area** (478/994-8181, info kiosk Mon.-Fri. 9am-5pm), a mile south of exit 181.

GETTING THERE AND AROUND

Macon is extraordinarily well served by the interstate highway system. I-75 passes through town north-south, and the western terminus of I-16 is here.

The small **Middle Georgia Regional Airport** (MCN, 1000 Terminal Dr., 478/788-3760, www.cityofmacon.net) hosts flights by Silver Airways to Atlanta and Orlando.

Macon is served by **Greyhound** (65 Spring St., 478/743-5411, www.greyhound.com). In town, the **Macon Transit Authority** (www.mta-mac.com, $1.25) runs buses and trolleys on various routes.

Indian Springs and Juliette

The short but often congested drive north from Macon on I-75 doesn't have to be a headlong rush into Atlanta's sprawl. There are several very interesting stops and stays along the way, including the nation's oldest state park.

INDIAN SPRINGS AND FLOVILLA
Indian Springs State Park

There's truth in advertising at **Indian Springs State Park** (678 Lake Clark Rd., 770/504-2277, www.gastateparks.org, daily 7am-10pm, parking $5, campsites $25-28, cottages $115-125), which centers on a natural spring well known to Native Americans for its heady taste and healing properties. A Civilian Conservation Corps masonry "spring house" from the 1930s showcases a rustic drinking fountain for guests to sample, and people often come to fill up jugs to take with them.

Georgia makes the case that this is technically the first state park in the country. The land was acquired in 1825 through the shady and controversial Second Treaty of Indian Springs, in which some Creek people were persuaded to sign over their entire community's rights to the remaining land in the area. By 1927 it was a "State Forest Park," and in 1931

Indian Springs and Vogel became the first two state parks in Georgia. Today, the park has 60 tent and RV campsites and 10 cottages, two of which are dog-friendly.

A bit north of Flovilla is one of Georgia's oldest restaurants and certainly one of its best, if not the best, 'cue joints, **◖ Fresh Air Barbecue** (1164 Hwy. 42, Jackson, 770/775-3182, www.freshairbarbecue.com, Mon.-Thurs. 8am-7:30pm, Fri.-Sat. 8am-8:30pm, Sun. 8am-8pm, $3-7), in business since before the Great Depression. The pit-cooked barbecue is generally served with a tangy North Carolina-style sauce. Significantly, they're open seven days a week.

JULIETTE AND VICINITY

Juliette was pretty neglected until a Hollywood scout decided it might be a great location for the 1991 film *Fried Green Tomatoes*. The town became a stand-in for Irondale, Alabama, with the old hardware store transformed into the film's Whistlestop Café.

The film crew is long gone, but somebody had the bright idea to keep the **◖ Whistlestop Café** (443 McCrackin St., 478/992-8886, www.thewhistlestopcafe.com, daily 11am-4pm, $10) going, and it became the centerpiece of a minor tourism renaissance in the little town. Clearly, you must have the fried green tomatoes, either as an appetizer or in the signature sandwich. Yup, Juliette has a **Fried Green Tomato Festival** (www.themiddleofeverywhere.com) in October.

Piedmont National Wildlife Refuge

The vast majority of federally run wildlife refuges in Georgia are on the coastal flyway, but a key exception is the 35,000-acre **Piedmont National Wildlife Refuge** (718 Juliette Rd., 478/986-5441, www.fws.gov, daily dawn-dusk, free). The backstory is interesting: With the land exhausted by the boll weevil beetle and poor farming practices, this was nearly a wasteland by the time of the Great Depression. In

the 1930s President Franklin Roosevelt made it a wildlife refuge, and since then the loblolly pine stands are back, along with a resident population of endangered red-cockaded woodpeckers, among much other flora and fauna.

Gray

Not much goes in the town of Gray, but folks drive from many miles around to enjoy what many connoisseurs consider Georgia's best barbecue: ◖ **Old Clinton BBQ** (4214 Gray Hwy., 478/986-3225, www.oldclintonbbq.com, Mon.-Thurs. 10am-8pm, Fri.-Sat. 10am-9pm, Sun. 10am-4pm, $5). This original location (there's another in nearby Milledgeville) has been dishing out masterfully smoked pork and ribs since 1958, and it looks every bit its age, with memorabilia and kitsch appeal to burn.

Milledgeville

Milledgeville may not get as much attention as some other cities in Georgia, but it's worth a visit and is actually vital to the state's history. It served as state capital during the antebellum era—Atlanta didn't get that title until after the Civil War—and so boasts more than its share of intriguing political shenanigans.

A cynic would say it's only fitting that a town famous for hosting so many politicians would also be famous as the site of one of the nation's earliest hospitals for the mentally ill. While the facility itself, now called Central State Hospital, has been dramatically downsized, it was once the largest mental hospital in the United States; in old Georgia lore "going to Milledgeville" was often slang for losing one's mind.

Milledgeville's eccentric combination of lively social gatherings and Southern Gothic darkness meant that it was the perfect breeding ground for writer Flannery O'Connor's brand of darkly humorous symbolic fiction.

SIGHTS
Old Capital Museum

Despite the ominously fortress-like

countenance of this Gothic Revival building on the quad of Georgia Military College, the **Old Capital Museum** (201 E. Greene St., 478/453-1803, www.oldcapitalmuseum.org, Tues.-Fri. 10am-4pm, Sat. noon-4pm, $5.50 adults, $4.50 children) was never a military site, but did serve as the meeting place for the state legislature. The sections detailing the area's often frightfully bloody early colonial history are the most interesting, as is the exhibit devoted to the building of the Georgia Lunatic Asylum, now Central State Hospital.

Stetson-Sanford House

A great example of the local "Milledgeville federal" architectural style, the **Stetson-Sanford House** (601 W. Hancock St., 478/453-1803, www.oldcapitalmuseum.org, Thurs.-Sat. visit via Milledgeville Trolley Tours) was originally on North Wilkinson Street and acted as a hotel to house dignitaries during Milledgeville's tenure as state capital. You can visit by taking a trolley tour; go to the Milledgeville Visitors Center (200 W. Hancock St.) to catch the trolley (Mon.-Fri. 10am, Sat. 2pm, $12 adults, $5 children).

© JIM MOREKIS

O'Connor family farm at Andalusia

Old Governor's Mansion

One of the preeminent examples of Greek Revival architecture in the country, the **Old Governor's Mansion** (120 S. Clark St., 478/445-4545, www.gcsu.edu, Tues.-Sat. 10am-4pm, Sun. 2pm-4pm, $10 adults, $2 children) was built in Georgia's antebellum heyday in the late 1830s. It hosted 10 Georgia governors and their families, until Atlanta became the state capital in 1868. It also briefly hosted General Sherman, who made it his headquarters during a portion of his March to the Sea. Tours begin at the top of each hour, and self-guided tours are not possible. There's a cute gift shop in a well-restored outbuilding to the mansion's rear.

◖ Andalusia

On a 550-acre plot of wooded land north of the city center, **Andalusia** (U.S. 441, 4 miles northwest of Milledgeville, 478/454-4029, www.andalusiafarm.org, Mon.-Tues. and Thurs.-Sat. 10am-4pm, $5 donation) is the name given to the family dairy farm of the O'Connor family, where iconic Southern writer Flannery

O'Connor lived most of her adult life. She wrote all her major works in a bedroom on the ground floor of the main house, actually a parlor converted so that the ailing Flannery, suffering from lupus, wouldn't have to climb the stairs (her crutches are right there by the bed).

Five rooms are open for viewing: Flannery's bedroom, the kitchen area, the dining room, a porch area with displays and a video, and an upstairs bedroom, plus there's a small reception area with a small but delightful selection of unique O'Connor-related items, some of them created by family members still in the area. Most of the furnishings are original, even the refrigerator.

Several outbuildings in various states of disrepair are also here to see, including a charming stable area where Flannery's beloved horse, Flossie, once roamed, and the restored cottage of the Hill family, African American workers featured in some of Flannery's letters. Of course, there's a pen for a family of peacocks, which have become living signatures of Flannery's life and works.

FINDING FLANNERY

Though born and raised in Savannah, Flannery O'Connor attended college in Milledgeville and did the bulk of her writing here. Her family had deep roots in the area and their imprint is felt all over town. Here are some related sites:

Her first home here is the **Cline-O'Connor-Florencourt House** (311 W. Greene St.), now a private residence, where she lived until her beloved father's early death from lupus (a hereditary disease which would later claim her life as well). As an aside, this handsome building briefly served as the governor's residence in the 1830s; indeed, it's a stone's throw from the grand old governor's mansion.

Flannery and family faithfully attended **Sacred Heart Catholic Church** (110 N. Jefferson St.), which was actually built on land donated to the church by her great-grandmother. After her father died, Flannery became quite close with her mother, Regina Cline O'Connor, and the two often lunched at the tearoom and enjoyed peppermint chiffon pie in the **Stetson-Sanford House** (601 W. Hancock St., 478/453-1803, www.oldcapitalmuseum. org), now a house museum.

During World War II, Flannery attended Georgia State College for Women, now Georgia College & State University. Visit the **Flannery O'Connor Room** of the college museum to see vintage photos and personal items, including the manual typewriter on which those amazing novels and short stories were written.

The major stop is at **Andalusia** (U.S. 441, 4 miles northwest of Milledgeville, 478/454-4029, www.andalusiafarm.org, Mon.-Tues. and Thurs.-Sat. 10am-4pm, $5 donation), the ancestral Cline-O'Connor family dairy farm. After studying at the prestigious University of Iowa Writer's Workshop writing program and a brief stay at the Yaddo writer's retreat in New York, O'Connor was diagnosed, as she feared, with lupus. She returned to Milledgeville under the burden of the pessimistic prognosis to live out her days with her mother and write in the downstairs parlor, converted into a bedroom.

However, Flannery defied expectations and lived another 14 years at Andalusia before passing away at the age of 39. Visit her simple gravesite at **Memory Hill Cemetery** (Liberty St. and Franklin St., www.friendsofcems. org, daily 8am-5pm). Well-wishers often leave a single peacock feather at her tomb in memory of Flannery's well-known fondness for "the king of the birds."

The entrance to Andalusia isn't particularly obvious; heading north out of Milledgeville, pass the Walmart on your left, then look for a Babcock furniture store on the right. The driveway entrance is directly across U.S. 441 on the left.

Central State Hospital

Fans of poignant abandoned sites will find themselves drawn to the evocative decay of the sprawling 1,700-acre Central State Hospital, one of the oldest in the United States and at one time the biggest. However, while you can drive around the buildings, you may not trespass within. You'll have to content yourself with a visit to the **Central State Hospital Museum** (620 Broad St., 478/445-4878, www.central-statehospital.org, by appointment, free) in the old 1891 depot on the hospital campus, which chronicles the history of this darkly fascinating institution.

In 1837 the state legislature authorized a "State Lunatic, Idiot, and Epileptic Asylum," which admitted its first patient in 1842. By the time it was renamed again in 1967 as Central State Hospital, it was the largest mental hospital in the country. Shock therapy was common, as was outright neglect and abuse.

Today, the vast bulk of the 150 years' worth of buildings, some of them oddly ornate, are vacant and unused, except for the tortured ghosts that many swear walk the halls and stairwells each night.

Memory Hill Cemetery

Flannery O'Connor isn't the only famous

person interred at the circa-1804 **Memory Hill Cemetery** (Liberty St. and Franklin St., www.friendsofcems.org, daily 8am-5pm), but her gravesite is the most visited. Native son, former congressman, and aircraft carrier namesake Carl Vinson, "father of the two-ocean navy," is also buried here, as is famed chemist and first University of Georgia football coach Charles Herty.

Georgia College & State University Museums

Georgia's dedicated public liberal arts university, which has a variety of buildings all over downtown, offers a trio of small but solid museums, all free of charge. **Georgia College Museum** (221 N. Clark St., 478/445-4391, www.gcsu.edu, Mon.-Sat. 10am-4pm, free) is primarily known for its standing Flannery O'Connor Room, a repository of personal items specific to the Milledgeville-based author, including mementos from her time at the college. The highlight is the manual typewriter on which she typed most of her works. The **Natural History Museum and Planetarium** (Herty Hall, W. Montgomery St. and N. Wilkinson St., 478/445-2395, www.gscu.edu, Mon.-Fri. 8am-4pm, first Sat. of month 10am-4pm, free) opened in 2004 and features a region-leading collection of fossils and other paleontology-related artifacts as well as a state-of-the-art digital planetarium. The **Museum of Fine Arts** (102 S. Columbia St., 478/445-4572, www.gcsu.edu, by appointment, free) is housed in the beautiful restored 1935 Napier-Underwood house.

ACCOMMODATIONS AND FOOD

The premier accommodations in Milledgeville are at the **☾ Antebellum Inn** (200 N. Columbia St., 478/453-3993, www.antebelluminn.com, rooms $110-150, cottage $170), which has five guest rooms in the Greek Revival main house plus an adorable pool cottage with a full-size pool, quite a rarity for B&Bs in these parts. Standard hotels in the area aren't very impressive, but you might try the **Holiday Inn Express** (1839 N. Columbia St., 877/859-5095, www.hiexpress.com, $80-110).

The "satellite location"—if that phrase can be used for such an old-school institution—of the original location in Gray, **☾ Old Clinton BBQ** (2645 N. Columbia St., 478/454-0084, www.oldclintonbbq.com, Mon.-Thurs. 10am-8pm, Fri.-Sat. 10am-9pm, Sun. 10am-4pm, $5) is considered one of Georgia's top-tier barbecue spots. Their sauce, atypical for Georgia, is of the tangier North Carolina variety. A full platter with the works is under $7, and a no-frills pulled-pork sandwich less than $3.

NORTH OF MILLEDGEVILLE
Eatonton

A short drive from Milledgeville in Putnam County is the small, neat town of Eatonton (http://eatonton.com), whose main claim to fame is as the birthplace of writers Joel Chandler Harris and Alice Walker. Don't be deceived by the moribund main drag of U.S. 441 through town; Eatonton has some magnificent antebellum architecture one block west, on Madison Avenue.

The **Uncle Remus Museum** (214 Oak St., 706/485-6856, www.uncleremusmuseum.org, Mon.-Sat. 10am-5pm, Sun. 2pm-5pm, free) is right on the main drag on the site of the original homestead of Joseph Sidney Turner, the "Little Boy" in the classic folk tales told by Uncle Remus and chronicled by Joel Chandler Harris. The small but charming museum is within a log cabin, which actually comprises three slave cabins moved from a nearby location and intended to simulate Remus's cabin.

There isn't a museum about Alice Walker, but Eatonton markets the **Alice Walker Driving Trail** that includes her girlhood church, Wards Chapel AME Church. Get the tour brochure at the **Eatonton-Putnam Chamber of Commerce** (305 N. Madison Ave., 706/485-7701, Mon.-Fri. 9am-5pm).

A few miles north of Eatonton off U.S. 441 within the grounds of the Georgia 4-H Center is the **Rock Eagle Effigy** (350 Rock Eagle Rd., 706/484-2899, www.rockeagle4H.org, daily 9am-5pm, free), an ancient Mississippian stone sculpture, one of the oldest Native American sites found in the state. Partially excavated and then restored during the 1930s by the Civilian Conservation Corps, the rock eagle can be viewed from a 1930s-era tower. Turn off U.S. 441 at the Georgia 4-H Center entrance and follow signs along the short drive to the effigy site.

INFORMATION AND SERVICES

Pick up your brochures and tour info at the friendly **Milledgeville Visitors Center** (200 W. Hancock St., 478/452-4687, Mon.-Fri. 9am-5pm, Sat. 10am-4pm). While you're picking up brochures, make sure you get the Milledgeville Historic Walking Tour brochure, a particularly well-done, user-friendly, and attractive little document. This is also where you can catch the **Guided Trolley Tour** (Mon.-Fri. 10am, Sat.

2pm, $12 adults, $5 children), including visits to the Old State Capitol and Lockerly Hall.

The paper of record in town is the *Union Recorder* (www.unionrecorder.com). Georgia College & State University has a high-quality, informative student newspaper, the *Colonnade* (www.gsunade.com).

Oconee Regional Medical Center (821 N. Cobb St., 478/454-3505, www.oconeeregional. com) provides a full range of emergency care.

GETTING THERE AND AROUND

U.S. 441 is the key route in and out of Milledgeville, and it can get crowded in the more sprawl-dominated northern and southern approaches to downtown. There is no public transportation, but you don't really need it because of the town's walkability.

FDR Country

As you'll quickly notice from all the things named after him here, to this day the entire area retains enormous impact of President Franklin D. Roosevelt (FDR). As governor of New York, FDR began visiting the town now called Warm Springs, eventually building his picturesque Little White House here, today a state historic site and museum. The expansive FDR State Park near Pine Mountain isn't only a mecca for area hikers, it also commemorates the president's legacy of community building and conservation, with some particularly well-preserved Depression-era Civilian Conservation Corps-built structures enjoyed by visitors to this day.

WARM SPRINGS

While Warm Springs owes its fame to FDR, the healing properties of its natural spring were well known to the indigenous Creek people. In the 18th and 19th centuries, the town, originally called Bullochville, was a familiar name to Southerners seeking relief from various ailments.

Franklin D. Roosevelt, at the time the governor of New York, began visiting the therapeutic springs in 1924, purchasing the historic Meriwether Inn and the 1,700 acres that the now-demolished building stood on. The 88°F water from sources deep within the surrounding hills (milder than the near-scalding water that some natural spas are known for) gave the town its more descriptive modern name. The gently warming, mineral-infused springs aided the management of Roosevelt's debilitation from polio, and the surrounding countryside extending north to Pine Mountain—much of which FDR also purchased—provided a restful getaway during the unprecedented four terms of his presidency, during which he faced the twin challenges of the Depression followed by World War II.

◖ FDR's Little White House

While Franklin D. Roosevelt began visiting Warm Springs in 1924, it wasn't until 1932—the year he was first elected president—that he had the charming six-room **Little White House** (401 Little White House Rd., 706/655-5870, www.gastateparks.org, daily 9am-4:45pm, $10 adults, $6 children) built from Georgia pine in a wooded area down the road from *the* town center. (The first building you'll see when walking toward the Little White House from the entrance building and museum is actually a servants quarters.)

While the president enjoyed all the amenities you'd expect, including a cook, a live-in secretary, servants, and constant U.S. Marine and Secret Service protection, the estate has a cozy and rustic feeling. Fascinating memorabilia are on hand, all arranged as they might have been during FDR's 16 visits here during his presidency.

While the Little White House itself is well worth seeing, the state of Georgia in 2004 completed the extensive **FDR Memorial Museum** on-site, contiguous with the entrance building and gift shop. Here you'll learn not only about FDR's political career but about his life and times in Warm Springs and how that community shaped some of his domestic policies.

Roosevelt Warm Springs Institute for Rehabilitation

Right around the corner from the Little White House on U.S. 27 is the **Roosevelt Warm Springs Institute for Rehabilitation** (6135 Roosevelt Hwy., 706/655-5670, www.roosevelt-rehab.org, daily 9am-5pm, free), on the site of FDR's first land purchase in the Warm Springs area. It's a working hospital, not an attraction, but you can take a free self-guided tour of the grounds. At the time of FDR the Meriwether Inn stood on this site, but it was soon demolished and replaced with the main entrance building of the institute, Georgia Hall.

Note the Roosevelt Warm Springs Institute is not the same as the FDR Historic Pools site. Both are on U.S. 27 and both have entrances on the same side of the road, which confuses a lot of visitors, but they are separate entities.

FDR Historic Pools and Springs

Just down the road from the Roosevelt Warm Springs Institute are the **FDR Historic Pools and Springs** (U.S. 27, 706/655-5870, www.gastateparks.org, daily 9am-4:45pm,

© JIM MOREKIS

FDR's Little White House in Warm Springs

$10, includes admission to the Little White House). At this simple, lovingly curated site, you can walk around the famous pools (usually empty) in which the president enjoyed the healing spring waters from beneath the nearby hills.

The pools are used occasionally, specifically on Labor Day each year, when they are open to the public. You have to sign up in advance, though, and swim time is limited to 90 minutes pp.

If you visit the Little White House, admission to the historic pools is included. Note the historic pools are not on the campus of the Roosevelt Warm Springs Institute, which is just down the road. Though both sites use the same spring water, they are unaffiliated and have completely separate entrances.

Accommodations and Food

The classic Warm Springs experience is a stay at the ◖ **Warm Springs Hotel** (47 Broad St., 706/655-2114, www.hotelwarmspringsbb.org, $65-160) on the little main block. During the Roosevelt era, this circa-1907 inn hosted luminaries from all over the world who came to visit the president at the Little White House, including the king and queen of Spain. The guest rooms are cute and come in all sizes, hence the wide range of rates. The associated Tuscawilla Soda Shop downstairs is a great place for a cool drink or some tasty ice cream and fudge, in addition to being historic in its own right: FDR often snacked here.

For other dining, I strongly recommend heading north a few minutes to Pine Mountain, which offers a much better and wider variety of food options. However, if you simply must eat in Warm Springs, try **Mac's Barbecue** (5711 Spring St., 706/655-2472, daily 11am-8pm, $5) about one minute's walk from the Warm Springs Hotel.

PINE MOUNTAIN

The thoroughly charming little burg of Pine Mountain, while owing much of its current success to the nearby Callaway Gardens attraction, is worth of a visit in and of itself. The main town area consists of a couple of well-restored blocks of shops and cafés, two very good barbecue spots, and the friendly little **Visitors Center** (101 Broad St., 706/663-4000, www.pinemountain.org, Mon.-Sat. 10am-5pm).

Callaway Gardens

It's a bit hard to describe **Callaway Gardens** (17800 U.S. 27, 800/225-5292, www.callawaygardens.com, daily 9am-5pm, $18 adults, $9 children) to those who don't know anything about it. Part nature preserve, part kids' theme park, part retiree playground, and part recreational dream, its 13,000 acres encompass all those pursuits as gracefully as could reasonably be expected.

Most visits start with a walk through the $12 million **Virginia Hand Callaway Discovery Center,** which features info kiosks and an orientation video in the big theater. A particular highlight at Callaway is the **Cecil B. Day Butterfly Center,** one of the largest butterfly observatories in North America. This LEED-certified building hosts at least 1,000 butterflies at any given time. The **John A. Sibley Horticultural Center** is a five-acre designed landscape featuring a hybrid garden-greenhouse-indoor waterfall area. Other offerings include a regular bird-of-prey show, a zip line, a beach, stocked fishing lakes, a nearly 10-mile bike trail, and miles of themed nature and garden walking trails. The annual Christmas lights show is always a huge hit.

Callaway Gardens' famous **Mountain View Golf Course** has hosted PGA events in the past and is a consistently high-rated course at the national level. The older course, **Lake View,** is less challenging but more scenic and quietly enjoyable.

Callaway Gardens' well-stocked lakes are known far and wide among anglers. **Mountain Creek Lake** is particularly known for its bass fishing; you can rent a boat or even go on a guided fishing trip. **Robin Lake** at Callaway Gardens bills itself as the world's largest artificial white-sand beach, stretching for a mile around the huge lake.

FDR State Park

It's fitting that **Franklin D. Roosevelt State Park** (2970 Hwy. 190, 706/663-4858, www.gastateparks.org, daily 7am-10pm, parking $5) would bear the president's name, since the circa-1935 park is one of the first built under the auspices of his now-legendary Civilian Conservation Corps (CCC). Of course, it had a head start; Roosevelt owned most of the land that the park now sits on.

Georgia's largest state park, the centerpiece is the 23-mile **Pine Mountain Trail.** The historic main building and ranger station offers numerous trail maps; you'll need one if you plan on doing any serious hiking. Pay a visit to **Dowdell's Knob,** the highest point in the park, where the president enjoyed picnics. A life-size sculpture of FDR sitting on his customized removable car seat is near the overlook; you can even sit next to him and have your picture taken with him.

Several of the cottages in the park are original CCC-era constructions. Take a dip in the historic **Liberty Bell Swimming Pool,** also a CCC project and a very enjoyable pool fed by natural springs.

Accommodations

UNDER $150

A surprisingly good stay for a low rate can be found at the **Days Inn & Suites** (368 S. Main Ave., 706/663-2121, www.daysinn.com, under $100) in Pine Mountain near Callaway Gardens. A nice B&B experience is in the heart of Pine Mountain proper at the charming **Chipley Murrah House** (207 W. Harris St., 706/663-9801, www.chipleymurrah.com, $95-150), with four guest rooms in the main house and three cottages.

$150-300

Callaway Gardens (17800 U.S. 27, 800/225-5292, www.callawaygardens.com) offers a variety of lodging, mostly geared for family getaways and often offering packages that include park admission. For larger families and groups, cottage and villa stays are available from about

$300 per night. The 150-room **C Lodge at Callaway Gardens** (4500 Southern Pine Dr., 706/489-3300, www.callawaygardens.com, from $220), actually a Marriott property, is the choice for swank upscale lodging, complete with a large beautiful pool area and the on-site Spa Prunifolia. Packages that include park admission are available.

CAMPING

If camping or cabin life is your thing, choose among the 22 cottages and 140 tent and RV campsites offered at historic **FDR State Park** (2970 Hwy. 190, 706/663-4858, www.gastateparks.org, parking $5, primitive campsites $9 pp, tent and RV sites $25, cottages $100-135, 5-night minimum). Many of the tent and RV sites are on scenic Lake Delanor, which also has canoe rental. There are 16 primitive campsites as well along the Pine Mountain Trail.

Food

I recommend dining in town rather than at the Callaway Gardens facilities if you can. If barbecue's your thing, head straight to **C The Whistlin' Pig Cafe** (572 S. Main Ave., 706/663-4647, Mon.-Sat. 10:30am-3pm, $7), a real local favorite that's also known far and wide for its pulled pork, absolutely out-of-this-world ribs, and excellent Brunswick stew. Don't confuse it with **Three Lil Pigs** (146 S. Main Ave., 706/307-7109, daily 11am-7pm, $7, cash only), which is not far away on the same side of the road and also has a local following. Stick with the pig that whistles.

If you must eat at Callaway Gardens, the best bet is the **Country Kitchen** (17800 U.S. 27, 800/225-5292, www.callawaygardens.com, Sun.-Thurs. 8am-8pm, Fri.-Sat. 8am-9pm, $12), inside the Country Store, with offerings a cut above the usual meat-and-three Southern fare at diners like this all over Georgia.

SPREWELL BLUFF WILDLIFE MANAGEMENT AREA

One of the great hidden gems of Georgia is the **Sprewell Bluff Wildlife Management**

Area (www.georgiawildlife.org, daily dawn-dusk, free), about 30 minutes' drive from Warm Springs. Once considered for the site of a dam—vetoed by then-governor Jimmy Carter—the area is now one of the best ways to enjoy the scenic and unique Flint River, whether by kayak and canoe, fly-fishing, or hiking along several miles of trails.

From April-September, **Flint River Outdoor Center** (4429 Woodland Rd., 706/647-2633, www.flintriveroutdoor-center.com) runs frequent half-day guided water tours that are just right. To get to Sprewell Bluff WMA from Warm Springs, take Highway 85 north to Woodbury. Take Highway 74 until you see Old Alabama Road; turn right and follow the signs.

INFORMATION AND SERVICES

The **Pine Mountain Visitors Center** (101 Broad St., 706/663-4000, www.pinemountain.org) provides a range of information for the entire area. The tiny **Warm Springs Welcome Center** (1 Broad St., 706/655-3322, hours vary) is in a restored train depot.

Oconee Regional Medical Center (821 N. Cobb St., Milledgeville, 478/454-3505, www.oconeeregional.com) provides a full range of emergency care.

GETTING THERE AND AROUND

U.S. 27 is the main route into and out of Warm Springs. The Pine Mountain area and all other FDR-related sites are along Highway 190.

Columbus

Unlike some of the more visually monotonous rural areas of Georgia, the state's western edge is scenically inviting and has a gently rolling landscape. Billing itself as the last city founded in the original 13 colonies and site of the last engagement of the Civil War, Columbus has retained a robust presence into the 21st century, due in no small part to its very close association with the massive U.S. Army installation at Fort Benning.

In recent years, downtown revitalization and the long, scenic Riverwalk on the Chattahoochee River have sparked visitor interest. To the world at large, however, Columbus is best known as the hometown of several key figures in Southern arts and commerce: author Carson McCullers *(The Heart Is a Lonely Hunter),* "Mother of the Blues" Ma Rainey, Coca-Cola inventor John Pemberton, and long-time Coca-Cola president and philanthropist extraordinaire Robert Woodruff.

SIGHTS
National Civil War Naval Museum

It surprises many people to hear that the **National Civil War Naval Museum** (1002 Victory Dr., 706/327-9798, www.portcolumbus.org, Tues.-Sat. 10am-4:30pm, Sun.-Mon. 12:30pm-4:30pm, $7.50 adults, $6 children) is located far away from the nearest ocean, but any Civil War buff will tell you that naval warfare during that conflict was mostly of a riverine nature, not out on the deep blue sea. That said, all maritime phases of the war are well represented here, from coastal to blue water.

Both the Civil War Naval Museum and the U.S. Infantry Museum at Fort Benning are located off Victory Parkway, a short drive from each other, so one can easily make an afternoon of visiting the pair.

◖ National Infantry Museum and Soldier Center

The **National Infantry Museum and Soldier Center** (1775 Legacy Way, 706/685-5800, www.nationalinfantrymuseum.org, Tues.-Sat. 9am-5pm, Sun. 11am-5pm, $5 donation) is a well-funded and well-designed extended love letter to the soldiers, paratroopers, and Rangers of the U.S. Army Infantry, a large portion of

To Staybridge Suites
Columbus

To Pine Mountain

To Atlanta

RIVER RD

AIRPORT

THRUWAY

BRITT-DAVID RD

27

COLUMBUS METRO AIRPORT

To Flat
Rock Park

80

WARM
SPRINGS RD

COLUMBUS

COLUMBUS-MANCHESTER EXPY

SHOPPING MALL

27A

85

45TH   ST

HAMILTON RD

WARM SPRINGS RD

COLUMBUS STATE UNIVERSITY

38TH ST

185

2ND   AVE

Golf
Course

AUBURN   AVE

MACON   RD

To Macon
Road BBQ

TALBOTTON RD

Weracoba
Park

WILDWOOD AVE

HOSPITAL

17TH   ST

CEMETERY

CARSON MCCULLERS CENTER FOR WRITERS AND MUSICIANS ★

COUNTRY'S ▼

SEE DETAIL

14TH   ST

Eagle
Falls

4TH   ST

10TH   ST

FRONT

COLUMBUS MUSEUM ★

10TH   ST

BROADWAY

WYNTON RD

8TH   ST

AVE

MARTIN LUTHER KING JR.   BLVD

Phenix
City

6TH   ST

AVE

4TH   ST

4TH   ST

CUSSETA RD

LUMPKIN BLVD

Bike   Path

Chattahoochee

NATIONAL CIVIL WAR NAVAL MUSEUM ★

27

280

To ⒸNATIONAL
INFANTRY MUSEM
AND SOLDIER CENTER
and Plains

River

VICTORY DR

ALABAMA

0   0.5 mi

0   0.5 km

© AVALON TRAVEL

Eagle
Falls

15TH   ST

14TH   ST

4TH   AVE

10TH   ST

COUNTRYS ■

13TH   ST

Riverwalk

12TH   ST

FRONT

THE CANNON BREWPUB ▼

11TH   ST

SPRINGER OPERA HOUSE ★

10TH   ST

RIVERCENTER ■

9TH   ST

BUS DEPOT ■

ROTHSCHILD-POUND HOUSE INN ●

8TH   ST

BROADWAY

7TH   ST

2ND   AVE

AVE

Phenix
City

6TH   ST

5TH   ST

4TH   ST

LUMPKIN BLVD

GOLDEN PARK ■

PORT COLUMBUS NAVAL MUSEUM ★

South
Commons

Bike   Path

whom received their training at Fort Benning, where the museum resides.

The grand entrance, featuring a giant statue of a World War II-era squad leader exhorting his men to attack, sets the tone. From there you enter a series of stimulating multimedia vignettes highlighting notable small-unit infantry actions from the Revolutionary War through the Vietnam War. From there, the bulk of the museum comprises separate galleries, each dealing with a specific period of U.S. Army history. As of this writing the Colonial-Revolutionary and Civil War galleries weren't completed, but the other galleries are well assembled and informative, featuring a range of uniforms, armaments, memorabilia, and instructional multimedia about individual campaigns and engagements through the present day.

An affiliated IMAX theater shows thematic movies in the IMAX format, in addition to special seasonal films. Check the website for showtimes and ticket prices.

Uptown Columbus

Most cities would call this "downtown," but in Columbus it's Uptown (www.uptown-columbusga.com). It's a National Historic District and the center of Columbus social and nightlife. The bulk of the activity centers on Broadway, which has a grassy median with a fountain.

Just a couple of blocks off Broadway is the renowned **Springer Opera House** (103 10th St., 706/324-5714, www.springeroperahouse. org), a handsome, cast iron, balcony-bedecked late-19th-century venue of 700 seats that has hosted luminaries such as Oscar Wilde, Will Rogers, Tom Thumb, Franklin D. Roosevelt, and Garrison Keilor (see the "Walk of Stars" on the sidewalk in front of the building). Built in 1871, the Springer was declared the official state theater of Georgia in the 1970s by then-governor Jimmy Carter. It continues to host a regular schedule of performances by its in-house theater company.

Directly adjacent to Uptown and overlooking the Chattahoochee River is the well-manicured RiverPark Campus of **Columbus State University** (www.columbusstate.edu), home of the university's art, music, and theater departments. The associated events, not to mention expenditures by students and faculty, are a big part of Uptown's revival and current success.

Columbus Museum

The **Columbus Museum** (1251 Wynnton Rd., 706/748-2562, www.columbusmuseum.com, Tues.-Wed. and Fri.-Sat. 10am-5pm, Thurs. 10am-8pm, Sun. 1pm-5pm, free) is among the best-curated museums I've seen in a medium-small city, with the not-trivial added benefit of having free admission every day. The space itself is bright, inviting, clean, and contemporary in feel, but without the sense of lonely emptiness that many such modern museums tend to evoke. The permanent collection boasts an excellent variety of stimulating American impressionists, and the third floor hosts rotating exhibits of national and international value and interest. There's a standing exhibit on Columbus history as well, with a particular focus on the Native American presence.

Carson McCullers Center for Writers and Musicians

Columbus State University now owns and operates the **Carson McCullers Center for Writers and Musicians** (1519 Stark Ave., 706/565-4021, www.mccullerscenter.org, by appointment, $5) based in the Smith-McCullers House, childhood home of the Columbus-born novelist. In a nice twist that McCullers herself would no doubt appreciate, not only is there a museum devoted to her life and an archive of her works and letters, there are continuing workshops and residencies for up-and-coming writers.

RECREATION

Most recreation in Columbus centers along the **Chattahoochee River.** The most obvious choice is a walk or ride along the **Chattahoochee River Trail,** a long stretch that extends roughly 15 miles from Uptown Columbus all the way to Fort Benning, concluding at Oxbow Meadows.

The trail includes the Riverwalk section adjacent to the popular Uptown area of restaurants and nightlife.

By far the biggest news in Columbus outdoors life is **Whitewater Express** (1000 Bay Ave., 706/321-4720, www.columbusgawhitewater.com daily 9am-6pm, raft trips $33-49), more popularly known as "River City Rush." Two antiquated earthen dams near the falls on the river have been demolished to reveal a magnificent 2.5-mile white-water run that goes from Class I all the way to Class IV. The city, which bills the white-water project as the longest urban white-water course in the world, hopes it will be a major spur for ecotourism development.

REBELS AT SEA

Though the Union blockaded the Southern coast almost immediately with war's outbreak, that didn't stop the Confederacy from embarking on a crash course to build its own navy. At its peak, the Confederate Navy counted only about 5,000 personnel—outnumbered literally 10 to 1 by the U.S. Navy in both vessels and sailors. However, what the rebels lacked in numbers they made up for in innovation and bravery.

Confederate subs made the first submarine attacks in history. The rebel raider CSS *Alabama* sank U.S. ships as far away as the coast of France. A particularly feared Southern innovation—as represented by the CSS *Virginia* or "Merrimac" in its epic fight with the USS *Monitor*—was the ironclad, a regular wooden warship stripped to its berth deck and topped with an impenetrable iron superstructure. By war's end a menagerie of bizarre-looking contraptions was the norm in both fleets. As awkward as some vessels were—many were simply too underpowered to drag around that extra metal—they were the forerunners of the sophisticated warships to come.

The best place to find out more is at the **National Civil War Naval Museum** (1002 Victory Dr., 706/327-9798, www.portcolumbus.org, Tues.-Sat. 10am-4:30pm, Sun.-Mon. 12:30pm-4:30pm, $7.50 adults, $6 children) in Columbus. You'll leave not only with a certain admiration for the ragtag but plucky Confederate Navy, but also with an appreciation of the profound paradigm shift in naval technology, which echoes in the present day.

ACCOMMODATIONS

The vast military presence in Columbus means there is plenty of inexpensive lodging. While quality can vary, generally speaking you can book a brand-name hotel for well under what you'd pay in other markets.

Under $150

The pet-friendly 🌑 **Staybridge Suites Columbus** (1678 Whittlesley Rd., 706/507-7700, www.sbscolumbus.com, $100) is close to I-185 and has a nice kitchen in each suite, and there is a hot breakfast each morning included in the rates. The **Hampton Inn Columbus** (7390 Bear Lane, 706/256-2222, www.hamptoninn.com, $100) is also off I-185 and is one of the least expensive Hampton Inns you'll find, with the guarantee of quality typical of the chain. There are no hidden charges here, and the Wi-Fi and parking really are included in the rates.

$150-300

The 🌑 **Rothschild-Pound House Inn** (201 7th St., 706/322-4075, www.thepoundhouseinn.com, $185-365) is the premier B&B in Columbus, set in an ornately appointed Second Empire-style home. There are four sumptuous suites in the main house, with another six spread out in three cottages that are part of the whole enterprise. Breakfast is in the grand (and rich) Southern style, with the added modern twist of Fair Trade coffee. Rates vary by season and the size of the cottage. Keep in mind that occupancy is capped at two guests, with the exception of the Garrett Suite in the main house, which has two queen beds.

FOOD

Every imaginable chain restaurant is available in the Columbus area. Otherwise, your best bet is to stick with pub food, which seems to set the standard here.

American

Also known for its lively bar scene, ☕ **The Cannon Brewpub** (1041 Broadway, 706/653-2337, www.thecannonbrewpub.com, Mon.-Thurs. 11am-10pm, Fri.-Sun. 11am-11pm, $15) is a linchpin of Uptown nightlife. All of the burgers are excellent, and you can get them with their signature sweet potato "sunspots." Of course, you have your selection of hand-crafted beers brewed on-site. Try the sampler flight of beers if you can't quite decide. Just down the street, a boisterous gastropub atmosphere is also the order of the day at **The Loft** (1032 Broadway, 706/596-8141, www.theloft. com, Tues.-Fri. 11:30am-2:30pm and 5pm-11pm, Sat. 5pm-11pm, $12), locally owned and one of the best all-around restaurants in town. There is live jazz every Friday night.

Barbecue

There are two major purveyors of Columbus 'cue, and each has its fan base. The best-known and the one with the longest tradition is ☕ **Country's** (3137 Mercury Dr., 706/563-7604, www.countrysbarbecue.com, Sun.-Thurs. 11am-10pm, Fri.-Sat. 11am-11pm, $8-12), which has a well-rounded menu featuring equally good pulled pork, grilled chicken, ribs, and brisket. Seasonal favorites are always welcomed by regular patrons. Tuesday night is all-you-can-eat barbecue chicken, and Friday and Saturday nights bring live bluegrass to the original location. There is also an Uptown location (1329 Broadway), a little closer to the action.

Some aficionados will tell you that the humble **Pepper's** (4620 Warm Springs Rd., 706/569-0051, Mon.-Tues. and Sat. 10:30am-2:30pm, Wed.-Fri. 10:30am-8pm, $7) is at least as good, with a leaner cut of meat, and offers a particularly tasty take on that Georgia side dish known as Brunswick stew.

INFORMATION AND SERVICES

The spacious and well-done **Columbus Visitors Center** (900 Front Ave., 706/322-1613, www. visitcolumbusga.com, Mon.-Fri. 8:30am-5:30pm, Sat. 10am-2pm) is conveniently located. For emergencies go to **The Medical Center** of the Columbus Regional Healthcare System (710 Center St., 706/571-1000, www. columbusregional.com). The newspaper of record is the *Ledger-Enquirer* (www.ledger-enquirer.com).

GETTING THERE AND AROUND

By Car

Columbus is on the Georgia-Alabama border, and several highways lead directly to and from both states over the Chattahoochee River. A major interstate highway doesn't pass through, but a spur of I-75 called I-185 takes you directly to Columbus. When driving in Columbus, keep in mind that Fort Benning in effect surrounds the city on the Georgia side. While highways going through that military facility are open to the public, traffic laws tend to be more strictly enforced.

By Air

Columbus Metropolitan Airport (CSG, 3250 W. Britt David Rd., 706/324-2449, www.flycolumbusga.com) has flights to Atlanta on Delta.

By Bus

Columbus is served by **Greyhound** (818 Veterans Pkwy., 706/322-7391, www.greyhound.com). There's a good public transportation service, **METRA** (www.columbusga.org, $1.30) with extensive routes throughout the city. It runs a charming trolley service through the Uptown-downtown-historic areas.

OUTSIDE COLUMBUS

Pasaquan

On the outskirts of Buena Vista about 20 miles outside Columbus is a very unique place, the folk-art compound of **Pasaquan** (238 Eddie Martin Rd., 229/649-9444, www.pasaquan.

blogspot.com, Apr.-Nov. first Sat. of the month 10am-4pm, $5). The sprawling collection of almost psychedelic pagoda-like temples, statues, and masonry walls, all of them brightly painted, is the product of the late visionary artist Eddie Owens Martin, known as "Saint EOM."

Sadly, Martin committed suicide in 1986.

Note the very limited hours, although for a $100 donation you can make an appointment for a private visit. To get here from the Buena Vista town square, drive north 1.5 miles on Highway 41, then veer left onto Highway 137. Go about 4.5 miles and take a right on Eddie Martin Road. Pasaquan is a 0.5 miles north.

Along I-16: Statesboro to Swainsboro

The stretch of I-16 between Macon and Savannah is relatively unexciting. While not really much less exciting than any other drive through a heavily rural area, there is a certain lonesome, nondescript feel to it. In any case, there are actually a few interesting things to do and see in the area. For a break, there's a state-run rest area at around mile marker 45 near Laurens.

POINTS NORTH
Statesboro
Cynics might say there's a good reason Blind Willie McTell wrote "Statesboro Blues" about his hometown, a tune later famously covered by the Allman Brothers. While it's true there's not much to do in "the 'Boro" (www.visitstatesboroga.com), the huge presence of **Georgia Southern University** (GSU, www.georgiasouthern.edu) does give this town, about 15 miles off I-16, an advantage over most in this often-overlooked area. Things have also spiced up a bit recently thanks to a referendum allowing the sale of alcoholic beverages in this formerly totally dry county.

The most interesting thing open to the public at GSU is the Center for Wildlife Education, specifically its **Lamar Q. Ball Jr. Raptor Center** (1461 Forest Dr., 912/478-0831, Mon.-Fri. 9am-5pm, Sat. 1pm-5pm, free), a research facility that stages frequent wildlife programs, generally daily at 3:30pm. (Georgia Southern sports teams are called the Eagles. Get it?) Highlights are the Thursday Flight Show in the amphitheater, involving various birds of

prey from the center. Friday afternoons usually bring a show devoted to the center's hawks.

One of the biggest things to happen in this neck of the woods was the $10 million **Splash in the 'Boro** (1388 Hwy. 24, 912/489-3000, www.splashintheboro.com, spring-fall Mon.-Sat. 10am-6pm, Sun. noon-6pm, $10-12), a waterpark that comes in very handy during Statesboro's extremely hot summers. There is a variety of slides for different age groups as well as a lazy river. Splash closes during the cooler months, so check ahead on the website.

A favorite downtown spot to get a tasty bite from breakfast on through dinner is **C Sugar Magnolia** (106 Savannah Ave., 912/764-2090, www.sugarmagnoliabakery.com, Tues.-Wed. 7am-4pm, Thurs.-Fri. 7am-8pm, Sat. 7am-9pm, Sun. 10am-2pm, $15). While its claim to fame is baked goods, they have a great all-around menu with no weak links. Pizza nights on Thursday and burger nights on Saturday in particular are big hits, with locals packing the place.

Ohoopee Dunes Natural Area
The entire coastal plain between Macon and Savannah was underwater 60 million years ago. To see the evidence, go to the Swainsboro vicinity and check out the **Ohoopee Dunes Natural Area** (www.georgiawildlife.com), white sandy deposits built up by wind as the water receded. This 3,000-acre area is but part of a 22,000-acre sandhill ecosystem stretching over 60 miles along the Ohoopee and Little Ohoopee Rivers to their meeting with the Altamaha River.

There are three separate tracts. To get to the McLeod Bridge Tract, go 1.5 miles west of Swainsboro on U.S. 80, then right on County Road 456 (McLeod Bridge Rd.). To get to the U.S. 80 Tract, go west of Swainsboro 4.1 miles on U.S. 80 until you see a small unpaved parking area and kiosk. To get to the Halls Bridge Tract, take U.S. 80 west of Swainsboro about one mile, then make a left on County Road 160 (Halls Bridge Rd.) to the crossing. You can launch a canoe or kayak from here.

Magnolia Springs State Park

One of the more interesting parks in Georgia, **Magnolia Springs State Park** (1053 Magnolia Springs Dr., 478/982-1660, www.gastateparks. org, daily 7am-10pm, parking $5, campsites $25-28, cottages $125-145) is named for a unique natural feature, a natural spring that still produces about seven million gallons per day and helps support a robust wetlands environment, which you can enjoy either from the boardwalk over the spring or by kayak and canoe. There's also a stocked 28-acre lake fed by the spring.

The spring is also indirectly responsible for the other really interesting thing about the park: its former role as the location of the largest POW camp in the Confederacy, **Camp Lawton.** Founded specifically to relieve overcrowding at the much more notorious camp at Andersonville, farther southwest, Camp Lawton actually held more prisoners during its brief six weeks of operation before the arrival of General Sherman's forces. Archaeology, mostly through ground-penetrating radar, is still ongoing; in 2010 a team from Georgia Southern University finally found the long-rumored location of the stockade wall. Despite its large size (1,000 acres), Magnolia Springs has comparatively few accommodations: only 26 tent and RV sites and eight cottages, one of which is dog-friendly.

POINTS SOUTH
Vidalia Onion Museum

One of Georgia's main exports is the delectable sweet onion. While Vidalia isn't the only place it's grown, the little town gave its name to the vegetable, memorialized at the **Vidalia Onion Museum** (100 Vidalia Sweet Onion Dr., 912/537-1918, www.vidaliaonion.org, Mon.-Fri. 9am-5pm, free), opened in 2011. Interactive displays explain the science behind the onion's sweetness and the economic benefits of the crop to the region. There's an on-site onion patch where you can see the little sweeties growing in the sandy soil, and, of course, onions are for sale.

Claxton

For reasons unknown to science, fruitcakes are a popular Christmas gift in some quarters. The acknowledged headquarters of this acquired taste is the little town of Claxton, "Fruitcake Capital of the World," specifically **Claxton Bakery** (203 W. Main St., 912/739-3441, www.claxtonfruitcake.com, Mon.-Sat. 8am-5pm), established over 100 years ago by an Italian immigrant. While you can't actually tour the facility, you can watch them being made through some large windows. And, of course, you can sample and buy them.

Jimmy Carter Country

With the notable exception of Providence Canyon, the deeply rural farm country around Americus isn't very scenically stimulating, but it contains some of the nation's most important and interesting history.

Many come just to see tiny Plains, population under 700, birthplace of the 39th U.S. president, Jimmy Carter. The president and his wife, Rosalynn, still live on the main road in the only house they've ever owned, and Carter himself still teaches Sunday School (open to the public) many times a year at his church on the outskirts of town.

Every American should visit the National Prisoner of War Museum, at the site of the notorious Andersonville POW Camp. The Civil War site is grimly fascinating, and the adjacent museum is deeply moving in its portrayal of the plight and ingenuity of U.S. prisoners of war throughout history.

AMERICUS

Americus is the best base of operations from which to explore Carter Country, and this cute town perched on a little hill offers a few things of its own worth seeing as well. Because it's home to Georgia Southwestern University and is the international headquarters of Habitat for Humanity, Americus is a little more resistant to the ups and downs of the economy than many comparatively hard-hit rural towns.

Habitat for Humanity Global Village and Discovery Center

Administrative offices are in Atlanta, but the global operations center for Habitat for Humanity and the associated **Global Village and Discovery Center** (721 W. Church St., 229/410-7937, www.habitat.org, Mon.-Fri. 9am-5pm, Sat. 10am-2pm, $4 adults, $3 children) is in its hometown of Americus. The centerpiece of the experience is seeing replicas of typical Third World housing, along with tours of 15 of the special low-cost sustainable

buildings that Habitat for Humanity seeks to build in those areas, each design customized for the particular area's climate and terrain.

Koinonia Farms

Before founding Habitat for Humanity, Millard and Linda Fuller met at **Koinonia Farms** (1324 Hwy. 49, 877/738-1741, www.koinoniapartners.org, Mon.-Sat. 9am-5pm, Sun. 1pm-5pm, free). This 70-year-old agricultural and ministerial institution was established by two couples, Clarence and Florence Jordan and Martin and Mabel England, specifically to embody what they saw as the ideals of early Christianity. By growing and providing food and spreading fellowship, they aimed to overcome the then-ingrained racism and economic disparity endemic to the South Georgia region and to be an example to other "intentional communities."

Today, visitors are always welcome at this working farm, especially at the weekday noon community lunches. The emphasis is on *working,* however, and Koinonia is mainly a place where people come to volunteer their labor on the farm or their trade skills, or even their musicianship, in exchange for a stay at the attached RV and lodging area, where people can stay for up to two weeks (longer during harvest time). Koinonia goods can be purchased on-site or at shops around the Americus and Plains area.

Georgia Rural Telephone Museum

About 20 minutes south of Americus in a restored cotton warehouse in tiny Leslie is one of the quirkiest and most fun little museums around, the **Georgia Rural Telephone Museum** (135 N. Bailey Ave., 229/874-4786, www.grtm.org, Mon.-Fri. 9am-3:30pm, nominal fee). We're not just talking rotary phones here; we're talking the old-timey phone exchanges with live operators who manually connected your call. In fact, this labor of love of Tommy Smith is the largest collection of such memorabilia in the country, with gear dating back to the very invention of the telephone in 1876, including the last operating old-fashioned switchboard of the Southern Bell Company.

Accommodations and Food

Your best bet for lodging in Americus is the historic **⬛ Windsor Hotel** (125 Lamar St., 229/924-1555, www.windsor-americus.com, $200), itself a landmark worth visiting. Now a Best Western property, it's a stirring image of Victoriana with its imposing turrets and broad balcony. Book in advance, as the Windsor often hosts dignitaries in the area to visit President Carter and Habitat for Humanity.

Another recommended lodging option is the well-run, clean, and recently upgraded **Jameson Inn** (1605 E. Lamar St., 229/924-2726, www.jamesoninns.com, $100), several blocks away, which offers a free full breakfast.

The Windsor also happens to be your best bet for food and adult beverages in this corner of the Bible Belt. The Windsor has two excellent dining options, the sit-down, farm-to-table **Rosemary & Thyme** (125 Lamar St., 229/924-1555, www.windsor-americus.com, Mon.-Fri. 6:30am-9:30am and 5pm-9pm, Sat. 6:30am-10am and 5pm-9pm, Sun. 6:30am-10am, $20) and the upstairs **⬛ Floyd's Pub** (125 Lamar St., 229/924-1555, www.windsor-americus. com, Mon.-Sat. from 5pm, $15), named after a longtime bellman. My favorite meal in Americus consists of sitting down at the bar at Floyd's and ordering the sublime gyro wrap; any of their sandwiches are excellent.

PLAINS

Plains (www.plainsgeorgia.com) itself is little more than a single block of businesses and a few houses and churches. For most intents and purposes, the entire town is the Jimmy Carter National Historic Site and can be enjoyed within a single day. It's surrounded by intensively cultivated farmland, which includes the exceptionally well-interpreted Jimmy Carter Boyhood Farm. All the Carter-oriented sites are free of charge.

As you'd expect from the place where a

peanut farmer became president, the big annual event is the **Plains Peanut Festival** (www. plainsgeorgia.com), happening each September, which almost always features appearances by the president and Rosalynn Carter.

Jimmy Carter National Historic Site

Start your visit at the Victorian-era **Plains Depot Museum and Presidential Campaign Headquarters** (Main St., 229/824-4104, www.nps.gov, daily 9am-4:30pm, free) on Main Street next to the block of shops comprising Plains's "downtown." Not just the train depot and oldest building in the area, it was where Jimmy Carter symbolically based his presidential campaign and is a must-stop for any political junkie. The interior of the depot (warning: no air-conditioning) features much memorabilia about Carter's insurgent run in the post-Watergate years, shocking not only the Democratic Party establishment but the entire globe, which marveled at a peanut farmer becoming leader of the free world.

Technically, the **Plains High School Visitors Center and Museum** (300 N. Bond St., 229/824-4104, www.nps.gov, daily 9am-5pm, free), housed in the old Plains High School, is the premier Carter-oriented site in Plains, but for those expecting an in-depth interpretation of his legacy and influential post-presidential activity, it might be underwhelming (for that, go to the Carter Center in Atlanta). But certainly, it's neat to walk around in the same school where both the future president and his future wife, Rosalynn, attended classes, and the museum does a good job in explaining the social and political circumstances of the times in which Carter grew up and his motivations for running for office after a successful career in the U.S. Navy submarine service.

Maranatha Baptist Church (148 Hwy. 45 N., 229/824-7896, www.mbcplains.com) isn't nearly the largest church in Plains (that distinction goes to Plains Baptist, which Jimmy and Rosalynn left decades ago in protest of their now-repudiated policy of refusing

© JIM MOREKIS

Jimmy Carter Boyhood Farm

African American congregants). But it's where the Carters still attend church each Sunday. Dozens of times a year the president himself gives an hour-long Sunday School lesson right before the regular 11am service. You can stay for the service or just attend the lesson; all you have to do is show up about 8am or 9am, get checked out quickly by the Secret Service, take a seat at a pew, listen to an orientation, and enjoy.

You won't be able to tour the **Carter Family Compound** on the town's main road, but you'll spot it instantly by the tall fence and the Secret Service checkpoint at the entrance. The simple 1961 ranch home is on 4.5 acres of land and is the only home the president and his wife have ever owned. There's a video tour at the museum in the old Plains High School.

◖ Jimmy Carter Boyhood Farm

It's not in Plains proper—it's actually in even smaller Archery—but the impeccably maintained **Jimmy Carter Boyhood Farm** (Old Plains Hwy., 229/824-4104, www.nps.gov, daily 10am-5pm, free) a few miles out of town, is a must-see, not only to get a better perspective on the president's boyhood but for a charming and educational slice-of-life of rural and agricultural Americana gone by.

While the centerpiece is the well-restored one-story farmhouse where Earl and Lillian Carter raised the future president and his siblings during the Depression era, there's plenty more to see, including lovingly tended native-plant gardens, the old Carter general store, domestic animals, and the restored home of the Clarks, an African American family who were often employed by the Carters and who provided a window on the real need for social justice in the Jim Crow-era South.

The farm itself is expertly maintained by the National Park Service, but keep in mind that there's no air-conditioning on-site, just as when the Carters lived here. There are restrooms and a water fountain at the entrance

© JIM MOREKIS

reconstructed POW tents at Andersonville

by the parking lot, and a park ranger is always around if you have any questions. Stay hydrated and use sunscreen. Walking tours of the farm are led on Saturday and Sunday at 11:30am and 3:30pm.

Get there by taking U.S. 280 west out of Plains for 0.5 miles, then bearing left on Old Plains Highway for 1.5 miles. The farm is on the right side of the road. The family burial ground in Lebanon Cemetery is along the same road; the president's parents and brother and sister are interred here.

SAM Shortline

The railroads are still very active in this part of Georgia, and the tracks through Plains host the tourist-oriented passenger shuttle **SAM Shortline** (877/427-2457, www.samshortline. com). These 1949 vintage cars are a fun way to get around from the Boyhood Farm with stops in Plains, Americus, and Leslie (site of the Georgia Rural Telephone Museum). Check the website for schedules and fares.

◖ NATIONAL PRISONER OF WAR MUSEUM

First off, don't be confused: The **National Prisoner of War Museum** (760 POW Rd., 229/924-0343, www.nps.gov, museum daily 9am-5pm, grounds and cemetery daily 8am-5pm, free), about 12 miles north of Americus, is also where you'll find the infamous Civil War prison camp now called Andersonville as well as Andersonville National Cemetery. The multiple nature of the site is deliberate and entirely appropriate.

The museum not only describes the history, atmosphere, and ensuing controversy of the Andersonville POW camp (called Camp Sumter at the time) through exhibits and an excellent short film, it also delves into the poignant human chronicle of American prisoners of war from all conflicts, from the Revolution to the world wars, the Korean War, the Vietnam War, and the Iraq War. Young children might find some of the exhibits disturbing, but I consider the museum

AMBIGUITY AND ANDERSONVILLE

The very word *Andersonville* is synonymous with harsh cruelty to captives, one reason the National Prisoner of War Museum was established a stone's throw from the notorious Confederate camp. From February 1864 to May 1865, 45,000 Union prisoners lived on this bare 26-acre plot, with no roof or shelter of any kind to shield them from the blistering South Georgia sun, nor from the winter cold. Nearly 13,000 died.

Within Andersonville's 20-foot stockade walls was a grotesque city all its own, with its own rules and rulers. Food was thrown into the compound to be fought over, sold, and resold by prisoners. The only drinking water was a fetid creek running through the middle of the camp, with the downstream portion the camp's only latrine.

The world's first war crimes trial came out of the Andersonville experience, as camp commandant Colonel Henry Wirz was hanged for his role after the war in a court martial presided over by Union general Lew Wallace, who would later write *Ben-Hur*.

As horrible as Andersonville was, however, the only reason the camp existed at all was because of a decision by Union general Ulysses S.

Grant to stop the practice of POW exchanges, previously the norm throughout the war. The concept was simple: Regular agreements were made to trade roughly equal numbers of prisoners, thus relieving the burden on both sides of feeding and caring for them. But the sudden halt in exchanges and the deterioration of Southern military and civilian standards meant that Confederates suddenly found themselves responsible for thousands of prisoners, but with dwindling supplies and people to devote to them.

Colonel Wirz sent a petition north asking that POW exchanges be reinstated; it was denied. By late 1864 the Confederacy even offered to release all prisoners if the Union would provide transportation; it refused.

So, as awful as it was, Andersonville represented a deeply flawed and imperfect response to a nearly impossible situation, a situation mirrored by similarly horrific POW camps in the north such as Camp Elmira, New York. Southerners were far from immune to the degrading effect of the prisoners' plight. Many Andersonville prison guards themselves broke down under the strain and guilt.

a must-visit for any American high schooler or older.

Behind the air-conditioned and fully appointed museum is the entrance to **Camp Sumter,** demarcated by a memorial wall and sculpture. You're greeted by an expanse of open space, split by a still-existing creek. At one point nearly 40,000 Union POWs were confined here, completely exposed to the elements, using the creek as both a toilet and for drinking water. The site was picked clean of artifacts decades ago, but the National Park Service has done a great job of maintaining replicas of the 18-foot stockade wall and associated "deadline," as well as facsimiles of the "she-bangs," or makeshift tents, of the otherwise sun-blasted prisoners. There are a series of ornate monuments erected by various Northern

states to memorialize their citizens' sacrifices while in captivity.

You can drive a small loop road around the entire Andersonville camp, but unless the afternoon sun is just too intense, I recommend walking the site to get the full impact of what actually went on here 150 years ago. Adjacent to Camp Sumter is **Andersonville National Cemetery,** which contains graves of POWs and Civil War veterans and was established specifically to keep the lessons of Andersonville in public memory.

Food

Really good food is hard to find in this area, but one notable exception is **⚑ Yoder's Deitsch Haus** (5252 Hwy. 26, 478/472-2024, Tues. and Thurs.-Sat. 11:30am-2pm and 5pm-8:30pm,

© JIM MOREKIS

Providence Canyon's dramatic features are actually human-made.

Wed. 11:30am-2pm, $8) near the otherwise bereft town of Montezuma a few miles from Andersonville. Yoder's menu—cooked and served by local Mennonites, a sizeable contingent in the surrounding area—draws people from miles around. The delectable, hearty Southern-meets-German cuisine is served in a clean, open, community-style buffet atmosphere. Save room for the amazing pies and other desserts, which are signature items. The only drinks are iced tea, coffee, and water. Dress conservatively.

POINTS WEST
◖ Providence Canyon State Outdoor Recreation Area

While at first glance it looks like a cluster of little canyons parachuted in from out west, the truth about **Providence Canyon State Outdoor Recreation Area** (8930 Canyon Rd., 229/838-6870, www.gastateparks.org, mid-Sept.-mid-Apr. daily 7am-6pm, mid-Apr.-mid-Sept. daily 7am-9pm, $5, backcountry campsites $9), a.k.a. "Georgia's Grand Canyon," is a bit more complicated. Though it doesn't look that way when you wander among these steep white walls dotted with trees and patrolled overhead by circling hawks, the canyons are actually products of human activity. Poor farming practices in the early 1800s in this soft-soil area led to topsoil erosion followed by dramatic washouts, carving the deep gulches that now form a picturesque attraction.

There are plenty of opportunities to drive or walk around the rim and look down into the fingers of Providence Canyon, but the best way to enjoy the 16 separate canyons that form the park is to take the short, pleasant hike onto the canyon floor. (It's strictly forbidden to climb the fragile walls once you're down here.) You might consider joining the **Canyon Climbers Club** (www.gastateparks.org, $10), which coordinates activity in Providence Canyon and two other Georgia parks with similar topography, Tallulah Gorge and Cloudland Canyon. Backpackers can camp on the seven-mile back-country trail.

While the **Visitors Center** (Sept. 1-Nov.

30 and Mar. 1-May 31 Sat.-Sun. 8am-5pm) at Providence Canyon is back in operation after an extended hiatus due to budget cuts, the attached museum remains closed for budgetary reasons.

Westville

Between Plains and Providence Canyon is the town of Lumpkin, and a very short drive south of the downtown area is the living history village of **Westville** (9294 Singer Rd., 888/733-1850, www.westville.org, Thurs.-Sat. 10am-5pm, $10 adults, $5 children), a compound of genuine 1850s buildings attended by volunteers in period dress doing all sorts of period things in true Williamsburg, Virginia, style. In a remarkable bargain, your admission entitles you to three separate 40-minute guided tours (each beginning at 15 minutes after the hour; call ahead to make sure they will be given that day).

INFORMATION AND SERVICES

The **Plains Welcome Center** (1763 U.S. 280 W., 229/824-7477) is a short way outside the tiny town, and as of this writing was facing budget issues. The best bet for information in Plains is at the **Plains High School Visitors Center and Museum** (300 N. Bond St., 229/824-4104, www.nps.gov, daily 9am-5pm,

free), also the main portal for exploring all Jimmy Carter-related sights.

If you pass through Americus, check out the **Americus Welcome Center** (123 W. Lamar St., 229/928-6059, www.visitamericusga.com) on the first floor of the town's Municipal Building.

The **Phoebe Putney Health System** (www.phoebeputney.com) is the largest health care provider in the region, serving several counties. The **North Campus** (2000 Palmyra Rd., Albany, 229/434-2000) in nearby Albany provides the nearest emergency care to the Americus-Plains area.

GETTING THERE AND AROUND

This part of South Georgia is very well served by roads and is fairly easy to get around by car. Americus, the best base of operations, is easily accessible from I-75 south of Atlanta. U.S. 280/27 heads due west out of Americus and takes you right through Plains, and on to Westville and Providence Canyon. To get to Andersonville, head north out of Americus on Highway 49.

A unique way to get around Carter County is by the **SAM Shortline** (877/427-2457, www.samshortline.com), a light passenger rail running a route from Plains to Cordele and points between. Check the website for frequently changing schedules and fares.

Southwest Georgia

Agriculture is the name of the game down here in this sparsely populated area, with peanuts, pecans, and cotton, including the state's dedicated agricultural college. Though largely free of fighting during the Civil War, this is where the Confederacy ended for good with the capture of Confederate president Jefferson Davis. The city of Albany played a key role in national civil rights, chiefly with the groundbreaking Albany Movement, orchestrated in part by Martin Luther King Jr. The main natural attraction is the scenic and intriguing Flint River.

ALBANY

South Georgia's largest city, Albany (www.visitalbanyga.com) owes its history to the scenic Flint River, one of the South's great waterways. The Flint's bounty sparked the city's founding as a trade center, named after the capital of New York State, in case anyone didn't get the hint.

Although the Food Network icon moved her operations to Savannah long ago, Paula Deen is actually an Albany native. By the way, locals like Paula pronounce it "all-BEN-ee," not "ALL-buh-ny." It ain't in New York, y'all!

Learn about the area's human and natural history at the **Thronateeska Heritage Center** (100 W. Roosevelt Ave., 229/432-6955, www.heritagecenter.org, Thurs.-Sat. 10am-4pm, free), named for the ancient Native American word for the area. There's a Museum of History, a Science Discovery Center, and a good model train layout within its cavernous interior—the main building is the repurposed 1913 rail depot—but for many the highlight is the **Wetherbee Planetarium** (showtimes vary, $3) in the adjacent building, which holds various themed shows on the night sky.

Albany's chief claim to fame to the world at large is as the boyhood home of the great Ray Charles, one of the first performers to move traditional gospel into the realm of popular R&B. He is commemorated in the neat **Ray Charles Plaza** (Front St.) on the Flint Riverwalk. The elaborate memorial features Charles at a rotating baby grand piano. He "plays" music through a discreet sound system, and each evening there is a light and fountain show. The audience sits in the round on huge piano keys.

The centerpiece of a recent public-private effort to revitalize downtown Albany is the **Flint RiverQuarium** (117 Pine Ave., 229/639-2650, www.flintriverquarium.com, Tues.-Sat. 10am-5pm, Sun. 1pm-5pm, $9 adults, $6.50 children), a 175,000-gallon, 22-foot-deep "Blue Hole" aquarium on the river—one of the few such open-air facilities you'll find—exploring the area's interesting riverine ecosystem.

Albany's key role in the national struggle for civil rights is documented at the **Albany Civil Rights Institute** (326 Whitney Ave., 229/432-1698, www.albanycivilrightsinstitute.org, Tues.-Sat. 10am-4pm, $6 adults, $5 students), a new facility next to the historic 1906 Mt. Zion Baptist Church, where Martin Luther King Jr. made speeches during the push to integrate Albany public facilities in the early 1960s. The entire history of the Albany Movement is chronicled in fascinating detail. The second Saturday of the month you can hear a

performance by the Freedom Singers, a group with roots going back to 1962.

The **Albany Museum of Art** (311 Meadowlark Dr., 229/439-8300, www.albanymuseum.com, Tues.-Sat. 10am-5pm, $4 adults, $2 children) has a solid collection of European and American art, but they're chiefly known for the Davis collection of sub-Saharan African art, one of the largest in the country. The museum recently began hosting a performance series by the Albany Symphony Orchestra.

WEST OF ALBANY
Kolomoki Mounds Historic Park

One of the best-preserved pre-Columbian mound-builder sites in the United States, **Kolomoki Mounds Historic Park** (205 Indian Mounds Rd., 229/724-2150, www.gastateparks.org, daily 7am-10pm, parking $5, campsites $25-27) is also Georgia's oldest, its sprawling complex inhabited from AD 350 to 750, nearly 1,000 years older than the Etowah Mounds up in Cartersville.

You'll see the mounds on the drive in, but you'll first want to go to the end of the road to the visitors center, which incorporates a theater and boardwalk within a partially excavated mound, opened in the less enlightened era of the 1930s. The film explores the history of the site and the culture of the Woodland people who built it, part of a thriving network of similar compounds across the Southeast.

The real highlight is a trip up the stairs to the top of the enormous great temple mound, tallest in Georgia at 57 feet over the surrounding vista and feeling much higher than that because of its dominant view overlooking a broad plain featuring two smaller burial mounds and several even smaller ceremonial mounds. Because this is a relatively isolated area, there are times you can have the entire top of the mound to yourself—quite a powerful experience.

Kolomoki offers 27 tent and RV sites. There are a couple of small lakes to boat and fish on, a boat ramp, and a swimming beach. Hikers will find a lake trail and a forest trail with a total of five miles of paths.

Colquitt, "Mural City"

With not even 2,000 residents and tucked away deep into some of Georgia's most productive farmland, Colquitt (www.colquitt-georgia. com) wouldn't seem to merit much attention from visitors. But over the last decade the tiny town has been rejuvenated through cultural tourism.

The most obvious aspect is the nearly 20 large-scale murals throughout the downtown area, seemingly on every flat surface. Initiated with the Millennium Mural Project and representing various aspects of regional life and history, the murals are of extremely high artistic quality and a photographer's dream. In 2010 Colquitt hosted the bi-annual Global Mural Conference.

The other component of Colquitt's vibrant cultural scene for its small size is *Swamp Gravy* (229/758-5450, www.swampgravy.com, $27), Georgia's "official folk-life play" performed at the historic **Cotton Hall** (158 E. Main St.), a renovated cotton warehouse turned into a 300-seat venue, which also hosts other productions throughout the year. *Swamp Gravy* is a humorous musical performed by a huge volunteer cast. A new edition premieres each October, portraying segments of local life, history, and culture, and is reprised each March.

EAST OF ALBANY

Irwinville

Technically speaking, the end of the Civil War didn't happen with Lee's surrender at Appomattox but instead with the capture of Confederate president Jefferson Davis in Irwinville under fairly unflattering circumstances (although he wasn't disguised as a woman, as Northern propaganda claimed at the time). While fleeing to link up with remaining Confederate forces and continue the fight in the western theater of battle, on May 9, 1865, Davis and his party were surrounded by two groups of Union cavalry who were unaware of each other. Two horsemen died under friendly fire, and Davis was taken prisoner.

The incident is commemorated at the **Jefferson Davis Memorial Historical Site**

(338 Jeff Davis Park Rd., 229/831-2335, www. gastateparks.org, Wed.-Sun. 9am-5pm, $2.75-4), a bit southeast of Tifton. It has a small but detailed museum and a marker at the site of his arrest, as well as a picnic area on the relaxing and scenic grounds. Once a state park, the facility was recently handed over to Irwin County due to budget issues; I strongly suggest calling ahead to confirm hours. Note that this site isn't to be confused with the site in Kentucky with a similar name, which marks Davis's birthplace.

Fitzgerald

Ironically, Fitzgerald (www.fitzgeraldga.org), less than 10 miles from the site of Davis's capture, was designed and founded after the Civil War by a former Union Army drummer. Its other main Civil War-themed claim to fame is the **Blue and Gray Museum** (116 N. Johnston St., 229/426-5069, www.fitzgeraldga. org, Tues.-Sat. 10am-4pm, Sun. 1pm-5pm, $3 adults, $2 children) in the baggage room of the ornate and historic train depot downtown, other portions of which also house the city hall.

Architecture buffs might enjoy Fitzgerald's unusual house designs. Primarily settled by migrating Midwesterners, the town boasts many examples of non-Southern styles such as the "T-house." Downtown Fitzgerald is also worth an architecture tour; go to the **Welcome Center** (116 N. Johnston St., 229/426-5033, Mon.-Fri. 10am-5pm), near the museum, for more friendly information. The highlight is the **Grand Theater** (115 S. Main St., 229/426-5090), an ornate art deco building, burned in the 1920s and rebuilt in the 1930s, which still hosts productions, including the locally themed musical about the unique circumstances of Fitzgerald's founding, *Our Friends, the Enemy.*

Walking around town, however, you'll see that Fitzgerald's real signature item is the horde of Burmese chickens wandering around, legacy of an ill-fated introduction by the state in the 1960s. Intended to stock the area as game birds, the plump, colorful fowl for whatever reason migrated to downtown Fitzgerald and don't want to leave, even blocking the street on occasion. So, of course, there's a **Wild Chicken**

HOW DO YOU SAY PECAN?

a south Georgia pecan orchard

PEA-can or pe-CON? The debate continues in South Georgia, where the meadows are dotted with picturesque pecan orchards and roadside stands sell bushels of the freshly harvested nut each autumn. What's the right way to pronounce pecan? Old-timers insist it ain't French, and the emphasis should be on the first syllable: PEA-can. More recent arrivals—perhaps enamored of the nut's newly acquired foodie cachet as a key part of reinvented Southern cuisine—say it's the more refined pe-CON. The Georgia Department of Agriculture has actually come up with a Solomonic answer to the debate. The official pronunciation of *pecan* for state agricultural purposes is with the emphasis on the first syllable: PEA-can. However, the Agriculture Department also says the original pronunciation of the word, derived from an ancient Native American tongue, was almost certainly pe-CON. So you're not nuts. You can say it any way you like.

Festival (www.wildchickenfestival.com) in March.

INFORMATION AND SERVICES

The **Albany Visitors Center** (112 N. Front St., 229/317-4760, www.visitalbanyga.com, Mon.-Fri. 9am-5pm, Sat. 10am-4pm, Sun. noon-4pm) in the historic Bridge Building downtown, is the best place in the area to get visitor info. The paper of record in town is the *Albany Herald* (www.albanyherald.com).

The **Phoebe Putney Health System** (www.phoebeputney.com) is the largest health care provider in the region, serving several counties. The **North Campus** (2000 Palmyra Rd., 229/434-2000) provides emergency care in Albany.

© JIM MOREKIS

GETTING THERE AND AROUND

Albany is easily accessible from I-75 via numerous exits from Cordele down to Tifton. **Greyhound** (300 W. Oglethorpe Blvd., 229/432-0511, www.greyhound.com) has a bus station downtown a couple of blocks from the Flint River. The **Albany Transit System** (www.albany.ga.us, fare $1.25) has bus routes around town.

Thomasville and Vicinity

This area borders the balmy, piney woods of north Florida, and has a different feel from most other parts of Georgia. Indeed, down here folks are more likely to root for the Seminoles of Florida State University in nearby Tallahassee than for the Bulldogs of the University of Georgia.

It's a high Victorian city, a legacy of the time when affluent Northerners came down to this railroad terminus seeking good weather, relaxation, and hunting; President Eisenhower enjoyed quail hunts down here. Many of their flamboyant "winter cottages" exist today and are part of the town's historic district. Its most famous native is actress Joanne Woodward, wife of the late Paul Newman.

SIGHTS

I recommend a stop at the **Visitors Center** (144 E. Jackson St.) at the side entrance of the circa-1940 Municipal Auditorium building to get brochures and information from the friendly folks there. They have a very well-done, handsome walking tour brochure that I highly recommend for a self-guided walking tour of downtown; or download it at www.thomasvillega.com.

The "Big Oak"

Yup, it's a live oak tree that's really big, and really old, over 300 years. It occupies its own lot at the corner of North Crawford and East Monroe Streets. The Big Oak measures nearly 30 feet in circumference, and its sprawling branches are now so long and heavy that they have to be suspended in some places with steel cables. While climbing on them is not allowed, you can have your picture taken with the tree through the **"Big Oak Cam"**; dial 229/236-0053 on your cell phone, look at the camera across the street, and follow the audio instructions. Find the photo online at www.bigoak.rose.net.

Thomas County Museum of History

The **Thomas County Museum of History** (725 N. Dawson St., 229/226-7664, www.thomascountyhistory.org, tours Mon.-Sat. 10am-11:30am and 2pm-3:30pm, closed late Aug., $5 adults, $1 children) has preserved local history for over a half century. This is a great place to learn about the area's somewhat unique background for this part of the country.

Jack Hadley Black History Museum

On the campus of a former black high school during the days of segregation, the **Jack Hadley Black History Museum** (214 Alexander St., 229/226-5029, www.jackhadleyblackhistorymuseum.com, Tues.-Sat. 10am-5pm, $5 adults, $3 children) is named for a leading local black historian whose copious collection of memorabilia is on display. There are exhibits about key local and regional African Americans. You can get info here on other key black history sites in Thomasville.

Lapham-Patterson House Historic Site

The whimsically handsome **Lapham-Patterson House Historic Site** (626 N. Dawson St., 229/226-7664, www.gastateparks.org, Fri. 1pm-5pm, Sat. 10am-5pm, Sun. 2pm-5pm, $5) is a great example of the "winter cottage" homes built by wealthy Northerners in the late 19th century as resort homes in the temperate climate of Thomasville. Chicago shoe merchant C. W. Lapham built this three-story gem in 1885, and it features some amazing artisanal work, from longleaf pine floors to fish-scale shingles, and a double-flue chimney with walk-through stairway.

Pebble Hill Plantation

Pebble Hill Plantation (1251 U.S. 319 S., www.pebblehill.com, Tues.-Sat. 10am-5pm, Sun. noon-5pm, plantation $5 adults, $2 children, with house tour adults $15, children $6) is a remarkable collection of a dozen early-1900s buildings—ranging from an ornate main house open for tours to a log cabin school to a dog hospital—all in the service of the Hanna and Ireland families. While the original plantation covered over 10,000 acres, it's down to a still-huge 3,000 acres now, of which about 75 well-manicured acres are open for relaxed visits.

ACCOMMODATIONS AND FOOD

The premier B&B in Thomasville is the **☾ 1884 Paxton House Inn** (445 Remington Ave., 229/226-5197, www.1884paxtonhouseinn.com, $175-275), an exquisitely restored, flamboyant Victorian that was one of the first and still best examples of homes built by wealthy Northerners for Thomasville's resort "winter season." In this case, Colonel J. W. Paxton of West Virginia had this house built complete with circular staircase, 13-foot ceilings, and 12 coal fireplaces, along with several outbuildings that also host guests today. There are four guest rooms in the main house, three in the garden cottage, and a suite in the carriage house and the pool house. It's located several blocks from downtown.

Wherever you stay in Thomasville, remember that its proximity to Tallahassee means many rooms are booked well in advance on Florida State University home football game weekends in the fall.

The most popular restaurant in town is **☾ Jonah's Fish and Grits** (109 E. Jackson St., 229/226-0508, www.jonahsfish.com, Mon.-Fri. 11am-2pm and 5pm-9pm, Sat. 11am-9pm, $12-15), which has an expansive seafood menu that offers a signature parmesan grouper entrée along with, of course, fish-and-chips and shrimp and grits.

The Okefenokee Swamp

Scientists often refer to Okefenokee as an "analogue," an accurate representation of a totally different epoch in the earth's history. In this case it's the Carboniferous Period, about 350 million years ago, when the living plants were lush and green and the dead plants simmered in a slow-decaying peat that would one day end up as the oil that powers our civilization. But for the casual visitor, Okefenokee might also be simply a wonderful place to get almost completely away from human influence and witness firsthand some of the country's most interesting wildlife in its natural habitat. Despite the enormous wildfires of the spring of 2007 and the summer of 2011—some of the largest the Southeast has seen in half a century, so large they were visible from space—the swamp has bounced back, for the most part, and is once again hosting visitors to experience its timeless beauty.

☾ OKEFENOKEE NATIONAL WILDLIFE REFUGE

It's nearly the size of Rhode Island and just a short drive off I-95, but the massive and endlessly fascinating **Okefenokee National Wildlife Refuge** (912/496-7836, www.fws.gov, Mar.-Oct. daily dawn-7:30pm, Nov.-Feb. daily dawn-5:30pm, $5 per vehicle) is one of the lesser-visited national public lands. The nearby old rail town of Folkston is the gateway to the swamp for most visitors off I-95.

History

The Okefenokee Swamp was created by an accident of geology. About 250,000 years ago, the Atlantic Ocean washed ashore about 70 miles farther inland from where it does today. Over time, a massive barrier island formed off this primeval Georgia coastline, running from what is now Jesup, Georgia, south to Starke, Florida. When the ocean level dropped during the Pleistocene Era, this sandy island became a topographical feature known today as the Trail Ridge, its height effectively creating a basin to its west. Approximately 90 percent of the Okefenokee's water comes from rainfall into that basin, which drains slowly via the Suwannee and St. Marys Rivers.

Ordinarily, what the summer heat evaporates from the Okefenokee is more than replenished by rain, unless there's a severe drought like the one that caused the recent wildfires. But even the fires can't hold the swamp back. In fact, the Okefenokee is a fire ecosystem, meaning some plant species, like the cypress, depend on heat generated by wildfires to open their seed cones and perpetuate their lifecycle. Portions of the massive Honey Prairie Fire of 2011 in the swamp's southwestern area, caused by a lightning strike, still smolder to this day under the surface.

Native Americans used the swamp as a hunting ground and gave us its current name, which means "Land of the Trembling Earth," a reference to the floating peat islands, called "houses," that dominate the landscape. The Spanish arrived in about 1600, establishing at least two missions. While trade had occurred on the outskirts for nearly a century earlier, it wasn't until the 1850s that the first nonnative settlers set up camp inside the swamp.

Sights and Wildlife

Contrary to the popular image of a nasty, dank swamp, the Okefenokee is anything but a monoculture. It features a wide variety of ecosystems, including peat bogs, sand hills, and black gum and bay forests. Perhaps most surprising is the wide open vista of the swamp's many prairies or extended grasslands, 22 in

great blue heron on the banks of the Suwanee River

© BRIAN LASENBY

all, which, besides being stirring to the eye, are also great places to see birds. So not all of the Okefenokee is wet. There is water aplenty here, though, with over 60 named lakes and 120 miles of boating trails. And as you kayak or canoe on one of the water trails or on the old **Suwanee Canal** from the logging era, you'll notice the water is all very dark. This blackwater is not black because of dirt or silt but rather natural tannic acid released into the water from the decaying vegetation that gave the swamp its name. While I don't recommend that you drink the water, it's actually very clean despite its color.

A great way to see the sandhill cranes and other birds of the Okefenokee is to hike the 0.75-mile boardwalk out to the 50-foot-tall **Chesser Island Observation Tower** on the eastern end of the swamp. Get here by driving or cycling the eight-mile round-trip **Wildlife Drive,** which also takes you by the old **Chesser Homestead,** the remnants of one of the oldest settlements in the swamp. You can also hike

OKEFENOKEE NATIONAL WILDLIFE REFUGE

Waycross

To Valdosta →

Laura S Walker State Park

OKEFENOKEE SWAMP PARK (NORTH ENTRANCE)

Cowhouse Island

MAUL HAMMOCK

KINGFISHER LANDING (LAUNCH)

Big Water Lake

Okefenokee National Wildlife Refuge

BIG WATER

Territory Prairie

Big Water Prairie

Floyd's Prairie

CRAVEN'S HAMMOCK

Minnie's Island

BLUFF LAKE

Pine Island

Floyd's Island

FOLKSTON INN B&B

Stephen C Foster State Park

(WEST ENTRANCE)

SUWANNEE RIVER SILL

ROUND TOP

CEDAR HAMMOCK

Folkston

Christie Prairie

TRADER'S HILL RECREATION AREA

Billy's Island

CANAL RUN

CHESSER ISLAND OBSERVATION TOWER

SUWANNEE CANAL RECREATION AREA (EAST ENTRANCE)

To I-95 →

Honey Island

Bugaboo Island

Buck Prairie

REFUGE OFFICE

Suwannee River

Okefenokee National Wildlife Refuge

Chesser Prairie

FLORIDA

SUWANNEE RIVER VISITOR CENTER

John's Negro Island

NATURE DRIVE

Fargo

St. Marys River

Blackjack Island

Grand Prairie

Soldier's Camp Island

St. George

| 0 | 6 mi |
| 0 | 6 km |

FLORIDA

Moniac

To I-10 →

© AVALON TRAVEL

out to Chesser; indeed, there are many miles of hiking trails through the upland areas of the swamp near the East Entrance.

Probably the first creature one thinks of when one thinks of a swamp is the alligator. Certainly Okefenokee has plenty of them, and no one who has heard the roar of a male alligator break the quiet of the night will ever forget the experience. Most of the time, though, alligators are quite shy.

Recreation

For most visitors, the best way to enjoy the Okefenokee is to book a guided tour through **Okefenokee Adventures** (866/843-7926, www.okefenokeeadventures.com), the designated concessionaire of the refuge. They offer a 90-minute guided boat tour ($18 adults, $11 children) that leaves each hour, and a 2.5-hour reservation-only sunset tour ($25 adults, $17 children) that takes you to see the gorgeous sunset over Chesser Prairie. Extended or custom tours, including multiday wilderness excursions, are also available. They also rent bikes, canoes, and camping gear, and even run a decent little café where you can either sit down and have a meal or take it to go on the trail.

Camping and Accommodations

If fire and water levels permit, it's possible to stay the night in the swamp, canoeing to one of the primitive camping "islands" in the middle of the refuge. You need to make reservations up to two months in advance, however, by calling the **U.S. Fish and Wildlife Service** (912/496-3331, Mon.-Fri. 7am-10am). A nonrefundable fee ($10 pp, includes entrance fee) must be received 16 days before you arrive (mailing address: Okefenokee National Wildlife Refuge, Route 2, Box 3330, Folkston, GA 31537). Campfires are allowed only at Canal Run and Floyds Island. A camp stove is required for cooking at all other shelters. Keep in mind that in times of extreme drought or fire threat, boat trips may not be allowed. Always check the website for the latest announcements.

Privately owned canoes and boats with motors under 10 hp may put in with no launch fee, but you must sign in and out. No ATVs are allowed on the refuge, and bicycles are allowed only on designated bike trails. Keep in mind that some hunting goes on in the refuge at designated times. Pets must be leashed at all times.

At the **Stephen Foster State Park** (17515 Hwy. 177, 912/637-5274, fall-winter daily 7am-7pm, spring-summer daily 6:30am-8:30pm, tent sites $24, cottages $100), a.k.a. the **West Entrance,** near Fargo, Georgia, there are 66 tent sites and nine cottages.

Information and Services

At the main East Entrance is the federally run **Richard S. Bolt Visitors Center** (912/496-7836, www.fws.gov, July-Aug. and Dec.-Jan. Mon.-Fri. 9am-5pm, Feb.-June and Sept.-Nov. daily 9am-5pm), which has some cool nature exhibits and a surround-sound orientation video. At the West Entrance is the state-run **Suwanee River Visitors Center** (912/637-5274, www.gastateparks.org, Wed.-Sun. 9am-5pm), a "green" building featuring an orientation video and exhibits.

Getting There and Around

The best way to access the Okefenokee is the **East Entrance** (912/496-7836, www.fws.gov, Mar.-Oct. daily dawn-7:30pm, Nov.-Feb. daily dawn-5:30pm, $5 per vehicle), otherwise known as the **Suwanee Canal Recreation Area.** This is the main U.S. Fish and Wildlife Service entrance and the most convenient way to hike, rent boating and camping gear, and observe nature. An easy way to get to the East Entrance is by taking the Kingsland exit off I-95 onto Highway 40 west. Go through Kingsland and into Folkston until it dead-ends. Take a right, then an immediate left onto Main Street. At the third light, make a left onto Okefenokee Drive (Hwy. 121) south.

Families with kids may want to drive a bit farther and hit the **North Entrance** at the privately run **Okefenokee Swamp Park** (U.S. 1, 912/283-0583, www.okeswamp.com, daily

9am-5:30pm, $12 adults, $11 ages 3-11) near Waycross. Here you will find a more touristy vibe, with a reconstructed pioneer village, a serpentarium, and animals in captivity. From here, you can take various guided tours for an additional fee. There's camping at the nearby but unaffiliated **Laura S. Walker State Park** (5653 Laura Walker Rd., 800/864-7275, www.gastateparks.org). Be aware that the state park is not in the swamp and isn't very swampy. Get to the North Entrance by taking I-95 exit 29 and going west on U.S. 82 about 45 miles to Highway 177 (Laura Walker Rd.). Go south through Laura S. Walker State Park; the Swamp Park is several miles farther.

If you really want that cypress-festooned, classic swamp look, go around the Okefenokee to **Stephen Foster State Park** (17515 Hwy. 177, 912/637-5274, fall-winter daily 7am-7pm, spring-summer daily 6:30am-8:30pm), a.k.a. the **West Entrance,** near Fargo, Georgia. Guided tours are available.

FOLKSTON

The chief attraction in Folkston, the little town right outside the refuge's East Entrance, is the excellent **◖ Inn at Folkston Bed and Breakfast** (509 W. Main St., 888/509-6246, www.innatfolkston.com, $120-170). There is nothing like coming back to its cozy Victorian charms after a long day out in the swamp. The four-room inn boasts an absolutely outstanding breakfast, an extensive reading library, and a whirlpool tub.

A five-minute drive from the Inn is another Folkston claim to fame, the viewing depot for the **Folkston Funnel** (912/496-2536, www.folkston.com), a veritable train watcher's paradise. This is the spot where the big CSX double-track rail line following the top of the ancient Trail Ridge hosts 60 or more trains a day. Railroad buffs from all over the South congregate here, anticipating the next train by listening to their scanners. The first Saturday each April brings buffs together for the all-day Folkston RailWatch.

WAYCROSS

Fans of the old *Pogo* will recall Waycross (www.waycrosstourism.com) from the comic strip; and yes, there's a real "Fort Mudge" nearby. Pogo was fictional, but real-life Waycross natives include musician Gram Parsons and actor Ossie Davis. Seat of Ware County, Waycross has a wide-open feel, a legacy of the fact that the city literally grew around the railroad, its design based on the tracks coming into town. Today, Waycross is still one of the South's busiest rail centers, and many of the trains that course through Folkston Funnel go through town.

So, of course, the centerpiece of Waycross's downtown renovation is the restored **Historic Passenger Rail Depot** (315 Plant Ave., 912/283-3744, Mon.-Fri. 10am-5pm), built in the early 1900s complete with Spanish Revival touches. It currently houses the town visitors center and Chamber of Commerce; get walking tour information to enjoy downtown Waycross's interesting and somewhat unusual architectural styles, some with Mediterranean flair.

The museum of note in Waycross is the **Okefenokee Heritage Center** (1460 N. Augusta Ave., 912/285-4260, http://okefenokeeheritagecenter.com, Tues.-Sat. 10am-4:30pm, $7 adults, $5 ages 6-18, free under age 5). Set on 20 acres of land, it features a historic locomotive, a recreated Waycross courthouse, an 1830s home, and an African American history exhibit.

A few miles south of town is **Obediah's Okefenok** (5115 Swamp Rd., 912/287-0090, www.okefenokeeswamp.com, daily 10am-5pm, $6.50 adults, $5 children), restored homestead of one of the first settlers and swamp guides in the Okefenokee: Henry "Obediah" Barber.

The best restaurant in town and, indeed, in the entire area for many, many miles around, is **◖ Pond View Fine Dining** (311 Pendleton St., 912/283-9300, www.pondviewinn.com, Wed.-Sat. 6pm-10pm, $20), in an attractively restored downtown storefront. What's more, there's a four-room inn ($100) upstairs, a nice break from the usual mediocre chain accommodations typical of the area.

SAVANNAH

Rarely has a city owed so much to the vision of one person than Savannah owes to General James Edward Oglethorpe. Given the mission by King George II to buffer Charleston from the Spanish, this reformer had a far more sweeping vision in mind. After befriending indigenous Creek people, Oglethorpe laid out his settlement in a deceptively simple plan that is still studied the world over as a model of nearly perfect urban design. Many of his other progressive ideas—such as prohibiting slavery and hard liquor, to name two—soon went by the wayside. But the legacy of his original plan lives on to this day.

Savannah was built as a series of rectangular "wards," each built around a central square. As the city grew, each square took on its own characteristics, depending on who lived on the square and how they made their livelihood. It is this individuality that is so well documented in John Berendt's *Midnight in the Garden of Good and Evil*. The squares of Savannah's downtown—since 1965 a National Landmark Historic District—are also responsible for the city's walkability, another defining characteristic.

Savannah is also known for being able to show you a rowdy good time, and not only during its massive, world-famous St. Patrick's Day celebration. Savannahians, like New Orleanians, will use any excuse for a party, and any excuse to drink in the full flavor of natural beauty here—whether in the heady glory of a spring day with all the flowers blooming, or the sweet release of the long-awaited autumn, brisk and bracing but not so crisp that you can't wear shorts.

© DREAMSTIME.COM

HIGHLIGHTS

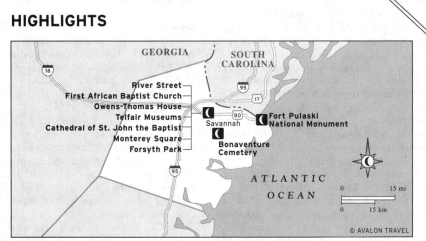

© AVALON TRAVEL

LOOK FOR ◖ TO FIND RECOMMENDED SIGHTS, ACTIVITIES, DINING, AND LODGING.

◖ **River Street:** Despite River Street's tourist tackiness, there's still nothing like strolling the cobblestones amid the old cotton warehouses, enjoying the cool breeze off the river, and watching the huge ships on their way to and from the bustling port (page 621).

◖ **First African Baptist Church:** The oldest black congregation in the United States still meets in this historic sanctuary, a key stop on the Underground Railroad (page 625).

◖ **Owens-Thomas House:** Possibly the country's best example of Regency architecture is an example of state-of-the-art historic preservation in action and Savannah's single greatest historical home (page 628).

◖ **Telfair Museums:** Old school meets new school in this museum complex that comprises the traditional collection of the Telfair Academy of Arts and Sciences and the ultra-modern Jepson Center for the Arts, both within a stone's throw of each other (page 630).

◖ **Cathedral of St. John the Baptist:** This soaring Gothic Revival edifice is complemented by its ornate interior and its matchless location on verdant Lafayette Square, stomping ground of the young Flannery O'Connor (page 632).

◖ **Monterey Square:** Perhaps Savannah's quintessential square has some of the best examples of local architecture and world-class ironwork all around its periphery (page 633).

◖ **Forsyth Park:** This verdant expanse ringed with old live oaks and chockablock with memorials is Savannah's backyard (page 639).

◖ **Bonaventure Cemetery:** This historic burial ground is the final resting place for some of Savannah's favorite citizens, including the great Johnny Mercer, and makes great use of its setting on the banks of the Wilmington River (page 642).

◖ **Fort Pulaski National Monument:** This well-run site, built with the help of a young Robert E. Lee, is not only historically significant; its beautiful setting makes it a great place for the entire family (page 645).

HISTORY

By the early 1700s, the land south of Charleston was a staging area for attacks by the Spanish and Native Americans. So in 1732, King George II granted a charter to the Trustees of Georgia, a proprietary venture that was the brainchild of a 36-year-old general and member of parliament, General James Edward Oglethorpe. On February 12, 1733, the *Anne* landed with 114 passengers along the high bluff on the south bank of the Savannah River. Oglethorpe bonded with Tomochichi, the local Creek Indian chief, and the colony prospered.

Oglethorpe had a plan for the new "classless society" in Savannah that prohibited slavery, rum, and—wait for it—lawyers! But as the settlers enviously eyed the dominance of Charleston's slave-based rice economy, the Trustees bowed to public pressure and relaxed restrictions on slavery and rum. By 1753, the crown reclaimed the charter, making Georgia the 13th colony.

Savannah's antebellum heyday was from 1800 to 1860, when for a time it outstripped Charleston as a center of commerce. Blockaded for most of the Civil War, Savannah didn't see much action other than the fall of Fort Pulaski in April 1862, when a Union force successfully laid siege using rifled artillery, a revolutionary new technology. War came to Savannah's doorstep when General William T. Sherman's March to the Sea concluded with his capture of the town in December 1864. Sherman sent a now-legendary telegram to President Lincoln granting him the city as a Christmas present with these words: "I beg to present you as a Christmas gift, the City of Savannah with 150 heavy guns and plenty of ammunition and also about 25,000 bales of cotton."

Savannah played a pioneering, though largely unsung, role in the civil rights movement. Ralph Mark Gilbert, pastor of the historic First African Baptist Church, launched one of the first black voter registration drives in the South. The opening of the Savannah College of Art and Design (SCAD) in 1979 ushered another important chapter in Savannah's renaissance.

After the publication of John Berendt's *Midnight in the Garden of Good and Evil* in 1994, nothing would ever be the same in Savannah. Old-money families cringed as idiosyncrasies and hypocrisies were laid bare in "The Book." Local merchants and politicians, however, delighted in the influx of tourists. A more recent driver of tourism to the area has been the arrival of Food Network star Paula Deen.

PLANNING YOUR TIME

Much more than just a parade, St. Patrick's Day in Savannah—an event generally expanded to include several days before and after it—is also a time of immense crowds, with the city's usual population of about 150,000 doubling with the influx of partying visitors. Be aware that lodging on and around March 17 fills up well in advance.

As in Charleston, you don't need a car to have a great time and see most sights worth enjoying. A strong walker can easily traverse the length and breadth of downtown in a day. To fully enjoy Savannah, however, you'll need access to a vehicle so you can go east to Tybee Island and south to various historical sights with spottier public transportation. Plan on two nights at an absolute minimum—not only to enjoy all the sights, but to fully soak in the local color and attitude.

ORIENTATION

The downtown area is bounded on the east by East Broad Street and on the west by Martin Luther King Jr. Boulevard (formerly W. Broad St.). For quick access to the south, take the one-way streets Price (on the east side of downtown) or Whitaker (on the west side of downtown). Conversely, if you want to make a quick trip north into downtown, three one-way streets taking you there are East Broad, Lincoln, and Drayton. Technically, Gwinnett Street is the southern boundary of the National Historic Landmark District, though in practice locals extend the boundary several blocks southward. When you're driving downtown and come to a square, the law says traffic within the square *always* has the right of way. In other words, if you haven't yet entered the square, you must yield to any vehicles already in the square.

Sights

It's best to introduce yourself to the sights of Savannah by traveling from the river southward. It's no small task to navigate the nation's largest contiguous Historic District, but when in doubt it's best to follow James Oglethorpe's original plan of using the five "monumental" squares on Bull Street (Johnson, Wright, Chippewa, Madison, and Monterey) as focal points.

WATERFRONT

It's only natural to start one's adventures in Savannah where Oglethorpe's adventures themselves began: on the waterfront, now dominated by scenic and historic River Street. Once the bustling center of Savannah's thriving cotton and naval stores export industry, the waterfront is also generally thought of as including Factor's Walk and Bay Street.

◖ River Street

If you have a car, park it somewhere else and walk. The cobblestones—actually old ballast stones from some of the innumerable ships that docked here over the years—are tough on the suspension, and much of River Street is dedicated to pedestrian traffic anyway.

THE WAVING GIRL

Begin your walking tour of River Street on the east end, at the statue of Florence Martus, a.k.a. *The Waving Girl,* set in the emerald green expanse of little Morrell Park. Beginning at the age of 19, Martus—who actually lived several miles downriver on Elba Island—took to greeting every passing ship with a wave of a handkerchief by day and a lantern at night, without fail for the next 40 years. Ship captains returned the greeting with a salute of their own on the ship's whistle, and word spread all over the world of the beguiling woman who waited on the balcony of that lonely house. Was she looking for a sign of a long lost love who went to sea and never returned? Was she trying to

get a handsome sea captain to sweep her off her feet and take her off that little island? No one knows for sure. Martus became such an enduring symbol of the personality and spirit of Savannah that a U.S. Liberty ship was named for her in 1943. She died a few months after the ship's christening at the age of 75.

WORLD WAR II MEMORIAL

Near the foot of the new Bohemian hotel on River Street, the newest addition to Savannah's public monuments, the World War II Memorial—fairly modernist by local standards—features a copper and bronze globe torn in half to represent the European and Pacific theaters of the war. The more than 500 local people who gave their lives in that conflict are memorialized by name.

FACTOR'S WALK

One level up from River Street, Factor's Walk has nothing to do with math, though a lot of money has been counted here. In arcane usage, a "factor" was a broker—a middleman for the sale of cotton, Savannah's chief export during most of the 1800s. Factors mostly worked in Factor's Row, the traditional phrase for the actual buildings on River Street, most all of which were used in various import-export activities before their current transformation into a mélange of shops, hotels, restaurants, and taverns. Factor's Walk is divided into Lower Factor's Walk, comprising the alleys and back entrances behind Factor's Row, and Upper Factor's Walk, the system of crosswalks at the upper levels of Factor's Row that lead directly to Bay Street.

BAY STREET

In front of the Hyatt Regency is a concrete bench marking the spot on which Oglethorpe pitched his first tent. But dominating Bay Street is **City Hall** (2 E. Bay St.) next door, with its gold-leaf dome. The 1907 building

SAVANNAH

SAVANNAH

Savannah   River

Emmet Park

RIVER STREET

THE WAVING GIRL

CHUCK'S BAR

KEVIN BARRY'S IRISH PUB

WWII MEMORIAL

FACTOR'S WALK

W FACTORS WALK

WILLIAMSON ST

BARNARD RAMP

HYATT

OLYMPIA CAFÉ

RIVER ST

E FACTORS WALK

CITY HALL

BAY STREET

E BAY

BOHEMIAN HOTEL

W BAY ST

CLUB ONE

OLDE PINK HOUSE

B. MATTHEW'S EATERY

MULBERRY INN

ANDAZ

FIRST AFRICAN BAPTIST CHURCH

W BRYAN ST

E BRYAN ST

WARREN SQUARE

WASHINGTON SQUARE

(W BROAD)

Franklin Square

CITY MARKET

Ellis Square

Johnson Square

Reynolds Square

VINNIE'S

W CONGRESS

LADY & SONS

E CONGRESS ST

SHIPS OF THE SEA MARITIME MUSEUM

LULU'S CHOCOLATE BAR

JINX

SAPPHIRE GRILL

CHRIST EPISCOPAL CHURCH

LUCAS THEATRE

LEOPOLD'S

To Trustees Garden

W BROUGHTON ST

E BROUGHTON ST

E BROUGHTON LN

ISAIAH DAVENPORT HOUSE MUSEUM

ANN ST

Liberty Square

TELFAIR MUSEUMS

OWENS-THOMAS HOUSE

W STATE ST

E STATE ST

Telfair Square

Wright Square

E PRESIDENT ST

Oglethorpe Square

KEHOE HOUSE

Columbia Square

Greene Square

TRINITY UNITED METHODIST CHURCH

ZUNZI'S

W YORK ST

MARTIN LUTHER KING JR BLVD

JEPSON CENTER

W YORK ST

JULIETTE GORDON LOW HOUSE

E YORK ST

E YORK LN

OGLETHORPE AVE

SCAD MUSEUM OF ART

ANGEL'S BBQ

W OGLETHORPE AVE

E OGLETHORPE AVE

MONTGOMERY ST

JEFFERSON ST

BARNARD ST

INDEPENDENT PRESBYTERIAN

WHITAKER ST

BULL ST

DRAYTON ST

ABERCORN ST

LINCOLN ST

PRICE ST

HOUSTON ST

COLONIAL CEMETERY

TURNER ST

Elbert Square

FOLEY HOUSE

W HULL ST

E HULL ST

VISITORS CENTER

Orleans Square

CIVIC CENTER

Chippewa Square

HISTORIC SAVANNAH THEATRE

Crawford Square

Battlefield Park

W PERRY ST

E PERRY ST

THE DISTILLERY

W LIBERTY ST

E LIBERTY ST

CATHEDRAL OF JOHN THE BAPTIST

LOUISVILLE RD

← To Muse Arts Warehouse

GREEN-MELDRIN HOUSE

PINKIE MASTERS

HABERSHAM ST

W HARRIS ST

E HARRIS ST

Pulaski Square

Madison Square

Lafayette Square

Troup Square

E MACON ST

W CHARLTON ST

ANDREW LOW HOUSE

E CHARLTON ST

W CHARLTON LN

E CHARLTON LN

W JONES ST

FLANNERY O'CONNOR CHILDHOOD HOME

E JONES ST

MRS. WILKES DINING ROOM

ELIZA THOMPSON HOUSE

W TAYLOR ST

TEMPLE MICKVE ISRAEL

E TAYLOR ST

16

RALPH MARK GILBERT CIVIL RIGHTS MUSEUM

MONTEREY SQUARE

Chatham Square

W GORDON ST

MERCER-WILLIAMS HOUSE

Calhoun Square

E WAYNE ST

E GORDON ST

Whitefield Square

W ALICE ST

E ALICE ST

W GASTON ST

GASTONIAN INN

E GASTON ST

MONTGOMERY ST

TATTNALL ST

DRAYTON ST

ABERCORN ST

0   200 yds

0   200 m

W HUNTINGDON ST

FORSYTH PARK

MANSION ON FORSYTH

E HUNTINGDON ST

LEOCI'S

To Carnegie Branch Library

W HALL ST

To The Legion

E HALL ST

© AVALON TRAVEL

statue of Florence Martus, *The Waving Girl*, by sculptor Felix de Weldon

was designed by acclaimed architect Hyman Witcover and erected on the site of Savannah's first town hall.

The large gray Greek Revival building directly across from City Hall is the **U.S. Custom House** (1 E. Bay St.), not "customs," regardless of what the tour guides may say. Within its walls was held the trial of the captain and crew of the notorious slave ship *Wanderer,* which illegally plied its trade after a national ban on the importation of slaves. Local newspaper publisher and educator John H. DeVeaux worked here after his appointment as the first African American U.S. Collector of Customs.

Directly adjacent to City Hall on the east is a small canopy sheltering two cannons, which together are the oldest monument in Savannah. These are the **Chatham Artillery Guns,** presented to the local militia group of the same name by President George Washington during his one and only visit to town in 1791. Today, locals use the phrase "Chatham Artillery" differently, to refer to

a particularly potent local punch recipe that mixes several hard liquors.

Look directly behind the cannons and you'll see the ornate **Savannah Cotton Exchange** (100 E. Bay St.), built in 1886 to facilitate the city's huge cotton export business. Once nicknamed "King Cotton's Palace" but now a Masonic lodge, this delightful building by William Gibbons Preston is one of Savannah's many great examples of the Romanesque style. You'll become well acquainted with Preston's handiwork during your stay in Savannah—the Boston architect built many of Savannah's finest buildings. The fanciful lion figure in front—sometimes mistakenly referred to as a griffin—represents Mark the Evangelist. However, it isn't original—the first lion was destroyed in 2009 in a bizarre traffic accident.

CITY MARKET

In local parlance, the phrase "City Market" refers not only to the refurbished warehouses that make up this tourist-friendly area of shops and restaurants in the Historic District's western portion but also its bookend squares as well—both of which had close scrapes with the bulldozer and wrecking ball before their current renaissance.

Ellis Square

Just across Bay Street on the western edge of the Historic District, Ellis Square has a history as Savannah's main open-air marketplace that goes back to 1755, when there was actually a single City Market building in the square itself. Three market buildings would come and go until the building of the fourth City Market in 1872, an ornate Romanesque affair with a 50-foot roofline. In 1954, the city, in the thrall of auto worship then sweeping the country, decided a parking garage in the square was more important than fresh food or a sense of community. So the magnificent City Market building—and Ellis Square—simply ceased to exist.

The eyesore that was the Ellis Square parking garage is now gone, and the square has been literally rebuilt as a pedestrian hangout, complete with a fountain, all atop a huge

SAVANNAH

SAVANNAH

OGLETHORPE: VISIONARY ARISTOCRAT

One of the greatest products of the Enlightenment, James Edward Oglethorpe was a study in contrasts, embodying all the vitality, contradiction, and ambiguity of that turbulent age. A stern moralist yet an avowed liberal, an aristocrat with a populist streak, an abolitionist and an anti-Catholic, a man of war who sought peace—the founder of Georgia would put his own inimitable stamp on the new nation to follow, a legacy personified to this day in the city he designed.

After making a name for himself fighting the Turks, the young London native and Oxford graduate would return home only to serve a two-year prison sentence for killing a man in a brawl. The experience was a formative one for Oglethorpe, scion of a large and upwardly mobile family now forced to see how England's underbelly really lived. Upon his release, the 25-year-old Oglethorpe ran for the "family" House of Commons seat once occupied by his father and two brothers, and won. He made a name for himself as a campaigner for human rights and an opponent of slavery. Another jail-related epiphany came when Oglethorpe saw a friend die of smallpox in debtors prison. More than ever, Oglethorpe was determined to right what he saw as a colossal wrong in the draconian English justice system. His crusade took the form of establishing a sanctuary for debtors in North America.

To that end, he and his friend Lord Perceval established the Trustees, a 21-member group who lobbied King George for permission to establish such a colony. The grant from the king—who was more interested in containing the Spanish than in any humanitarian concerns—would include all

land between the Altamaha and Savannah Rivers and from the headwaters of these rivers to the "south seas." Ironically, there were no debtors among Savannah's original colonists. Nonetheless, the new settlement was indeed a reflection of its founder's core values, banning rum as a bad influence (though beer and wine were allowed), prohibiting slavery, and eschewing lawyers on the theory that a gentleman should always be able to defend himself.

Nearing 40 and distracted by war with the Spanish, Oglethorpe's agenda gradually eroded in the face of opposition from settlers, who craved not only the more hedonistic lifestyle of their neighbors to the north in Charleston but the economic advantage that city enjoyed in the use of slave labor. In nearly the same hour as his greatest military victory, crushing the Spanish at the Battle of Bloody Marsh on St. Simons Island, Oglethorpe also suffered an ignominious defeat: being replaced as head of the 13th colony, which he had founded.

He went back to England, never to see the New World again. But his heart was always with the colonists. After successfully fending off a political attack and a court-martial, Oglethorpe married and commenced a healthy retirement. He supported independence for the American colonies, making a point to enthusiastically receive the new ambassador from the United States, one John Adams. The old general died on June 30, 1785, at age 88. Fittingly for this lifelong philanthropist and humanitarian, his childhood home in Godalming, Surrey, is now a nursing home.

underground parking garage. It cost taxpayers millions of dollars, but as any Savannahian will tell you, the return of one of their precious squares is priceless. Be sure to check out the smallish bronze of native Savannahian and Oscar-winning lyricist Johnny Mercer on the square's western edge.

Franklin Square

Just west of City Market is Franklin Square,

once known simply as "Water Tank Square" because that's where the city reservoir was back in the day. Don't be alarmed by the numbers of men hanging out in the square. Scruffy heirs to an old Savannah tradition, most of them are day laborers for hire. Until recently, Franklin Square was, like Ellis Square, a victim of "progress," this time in the form of a highway going right through the middle of it. But as part of the city's effort to reclaim its history, Franklin

Square was returned to its integral state in the mid-1980s.

◀ FIRST AFRICAN BAPTIST CHURCH

Without a doubt the premier historic attraction on Franklin Square—and indeed one of the most significant historic sites in Savannah—is the **First African Baptist Church** (23 Montgomery St., 912/233-2244, www.firstafricanbc.com, tours Sun. 1pm, $7). It's the oldest black congregation in North America, dating from 1777. The present building dates from 1859 and was built almost entirely by members of the congregation themselves, some of whom redirected savings intended to purchase their freedom toward the building of the church. It houses the oldest church organ in Georgia. A key staging area for the fabled Underground Railroad, First African Baptist still bears the scars of that turbulent time. In the floor of the fellowship hall—where many civil rights meetings were held, because it was safer for white citizens to go there instead of black activists going outside the church—you'll see breathing holes, drilled for use by escaped slaves hiding in a cramped crawlspace.

HISTORIC DISTRICT
Johnson Square

Due east of City Market, Oglethorpe's very first square is named for Robert Johnson, governor of South Carolina at the time of Georgia's founding. It was here that Savannah's Liberty Pole was erected in 1774 to celebrate a new nation. And it was here that a gathering in 1861 celebrated Georgia's secession, ironically with a huge banner draped over the Greene Monument bearing the words "Don't Tread on Me"—a slogan used in the founding of the very union they sought to dissolve.

The roomy, shady square, ringed with major bank branches and insurance firms, is dominated by the **Nathanael Greene Monument** in honor of George Washington's second-in-command. Marquis de Lafayette dedicated the towering obelisk during his one and only visit to Savannah in 1825. At the time it did not honor any one person. Its

dedication to Greene came in 1886, followed by the reinterment of Greene's remains underneath the monument in 1901. (In typically maddening Savannah fashion, there is a separate square named for Greene, which has no monument to him at all.)

CHRIST EPISCOPAL CHURCH

The southeast corner of Johnson Square is dominated by **Christ Episcopal Church** (18 Abercorn St., 912/232-4131, www.christchurchsavannah.org), a.k.a. Christ Church, a historic house of worship also known as the "Mother Church of Georgia" because its congregation traces its roots to that first Anglican service in Savannah, held the same day Oglethorpe landed.

Reynolds Square

Walk directly east of Johnson Square to find yourself at Reynolds Square, named for John Reynolds, the first (and exceedingly unpopular) royal governor of Georgia. First called "Lower New Square," Reynolds originally served as site of the filature, or cocoon storage warehouse, during the fledgling colony's ill-fated flirtation with the silk industry (a federal building now occupies the site). The monument in Reynolds Square has nothing to do with its namesake, but is a likeness of John Wesley dedicated in 1969 near the spot believed to have been his home. On the northeast corner of the square is the parish house of Christ Church, Wesley's congregation.

A Reynolds Square landmark, the **Olde Pink House** (23 Abercorn St.), is the oldest Savannah mansion from the 18th century still standing as well as the first place in Savannah where the Declaration of Independence was read aloud. Pink inside as well as out, the Georgian mansion was built in 1771 for rice planter James Habersham Jr., one of America's richest men at the time and a member of the "Liberty Boys" who plotted revolution. The building's pink exterior was a matter of serendipity, resulting from its core redbrick seeping through the formerly white stucco outer covering.

SAVANNAH

SAVANNAH

LUCAS THEATRE FOR THE ARTS

The other major Savannah landmark on Reynolds Square is the **Lucas Theatre for the Arts** (32 Abercorn St., 912/525-5040, www.lucastheatre.com). Built in 1921 as part of Arthur Lucas's regional chain of movie houses, the Lucas also featured a stage for road shows. Ornate and stately but with cozy warmth to spare, the venue was a hit with Savannahians for four decades, until the advent of TV and residential flight from downtown led to financial disaster. In 1976, the Lucas closed after a screening of *The Exorcist*. When the building faced demolition in 1986, a group of citizens created a nonprofit to save it. Despite numerous starts and stops, the 14-year campaign finally paid off in a grand reopening in 2000, an event helped immeasurably by timely donations from *Midnight* star Kevin Spacey and the cast and crew of the locally shot *Forrest Gump*.

Columbia Square

Named for the mythical patroness of America, this square features at its center not an expected portrait of that female warrior figure but the original fountain from Noble Jones's Wormsloe Plantation, placed there in 1970.

ISAIAH DAVENPORT HOUSE MUSEUM

Columbia Square is the home of the **Isaiah Davenport House Museum** (324 E. State St., 912/236-8097, www.davenporthousemuseum.org, Mon.-Sat. 10am-4pm, Sun. 1pm-4pm, $8 adults, $5 children). The house museum is a delightful stop in and of itself because of its elegant simplicity, sweeping double staircase, and near-perfect representation of the federalist style. But the Davenport House occupies an exalted place in Savannah history as well, because the fight to save it began the preservation movement in Savannah in 1955.

Most Octobers, the Davenport House hosts living history dramatizations based on Savannah's yellow fever plague of the 1820s. Despite the grim subject matter, the little playlets are usually quite entertaining.

Across the corner from the Davenport House is the Classical Revival masterpiece **Kehoe**

House (123 Habersham St.), designed for local ironworks owner William Kehoe in 1892 by DeWitt Bruyn, and now one of Savannah's premier bed-and-breakfasts.

Warren and Washington Squares

Warren Square and its neighbor Washington Square formed the first extension of Oglethorpe's original four and still boast some of the oldest houses in the Historic District. Both squares are lovely little garden spots, ideal for a picnic in the shade. Two houses near Washington Square were restored by the late Jim Williams of *Midnight* fame: The **Hampton Lillibridge House** (507 E. St. Julian St.), which once hosted an Episcopal exorcism, and the **Charles Oddingsells House** (510 E. St. Julian St.). Now a hotel, **The Brice** on Washington Square was once a cotton warehouse and subsequently one of the nation's first Coca-Cola bottling plants.

Greene Square

Named for Revolutionary War hero Nathanael Greene, but bearing no monument to him whatsoever, this square is of particular importance to local African American history. At the corner of Houston (pronounced "HOUSE-ton") and East State Streets is the 1810 **Cunningham House,** built for Henry Cunningham, former slave and founding pastor of the **Second African Baptist Church** (124 Houston St., 912/233-6163) on the west side of the square, in which General Sherman made his famous promise of "40 acres and a mule." In 1818, the residence at 542 East State Street was constructed for free blacks Charlotte and William Wall. The property at 513 East York Street was built for the estate of Catherine DeVeaux, part of a prominent African American family.

Trustees Garden

At the east end of Bay Street where it meets East Broad Street rises a bluff behind a masonry wall. This is Trustees Garden, the nation's first experimental garden. Modeled on the Chelsea Botanical Garden in London, it was intended

THE IRISH IN SAVANNAH

It seems Savannah's close connection to St. Patrick's Day was ordained from the beginning. The very first baby born here, Georgia Close, came into the world on March 17, 1733. Two hundred and fifty years later, Savannah holds the second-largest St. Patrick's Day celebration in the world, second only to New York City's. Three presidents have visited during the shindig—William Howard Taft, Harry Truman, and Jimmy Carter. With its fine spring weather and walkability—not to mention its liberal "to-go cup" rules allowing you to carry an adult beverage on the street—Savannah is tailor-made for a boisterous outdoor celebration. But most of all, what makes it a perfect fit is the city's large Irish-American population.

The earliest Irish in Georgia were descendants of the Calvinist Scots who "planted" Ireland's northern province of Ulster in the 1600s. Often called "crackers"—perhaps from the Gaelic *craic*, "enjoyable conversation"—these early Irish entered Georgia from upstate South Carolina and made their living trading, trapping, or soldiering. One such "cracker" was Sergeant William Jasper, mortally wounded leading the charge to retake Savannah from the British in 1779.

The main chapter in local Irish history began in the 1830s with the arrival of the first wave of Irish to build the Central of Georgia Railway. The story goes that Irish were employed on the railroad because, unlike slaves, their bodies had no commercial value and could be worked to exhaustion with impunity. A second wave of Irish immigration followed two decades later when the potato famine in the old country forced many to seek new shores.

Though the Irish were initially subject to prejudice, their willingness to work long hours for low pay soon made them irreplaceable in Savannah's economy. And as in New York, in short order the Irish became major players in politics and business. In the early days, Irish neighborhoods were clustered around East Broad Street in the Old Fort area, and on the west side near West Broad Street (now MLK Jr. Blvd.). It's no coincidence that those areas also had large African American populations. Because of their shared links of poverty and prejudice, in the early days Savannah's Irish tended to live near black neighborhoods, often socializing with them after-hours—much to the chagrin of Savannah's elite.

Ironically, given St. Patrick's Day's current close association with the Roman Catholic faith, the first parade in Savannah was organized by Irish Protestants. Thirteen members of the local Hibernian Society—the country's oldest Irish society—took part in a private procession to Independent Presbyterian Church in 1813. The first public procession was in 1824, when the Hibernians invited all local Irishmen to parade through the streets. The first recognizably modern parade, with bands and a "grand marshal," happened in 1870.

Today's parade is a far cry from those early beginnings. Organized by a "committee" of about 700 local Irishmen—with but a tiny sprinkling of women—the three-hour procession includes marchers from all the local Irish organizations, in addition to marching bands and floats representing many local groups. Rain or shine, the assembled clans march—*amble* is perhaps a more accurate word—wearing their kelly green blazers, brandishing their walking canes and to-go cups, some pushing future committee members in strollers, fair skin gradually getting redder in the Georgia sun.

to be the epicenter of Savannah's silk industry. Alas, the colonists had little knowledge of native soils or climate—they thought the winters would be milder—and the experiment was not as successful as hoped. The area fell from grace and became known for its illegal activity and as the haunt of sea salts such as the ones who frequented what is now the schlocky Pirates' House restaurant. That building began life in 1753 as a seamen's inn and was later chronicled by Robert Louis Stevenson in *Treasure Island* as a rogue's gallery of pirates and nautical ne'er-do-wells.

Find the **Herb House** on East Broad Street,

SAVANNAH

the older-looking clapboard structure next to the Pirates' House entrance. You're looking at what is considered the single oldest building in Georgia and one of the oldest in the United States. Constructed in 1734, it was originally the home of Trustees Garden's chief gardener.

To the rear of Trustees Garden is the 1881 Hillyer building, now the **Charles H. Morris Center,** a mixed-use performing arts and meeting space that is heavily used during the springtime Savannah Music Festival.

Broughton Street

Downtown's main shopping district for most of the 20th century, Broughton Street once dazzled shoppers with decorated gaslights, ornate window displays, and fine examples of terrazzo, a form of mosaic that still adorns many shop entrances. Postwar suburbs and white flight brought neglect to the area by the 1960s, and many thought Broughton was gone for good. But with the downtown renaissance brought about largely by the Savannah College of Art and Design (SCAD), Broughton was able not only to get back on its feet but to thrive as a commercial center once again.

Around the corner from the Lucas Theatre on Reynolds Square is the art moderne **Trustees Theatre** (216 E. Broughton St., 912/525-5051, www.scad.edu), a SCAD-run operation that seats 1,200 and hosts concerts, film screenings, and the school's much-anticipated spring fashion show. It began life in the postwar boom of 1946 as the Weis Theatre, another one of those ornate Southern movie houses that took full commercial advantage of being the only buildings at the time to have air conditioning.

Wright Square

By now you know the drill. The big monument in Wright Square, Oglethorpe's second square, has nothing to do with James Wright, royal governor of Georgia before the Revolution, for whom it's named. Instead the monument honors **William Gordon,** former mayor and founder of the Central of Georgia Railway. More importantly, Wright Square

is the final resting place of Yamacraw chief **Tomochichi,** buried in 1737 in an elaborate state funeral at James Oglethorpe's insistence. A boulder of North Georgia granite honoring the chief was placed in a corner of the square. However, Tomochichi is not buried under the boulder, but somewhere underneath the Gordon monument. So why not rename it Tomochichi Square? Old ways die hard down here.

JULIETTE GORDON LOW BIRTHPLACE

Around the corner from Wright Square at Oglethorpe and Bull is the **Juliette Gordon Low Birthplace** (10 E. Oglethorpe Ave., 912/233-4501, www.juliettegordonlowbirthplace.org, Mar.-Oct. Mon.-Sat. 10am-4pm, Sun. 11am-4pm, Nov.-Feb. Mon.-Tues. and Thurs.-Sat. 10am-4pm, Sun. 11am-4pm, $9 adults, $8 children, $7 Girl Scouts under age 19), declared the city's very first National Historic Landmark in 1965. The founder of the Girl Scouts of the USA lived here from her birth in 1860 until her marriage, returning home to stay until her mother's death.

Also called the Girl Scout National Center, the Low birthplace is probably Savannah's most festive historic site because of the heavy traffic of Girl Scout troops from across the United States. You don't have to be affiliated with the Girl Scouts to tour the home. Tours are given every 15 minutes, and tickets are available at the Oglethorpe Avenue entrance. Be aware that the site is closed most holidays, sometimes for extended periods; be sure to check the website for details.

Oglethorpe Square

Don't look for a monument to Georgia's founder in the square named for him. That would be way too easy, so of course his monument is in Chippewa Square. Originally called "Upper New Square," Oglethorpe Square was created in 1742.

◪ OWENS-THOMAS HOUSE

The square's main claim to fame, the **Owens-Thomas House** (124 Abercorn St.,

SAVANNAH

SCOUT'S HONOR: JULIETTE GORDON LOW

Known as "Daisy" to family and friends, Juliette Magill Kinzie Gordon was born to be a pioneer. Her father's family took part in the original settlement of Georgia, and her mother's kin were among the founders of Chicago. Mostly known as the founder of the Girl Scouts of the USA, Daisy was also an artist, adventurer, and healer. Born and raised in the house on Oglethorpe Avenue in Savannah known to Girl Scouts across the nation as simply "The Birthplace," she was an animal lover with an early penchant for theater, drawing, and poetry.

After school she traveled, returning home to marry wealthy cotton heir William Mackay Low, son of the builder of Savannah's exquisite Andrew Low House. A harbinger of her troubled marriage happened on her wedding day on the steps of Christ Church. A grain of rice, thrown for good luck, struck her eardrum and led to a painful infection and loss of hearing. Daisy and her husband moved to England, using the Andrew Low House as a rental property and winter residence. She maintained a home in England until her death, spending much of the year traveling in the United States and abroad.

Daisy returned to Savannah with the outbreak of the Spanish-American War in 1898. Because of the city's proximity to Cuba, one of the main theaters of the war, it became a staging area for U.S. Army troops from all over the country. For Savannah, taking such an active role was an opportunity to make amends for the alienation of the Civil War and effectively rejoin the Union again. For the first time since Sherman's March to the Sea, Savannahians proudly displayed the Stars and Stripes in an honest show of patriotism of which Daisy was a part, tending to wounded soldiers returning from Cuba. After the war, Daisy returned to England to spend the last days of her marriage, which existed in name only until her husband's death in 1905. After settling his estate, she used the proceeds to fund some traveling.

In 1911, while in England, she met another man who would change her life: Robert Baden-Powell, founder of the Boy Scouts and Girl Guides in Britain. Struck by the simplicity and usefulness of his project, she carried the seeds of a similar idea back with her to the United States. "I've got something for the girls of Savannah, and all of America, and all the world, and we're going to start it tonight," were her famous words in a phone call to a cousin after meeting Baden-Powell. So on March 12, 1912, Daisy gathered 18 girls to register the first troop of American Girl Guides, later the Girl Scouts of the USA.

Juliette "Daisy" Gordon Low died of breast cancer in her bed in the Andrew Low House on January 17, 1927. She was buried in Laurel Grove Cemetery on the city's west side. Girl Scout troops from all over the United States visit her birthplace, the Andrew Low House, and her gravesite to this day, often leaving flowers and small personal objects near her tombstone as tokens of respect and gratitude.

912/233-9743, www.telfair.org, Mon. noon-5pm, Tues.-Sat. 10am-5pm, Sun. 1pm-5pm, last tour 4:30pm, $15 adults, $5 children, $20 multisite ticket), widely known as the finest example of Regency architecture in the United States, was designed by brilliant young English architect William Jay. One of the first professionally trained architects in the United States, Jay was only 24 when he designed the home for cotton merchant or "factor" Richard Richardson, who lost the house in the depression of 1820 (all that remains of Richardson's tenure are three marble-top tables). The house's current name is derived from Savannah Mayor George Owens, who bought the house in 1830. It remained in his family until 1951, when his granddaughter Margaret Thomas bequeathed it to the Telfair Academy of Arts and Sciences, which currently operates the site.

It is constructed mostly of tabby, a mixture of lime, oyster shells, and sand. Perhaps most interestingly, a complex plumbing system features rain-fed cisterns, flushing toilets, sinks, bathtubs, and a shower. When built, the

Owens-Thomas House in fact had the first indoor plumbing in Savannah.

While inside the house, notice the little touches like the unusual curved walls, with doors bowed to match, and the recessed skylights. On the south facade is a beautiful cast-iron veranda from which Revolutionary War hero Marquis de Lafayette addressed a crowd during his visit in 1825. The 1990s marked the most intensive phase of restoration for the home, which began with a careful renovation of the carriage house and the associated slave quarters—discovered in a surprisingly intact state, including the original "haint blue" paint. The carriage house, where all tours begin, is now the home's gift shop.

Telfair Square

One of the few Savannah squares to show consistency in nomenclature, Telfair Square was indeed named for Mary Telfair, last heir of a family that was one of the most important in Savannah history. Mary bequeathed the family mansion to the Georgia Historical Society upon her death in 1875 to serve as a museum. Originally called St. James Square after a similar square in London, Telfair is the last of Oglethorpe's original four squares.

🅒 TELFAIR MUSEUMS

Also consistent with its name, Telfair Square indeed hosts two of the three buildings operated by the **Telfair Museums** (912/790-8800, www.telfair.org, $20 adults, $5 children, $12 Jepson Center and Telfair Academy, $15 Owens-Thomas House, free under age 5), an umbrella organization that relies on a combination of private and public funding and has driven much of the arts agenda in Savannah for the last 125 years. The original part of the complex and in fact the oldest public art museum in the South, the **Telfair Academy of Arts and Sciences** (121 Barnard St., Mon. noon-5pm, Tues.-Sat. 10am-5pm, Sun. 1pm-5pm) was built in 1821 by the great William Jay for Alexander Telfair, scion of that famous Georgia family. The five statues in front are of Phidias, Raphael, Rubens,

Michelangelo, and Rembrandt. Inside, the sculpture gallery and rotunda were added in 1885, the year before the building's official opening as a museum. As well as displaying Sylvia Judson Shaw's now-famous *Bird Girl* sculpture, originally in Bonaventure Cemetery (actually the third of four casts by the sculptor), the Telfair Academy features an outstanding collection of primarily 18th- and 20th-century works, most notably the largest public collection of visual art by Khalil Gibran. Major paintings include work by Childe Hassam, Frederick Frieseke, Gari Melchers, and the massive *Black Prince of Crécy* by Julian Story.

The latest and proudest addition to the Telfair brand is the striking, 64,000-square-foot **Jepson Center for the Arts** (207 W. York St., Tues.-Wed. and Fri.-Sat. 10am-5pm, Thurs. 10am-8pm, Sun.-Mon. noon-5pm), whose ultramodern exterior sits catty-corner from the old Telfair. Promoting a massive, daringly designed new facility devoted to nothing but modern art was a hard sell in this traditional town, especially when renowned architect Moshe Safdie insisted on building a glassed-in flyover across a lane between two buildings. After a few delays in construction, Jepson opened its doors in 2006 and has since wowed locals and visitors alike with its cutting-edge traveling exhibits and rotating assortment of late-20th-century and 21st-century modern art. If you get hungry, you can enjoy lunch in the expansive atrium café, and, of course, there's a nice gift shop.

Paying admission to one site also gets you a one-time visit to the other two sites for a week following purchase.

TRINITY UNITED METHODIST CHURCH

Directly between the Telfair and the Jepson stands **Trinity United Methodist Church** (225 W. President St., 912/233-4766, www.trinitychurch1848.org, sanctuary daily 9am-5pm, services Sun. 8:45am and 11am), Savannah's first Methodist church. Built in 1848 on the site of the Telfair's family garden, its masonry walls are of famous "Savannah Gray" bricks—a lighter, more porous, and elegant variety—under stucco. Virgin longleaf pine was used for most of the interior, fully restored in 1969. Call ahead for a tour.

Chippewa Square

Named for a battle in the War of 1812, Chippewa Square has a large monument not to the battle, natch, but to James Oglethorpe, clad in full soldier's regalia. Notice the general is still facing south, toward the Spanish.

Yes, the bench on the square's north side is in the same location as the one Tom Hanks occupied in *Forrest Gump,* but it's not the same bench that hosted the two-time Oscar winner's backside—that one was donated by Paramount Pictures to be displayed in the Savannah History Museum on MLK Jr. Boulevard.

HISTORIC SAVANNAH THEATRE

At the northeast corner is the **Historic Savannah Theatre** (222 Bull St., 912/233-7764, www.savannahtheatre.com), which

statue of General James Oglethorpe in Chippewa Square

claims to be the oldest continuously operating theater in the United States. Designed by William Jay, it opened in 1818 with a production of *The Soldier's Daughter.* In the glory days of gaslight theater in the 1800s, some of the nation's best actors, including Edwin Booth, brother to Lincoln's assassin, regularly trod the boards of its stage. Other notable visitors were Sarah Bernhardt, W. C. Fields, and Oscar Wilde. Due to a fire in 1948, little remains of Jay's original design except a small section of exterior wall. It's currently home to a semiprofessional revue company specializing in oldies shows.

INDEPENDENT PRESBYTERIAN CHURCH

Built in 1818, possibly by William Jay—scholars are unsure of the scope of his involvement—**Independent Presbyterian Church** (207 Bull St., 912/236-3346, www.ipcsav.org, services Sun. 11am and Wed. noon) is called the "mother of Georgia Presbyterianism." A fire destroyed most of Independent Presbyterian's original structure in 1889, but the subsequent rebuilding was a very faithful rendering of the original design, based on London's St. Martin-in-the-Fields. The marble baptismal font survived the fire and is still used today. Note also the huge mahogany pulpit, another original feature. The church's steeple made a cameo appearance in *Forrest Gump* as a white feather floated by.

Lowell Mason, composer of the hymn "Nearer My God to Thee," was organist at Independent Presbyterian. In 1885 President Woodrow Wilson married local parishioner Ellen Louise Axson in the manse to the rear of the church.

COLONIAL CEMETERY

Just north of Chippewa Square is Oglethorpe Avenue, originally called South Broad and the southern boundary of the original colony. At Oglethorpe and Abercorn Streets is Colonial Cemetery, first active in 1750. You'd be forgiven for assuming it's the "DAR" cemetery; the Daughters of the American Revolution contributed the ornate iron entranceway in 1913,

© JIM MOREKIS

thoughtfully dedicating it to themselves instead of the cemetery itself.

Unlike the picturesque beauty of Bonaventure and Laurel Grove cemeteries, Colonial Cemetery has a morbid feel. The fact that burials stopped here in 1853 plays into that desolation, but maybe another reason is because it's the final resting ground of many of Savannah's yellow fever victims. Famous people buried here include Button Gwinnett, one of Georgia's three signers of the Declaration of Independence. Vandalism through the years, mostly by Union troops, took a toll on the old gravestones. Many line the east wall of the cemetery, with no one alive able to remember where they originally stood.

Madison Square

Named for the nation's fourth president, Madison Square memorializes a local hero who gave his life for his city during the American Revolution. Irish immigrant Sergeant William Jasper, hero of the Battle of Fort Moultrie in Charleston three years earlier, was killed leading the American charge during the Siege of Savannah, when an allied army failed to retake the city from the British. The monument in the square honors Jasper, but he isn't buried here; his body was interred in a mass grave near the battlefield along with other colonists and soldier-immigrants killed in the one-sided battle.

GREEN-MELDRIM HOUSE

Given the house's beauty and history, visitors will be forgiven for not immediately realizing that the **Green-Meldrim House** (1 W. Macon St., 912/232-1251, tours every 30 minutes Tues. and Thurs.-Fri. 10am-4pm, Sat. 10am-1pm, $7 adults, $2 children) is also the rectory of the adjacent St. John's Episcopal Church, which acquired it in 1892. Though known primarily for serving as General William T. Sherman's headquarters during his occupation of Savannah, visitors find the Green-Meldrim House a serene location in and of itself. A remarkably tasteful example of Gothic Revival architecture, this 1850 design by John Norris features a beautiful

external gallery of filigree ironwork. The interior is decorated with a keen and rare eye for elegant minimalism in this sometimes rococo-minded town.

Lafayette Square

Truly one of Savannah's favorite squares, especially on St. Patrick's Day, verdant Lafayette Square boasts a number of important sights and attractions.

◖ CATHEDRAL OF ST. JOHN THE BAPTIST

Spiritual home to Savannah's Irish community and the oldest Roman Catholic church in Georgia, the **Cathedral of St. John the Baptist** (222. E. Harris St., 912/233-4709, www.savannahcathedral.org, daily 9am-noon and 12:30pm-5pm, mass Sun. 8am, 10am, 11:30am, Mon.-Sat. noon, Latin mass Sun. 1pm) was initially known as Our Lady of Perpetual Help. It's the place to be for mass the morning of March 17 at 8am, as the clans gather in their green jackets and white dresses to take a sip of communion wine before moving on to harder stuff in honor of St. Patrick.

Despite its overt Celtic character today, the parish was originally founded by French Catholics who arrived after an uprising in the colony of Haiti in the late 1700s. The first sanctuary on the site was built in 1873, after the diocese traded a lot at Taylor and Lincoln Streets to the Sisters of Mercy in exchange for this locale. In a distressingly common event back then in Savannah, fire swept through the edifice in 1898, leaving only two spires and the external walls. In an amazing story of determination and skill, the cathedral was completely rebuilt within a year and a half. The most recent renovation, from 1998 to 2000, involved the intricate removal, cleaning, and releading of more than 50 of the cathedral's stained-glass windows, a roof replacement, and an interior makeover.

ANDREW LOW HOUSE MUSEUM

Another major landmark on Lafayette Square is the **Andrew Low House Museum**

(329 Abercorn St., 912/233-6854, www.an-drewlowhouse.com, Mon.-Sat. 10am-4pm, Sun. noon-4pm, last tour 4pm, $8 adults, $6 children), once the home of Juliette "Daisy" Gordon Low, the founder of the Girl Scouts of the USA, who was married to cotton heir William "Billow" Low, Andrew Low's son. Despite their happy-go-lucky nicknames, the union of Daisy and Billow was a notably unhappy one. Still, divorce was out of the question, so the couple lived separate lives until William's death in 1905. The one good thing that came out of the marriage was the germ for the idea for the Girl Scouts, which Juliette got from England's "Girl Guides" while living there with her husband, Savannah being the couple's winter residence.

Designed by the great New York architect John Norris, the Low House is a magnificent example of the Italianate style. Check out the cast-iron balconies on the long porch, a fairly rare feature in historic Savannah homes. Antiques junkies will go nuts over the furnishings, especially the massive secretary in the parlor, one of only four of this type in existence (a sibling is in the Metropolitan Museum of Art). Author William Makepeace Thackeray ate in the dining room, now sporting a full French porcelain service, and slept in an upstairs room; he also wrote at the desk by the bed. Also on the second floor you'll see the room where Robert E. Lee stayed during his visit and the bed where Juliette Gordon Low died.

FLANNERY O'CONNOR CHILDHOOD HOME
On the other corner of Lafayette Square stands the rather Spartan facade of the **Flannery O'Connor Childhood Home** (207 E. Charlton St., 912/233-6014, www.flan-neryoconnorhome.org, Fri.-Wed. 1pm-4pm, $6 adults, $5 students, free under age 15). The Savannah-born novelist lived in this three-story townhome from her birth in 1925 until 1938 and attended church at the cathedral across the square. A recent round of renovations has returned the two main floors to the state Flannery would have known, including an

extensive library. A nonprofit association sponsors O'Connor-related readings and signings. While the current backyard garden dates to 1993, it's the place where five-year-old Flannery is said to have taught a chicken to walk backward, foreshadowing the eccentric, Gothic flavor of her writing.

Across from the O'Connor house is the **Hamilton-Turner Inn** (330 Abercorn St., 912/233-1833, www.hamilton-turnerinn.com). Now a privately owned bed-and-breakfast, this 1873 Second Empire mansion is best known for the showmanship of its over-the-top Victorian appointments and its role in "The Book" as the home of Joe Odom's girlfriend "Mandy Nichols" (real name Nancy Hillis).

Troup Square

Troup Square is the home of the historic **Unitarian Universalist Church of Savannah** (313 E. Harris St., 912/234-0980, www.jinglebellschurch.org, services Sun. 11am). This original home of Savannah's Unitarians, who sold the church when the Civil War came, was recently reacquired by the congregation. It is where James L. Pierpont first performed his immortal tune "Jingle Bells." When he did so, however, the church was actually on Oglethorpe Square. The entire building was moved to Troup Square in the mid-1800s.

Just east of Troup Square, near the intersection of Harris and Price Streets, is the **Beach Institute** (502 E. Harris St., 912/234-8000, www.kingtisdell.org, Tues.-Sun. noon-5pm, $4). Built as a school by the Freedmen's Bureau soon after the Civil War, it was named after its prime benefactor, Alfred Beach, editor of *Scientific American*.

Monterey Square

For many, this is the ultimate Savannah square. Originally named "Monterrey Square" to commemorate the local Irish Jasper Greens' participation in a victorious Mexican-American War battle in 1846, the spelling morphed into its current version somewhere along the way. But Monterey Square remains one of the most visually beautiful and serene spots in all

THE STORY OF "JINGLE BELLS"

Long after the Civil War, a North-South feud of a more harmless kind still simmers, as Boston and Savannah vie over bragging rights as to where the classic Christmas song "Jingle Bells" was written. The song's composer, James L. Pierpont, led a life at times as carefree as his song itself. Born in Boston as the son of an abolitionist Unitarian minister, Pierpont's wanderlust manifested early, when he ventured from his new wife and young children to follow the 1849 gold rush to San Francisco, coming back east after one of that city's periodic enormous fires. When his brother John was named minister of the new Unitarian congregation in Savannah in 1853—a novelty down south at the time—Pierpont followed him, becoming music director and organist, again leaving behind his wife and children in Boston. During this time Pierpont became a prolific composer of secular tunes, including polkas, ballads, and minstrel songs.

Pierpont's first wife died of tuberculosis in 1856. By August 1857 he had remarried the daughter of the mayor of Savannah. That same month, a Boston-based publisher, Oliver Ditson and Co., published his song "One Horse Open Sleigh." Two years later it was rereleased with the current title, "Jingle Bells." At neither time, however, was the song a popular hit. In 1859, with slavery tearing the country apart, the Unitarian Church in Savannah closed due to its abolitionist stance. By the outbreak of war, Pierpont's brother John had gone back up north. James Pierpont, however, opted to stay in Savannah with his second wife, Eliza Jane, going so far as to sign up with the Isle of Hope Volunteers (he served as a company clerk) of the Confederate Army.

It took action by his son Juriah in 1880 to renew the copyright to what would become one of the most famous songs of all time. Pierpont died in 1883 in Winter Haven, Florida, and by his own request was buried in Savannah's Laurel Grove Cemetery. The provenance of his now-famous song is more in doubt. In Massachusetts, they swear Pierpont wrote the song while at the home of one Mrs. Otis Waterman. In Georgia, scholars assure us a homesick Pierpont wrote the tune during a winter at a house at Oglethorpe and Whitaker Streets, long since demolished. The Savannah contingent's ace in the hole is the fact that "Jingle Bells" was first performed in public at a Thanksgiving program at the local Unitarian Universalist Church in 1857. And despite persistent claims in Massachusetts that he wrote the song there in 1850, Southern scholars point out that Pierpont was actually in California in 1850. So in this case, at least, it appears the South can claim victory over the Yankees.

In one of those delightful happenstances of serendipity, Pierpont's old church—moved to Troup Square from its original site on Oglethorpe Square—went on the market in the 1990s, and the local Unitarian Universalist congregation was able to raise enough money to buy it. It remains there to this day.

of Savannah. At the center of the square is a monument not to the victory for which it is named but to Count Casimir Pulaski, killed while attempting to retake the city from the British, and whose remains supposedly lie under the 55-foot monument. As early as 1912, people began noticing the disintegration of the monument due to substandard marble used in some key parts, but it wasn't until the 1990s that a full restoration was accomplished. The restoration company discovered that one of the monument's 34 sections had accidentally been installed upside down. So in the true spirit of preservation, they dutifully put the section back—upside down. The *Goddess of Liberty* atop the monument, however, is not original; you can see her in the Savannah History Museum. Fans of ironwork will enjoy the ornate masterpieces in wrought iron featured at many houses on the periphery of the square.

Mercer-Williams House Museum on Monterey Square

SAVANNAH

MERCER-WILLIAMS HOUSE MUSEUM

Many visitors come to see the **Mercer-Williams House Museum** (429 Bull St., 912/236-6352, www.mercerhouse.com, Mon.-Sat. 10:30am-4pm, Sun. noon-4pm, $12.50 adults, $8 students). While locals never begrudge the business Savannah has enjoyed since "The Book," it's a shame that this grand John Norris building is now primarily known as a crime scene involving antiques dealer Jim Williams and his lover. Therefore it might come as no surprise that if you take a tour of the home, you might hear less about "The Book" than you may have expected. Now proudly owned by Jim Williams's sister Dorothy Kingery, an established academic in her own right, the Mercer-Williams House deliberately concentrates on the early history of the home and her brother's prodigious talent as a collector and conservator of fine art and antiques.

Built for General Hugh W. Mercer, Johnny Mercer's great-grandfather, in 1860 the war interrupted construction. General Mercer—descendant of the Revolutionary War general and George Washington's close friend Hugh Mercer—survived the war, in which he was charged with the defense of Savannah. But he soon fell on hard times and was forced to sell the house to John Wilder, who moved in after completion in 1868. Just so you know, and despite what any tour guide might tell you, the great Johnny Mercer himself never lived in the house. Technically, no member of his family ever did.

Tours of the home's four main rooms begin in the carriage house to the rear of the mansion. They're worth it for art aficionados even though the upstairs, Dr. Kingery's residence, is off-limits. Be forewarned that if you're coming just to see things about the book or movie, you might be disappointed.

TEMPLE MICKVE ISRAEL

Directly across Monterey Square from the Mercer House is **Temple Mickve Israel** (20 E. Gordon St., 912/233-1547, www.mickveisrael.

org), a notable structure for many reasons: It's Georgia's first synagogue; it's the only Gothic synagogue in the country; and it's the third-oldest Jewish congregation in North America (following those in New York and Newport, Rhode Island). Notable congregants have included Dr. Samuel Nunes Ribeiro, who helped stop an epidemic in 1733; his descendant Raphael Moses, considered the father of the peach industry in the Peach State; and current Mickve Israel rabbi Arnold Mark Belzer, one of Savannah's most beloved community leaders. A specialist in the study of small, often-persecuted Jewish communities around the world, Belzer met Pope John Paul II in 2005 as a part of that pontiff's historic rapprochement between the Roman Catholic Church and Judaism.

Mickve Israel offers 30-45 minute tours of the sanctuary and museum (Mon.-Fri. 10am-1pm and 2pm-4pm, closed Jewish holidays).

Calhoun Square

The last of the 24 squares in Savannah's original grid, Calhoun Square is also the only square with all its original buildings intact—a rarity indeed in a city ravaged by fire so many times in its history.

Dominating the south side of the square is Savannah's first public elementary school and spiritual home of Savannah educators, the **Massie Heritage Center** (207 E. Gordon St., 912/201-5070, www.massieschool.com, Mon.-Sat. 10am-4pm, Sun. noon-4pm, self-guided tour $7 adults, $5 children). In 1841, Peter Massie, a Scots planter with a populist streak, endowed the school to give poor children as good an education as the children of rich families, like Massie's own, received. Another of Savannah's masterpieces by John Norris—whose impressive oeuvre includes the Low House, the Mercer House, and the Green-Meldrim House—the central portion of the trifold building was completed in 1856 and is a great example of Greek Revival architecture. After the Civil War, the "Massie school," as it's known locally, was designated as the area's African American public school.

Classes ceased in 1974, and it now operates as a living history museum, centering on the period-appointed one-room "heritage classroom." A recent $1 million renovation includes an interactive model of Oglethorpe's urban design and several interesting exhibits on aspects of Savannah architecture and history.

Catty-corner to the Massie School is the **Wesley Monumental United Methodist Church** (429 Abercorn St., 912/232-0191, www.wesleymonumental.org, sanctuary daily 9am-5pm, services Sun. 8:45am and 11am). This home of Savannah's first Methodist parish was named not only for movement founder John Wesley but for his musical younger brother Charles. Built in 1875 on the model of Queen's Kirk in Amsterdam and the fourth incarnation of the parish home, this is another great example of Savannah's Gothic churches. Its acoustically wonderful sanctuary features a magnificent Noack organ, which would no doubt please the picky ears of Charles Wesley himself, author of the lyrics to "Hark! The Herald Angels Sing."

Martin Luther King Jr. Boulevard

Originally known as West Broad Street (you'll still hear old-timers refer to it that way), Martin Luther King Jr. Boulevard is the spiritual home of Savannah's African American community, though it has gone through several transformations. In the early 1800s, West Broad was a fashionable address, but during the middle of that century its north end got a bad reputation for crime and blight as thousands of Irish immigrants packed in right beside the area's poor black population.

RALPH MARK GILBERT
CIVIL RIGHTS MUSEUM

One of the former black-owned bank buildings on MLK Jr. Boulevard is now home to the **Ralph Mark Gilbert Civil Rights Museum** (460 MLK Jr. Blvd., 912/231-8900, Mon.-Sat. 9am-5pm, $8 adults, $4 children). Named for the pastor of the First African Baptist Church and a key early civil rights organizer, the building was also the local NAACP headquarters for a time. Three floors of exhibits here include photos and interactive exhibits, the highlight for historians being a fiber-optic map of nearly 100 significant civil rights sites. The first floor features a re-creation of the Azalea Room of the local Levy's department store, an early boycott diner where blacks were not allowed to eat, though they could buy goods from the store. The second floor is more for hands-on education, with classrooms, a computer room, and a video and reading room. A film chronicles mass meetings, voter registration drives, boycotts, sit-ins, kneel-ins (the integration of churches), and wade-ins (the integration of beaches).

SHIPS OF THE SEA MARITIME MUSEUM

One of Savannah's more unique museums is the quirky **Ships of the Sea Maritime Museum** (41 MLK Jr. Blvd., 912/232-1511, http://shipsofthesea.org, Tues.-Sun. 10am-5pm, $8.50 adults, $6.50 students). The stunning Greek Revival building in which it resides is known as the Scarbrough House because it was initially built in 1819 by the great William Jay for local shipping merchant William Scarbrough, owner of the SS *Savannah,* the first steamship to cross the Atlantic. After the Scarbroughs sold the property, it became the West Broad School for African Americans from Reconstruction through integration.

One of the Historic Savannah Foundation's key restoration projects in the 1970s, the museum got another major facelift in 1998, including a roof based on the original Jay design and a delightful enlargement of the mansion's garden out back. Inside, children, maritime buffs, and crafts connoisseurs can find intricate and detailed scale models of various historic vessels, such as Oglethorpe's *Anne,* the SS *Savannah,* and the NS *Savannah,* the world's first nuclear-powered surface vessel. There's even a model of the *Titanic.*

BATTLEFIELD PARK COMPLEX

Three important sites are clustered together on MLK Jr. Boulevard under the auspices of the Coastal Heritage Society: the Savannah History Museum, the Roundhouse Railroad Museum, and the Siege of Savannah battlefield.

The **Savannah History Museum** (303 MLK Jr. Blvd., 912/651-6825, www.chsgeorgia.org, Mon.-Fri. 8:30am-5pm, Sat.-Sun. 9am-5pm, $5 adults, free for children), first stop for many a visitor to town because it's in the same restored Central of Georgia passenger shed as the visitors center, contains many interesting exhibits on local history, concentrating mostly on colonial times. Toward the rear of the museum is a room for rotating exhibits, as well as one of Johnny Mercer's two Oscars and, of course, the historic "*Forrest Gump* bench" that Tom Hanks sat on during his scenes in Chippewa Square.

The **Roundhouse Railroad Museum** (601 W. Harris St., 912/651-6823, www.chsgeorgia.org, daily 9am-5pm, $10 adults, $4 students) is an ongoing homage to the deep and strangely underreported influence of the railroad industry on Savannah. Constructed in 1830 for the brand-new Central of Georgia line, the Roundhouse's design was cutting-edge for the time, the first facility to put all the railroad's key facilities in one place. Spared by General Sherman, the site saw its real heyday after the Civil War. But as technology changed, so did the Roundhouse, which gradually fell further into neglect until the 1960s, when preservation-minded buffs banded together to raise enough money to save it. The real highlight of the Roundhouse is the thing in the middle that gave it its name, a huge central turntable for positioning rolling stock for repair and maintenance. Frequent demonstrations occur with an actual steam locomotive firing up and taking a turn on the turntable.

Next to the Railroad Museum is the new **Savannah Children's Museum** (655 Louisville Rd., 912/651-6823, www.savannahchildrensmuseum.org, Tues.-Sat. 10am-4pm, Sun. 11am-4pm, $7.50), a work in progress that currently has an "Exploration Station" and a planned larger facility.

Right off MLK Jr. Boulevard is the **Battlefield Park** (dawn-dusk, free), a.k.a. the Spring Hill Redoubt, a reconstruction of the

SAVANNAH

© JIM MOREKIS

Battlefield Park off MLK Jr. Boulevard

British fortifications at the Siege of Savannah with an interpretive site. Note that the redoubt is not at the actual location of the original fort; that lies underneath the nearby Sons of the Revolution marker. Eight hundred granite markers signify the battle's casualties, most of whom were buried in mass graves soon afterward. Sadly, most of the remains of these brave men were simply bulldozed up and discarded without ceremony during later construction projects.

SCAD MUSEUM OF ART

The Savannah College of Art and Design recently concluded a massive expansion of this handsome building into an old railroad facility immediately behind it, more than doubling exhibition space and adding the impressive Walter O. Evans Collection of African American Art. The **SCAD Museum of Art** (601 Turner Blvd., 912/525-5220, www.scad.edu, Tues.-Wed. and Fri. 10am-5pm, Thurs. 10am-8pm, Sat.-Sun. noon-5pm, $10, $5 students) now hosts a rotating series of exhibits, from standard painting to video installations, many of them commissioned by the school itself.

VICTORIAN DISTRICT

Boasting 50 blocks of fine Victorian and Queen Anne frame houses, Savannah's Victorian district gets nowhere near the media attention that the older, more stately homes closer to the river get. But it is truly magnificent in its own right, and nearly as expansive. The city's first suburb, built between 1870 and 1910, it runs from roughly Gwinnett Street south to Anderson Street, with Montgomery and Price Streets as eastern and western boundaries.

In addition to the glories of Forsyth Park, some key areas for connoisseurs of truly grand Victorian architecture are the residential blocks of East Hall Street between Lincoln and Price Streets—one of the few street sections in town with the original paving. Some other nice examples are in the 1900-2000 blocks of Bull Street near the large Bull Street Public Library, including the famous "Gingerbread House" at 1917 Bull Street, now a private bridal design studio.

SAVANNAH

© JIM MOREKIS

Forsyth Fountain

◖ Forsyth Park

A favorite with locals and visitors alike, the vast, lush expanse of Forsyth Park is a center of local life, abuzz with activity and events year-round. The park owes its existence to William B. Hodgson, who donated its core 10 acres to the city for use as a park. Deeply influenced by the then-trendy design of green-space areas in France, Forsyth Park's landscape design by William Bischoff dates to 1851. Named for Georgia Governor John Forsyth, the park covers 30 acres, and its perimeter is about a mile. The park is a center of activities all year long, from free festivals to concerts to Ultimate Frisbee games to the constant circuit around the periphery of walkers, joggers, dog owners, and bicyclists. The only time you shouldn't venture into the park is after midnight; otherwise, enjoy.

A WALKING TOUR OF FORSYTH PARK

Here's a walking tour of Savannah's backyard, the one-of-a-kind Forsyth Park, beginning at the north end at Gaston and Bull Streets: As you approach the park, don't miss the ornate ironwork on the west side of Bull street marking the **Armstrong House,** designed by Henrik Wallin. It was featured in the 1962 film *Cape Fear* as well as 1997's *Midnight in the Garden of Good and Evil.*

As you enter the park's north side, look west at the corner of Whitaker and Gaston Streets; that's **Hodgson Hall,** home of the Georgia Historical Society. This 1876 building was commissioned by Margaret Telfair to honor her late husband, William Hodgson, chief benefactor of the park the house overlooks.

Looking east at the corner of Drayton and Gaston Streets, you'll see the old **Poor House and Hospital,** in use until 1854, when it was converted to serve as the headquarters for the Medical College of Georgia. From 1930 to 1980 the building was the site of Candler Hospital. Today it's a private law school. Behind cast-iron fence, you can soak in the venerable beauty of Savannah's most famous tree, the 300-year-old **Candler Oak.**

Walking south into the park proper, you

can't miss the world-famous **Forsyth Fountain,** an iconic Savannah sight if there ever was one. Cast in iron on a French model, the fountain was dedicated in 1858. Its water is typically dyed green a few days before St. Patrick's Day.

Continuing south, you'll encounter two low buildings in the center of the park. The one on the east side is the so-called "Dummy Fort," circa 1909, formerly a training ground for local militia. Now it's the **Forsyth Park Café** (daily 7am-dusk, open later on festival evenings) managed by the hotel Mansion on Forsyth Park just across Drayton Street. To the west is the charming **Fragrant Garden for the Blind.** One of those precious little Savannah gems that is too often overlooked in favor of other attractions, the Fragrant Garden was initially sponsored by the local Garden Club and based on others of its type throughout the United States.

The tall monument dominating Forsyth Park's central mall area is the **Confederate Memorial,** which recently received a major facelift. Dedicated in 1875, it wasn't finished in its final form until several years later. A New York sculptor carved the Confederate soldier atop the monument.

We'll close the walking tour with the Memorial to Georgia Veterans of the Spanish-American War, more commonly known as *The Hiker* because of the subject's almost casual demeanor and confident stride. Sculpted in 1902 by Alice Ruggles Kitson, more than 50 replicas of *The Hiker* were made and put up all over the United States; because the same bronze formula was used for all 50 of them, the statues are used by scientists today to gauge the effects of acid rain across the nation.

EASTSIDE
Old Fort Jackson
The oldest standing brick fort in Georgia, **Old Fort Jackson** (Fort Jackson Rd., 912/232-3945, http://chsgeorgia.org, daily 9am-5pm, $6, free under age 7), named for Georgia Governor James Jackson, is also one of eight remaining examples of the so-called Second System of American forts built prior to the War of 1812. Its main claim to fame is its

supporting role in the saga of the CSS *Georgia,* a Confederate ironclad now resting under 40 feet of water directly in front of the fort. Built with $115,000 in funds raised by the Ladies Gunboat Society, the *Georgia*—wrapped in an armor girdle of railroad ties—proved too heavy for its engine. So it was simply anchored in the channel opposite Fort Jackson as a floating battery. With General Sherman's arrival in 1864, Confederate forces evacuating to South Carolina scuttled the vessel to keep it out of Yankee hands.

Inside the fort's casemates under the ramparts you'll find well-organized exhibits. Most visitors especially love the daily cannon firings during the summer. If you're really lucky, you'll be around when Fort Jackson fires a salute to passing military vessels on the river—the only historic fort in the United States that does so.

To get to Fort Jackson, take President Street Extension (Islands Expressway) east out of downtown. The entrance is several miles down on the left.

Oatland Island Wildlife Center
The closest thing Savannah has to a zoo is the vast, multipurpose **Oatland Island Wildlife Center** (711 Sandtown Rd., 912/898-3980, www.oatlandisland.org, daily 10am-5pm, $5 adults, $3 children). The main attractions here are the critters, located at various points along a meandering two-mile nature trail through the woods and along the marsh. All the animals at Oatland are there because they're somehow unable to return to the wild. Highlights include a tight-knit pack of Eastern wolves, a pair of bison, cougars (once indigenous), some cute foxes, and an extensive raptor aviary.

To get here from downtown, take President Street Extension (Islands Expressway) about five miles. Begin looking for the Oatland Island sign on the right. You'll go through part of a residential neighborhood until you take a bend to the right; Oatland's gate is then on the left. To get here from Bonaventure Cemetery, go straight out the gate on Bonaventure Road and take a right on Pennsylvania Avenue. As you dead-end on Islands Expressway, take a

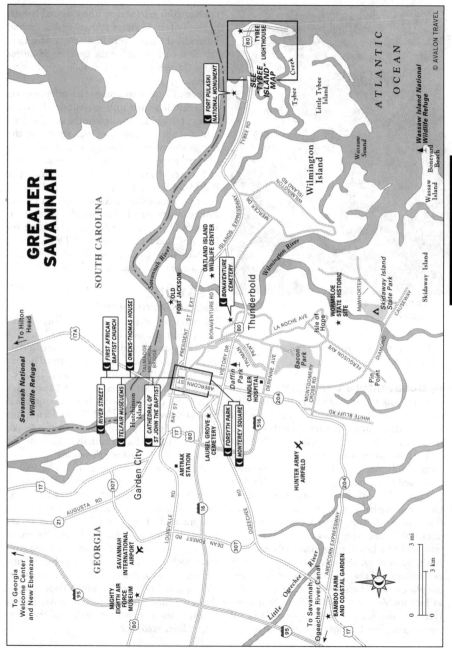

© AVALON TRAVEL

SAVANNAH

GREATER SAVANNAH

SOUTH CAROLINA

GEORGIA

ATLANTIC OCEAN

To Hilton Head

To Georgia Welcome Center and New Ebenezer

RIVER STREET

FIRST AFRICAN BAPTIST CHURCH

OWENS-THOMAS HOUSE

TELFAIR MUSEUMS

CATHEDRAL OF ST. JOHN THE BAPTIST

LAUREL GROVE CEMETERY

FORSYTH PARK

MONTEREY SQUARE

FORT PULASKI NATIONAL MONUMENT

SEE TYBEE ISLAND MAP

TYBEE LIGHTHOUSE

OATLAND ISLAND WILDLIFE CENTER

BONAVENTURE CEMETERY

WORMSLOE STATE HISTORIC SITE

MIGHTY EIGHTH AIR FORCE MUSEUM

BAMBOO FARM AND COASTAL GARDEN

Savannah National Wildlife Refuge

Wassaw Island National Wildlife Refuge

SAVANNAH INTERNATIONAL AIRPORT

AMTRAK STATION

HUNTER ARMY AIRFIELD

CANDLER HOSPITAL

Garden City

Thunderbolt

Wilmington Island

Skidaway Island

Skidaway Island State Park

Tybee Island

Little Tybee Island

Wassaw Island

Boneyard Beach

Wassaw Sound

Savannah River

Wilmington River

Little Ogeechee River

Ogeechee River Canal

To Savannah-Ogeechee River Canal

Old Fort Jackson

Hutchinson Island

Pin Point

Isle of Hope

Bacon Park

Daffin Park

Tybee Creek

3 mi

3 km

SAVANNAH

© JIM MOREKIS

memorial to "Gracie" in Bonaventure
Cemetery

right and look for the entrance farther along
on the right.

❰ Bonaventure Cemetery

On the banks of the Wilmington River just
east of town lies one of Savannah's most
unique sights, **Bonaventure Cemetery** (330
Bonaventure Rd., 912/651-6843, daily 8am-
5pm). John Muir, who went on to found the
Sierra Club, wrote of Bonaventure's Spanish
moss-bedecked beauty in his 1867 book *A
Thousand-Mile Walk to the Gulf*, marveling at
the screaming bald eagles that then frequented
the area. While its pedigree as Savannah's premier public cemetery goes back 100 years, it
was used as a burial ground as early as 1794.
In the years since, this achingly poignant vista
of live oaks and azaleas has been the final resting place of such local and national luminaries
as Johnny Mercer, Conrad Aiken, Wormsloe
Historic Site founder Noble Jones, and, of
course, the Trosdal plot, former home of the

famous *Bird Girl* statue (the original is now
in the Telfair Academy of Arts and Sciences).
Fittingly, the late, great Jack Leigh, who took
the *Bird Girl* photo for the cover of *Midnight
in the Garden of Good and Evil*, is interred here
as well.

Several local tour companies offer options
that include a visit to Bonaventure. If you're
doing a self-guided tour, go by the small visitors
center at the entrance and pick up one of the
free guides to the cemetery, assembled by the
local volunteer Bonaventure Historical Society.

To get here from downtown, take
President Street Extension east and take a
right on Pennsylvania Avenue, then a left on
Bonaventure Road. Alternately, go east on
Victory Drive (U.S. 80) and take a left on
Whatley Road in the town of Thunderbolt.
Veer left onto Bonaventure Road. The ceme-
tery is one mile ahead on the right.

WESTSIDE
Laurel Grove Cemetery

Its natural vista isn't as alluring as
Bonaventure's, but Laurel Grove Cemetery
boasts its own exquisitely carved memorials
and a distinctly Victorian type of surreal beauty
that not even Bonaventure can match. In keeping with the racial apartheid of Savannah's
early days, there are actually two cemeteries:
Laurel Grove North (802 W. Anderson St.,
daily 8am-5pm) for whites, and **Laurel Grove
South** (2101 Kollock St., daily 8am-5pm) for
blacks. Both are well worth visiting.

By far the most high-profile site in the
North Cemetery is that of Juliette Gordon
Low, founder of the Girl Scouts of the USA.
Other historically significant sites there include
the grave of "Jingle Bells" composer James
Pierpont. But it's the graves of the anonymous
and near-anonymous that are the most poignant sights. The various sections for infants,
known as "babylands," cannot fail to move.
"Mr. Bones," a former Savannah Police dog, is
the only animal buried at Laurel Grove. There's
an entire site reserved for victims of the great
yellow fever epidemic.

JOHNNY MERCER'S BLACK MAGIC

Visitors might be forgiven for thinking Paula Deen is Savannah's most famous native, but the Food Network star, born 200 miles away in Albany, Georgia, technically cannot claim that title. The great Johnny Mercer was one of the greatest lyricists music has ever known. He grew up on a small river then called the Back River but since renamed Moon River in honor of his best-known song. Armed with an innate talent for rhythm and a curious ear for dialogue, Mercer moved away from Savannah to New York when he was only 19 to try his hand in Tin Pan Alley, then the world center of popular music.

There he met the woman who would be his wife, Ginger Meehan (real name Elizabeth Meltzer). This Brooklyn Jewish chorus girl—once Bing Crosby's lover—would be both muse and foil for Mercer in the decades to follow. Mutual infidelity and a partying lifestyle combined for a stormy marriage, yet both remained together until Mercer's death from a brain tumor in 1976 (Ginger died in 1994). During the 1930s, the show business center of gravity was moving toward Hollywood, and Mercer—ahead of his time as usual—sensed the shift early and moved to the West Coast to write musicals for RKO. The advent of high-quality microphones was tailor-made for Mercer's nuanced lyrics. During his long and productive Hollywood career in the 1930s

and 1940s, he wrote such classics as "Jeepers Creepers," "That Old Black Magic," "Come Rain or Come Shine," "Skylark," and "Ac-Cent-Tchu-Ate the Positive."

Mercer embarked on an affair with the young Judy Garland in 1941, a dalliance that he later said inspired the song "I Remember You." While the advent of rock and roll in the postwar era signaled the decline of Mercer's career, he wrote what is arguably his greatest song, "Moon River," in 1961. The song, debuted by Audrey Hepburn in the film *Breakfast at Tiffany's*, won an Academy Award for Best Original Song. In addition to "Moon River," Mercer won three other Oscars, for "On the Atchinson, Topeka and the Santa Fe" (1946), "In the Cool, Cool, Cool of the Evening" (1951), and "Days of Wine and Roses" (1962).

Today you can pay your respects to Mercer in three places: his boyhood home (509 E. Gwinnett St.; look for the historical marker in front of this private residence); the bronze sculpture of Mercer in the newly revitalized Ellis Square near City Market, erected in 2009 in honor of the centennial of his birth; and, of course, at his gravesite in beautiful Bonaventure Cemetery. And regardless of what anyone tells you, neither Johnny Mercer nor any member of his family ever lived in the Mercer-Williams House on Monterey Square, of *Midnight in the Garden of Good and Evil* fame.

SAVANNAH

To get to Laurel Grove North, take MLK Jr. Boulevard to Anderson Street and turn west. To get to Laurel Grove South, take Victory Drive (U.S. 80) west to Ogeechee Road. Take a right onto Ogeechee, then a right onto West 36th Street. Continue on to Kollock Street.

Mighty Eighth Air Force Museum

Military and aviation buffs mustn't miss the **Mighty Eighth Air Force Museum** (175 Bourne Ave., 912/748-8888, www.mightyeighth.org, daily 9am-5pm, $10 adults, $6 children and active duty military) in Pooler,

Georgia, right off I-95. The 8th Air Force was born at Hunter Field in Savannah as the 8th Bomber Command in 1942, becoming the 8th Air Force in 1944; it is now based in Louisiana.

A moving testament to the men and machines who conducted those strategic bombing campaigns over Europe in World War II, the museum also features later 8th Air Force history such as the Korean War, the Linebacker II bombing campaigns over North Vietnam, and the Persian Gulf. Inside you'll find not only airplanes like the P-51 Mustang and the German

© DNDAVIS/123RF.COM

Wormsloe State Historic Site

ME-109, there's also a restored B-17 bomber, the newest jewel of the collection.

To get to the Mighty Eighth Museum from downtown, take I-16 west until it intersects I-95. Take I-95 north, take exit 102, and follow the signs.

Savannah-Ogeechee River Canal

A relic of the pre-railroad days, the **Savannah-Ogeechee River Canal** (681 Ft. Argyle Rd., 912/748-8068, www.savanna-hogeecheecanalsociety.org, Fri. and Mon. 10am-4pm, Sat. 9am-5pm, Sun. 1pm-5pm, $3 adults, $1 students) is a 17-mile barge route joining the two rivers. Finished in 1830, it saw three decades of prosperous trade in cotton, rice, bricks, guano, naval stores, and agriculture before the coming of the railroads finished it off. You can walk some of its length today near the Ogeechee River terminus. Do bring mosquito repellent, although often there's a community spray can at the front door of the little visitors center-museum where you pay your fee.

To get here, get on I-95 south and take exit 94. The canal is a little over two miles west.

SOUTHSIDE
Wormsloe State Historic Site

The one-of-a-kind **Wormsloe State Historic Site** (7601 Skidaway Rd., 912/353-3023, www.gastateparks.org/info/wormsloe, Tues.-Sun. 9am-5pm, $9 adults, $4.50 children) was first settled by Noble Jones, who landed with Oglethorpe on the *Anne* and fought beside him in the War of Jenkin's Ear. One of the great renaissance men of history, this soldier was also an accomplished carpenter, surveyor, forester, botanist, and physician. Jones's descendants donated 822 acres to the Nature Conservancy, which transferred the property to the state. The house, dating from 1828, and 65.5 acres of land are still owned by his family, and no, you can't visit them.

The stunning entrance canopy of 400 live oaks, Spanish moss dripping the entire length, is one of those iconic images of Savannah. A small interpretive museum, a one-mile nature walk, and occasional living history demonstrations make this a great site for the entire family.

Pin Point

Off Whitfield Avenue (Diamond Causeway) on the route to Skidaway Island is tiny **Pin Point, Georgia,** a predominantly African American township better known as the boyhood home of Supreme Court Justice Clarence Thomas. Pin Point traces its roots to a community of former slaves on Ossabaw Island. Displaced by a hurricane, they settled at this idyllic site overlooking the Moon River, itself a former plantation. Many new residents made their living by shucking oysters at the Varn Oyster Company, the central shed of which still remains and forms the basis of the new **Pin Point Heritage Museum** (9924 Pin Point Ave., 912/232-3945, www.pinpointheritagemuseum.com, Thurs. and Sat. 9am-5pm, free). The museum tells the story of the Pin Point community through exhibits, a film, and demonstrations of some of the maritime activities at the Varn Oyster Company through the decades, such as crabbing, canning, shucking, and shrimp net making.

Skidaway Island

Skidaway Island is notable for two beautiful and educational nature-oriented sites. The first, the **University of Georgia Marine Educational Center and Aquarium** (30 Ocean Science Circle, 912/598-3474, www.marex.uga.edu, Mon.-Fri. 9am-4pm, Sat. 10am-5pm, $6 adults, $3 children, cash only) shares a scenic 700-acre campus on the scenic Skidaway River with the research-oriented **Skidaway Institute of Oceanography,** also affiliated with the University of Georgia (UGA). It hosts scientists and grad students from around the nation, often on trips on is research vessel, the RV *Sea Dawg.* The main attraction of the Marine Center is the small but well-done and recently upgraded aquarium featuring 14 tanks with 200 live animals.

The second site of interest to visitors is **Skidaway Island State Park** (52 Diamond Causeway, 912/598-2300, www.gastateparks.

org/info/skidaway, daily 7am-10pm, parking $2). Yeah, you can camp here ($25-28), but the awesome nature trails leading out to the marsh—featuring an ancient Native American shell midden and an old whiskey still—are worth a trip just on their own, especially when combined with the Marine Education Center Aquarium. To get here, take Victory Drive (U.S. 80) until you get to Waters Avenue and continue south as it turns into Whitefield Avenue and then the Diamond Causeway. The park is on your left after the drawbridge. An alternate route from downtown is to take the Truman Parkway all the way to its dead end at Whitefield Avenue; take a left and continue as it turns into Diamond Causeway into Skidaway.

TYBEE ISLAND

Its name means "salt" in the old Euchee tongue, indicative of the island's chief export in those days. And Tybee Island—"Tybee" to locals—is indeed one of the essential seasonings of life in Savannah. First incorporated as Ocean City and then Savannah Beach, the island has since reclaimed its original name. Eighteen miles from Savannah, in truth Tybee is part and parcel of the city's social and cultural fabric.

【 Fort Pulaski National Monument

There's one must-see before you get to Tybee Island proper. On Cockspur Island you'll find **Fort Pulaski National Monument** (U.S. 80 E., 912/786-5787, www.nps.gov/fopu, fort Sept.-May daily 9am-5pm, June-Aug. daily 9am-6:30pm, visitors center Sept.-May daily 9am-5pm, June-Aug. daily 9am-6:45pm, $5, free under age 16). Not only a delight for any history buff, the fort's also a fantastic place to take the kids. They can climb on the parapets, earthworks, and cannons, and burn off calories on the great nature trail nearby. Along the way they'll no doubt learn a few things as well.

Perhaps prophetically named for Count Casimir Pulaski, who died leading an ill-fated charge on the British in 1779, Fort Pulaski is also symbolic of a catastrophic defeat, this one

SAVANNAH

in 1862 when Union forces using new rifled cannons reduced much of it to rubble in 30 hours. Robert E. Lee—yes, *that* Robert E. Lee—helped build the fort while a lieutenant with the U.S. Army Corps of Engineers. Based on state-of-the-art European design forged in the cauldron of the Napoleonic Wars, Fort Pulaski was considered invincible.

When Georgia seceded in January 1861, Confederates took control of two Savannah area fortifications, Fort Pulaski and Fort

Jackson. However, in early 1862 a Union sealand force came to covertly lay the groundwork for a siege of Fort Pulaski. The Union barrage began at 8:15am on April 10, 1862, and Fort Pulaski's walls immediately began to crumble under the withering Union fire. At least one shell struck a powder magazine, igniting an enormous explosion. After a mere 30 hours, Confederate colonel Charles H. Olmstead surrendered the "invincible" fortress.

The fort was occupied mostly by troops of

© JIM MOREKIS

Fort Pulaski

the 48th New York Volunteers, who sometimes relieved the boredom of garrison duty by playing the brand-new game of baseball on the fort's vast, grassy parade ground. One of the first photographs of a baseball game was taken at Fort Pulaski in 1863.

By all means, visit the visitors center, a few hundred yards from the fort itself—but the palpable pleasure starts when you cross the drawbridge over the moat and see a cannon pointed at you from a narrow gun port. Enter the inside of the fort and take in just how big it is. Take a walk around the perimeter, underneath the ramparts. This is where the soldiers lived and worked, and you'll see re-creations of officer's quarters, meeting areas, sick rooms, and prisoners' bunks among the cannons, where Confederate prisoners of war were held after the fort's surrender. Cannon firings happen most Saturdays. Take the steep corkscrew staircase up to the ramparts themselves and take in the jaw-dropping view of the lush marsh, the Savannah River and Tybee Island spreading out in the distance.

Tybee Lighthouse

Reaching Tybee proper on U.S. 80, you'll soon arrive at the intersection with North Campbell Avenue. This is the entrance to the less-populated, more historically significant north end of the island, once almost entirely taken up by Fort Screven, a coastal defense fortification of the early 1900s. Take a left onto North Campbell Avenue then left again on Van Horne Street. Take an immediate right onto Meddin Drive. Continue until you see a lighthouse on the left and a parking lot on the right.

Rebuilt several times in its history, the **Tybee Island Light Station and Museum** (30 Meddin Ave., 912/786-5801, www.tybeelighthouse.org, Wed.-Mon. 9am-5:30pm, last admission 4:30pm, $9 adults, $7 children) traces its construction to the first year of the colony, based on a design by the multitalented Noble Jones. At its completion in 1736, it was the tallest structure in the United States. One of a handful of working 18th-century lighthouses today, the facility

THE TYBEE BOMB

On a dark February night in 1958 at the height of the Cold War, a USAF B-47 Stratojet bomber based at Homestead, Florida, made a simulated nuclear bombing run somewhere over southeast Georgia. A Charleston-based F-86 fighter on a mock intercept came too close, clipping the big bomber's wing. Before bringing down the wounded B-47 at Savannah's Hunter Airfield—then a Strategic Air Command base—Commander Howard Richardson decided he first had to jettison his lethal cargo: a 7,000-pound Mark 15 hydrogen bomb, serial number 47782. We know for sure that he jettisoned it over water; Richardson, who won the Distinguished Flying Cross for his efforts that night, said so himself. What no one knows is exactly where. And thus began the legend of "the Tybee bomb." Go in any Tybee watering hole and ask 10 people where they think it is and you'll get 10 different answers. Some say it's in the north side of Wassaw Sound, some say the south. Some say it's in the shallows, some in deep water. Many locals who work in shrimping, crabbing, and fishing have claimed at various times to have ripped their nets on the bomb. Or on something.... Speculation ran wild, with some locals fearing a nuclear explosion, radioactive contamination, or even that a team of scuba-diving terrorists would secretly retrieve the ancient weapon.

Former Army colonel and present-day raconteur and soldier of fortune Derek Duke took it as his personal mission to find the bomb. He says the Air Force could easily find it but won't do so either because they don't want to go to the expense of finding it or they don't want to admit they lost a thermonuclear weapon for half a century. Duke claims to have found a radiation-emitting object off Little Tybee Island during a search in 2004.

Commander Richardson, now retired and living in Jackson, Mississippi, says the point is moot because the bomb wasn't armed when he jettisoned it. Environmentalists say that doesn't matter, because the enriched uranium the Air Force admits was in the bomb is toxic whether or not there's the risk of a nuclear detonation. People who work in the fishing industry on Tybee say the fact that the bomb also had 400 pounds of high explosive "nuclear trigger" is reason enough to get it out of these waterways, which hosted the 1996 Olympic yachting competition. And what of the owners of the Tybee Bomb, the Air Force? In 2000, they sent a team to Savannah to find the bomb, concluding it was buried somewhere off the coast in 5 to 15 feet of mud. In 2005, in another attempt to find the weapon—and also to shut down the rampant conspiracy theories, most of them propagated by Duke—they sent another team of experts down to look one last time. Their verdict: The bomb's still lost. That won't stop local speculation about its whereabouts, however. Who can resist a real-life cloak-and-dagger story? Certainly few people around here.

Postscript: No one was injured that night in 1958, except for some frostbite the F-86 pilot suffered as a result of ejecting from his damaged plane. In an interesting bit of synchronicity, the fighter pilot, Clarence Wilson, and the B-47 commander, Howard Richardson, grew up miles away from each other in Winston County, Mississippi.

has been restored to its 1916-1964 incarnation, featuring a nine-foot-tall first-order Fresnel lens installed in 1867.

The entrance fee gives you admission to the lighthouse, the lighthouse museum, and the nearby Tybee Island Museum. All the outbuildings on the lighthouse grounds are original, including the residence of the lighthouse keeper, also the oldest building on the island.

If you've got the legs and the lungs, definitely take all 178 steps up to the top of the lighthouse for a stunning view of Tybee, the Atlantic, and Hilton Head Island.

TOURS

Savannah's tourism boom has resulted in a similar explosion of well over 50 separate tour services, including simple guided trolley journeys,

Old Town Trolley Tours on the streets of Savannah

horse-drawn carriage rides, specialty tours, and ecotourism adventures.

Trolley Tours

The vehicle of choice for the bulk of the masses visiting Savannah, trolley tours allow you to sit back and enjoy the views in reasonable comfort. As in other cities, the guides provide commentary while attempting, with various degrees of success, to navigate the cramped downtown traffic environment. The main trolley companies in town are **Old Savannah Tours** (912/234-8128, www.old-savannahtours.com, basic on-off tour $25 adults, $11 children), **Old Town Trolley Tours** (800/213-2474, www.trolleytours.com, basic on-off tour $23 adults, $10 children), and **Oglethorpe Trolley Tours** (912/233-8380, www.oglethorpetours.com, basic on-off tour $22.50 adults, $10 children). All embark from the Savannah Visitors Center on Martin Luther King Jr. Boulevard about every 20-30 minutes on the same schedule, daily 9am-4:30pm.

Specialty Tours

Besides the standard narrated Historic District tours, all the above companies also offer a number of spin-off tours. Samples include the Pirate's House Dinner & Ghost Tour, Belles of Savannah, the Evening Haunted Trolley, and multiple Paula Deen tours.

The copious ghost tours, offered by all the companies, can be fun for the casual visitor who wants entertainment rather than actual history. Students of the paranormal are likely to be disappointed by the cartoonish, Halloween aspect of some of the tours. A standout in the ghost field is the **Hearse Ghost Tours** (912/695-1578, www.hearseghosttours.com, $15), a unique company that also operates tours in New Orleans and St. Augustine, Florida. Up to eight guests at a time ride around in the open top of a converted hearse, painted all black, of course, and get a 90-minute, suitably over-the-top narration from the driver-guide. It's still pretty cheesy, but a hip kind of cheesy. Two very popular ghostly walking tours are found with **Cobblestone Tours** (912/604-3007, www.cobblestone-tours.com, $20), a "Haunted History" tour and a "Haunted Pub Crawl." Another fun paranormal-ghost tour is at **Blue Orb Tours** (912/665-4258, www.blueorbtours. com, $25-50), which offers—you guessed it—a "Zombie Tour."

Storyteller and author Ted Eldridge leads **A Walk Through Savannah Tours** (912/921-4455, www.awalkthroughsavannah.brave-host.com, $15 adults, $5 ages 6-12, free under age 6) and offers all kinds of specialty walking tours. To learn about Savannah's history of filmmaking and to enjoy the best of local cuisine, try a **Savannah Movie Tour** (912/234-3440, www.savannahmovietours. net, $25 adults, $15 children), taking you to various film locations in town, and a newer **Savannah Foody Tour** (912/234-3440, www. savannahmovietours.net, $48) featuring six to nine local eateries.

To see downtown Savannah by bicycle—quite a refreshing experience—try **Savannah Bike Tours** (41 Habersham St., 912/704-4043, www.savannahbiketours.com, $15 adults, $10 under age 12), two-hour trips through all 19 squares and Forsyth Park with your "rolling concierge." They leave daily at 9:30am, 12:30pm, and 4pm. Rent bikes from them or ride your own.

The unique **Negro Heritage Trail Tour** (912/234-8000, $19 adults, $10 children) takes you on a 90-minute air-conditioned bus tour of over 30 of Savannah's key African American history sites. Pick up the Negro Heritage Tour at the Visitors Center downtown (301 MLK Jr. Blvd.) Tuesday-Saturday at 10am and noon.

Carriage Tours

Ah, yes—what could be more romantic and more traditional than enjoying downtown Savannah the way it was originally intended to be traveled, by horse-drawn carriage? Indeed, this is one of the most fun ways to see the city, for couples as well as for those with horse-enamored children. Yes, the horses sometimes look tired, but the tour operators generally take great care to keep the horses hydrated and out of the worst of the heat. There are three main purveyors of equine tourism in town: **Carriage Tours of Savannah** (912/236-6756, www.carriagetoursofsavannah.com, pickup in City Market), **Historic Savannah Carriage Tours** (888/837-1011, www.savannahcarriage.com, pickup at the Hampton Inn), and **Plantation Carriage Company** (912/201-0001, pickup in City Market). As with the trolleys, the length of the basic tour and the price is about the same for all—45 to 60 minutes, about $20 adults and $10 children. All offer specialty tours as well, from ghost tours to evening romantic rides with champagne. Some will pick you up at your hotel.

Ecotours

The 35-year-old nonprofit **Wilderness Southeast** (912/897-5108, www.wilderness-southeast.org, $10-35) offers guided trips, including paddles to historic Mulberry Grove, birding trips, and beach explorations. Regularly scheduled "Walks on the Wild Side" run the gamut from "Alligators to Anhingas" to the "Urban Forest" to "Explore the Night Sky" to the "Blackwater River Float." Custom tours are also available.

Entertainment and Events

If you like to have a good time, you're in the right place. Savannah is known for its heavy year-round schedule of festivals, many of them outdoors, as well as its copious variety of watering holes hosting a diverse range of local residents and adventurous visitors.

NIGHTLIFE

Savannah is a hard-drinking town, and not just on St. Patrick's Day. The ability to legally walk downtown streets with beer, wine, or a cocktail in hand also contributes to the overall joie de vivre. Bars close in Savannah at 3am, a full hour later than in Charleston. A citywide indoor smoking ban is in effect, and you may not smoke in any bar in Savannah.

Bars and Pubs

Uncharacteristically, Savannah now sports several good hotel bars, and chief among them is no doubt **Rocks on the Roof** (102 W. Bay St., 912/721-3800, daily 11am-3pm) atop the Bohemian Hotel Savannah on the waterfront. In good weather the exterior walls are opened up to reveal a large wraparound seating area with stunning views of downtown on one side and of the Savannah River on the other. The crowd is a fun mix of locals and visitors.

Savannah's old-school dive is **Pinkie Masters** (318 Drayton St., 912/238-0447, Mon.-Fri. 4pm-3am, Sat. 5pm-3am). Named for a legendary local political kingmaker, Pinkie's is a favorite not only with students, artists, and professors but also with lawyers, journalists, and grizzled war vets. This is where Jimmy Carter, ironically a teetotaler, stood on the bar and announced his candidacy for Georgia governor.

The real hipster hangout, in ironic fashion drinking PBRs, is the **American Legion Bar** (1108 Bull St., 912/233-9277, http://al-post135.com, Mon.-Sat. 4pm-2am), located in, yes, an actual American Legion post. While the Legionnaires themselves are a straight-laced patriotic bunch, the patrons of "the Legion," as the bar is colloquially known, tend toward the counterculture. Fun historical fact: The building housing the Legion was the birthplace of the U.S. 8th Air Force during World War II.

The Distillery (416 W. Liberty St., 912/236-1772, www.distillerysavannah.com) is located in, yes, a former distillery. As such, the atmosphere isn't exactly dark and romantic—it's one big open room—but the excellent location at the corner of MLK Jr. Boulevard and Liberty Street, the long vintage bar, and the great selection of beers on tap combine to make this a happening spot.

The main landmark on the west end of River Street is the famous (or infamous, depending on which side of "The Troubles" you're on) **Kevin Barry's Irish Pub** (117 W. River St., 912/233-9626, www.kevinbarrys.com, daily 11am-3am), one of Savannah's most beloved establishments. KB's is open seven days a week, with evenings seeing performances by a number of Irish troubadours, all veterans of the East Coast trad circuit. An eclectic mix of travelers, local Irish, military, and sailors keeps this place always interesting and alive.

The only brewpub in Savannah, **Moon River Brewing Company** (21 W. Bay St., 912/447-0943, www.moonriverbrewing.com, Mon.-Thurs. 11am-11pm, Fri.-Sat. 11am-midnight, Sun. 11am-10pm), directly across from the Hyatt Regency, offers half a dozen handcrafted beers.

Live Music and Karaoke

Despite its high-volume offerings, the hardcore and heavy metal club **The Jinx** (127 W. Congress St., 912/236-2281, www.thejinx.net, Mon.-Sat. 4pm-3am) is a friendly watering hole and probably the closest thing Savannah has to a full-on Athens, Georgia-style music club. Shows start *very* late here, never before 11pm and often later than that. If you're here for the show, bring earplugs.

Savannah's undisputed karaoke champion is **McDonough's** (21 E. McDonough St., 912/233-6136, www.mcdonoughsofsavannah. com, Mon.-Sat. 8pm-3am, Sun. 8pm-2am), an advantage compounded by the fact that a lot more goes on here than karaoke. The kitchen at McDonough's is quite capable, and many locals swear you can get the best burger in town. Despite the sports bar atmosphere, the emphasis here is on the karaoke, which ramps up every night at 9:30pm.

Gay and Lesbian

Any examination of gay and lesbian nightlife in Savannah must, of course, begin with **Club One Jefferson** (1 Jefferson St., 912/232-0200, www.clubone-online.com) of *Midnight in the Garden of Good and Evil* fame, with its famous drag shows, including the notorious Lady Chablis, upstairs in the cabaret, and its rockin' 1,000-square-foot dance floor downstairs. Cabaret showtimes are Thursday-Saturday 10:30pm and 12:30am, Sunday 10:30pm, and Monday 11:30pm. Call for Lady Chablis's showtimes. As with all local gay nightclubs, straights are more than welcome.

A friendly, kitschy little tavern at the far west end of River Street near the Jefferson Street ramp, **Chuck's Bar** (301 W. River St., 912/232-1005, Mon.-Wed. 8pm-3am, Thurs.-Sat. 7pm-3am) is a great place to relax and see some interesting local characters. Karaoke at Chuck's is especially a hoot, and they keep the Christmas lights up all year.

PERFORMING ARTS
Theater

The multiuse venue **Muse Arts Warehouse** (703D Louisville Rd., 912/713-1137, www. musesavannah.org) hosts a variety of community-based plays and performances within a well-restored historic train depot. Get there by taking Liberty Street west from downtown, where it turns into Louisville Road.

The semipro troupe at the **Historic Savannah Theatre** (222 Bull St., 912/233-7764, www.savannahtheatre.com) performs a busy rotating schedule of oldies revues (a typical title: *Return to the '50s*), which make up for their lack of originality with the tightness and energy of their talented young cast of regulars.

Music

The **Savannah Philharmonic** (800/514-3849, www.thesavannahphil.org) is a professional troupe that performs concertos and sonatas

---

THE TO-GO CUP TRADITION

Arguably the single most civilized trait of Savannah, and certainly one of the things that most sets it apart, is the glorious old tradition of the "to-go cup." True to its history of hard-partying and general open-mindedness, Savannah, like New Orleans, legally allows you to walk the streets downtown with an open container of your favorite adult beverage. Of course, you have to be 21 and over, and the cup must be Styrofoam or plastic, never glass or metal, and no more than 16 ounces. While there are boundaries to where to-go cups are legal, in practice this includes almost all areas of the Historic District frequented by visitors. The quick and easy rule of thumb is, keep your to-go cups north of Jones Street.

Every other election year, some local politician tries to get the church folk all riled up and proposes doing away with to-go cups in the interest of public safety, and he or she is inevitably shouted down by the outcry from the tourism-conscious Chamber of Commerce and from patriotic Savannahians defending their way of life. Every downtown watering hole has stacks of cups at the bar for patrons to use. You can either ask the bartender for a to-go cup—alternately a "go cup"—or just reach out and grab one yourself. Don't be shy; it's the Savannah way.

at various venues around town and is always worth checking out.

CINEMA

The closest multiplex to downtown is the **Victory Square Stadium 9** (1901 E. Victory Dr., 912/355-5000). The historic **Lucas Theatre for the Arts** (32 Abercorn St., 912/525-5040, www.lucastheatre.com) downtown is a great place to see a movie and has screenings throughout the year; check the website for schedules. The **Sentient Bean Coffeehouse** (13 E. Park Ave., 912/232-4447, www.sentientbean.com) hosts countercultural and political documentaries and kitsch classics.

FESTIVALS AND EVENTS

Savannah's calendar fairly bursts with festivals, many outdoors. Dates shift from year to year, so it's best to consult the listed websites for details.

February

Definitely not to be confused with St. Patrick's Day, the **Savannah Irish Festival** (912/232-3448, www.savannahirish.org) focuses on Celtic music. A regular performer and Savannah's most popular "Irishman at large" is folk singer Harry O'Donoghue, a native of Ireland who regularly plays at Kevin Barry's Irish Pub on River Street and hosts his own Celtic music show, "The Green Island," on local public radio (91.1 FM) Saturday evenings.

Hosted by the historically black Savannah State University at various venues around town, the monthlong **Black Heritage Festival** (912/691-6847) is tied into Black History Month and boasts name entertainers like the Alvin Ailey Dance Theatre (performing free!). This event also usually features plenty of historical lectures devoted to the very interesting and rich history of African Americans in Savannah.

Also in February is the **Savannah Book Festival** (www.savannahbookfestival.org), modeled after a similar event in Washington DC and featuring many local and regional authors at various venues.

March

One of the most anticipated events for house-proud Savannahians, the **Tour of Homes and Gardens** (912/234-8054, www.savannahtourofhomes.org) offers guests the opportunity to visit six beautiful sites off the usual tourist-trod path. This is a great way to expand your understanding of local architecture and hospitality beyond the usual house museums.

More than just a day, the citywide **St. Patrick's Day** (www.savannahsaintpatricksday.com) celebration generally lasts at least half a week and temporarily triples the population. The nearly three-hour parade—the second-biggest in the United States—always begins at 10am on St. Patrick's Day (unless that falls on a Sunday, in which case it's generally on the previous Saturday) and includes a mix of bands, wacky floats, and sauntering local Irishmen in kelly green jackets. While the parade itself is very family-friendly, afterward hard-core partiers generally head en masse to River Street, which is blocked off for the occasion and definitely not where you want to take small children.

Savannah's answer to Charleston's Spoleto, the three-week **Savannah Music Festival** (912/234-3378, www.savannahmusicfestival.org) is held at various historical venues around town and begins right after St. Patrick's Day. Past festivals have featured Wynton Marsalis, the Beaux Arts Trio, and Diane Reeves. The most economical way to enjoy the Music Festival is to purchase tickets online before December of the previous year at a 10 percent discount. However, if you just want to take in a few events, individual tickets are available at a tiered pricing system that allows everyone to enjoy this popular event. You can buy tickets to individual events in town at the walk-up box office beside the Trustees Theatre on Broughton Street.

April

Short for "North of Gaston Street," the **NOGS Tour of Hidden Gardens** (912/961-4805, www.gcofsavnogstour.org, $30) is available two days in April and focuses on Savannah's amazing selection of private gardens selected for excellence of design, historical interest, and beauty.

Everyone loves the annual free **Sidewalk Arts Festival** (912/525-5865, www.scad.edu) presented by the Savannah College of Art and Design in Forsyth Park. Contestants claim a rectangular section of sidewalk on which to display their chalk art talent. There's a noncontest section with chalk provided.

May

The SCAD-sponsored **Sand Arts Festival** (www.scad.edu) on Tybee Island's North Beach centers on a competition of sand castle design, sand sculpture, sand relief, and wind sculpture. You might be amazed at the level of artistry lavished on the sometimes-wondrous creations only for them to wash away with the tide.

September

Though the quality of the acts has been overshadowed lately by the Savannah Music Festival in the spring, the **Savannah Jazz Festival** (www.savannahjazzfestival.org) has two key things going for it: It's free, and it's outside in the green expanse of Forsyth Park. Generally spread out over several nights, the volunteer-run festival draws a good crowd regardless of the lineup, and food and drink are available.

October

If pickin' and grinnin' is your thing, don't miss the low-key but always entertaining **Savannah Folk Music Festival** (www.savannahfolk.org). The main event of the weekend is held on a Sunday night in the historic Grayson Stadium in Daffin Park, but a popular Old-Time Country Dance is usually held the previous Saturday. Members of the Savannah Folk Music Society will help you learn how to do the dance, so don't be shy!

Despite its generic-sounding name, the **Fall Festival** (www.bamboo.caes.uga.edu) is actually quite interesting, given its location in the unique Bamboo Farm and Coastal Garden. A joint project of the University of Georgia and Chatham County, the Bamboo Farm features a wide array of native species, all lovingly tended. The festival features tours, displays, arts and crafts, food, and lots of kids' activities. The event is free, but parking is $1. To get here, take I-95 exit 94 and take Highway 204 east toward Savannah. Turn right on East Gateway Boulevard, then left on Canebrake Road. Enter at the Canebrake gate.

Hosted by the Savannah College of Art and Design, the weeklong **Savannah Film Festival** (www.scad.edu) beginning in late October is rapidly growing not only in size but in prestige. Lots of older, more established Hollywood names appear as honored guests for the evening events, while buzz-worthy up-and-coming actors, directors, producers, writers, and animators give excellent workshops during the day. Many of these usually jaded showbiz types really let their hair down for this festival, because, as you'll see, Savannah is the real star. The best way to enjoy this excellent event is to buy a pass, which enables you to walk from event to event.

Shopping

Downtown Savannah's main shopping district is Broughton Street, which is included here along with several other key shopping areas of note.

BROUGHTON STREET

The historic center of downtown shopping has recently seen a major renaissance and is once again home to the most vibrant shopping scene in Savannah, just like it was in the 1940s and 1950s. While several chain stores have made inroads onto the avenue, here are some of the most notable independent shops.

Clothes and Fashion

Perhaps Broughton's most beloved old shop is

SAVANNAH

© JIM MOREKIS

The Paris Market & Brocante

Globe Shoe Co. (17 E. Broughton St., 912/232-8161), a Savannah institution and a real throwback to a time of personalized retail service. They have no website and no Facebook page—they're all about simple one-to-one service, like in the old days. Easily one of the coolest women's stores in town is **Go Fish** (106 W. Broughton St., 912/231-0609, www.gofishretail.com). This regional franchised operation provides for a lot of independence on the part of the owners; Debbie and Lloyd Ryysylainen offer a sharply curated range of upscale-looking clothes and shoes at reasonable prices. **Gaucho** is another popular choice for women, with a strong emphasis on accessories, jewelry, and shoes. There are two locations: 18 East Broughton Street (912/234-7414, Mon.-Sat. 10am-6pm) and the original location at 250 Bull Street (912/232-7414, Mon.-Sat. 10am-6pm, Sun. 1pm-5pm). **Copper Penny** (22 W. Broughton St., 912/629-6800, www.shopcopperpenny.com) is easily the premier women's shoe showcase on the historic avenue. Vintage shoppers will enjoy **Civvies** (22 E. Broughton

St., 912/236-1551), a second-floor shop with a nice selection of previously owned clothing.

Home Goods

While Savannah is an Anglophile's dream, Francophiles will enjoy **The Paris Market & Brocante** (36 W. Broughton St., 912/232-1500, www.theparismarket.com, Mon.-Sat. 10am-6pm, Sun. 11am-4pm) on a beautifully restored corner of Broughton Street. Home and garden goods, bed and bath accoutrements, and a great selection of antique and vintage items combine for a rather opulent shopping experience. Plus there's an old-school Euro café inside where you can enjoy a coffee, tea, or hot chocolate.

Those looking for great home decorating ideas with inspiration from both global and Southern aesthetics, traditional as well as sleekly modern, should check out **24e Furnishings at Broughton** (24 E. Broughton St., 912/233-2274, www.twentyfoure.com, Mon.-Thurs. 10am-6pm, Fri.-Sat. 10am-7pm, Sun. noon-5pm), located in an excellent restored 1921 storefront. Be sure to check out the expansive second-floor showroom.

One of the more unique Savannah retail shops is the **Savannah Bee Company** (104 W. Broughton St., 912/233-7873, www.savannahbee.com, Mon.-Sat. 10am-7pm, Sun. 11am-5pm), which, as the name implies, carries an extensive line of honey-based merchandise, from foot lotion to lip balm. All the honey comes from area hives owned by company founder and owner Ted Dennard. The company now has a sizeable national presence since being picked up for the Williams-Sonoma catalogue 10 years ago. The flagship Broughton location provides plenty of sampling opportunities at the little café area and even boasts a small theater space for instructional films.

Outdoor Outfitters

Outdoors lovers should make themselves acquainted with **Half Moon Outfitters** (15 E. Broughton St., 912/201-9313, www.halfmoonoutfitters.com, Mon.-Sat. 10am-7pm, Sun. noon-6pm), a full-service camping, hiking, skiing, and kayaking store. Half Moon is part of a regional chain that also has two locations in Charleston.

CITY MARKET

A borderline tourist trap, City Market strongly tends toward more touristy, less unique items. Here are a couple of exceptions: The whimsical **A. T. Hun Gallery** (302 W. St. Julian St., 912/233-2060, www.athun.com, Mon.-Thurs. 10am-6pm, Fri.-Sat. 10am-10pm, Sun. 11am-5pm) is one of the first true art galleries in town and features a variety of adventurous art from local and regional favorites. **Kobo Gallery** (33 Barnard St., 912/201-0304, http://kobogallery.com, Mon.-Sat. 10:30am-5:30pm, Sun. 11am-5pm) is a local artists cooperative and offers a nice range of adventurous artwork in a variety of media.

BOOKS

The fact that **E. Shaver Bookseller** (326 Bull St., 912/234-7257, Mon.-Sat. 9am-6pm) is one of the few locally owned independent bookstores left in town should not diminish the fact that it is also one of the best bookstores in town. The well-read staff can help you around the rambling old interior of their ground-level store and its generous stock of regionally themed books. Don't miss the rare map room, with some gems from the 17th and 18th centuries.

Specializing in "gently used" books in good condition, **The Book Lady** (6 E. Liberty St., 912/233-3628, Mon.-Sat. 10am-5:30pm) on Liberty Street features many rare first editions. Enjoy a gourmet coffee while you browse the stacks. The beautiful Monterey Square location and a mention in *Midnight in the Garden of Good and Evil* combine to make **V&J Duncan** (12 E. Taylor St., 912/232-0338, www.vjduncan.com, Mon.-Sat. 10:30am-4:30pm) a Savannah "must-shop." Owner John Duncan and his wife Virginia ("Ginger" to friends) have collected an impressive array of prints, books, and maps over the past quarter-century, and are themselves a treasure trove of information.

OTHER UNIQUE STORES

Not only a valuable outlet for SCAD students and faculty to sell their artistic wares, **shopSCAD** (340 Bull St., 912/525-5180, www.shopscadonline.com, Mon.-Wed. 9am-5:30pm, Thurs.-Fri. 9am-8pm, Sat. 10am-8pm, Sun. noon-5pm) is also one of Savannah's most unique boutiques. You never really know what you'll find, but whatever it is, it will be one-of-a-kind. The jewelry in particular is always cutting-edge in design and high-quality in craftsmanship. The designer T-shirts are a hoot as well.

Possibly the most beloved antiques store in town is **Alex Raskin Antiques** (441 Bull St., 912/232-8205, Mon.-Sat. 10am-5pm) in Monterey Square, catty-corner from the Mercer-Williams House. Set in the historic Hardee mansion, a visit is worth it just to explore the home. But the goods Alex lovingly curates are among the best and most tasteful in the region.

And in this town so enamored of all things Irish, a great little locally owned shop is **Saints** and **Shamrocks** (309 Bull St., 912/233-8858, www.saintsandshamrocks.org, Mon.-Sat. 9:30am-5:30pm, Sun. 11am-4pm). Pick up your St. Patrick's-themed gear and gifts to celebrate Savannah's highest holiday along with high-quality Irish imports.

MALLS

The mall closest to downtown—though not that close, at about 10 miles south—is **Oglethorpe Mall** (7804 Abercorn St., 912/354-7038, www.oglethorpemall.com, Mon.-Sat. 10am-9pm, Sun. noon-6pm). Its anchor stores are Sears, Belk, J. C. Penney, and Macy's.

GROCERIES AND MARKETS

Savannah's first and still premier health-food market, **Brighter Day Natural Foods** (1102 Bull St., 912/236-4703, www.brighterday-foods.com, Mon.-Sat. 9am-7pm, Sun. noon-5:30pm) has been the labor of love of Janie and Peter Brodhead for 30 years, all of them in the same location at the southern tip of Forsyth Park. Boasting organic groceries, regional produce, a sandwich and smoothie bar with a takeout window, and an extensive vitamin, supplement, and herb section, Brighter Day is an oasis in Savannah's sea of chain supermarkets.

For a more corporate health food experience, Savannah just got a new **Whole Foods Market** (1815 E. Victory Dr., www.wholefoodsmarket. com, daily 8am-9pm) on the Eastside of town on Victory Drive/Hwy 80, which eventually takes you to Tybee Island.

Fairly new but already thriving, the **Forsyth Park Farmers Market** (www.forsythfarmers-market.org, Sat. 9am-1pm) happens in the south end of Forsyth Park. You'll find fresh fruit and produce, as well as organic dairy and meat products, from a variety of fun and friendly regional farmers.

If you need some good quality groceries downtown—especially after-hours—try **Parker's Market** (222 E. Drayton St., 912/231-1001, daily 24 hours). In addition to a pretty wide array of gourmet-style victuals inside, there are gas pumps outside to fuel your vehicle.

A local tradition for 20 years, **Keller's Flea Market** (5901 Ogeechee Rd., I-95 exit 94, 912/927-4848, www.ilovefleas.com, Sat.-Sun. 8am-6pm, free) packs in about 10,000 shoppers over the course of a typical weekend, offering a range of bargains in antiques, home goods, produce, and general kitsch. Food and drink are available on-site.

Sports and Recreation

Savannah more than makes up for its sad organized sports scene with copious outdoor options that take full advantage of its temperate climate and the natural beauty of its marshy environment next to the Atlantic Ocean.

ON THE WATER
Kayaking and Canoeing

Maybe the single best kayak or canoe adventure in Savannah is the run across the Back River from Tybee to **Little Tybee Island,** an undeveloped State Heritage Site that despite its name is actually twice as big as Tybee, albeit mostly marsh. Many kayakers opt to camp on the island. Begin the paddle at the public boat ramp

on the Back River. To get here, take Butler Avenue all the way to 18th Street and take a right, then another quick right onto Chatham Avenue. The parking lot for the landing is a short way up Chatham Avenue on the left. Warning: Do not attempt to swim to Little Tybee, no matter how strong a swimmer you think you are—the currents are exceptionally vicious. Also, do not be tempted to walk far out onto the Back River beach at low tide. The tide comes in very quickly and often strands people on the sandbar.

One of the great overall natural experiences in the area is the massive **Savannah National Wildlife Refuge** (912/652-4415, www.fws. gov/savannah, daily dawn-dusk, free). This

30,000-acre reserve—half in Georgia, half in South Carolina—is on the Atlantic Flyway, so you'll be able to see birdlife in abundance, in addition to alligators and manatees. Earthen dikes crisscrossing the refuge are vestigial remnants of paddy fields from plantation days. You can kayak on your own, but many opt to take guided tours offered by **Wilderness Southeast** (912/897-5108, www.wilderness-southeast.org, 2-hour trips from $37.50 for 2 people), **Sea Kayak Georgia** (888/529-2542, www.seakayakgeorgia.com, $55 pp), and **Swamp Girls Kayak Tours** (843/784-2249, www.swampgirls.com, $45). To get here, take U.S. 17 north over the big Talmadge Bridge, over the Savannah River into South Carolina. Turn left on Highway 170 south and look for the entrance to Laurel Hill Wildlife Drive on the left.

Another pleasant kayaking route is the **Skidaway Narrows.** Begin this paddle at the public boat ramp, which you find by taking Waters Avenue all the way until it turns to Whitefield Avenue and then Diamond Causeway. Continue all the way over the Moon River to a drawbridge; park at the foot of the bridge. Once in the water, paddle northeast. Look for the osprey nests on top of the navigational markers in the narrows as you approach Skidaway Island State Park. Continuing on, you'll find scenic Isle of Hope high on a bluff to your left, with nearly guaranteed dolphin sightings around marker 62.

The best guided water tour in the area is Captain Rene Heidt's **Sundial Nature Tours** (912/786-9470, www.sundialcharters.com). Rene is an expert in local marine life and offers a variety of tours, including dolphin watches, fossil hunts, and trips to various barrier islands. Rates start at about $160 for two people. A great one-stop shop for local kayaking information, tours, and equipment is **Savannah Canoe & Kayak** (414 Bonaventure Rd., 912/341-9502, www.savannahcanoeandkayak.com, tours from $55/half-day), run by the husband-wife team of Nigel and Kristin Law. To rent an ocean-worthy kayak on Lazaretto Creek, stop by **North Island Surf and Kayak** (1C Old Hwy. 80,

912/786-4000, www.northislandkayak.com, Mon.-Fri. 10am-5pm, Sat.-Sun. 9am-6pm, $45), located at Tybee Marina. Reservations are recommended.

ON THE LAND
Golf
There are a couple of strong public courses in Savannah that are also very good bargains. Chief among these has to be the **Henderson Golf Club** (1 Al Henderson Blvd., 912/920-4653, www.hendersongolfclub.com), an excellent municipal course with very reasonable greens fees (Mon.-Fri. $28, Sat.-Sun. $33) that include a half-cart. A relatively new course but not one you'd call a bargain is the **Club at Savannah Harbor** (2 Resort Dr., 912/201-2007, www.theclubatsavannahharbor.com, greens fees $135, twilight $70) across the Savannah River on Hutchinson Island, adjacent to the Westin Savannah Harbor Resort. Home to the Liberty Mutual Legends of Golf Tournament each spring, the Club's tee times are 7:30am-3pm.

Cycling
Plenty of folks ride their bikes downtown, and it is particularly enriching and fun to pedal around the squares. Legally, however, you're not allowed to ride through the squares; you're supposed to stay on the street around them. And always yield to traffic already within the square as you enter. For a guided two-hour tour of downtown, try **Savannah Bike Tours** (41 Habersham St., 912/704-4043, www.savannahbiketours.com, $15 adults, $10 under age 12), leaving every day at 9:30am, 12:30pm, and 4pm.

SPECTATOR SPORTS
Topping the list of local spectator sports is the **Savannah Sand Gnats** (912/351-9150, www.sandgnats.com, season Apr.-Sept.) baseball franchise, currently a single-A affiliate of the New York Mets. The attraction here is not the level of play but the venue itself: Grayson Stadium (1401 E. Victory Dr.) in Daffin Park in the city's midtown area, a historic venue that

SAVANNAH BASEBALL

Savannah has a long and significant history with the national pastime. In fact, the first known photograph of a baseball game was taken in Fort Pulaski, of Union occupation troops at play on the parade ground.

A pivotal figure in baseball history also has a crucial association with Savannah. Long before gaining notoriety for his role on the infamous Chicago "Black Sox" that threw the 1919 World Series, baseball legend **Shoeless Joe Jackson** was a stalwart on the South Atlantic or "Sally" League circuit. Playing for the Savannah Indians in 1909, Joe played ball predominantly at Bolton Street Park, off what's now Henry Street. After retirement Joe returned to town, began a thriving dry-cleaning business, and lived with his wife at 143 Abercorn Street and then on East 39th Street.

Another early great who played in Savannah was Georgia native Ty Cobb, who visited in 1905 with an Augusta team. He's remembered, typically enough, for getting into a fistfight with a teammate who voiced his displeasure at Cobb eating popcorn in the outfield and muffing an easy catch.

Savannah got a proper ballpark in 1926, named Municipal Stadium. After a hurricane destroyed it in 1940, rebuilding began but abruptly stopped when Pearl Harbor was attacked the next year and all the laborers rushed off to enlist. So abruptly did they drop their tools, in fact, that to this day behind third base you can still clearly see the jagged line indicating where construction halted.

The great **Babe Ruth** played in the stadium once in 1935 in his final year as a major leaguer, as his Boston Braves beat the South Georgia Teachers College (now Georgia Southern University) 15 to 1 in an exhibition game. Ruth, of course, hit a home run.

Mickey Mantle and the defending world champion New York Yankees played the Cincinnati Reds in a 1959 exhibition game in Savannah. The switch-hitting slugger hit two of his trademark mammoth home run shots during the game—both left-handed and each over 500 feet, according to witnesses.

Atlanta Braves great **Hank Aaron**, then a skinny second baseman with a Jacksonville club, played in Grayson's first game with both black and white players in 1953. Jackie Robinson stole home base in an exhibition game.

But in a way, all these names pale in comparison to one Savannah player whose influence can be felt to this day, not only in sports but in the business world at large: **Curt Flood,** who gave the world free agency. Flood, who played for the Savannah Redlegs in 1957, refused to report to the Phillies after the Cardinals traded him in 1969. Flood sued Major League Baseball the next year, saying the so-called "reserve clause" allowing the trade violated antitrust laws. While Flood would lose the lawsuit in the U.S. Supreme Court, the narrowly worded decision left the way open for collective bargaining and today's massive free agent salaries.

The **Savannah Braves**, a double-A team, began a successful run in 1971 (including a 12-game winning season by pitcher and controversial *Ball Four* writer Jim Bouton), followed in 1984 by the Savannah Cardinals.

The current single-A team, the **Savannah Sand Gnats**, had their name chosen by a poll of daily newspaper readers. While their level of play rarely conjures mental images of Shoeless Joe or the Babe, Grayson Stadium itself has just been given an impressive new facelift courtesy of the city, with a new scoreboard and upgraded seating. By far the Sand Gnats' most famous face so far has been Cy Young Award-winning pitcher Éric Gagné, who pitched his very first professional game with the local club.

has hosted such greats as Babe Ruth, Jackie Robinson, and Mickey Mantle over the years. There's not a bad seat in the house, so your best bet by far is to just buy a $7 general admission ticket. The games never sell out, so there's no need to stress. Entertainment runs the usual gamut of minor league shenanigans, including frequent fireworks displays after the games.

For sports action that's a good bit more hard-hitting and comes with a certain hipster kitsch quotient, check out the bruising bouts of the women of the **Savannah Derby Devils** (www. savannahderby.com), who bring the Roller Derby thunder against other regional teams.

They skate downtown at the Savannah Civic Center (301 W. Oglethorpe Ave., 912/651-6556), and the matches are usually quite well attended.

Accommodations

The hotel scene in Savannah, once notorious for its absurdly high price-to-service ratio, has improved a great deal in the past few years. Perhaps ironically, several stylish new downtown hotels opened concurrently with the recent economic downturn. Their appearance means increased competition, and therefore marginally lower prices, across the board. Savannah's many historic bed-and-breakfasts are competitive with the hotels on price, and often outperform them on service and ambience. If you don't need a swimming pool and don't mind climbing some stairs every now and

© JIM MOREKIS

The Bohemian is one of Savannah's favorite new hotels.

then, a B&B is usually your best bet. And the breakfasts, of course, are great too.

CITY MARKET
$150-300

Providing a suitably modernist decor to go with its somewhat atypical architecture for Savannah, the new **Andaz Savannah** (14 Barnard St., 912/233-2116, www.savannah. andaz.hyatt.com, from $200) overlooks restored Ellis Square and abuts City Market with its shopping, restaurants, and nightlife. The guest rooms and suites feature top-of-the-line linens, extra-large and well-equipped baths, in-room snack bars, and technological features such as MP3 docking stations, free Wi-Fi, and, of course, the ubiquitous flat-screen TV. Off the lobby is a very hip bar that attracts locals as well as hotel guests to enjoy its high-end, masterfully made cocktails.

WATERFRONT
$150-300

It's not exactly brand-new—it occupies the space formerly occupied by the well-regarded Mulberry Inn—but ☾ **The Brice** (601 E. Bay St., 912/238-1200, www.thebricehotel.com, $220-370) features a complete boutique-style upgrade to this historic building, which formerly housed Savannah's first Coca-Cola bottling plant, on the eastern edge of the Historic District. With great service and 145 rooms, most complete with a modernized four-poster bed, The Brice also features Pacci Italian Kitchen + Bar (breakfast daily 7am-10am, lunch daily 11am-3pm, brunch 10am-3pm Sat.-Sun., dinner 5pm-10pm Mon.-Thu. and Sun., 5pm-10:30pm Sat., $15-25), one of the better hotel restaurant/bar combos in town.

Executive chef Roberto Leoci also runs the popular Italian restaurant Leoci's Trattoria, also in the Historic District.

Although it's new, the **C Bohemian Hotel** (102 W. Bay St., 912/721-3800, www.bohemianhotelsavannah.com, $279-350) is already gaining a reputation as one of Savannah's premier hotels, both for the casual visitor as well as visiting celebrities. Located between busy River Street and bustling City Market, this isn't the place for peace and quiet, but its combination of boutique-style retro-hip decor and happening rooftop bar scene (swank and quite popular with local scenesters) make it a great place to go for a fun stay that's as much Manhattan as Savannah. Valet parking is available, which you will come to appreciate.

Over $300

For years, critics have called it an insult to architecture and to history. That said, one of the few name-brand hotels in Savannah worth the price and providing a consistent level of service is one of its original chain hotels, the **C Hyatt Regency Savannah** (2 E. Bay St., 912/238-1234, www.savannah.hyatt.com, $379). It is more than three decades old, but a competent renovation means that the Hyatt—a sort of exercise in cubism straddling an entire block of River Street—has avoided the neglect of many older chain properties downtown. While the price may seem daunting, consider the location: literally smack-dab on top of River Street, mere blocks from the bulk of the important attractions downtown and some of its best restaurants. Three sides of the hotel offer views of the bustling Savannah waterfront, with its massive ships coming in from all over the world.

HISTORIC DISTRICT
$150-300

Easily the best bed-and-breakfast for the price in Savannah is the **Green Palm Inn** (546 E. President St., 912/447-8901, www.green-palminn.com, $159-189), a folksy and romantic little Victorian number with some neat

gingerbread exterior stylings and four cute guest rooms, each named after a species of palm tree. It's situated on the very easternmost edge of the Historic District—hence it's reasonable rates—but let's face it, being right next to charming little Greene Square is far from the worst place you could be. Delightful innkeeper Diane McCray provides a very good and generous breakfast plus a pretty much constant dessert bar.

One of Savannah's original historic B&Bs, the **C Eliza Thompson House** (5 W. Jones St., 912/236-3620, www.elizathompsonhouse.com, $180-225) is a bit out of the bustle on serene, beautiful Jones Street but still close enough to get involved whenever you feel the urge. You can enjoy the various culinary offerings—breakfast, wine and cheese, nighttime munchies—either in the parlor or on the patio overlooking the house's classic Savannah garden. One of the half-dozen lodging properties owned by the locally based HLC group, the Eliza Thompson House hews to their generally high standard of service.

The circa-1896 **Foley House Inn** (14 W. Hull St., 912/232-6622, www.foleyinn.com, $199-375) is a four-diamond B&B with some guest rooms available at a three-diamond price. Its 19 individualized, Victorian-decor guest rooms, in two town houses, range from the smaller Newport overlooking the "grotto courtyard" to the four-poster, bay-windowed Essex room, complete with a fireplace and a whirlpool bath. The location on Chippewa Square is pretty much perfect: well off the busy east-west thoroughfares but in the heart of Savannah's active theater district and within walking distance of anywhere.

One of Savannah's favorite bed-and-breakfasts, **The Kehoe House** (123 Habersham St., 912/232-1020, www.kehoehouse.com, $215-315) is a great choice for its charm and attention to guests. Its historic location, on quiet little Columbia Square catty-corner to the Isaiah Davenport House, is within walking distance to all the downtown action, but far enough from the bustle to get some peace out on one of the rocking chairs on the veranda.

VICTORIAN DISTRICT
$150-300

A short walk from Forsyth Park, the **Dresser-Palmer House** (211 E. Gaston St., 912/238-3294, www.dresserpalmerhouse.com, $189-319) features 15 guest rooms in two wings but still manages to make things feel pretty cozy. Garden-level rooms go for a song (under $200).

The 1868 [(**Gastonian Inn** (220 E. Gaston St., 912/232-2869, www.gastonian.com, $245-455) got a major renovation in 2005 and remains a favorite choice for travelers to Savannah, mostly for its 17 sumptuously decorated guest rooms and suites, all with working fireplaces, and the always outstanding full breakfast. They pile on the epicurean delights with teatime, evening nightcaps, and complimentary wine. This is one of the six properties owned by the local firm HLC, which seems to have consistently higher standards than most out-of-town chains.

Over $300

How ironic that a hotel built in a former mortuary would be one of the few Savannah hotels not to have a resident ghost story. But that's the case with **Mansion on Forsyth Park** (700 Drayton St., 912/238-5158, www.mansiononforsythpark.com, $339-419), which dominates an entire block alongside Forsyth Park, including partially within the high-Victorian former Fox & Weeks Mortuary building. Its sumptuous guest rooms, equipped with big beds, big baths, and big-screen TVs, scream "boutique hotel," as does the swank little bar and the alfresco patio area. The Mansion's Addams Family decor of thick velvet and vaguely Dadaist artwork isn't for everyone, but still, it certainly beats seagulls and pink flamingos.

TYBEE ISLAND

Most of the hotels on the main drag, Butler Avenue, are what we describe in the South as "rode hard and put away wet," meaning that they see a lot of wear and tear from eager vacationers. For that reason it's difficult for me to recommend any of them in good conscience. Also be aware that any place on Butler Avenue, even the substandard places, charges a premium during the high season (Mar.-Oct.). For long-term stays, weekly rentals are the name of the game. Though not cheap—expect to pay roughly $1,000 per week in the summer—they provide a higher level of accommodations than some hotels on the island. For weekly rentals, try **Oceanfront Cottage Rentals** (800/786-5889, www.oceanfrontcottage.com), **Tybee Island Rentals** (912/786-4034, www.tybeeislandrentals.com), or **Tybee Vacation Rentals** (866/359-0297, www.tybeevacationrentals.com).

Here are a few other places that are a cut above. One of Tybee's most worthwhile lodging experiences for the money, the single-suite [(**Bluebird Bed and Breakfast** (1206 Venetian Dr., 912/786-0786, www.tybeebandb.com, $125) is tucked away on Horsepen Creek and the Back River, away from the general beach-town hubbub—but that's what makes it all the more romantic, in a whimsical sort of way. Its spacious and charming interior comprises a master bedroom, a large kitchen-den area, and a delightful breakfast nook overlooking the marsh. There's even a resident dock if you want to put in your kayak or canoe. There is a two-night minimum on weekends.

Available for daily or weekly rentals, the delightful and well-appointed upstairs apartment of **The Octopus Lair** (12th St., 912/660-7164, www.octopuslair.com, $125) is tucked away on the south side of the island, equidistant from both the beach and the more active areas. There's even a propane grill on the porch so you can cook out. Another good B&B-style experience can be found at **The Georgianne Inn** (1312 Butler Ave., 912/786-8710, $125-235), a short walk off the beach.

CAMPING

The best overall campground in town is at the well-managed and rarely crowded **Skidaway Island State Park** (52 Diamond Causeway, 912/598-2300, www.gastateparks.org, parking

$2 per vehicle per day, tent and RV sites $24, group camping $35). There are 88 sites with 30-amp electric hookups.

There's one campground on Tybee Island, the **River's End Campground and RV Park** (915 Polk St., 912/786-5518, www.cityoftybee. org, water and electric sites $34, 50-amp full hookup sites $45) on the north side. Owned by the city of Tybee Island, River's End offers 100 full-service sites plus some primitive tent sites.

Food

Although Charleston's cuisine scene is clearly a cut or two above Savannah's, the Georgia city is still a foodie's paradise, with a big-city selection of cuisine concocted by a cast of executive chefs who, despite their many personal idiosyncrasies, tend to go with what works rather than experimenting for the sake of experimentation. Here's a breakdown of the most notable offerings, by area and by type of cuisine. You'll note there's rarely a separate *Seafood* section listed; that's because seafood is an intrinsic part of most restaurant fare in Savannah, whether through regular menu offerings or through specials.

CITY MARKET
Classic Southern
Every year, thousands of visitors come to Savannah for the privilege of waiting for hours outside in all weather, the line stretching a full city block, for a chance to eat at **The Lady & Sons** (102 W. Congress St., 912/233-2600, www.ladyandsons.com, lunch Mon.-Sat. 11am-3pm, dinner Mon.-Sat. from 5pm, buffet Sun. 11am-5pm, $17-25) and sample some of local celebrity Paula Deen's "home" cooking—actually a fairly typical Southern buffet with some decent fried chicken, collard greens, and mac-and-cheese. For the privilege, you must begin waiting in line as early as 9:30am for lunch and as early as 3:30pm for dinner in order to be assigned a dining time. You almost assuredly will never see Paula, who has precious little to do with the restaurant these days.

Coffee, Tea, and Sweets
Combine a hip bar with outrageously tasty dessert items and you get **Lulu's Chocolate Bar** (42 MLK Jr. Blvd., 912/238-2012, www.lulus-chocolatebar.net, Sun.-Thurs. noon-midnight, Fri.-Sat 2pm-2am). While the whole family is welcome before 10pm to enjoy chocolate chip cheesecake and the like, after that it's strictly 21-and-over. The late crowd is younger and trendier and comes mostly for the unique specialty martinis, including the pineapple upside-down martini.

Italian
One would never call Savannah a great pizza town, but the best pizza here is **Vinnie VanGoGo's** (317 W. Bryan St., 912/233-6394, www.vinnievangogos.com, Mon.-Thurs. 4pm-11:30pm, Fri. 4pm-1am, Sat. noon-1am, Sun. noon-11:30pm, $3-13, cash only) at the west end of City Market on Franklin Square. Featuring some of the best local characters both in the dining area and behind the counter, Vinnie's is a classic Savannah hangout, due in no small part to its excellent beer selection and late hours on weekends. Their pizza is a thin-crust Neapolitan style—although the menu claims it to be New York style—with a delightful tangy sauce and fresh cheese. Individual slices are huge, so don't feel obliged to order a whole pie. The waiting list for a table can get pretty long, but take heart: Vinnie's offers free delivery throughout downtown, delivered by bicycle courier. Remember, cash only.

New Southern
Accomplishing the difficult task of being achingly hip while also offering some of the best food in town, **Sapphire Grill** (110 W. Congress St., 912/443-9962, www.sapphiregrill.com, Fri.-Sat. 5:30pm-11:30pm,

Sun.-Thurs. 6pm-10:30pm, $25-40) comes closer than any other Savannah restaurant to replicating a high-class trendy Manhattan eatery—at prices to match. With its bare stone walls, lean ambience, and romantically dark interior, you'd be tempted to think it's all sizzle and no steak. But executive chef Chris Nason, former exec at Charleston's Anson Restaurant, has a way with coastal cuisine, relying on the freshest local seafood. His classic meat dishes like lamb, filet mignon, and veal are equally skillful. The lobster bisque is a must-have.

WATERFRONT
Breakfast
If you're downtown and need something more than your hotel breakfast—and you will!—go to (**B. Matthew's Eatery** (325 E. Bay St., 912/233-1319, www.bmatthewseatery. com, Mon.-Thurs. 8am-9pm, Fri.-Sat. 8am-10pm, brunch Sun. 9am-3pm, $15), widely considered the best breakfast in the entire Historic District. The omelets—most under $10—are uniformly wonderful, and the sausage and bacon are excellent and not greasy. There is a range of healthier selections as well, and you can actually get a decent bowl of oatmeal—but I suggest something more decadent. Sunday brunch is incredible. And they don't just do breakfast—lunch sandwiches and salads are of similarly high quality, and dinner entrées (from $17) include killer osso buco, lamb, and seafood.

Classic Southern
Very few restaurants on River Street rise above tourist schlock, but a standout is **Vic's on the River** (16 E. River St., 912/721-1000, www. vicsontheriver.com, Sun.-Thurs. 11am-10pm, Fri.-Sat. 11am-11pm, $22-40). Hewing more to Charleston-style fine dining than most Savannah restaurants—with dishes like wild Georgia shrimp, stone-ground grits, and blue crab cakes with a three-pepper relish—Vic's combines a romantic old Savannah atmosphere with an adventurous take on Lowcountry cuisine. Note the entrance to the dining room is

not on River Street but on the Bay Street level on Upper Factor's Walk.

Greek
Another worthwhile place to stop for a relaxing and tasty meal on River Street is **Olympia Café** (5 E. River St., 912/233-3131, www.olympia-cafe.net, daily 11am-10pm, $15), which serves a variety of Greek dishes such as dolmades, spanakopita, seafood and lemon chicken in a friendly atmosphere. The standard menu items aren't particularly cheap, but the daily specials often offer a surprisingly good deal.

HISTORIC DISTRICT
Barbecue
A great local barbecue joint tucked away in a lane is **Angel's BBQ** (21 W. Oglethorpe Lane, 912/495-0902, www.angels-bbq.com, Tues. 11:30am-3pm, Wed.-Sat. 11:30am-6pm, $5-9), which was featured on an episode of Travel Channel's *Man v. Food*. Get there by finding Independent Presbyterian Church at the northwest corner of Chippewa Square and walking down the lane next to the church. Angel's offers a particularly Memphis-style take on barbecue, but you might try the unique house specialty, the barbecued bologna. Don't miss the peanuts-and-greens on the side. Vegetarians can opt for the "Faux-Q," barbecue-flavored tofu.

Classic Southern
The meteoric rise of Paula Deen and her Lady & Sons restaurant has only made local epicures even more exuberant in their praise for (**Mrs. Wilkes' Dining Room** (107 W. Jones St., 912/232-5997, www.mrswilkes.com, Mon.-Fri. 11am-2pm, $13), Savannah's original comfort-food mecca. President Obama's impromptu lunchtime visit with the local mayor in 2010 further raised the restaurant's already legendary profile. The delightful Sema Wilkes herself has passed on, but nothing has changed—not the communal dining room, the cheerful service, the care taken with take-out customers, and, most of all, the food—a succulent mélange of the South's greatest hits, including the best fried chicken in town, snap beans, black-eyed

SAVANNAH

© JIM MOREKIS

Angel's BBQ is hard to find, but well worth the effort.

peas, and collard greens. While each day boasts a different set menu, almost all of the classics are on the table at each meal.

Once the home of General James Habersham and the first place the Declaration of Independence was read aloud in Savannah, the **Olde Pink House** (23 Abercorn St., 912/232-4286, Sun.-Thurs. 5:30pm-10:30pm, Fri.-Sat. 5:30pm-11pm, $15-30) is still a hub of activity in Savannah, as visitors and locals alike frequent the classic interior of the dining room and the downstairs Planter's Tavern. The Pink House is known for its savvy (and often sassy) service and the uniquely regional flair it adds to traditional dishes, with liberal doses of pecans, Vidalia onions, shrimp, and crab. The she-crab soup and lamb chops in particular are crowd-pleasers, and the scored crispy flounder stacks up to similar versions of this dish at several other spots in town. Reservations are recommended.

Coffee, Tea, and Sweets

He helped produce *Mission Impossible III* and other Hollywood movies, but Savannah native Stratton Leopold's other claim to fame is running the 100-year-old family business at ◖**Leopold's Ice Cream** (212 E. Broughton St., 912/234-4442, www.leopoldsicecream.com, Sun.-Thurs. 11am-10pm, Fri.-Sat. 11am-11pm). Now in a new location but with the same delicious family ice cream recipe, Leopold's also offers soup and sandwiches to go with its delicious sweet treats. Memorabilia from Stratton's various movies is all around the shop, which stays open after every evening performance at the Lucas Theatre around the corner. You can occasionally find Stratton himself behind the counter doling out scoops.

For a more upscale take on sweets, check out the chocolate goodies at **Wright Square Cafe** (21 W. York St., 912/238-1150, Mon.-Fri. 7:30am-5:30pm, Sat. 9am-5:30pm). While they do offer tasty wraps and sandwiches, let's not kid ourselves; the draw here is the outrageous assortment of high-quality European-style brownies, cookies, cakes, and other sweet treats.

Leopold's Ice Cream is in the heart of the theater district.

French

One of only two honest-to-goodness French restaurants in town is 🄲 **Brasserie 529** (529 E. Liberty St., 912/238-0045, Tues.-Sat. 11am-3pm and 5pm-10pm, from $20). The interior is renovated in contemporary bistro. The food is splendid and authentically French in both flavor and cost. House specialties include *côtes de boeuf* (a bone-in rib eye for two), rabbit stew, and steak frites, featuring a hanger steak and the best french fries you'll ever enjoy. My favorite dish, however, is the Fish Normande, a succulently cooked piece of halibut that is the best whitefish entrée I've eaten anywhere. As mundane as this sounds after all that buildup, the fact that Brasserie 529 has a dedicated parking lot is another huge plus given the general dearth of parking spaces in downtown Savannah.

Italian

The hot Italian place in town is **Leoci's Trattoria** (606 Abercorn St., 912/335-7027, www.leocis.com, daily 11am-10pm, $10-20), named for its skillful and personable young executive chef, Roberto Leoci. His compact but diverse menu offers delights such as a crispy delicious pizza, excellent paninis, and a wild-mushroom risotto. The room is small and intimate, and the restaurant is quite popular, so a wait is not unusual.

South African

Look for the long lunchtime line outside the tiny storefront that is **Zunzi's** (108 E. York St., 912/443-9555, Mon.-Sat. 11am-6pm, $5-10). This takeout joint is one of Savannah's favorite lunch spots, the labor of love of South African expatriates Gabby and Johnny DeBeer, who've gotten a lot of national attention for their robust, rich dishes like the exquisite South African-style sausage.

VICTORIAN DISTRICT

This pretty, quiet, but up-and-coming area—occasionally referred to by the somewhat precious new term SoFo, for South of Forsyth—spans Forsyth Park south to Victory Drive (U.S. 80).

Burgers

Cozy 🄲 **Green Truck Neighborhood Pub** (2430 Habersham St., 912/234-5885, http://greentruckpub.com, Tues.-Sat. 11am-11pm, $10) earns its raves on the basis of delicious regionally sourced meat and produce offered at reasonable prices. (The large selection of craft beers on tap is a big draw too). The marquee item is the signature five-ounce grass-fed burger. A basic burger is $7, but several other, increasingly more dressed-up versions are offered, none over $12.50. Burgers are also offered with chicken or veggie patties. The salads are also particularly awesome, all with the option of an added burger, chicken, or veggie patty to any salad for $4.50 extra. It's a small room that often has a big line, and they don't take reservations, so be prepared.

Coffee, Tea, and Sweets

The coffee at **The Sentient Bean** (13 E. Park Ave., 912/232-4447, www.sentientbean.com, daily 7:30am-10pm) is all fair-trade and organic, and the all-vegetarian fare is a major upgrade above the usual coffeehouse offering. But "The Bean" is more than a coffeehouse—it's a community. Probably the best indie film venue in town, The Bean regularly hosts screenings of cutting-edge left-of-center documentary and kitsch films, as well as rotating art exhibits. When there's no movie, there's usually some low-key live entertainment or spoken word open-mike action.

Primarily known for its sublime sweet treats, **Back in the Day Bakery** (2403 Bull St., 912/495-9292, www.backinthedaybakery.com, Tues.-Fri. 9am-5pm, Sat. 8am-3pm, $7), on the southern edge of the Victorian District, also offers a small but delightfully tasty (and tasteful) range of lunch soups, salads, and sandwiches (11am-2pm). Lunch highlights are the baguette with camembert, roasted red peppers, and lettuce; and the *caprese,* the classic tomato, mozzarella, and basil trifecta on a perfect *ciabatta.* But whatever you do, save room for dessert, which runs the full sugar spectrum: red velvet cupcakes, lemon bars, macaroons, carrot cake, Cosmopolitan Cake, Nana's Pudding, and my favorite, Omar's Mystic Espresso Cheesecake.

New Southern

Before there was Paula Deen, there was Elizabeth Terry, Savannah's first well-known high-profile chef and founder of this most elegant of all Savannah restaurants, **❰ Elizabeth on 37th** (105 E. 37th St., 912/236-5547, daily 6pm-10pm, from $25). Terry has since sold the place to two of her former waiters, Greg and Gary Butch, but this restaurant has, for the most part, continued to maintain her high standards. Executive chef Kelly Yambor uses eclectic, seasonally shifting ingredients that blend the South with the south of France. Along with generally attentive service, it makes for a wonderfully old-school fine-dining experience. Reservations are recommended.

EASTSIDE
Classic Southern

Located just across the Wilmington River from the fishing village of Thunderbolt, **❰ Desposito's** (187 Old Tybee Rd., 912/897-9963, www.despositosseafood.com, Tues.-Fri. 5pm-10pm, Sat. noon-10pm, $15-25) is a big hit with locals and visitors alike, although it's not in all the guidebooks. The focus here is on crab, shrimp, and oysters, and lots of them, all caught wild in local waters and served humbly on tables covered with newspapers.

TYBEE ISLAND
Breakfast and Brunch

Considered the best breakfast in the Savannah area for 30 years and counting, **❰ The Breakfast Club** (1500 Butler Ave., 912/786-5984, http://tybeeisland.com/breakfast-club, daily 6:30am-1pm, $5-15), with its brisk diner atmosphere and hearty Polish sausage-filled omelets, is like a little bit of Chicago in the South. Lines start early for a chance to enjoy such house specialties as Helen's Solidarity, the Athena Omelet, and the Chicago Bear Burger, but don't worry—you'll inevitably strike up a conversation with someone interesting while you wait.

Casual Dining

One of Tybee's most cherished restaurants is on the north end in the shadow of the Tybee Lighthouse. Like a little slice of Jamaica near the dunes, the laid-back **North Beach Grill** (33 Meddin Ave., 912/786-4442, lunch and dinner daily, $8-17) deals in tasty Caribbean fare such as its signature jerk chicken, fish sandwiches, and, of course, delicious fried plantain, all overseen by chef-owner "Big George" Spriggs. Frequent live music adds to the island vibe.

For a leisurely and tasty dinner, try **Tybee Island Social Club** (1311 Butler Ave., 912/472-4044, http://tybeeislandsocialclub.com, Tues. 5pm-9:30pm, Wed.-Fri. noon-9:30pm, Sat.-Sun. 11:30am-10pm, brunch Sun. 11:30am-2pm, $15). Their menu is somewhat unusual for this seafood-heavy island: Primarily an assortment of gourmet-ish tacos, including fish, duck, and lime- and tequila-marinated steak, all under $10 each. The beer and wine list is accomplished, and the live entertainment usually very good—which is fortunate, since the service here can be on the slow side.

Known far and wide for its sublime pizza is ⓒ **Huca Poo's Bites & Booze** (1213 E. U.S. 80, 912/786-5900, http://hucapoos.com, daily 11am-11pm, $10). Individual slices run about four bucks, can easily feed two, and are quite delicious. Out of the tourist ruckus and tucked away within a small shopping center just as you arrive onto Tybee proper, Huca Poo's also has a lively bar scene.

Set in a large former fishing camp overlooking Chimney Creek, **The Crab Shack** (40 Estill Hammock Rd., 912/786-9857, www.thecrabshack.com, Mon.-Thurs. 11:30am-10pm, Fri.-Sun. 11:30am-11pm, $6-30) is a favorite local seafood place and also something of an attraction in itself. Don't expect gourmet fare or quiet seaside dining; the emphasis is on mounds of fresh, tasty seafood, heavy on the raw-bar action. Getting there is a little tricky: Take U.S. 80 to Tybee, cross the bridge over Lazaretto Creek, and begin looking for Estill Hammock Road to Chimney Creek on the right. Take Estill Hammock Road and veer right. After that, it's hard to miss.

Information and Services

VISITORS CENTERS

The main clearinghouse for visitor information is the downtown **Savannah Visitors Center** (301 MLK Jr. Blvd., 912/944-0455, Mon.-Fri. 8:30am-5pm, Sat.-Sun. and holidays 9am-5pm). The newly revitalized Ellis Square features a small visitors kiosk (Mon.-Fri. 8am-6pm), at the northwest corner of the square, with public restrooms and elevators to the underground parking garage beneath the square.

Other visitors centers in the area include the **River Street Hospitality Center** (1 River St., 912/651-6662, daily 10am-10pm), the **Tybee Island Visitors Center** (S. Campbell Ave. and U.S. 80, 912/786-5444, daily 9am-5:30pm), and the **Savannah Airport Visitors Center** (464 Airways Ave., 912/964-1109, daily 10am-6pm).

Visit Savannah (101 E. Bay St., 877/SAVANNAH—877/728-2662, www.savannahvisit.com), the local convention and visitors bureau, maintains a list of lodgings on its website.

HOSPITALS

Savannah has two very good hospital systems. Centrally located near midtown, **Memorial Health University Hospital** (4700 Waters Ave., 912/350-8000, www.memorialhealth.com) is the region's only Level I Trauma Center and is one of the best in the nation. The St. Joseph's-Candler Hospital System (www.sjchs.org) has two units, **St. Joseph's Hospital** (11705 Mercy Blvd., 912/819-4100), on the extreme south side, and **Candler Hospital** (5401 Paulsen St., 912/819-6000), closer to midtown.

MEDIA
Newspapers

The daily newspaper of record is the *Savannah Morning News* (912/525-0796, www.savannahnow.com). It puts out an entertainment insert, called "Do," on Thursday. The free weekly newspaper in town is *Connect Savannah* (912/721-4350, www.connectsavannah.com), hitting stands each Wednesday. Look to it for culture and music coverage as well as an alternative take on local politics and issues.

Two glossy magazines compete: the hipper *The South* (912/236-5501, www.thesouthmag.com) and the more establishment *Savannah* (912/652-0293, www.savannahmagazine.com).

Radio and Television

The National Public Radio affiliate is the Georgia Public Broadcasting station WSVH (91.1 FM). Savannah State University offers jazz, reggae, and Latin music on WHCJ (90.3 FM). Georgia Public Broadcasting is on WVAN. The local NBC affiliate is WSAV, the

CBS affiliate is WTOC, the ABC affiliate is WJCL, and the Fox affiliate is WTGS.

LIBRARIES

The **Live Oak Public Library** (www.liveoakpl. org) is the umbrella organization for the libraries of Chatham, Effingham, and Liberty Counties. By far the largest branch is south of downtown Savannah, the **Bull Street Branch** (222 Bull St., 912/652-3600, Mon.-Tues. 9am-8pm, Wed.-Fri. 9am-6pm, Sun. 2pm-6pm, closed Sat.). In midtown Savannah is the historic **Carnegie Branch** (537 E. Henry St., 912/231-9921, Mon. 10am-8pm, Tues.-Thurs. 10am-6pm, Fri. 2pm-6pm, Sat. 10am-6pm).

The **Georgia Historical Society** (501 Whitaker St., 912/651-2128, www.georgiahistory.com, Tues.-Sat. 10am-5pm) has an extensive collection of clippings, photos, maps, and other archived material at its headquarters at the corner of Forsyth Park in Hodgson Hall.

The **Jen Library** (201 E. Broughton St., 912/525-4700, www.scad.edu, Mon.-Fri. 7:30am-1am, Sat. 10am-1am, Sun. 11am-1am, shorter hours during school breaks), run by the Savannah College of Art and Design, features 3,000 Internet connections in its cavernous 85,000-square-foot space. Its main claim to fame is the remarkable variety of art periodicals to which it subscribes, nearly 1,000 at last count. Nonstudents can use the facility with a photo ID (you just can't check anything out).

GAY AND LESBIAN RESOURCES

Visitors often find Savannah to be surprisingly cosmopolitan and diverse for a Deep South city, and nowhere is this truer than in its sizeable and influential gay and lesbian community. In line with typical Southern protocol, the community is largely apolitical and more concerned with integration than provocation. But they're still very much aware of their growing impact on the local economy and are major players in art and commerce.

The **Savannah Pride Festival** is held every September at various venues in town. Top-flight dance-oriented musical acts perform, restaurants show off their creativity, and activists staff information booths. The chief resource for local gay and lesbian information and concerns is the First City Network, whose main website (www.firstcitynetwork. org) features many useful links, though many might find its MySpace page (www. myspace.com/firstcitynetwork) useful as well. Another great Internet networking resource is Gay Savannah (www.gaysavannah. com). For specifically gay-friendly accommodations, try the **Under the Rainbow Inn** (104-106 W. 38th St., 912/790-1005, www. under-the-rainbow.com, $109-155), a great B&B in the historic Thomas Square district, a former streetcar suburb of Savannah.

Getting There and Around

BY AIR

Savannah is served by the fairly new and efficient **Savannah/Hilton Head International Airport** (SAV, 400 Airways Ave., 912/964-0514, www.savannahairport.com), directly off I-95 at exit 104. The airport is about 20 minutes from downtown Savannah and an hour from Hilton Head Island. Airlines with routes to SAV include American Airlines (www.aa.com), Delta (www.delta.com), JetBlue (www.jetblue.com), United Express (www.ual.com), and US Airways (www.us-airways.com).

Taxi stands provide taxi transportation to Savannah at the following regulated fares and conditions: The cost is $2 for the first one-sixth of a mile and $0.32 per sixth of a mile thereafter, not to exceed $3.60 for the first mile and $1.92 per mile thereafter. Waiting charge is $21 per hour. No charge for baggage. The maximum fare for destinations in the Historic District is $25.

BY CAR

Savannah is the eastern terminus of I-16, and that interstate is the most common entrance to the city. However, most travelers get to I-16 via I-95, taking the exit for downtown Savannah (Historic District). Once on I-16, the most common entry points into Savannah proper are via the Gwinnett Street exit, which puts you near the southern edge of the Historic District near Forsyth Park, or more commonly, the Montgomery Street exit farther into the heart of downtown.

Paralleling I-95 is the old coastal highway, now U.S. 17, which goes through Savannah. U.S. 80 is Victory Drive for most of its length through town; after you pass through Thunderbolt on your way to the islands area, however, including Tybee, it reverts to U.S. 80.

BY TRAIN

Savannah is on the New York-Miami *Silver Service* of **Amtrak** (2611 Seaboard Coastline Dr., 912/234-2611, www.amtrak.com). To get to the station on the west side of town, take I-16 west and then I-516 north. Immediately take the Gwinnett Street-Railroad Station exit and follow the "Amtrak" signs.

BY BUS

Chatham Area Transit (www.catchacat.org, Mon.-Sat. 5:30am-11:30pm, Sun. 7am-9pm, $1.50, includes one transfer, free for children under 41 inches tall, exact change only), Savannah's publicly supported bus system, is quite thorough and efficient considering Savannah's relatively small size. Plenty of routes crisscross the entire area.

Of primary interest to visitors is the free **Dot Express Shuttle** (daily 7am-9pm), which travels a continuous circuit route through the Historic District with 11 stops at hotels, historic sites, and the Savannah Visitors Center. The Shuttle is wheelchair-accessible.

If you're on River Street, a neat experience is to jump on the free **River Street Trolley** (www.catchacat.org, Thurs.-Sun.). This restored historical trolley moves on the old trolley lines on

River Street, and while it only goes a short distance, serving six stops, it's certainly fun.

BY RENTAL CAR

The majority of rental car facilities are at the Savannah/Hilton Head International Airport, including **Avis** (800/831-2847), **Budget** (800/527-0700), **Dollar** (912/964-9001), **Enterprise** (800/736-8222), **Hertz** (800/654-3131), **National** (800/227-7368), and **Thrifty** (800/367-2277). Rental locations away from the airport are **Avis** (7810 Abercorn St., 912/354-4718), **Budget** (7070 Abercorn St., 912/355-0805), and **Enterprise** (3028 Skidaway Rd., 912/352-1424; 9505 Abercorn St., 912/925-0060; 11506-A Abercorn Expressway, 912/920-1093; 7510 White Bluff Rd., 912/355-6622).

BY TAXI

Taxi services in Georgia tend to be less regulated than in other states, but service is plentiful in Savannah. The chief local provider is **Yellow Cab** (866/319-9646, www.savannahyellowcab.com). Other providers include **Adam Cab** (912/927-7466), **Magikal Taxi Service** (912/897-8294), and **Sunshine Cab** (912/272-0971).

If you're not in a big hurry, it's always fun to take a **Savannah Pedicab** (912/232-7900, www.savannahpedicab.com) for quick trips around downtown. Your friendly driver will pedal one or two passengers anywhere within the Historic District for a reasonable price.

PARKING

Parking is at a premium in downtown Savannah. Traditional coin-operated meter parking is available throughout the city, but more and more the city is going to self-pay kiosks where you purchase a stamped receipt to display inside your car's dashboard. The city operates several parking garages at various rates and hours: the **Bryan Street Garage** (100 E. Bryan St.), the **Robinson Garage** (132 Montgomery St.), the **State Street Garage** (100 E. State St.), the **Liberty Street Garage** (401 W. Liberty St.), and the new **Whitaker Street Garage** underneath revitalized Ellis Square.

Outside Savannah

As is the case with Charleston, Savannah's outlying areas still bear the indelible marks of the plantation era. The marsh still retains traces of the old paddy fields, and the economics of the area still retain a similar sense of class and racial stratification. While history is no less prominent, it is more subtle in these largely semirural areas, and the tourist infrastructure is much less well-developed than Savannah proper. This area contains some of the most impoverished communities in Georgia, so keep in mind that the locals may have more on their minds than keeping you entertained—though certainly at no point will their Southern manners fail them. And also keep in mind that you are traveling in one of the most unique ecosystems in the country, and natural beauty is never far away.

MIDWAY AND LIBERTY COUNTY

In seeking to pacify the local Creek people, the Council of Georgia in 1752 granted a group of Massachusetts Puritans then residing in Dorchester, South Carolina, a 32,000-acre land grant as incentive to move south. After moving into Georgia and establishing New Dorchester, they soon founded a nearby settlement known as Midway. Midway's citizens were aggressive early on in the cause for American independence, which is why the area's three original parishes were combined and named Liberty County in 1777.

Sights

Tourism in this area has been made much more user-friendly by the liberal addition of signage for the "Liberty Trail," a collection of key attractions. When in doubt, follow the signs.

In Midway proper is the charming **Midway Museum** (U.S. 17, 912/884-5837, www.themidwaymuseum.org, Tues.-Sat. 10am-4pm, $3) and the adjacent **Midway Church,** sometimes called the Midway meetinghouse. The

museum contains a variety of artifacts, most from the 18th and 19th centuries. The Midway Church, built in 1756, was burned during the Revolution but rebuilt in 1792. Both Button Gwinnett and Lyman Hall attended services here, and during the Civil War some of General Sherman's cavalry set up camp. The cemetery across the street is wonderfully poignant. The museum, church, and cemetery are easy to find: take exit 76 from I-95 south, and take a right on U.S. 84 (Oglethorpe Hwy.). Turn right on U.S. 17, and they're just ahead on the right.

Farther west off Islands Highway is **Seabrook Village** (660 Trade Hill Rd., 912/884-7008, www.discoverlibertyga.com, Tues.-Sat. 10am-4pm, $3), a unique living-history museum chronicling the everyday life of Liberty County's African Americans, with a direct link to Sherman's famous "40 acres and a mule" Field Order No. 15.

Built to defend the once-proud port of Sunbury, **Fort Morris State Historic Site** (2559 Ft. Morris Rd., 912/884-5999, www.gastateparks.org/info/ftmorris, Tues.-Sat. 9am-5pm, Sun. 2pm-5:30pm, $3) was reconstructed during the War of 1812 and was an encampment during the Civil War. It was here that Colonel John McIntosh gave his famous reply to the British demand for his surrender: "Come and take it." The museum has displays of military and everyday life of the era. Reenactments and cannon firings are highlights. To get here, take exit 76 from I-95 south. Go east on Islands Highway and take a left on Fort Morris Road; the site is two miles along.

Accommodations and Food

While industry is coming quickly to Liberty County, it's still a small self-contained community with not much in the way of tourism amenities (many would say that is part of its charm). A great choice for a stay is **(Dunham Farms** (5836 Islands Hwy., Midway,

SAVANNAH

© JIM MOREKIS

reenactors at Fort Morris

912/880-4500, www.dunhamfarms.com). The B&B ($165-205) is in the converted 1940s Palmyra Barn, and the self-catered circa-1840 Palmyra Cottage ($300) nearby is right on the river, with plenty of kayaking and hiking opportunities. Your hosts, Laura and Meredith Devendorf, couldn't be more charming or informed about the area, and the breakfasts are absurdly rich and filling in that hearty and deeply comforting Southern tradition.

Restaurants of note include the **Sunbury Crab Company** (541 Brigantine Dunmore Rd., Midway, 912/884-8640, lunch Sat.-Sun., dinner Wed.-Sun., $10-30), providing, you guessed it, great crab cakes in a casual atmosphere on the Midway River. Get here by taking Highway 38 east of Midway and then a left onto Fort Morris Road. Many locals eat at least once a week at **Holton's Seafood** (13711 E. Oglethorpe Hwy., Midway, 912/884-9151, daily lunch and dinner, $7-17), an unpretentious and fairly typical family-run fried seafood place just off I-95 at the Midway exit.

NEW EBENEZER

Few people visit New Ebenezer today, west of Savannah in Effingham County. Truth is, there's not much there anymore except for one old church. But, oh, what a church. The **Jerusalem Evangelical Lutheran Church** (2966 Ebenezer Rd., Rincon, 912/754-3915, www.effga.com/jerusalem) hosts the oldest continuous congregation in the United States. Built of local clay brick in 1769, its walls are 21 inches thick. Some original panes of glass remain, and its European bells are still rung before each service (Sun. 11am). Several surrounding structures are also heirs to New Ebenezer's Salzburg legacy. Around the corner from the church is a much newer spiritually themed site, the **New Ebenezer Retreat and Conference Center** (2887 Ebenezer Rd., Rincon, 912/754-9242, www.newebenezer. org). Built in 1977, the Retreat provides acres of calm surroundings, lodging, and meals in an ecumenical Christian setting.

Scenic blackwater **Ebenezer Creek** is best experienced by putting in at the

NEW EBENEZER AND THE SALZBURGERS

Perhaps the most unsung chapter in Europe's great spiritual diaspora of the 1700s, the Salzburgers of New Ebenezer–a thrifty, peaceful, and hard-working people–were Georgia's first religious refugees and perhaps the most progressive as well. The year after Oglethorpe's arrival, a contingent of devout Lutherans from Salzburg in present-day Austria arrived after being expelled from their home country for their beliefs. Oglethorpe, mindful of Georgia's mission to provide sanctuary for persecuted Protestants and also wishing for a military buffer to the west, eagerly welcomed them. Given land about 25 miles west of Savannah, the Salzburgers named their first settlement Ebenezer ("stone of help" in Hebrew). Disease prompted them to move the site to better land nearer to the river and call it–in pragmatic Germanic style–New Ebenezer, and so it remains to this day.

Because they continued to speak German instead of English, the upriver colony maintained its isolation. Still, the Salzburgers were among Oglethorpe's most ardent and loyal supporters. Their pastor and de facto political leader, Johann Martin Boltzius, seeking to build an enlightened agrarian utopia of small farmers, was an outspoken foe of slavery and the exploitative plantation system of agriculture. His system largely worked: The fragile silk industry thrived in New Ebenezer while it had failed miserably in Savannah, and the nation's first rice mill was built here. However, don't get the idea that the Salzburgers were all work and no play. They en-

joyed their beer–so much so that Oglethorpe was forced to send regular shipments, rationalizing that "cheap beer is the only means to keep rum out."

For 10 years, Georgia hosted another progressive Lutheran sect, the Moravians, whom John Wesley called the only genuine Christians he'd ever met. Despite their professed pacifism, however, they had to leave New Ebenezer because they didn't get along with the Salzburgers, and their communal living arrangements led to internal discord.

The Trustees' turnover of Georgia back to the crown in 1750 signaled the final victory of pro-slavery forces–so much so that even Pastor Boltzius acquired a couple of slaves as domestic servants. New Ebenezer's influence began a decline that rapidly accelerated when British forces pillaged much of the town in the Revolution, even burning pews and Bibles. Fifty years later, nothing at all remained except the old Jerusalem Church, now the Jerusalem Evangelical Lutheran Church. Built in 1769, it still stands today and hosts regular worship services. Right around the corner is the New Ebenezer Retreat, nestled along the banks of the Savannah River, providing an ecumenical meeting and natural healing space for those of all faiths.

Although New Ebenezer is often called a "ghost town," this is a misnomer. Extensive archaeological work continues in the area, and the Georgia Salzburger Society works hard to maintain several historic buildings and keep the legacy alive through special events.

private Ebenezer Landing ($5). To get to New Ebenezer, take exit 109 from I-95. Go north on Highway 21 through Rincon, Georgia, then east on Highway 275 (Ebenezer Rd.). The New Ebenezer Retreat and Conference Center offers a range of very reasonably priced lodgings, most including meals, in a beautiful setting. The extremely fast-growing town of Rincon, through which you will most likely drive on your way to New Ebenezer, offers an assortment of the usual chain food and lodging establishments.

WASSAW ISLAND NATIONAL WILDLIFE REFUGE

Totally unique in that it's the only Georgia barrier island never cleared for agriculture or development, the 10,000-acre **Wassaw Island National Wildlife Refuge** (www.fws.gov/wassaw) is accessible only by boat. There are striking driftwood-strewn beaches, and the interior of the island has some beautiful old-growth stands of longleaf pine and live oak. Wassaw is a veritable paradise for nature lovers and bird-watchers, with migratory activity in the spring and fall, waterfowl in abundance in the summer, and manatee and loggerhead turtle activity (about 10 percent of Georgia's transient loggerhead population makes use of Wassaw for nesting).

It's easiest to get to Wassaw Island from Savannah. Charters and scheduled trips are available from **Captain Walt's Charters** (Thunderbolt Marina, 3124 River Dr., 912/507-3811, www.waltsadventure.com/charters), the **Bull River Marina** (8005 E. U.S. 80, 912/897-7300), **Delegal Marina** (1 Marina Dr., 912/598-0023), **Captain Joe Dobbs** (Delegal Marina, 1 Marina Dr., 912/598-0090, www.captjdobbs.com), and **Isle of Hope Marina** (50 Bluff Dr., 912/354-8187, www.isleofhope-marina.com). There's no camping allowed on Wassaw Island; it's for day use only.

THE GOLDEN ISLES

More than any other area in the region, the Georgia coast retains a timeless mystique evocative of a time before the coming of Europeans, even before humankind itself. They're called the Golden Isles because of the play of the afternoon sun on the vistas of marsh grass; another nickname, "the Debatable Land," is a nod to a centuries-long role as a constantly shifting battleground of European powers.

On the map it looks relatively short, but Georgia's coastline is the longest contiguous salt marsh environment in the world—a third of the country's remaining salt marsh. Ancient Native Americans held the area in special regard, intoxicated not only by the easy sustenance it offered but its spiritual solace. Avaricious for gold as they were, the Spanish also admired the almost monastic enchantment of Georgia's coast, choosing it as the site of their first colony in North America. Their subsequent chain of Roman Catholic missions are now long gone but certainly testified to their quest here.

HISTORY

For over 5,000 years, the Golden Isles of what would become Georgia were an abundant food and game source for Native Americans. But all that changed in 1526 when the Golden Isles became the site of the first European settlement in what is now the continental United States, the fabled San Miguel de Gualdape, founded nearly a century before the first English settlements in Virginia. San Miguel disintegrated within a couple of months, but it set the stage for

© JIM MOREKIS

THE GOLDEN ISLES

HIGHLIGHTS

■ **Jekyll Island Historic District:** Relax and soak in the salty breeze at this onetime playground of the country's richest people (page 685).

■ **The Village:** The center of social life on St. Simons Island has shops, restaurants, a pier, and a beachside playground (page 693).

■ **Fort Frederica National Monument:** This tabby fortress from the first days of English settlement in Georgia is excellently preserved (page 694).

■ **Harris Neck National Wildlife Refuge:** This former wartime airfield is now one of the East Coast's best birding locations (page 698).

■ **Cumberland Island National Seashore:** Wild horses—such as the ones that live here—might not be able to drag you off this evocative, undeveloped island paradise (page 705).

LOOK FOR ■ TO FIND RECOMMENDED SIGHTS, ACTIVITIES, DINING, AND LODGING.

a lengthy Spanish presence on the Georgia coast that culminated in the mission period (1580-1684). The missions began retreating with the English incursion into the American Southeast in the 1600s.

Sherman's March to the Sea came down as far as Darien, a once-vital trading port that was burned to the ground by Union troops. With slavery gone and the plantation system in disarray, the coast's African American population was largely left to its own devices. Although the famous "40 acres and a mule" land and wealth redistribution plan for freed slaves was not to see fruition, the black population of Georgia's Sea Islands, like that of South Carolina's, developed an inward-looking culture that persists to this day. The generic term for this culture is Gullah, but in Georgia you'll also hear it referred to as Geechee, local dialect for the nearby Ogeechee River.

PLANNING YOUR TIME

Generally speaking, the peak season in this area is March-Labor Day. With the exception of some resort accommodations on St. Simons Island, Little St. Simons Island, and Sea Island, lodging is generally far more affordable than up the coast in either Savannah or Charleston.

Many travelers take I-95 south from Savannah to the Golden Isles, but U.S. 17 roughly parallels the interstate—in some cases

THE
GOLDEN
ISLES

SMALLEST CHURCH
IN NORTH AMERICA
★
South Newport

HARRIS NECK NATIONAL
WILDLIFE REFUGE

St.
Catherines
Island

Shellman
Bluff

Blackbeard
Island
NWR

Eulonia

Sapelo
Island

Sapelo Island
National
Estuarine
Research
Reserve

Meridian

Darien

BUTLER ISLAND/
ALTAMAHA WMA
★

FORT KING
GEORGE STATE
HISTORIC SITE
★

Wolf Island

Wolf Island NWR

HOFWYN-BROADFIELD
PLANTATION
★

Sterling

Little
St. Simons
Island

Waynesville

FORT FREDERICA
NATIONAL MONUMENT

Nahunta

Sea Island

Brunswick

St. Simons
Island
★

Waverly

THE
VILLAGE

JEKYLL ISLAND
HISTORIC DISTRICT

Jekyll
Island

ATLANTIC

OCEAN

St. Andrew Sound

Satilla   River

Cumberland
Island

CUMBERLAND
ISLAND NATIONAL
SEASHORE

Folkston

Crooked
River State
Park

Kingsland

GEORGIA

St. Marys River

St. Marys

Hilliard

Fernandina
Beach

FLORIDA

Yulee

Amelia
Island

Altamaha   River

Jesup

0   10 mi
0   10 km

© AVALON TRAVEL

so closely that drivers on both roads can see each other—and is a far more scenic and enriching drive.

Getting to the undeveloped barrier islands, Sapelo and Cumberland, takes planning in advance because there is no bridge to either. Both require a ferry booking and hence a more substantial commitment of time. There are no real stores and few facilities on these islands, so pack along whatever you think you'll need, including be food, water, medicine, suntan lotion, insect repellent, and so on. Sapelo Island is limited to day use unless you have prior reservations, with the town of Darien in McIntosh County as the gateway. The same is true for Cumberland Island National Seashore, with the town of St. Marys in Camden County as the gateway.

Brunswick and Glynn County

Consider Brunswick sort of a junior Savannah, sharing with that city twice its size to the north a heavily English flavor, great manners, a city plan with squares courtesy of General James Oglethorpe, a thriving but environmentally intrusive seaport, and a busy shrimping fleet. While Brunswick never became the dominant commercial center, à la Savannah, that it was envisioned to be, it has followed the Savannah model in modern times, both in terms of downtown revitalization and an increasing emphasis on port activity. Sadly, unlike Savannah, Brunswick has not seen fit to preserve the integrity of its six existing squares, all but one of which (Hanover Square) have been bisected by streets or built on.

Hit hard by the recent economic downturn, Brunswick has seen better days. Despite an admirable effort at downtown revitalization centering on Newcastle Street, most visitors to the area seem content to employ Brunswick, as its nickname implies, as a "Gateway to the Golden Isles" rather than as a destination in itself.

SIGHTS
Brunswick Historic District
Technically, Brunswick has an "Old Town" district on the National Register of Historic Places as well as an adjacent district called "Historic Brunswick" centering on the storefronts of Newcastle Street. Since it's all pretty close together, we'll consider it all one nice package. Unlike Savannah, which renamed many of its streets in a fit of patriotism after the American Revolution, Brunswick's streets bear their original Anglophilic names, like Gloucester, Albemarle, and Norwich. You'd be forgiven for thinking that Brunswick's Union Street is a post-Civil War statement of national unity, but the name actually commemorates the union of Scotland and England in 1707. Most of the visitor-friendly activity centers on **Newcastle Street,** where you'll find the bulk of the galleries, shops, and restored buildings. Adjacent in the more historic areas are some nice residential homes.

The new pride of downtown is **Old City Hall** (1212 Newcastle St.), an amazing circa-1889 Richardsonian Romanesque edifice designed by noted regional architect Alfred Eichberg, who also planned many similarly imposing buildings in Savannah. City Hall reopened in 2004 after extensive renovations, bringing back to life its great vintage fireplaces and refitting its original gaslight fixtures.

Another active restored building is the charming **Ritz Theatre** (1530 Newcastle St., 912/262-6934, www.goldenislearts.org), built in 1898 to house the Grand Opera House and the offices of the Brunswick and Birmingham Railroad. This ornate three-story Victorian transitioned with the times, becoming a vaudeville venue, then a movie house. Under the management of the Golden Isles Arts and Humanities Association since 1989, the Ritz now hosts performances, studios, an art gallery, and classes.

© AVALON TRAVEL

THE GOLDEN ISLES

© JIM MOREKIS

Lanier Oak, near the fabled Marshes of Glynn

Mary Ross Waterfront Park

This downtown gathering place at Bay and Gloucester Streets also has economic importance as a center of local economic activity—it's here where Brunswick's shrimp fleet is moored and the town's large port facilities begin. Unfortunately, nearby is a huge factory, dispensing its unpleasant odor over the waterfront 24-7. In 1989 the park was dedicated to Mary Ross, member of a longtime Brunswick shrimping family and author of the popular Georgia history book *The Debatable Land*. While the book is still a great read, sadly Ross was wrong when she wrote that the tabby ruins in the area were of Spanish origin. Devastated by the discovery that they actually dated from later and were of English construction, she vowed never to publish another word again.

At the entrance to the park is a well-done model of a Liberty ship, like the thousands that were built in Brunswick during World War II.

Lover's Oak

At the intersection of Prince and Albany Streets, you'll find the Lover's Oak, a nearly 1,000-year-old tree. Local lore tells us that it has been a secret meeting place for young lovers for centuries (though one does wonder how much of a secret it actually could have been). It's about 13 feet in diameter and has 10 sprawling limbs.

Marshes of Glynn

Amid the light industrial sprawl of this area of the Golden Isles Parkway is the interesting little **Overlook Park,** just south of the visitors center on U.S. 17—a good, if loud, place for a picnic. From the park's picnic grounds or overlook you can see the fabled Marshes of Glynn, which inspired Georgia poet Sidney Lanier to write his famous poem of the same title under the **Lanier Oak,** located a little farther up the road in the median.

Hofwyl-Broadfield Plantation

South Carolina doesn't own the patent on well-preserved old rice plantations, as the **Hofwyl-Broadfield Plantation** (5556 U.S. 17,

912/264-7333, www.gastateparks.org, Thurs.-Sat. 9am-5pm, last main house tour 4:45pm, $7 adults, $4 children), a short drive north of Brunswick, proves. With its old paddy fields along the gorgeous and relatively undeveloped Altamaha River estuary, the plantation's main home is an antebellum wonder, with an expansive porch and a nice house museum inside, with silver, a model of a rice plantation, and a slide show. There's also a nice nature trail.

William Brailsford of Charleston finished the plantation in 1807, and it soon passed into the hands of the Troup family, who expanded the holdings to over 7,000 acres. Rice finally became financially unfeasible in the early 20th century, and the plantation turned to dairy farming, a pursuit that lasted until World War II. Ophelia Troup Dent would finally will the site to the state of Georgia in 1973.

The best way to get here is by taking U.S. 17 north of Brunswick until you see the signs; the plantation entrance is on the east side of the road.

ENTERTAINMENT AND EVENTS

The **Golden Isles Arts and Humanities Association** (1530 Newcastle St., 912/262-6934, www.goldenislesarts.org) is an umbrella organization for many arts activities in the Brunswick, Jekyll, and St. Simons area. They also manage the historic **Ritz Theatre** (1530 Newcastle St., 912/262-6934) in downtown Brunswick, which offers a yearly performance season that's worth checking out if you have a free weekend night.

Nightlife

Brunswick is a conservative place with little bar scene to speak of. But a few miles offshore is quite a different story when the **Emerald Princess Dinner and Casino Cruises** (Gisco Point, 912/265-3558, www.emeraldprincess-casino.com, Mon.-Thurs. 7pm-midnight, Fri.-Sat. 11am-4pm and 7pm-1am, Sun. 1pm-6pm, $10) is operating. This is the classic gambling and party boat experience, with the action starting when the *Emerald Princess* slips into

international waters and out of domestic gambling regulations. Ten bucks for the cruise gets you a light dinner. Drinks and chips, of course, are on you. No one under age 21 is allowed, and minimum and maximum bets vary by table. Reservations are required. To get to the dock, take U.S. 17 over the massive Sidney Lanier Bridge. Take a left onto the Jekyll Island Causeway and then an immediate left onto Gisco Point Drive. Follow signs into the parking lot.

Performing Arts

Based in St. Simons Island, the **Coastal Symphony of Georgia** (912/634-2006, www.coastalsymphonyofgeorgia.org), under the baton of Vernon Humbert, plays concerts in Brunswick during its season at different venues. Check the website for details. **Art Downtown** (209 Gloucester St., 912/262-0628, www.art-downtowngallery209.com) hosts locally written shows performed by the Brunswick Actors Theatre in its black box space and showcases local visual artists in its attached Gallery 209. The **Brunswick Community Concert Association** (912/638-5616, www.brunswickcommunityconcert.org, $25 adults, $10 students) brings an eclectic variety of high-quality national and regional vocal acts to various venues. The **C.A.P.E. Theater** (916 Albany St., 912/996-7740, www.capetheater.org), short for Craft, Appreciation, Performance, and Education, is a community group that performs a mix of classics and musicals at various venues. No reservations are necessary unless you're attending a dinner theater show, which is about $30 adults, $15 students. The town's main dance group is **Invisions Dance Company,** which performs out of **Studio South** (1307 Grant St., 912/265-3255, www.studiosouthga.com).

Festivals

Each Mother's Day at noon, parishioners of the local St. Francis Xavier Church hold the **Our Lady of Fatima Processional and Blessing of the Fleet** (www.brunswick.net), begun in 1938 by the local Portuguese fishing community.

After the procession, at about 3pm at Mary Ross Waterfront Park, comes the actual blessing of the shrimp-boat fleet.

Foodies will enjoy the **Brunswick Stewbilee** ($9 adults, $4 children), held on the second Saturday in October 11:30am-3pm. Pro and amateur chefs match skills in creating the local signature dish and vying for the title of "Brunswick Stewmaster." There are also car shows, contests, displays, and much live music.

SHOPPING

Right in the heart of the bustle on Newcastle is a good indie bookstore, **Hattie's Books** (1531 Newcastle St., 912/554-8677, www.hatties-books.net, Mon.-Fri. 10am-5:30pm, Sat. 10am-4pm). Not only do they have a good selection of local and regional authors, you can also get a good cup of coffee.

Like Beaufort, South Carolina, Brunswick has made the art gallery a central component of its downtown revitalization, with nearly all of them on Newcastle Street. Near Hattie's you'll find the eclectic **Kazuma Gallery** (1523 Newcastle St., 912/279-0023, Mon.-Fri. 10am-5:30pm, Sat. 10am-2pm) as well as the **Ritz Theatre** (1530 Newcastle St., 912/262-6934, Tues.-Fri. 9am-5pm, Sat. 10am-2pm), which has its own art gallery inside. Farther down is **The Gallery on Newcastle Street** (1626 Newcastle St., 912/554-0056, Thurs.-Sat. 11am-5pm), showcasing the original oils of owner Janet Powers.

SPORTS AND RECREATION
Hiking, Biking, and Bird-Watching
As one of the Colonial Coast Birding Trail sites, **Hofwyl-Broadfield Plantation** (5556 U.S. 17, 912/264-7333, www.gastateparks.org, Thurs.-Sat. 9am-5pm) offers a great nature trail along the marsh. Clapper rails, marsh wrens, and a wide variety of warblers come through the site regularly.

Birders and hikers will also enjoy the **Earth Day Nature Trail** (1 Conservation Way, 912/264-7218), a self-guided, fully accessible walk where you can see such comparative rarities as the magnificent wood stork and

other indigenous and migratory waterfowl. There are observation towers and binoculars available for checkout. To get here, take U.S. 17 south through Brunswick. Just north of the big Sidney Lanier Bridge, turn left on Conservation Way; you'll see signage and come to a parking lot.

Kayaking and Boating
Most recreational adventurers in the area prefer to launch from St. Simons Island. The key public landing in Brunswick, however, is **Brunswick Landing Marina** (2429 Newcastle St., 912/262-9264). You can also put in at the public boat ramps at **Blythe Island Regional Park,** which is on the Brunswick River, or the **Altamaha Park of Glynn County** (1605 Altamaha Park Rd., 912/264-2342), on the Altamaha River slightly north.

For expert guided tours at a reasonable price, check out **South East Adventures** (1200 Glynn Ave./U.S. 17, 912/265-5292, www.southeastadventure.com), which has a dock right on the fabled "Marshes of Glynn."

ACCOMMODATIONS
In addition to the usual variety of chain hotels—most of which you should stay far away from—there are some nice places to stay in Brunswick, if you want to make it a base of operations, at very reasonable prices. In the heart of Old Town in a gorgeous Victorian is the **◖ McKinnon House** (1001 Egmont St., 912/261-9100, www.mckinnonhousebandb.com, $125), which had a cameo role in the 1974 film *Conrack*. Today, this bed-and-breakfast is Jo Miller's labor of love, a three-suite affair with some plush interiors and an exterior that is one of Brunswick's most photographed spots. Surprisingly affordable for its elegance, the **WatersHill Bed & Breakfast** (728 Union St., 912/264-4262, www.watershill.com, $100) serves a full breakfast and offers a choice of five themed suites, such as the French country Elliot Wynell Room or the large Mariana Mahlaney Room, way up in the restored attic.

The most unique lodging in the area is the

BRUNSWICK STEW

Of course, Virginians being Virginians, they'll insist that the distinctive Southern dish known as Brunswick stew was named for Brunswick County, Virginia, in 1828, where a political rally featured stew made from squirrel meat. But all real Southern foodies know the dish is named for Brunswick, Georgia. Hey, there's a plaque to prove it in downtown Brunswick—although it says the first pot was cooked on July 2, 1898, on St. Simons Island, not in Brunswick at all. However, I think we can all agree that "Brunswick stew" rolls off the tongue much more easily than "St. Simons stew."

In any case, it seems likely that what we now know as Brunswick Stew is based on an old colonial recipe, adapted from Native Americans, that relied on the meat of small game—originally squirrel or rabbit but nowadays mostly chicken or pork—along with vegetables like corn, onions, and okra simmered over an open fire. Today, this tangy, thick, tomato-based delight is a typical accompaniment to barbecue along the Lowcountry and Georgia coasts, as well as a freestanding entrée on its own. Done traditionally and correctly, a proper pot of Brunswick Stew is an involved kitchen project taking most of a day, but it's worth it. Here's a typical recipe from Glynn County, home of the famous Brunswick Stewbilee festival held the second Saturday of October:

SAUCE
Melt ¼ cup butter over low heat, then add:
1¾ cups ketchup
¼ cup yellow mustard
¼ cup white vinegar
Blend until smooth, then add:
½ tablespoon chopped garlic
1 teaspoon ground black pepper
½ teaspoon crushed red pepper
½ ounce Liquid Smoke
1 ounce Worcestershire sauce
1 ounce hot sauce
½ tablespoon fresh lemon juice
Blend until smooth, then add:
¼ cup dark brown sugar

Stir constantly and simmer for 10 minutes, being careful not to boil. Set aside.

STEW
Melt ¼ pound butter in a two-gallon pot, then add:
3 cups diced small potatoes
1 cup diced small onion
2 14½-ounce cans chicken broth
1 pound baked chicken
8-10 ounces smoked pork
Bring to a boil, stirring until potatoes are nearly done, then add:
1 8½-ounce can early peas
2 14½-ounce cans stewed tomatoes
1 16-ounce can baby lima beans
¼ cup Liquid Smoke
1 14½-ounce can creamed corn
Stir in sauce. Simmer slowly for two hours. Makes one gallon of Brunswick Stew.

The first Brunswick Stew was cooked in this pot.

© JIM MOREKIS

THE GOLDEN ISLES

◀ **Hostel in the Forest** (U.S. 82, 912/264-9738, www.foresthostel.com, $25 pp, cash only), essentially a group of geodesic domes and whimsical tree houses a little way off the highway. Formed over 30 years ago as an International Youth Hostel, the place initially gives off a hippie vibe, with an evening communal meal (included in the rates) and a near-total ban on cell phones. There's even a sweat lodge. But don't expect a wild time: No pets are allowed, the hostel discourages young children, and quiet time is strictly enforced at 11pm. To reach the hostel, take I-95 exit 29 and go west for two miles. Make a U-turn at the intersection at mile marker 11. Continue east on U.S. 82 for 0.5 miles. Look for a dirt road on the right with a gate and signage.

FOOD

Brunswick isn't known for its breadth of cuisine options, and, frankly, most discriminating diners make the short drive over the causeway to St. Simons Island. One exception in Brunswick that really stands out, however, is **Indigo Coastal Shanty** (1402 Reynolds St., 912/265-2007, www.indigocoastalshanty.com, Tue.-Fri. 11am-3pm, Fri.-Sat. also open 5pm-10pm, $12). This friendly, smallish place specializes in creative coastal themes, with dishes like the Charleston Saute (shrimp and ham with peppers), Fisherman's Bowl (shrimp and fish in a nice broth), and even that old Southern favorite, a pimento cheeseburger.

INFORMATION AND SERVICES

The **Brunswick-Golden Isles Visitors Center** (2000 Glynn Ave., 912/264-5337, daily 9am-5pm) is at the intersection of U.S. 17 and the Torras Causeway to St. Simons Island. It features the famous pot in which the first batch of Brunswick stew was cooked over the bridge on St. Simons. A downtown **information station** is in the Ritz Theatre (1530 Newcastle St., 912/262-6934, Tues.-Fri. 9am-5pm, Sat. 10am-2pm).

GETTING THERE AND AROUND

Brunswick is directly off I-95. Take exit 38 to the Golden Isles Parkway, and take a right on U.S. 17. The quickest way to the historic district is to make a right onto Gloucester Street. Plans and funding for a citywide public transit system are pending, but currently Brunswick has no public transportation.

Jekyll Island

Few places in the United States have as paradoxical a story as Jekyll Island. Once the playground of the world's richest people—whose indulgence allowed it to escape the overdevelopment that plagues nearby St. Simons—Jekyll then became a dedicated vacation area for Georgians of modest means, by order of the state legislature. Today, it's somewhere in the middle—a great place for a relaxing nature-oriented vacation with some of the perks of luxury owing to its Gilded Age pedigree.

HISTORY

In prehistoric times, Jekyll was mainly a seasonal getaway for Native Americans. The Spanish also knew it well, calling it Isla de Las Ballenas (Island of the Whales) for the annual gathering of calving right whale families directly off the coast every winter—a mystical event that happens to this day. After securing safe access to the island from the Creek people in 1733, Georgia's founder, General James Oglethorpe, gave the island its modern name, after his friend Sir Joseph Jekyll.

As a home away from home for the country's richest industrialists—including J. P. Morgan, William Rockefeller, and William Vanderbilt—in the late 1800s and early 1900s, Jekyll Island was the unlikely seat of some of the most crucial events in modern American history. It was at the Jekyll Island Club that the Federal Reserve banking system was set up, in a secret convocation of investors and tycoons, in 1910. Five years later, AT&T President Theodore Vail, on the grounds of the club, would listen in on the first transcontinental phone call.

Jekyll's unspoiled beauty prompted the state legislature in 1947 to purchase the island and—ironically, considering the island's former history—declare it a totally accessible "playground" for Georgians of low to middle income (a causeway wasn't completed until the mid-1950s).

ORIENTATION

You'll have to stop at the entrance gate and pay a $6 "parking fee" to gain access to this state-owned island (bicyclists and pedestrians don't pay the fee). A friendly attendant will give you a map and newsletter, and from there you're free to enjoy the whole island at your leisure.

As you dead-end into Beachview Drive, you're faced with a decision to turn either left or right. Most scenic and social activity is to the north, a left turn. For more peaceful beach-oriented activity with few services, turn right and head south. One historical reason for the lesser development at the south end is the fact that segregation laws were still in effect after the state's purchase of Jekyll in 1947; African American facilities were centered on the south end, while white activities were in the north.

SIGHTS
◖ Jekyll Island Historic District

A living link to one of the most glamorous eras of American history, the Jekyll Island Historic District is also one of the largest ongoing restoration projects in the southeastern United States. A visit to this 240-acre riverfront area is like stepping back in time to the Gilded Age, with croquet grounds, manicured gardens, and even ferry boats with names like the *Rockefeller* and the *J. P. Morgan.* The Historic District essentially comprises the buildings and grounds of the old **Jekyll Island Club,** not only a full-service resort complex—consisting of the main building and several amazing "cottages" that

© AVALON TRAVEL

are mansions themselves—but a sort of living history exhibit chronicling that time when Jekyll was a gathering place for the world's richest and most influential people.

The Queen Anne-style main clubhouse, with its iconic turret, dates from 1886. Within a couple of years the club had already outgrown it, and the millionaires began building the ornate cottages on the grounds surrounding it. The Chicora cottage is gone, demolished after the supposedly accidental gunfire death of Edwin Gould in 1917, with only a hole in the ground remaining, but most of the others have been fully restored as lodgings. In 2000 a renovation took place for the most magnificent outbuilding, the 24-bedroom Crane Cottage, a Mediterranean villa that also hosts a fine restaurant. The most recent renovation was the 2010 reopening of the Indian Mound Cottage, once William Rockefeller's vacation getaway, to tours.

The **Jekyll Island Museum** (100 Stable Rd., 912/635-4036, www.jekyllisland.com, daily 9am-5pm, free), in the Historic District at the old club stables, houses some good history exhibits. The museum also provides a number of guided themed tours (daily 11am, 1pm, and 3pm, $16 adults, $8 ages 6-12) focusing on the Historic District. You can also purchase a guidebook for self-guided tours of the Historic District.

Georgia Sea Turtle Center

Within the grounds of the Historic District in a whimsically renovated historic 1903 building is the **Georgia Sea Turtle Center** (214 Stable Rd., 912/635-4444, www.georgiaseaturtlecenter.org, Mon. 10am-2pm, Tues.-Sun. 9am-5pm, $6 adults, $4 children), which features interactive exhibits on these important marine creatures, for whom Jekyll Island is a major nesting ground. Don't miss the attached rehabilitation building, where you can see the center's turtles in various states of treatment and rehabilitation before being released into the wild. Children and adults alike will enjoy this unique opportunity to see these creatures up close and learn about the latest efforts to protect them.

Driftwood Beach

Barrier islands like Jekyll are in a constant state of southward flux as currents erode the north end and push sand down the beach to the south end. Hence the creation of Driftwood Beach, as the soil erodes from under the large trees, causing them to fall and settle into the sand. In addition to a naturalist's wonderland, it's also a starkly beautiful and strangely romantic spot. The newsletter you get as you enter the island has a map with Driftwood Beach on it, but here's a tip: Drive north on Beachview Drive until you see a pullover on your right immediately after the Villas by the Sea (there's no signage). Park and take the short trail through the maritime forest, and you'll find yourself right there among the fallen trees and sand.

Horton House Tabby Ruins

Round the curve and go south on Riverview Drive, and you'll see the large frame of a two-story house on the left (east) side of the road. That is the ruins of the old Horton House, built by Jekyll's original English-speaking settler, William Horton. Horton's house has survived two wars, a couple of hurricanes, and a clumsy restoration in 1898 to its current state of preservation at the hands of the Jekyll Island Authority and various federal, state, and local partners.

ENTERTAINMENT AND EVENTS

There's no real nightlife to speak of on Jekyll, it being intended for quiet, affordable daytime relaxation. The focus instead is on several annual events held at the **Jekyll Island Convention Center** (1 N. Beachview Dr., 912/635-3400, hwww.jekyllislandconventioncenter.com), which has undergone a massive restoration to bring it in line with modern convention standards.

In the beginning of January comes one of the area's most beloved and well-attended events, the **Jekyll Island Bluegrass Festival** (www.adamsandandersonbluegrass.com). Many of the genre's biggest traditional names come to play at this casual multiday gathering. The focus

JEKYLL ISLAND'S MILLIONAIRES CLUB

After the Civil War, as the Industrial Revolution gathered momentum seemingly everywhere but Georgia's Golden Isles, a couple of men decided to do something to break the foggy miasma of Reconstruction that had settled into the area and make some money in the process. In the late 1870s, John Eugene DuBignon and his brother-in-law Newton Finney came up with a plan to combine DuBignon's long family ties to Jekyll with Finney's extensive Wall Street connections in order to turn Jekyll into an exclusive winter hunting club. Their targeted clientele was a no-brainer: the newly minted American mega-tycoons of the Industrial Age. Finney found 53 such elite millionaires willing to pony up to become charter members of the venture, dubbed the Jekyll Island Club. Among them were William Vanderbilt, J.P. Morgan, and Joseph Pulitzer. As part of the original business model, in 1886 Finney purchased the island from DuBignon for $125,000.

With the formal opening two years later began Jekyll Island's half-century as a premier playground for the country's richest citizens, centered on the Victorian winter homes, called "cottages," built by each member and preserved today in the Historic District. While it was formed as a hunt club, the Jekyll Island Club welcomed the millionaires' families. In the 1920s, the focus began shifting to golf, and you can still play a portion of the historic course at the club today. By 1900 the club's membership represented one-sixth of the world's wealth. And the word *exclusive* has never been more appropriate: Nonmembers were not allowed to enjoy the facilities, regardless of social stature. Winston Churchill and even President McKinley were refused admission.

As the mega-rich are wont to do even today, these influential men often mixed business with pleasure. In 1910, secret meetings of the so-called "First Name Club" led to the development of the Aldrich Plan, which laid the groundwork for the modern Federal Reserve System.

Under assumed names, Senator Nelson Aldrich, Assistant Treasury Secretary A. Piatt Andrew, Banker's Trust vice president Benjamin Strong, National City Bank president Frank Vanderlip, investment banker Paul Warburg, and J. P. Morgan partner Henry P. Davison came into the Club with the cover story of participating in a duck hunt. After they arrived by train at Brunswick, the stationmaster told them the cat was out of the bag and a gaggle of reporters had already gathered. But Davison took the stationmaster aside, saying, "Come out, old man, I will tell you a story." Returning a few minutes later, Davison told his colleagues, "That's all right. They won't give us away." What Davison's "story" was remains a mystery, but it must have been a pretty compelling one.

A few years later, AT&T president Theodore Vail, nursing a broken leg at his Mound Cottage on Jekyll, participated in the first transcontinental telephone call on January 25, 1915, among New York City, San Francisco, and the special line strung down the coast from New York and across Jekyll Sound to the club grounds. Also on the line were the telephone's inventor, Alexander Graham Bell, his assistant Thomas Watson, the mayors of New York and San Francisco, and President Woodrow Wilson.

The millionaires continued to frolic on Jekyll through the Great Depression, but worsening international economic conditions reduced membership, even though the cost of membership was lowered in 1933. The outbreak of World War II and the resulting drain of labor into the armed forces put a further cramp in the club's workings, and it finally closed for good in 1942. By the time prowling German U-boats began appearing off the Georgia coast, prompting island-wide blackouts, the Jekyll Island Club era already seemed like ancient history. The state would acquire the island after the war in 1947, turning the once-exclusive playground of millionaires into a playground for all the people.

THE GOLDEN ISLES

© JIM MOREKIS

Jekyll Island's Driftwood Beach

here is on the music, not the trappings, so come prepared to enjoy wall-to-wall bluegrass played by the best in the business. Keep in mind that during this weekend the island is awash in RVs from all over the country, so if you're camping, you'd better make reservations.

In September, as the harvest comes in off the boats, the **Wild Georgia Shrimp and Grits Festival** (www.jekyllisland.com, free), seeks to promote the value of the Georgia shrimping industry by focusing on how good the little critters taste in various regional recipes.

SPORTS AND RECREATION
Hiking and Biking

Quite simply, Jekyll Island is a paradise for bicyclists and walkers, with a very well-developed and very safe system of paths, totaling about 20 miles, running the entire circumference of the island, going by all major sights, including the Jekyll Island Club in the Historic District. In addition, walkers and bicyclists can enjoy much of the seven miles of beachfront at low tide.

Rent your bikes at **Jekyll Island Miniature**

Golf (100 James Rd., 912/635-2648, daily 9am-8pm, $5.25 per hour, $11.50 per day). Take a left at the dead-end after the entrance gate, then another left.

Golf and Tennis

True to Jekyll Island's intended role as a playground for Georgians of low to medium income, its golf and tennis facilities—all centrally located at the middle of the island—are quite reasonably priced. The **Jekyll Island Golf Resort** (322 Captain Wylly Rd., 912/635-2368, www.jekyllisland.com, greens fees $40-60) is the largest public golf resort in Georgia. A total of 63 holes on four courses—Pine Lakes, Indian Mound, Oleander, and Ocean Dunes (nine holes)—await. Check the website for "golf passport" packages that include local lodging.

The adjacent **Jekyll Island Tennis Center** (400 Captain Wylly Rd., 912/635-3154, $25 per hour) boasts 13 courts, seven of them lighted, as well as a pro shop (daily 9am-6pm).

If a different kind of golf is your thing, try

Jekyll Island Miniature Golf (100 James Rd., 912/635-2648, Sun.-Thurs. 9am-8pm, Fri.-Sat. 9am-10pm, $6).

Kayaking and Boating
Most kayaking activity in the area centers on St. Simons, across the sound. But **Tidelands 4-H Nature Center** (100 Riverview Dr., 912/635-5032, www.tidelands4h.org) offers a variety of Jekyll-oriented guided kayak tours and also rents kayaks and canoes March-October.

Water Parks
Summer Waves (210 S. Riverview Dr., 912/635-2074, www.jekyllisland.com, Memorial Day-Labor Day, $20 adults, $16 children under 48 inches tall) is just what the doctor ordered for kids with a surplus of energy. The 11-acre facility has a separate section for toddlers to splash around in, with the requisite more daring rides for hard-charging preteens. Hours vary, so call ahead.

Horseback Riding and Tours
Victoria's Carriages and Trail (100 Stable Rd., 912/635-9500, Mon.-Sat. 11am-4pm) offers numerous options, both on horseback as well as in a horse-drawn carriage, including carriage tours of the island (Mon.-Sat. hourly 11am-4pm, $15 adults, $7 children). There's a 6pm-8pm night ride ($38 per couple). Horseback rides include a one-hour beach ride ($55) that leaves at 11am, 1pm, and 3pm and a sunset ride (6:30pm, $65) that lasts a little over an hour. Victoria's is at the entrance to the Clam Creek Picnic Area on the north end of the island, directly across the street from the Jekyll Island campground.

The **Tidelands 4-H Center** (912/635-5032) gives 1.5- to 2-hour Marsh Walks (Mon. 9am, $5 adults, $3 children) leaving from Clam Creek Picnic Area, and Beach Walks ($5 adults, $3 children) Wednesday at 9am leaving from the St. Andrews Picnic area, and Friday at 9am from South Dunes Picnic Area.

Captain Vernon Reynolds's **Coastal Expeditions** (3202 E. 3rd St., 912/265-0392, www.coastalcharterfishing.com, $24 adults, $10 children) provides dolphin tours March-May Tuesday-Saturday at 1:30pm, and three trips daily June-August.

ACCOMMODATIONS
Under $150
The **Days Inn** (60 S. Beachview Dr., 912/635-9800, www.daysinnjekyll.com, $100) has seen a remodeling and is the best choice if budget is a concern (and you don't want to camp, that is). It has a good location on the south side of the island with nice ocean views.

$150-300
Any discussion of lodging on Jekyll Island begins with the legendary ◖ **Jekyll Island Club** (371 Riverview Dr., 800/535-9547, www.jekyllclub.com, $199-490), which is reasonably priced considering its history, postcard-perfect setting, and delightful guest rooms. Some of its 157 guest rooms in the club and annex areas are available for under $200, and even the finest, the Presidential Suite, tops out at under $500 in high season (Mar.-Oct.). There are 60 guest rooms in the main club building and several outlying cottages. All rates include use of the big outdoor pool overlooking the river, and a neat amenity is a choice of meal plans for an extra daily fee.

The first new hotel on the island in 35 years, ◖ **Hampton Inn & Suites Jekyll Island** (200 S. Beachview Dr., 912/635-3733, www.hamptoninn.com, $180-210) was built according to an exacting set of conservation guidelines, conserving much of the original tree canopy and various low-impact design and building techniques. Quite simply, it's one of the best ecofriendly hotel designs I've experienced. An elevated wooden walkway to the beach preserves as much of the natural dune-scape as possible, though keep in mind that the tradeoff is that you can't see the ocean from the hotel.

Camping
One of the niftiest campgrounds in the entire area is the **Jekyll Island Campground** (197 Riverview Dr., 912/635-3021, tent sites $25, RV sites $32). It's a friendly place with

an excellent location at the north end of the island—a short drive or bicycle ride from just about anywhere and directly across the street from the Clam Creek Picnic Area, with easy beach access. There are more than 200 sites, from tent to full-service pull-through RV sites. There's a two-night minimum on weekends and a three-night minimum on holiday and special-event weekends; reservations are recommended.

FOOD

Cuisine offerings are few and far between on Jekyll. I'd suggest you patronize one of the three dining facilities at the **Jekyll Island Club** (371 Riverview Dr.), which are all open to nonguests. They're not only delicious but pretty reasonable as well, considering the swank setting. My favorite is the **Courtyard at Crane** (912/635-2400, lunch Sun.-Fri. 11am-4pm, Sat. 11am-2pm, dinner Sun.-Thurs. 5:30pm-9pm, $27-38). In the beautifully restored circa-1917 Crane

Cottage, one of the old tycoon villas, the Courtyard offers romantic evening dining (call for reservations) as well as tasty and stylish lunch dining in the alfresco courtyard area or inside. The lunch menu—a great deal for the quality—is Mediterranean-heavy, with wraps, sandwiches, and soups. The dinner menu moves more toward wine-country casual chic, with a lot of pork, veal, and beef dishes to go with the requisite fresh seafood. As a plus, the coffee is great—not at all a given in Southern restaurants. Casual dress is OK.

For a real and figurative taste of history, make a reservation at the **Grand Dining Room** (912/635-2400, breakfast Mon.-Sat. 7am-11am, Sun. 7am-10am, lunch Mon.-Sat. 11:30am-2pm, brunch Sun. 10:45am-2pm, dinner daily 6pm-10pm, dinner $26-35), the club's full-service restaurant. Focusing on continental cuisine—ordered either à la carte or as a prix fixe "sunset dinner"—the Dining Room features a pianist each evening

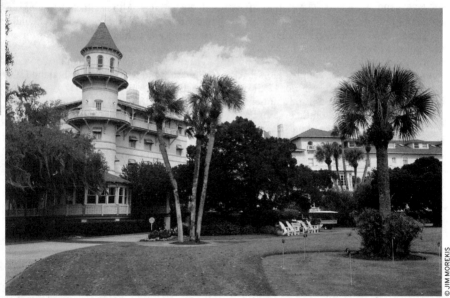

Jekyll Island Club

© JIM MOREKIS

and for Sunday brunch. Jackets or collared shirts are required for men.

INFORMATION AND SERVICES

The **Jekyll Island Visitors Center** (901 Downing Musgrove Causeway, 912/635-3636, daily 9am-5pm) is on the long causeway along the marsh before you get to the island. Set in a charming little cottage it shares with the Georgia State Patrol, the center has a nice gift shop and loads of brochures on the entire Golden Isles region. Don't hesitate to ask questions of the person taking your entrance fee when you get to the island itself.

GETTING THERE AND AROUND

Jekyll Island is immediately south of Brunswick. Take I-95 exit 38 to the Golden Isles Parkway. Take a right onto U.S. 17 and keep going until you cross the huge Sidney Lanier Bridge over the Brunswick River. Take an immediate left at the foot of the bridge onto the Downing Musgrove Causeway (Jekyll Island Rd.). This long, scenic route over the beautiful marshes eventually takes you directly onto Jekyll, where you'll have to pay a $6 per vehicle fee to get onto the island. Once on the island, most sites are on the north end (a left as you reach the dead-end at Beachview Dr.). The main circuit route around the island is Beachview Drive, which suitably enough changes into Riverview Drive as it rounds the bend to landward at the north end.

Many visitors choose to bicycle around the island once they're here, which is certainly the best way to experience both the sights and the beach itself at low tide.

St. Simons Island

Despite a certain reputation for aloof affluence, the truth is that St. Simons Island is also very visitor-friendly, and there's more to do here than meets the eye. Think of St. Simons—with a year-round population of about 13,000—as a smaller, less-hurried Hilton Head and you've got the right idea. For those looking for island-style relaxation with no high-rise cookie-cutter development—but still all the modern amenities and luxuries—St. Simons fits the bill perfectly. A major difference from Hilton Head is that St. Simons respects much of its history, and a lot of it is still left to enjoy, particularly the expansive and archaeologically significant Fort Frederica National Monument.

HISTORY

St. Simons Island and its much smaller, symbiotic neighbor Sea Island (originally Long Island) were well known to Native Americans as a hunting and fishing ground. Eventually the Spanish would have two missions on St. Simons. A lasting European influence didn't come until 1736 with General James Oglethorpe's construction of Fort Frederica. The fort and surrounding town was a key base of operations for the British struggle to evict the Spanish from Georgia, which culminated in the decisive Battle of Bloody Marsh south of the fort.

In the years after American independence, St. Simons woke up from its slumber as acre after acre of virgin live oak were felled to make the massive timbers of new warships for the U.S. Navy, including the USS *Constitution*. In their place was planted a new crop—cotton. The island's antebellum plantations boomed to world-class heights of profit and prestige when the superior strain of the crop known as Sea Island Cotton came in the 1820s.

The building of the first causeway in 1924 led directly to the island's resort development by the mega-rich industrialist Howard Coffin of Hudson Motors fame, who also owned nearby Sapelo Island to the north. By 1928, Coffin had completed the Sea Island

THE GOLDEN ISLES

GOLDEN ISLES ON THE PAGE

*And now from the Vast of the Lord will the
    waters of sleep
Roll in on the souls of men,
But who will reveal to our waking ken
The forms that swim and the shapes that
    creep
Under the waters of sleep?
And I would I could know what swimmeth
    below when the tide comes in
On the length and the breath of the marvel-
    ous marshes of Glynn.*

                                    –Sidney Lanier

Many authors have been inspired by their time in the Golden Isles, whether to pen flights of poetic fancy, page-turning novels, or politically oriented chronicles. Here are a few of the most notable names:

• **Sidney Lanier:** Born in Macon, Georgia, Lanier was a renowned linguist, mathematician, and legal scholar. Fighting as a Confederate during the Civil War, he was captured while commanding a blockade runner and taken to a POW camp in Maryland, where he came down with tuberculosis. After the war, he stayed at his brother-in-law's house in Brunswick to recuperate, and it was during

that time that he took up poetry, writing the famous "Marshes of Glynn," quoted above.

• **Eugenia Price:** Although not originally from St. Simons, Price remains the best-known local cultural figure, setting her *St. Simons Trilogy* here. After relocating to the island in 1965, she stayed here until her death in 1996. She's buried in the Christ Church cemetery on Frederica Road.

• **Tina McElroy Ansa:** Probably the most notable literary figure currently living on St. Simons Island is award-winning African American author Tina McElroy Ansa. Few of her books deal with the Golden Isles region, but they all deal with life in the South, and Ansa is an ardent devotee of St. Simons and its relaxed, friendly ways.

• **Fanny Kemble:** In 1834, this renowned English actress married Georgia plantation heir Pierce Butler, who would become one of the largest slave owners in the United States. Horrified by the treatment of Butler's slaves at Butler Island, just south of Darien, Georgia, Kemble penned one of the earliest anti-slavery chronicles, *Journal of a Residence on a Georgian Plantation in 1838-1839*. Kemble's disagreement with her husband over slavery hastened their divorce in 1849.

Golf Club on the grounds of the old Retreat Plantation on the south end of St. Simons Island. He would move on to develop the famous Cloisters resort on Long Island (later Sea Island) itself.

ORIENTATION

Because it's only a short drive from downtown Brunswick on the Torras Causeway, St. Simons has much less of a remote feel than most other Georgia barrier islands and is much more densely populated than any other Georgia island except for Tybee. Most visitor-oriented activity on this 12-mile-long, heavily residential island, about the size of Manhattan, is clustered at the south end, where St. Simons Sound meets the Atlantic.

The main reasons to travel north on the island are to golf or visit the historic site of Fort Frederica on the landward side.

The main roads to remember are Kings Way, which turns into Ocean Boulevard as it nears the active south end of the island, called "The Village"; Demere ("DEM-er-ee") Road, which loops west to east around the little island airport and then south, joining up with Ocean Boulevard down near the lighthouse; Frederica Road, the dominant north-south artery; and Mallory Street, which runs north-south through the Village area and dead-ends at the pier on St. Simons Sound. (You'll notice that Mallory Street is sometimes spelled "Mallery," which is actually the correct spelling of the avenue's namesake: Mallery King, child

The Village is the center of activity on St. Simons Island.

© JIM MOREKIS

of Thomas King, owner of the historic Retreat Plantation.)

SIGHTS
◖ The Village

Think of "The Village" at the extreme south end of St. Simons as a mix of Tybee's downscale accessibility and Hilton Head's upscale exclusivity. This compact, bustling area only a few blocks long offers not only boutiques and stylish cafés but vintage stores and busking musicians. It's fun to meander down Mallory Drive, casually shopping or noshing, and then make your way out onto the short but fun **St. Simons Pier** to enjoy the breeze and occasional spray coming off the sound. The long, low, sprawling building immediately to the north overlooking the expanse of Massengale Park is the old casino building, now used for local government offices and community meetings.

St. Simons Lighthouse Museum

Unlike many East Coast lighthouses, which tend to be in hard-to-reach places, anyone can walk right up to the **St. Simons Lighthouse Museum** (101 12th St., 912/638-4666, www. saintsimonslighthouse.org, Mon.-Sat. 10am-5pm, Sun. 1:30pm-5pm, $10 adults, $5 children). Once inside, you can enjoy the museum's exhibit and take the 129 steps up to the top of the 104-foot beacon—which is, unusually, still active—for a gorgeous view of the island and the ocean beyond.

The museum offers a "Family of Four" package admission ($25) for two adults and two children as well as a combo ticket to the nearby Maritime Center ($10 adults, $5 children).

Maritime Center

A short walk from the lighthouse and also administered by the Coastal Georgia Historical Society, the **Maritime Center** (4201 1st St., 912/638-4666, www.saintsimonslighthouse. org, Mon.-Sat. 10am-5pm, Sun. 1:30pm-5pm, $10 adults, $5 children) is at the historic East Beach Coast Guard Station. Authorized by President Franklin Roosevelt in 1933 and completed in 1937 by the Works Progress

Administration, the East Beach Station took part in military action in World War II, an episode chronicled in exhibits at the Maritime Center. On April 8, 1942, the German U-boat U-123 torpedoed and sank two cargo ships off the coast of St. Simons Island.

The Maritime Center offers a "Family of Four" package admission ($25) for two adults and two children as well as a combo ticket to the St. Simons Lighthouse ($10 adults, $5 children).

◖ Fort Frederica National Monument

The expansive and well-researched **Fort Frederica National Monument** (Frederica Rd., 912/638-3639, www.nps.gov/fofr, daily 9am-5pm, $3 adults, free under age 15) lies on the landward side of the island. Established by General James Oglethorpe in 1736 to protect Georgia's southern flank from the Spanish, the fort (as well as the village that sprang up around it, in which the Wesley brothers preached for a short time) was named for Frederick Louis, the Prince of Wales. The feminine suffix *-a* was added to distinguish it from the older Fort Frederick in South Carolina.

You don't just get to see a military fort here (actually the remains of the old powder magazine; most of the fort itself eroded into the river long ago); this is an entire colonial town site a mile in circumference, originally modeled after a typical English village. A self-guided walking tour through the beautiful grounds—the oak trees here have the longest, most luxurious Spanish moss I've ever seen—shows foundations of building sites that have been uncovered, including taverns, shops, and the private homes of influential citizens. Closer to the river is the large tabby structure of the garrison barracks.

Bloody Marsh Battlefield

There's not a lot to see at **Bloody Marsh Battlefield** (Frederica Rd., 912/638-3639, www.nps.gov/fofr, daily 8am-4pm, free), the site of the Battle of Bloody Marsh, but imagination fills in the gaps. Essentially just a few interpretive signs overlooking a beautiful piece of salt marsh, the site is believed to be near the place where British soldiers from nearby Fort Frederica ambushed a force of Spanish regulars on their way to besiege the fort. The battle wasn't actually that bloody—some accounts say the Spanish lost only seven men—but the stout British presence convinced the Spanish to leave St. Simons a few days later, never again to project their once-potent military power that far north in the New World.

While the Battle of Bloody Marsh site is part of the National Park Service's Fort Frederica site, it's not at the same location. Get to the battlefield from the fort by taking Frederica Road south, and then a left (east) on Demere Road. The site is on the left as Demere Road veers right, in the 1800 block.

Christ Church

Just down the road from Fort Frederica is historic **Christ Church** (6329 Frederica Rd., 912/638-8683, www.christchurchfrederica.org, daily 2pm-5pm). The first sanctuary dates from 1820, but the original congregation at the now-defunct town of Frederica held services under the oaks at the site as early as 1736. The founder of Methodism, John Wesley, and his brother Charles both ministered to island residents during 1736-1737.

The original church was rendered unusable by Union occupation during the Civil War. A handsome new church, the one you see today, was funded and built in 1883 by a local mill owner, Anson Dodge, as a memorial to his first wife.

Tours

St. Simons Island Trolley Tours (912/638-8954, www.stsimonstours.com, daily 11am, $22 adults, $10 ages 4-12, free under age 4) offers just that, a ride around the island in comparative comfort, leaving from the pier.

ENTERTAINMENT AND EVENTS
Nightlife

St. Simons is far from Charleston's or

Savannah's league when it comes to partying, but there is a fairly active nightlife scene, with a strong dose of island casual. Unlike some areas this far south on the Georgia coast, there's usually a sizeable contingent of young people out looking for a good time. The island's premier club, **Rafters Blues and Raw Bar** (315½ Mallory St., 912/634-9755, www.raftersblues.com, Mon.-Sat. 4:30pm-2am), known simply as "Rafters," brings in live music most Thursday-Saturday nights, focusing on the best acts on the regional rock circuit.

My favorite spot on St. Simons for a drink or an espresso—or a panini for that matter—is **Palm Coast Coffee, Cafe, and Pub** (316 Mallory St., 912/634-7517, www.palmcoastssi.com, daily 8am-10pm). This handy little spot, combining a hip, relaxing coffeehouse with a hearty menu of brunchy items, is in the heart of the village. The kicker, though, is the cute little bar the size of a large walk-in closet right off the side of the main room—a little bit of Key West on St Simons. Monday is open-mike night.

Inside the Village Inn is the popular nightspot the **Village Pub** (500 Mallory St., 912/634-6056, www.villageinnandpub.com, Mon.-Sat. 5pm-midnight, Sun. 5pm-10pm). Slightly more upscale than most watering holes on the island, this is the best place for a quality martini or other premium cocktail.

SHOPPING

Most shopping on St. Simons is centered in the Village and is a typical beach-town mix of hardware and tackle, casual clothing, and souvenir stores. A funky highlight is **Beachview Books** (215 Mallory St., 912/638-7282, Mon.-Sat. 10:30am-5:30pm, Sun. 11:30am-3pm), a rambling used bookstore with lots of regional and local goodies, including books by the late great local author Eugenia Price. Probably the best antiques shop in this part of town is **Village Mews** (504 Beachview Dr., 912/634-1235, Mon.-Sat. 10am-5pm).

SPORTS AND RECREATION
Beaches
Keep going from the pier past the lighthouse to find **Massengale Park** (daily dawn-dusk), with a playground, picnic tables, and restrooms right off the beach on the Atlantic side. The beach itself on St. Simons is underwhelming compared to some in these parts, but nonetheless it's easily accessible from the pier area and good for a romantic stroll if it's not high tide. There's a great playground, Neptune Park, right next to the pier overlooking the waterfront.

Kayaking and Boating
With its relatively sheltered landward side nestled in the marsh and an abundance of wildlife, St. Simons Island is an outstanding kayaking site, attracting connoisseurs from all over. A good spot to put in on the Frederica River is the **Golden Isles Marina** (206 Marina Dr., 912/634-1128, www.gimarina.com), which is actually on little Lanier Island on the Torras Causeway right before you enter St. Simons proper. For a real adventure, put in at the ramp at the end of South Harrington Street off Frederica Road, which will take you out Village Creek on the seaward side of the island.

The best kayaking outfitter and tour operator in this part of the Golden Isles is **SouthEast Adventure Outfitters** (313 Mallory St., 912/638-6732, www.southeastadventure.com, daily 10am-6pm), which also has a location in nearby Brunswick. Michael Gowen and company offer an extensive range of guided tours all over the St. Simons marsh and sound area as well as trips to undeveloped Little St. Simons Island to the north.

Hiking and Biking
Like Jekyll Island, St. Simons is a great place for bicyclists. Bike paths go all over the island, and a special kick is riding on the beach almost the whole length of the island (but only at low tide). There are plenty of bike rental spots, with rates generally $15-20 per day, depending on the season. The best place to rent bikes is **Monkey Wrench Bicycles** (1700 Frederica Rd., 912/634-5551). You can rent another kind of pedal-power at **Wheel Fun Rentals** (532 Ocean

Blvd., 912/634-0606), which deals in four-seat pedaled carts with steering wheels.

Golf and Tennis

A popular place for both sports is the **Sea Palms Golf and Tennis Resort** (5445 Frederica Rd., 800/841-6268, www.seapalms.com, greens fees $70-80) in the middle of the island, with three nine-hole public courses and three clay courts. The **Sea Island Golf Club** (100 Retreat Rd., 800/732-4752, www.seaisland.com, greens fees $185-260) on the old Retreat Plantation as you first come onto the island has two award-winning 18-hole courses, the Seaside and the Plantation. Another public course is the 18-hole **Hampton Club** (100 Tabbystone Rd., 912/634-0255, www.hamptonclub.com, greens fees $95) on the north side of the island, part of the King and Prince Beach and Golf Resort.

ACCOMMODATIONS
Under $150

A charming and reasonable place a stone's throw from the Village is **C Queens Court** (437 Kings Way, 912/638-8459, $85-135), a traditional roadside motel from the late 1940s, with modern upgrades that include a nice outdoor pool in the central courtyard area. Despite its convenient location, you'll feel fairly secluded.

One of the most interesting lodgings in the Lowcountry and Georgia coast is **Epworth by the Sea** (100 Arthur J. Moore Dr., 912/638-8688, www.epworthbythesea.org, $90-100). This Methodist retreat in the center of the island boasts an entire complex of freestanding motels and lodges on its grounds, in various styles and configurations.

You couldn't ask for a better location than the **St. Simons' Inn by the Lighthouse** (609 Beachview Dr., 912/638-1101, www.saintsimonsinn.com, $120-300), which is indeed in the shadow of the historic lighthouse and right next to the hopping Village area. A so-called "condo-hotel," each of the standard and deluxe suites at the Inn are individually owned by off-site owners—however, each guest gets full maid service and a complimentary breakfast.

$150-300

The best-known lodging on St. Simons Island is the **C King and Prince Beach and Golf Resort** (201 Arnold Rd., 800/342-0212, $249-320). Originally opened as a dance club in 1935, the King and Prince brings a swank old-school glamour similar to the Jekyll Island Club (though less imposing). And like the Jekyll Island Club, the King and Prince is also designated as one of the Historic Hotels of America. Its nearly 200 guest rooms are spread over a complex that includes several buildings, including the historic main building, beach villas, and freestanding guesthouses. Some standard rooms can go for under $200 even in the spring high season. Winter rates for all guest rooms are appreciably lower and represent a great bargain. For a dining spot overlooking the sea, try the **Blue Dolphin** (lunch daily 11am-4pm, dinner daily 5pm-10pm, $15-30). The Resort's Hampton Club provides golf for guests and the public.

Over $300

Affiliated with the Sea Island Resort, the **Lodge at Sea Island** (100 Retreat Ave., 912/638-3611, $650-2,500) is actually on the south end of St. Simons Island on the old Retreat Plantation. Its 40 grand guest rooms and suites all have great views of the Atlantic Ocean, the associated Plantation Course links, or both. Full butler service makes this an especially pampered and aristocratic stay.

FOOD

While the ambience at St. Simons has an upscale feel, don't feel like you have to dress up to get a bite to eat—the emphasis is on relaxation and having a good time.

Breakfast and Brunch

C Palmer's Village Cafe (223 Mallory St.,

912/634-5515, www.palmersvillagecafe.com, Tues.-Sun. 7:30am-2pm, $10-15), formerly called Dressner's, is right in the middle of the Village's bustle. It's one of the island's most popular places but still with enough seats so you usually don't have to wait. Sandwiches and burgers are great, but breakfast all day is the real attraction and includes lovingly crafted omelets, hearty pancakes, and a "build your own biscuit" menu.

Named for the birthday that the original three co-owners share, **Fourth of May Deli** (444 Ocean Blvd., 912/638-5444, breakfast daily 7am-1pm, lunch daily 11am-9pm, $8-20) is a popular breakfast and lunch place in the Village. Breakfast focuses on specialties like eggs benedict and huevos rancheros, along with some fantastic breakfast burritos, a comparative rarity in the South.

Seafood

Despite its somewhat unappetizing name, **Mullet Bay** (512 Ocean Blvd., 912/634-9977, daily 11:30am-10pm, $7-18) in the Village is a favorite good old-fashioned Southern seafood place, the kind where you get a big fried platter with two sides and hush puppies. A popular seafood place right in the action in the Village is **Barbara Jean's** (214 Mallory St., 912/634-6500, www.barbarajeans.com, Sun.-Thurs. 11am-9pm, Fri.-Sat. 11am-10pm, $7-20), which also has a great variety of imaginative veggie dishes to go along with its formidable seafood menu, including some excellent she-crab soup and crab cakes. They also have plenty of good landlubber treats for those not inclined to the marine critters.

Fine Dining

(J. Mac's Island Restaurant (407 Mallory St., 912/634-0403, www.jmacsislandrestaurant.com, Tues.-Sat. 6pm-9pm, $20-30) is the Village's high-end restaurant, one that wouldn't be out of place in downtown Charleston or Savannah. Owner J. Mac Mason and head chef Connor Rankin conspire to bring a fresh take on Southern and seafood classics, with adventurous entrées like seared "Creamsicle" marlin with jumbo asparagus and sweet corn puree-seared filet with gorgonzola and herb gratin.

INFORMATION AND SERVICES

The **St. Simons Visitors Center** (530-B Beachview Dr., 912/638-9014, www.bgivb.com, daily 9am-5pm) is in the St. Simons Casino Building near Neptune Park and the Village.

GETTING THERE AND AROUND

Get to St. Simons through the gateway city of Brunswick. Take I-95 exit 38 for Golden Isles, which will take you to the Golden Isles Parkway. Take a right onto U.S. 17 and look for the intersection with the Torras Causeway, a toll-free road that takes you the short distance onto St. Simons.

Immediately as you cross the Frederica River onto the island, look for a quick right onto Kings Way to take you directly to the Village area. You can also take a quick left onto Demere Road to reach Frederica Road and the more northerly portion of the island, where you'll find Fort Frederica and Christ Church.

LITTLE ST. SIMONS ISLAND

This 10,000-acre privately owned island, accessible only by water, is almost totally undeveloped—thanks to its salt-stressed trees, which discouraged timbering—and boasts seven miles of beautiful beaches. All activity centers on the circa-1917 **(Lodge on Little St. Simons Island** (1000 Hampton Point Dr., 888/733-5774, www.littlestsimonsisland.com, from $625), named by *Condé Nast Traveler* as the top U.S. mainland resort in 2007. Within it lies the famed Hunting Lodge, where meals and cocktails are served. With 15 ultra-plush guest rooms and suites in an assortment of historic buildings, all set amid gorgeous natural beauty—there are five full-time naturalists on staff—the Lodge is a reminder of what

St. Simons proper used to look like. The guest count is limited to 30 people.

Getting There and Around

Unless you enlist the aid of a local kayaking charter company, you have to be a guest of the Lodge to have access to Little St. Simons. The ferry, a 15-minute ride, leaves from a landing at the northern end of St. Simons at the end of Lawrence Road. Guests have full use of bicycles once on the island and can also request shuttle transportation just about anywhere.

SEA ISLAND

The only way to enjoy Sea Island—basically a tiny appendage of St. Simons facing the Atlantic Ocean—is to be a guest at ◖ The **Sea Island Resort** (888/732-4752, www. seaisland.com, from $700). And guests visiting now are truly lucky; the legendary facility, routinely ranked as one of the best resorts on the planet, completed extensive renovations in 2008. The rooms at the Resort's premier lodging institution, **The Cloister,** nearly defy description and the service is equally world-class, featuring 24-hour butler service in the European tradition.

Getting There and Around

Get to Sea Island by taking Torras Causeway onto the island and then making a left onto Sea Island Causeway, which takes you all the way to the gate marking the only land entrance to Sea Island.

Darien and McIntosh County

Unlike Anglophilic Savannah to the north, in 1736 Scottish Highlanders established a settlement at the mouth of the Altamaha River at the bequest of General James Oglethorpe, who wanted the tough Scots protecting his southern border. They called it Darien, honoring the failed 1697 settlement in Panama.

A prosperous rice culture grew up around the Altamaha estuary. Almost nothing from this period remains, however, because on June 11, 1863, a force of mostly African American Union troops under the command of Colonel Robert G. Shaw (portrayed in the movie *Glory*) burned Darien to the ground.

In pre-interstate highway days, U.S. 17 was the main route south to booming Florida. McIntosh County got a bad reputation for "clip joints," which would fleece gullible travelers with a variety of illegal schemes. This period is recounted in the best-seller *Praying for Sheetrock* by Melissa Fay Greene.

Right where U.S. 17 crosses the Darien River, find the **Darien Welcome Center** (U.S. 17 and Fort King George Dr., 912/437-6684, daily 9am-5pm).

SIGHTS
Smallest Church in North America

While several other churches claim that title, in any case fans of the devout and of roadside kitsch alike will enjoy the tiny and charming little **Memory Park Christ Chapel** (U.S. 17, daily 24 hours). Built in 1949 by local grocer Agnes Harper, the church—which contains a pulpit and chairs for a dozen people—was intended as a round-the-clock travelers' sanctuary on what was then the main coastal road, U.S. 17. Upon her death, Harper simply willed the church to Jesus Christ. The stained-glass windows are imported from England, and there's a guestbook so you can leave any note of appreciation. Get there by taking I-95 exit 67 and going south a short way on U.S. 17; the church is on the east side of the road.

◖ Harris Neck National Wildlife Refuge

Literally a stone's throw away from the "Smallest Church" is the turnoff east onto the seven-mile Harris Neck Road leading to

© JIM MOREKIS

Memory Park Christ Chapel, the "Smallest Church in North America"

the **Harris Neck National Wildlife Refuge** (912/832-4608, www.fws.gov/harrisneck, daily dawn-dusk, free). In addition to being one of the single best sites in the South from which to view wading birds and waterfowl in their natural habitat, Harris Neck also has something of a poignant backstory. For generations after the Civil War, an African American community struggled to eke out a living fishing and farming. But their land was taken by the federal government in World War II to build a U.S. Army Air Force base.

Now a nearly 3,000-acre nationally protected refuge, Harris Neck gets about 50,000 visitors a year to experience its mix of marsh, woods, and grassland ecosystems and for its nearly matchless bird-watching. Its former life as a military base has the plus of leaving behind a decent system of roads, many of them based on old runways. Most visitors use the four-mile "wildlife drive" to travel through the refuge, stopping occasionally for hiking or bird-watching.

Kayaks and canoes can put in at the public boat ramp on the Barbour River. Near the landing is an old African American cemetery, publicly accessible, with some charming handmade tombstones that evoke the post-Civil War era of Harris Neck before the displacement of local citizens to build the airfield.

To get here, take I-95 exit 67 and go south on U.S. 17 about one mile, then east on Harris Neck Road (Hwy. 131) for seven miles to the entrance gate on the left.

Shellman Bluff

Just northeast of Darien is the old oystering community of Shellman Bluff. It's notable not only for the stunning views from the high bluff but for fresh seafood. Go to **Shellman's Fish Camp** (912/832-4331) to put in for a kayak or canoe ride. Save room for some food; there are some great seafood places here.

To get to Shellman Bluff, take I-95 exit 67 for South Newport and get on U.S. 17 south. There are two easy ways to get to Shellman

Bluff from U.S. 17: East on Minton Road and then left onto Shellman Bluff Road, or east on Pine Harbor Road followed by an immediate left onto Shellman Bluff Road. In either case, take Shellman Bluff Road until it dead-ends, then a right onto Sutherland Bluff Drive.

Vernon Square

Right around the corner from the Welcome Center on Washington Street is Vernon Square, a charming little nook of live oaks and Spanish moss that was the social center of Darien in the town's antebellum heyday. The **Darien Methodist Church** on the square was built in 1843, damaged during the Civil War, then rebuilt in 1884 using materials from the first church. The nearby **St. Andrews Episcopal Church,** built in 1878, was once the site of the powerful Bank of Darien. Nearby is the affiliated and equally historic **St. Cyprian's Episcopal Church** (Fort King George Rd. and Rittenouse St.) built by an African American congregation and one of the largest tabby structures still in use anywhere.

Fort King George State Historic Site

The oldest English settlement in what would become Georgia, **Fort King George State Historic Site** (1600 Wayne St., 912/437-4770, www.gastateparks.org/fortkinggeorge, Tues.-Sun. 9am-5pm, $7 adults, $4 children) for a short time protected the Carolinas from attack, from its establishment in 1721 until its abandonment in 1727. In addition to chronicling the ill-fated English occupation of the area, the site also has exhibits about the indigenous Guale people, the Spanish missionary presence, and the era of the great sawmills. Fort King George holds regular reenactments, living history demonstrations, and cannon firings; go to the website for details.

To get here, take U.S. 17 to the Darien River Bridge, and then go east on Fort King George Drive. There's a bike route to the fort if you want to park in town.

Butler Island

South of Darien is the Altamaha River, Georgia's largest and only undammed river as well as one of the country's great estuarine habitats, with the second-largest watershed on the East Coast. A great way to enjoy the river ecosystem is at the **Altamaha Waterfowl Management Area** (912/262-3173, http://georgiawildlife.dnr.state.ga.us, $3). This was the site of Butler Island Plantation, one of the largest and most successful tidewater plantations in the antebellum era. (The 75-foot brick chimney just off U.S. 17 is part of an old rice mill belonging to the plantation.)

Kayaks and canoes can easily put in at the state-run landing at **Champney River Park** right where U.S. 17 crosses the Champney River. There are a variety of fish camps up and down this entire riverine system, providing fairly easy launching and recovery.

TOURS

Altamaha Coastal Tours (229 Ft. King George Rd., 912/437-6010, www.altamaha.com) is your best bet to take a guided kayak tour (from $50) or rent a kayak (from $20 per day) to explore the beautiful Altamaha River, Georgia's longest.

ACCOMMODATIONS

If you want to stay in McIntosh County, I strongly recommend booking one of the five charming guest rooms at **❰ Open Gates Bed and Breakfast** (301 Franklin St., Darien, 912/437-6985, www.opengatesbnb.com, $125-140). This lovingly restored and reasonably priced inn is on historic and relaxing Vernon Square in downtown Darien. Owners Kelly and Jeff Spratt are not only attentive innkeepers who rustle up a mean breakfast, they're also biologists who can hook you up with the best nature-oriented experiences and tours on this part of the coast.

FOOD

McIntosh County is a powerhouse in the food department, and as you might expect, fresh and delicious seafood in a casual atmosphere is the order of the day here. A Shellman Bluff favorite is **Speed's Kitchen** (Shellman Bluff, 912/832-4763, Thurs.-Sat. 5pm-close, Sun. noon-close, $10-20), where people move anything but fast and the fried fish and crab-stuffed flounder are out of this world. Take a right off Shellman Bluff Road onto Sutherland Bluff Drive; then take a right onto Speed's Kitchen Road.

One of my favorite restaurants is the **Old School Diner** (1080 Jesse Grant Rd. NE, Townsend, 912/832-2136, http://old-schooldiner.com, Wed.-Fri. 5:30pm-9:30pm, Sat.-Sun. noon-9:30pm, $15-30, cash only), located in a whimsical semirural compound seven miles off U.S. 17 just off Harris Neck Road on the way to the wildlife refuge. Run by the gregarious comfort-food culinary genius Jerome Brown, the restaurant is a reflection of the man himself—warm, inviting, eccentric, and full of life. People drive here literally from all over the state to enjoy succulent fresh seafood in the coastal Georgia tradition—delicately fried and imbued with the subtle, inviting flavors of soul food. Not a seafood fan? Jerome's ribs are also some of the best anywhere. Reservations are recommended, and remember, it's cash only. They take no plastic of any kind, and there are no ATMs nearby.

Even farther off the main roads than the Old School Diner, the community of Shellman Bluff is also well worth the drive. Find **Hunter's Café** (Shellman Bluff, 912/832-5771, lunch Mon.-Fri. 11am-2pm, dinner Mon.-Fri. 5pm-10pm, Sat.-Sun. 7am-10pm, $10-20) and get anything that floats your boat—it's all fresh and local. Wild Georgia shrimp are a particular specialty, as is the hearty cream-based crab stew. Take a right off Shellman Bluff Road onto Sutherland Bluff Drive, then a left onto New Shellman Road. Take a right onto the unpaved River Road and you can't miss it.

GETTING THERE AND AROUND

U.S. 17 goes directly through Darien. The closest I-95 exit is exit 49. Once you get off U.S. 17, Darien is a pretty bike-friendly place; you

THE GOLDEN ISLES

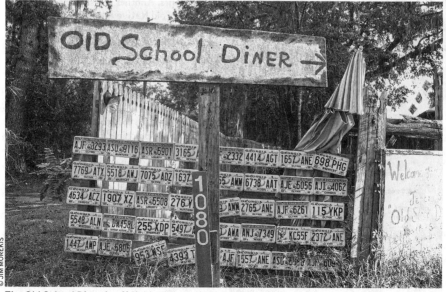

© JIM MOREKIS

The Old School Diner is off the beaten path, but well worth it.

can park the car downtown and ride your bike east on Fort King George Drive to visit Fort King George.

SAPELO ISLAND

Another of those amazing, undeveloped Georgia barrier islands that can only be reached by boat, Sapelo also shares with some of those islands a link to the Gilded Age.

The Spanish established a Franciscan mission on the north end of the island in the 1500s. Sapelo didn't become fully integrated into the Lowcountry plantation culture until its purchase by Thomas Spalding in the early 1800s. After the Civil War, many of the nearly 500 former slaves on the island remained, with a partnership of freedmen buying land as early as 1871.

Hudson Motors mogul Howard Coffin bought all of Sapelo, except for the African American communities, in 1912, building a palatial home and introducing a modern infrastructure. In 1934, Coffin sold Sapelo to tobacco heir R. J. Reynolds, who consolidated the island's African Americans into the single Hog Hammock community. By the mid-1970s the Reynolds family had sold the island to the state, again with the exception of the 430 acres of Hog Hammock, at the time with slightly more than 100 residents. Today, most of the island is administered for marine research purposes under the designation of **Sapelo Island National Estuarine Research Reserve** (www.sapelonerr.org).

Sights

Once on the island, you can take guided tours under the auspices of the Georgia Department of Natural Resources. Wednesday 8:30am-12:30pm is a tour of the **R. J. Reynolds Mansion** (www.reynoldsonsapelo.com) on the south end, along with the rest of the island, including Hog Hammock and the Long Tabby ruins. Saturday 9am-1pm is a tour of the historic **Sapelo Lighthouse** on the north end, along with the rest of the island. Call 912/437-3224 for reservations. You can also arrange private tours. Another key sight on Sapelo is a 4,500-year-old **Native American shell ring** on the north end, one of the oldest and best preserved anywhere. Beach-lovers will especially enjoy the unspoiled strands on Sapelo, including the famous **Nannygoat Beach.**

Accommodations

While it's theoretically possible to stay overnight at the **R. J. Reynolds Mansion** (www.reynoldsonsapelo.com), it is limited to groups of at least 16 people. Realistically, to stay overnight on Sapelo you need a reservation with one of the locally owned guesthouses. One recommendation is Cornelia Bailey's six-room **The Wallow** (912/485-2206, call for rates) in historic Hog Hammock. The Baileys also run a small campground, **Comyam's Campground** (912/485-2206, $10 pp). Another option is **The Weekender** (912/485-2277, call for rates).

Getting There

Visitors to Sapelo must embark on the ferry at

SAPELO ISLAND

Sapelo Sound

SAPELO LIGHTHOUSE ★

NATIVE AMERICAN SHELL RING ★

■ DUCK PONDS

Blackbeard Island National Wildlife Refuge

CHOCOLATE RUINS ■

Blackbeard Island

MOSES HAMMOCK BOARDWALK (RESEARCH SITE) ■

Duplin River

PERIMETER RD

WEST

DOGPATCH

EAST PERIMETER RD

RACCOON BLUFF CHURCH ■

ATLANTIC OCEAN

LONG TABBY/ POST OFFICE ■

AUTOBAHN

▲ CABRETTA ISLAND

DNR HOUSING ■

CABRETTA RD

DNR HEADQUARTERS ■

CEMETERY ■

★ HOG HAMMOCK

FERRY TO MERIDIAN ■

R.J. REYNOLDS ■ MANSION

Sapelo Island National Estuarine Research Reserve

Nannygoat Beach

UNIVERSITY OF GEORGIA MARINE INSTITUTE

BEACH RD

Doboy Sound

0   2 mi

0   2 km

© AVALON TRAVEL

the **Sapelo Island Visitors Center** (912/437-3224, www.sapelonerr.org, various times daily, $15 adults, $10 ages 6-18) in little Meridian, Georgia, on Highway 99 north of Darien. Keep in mind you must call in advance for reservations before showing up at the visitors center. April-October it's recommended to call at least a week in advance.

BLACKBEARD ISLAND

While no one is positive if the namesake of Blackbeard Island actually landed here, the legends tell us he used it as a layover—even leaving some treasure here. Now federally administered as **Blackbeard Island National Wildlife Refuge** (912/652-4415, www.fws.gov/blackbeardisland), the island is accessible to the public by boat and gets about 10,000 visitors a year. Plenty of hiking trails exist, and the bird-watching is fantastic. It's also a major nesting ground for the endangered loggerhead turtle. Cycling is permitted, but overnight camping is not. For charters to Blackbeard, I recommend **SouthEast Adventures** (313 Mallory St., St. Simons, 912/638-6732) on St. Simons Island.

Cumberland Island and St. Marys

Actually two islands—Great Cumberland and Little Cumberland—Cumberland Island National Seashore is the largest and one of the oldest of Georgia's barrier islands, and also one of its most remote and least developed. Currently administered by the National Park Service, it's accessible only by ferry or private boat. Most visitors to Cumberland get here from the gateway town of St. Marys, Georgia, a nifty little fishing village that has so far managed to defy the increasing residential sprawl coming to the area.

ST. MARYS

Much like Brunswick to the north, the fishing town of St. Marys plays mostly a gateway role, in this case to the Cumberland Island National Seashore. During the colonial period, St. Marys was the southernmost U.S. city. A hotel was built in 1916 (and hosted Marjorie Kinnan Rawlings, author of *The Yearlings*), but travelers didn't discover the area until the 1970s. It was also then that the U.S. Navy built the huge nuclear submarine base at Kings Bay, currently the area's largest employer with almost 10,000 workers.

As in Brunswick, the waterfront faces opposite the ocean and is instead oriented west, toward a river, in this case the St. Marys River. Most activity in downtown St. Marys happens up and down Osborne Street, which, perhaps not coincidentally, is also how you get to the **Cumberland Island Visitors Center** (113 St. Marys St., 912/882-4335, daily 8am-4:30pm) and from there board the *Cumberland Queen* for the trip to the island.

Sights

Tying the past to the present, it's only fitting that the home of the Kings Bay Submarine Base (not open to the public) has a museum dedicated to the "Silent Service." The **St. Marys Submarine Museum** (102 St. Marys St., 912/882-2782, www.stmaryssubmuseum.com, Tues.-Sat. 10am-4pm, Sun. 1pm-5pm, $5 adults, $3 children) on the riverfront has a variety of exhibits honoring the contribution of American submariners. There's a neat interactive exhibit where you can look through the genuine sub periscope that sticks out of the roof of the museum.

The most notable historic home in St. Marys is the **Orange Hall House Museum** (311 Osborne St., 912/576-3644, www.orangehall.org, Tues.-Sat. 9am-4pm, Sun. 1pm-4pm, $3 adults, $1 children). This beautiful Greek Revival home, circa 1830, survived the Civil War and was the center of town social life during the Roaring '20s, when it was owned by a succession of socialites from up north. The home is gorgeous inside and

THE GOLDEN ISLES

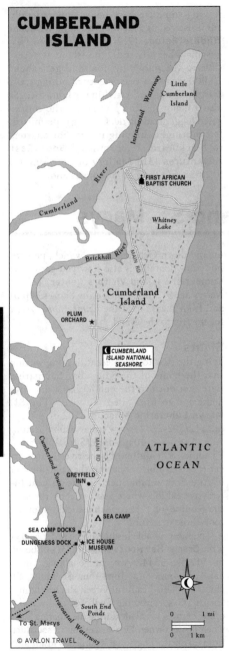

CUMBERLAND ISLAND

Little Cumberland Island

Intracoastal Waterway

Cumberland River

River

FIRST AFRICAN BAPTIST CHURCH

Whitney Lake

MAIN RD

Brickhill River

Cumberland Island

PLUM ORCHARD ★

CUMBERLAND ISLAND NATIONAL SEASHORE

Cumberland Sound

MAIN RD

GREYFIELD INN ●

ATLANTIC OCEAN

▲ SEA CAMP

SEA CAMP DOCKS
DUNGENESS DOCK ■ ★ ICE HOUSE MUSEUM

South End Ponds

To St. Marys

Intracoastal Waterway

© AVALON TRAVEL

0   1 mi
0   1 km

out, particularly during the holidays when it gets the full decorative treatment.

Events and Recreation

For outdoor recreation near St. Marys, go to **Crooked River State Park** (6222 Charlie Smith Sr. Hwy., 912/882-5256, www.gastateparks.org, office Fri.-Wed. 8am-10pm, Thurs. 8am-5pm), which is not only a great place to put in for kayaking trips, including jaunts to Cumberland Island, but also has a wide range of lodging options as well. A key stop on the Colonial Coast Birding Trail, Crooked River features its own nature center and is near a historic site just upriver, the tabby ruins of the McIntosh Sugar Works—actually a lumber mill from the early 1800s. The easiest way to get here is to take I-95 exit 3 and go about eight miles east. To rent kayaks or book kayak and ecotours, try **Up the Creek Xpeditions** (111 Osborne St., 912/882-0911, www.upthecreekx.com), which can take you all around the area, including out to Cumberland Island.

Accommodations

UNDER $150

Don't even think about staying at a chain hotel when you're in St. Marys. Stay at one of these cute historic inns for a song. The most notable lodging for historic as well as economic value is the 18-room **Riverview Hotel** (105 Osborne St., 912/882-3242, www.riverviewhotelstmarys.com, under $100). The waterfront locale, like many old hotels in this area, has a great retro feel. It was built in the 1920s and has hosted such notables as author Marjorie Rawlings, John Rockefeller, poet Sidney Lanier, and Andrew Carnegie.

More outdoorsy visitors can stay at cottage, tent, or RV sites at **Crooked River State Park** (6222 Charlie Smith Sr. Hwy., 912/882-5256, www.gastateparks.org). There are 62 tent and RV sites (about $22) and 11 cottages ($85-110) as well as primitive camping ($25).

$150-300

Emma's Bed and Breakfast (300 West Conyers St., 912/882-4199, www.emmasbedandbreakfast.com, under $200) is situated on four beautiful acres in downtown St. Marys in a grand Southern-style mansion with all the trappings and hospitality you'd expect. You can also hang out on the stunning veranda at the historic **◖ Goodbread House** (209 Osborne St., 912/882-7490, www.goodbreadhouse.com, under $200), which offers rates below $100 in the off-season. The 1870 house features sumptuous interiors, including a classic dining room in which awesome breakfasts are served.

Food
One of the best places to eat seafood on the waterfront in St. Marys is at **Lang's Marina Restaurant** (307 W. St. Marys St., 912/882-4432, lunch Tues.-Fri. 11am-2pm, dinner Wed.-Sat. 5pm-9pm, $15-20). The other premier seafood place is **Trolley's** (109 W. St. Marys St., 912/882-1525, Sun.-Thurs. 11am-9pm, Fri.-Sat. 11am-10pm, $15-20).

Information and Services
The **St. Marys Convention and Visitors Bureau** (406 Osborne St., 912/882-4000, www.stmaryswelcome.com) is a good source of information not only for the town but for Cumberland Island, but keep in mind that this is not actually where you catch the ferry to the island.

Getting There and Around
Take I-95 exit 3 for Kingsland-St. Marys Road (Hwy. 40). This becomes Osborne Road, the main drag of St. Marys, as it gets closer to town. The road by the waterfront is St. Marys Street.

◖ CUMBERLAND ISLAND NATIONAL SEASHORE
Not only one of the richest estuarine environments in the world, **Cumberland Island National Seashore** (912/882-4335, www.nps.gov/cuis) is quite simply one of the most beautiful and romantic places on the planet, as everyone learned when the "it" couple of their day, John F. Kennedy Jr. and Carolyn Bessette, were wed on the island in 1996. With more than 16 miles of gorgeous beach and an area of

over 17,000 acres, there's no shortage of beauty either.

History
Like modern-day Americans, the indigenous Timucuan people also revered this site, visiting it often for shellfish and for sassafras, a medicinal herb common on the island. Cumberland's size and great natural harbor made it a perfect base for Spanish missionaries, who established the first mission on the island, San Pedro de Mocama, in 1587. In fact, the first Roman Catholic martyr in Georgia was on Cumberland, when the missionary Pedro Martínez was killed by indigenous people.

While land grants were made in the 1760s, they saw little follow-through, and by the time of naturalist William Bartram's visit in 1774, Cumberland Island was almost uninhabited. But inevitably, the Lowcountry planters' culture made its way down to Cumberland. After the Revolution, the heirs of one of its heroes, General Nathanael Greene, established Dungeness Plantation in 1802, its central building a now-gone tabby structure.

The Industrial Revolution came to Cumberland in the form of a vacation getaway for a mega-tycoon, in this case Thomas Carnegie, industrialist and brother of the better-known Andrew Carnegie of Carnegie Library fame. Carnegie built a new, even grander Dungeness, which suffered the same fate as its predecessor in a 1959 fire. The Carnegies joined with the Georgia Conservancy to broker an agreement that resulted in dubbing Cumberland a National Seashore in 1972, saving it from further development.

Sights
The ferry typically stops at two docks a short distance from each other, the Sea Camp Dock and the Dungeness Dock. At 4pm, Rangers offer a "Dockside" interpretive program at the Sea Camp. A short way farther north at the Dungeness Dock, Rangers offer a "Dungeness Footsteps Tour" at 10am and 12:45pm, concentrating on the historic sites at the southern end of the island. Also at the Dungeness

WILD HORSES OF CUMBERLAND

Cumberland Island's famous wild horses are not actually direct descendants of the first horses brought to the island by Spanish and English settlers, although certainly feral horses have ranged the island for most of recorded history. The current population of 250 or so is actually descended from horses brought to the island by the Carnegie family in the 1920s.

Gorgeous and evocative though these mag-nificent animals are, they have a big appetite for vegetation and are frankly not the best thing for this sensitive barrier island ecosys-tem. But their beauty and visceral impact on the visitor is undeniable, which means the horses are likely to stay as long as nature will have them. And yes, these really are *wild* horses, meaning you shouldn't feed them even if they approach you for food, and you certainly won't be riding them.

Dock is the little **Ice House Museum** (912/882-4336, daily 9am-5pm, free) containing a range of exhibits on the island's history from Native American times to the present day.

Down near the docks are also where you'll find the spooky **Dungeness Ruins** and the nearby grave marker of Light-Horse Harry Lee. Moving north on the Main Road (Grand Ave.) you come to **Greyfield Inn** (904/261-6408, www.greyfieldinn.com). Because it is a pri-vately owned hotel, don't trespass through the grounds. A good way farther north, just off the main road, you'll find the rambling 20-room mansion **Plum Orchard,** another Carnegie legacy. Guided tours of Plum Orchard ($6 plus ferry fare) are available on the second and fourth Sunday of the month; reserve a place at 912/882-4335.

At the very north end of the island, acces-sible only on foot or by bicycle, is the former freedmen's community simply known as **The Settlement,** featuring a small cemetery and the now-famous **First African Baptist Church** (daily dawn-dusk)—a 1937 version of the 1893 original—a humble and rustic one-room church made of whitewashed logs in which the 1996 Kennedy-Bessette marriage took place.

Sports and Recreation

There are more than 50 miles of trails all over Cumberland, about 17 miles of nearly isolated beach to comb, and acres of maritime forest to explore—the latter an artifact of Cumberland's unusually old age for a barrier island. Upon arrival, you might want to rent a bicycle at the **Sea Camp docks** (no reservations, arrange rentals on the ferry, adult bikes $16 per day, youth bikes $10, $20 overnight).

Shell and sharks-teeth collectors might want to explore south of Dungeness Beach as well as between the docks. Unlike some parks, you are allowed to take shells and fossils off the island. Wildlife enthusiasts will be in heaven. More than 300 species of birds have been recorded on the island, which is also a favorite nesting ground for female loggerhead turtles in the late summer. Of course, the most iconic image of Cumberland Island is its famous **wild horses,** a free-roaming band of feral equines who traverse the island year-round, grazing as they please.

Accommodations
OVER $300
The only "civilized" lodging on Cumberland is the 13-room **(Greyfield Inn** (Grand Ave., 904/261-6408, www.greyfieldinn.com, $475), ranked by the American Inn Association as one of the country's "Ten Most Romantic Inns." Opened in 1962 as a hotel, the Greyfield was originally built in 1900 as the home of the Carnegies. The room rates includes meals, transportation, tours, and bicycle usage.

CAMPING
Many visitors opt to camp on Cumberland (reservations 877/860-6787, maximum 7

nights, $4) in one of three basic ways: at the **Sea Camp,** which has restrooms and shower facilities and allows fires; the remote **Stafford Beach,** a good hike from the docks and with no facilities; and pure wilderness camping farther north at **Hickory Hill, Yankee Paradise,** and **Brickman Bluff,** all of which are a several-mile hike away, do not permit fires, and have no facilities of any kind. Reservations are required for camping. All trash must be packed out on departure.

Getting There and Around

The most vital information about Cumberland is how to get ashore in the first place. Most visitors do this by purchasing a ticket on the *Cumberland Queen* at the **Cumberland Island Visitors Center** (113 St. Marys St., St. Marys,

912/882-4335, daily 8am-4:30pm, $20 adults, $18 seniors, $12 under age 13) on the waterfront at St. Marys. The ferry ride is 45 minutes each way. You can call for reservations Monday-Friday 10am-4pm. The ferry does not transport pets, bicycles, kayaks, or cars. However, you can rent bicycles at the Sea Camp docks once you're there. Every visitor to Cumberland over age 16 must pay a $4 entry fee, including campers.

March 1-November 30, the ferry leaves St. Marys at 9am and 11:45am, returning from Cumberland at 10:15am and 4:45pm. March 1-September 30 Wednesday-Saturday, there's an additional 2:45pm departure from Cumberland back to St. Marys. December 1-February 28 the ferry operates only Thursday-Monday.

BACKGROUND

The Land

GEOGRAPHY

The Carolinas and Georgia are linked by more than history and shared experience. All three states are made up of the same three distinct geographical regions. The most easily identified is the **mountain region,** which forms the western edge of North and South Carolina and the extreme northern portion of Georgia.

The ridges of the Blue Ridge and Great Smoky Mountains run in a general northeast-southwest configuration, from the Virginia line to the farthest southwestern corner where the toe of North Carolina tickles Georgia and Tennessee. Six of the 10 highest mountains in the eastern United States are found in North Carolina, including the very highest, 6,684-foot Mount Mitchell.

Since the mid-19th century, the **Piedmont** has been the primary locus of population and industry in all three states. Most of the major cities are in the Piedmont, including Atlanta, Augusta and Athens in Georgia, the Raleigh-Durham metro area, Charlotte, Winston-Salem, and Greensboro in North Carolina, and the Greenville-Spartanburg metro area and Columbia in South Carolina.

The **Coastal Plain** is the third region, with a name that's fairly self-explanatory. Generally

© DREAMSTIME.COM

GEOGRAPHICAL VOCABULARY

The region has some unusual landscapes and environments, and some unusual vocabulary to describe them. As you explore the area, you may encounter the following terms.

POCOSIN

Pronounced "puh-CO-sin," the word is said to come from the Algonquin for "swamp on a hill." A pocosin is a moist peat bog of a kind unique to the Southeast. The peat layer is thinnest around the edges, and usually supports communities of pine trees. Moving toward the center of the bog, the ground becomes slightly higher, the peat thicker, more acidic, and less welcoming of plant species. Because the soil is so poor and bereft of nutrients, carnivorous plants, who have their meals delivered rather than depending on the soil's bounty, are particularly well suited to life in pocosins.

CAROLINA BAY

The word *bay* here refers not to an inlet on the coast but to another kind of upland swamp—sort of like an inside-out pocosin. The bays' origins are mysterious, and their regularity of form and commonness in this region are most uncanny. If you look down at eastern North and South Carolina from an airplane, or in a satellite image, the bays are unmistakable. They're oval-shaped depressions, varying in size from Lake Waccamaw to mere puddles, and are always aligned in a northeast-southwest configuration. Unlike ponds and regular swamps, Carolina bays are usually unconnected to any groundwater source and are fed solely by rainwater. Like pocosins, bays attract colonies of carnivorous plants, which love to establish their dens of iniquity in such unwholesome soil.

SANDHILLS

If you're in Wilmington, Southport, Vidalia, or the Pee Dee region of South Carolina, or somewhere else along the Southeastern coast, take note of what the soil beneath your feet looks like. Then, turn your back to the ocean and head inland. Travel 100 miles west and then look down again. What you'll see is very similar—sandy, light-colored ground, wiry vegetation (and a few carnivorous plants), maybe even some scattered shells. About 20 million years ago, during the Miocene Epoch, parts of the modern coastal plain were sand dunes on the shores of an ocean that covered what is now North Carolina's coastal plain.

HOLLER

Here's a term that's really more of a regional pronunciation than a unique word. A holler is what is on paper termed a "hollow"—a mountain cove—it's just that we in the South aren't much for rounding words that end in "ow." If you don't believe me, just beller out the winda to that feller wallering in yonder meada.

BALD

An ecological mystery, the Appalachian bald is a mountaintop area on which there are no trees, even though surrounding mountaintops of the same elevation may be forested. Typically a bald is either grassy or a heath. Heaths are more easily explicable, caused by soil conditions that don't support forest. Grassy balds, though, occur on land where logically one would expect to find trees. Some theories hold that grassy balds were caused by generations of livestock grazing, but soil studies show that they were grassy meadows before the first mountain farmer turned cattle or sheep out to pasture. Grazing may still be the answer, though. The balds may originally have been chomped and trampled down by prehistoric megafauna—ancient bison, mastodons, and mammoths. Today, in the absence of mammoths as well as free-ranging cattle, some balds are gradually sealing up in woodland, except where deliberately maintained.

speaking, the basic western edge of the Coastal Plain runs roughly parallel to I-95, a major traffic artery through all three states.

The region's big **alluvial,** or sediment-bearing, rivers originate in the Appalachian mountain chain. Key examples are the Savannah River, the Cape Fear River, and the Pee Dee River. The **blackwater river** is a particularly interesting Southern phenomenon, duplicated elsewhere only in South America and one example each in New York and Michigan. While alluvial rivers generally originate in highlands and carry with them a large amount of sediment, blackwater rivers—the Edisto River in South Carolina being the most remarkable example—tend to originate in low-lying areas and move slowly toward the sea, carrying with them very little sediment. Their dark tea color comes from the tannic acid of decaying vegetation all along the banks, washed out by the slow, inexorable movement of the river toward the sea.

Most biologists will tell you that the coastal

© JIM MOREKIS

The Edisto River is the longest blackwater river in the world.

plain is where things get interesting. The place where a river interfaces with the ocean is called an **estuary,** and it's perhaps the most interesting place of all. Estuaries are heavily tidal in nature (indeed, the word derives from *aestus,* Latin for "tide"), and feature brackish water and heavy silt content.

This portion of the U.S. East Coast has about a 6- to 8-foot tidal range, and the coastal ecosystem depends on this steady ebb and flow for life itself. At high tide, shellfish open and feed. At low tide, they literally clam up, keeping saltwater inside their shells until the next tide comes.

Waterbirds and small mammals feed on shellfish and other animals at low tide, when their prey is exposed. High tide brings an influx of fish and nutrients from the sea, in turn drawing predators like dolphins, who often come into tidal creeks to feed.

All this water action in both directions—freshwater coming from inland, saltwater encroaching from the Atlantic—results in the phenomenon of the **salt marsh.** (Freshwater marshes are rarer, Florida's Everglades being perhaps the premier example.)

Far more than just a transitional zone between land and water, marshes are also nature's nursery. Plant and animal life in marshes tends not only to be diverse but to encompass multitudes. You may not see its denizens easily, but on close inspection you'll find the marsh absolutely teeming with creatures. Visually, the main identifying feature of a salt marsh is its distinctive reedlike marsh grasses, adapted to survive in brackish water.

All three states feature distinctive island formations. The **Outer Banks** of North Carolina form a magnificent, sweeping arc from the Virginia line at the north, out to its eastern ultima Thule at Cape Hatteras, to the edge of the Croatan Forest and Bogue Banks at the south. South of Bogue Banks, a crazed margin of marshes and barrier islands shelter the coast. An ever-changing sandbar, the Outer Banks shift imperceptibly from day to day as the tides nudge them back and forth, but in a hurricane can be transformed in just a few hours.

The South Carolina and Georgia coasts boast a series of barrier islands often just called the **Sea Islands.** After the Civil War, the Sea Islands remained ancestral homes to formerly enslaved people who stayed on the islands, retaining many traditional folkways. Their somewhat isolated culture is generally referred to as **Gullah,** though in parts of Georgia you'll still hear the phrase **Geechee** used to refer to the same cultural tradition.

CLIMATE

This is a large region of the country and therefore has a wide range of climatic conditions. While summers are generally long, hot, and humid, with winters being quite mild, a clear exception exists anywhere in the mountainous regions.

Asheville and Boone in North Carolina can get snow when the trees down in the Piedmont are already green and leafy, but the average winter temperatures in the mountains stay mostly above freezing. In the summer it can be chilly in the mountains, especially in the evening, but plenty of days hit the 80s.

The central portions of the Carolinas and most of Georgia can be incredibly hot in the summer, and plenty hot in the spring and fall. Towns like Fayetteville, North Carolina, Columbia, South Carolina, and Americus, Georgia, can feel like the hottest places on earth. The Piedmont sees snow, though not nearly so much as the mountains, and the counties east of I-95 are virtually snow-free and much likelier to have rain during winter storms.

In the Outer Banks, the warm Gulf Stream keeps the air from getting too frigid in the winter, while the circulation of sea breezes makes it ever so slightly less steamy in the summer. The difference is subtle, though, and chances are that on the coldest day in January or the hottest day in August, the relief won't be perceptible.

The coastal region of all three states is subject to **hurricanes** on a fairly regular basis. The Outer Banks in particular are terribly vulnerable. Hurricane season lasts from June through November, and it's toward the end of the summer that people really start to be watchful.

Tornadoes, though most common in the spring, can whip up trouble any time of year in the central portions of the states. Plain old **thunderstorms** can be dangerous too, bringing lightning, flash flooding, and difficult driving conditions. **Snowstorms** with significant accumulation are more likely in the North Carolina mountains than at lower elevations.

Flora

In the early 1700s, John Lawson, an English explorer who would soon be the first victim of the Tuscarora War, recorded a fanciful tale he'd picked up in the very young colony of North Carolina. "I have been informed of a Tulip-Tree," he wrote, "that was ten Foot Diameter; and another, wherein a lusty Man had his Bed and Household Furniture, and liv'd in it, till his Labour got him a more fashionable Mansion. He afterwards became a noted Man, in his Country, for Wealth and Conduct." Whether or not there was ever really a tulip poplar large enough to serve as a furnished bachelor pad, the region's colonial virgin forests must have seemed miraculous to the first Europeans to happen upon them.

However, contrary to Hollywood portrayals, no one ever needed a machete to tear their way through an old-growth forest. Because the high, thick tree canopy blocks enough light to allow little to grow on the forest floor, Native Americans and early settlers could walk through these primordial forests with ease.

Few old-growth forests exist today, after generations of logging and farming throughout the state, but those enclaves of virgin woods, like the Joyce Kilmer Forest in the Smoky Mountains or the Congaree National Monument outside Columbia, South Carolina, are a sight to behold and make Lawson's anecdote seem like a fairy tale that might actually

© JIM MOREKIS

Longleaf pine once covered most of the southeast.

live oak is one of nature's most magnificent creations. The timber value of live oaks has been well known since the earliest days of the American shipbuilding industry—when the oak dominated the entire coast inland of the marsh—but their value as a canopy tree has finally been widely recognized by local and state governments.

Fittingly, the other iconic plantlife of the coast grows on the branches of the live oak. Contrary to popular opinion, **Spanish moss** is neither Spanish nor moss. It's an air plant, a wholly indigenous cousin to the pineapple. Also contrary to folklore, Spanish moss is not a parasite nor does it harbor parasites while living on an oak tree—although it can after it has already fallen to the ground.

Cotton or tobacco aside, you could make the case that the most important plant in the history of the Carolinas and Georgia is the **longleaf pine,** also called the pitch pine. Though something of a rarity today, the vast stands of longleaf pine that formerly blanketed the region enabled a globally important naval stores industry in the 18th and 19th centuries, producing turpentine, pitch, tar, and lumber for the world's navies and shipping fleets. Today, what's left of the longleaf piney woods are crucial habitats for several endangered species, including the red cockaded woodpecker and the pine barrens tree frog.

The acres of **smooth cordgrass** for which the Georgia Golden Isles are named are plants of the *Spartina alterniflora* species. (A cultivated cousin, *Spartina anglica,* is considered invasive.) Besides its simple natural beauty, *Spartina* is also a key food source for marsh denizens. Playing a key environmental role on the coast are **sea oats.** This wispy, fast-growing perennial grass anchors sand dunes and hence is a protected species (it's a misdemeanor to pick them).

South Carolina isn't called the Palmetto State for nothing. Palm varieties are not as common here as in Florida, but you'll definitely encounter several types along the coast. The **cabbage palm,** for which South Carolina is nicknamed, is the largest variety, up to 50-60

be true. Scores of specialized ecosystems host a marvelous diversity of plant and animal life, from the cypress swamps in the east to the longleaf pine forests in the Sandhills to the fragrant balsam forests of the high country.

Coastal forests are dominated by hardwoods—**oaks** of many varieties, and **gum** and **cypress,** species that thrive in wetlands. There are also vast swathes of loblolly **piney woods** along the coast.

In the Piedmont, oak and **hickory** predominate, but share their range with smaller bands of piney woods. In the mountains too, oak and hickory woods are the rule. **Pine, balsam,** and other conifers put in appearances as well.

The most iconic plant life of the coastal region is the **Southern live oak.** Named because of its evergreen nature, a live oak is technically any one of a number of evergreens in the *Quercus* genus, but in local practice the name almost always refers to the Southern live oak. Capable of living over 1,000 years and possessing wood of legendary resilience, the Southern

© JIM MOREKIS

Venus flytrap

feet tall. Its "heart of palm" is an edible delicacy, which coastal Native Americans boiled in bear fat as porridge. In dunes and sand hills you'll find clumps of the low-lying **saw palmetto**. The **bush palmetto** has distinctive fan-shaped branches. The common **Spanish bayonet** looks like a palm, but it's actually a member of the agave family.

You've probably seen **Venus flytraps** for sale in nurseries, and maybe you've even bought one and brought it home to stuff with kitchen bugs. Venus flytraps grow in the wild only in one tiny corner of the world, and that happens to be here, in a narrow band of counties between Wilmington, North Carolina, and Myrtle Beach, South Carolina. They and their dozens of carnivorous local kin, like pitcher plants, abattoirs of the bug world, and Dr. Seussian sundews, are fondest of living in places with nutrient-starved soil, like pine savannas and pocosins, where they have little competition for space and sunlight and can feed handsomely on meals that come right to them.

There are many species of **pitcher plants** here, a familiar predator of the plant world. Shaped like tubular vases, with a graceful elfin flap shading the mouth, pitcher plants attract insects with an irresistible brew. Unsuspecting bugs pile in, thinking they've found a keg party, but instead find themselves paddling in a sticky mess from which they're unable to escape, pinned down by spiny hairs that line the inside of the pitcher. Enterprising frogs and spiders that are either strong or clever enough to come and go safely from inside the pitcher will often set up shop inside a plant and help themselves to stragglers.

FALL FOLIAGE

Arriving as early as mid-September at the highest elevations, and gradually sliding down the mountains through late October, autumn colors bring a late-season wave of visitors to western North and South Carolina and North Georgia. The latter weeks of October tend to be the peak, however. During those weeks it can be very difficult to find lodging in the mountains, so be sure to plan ahead. Some of the best places for leaf peeping are along the Blue Ridge Parkway and in the Great Smoky Mountains National Park.

Fauna

ON LAND

Perhaps the most iconic land animal—or semi-land animal, anyway—of the South is the legendary **American alligator,** the only species of crocodilian native to the area. Contrary to their fierce reputation, locals know these massive reptiles, 6-12 feet long as adults, to be quite shy. If you come in the colder months, you won't see them at all, since alligators require an outdoor temperature over 70°F to become active and feed (indeed, the appearance of alligators was once a well-known symbol of spring in the area). Often all you'll see is a couple of eyebrow ridges sticking out of the water, and a gator lying still in a shallow creek can easily be mistaken for a floating log. But should you see one or more gators basking in the sun—a favorite activity on warm days for these cold-blooded creatures—it's best to admire them from afar. A mother alligator, in particular, will destroy anything that comes near her nest. Despite the alligator's short, stubby legs, they run amazingly fast on land—faster than you, in fact.

The region hosts large populations of playful **river otter.** Not to be confused with the larger sea otters off the West Coast, these fast-swimming members of the weasel family inhabit inland waterways and marshy areas, with dominant males sometimes ranging as much as 50 miles within a single waterway. As strict carnivores, usually of fish, otters are a key indicator of the health of their ecosystem. If they're thriving, water and habitat quality are likely to be pretty high. If they're not, something's going badly wrong.

While you're unlikely to encounter an otter, if you're camping, you might easily run into the **raccoon,** an exceedingly intelligent and crafty relative of the bear, sharing that larger animal's resourcefulness in stealing your food. Though nocturnal, raccoons will feed whenever food is available. Raccoons can grow so accustomed to the human presence as to almost consider themselves part of the family, but resist the temptation to get close to them. Rabies is prevalent in the raccoon population, and you should always, always keep your distance.

Another common campsite nuisance, the **opossum** is a shy, primitive creature that is much more easily discouraged. North America's only marsupial, an opossum's usual "defense" against predators is to play dead. That said, however, they have an immunity to snake venom and often feed on the reptiles, even the most poisonous ones.

IN THE WATER

Humankind's aquatic cousin, the **Atlantic bottle-nosed dolphin** is a well-known and frequent visitor to the coast, coming far upstream into creeks and rivers to feed. Children, adults, and experienced sailors alike all delight in encounters with the mammals, sociable creatures who travel in family units. When not occupied with feeding or mating activities—both of which can get surprisingly rowdy—dolphins show great curiosity about human visitors to their habitat. They will gather near boats, surfacing often with the distinctive chuffing sound of air coming from their blowholes. Occasionally they'll even lift their heads out of the water to have a look at you; consider yourself lucky indeed to have such a close encounter. Don't be fooled by their cuteness, however. Dolphins live life with gusto and aren't scared of much. They're voracious eaters of fish, amorous and energetic lovers, and will take on an encroaching shark in a heartbeat.

Another beloved part-time marine creature of the barrier islands of the coast is the **loggerhead turtle.** Though the species prefers to stay well offshore the rest of the year, females weighing up to 300 pounds come out of the sea each May-July to dig a shallow hole in the dunes and lay over 100 leathery eggs, returning to the ocean and leaving the eggs to hatch on their own after two months. Interestingly, the mothers prefer to nest at the same spot on

© BRIAN LASENBY/123RF.COM

alligator in the Okefenokee

the same island year after year. After hatching, the baby turtles then make a dramatic, extremely dangerous (and extremely slow) trek to the safety of the waves, at the mercy of various predators. A series of dedicated research and conservation efforts are working hard to protect the loggerheads' traditional nursery grounds to ensure the survival of this fascinating, loveable, and threatened species. Cape Island within the Cape Romain National Wildlife Refuge in South Carolina is the leading nesting site north of Florida. Other key sites include Kiawah, Edisto, Hilton Head, and Tybee Islands.

Of course, the coastal waters and rivers are chockablock with fish. The most abundant and sought-after recreational species in the area is the **spotted sea trout,** followed by the **red drum.** Local anglers also pursue many varieties of **bass, bream, sheepshead,** and **crappie.** It may sound strange to some accustomed to considering it a "trash" fish, but many types of **catfish** are not only plentiful here but are a common and well-regarded food source. Many species of **flounder** inhabit the silty bottoms of estuaries all along the coast. Farther offshore are game and sport fish like **marlin, swordfish, shark, grouper,** and **tuna.**

Crustaceans and shellfish have been a key food staple in the area for thousands of years, with the massive shell middens of the coast being testament to Native Americans' healthy appetite for them. The beds of the local variant, the **oyster,** aren't what they used to be due to overharvesting, water pollution, and disruption of habitat. In truth, these days most local restaurants import the little filter-feeders from the Gulf of Mexico. Oysters spawn May-August, hence the old folk wisdom about eating oysters only in months with the letter *r* so as not to disrupt the breeding cycle.

Each year from April to January, shrimp boats up and down the Southeastern coast trawl for **shrimp;** two local species, the white shrimp, and the brown shrimp, are the most commercially viable. Shrimp are the most popular seafood item in the United States and account for bringing hundreds of millions of dollars in revenue into the coastal economy.

While consumption won't slow down anytime soon, the South Carolina shrimping industry is facing serious threats, both from species decline due to pollution and overfishing and from competition from shrimp farms and the Asian shrimp industry.

Another important commercial crop is the **blue crab,** the species used in such Lowcountry delicacies as crab cakes. You'll often see floating markers bobbing up and down in rivers throughout the region. These signal the presence directly below of a crab trap, often of an amateur crabber. A true living link to primordial times, the alien-looking **horseshoe crab** is frequently found on beaches of the coast during the spring mating season (it lives in deeper water the rest of the year). More closely related to scorpions and spiders than crabs, the horseshoe has evolved hardly a lick in hundreds of millions of years. Any trip to a local salt marsh at low tide will likely uncover hundreds of **fiddler crabs,** so-named for the way the males wave their single enlarged claws in the air to attract mates. (Their other, smaller claw is the one they actually eat with.) The fiddlers make distinctive burrows in the pluff mud for sanctuary during high tide, recognizable by the little balls of sediment at the entrances (the crabs spit out the balls after sifting through the sand for food).

IN THE AIR

When enjoying the marshlands of the coast, consider yourself fortunate to see an endangered **wood stork,** although their numbers are on the increase. The only storks to breed in North America, these graceful long-lived birds (routinely living over 10 years) are usually seen on a low flight path across the marsh, although at some birding spots beginning in late summer you can find them at a **roost,** sometimes numbering over 100 birds. Resting at high tide, they fan out over the marsh to feed at low tide on foot. Old-timers sometimes call them "Spanish buzzards" or simply "the preacher." Often confused with the wood stork is the gorgeous **white ibis,** distinguishable by its orange bill and black wingtips. Like the wood stork, the

ibis is a communal bird that roosts in colonies. Other similar-looking coastal denizens are the white-feathered **great egret** and **snowy egret,** the former distinguishable by its yellow bill and the latter by its black bill and the tuft of plumes on the back of its head. Egrets are in the same family as herons. The most magnificent is the **great blue heron.** Despite their imposing height—up to four feet tall—these waders are shy. Often you hear them rather than see them, a loud shriek of alarm that echoes over the marsh. So how to tell the difference between all these wading birds at a glance? It's actually easiest when they're in flight. Egrets and herons fly with their necks tucked in, while storks and ibis fly with their necks extended.

The chief raptor of the salt marsh is the fish-eating **osprey.** These large grayish birds of prey are similar to eagles but are adapted to a maritime environment, with a reversible outer toe on each talon (the better for catching wriggly fish) and closable nostrils so they can dive into the water after prey. Very common all along the coast, they like to build big nests on top of buoys and channel markers in addition to trees. The **bald eagle** is making a comeback in the area thanks to increased federal regulation and better education of trigger-happy locals. Of course, as we all should have learned in school, the bald eagle is not actually bald but has a head adorned with white feathers. Like the osprey, they prefer fish, but unlike the osprey will settle for rodents and rabbits.

Inland among the pines you'll find the most common area woodpecker, the huge **pileated woodpecker** with its huge crest. Less common is the smaller, more subtly marked **red-cockaded woodpecker.** Once common in the vast primordial pine forests of the Southeast, the species is now endangered, its last real refuge being the big tracts of relatively undisturbed land on military bases and national wildlife refuges.

INSECTS

Down here they say that God invented bugs to keep the Yankees from completely taking over the South. And insects are probably the most unpleasant fact of life in the Southeastern coastal region. The list of annoying indigenous insects must begin with the infamous **sand gnat,** scourge of the lowlands. This tiny and persistent nuisance, a member of the midge family, lacks the precision of the mosquito with its long proboscis. No, the sand gnat is more torture master than surgeon, brutally gouging and digging away its victim's skin until it hits a source of blood. Most prevalent in the spring and fall, the sand gnat is drawn to its prey by the carbon dioxide trail of its breath. While long sleeves and long pants are one way to keep gnats at bay, that causes its own discomfort because of the region's heat and humidity. The only real antidote to the sand gnat's assault—other than never breathing—is the Avon skincare product Skin So Soft, which has taken on a new and wholly unplanned life as the South's favorite antignat lotion.

Running a close second to the sand gnat are the over three dozen species of highly aggressive **mosquito,** which breeds anywhere a few drops of water lie stagnant. Not surprisingly, massive populations blossom in the rainiest months, in late spring and late summer. Like the gnat, the mosquito—the biters are always female—homes in on its victim by trailing the plume of carbon dioxide exhaled in the breath. Alas, Skin So Soft has little effect on the mosquito. Try over-the-counter sprays, anything smelling of citronella, and wearing long sleeves and long pants when weather permits.

But undoubtedly the most viscerally loathed of all pests on the Lowcountry and Georgia coasts is the so-called "palmetto bug," or **American cockroach.** These black, shiny, and sometimes grotesquely massive insects—up to two inches long—are living fossils, virtually unchanged over hundreds of millions of years. And perfectly adapted as they are to life in and among wet, decaying vegetation, they're unlikely to change a bit in 100 million more years. Popular regional use of the term *palmetto bug* undoubtedly has its roots in a desire for polite Southern society to avoid using the ugly word *roach* and its connotations of filth and unclean environments.

History

BEFORE THE EUROPEANS

Based on studies of artifacts found throughout the state, anthropologists know that the first humans arrived in South Carolina at least 13,000 years ago, at the tail end of the last ice age. However, a still-controversial archaeological dig in the state, the Topper Site on the Savannah River near Allendale, has found artifacts that some scientists say are about 50,000 years old.

In any case, during this **Paleo-Indian Period,** sea levels were over 200 feet lower than present levels, and large mammals such as woolly mammoths, horses, and camels were hunted for food and skins. However, rapidly increasing temperatures, rising sea levels, and efficient hunting techniques combined to quickly kill off these large mammals, ushering in the **Archaic Period.** It's during this time that the great **shell middens** of the Georgia and South Carolina coasts trace their origins. Basically serving as trash heaps for discarded oyster shells, as the middens grew in size they also took on a ceremonial status, often being used as sites for important rituals and meetings.

The introduction of agriculture and improved pottery techniques about 3,000 years ago led to the **Woodland Period** of Native American settlement. Native Americans had been cremating or burying their dead for years, a practice that eventually gave rise to the construction of the first mounds during the Woodland Period.

Increased agriculture led to increased population, and with that population growth came competition over resources and a more formal notion of warfare. This period, about AD 800-1600, is termed the **Mississippian Period.** It was the Mississippians who would be the first Native Americans in what's now the continental United States to encounter European explorers and settlers after Columbus. The Native Americans who would later be called the **Creek people** were the direct descendants of the Mississippians in lineage, language, and lifestyle.

THE SPANISH ARRIVE

The first known contact by Europeans on the Southeastern coast came in 1521, roughly concurrent with Cortés's conquest of Mexico. A party of Spanish slavers ventured into what's now Port Royal Sound in South Carolina. They kidnapped a few Native American slaves and left, ranging as far north as the Cape Fear River in present-day North Carolina, and by some accounts even farther up the coast.

The first serious exploration of the coast came in 1526, when Lucas Vázquez de Ayllón and about 600 colonists made landfall at Winyah Bay near present-day Georgetown, South Carolina. They didn't stay long, however, immediately moving down the coast and trying to set down roots in the St. Catherine's Sound area of modern-day Liberty County, Georgia. That colony—called San Miguel de Gualdape—was the first European colony in North America (the continent's oldest continuously occupied settlement, St. Augustine, Florida, wasn't founded until 1565). The colony also brought with it the seed of a future nation's dissolution: enslaved people from Africa. San Miguel lasted only six weeks due to political tension and a slave uprising.

Hernando de Soto's infamous expedition of 1539-1543 began in Florida and went through southwest Georgia before crossing the Savannah River somewhere near modern-day North Augusta, South Carolina. Long after his departure and eventual death from fever in Alabama, De Soto's legacy was felt throughout the Southeast in the form of various diseases for which the indigenous Mississippian people had no immunity whatsoever.

The next serious Spanish expedition into South Carolina began on the coast in 1566,

when Juan Pardo set out from Santa Elena on Parris Island. Pardo and his party of 125 soldiers were on a mission to explore the hinterland and scout a location for a road to the main Spanish silver mines in Mexico. Along the way Pardo established several short-lived forts in what are now the Carolinas and Tennessee. One of these forts, called San Juan, has been identified by archaeologists outside present-day Morganton, North Carolina, in a community called Worry Crossroads.

THE LOST COLONY

The next major episode in the nonnative settlement of the region is one of the strangest mysteries in American history, that of the Lost Colonists of Roanoke. After two previous failed attempts to establish an English stronghold on the island of Roanoke, fraught by poor planning and even worse diplomacy, a third group of English colonists tried their luck.

Sometime between being dropped off in the New World in 1585, and one of their leaders returning three years later to resupply them, all of the colonists—including Virginia Dare, the first English-speaking person born in the Americas—had vanished. (North Carolina at that time was part of the colony of Virginia.) A subsequent expedition found only "CROATOAN" carved into a fence and "CRO" carved into a tree.

To this day, the fate of the 90 men, 17 women, and 11 children is unknown, although a host of fascinating theories are still debated, and probably always will be. Were they murdered by Native Americans? The Spanish? Or did they simply integrate into local Native American communities, who were much better equipped to feed themselves than the woefully prepared settlers?

THE MISSION ERA

It's rarely mentioned as a key part of U.S. history, but the Spanish missionary presence on the Georgia coast was longer and more comprehensive than its much more widely known counterpart in California.

St. Augustine governor Pedro Menéndez

HENRY WOODWARD, COLONIAL INDIANA JONES

He's virtually unsung in the history books, and there are no movies made about him, but Dr. Henry Woodward, the first English settler in South Carolina, lived a life that is the stuff of novels and screenplays. Educated in medicine in London, Woodward first tried his hand in the colony of Barbados. But Barbados, crowded and run by an elite, was no place for a young man with a sense of adventure but no contacts in the sugar industry. Still in his teens, Woodward left Barbados in Captain Robert Sandford's 1664 expedition to Carolina. Landing in the Cape Fear region, Sandford's cohort made its way down to Port Royal Sound to contact the Cusabo Indians. In 1666, in what is perhaps the New World's first "cultural-exchange program," Woodward volunteered to stay behind while the rest of the expedition returned to England with a Native American named Shadoo.

Woodward learned the local language and established political relations with surrounding Native American groups, actions for which the Lords Proprietors granted him temporary "formall possession of the whole Country to hold as Tennant att Will." The Spanish had different plans, however. They came and kidnapped the young Englishman, taking him to what turned out to be a very permissive state of house arrest at the Spanish stronghold of St. Augustine in Florida. Surprising the Spanish with his request—in Latin, no less—to convert to Catholicism, Woodward was popular and well treated. An excellent student of the Catechism, Woodward became a favorite of the Spanish governor and was even promoted to official surgeon. During that time, he studied Spanish government, commerce, and culture, with the same diligence with which he studied the Indians a year earlier. In 1668, Woodward was "rescued" by English privateers—pirates, really—under the command of Robert Searle, who'd come to sack St. Augustine. Woodward's sojourn with the pirates would last two years, during which he was kept on board as ship's surgeon. Was the pirate raid a coincidence? Or, as some scholars suggest, was Woodward really one of history's greatest spies? We will probably never know.

Incredibly, the plot thickens. In another coincidence, in 1670 Woodward was rescued when the pirates shipwrecked on the Caribbean island of Nevis. His rescuers were none other than the settlers on their way to found Charles Towne. On landfall, Woodward asserted his previous experience in the area to direct the colonists away from Port Royal to an area of less Spanish influence. That same year he began a series of expeditions to contact indigenous people in the Carolina interior—the first non-Spanish European to set foot in the area. Using economic espionage gained from the Spanish, Woodward's goal was to jumpstart the trade in deerskins that would be the bulwark of the Charles Towne colony. Woodward's unlikely 1674 alliance with the aggressive Westo people was instrumental in this burgeoning trade. As if all this weren't enough, in 1680 Woodward, now with property of his own on Johns Island, would introduce local farmers to a certain strange crop recently imported from Madagascar: rice.

Woodward made enemies, however, of settlers who were envious of his growing affluence and suspicious of his friendship with the Westo. His outspoken disgust with the spread of Indian slavery brought a charge against him of undermining the interests of the crown. But Woodward, by now a celebrity of sorts, returned to England to plead his case directly to the Lords Proprietors. They not only pardoned him but made him their official Indian agent—with a 20 percent share of the profits. Woodward would never again see the land of his birth. He returned to the American colonies to trek inland, making alliances with groups of Creek Indians in Spanish-held territory. Hounded by Spanish troops, Woodward fell ill of a fever somewhere in the Savannah River valley. He made it to Charleston and safety but never fully recovered and died around 1690—after living the kind of life you usually only see in the movies.

de Avilés, over "biscuits with honey" on the beach at St. Catherine's Island in Georgia with a local Native American chief, negotiated for the right to establish a system of Jesuit missions in two coastal chiefdoms: the Mocama on and around Cumberland Island, and the Guale (pronounced "wallie") to the north. Those early missions, the first north of Mexico, were largely unsuccessful. But a renewed, organized effort by the Franciscan Order came to fruition during the 1580s. Missions were established all along the Georgia coast, from the mainland near St. Simons and Sapelo Islands to the Altamaha River.

Spanish power waned under the English threat, however. But even as late as 1667, right before the founding of Charleston, there were still 70 missions on the Georgia coast. Pirate raids and slave uprisings finished off the Georgia missions for good by 1684.

THE COLONY OF CAROLINA

The Carolinas are a product of the **English Restoration,** when the monarchy returned to power after the grim 11-year tenure of Oliver Cromwell. The attitudes of the Restoration era—expansionist, confident, mercantile—are key to understanding the character of South Carolina even today. Historians dispute exactly how close-minded Cromwell was, but there's no debating the puritanical tone of his reign as English head of state. Theater was banned, as was most music, except for hymns. Hair was close-cropped, and dress was extremely conservative. Most disturbing of all for the holiday-loving English, the observation of Christmas and Easter was strongly discouraged because of their supposedly pagan origins.

Enter Charles II, son of the beheaded Charles I. His ascent to the throne in 1660 signaled a release of all the pent-up creativity and energy of the English people, stagnant under Cromwell's repression. In 1665 King Charles II gave a charter to eight **Lords Proprietors** to establish a colony, generously to be named Carolina after the monarch himself. Remarkably, none of the Proprietors ever

set foot in the colony they established for their own profit.

In 1666 explorer Robert Sandford officially claimed Carolina for the king, in a ceremony on modern-day Seabrook or Wadmalaw Island. The Proprietors then sent out a fleet of three ships from England, only one of which, the *Carolina,* would make it the whole way. After stops in the thriving English colonies of Barbados and Bermuda, the ship landed in Port Royal. They were greeted without violence, but the fact that the local indigenous people spoke Spanish led the colonists to conclude that perhaps the site was too close for comfort to Spain's sphere of influence. A Kiawah chief, eager for allies against the fierce, slave-trading Westo people, invited the colonists north to settle instead. So the colonists—148 of them, including three enslaved Africans—moved 80 miles up the coast and in 1670 pitched camp on the Ashley River at a place they dubbed Albemarle Point, after one of their lost ships.

A few years later some colonists from Barbados, which was beginning to suffer the effects of overpopulation, joined the Carolinians. The Barbadian influence, with an emphasis on large-scale slave labor and a caste system, would have an indelible imprint on the colony. Indeed, within a generation a majority of settlers in the new colony would be enslaved Africans. By 1680, however, Albemarle Point was feeling growing pains as well, and the Proprietors ordered the site moved to Oyster Point at the confluence of the Ashley and Cooper Rivers (the present-day Battery). Within a year, Albemarle Point was abandoned, and the walls of Charles Towne were built a few hundred yards up from Oyster Point on the banks of the Cooper River.

The English settlements quickly gained root as the burgeoning deerskin trade increased exponentially. Traders upriver, using an ancient network of trails, worked with local Native Americans, mostly Cherokee people, to exploit the massive numbers of deer in the American interior. By the mid-1700s, the deer population had been so overharvested that the Cherokees had trouble feeding themselves. This led to the need to purchase or barter for food from the

English, a dependency that would lead inexorably to violence in years to come.

Around this time German and Scots-Irish settlers from Pennsylvania and Virginia came down the **Great Wagon Road** along the Appalachians to enter the interior of the Carolinas in great numbers. Although many of these independent farmers owned slaves, generally they were far less sympathetic to slavery than coastal residents, and certainly much less dependent on it.

OGLETHORPE'S VISION

In 1712, the colony of Carolina was divided into north and south after a building period of political and economic estrangement. What would be South Carolina was increasingly identified with large rice plantations dependent on slave labor. Other than a band of plantations on its southeast coast near Wilmington, North Carolina's economy evolved to be somewhat less dependent on slavery.

In 1731, a colony to be known as Georgia, after the new English king, was carved out of the southern part of the original Carolina land grant specifically to buffer the wealthy plantations in South Carolina from the Spanish. A young general, aristocrat, and humanitarian named James Edward Oglethorpe gathered together a group of trustees to take advantage.

On February 12, 1733, after stops in Beaufort and Charleston, the ship *Anne* with its 114 passengers made its way to the highest bluff on the Savannah River. The area was controlled by the peaceful Yamacraw people. Oglethorpe struck up a treaty and eventually a genuine friendship with the elderly chief Tomochichi. In negotiations with local Native Americans, the persuasive Oglethorpe convinced the coastal Creek people to cede to the crown all Georgia land to the Altamaha River "which our Nation hath not occasion for to use" in exchange for goods.

While the trustees' utopian vision was largely economic in nature, like Carolina, the Georgia colony also emphasized religious freedom. While to modern ears Oglethorpe's original ban of Roman Catholics from Georgia might seem incompatible with this goal, the reason was a coldly pragmatic one for the time: England's two main global rivals, France and Spain, were both staunchly Roman Catholic.

The conflict came to a head on the coast in 1739 with the so-called War of Jenkins' Ear. A year later Oglethorpe cobbled together a force of settlers, Native American allies, and Carolinians to reduce the Spanish fortress at St. Augustine, Florida.

The siege failed, and Oglethorpe retreated to St. Simons Island, Georgia, to await the inevitable counterattack. In 1742 a massive Spanish force invaded the island but was eventually turned back for good with heavy casualties at the **Battle of Bloody Marsh.** That clash marked the end of Spanish overtures on England's colonies in America. The stage was set for an internal battle between England and its burgeoning colonies across the Atlantic.

REVOLUTION AND A NEW NATION

While the New England area gets most of the press when people talk about the American Revolution, the Carolinas and Georgia were key theaters of the war.

After the battles of Lexington and Concord, Governor Martin of North Carolina removed himself from the then-capital of New Bern, the first colonial governor to buck his post. North Carolina's Mecklenburg County (the Charlotte area) also made history by passing the first colonial declaration in rejection of the crown's authority.

At war's outbreak, the British failed to take Charleston—fourth-largest city in the colonies—in June 1776. The episode gave South Carolina its "Palmetto State" moniker when redcoat cannonballs bounced off the palm tree-lined walls of Fort Moultrie on Sullivan's Island. The British successfully took the city, however, in 1780, holding it until 1782. The area's two major cities were captured—Savannah fell to the British in 1778—but the war raged on in the surrounding area. The struggle became a guerrilla war of colonists versus the British as well as a civil war between Patriots and Loyalists, or **Tories.** Patriots of the South Carolina Lowcountry formed a group of deadly guerrilla soldiers under legendary leaders such as Francis Marion, "the Swamp Fox," and Thomas Sumter, "the Gamecock."

In South Carolina, militiamen would defeat Loyalist forces in two pivotal battles of the war, at Cowpens and Kings Mountain. The unexpected show of patriotism from noncoastal settlers put a dagger in General Cornwallis's ill-fated Southern Strategy and led inevitably to the British retreat through North Carolina. Cornwallis received another blow at the Battle of Guilford Courthouse, which, though technically a British victory, weakened his forces considerably, leading to his eventual final defeat at Yorktown, Virginia.

THE GOLD RUSHES

Cotton and tobacco weren't the only moneymakers in the Carolinas and Georgia in the antebellum era. Two gold rushes, one in North Carolina and one in Georgia, were America's first. In Cabarrus County, North Carolina, gold nuggets were found in large numbers in the late 1790s. By the 1830s, there was so much gold that the U.S. Mint opened a branch in Charlotte.

The North Georgia strike near Dahlonega was even bigger. By 1830 there were 4,000 miners panning for gold on one Georgia creek alone. As in North Carolina, the amount and quality of gold was so extravagant that the U.S. Mint opened a branch office in Dahlonega in 1838. Before closing at the outbreak of the Civil War, it had produced 1.5 million gold coins.

Of course, the original inhabitants of the gold rush land in both states were the Cherokee people. Writing in a Cherokee newspaper, one said of the rush, "Our neighbors who regard no law and pay no respects to the laws of humanity are now reaping a plentiful harvest. . . . We are an abused people." Those words were prophetic, and decades of government activity oriented toward removing Creek and Cherokee from the region came to a head when gold was used as an excuse to take final action.

Andrew Jackson's administration presided over the passage of the Indian Removal Act in 1830, which assigned reservations in the Indian Territory of present-day Oklahoma to the "Five Civilized Tribes" of the southeastern United States—the Cherokee, Choctaw, Creek, Chickasaw, and Seminole. Thousands upon thousands of Cherokee people were forced out of western North Carolina, North Georgia, eastern Tennessee, and Alabama and marched west on the Trail of Tears. About 4,000 died along the way.

Another 1,000 or so Cherokee people, through hiding, fighting, and negotiation, managed to win the right to stay in North Carolina—an act of resistance that was the birth of the modern Eastern Band of the Cherokee, which is still centered in and around the town of Cherokee on the Qualla Boundary in North Carolina's Great Smoky Mountains.

SECESSION

Much of the lead-in to the Civil War focused on whether slavery would be allowed in the newest U.S. territories in the West, but there's no doubt that all figurative roads eventually led to South Carolina. During Andrew Jackson's presidency in the 1820s, his vice president, South Carolina's John C. Calhoun, became a thorn in Jackson's side with his aggressive advocacy for the concept of **nullification,** which Jackson strenuously rejected. In a nutshell, Calhoun said that if a state decided that the federal government wasn't treating it fairly—in this case with regard to tariffs that were hurting the cotton trade in the Palmetto State—it could simply nullify the federal law, superseding it with law of its own.

In 1860 the national convention of the Democratic Party, then the dominant force in U.S. politics, was held in—where else?—Charleston. Rancor over slavery and state's rights was so high that they couldn't agree on a single candidate to run to replace President James Buchanan. Reconvening in Maryland, the party split along sectional lines, with the Northern wing backing Stephen A. Douglas. The Southern wing, fervently desiring secession, deliberately chose its own candidate, John

OLD HICKORY'S LEGACY

Although many histories of Andrew Jackson, seventh president of the United States, say he was born in North Carolina, don't tell that to South Carolinians. They're sure Old Hickory is one of their own. If you don't believe them, get into your time machine and ask Andrew Jackson himself. He always insisted he was born in a log house in South Carolina a couple of miles from the border with the Tar Heel State.

In any case, we know that Old Hickory was born in what's called the Waxhaws region, straddling the border of the Carolinas roughly in the area of modern-day Charlotte and its suburbs to the south. Like much of the Upstate, the area was generally immune to the charms of the Lowcountry planters, whom they thought of as a pampered elite. While owning slaves was certainly a part of the entire state's economy, it was noticeably less important in the Upstate.

This sensitivity to the needs and basic dignity of the common man would go on to inform Jackson's time in the White House. Prior to Jackson's presidency, only white male landowners could vote in the United States. Setting the stage for gradually increasing suffrage gains—such as for African American men, and later for all women—Jackson changed the system so that owning land was not a requirement to vote.

Jackson had noticeably less populist sympathy for Native Americans, however. As a product of the rough Carolina frontier, the site of generations of savage wars between settlers and local indigenous people, he grew up with a strong bias against the region's original inhabitants. This enmity would see its awful height in the Trail of Tears, a direct result of Jackson's Indian Removal Act of 1830. The most famous—and possibly apocryphal—example of Jackson's literal "my way or the highway" approach came in 1831, when the Supreme Court, under Chief Justice John Marshall, ruled against the state of Georgia's action to take Cherokee land. In response, Jackson supposedly said, "John Marshall has made his decision—now let him enforce it."

Another development that didn't necessarily have such sanguine results was his introduction of the patronage system, in other words, "to the victor go the spoils." Before Jackson, civil servants kept their jobs regardless of which team was in the White House. Afterward, bureaucrats became political appointees. While today patronage is generally thought of as leading to corruption and cronyism, at the time Jackson intended it as an antidote to what he saw as a creeping aristocracy in the government and another example of the venal self-centered nature of the Lowcountry planter elite.

One of Jackson's key philosophies, a sharp distrust of banks, did not survive his time in office. Although he fought strenuously against the undue influence of the banking industry on the American body politic, no one could say he was successful in light of their power today.

Learn more about Old Hickory when you're in the state of his birth (according to the man himself, anyway) by visiting **Andrew Jackson State Park** (196 Andrew Jackson Park Rd., 803/285-3344, www.southcarolinaparks.com, during daylight saving time daily 9am-9pm, other seasons daily 8am-6pm, $2 adults, free under age 16).

Andrew Jackson's main protégé, James K. Polk, is widely considered by historians to be the most influential and important one-term president in American history, dramatically expanding the borders of the country to the Pacific Ocean through a Jacksonian combination of hard-nose diplomacy and outright warfare. Outside Charlotte, North Carolina, you can visit his restored homestead and birthplace at the **James K. Polk Historic Site** (12031 Lancaster Hwy., Pineville, 704/889-7145, www.nchistoricsites.org, Tues.-Sat. 9am-5pm, free).

Breckenridge, in order to split the Democratic vote and throw the election to Republican Abraham Lincoln, an outspoken opponent of the expansion of slavery. During that so-called **Secession Winter** before Lincoln took office, seven states seceded from the union, first among them the Palmetto State, followed by Mississippi, Florida, Alabama, Georgia, Louisiana, and Texas.

Politically moderate compared to South Carolina and some other Southern states, and less invested economically and politically in slavery, North Carolinians were painfully divided as war approached. The state's voters rejected a ballot measure to authorize a secession convention, but North Carolina's hand was forced when fighting erupted at Fort Sumter in Charleston harbor. North Carolina seceded on May 20, 1861.

THE CIVIL WAR

Five days after South Carolina's secession on December 21, 1860, U.S. Army Major Robert Anderson moved his garrison from Fort Moultrie in Charleston harbor to nearby Fort Sumter. Over the next few months and into the spring, Anderson would ignore many calls to surrender, and Confederate forces would prevent any Union resupply or reinforcement. Shortly before dawn on April 12, 1861, Confederate batteries around Charleston—ironically none of which were at the Battery itself—opened fire on Fort Sumter for 34 straight hours, until Anderson surrendered on April 13.

Far from prodding the North to sue for peace, the fall of Fort Sumter instead caused the remaining states in the union to rally around the previously unpopular tall man from Illinois. Lincoln's skillful—some would say cunning—management of the Fort Sumter standoff meant that from then on, the South would bear history's blame for initiating the conflict that would claim over half a million American lives.

In summer 1861, the Union blockade of the Southeast coast began. New Bern, North Carolina, fell in the spring of 1862 and became a major locus of strategic operations for the Union military, as well as a thriving political base for free African Americans and escaped slaves. To the south, Fort Fisher on Cape Fear, near Wilmington, was a crucial outlet for blockade runners. It kept the city of Wilmington in Confederate hands until nearly the end of the war, and when it finally did fall to Union forces in late February 1865, it required what would remain the largest amphibious assault in American military history until World War II.

In November 1861, a massive Union invasion armada landed in Port Royal Sound in South Carolina, effectively taking the entire Lowcountry and Sea Islands out of the war. Charleston, however, did host two battles in the conflict. The **Battle of Secessionville** came in June 1862, when a Union force attempting to take Charleston was repulsed on James Island with heavy casualties. The next battle, an unsuccessful Union landing on Morris Island in July 1863, was immortalized in the movie *Glory*.

The 54th Massachusetts Regiment, an African American unit with white commanders, performed so gallantly in its failed assault on the Confederate Battery Wagner that it inspired the North and was cited by abolitionists as further proof that African Americans should be given freedom and full citizenship rights. Another invasion attempt on Charleston would not come, but it was besieged and bombarded for nearly two years (devastation made even worse by a massive fire, unrelated to the shelling, that destroyed much of the city in 1861).

Large-scale fighting didn't hit Georgia until the Union pushed down from Chattanooga, Tennessee. The last major Confederate victory of the war came at Chickamauga in September 1863, when Confederate general Braxton Bragg, with considerable assistance from General James Longstreet, a Georgia native, pushed Union troops under General William Rosecrans back into Tennessee after three days of brutal fighting. However, the Union Army still held Chattanooga and continued to consolidate their forces for General

William T. Sherman's eventual push to capture the real prize, Atlanta, and deal a dual blow to the Confederacy by seizing a major transportation and commercial hub as well as likely guaranteeing Lincoln's reelection later in 1864.

The spring was a fateful one for the South, as Sherman's initial forays into the area north of Atlanta were successful. Unrest in the top Confederate ranks led to Jefferson Davis firing General Joseph Johnston and replacing him with General John B. Hood, even as Sherman's army was gathering for the final assault only five miles from the city. Hood's attacks against the Union lines were too little, too late, and by the end of the summer of 1864 Hood had evacuated Atlanta and left it to its fate. Sherman telegraphed Lincoln, "Atlanta is ours and fairly won."

It was during roughly the same period that the notorious Camp Sumter POW camp operated near Andersonville, the name by which it's mostly known today. At its height of prisoner population, so many captured Union troops roasted in the sun within its unsheltered, stockaded space that it would have been the Confederacy's fifth-largest city.

After three months of occupying Atlanta, Sherman was set to begin his fabled "March to the Sea" in an attempt to break the Southern will to fight for good, by destroying the means of supporting an army. On his way out of Atlanta in November, he gave the order to burn everything in the city that might be useful to the Southern war effort. The arson extended to private residences, and the entire downtown area burned in a massive and controversial conflagration.

The March to the Sea was made easier by Hood's removal of his forces to the west in an effort to draw Sherman toward Tennessee again. Sherman didn't take the bait, and with the way clear to the coast, he broke standard protocol not only by splitting his forces, but by operating without a supply line, instead wanting his army to forage off the land and whatever supplies they could obtain from the populace. He divided his 60,000-man army into two equal wings: one would head toward Augusta and the other toward Macon. They both met at the state capital of Milledgeville, where the statehouse was ransacked and anything of remote military value was put to the torch. A Confederate cavalry force under General Joseph Wheeler harried Union forces the whole way, but to little effect. Union "bummers" took what they wanted from local farms, and railroad-wrecking crews heated railroad tracks into twisted messes called "Sherman's neckties."

In Savannah, Sherman concluded his March to the Sea in December 1864, famously giving the city to Lincoln as a Christmas present, along with 25,000 bales of cotton.

The only military uncertainty left was in how badly Charleston, the "cradle of secession," would suffer for its sins. Historians and local wags have long debated why Sherman spared Charleston, the hated epicenter of the Civil War. Did he fall in love with the city during his brief posting there as a young lieutenant? Did he literally fall in love there, with one of its legendarily beautiful and delicate local belles? We may never know for sure, but it's likely that the Lowcountry's marshy, mucky terrain simply made it too difficult to move large numbers of men and supplies from Savannah to Charleston proper. So Sherman turned his terrifying battle-hardened army inland toward the state capital, Columbia, which would not be so lucky. Most of Charleston's once-great plantation homes were also put to the torch.

For the African American population of the region, however, it was not a time of sadness but the great Day of Jubilee. Soon after the Confederate surrender, black Charlestonians held one of the largest parades the city has ever seen, with one of the floats being a coffin bearing the sign "Slavery is dead."

As for the place where it all began, a plucky Confederate garrison remained underground at Fort Sumter throughout the war, as the walls above them were literally pounded into dust by the long Union siege. The garrison quietly left the fort under cover of night on February 17, 1865. Major Robert Anderson, who surrendered the fort at war's beginning, returned to Sumter in April 1865 to raise the same flag he'd lowered exactly four years earlier. Later that same night, on Good Friday, Abraham Lincoln was assassinated in Washington DC.

The last major battle of the war was fought in North Carolina, when Sherman and Confederate general Joseph Johnston engaged at Bentonville. Johnston surrendered to Sherman in Durham in April 1865.

President Jefferson Davis met with his cabinet for the last time on May 5, 1865, in Washington, Georgia, essentially dissolving the Confederate government. Five days later, still on the run, he was captured by Union cavalry near Irwinville, Georgia, in the center of the state.

RECONSTRUCTION AND THE NEW SOUTH

The years immediately after the war were painful, as a vast population of newly free African Americans tried to make a new life for themselves economically and politically in the face of tremendous opposition, and often violence, from whites. The Ku Klux Klan was born during this era, inaugurating an era of horror for African Americans throughout the South and beyond. Federal occupation and domination of the Southern states' political and legal systems also exacerbated resentment toward the North.

For a brief time, General Sherman's benevolent dictatorship on the coast held promise for an orderly postwar future. In 1865 he issued his sweeping "40 acres and a mule" order seeking dramatic economic restitution for coastal Georgia's free blacks. Politics reared its ugly head in the wake of Lincoln's assassination, however, and the order was rescinded, ushering in the chaotic Reconstruction era, echoes of which linger to this day. Nonetheless, that period of time in the South Carolina and Georgia Sea Islands served as an important incubator of sorts for the indigenous African American culture of the coast—called Gullah in South Carolina and Geechee in Georgia. Largely left to their own devices, these insulated farming and oystering communities held to their old folkways, many of which exist today.

The late 1800s saw large-scale investment in North Carolina's railroad system, enabling an industrial boom in the New South. Agriculture changed in this era too, as the rise of tenancy created a new form of enslavement for many farmers—black, white, and Native American. R. J. Reynolds, Washington Duke, and other entrepreneurs built a massively lucrative empire of tobacco production from field to factory. Textile and furniture mills sprouted throughout the Piedmont of the Carolinas, creating a new cultural landscape as rural Southerners migrated to mill towns.

Atlanta was gradually rebuilt and quickly regained its dominant transportation status. In an acknowledgement of the city's overriding importance to the state, the Georgia capital was moved there from Milledgeville in 1868, a scant four years after it was burned to the ground. By 1880, Atlanta had surpassed Savannah as Georgia's largest city. The "New South" movement, spearheaded by *Atlanta Journal-Constitution* editor Henry W. Grady, posited a region less about agriculture than about industry and progressive thought.

Despite the upheaval of Reconstruction, the Victorian era in the Carolinas and Georgia was remarkably robust, with fortunes being made and glittering downtowns and residential areas rebuilt. A number of newly minted African American millionaires gained prominence during this time as well, most notably in Atlanta. The exclusive Jekyll Island Club opened in 1886, bringing the world's wealthiest people to the Georgia coast to play. In Horry County, South Carolina, the town of Conway exploded as a commercial center for the area logging industry. By 1901 the first modest resort had been built on nearby Myrtle Beach, and the area rapidly became an important vacation area—a role it serves to this day.

THE 20TH CENTURY

The arrival of the tiny but devastating boll weevil all but wiped out the cotton trade on the coast after the turn of the 20th century, forcing the economy to diversify. Naval stores and lumbering were the order of the day at the advent of

World War I, the patriotic effort of which did wonders in repairing the wounds of the Civil War, still vivid in many local memories.

The New Deal

Beginning in 1915 the old cotton-growing states of the South saw the arrival of the tiny but devastating boll weevil, which all but wiped out the cotton trade. Sharecroppers, a large percentage of the population and never far from economic disaster in the best of times, were hit especially hard. Old tensions flared as the Ku Klux Klan was revived on Stone Mountain, Georgia.

During the 1920s, then-New York governor Franklin D. Roosevelt began visiting the Warm Springs area of Georgia to seek relief for his worsening polio symptoms. He saw firsthand the struggle of rural Southerners, and these experiences would influence many domestic initiatives, such as the Rural Electrification program, after he was elected president in 1932.

The coming of the Great Depression in the early 1930s was for most Southerners just a worsening of an already bad economic situation. While FDR's New Deal programs had some positive effect, they were later in coming to the South and were less effective because of resistance on the part of state politicians such as Governor Eugene Talmadge of Georgia, who was a staunch segregationist and sought to limit any benefits of Roosevelt's largesse to white citizens only.

The cities fared a good bit better due to their transportation and manufacturing importance. Atlanta in particular weathered the Great Depression well, at the same time seeing a robust growth in the black middle class, a background that nurtured a young Martin Luther King Jr. in the then-prosperous black neighborhood called Sweet Auburn. The auto bug bit Atlanta hard (it's still felt there today) and the first car suburbs were built.

The chief legacy today of the Depression era in the region is the work of the Civilian Conservation Corps (CCC), a 10-year jobs program that resulted in the construction of many of the area's state parks, many of which feature original structures built by "Roosevelt's Tree Army" that are still very much in use today. Parts of the great Appalachian Trail were also cleared by the CCC, with many of the shelters used by through-hikers still in steady use today.

World War II

The modern-day military importance of the Carolinas and Georgia largely dates to the era of World War II. Installations at Fort Bragg, Camp Lejeune, Fort Jackson, Parris Island, and other still-vital bases in the Carolinas were constructed or expanded.

In Georgia, the enormous Bell Bomber plant was built in Marietta, near Atlanta, producing thousands of B-29 bombers for the final air offensive against the empire of Japan. Fort Benning in Columbus became the U.S. Army's main infantry, paratrooper, and Ranger training base. The "Mighty Eighth" Air Force was founded in Savannah, and enormous Fort Stewart was built in nearby Hinesville. In shipyards in Savannah and Brunswick, hundreds of Liberty ships were built to transport cargo to the citizens and allied armies of Europe.

In Aiken, South Carolina, the construction of the sprawling Savannah River Site hydrogen-bomb plant in the early 1950s forced the relocation of thousands of citizens, mostly low-income African Americans. Although environmentally problematic, the site has continued to provide many jobs to the area.

Civil Rights

In the 1950s and 1960s, African Americans in North Carolina, and throughout the United States, struggled against the monolithic system of segregation and racism. The Ku Klux Klan stepped up its efforts in political and physical violence—against Native Americans as well as blacks, as in the famous 1958 "Battle of Maxton" in North Carolina, in which 500 armed Lumbee people foiled a Klan rally and sent the Knights running for their lives.

Change arrived slowly. The University of North Carolina accepted its first African American graduate student in 1951, and the first black undergraduates four years later. The

University of Georgia enrolled its first black students in 1961.

Lunch counter sit-ins happened all over the region, including the episode of the "Friendship Nine" in Rock Hill, South Carolina, and the "Albany Movement" in Albany, Georgia. Martin Luther King Jr. visited South Carolina in the late 1960s, speaking in Charleston in 1967 and helping reestablish the Penn Center on St. Helena Island as not only a cultural center but a center of political activism as well.

In 1965, Atlanta, "the city too busy to hate," would elect its first black alderman, and 11 African Americans were elected to the state legislature. Julian Bond, Georgia's first black Congressman, was sent to Washington in 1967. Atlanta's first African American mayor, Maynard Jackson, was elected in 1969.

The civil rights era would spawn another political career when a peanut farmer in tiny Plains, Georgia, was inspired to fight for social justice and equality by running for the Georgia State Senate. Jimmy Carter would go on to be governor in 1971 and then U.S. president in 1976. In an intriguing and somewhat prophetic blend of the forces that would shape American politics into the Obama era, Carter was both the first statewide Southern officeholder to publicly embrace full civil rights as well as the first evangelical Christian president.

CONTEMPORARY TIMES

Throughout the 1980s, the region, especially Atlanta, underwent an economic surge driven by many of the same factors contributing to similar success stories throughout the U.S. Sun Belt. When the economic boom of the 1990s came, Atlanta and Charlotte were firmly cemented as a major convention and corporate business centers. Atlanta hosted the 1996 Summer Olympics, which, though marred by a bombing in Centennial Olympic Park, was pulled off quite successfully and signaled Atlanta's emergence as a truly global city—not that there was ever really any doubt.

But outside the massive twin economic engines of Atlanta and Charlotte, global trade has been a largely destructive force in the region during the past two decades. The textile industry has collapsed. This, combined with the ongoing slow death of tobacco in North Carolina and the loss of the fishing industry to international commerce, is causing the government and people of the region to look more and more toward tourism, the biotech field, and new approaches to agriculture to define their role in a changing world.

Lured by cheap labor and generous tax incentives, Hollywood has discovered the Carolinas and Georgia in a big way. Wilmington, North Carolina, has been a popular film location for decades now, including *Blue Velvet* and the TV series *Dawson's Creek*. Savannah, Georgia, has followed suit, hosting film shoots such as Forrest Gump, Glory, and, of course, *Midnight in the Garden of Good and Evil*. Beaufort, South Carolina, emerged from its stately slumber as the location of *The Great Santini* and *The Big Chill*.

Government and Economy

POLITICAL LIFE

For many decades, the South was completely dominated by the Democratic Party. Originally the party of slavery, segregation, and Jim Crow, the Democratic Party began attracting Southern African American voters in the 1930s with the election of Franklin D. Roosevelt. The allegiance of black voters was further cemented in the Truman, Kennedy, and Johnson administrations.

The region would remain solidly Democratic until a backlash against the civil rights movement of the 1960s drove many white Southerners, ironically enough, into the party of Lincoln, the Republicans. This added racial element, so confounding to Americans from other parts of the country, remains just as potent today.

The default mode in the South is that white voters are massively Republican and black voters massively Democratic. The GOP currently controls the governor's mansion and both houses of the state legislature in both Carolinas and Georgia. However, plenty of progressive enclaves exist, particularly in Atlanta, Athens, and Savannah in Georgia, Asheville and Chapel Hill in North Carolina, and to a lesser extent Charleston in South Carolina.

ECONOMY
The industries largely responsible for the wealth and development of the region in the preceding centuries have fallen by the wayside in the new world. The **tobacco** industry dominated North Carolina's economy for generations, employing countless Carolinians from field to factory and funding an inestimable portion of the state's fundamental physical and cultural infrastructure. The gradual decline of the worldwide tobacco industry from the 1980s on has changed the state forever, particularly in the rural east.

Likewise, the **textile** industry, an industrial giant from the late 19th century until the late 20th century, and the **furniture** businesses of the Piedmont have fallen off to nearly nothing as manufacturers send their work to overseas labor. The once-thriving **fishing** industry is

HOW CAN YOU TELL A TAR HEEL?

What manner of man is a North Carolinian? How can you tell a Tar Heel? What ingredients went into his making? Is he different, and if so, how and why?

There is no slide-rule answer to these questions, but it may be interesting to explore them. The Tar Heel is not a distinct species, but he may have some distinguishing marks.

[We are] independent, courageous, resourceful, democratic, gregarious and individualistic, although we would use plainer words than these Latin terms to describe ourselves....

There is a progressive strain in this Tar Heel, a realistic and resourceful determination to get ahead with the work for a better way of life for himself and his fellows...There is often a kindness in the voice which covers a lot of humanity in its acceptance of all sorts and conditions of men...

But there is no pouring Tar Heels into a mold. The point is that we are by preference and habit individualists, or what we call "characters."

So much for our good side. Generally, we are liable to be pretty good folks, but we have a bad side too, and the truth is that we can be, when we take a notion or for no reason at all, as violent, ornery, cantankerous, stubborn, narrow and lazy as any people anywhere on earth, civilized or uncivilized.

We cut and shoot one another at a rate not even equaled in the centers of urban civilization. True, we consider our violence too valuable to waste on outsiders and so confine it to ourselves.... Tar Heels hardly ever kill or maim anybody unless he is either an old friend or a close relative.

Blackwell P. Robinson, editor, *The North Carolina Guide* (UNC Press, 1955)

UNDERSTANDING LOCAL LINGO

Regional speech features all sorts of delightful and sometimes perplexing regional vocabulary and grammar. Following are a selection of some of the common phrases most likely to stump the traveler or newcomer.

- **Bless your/his/her heart:** A complex declaration with infinitely varied intentions, interpreted depending on context or tone. In its most basic use, "Bless your heart" is a sincere thank-you for a favor or a kindness paid. It's also an exclamation of affection, usually applied to children and the elderly, as in, "You are *not* 92 years old! You are? Well, bless your heart." Frequently, though, hearts are blessed to frame criticism in a charitable light, as in, "Bless his heart, that man from New York don't know not to shout."

- **buggy:** a shopping cart, as at a grocery store.

- **carry:** convey, escort, give a ride to. "I carried my mother up to the mountains for her birthday."

- **cattywompus:** topsy-turvy and mixed up. Used especially in the Piedmont and farther west.

- **Coke:** any soft drink; may be called "pop" in the mountains.

- **Come back:** often uttered by shopkeepers as a customer leaves, not to signify that something was left behind for which one should return immediately, but simply an invitation to patronize the establishment again someday.

- **dinner:** the midday meal.

- **evening:** not just the twilight hours, but all the hours between about 3pm and nightfall.

- **ever-how:** however; similarly, "ever-when," "ever-what," and "ever-who."

- **fair to middling:** so-so, in response to "How you?"

- **fixing:** about to or preparing to do something. "She's fixing to have a baby any day now."

- **holler:** hollow, a mountain cove.

- **Kakalak:** Carolina. (Also Kakalaky, Cakalack).

- **mash:** press, as a button. "I keep mash-

---

also in steep decline due to globalization and pollution.

New industries and fields have taken up where the former staples left off. **Pharmaceutical** and **high-tech** corporations are an important draw of labor and revenue to the area around the North Carolina Triangle. Charlotte is second only to New York City among the United States' largest **banking** centers. Thanks largely to Atlanta's economic importance, Georgia hosts over 25 Fortune 1,000 company headquarters, including Home Depot, UPS, Coca-Cola, Delta Airlines, Gulfstream Aerospace (in Savannah), and Aflac (in Columbus). Kia Motors recently opened its first U.S. assembly plant in West Point, near Atlanta. **Tourism** is absolutely crucial, from the cobblestones of historic Wilmington, Charleston, and Savannah, to the beach-resort locales of Nag's Head, Myrtle Beach, and Hilton Head.

One old standby remains, however. **Agriculture** continues to be very important, from the hog farms of eastern North Carolina to the chicken processing plants of North Georgia to the peanut and pecan and sweet-onion farms of South Georgia. But the Peach State isn't actually the nation's largest producer of peaches anymore—that would be South Carolina.

ing the button, but that elevator just won't come."

- **mess:** discombobulated, in a rut, not living right. "I was a mess until I joined the church."

- **might could/should/would:** could/should/would perhaps. "Looks like it's fixing to rain. You might should go roll up your car windows."

- **mommocked:** see *cattywompus*. Used especially on the Outer Banks and in rural southeastern North Carolina.

- **piece:** a vague measure of distance, as in, "down the road a piece" (a little ways down the road) or "a fair piece" (a long way).

- **poke:** a bag, such as a paper shopping bag. Used especially in the mountains.

- **reckon:** believe, think. Often used in interrogative statements that end with falling intonation, as in, "Reckon what we're having for dinner." (That is, "What do you suppose is for lunch?")

- **right:** quite, very. Variations include "right quick" (soon, hurriedly), "right much" (often),

and "a right many" or "a right smart of" (a great quantity).

- **sorry:** worthless, lame, shoddy. "I wanted to play basketball in college, but I was too sorry of an athlete."

- **speck so:** "I expect so," or, "Yes, I guess that's correct."

- **supper:** the evening meal (as opposed to "dinner," meaning lunch)

- **sy-goggling:** see *cattywompus, mommocked*. Used especially in the mountains.

- **ugly:** mean or unfriendly, spiteful. Sometimes referred to as "acting ugly." "Hateful" is a common synonym. The favorite Southern injunction that "God don't like ugly" does not mean that God wants us to be pretty (except inasmuch as pretty is as pretty does), but rather that we should be nice.

- **wait on:** to wait for.

- **Y'all:** pronoun used to address any group of two or more people.

- **yonder:** over there.

- **Y'uns:** y'all, used in the mountains.

People and Culture

DEMOGRAPHICS

Georgia is the ninth most populous state in the union, with nearly 10 million people. Atlanta, of course, is by far its biggest city, its metro area accounting for half that total. The demographic breakdown shows that whites make up 63 percent of Georgia's population and African Americans 31 percent. While the Latino population is under 10 percent, it is the most rapidly growing demographic.

North Carolina is nearly a mirror image of the Peach State. The 10th most populous state in the union, North Carolina has nine million residents. Charlotte is easily its biggest metro area. More than two-thirds of

North Carolinians are white, and not quite one-third are African American. The state's population is about 6 percent Latino, and it has the sixth-largest Native American population of any state, behind only California, Arizona, Oklahoma, New Mexico, and Texas.

South Carolina is significantly smaller than its neighbors. The 24th most populous state, South Carolina is home to just under five million people. Its largest population center is the Greenville-Spartanburg metro area, closely followed by the state capitol, Columbia. Like the Tar Heel State, South Carolina is about two-thirds white, one-third black, with a smaller

Latino population than either North Carolina or Georgia.

MANNERS

The prevalence and importance of good manners is the main thing to keep in mind about the South. While it's tempting for folks from more outwardly assertive parts of the world to take this as a sign of weakness, that would be a major mistake. Bottom line: Good manners will take you a long way here. Southerners use manners, courtesy, and chivalry as a system of social interaction with one goal above all: to maintain the established order during times of stress. A relic from a time of extreme class stratification, etiquette and chivalry are ways to make sure that the elites are never threatened—and, on the other hand, that even those on the lowest rungs of society are afforded at least a basic amount of dignity. But as a practical matter, it's also true that Southerners of all classes, races, and backgrounds rely on the observation of manners as a way to sum up people quickly. To any Southerner, regardless of class or race, your use or neglect of basic manners and proper respect indicates how seriously they should take you—not in a socioeconomic sense, but in the big picture overall.

The typical Southern sense of humor—equal parts irony, self-deprecation, and good-natured teasing—is part of the code. Southerners are loath to criticize another individual directly, so often they'll instead take the opportunity to make an ironic joke. Self-deprecating humor is also much more common in the South than in other areas of the country. Because of this, you're also expected to be able to take a joke yourself without being too sensitive.

Etiquette

It's rude here to inquire about personal finances, along with the usual no-go areas of religion and politics. Here are some other specific etiquette tips:

• **Basics:** Be liberal with "please" and "thank

you," or conversely, "no, thank you" if you want to decline a request or offering.

• **Eye contact:** With the exception of very elderly African Americans, eye contact is not only accepted in the South, it's encouraged. In fact, to avoid eye contact in the South means you're likely a shady character with something to hide.

• **Handshake:** Men should always shake hands with a *very* firm, confident grip and appropriate eye contact. It's OK for women to offer a handshake in professional circles, but otherwise not required.

• **Chivalry:** When men open doors for women here—and they will—it is not thought of as a patronizing gesture but as a sign of respect. Accept graciously and walk through the door. Also, if a female of any age or appearance drops an object on the floor, don't be surprised if several nearby males jump to pick it up. This is considered appropriate behavior and not at all unusual.

• **The elderly:** Senior citizens—or really anyone obviously older than you—should be called "sir" or "ma'am." Again, this is not a patronizing gesture in the South but is considered a sign of respect. Also, in any situation where you're dealing with someone in the service industry, addressing them as "sir" or "ma'am" regardless of their age will get you far.

• **Bodily contact:** Interestingly, though public displays of affection by romantic couples are generally frowned upon here, Southerners are otherwise pretty touchy-feely once they get to know you. Full-on body hugs are rare, but Southerners who are well acquainted often say hello or good-bye with a small hug.

• **Driving:** With the exception of the interstate perimeter highways around the larger cities, drivers in the South are generally less aggressive than in other regions. Cutting sharply in front of someone in traffic is taken as a personal offense. If you need to cut in front of someone, poke the nose of your car a little bit in that direction and wait for a car to slow down and wave you in front. Don't forget to wave back as a thank-you. Similarly, using a car horn can also be taken as a personal affront, so use your horn sparingly, if at all. In rural areas, don't be surprised to see the driver of an oncoming car offer a little wave. This is an old custom, sadly dying out. Just give a little wave back; they're trying to be friendly.

ESSENTIALS

Getting There and Around

BY AIR
North Carolina

North Carolina's international airports are in Charlotte, Greensboro, and Raleigh-Durham (with Wilmington qualifying as a major airport with more limited service). The 10th busiest airport in the country and 30th in the world, **Charlotte-Douglas International Airport** (CLT, 5501 Josh Birmingham Pkwy., 704/359-4000, www.clt.com) has more than 600 daily departures and is served by dozens of airlines. There are direct nonstop flights to over 100 domestic destinations as well as international flights between Charlotte and many cities in Latin America and the Caribbean as well as London, Frankfurt, Munich, and Toronto. Parking is abundant and inexpensive, with parking shuttles running from 5am.

Raleigh-Durham International Airport (RDU, 2600 W. Terminal Blvd., Morrisville, 919/840-2123, www.rdu.com), located in Wake County about midway between Raleigh and Durham, offers service to most major domestic air hubs as well as to London, Toronto, and Cancún. Hourly and daily parking is available for reasonable rates within walking distance of the terminals, and in satellite lots linked by shuttles.

© DREAMSTIME.COM

Piedmont Triad International Airport (GSO, 1000 A. Ted Johnson Pkwy., Greensboro, 336/665-5600, www.flyfrompti.com) serves the Greensboro and Winston-Salem area, with flights to and from many domestic destinations, particularly in the South, Midwest, and mid-Atlantic. There are several smaller airports around the state, including **Wilmington International Airport** (ILM, 1740 Airport Blvd., Wilmington, 910/341-4125, www.flyilm.com), **Asheville Regional Airport** (AVL, 61 Terminal Dr., Fletcher, 828/684-2226, www.flyavl.com), and **Fayetteville Regional Airport** (FAY, 400 Airport Rd., Fayetteville, 910/433-1160, www.flyfay.com). Smaller airports with regularly scheduled passenger service are in Greenville, New Bern, and Jacksonville/Richland; you can fly Delta to any of them.

South Carolina

There are six key airports serving South Carolina. **Charleston International Airport** (CHS, 5500 International Blvd., 843/767-1100, www.chs-airport.com) is served by the major national airlines and is a primary gateway to the entire coast. **Columbia Metropolitan Airport** (CAE, 3000 Aviation Way, 803/822-5000, www.columbiaairport.com) is a good access point for the center of the state, and **Greenville-Spartanburg International Airport** (GSP, 2000 GSP Dr., 864/877-7426, www.gspairport.com) is a good point of entry for the upper half of the state.

Because of the lack of interstate highway coverage in this area, **Myrtle Beach International Airport** (MYR, 1100 Jetport Rd., 843/448-1589, www.flymyrtlebeach.com) is best used only if Myrtle Beach is your primary destination. **Savannah/Hilton Head International Airport** (SAV, 400 Airways Ave., 912/964-0514, www.savannahairport.com), off I-95 in Savannah, Georgia, is perhaps the best access point to enjoy the lower portion of the South Carolina coast, and definitely Hilton Head.

Charlotte-Douglas International Airport (CLT, 5501 Josh Birmingham Pkwy., 704/359-4000, www.clt.com) is by far the busiest airport

in the state. Its location just across the North Carolina border and on I-77 makes it a fairly convenient point of entry unless your goal is to head for the coast.

Georgia

While some may be tempted to fly into Atlanta's Hartsfield-Jackson International Airport because of the sheer number of flights into that facility, unless your destination is Atlanta, I strongly advise against it because of the massive congestion in the area. **Hartsfield-Jackson Atlanta International Airport** (ATL, 6000 North Terminal Pkwy., 404/530-6600, www.atlanta-airport.com) is the world's busiest, serving nearly 100 million passengers a year. Its flagship airline is Delta, with 60 percent of the airport's traffic. In all, about two dozen airlines fly in and out to domestic destinations as well as Europe, Asia, and South America.

The state's second most comprehensive airport is **Savannah/Hilton Head International Airport** (SAV, 400 Airways Ave., 912/964-0514, www.savannahairport.com), directly off I-95 at exit 104, about 20 minutes from downtown Savannah.

The only other major airport in Georgia is **Augusta Regional Airport** (AGS, 1501 Aviation Way, 706/798-3236, www.flyags.com). Another option for coastal and southeast Georgia is **Jacksonville International Airport** (JAX, 2400 Yankee Clipper Dr., 904/741-4902, www.jia.com) about 20 miles north of Jacksonville, Florida. While it's a two-hour drive from Savannah, this airport's proximity to the attractions south of Savannah makes it attractive for visitors to the region.

BY CAR
North Carolina

Several major interstate highways spider across North Carolina, so if you're driving here and would prefer that your trip be efficient rather than scenic, you've got several convenient choices. If you're coming from most anywhere along the eastern seaboard, you'll likely be on I-95 for much of the trip. I-95 slices through the eastern third of the state, making for easy access to the beaches (most are 1-2 hours east of I-95) and to the Triangle area (just under an hour west via U.S. 64, U.S. 70, or I-40). If you're coming to the Triangle from the north, you might also choose to veer southwest at Richmond, Virginia, on I-85; this is a particularly efficient route to Durham and Chapel Hill, as well as to the Triad and Charlotte regions.

I-40 starts near Los Angeles and runs east all the way to Wilmington, paring the state in half horizontally much as it does the continent. It's a fast road all the way through North Carolina, although weather (ice in the fall, winter, and spring; fog any time of year) might slow you down considerably between Knoxville, Tennessee, and Asheville.

U.S. 64 and I-77 connect North Carolina to the Midwest. I-77 cuts through the toe of Virginia, in the mountains, for a straight shot to Charlotte, while U.S. 64 meanders east through the Triangle and all the way to Roanoke Island and the Outer Banks. If you're coming from the Deep South or Texas, your best bet is probably to catch I-20 to Atlanta, and from there pick up I-85 to Charlotte (or U.S. 19 or U.S. 23 if you're going to the mountains).

South Carolina

South Carolina is extremely well-served by the U.S. interstate highway system. The main interstate arteries into the region are the north-south I-95, I-77, and I-85, and the east-west I-20 and I-26. Charleston has a perimeter interstate, I-526 (the Mark Clark Expressway). Columbia's perimeter is I-126. Greenville has two, I-185 and I-386; Spartanburg's is I-585.

Keep in mind that despite being heavily traveled, the Myrtle Beach area is not served by any interstate highway. A common landmark road through the coastal region is U.S. 17, which used to be known as the Coastal Highway and currently goes by a number of local incarnations as it winds its way along the coast.

Unfortunately, the stories you've heard about speed traps in small South Carolina towns are correct. Always strictly obey the speed limit, and if you're pulled over, always deal with the police respectfully and truthfully, whether or not you agree with their judgment.

Winter driving in South Carolina is generally easy, since it rarely snows. During periods of heavy rainfall, however, unpaved roads can become quite muddy. Should you be unlucky enough to be on the coast during a mandatory hurricane evacuation, be aware that some roads, especially interstate highways, will become one-way westbound for all lanes to streamline the evacuation. In any case, always follow all law enforcement directions. For updates on planned slowdowns due to construction projects, go to www.dot.state.sc.us.

South Carolina's copious network of interstate highways offers numerous **rest stops.** They are often a very welcome sight, since the state's heavily rural nature means services can be hard to come by on the road. The following is a list of rest areas.

- **I-95:** Mile markers 5 (northbound near the Georgia border), 17 (Ridgeland, no facilities), 47 (south of Walterboro), 99 (Santee), 139 (south of Florence), 171 (north of Florence), and 195 (southbound at the North Carolina border).

- **I-26:** Mile markers 63 (north of Newberry), 123 (south of Columbia), 150 (eastbound at Orangeburg), 152 (westbound at Orangeburg), 202 (westbound at Summerville), and 204 (eastbound at Summerville).

- **I-85:** Mile markers 17 (northbound at Anderson), 24 (southbound at Anderson), and 89 (Gaffney).

- **I-20:** Mile marker 93 (Camden).

- **I-77:** Mile marker 66 (south of Rock Hill).

While all rest stops are clean, safe, and well-equipped, remember there is no gasoline sold at any of them.

Georgia

The road-building lobby is politically very powerful in Georgia, and as a result the state and county highways are appreciably better funded and maintained than in many other states. When possible I always choose the local highways over the interstates because they are comparatively less crowded and in many cases are of equal or better quality to get me where I want to go at least as quickly.

But if you prefer traveling on the interstate highway system, Georgia is very well served; it includes north-south I-95, north-south I-75 and I-85 (which combine through Atlanta), the east-west I-20 across the northern half of the state, and the least-traveled example, east-west I-16 between Savannah and Macon. Shorter connecting interstate highways include the notorious I-285 around Atlanta, I-575 through North Georgia, I-185 from Columbus to I-85 proper, the small loop of I-516 in Savannah, and two "shortcut" segments, I-675 south of Atlanta and I-475 around Macon.

A common landmark road throughout the coastal region is U.S. 17, which used to be known as the Coastal Highway and which currently goes by a number of local incarnations as it winds its way down the coast, roughly paralleling I-95.

Car Rentals

Renting a car is easy and fairly inexpensive as long as you play by the rules, which are simple. You need either a valid driver's license from any U.S. state or a valid International Driving Permit from your home country, and you must be at least 25 years old.

If you do not either purchase insurance coverage from the rental company or already have insurance coverage through the credit card you rent the car with, you will be 100 percent responsible for any damage caused to the car during your rental period. While purchasing insurance at the time of rental is by no means mandatory, it might be worth the extra expense just to have that peace of mind.

Key rental car companies in the region include **Hertz** (www.hertz.com), **Avis** (www.avis.

com), **Thrifty** (www.thrifty.com), **Enterprise** (www.enterprise.com), and **Budget** (www.budget.com). Some rental car locations are in the cities, but the vast majority of outlets are at airports, so plan accordingly. The airport locations have the bonus of generally being open for longer hours than their in-town counterparts.

BY TRAIN

Passenger rail service in the car-dominated United States is far behind that in other developed nations, both in quantity and quality. Many towns and cities in the Carolinas and Georgia are served by the national rail system, **Amtrak** (www.amtrak.com), which is pretty good, if erratic at times—though it certainly pales in comparison with European rail transit.

Although it does not currently serve the mountains or the coast, Amtrak is a great way to get to and around central North Carolina. The Washington DC-Florida *Auto Train* and the two main New York-Florida routes—the *Silver Meteor* and the *Silver Star*—pass through North Carolina. The first two follow roughly the I-95 corridor, while the *Silver Star* makes a dogleg west to Raleigh before continuing south. The New York-New Orleans route, the *Crescent*, goes through both Raleigh and Charlotte. Two interstate routes serve the Carolinas as their primary destinations; the *Carolinian* runs from New York to Charlotte, by way of Raleigh, and the *Palmetto* goes from New York to Savannah, crossing the eastern third of both Carolinas.

With the notable exception of the Grand Strand, South Carolina is well served by Amtrak. You'll find stations in Camden, Charleston, Clemson, Columbia, Florence, Greenville, and Spartanburg. The closest Amtrak station to the Beaufort-Hilton Head area is in Yemassee.

Two areas of Georgia, the southeast coastal portion and the northern portion, are served by two Amtrak lines. Amtrak stations on the northern route are in Atlanta, Gainesville, and Toccoa. Stations on the southeast route are in Savannah and Jesup.

BY BUS

Travel to and through the region can be accomplished easily and cheaply by bus. **Greyhound** (800/229-9424, www.greyhound.com) offers daily service to a long list of towns and cities. In North Carolina, Greyhound runs to Ahoskie, Asheville, Burlington, Camp Lejeune, Charlotte, Concord, Durham, Edenton, Elizabeth City, Fayetteville, Gastonia, Goldsboro, Greensboro, Greenville, Henderson, High Point, Jacksonville, Kinston, New Bern, Raleigh, Rocky Mount, Salisbury, Smithfield, Wallace, Washington, Waynesville, Williamston, Wilmington, Wilson, and Winston-Salem. There is currently no Greyhound service to the Outer Banks, or to mountain locations in North Carolina other than Asheville and Waynesville, but you can sneak around the back way by coming through one of the Tennessee cities close to the state line, like Knoxville or Johnson City.

South Carolina has Greyhound stops throughout the state, including Aiken, Anderson, Beaufort, Camden, Charleston, Columbia, Florence, Georgetown, Greenville, Myrtle Beach, Orangeburg, Spartanburg, Sumter, and Walterboro.

Georgia is the largest of the three states in this book, so keep in mind that distances are longer and so are the bus rides. There are several Greyhound stations in the Atlanta metro area, including at the airport, Marietta, Norcross, and LaGrange. Other stations are in Albany, Macon, Savannah, Columbus, Valdosta, and Hinesville (Ft. Stewart).

While rates are reasonable and the vehicles are high-quality, this is by far the slowest possible way to travel, as buses stop frequently and sometimes for lengthy periods of time.

BY BOAT

One of the coolest things about the South Carolina coast is the prevalence of the Intracoastal Waterway, a combined artificial and natural sheltered seaway from Miami to Maine. Many boaters enjoy touring the coast by simply meandering up or down the Intracoastal, putting in at marinas along the way.

Recreation

STATE PARKS AND NATURAL AREAS

The Carolinas have some of the best state park systems in the United States. Many of the older parks were built by the Civilian Conservation Corps (CCC) during FDR's New Deal and boast distinctive, rustic, and well-made architecture. In all, there are nine CCC-era parks in North Carolina, 17 in South Carolina, and 11 in Georgia.

Many state parks offer fully equipped rental cabins with modern amenities that rival a hotel's. Generally speaking, such facilities tend to book up early, so make reservations as soon as you can. Keep in mind that during the high season (Mar.-Nov.) there are often minimum rental requirements. While I encourage camping in the Blue Ridge, be aware that the closer you are to the Appalachian Mountains, the higher the rainfall. Be prepared to camp wet. Dogs are allowed in state parks, but they must be leashed at all times.

Currently, only three North Carolina state parks charge an entrance fee: Falls Lake, Jordan Lake, and Kerr Lake. Entrance fees vary in South Carolina, from free to $5 pp, depending on the park. Long-term visitors can save money on frequent visits by purchasing a **State Park Passport** ($75), which covers a full year of admission from the date of purchase. Get on online at www.southcarolinaparks.com.

Georgia State Parks (www.gastateparks. org) charge a $5 per vehicle parking fee per day on top of whatever the camping fees are, generally around $25. However if you plan on visiting multiple parks in one day—entirely possible in some areas with a high volume of parks, such as North Georgia—that one-day $5 pass gets you into all parks for that day. There are plenty of private campgrounds as well, but if at all possible utilize the state parks system, not only because it's great, but because increased use will help ensure adequate future funding.

NATIONAL WILDLIFE REFUGES

There are 10 federally administered National Wildlife Refuges (NWR) in North Carolina:

• **Alligator River NWR** (www.fws.gov/ alligatorriver)

• **Cedar Island NWR** (www.fws.gov/ cedarisland)

• **Currituck NWR** (www.fws.gov/currituck)

• **Mackay Island NWR** (www.fws.gov/ mackayisland)

• **Mattamuskeet NWR** (www.fws.gov/ mattamuskeet)

• **Pea Island NWR** (www.fws.gov/peaisland)

• **Pee Dee NWR** (www.fws.gov/peedee)

• **Pocosin Lakes NWR** (www.fws.gov/ pocosinlakes)

• **Roanoke River NWR** (www.fws.gov/ roanokeriver)

• **Swanquarter NWR** (www.fws.gov/ swanquarter)

There are seven National Wildlife Refuges in South Carolina:

• **ACE Basin NWR** (www.fws.gov/acebasin)

• **Cape Romain NWR** (www.fws.gov/ caperomain)

• **Carolina Sandhills NWR** (www.fws.gov/ carolinasandhills)

• **Pinckney NWR** (www.fws.gov/ pinckneyisland)

• **Santee NWR** (www.fws.gov/santee)

• **Savannah NWR** (www.fws.gov/savannah)

• **Waccamaw NWR** (www.fws.gov/waccamaw)

There are eight National Wildlife Refuges in Georgia:

• **Banks Lake NWR** (www.fws.gov/bankslake)

• **Blackbeard Island NWR** (www.fws.gov/ blackbeard)

• **Bond Swamp NWR** (www.fws.gov/ bondswamp)

• **Harris Neck NWR** (www.fws.gov/harrisneck)

• **Okefenokee NWR** (www.fws.gov/ okefenokee)

• **Piedmont NWR** (www.fws.gov/piedmong)

• **Wassaw NWR** (www.fws.gov/wassaw)

• **Wolf Island NWR** (www.fws.gov/wolfisland)

Admission is generally free. Access is limited to daytime hours (sunrise-sunset). Keep in mind that some hunting is allowed on some refuges.

BEACHES

Some of the best beaches in the country are in the region covered in this guide. While the upscale amenities aren't always there and they aren't very surfer-friendly, the area's beaches are outstanding for anyone looking for a relaxing scenic getaway. By law, beaches in these states are fully accessible to the public up to the high-tide mark during daylight hours, even if the beach fronts are private property and even if the only means of public access is by boat.

It is a misdemeanor to disturb sea oats, those wispy, waving, wheat-like plants among the dunes. Their root system is vital to keeping the beach intact. Also never disturb a turtle nesting area, whether it is marked or not.

Rip Currents

More than 100 people die every year on American beaches because of rip currents. Also called riptides, these dangerous currents can occur on any beach and can be very difficult to identify by sight. In rip current conditions, channels of water flow swiftly out toward deep water, and even if you are standing in relatively shallow water, you can in a matter of moments be swept under and out into deep water. Rip current safety tips are available on the National Oceanic and Atmospheric Administration (NOAA) website (www.ripcurrents.noaa.gov). Among NOAA's advice: "Don't fight the current. Swim out of the current, and then to shore. If you can't escape, float or tread water. If you need help, call or wave for assistance." Heed riptide warnings, and try to swim within sight of a lifeguard. Even good swimmers can drown in a rip current, so if you have any doubts about your swimming abilities or beach conditions, play it safe and stay close to shore.

Tips for Travelers

WOMEN TRAVELING ALONE

Women should take the same precautions they would take anywhere else in the United States. Many women traveling to this region have to adjust to the prevalence of traditional chivalry. In the South, if a man opens a door for you, it's considered a sign of respect, not condescension.

Another adjustment is the possible assumption that two or three women who go to a bar or tavern together might be there to invite male companionship. This misunderstanding can happen anywhere, but in some parts of the South it might be more prevalent.

While small towns in the Carolinas and Georgia are generally very friendly and law-abiding, some are more economically depressed than others and hence prone to more crime. Always take commonsense precautions no matter how bucolic the setting may be.

TRAVELERS WITH DISABILITIES

While the vast majority of attractions and accommodations make every effort to comply with federal law regarding those with disabilities, as they're obligated to do, the historic nature of much of this region means that some structures simply cannot be retrofitted for maximum accessibility. This is something you'll need to find out on a case-by-case basis, so call ahead.

Call 919/855-3500 or TTY 919/855-3579 or visit http://dvr.dhhs.state.nc.us for the current edition of **Access North Carolina,** published by the state Department of Health and Human Services. The guide is divided into Mountains, Foothills, Piedmont, Coastal Plain, and Coast divisions, and broken down by counties within each division. All sites are described, with addresses, phone numbers, websites, hours of operation, admissions costs, and other types of information, and then rated in terms of accessibility.

GAY AND LESBIAN TRAVELERS

Despite the region's essential conservatism, many of the areas in this guide can be considered quite gay-friendly, with the most obvious examples being Atlanta, Asheville, Charlotte, Savannah, and Charleston, in addition to the college towns of Athens, Chapel Hill, and Durham.

Gay, lesbian, bisexual, and transgendered travelers planning to visit North Carolina can learn a great deal online about community resources and activities. Check out **Carolina Purple Pages** (www.carolinapurplepages.com), serving Charlotte, Asheville, and the Triangle, **Gay Triad** (http://gaytri-adnc.homestead.com), the **Out Wilmington Community Center** (www.outwilmington.com), and **Out in Asheville** (http://outinasheville.com).

Visit **QNotes** (www.q-notes.com) for info on South Carolina and Georgia as well. Atlanta in particular has a large and thriving LGBT community. The "official" guide is *GA Voice* (www.gay-atlanta.com).

SENIOR TRAVELERS

Both because of the large proportion of retirees in the region and because of the South's traditional respect for the elderly, the area is quite friendly to senior citizens. Many accommodations and attractions offer a seniors discount, which can add up over the course of a trip. Always inquire before making a reservation, however, as check-in time is sometimes too late.

TRAVELING WITH PETS

While the United States is very pet-friendly, that friendliness rarely extends to restaurants and other indoor locations. More and more accommodations are allowing pet owners to bring pets, often for an added fee, but inquire before you arrive. In any case, keep your dog on a leash at all times. Some beaches in the area permit dog-walking at certain times of the year, but as a general rule, keep dogs off beaches unless you see signs saying otherwise.

Health and Safety

CRIME

While crime rates are generally above national averages in much of this region, especially in inner-city areas, incidents of crime in the more heavily touristed areas are no more common than elsewhere. In fact, these areas might be safer because of the amount of foot traffic and police attention.

By far the most common crime against visitors is simple theft, primarily from cars. (Pickpocketing, thankfully, is quite rare in the United States). Always lock your car doors. Conversely, only leave them unlocked if you're absolutely comfortable living without whatever's inside at the time. As a general rule, I try to lock valuables—such as CDs, a recent purchase, or my wife's purse—in the trunk. (Just make sure the "valet" button, allowing the trunk to be opened from the driver's area, is disabled.)

Should someone corner you and demand your wallet or purse, just give it to them. Unfortunately, the old advice to scream as loud as you can is no longer the deterrent it once was, and in fact may hasten aggressive action by the robber.

A very important general rule to remember is not to pull over for cars you do not recognize as law enforcement, no matter how urgently you might be asked to do so. This is not a common occurrence, but a possibility you should be aware of. A real police officer will know the correct steps to take to identify him or herself. If you find yourself having to guess, then do the safe thing and refuse to stop.

If you are the victim of a crime, *always call the police.* Law enforcement wants more information, not less, and at the very least you'll have an incident report in case you need to make an insurance claim for lost or stolen property.

Remember that in the United States as elsewhere, no good can come from a heated argument with a police officer. The place to prove a police officer wrong is in a court of law, perhaps with an attorney by your side, not at the scene.

For emergencies, always call 911.

AUTO ACCIDENTS

If you're in an auto accident, you're bound by law to wait for police to respond. Failure to do so can result in a "leaving the scene of an accident" charge or worse. In the old days, cars in accidents had to be left exactly where they came to rest until police gave permission to move or tow them. However, the states in this guide have recently loosened regulations so that if a car is blocking traffic as a result of an accident, the driver is allowed to move it enough to allow traffic to flow again. That is, if the car can be moved safely. If not, you're not required to move it out of the way.

Since it's illegal to drive without auto insurance, I'll assume you have some. And because you're insured, the best course of action in a minor accident, where injuries are unlikely, is to patiently wait for the police and give them your side of the story. In my experience, police react negatively to people who are too quick to start making accusations against other people. After that, let the insurance companies deal with it; that's what they're paid for.

If you suspect any injuries, call 911 immediately.

ILLEGAL DRUGS

Marijuana, heroin, methamphetamine, and cocaine and all its derivatives are illegal in the United States with only a few exceptions, none of which apply to the areas covered by this guide. The use of ecstasy and similar mood-elevators is also illegal. The penalties for illegal drug possession and use in South Carolina are extremely severe. Just stay away from them entirely.

ALCOHOL

The drinking age in all of the United States is 21. Most restaurants that serve alcoholic beverages allow those under 21 inside. Generally speaking, if only those over 21 are allowed inside, you will be greeted at the door by someone asking to see identification. These people are often poorly trained, and anything other than a state driver's license may confuse them, so be forewarned.

Drunk driving is a problem on U.S. roads. Always drive defensively, especially late at night, and obey all posted speed limits and road

signs—and never assume the other driver will do the same. You may never drive with an open alcoholic beverage in the car, even if it belongs to a passenger.

GETTING SICK

Unlike most developed nations, the United States has no comprehensive national health care system. Visitors from other countries who need nonemergency medical attention are best served by going to freestanding medical clinics. The level of care is typically very good, but unfortunately you'll be paying out of pocket for the service.

For emergencies, however, do not hesitate to go to the closest hospital emergency room, where the level of care is generally also quite good, especially for trauma. Worry about payment later; emergency rooms in the United States are required to take true emergency cases whether or not the patient can pay for services.

Pharmaceuticals

Unlike in many other countries, antibiotics are available in the United States only on a prescription basis and are not available over the counter. Most cold, flu, and allergy remedies are available over the counter. While homeopathic remedies are gaining popularity in the United States, they are nowhere near as prevalent as in Europe.

Medications with the active ingredient ephedrine are available in the United States without a prescription, but their purchase is now tightly regulated to cut down on the use of these products to make the illegal drug methamphetamine.

NOT GETTING SICK
Vaccinations

As of this writing, there are no vaccination requirements to enter the United States. Contact your embassy before coming to confirm this before arrival, however.

In the autumn, at the beginning of flu season, preventive influenza vaccinations, simply called "flu shots," often become available at easily accessible locations like clinics, health departments, and even supermarkets.

Humidity, Heat, and Sun

There is only one way to fight the South's high heat and humidity, and that's to drink lots of fluids. A surprising number of people each year refuse to take this advice and find themselves in various states of dehydration, some of which can land you in a hospital. Remember: If you're thirsty, you're already suffering from dehydration. The thing to do is keep drinking fluids before you're thirsty, as a preventative action rather than a reaction.

Always use sunscreen, even on a cloudy day. If you do get a sunburn, get a pain relief product with aloe vera as an active ingredient. On extraordinarily sunny and hot summer days, don't even go outside between the hours of 10am and 2pm.

HAZARDS
Insects

Because of the recent increase in the mosquito-borne West Nile virus, the most important step to take in staying healthy in the Lowcountry and Southeast coast—especially if you have small children—is to keep mosquito bites to a minimum. Do this with a combination of mosquito repellent and long sleeves and long pants, if possible. Not every mosquito bite will give you the virus; in fact, chances are quite slim that one will. But don't take the chance if you don't have to.

The second major step in avoiding insect nastiness is to steer clear of **fire ants,** whose large gray or brown-dirt nests are quite common in this area. They attack instantly and in great numbers, with little or no provocation. They don't just bite; they inject you with poison from their stingers. In short, fire ants are not to be trifled with. While the only real remedy is the preventative one of never coming in contact with them, should you find yourself being bitten by fire ants, the first thing to do is to stay calm. Take off your shoes and socks and get as many of the ants off you as you can. Unless you've had a

truly large number of bites—in which case you should seek medical help immediately—the best thing to do next is wash the area to get any venom off, and then disinfect it with alcohol if you have any handy. Then a topical treatment such as calamine lotion or hydrocortisone is advised. A fire ant bite will leave a red pustule that lasts about a week. Try your best not to scratch it so that it won't get infected.

Outdoor activity, especially in woodsy, undeveloped areas, may bring you in contact with another unpleasant indigenous creature, the tiny but obnoxious **chigger,** sometimes called the redbug. The bite of a chigger can't be felt, but the enzymes it leaves behind can lead to a very itchy little red spot. Contrary to folklore, putting fingernail polish on the itchy bite will not "suffocate" the chigger, because by this point the chigger itself is long gone. All you can do is get some topical itch or pain relief and go on with your life. The itching will eventually subside.

For **bee stings,** the best approach for those who aren't allergic to them is to immediately pull the stinger out, perhaps by scraping a credit card over the bite, and apply ice if possible. A topical treatment such as hydrocortisone or calamine lotion is advised. In my experience, the old folk remedy of tearing apart a cigarette and putting the tobacco leaves directly on the sting does indeed cut the pain. But that's not a medical opinion, so do with it what you will. A minor allergic reaction can be quelled by using an over-the-counter antihistamine. If the victim is severely allergic to bee stings, go to a hospital or call 911 for an ambulance.

Threats in the Water

While enjoying area beaches, a lot of visitors become inordinately worried about **shark attacks.** Every couple of summers there's a lot of hysteria about this, but the truth is that you're much more likely to slip and fall in a bathroom than you are even to come close to being bitten by a shark in these shallow Atlantic waters.

A far more common fate for area swimmers

is to get stung by a **jellyfish,** or sea nettle. They can sting you in the water, but most often beachcombers are stung by stepping on beached jellyfish stranded on the sand by the tide. If you get stung, don't panic; wash the area with saltwater, not freshwater, and apply vinegar or baking soda.

Lightning
The southeastern United States is home to vicious, fast-moving thunderstorms, often with an amazing amount of electrical activity. Death by lightning strike occurs often in this region and is something that should be taken quite seriously. The general rule of thumb is that if you're in the water, whether at the beach or in a swimming pool, and hear thunder, get out of the water immediately until the storm passes. If you're on dry land and see lightning flash a distance away, that's your cue to seek safety indoors. Whatever you do, do not play sports outside when lightning threatens.

Information and Services

MONEY
Automated Teller Machines (ATMs) are available in all the urban areas covered in this guide. Be aware that if the ATM is not owned by your bank, not only will that ATM likely charge you a service fee, but your bank may charge you one as well. While ATMs have made traveler's checks less essential, traveler's checks do have the important advantage of accessibility, as some rural and less-developed areas have few or no ATMs. You can purchase traveler's checks at just about any bank.

Establishments in the United States only accept the national currency, the U.S. dollar. To exchange foreign money, go to any bank.

Generally, establishments that accept credit cards will feature stickers on the front entrance with the logo of the particular cards they accept, although this is not a legal requirement. The use of debit cards has dramatically increased in the United States. Most retail establishments and many fast-food chains are now accepting them. Make sure you get a receipt whenever you use a credit card or a debit card.

Tipping
Unlike many other countries, service workers in the United States depend on tips for the bulk of their income. In restaurants and bars, the usual tip is 15 percent of the pretax portion of the bill for acceptable service, 20 percent (or more) for excellent service. For large parties, usually six or more, a 15-18 percent gratuity is sometimes automatically added to the bill.

It's also customary to tip hotel bell staff about $2 per bag when they assist you at check-in and checkout of your hotel; some sources recommend a minimum of $5.

For taxi drivers, 15 percent is customary as long as the cab is clean, smoke-free, and you were treated with respect and taken to your destination with a minimum of fuss.

INTERNET ACCESS
Visitors from Europe and Asia are likely to be disappointed at the quality of Internet access in the United States, particularly the area covered in this guide. Fiber-optic lines are still a rarity, and while many hotels and B&Bs now offer in-room Internet access—some charge, some don't, so make sure to ask ahead—the quality and speed of the connection might prove poor.

Wireless (Wi-Fi) networks also are less than impressive, although that situation continues to improve on a daily basis in coffeehouses, hotels, and airports. Unfortunately, many Wi-Fi access points in private establishments are for rental only.

PHONES
Generally speaking, the United States is behind Europe and much of Asia in terms of

cell phone technology. Unlike Europe, where "pay-as-you-go" refills are easy to find, most American cell phone users pay for monthly plans through a handful of providers. Still, you should have no problem with cell phone coverage in urban areas. Where it gets much less dependable is in rural areas and on beaches. Bottom line: Don't depend on having cell service everywhere you go. As with a regular landline, any time you face an emergency, call 911 on your cell phone.

All phone numbers in the United States are seven digits preceded by a three-digit area code. You may have to dial a 1 before a phone number if it's a long-distance call, even within the same area code.

RESOURCES

Suggested Reading

NONFICTION

Blythe, Will. *To Hate Like This Is to Be Happy Forever: A Thoroughly Obsessive, Intermittently Uplifting, and Occasionally Unbiased Account of the Duke-North Carolina Basketball Rivalry.* New York: Harper-Collins, 2006. Entertaining book about the hatred that exists between partisans of UNC and Duke, and how the famous basketball rivalry brings out the best and worst in people.

Bryson, Bill. *A Walk in the Woods: Rediscovering America on the Appalachian Trail.* New York: Anchor, 2006. Entertaining and affecting tales from the length of the Appalachian Trail.

Carter, Jimmy. *Keeping Faith: Memoirs of a President.* Fayetteville, AR: University of Arkansas Press, 1995. The 39th president's own account of his time in the White House from Plains, Georgia.

Cecelski, David. *The Waterman's Song: Slavery and Freedom in Maritime North Carolina.* Chapel Hill, NC: UNC Press, 2000. A marvelous treatment of the African American heritage of resistance in eastern North Carolina, and how the region's rivers and sounds were passages to freedom for many enslaved people.

Duncan, Barbara and Brett Riggs. *Cherokee Heritage Trails.* Chapel Hill, NC: UNC Press, 2003 (online companion at www.cherokeeheritage.org). A fascinating guide to both the historic and present-day home of the Eastern Band of the Cherokee in North Carolina, Tennessee, and Georgia, from ancient mounds and petroglyphs to modern-day arts co-ops and sporting events.

Ferling, John E. *Almost a Miracle: The American Victory in the War of Independence.* New York: Oxford University Press, 2007. Not only perhaps the best single volume detailing the military aspects of the Revolutionary War, but absolutely indispensable for learning about the key role of the Carolinas and Georgia in it.

Fussell, Fred, with photographs by Cedric N. Chatterley. *Blue Ridge Music Trails: Finding a Place in the Circle.* Chapel Hill, NC: UNC Press, 2003 (http://uncpress.unc.edu, www.ncfolk.org, online companion at www.blueridgemusic.org). A guide to destinations—festivals, restaurants, oprys, church singings—in the North Carolina and Virginia mountains where great authentic bluegrass, old-time, and sacred music can be experienced by visitors.

Gray, Marcus. *It Crawled from the South: An R.E.M. Companion.* Cambridge, MA: Da Capo Press, 1997. The complete guide to the band R.E.M., from personal histories to lyrics.

Greene, Melissa Fay. *Praying for Sheetrock.* New York: Ballantine, 1992. Greene explores the racism and corruption endemic in McIntosh County, Georgia, during the civil rights movement.

Hannon, Lauretta. *The Cracker Queen: A Memoir of a Jagged, Joyful Life.* New York: Gotham, 2010. A humorous recounting of the more dysfunctional aspects of the author's life in middle Georgia and Savannah.

Jones, Bobby. *Down the Fairway.* Latham, NY: British American Publishing, 1995. Golf history, lore, and lessons from the great Atlantan who founded Augusta National Golf Club.

Kemble, Fanny. *Journal of a Residence on a Georgian Plantation in 1838-1839.* Athens, GA: University of Georgia Press, 1984. English actress's groundbreaking account of her stay on a rice plantation in McIntosh County, Georgia.

Klein, Maury. *Days of Defiance: Sumter, Secession, and the Coming of the Civil War.* New York: Vintage, 1999. A gripping and vivid account of the lead-up to war, with Charleston as the focal point.

Ray, Janisse. *Ecology of a Cracker Childhood.* Minneapolis: Milkweed Editions, 2000. Heartfelt memoir of growing up amid the last stands of the longleaf pine ecosystem in southeast Georgia.

Robinson, Sally Ann. *Gullah Home Cooking the Daufuskie Island Way.* Chapel Hill, NC: UNC Press, 2007. Subtitled *Smokin' Joe Butter Beans, Ol' 'Fuskie Fried Crab Rice, Sticky-Bush Blackberry Dumpling, and Other Sea Island Favorites,* this cookbook by a native Daufuskie Islander features a foreword by Pat Conroy.

Todd, Leonard. *Carolina Clay: The Life and Legend of the Slave Potter Dave.* New York: W. W. Norton, 2008. A fascinating exploration of the world of the largely anonymous African American artisans who created the now-hot genre known as Edgefield pottery. We know the story of one of them, the man simply known as Dave, because he was literate enough to sign his name to his amazing works—an extremely unusual (and dangerous) act for the time.

Washington, James Melvin, ed. *A Testament of Hope: The Essential Writings and Speeches of Martin Luther King, Jr.* New York: HarperOne, 1990. A collection of work by the Atlanta native and civil rights icon.

Woodward, C. Vann, ed. *Mary Chesnut's Civil War.* New Haven, CT: Yale University Press, 1981. The Pulitzer Prize-winning classic compilation of the sardonically funny and quietly heartbreaking letters of Charleston's Mary Chesnut during the Civil War.

FICTION

Berendt, John. *Midnight in the Garden of Good and Evil.* New York: Vintage, 1994. Not exactly fiction but far from completely true, this modern crime classic definitely reads like a novel while remaining one of the unique travelogues of recent times.

Caldwell, Erskine. *God's Little Acre.* Athens, GA: University of Georgia Press, 1995. Scandalous in its time for its graphic sexuality, Caldwell's best-selling 1933 novel chronicles socioeconomic decay in the mill towns of South Carolina and Georgia during the Great Depression.

Caldwell, Erskine. *Tobacco Road.* Athens, GA: University of Georgia Press, 1932. Lurid and sensationalist, this portrayal of a shockingly dysfunctional rural Georgia family during the Depression paved the way for *Deliverance.*

Conroy, Pat. *The Lords of Discipline.* New York: Bantam, 1985. For all practical purposes set at the Citadel, this novel takes you behind the scenes of the notoriously insular Charleston military college.

Conroy, Pat. *The Water Is Wide.* New York: Bantam, 1987. Immortal account of Conroy's time teaching African American children in a two-room schoolhouse on "Yamacraw" (actually Daufuskie) Island.

Dickey, James. *Deliverance.* New York: Delta, 1970. Gripping and socially important tale of a North Georgia rafting expedition gone horribly awry.

Harris, Joel Chandler. *The Complete Tales of Uncle Remus.* New York: Houghton Mifflin, 2002. The Atlanta author broke new ground in oral history by compiling these African American folk stories.

Kinsella, W. P. *Shoeless Joe.* New York: Houghton Mifflin, 1982. Magical realist novel about a man who hears a voice telling him to "build it and they will come" and constructs a baseball diamond in an Iowa cornfield. Later adapted into the hit film *Field of Dreams* starring Kevin Costner and—with a totally out-of-place New York accent—Ray Liotta as Greenville, South Carolina, native "Shoeless" Joe Jackson.

Mitchell, Margaret. *Gone with the Wind.* New York: MacMillan, 1936. The Atlanta author's immortal tale of Scarlett O'Hara and Rhett Butler and one of the most popular books of all time.

O'Connor, Flannery. *Flannery O'Connor: Collected Works.* New York: Library of America, 1988. A must-read volume for anyone wanting to understand the South and the Southern Gothic genre of literature.

Poe, Edgar Allan. *The Gold Bug.* London: Hesperus Press, 2007. Inspired by his stint there with the U.S. Army, the great American author set this classic short story on Sullivan's Island, South Carolina, near Charleston.

Internet Resources

TOURISM AND RECREATION
North Carolina
Visit North Carolina
www.visitnc.com
The state's official tourism website.

North Carolina State Parks
http://ncparks.gov
Info on how to enjoy North Carolina's network of state park sites and recreation areas, including camping reservations.

South Carolina
Discover South Carolina
www.discoversouthcarolina.com
The state's official tourism website.

South Carolina State Parks
www.southcarolinaparks.com
This site offers vital historical and visitor information for South Carolina's excellent network of state park sites, including camping reservations.

Georgia
Explore Georgia
www.exploregeorgia.com
The state's official tourism website.

Georgia State Parks
www.gastateparks.org
Vital historical and visitor information for Georgia's underrated network of historical state park sites, including camping reservations.

NATURE

North Carolina

North Carolina Wildlife Resources Commission
www.ncwildlife.org
Practical information about outdoor recreation in the Tarheel State.

CanoeNC
www.canoenc.org
This is a nice starting point for planning a flat-water paddling trip in eastern North Carolina.

South Carolina

South Carolina Department of Natural Resources
www.dnr.sc.gov
Practical advice on how best to enjoy South Carolina's great outdoors, whether you're an angler, a kayaker, a bird-watcher, a hiker, or a biker.

Georgia

Georgia Department of Natural Resources Wildlife Resources Division
www.georgiawildlife.com
Lots of specific information hunting, fishing, and outdoor recreation in Georgia's various regions.

Paddle Georgia
www.garivers.org
Georgia River Network site that clues you in on guided trips and tours of the state's rivers, creeks, and marshes.

HISTORY AND CULTURE

Blue Ridge Heritage Area
www.blueridgeheritage.com
A resource that not only has a huge amount of mountain-area travel information but an ever-growing directory of traditional artists of all kinds in the Carolina mountains.

Foxfire
www.foxfire.org
Website of the longstanding nonprofit cultural organization based in Rabun, Georgia, that seeks to preserve Appalachian folkways.

Lostworlds
www.lostworlds.org
Well-researched and readable exploration of Georgia's extensive pre-Columbian Native American history.

New Georgia Encyclopedia
www.georgiaencyclopedia.org
A mother lode of concise, neutral, and well-written information on the natural and human history of Georgia from prehistory to the present.

North Carolina Folklife Institute
www.ncfolk.org
The website will fill you in on the many organizations across the state that promote traditional music, crafts, and folkways. You'll also find a calendar of folklife-related events in North Carolina, and travel itineraries for weekends exploring Core Sound, the Seagrove potteries, and Cherokee heritage in the Smokies.

South Carolina Information Highway
www.sciway.net
An eclectic cornucopia of interesting South Carolina history and assorted background facts makes for an interesting Internet portal into all things Palmetto State.

Southern Highland Craft Guild
www.southernhighlandguild.org
An Asheville-based regional arts giant with an extensive online guide to craftspeople throughout the region.

Index

First National Bank Building: 443-444
fish/fishing: general discussion 715; Charleston
313, 331-332; Columbia and the Midlands
413, 419, 420, 424-425, 431; Greenville and
the Upstate 457-458, 464; Hilton Head and
the Lowcountry 369, 384, 389; Middle and
South Georgia 593, 595; Myrtle Beach and
the Grand Strand 241, 252; North Georgia
535, 536, 546, 552, 563, 570, 571
Fitzgerald: 610-611
Flannery O'Connor Childhood Home: 633
Flannery O'Connor Room: 589
Flat Rock: 25, 201
Flat Rock Playhouse: 201
Flint RiverQuarium: 609
flora: 711-713
Flovilla: 586
Flowertown Festival: 351
Foley House Inn: 24, 661
Folk Art Center: 19, 22, 187
Folk Pottery Museum of Northeast
Georgia: 538
Folkston: 617
Folly Beach: 312-313
Folly Beach County Park: 330
Folly Beach Fishing Pier: 331
Fontana Dam and Lake: 20, 220
Footlight Players: 319-320
Ford Conger Field: 431
Forsyth Fountain: 640
Forsyth Park: 639-640
Fort Anderson: 100
Fort Defiance: 178
Fort Fisher State Park: 96-98
Fort Frederica: 375
Fort Frederica National Monument: 694
Fort Fremont Preserve: 372
Fort King George State Historic Site: 700
Fort Macon State Park: 62
Fort Morris State Historic Site: 671
Fort Moultrie: 26, 312
Fort Mountain State Park: 545
Fort Pulaski National Monument: 21, 24,
645-647
Fort Raleigh National Historic Site: 23, 40-41
Fort Sumter: 24, 291
Fort Watson: 282
40 Watt Club: 20, 556, 557
Four Corners of Law: 289
Foxfire Mountaineer Festival: 534
Foxfire Museum & Heritage Center: 534
Fox Theatre: 20, 483-484, 492
Fragrant Garden for the Blind: 640

Francis Beidler Forest: 424
Francis Hext House: 366
Francis Marion National Forest: 274-275
Francis Marion Square: 300
Franklin D. Roosevelt State Park: 20, 594
Franklin Square: 624-625
Freedom Park: 502
French Broad Brewery: 189
French Huguenot Church: 294
French Huguenots: 295
French Quarter: 21, 291-292, 294, 296-297
Freshwater Coast Discovery Center: 433
Frogtown Cellars: 544-545
Front Street Brewery: 90
Full Frame Documentary Festival: 120-121
Full Radius Dance: 494
Fuqua Orchid Center: 482

G
Gainesville: 528
Gatesville: 64-65
gay and lesbian travelers: 740-741
geography: 708, 709, 710-711
Georgetown: 267-277; map 268
Georgetown County Museum: 269
Georgetown Lighthouse: 272
George Washington Statue: 407
Georgia Apple Festival: 545
Georgia Aquarium: 20, 474
Georgia Children's Museum: 580
Georgia College & State University: 25, 589
Georgia College Museum: 590
Georgia Governor's Mansion: 487
Georgia Guidestones: 571-572
Georgia Institute of Technology (Georgia
Tech): 488
Georgia Mountain Fairgrounds: 542
Georgia Mountain Fall Festival: 542
Georgia Museum of Art: 554-555
Georgian Terrace Hotel: 20, 25, 506-507
Georgia Rural Telephone Museum: 602-603
Georgia Sea Turtle Center: 686
Georgia Shakespeare: 494
Georgia Southern University: 600
Georgia Sports Hall of Fame: 580
Georgia State Capitol: 478
Georgia State Panthers (football): 505
Georgia State University: 489
Georgia State University Symphony
Orchestra: 493
Georgia Symphony Orchestra: 493
Georgia Tech athletics: 504-505
Georgia Theatre: 555, 557

List of Maps

JOIN OUR TRAVEL COMMUNITY
AND SIGN UP FOR OUR NEWSLETTER

MOON.COM

MAP SYMBOLS

▒▒▒ Expressway	**⦗** Highlight	✗ Airfield	⚲ Golf Course
▒▒▒ Primary Road	○ City/Town	✈ Airport	🅿 Parking Area
▒▒▒ Secondary Road	◎ State Capital	▲ Mountain	⛩ Archaeological Site
═ ═ ═ Unpaved Road	⊛ National Capital	✛ Unique Natural Feature	⛪ Church
- - - - Trail	★ Point of Interest		
·········· Ferry	• Accommodation	⚑ Waterfall	⛽ Gas Station
▬·▬·▬ Railroad	▼ Restaurant/Bar	♠ Park	🍪 Glacier
▒▒▒ Pedestrian Walkway	■ Other Location	⬧ Trailhead	🗺 Mangrove
⊓⊓⊓⊓ Stairs	⋀ Campground	⛷ Skiing Area	🗻 Reef
			Swamp

CONVERSION TABLES

°C = (°F - 32) / 1.8
°F = (°C x 1.8) + 32
1 inch = 2.54 centimeters (cm)
1 foot = 0.304 meters (m)
1 yard = 0.914 meters
1 mile = 1.6093 kilometers (km)
1 km = 0.6214 miles
1 fathom = 1.8288 m
1 chain = 20.1168 m
1 furlong = 201.168 m
1 acre = 0.4047 hectares
1 sq km = 100 hectares
1 sq mile = 2.59 square km
1 ounce = 28.35 grams
1 pound = 0.4536 kilograms
1 short ton = 0.90718 metric ton
1 short ton = 2,000 pounds
1 long ton = 1.016 metric tons
1 long ton = 2,240 pounds
1 metric ton = 1,000 kilograms
1 quart = 0.94635 liters
1 US gallon = 3.7854 liters
1 Imperial gallon = 4.5459 liters
1 nautical mile = 1.852 km

MOON CAROLINAS & GEORGIA
Avalon Travel
a member of the Perseus Books Group
1700 Fourth Street
Berkeley, CA 94710, USA
www.moon.com

Series Manager: Kathryn Ettinger
Editors: Kathryn Ettinger, Nikki Ioakimedes
Copy Editor: Christopher Church
Graphics and Production Coordinator: Lucie Ericksen
Cover Design: Faceout Studios, Charles Brock
Moon Logo: Tim McGrath
Map Editor: Kat Bennett
Cartographers: Kat Bennett, Stephanie Poulain
Indexer: Greg Jewett

ISBN-13: 978-1-61238-779-6
ISSN: 2372-9368

Printing History
1st Edition – September 2014
5 4 3 2 1

Text © 2014 by Jim Morekis and Avalon Travel.
Maps © 2014 by Avalon Travel.
All rights reserved.

Some photos and illustrations are used by permission
and are the property of the original copyright
owners.
Front cover photo: Morris Island Park, South Carolina
© Richard Ellis/GettyImages
Title page photo: Bodie Island Lighthouse in North
Carolina's Outer Banks © Dreamstime.com
Interior color photos: pg. 8: Tryon Palace, New Bern ©
Jim Morekis; pg. 9: wild horses on a beach © Paula
Stephenes/123RF; page 10 top-left: Blue Ridge vista
© Jim Morekis; top-right: Brookgreen Gardens ©
Sophia Morekis; bottom: Cades Cove, Great Smoky
Mountains National Park © daveallenphoto/123rf.com
page 11 top: great egret at Lake Mayer in Savannah ©
Rose Waddell/Dreamstime.com; bottom-left: Trinity
Episcopal Church, Columbia © Jim Morekis; bottom
right: Reedy Falls, Greenville © Janice Smith/123RF
page 12: Hunting Island © Jim Morekis; page 13 top:
the Unitarian Universalist cemetery in Charleston
© Sophia Morekis; bottom-left: site of the Wright
Brothers' first flight © Jim Morekis; bottom-right:
flamingos at Columbia's Riverbanks Zoo © Sophia
Morekis; pgs. 14-17, 21, 22-25: © Jim Morekis; pg. 18: ©
Liane Harrold/123RF, pg. 19: © Alex Grichenko/123RF;
pg. 20: Dean Fikar/123RF; pg. 28: photo courtesy of
nps.gov

Printed in Canada by Friesens

Moon Handbooks and the Moon logo are the property
of Avalon Travel. All other marks and logos depicted
are the property of the original owners. All rights
reserved. No part of this book may be translated or
reproduced in any form, except brief extracts by a
reviewer for the purpose of a review, without written
permission of the copyright owner.

All recommendations, including those for sights,
activities, hotels, restaurants, and shops, are based
on each author's individual judgment. We do not
accept payment for inclusion in our travel guides,
and our authors don't accept free goods or services
in exchange for positive coverage.

Although every effort was made to ensure that
the information was correct at the time of going
to press, the author and publisher do not assume
any liability to any party for any loss or damage caused by errors, omissions, or any
potential travel disruption due to labor or financial
difficulty, whether such errors or omissions result
from negligence, accident, or any other cause.

KEEPING CURRENT

If you have a favorite gem you'd like to see included in the next edition, or see anything
that needs updating, clarification, or correction, please drop us a line. Send your com-
ments via email to feedback@moon.com, or use the address above.